ELIZABETHAN CRITICAL ESSAYS

ELIZABETHAN CRITICAL ESSAYS

EDITED WITH AN INTRODUCTION

BY

G. GREGORY SMITH

VOLUME I

OXFORD UNIVERSITY PRESS
LONDON : HUMPHREY MILFORD

First edition 1904
Reprinted photographically in Great Britain in 1937
by LOWE & BRYDONE, LONDON, from sheets of the
First edition

PREFACE

THE purpose of these volumes is to collect the writings of the Elizabethan age which are concerned with Literary Criticism. The term is used in its most comprehensive sense, and permits the inclusion not merely of academic treatises on the nature of poetry or on more special problems of form, but of tracts and prefaces which express contemporary taste. Some of the texts, such as Harvey's and Nash's, are reproduced less for their matter than for their manner of approach. The work is therefore an attempt to recover, primarily in the words of the Elizabethans themselves, what then passed for critical opinion in literary circles. I hope the collection will commend itself as being fairly complete: the ingenious repetition of argument and illustration which runs throughout would show at least that we are in possession of the abiding topics.

Several of the texts have been reprinted, either individually or as parts of works, during the late century, and notably by Haslewood, Grosart, and Mr. Arber. In these, it may be said, the interest has been exclusively bibliographical and historical—a restriction perhaps inevitable in the plan of separate reprints. The advance in the study of Criticism has proved, however, that there are other, and perhaps more important, interests in this material, and that these are best served by treating it as a whole. In no other way can we find the historical perspective of what appears to be a 'mingle-mangle' of ill-considered, off-hand sayings, or better appreciate the fact that in these we have the true beginnings of English Criticism as a separate literary 'kind,' or adequately understand how much of the classical mood expressed in Dryden and his successors is the natural and native outcome of these early speculations. I have endeavoured, in the Introduction, to discuss these general problems, and to show that the texts here reprinted supply evidence for certain conclusions.

It has been found convenient to use the epithet 'Elizabethan' in the strictest chronological sense, and to exclude the earlier treatises of Coxe, Wilson, and Sherry, and, with them, Fulwood's book of 1568, which are either entirely rhetorical or merely anthological. By ending with Elizabeth's death-year, we are denied the critical work of Ben Jonson,—other than the earlier pieces which appear in the Appendix to Vol. ii,—and all the work of Bacon: for though the first edition of the *Essays* appeared in 1597, the important reissues fall well within James's reign. Moreover—considerations of space apart—Jonson's and Bacon's *milieu* is Jacobean, and their work introduces us to a later stage in the history of criticism. In that work, with Bolton's *Hypercritica*, Stirling's *Anacrisis*, Drayton's *Epistle to Reynolds*, and others, there is ample material for another volume. Yet we need not concern ourselves overmuch with the chronological division. The defence of the limits here chosen must be the mutual dependence of the essays between Ascham's chapter on *Imitation* and Daniel's *Defence*. It so happens that the date of the latter falls in or about 1603.

Preface

All the writings in the body of the book are in prose. The contributions in verse, such as Daniel's *Musophilus*, Hall's *Satires*, or Peele's judgements on contemporaries, are either plainly supplementary or too occasional for the present purpose. These have been incorporated by way of illustration in the Notes. The extracts from Jonson's earlier criticism in verse and a passage from the *Returne from Parnassus* have been printed as an Appendix to Vol. ii, partly to elucidate certain matters, partly to make a link with the next period of English criticism.

In every case the texts have been taken from the originals, and have been carefully collated. I am responsible for the punctuation, and in several places for editorial emendation. The errors and confusion, which it is easier to note than to put right, are partly due to the carelessness or poor scholarship of some of the authors, but more frequently to the fact that the essays were printed without their consent, and were issued without correction, or were 'edited' by the compositors. Printer Jaggard once rounded on an author who had dared to complain, that he regretted his workmen had not been 'so madly disposed' as to 'have given him leave to print his own English.' For then, thought Jaggard (with what truth, it matters not), the complainer would have proved his incompetence. There is good reason to believe that in most cases the author never saw a proof of his work, and that in some no proof was pulled. Only in this way can we explain the appearance, if not always the meaning, of the gibberish in Lodge's *Defence*, or the eccentricities of Webbe and Meres, which are not unworthy of the genius whose *Butyrum et Caseum* disguised the names of Caesar's murderers. In one or two places the correction or suggested emendation of errors in the originals, which had escaped my scrutiny, will be found in the Notes. There must be others. For the transcription and collation of the texts in the Bodleian I am indebted to Miss L. Toulmin Smith, and of those in the British Museum to Mrs. Salmon.

As for the Notes, I hope I may claim for them, as Sir John Harington does for his, that they are not a 'work of supererogation'; though it is perhaps no defence or extenuation to state that the majority of the texts are here annotated for the first time. I shall be sorry if they are not explicit in showing my indebtedness to those who have helped me personally or by their writings. No venturer in this subject dare reckon without the learned author of the *History of Criticism*, or the American scholar who broke fresh ground in the remarkable volume on *Literary Criticism in the Renaissance*. To the thanks which I owe to them for my share of these public gifts, I add my hearty acknowledgement of not a few happy suggestions which our friendship has made possible. Mr. Nichol Smith, who very kindly read all the proofs, has supplied me with many interesting references, especially to the French critics. I would also thank the Secretary and Staff of the Clarendon Press for their ready co-operation at every stage of the work, and Mr. Doble, in particular, for helping me to the solution of some textual difficulties.

December 29, 1903.

CONTENTS OF VOL. I

INTRODUCTION.   PAGE
    I. Preliminary, pp. xi–xiv; II. The Puritan Attack, pp. xiv–xxi; III. The Defence, pp. xxi–xxxi; IV. The Classical Purpose, pp. xxxi–xli; V. The Special Problems: 1. Decorum, pp. xli–xlvi; 2. Prosody, pp. xlvi–lv; 3. Diction, pp. lv–lx; VI. The Romantic Qualities, pp. lx–lxvi; VII. The Critical Temper, pp. lxvi–lxxi; VIII. The Sources: 1. Classical and Mediaeval, pp. lxxi–lxxvii; 2. Italian, pp. lxxvii–lxxxvii; 3. French, pp. lxxxvii–lxxxix; 4. Spanish, pp. lxxxix–xc; 5. English Predecessors: Inter-borrowings, pp. xc–xcii . . . . . .

ROGER ASCHAM.
    'Of Imitation': *The Scholemaster* (Book II). 1570.   1–45

RICHARD WILLES.
    From *Poematum Liber*. 1573.   Footnote.   46–47

GEORGE GASCOIGNE.
    Certayne Notes of Instruction. 1575 . . .   46–57

GEORGE WHETSTONE.
    The *Dedication* to *Promos and Cassandra*. 1578 .   58–60

THOMAS LODGE.
    A Defence of Poetry. 1579.   61–86
    Bibliographical List of Pamphlets for and against the Stage. 1577–87 . . .   61–63

Contents

Spenser-Harvey Correspondence. 1579–80.

	PAGE
Edmund Spenser to Gabriel Harvey. [I]	87–92
Gabriel Harvey to Edmund Spenser. [II]	93–97
Edmund Spenser to Gabriel Harvey. [III]	98–101
Gabriel Harvey to Edmund Spenser. [IV]	101–122
From Gabriel Harvey's Letter-Book	123–126

'E. K.'

Epistle Dedicatory to *The Shepheards Calender*. 1579 127–134

Richard Stanyhurst.

From the Dedication and Preface to the Translation of the *Aeneid*. 1582 135–147

Sir Philip Sidney.

An Apologie for Poetrie. c. 1583 (printed 1595) . 148–207

King James VI.

Ane Schort Treatise conteining some Reulis and Cautelis to be obseruit and eschewit in Scottis Poesie. 1584 208–225

William Webbe.

A Discourse of English Poetrie. 1586 . . . 226–302

Abraham Fraunce.

From *The Arcadian Rhetorike*. 1588 . . . 303–306

Thomas Nash.

I. Preface to Greene's *Menaphon*. 1589 . . 307–320
II. From *The Anatomie of Absurditie*. 1589 . . 321–337

Appendix.

From E. Hoby's translation of Coignet's *Politique Discourses*. 1586 339–344

Notes to Texts in Volume I 345–431

INTRODUCTION

I.

IT is a commonplace that the age of Elizabeth was too great in creation to be even respectable in criticism. Many who see the bad logic and bad history of this popular formula have concluded not less adversely from a survey of the literary evidence. It is shown that the 'critical' writings are a mere miscellany of stray pamphlets, a 'gallimaufry' of treatises in the old rhetorical vein, tracts on prosody, or prefaces of abuse: and that the writers who disclose something of the critical temper were indifferent to the things which interest modern criticism, or indeed interested their own generation. For is it not remarkable that when Spenser and Sidney, not to speak of the lesser, turn critic, they have no eyes for the pageant of their stage, and but careless ears for the immortal music of contemporary verse; that they find the measure of dramatic excellence in Buchanan's *Jephthes* or Watson's *Absolon*, or the secret of English poetry in hobbling hexameters? And if Spenser redeemed his honour by giving us the *Faerie Queene* and Campion his in the *Books of Airs*, they have proved not so much how great they were as poets as how poor they were as critics. Sidney in his *Apologie*, to which of all these writings least exception can be taken, commends himself most when he strays from academic argument to raptures on the nobility of the Poet's calling.

This is altogether a superficial estimate. It is inadequate as a description of the critical activities which are crowded into the work of a single generation. The mere volume of the texts is evidence against the occasional character of the reflections; and their variety, far from showing the inconsequence of the amateur, proves a vitality of critical purpose. The persistent effort towards the understanding of the principles of Poetry is in itself an important fact which must prompt us, if it do nothing else, to discover its cause. Moreover, the modern dislike of the classical elements in the essays leaves unanswered the very pertinent question why Elizabethan criticism is apparently out of touch with the literature of its age. And it passes by the important consideration of the bearing of this pre-Jonsonian material upon the doctrine of Dryden and his successors, who inherited more of Elizabethan tradition than it has been the custom to allow. Further, the experimental character of the work, taken as a whole, the tentative conclusions, the borrowings and reborrowings, the inconsistencies, are not without their positive value, especially as the age was itself conscious that it was but seeking its way. Nor must it be forgotten that English criticism had no English tradition, and little, if any, English material on which it could found a Poetic; and that it was at this time in England, and hardly earlier in Renaissance Europe, that Criticism *per se* first laid claim to rank as a literary 'kind' in the vernacular. It appears therefore more reasonable to look upon this extensive and mixed collection of documents as an important body of evidence in the study of literary origins. In the perspective of these essays we may find something of that critical temper which is first made clear in Dryden, so justly named the Father of English Criticism; but we must not measure the quality of these early efforts, and even of Jonson's, by later experience, any more than we may look for a general canon governing the exercise of that temper. All is in the making: these remains are *Explorata* or *Discoveries—Timber* for the building of the later edifice, of which Jonson drew the plans, but which he could not complete.

It may be said that the recognition of this inchoate, and to some extent irregular, character of Elizabethan criticism is a serious objection to the treatment of the essays as a whole, and makes their association in these volumes a mere matter of convenience. What is common, it will be asked, to Ascham on the imitation of classical authors, Gascoigne on the making of verses, Nash on Gabriel Harvey, Sidney in defence of 'poor Poetry,' Puttenham on rhetorical figures, and Meres in his directory of writers? Can we reconcile the purposes of the practical educationist, the Bohemian, the college pedant, the rhapsodist, the courtier who writes for courtiers? And what is the critical utility of making neighbours of Gascoigne's random notes and Puttenham's 'whole receipt of Poetry,' or King James's *juvenilia* and Daniel's great *Defence*? The objection is less valid than it would appear to be, though it may be useful as a caution against making a too absolute 'composite' out of the variety. Recent study, especially on the comparative side, has greatly increased our knowledge of the relationship of phases which appear to be individual and incoherent. We have outlived the merely antiquarian taste which happily prompted Haslewood to collect certain of these tracts in his *Ancient Critical Essays*; though there is in him some hint of their value as a corporate study. 'Perhaps it may be confidently said,' he wrote, 'that such a body of criticism as these tracts collectively present, although few in number, is not anywhere to be found. Independent of rarity, intrinsic value may justly entitle this volume, although a humble reprint, to range with those of the Elizabethan æra[1].' This was written nearly a century ago, and since then the editorial

---

[1] *Ancient Critical Essays upon English Poets and Poësy*, edited by Joseph Haslewood (2 vols., 1811, 1815), II. xxii.

interest has been confined to the publication of some of these tracts either individually or in popular gatherings of kindred prose. The present collection brings these together again, and recovers others of not less importance. What justification there may be for restoring this comradeship, and for reasons other than that the Essays were written about the same time, the following pages will endeavour to show.

II. THE PURITAN ATTACK.

Elizabethan criticism arose in controversy. The early Essays are 'Apologies' for Poets and Poetry against the attacks of a vigorous Puritanism. Some are direct answers to onslaughts on special forms or on individuals; all have the common purpose of upholding the usefulness and pleasure-giving power of Poetry. It is noteworthy that the greater forces which stimulated this literary defence were themselves unliterary. They are not represented in these volumes, except in the answers of their adversaries[1]. They denounce Poetry because it is often lewd, the theatre because it is a school of abuse: their argument is social, political, personal. Their importance—and it should not be underestimated—lies in the fact that they called forth a reasoned defence, and compelled their opponents to examine the principles of Poetry. They thus defined the first problem for English criticism. But they did more, by helping the critics, in their investigation of the bases of Poetry, to see that there was some excuse for the obloquy cast upon what had been written, and that some reform from within was necessary. The problem as it presented itself to Sidney and his friends was in general terms. Poetry is a good thing in itself: 'it is abused and does not abuse': if there be vice in it, it is the fault of 'poet-apes,' not of

---

[1] Occasional passages from Gosson are given in the notes to Lodge's reply. See the bibliography of the pamphlets, i. 61-3.

poets: let the vice be taken away. Thus, to a degree, the spirit of the extremer sort who would banish poets from the commonwealth passed into their opponents and made them severe judges of the literature which fell short of their ideal. There was not as yet any serious thought of the fixing of a canon, but the scrutiny of English habit which proceeded apace was, in the nature of things, the sure forerunner of a critical system. The achievement of this is, however, the tale of a later period. The Elizabethan mind was not, could not be, resolved on such discipline. Yet its efforts, though tentative, were not chaotic, for it established the preliminary positions that Poetry can justify herself, and that English Poetry must. And if the reader will keep this in view, he may escape some of the confusion which surrounds the double argument of the defenders against the 'Misomousoi' or Poet-haters, and against the 'rakehelly rout' of English rhymers.

The Puritan arguments fall into two main groups—the historical and moral. The former was the less urgent, though it may be undervalued because the other was debated with greater noise and persistency. There was, in the first place, the patristic tradition of the iniquity of stage-plays, songs, and merry tales, wrested with more or less exaggeration from Augustine, Tertullian, Cyprian, Lactantius, and Chrysostom. Passages of this mediaeval protest are quoted and requoted, not because Renaissance or Reformed England was in sympathy with the Fathers, or even knew their work at first hand, but because these satisfied the perennial instinct of that half of the nation which must be ascetic. The marked Puritanism of the Elizabethan age, to be traced alike in the *Faerie Queene* and in the abhorred plays, was but one phase of a condition which was constitutional rather than the literary infection of earlier theology and philosophy. It found support for its purposes in the alien and misunderstood past, and readily borrowed its phrases to clinch the argument. So, too, it turned to classical literature, and confounded the scholars and lovers of vain things with the dicta of Aristotle, or of Plato, the accredited expeller of poets from the ideal Commonwealth. It was a partisan selection; and opponents of no greater scholarship found it easy to marshal other holy and learned adversaries, or to turn these very mentors to their own account. The Precisians, however, made a stronger point when they appealed to the Protestant antipathy to the so-called Dark Ages. It is clear to us that the blindness to the merits of the mediaeval romances is due less to a crazy dislike of what they chose to call their 'bold bawdry,' than to the fact that they were the work of 'abbey-lubbers' and 'wanton canons.' Even the courtier Puttenham boldly concludes: 'Thus what in writing of rhymes and registering of lies was the clergy of that fabulous age wholly occupied[1].' The Humanists joined with them in condemnation of the 'standing pool' of English literature, though their nicer noses smelt ignorance rather than Papistry in its stagnant waters. But the chief support to this hatred of the fooleries and lies of the Muse lay in the record of English poetry. With the exception of Chaucer, and there was no reason why the sterner minds should except even him, there was little or nothing of poetry, as they knew it, to be commended, except by professional friendship, and certainly nothing sufficiently outstanding to win over the more open-minded of that party. The defenders are the first to admit this, but on that admission they founded an argument for the revival, not for the suppression of the Art.

The attack was, however, keener on the side of Morality, and it was led in two directions—against the playhouse and its associations, and against the foreign, especially the Italian, influences in society. The former

[1] i. 15.

are the immediate object. The Puritan pamphleteers inveigh rather than argue; they are more concerned with the social bearings of the playhouse than with the intrinsic immorality of the plays. They seldom condescend to the literary question; in their condemnation they are but

> 'Rude foggie squires
> That knowe not to esteeme of witt or arte[1],'

and they are not too explicit in their production of evidence against the theatre as a social institution. Gosson, who has the exceeding enthusiasm of the pervert, defends his position thus: 'Now if any man ask me why myself have penned comedies in time past, and inveigh so eagerly against them here, let him know that *semel insaniuimus omnes*: I have sinned, and am sorry for my fault: he runs far that never turns; better late than never[2].' Such a plea, however effective it may have proved by reason of its confidence, and however welcome it must have been to cherished sentiments, was clearly inadequate for the settlement of even the narrowest issues. It was not difficult for the opponents of the Puritans to point out that all the vices of the playhouse, which they themselves were not slow to condemn, were not an argument against its continuation, much less against plays and poetry.

There was more force in the protest against the Italianate Englishman. Yet the Precisians state it in an indifferent or occasional way, and do not see that it was perhaps the best weapon in their armoury. Their more clear-sighted opponents wrested it from their hands and used it for their own purposes. To these, and not to the Puritans, we must go for the best estimate of the risks which came to English life and art from 'diabolical ruffs and wicked great breeches full of sin.' The Puritans hate the over-sea

---

[1] *Pilgrimage to Parnassus*, v. (536–7).   [2] i. 369.

affectation because they find in it certain glaring evidences of Renaissance degeneracy, of loose living and filthy reading. They hardly touch the old problem whether Art may not, by its very exercise, tend to destroy itself. Ascham, the least bigoted in his Puritan sympathies, sees in the Italian books the undoing of both true doctrine and honest living, the opening of 'not fond and common ways to vice, but such subtle, cunning, new, and diverse shifts ... as the simple head of an Englishman is not able to invent[1].' When he approaches nearest to the literary intention, as in his denunciation of rhyming, he vaguely concludes: 'And you that be able to understand no more than ye find in the Italian tongue, and never went farther than the school of Petrarch and Ariosto abroad, or else of Chaucer at home, though you have pleasure to wander blindly still in your foul wrong way, envy not others that seek, as wise men have done before them, the fairest and rightest way; or else, beside the just reproach of malice, wise men shall truly judge that you do so, as I have said and say yet again unto you, because either for idleness ye will not, or for ignorance ye cannot, come by no better yourself[2].' There is no criticism in these things: merely the old war against the Devil and his works, be he Italian or Englishman, rhymer or not, and the longing of saints and philosophers for the old simplicity. The constant appeal to the days of yore, when men were not yet schooled in abuse—to the England 'of our forefathers' time,' ere monkish tales of Sir Lancelot and Sir Tristram had infected our chivalry—is but the cry of the Gossons of every generation. In their zeal against playhouse ribaldry and Italian luxury some prayed for the Scriptural pastures, some for a new Scythia, where among valorous men even Poetry would be 'without vice, as the Phoenix in Arabia without a fellow[3].'

[1] i. 4. [2] i. 33. [3] i. 368.

Introduction

It would, however, be an error to consider the Puritan attack as ineffectual zealotry. Though it was badly managed, though it erred by exaggeration, and was ignorant of the working values of the pleas which it advanced though (in Sidney's words), it fell out 'with these Poet-whippers, as with some good women, who often are sick, but in faith they cannot tell where[1],' it has more than an accidental bearing upon the development of Elizabethan criticism. That it was taken so seriously by the writers who had the cause of literature at heart gives it the importance of having to some extent determined the lines of their defence. Not merely were the Puritan positions, such as the appeal to history, directly met, but others of more specific character, such as the charges against the theatre and the denunciation of Italian influence, were transformed into essential topics in the ensuing discussion of literary principles. And, further, the Puritans called forth, and perhaps intensified, a latent sympathy with their ideals in some of the best and keenest of their professed opponents, even though their overstrainings prompted not a few hard sayings about the 'senseless stoical austerity,' and the inconsistency and confidence of the 'sour reforming enemies of art[2].' Ascham is strongly sympathetic; Sidney, who represents the most complete and positive qualities of Elizabethan criticism, gives a courtly hearing; Harington, who sees but a weak faction in those who from malice love not Poetry or from folly understand it not[3], must say that 'to us that are Christians, in respect of the high end of all, which is the health of our souls, not only Poetry but all other studies of Philosophy are in a manner vain and superfluous[4].' And William Vaughan, who will not have plays suffered in a Commonwealth, but defends Poetry,

---

[1] i. 180. [2] The hardest hit (of many) at the Puritan is Jonson's. See *Discoveries* xii, '*Hypocrita*.' [3] ii. 195. [4] ii. 197.

must yet have it after the purest pattern. 'Sundry times,' he says, 'have I been conversant with such as blasphemed Poetry, by calling it mincing and lying Poetry. But it is no marvel that they thus deride Poetry, since they stick not in this out-worn age to abuse the ministers of God by terming them bookish fellows and Puritans, they themselves not knowing what they mean[1].' There is likely to be some confusion here, in this enthusiasm for Poetry *and* Puritans.

It must be admitted that the main thesis of the Poet-whippers was not fully met by the Apologists. The controversy was carried on from different standpoints. The Puritans had in view the popular literature of the play-house and of Paul's. As men of the people they spoke only of what interested the people. 'Poetry' with them meant Elderton and Tarlton, or bawdy sonnets; 'books' translations of the naughty tales of Italy; 'playgoing' the noisy delights of Shoreditch. The defence of Poetry was in the hands of courtiers and scholars who lived beyond the pale of Bohemia. To Sidney, Puttenham, or Harington those things which they admitted were pleasing neither to gentlemen nor Christians were not the sum of the matter. If Poetry was to be denounced because of this popular travesty, of which they professed to know little and for which perhaps they cared as little, it was necessary to show that she could be defended on broader and better grounds. Hence it is that each party, though in amiable agreement on the viciousness of Vice, argue for and against the claims of Poetry from different premises. And hence, too, our earlier critical literature presents the double paradox—that culture and learning, which were both the most competent force and the real agent in the development of criticism, took no serious heed to the truly national literature with which in the future that

[1] ii 326.

Introduction xxi

criticism must primarily concern itself: and, in the second place, that the defence was based largely on over-sea tradition and Italian practice, which in its more popular application was contemned by both sides. Thus Ascham, who hates things Italianate not less than the monkish *Morte Arthur*, justifies his literary theory by the canons of Italian Humanism in which he had been schooled. The Puritans in their anxiety to exile the too amorous Tuscan were the means of calling in his more learned, perhaps more respectable, brother to defend him against themselves.

III. THE DEFENCE.

The argument for the Defence falls into two main divisions—the historical testimony in favour of Poetry, and the excellence of its nature or character. There is, as we shall see, little originality in the general drift or in the illustrations. It is obvious that the Essayists are constantly borrowing from each other, and often verbatim: it is not less obvious from their selection and arrangement of the leading reasons that they are drawing from outside opinion[1]. There are of course degrees of adaptation—from the absolute 'scissors-and-paste' method of the *Palladis Tamia* to the happily disguised borrowings of the *Apologie for Poetrie*.

On the historical side there are three proofs of the goodness of Poetry: for when it is of hoary antiquity, is found with all peoples, and has enjoyed the favour of the greatest, it is surely good. To those who hold that in the earliest period of the national life men were rather doing things worthy to be written than writing things fit to be done[2], Sidney says, 'What that before time was, I think scarcely *Sphinx* can tell[3].' So thinks Lodge, when reflecting on the drama[4]; so Nash, quoting from Cicero[5]; so Puttenham,

---

[1] See infra, p. lxxi et seq.   [2] i. 187.   [3] Ibid.
[4] i. 80.   [5] i. 328.

when he says that the 'profession and use of Poesy is most ancient from the beginning, and not, as many erroneously suppose, after, but before any civil society was among men[1].' The Poets were the first lawgivers, the first philosophers, and, in due course, the first historians. It is a later refinement, specially commendable to King James VI and the courtier Puttenham, which denies them the right to treat of the grave matters of princes[2].

In all nations, too, there has been 'some feeling of Poetry[3].' As it was the most ancient, so was it the most universal. 'Which two points,' adds Puttenham, 'give to all human inventions and affairs no small credit[4].' Sidney and he have little difficulty in illustrating this by accounts of the poet-loving Turk, Indian, Dane, 'the Perusine, and the very cannibal[5].'

As for the approbation of Poetry by princes and the learned, the citations are certainly ample in Lodge[6], Sidney[7], Webbe[8], Puttenham[9], Harington[10], Chapman[11], and Meres[12]. 'But to speak of all those ... were tedious, and would require a rehearsal of all such in whose time there grew any to credit and estimation in that faculty[13].' This favourite argument by testimonial[14] received an exaggerated importance from the fact that the Puritans had made so much of the opinions of the theologians and philosophers. The obvious retort was to count the votes on the other side: yet the defenders were not whole-hearted in the business. Harington, who feels that the defence of poetry is a supererogation, is content to say that he could bring in such an army of approvers 'as not only the sight but the very sound of them were able to vanquish and dismay the final forces of our adversaries[15].'

---

[1] ii. 6.   [2] i. 221, ii. 33.   [3] i. 153.   [4] ii. 10.   [5] Ibid.
[6] i. 70-1.   [7] i. 192-3.   [8] i. 232-3.   [9] ii. 16-23.   [10] ii. 195.
[11] ii. 302.   [12] ii. 321-2.   [13] i. 233.
[14] Of which Boccaccio's *De Genealogia Deorum* gives an early model. See infra, pp. lxxviii-ix.   [15] ii. 195.

Introduction

They based their defence with more confidence on the nature of Poetry, on its claims as a moral force and as an artistic pleasure. In this section of their Apology they made their first critical experiments. The argument is worked out on different lines; but in no single author, with perhaps the exception of Sidney, is a complete statement attempted. The main points are these:—

(1) Poetry is of divine origin. 'Who thinketh not,' says Lodge, 'that it proceedeth from above?... It is a pretty sentence, yet not so pretty as pithy, *Poeta nascitur, orator fit*[1].' All poets may not be holy[2], yet the poet, *per se*, is *vates*, diviner, foreseer, prophet[3]. He is possessed of the Platonic *furor*[4], or divine rapture[5]. Homer's poems were written 'from a free fury[6].' *Est deus in nobis: agitante calescimus illo*[7]. Harington quizzically refuses to admit the point to debate by saying that Puttenham's 'parcels' of his own verse quoted in his treatise are themselves the best proof that poetry is a gift, not an art[8].

(2) Poetry is an art of imitation, and not a mere empiric of sound and form or the refashioning of traditional material. It is, as Sidney and others claim, ποίησις and μίμησις in a fuller sense than is allowed by their extremer opponents, or understood by the ordinary practitioners, or by young critics who could accept James VI's 'deciphering' of the perfect poet[9]. This appeal to Aristotelian doctrine, through Horace and especially through Scaliger and the Renaissance critics, is of first importance in its effect on the development of criticism in England. It breaks fresh ground for the study of the bases of poetry: and it foreshadows the introduction of aesthetic theory. Though the argument was classical in origin and classical in its first application, it contained *in gremio* the justification of romantic freedom[10].

[1] i. 70–1. [2] e.g. i. 71 [3] i. 154. [4] ii. 3. [5] ii. 297.
[6] ii. 298. [7] See i. 232. [8] ii. 197. [9] i. 211. [10] Infra, p. lx et seq.

(3) The argument of the moral value of Poetry is to a great extent based on the mediaeval doctrine of the Allegory. 'For undoubtedly,' Wilson had said in his *Arte of Rhetorique*, 'there is no one tale among all the Poets, but under the same is comprehended some thing that pertaineth either to the amendment of manners, to the knowledge of truth, to the setting forth of Nature's work, or else to the understanding of some notable thing done. . . . The Poets were wise men and wished in heart the redress of things[1].' This idea runs throughout the essays, alike in the general theory, and in the method used in the interpretation of literary examples. There is, on the one hand, the plain statements of Lodge, following Campanus[2], or of Stanyhurst[3], or the more extreme attitude of Chapman, who upholds the views of Spondanus[4]: on the other, the more reasonable and historical explanation offered by Sidney and Harington. Between these two extremes there is perhaps more than a question of degree. In a sense there is a *volte-face*: or at least the turn has begun. The older view assumes that the *moralitas* is the kernel, and that the fable and poetic imaginings are an outside means to attract the reader to some hidden good. Or, to borrow the familiar Renaissance metaphors, common with the Elizabethans, Poetry is the sugar-coating of the pill, the candy with the dose of rhubarb. The sugar-coating or the candy is there, because there is the necessary pill or rhubarb. In other words, the allegorical usefulness of poetry is its *rationale*, and for that reason it is to be defended as a good thing. On the other hand, it is clear that with the progress of the general defence of Poetry this view becomes less important. Thus Sidney, though he refers to it in his claim for the poet as the right popular philosopher[5], makes little of it: and Harington, in his analysis of the allegorical senses in

---

[1] ed. 1562, f. 99ᵛ.   [2] i. 65.   [3] i. 136.   [4] ii. 297.   [5] i. 167.

which poetry may be read[1], rather emphasizes the attitude of the weaker capacities who take but the pleasantness of the story and the sweetness of the verse. The quite contrary position that imagination first constructs the fable, and thereafter the poet or his commentator or his reader finds the moral, could hardly be established until aesthetic criticism had found its axioms. But we are not far from it, certainly not far from the later theory of poetic freedom. The change was undoubtedly furthered by the increasing attention by the critics to the pleasure-giving function of Poetry. Nor must it be forgotten that the allegorical enthusiasm of the age was of a secondary kind, and that in so far as the majority of writers are interested in the 'rind within the rind,' they often show no more than emblematic or anagrammatic curiosity.

(4) In their rough definitions of the purpose of Poetry the defenders are careful not to subordinate the *dulce* to the *utile*. The end of Poetry is, with Sidney, 'to teach and delight[2].' It is well known, says Nash, 'that delight doth prick men forward to the attaining of knowledge, and that true things are rather admired if they be included in some witty fiction, like to pearls that delight more if they be deeper set in gold[3].' Webbe's plea, which he borrows by admission from Horace, is generally accepted. 'The perfect perfection of poetry is this, to mingle delight with profit in such wise that a reader might by his reading be partaker of both[4].' Puttenham goes further in his account of the subject or matter of Poetry[5] when he names, as one of its functions, 'the common solace of mankind in all his travails and cares of this transitory life'; and claims that 'in this last sort, being used for recreation only, it may allowably bear matter not always of the gravest or of any great commodity or profit, but rather in some sort vain, dissolute,

---

[1] ii. 202-3. [2] i. 158. [3] i. 329. [4] i. 250. [5] ii. 25.

or wanton, so it be not very scandalous and of evil example[1].' Here the friends of poetry found their chief argument: and here too their adversaries, ever suspicious of pleasure, in argument or in practice, found the heresy. For this seductive power as readily leads men to like obscenity as to love honesty. Yet the defenders, though heartily admitting the danger, are in no doubt that the abuse cannot discredit the function or the excellence of its effects. 'In this their argument of abuse,' says Sidney, 'they prove the commendation[2].' The result of this consideration by the defence was that, though they did not go quite so far as to separate the *dulce* from the *utile*, they appeared to give a primary importance to the former. In Sidney's reiteration of the 'delightful teaching[3]' he appears to be laying more stress on the pleasure than on the profit, and in the memorable passage on the Poet as Monarch he is still less equivocal. The Poet 'cometh to you with words sent in delightful proportion, either accompanied with, or prepared for, the well enchanting skill of music; and with a tale forsooth he cometh unto you, with a tale which holdeth children from play, and old men from the chimney corner[4].' Moreover, in Webbe's opinion, 'as the very sum or chiefest essence of Poetry did always for the most part consist in delighting the readers or hearers with pleasure, so, as the number of Poets increased, they still inclined this way rather than the other, so that most of them had special regard to the pleasantness of their fine conceits, whereby they might draw men's minds into admiration of their inventions, more than they had to the profit or commodity that the readers should reap by their works[5].' Puttenham caps his fore-quoted defence of toys by a more remarkable passage at the con-

[1] ii. 25.   [2] i. 187.   [3] e.g. i. 197, 200.
[4] i. 172.   [5] i. 235-6.

clusion of his quaint chapter on 'Proportion in Figure[1],' and pushes the Puritan's logic *ad absurdum*.

'All is but a iest, all dust, all not worth two peason:
For why in mans matters is neither rime nor reason.'

The effect of this separation, or emphasis, of the pleasure-giving function was undoubtedly to quicken the theory of Poetry as an Art. We find hints of this in Sidney[2], even in writers like Nash, who lay stress on the 'profit' in the poetical account. 'Nothing is more odious,' says the latter, 'than the artless tongue of a tedious dolt, which dulleth the delight of hearing, and slacketh the desire of remembering[3].' Yet the expression of a general theory is but half-conscious: we shall see the underlying principle more clearly in their practical schemes of reform. Sidney, who reaches nearest to the root of this matter, comes to it by natural sympathy rather than by critical insight. When he points to the danger of poesy which 'by the reason of his sweet charming force can do more hurt than any other army of words[4],' he has no inkling of the problem of the self-destruction of Art[5]. He is merely admitting that abuse is possible.

In support of these views of the character of Poetry the writers added the well-worn comparisons with Philosophy and History, and answered, in more or less stereotyped fashion, the charges of Agrippa[6], that poets are liars, wantons, and wasters of wise men's time. The persistency of these comparisons is not less striking than their lack of originality. The defensive character of the Essays probably gave an undue importance to this line of argu-

---

[1] ii. 115–16.   [2] e.g. i. 183.   [3] i. 335.   [4] i. 187.
[5] Supra, p. xviii.
[6] Agrippa, who is named by Sidney, was not the first framer of these, as Boccaccio's writings show. See infra, p. lxxix.

ment, by which they sought to make clear that the Poet must be worthy of honour, if he can be shown to be better than the honoured Philosopher or the honoured Historian. So Sidney makes bold to prove that he is the monarch of all sciences[1]; and Puttenham that he is 'above all other artificers scientific or mechanical[2].' We have perhaps lost the perspective of this interminable squabble from the days of Aristotle; but, though we may think lightly of the whole retort, we must at least acknowledge its historical propriety. We have only to look at the authors represented in such collections as the *Artis Penus Historicae*[3] to see how the defenders of 'poor Poetry' were forced, even as a matter of form, to set the balance aright.

It was probably this historical craze which gave point to the old charge that Poets are liars, and compelled the critics' reply. Lodge, who finds the imputation supported 'by no small bird, even Aristotle himself,' and by 'severe Cato,' answers by the aid of his Lactantius[4]. Sidney in his reply is again comparative; 'the poet is the least liar[5],' certainly less so than the Historian, who can 'hardly escape from many lies[6].' The Poet 'never affirmeth[7]': he 'never maketh any circles about your imagination, to conjure you to believe for true what he writes[8].' This is endorsed by Harington, who enlarges on the importance of invention or fiction as one of the main components, and the glory, of Poetry. And after all, as Sidney had said, 'a feigned example hath as much force to teach as a true example[9].' Yet the taunt is ever recurring, not only from the natural Puritan who finds consolation in Socrates's being 'ill brought up to poesy, because he loved the truth[10],' but from others of more generous mind, who are yet strongly prejudiced on some particular point. Thus Nash

---

[1] i. 172. [2] ii. 3. [3] 2 vols., Basle, 1579. [4] i. 73. [5] i. 184.
[6] Ibid. [7] i. 185. [8] Ibid. [9] i. 169. [10] i. 342.

is seldom more angry than when he is speaking of mediaeval Romance as 'that forgotten legendary licence of lying[1].'

That poets are wanton is of course one of the main topics of the Gosson-Lodge controversy[2], and is fully met by Sidney[3], Nash[4], and Harington[5], who readily admit the danger when Cupido is lawlessly crept in. Gosson's plea that Poetry makes men effeminate directly inspires Sidney's memorable countercuff that it, above all things, is the companion of camps[6]. Harington, with Ariosto as his illustration to hand, shows that there may be even literary *decorum* in 'the persons of those that speak lasciviously,' that 'obscenousness' may be altogether a matter of good or bad interpretation of the poems, and that the Puritans who so disregard the context convict themselves of the failing of the chaste wife of Brutus[7]. The hackneyed statement that Plato banished poets, so that youth might not be corrupted, is easily answered by several of the writers[8].

To the third, that the study of poetry is a waste of time and a pleasure to fools, Sidney and Harington reply with some word-chopping and sarcasm, which, though not a convincing reply to a Precisian, is reasonably sufficient. Sidney ends the controversy curtly—'but I still and utterly deny that there is sprung out of earth a more fruitful knowledge[9]'; and Harington concludes his answer by expressing the doubt whether the charge be worth the answering[10]. Puttenham, who is firmly convinced of the dignity of Poesy and approves all manner of toys, even 'pillars' and 'fuzies,' has of course no doubt of the silliness of the proposition.

The pleas for Poetry in the general are supplemented by others dealing with special forms or subjects, or with

---

[1] i. 323. [2] i. 73, &c. [3] i. 183, 186. [4] i. 332. [5] ii. 209.
[6] i. 188. [7] ii. 209. [8] Cf. infra, lxxii, lxxix. [9] i. 184. [10] ii. 208.

topics arising from the consideration of them. The chief interest of these more particular discussions lies, as we shall see, in their critical intention. The essayists, unhampered by the necessity of answering a vaguely expressed attack on the whole art, condescend to the more detailed examination of one or other form; and in these separate studies they give us the positive side of Elizabethan criticism. It is thus in the special analyses of the dramatic forms, or heroic poetry, or the art of translation, that they, to our eyes, not only best express the character of the onslaught of the poet-whippers, but lay the foundations of later speculation on literary principles. In the drama, for example, which is the chief area of conflict, it is a minor matter to learn how they met Gosson's pronouncement that morality is impossible in the play-house, or the quasi-literary absurdity that the plays of Buchanan or the *Christus* ascribed to Nazianzen were written 'dialoguewise' for the closet. On the other hand, it is clear that the purpose of the essayists in the detailed treatment of certain portions was less in the interest of critical theory than in support of their side in the controversy with the poet-haters. For they argued that the excellence possible in each and all, whether tragedy, comedy, heroic poetry, pastoral, elegy, satire, epigram, or anagram, had a cumulative value in proving the excellence of Poetry itself. Sidney, Webbe, and the others distinctly imply that the poet is not merely the monarch of all the arts, but that his empire is wide and self-sufficing. Poetry, says Webbe, 'is not debarred from any matter which may be expressed by pen or speech[1].' The consuming sense of the dignity and compass of the art is the most striking characteristic of its most eloquent defenders, who seldom, if ever, forget to refer to these things, even when they bury themselves in professional

[1] i. 249. Cf. Chapman, *Epist.* to *First XII Books of Homer*, ll. 118-19.

problems of technique. Though their large assurance sometimes led them into critical blind-alleys, as in their confusion of the functions of verse and prose, it supplied the staying power to these beginnings in criticism, and moreover was thoroughly appropriate to the circumstances. Nor was their superior manner of debate, and an occasional irritation at their opponents, less appropriate to the occasion. In feeling with Harington that the whole matter was but the Sophister's praise of Hercules [1], they intimated an intellectual confidence which promised well for an English doctrine of taste.

IV. THE CLASSICAL PURPOSE.

The apologetic character of the essays is, however, of less importance to the present purpose. It is at most only of historical interest, as a clue to the cause of the remarkable attention to a great literary problem. Their true value lies in the evidence which they give of an incipient, and to some extent unconscious, effort towards an appreciation of the principles of literature, and towards a systematic investigation of the capabilities of the craft of English.

Proof of the conviction of the critics that their house must be put in order need not be sought in their classification of literary types and forms. The favourite groupings by style, as in Ascham [2], Sidney [3], Webbe [4], or Puttenham [5], by subject, most elaborately in Meres's *Comparative Discourse*, or by prosodic forms, are little else than the accentuation of a mediaeval fashion which is observed in the earlier Renaissance stages of all European literatures. We find the first positive evidence of the awakening criticism in the dissatisfaction with certain

[1] ii. 194. [2] i. 23-6. [3] i. 175. [4] i. 249. [5] ii. 155.

existing conditions and in the acknowledgement that English is in transition.

The persistency of contemporary reference to this chaos and to the necessity of some immediate interference is perhaps the most striking feature of these early efforts. They are the topic of every writer, and they supply the *motif* for reform, however much the ultimate purpose of each critic may differ. The vocabulary of denunciation has the Elizabethan fullness. Ascham laments the 'fond books,' the 'lewd and rude rhymes,' sold in every shop[1]. 'Good God,' says Stanyhurst, 'what a fry of *wooden rythmours* doth swarm in stationers' shops[2]': and Webbe thinks sadly of the 'infinite fardels of printed pamphlets wherewith this country is pestered[3].' 'E. K.' anathematizes 'the rakehelly rout of ragged rhymers[4],' and Sidney, who mourns that 'an over-faint quietness should seem to strew the house for poets[5],' candidly admits, 'I that, before ever I durst aspire unto the dignity, am admitted into the company of the paper-blurrers, do find the very true cause of our wanting estimation in wanting desert; taking upon us to be poets in despite of Pallas[6].' It is a world of 'rude smatterers[7],' 'brainless bussards[8],' 'pottical, poetical heads,' who rhyme 'in commendation of Copper noses or Bottle Ale[9]'; and full enough of fooleries, without these 'new-new writers, the loadstones of the press, wonderfully beholden to the Ass[10].' 'Such is this golden age wherein we live,' quoth Nash, who elsewhere bids the poets put out their rush-candles[11], 'and so replenished with golden asses of all sorts, that, if learning had lost itself in a grove of genealogies, we need do no more but set an old goose over half a dozen pottle pots (which are as it were

[1] i. 2, 4, 31.   [2] i. 141.   [3] i. 226.   [4] i. 131.
[5] i. 194.   [6] i. 195.   [7] i. 229.   [8] i. 322.
[9] i. 246.   [10] ii. 231, 238.   [11] ii. 225.

the eggs of invention) and we shall have such a breed of books within a little while after, as will fill all the world with the wild fowl of good wits¹.' Nor does the verse lag behind the prose in hunting down the abuse: witness Jonson in his *Every Man in his Humour*², as in his *Discoveries*; or Daniel in his *Musophilus*³, and in his dedication to the Countess of Pembroke, who is to preserve the Muses from 'these hideous beasts Oblivion and Barbarism⁴.' So fly the words: yet the censors claim that they are not severe. When Webbe has recorded the 'pottical, poetical' gibe, he amiably quotes 'E.K.'s censure, because he would not be 'too broad' with them in his own speech⁵. Though it may be suspected that this long-drawn denunciation is directed chiefly against the vulgar crowd of Martinist and Eldertonian pamphlets, it will be found, on closer examination, that such an assumption is too narrow.

Their explanation of this barbarism and their suggestion for its cure are not less clearly stated. 'Marry,' says Sidney, 'they that delight in Poesy itself should seek to know what they do, and how they do. . . . A Poet no industry can make, if his own genius be not carried unto it. . . . Yet confess I always that as the fertilest ground must be manured, so must the highest flying wit have a Daedalus to guide him. That Daedalus, they say, both in this and in other, hath three wings to bear itself up into the air of due commendation: that is, Art, Imitation, and Exercise. But these, neither artificial rules nor imitative patterns, we much cumber ourselves withal⁶.' Classicists like Harvey plead for the bringing of our language 'into Art⁷,' and protest that 'right artificiality is not mad-brained, or ridiculous, or absurd, or blasphemous, or monstrous⁸.' Webbe is con-

---

¹ i. 227. ² ii. 388. ³ Ed. Grosart, i. ll. 227, 239, 446-9.
⁴ Ibid. i. p. 53. ⁵ i. 246. ⁶ i. 195. ⁷ i. 102. ⁸ ii. 234.

vinced that cure is possible, and that reformation can come only when English literature is freed from the 'cankered enmity of curious custom[1].' With Puttenham Poetry must be 'corrected and reformed by discreet judgments,' and with no less cunning and curiosity than Greek and Latin. To disallow this improvement in the most ancient of arts is but to admit that Adam and Eve's aprons were the gayest garments, and the shepherd's tent the best housing[2]. Poetry, he believes, may be an Art in our vulgar, and that very methodical and commendable: indeed, the whole aim of the author of the *Arte of English Poesie* is to bring order into the literary chaos, and to show, in Nash's words, 'what an obloquy these impudent incipients in Arts are unto Art[3].' In the 'rabblement' of English the critics see a cause why Poetry is in disrepute, and why their general defence, which they feel to be somewhat of a supererogation, is justified. But they do not rest there. Their confidence that all will yet be well with English Poetry, the immediate recognition by all groups of critics of the first signs of revival in contemporary work—a recognition which has proved to be historically just,—their enthusiasm in experiment, and their general good sense in the discussion of its results, show that the Matter of English Literature was now acknowledged to be a subject for profitable reflection. The very seriousness with which they approach the problem, and their own never-ending protests that the Essays are too haphazard and unworthy of the occasion, are symptoms of vital importance.

It is not too much to say that the intention is strongly *classical*. When 'E. K.' in his eulogy of Spenser takes upon himself to tell how the New Poet differs from most English writers, he points out that his work is 'well grounded, finely framed, and strongly trussed up together[4].' This

[1] i. 228.   [2] ii. 24.   [3] i. 334.   [4] i. 131.

Introduction

is somewhat inconsistent with the accepted judgement on the author of the *Faerie Queene* (though it must be remembered that it is with the *Shepheards Calender* that the critics are chiefly concerned), but the rightness or wrongness of it is of less importance than the fact that they looked for these qualities as an explanation of superiority. In other words, what was disorder in mediaeval and contemporary literature is in Spenser changed to order. Poetry, they believe, cannot be good, unless it show the discipline of Art. This admitted, it was the function of criticism to teach that discipline, to tell lovers of poetry 'what they do, and how they do.'

Ascham appears to be the first in English to give definite expression to this doctrine in the notable passage on Εὐφυής[1], which supplied the *motif* and title to Lyly's work, and through that, as well as directly, left its mark on Elizabethan literature. The idea is of course not original[2], but the credit for its more complete expression and its introduction to English letters is undoubtedly Ascham's[3]. It must be noted that the proposition is not exclusively literary, or rather that its literary application is but part of a more comprehensive conception. For literature is to be 'well-grown,' to show the just proportions of art in subject, technique, and intention, just as the human body and the body politic are to express the ideal harmony of line and plan. The larger notion runs throughout the Essays, from Ascham's own reflections on the rude writing of men who are themselves rude[4] and his reminiscences of Cheke's conversations[5] to Puttenham's defence of his inclusion in his *Arte of Poesie*[6] of the question of decencies in general conduct.

The acknowledgement of the necessity of discipline, implied in this classical argument, gives a point of contact

---

[1] i. 1-2.   [2] See infra, lxxii; i. 349.   [3] See note to i. 349.   [4] i. 6-7.
[5] i. 40-1.   [6] See the opening sentence of chap. xxiv, ii. 181.

between the critics and their Puritan adversaries. But they approach from quite opposite directions, and their agreement is, after all, merely accidental. It is more important to note that in the acceptance of this principle we find the explanation of the strong dislike of mediaeval literature and Italian fashions, two of the most remarkable of the *idées fixes* of the Elizabethans[1]. Other causes, as we have seen, contributed to the unpopularity of the Romances: they were 'bold bawdry,' they were the amusement of abbey-lubbers, they were jingles of rhymes; but they were also the disordered product of a disordered literary age. They had no decency in proportions, no coherence of episodes. The Italian, if he could not be charged with barbarousness, was, apart from being a danger to English morals, an extravagant in his literary motives and literary forms, as he was in his dress and social habits. And the Italianate Englishman, whether a mere adventurer or an enthusiast for Italian tales and sonnets, if not always a *diavolo incarnato*, was at least bad company. It is quite clear that beyond the growing national feeling against foreign affectations in public and private life—which must have had its effect in the determination of literary taste—there was the more purely critical dislike of the licence and curiosity of Italian romanticism. The combination of these impressions, that the Middle Ages were discredited because they were barbarous and Gothic, and that the contemporary inflow of Italianate habits and ideas was no less disorderly and dangerous, supplemented by the full confidence in the sufficiency and possibilities of English, forced the critics to some immediate consideration of the cure, especially as they found ready to hand, in Renaissance literature, an apparently perfect rule of health.

It may be premised that the first endeavours towards

---

[1] See supra, xvi, xvii.

reform would be concerned with technical details rather than with general principles. Criticism could not begin otherwise, and a criticism which was to a great extent derived was at first attracted to the nicer points of the canon. Yet despite the attention to the things of vocabulary and prosody, it is possible to unravel the general principles which are threaded through these miscellanies, and thereafter to show how one or other of these minor problems relates itself to a larger critical purpose.

The saving quality of this incipient classicism, for so let us call it, is that it is not extreme. There is much good sense, even in the most partisan discussions on the reformation of English prosody, and in the most ample borrowings from the rules of the Italian critics. Not only is the whole matter tentative, as the historical eye cannot fail to see, but it is acknowledged to be so by the essayists themselves. They have a genuine conviction of their inefficiency, and though they play with dogma, which in the immediate future became the creed of a militant criticism, they seldom forget that they cannot claim to be more than experimenters. 'God help us,' says Harvey to Spenser, after recitation of a set of 'pawlting bungrely' verses, 'you and I are wisely employed (are we not?) when our pen and ink, and time and wit, and all runneth away in this goodly yonkerly vein: as if the world had nothing else for us to do, or we were born to be the only Nonproficients and Nihilagents of the world[1].' So far as the critics are minded to expound the classical reform of English, they are content to prove its necessity rather than to be dictatorial in defining a new body of laws. 'And that is enough for me,' says Puttenham, 'seeking but to fashion an art, and not to finish it: which time only and custom have authority to do[2].' The moderation of the Elizabethan view is the more remarkable, since it was

[1] i. 116.   [2] ii. 130.

held that the time had come to English when she must prove that she can match the greatness of Greece and Rome, and not less clearly admitted that in these rivals were to be found the alpha and omega of literary perfection.

The classical quality of Elizabethan criticism is disclosed in its main theses that English literature must improve itself by attention to suitable models, and that the most absolute matters for consideration are restraint and symmetry. The necessity of studying and imitating the masterpieces begins with Ascham's plea in his *Scholemaster*. His memorable account of a conversation with Cheke[1] defines the character of the new discipline. The 'ancients' offer 'experience,' which cannot but be useful to a youthful vernacular: but there is to be no blind imitation of them, and certainly no superficial copy of what is after all but mannerism. Writing is not to be 'more Art than nature and more labour than Art[2],' for a writer's uncontented care to write better than he can is as hateful as disorder. This qualification is but the general expression of that dislike of unnatural effort which they found grown to such enormity in the archaic, inkhorn, and over-sea affectations of the age[3]. Imitation must be reasonable[4]; it is a training of the judgement, for writers must not be common porters and carriers[5]; there is in this doctrine no shackling of the wit, no hindering of the course of a man's good nature[6]. Rome herself had her 'unmeasurable confluence of scribblers[7].' In all this there is good sense, and it was well for the future that Cheke and Ascham, who gave the password to their contemporaries, had put it so. Harvey, though he knows the value of a 'good pattern' to the Poet[8], shows not less clearly than they do that the adaptation of Method must

[1] i. 40, &c. [2] i. 40. [3] See infra, lv et seq. [4] i. 9–10.
[5] i. 19. [6] i. 10. [7] ii. 363. [8] i. 109.

proceed with a lively knowledge of its propriety to the case in hand, and that the vitality of the model, and not its mere *corpus*, must be transferred to the canvas. 'He must not dream of perfection that improveth not the perfectest Art with the most perfect industry[1].' 'Perfect use worketh masteries ... : singular practice [is] the only singular and admirable workman of the world[2].' There is no mistaking the deep purpose of this classical appeal: it is at bottom that English may draw upon the life and spirit of the great things of antiquity, not that she should become the ape of Greece and Rome, simply because she is heartily sick of her present confusion. When Chapman sees in Homer a means to the absolute redress of all the unmanly degeneracies of his age, he is thinking only of the direct vigour and free soul of the old poet which will cure the fantasies of a transposed and Italianate England[3]. And though Campion rather spoiled by bad logic his excellent aphorism that the world is made by symmetry and proportion[4], his error was confined to the technical details of prosody. The critics had convinced themselves that symmetry and proportion must be the corner-stones of the new edifice: they saw how Greece and Rome had builded. So far they were wise: but they were wiser in refusing to be mere copyists.

The essayists are explicit on this point. Indeed, there is nothing which is so often and so strenuously urged throughout these pages than their repugnance to a rigid classical canon. They are suspicious of 'ram's-horn rules of direction[5],' of a 'rabble of scholastical precepts[6],' of 'strict and regular forms[7],' of the cumber of 'artificial rules and imitative patterns[8].' Even in the narrower problem of the reformed versifying we find Harvey disclaiming any intention to lay down a general Art[9]: and

[1] ii. 237. [2] ii. 236. [3] ii. 302-3. [4] ii. 329. [5] i. 336.
[6] ii. 176. [7] ii. 393. [8] i. 195. [9] i. 103, 122.

Stanyhurst[1] and King James VI[2] are against a final judgement. Daniel, who perhaps reaches deepest to the philosophical bases of criticism, enters a general caveat against arrogance, and draws attention to the 'unnecessary intrications' which confound the understanding—'as if Art were ordained to afflict Nature[3].' So open-minded is this defender of rhyme against the attacks by one of its happiest exponents, that he can admit that it should be used with great moderation. He sees that the tyranny of licence may be as great as the tyranny of a code[4].

If the main interest of this criticism is that it is classical, whether as a preliminary symptom of later academic theory or as an instrument for the reform of contemporary literature, we must note that, taken in its most general bearings, this criticism is as yet quite unprejudiced. In other words, we should have had no reason to assume, had we been ignorant of later history, that the forces of classicism were destined to become paramount. On the other hand, our knowledge of later developments makes it clear that we have in these propositions the true awakening of the classical spirit in English literature. And it is only when we have searched these beginnings and the work of the neglected successors of these essayists in the first half of the seventeenth century that we find ourselves in a position to interpret aright Johnson's dictum that Dryden is the Father of English Criticism. Then, and then only, do we know how much Dryden and his age drew from later continental sources through French channels, and how much from earlier English critical tradition, however or whenever his Elizabethan masters had been themselves inspired[5].

Though the classical quality of these Essays is sug-

---

[1] i. 144.   [2] i. 210.   [3] ii. 365.
[4] See infra, 'Romantic Qualities,' p. lx et seq.
[5] It is probably more than a coincidence that makes the questions of

gested rather than carefully defined, it is none the less true that, even in their brief compass, some progression in its application may be observed. Jonson's criticism is not Sidney's, nor is it Ascham's: and the difference between these must be expressed in terms of a greater or less classical intention. Jonson marks the close of the first stage; but the full statement of his position is outside the scope of these volumes, and more fitly belongs to Jacobean and Caroline criticism, to which it is the natural introduction.

While therefore the leading propositions of Elizabethan criticism are classical only in a general sense, there are certain special problems in which, through the heat of controversy or the narrow area of argument, the classical character is thrown into stronger relief. These discussions have a value of their own, for though their relation to fundamental principles was not readily, if at all, recognized, and though some, such as the question of the hexameter, could not but be of passing interest, they represent the laboratory experience of independent workers in a young science.

V. THE SPECIAL PROBLEMS.

1. *Decorum*.

One of the most persistent topics is the adjustment of the classical notion of *Decorum* to English style. It recurs in the discussion of almost every 'kind,' but chiefly of the dramatic forms. In its most general acceptation it is identical with what has been understood by proportion, 'decency,' the truly euphuistic, or, as Puttenham puts

---

'Barbarism,' 'Monosyllables,' and 'Prosody' interesting to Dryden in his *Discourse concerning the Original and Progress of Satire*, his *Dedication of the Aeneis*, and his Preface to *Albion and Albanius*; and, later, to Shaftesbury in his *Advice to an Author*.

it excellently in his chapter on this subject[1], 'the good grace of everything in his kind.' 'We in our vulgar,' he says, 'call it by a scholastical term *decency*; our own Saxon English term is *seemliness*. . . .: we call it also *comeliness*, for (so runs Puttenham's philology) the delight it bringeth coming towards us, and to that purpose may be called *pleasant approach*[2].' In an earlier chapter he points out the necessity of style being fashioned to the matter, so that '*decorum* and good proportion' be kept in every respect[3]. This notion appears in nearly all the Essays. Ascham shows its importance in his scheme of perfect imitation of classical authors[4]; Gascoigne sees its breach in the mingling of merry jests in serious matter[5]; 'E. K.' notes its due observance in the construction and details of the *Shepheards Calender*[6], as Stanyhurst does in the *Aeneid*[7]; and Puttenham fails to find it in parts of Stanyhurst's translation[8]. It is intended in King James's plea for *vocabula artis*[9]. The term is of course not understood in the modern restricted sense. Harington defends the naughty passages in Ariosto at the expense of Virgil, and shows that there may be *decorum* 'in the persons of those that speak lasciviously[10].' All are but re-expressing the Horatian maxims, either directly or through media such as Fabricius's *Catholica*, which Webbe has translated[11].

As a problem of dramatic style it assumes greater importance, and is the common element in the varied discussions on the character and *differentia* of tragedy and comedy, on the mixed tragi-comedy, on the doctrine of the Unities, on the development of the notion of the Humours. The main charge against contemporary stagecraft, in the few places where the critics refer to the

[1] ii. 173, et seq. [2] ii. 174. [3] i. 155. [4] i. 23. [5] i. 48.
[6] i. 128. [7] i. 137. [8] ii. 178. [9] i. 218.
[10] ii. 215. [11] i. 290, &c.

romantic drama, is its lack of *decorum* in one or more ways; and the attempts at positive criticism of the English examples of the classical type are concerned with the exposition of their observance or neglect of 'true decency.' Robert Wilmot exactly expresses the critical attitude in the Address prefixed to *Tancred and Gismund* (1591), where he warns his Gismund not to 'straggle in her plumes abroad, but to contain herself within the walls of your house; so I am sure she shall be safe from the tragedian tyrants of our time.' Gascoigne, who for *decorum's* sake divided his *Discourse of Promos and Cassandra* into two comedies[1], shows how the Englishman in his play-making is 'out of order'; Sidney follows suit[2]; and Jonson condemns these 'ill customs of the age[3],' as he does later its 'scenical strutting and furious vociferation[4].'

The criticism of the mixed kinds of Drama is the effect of a double set of influences—classical example, enforced by the definitions of the Renaissance commentators, and distrust of the contemporary Romantic Drama in England. The domination of the former is first indicated by Ascham, who bases his judgement of the excellence of plays on the 'precepts' of Aristotle and Horace and the examples of Euripides, Sophocles, and Seneca[5]; but it receives its fuller acknowledgement from Sidney, who may be said to be the first to enuntiate the formulae of Elizabethan dramatic criticism. He and his contemporaries, excepting Ascham, are in their views on tragedy more exclusively Aristotelian and Senecan: for comedy their models are Plautus and Terence or the Terentian Scholia. The hard-and-fast distinction between tragedy and comedy, which is a Renaissance tradition, appears

---

[1] i. 58.   [2] i. 199.
[3] ii. 389. For other references, see notes to this and the preceding passages.   [4] *Discoveries*, lxv, '*Ingeniorum Discrimina.*'   [5] i. 23.

in the definitions given in Webbe and Puttenham, and is suggested in Sidney. It is probably unnecessary here to restate these well-known differences, especially as the texts are quite explicit[1], but it is important to note that the rigidity of these canons, as incorporated in the English *ars poetica*, was one of the main causes of the not less rigid censure of English dramatic practice. The objections which came most naturally to the classicists were that English was not careful in its differentiation of kinds, that it mixed the tragic and comic purposes, that it neglected the propriety of the characters and the relationship of each with its neighbours, and that it was careless of the so-called Unities in the development of the plot. It is interesting to observe that this criticism is to some extent an academic anticipation of what became later a practical problem to English dramatists in the Comedy of Humours, and in the Rules of the Dramatic Unities. Indeed, all the later classical manner, as all this Elizabethan criticism, was based on a more or less acute appreciation of the virtues of *decorum*. Sidney is somewhat inconsistent in his argument against mixed kinds, for he says in one passage that 'if severed they be good, the conjunction cannot be hurtful[2]'; but it is easy to see from his later utterances, despite a certain romantic predisposition, hinted rather than expressed, that his sense of literary decency is jarred by the matching of hornpipes and funerals, and by the intrusion of the clownish element in the so-called tragi-comedy. There is a suspicion in his case that it is less a reasoned objection against the combination of the different elements than a courtly dislike of the vulgar buffoon *per se* and of the vulgar associations of the contemporary stage. He

---

[1] See Spingarn, *Lit. Crit.*, pp. 283-90; H. Symmes, *Les Débuts de la Critique Dramatique*, &c., Paris, 1903, passim; and infra, i. pp. 391-2, 398-400, &c.   [2] i. 174.

more readily disapproves these forms because they do not appear to be countenanced in the statelier drama and more learned criticism to which he is of necessity attracted. In his pronouncement on the Unities, the neglect of which is his chief fault with the well-esteemed *Gorboduc*, he formulates a doctrine which, though disregarded by the Elizabethan Romantic Drama, passed into English criticism, and is always present, in a more or less definite way, in the later history of that criticism. The fruit of the doctrine which required *decorum* in character came early in the Humorous Comedy of Ben Jonson, and lingered for a time in the seventeenth century[1]. It too, though discredited by later playwrights, has never lost its influence in later criticism, even outside the more strictly classical eighteenth century.

In the other literary forms Elizabethan criticism finds small opportunity: but in so far as it defines or ventures on commentary it is essentially classical. Thus in the references to Heroic Poetry, such as are given by Sidney, Webbe, Puttenham, Harington, and Campion, there is the restatement, at second or third hand, and probably without knowledge of the source, that it is 'the most accomplished kind of Poetry,' i.e. στασιμώτατον καὶ ὀγκωδέστατον[2]. But Harington goes further and makes the first contact between English criticism and Aristotle on this topic. He is not content in his panegyric of Ariosto with the expected comparison with Virgil, in which Ariosto would have had the better of the Roman, but he meets those who 'reduce all heroical poems unto the method of Homer and certain precepts of Aristotle' by showing how Ariosto fulfils every requirement. With regard to the latter he is quite certain. 'As for Aristotle's rules, I take it he hath followed them very strictly[3]': and he proceeds to prove this by Ariosto's

---

[1] See note, ii. p. 462.
[2] See notes, ii. pp. 43 (l. 21), 338 (l. 2).   [3] ii. 216.

attention to three things, the historical basis, the credibility of the narrative, and the περιπέτεια[1]. Yet the main interest of Heroic Poetry to these defenders of Poetry is that it offers a standing refutation of the charge of wantonness, for 'of all kind of poesy the heroical is least infected therewith[2].' It at least satisfied the broader claims of *decorum*. It was left to a later period of English criticism, to Dryden and his age, to feel the professional classical influence of Le Bossu, Rapin, and the French specialists in epical theory. The comments on the Pastoral, Elegy, Lyric, Satire, Epigram, and other kinds are slight, and are, especially in Sidney's *Apologie* and the more formal *artes poeticae* of Webbe and Puttenham, a mere echo of Latin and neo-Latin opinion. When Webbe gives his list, he appears to be not less concerned to illustrate his view that 'Poetry is not debarred from any matter which may be expressed by pen or speech[3]' than to discuss the differences of the kinds.

It is, however, in the discussions of problems of even more detailed and technical interest that the real force of the classical influence is felt. These arguments are concerned with two main topics, the reconstruction of English Prosody—the 'reform of English versifying,' as the pioneers of the Areopagus called it, and the purification of English from archaism, inkhornism, and over-sea affectation.

2. *Prosody*.

No subject obtrudes itself more than Prosody. Even in the Essays which are not intended to be exclusively interested in it, there are continual references and digressions to some part of it, and in especial to the establishment of the so-called Hexameter. This matter is indeed an obsession of the Elizabethan mind; and in it we find the most positive evidence of a classicizing purpose. It

---

[1] ii. 216. [2] ii. 209. [3] Supra, p. xxx and note.

is confessed that here, if anywhere, something must be done by way of reform, and it is as readily taken for granted by the greater number of the writers that something can be done. Their grievances were more patent. To them the older verse, Chaucer's excepted, was poor enough, and the Eldertonian doggerel plentiful enough: and the revel of even the better poets in Italian stanzas was the despair of the least censorious. The cure was at hand, though the measure of its success on the continent was not considered in the hurry to stay the spasms of ingenuity[1] and restore English to prosodic *decorum*. Not the least remarkable feature of this special controversy, and of the poets' experimental interest in it, is its brief life, which begins and ends within the limits of these volumes. When Daniel struck his blow the craze was at the point of death, for Campion, who incited Daniel, was a belated theorist; and the curious preface to the *First Booke of the Preservation of King Henry the VII*[2] is the enthusiasm of a monomaniac out of touch with the times. The effects of the discussion continued to be felt, and may be seen in later experiments in better though not less inappropriate hexameters, down to our own day: but the problem over which the Elizabethans fought so well must be considered, both in its intention and in its specific terms, as a strictly Elizabethan matter—an episode in critical development which derives its meaning from Elizabethan conditions.

The proposition of the classicists resolved itself into three parts: that the metrical chaos was due largely to the use of rhyme; that the accentual structure of the line was monotonous and should be changed for quantitative variety; and that a uniform orthography and a rule of pronunciation was necessary. They are mixed up in the different arguments of the classicists. Not a few of the writers make the discrediting of rhyme a necessary

[1] Cf. i. 224, 225.   [2] See i. pp. 377-8.

preliminary to their reform of the measures. Harvey sees the honour of the hexameter in being the 'high controller of rhymes[1].' It is not impossible that the philological confusion of rhyme and rhythm, as shown in Puttenham[2] and others, may have put some of those who honoured the hexameter in a false position towards the function of rhyme.

Ascham, in repeating Cheke's opinion, set the fashion of abuse, and he also to a great extent prescribed the terms to his successors. To them the 'rude beggarly rhyming' was a foreign thing, and the heritage of the Goths and Huns; and English poets in following it rather than the 'true versifying' of the Greeks had eaten acorns with swine, when they might have freely eaten wheaten bread amongst men[3]. There can be no doubt that much of the dislike of rhyme had been nourished by the rhyming Latin verses of the mediaeval church. Webbe[4] and Puttenham[5] say as much, and the latter, though he is by no means an opponent, recognizes the impropriety of this Gothic intrusion in Latin poetry. Moreover, as such lines were generally the 'idle invention of monastical men[6],' they were less commendable to the Renaissance temper. To a man of Harvey's turn of mind there could be no allowance, but he is less severe in his attack on rhyme than on the loose rhythm of the line; and this gives some point to Nash's taunt that he was clapped in the Fleet for a rhymer[7]. The details of the arguments for and against rhyme do not concern us in this place: all that can be said against it will be found in Campion's Essay, and all for it, and in the best possible manner, in Daniel's reply. Not a few cast side glances of reproof at rhyme, as if it were responsible for the mischief in metre; but the historical writers, and especially Puttenham, are inclined in its

[1] ii. 230.   [2] ii. 81.   [3] i. 30.   [4] i. 240.   [5] ii. 11–15.
[6] ii. 14.   [7] ii. 241.

favour. The most curious fact in the whole controversy is Spenser's and Campion's rôles as anti-rhymers. Fortunately in both cases theory was divorced from their general practice; and it is possible to make too much of Spenser's college gossip with Harvey[1], for he appears to be but half-hearted in his critical interest in their burlesque toys. Campion's attitude is, as Daniel himself hints, difficult to understand, though it is the extremeness of his special pleading rather than his demand for prosodic revision that is unintelligible. Later criticism has been seldom more superficial than when it has condemned these critical experiments as foolishness. Their value is not to be measured by the metrical illustrations which accompanied them, perhaps between jest and earnest[2]. Daniel's judgement set the matter at rest for a while: when rhyme again involves the critics, in the seventeenth century, the problem is restricted to its usefulness in one literary form. To the historical student the controversy has another and all-important interest of which the Elizabethans were quite unconscious. It does not appear to have been suggested to any one of them that in their efforts to be rid of the jingle of English metres they were working for the recognition of blank verse, and were in reality justifying it on the side of theory. They are not at fault because they had not the gift of prophecy, nor because they lacked insight in connecting their plans with the beginnings of that later triumph of English. Yet so far were they out that they did not understand Surrey's 'strange metre.' Not only did they fail to perceive how different it was from the metre of such a piece as Gascoigne's *Steele Glas*; but the stumbling Webbe thought it was written in *hexametrum epicum*[3].

The plea for the 'new versifying' shows the classical influence in a more constructive way. It follows naturally

[1] See i. 380 (note). [2] i. 245. [3] i. 283.

on the attack on rhyme, for by the law of compensation it was necessary to find some new rhythm within the line to make good the loss: and the absence of unrhymed verse, or the ignorance of the possibilities of Surrey's example, made the transition to out-and-out classicism not only probable but quite reasonable. The first symptoms of the 'hexameter fury[1]' appear in Ascham[2], who, while admitting that the dactyl is difficult to manage in English on account of the monosyllabic richness of the language, thinks that the *carmen iambicum* may be naturalized[3]. But the impetus to the movement came from the Areopagus, of which we have a vague account in the Spenser-Harvey correspondence[4]. The inspirer of these deliberations, 'gorbellied' Archdeacon Drant, is a mere shadow to us. It is doubtful whether his famous 'rules' were committed to writing, and whether it was not certain of his experiments, like Thomas Watson's, rather than any critical argument, which had fired Harvey to be a reformer and had created an interest in the circle of Spenser, Sidney, and Dyer. The earlier efforts of Ascham, Watson, and Blenerhasset (in his *Complaint of Cadwallader*[5]), are accentual hexameters, as not a few of the later examples are; but the difference which the Areopagites, excepting Harvey, endeavoured to establish was that English verse should be quantitative. Between Drant's system (in so far as we know it) and Harvey's there is a serious disagreement. The first is an uncompromising imitation of classical usage, which accepts the rule of 'position' and gives absolute values to monosyllables and word-endings. When accentuation and long quantity coincide, as they frequently do, the agreement is treated

[1] i. 315.
[2] The first known examples are his (see *Toxophilus*): and he is the first to give the oft-quoted lines by Thomas Watson.
[3] i. 30–1.   [4] i. 87 et seq.
[5] In the *Mirror for Magistrates*.

as an accident. Harvey, on the other hand, sees that what appears to be an accident in the system is really an insidious proof that it cannot reckon without accent. 'I dare swear,' he says to Spenser, '... that it is not either Position, or Diphthong, or Diastole, or any like grammar-school device that doth or can indeed either make long or short, or increase, or diminish the number of syllables, but only the common allowed and received Prosody, taken up by a universal consent of all, and continued by a general use and custom of all. Wherein nevertheless I grant, after long advice and diligent observation of particulars, a certain uniform analogy and concordance being in process of time espied out, sometime this, sometime that, hath been noted by good wits in their analyses to fall out generally alike, and as a man would say, regularly, in all or most words: as Position, Diphthong, and the like: *not as first and essential causes of this or that effect* (here lieth the point), *but as secondary and accidental signs of this or that quality*'.' Harvey, therefore, though an hexametrist [2], and the traditional standard-bearer of the faction, does not hesitate to make certain qualifications. His conception of the importance of accent, which was left to Puttenham and others to develop, shows that he would be no party to the mere 'dranting' of verses. What he appears to have fully recognized, and this is the sum of his reform, is that something should be done to extend the possibilities of English verse, and that the hints towards effecting that lay to hand in classical practice: and, having committed himself to the party which loved not rhyme, he saw the necessity of compensating the loss by a rearrangement and elaboration of the rhythm. It is perhaps

[1] i. 120-1.
[2] See note on Nash's epithet and Harvey's acceptance of it (ii. 230, 239).

not remarkable that he and the extremer critics who were so blind to the meaning of Surrey's experiment did not observe that they entirely failed in practice to secure rhythm in their hexameters, except in those places where accent agreed with quantity. Harvey did not see that his acute criticism of Drant's verses was perhaps not less valid against his own. Yet, despite this limitation, he was the truer classicist, in that he adapted rather than adopted direct. He shows this in his subsidiary plea for a uniform orthography, by which he hoped to exorcise the spirits of confusion which had undone English Prosody.

Harvey's argument proved of greater force. Stanyhurst shows his agreement in the deliberate attempt to define orthography, and in his protest against being too 'stiffly tied to the ordinances of the Latins[1],' though it may be said he went somewhat further than some of the Priscianists in his devotion to quantity[2]. Sidney reveals but a courteous interest in the topic, and, notwithstanding the use of quantity in his early verses in the *Arcadia*, is not partisan in his *Apologie*. There he holds the balance fairly, speaks kindly of both, and even shows how admirably suited English is for rhyme[3]. Of Webbe, who has not even the merit of respectable scholarship, little need be said beyond this, that he is 'fully and certainly persuaded' that had English submitted early to the rigid discipline of classical quantity, it would by his time have enjoyed a reputation with the best[4]. So fast does this Procrustes stand for 'position' that he would that words and syllables which do not suit 'be a little wrested[5].' He is sadly out in his interpretation of Surrey's 'strange metre,' and his own experiments are not in his favour. We can

[1] i. 141.
[2] See the paper by Mr. R. B. McKerrow in *Mod. Lang. Quart.* (v. 6) for Stanyhurst's treatment of the accentual values of the last two feet.
[3] i. 204–5. [4] i. 278. [5] i. 282.

only guess that Fraunce, perhaps the most active practitioner of the new versification, was on the same side, for he has left no record of critical opinion. Yet the domination of accent, or rather its coincidence, in his so-called hexameters, shows that he was no Dranter: and his heresy of 'rhythming' or rhyming[1] hexameters must have disturbed the archdeacon. Harvey's triumph came with Puttenham, who, while recognizing the usefulness of Latin models, is all for accent[2]. He explains his attitude with a pretty condescension to young poets and others who delight in novelty, and refers to the problem that he 'may not seem by ignorance or oversight to omit any point of subtlety.' He points out the essential antipathies between Classical and English prosody[3], and feels that if anything must be done it must be in the English way of compromise. His general plan amounts to the substitution of accent for quantity. Some minor allowances which he offers as a sacrifice to 'position' are the only blemishes in a thoroughly common-sense judgement. At the close of the discussion he frankly states that he thinks them 'but vain and superstitious observations, nothing at all furthering the pleasant melody of our English metre,' and so will say no more of them, rather wishing 'the continuance of our old manner of poesy[4].' Though the experiments continued, the next critical opinion is Campion's on the eve of the dissolution of the whole craze. He is of course chiefly concerned with rhyme; and he holds that the classical rhythms have been attempted with 'passing pitiful success.' He thinks that accent must be diligently observed, 'for chiefly by the accent in any language the true value of the syllables is to be measured[5]'; but 'position' must be

[1] Not necessarily 'rhyming' in the modern sense, but showing *some* likeness in the last syllables.   [2] ii. 117 et seq.   [3] ii. 122.
[4] ii. 134.   [5] ii. 351.

a rule¹, and we must take our syllables as we speak them, not as we write them, because our English orthography differs from our common pronunciation². As far as rhythm is concerned he is hardly at variance with Puttenham; indeed, as Daniel points out, he admits that his feet are but the old English 'apparelled in foreign titles³.' If he is aiming at anything tangible it is at equality in the reading length of the lines, and his rules to this end assume the propriety of syllabic equivalence⁴. As our period closes, the scheme in both its extremer and more elastic forms is already discredited by the critics, as it had been neglected by the great body of poets. The discussion had gradually resolved itself to the conclusion that

> 'Sweet Poesy
> Will not be clad in her supremacy
> With those strange garments (Rome's hexameters),
> As she is English; but in right prefers
> Our native robes (put on with skilful hands—
> English heroics) to those antic garlands⁵.'

So the poet. And so the satirist, who wrote:—

> 'Manhood and garboils shall be chaunt "with changed feet,
> And head-strong dactyls making music meet⁶."'

And so, too, the philosopher, when the matter was ended: 'Illud reprehendendum, quod quidam antiquitatis nimium studiosi linguas modernas ad mensuras antiquas (heroïcas, elegiacas, sapphicas, etc.) traducere conati sunt; quas ipsarum linguarum fabrica respuit, nec minus aures exhorrent. In huiusmodi rebus sensus iudicium artis praeceptis praeponendum . . . Neque vero ars est, sed artis abusus, cum illa naturam non perficiat sed pervertat⁷.'

We must not, however, fail to observe that this criticism

---

[1] ii. 352. [2] Ibid. [3] ii. 350, 377. [4] See McKerrow, u.s., p. 12.
[5] Chapman, *The Shadow of Night* (*Hymnus in Cynthiam*, ll. 86-91).
[6] Hall, i. vi. [7] Bacon, *De Dign. & Augm. Scient.* vi. i.

of rhyme and rhythm is touched by the shyness which characterizes all the critical work of the age. If Drant did seek to establish a tyranny, he has been badly served by history. Harvey, whom posterity would make godfather to every pedantry, and in this matter to the most ridiculous of codes, is careful to disclaim any 'general certainty[1].' 'Credit me,' he says, 'I dare give no precepts nor set down any certain general art[2].' Stanyhurst tells us that his preface was written to explain his own verses, not to publish a 'directory' to the learned[3]. Puttenham gently persuades to discipline by showing the discredit of a rhymer 'that will be tied to no rules at all[4],' and, after showing the danger of inventing a new prosody and the folly of thinking that it will please everybody, proceeds to his account, only that the subject may be 'pleasantly scanned upon[5].' If the details of this controversy are less important to us than the general principle for which the writers strove, that general principle is in its turn of subsidiary interest in the history of criticism to the temper in which it was presented and handled. And here as elsewhere the Elizabethan critics showed something of the true classical spirit, not less in the manner of their argument than in their predisposition to certain lines of thought.

3. *Diction.*

The plans for the reform of the vocabulary of English poetry deal with three varieties of excess, archaism, inkhornism, and over-sea language; that is, with the affectation of antique forms, latinized terms of Humanist study, and foreign, especially Italian, words and phrases. They may be conveniently grouped together in this place, as the critical problem involved is, despite obvious differences, fundamentally the same in all. Here, again, the

[1] i. 122. [2] i. 102. [3] i. 147. [4] ii. 79. [5] ii. 124.

intention is classical—a desire to restrain the curiosity and eclecticism which had shown such scant respect to the 'sufficiency' of English. In a sense the disease itself was classical in origin—an attempt to bring order and to add ornament in the transitional and dialectal confusion of the language by borrowing from more fully developed literatures; to do for English what the Burgundian *Rhétoriqueurs* had done, with less reason, for French. But excess was inevitable, and the English 'despumation of the Latial verbocination' and the craze for antiquity required correction. So it fell out that while English at one stage sought to imitate the more learned and rhetorical style of Latin and the greater vernaculars, in the next she felt that she had but substituted one disorder for another, and that she must return to simplicity. The first conviction of the English poet was that he must write better than he had done; the later, that he had an uncontented care to write better than he could [1].

The discussion of Diction [2] was due to several causes, and was not primarily literary. The growing feeling of nationality, which was stimulated by the dislike of Italian influences, had already found voice in literature, and had urged writers like the author of *Toxophilus*, for purely patriotic reasons, to write English matters in the English tongue for Englishmen [3]. On this there naturally followed a defence of the mother-speech, to prove its sufficiency as well as its right to be heard. Some of the more deliberate vindications appear to have been prompted by continental examples, as Carew's was by Henri Estienne's [4]; or to have been suggested by the argument of continental purists, as Harvey's was by Bembo's teaching. But the defence was not complete until there had been a critical inquiry into the possible reasons for the delay or undoing of the vernacular triumph. These the

[1] i. 40.   [2] Cf. Sidney, i. 201.   [3] *Toxophilus (Dedication)*.   [4] ii. 444.

critics found in the outworn, outlandish, and pedantic licence of their age. The protest had been made before the appearance of the *Scholemaster*. Wilson, in the first pages of his *Arte of Rhetorique*, had reminded his reader how the philosopher Favorinus had served a youth for using words too old and strange. Cheke had told Thomas Hoby that English by ever borrowing would fain keep her house as bankrupt[1]. Ascham, despite his enthusiasm for Latin as an instrument of culture, is with them in pointing out that English must not ape foreign fashions, old or new. Mulcaster, too, loves Rome, but London better : ' I favour Italy, but England more ; I honour the Latin, but I worship the English.' And he adds : 'If we must cleave to the eldest and not the best, we should be eating acorns and wearing old Adam's pelts. But why not all in English ? I do not think that any language, be it whatsoever, is better able to utter all arguments either with more pith or greater plainness than our English tongue is[2].' Puttenham in his shrewd chapter on language[3] argues that nothing is to be added or changed in a national speech 'but by extraordinary occasions, by little and little ' ; and he gives warning of the evils which have come from preachers, schoolmasters, secretaries, merchants, and travellers[4]. To Daniel these affectations of antiquity and novelty are a deformity next to the folly of the reformed versifying[5]. Nash notes the fault of this ' overracked absonism[6].' But no one sees it more clearly than Jonson in his *Poetaster*[7]. His counsel of 'fair abstinence' is the sum of the classicists' purpose, fittingly delivered by the greatest of their company.

It would be wrong to interpret this critical propaganda as the mere backwash of Humanism. Far from being a tired reaction after the enthusiasm of the past century, it

[1] i. 357. [2] *First Part of the Elementarie* (1582). [3] ii. 149.
[4] Ibid. 151, 159. [5] ii. 384. [6] ii. 242. [7] ii. 397.

was the intelligent application of the principles of classicism to the disorders which had come upon English from different quarters. There was, in the first place, the glut of translations which, though they did inestimable good to the literature and language, if only by way of exercise, showed many serious symptoms of excess. The 'trade of glose or translations[1]' was so enlarged, that the charge of insular ignorance which Hoby had brought against his countrymen had lost its meaning. Now Nash could wish nothing worse to those who 'feed on nought but the crumbs that fall from the translators' trencher' than that they be left to the mercy of their mother-tongue[2]. To such a pass had it come that Harington and others thought it necessary to defend the craft of the translator. There was, in the second place, the remarkable interest in Chaucer and in the pseudo-Chaucerian pieces of the fifteenth century, of which the more aureate examples were greedily gorged in the general hunger. They were at least English, and so far would escape the censure directed against foreign influences. Nash saw the danger of this insidious argument, and in brave language maintained that Chaucer, had he lived, would have been scandalized by these 'balductums'; and, further, in a brief historical argument, that there was then no reason that English, 'when she hath recovered her state,' should be compelled to 'wear the robes of adversity and jet it in her old rags[3].' Later, Drayton showed that the enthusiasm must be for Chaucer's genius, not for the assumed perfection of his form:—

> 'As much as then
> The English language could express to men
> He made it do[4].'

And in the third place, there was the effect, also native

---

[1] i. 315.   [2] i. 308.   [3] ii. 242-3.   [4] *Epistle to Henry Reynolds.*

in process, of the artificial style of Euphuism. This was as alien in the eyes of the more reasonable purists as the most foreign, inkhornish, or antique affectation. Sidney, taking his metaphor from the Italianate folly, calls it a transformed and awry thing. Lyly, though he deserved, and received, full allowance for his aid in the betterment of English style, must take his share of blame with the imitators of 'his ridiculous tricks[1].' English had outgrown the youthful fervour when *Euphues* was *ipse ille*[2].

Definite as this criticism is in its exposure of the causes of disorder, and in its conviction of the ' equipollence' and individuality of English[3], it too is tempered by that fine discretion which Horace exhorted the poet to observe[4]. The writers who are most sensible of the dangers of eclecticism are just those who admit that English must be a borrower. But the poet must borrow as the translators do, or should do, by making his adornments appear natural and fitting to the tongue which receives them[5]. Gascoigne enters a caveat against strange words, but admits, as Ronsard had done, that in some places they may 'draw attentive reading[6].' Spenser's panegyrist naturally, and yet with stated reasons, is sure that ancient solemn words are a great ornament[7]. Though Sidney disapproves of the 'dictionary' method[8], he understands the proposition that English is a mingled language[9]. Chapman in defence of his translation craves Englishmen to accept his variety of new words as a compromise between 'discountryed affection' and the nakedness of ordinary table-talk[10]. And Daniel denounces foreign words not because they are altogether

---

[1] Drayton, *Epistle to Henry Reynolds.*   [2] ii. 243.
[3] See, in addition, i. 138, 142, 159, &c.; ii. 122, &c., 285, 297, 300, &c. And cf. Fletcher's *Licia* and Daniel's *Cleopatra.*
[4] Cf. i. 300.   [5] Cf. ii. 296.   [6] i. 53.   [7] i. 129.   [8] i. 202.
[9] Ibid. 204.   [10] ii. 305.

bad, but because they are established free-denizens 'without a Parliament, without consent or allowance[1].' It was Peele's praise of Harington (the 'well-lettered and discreet') that he had

> 'So purely naturalized
> Strange words and made them all free-denizens[2].'

So that here again, as in the discussion on Prosody, we have not only in the direct attack but also in the tone and terms of the reformers the true expression of the classical temper.

VI. THE ROMANTIC QUALITIES.

It is not inconsistent with what has been said about the marked classical tendency in Elizabethan criticism to find hints of a contrary movement in the direction of romantic taste. In the first place, it is fair to assume that however much criticism was indifferent to the fervours of the age—by which that age has commended itself to posterity—it could not altogether escape the influence of the popular manner. And, in the second place, we are reminded that the two apparently opposite moods of Classicism and Romanticism are always found co-existing in the greatest periods and greatest writers. Indeed, if we look for a too strong antithesis, and certainly if we expect exclusiveness for the one or the other, the distinction must entirely fail as a critical instrument. It is not necessary to defend the paradox of the classicism of Shakespeare, or of the romanticism of Virgil; or to show in cases of minor importance that the 'placing' of an author or of his period may be difficult and inconclusive, and indeed that the choice of the epithet largely depends on the point of view of the critic. We have illustration of this in these essays. The persistent plea of Harvey and others that

---

[1] ii. 384. [2] *Ad Maecenatem Prologus*, 1593.

custom, common usage, or 'natural instinct' must rule in the shaping of style, is in one sense the romantic claim for freedom from the tyranny of the canon, in another an admission that the writer, far from enjoying individual liberty, is conditioned by practice, which is not less exacting than classical convention. Daniel's hearty counsel that the world is to be suffered 'to enjoy that which it knows and what it likes[1]' may quite reasonably be accepted by the classicists, or prove irksome to the romanticists. Experience, another of Harvey's favourites, commends itself to his party, because it hits at tradition and deals with things known to, or felt by, the poet. Experience, say the opponents, especially perfected experience, gives the 'Ancients' and the Great Patterns their claim upon the obedience of their successors. To the first, it makes the individual writer and creates the living pages of literature; to the others, it is the sum of the past, discovered of old, and handed on by the 'classics' as the unsurpassed, perhaps unsurpassable, expression of the wisdom of life and beauty of art. When Harington, in his critique on Ariosto, answers certain objections with the striking words, 'Methinks it is a sufficient defence to say Ariosto doth it[2],' what appears so modern and aesthetic in its tone is after all but the masked admiration of the classicist for another Homer or Virgil. And so our signposts may be Knights or Saracens, according as we look upon them; for much may be said on both sides.

The unwillingness to have rigid rules, whether in the choice of subject, in language, or in prosody, has been already noted. The caution against interference with existing habit, against drawing Poetry by the ears[3], is not only Sidney's and Daniel's, but the commonplace of this collection of essays. The dictum, too, that Poetry has no limita-

[1] ii. 363.   [2] ii. 217.   [3] i. 195.

tions, which is urged hardly less frequently, is on the side of eclecticism, though the critics may not have quite realized the fact. So much freedom is allowed to the writer that he is advised not to 'compose of seen subjects[1],' but to rely on his own invention. In a sense, this unwillingness is an effect of the classical restraint and discretion, a transference of method from literary practice to criticism *per se*, though it is in time lost when critics have made up their minds as to what is orthodoxy, and how it is to be enforced. Or it may be to some extent due to timidity or confusion in interpreting the relationship of the classical canon to English use and wont. But if there be little or no evidence of romantic bias in the call for discretion, it is otherwise when the critics condescend to discuss the reasons. Thus Puttenham says, 'Since the actions of man with their circumstances be infinite, and the world likewise replenished with many judgements, it may be a question who shall have the determination of such controversy as may arise whether this or that action or speech be decent or indecent[2].' And Daniel, who in many places speaks strongly against arrogance in judging the positive though varying virtues of 'this manifold creature man[3],' advances a step further when he admits that he dare not take upon himself to dictate to his fellows, because he holds a fixed view and thinks it right; for 'indeed there is no right in these things that are continually in a wandering motion, carried with the violence of uncertain likings, being but only the time that gives them their power[4].' Here there is no truce with either the stricter discipline, or with the good-mannered discretion of the classicist.

Daniel's remark foreshadows the modern conception of historical process in literature. There is no hint of it in the generality of Elizabethan writings, which tacitly

[1] i. 48, 220.   [2] ii. 175.   [3] ii. 367.   [4] ii. 383.

accept the restricted Mediaeval tradition or substitute for
it the not less exclusive views of the Renaissance. There
is nothing more remarkable in the Elizabethans than their
neglect of the earlier literary conditions in England, as
bearing on the problems which interested them so much.
It was indeed more than neglect, for the reformers, and
those who had hopes of a great English revival, made it
a preliminary to their argument to abuse the lack-learning
times, and on every occasion to scoff at the Amadises and
Arthurs. Sidney, in notable exception to Ascham and his
friends, shows a genuine, though reserved, appreciation
of Romance, but he does not make any effort to justify
his catholicity. And Puttenham, who in one place appears
to think kindly of the old stuff[1], is neither acute nor consistent, and is perhaps thinking most of his own historical
ditty. There is a hint of the later attitude in Blenerhasset's
Epistle in the Second Part of the *Mirror for Magistrates*,
where he excuses his style by pointing out that those
whose falls he has described lived not 'of late time,'
and that he had not thought it decent 'that the men
of the old world should speak with so garnished a style,
as they of the latter time[2].' We have here the superior
manner of Renaissance criticism, but there is also the
confession that ages differ, and that each has its own
mode. And the importance of this allowance is not
diminished, although his attitude may be reasonably explained as the application of the classical doctrine of
decorum in the representation of different times as in
that of different characters. In Daniel, however, the expression of the modern idea is, for the first time in
English, unequivocal. His apology for the Middle Ages
and his demurrer to the infallibility of Latin are a direct
retort to the classicists. As different conceptions of
wisdom throughout the world are but one, 'apparelled

[1] ii. 44; contrast ii. 15. 87, 166.   [2] Haslewood, i. 349.

according to the fashion of every nation[1],' so the tastes of different ages but express 'that perpetual revolution which we see to be in all things that never remain the same[2].' He speaks of this continuity as 'the law of time[3],' and sees in its process the passing of all things—including Campion's craze against rhyme. What matters it, when this 'will make all that for which we now contend *Nothing*'? There is more in this than in Puttenham's commonplace that all old things soon wax stale[4]; it is, as it were, the exaltation of fate and the refutation of finality in Art. The practical application therefore is, to the artist, that he shall take such opportunity as comes by mood rather than by convention; and to the critic, that he shall not arrogantly find perfection in one phase of artistic experience. Daniel is but further expounding this larger doctrine when he brings home the difficulty of finding the true perspective of an age which shall stand the test when 'after-times shall make a quest of inquiry[5].' If it be claimed for this historical sense, which is the flower of Elizabethan criticism, that it is but the perception of a larger unity, and the extension of the old bounds, and is therefore nothing more nor less than a transcendent classicism, we must bear in mind that it shows the building up of the whole by its parts, not the illustration of that unity by certain forms and works. The Renaissance allowed little to the individual except in his relationship to the general principle which it had accepted; here criticism accepted the individual works on their own merits, and thereafter based its conception of unity and continuity on the evidence of their essential qualities. Daniel's essay, even considered in the narrowest sense of re-establishing the literary credit of the Middle Ages, was an important document on the side of romanticism.

The Renaissance individualism which stimulated this

[1] ii. 372. [2] ii. 384. [3] Ibid. [4] ii. 166. [5] ii. 380.

Introduction

sense by giving to each age, or literary kind, or writer, the consideration which it accorded to each *man*, shows other immediate effects in the critical work of the time. And these further illustrate the coincidence of classical and romantic purpose, to which reference has already been made. For the plea, as expressed by Puttenham, that criticism shall give 'special regard to all circumstances of the person, place, time, cause, and purpose[1],' or by Chapman, that 'the whole drift, weight, and height' of a poet's works shall be set before the 'apprehensive eyes of his judge[2],' is a classical conception, at base but the familiar *decorum*; and it is here applied to criticism *per se*, as it was later, and with fuller meaning, by Dryden, Pope, and Johnson. But it also meant the recognition of individual workmanship, and the giving of fair treatment even to inferior writers[3]. In other words, it broke with the Renaissance habit of judging works only as part of a system or as examples of a certain kind.

There could be as yet but little aesthetic criticism in the modern acceptation of the term; but there are hints of it in the claim by the critics for a freer expression of their personal liking. Puttenham speaks of his 'singular opinion[4],' and admits that it may be disputed. Chapman says that his chief pleasure of his labours is in his own profit, and that he does not tremble before the feverish censure of a 'young prejudicate or castigatory brain[5].' Daniel's 'own ease' is his guide in certain questions. Yet he and the others admit that though such are their own conclusions, they may not be commendable to others. 'I must not out of mine own daintiness condemn this kind of writing, which peradventure to another may seem most delightful[6].' This then is more than unwillingness to accept the authority of a

---

[1] ii. 161.　　[2] ii. 299.　　[3] ii. 282.　　[4] ii. 126.
[5] ii. 306.　　[6] ii. 382.

body of rules: it grants the reasonableness of individual criticism, and by allowing that criticism may be based on impression, whether fixed or tentative, hits at the heart of convention. Jonson, as a classicist, saw the danger of this unloosing in the insidious working of the pathetic fallacy[1]; but the tendency made for critical sympathy, and was not without good influence in the strictest age of classical orthodoxy.

VII. THE CRITICAL TEMPER.

In this period, in which Criticism first claims, or is preparing to claim, the right to be recognized as a 'kind' in English letters, the method, tone, and craftsmanship of the critic are hardly less important than the general principles by which he is guided. It might not be too much to say that it is by reason of these qualities that this *olla* of treatise, preface, and letter deserves the name of criticism in the accepted sense. For it is clear that such general questions as the origin of poetry, or its defence, or the respective advantages of a classical or romantic theory of Art, may remain entirely academic, and may neither help nor harm the critic in his efforts to interpret individual genius or record his impressions of a literary group. The additional interest of these essays, therefore, is that in them we have the first hints in English of the Critical Temper.

The evidence of this is scattered; and there are many passages and points of views which on analysis must lose their apparent claims to novelty in this respect. This is especially true of the judgements on Classical and Renaissance writers. With perhaps the exception of Cheke's ingenious explanation of Sallust's style[2], or Chapman's assault on Scaliger[3], nothing is said in appreciation of the gods of the Old and the New Rome which had not been

---

[1] ii. 396.   [2] i. 40.   [3] ii. 301.

said before, or might have been said. The historical sketches of classical literature by Sidney, or Webbe, or Puttenham, or even Jonson, are but shreds of Horatian tradition or patchwork of Renaissance commentary. In their references to the later material, down even to their own time, the critics wield the weapons and give the cries of the Aristotelian and Ciceronian wars of the previous century. Harvey's panegyric on Petrarch is but a heap of epithetic scrap-iron; Harington's special pleading for Ariosto at the expense of Virgil discloses little more than the wisdom of Renaissance commonplace.

When we come to their treatment of contemporaries, there are signs of vitality, though they are occasional, and appear in a phrase here and there rather than in the complete argument. It may not be difficult to see that at times the purpose and method of these references to writers of their day have been suggested by such Renaissance models as Scaliger or Lilius Gyraldus, or have been devised as the appropriate retort to the Puritan attack; yet their frequency is a new and noteworthy feature. Jonson, himself a ready censurer and gossip on fellow-authors, drew attention, a few years later, to these 'running judgements upon poetry and poets[1].' That they were in the main preposterous, as Jonson holds, does not lessen the historical importance of the activity of such early experiment. It may be said that the heat of controversy which gave the critics their opportunity, did not at the same time give them a keener judicial faculty. Their praise and blame, their descriptions and groupings, appear in the false relief which is familiar in the argument of the special pleader. They cite and quote to prove or illustrate some definite thesis; less frequently do they attempt to give an independent appreciation. Thus there is a certain historical value in the lucubrations of Lodge on

[1] *Discoveries*, lxiii, '*Censura de Poetis.*'

Gosson, Stanyhurst on Phaer, Harvey on Nash, or Nash on Kyd, which may or may not be negligible in a later critical estimate of Gosson, Phaer, Nash, or Kyd. Occasionally, as in the uniform correctness of their judgement of Spenser, they have anticipated the verdict of posterity; but it is no disrespect to either the intelligence or humanity of any of them to say that their opinion might have been different had Spenser been less a free and uncontentious person.

Two of the more striking features of their work they owed to humanistic culture; the one of method, the other of manner: and their chief claim to originality is shown in the way which they modified these. The former, the Comparative Method, was a choice of necessity; but it was the surest beginning. At first an author is good or bad according as he stands comparison with some accepted pattern; English is a noble and self-sufficing language because it is as rich and subtle as other honoured vernaculars; English prosody is at fault because it does not carry the Latin measures. This is but the humanistic pitting of the one against the other, without due consideration of the fairness of the encounter, or indeed of the necessity of their fighting at all. The habit was doubtless confirmed by the anthological craze of the age, and by the prevalence of the Euphuistic mood, by which accidental or far-fetched similitudes and antipathies had acquired a false importance. The extreme is found in Meres's fantastic catalogue; there is much that appears meaningless in the more scholarly Harvey, and perhaps not less in Nash and others. But it is not difficult to see that, by some, comparison is less and less used as an instrument for shaping forth a prejudice, and more as an exercise for widening the literary horizon. Daniel, at the close, hits at the narrow scholastic method when he says: 'It is our weakness that makes us mistake or misconceive in these delineations of men the true figure of their worth. And our passion and belief is so apt to lead us beyond truth, that unless we try them by the just compass of humanity, and as they were men, we shall cast their figures in the air, when we should make their models upon earth[1].' He argues that differences between nations and individuals are of fashion rather than of degree, and that in the 'collation of writers' men rather weigh the accidents than the positive merit[2]. This is but another expression of the romantic argument for toleration; and evidence of its more direct application to critical method.

A like tendency is recognizable in the change in the tone of Elizabethan criticism. The earlier critics are not less humanist in their manner of censure than they are in their erudition. They have a fine genius for denunciation and personality, which would do credit to the noisiest of the Ciceronians. In their statement of general principles they are tolerably meek, but they show small measure of 'decency' when an opponent is to be damned. Yet scholars' quarrels have always been lively; and it is perhaps no accident, though it is not a primary cause, that as scholarship decreases in Elizabethan criticism a gentler habit begins to rule. There is of course no lack of biting speeches in the later writers, but these are to be treated on their individual merits, and as idiosyncrasies of the authors. Thus Nash's 'declamatory vein' is Nash's own: much more so than Harvey's is his own natural rudeness, unaffected by his pedantic training and recreation. Yet it would be too fine and unprofitable a discussion to distinguish between these kinds of 'flyting.' There is poor sport for the modern in this cockpit of abuse. We feel a change when we pass from Ascham to Sidney, or from Harvey to Daniel. How much of the difference is directly due to Sidney it might be difficult to say, but it

[1] ii. 371.   [2] ii. 380.

is at least reasonable to assume that his reputation and his literary tone had some effect, else the multitudinous references to the 'Sidnaean showers of sweet discourse[1]' have no meaning. The fact that he and Puttenham and Harington and others are courtiers—by profession, let us say —could not fail to ameliorate the harshness of the mere scholar or the Martinist, though it was on the other hand a barrier to their critical appreciation of the great work of the Bohemians. Yet mere courtliness will not explain the enthusiasm, the generous wisdom, and, above all, the absolute temper of his *Apologie*, or account for its influence on contemporaries. Nor can it have been altogether a personal quality, for in the Italian sources, from which Sidney and the others drew not a little, already something of the old harshness had been lost.

It is to be observed that this change, both in the outlook and manner of English criticism, is first associated with those whose sympathies are on the romantic side, and especially with Sidney and Daniel, the most striking exponents of that turn in taste. It is they who establish the claim of English criticism as a separate literary kind, as an instrument of power outside the craft of rhetoricians and scholars. For though it was for classical ends that this criticism was first turned to account, and though it was later by classical hands made perfect, it was by the genius of those who were least trammelled by classical tradition that it first found its cunning. There are many passages in Sidney, and more than enough in Daniel, of inspired knowledge, happy suggestion, and generous common sense, to show how far the best of the Elizabethans had wandered from the old ways, and how very near they could come to some of the best of their later successors. And in other places, in essays of less sustained power, as in Puttenham's definition of style[2], or

[1] Crashaw, *Wishes*. [2] ii. 153.

Introduction

Chapman's defence of Homer's 'ascential muse[1],' or in Harvey's spasms of phrase, there is no lack of critical intelligence, which more than balances all the dreary pages of the 'most threatening slashers[2]' and pedants.

VIII. THE SOURCES.

There remains the question of origins: how much of Elizabethan criticism expresses a general tendency or deals with matters which are as English as they are Italian or French, and how much is directly drawn from foreign sources. It is of course impossible to measure the latter with accuracy, and it is easy to err in over-estimating its extent. Yet it is not the less true that Elizabethan criticism, especially on its theoretical side, shows, and to some extent admits, a considerable assimilation of argument and illustration from without. Whatever may be said of the original qualities of these essays, it is clear that their authors, like certain wits described by Jonson, usurped freely from others; but it must be put to their credit that, unlike these, they did not protest against all reading, or make a 'false venditation of their own naturals[3].' The notes will show how handsomely some of them borrowed.

We shall confine ourselves here to a general statement of that indebtedness, and in attempting to estimate its extent we shall assume that the essayists drew from one or more of three main sources, (1) from Classical canon, either directly or through the medium of the mediaeval recensions of Plato, Aristotle, Horace, and others, (2) from Italian and French criticism, Latin and vernacular, of the sixteenth century, and (3) from English writers before 1570 and from contemporaries.

It is hardly necessary to remark on the persistence of

---

[1] ii. 301.   [2] ii. 252.   [3] *Discoveries*, lxv. § 8.

classical tradition in criticism, at all stages of its history, whether in the theory of poetry or in the regulation of poetic form. The chief guides had been Plato, Aristotle, and Horace, or what passed for them at the hands of the grammarians. Of these, Plato is of least account. There is nothing in Elizabethan criticism corresponding to the influence exerted by the Platonic philosophy in the works of contemporary poets and thinkers. The all-important notion of εὐφυής is an adaptation to literature from philosophy, and, though Platonic in origin, was most probably known to the Renaissance writers and the Elizabethans through later works, such as Plutarch's *Moralia*[1]. The direct references to Plato (and their directness is sometimes disputable) are almost without exception to the passage dealing with the expulsion of poets from the commonwealth: and in these the critics more often discuss the plain question of Plato's intention[2] than his general views on the fable and the relation of poetry to philosophy, by which he appeared to conclude against the poets[3]. Though the critics strain to prove that Plato was no enemy to poetry, they show that they bear him some grudge. Sidney is careful to say that he reverences him as a philosopher[4]; and Puttenham, on his first page, challenges the 'Platonists with their Ideas[5].' Webbe's references to the Platonic explanation of rhythm[6] are unimportant. It is perhaps possible, with the aid of the Italians, to find some threads of Plato's doctrine in the Elizabethan application of the arguments in favour of the philosopher to the defence of the poet; or in the assumption that the Platonic theory of beauty can be extended as a justification of poetry. There is certainly something

[1] See i. 349.
[2] e.g. Lodge, i. 67; Sidney, i. 184, and especially 190-2; Nash, i. 328; Hoby, i. 341; Harington, ii. 204. See infra, p. lxxix.
[3] e.g. Sidney, i. 152; Harington, ii. 203.
[4] i. 190.   [5] ii. 3.   [6] i. 231, 248.

Introduction

Platonic in Sidney's conception of the golden world of art beyond the brazen world of nature[1]. But it would be pushing the historical method too far to explain such positions as direct borrowings, even from the Renaissance Platonists. And it would be not less extreme to connect the romantic feeling for freedom in the exercise of the imagination with any special system or dictum. If these things were originally Plato's, Plato had been absorbed in European thought; and the impulses, though first expressed by him, were, in every valid sense, each thinker's own.

With Aristotle, and especially with Horace, the case is otherwise. As formalists they more readily commended themselves to a young criticism which was concerned before everything with practical matters of form. Ascham puts it on record, that he, Cheke, and Watson, the author of *Absolon*, 'had many pleasant talks together in comparing the precepts of Aristotle and Horace *de Arte Poetica* with the examples of Euripides, Sophocles, and Seneca[2].' The passage has the additional interest of containing, as far as we know, the first allusion in English to the *Poetics*[3]. Hitherto all the Aristotelian borrowings had been from the philosophical works, the *Politics*, and the *Rhetoric*; and, indeed, for some time to come the tradition of the scholastic discipline was paramount in English letters, or at least the writers show by their allusions to the *Politics*, *Ethics*[4], and *Analytics* greater intimacy with these works. Of the ten or twelve passages in these essays which are based on the *Poetics*, only a few imply any knowledge of the text or discuss its doctrine; and nearly all of them are to be found in Sidney's *Apologie*, in which the *Poetics*

---

[1] i. 156.   [2] i. 23.

[3] The recovery of the *Poetics* in Italy, France, and England inaugurated the critical reputation of Aristotle, just at the time when his long-established authority in philosophy was on the decline.

[4] e.g. Sidney, i. 161, 20 (note).

takes its place in the list of literary testimonies in favour of poetry[1]. They refer to the commonplace on μίμησις[2], to the comparison of poetry with history[3], to the Unity of Time[4], and to τὸ γελοῖον[5]. But there is a suspicion even in these that Sidney had reached Aristotelian theory in a roundabout way—a suspicion which is confirmed by other vague and unauthenticated references[6], and is but slightly removed by his recommendation in his correspondence that Aristotle should be studied in the original[7]. The passage on the 'Unity of Time,' for example, derives its importance from its relationship to recent Italian views rather than to the original[8]. Of the other writers, Harington, who owes so much to Sidney, merely alludes to μίμησις[9], and to the fable[10], though he elsewhere speaks approvingly of 'Aristotle and the best censurers of Poetry[11].' Webbe's allusions are accidental, and as valueless as his references to Plato[12]. Puttenham refers to Aristotle thrice, but does not seem to have known the *Poetics*; and Daniel makes mention at second-hand of some Latin account of Aristotle's views on rhythm[13]. There are but few traces of other Greek critics in the Essays. Demetrius Phalereus and Dionysius of Halicarnassus are known to Ascham, and possibly to Puttenham, whose strangely mixed list of points of 'good utterance' would appear to be based upon them, though perhaps indirectly[14]. From Longinus little or nothing has been borrowed.

The vitality of Horatian tradition in late classical and mediaeval times, and especially throughout the Renais-

---

[1] i. 192.   [2] i. 158, 173.   [3] i. 167.
[4] i. 197.   [5] i. 200.   [6] e.g. i. 206. See note.
[7] Ed. Pears, pp. 28, 195, 208.
[8] See note to i. 398. Yet Sidney has the credit, however much he may have drawn from Scaliger and others, of infusing the Aristotelian elements into English criticism, especially on the dramatic side.
[9] ii. 200.   [10] ii. 203.   [11] ii. 216.   [12] i. 231, 236, 248.
[13] ii. 360.   [14] See note to ii. p. 162, l. 4, &c.

sance, is one of the most remarkable facts of literary history. An essentially derivative criticism such as the Elizabethan could not but draw freely from this storehouse; and it did so from the first, before it had acquired anything from Aristotle, directly or indirectly. The Horatian notion of the original function of the poet as the legislator and *vates* commended itself to the English mind, and would have done so hardly less easily had there been no predisposing cause in mediaeval and Renaissance habit. Horace, too, in his body of general rules, met the taste and practical needs of the defenders of poetry; Aristotle, in a sense a new acquaintance, offered theory and canon for the drama, which was but one of their interests, and not the most important. The debt to Horace is certainly greater than would appear at the first estimate, for much that stands to the credit of Aristotle and others is really his, or is at least Horatian. The *Ars Poetica* had usurped the place of mentor, not only to many who would write poetry, but to all who would write about it. Though the direct references in these essays to it or its author are not frequent, and though Webbe's inclusion in his *Discourse* of a complete translation of Fabricius's *vademecum*[1] is an exceptional proof of enthusiasm by one of the least scholarly of the critics, there is no lack of borrowing of Horatian doctrine and rule, not to speak of innumerable tags of quotation in Latin. But the matter need not be laboured further; and the many references in the Notes may be accepted as evidence.

The critical influence of Cicero and Quintilian was, as might be expected, confined almost exclusively to rhetorical matters. When it is found outside these, it is merely illustrative or analogical; that is, it occasionally applies arguments in favour of poetry which were familiar in the Rhetorics. This is, however, more noticeable in the Italians,

[1] i. 290-301.

as in Minturno¹, than in the Elizabethans who are indebted to them. Cicero's sole claim on English, as a critic and not as the educational demi-god of the Ciceronians, is based on an error; for the credit of the definition of comedy given by Lodge² and others belongs to Donatus. Quintilian has some share in the genesis of the doctrine of imitation upheld by Ascham. The latter was directly inspired by Sturm³, and by Cheke, too, we may be certain; and they, with Melanchthon and others, had well digested the chapter on imitation in the *Institutes*⁴. Though Ascham criticizes Quintilian, and even qualifies Sturm's view, which he thinks is 'far best of all⁵,' he helps us to trace the genealogy of the argument. Yet Quintilian's influence was never active, then or later. The frequent quotations and allusions in the *Discoveries* prove nothing more than that the rhetorician was one of Jonson's favourites.

Plautus, Terence, and Seneca are referred to merely as models of dramatic form. Aelius Donatus, the scholiast of the second, was too well known, even to schoolboys, to escape being pilfered from by some. His characterization of comedy was a commonplace, though nobody gave him the credit of its authorship. Lodge evidently knew his tract⁶, and it is plausible that not a little of what passes for older dramatic theory and history in these essays is not more ancient⁷. Plutarch, whose *Moralia* was not less popular than his *Lives*, stands sponsor for

---

¹ For example: 'Nam, ut id quoque de oratore ad poetam, ex M. Tullio in hunc locum, quemadmodum et alia non pauca transferamus, hic noster Heroicus, quem . . .,' &c. (*De Poeta*, p. 105). Cf. the application of the Platonic eulogy of the philosopher to the poet, supra.

² i. 81, 1, and note.   ³ i. 9.   ⁴ X. ii.   ⁵ i. 13.

⁶ See notes to i. 68, 25, and 80, 7.

⁷ We may go even further, though with less truth here than in the next century, and say that not a little which comes originally from Donatus was known only through Scaliger.

Simonides' metaphor of the speaking picture[1], but for little else.

Virgil is used but sparingly as a critical aid, though there is ample proof in the quotations and references that mediaeval Maronism was still a living faith, now disciplined by Humanism. When he is alluded to, it is to point a comparison with some later author; or his verses are treated as practical models by the reformers of English measures. The comparative passages, somewhat in the Macrobian vein, are of no critical value, except when Harington turns the balance in favour of Ariosto, and Chapman in favour of Homer; and there the critical interest lies, not in what they say in behalf of their literary gods, but in the one's daring so bravely for Ariosto, and in the other's trouncing Scaliger so roundly.

These classical authorities, and, we may add, the 'classics' of early patristic literature [2] are the general quarries where every man who would build his house found his stone. So far the borrowing is inevitable, and its extent cannot be satisfactorily determined. The difficulty is perhaps not less when we endeavour to estimate the debt to immediate predecessors and contemporaries. There the detective of plagiarism must carry himself with the greatest circumspection, even though it be clear that the borrowings have a more individual character and deal with narrower issues, instead of being the consensus of long-established opinion. At the same time it must be kept in mind that not a few of these appropriations, of which the writers make full confession, are of value only as indicating the personal liking, or perhaps the recent reading of the critic, and have little or no bearing on the general critical process. For example, it is easy to exaggerate the importance of Harvey's lists and

[1] See i. 386. [2] Supra, xv.

interesting allusions as evidence of the debt of the Elizabethans to Italian literature; perhaps even to overestimate the influence of that literature on Harvey himself.

The difficulty lies in tracing the original owners of the contents of these 'packets of pilferies,' not in proving that they are stolen goods. Whatever objections may be taken to the detailed evidence advanced by enthusiasts for the Italian origin of Elizabethan criticism, there can be no doubt as to the validity of the general contention. Its truth will be apparent to every one who reads, more or less carefully, the series of critical essays between Giraldi Cintio's *Discorsi* (1554) and Castelvetro's version of Aristotle's *Poetics* (1570). The identities and parallelisms recorded in the notes to this collection may be taken as merely illustrative; they are not an adequate estimate of the evidence in some cases. If their cumulative strength does not bring conviction, let us admit that the proofs have been indifferently marshalled, or but partially stated; or, as we incline to believe, that they are of a kind that must be judged by general impression rather than by painful statistics. It would be an easy matter for the historical critic were all plagiarists, and especially Elizabethan plagiarists, to disclose where and how they borrowed. Yet, even if we neglect the occasional clues which the essays themselves afford, it would be difficult to escape the impression that they had been written with an intimate knowledge of Italian criticism.

It may be at times a question how much of the borrowing from Italian sources is taken direct from Boccaccio's *De Genealogia Deorum* or from the sixteenth-century critics who were undoubtedly inspired by that work. Its great popularity throughout Europe, especially between 1500 and 1600, must have established a critical tradition; and it is plausible to find in it, in the fourteenth and fifteenth books, the originals of some of the propositions

Introduction

which were in vogue in the later Renaissance. Thus, to give but one or two illustrations, we have an anticipation of the Agrippan argument and of its answer in the chapter 'Poetas non esse mendaces,' in a second beginning 'Porro zelantes hi suasores criminum Poetas affirmant,' and in another, entitled 'Philosophorum simias minime Poetas esse[1].' So, too, the comparison of the Poet with the Historiographer[2], and the interpretation of Plato's much quoted dictum about the danger of Poetry[3], at once connect themselves with passages in Sidney's *Apologie*[4]. The assumption that Sidney not merely knew but used the book comes in one place as near as possible to proved fact[5]. Yet in whatever way future research may adjust the claims of Boccaccio and of his successors, the Elizabethan debt to Renaissance Italy will remain undisputed.

The period between Cintio and Castelvetro is but a portion of a full century of critical activity in Italy, which begins with Vida's *De Arte Poetica* (1527), but it contains nearly all the material which was used by the Elizabethans. Important as Vida was to Renaissance criticism generally, as the high-priest of *decorum*, the upholder of the Horatian canon, and the panegyrist of classical culture, he appears to have had no influence in England at this stage[6]. He is neither named nor quoted. It may be that the extremeness of his view did not readily attract the more moderate English mind, as it did Du Bellay and

---

[1] Bk. xiv. chaps. xiii, xv, xvii (Basle edition of Hervagius, 1532, pp. 369 et seqq.).

[2] ib. p. 371.   [3] ib. p. 381.   [4] Infra, i. p. 191.

[5] See note to i. p. 206, ll. 6–7. References like that to Robert of Sicily (ed. u. s., p. 385) may be the sources of some of the Elizabethan allusions.

[6] In the late seventeenth century, and especially in the eighteenth, Vida's 'honour'd brow' is reverently crowned with the 'critic's ivy.' (Cf. Pope, *Essay on Criticism*, 704.)

Vauquelin in France[1]; it is probable that he was forgotten in the crush of immediate interests. Minturno and Scaliger barely preceded the earlier Elizabethans, and were, with certain others, apart from any intrinsic value or reputation, the writers who would most naturally come under the notice of Englishmen who knew Italy and her literature. This chronological fact, and another not less important, that the general defence of poetry, which was the first pressing problem of English criticism, was the main topic with these Italians, compel us to assume that some interconnexion was not merely possible, but almost inevitable. It is a question whether the Elizabethans would have been attracted by Italian criticism had their needs not been so happily met by the Italian discussion of the general principles. The other matters dealt with in the complex body of Italian criticism could have had but little interest for them. Its unbounded confidence in Italian and supercilious neglect of other literatures, its business in ordering the minutiae of Italian vocabulary and grammar, its over-elaboration of strict classical canon were more or less outside the English purpose. The only exception might be found in metrical theory, which would interest the English hexametrists. Yet Daniel's reference to Tolomei's treatise[2] (1539) does not imply more than that he had heard of it, and knew its drift. Ascham is interested in Tomitano[3], not as a prosodist, but as a critic of the Aristotelian logic. The various allusions to Italian prosody[4] have but a secondary importance, and are merely illustrative

---

[1] It is possible that the accepted view that Vida exercised a strong influence on the continent, especially in the sixteenth and seventeenth centuries, is an exaggeration. At least it is difficult to prove it. For beyond the testimony of Scaliger, inspired by a common enthusiasm for Virgil, there is little of sincere discipleship.

[2] *Versi e Regole della Nuova Poesia.*   [3] i. 21, and note.

[4] As in Puttenham, ii. 73, 90, 91, 92, &c.

of the Italianate practice of contemporary English verse. Ascham's mention of Pigna[1], though interesting evidence of an Englishman's knowledge of one of the most original of sixteenth-century critics, is provokingly disappointing by its narrow concern in the Italian's views on Horace's 'golden' Epistle, Aristotle's *Rhetoric*, and the plays of Sophocles. If any one wandered beyond the limits which we have chosen, it is Sidney, in his reference to Cristofero Landino[2], and perhaps in his echoes of Daniello. But the latter[3] are merely conjectural.

After all, the more important question is not whether Italian influence can be found in English criticism, but why it is not more active. There were strong predisposing causes to borrow other things than an academic defence of Poetry. Italy had for some time supplied the models to English letters, as it had to art and music. We know what the pastoral owed to Tasso and Guarini, or satire to Alamanni, or the epic to Ariosto; how much Wyatt, Surrey, Sidney, and Spenser owed in the structure of their verse; how much, in fact, of the *form* of Elizabethan literature was defined by Italian practice. For great as is the debt to the *matter* of Italian literature, it is small and accidental compared with the debt to its rules and artistic habit. The poets 'tasted the sweet and stately *measures and style* of the Italian Poesy[4]': the courtly ordered themselves by the etiquette of Della Casa, Castiglione, and Guazzo[5]. The entire Italianate controversy resolves itself into a discussion of *ways* and *manner*. Further, English by its translating fury had established the custom of going to Italy for everything, even for learn-

[1] See i. 349.   [2] i. 206, and note.
[3] i. 151, 13, note; i. 164, 11-13, note.   [4] ii. 62.
[5] Note, too, that the epithetic habit of the Elizabethans, including the critics, was most generally Italian: e.g. Harvey's 'Petrarchize,' and his calling of Nash the 'English Aretine.' Spenser to others is the 'English Petrarch.'

ing, which it might have had direct through native scholarship. How reasonable, therefore, to assume that when the Elizabethans turned their attention to criticism they should look first to the literature from which they had drawn their formal experience, and in which the principles of the art of writing had already been fully discussed. And it might not be less reasonable to assume that the rise and activity of critical writing in Italy not merely defined the content of English criticism, but was the immediate cause of its appearance at this time. When the essayists show an acquaintance with even the lesser-known Italian poets and prose-writers, and refer to books like Celiano's which had just been published[1], it is unlikely that they passed by the critics. There was, of course, greater temptation to be silent when plagiarizing from the latter than when praising or damning a Tuscan poet.

This relationship to Italian may be traced in several ways. There is, in the first place, the more specific indebtedness to individual authors, either expressly admitted by the essayists or reasonably certain to the reader who makes the comparison. This evidence[2] is drawn mainly from Minturno and Scaliger, but not entirely. Thus Daniel's statement about *Remensi*, which has disturbed his editors and tempted them to an absurd correction, is Giraldi Cintio's, and is fixed down by Daniel's parenthesis 'as some Italians hold[3].' Sidney's explanation of the function of comedy is strangely like Trissino's[4], as is his comparison of poetry with ethics and law like Varchi's[5]; and there is a temptation to think that he knew Castelvetro's opinion when he enlarged on verse's 'being

---

[1] i. 428.
[2] The citations on the following pages are, as stated above, merely illustrative. The index will help the reader to further references in the Notes.
[3] ii. 360, note.   [4] See note to i. 176, 30.
[5] See note to i. 163, 29; and Spingarn, *Lit. Crit.*, p. 51.

but an ornament and no cause of Poetry[1],' and that he may have been helped by that critic to his extension of the notion of the Dramatic Unities[2]. Such points are of minor importance by themselves, but they strengthen the general impression that the Elizabethan critics, and especially Sidney, were in one way or another conversant with the work of their Italian contemporaries.

In the case of Minturno and Scaliger the claim might be urged on the side of general theory alone, by the terms of the defence of poetry, the view as to its origin, and the history of its development. Minturno is not named by any of the essayists: Scaliger is frequently cited by them, and at least four times by Sidney. The contrast may be explained by the fact that Minturno was almost exclusively a critic[3], known to critics by two works, while Scaliger had already a European reputation, based on a long series of treatises, of which the *Poetice* was but a part. It was easier to draw silently from Minturno than from imperial Scaliger, a name to be conjured with even in the *Pueriles* of the schools.

Minturno's earlier work *De Poeta* (1559)[4] shows nearly all the points of contact. Harington may have his *Arte Poetica* (1564)[5] in mind when he refers to the opinion of

[1] See note to i. 159, 35.   [2] i. 398.

[3] He wrote verses in Latin and Italian. He is the author of *L'amore innamorato* (1559).

[4] ANTONII | SEBASTIANI MINTVRNI | DE POETA, AD HECTOREM | PIGNATELLVM, VIBONEN- | SIVM DVCEM, | LIBRI SEX | . . | VENETIIS, ANN. MDLIX.   4to. pp. v + 567.

[5] L'ARTE POETICA | DEL SIG. ANTONIO | MINTVRNO, | NELLA QVALE SI CONTENGONO | *i precetti Heroici, Tragici, Comici, Saty|r-ici, e d'ogni altra Poesia:* | CON LA DOTTRINA DE' SONETTI, CANZO-|ni, *& ogni sorte di Rime Thoscane, doue s'insegna il mo-|do, che tenne il Petrarca nelle sue opere.* | *Et si dichiara a' suoi luoghi tutto quel, che da Aristotele, Horatio,* | *& altri auttori Greci, e Latini è stato scritto per* | *ammaestramento di Poeti.* | CON LE POSTILLE DEL DOTTOR VALVASSORI, ... || *Per Gio. Andrea Valuassori del* M.D.LXIIII.   4to. x + 48 (Contents and Index) + 453 + 2 (unnumbered).

'Aristotle and the best censurers of Poesy' on the 'period' of the Epic[1]. There is less doubt about Sidney's connexion with the *De Poeta*. Almost all the references are to be found in the *Apologie*, and there in the first instance; for, as we shall see, Sidney was in turn freely copied by his English contemporaries. Yet his disciple Harington, who had stronger Italian interests than any, must have known it at first hand, if only because of the very guilty passage on 'Peripeteia' and 'Agnition[2].' The traces of Minturno are more obvious in the earlier portion of Sidney's essay, where indeed they should occur, as the portion is concerned with general doctrine and allows less opportunity for original and English matter. Of these may be mentioned the terms of his plea for the antiquity of poetry[3], and for its being found in all nations[4]; the order of the illustrative details in the passage on the works of Nature as the principal object of art[5]; the view that the poet feigns notable images of virtues and vices[6]; the criticism of the 'thorny argument' of the philosopher[7], which, though found in Daniello, probably takes its true place with the subsequent passage comparing the poet with the philosopher[8]. These and the important reference to 'Admiration[9]' are seven: the Notes will supply as many more; and others may be discoverable. It is open to any one to dispute Sidney's debt in each case, but we cannot escape the lesson of the whole body, even if they are only possibilities. A dozen possible indications of borrowing constitute the best of circumstantial evidence.

The case for Scaliger[10] is still more clear, partly be-

---

[1] See note to ii. 216, 17-18.   [2] Note to ii. 216, 18, &c.
[3] i. 151, 22. See the notes to this passage and the following for the references to Minturno's text.
[4] i. 153, 12.   [5] i. 155, 34, &c.   [6] i. 160, 13-16.
[7] i. 164, 12-13.   [8] i. 164, 25, &c.   [9] See note, i. 392.
[10] IVLII CAESARIS | SCALIGERI, VIRI | CLARISSIMI, |

cause the writers have on not a few occasions admitted their knowledge of his treatise. It is not difficult, for example, to see that Sidney's dramatic theory, though Aristotelian, is derived through the medium of Scaliger, and that his illustrations[1] and his 'lists' are reminiscent of the *Poetice*. Passages such as that on the poet as maker[2], on imitation[3], on the three several kinds[4], and on the very end of poetry[5], give point to the direct reference in Sidney's peroration[6]. He is, by his own admission, brought to the question of the necessity of verse to poetry by a passage in Scaliger[7]. Webbe may be echoing Scaliger when he points to the *Iliad* and *Odyssey* as fixing the distinction of the dramatic kinds[8], though the idea was widely diffused[9], and may have been borrowed from Donatus. Puttenham, who had lived abroad and refers to Italian and French matters in his *Arte*, is distinctly Scaligerian in his general notion of poetry and the function of the poet, and comes perilously near direct copying in details of the more rhetorical kind; e.g. in his treatment of the 'figured' verses[10], and perhaps in his definition of *Energia* and *Enargia*[11]. Harington refers to Scaliger's Maronism[12], a topic which gives Chapman an opportunity for vigorous denunciation. Yet in the latter's epithets and taunts there is something more

---

POETICES LIBRI SEPTEM: || I. *Historicus*. II. *Hyle*. III. *Idea*. IV. *Parasceve*. V. *Criticus*. VI. *Hypercri-ticus*. VII. *Epinomis*. | *Ad Sylvium Filium*. || *Apud Ioannem Crispinum* | M.D.LXI. Fol., 364 pp. double columns +36 pp. of Index (triple columns). The second edition appeared in 1581 ('*Apud Petrum Santandreanum*'). The fifth, which is now the most easily procurable, was issued in 1617 ('*In Bibliopolio Commeliano*').

[1] e.g. Theagines and Cariclea, i. 160, 8, note.

[2] i. 155, 26. See the notes to this passage and the others for the references to Scaliger's text.

[3] i. 158, 5, &c.   [4] i. 158, 9.   [5] i. 197, 3.   [6] i. 206, 9–11.
[7] i. 182.   [8] i. 249. See note to i. 248, 26, &c.   [9] Cf. Puttenham.
[10] ii. 95; ch. xiii, note.   [11] ii. 148, 9–12, note.   [12] ii. 210, 11.

than angry froth: 'Thou soule-blind Scaliger, that neuer hadst anything *but place, time, and termes* to paint thy proficiencie in learning[1].'

The relationship may, however, be illustrated in other ways than by chapter and page in specified authors. There are certain common topics, and metaphors and phrases, and methods, which, though they cannot be ascribed to any one, were first formulated in Italian, or at least came from it to English criticism. The evergreen antithesis of the soldier and scholar[2] is an Italian commonplace, which is used to some purpose in Sidney's plea for poetry as the companion of the camps. The notion of the speaking picture, though as old as Simonides, was discovered by English critics in Renaissance Italy. So too was the culinary metaphor by which poetry is a dainty dish of divers ingredients; and so the nursery figure of coated pills, and rhubarb and candy, which do so much for the allegorical part of the argument. And the bee which distilled honey and the spider which sucked poison, for the benefit of controversialists on the goodness or badness of poetry, were creatures of the South. We may reasonably suspect that Sidney's metaphor of the ulcer[3] discovers a trace of that Italian tradition which expresses the original medical sense of κάθαρσις. Minturno clearly leans to this view[4], though he is, with the majority of his countrymen, as with Milton in English[5], medical rather than surgical. Again, in regard to the form and literary manner, apart from the material of the essays, there are salient likenesses which are best explained by some sort of kinship. The conception of the treatise, whether 'art' or 'apology,' its ordonnance, its restriction to poetry, its

---

[1] ii. 301. [2] See note, i. 395. [3] i. 177. [4] *De Poeta*, especially p. 64.
[5] *Preface* to *Samson Agonistes*. See Mr. Bywater's article on 'Milton and the Aristotelian Definition of Tragedy' in the *Journal of Philology*, xxvii. 54 (1900), pp. 267-75.

monotony in title, give these essays a familiar look to the reader who knows the Italian predecessors, and is yet willing to make full allowance for the English quality of such a writer as Sidney. Of the mere cataloguing manner, shown at its best, or worst, in the *Palladis Tamia*, it is reasonable, and certainly generous, to think of the models supplied by Lilius Gyraldus and others. And as for the 'trade of glose,' which Nash saw to be as painfully enlarged as that of translation, it is not fantastical to find some clue in the well-strewn *postilli* and *sposizioni* of the Italian critics and poets [1]—even if we had not had 'E. K.'s frank statement that the manner then seemed 'strange and rare in our tongue [2].'

The 'filcheries' from French criticism are unimportant and would appear to be confined to the contemporary prefaces of Du Bellay and Ronsard [3]. The earlier dissertations from Deschamps to Sibilet, had they been known, would have given little to the theorists of Poetry, and would have been useless to English prosodists. Interesting as it is to find the old lines of argument on the antiquity of poetry in Sibilet [4], Pelletier [5], Fauchet [6], or De Laudun [7]; or Sidney's comparison of the poet with the orator in Pelletier [8], or his views on poets' being more than rhymers in Sibilet [9]; or to read the general defence of French against 'outlandish' and 'inkhorn' dangers such as beset English; or to be reminded in Fauchet [10] of Ascham's

---

[1] Self-commentators, like Watson in his 'Ἑκατομπαθία, had many patterns in the Italian poets, from the author of the *Vita Nuova* onwards.

[2] i. 132.   [3] See the bibliographical notes, i. 404.

[4] Thomas Sibilet, *Art Poétique François* (1548), I. 1.

[5] Jacques Pelletier, *L'Art Poëtique* (1555), I.

[6] Claude Fauchet, *Recueil de l'Origine de le Langue et Poesie Françoise, ryme et romans*, 1581 (*Œuvres*, 1610, p. 545).

[7] Pierre de Laudun, *L'Art Poétique François* (1598), I.

[8] u. s.   [9] u. s., II. 2.   [10] u. s., pp. 548⁰, 549.

account of the origin of rhyme, or in Jean de la Taille[1] of Sidney's advance in the conception of the Dramatic Unities—nothing but parallelism can be proved, or is likely. This is perhaps remarkable, when we consider how much of French literature was known to the Elizabethans, and how even these essays show some knowledge of French authors. On the other hand, it need not be pointed out that though this fact makes French criticism of small account for our present purpose, that criticism is of the greatest importance to the comparative study of critical development. For a spontaneous parallelism in idea in two literatures may give a better clue to first principles than a parallelism which is merely, or largely, derivative. So it would appear that though the French Arts of Poetry are not very helpful in explaining the genealogy of English doctrine, their interpretative value in the study of Renaissance theory in England is not inferior to that of the Italian models. And, it may be added, this would appear to be the true lesson of the French analogies in later periods and in other 'kinds,' where direct influence, though stronger than here, has without doubt been exaggerated.

The French influence showed itself in borrowings of words, as noted by 'E. K.'[2] and Puttenham[3]—quaffings of the 'cup of Frenchman's Helicon' as the *Returne from Parnassus* has it[4]—and in certain plagiarisms of conceits and verse-forms from the literature of the *Pléiade*[5]; or it acted in the more general way of suggesting a topic, as is shown in Carew's acknowledgements to Henri Estienne[6]. The technical concern of Du Bellay and Ronsard in matters of poetic diction and metre per-

---

[1] *De l'Art de la Tragedie*, the preface to *Paul le Furieux* (1572).
[2] i. 130.   [3] ii. 171.   [4] ii. 402.
[5] See Mr. Bullen's note in *Lyrics from Elizabethan Dramatists*, 1891, p. 288.   [6] ii. 285, note.

Introduction

force restricted their effect to a small part of English criticism. Indeed, if any critical debts or parallelisms are to be found we must look for them in metrical essays of the type of Gascoigne's and King James's. An agreement such as appears between Sidney[1] and Ronsard is reached independently, and most probably from Scaliger or other Italian sources.

The hard characterization of the poet by Gascoigne, and especially by James[2], is in marked contrast with the Italian view, and is strongly reminiscent of Du Bellay and Ronsard. The former is named by James in his tract, when he explains his reasons for undertaking an Art of Scots Poetry, and excuses himself for repeating second-hand observations. His seventh chapter[3], on the difference between the attitude of the translator and of the poet, may be part of his debt. Puttenham's theft from the *Defense*[4], though not of critical importance, shows at least that he was familiar with its text. The suggestions of indebtedness to Ronsard are perhaps more numerous. These may be found in the remarks on invention[5], on the musical value of the caesura[6], and on the use of 'comparisons[7].' Puttenham's reference to the metre of twelve syllables, which 'the Frenchman calleth a verse *Alexandrine*[8],' may well have come from Ronsard's chapter, ' Des vers Alexandrins' in the *Abrégé*.

Great as is the debt of Elizabethan literature to Spain[9], it would appear that criticism owes nothing. Occasional references, such as Ascham's to Gonçalvo Perez's translation of Homer[10], or Puttenham's to Vargas[11], or

---

[1] i. 182, 17-18, note.   [2] See i. 211, 19-32, note.
[3] i. 221. See the notes to this and the other passages for the references to Du Bellay and Ronsard.   [4] See ii. 417.   [5] i. 47, &c.
[6] i. 54, 216.   [7] i. 219, 9 and perhaps 18.   [8] 11 ii. 75.
[9] Cf. e. g. ii. p. 440.   [10] i. 32.   [11] ii. 18.

Puttenham's and Harvey's to Guevara[1], show but a more or less direct knowledge of certain Spanish books. It could not well be otherwise, for Spanish criticism, if we exclude the older rhetorical treatises, does not begin before the close of the century, in Rengifo (1592) and Alonzo Lopez (1596); and these do not appear to have been known in England. Even the excusable suspicion that something of the Spanish dramatic heresies of the mixture of kinds and of indifference to the Unities may have affected English criticism, and perhaps Sidney himself, is dispelled when we find that the earlier Spanish examples were not yet available. All that is allowed to us is to speculate on the change of attitude which might have taken place in English dramatic criticism had chronology been other than it was.

The tale of indebtedness is not complete until we know how much the Elizabethans borrowed from each other. That it can be proved that they plagiarized may strengthen the contention that they would not be less inclined to draw from such foreign writers as were accessible; but at the same time it compels us to guard against overestimating the extent of that draught. For it is clear that not a few of the statements, which are obviously non-English in origin, are taken from English writers who had already made them their own. We are helped to this in some places by the greater frankness of the borrowers (partly due to the growing pride in the sufficiency of English letters), and in others by the forced confession of the texts.

We have an interesting side-light on this literary habit in the frequent efforts to apportion what is, in Puttenham's words, 'as borrowed, and what as of our own peculiar[2].' It is one of 'E. K.'s commendations of Spenser that he follows the 'footing' of many poets, 'yet so as few, but

[1] Haslewood, p. 176; Arber, p. 220; ii. 276.   [2] ii. 26.

they be well scented, can trace him out¹.' The Sidney of
the *Apologie* can protest, as the poet lover of Stella,

> 'Some doe I heare of Poets fury tell,
> But God wot, wot not what they meane by it:
> And this I sweare by blackest brooke of hell,
> I am no Pickepurse of an others wit².'

Nash resents the charge that he has borrowed from
Greene, or Tarlton, or Lyly: 'the vein which I have ...
is of my own begetting, and calls no man father in
England but myself³.' As things went, each critic, like
each poet, might well suspect his neighbour. Harington's
preface takes a different place when we discover how
inadequately his acknowledgement to Sidney covers his
debt to the *Apologie*. Meres, obviously a dullard to the
most casual reader, discloses an editorial cunning which
does him credit, and indeed makes his *Comparative Discourse* not the least important of these documents. For by
having no mind of his own, and only a plodding interest
in the whims of others, he has given us a digest of contemporary history and opinion which is of positive value.

Not a little comes to these essayists from writers of the
earlier part of the century: notably from the different
editions of Wilson's *Arte of Rhetorique* (1553) and his
Rule of Reason, conteinyng the Art of Logique (1551),
and from Sir Thomas Elyot's *Governour* (1531)⁴. Yet
the relationship is one of general agreement rather than
of literal copying. We can see, for example, in Wilson's
view that 'eloquence itself came not up first by the art,
but the art rather was gathered upon eloquence⁵' something of his successors' dislike of a critical tyranny.
Of their own number, Ascham and Sidney are the
favourite quarries. Ascham's 'dead advertisement and

---
¹ i. 132.   ² *Astrophel and Stella*, lxxiv. 5-8.   ³ ii. 243.
⁴ e.g. i. 360, 388, 413. No influence from Coxe's earlier work on
Rhetoric (*c.* 1530) is recognizable.   ⁵ Fol. 3.

persuasion,' as Harvey calls it[1], in behalf of artificial verses, is kindly remembered by the reformers. Stanyhurst cites the 'golden pamphlet entitled *The Scholemaster*' on this point[2]; and Webbe repeats its views on the barbarous origin of rhyming[3], and incorporates at least one passage *verbatim*[4]. Nash refers his reader to its excellent censures on Greek and Latin authors[5]. The debt to Sidney is greater—a fact the more striking when we remember that the *Apologie* remained in MS. till 1595. He is known to everybody, and cited by nearly all, but never so greedily as by his admirer Harington[6]. Puttenham, however, is not far behind[7]. And Harington is in turn indebted to Puttenham[8]; as James VI and Webbe are to Gascoigne[9]. But we cannot thread this labyrinth. The Notes will supply clues to what each author has taken from his contemporaries. There is some recompense in this discounting of the originality of these essayists. It may minimize their individual value, but it at least shows that a critical interest had arisen, and that by it not only many, but the best of them, had been attracted. The activity discloses, as it were, a rude concerted plan for the recognition of the Art of Criticism as a separate branch of English literature. It matters not how much was copied, or how much was inappropriate to English needs, if we acknowledge the vitality of the Elizabethan endeavour which lies behind old argument and metaphor, and see in these registers the genuine beginnings of a literary 'kind' in England, and the first hints of the true temper of English criticism.

[1] i. 101. [2] i. 137. [3] i. 240. [4] i. 267. [5] i. 337.
[6] ii. 196, and notes from p. 422 onwards. [7] e.g. ii. 408, 410, &c.
[8] ii. 196, &c. [9] i. 414, &c.; and see the notes to James VI's *Schort Treatise*, i. 403 et seq.

ROGER ASCHAM

(FROM *THE SCHOLEMASTER*)

1570

[THE First Book of *The Scholemaster* (London, John Daye: 1570) deals with 'the bringyng up of youth,' and is only incidentally concerned with matters of literary interest; but it supplies hints of certain topics which are discussed more fully elsewhere. Ascham defines the Platonic εὐφυής, the first of the seven 'trewe notes of a good witte'; he interpolates a recommendation of the new 'versifying,' on which he promises to speak 'more at large hereafter'; and, in the well-known passage on the evil influence of Italian travel and Italian books (especially in English translation), he shows his sympathy with the Puritanical principles of Gosson and the anti-stage pamphleteers. In introducing the seven 'trewe notes' he says:

'And bicause I write English, and to Englishemen, I will plainlie declare in Englishe both what thies wordes of *Plato* meane, and how aptlie they be linked and how orderlie they folow one an other.'

He then proceeds:

'Εὐφυής is he that is apte by goodnes of witte, and appliable by readines of will, to learning, hauing all other qualities of the minde and partes of the bodie, that must an other day serue learning, not trobled, mangled, and halfed, but sounde, whole, full, and hable to do their office: as, a tong, not stamering, or ouer hardlie drawing forth wordes, but plaine, and redie to deliuer the meaning of the minde; a voice, not softe, weake, piping, womannishe, but audible, stronge, and manlike; a countenance, not werishe and crabbed, but faire and cumlie; a personage, not wretched and deformed, but taule and

'goodlie: for surelie a cumlie countenance, with a goodlie
stature, geueth credit to learning, and authoritie to the
person; otherwise, commonlie, either open contempte or
priuie disfauour doth hurte, or hinder, both person and
learning. And euen as a faire stone requireth to be sette
in the finest gold with the best workmanshyp, or else it
leseth moch of the Grace and price, euen so excellencye
in learning, and namely Diuinitie, ioyned with a cumlie
personage, is a meruelous Iewell in the world. And how
can a cumlie bodie be better employed than to serue the
fairest exercise of Goddes greatest gifte, and that is learning?
But commonlie the fairest bodies ar bestowed on the foulest
purposes. I would it were not so, and with examples herein
I will not medle: yet I wishe that those shold both mynde
it and medle with it, which haue most occasion to looke to
it, as good and wise fathers shold do, and greatest authoritie
to amend it, as good and wise magistrates ought to do.
And yet I will not let openlie to lament the vnfortunate
case of learning herein.

'For, if a father haue foure sonnes, three faire and well
formed both mynde and bodie, the fourth wretched, lame,
and deformed, his choice shalbe to put the worst to learning,
as one good enoughe to becum a scholer. I haue spent the
most parte of my life in the Vniuersitie, and therfore I can
beare good witnes that many fathers commonlie do thus;
wherof I haue hard many wise, learned, and as good men
as euer I knew make great and oft complainte: a good
horseman will choise no soch colte, neither for his own
nor yet for his masters sadle.'

Further over, Ascham enlarges on the moral weakness of
Italianate Englishmen, and concludes:

'These be the inchantementes of *Circes*, brought out of
Italie, to marre mens maners in England; much by example of ill life, but more by preceptes of fonde bookes,
of late translated out of *Italian* into English, sold in
euery shop in London, commended by honest titles the
soner to corrupt honest maners, dedicated ouer boldlie
to vertuous and honorable personages the easielier to
begile simple and innocent wittes. It is pitie that those
which haue authoritie and charge to allow and dissalow

'bookes to be printed be no more circumspect herein than they are. Ten Sermons at Paules Crosse do not so moch good for mouyng men to trewe doctrine as one of those bookes do harme with inticing men to ill liuing. Yea, I say farder, those bookes tend not so moch to corrupt honest liuing as they do to subuert trewe Religion. Mo Papistes be made by your mery bookes of *Italie* than by your earnest bookes of *Louain*. And bicause our great Phisicians do winke at the matter, and make no counte of this sore, I, though not admitted one of their felowshyp, yet hauyng bene many yeares a prenfice to Gods trewe Religion, and trust to continewe a poore iorney man therein all dayes of my life, for the dewtie I owe, and loue I beare, both to trewe doctrine and honest liuing, though I haue no authoritie to amend the sore my selfe, yet I will declare my good will to discouer the sore to others.

' S. Paul saith that sectes and ill opinions be the workes of the flesh and frutes of sinne: this is spoken no more trewlie for the doctrine than sensiblie for the reason. And why? For ill doinges breed ill thinkinges. And of corrupted maners spryng peruerted iudgementes. And how? There be in man two speciall thinges: Mans will, mans mynde. Where will inclineth to goodnes, the mynde is bent to troth: Where will is caried from goodnes to vanitie, the mynde is sone drawne from troth to false opinion. And so the readiest way to entangle the mynde with false doctrine is first to intice the will to wanton liuyng. Therfore, when the busie and open Papistes abroad could not, by their contentious bookes, turne men in England fast enough from troth and right iudgement in doctrine, than the sutle and secrete Papistes at home procured bawdie bookes to be translated out of the *Italian* tonge, whereby ouer many yong willes and wittes allured to wantonnes do now boldly contemne all seuere bookes that sounde to honestie and godlines. In our forefathers tyme, whan Papistrie, as a standyng poole, couered and ouerflowed all England, fewe bookes were read in our tong, sauyng certaine bookes of Cheualrie, as they sayd, for pastime and pleasure, which, as some say, were made in Monasteries, by idle Monkes or wanton Chanons: as 'one for example, *Morte Arthure*; the whole pleasure of which booke standeth in two speciall poyntes, in open mans slaughter and bold bawdrye: In which booke those be counted the noblest Knightes that do kill most men without any quarell, and commit fowlest aduoulteres by sutlest shiftes; as Sir *Launcelote*, with the wife of king *Arthure*, his master: Syr *Tristram*, with the wife of kyng *Marke*, his vncle: Syr *Lamerocke*, with the wife of king *Lote*, that was his own aunte. This is good stuffe for wise men to laughe at, or honest men to take pleasure at. Yet I know when Gods Bible was banished the Court, and *Morte Arthure* receiued into the Princes chamber. What toyes the dayly readyng of such a booke may worke in the will of a yong ientleman, or a yong mayde, that liueth welthelie and idlelie, wise men can iudge, and honest men do pitie. And yet ten *Morte Arthures* do not the tenth part so much harme as one of these bookes made in *Italie* and translated in England. They open, not fond and common wayes to vice, but such subtle, cunnyng, new, and diuerse shiftes, to cary yong willes to vanitie, and yong wittes to mischief, to teach old bawdes new schole poyntes, as the simple head of an English man is not hable to inuent, nor neuer was hard of in England before, yea when Papistrie ouerflowed all. Suffer these bookes to be read, and they shall soone displace all bookes of godly learnyng. For they, caryng the will to vanitie and marryng good maners, shall easily corrupt the mynde with ill opinions and false iudgement in doctrine; first to thinke ill of all trewe Religion, and at last to thinke nothyng of God hym selfe, one speciall pointe that is to be learned in *Italie* and *Italian* bookes. And that which is most to be lamented, and therfore more nedefull to be looked to, there be moe of these vngratious bookes set out in Printe within these fewe monethes than haue bene sene in England many score yeare before. And bicause our English men made *Italians* can not hurt but certaine persons, and in certaine places, therfore these *Italian* bookes are made English, to bryng mischief enough openly and boldly to all states, great and meane, yong and old, euery where.'

The Second Book, 'teachyng the ready way to the Latin tong,' begins with some general remarks on the practical value of 'double translation,' and then proceeds to discuss the 'six wayes appointed by the best learned men for the learning of tonges and encreace of eloquence,' viz. *Translatio linguarum, Paraphrasis, Metaphrasis, Epitome, Imitatio, Declamatio*. The more important matter for our present purpose is found in the fifth and concluding section[1] (fol. 45 v⁰ to the end), which is here printed from the copy in the Bodleian Library (Malone, 645).]

IMITATIO

IMITATION is a facultie to expresse liuelie and perfitelie that example which ye go about to folow. And of it selfe it is large and wide: for all the workes of nature in a maner be examples for arte to folow.

5 But to our purpose: all languages, both learned and mother tonges, be gotten, and gotten onelie by *Imitation*. For as ye vse to heare, so ye learne to speake: if ye heare no other, ye speake not your selfe: and whome ye onelie heare, of them ye onelie learne.

10 And therefore, if ye would speake as the best and wisest do, ye must be conuersant where the best and wisest are: but if yow be borne or brought vp in a rude contrie, ye shall not chose but speake rudelie: the rudest man of all knoweth this to be trewe.

15 Yet neuerthelesse, the rudenes of common and mother tonges is no bar for wise speaking. For in the rudest contrie, and most barbarous mother language, many be found [that] can speake verie wiselie: but in the Greeke and Latin tong, the two onelie learned tonges, which be 20 kept not in common taulke but in priuate bookes, we finde alwayes wisdome and eloquence, good matter and good vtterance, neuer or seldom asonder. For all soch Authors as be fullest of good matter and right iudgement in

---

[1] Ascham omits the sixth section. It was perhaps never written. See the Notes for his account of his original scheme.

doctrine be likewise always most proper in wordes, most
apte in sentence, most plaine and pure in vttering the
same.

And, contrariwise, in those two tonges, all writers, either
in Religion or any sect of Philosophie, who so euer be
founde fonde in iudgement of matter, be commonlie found as
rude in vttering their mynde. For Stoickes, Anabaptistes,
and Friers, with Epicures, Libertines, and Monkes, being
most like in learning and life, are no fonder and pernicious
in their opinions than they be rude and barbarous in their
writinges. They be not wise therefore that say, 'What
care I for a mans wordes and vtterance, if his matter and
reasons be good.' Soch men say so, not so moch of
ignorance, as eyther of some singular pride in themselues
or some speciall malice or other, or for some priuate and
parciall matter, either in Religion or other kinde of learning. For good and choice meates be no more requisite
for helthie bodies than proper and apte wordes be for
good matters, and also plaine and sensible vtterance for
the best and depest reasons: in which two pointes standeth
perfite eloquence, one of the fairest and rarest giftes that
God doth geue to man.

Ye know not what hurt ye do to learning, that care not
for wordes but for matter, and so make a deuorse betwixt
the tong and the hart. For marke all aiges: looke vpon
the whole course of both the Greeke and Latin tonge, and
ye shall surelie finde that, whan apte and good wordes
began to be neglected, and properties of those two tonges
to be confounded, than also began ill deedes to spring,
strange maners to oppresse good orders, newe and fond
opinions to striue with olde and trewe doctrine, first in
Philosophie and after in Religion, right iudgement of all
thinges to be peruerted, and so vertue with learning is
contemned, and studie left of: of ill thoughtes cummeth
peruerse iudgement, of ill deedes springeth lewde taulke.

Of Imitation

Which fower misorders, as they mar mans life, so destroy they good learning withall.

But behold the goodnesse of Gods prouidence for learning: all olde authors and sectes of Philosophy, which were fondest in opinion and rudest in vtterance, as Stoickes and Epicures, first contemned of wise men and after forgotten of all men, be so consumed by tymes, as they be now not onelie out of vse but also out of memorie of man: which thing, I surelie thinke, will shortlie chance to the whole doctrine and all the bookes of phantasticall Anabaptistes and Friers, and of the beastlie Libertines and Monkes.

Againe, behold on the other side how Gods wisdome hath wrought, that of *Academici* and *Peripatetici*, those that were wisest in iudgement of matters and purest in vttering their myndes, the first and chiefest that wrote most and best in either tong, as *Plato* and *Aristotle* in Greeke, *Tullie* in Latin, be so either wholie or sufficiently left vnto vs, as I neuer knew yet scholer that gaue himselfe to like, and loue, and folowe chieflie those three Authors, but he proued both learned, wise, and also an honest man, if he ioyned with all the trewe doctrine of Gods holie Bible, without the which the other three be but fine edge tooles in a fole or mad mans hand.

But to returne to *Imitation* agayne: There be three kindes of it in matters of learning.

The whole doctrine of Comedies and Tragedies is a perfite *imitation*, or faire liuelie painted picture of the life of euerie degree of man. Of this *Imitation* writeth *Plato* at large in 3. *de Rep.*, but it doth not moch belong at this time to our purpose.

The second kind of *Imitation* is to folow for learning of tonges and sciences the best authors. Here riseth, emonges proude and enuious wittes, a great controuersie, whether one or many are to be folowed: and, if one, who is that one; *Seneca* or *Cicero*; *Salust* or *Cæsar*; and so forth in Greeke and Latin.

The third kinde of *Imitation* belongeth to the second: as, when you be determined whether ye will folow one or mo, to know perfitlie, and which way to folow, that one; in what place; by what meane and order; by what tooles and instrumentes ye shall do it; by what skill and iudgement ye shall trewelie discerne whether ye folow rightlie or no.

This *Imitatio* is *dissimilis materiei similis tractatio*; and, also, *similis materiei dissimilis tractatio*, as *Virgill* folowed *Homer*: but the Argument to the one was *Vlysses*, to the other *Æneas*. *Tullie* persecuted *Antonie* with the same wepons of eloquence that *Demosthenes* vsed before against *Philippe*.

Horace foloweth *Pindar*, but either of them his owne Argument and Person; as the one, *Hiero* king of *Sicilie*, the other, *Augustus* the Emperor: and yet both for like respectes, that is, for their coragious stoutnes in warre and iust gouernment in peace.

One of the best examples for right *Imitation* we lacke, and that is *Menander*, whom our *Terence* (as the matter required), in like argument, in the same Persons, with equall eloquence, foote by foote did folow.

Som peeces remaine, like broken Iewelles, whereby men may rightlie esteme and iustlie lament the losse of the whole.

Erasmus, the ornament of learning in our tyme, doth wish that som man of learning and diligence would take the like paines in *Demosthenes* and *Tullie* that *Macrobius* hath done in *Homer* and *Virgill*, that is, to write out and ioyne together where the one doth imitate the other. *Erasmus* wishe is good, but surelie it is not good enough: for *Macrobius* gatherings for the *Æneados* out of *Homer*, and *Eobanus Hessus* more diligent gatherings for the

Of Imitation

Bucolikes out of *Theocritus*, as they be not fullie taken out of the whole heape, as they should be, but euen as though they had not sought for them of purpose but fownd them scatered here and there by chance in their way, euen so, onelie to point out and nakedlie to ioyne togither their sentences, with no farder declaring the maner and way how the one doth folow the other, were but a colde helpe to the encrease of learning.

But if a man would take his paine also, whan he hath layd two places of *Homer* and *Virgill* or of *Demosthenes* and *Tullie* togither, to teach plainlie withall, after this sort:

1. *Tullie* reteyneth thus moch of the matter, thies sentences, thies wordes:

2. This and that he leaueth out, which he doth wittelie to this end and purpose.

3. This he addeth here.

4. This he diminisheth there.

5. This he ordereth thus, with placing that here, not there.

6. This he altereth and changeth, either in propertie of wordes, in forme of sentence, in substance of the matter, or in one or other conuenient circumstance of the authors present purpose.

In thies fewe rude English wordes are wrapt vp all the necessarie tooles and instrumentes, where with trewe *Imitation* is rightlie wrought withall in any tonge. Which tooles, I openlie confesse, be not of myne owne forging, but partlie left vnto me by the cunningest Master, and one of the worthiest Ientlemen that euer England bred, Syr *Iohn Cheke*, partelie borowed by me out of the shoppe of the dearest frende I haue out of England, *Io. St.* And therefore I am the bolder to borow of him, and here to leaue them to other, and namelie to my Children: which tooles, if it please God that an other day they may be able to vse rightlie, as I do wish and

daylie pray they may do, I shal be more glad than if
I were able to leaue them a great quantitie of land.

This foresaide order and doctrine of *Imitation* would
bring forth more learning, and breed vp trewer iudgement, than any other exercise that can be vsed, but not for
yong beginners, bicause they shall not be able to consider
dulie therof. And, trewelie, it may be a shame to good
studentes, who, hauing so faire examples to follow, as
Plato and *Tullie*, do not vse so wise wayes in folowing
them for the obteyning of wisdome and learning as rude
ignorant Artificers do for gayning a small commoditie.
For surelie the meanest painter vseth more witte, better
arte, greater diligence, in hys shoppe, in folowing the
Picture of any meane mans face, than commonlie the best
studentes do, euen in the vniuersitie, for the atteining of
learning it selfe.

Some ignorant, vnlearned, and idle student, or some
busie looker vpon this litle poore booke, that hath neither
will to do good him selfe, nor skill to iudge right of others,
but can lustelie contemne, by pride and ignorance, all
painfull diligence and right order in study, will perchance
say that I am to precise, to curious, in marking and
piteling thus about the imitation of others; and that the
olde worthie Authors did neuer busie their heades and
wittes in folowyng so preciselie, either the matter what
other men wrote, or els the maner how other men wrote.
They will say it were a plaine slauerie, and iniurie to,
to shakkle and tye a good witte, and hinder the course of
a mans good nature, with such bondes of seruitude, in
folowyng other.

Except soch men thinke them selues wiser then *Cicero*
for teaching of eloquence, they must be content to turne
a new leafe.

The best booke that euer *Tullie* wrote, by all mens
iudgement, and by his owne testimonie to, in wrytyng

wherof he employed most care, studie, learnyng, and
iudgement, is his booke *de Orat. ad Q. F.* Now let vs see
what he did for the matter, and also for the maner of
writing therof. For the whole booke consisteth in these
two pointes onelie: In good matter, and good handling of
the matter. And first, for the matter, it is whole *Aristotles*,
what so euer *Antonie* in the second and *Crassus* in the
third doth teach. Trust not me, but beleue *Tullie* him
selfe, who writeth so, first, in that goodlie long Epistle *ad
P. Lentulum*, and after in diuerse places *ad Atticum*. And
in the verie booke it selfe Tullie will not haue it hidden,
but both *Catulus* and *Crassus* do oft and pleasantly lay that
stelth to *Antonius* charge. Now, for the handling of the
matter, was *Tullie* so precise and curious rather to follow
an other mans Paterne than to inuent some newe shape
him selfe, namelie in that booke, wherein he purposed to
leaue to posteritie the glorie of his witte? yea forsoth, that
he did. And this is not my gessing and gathering, nor
onelie performed by *Tullie* in verie deed, but vttered also
by *Tullie* in plaine wordes: to teach other men thereby
what they should do in taking like matter in hand.

And that which is especially to be marked, *Tullie* doth
vtter plainlie his conceit and purpose therein, by the
mouth of the wisest man in all that companie: for sayth
Scaeuola him selfe, *Cur non imitamur, Crasse, Socratem
illum, qui est in Phaedro Platonis? etc.*

And furder to vnderstand that *Tullie* did not *obiter* and
bichance, but purposelie and mindfullie, bend him selfe to
a precise and curious Imitation of *Plato*, concernyng the
shape and forme of those bookes, marke, I pray you, how
curious *Tullie* is to vtter his purpose and doyng therein,
writing thus to *Atticus*.

*Quod in his Oratoriis libris, quos tantopere laudas, per-
sonam desideras Scaeuolae, non eam temere dimoui: sed
feci idem, quod in πολιτείᾳ deus ille noster Plato, cum in*

Piraeeum Socrates venisset ad Cephalum locupletem et festi-
uum senem, quoad primus ille sermo haberetur, adest in
disputando senex: deinde, cum ipse quoque commodissime
locutus esset, ad rem diuinam dicit se velle discedere, neque
postea reuertitur. Credo Platonem vix putasse satis con-
sonum fore, si hominem id aetatis in tam longo sermone
diutius retinuisset. Multo ego satius hoc mihi cauendum
putaui in Scaeuola, qui et aetate et valetudine erat ea qua [*esse*]
meministi, et his honoribus, vt vix satis decorum videretur,
eum plures dies esse in Crassi Tusculano. Et erat primi
libri sermo non alienus a Scaeuolae studiis: reliqui libri
τεχνολογίαν *habent, vt scis. Huic ioculatoriae disputationi*
senem illum, vt noras, interesse sane nolui.

If *Cicero* had not opened him selfe and declared hys owne thought and doynges herein, men that be idle, and ignorant, and enuious of other mens diligence and well doinges, would haue sworne that *Tullie* had neuer mynded any soch thing, but that of a precise curiositie we fayne and forge and father soch thinges of *Tullie* as he neuer ment in deed. I write this not for nought; for I haue heard some both well learned and otherwayes verie wise, that by their lustie misliking of soch diligence haue drawen back the forwardnes of verie good wittes. But euen as such men them selues do sometymes stumble vpon doyng well by chance and benefite of good witte, so would I haue our scholer alwayes able to do well by order of learnyng and right skill of iudgement.

Concernyng *Imitation* many learned men haue written, with moch diuersitie for the matter, and therfore with great contrarietie and some stomacke amongest them selues. I haue read as many as I could get diligentlie, and what I thinke of euerie one of them I will freelie say my mynde. With which freedome I trust good men will beare, bicause it shall tend to neither spitefull nor harmefull controuersie.

Of Imitation

In *Tullie*, it is well touched, shortlie taught, not fullie declared by *Ant.* in 2. *de Orat.*: and afterward in *Orat. ad Brutum*, for the liking and misliking of *Isocrates*: and the contrarie iudgement of *Tullie* agaynst *Caluus*, *Brutus*, and *Calidius*, *de genere dicendi Attico et Asiatico*.

Dionis. Halic. περὶ μιμήσεως I feare is lost: which Author, next *Aristotle*, *Plato*, and *Tullie*, of all other that write of eloquence, by the iudgement of them that be best learned, deserueth the next prayse and place.

Quintilian writeth of it, shortly and coldlie for the matter, yet hotelie and spitefullie enough agaynst the Imitation of *Tullie*.

Erasmus, beyng more occupied in spying other mens faultes than declaryng his owne aduise, is mistaken of many, to the great hurt of studie, for his authoritie sake. For he writeth rightlie, rightlie vnderstanded: he and *Longolius* onelie differing in this, that the one seemeth to giue ouermoch, the other ouer litle, to him whom they both best loued and chiefly allowed of all other.

Budæus in his Commentaries roughlie and obscurelie, after his kinde of writyng: and for the matter, caryed somewhat out of the way in ouermuch misliking the Imitation of *Tullie*.

Phil. Melancthon learnedlie and trewlie.

Camerarius largely with a learned iudgement, but somewhat confusedly, and with ouer rough a stile.

Sambucus largely, with a right iudgement but somewhat a crooked stile.

Other haue written also, as *Cortesius* to *Politian*, and that verie well: *Bembus ad Picum* a great deale better: but *Ioan. Sturmius*, *de Nobilitate literata et de Amissa dicendi ratione*, farre best of all, in myne opinion, that euer tooke this matter in hand. For all the rest declare chiefly this point, whether one, or many, or all are to be followed: but *Sturmius* onelie hath most learnedlie declared who is to be followed, what is to be followed, and, the best point of all, by what way and order trew Imitation is rightlie to be exercised. And although *Sturmius* herein doth farre passe all other, yet hath he not so fullie and perfitelie done it as I do wishe he had, and as I know he could. For though he hath done it perfitelie for precept, yet hath he not done it perfitelie enough for example: which he did, neither for lacke of skill, nor by negligence, but of purpose, contented with one or two examples, bicause he was mynded in those two bookes to write of it both shortlie, and also had to touch other matters.

Barthol. Riccius Ferrariensis also hath written learnedlie, diligentlie, and verie largelie of this matter, euen as hee did before verie well *de Apparatu linguae Lat.* He writeth the better in myne opinion, bicause his whole doctrine, iudgement, and order semeth to be borowed out of *Io. Stur.* bookes. He addeth also examples, the best kinde of teaching: wherein he doth well, but not well enough: in deede, he committeth no faulte, but yet deserueth small praise. He is content with the meane, and followeth not the best: as a man that would feede vpon Acornes, whan he may eate as good cheape the finest wheat bread. He teacheth, for example, where and how two or three late *Italian* Poetes do follow *Virgil*; and how *Virgil* him selfe in the storie of *Dido* doth wholie imitate *Catullus* in the like matter of *Ariadna*: Wherein I like better his diligence and order of teaching than his iudgement in choice of examples for *Imitation*. But, if he had done thus, if he had declared where and how, how oft and how many wayes, *Virgil* doth folow *Homer*, as for example the comming of *Vlysses* to *Alcynous* and *Calypso*, with the comming of *Æneas* to *Cartage* and *Dido*; Likewise the games, running, wrestling, and shoting, that *Achilles* maketh in *Homer*, with the selfe same games that *Æneas* maketh in *Virgil*; The harnesse of *Achilles*, with the harnesse of

Æneas, and the maner of making of them both by *Vulcane*; The notable combate betwixt *Achilles* and *Hector*, with as notable a combate betwixt *Æneas* and *Turnus*; The going downe to hell of *Vlysses* in *Homer*, with the going downe to hell of *Æneas* in *Virgil*; and other places infinite mo, as similitudes, narrations, messages, discriptions of persons, places, battels, tempestes, shipwrackes, and common places for diuerse purposes, which be as precisely taken out of *Homer* as euer did Painter in London follow the picture of any faire personage; And when thies places had bene gathered together by this way of diligence, than to haue conferred them together by this order of teaching, as diligently to marke what is kept and vsed in either author, in wordes, in sentences, in matter, what is added, what is left out, what ordered otherwise, either *praeponendo*, *interponendo*, or *postponendo*, and what is altered for any respect, in word, phrase, sentence, figure, reason, argument, or by any way of circumstance: If *Riccius* had done this, he had not onely bene well liked for his diligence in teaching, but also iustlie commended for his right iudgement in right choice of examples for the best *Imitation*.

Riccius also for *Imitation* of prose declareth where and how *Longolius* doth folow *Tullie*; but, as for *Longolius*, I would not haue him the patern of our *Imitation*. In deede, in *Longolius* shoppe be proper and faire shewing colers, but as for shape, figure, and naturall cumlines, by the iudgement of best iudging artificers he is rather allowed as one to be borne withall than especially commended as one chieflie to be folowed.

If *Riccius* had taken for his examples where *Tullie* him selfe foloweth either *Plato* or *Demosthenes*, he had shot than at the right marke. But to excuse *Riccius* somwhat, though I can not fullie defend him, it may be sayd his purpose was to teach onelie the Latin tong; when thys way that I do wish, to ioyne *Virgil* with *Homer*, to read

Tullie with *Demosthenes* and *Plato*, requireth a cunning and perfite Master in both the tonges. It is my wish in deede, and that by good reason: For who so euer will write well of any matter must labor to expresse that that is perfite, and not to stay and content himselfe with the meane: yea, I say farder, though it be not vnposible, yet it is verie rare, and meruelous hard, to proue excellent in the Latin tong for him that is not also well seene in the Greeke tong. *Tullie* him selfe, most excellent of nature, most diligent in labor, brought vp from his cradle in that place and in that tyme where and whan the Latin tong most florished naturallie in euery mans mouth, yet was not his owne tong able it selfe to make him so cunning in his owne tong, as he was in deede, but the knowledge and *Imitation* of the Greeke tong withall.

This he confesseth himselfe; this he vttereth in many places, as those can tell best that vse to read him most.

Therefore thou that shotest at perfection in the Latin tong think not thy selfe wiser than *Tullie* was, in choice of the way that leadeth rightlie to the same: thinke not thy witte better than *Tullies* was, as though that may serue thee that was not sufficient for him. For euen as a hauke flieth not hie with one wing, euen so a man reacheth not to excellency with one tong.

I haue bene a looker on in the Cokpit of learning thies many yeares: And one Cock onelie haue I knowne, which with one wing, euen at this day, doth passe all other, in myne opinion, that euer I saw in any pitte in England, though they had two winges. Yet neuerthelesse, to flie well with one wing, to runne fast with one leg, be rather rare Maistreis moch to be merueled at than sure examples safelie to be folowed. A Bushop that now liueth, a good man, whose iudgement in Religion I better like than his opinion in perfitnes in other learning, said once vnto me: 'We haue no nede now of the Greeke tong,

Of Imitation

when all thinges be translated into Latin.' But the good man vnderstood not that euen the best translation is, for mere necessitie, but an euill imped wing to flie withall, or a heuie stompe leg of wood to go withall: soch, the hier they flie, the sooner they falter and faill: the faster they runne, the ofter they stumble, and sorer they fall. Soch as will nedes so flie, may flie at a Pye and catch a Dawe: And soch runners, as commonlie they shoue and sholder to stand formost, yet in the end they cum behind others and deserue but the hopshakles, if the Masters of the game be right iudgers.

Therefore, in perusing thus so many diuerse bookes for *Imitation*, it came into my head that a verie profitable booke might be made *de Imitatione*, after an other sort than euer yet was attempted of that matter, conteyning a certaine fewe fitte preceptes, vnto the which should be gathered and applied plentie of examples, out of the choisest authors of both the tonges. This worke would stand rather in good diligence for the gathering, and right iudgement for the apte applying of those examples, than any great learning or vtterance at all.

The doing thereof would be more pleasant than painfull, and would bring also moch proffet to all that should read it, and great praise to him [that] would take it in hand, with iust desert of thankes.

Erasmus, giuyng him selfe to read ouer all Authors, *Greke* and *Latin*, seemeth to haue prescribed to him selfe this order of readyng, that is, to note out by the way three speciall pointes, All Adagies, all similitudes, and all wittie sayinges of most notable personages: And so, by one labour, he left to posteritie three notable bookes, and namelie two, his *Chiliades*, *Apophthegmata*, and *Similia*. Likewise, if a good student would bend him selfe to read diligently ouer Tullie, and with him also at the same tyme as diligently *Plato* and *Xenophon* with his bookes of

Philosophie, *Isocrates* and *Demosthenes* with his orations, and *Aristotle* with his Rhetorickes, which fiue of all other be those whom *Tullie* best loued and specially followed, and would marke diligently in *Tullie* where he doth *exprimere* or *effingere* (which be the verie proper wordes of Imitation) either *copiam Platonis* or *venustatem Xenophontis, suauitatem Isocratis*, or *vim Demosthenis, propriam et puram subtilitatem Aristotelis*, and not onelie write out the places diligentlie, and lay them together orderlie, but also to conferre them with skilfull iudgement by those few rules which I haue expressed now twise before: if that diligence were taken, if that order were vsed, what perfite knowledge of both the tonges, what readie and pithie vtterance in all matters, what right and deepe iudgement in all kinde of learnyng would follow, is scarse credible to be beleued.

These bookes be not many, nor long, nor rude in speach, nor meane in matter, but, next the Maiestie of Gods holie word, most worthie for a man, the louer of learning and honestie, to spend his life in. Yea, I haue heard worthie *M. Cheke* many tymes say: I would haue a good student passe and iorney through all Authors both *Greke* and *Latin*; but he that will dwell in these few bookes onelie, first in Gods holie Bible, and than ioyne with it *Tullie* in *Latin, Plato, Aristotle, Xenophon, Isocrates*, and *Demosthenes* in *Greke*, must nedes proue an excellent man.

Some men alreadie in our dayes haue put to their helping handes to this worke of Imitation: As *Perionius, Henr. Stephanus in dictionario Ciceroniano*, and *P. Victorius* most praisewortheliе of all, in that his learned worke conteyning xxv. bookes *de varia lectione*: in which bookes be ioyned diligentlie together the best Authors of both the tonges where one doth seeme to imitate an other.

But all these, with *Macrobius, Hessus*, and other, be no

Of Imitation

more but common porters, caryers, and bringers of matter and stuffe togither. They order nothing. They lay before you what is done: they do not teach you how it is done. They busie not them selues with forme of buildyng. They do not declare, this stuffe is thus framed by *Demosthenes*, and thus and thus by *Tullie*, and so likewise in *Xenophon*, *Plato*, and *Isocrates*, and *Aristotle*. For ioyning *Virgil* with *Homer* I haue sufficientlie declared before.

The like diligence I would wish to be taken in *Pindar* and *Horace*, an equall match for all respectes.

In Tragedies (the goodliest Argument of all, and, for the vse either of a learned preacher or a Ciuill Ientleman, more profitable than *Homer*, *Pindar*, *Virgill*, and *Horace*, yea comparable in myne opinion with the doctrine of *Aristotle*, *Plato*, and *Xenophon*), the *Grecians Sophocles* and *Euripides* far ouer match our *Seneca* in Latin, namely in Οἰκονομίᾳ *et Decoro*, although *Senacaes* elocution and verse be verie commendable for his tyme. And for the matters of *Hercules*, *Thebes*, *Hippolytus*, and *Troie*, his Imitation is to be gathered into the same booke, and to be tryed by the same touchstone, as is spoken before.

In histories, and namelie in *Liuie*, the like diligence of Imitation could bring excellent learning, and breede stayde iudgement, in taking any like matter in hand. Onely *Liuie* were a sufficient taske for one mans studie, to compare him, first with his fellow for all respectes, *Dion. Halicarnassaeus*; who both liued in one tyme, tooke both one historie in hande to write, deserued both like prayse of learnynge and eloquence: Than with *Polybius* that wise writer, whom *Liuie* professeth to follow; and, if he would denie it, yet it is plaine that the best part of the thyrd *Decade* in *Liuie* is in a maner translated out of the thyrd and rest of *Polibius*: Lastlie with *Thucydides*, to whose Imitation *Liuie* is curiouslie bent, as may well appeare by that one Oration of those of *Campania*, asking aide of the *Romanes* agaynst the *Samnites*, which is wholie taken, Sentence, Reason, Argument, and order, out of the Oration of *Corcyra*, asking like aide of the *Athenienses* against them of *Corinth*. If some diligent student would take paynes to compare them togither, he should easelie perceiue that I do say trew. A booke thus wholie filled with examples of Imitation, first out of *Tullie*, compared with *Plato, Xenophon, Isocrates, Demosthenes,* and *Aristotle*, than out of *Virgil* and *Horace*, with *Homer* and *Pindar*, next out of *Seneca*, with *Sophocles* and *Euripides*, lastlie out of *Liuie*, with *Thucydides, Polibius,* and *Halicarnassaeus*, gathered with good diligence, and compared with right order, as I haue expressed before, were an other maner of worke for all kinde of learning, and namely for eloquence, than be those cold gatheringes of *Macrobius, Hessus, Perionius, Stephanus,* and *Victorius*, which may be vsed, as I sayd before, in this case, as porters and caryers, deseruing like prayse, as soch men do wages; but onely *Sturmius* is he, out of whom the trew suruey and whole workemanship is speciallie to be learned.

I trust this my writyng shall giue some good student occasion to take some peece in hand of this worke of Imitation. And as I had rather haue any do it than my selfe, yet surelie my selfe rather than none at all. And by Gods grace, if God do lend me life, with health, free laysure, and libertie, with good likyng and a merie heart I will turne the best part of my studie and tyme to toyle in one or other peece of this worke of Imitation.

This diligence to gather examples, to giue light and vnderstandyng to good preceptes, is no new inuention, but speciallie vsed of the best Authors and oldest writers. For *Aristotle* him selfe (as *Diog. Laertius* declareth), when he had written that goodlie booke of the *Topickes*, did gather out of stories and Orators so many examples as filled xv. bookes, onelie to expresse the rules of his

Of Imitation

Topickes. These were the Commentaries that *Aristotle* thought fit for hys *Topickes*: And therfore to speake as I thinke, I neuer saw yet any Commentarie vpon *Aristotles* Logicke, either in *Greke* or *Latin*, that euer I lyked, bicause they be rather spent in declaryng scholepoynt rules than in gathering fit examples for vse and vtterance, either by pen or talke. For preceptes in all Authors, and namelie in *Aristotle*, without applying vnto them the Imitation of examples, be hard, drie, and cold, and therfore barrayn, vnfruitfull, and vnpleasant. But *Aristotle*, namelie in his *Topickes* and *Elenches*, should be not onelie fruitfull but also pleasant to, if examples out of *Plato* and other good Authors were diligentlie gathered and aptlie applied vnto his most perfit preceptes there. And it is notable that my frende *Sturmius* writeth herein, that there is no precept in *Aristotles Topickes* wherof plentie of examples be not manifest in *Platos* workes. And I heare say, that an excellent learned man, *Tomitanus* in *Italie*, hath expressed euerie fallacion in *Aristotle* with diuerse examples out of *Plato*. Would to God I might once see some worthie student of *Aristotle* and *Plato* in Cambrige, that would ioyne in one booke the preceptes of the one with the examples of the other. For such a labor were one speciall peece of that worke of Imitation, which I do wishe were gathered together in one Volume.

Cambrige, at my first comming thither, but not at my going away, committed this fault in reading the preceptes of *Aristotle* without the examples of other Authors: But herein, in my time, thies men of worthie memorie, *M. Redman, M. Cheke, M. Smith, M. Haddon, M. Watson*, put so to their helping handes, as that vniuersitie, and all studentes there, as long as learning shall last, shall be bounde vnto them, if that trade in studie be trewlie folowed which those men left behinde them there. . . . .

Now to returne to that Question, whether one, a few, many, or all are to be followed, my aunswere shalbe short: All, for him that is desirous to know all: yea, the worst of all, as Questionistes, and all the barbarous nation of scholemen, helpe for one or other consideration: But in euerie separate kinde of learnyng, and studie by it selfe, ye must follow choselie a few, and chieflie some one, and that namelie in our schole of eloquence, either for penne or talke. And as in port[r]aicture and paintyng wise men chose not that workman that can onelie make a faire hand, or a well facioned legge, but soch one as can furnish vp fullie all the fetures of the whole body of a man, woman, and child, and with all is able to, by good skill, to giue to euerie one of these three, in their proper kinde, the right forme, the trew figure, the naturall color, that is fit and dew to the dignitie of a man, to the bewtie of a woman, to the sweetnes of a yong babe; euen likewise do we seeke soch one in our schole to folow, who is able alwayes, in all matters, to teach plainlie, to delite pleasantlie, and to cary away by force of wise talke, all that shall heare or read him, and is so excellent in deed as witte is able or wishe can hope to attaine vnto: And this not onelie to serue in the *Latin* or *Greke* tong, but also in our own English language. But yet, bicause the prouidence of God hath left vnto vs in no other tong, saue onelie in the *Greke* and *Latin* tong, the trew preceptes and perfite examples of eloquence, therefore must we seeke in the Authors onelie of those two tonges the trewe Paterne of Eloquence, if in any other mother tongue we looke to attaine either to perfit vtterance of it our selues or skilfull iudgement of it in others.

And now to know what Author doth medle onelie with some one peece and member of eloquence, and who doth perfitelie make vp the whole bodie, I will declare, as I can call to remembrance the goodlie talke that I haue had oftentymes of the trew difference of Authors with that Ientleman of worthie memorie, my dearest frend, and teacher of all the litle poore learning I haue, Syr *Iohn Cheke.*

The trew difference of Authors is best knowne *per diuersa genera dicendi* that euerie one vsed. And therfore here I will deuide *genus dicendi*, not into these three, *Tenue, mediocre, et grande,* but as the matter of euerie Author requireth, as

in Genus { *Poeticum, Historicum, Philosophicum, Oratorium.* }

These differre one from an other in choice of wordes, in framyng of Sentences, in handling of Argumentes, and vse of right forme, figure, and number, proper and fitte for euerie matter; and euerie one of these is diuerse also in it selfe, as the first,

Poeticum, in { *Comicum, Tragicum, Epicum, Melicum.* }

And here, who soeuer hath bene diligent to read aduisedlie ouer *Terence, Seneca, Virgil, Horace,* or els *Aristophanes, Sophocles, Homer,* and *Pindar,* and shall diligently marke the difference they vse, in proprietie of wordes, in forme of sentence, in handlyng of their matter, he shall easelie perceiue what is fitte and *decorum* in euerie one, to the trew vse of perfite Imitation. Whan *M. Watson* in S. Iohns College at Cambrige wrote his excellent Tragedie of *Absalon, M. Cheke,* he, and I, for that part of trew Imitation, had many pleasant talkes togither, in comparing the preceptes of *Aristotle* and *Horace de Arte Poetica* with the examples of *Euripides,*

Sophocles, and *Seneca*. Few men, in writyng of Tragedies in our dayes, haue shot at this marke. Some in *England*, moe in *France, Germanie*, and *Italie* also, haue written Tragedies in our tyme: of the which not one I am sure is able to abyde the trew touch of *Aristotles* preceptes and *Euripides* examples, saue onely two that euer I saw, M. *Watsons Absalon* and *Georgius Buckananus Iephthe*. One man in Cambrige, well liked of many, but best liked of him selfe, was many tymes bold and busie to bryng matters vpon stages, which he called Tragedies. In one, wherby he looked to wynne his spurres, and whereat many ignorant felowes fast clapped their handes, he began the *Protasis* with *Trochoeiis Octonariis*: which kinde of verse, as it is but seldome and rare in Tragedies, so it is neuer vsed, saue onelie *in Epitasi*: whan the Tragedie is hiest and hotest, and full of greatest troubles. I remember ful well what *M. Watson* merelie sayd vnto me of his blindnesse and boldnes in that behalfe, although otherwise there passed much frendship betwene them. *M. Watson* had an other maner care of perfection, with a feare and reuerence of the iudgement of the best learned: Who to this day would neuer suffer yet his *Absalon* to go abroad, and that onelie bicause, *in locis paribus, Anapestus* is twise or thrise vsed in stede of *Iambus*: A smal faulte, and such one as perchance would neuer be marked, no neither in *Italie* nor *France*. This I write, not so much to note the first, or praise the last, as to leaue in memorie of writing, for good example to posteritie, what perfection, in any tyme, was most diligentlie sought for in like maner, in all kinde of learnyng, in that most worthie College of S. Iohns in Cambrige.

Historicum, in { *Diaria,*
Annales,
Commentarios,
Iustam Historiam. }

For what proprietie in wordes, simplicitie in sentences, plainnesse and light, is cumelie for these kindes, *Cæsar* and *Liuie*, for the two last, are perfite examples of Imitation: And for the two first the old paternes be lost, and as for some that be present and of late tyme, they be fitter to be read once for some pleasure than oft to be perused for any good Imitation of them.

Philosophicum, in { *Sermonem*, as *Officia Cic. et Eth. Arist.* *Contentionem*, as the Dialoges of *Plato, Xenophon,* and *Cicero*: }

Of which kinde of learnyng, and right Imitation therof, *Carolus Sigonius* hath written of late, both learnedlie and eloquentlie: but best of all my frende *Ioan. Sturmius* in hys Commentaries vpon *Gorgias Platonis*, which booke I haue in writyng, and is not yet set out in Print.

Oratorium, in { *Humile, Mediocre, Sublime.* }

Examples of these three, in the *Greke* tong, be plentifull and perfite, as *Lycias, Isocrates,* and *Demosthenes*: and all three in onelie *Demosthenes,* in diuerse orations, as *contra Olimpiodorum, in Leptinem, et pro Ctesiphonte*. And trew it is that *Hermogenes* writeth of *Demosthenes* that all formes of Eloquence be perfite in him. In *Ciceroes* Orations *Medium et sublime* be most excellentlie handled, but *Humile* in his Orations is seldome sene. Yet neuerthelesse in other bookes, as in some part of his Offices, and specially *in Partitionibus*, he is comparable *in hoc humili et disciplinabili genere,* euen with the best that euer wrote in *Greke*. But of *Cicero* more fullie in fitter place. And thus the trew difference of stiles, in euerie Author

and euerie kinde of learnyng, may easelie be knowne by
this diuision:

in Genus { *Poeticum,*
Historicum,
Philosophicum,
Oratorium.

Which I thought in this place to touch onelie, not to
prosecute at large, bicause, God willyng, in the *Latin* tong,
I will fullie handle it in my booke *de Imitatione*.

Now, to touch more particularlie which of those Authors,
that be now most commonlie in mens handes, will some
affourd you some peece of Eloquence, and what maner a
peece of eloquence, and what is to be liked and folowed,
and what to be misliked and eschewed in them, and how
some agayne will furnish you fully withall, rightly, and
wisely considered, somwhat I will write as I haue heard
Syr *Iohn Cheke* many tymes say.

The Latin tong, concerning any part of purenesse of it,
from the spring to the decay of the same, did not endure
moch longer than is the life of a well aged man, scarse
one hundred yeares from the tyme of the last *Scipio
Africanus* and *Laelius* to the Empire of *Augustus*. And
it is notable that *Vellius Paterculus* writeth of *Tullie*, how
that the perfection of eloquence did so remayne onelie in
him and in his time, as before him were few which might
moch delight a man, or after him any worthy admiration,
but soch as *Tullie* might haue seene, and such as might
haue seene *Tullie*. And good cause why: for no perfection
is durable. Encrease hath a time, and decay likewise,
but all perfit ripenesse remaineth but a moment: as is
plainly seen in fruits, plummes, and cherries, but more
sensibly in flowers, as Roses and such like; and yet as
trewlie in all greater matters. For what naturallie can
go no hier must naturallie yeld and stoupe againe.

Of this short tyme of any purenesse of the Latin tong,

Of Imitation

for the first fortie yéare of it, and all the tyme before, we haue no peece of learning left, saue *Plautus* and *Terence*, with a litle rude vnperfit pamflet of the elder *Cato*. And as for *Plautus*, except the scholemaster be able to make wise and ware choice, first in proprietie of wordes, than in framing of phrases and sentences, and chieflie in choice of honestie of matter, your scholer were better to play then learne all that is in him. But surelie, if iudgement for the tong, and direction for the maners, be wisely ioyned with the diligent reading of *Plautus*, than trewlie *Plautus* for that purenesse of the Latin tong in Rome, whan Rome did most florish in well doing, and so thereby in well speaking also, is soch a plentifull storeho[u]se for common eloquence, in meane matters, and all priuate mens affaires, as the Latin tong, for that respect, hath not the like agayne. Whan I remember the worthy tyme of Rome wherein *Plautus* did liue, I must nedes honor the talke of that tyme which we see *Plautus* doth vse.

Terence is also a storehouse of the same tong, for an other tyme, following soone after; and although he be not so full and plentiful as *Plautus* is, for multitude of matters and diuersitie of wordes, yet his wordes be chosen so purelie, placed so orderly, and all his stuffe so neetlie packed vp and wittely compassed in euerie place, as, by all wise mens iudgement, he is counted the cunninger workeman, and to haue his shop, for the rowme that is in it, more finely appointed and trimlier ordered than *Plautus* is.

Three thinges chiefly, both in *Plautus* and *Terence*, are to be specially considered: The matter, the vtterance, the words, the meter. The matter in both is altogether within the compasse of the meanest mens maners, and doth not stretch to any thing of any great weight at all, but standeth chiefly in vtteryng the thoughtes and conditions

of hard fathers, foolish mothers, vnthrifty yong men, craftie
seruantes, sotle bawdes, and wilie harlots, and so is moch
spent in finding out fine fetches and packing vp pelting
matters, soch as in London commonlie cum to the hearing
of the Masters of Bridewell. Here is base stuffe for that
scholer that should becum hereafter either a good minister
in Religion or a Ciuill Ientleman in seruice of his Prince
and contrie (except the preacher do know soch matters to
confute them), whan ignorance surelie in all soch thinges
were better for a Ciuill Ientleman than knowledge. And
thus, for matter, both *Plautus* and *Terence* be like meane
painters, that worke by halfes, and be cunning onelie in
making the worst part of the picture, as if one were skilfull
in painting the bodie of a naked person from the nauell
downward, but nothing else.

  For word and speach *Plautus* is more plentifull, and
Terence more pure and proper: And for one respect *Terence*
is to be embraced aboue all that euer wrote in hys kinde
of argument: Bicause it is well known by good recorde of
learning, and that by *Ciceroes* owne witnes, that some
Comedies bearyng *Terence* name were written by worthy
Scipio and wise *Laelius*, and namely *Heauton* and *Adelphi*.
And therefore, as oft as I reade those Comedies, so oft doth
sound in myne eare the pure fine talke of Rome, which
was vsed by the floure of the worthiest nobilitie that euer
Rome bred. Let the wisest man, and best learned that
liueth, read aduisedlie ouer the first scene of *Heauton* and
the first scene of *Adelphi*, and let him consideratlie iudge
whether it is the talke of the seruile stranger borne, or
rather euen that milde eloquent wise speach which *Cicero*
in *Brutus* doth so liuely expresse in *Laelius*. And yet,
neuerthelesse, in all this good proprietie of wordes and
purenesse of phrases which be in *Terence*, ye must not
follow him alwayes in placing of them, bicause for the
meter sake some wordes in him somtyme be driuen

awrie, which require a straighter placing in plaine prose, if ye will forme, as I would ye should do, your speach and writing to that excellent perfitnesse which was onely in *Tullie*, or onelie in *Tullies* tyme.

5 The meter and verse of *Plautus* and *Terence* be verie meane, and not to be followed : which is not their reproch, but the fault of the tyme wherein they wrote, whan no kinde of Poetrie in the Latin tong was brought to perfection, as doth well appeare in the fragmentes of *Ennius*, 10 *Cecilius*, and others, and euidentlie in *Plautus* and *Terence*, if thies in Latin be compared with right skil with *Homer*, *Euripides*, *Aristophanes*, and other in Greeke of like sort. *Cicero* him selfe doth complaine of this vnperfitnes, but more plainly *Quintilian*, saying, *in Comoedia maxime claudi-* 15 *camus, et vix leuem consequimur vmbram*: and most earnestly of all *Horace in Arte Poetica*, which he doth namely *propter carmen Iambicum*, and referreth all good studentes herein to the Imitation of the Greeke tong, saying,

Exemplaria Graeca
20 *nocturna versate manu, versate diurna.*

This matter maketh me gladly remember my sweete tyme spent at Cambrige, and the pleasant talke which I had oft with *M. Cheke* and *M. Watson* of this fault, not onely in the olde Latin Poets, but also in our new English 25 Rymers at this day. They wished as *Virgil* and *Horace* were not wedded to follow the faultes of former fathers (a shrewd mariage in greater matters) but by right *Imitation* of the perfit Grecians had brought Poetrie to perfitnesse also in the Latin tong, that we Englishmen likewise would 30 acknowledge and vnderstand rightfully our rude beggerly ryming, brought first into Italie by *Gothes* and *Hunnes*, whan all good verses and all good learning to were destroyd by them, and after caryed into France and Germanie, and at last receyued into England by men of excellent wit in deede, but of small learning and lesse iudgement in that behalfe.

But now, when men know the difference, and haue the examples, both of the best and of the worst, surelie to follow rather the *Gothes* in Ryming than the *Graekes* in trew versifiyng were euen to eate ackornes with swyne, when we may freely eate wheate bread emonges men. In deede, *Chauser, Th. Norton* of Bristow, my L. of Surrey, *M. Wiat, Th. Phaer,* and other Ientlemen, in translating *Ouide, Palingenius,* and *Seneca,* haue gonne as farre to their great praise as the copie they followed could cary them; but, if soch good wittes and forward diligence had bene directed to follow the best examples, and not haue bene caryed by tyme and custome to content themselues with that barbarous and rude Ryming, emonges their other worthy praises, which they haue iustly deserued, this had not bene the least, to be counted emonges men of learning and skill more like vnto the Grecians than vnto the Gothians in handling of their verse.

In deed, our English tong, hauing in vse chiefly wordes of one syllable which commonly be long, doth not well receiue the nature of *Carmen Heroicum,* bicause *dactylus,* the aptest foote for that verse, conteining one long and two short, is seldom therefore found in English; and doth also rather stumble than stand vpon *Monasyllabis.* *Quintilian,* in hys learned Chapiter *de Compositione,* geueth this lesson *de Monasyllabis* before me; and in the same place doth iustlie inuey against all Ryming; that if there be any who be angrie with me for misliking of Ryming may be angry for company to with *Quintilian* also for the same thing. And yet *Quintilian* had not so iust cause to mislike of it than as men haue at this day.

And although *Carmen Exametrum* doth rather trotte and hoble than runne smothly in our English tong, yet I am sure our English tong will receiue *carmen Iambicum*

Of Imitation

as naturallie as either *Greke* or *Latin*. But for ignorance
men can not like, and for idlenes men will not labor, to
cum to any perfitenes at all. For, as the worthie Poetes
in *Athens* and *Rome* were more carefull to satisfie the
iudgement of one learned than rashe in pleasing the
humor of a rude multitude, euen so if men in England
now had the like reuerend regard to learning, skill, and
iudgement, and durst not presume to write except they
came with the like learnyng, and also did vse like diligence
in searchyng out not onelie iust measure in euerie meter,
as euerie ignorant person may easely do, but also trew
quantitie in euery foote and sillable, as onelie the learned
shalbe able to do, and as the *Grekes* and *Romanes* were
wont to do, surelie than rash ignorant heads, which now
can easely recken vp fourten sillabes, and easelie stumble
on euery Ryme, either durst not, for lacke of such learnyng,
or els would not, in auoyding such labor, be so busie
as euerie where they be; and shoppes in London should
not be so full of lewd and rude rymes, as commonlie they
are. But now the ripest of tong be readiest to write: And
many dayly in setting out bookes and balettes make great
shew of blossomes and buddes, in whom is neither roote
of learning nor frute of wisedome at all. Some that make
Chaucer in English and *Petrarch* in Italian their Gods in
verses, and yet be not able to make trew difference, what
is a fault and what is a iust prayse in those two worthie
wittes, will moch mislike this my writyng. But such men
be euen like followers of *Chaucer* and *Petrarke*, as one
here in England did folow Syr *Tho. More*, who, being
most vnlike vnto him in wit and learnyng, neuertheles
in wearing his gowne awrye vpon the one shoulder, as
Syr *Tho. More* was wont to do, would nedes be counted
lyke vnto him.

This mislikyng of Ryming beginneth not now of any
newfangle singularitie, but hath bene long misliked of

many, and that of men of greatest learnyng and deepest
iudgement. And soch that defend it do so, either for
lacke of knowledge what is best, or els of verie enuie that
any should performe that in learnyng, whereunto they, as
I sayd before, either for ignorance can not, or for idlenes
will not, labor to attaine vnto.

And you that prayse this Ryming, bicause ye neither
haue reason why to like it nor can shew learning to
defend it, yet I will helpe you with the authoritie of the
oldest and learnedst tyme. In *Grece*, whan Poetrie was
euen as the hiest pitch of perfitnes, one *Simmias Rhodius*
of a certaine singularitie wrote a booke in ryming *Greke*
verses, naming it ᾠόν, conteyning the fable how *Iupiter*
in likenes of a swan gat that egge vpon *Leda*, whereof
came *Castor, Pollux*, and faire [*H*]*elena*. This booke was
so liked that it had few to read it, but none to folow
it: But was presentlie contemned: and, sone after, both
Author and booke so forgotten by men, and consumed
by tyme, as scarse the name of either is kept in memorie
of learnyng. And the like folie was neuer folowed of any
many hondred yeares after, vntill the *Hunnes* and *Gothians*
and other barbarous nations of ignorance and rude
singularitie did reuiue the same folie agayne.

The noble Lord *Th.* Earle of Surrey, first of all English
men in translating the fourth booke of *Virgill*, and *Gonsaluo
Periz*, that excellent learned man, and Secretarie to kyng
Philip of *Spaine*, in translating the *Vlisses* of *Homer* out
of *Greke* into *Spanish*, haue both, by good iudgement,
auoyded the fault of Ryming, yet neither of them hath
fullie hit[t]e perfite and trew versifying. In deede, they
obserue iust number, and euen feete: but here is the
fault, that their feete be feete without ioyntes, that is to
say, not distinct by trew quantitie of sillabes: And so
soch feete be but numme feete, and be euen as vnfitte
for a verse to turne and runne roundly withall as feete

Of Imitation

of brasse or wood be vnweeldie to go well withall. And as a foote of wood is a plaine shew of a manifest maime, euen so feete in our English versifing without quantitie and ioyntes be sure signes that the verse is either borne deformed, vnnaturall, and lame, and so verie vnseemlie to looke vpon, except to men that be gogle eyed them selues.

The spying of this fault now is not the curiositie of English eyes, but euen the good iudgement also of the best that write in these dayes in *Italie*: and namelie of that worthie *Senese Felice Figliucci*, who, writyng vpon *Aristotles Ethickes* so excellentlie in *Italian*, as neuer did yet any one in myne opinion either in *Greke* or *Latin*, amongest other thynges doth most earnestlie inuey agaynst the rude rymyng of verses in that tong: And whan soeuer he expresseth *Aristotles* preceptes with any example out of *Homer* or *Euripides*, he translateth them, not after the Rymes of *Petrarke*, but into soch kinde of perfite verse, with like feete and quantitie of sillabes, as he found them before in the *Greke* tonge; exhortyng earnestlie all the *Italian* nation to leaue of their rude barbariousnesse in rymyng, and folow diligently the excellent *Greke* and *Latin* examples in trew versifiyng.

And you that be able to vnderstand no more then ye finde in the *Italian* tong, and neuer went farder than the schole of *Petrarke* and *Ariostus* abroad, or els of *Chaucer* at home, though you haue pleasure to wander blindlie still in your foule wrong way, enuie not others that seeke, as wise men haue done before them, the fairest and rightest way; or els, beside the iust reproch of malice, wisemen shall trewlie iudge that you do so, as I haue sayd and say yet agayne vnto you, bicause either for idlenes ye will not, or for ignorance ye can not, cum by no better your selfe.

And therfore, euen as *Virgill* and *Horace* deserue most

worthie prayse, that they, spying the vnperfitnes in *Ennius* and *Plautus*, by trew Imitation of *Homer* and *Euripides* brought Poetrie to the same perfitnes in *Latin* as it was in *Greke*, euen so those that by the same way would benefite their tong and contrey deserue rather thankes than disprayse in that behalfe.

And I reioyce that euen poore England preuented *Italie*, first in spying out, than in seekyng to amend this fault in learnyng.

And here for my pleasure I purpose a litle by the way to play and sporte with my Master *Tully*; from whom commonlie I am neuer wont to dissent. He him selfe, for this point of learnyng, in his verses doth halt a litle, by his leaue. He could not denie it, if he were aliue, nor those defend hym now that loue him best. This fault I lay to his charge: bicause once it pleased him, though somwhat merelie, yet oueruncurteslie, to rayle vpon poore England, obiecting both extreme beggerie and mere barbariousnes vnto it, writyng thus vnto his frend *Atticus*: There is not one scruple of siluer in that whole Isle, or any one that knoweth either learnyng or letter.

But now, master *Cicero*, blessed be God and his sonne Iesus Christ, whom you neuer knew, except it were as it pleased him to lighten you by some shadow, as couertlie in one place ye confesse saying, *Veritatis tantum vmbram consectamur*, as your Master *Plato* did before you: blessed be God, I say, that sixten hundred yeare after you were dead and gone it may trewly be sayd, that for siluer there is more cumlie plate in one Citie of England than is in foure of the proudest Cities in all *Italie*, and take *Rome* for one of them. And for learnyng, beside the knowledge of all learned tongs and liberall sciences, euen your owne bookes, *Cicero*, be as well read, and your excellent eloquence is as well liked and loued, and as trewlie folowed, in England at this day, as it is now, or euer was, sence

Of Imitation

your owne tyme in any place of *Italie*, either at *Arpinum*, where ye were borne, or els at *Rome*, where ye were brought vp. And a litle to brag with you, *Cicero*, where you your selfe, by your leaue, halted in some point of learnyng in your owne tong, many in England at this day go streight vp, both in trewe skill and right doing therein.

This I write, not to reprehend *Tullie*, whom aboue all other I like and loue best, but to excuse *Terence*, because in his tyme, and a good while after, Poetrie was neuer perfited in *Latin*, vntill by trew *Imitation* of the Grecians it was at length brought to perfection: And also thereby to exhorte the goodlie wittes of England, which, apte by nature and willing by desire, geue them selues to Poetrie, that they, rightly vnderstanding the barbarous bringing in of Rymes, would labor, as *Virgil* and *Horace* did in Latin, to make perfit also this point of learning in our English tong.

And thus much for *Plautus* and *Terence*, for matter, tong, and meter, what is to be followed, and what to be exchewed in them.

After *Plautus* and *Terence* no writing remayneth vntill *Tullies* tyme, except a fewe short fragmentes of *L. Crassus* excellent wit, here and there recited of *Cicero* for example sake, whereby the louers of learnyng may the more lament the losse of soch a worthie witte.

And although the Latin tong did faire blome and blossome in *L. Crassus* and *M. Antonius*, yet in *Tullies* tyme onely, and in *Tullie* himselfe chieflie, was the Latin tong fullie ripe and growne to the hiest pitch of all perfection.

And yet in the same tyme it began to fade and stoupe, as *Tullie* him selfe, in *Brutus de Claris Oratoribus*, with weeping wordes doth witnesse.

And bicause emongs them of that tyme there was some difference, good reason is that of them of that tyme should

be made right choice also. And yet let the best *Ciceronian*
in Italie read *Tullies* familiar epistles aduisedly ouer, and
I beleue he shall finde small difference for the Latin tong,
either in propriety of wordes or framing of the stile,
betwixt *Tullie* and those that write vnto him: As *Ser.*
Sulpitius, A. Cecinna, M. Cael[i]us, M. et D. Bruti, A. Pollio,
L. Plancus, and diuerse other. Read the epistles of
L. Plancus in *x. Lib.*, and for an assay that Epistle namely
to the *Coss.* and whole *Senate*, the eight Epistle in number;
and what could be eyther more eloquentlie or more
wiselie written, yea by *Tullie* himselfe, a man may iustly
doubt. Thies men and *Tullie* liued all in one tyme, were
like in authoritie, not vnlike in learning and studie, which
might be iust causes of this their equalitie in writing:
And yet surely they neyther were in deed, not yet were
counted in mens opinions, equall with *Tullie* in that facultie.
And how is the difference hid in his Epistles? verelie,
as the cunning of an expert Seaman in a faire calme fresh
Ryuer doth litle differ from the doing of a meaner workman therein, euen so, in the short cut of a priuate letter,
where matter is common, wordes easie, and order not
moch diuerse, small shew of difference can appeare. But
where *Tullie* doth set vp his saile of eloquence, in some
broad deep Argument, caried with full tyde and winde of
his witte and learnyng, all other may rather stand and
looke after him than hope to ouertake him, what course
so euer he hold, either in faire or foule. Foure men
onely, whan the Latin tong was full ripe, be left vnto vs,
who in that tyme did florish, and did leaue to posteritie the
fruite of their witte and learning: *Varro, Salust, Caesar,*
and *Cicero*. Whan I say these foure onely, I am not
ignorant that euen in the same tyme most excellent Poetes,
deseruing well of the Latin tong, as *Lucretius, Catullus,*
Virgill, and *Horace*, did write, but bicause in this litle
booke I purpose to teach a yong scholer to go, not to

daunce, to speake, not to sing (whan Poetes in deed, namelie *Epici* and *Lyrici*, as these be, are fine dauncers and trime singers): but *Oratores* and *Historici* be those cumlie goers, and faire and wise speakers, of whom I wishe my scholer to wayte vpon first, and after in good order and dew tyme to be brought forth to the singing and dauncing schole: And for this consideration do I name these foure to be the onelie writers of that tyme.

VARRO.

Varro, in his bookes *de lingua Latina et Analogia*, as these be left mangled and patched vnto vs, doth not enter there in to any great depth of eloquence, but as one caried in a small low vessell him selfe verie nie the common shore, not much vnlike the fisher men of Rye and Hering men of Yarmouth, who deserue, by common mens opinion, small commendacion for any cunning sailing at all, yet neuertheles in those bookes of *Varro* good and necessarie stuffe, for that meane kinde of Argument, be verie well and learnedlie gathered togither.

His bookes of Husbandrie are moch to be regarded and diligentlie to be read, not onelie for the proprietie, but also for the plentie of good wordes, in all contrey and husbandmens affaires: which can not be had by so good authoritie out of any other Author, either of so good a tyme, or of so great learnyng, as out of *Varro*. And yet, bicause he was fourscore yeare old whan he wrote those bookes, the forme of his style there compared with *Tullies* writyng is but euen the talke of a spent old man: whose wordes commonlie fall out of his mouth, though verie wiselie, yet hardly and cold[l]ie, and more heauelie also than some eares can well beare, except onelie for age and authorities sake. And, perchance, in a rude contrey argument, of purpose and iudgement he rather vsed the speach of the contrey than talke of the Citie.

And so, for matter sake, his wordes sometyme be somewhat rude, and, by the imitation of the elder *Cato*, old and out of vse: And beyng depe stept in age, by negligence some wordes do so scape and fall from him in those bookes, as be not worth the taking vp by him that is carefull to speak or write trew Latin, as that sentence in him, *Romani in pace a rusticis alebantur, et in bello ab his tuebantur.* A good student must be therfore carefull and diligent to read with iudgement ouer euen those Authors which did write in the most perfite tyme: and let him not be affrayd to trie them, both in proprietie of wordes and forme of style, by the touch stone of *Caesar* and *Cicero*, whose puritie was neuer soiled, no not by the sentence of those that loued them worst.

All louers of learnyng may sore lament the losse of those bookes of *Varro* which he wrote in his yong and lustie yeares with good leysure and great learnyng of all partes of Philosophie : of the goodliest argumentes perteyning both to the common wealth and priuate life of man, as *de Ratione studii et educandis liberis*, which booke is oft recited and moch praysed in the fragmentes of *Nonius*, euen for authoritie sake. He wrote most diligentlie and largelie also the whole historie of the state of *Rome*; the mysteries of their whole Religion ; their lawes, customes, and gouernement in peace ; their maners, and whole discipline in warre. And this is not my gessing, as one in deed that neuer saw those bookes, but euen the verie iudgement and playne testimonie of *Tullie* him selfe, who knew and read those bookes, in these wordes :—*Tu aetatem patriae: tu descriptiones temporum: tu sacrorum, tu sacerdotum iura: tu domesticam, tu bellicam disciplinam: tu sedem regionum, locorum ; tu omnium diuinarum hu-*

manarumque rerum nomina, genera, officia, causas aperuisti,
etc.

But this great losse of *Varro* is a litle recompensed by the happy comming of *Dionysius Halicarnassaeus* to *Rome* in *Augustus* dayes: who, getting the possession of *Varros* librarie, out of that treasure house of learning did leaue vnto vs some frute of *Varros* witte and diligence; I meane his goodlie bookes *de Antiquitatibus Romanorum*. *Varro* was so estemed for his excellent learnyng, as *Tullie* him selfe had a reuerence to his iudgement in all doutes of learnyng. And *Antonius Triumuir*, his enemie, and of a contrarie faction, who had power to kill and bannish whom he listed, whan *Varros* name amongest others was brought in a schedule vnto him to be noted to death, he tooke his penne and wrote his warrant of sauegard with these most goodlie wordes, *Viuat Varro, vir doctissimus*. In later tyme, no man knew better, nor liked and loued more *Varros* learnyng than did *S. Augustine*, as they do well vnderstand that haue diligentlie read ouer his learned bookes *de Ciuitate Dei*: Where he hath this most notable sentence: 'Whan I see how much *Varro* wrote, I meruell much that euer he had any leasure to read; and, whan I perceiue how many thinges he read, I meruell more that euer he had any leasure to write,' etc.

And, surelie, if *Varros* bookes had remained to posteritie, as by Gods prouidence the most part of *Tullies* did, than trewlie the *Latin* tong might haue made good comparison with the *Greke*.

SALUSTE.

Salust is a wise and worthy writer; but he requireth a learned Reader, and a right considerer of him. My dearest frend, and best master that euer I had or heard in learning, Syr *I. Cheke*, soch a man as, if I should liue to see England breed the like againe, I feare I should liue ouer long, did once giue me a lesson for *Salust*, which, as I shall neuer forget my selfe, so is it worthy to be remembred of all those that would cum to perfite iudgement of the Latin tong. He said that *Salust* was not verie fitte for yong men to learne out of him the puritie of the Latin tong, because he was not the purest in proprietie of wordes, nor choisest in aptnes of phrases, nor the best in framing of sentences; and therefore is his writing, sayd he, neyther plaine for the matter, nor sensible for mens vnderstanding. 'And what is the cause thereof, Syr?' quoth I. 'Verilie,' said he, 'bicause in *Salust* writing is more Arte than nature, and more labor than Arte: and in his labor also to moch toyle, as it were, with an vncontented care to write better than he could, a fault common to very many men. And therefore he doth not expresse the matter liuely and naturally with common speach, as ye see *Xenophon* doth in Greeke; but it is caried and driuen forth artificiallie, after to learned a sorte, as *Thucydides* doth in his orations.' 'And how cummeth it to passe,' sayd I, 'that *Caesar* and *Ciceroes* talke is so naturall and plaine, and *Salust* writing so artificiall and darke, whan all they three liued in one tyme?' 'I will freelie tell you my fansie herein,' said he: 'surely *Caesar* and *Cicero*, beside a singular prerogatiue of naturall eloquence geuen vnto them by God, both two, by vse of life, were daylie orators emonges the common people and greatest councellers in the Senate house, and therefore gaue themselues to vse soch speach as the meanest should well vnderstand and the wisest best allow, folowing carefullie that good councell of *Aristotle, loquendum vt multi, sapiendum vt pauci*. *Salust* was no soch man, neyther for will to goodnes nor skill by learning; but, ill geuen by nature, and made worse by bringing vp, spent the most part of his yougth very misorderly in ryot and lechery, in the company of soch, who, neuer geuing theyr mynde to honest doyng, could neuer inure their tong to wise speaking; but at last cummyng to better yeares, and bying witte at the dearest hand, that is by long experience of the hurt and shame that commeth of mischeif, moued by the councell of them that were wise, and caried by the example of soch as were good, first fell to honestie of life, and after to the loue of studie and learning; and so became so new a man that *Caesar*, being dictator, made him Pretor in *Numidia*, where he, absent from his contrie and not inured with the common talke of Rome, but shut vp in his studie and bent wholy to reading, did write the storie of the Romanes. And for the better accomplishing of the same, he red *Cato* and *Piso* in Latin for gathering of matter and troth, and *Thucydides* in Greeke for the order of his storie and furnishing of his style. *Cato* (as his tyme required) had more troth for the matter than eloquence for the style. And so *Salust*, by gathering troth out of *Cato*, smelleth moch of the roughnes of his style: euen as a man that eateth garlike for helth shall cary away with him the sauor of it also, whether he will or not. And yet the vse of old wordes is not the greatest cause of *Salustes* roughnes and darknesse: There be in *Salust* some old wordes in deed as *patrare bellum, ductare exercitum*, well noted by *Quintilian*, and verie much misliked of him; and *supplicium* for *supplicatio*, a word smellyng of an older store than the other two so misliked by *Quint.* And yet is that word also in *Varro*, speaking of Oxen thus, *boues ad victimas faciunt, atque ad Deorum supplicia*: and a few old wordes mo. Read *Saluste* and *Tullie* aduisedly together, and in wordes ye shall finde small difference; yea *Salust* is more geuen to new wordes than to olde, though som olde writers say the contrarie: as *Claritudo* for *Gloria*, *exacte* for *perfecte*, *Facundia* for *eloquentia*. Thies two last wordes *exacte* and *facundia*, now in euery mans mouth, be neuer (as I do remember) vsed of *Tullie*, and therefore I thinke they be not good: For surely *Tullie* speaking euery where so moch of the matter of eloquence would not so precisely haue absteyned from the word *Facundia* if it had bene good, that is proper for the tong, and common for mens vse. I could be long in reciting many soch like, both olde and new wordes in *Salust*, but in very dede neyther oldnes nor newnesse of wordes maketh the greatest difference betwixt *Salust* and *Tullie*, but first strange phrases made of good Latin wordes but framed after the Greeke tonge, which be neyther choisly borowed of them, nor properly vsed by him; than a hard composition and crooked framing of his wordes and sentences, as a man would say, English talke placed and framed outlandish like. As for example first in phrases, *nimius et animus* be two vsed wordes, yet *homo nimius animi* is an vnused phrase. *Vulgus, et amat, et fieri*, be as common and well known wordes as may be in the Latin tong, yet *id quod vulgo amat fieri*, for *solet fieri*, is but a strange and Grekysh kind of writing. *Ingens et vires* be proper wordes, yet *vir ingens virium* is an vnproper kinde of speaking; and so be likewise *aeger consilii, promptissimus belli, territus animi*, and many soch like phrases in *Salust*, borowed, as I sayd, not choisly out of Greeke, and vsed therefore vnproperlie in. Latin. Againe, in whole sentences, where the matter is good, the wordes proper and plaine, yet the sense is hard and darke, and namely in his prefaces and oration[s], wherein he vsed most labor, which fault is likewise in *Thucydides* in Greeke, of whom *Salust* hath taken the greatest part of his darkenesse. For *Thucydides* likewise wrote his storie, not at home in Grece, but abrode in Italie, and therefore smelleth of a certaine outlandish kinde of talke, strange to them of *Athens*, and diuerse from their writing that liued in Athens and Grece, and

Of Imitation

wrote the same tyme that *Thucydides* did, as *Lysias*, *Xenophon*, *Plato*, and *Isocrates*, the purest and playnest writers that euer wrote in any tong, and best examples for any man to follow whether he write Latin, Italian, French, or English. *Thucydides* also semeth in his writing not so much benefited by nature as holpen by Arte, and caried forth by desire, studie, labor, toyle, and ouer great curiositie; who spent xxvii. yeares in writing his eight bookes of his history. *Salust* likewise wrote out of his contrie, and followed the faultes of *Thuc.* to moch; and boroweth of him som kinde of writing which the Latin tong can not well beare, as *Casus nominatiuus* in diuerse places *absolute positus*, as in that place of *Iugurth*, speaking *de Leptitanis, Itaque ab imperatore facile quae petebant adepti, missae sunt eo cohortes Ligurum quatuor*. This thing in participles, vsed so oft in *Thucyd.* and other Greeke authors to, may better be borne with all, but *Salust* vseth the same more strangelie and boldlie, as in thies wordes, *Multis sibi quisque imperium petentibus*. I beleue the best Grammarien in England can scarse giue a good reule why *quisque*, the nominatiue case, without any verbe, is so thrust vp amongest so many oblique cases.' Some man perchance will smile, and laugh to scorne this my writyng, and call it idle curiositie thus to busie my selfe in pickling about these small pointes of Grammer, not fitte for my age, place, and calling to trifle in: I trust that man, be he neuer so great in authoritie, neuer so wise and learned, either by other mens iudgement or his owne opinion, will yet thinke that he is not greater in England than *Tullie* was at *Rome*, not yet wiser nor better learned than *Tullie* was him selfe, who, at the pitch of three score yeares, in the middes of the broyle betwixt *Caesar* and *Pompeie*, whan he knew not whither to send wife and children, which way to go, where to hide him selfe, yet, in an earnest letter, amongest his earnest

councelles for those heuie tymes concerning both the
common state of his contrey and his owne priuate great
affaires, he was neither vnmyndfull nor ashamed to reason
at large, and learne gladlie of *Atticus*, a lesse point of
Grammer than these be, noted of me in *Salust*, as whether
he should write *ad Piraeea, in Piraeea,* or *in Piraeeum,* or
Piraeeum, sine praepositione : And in those heuie tymes he
was so carefull to know this small point of Grammer
that he addeth these wordes, *Si hoc mihi* ζήτημα *persolueris,
magna me molestia liberaris.* If *Tullie*, at that age, in that
authoritie, in that care for his contrey, in that ieoperdie
for him selfe and extreme necessitie of hys dearest
frendes, beyng also the Prince of Eloquence hym selfe,
was not ashamed to descend to these low pointes of
Grammer, in his owne naturall tong, what should scholers
do, yea what should any man do, if he do thinke well
doyng better than ill doyng: And had rather be perfite
than meane, sure than doutefull, to be what he should be
in deed, not seeme what he is not in opinion. He that
maketh perfitnes in the *Latin* tong his marke must cume
to it by choice and certaine knowledge, not stumble vpon
it by chance and doubtfull ignorance. And the right
steppes to reach vnto it be these, linked thus orderlie
together, aptnes of nature, loue of learnyng, diligence in
right order, constancie with pleasant moderation, and
alwayes to learne of them that be best; and so shall you
iudge as they that be wisest. And these be those reules
which worthie Master *Cheke* dyd impart vnto me concernyng *Salust* and the right iudgement of the *Latin*
tong.

CAESAR.

Caesar, for that litle of him that is left vnto vs, is
like the halfe face of a *Venus*, the other part of the head

Of Imitation

beyng hidden, the bodie and the rest of the members vnbegon, yet so excellentlie done by *Apelles*, as all men may stand still to mase and muse vpon it, and no man step forth with any hope to performe the like.

5 His seuen bookes *de bello Gallico* and three *de bello ciuili* be written so wiselie for the matter, so eloquentlie for the tong, that neither his greatest enemies could euer finde the least note of parcialitie in him (a meruelous wisdome of a man, namely writyng of his owne doynges),
10 nor yet the best iudegers of the *Latin* tong, nor the most enuious lookers vpon other mens writynges, can say any other but all things be most perfitelie done by him.

Brutus, *Caluus*, and *Calidius*, who found fault with
15 *Tullies* fulnes in woordes and matter, and that rightlie, for *Tullie* did both confesse it and mend it, yet in *Caesar* they neither did, nor could, finde the like or any other fault.

And therfore thus iustlie I may conclude of *Caesar*,
20 that where, in all other, the best that euer wrote, in any tyme, or in any tong, in *Greke* or *Latin* (I except neither *Plato*, *Demosthenes*, nor *Tullie*), some fault is iustlie noted, in *Caesar* onelie could neuer yet fault be found.

Yet neuertheles, for all this perfite excellencie in him,
25 yet it is but in one member of eloquence, and that but of one side neither, whan we must looke for that example to folow, which hath a perfite head, a whole bodie, forward and backward, armes and legges and all.

GEORGE GASCOIGNE

(*CERTAYNE NOTES OF INSTRUCTION*)

1575[1]

[Gascoigne's *Certayne Notes of Instruction* first appeared in the quarto edition of *The Posies of George Gascoigne, Esquire, corrected, perfected, and augmented by the Author*, London (Feb.) 1575, and was reprinted in the *Whole Woorkes* (1587). The text is taken from the copy of the *Posies* in the Bodleian Library (Malone, 792), which is freely annotated in the handwriting of Gabriel Harvey (see notes *passim*). The *Notes* occupy five leaves, in black-letter (sig. Tij—Uij).]

CERTAYNE NOTES OF INSTRUCTION CONCERNING THE MAKING OF VERSE OR RYME IN ENGLISH, WRITTEN AT THE REQUEST OF MASTER *EDOUARDO DONATI*.

SIgnor Edouardo, since promise is debt, and you (by the lawe of friendship) do burden me with a promise that I shoulde lende you instructions towards the making of English verse or ryme, I will assaye to discharge the same, though not so perfectly as I would, yet as readily as I may: and therwithall I pray you consider that *Quot*

---

[1] In 1573 Richard Willes published (*a*) *Poematum Liber* (London, Tottell), and (*b*) *In suorum Poemat. librum Ricardi Willeii Scholia* (London, Tottell), a separate issue, though also contained in (*a*). The second book, which is dedicated to the Warden and Scholars of Wykeham's College at Winchester, is divided into (1) *De Re Poetica Disputatio* (Aj—Cj), and (2) *Scholia* (Cj v°—E iiij). It is prefaced by an *Epistola* (three leaves) and by two pages of introduction to the *Disputatio* praising Wykeham's domicile (the school) and exalting the study of poetry. 'Erunt igitur nostrae disputationis partes tres.

homines, tot Sententiae, especially in Poetrie, wherein (neuerthelesse) I dare not challenge any degree, and yet will I at your request aduenture to set downe my simple skill in such simple manner as I haue vsed, referring the same hereafter to the correction of the *Laureate*. And you shall haue it in these few poynts followyng.

The first and most necessarie poynt that euer I founde meete to be considered in making of a delectable poeme is this, to grounde it upon some fine inuention. For it is not inough to roll in pleasant woordes, nor yet to thunder in *Rym, Ram, Ruff* by letter (quoth my master *Chaucer*), nor yet to abounde in apt vocables or epythetes, vnlesse the Inuention haue in it also *aliquid salis*. By this *aliquid salis* I meane some good and fine deuise, shewing the quicke capacitie of a writer: and where I say some *good and fine inuention* I meane that I would haue it both fine and good. For many inuentions are so superfine that they are *Vix good*. And, againe, many Inuentions are good, and yet not finely handled. And for a general for-

---

Primo commentarium de Poeticae natura atque ortu, de Poeticae significatione, diversisque Poetarum generibus, de origine metri atque usu carminum diversis ex auctoribus colligam': and he goes on to explain his plan. He has three theses, viz. (1) *Poeticam esse praestantiorem caeteris artibus* (four pages); (2) *Poeticen artem esse fructuosam* (one and a half pages); and (3) *Poeticen esse iucundissimam*, with a sub-section, *Quae obiici contra Poeticam solent, illa modo erunt diluenda*, containing *calumnia* and *resp[onsiones]* (about six leaves). The *Scholia* explain and expound various words, figures, and technical matters used in poetry (about a page to each), such as *Donat atque dedicat* (being the first title), *Quincunx, Ara, Gladius, Paruum ovum, Pyrum, Pastoricia fistula, Alae, Cantuariensis ecclesiae insignia, Pyramis inversa, Securis, Cento, Rhapsodia*, &c. Willes is not tempted to refer to contemporary English verse, or to any of the problems of versification. The volume concludes with a poem on the life of William of Wykeham and a number of distichs on the Wardens of the School, and with a 'didascalorum elenchus.' [From the copy preserved in the Bodleian Library (Wood, 105).]

warning: what Theame soeuer you do take in hande, if
you do handle it but *tanquam in oratione perpetua*, and
neuer studie for some depth of deuise in the Inuention,
and some figures also in the handlyng thereof, it will
appeare to the skilfull Reader but a tale of a tubbe. To
deliuer vnto you generall examples it were almoste vnpossible, sithence the occasions of Inuentions are (as it were)
infinite; neuerthelesse, take in worth mine opinion, and
perceyue my furder meanyng in these few poynts. If
I should vndertake to wryte in prayse of a gentlewoman,
I would neither praise hir christal eye, nor hir cherrie
lippe, etc. For these things are *trita et obuia*. But I would
either finde some supernaturall cause wherby my penne
might walke in the superlatiue degree, or els I would
vndertake to aunswere for any imperfection that shee
hath, and therevpon rayse the prayse of hir commendacion. Likewise, if I should disclose my pretence in
loue, I would eyther make a strange discourse of some
intollerable passion, or finde occasion to pleade by the
example of some historie, or discouer my disquiet in
shadowes *per Allegoriam*, or vse the couertest meane that
I could to auoyde the vncomely customes of common
writers. Thus much I aduenture to deliuer vnto you
(my freend) vpon the rule of Inuention, which of all other
rules is most to be marked, and hardest to be prescribed
in certayne and infallible rules; neuerthelesse, to conclude
therein, I would haue you stand most vpon the excellencie
of your Inuention, and sticke not to studie deepely for
some fine deuise. For, that beyng founde, pleasant woordes
will follow well inough and fast inough.

2. Your Inuention being once deuised, take heede that
neither pleasure of rime nor varietie of deuise do carie
you from it: for as to vse obscure and darke phrases in
a pleasant Sonet is nothing delectable, so to entermingle
merie iests in a serious matter is an *Indecorum*.

The Making of Verse

3. I will next aduise you that you hold the iust measure wherwith you begin your verse. I will not denie but this may seeme a preposterous ordre; but, bycause I couet rather to satisfie you particularly than to vndertake a generall tradition, I wil not somuch stand vpon the manner as the matter of my precepts. I say then, remember to holde the same measure wherwith you begin, whether it be in a verse of sixe syllables, eight, ten, twelue, etc.: and though this precept might seeme ridiculous vnto you, since euery yong scholler can conceiue that he ought to continue in the same measure wherwith he beginneth, yet do I see and read many mens Poems now adayes, whiche beginning with the measure of xij. in the first line, and xiiij. in the second (which is the common kinde of verse), they wil yet (by that time they haue passed ouer a few verses) fal into xiiij. and fourtene, *et sic de similibus*, the which is either forgetfulnes or carelesnes.

4. And in your verses remembre to place euery worde in his natural *Emphasis* or sound, that is to say, in such wise, and with such length or shortnesse, eleuation or depression of sillables, as it is commonly pronounced or vsed. To expresse the same we haue three maner of accents, *grauis, leuis, et circumflexa*, the whiche I would english thus, the long accent, the short accent, and that whiche is indifferent: the graue accent is marked by this caracte \, the light accent is noted thus /, and the circumflexe or indifferent is thus signified ⌢: the graue accent is drawen out or eleuate, and maketh that sillable long wherevpon it is placed; the light accent is depressed or snatched vp, and maketh that sillable short vpon the which it lighteth; the circumflexe accent is indifferent, sometimes short, sometimes long, sometimes depressed and sometimes eleuate. For example of th' emphasis or natural sound of words, this word *Treasure* hath the graue accent vpon the first sillable; whereas if it shoulde be written in

this sorte *Treasúre*, nowe were the second sillable long, and that were cleane contrarie to the common vse wherwith it is pronounced. For furder explanation hereof, note you that commonly now a dayes in English rimes (for I dare not cal them English verses) we vse none other order but a foote of two sillables, wherof the first is depressed or made short, and the second is eleuate or made long; and that sound or scanning continueth throughout the verse. We haue vsed in times past other kindes of Meeters, as for example this following:

No wight in this world, that wealth can attayne,
Vnlèsse hè belèue, thàt àll ìs bùt vàyne.

Also our father *Chaucer* hath vsed the same libertie in feete and measures that the Latinists do vse: and who so euer do peruse and well consider his workes, he shall finde that although his lines are not alwayes of one selfe same number of Syllables, yet, beyng redde by one that hath vnderstanding, the longest verse, and that which hath most Syllables in it, will fall (to the eare) correspondent vnto that whiche hath fewest sillables in it: and like wise that whiche hath in it fewest syllables shalbe founde yet to consist of woordes that haue suche naturall sounde, as may seeme equall in length to a verse which hath many moe sillables of lighter accentes. And surely I can lament that wee are fallen into suche a playne and simple manner of wryting, that there is none other foote vsed but one; wherby our Poemes may iustly be called Rithmes, and cannot by any right challenge the name of a Verse. But, since it is so, let vs take the forde as we finde it, and lette me set downe vnto you suche rules or precepts that euen in this playne foote of two syllables you wreste no woorde from his natural and vsuall sounde. I do not meane hereby that you may vse none other wordes but of twoo sillables, for therein you may vse discretion according to occasion of matter, but my meaning is, that all the wordes in your verse be so placed as the first sillable may sound short or be depressed, the second long or eleuate, the third shorte, the fourth long, the fifth shorte, etc. For example of my meaning in this point marke these two verses:

I vnderstand your meanying by your eye.
Your meaning I vnderstand by your eye.

In these two verses there seemeth no difference at all, since the one hath the very selfe same woordes that the other hath, and yet the latter verse is neyther true nor pleasant, and the first verse may passe the musters. The fault of the latter verse is that this worde *vnderstand* is therein so placed as the graue accent falleth upon *der*, and therby maketh *der* in this worde *vnderstand* to be eleuated; which is contrarie to the naturall or vsual pronunciation, for we say *vnderstand*, and not *vnderstand*.

5. Here by the way I thinke it not amisse to forewarne you that you thrust as few wordes of many sillables into your verse as may be: and herevnto I might alledge many reasons. First, the most auncient English wordes are of one sillable, so that the more monasyllables that you vse the truer Englishman you shall seeme, and the lesse you shall smell of the Inkehorne: Also wordes of many syllables do cloye a verse and make it vnpleasant, whereas woordes of one syllable will more easily fall to be shorte or long as occasion requireth, or wilbe adapted to become circumflexe or of an indifferent sounde.

6. I would exhorte you also to beware of rime without reason: my meaning is hereby that your rime leade you not from your firste Inuention, for many wryters, when they haue layed the platforme of their inuention, are yet

drawen sometimes (by ryme) to forget it or at least to alter it, as when they cannot readily finde out a worde whiche maye rime to the first (and yet continue their determinate Inuention) they do then eyther botche it vp with a worde that will ryme (howe small reason soeuer it carie with it), or els they alter their first worde and so percase decline or trouble their former Inuention: But do you alwayes hold your first determined Inuention, and do rather searche the bottome of your braynes for apte wordes than chaunge good reason for rumbling rime.

7. To help you a little with ryme (which is also a plaine yong schollers lesson), worke thus: when you haue set downe your first verse, take the last worde thereof and coumpt ouer all the wordes of the selfe same sounde by order of the Alphabete: As, for example, the laste woorde of your firste line is *care*, to ryme therwith you haue *bare, clare, dare, fare, gare, hare,* and *share, mare, snare, rare, stare,* and *ware, &c.* Of all these take that which best may serue your purpose, carying reason with rime: and if none of them will serue so, then alter the laste worde of your former verse, but yet do not willingly alter the meanyng of your Inuention.

8. You may vse the same Figures or Tropes in verse which are vsed in prose, and in my iudgement they serue more aptly and haue greater grace in verse than they haue in prose: but yet therein remembre this old adage, *Ne quid nimis*, as many wryters which do not know the vse of any other figure than that whiche is expressed in repeticion of sundrie wordes beginning all with one letter, the whiche (beyng modestly vsed) lendeth good grace to a verse, but they do so hunte a letter to death that they make it *Crambe*, and *Crambe bis positum mors est*: therfore *Ne quid nimis*.

9. Also, asmuche as may be, eschew straunge words, or *obsoleta et inusitata*, vnlesse the Theame do giue iust occa-

sion : marie, in some places a straunge worde doth drawe attentiue reading, but yet I woulde haue you therein to vse discretion.

10. And asmuch as you may, frame your stile to *perspicuity* and to be sensible, for the haughty obscure verse doth not much delight, and the verse that is to easie is like a tale of a rosted horse; but let your Poeme be such as may both delight and draw attentiue readyng, and therewithal may deliuer such matter as be worth the marking.

11. You shall do very well to vse your verse after thenglishe phrase, and not after the maner of other languages. The Latinists do commonly set the adiectiue after the Substantiue: As, for example, *Femina pulchra, aedes altae, &c.*; but if we should say in English a woman fayre, a house high, etc. it would haue but small grace, for we say a good man, and not a man good, etc. And yet I will not altogether forbidde it you, for in some places it may be borne, but not so hardly as some vse it which wryte thus:

Now let vs go to Temple ours.
I will go visit mother myne &c.

Surely I smile at the simplicitie of such deuisers which might aswell haue sayde it in playne Englishe phrase, and yet haue better pleased all eares, than they satisfie their owne fancies by suche *superfinesse*. Therefore euen as I haue aduised you to place all wordes in their naturall or most common and vsuall pronunciation, so would I wishe you to frame all sentences in their mother phrase and proper *Idióma*; and yet sometimes (as I haue sayd before) the contrarie may be borne, but that is rather where rime enforceth, or *per licentiam Poëticam*, than it is otherwise lawfull or commendable.

12. This poeticall licence is a shrewde fellow, and couereth many faults in a verse; it maketh wordes longer, shorter, of mo sillables, of fewer, newer, older, truer,

falser; and, to conclude, it turkeneth all things at pleasure, for example, *ydone* for *done*, *adowne* for *downe*, *orecome* for *ouercome*, *tane* for *taken*, *power* for *powre*, *heauen* for *heaun*, *thewes* for good partes or good qualities, and a numbre of other, whiche were but tedious and needelesse to rehearse, since your owne iudgement and readyng will soone make you espie such aduauntages.

13. There are also certayne pauses or restes in a verse, whiche may be called *Ceasures*, whereof I woulde be lothe to stande long, since it is at discretion of the wryter, and they haue bene first deuised (as should seeme) by the Musicians: but yet thus much I will aduenture to wryte, that in mine opinion in a verse of eight sillables the pause will stand best in the middest; in a verse of tenne it will best be placed at the ende of the first foure sillables; in a verse of twelue, in the midst; in verses of twelue in the firste and fouretene in the seconde wee place the pause commonly in the midst of the first, and at the ende of the first eight sillables in the second. In Rithme royall it is at the wryters discretion, and forceth not where the pause be vntill the ende of the line.

14. And here, bycause I haue named Rithme royall, I will tell you also mine opinion aswell of that as of the names which other rymes haue commonly borne heretofore. Rythme royall is a verse of tenne sillables; and seuen such verses make a staffe, whereof the first and thirde lines do aunswer (acrosse) in like terminations and rime, the second, fourth, and fifth do likewise answere eche other in terminations, and the two last do combine and shut vp the Sentence: this hath bene called Rithme royall, and surely it is a royall kinde of verse, seruing best for graue discourses. There is also another kinde, called Ballade, and thereof are sundrie sortes: for a man may write ballade in a staffe of sixe lines, euery line conteyning eighte or sixe sillables, whereof the firste and

third, second and fourth do rime acrosse, and the fifth and sixth do rime togither in conclusion. You may write also your ballad of tenne sillables, rimyng as before is declared; but these two were wont to be most commonly vsed in ballade, which propre name was (I thinke) deriued of this worde in Italian *Ballare*, whiche signifieth to daunce. And in deed those kinds of rimes serue beste for daunces or light matters. Then haue you also a rondlette, the which doth alwayes end with one self same foote or repeticion, and was thereof (in my iudgement) called a rondelet. This may consist of such measure as best liketh the wryter. Then haue you Sonnets: some thinke that all Poemes (being short) may be called Sonets, as in deede it is a diminutiue worde deriued of *Sonare*, but yet I can beste allowe to call those Sonnets whiche are of fouretene lynes, euery line conteyning tenne syllables. The firste twelue do ryme in staues of foure lines by crosse meetre, and the last two ryming togither do conclude the whole. There are Dyzaynes, and Syxaines, which are of ten lines, and of sixe lines, commonly vsed by the French, which some English writers do also terme by the name of Sonettes. Then is there an old kinde of Rithme called Ver layes, deriued (as I haue redde) of this worde *Verd*, whiche betokeneth Greene, and *Laye*, which betokeneth a Song, as if you would say greene Songes: but I muste tell you by the way that I neuer redde any verse which I saw by aucthoritie called *Verlay* but one, and that was a long discourse in verses of tenne sillables, whereof the foure first did ryme acrosse, and the fifth did aunswere to the firste and thirde, breaking off there, and so going on to another termination. Of this I could shewe example of imitation in mine own verses written to the right honorable the Lord *Grey* of *Wilton* upon my iourney into *Holland*, etc. There are also certaine Poemes deuised of tenne syllables, whereof the first aunswereth in termination with the fourth, and the second and thirde answere eche other: these are more vsed by other nations than by vs, neyther can I tell readily what name to giue them. And the commonest sort of verse which we vse now adayes (*viz.* the long verse of twelue and fourtene sillables) I know not certainly howe to name it, vnlesse I should say that it doth consist of Poulters measure, which giueth xii. for one dozen and xiiij. for another. But let this suffise (if it be not to much) for the sundrie sortes of verses which we vse now adayes.

15. In all these sortes of verses, when soeuer you vndertake to write, auoyde prolixitie and tediousnesse, and euer, as neare as you can, do finish the sentence and meaning at the end of euery staffe where you wright staues, and at the end of euery two lines where you write by cooples or poulters measure: for I see many writers which draw their sentences in length, and make an ende at latter Lammas: for, commonly, before they end, the Reader hath forgotten where he begon. But do you (if you wil follow my aduise) eschue prolixitie and knit vp your sentences as compendiously as you may, since breuitie (so that it be not drowned in obscuritie) is most commendable.

16. I had forgotten a notable kinde of ryme, called ryding rime, and that is suche as our Mayster and Father *Chaucer* vsed in his Canterburie tales, and in diuers other delectable and light enterprises; but, though it come to my remembrance somewhat out of order, it shall not yet come altogether out of time, for I will nowe tell you a conceipt whiche I had before forgotten to wryte: you may see (by the way) that I holde a preposterous order in my traditions but, as I sayde before, I wryte moued by good wil, and not to shewe my skill. Then to returne too my matter, as this riding rime serueth most aptly to wryte a merie tale, so Rythme royall is fittest for a graue discourse. Ballades

are beste of matters of loue, and rondlettes moste apt for
the beating or handlyng of an adage or common prouerbe:
Sonets serue aswell in matters of loue as of discourse:
Dizaynes and Sixaines for shorte Fantazies: Verlayes
for an effectual proposition, although by the name you
might otherwise iudge of Verlayes; and the long verse
of twelue and fouretene sillables, although it be now adayes
vsed in all Theames, yet in my iudgement it would serue
best for Psalmes and Himpnes.

I woulde stande longer in these traditions, were it not
that I doubt mine owne ignoraunce; but, as I sayde before,
I know that I write to my freende, and, affying my selfe
therevpon, I make an ende.

GEORGE WHETSTONE

(*The Dedication to Promos and Cassandra*)

1578

[The text of the *Dedication* to *The right excellent and famous Historye of Promos and Cassandra*, 1578, is printed from the copy in the British Museum (C 34. e. 42).]

TO HIS WORSHIPFVLL FRIENDE AND KINSEMAN, *WILLIAM FLEETEWOODE ESQUIER, RECORDER OF LONDON.*

SYR, (desirous to acquite your tryed frendships with some token of good will) of late I perused diuers of my vnperfect workes, fully minded to bestowe on you the trauell of some of my forepassed time. But (resolued to accompanye the aduenturous Captaine Syr *Humfrey Gylbert* in his honorable voiadge) I found my leysure too littel to correct the errors in my sayd workes. So that (inforced) I lefte them dispersed amonge my learned freendes, at theyr leasure to polish, if I faild to returne: spoyling (by this meanes) my studdy of his necessarye furnyture. Amonge other vnregarded papers I fownde this Discource of *Promos* and *Cassandra*; which for the rarenesse (and the needeful knowledge) of the necessary matter contained therein (to make the actions appeare more liuely) I deuided the whole history into two Commedies, for that, *Decorum* vsed, it would not be conuayed in one. The effects of both are good and bad: vertue intermyxt with vice, vnlawfull desyres (yf it were possible) queancht with chaste denyals: al needeful actions (I

thinke) for publike vewe. For by the rewarde of the
good the good are encouraged in wel doinge: and with
the scowrge of the lewde the lewde are feared from euill
attempts : mainetayning this my oppinion with *Platoes*
auctority. *Nawghtinesse commes of the corruption of nature,
and not by readinge or hearinge the liues of the good or lewde
(for such publication is necessarye), but goodnesse (sayth he)
is beawtifyed by either action.* And to these endes *Menander*,
Plautus, and *Terence*, them selues many yeares since in-
tombed, (by their Commedies) in honour liue at this daye.
The aunctent *Romanes* heald these showes of suche prise
that they not onely allowde the publike exercise of them,
but the graue Senators themselues countenaunced the
Actors with their presence: who from these trifles wonne
morallytye, as the Bee suckes honny from weedes. But
the aduised deuises of aunctent Poets, disc[r]edited with
tryfels of yonge, vnaduised, and rashe witted wryters, hath
brought this commendable exercise in mislike. For at
this daye the *Italian* is so lasciuious in his commedies that
honest hearers are greeued at his actions: the *Frenchman*
and *Spaniarde* folowes the *Italians* humor: the *Germaine*
is too holye, for he presentes on euerye common Stage
what Preachers should pronounce in Pulpets. The *Englishman* in this quallitie is most vaine, indiscreete, and
out of order: he fyrst groundes his worke on impossi-
bilities; then in three howers ronnes he throwe the
worlde, marryes, gets Children, makes Children men,
men to conquer kingdomes, murder Monsters, and bringeth
Gods from Heauen, and fetcheth Diuels from Hel. And
(that which is worst) their ground is not so vnperfect as
their workinge indiscreete: not waying, so the people
laugh, though they laugh them (for theyr follyes) to scorne.
Manye tymes (to make mirthe) they make a Clowne companion with a Kinge; in theyr graue Counsels they allow
the aduise of fooles; yea, they vse one order of speach for

all persons: a grose *Indecorum*, for a Crowe wyll yll counterfet the Nightingale's sweete voice; euen so affected speeche doth misbecome a Clowne. For, to worke a Commedie kindly, graue olde men should instruct, yonge men should showe the imperfections of youth, Strumpets should be lasciuious, Boyes vnhappy, and Clownes should speake disorderlye: entermingling all these actions in such sorte as the graue matter may instruct and the pleasant delight; for without this chaunge the attention would be small, and the likinge lesse.

But leaue I this rehearsall of the vse and abuse of Commedies, least that I checke that in others which I cannot amend in my selfe. But this I am assured, what actions so euer passeth in this History, either merry or morneful, graue or lasciuious, the conclusion showes the confusion of Vice and the cherising of Vertue. And sythe the end tends to this good, although the worke (because of euel handlinge) be vnworthy your learned Censure, allowe (I beseeche you) of my good wyll, vntyl leasure serues me to perfect some labour of more worthe. No more, but that almightye God be your protector, and preserue me from dainger in this voiadge, the xxix of July, 1578.

        Your Kinsman to vse,

            GEORGE WHETSTONE.

THOMAS LODGE

(*DEFENCE OF POETRY*)

1579

[Of Lodge's 'Defence of Poetry, Music, and Stage Plays,' written in reply to Stephen Gosson's *Schoole of Abuse*, only two copies are known, one being in the Bodleian, the other in the Britwell Collection. Neither copy has a title-page. The book was issued privately in 1579, and was withdrawn immediately. It was reprinted by the Shakespeare Society in 1853. The present version, which has been transcribed from the Bodleian copy (Malone, Add. 896), restores a few words and spellings which had been mistaken in the reprint. The text is very corrupt, and in some places defies emendation. Many of the errors seem to be due to the printer's ignorance of MS. contractions. In the original there are only two paragraph-breaks.

The accompanying table gives the earlier contributions to the anti-stage controversy.

- 1577. John Northbrooke enters his *Treatise wherein Dicing, Dauncing, vaine Playes or Enterluds, with other idle Pastimes, &c., commonly vsed on the Sabaoth Day, are reproued by the Authoritie of the Word of God and auntient Writers* (ed. Collier, Shakes. Soc., 1843).

- 1579. *The Schoole of Abuse. Conteining a plesaunt invectiue against Poets, Pipers, Plaiers, Jesters and such like Catterpillers of a Commonwelth; setting vp the Flagge of Defiance to their mischieuous exercise, and ouerthrowing their Bulwarkes, by Prophane Writers, Naturall reason, and common Experience. . . . By Stephan Gosson. Stud. Oxon.* Dedicated to Sir Philip Sidney (See Spenser's letter, 16th Oct., *infra*, p. 89) The pamphlet has been reprinted in Somers's *Collection* (1810, iii. 552), by the Shakespeare Society (ed. Collier), and by Mr. Arber in his *English Reprints* (New Issue, 1895).

1579. *Straunge News out of Affrick.* A Defence of the stage, of which nothing is known except the account given by Gosson in his *Ephemerides* (see Arber's edit. *u. s.* pp. 62–3).

1579. *A Short Apologie of the Schoole of Abuse, against Poets, Pipers, Players, and their Excusers,* by Gosson. Added to his *Ephemerides of Phialo.* The *Apologie* is dedicated to Sir Philip Sidney. Reprinted by Arber, *u. s.* pp. 64–75.

Towards the close Gosson writes: 'It is tolde mee that they haue got one in London to write certain *Honest excuses*, for so they tearme it, to their dishonest abuses which I reuealed . . . . How he frames his excuses, I know not yet, because it is doone in hudder mudder. Trueth can neuer be Falsehods Visarde, which maketh him maske without a torch, and keepe his papers very secret.' It is doubtful whether this passage, and especially the allusion to secrecy, refers to the next work.

1579. Lodge's *Defence* (here reprinted).

1579. *The Play of Playes,* an unknown 'Defence,' described by Gosson in the Fourth 'Action' of his *Playes Confuted.*

1580. Henry Denham enters his tract, *A Second and Third Blast of Retreat from Plays and Theatres.*

1581. *A Treatise of Daunses, wherein it is showed, that they are as it were accessories and dependants* (*or things annexed*) *to whoredom: where also by the way is touched and proved, that Playes are ioyned and knit together in a ranck or rowe with them* (see Chatsworth Library Catalogue, vol. iv. p. 49).

? 1582. *Playes confuted in five Actions* &c., by Gosson, in answer to Lodge's *Defence* and the *Play of Playes.* Dedicated to Sir Francis Walsingham. (Reprinted by Mr. W. C. Hazlitt in the Roxburghe Library, 1868.)

1581–3. Sidney writing his *Apologie* or *Defence.* Published in 1595 (see p. 148).

1583. *The Anatomie of Abuses*, by Philip Stubbes. (Reprinted by the New Shaks. Soc. 1877, ed. F. J. Furnivall.)

1584. *A Touchstone for the Time*, by George Whetstone. (Added to *A Mirour for Magestrates of Cyties*.)

1587. *A Mirrour of Monsters*, by William Rankins.

} All anti-stage.

There is but little material of literary interest in these controversial works (excluding Sidney's *Apologie* or *Defence*); they are almost exclusively devoted to partisan discussion of the social influence of the playhouse. Gosson's essays have not been reprinted here, for though he is the best known and the most active of the Puritan pamphleteers, and though he prompted Lodge to write his rhetorical answer and may have inspired Sidney's essay, he but rarely ventures to touch on the art or theory of poetry and the drama. The more important passages in his works are printed in the notes to Lodge and others, by way of illustration and commentary. Lodge's *Defence*, even in the portion here printed, is almost as uncritical as Gosson's attack, but it has a superior historical importance in defining a special trend in the later development of Elizabethan criticism.]

PROTOGENES can know Apelles by his line though he se him not, and wise men can consider by the Penn of aucthoritie of the writer thoughe they know him not. The Rubie is discerned by his pale rednes; and who hath not hard that the Lyon is knowne by hys clawes? Though Æsopes craftie crowe be neuer so deftlye decked, yet is his double dealing esely desiphered: & though men neuer so perfectly pollish there wrytings with others sentences, yet the simple truth wil discouer the shadow of ther follies: and bestowing euery fether in the bodye of the right M. tourne out the naked dissembler into his owen cote, as a spectacle of follye to all those which can rightlye Iudge what imperfections be.

There came to my hands lately a litle (woulde God a wittye) pamphelet, baring a fayre face as though it were the scoole of abuse; but, being by me aduisedly wayed, I fynd it the oftscome of imperfections, the writer fuller of wordes then iudgement, the matter certainely as ridiculus as serius. Assuredly his mother witte wrought this wonder, the child to dispraise his father, the dogg to byte his mayster for his dainty morcell: but I se (with Seneca) that the wrong is to be suffered, since he dispraiseth, who by costome hath left to speake well. But I meane to be short, and teach the Maister what he knoweth not, partly that he may se his own follie, and partly that I may discharge my promise,—both binde me: therefore I would wish the good scholmayster to ouer looke his abuses againe with me, so shall he see an ocean of inormities which begin in his first prinsiple in the dispraise of poetry. And first let me familiarly consider with this find faulte what the learned haue alwayes esteemed of poetrie. Seneca, thoughe a stoike, would haue a poeticall sonne, and, amongst the auncientest, Homer was no les accompted then *Humanus deus.* What made Alexander, I pray you, esteme of him so much? why allotted he for his works so curious a closset? was ther no fitter vnderprop for his pillow then a simple pamphelet? in all Darius cofers was there no iewell so costly? Forsoth, my thinks, these two (the one the father of Philosophers, the other the cheftaine of chiualrie) were both deceiued if all were as a GOSSON would wish them; yf poets paynt naughte but palterie toyes in vearse, their studies tended to foolishnesse, and in all their indeuors they did naught els but *agendo nihil agere.* Lord, howe Virgil's poore gnatt pricketh him, and how Ouid's fley byteth him! he can beare no bourde, he hath raysed vp a new sect of serius stoikes, that can abide naught but their owen shadowe, and alow nothing worthye but what they conceaue. Did you neuer reade (my ouer wittie frend) that vnder the persons of beastes many abuses were dissiphered? haue you not reason to waye that whatsoeuer ether Virgil did write of his gnatt or Ouid of his fley was all couertly to declare abuse? but you are *homo literatus*, a man of the letter, little sauoring of learning; your giddy brain made you leaue your thrift, and your abuses in London some part of your honestie. You say that Poets are subtil; if so, you haue learned that poynt of them; you can well glose on a trifeling text. But you haue dronke perhaps of Lethe; your gramer learning is out of your head; you forget your Accidence; you remember not that vnder the person of Æneas in Virgil the practice of a dilligent captaine is discribed, vnder the shadow of byrds, beastes, and trees the follies of the world were disiphered; you know not that the creation is signified in the Image of Prometheus, the fall of pryde in the person of Narcissus; these are toyes, because they sauor of wisedome which you want. Marke what Campanus sayth: *Mira fabularum vanitas, sed quae si introspiciantur videri possunt non vanae.* The vanitie of tales is wonderful; yet if we aduisedly looke into them they wil seme and proue wise. How wonderful are the pithie poemes of Cato? the curious comedies of Plautus? how brauely discouereth Terence our imperfection in his Eunuch? how neatly dissiphereth he Dauus? how pleasauntly paynteth he out Gnatho? whom if we shoulde seeke in our dayes, I suppose he would not be farr from your parson.

But I see you would seeme to be that which you are not, and, as the prouerb sayth, *Nodum in* [s]*cirpo quaerere*. Poetes, you say, vse coullors to couer their inco[n]u[en]iences, and wittie sentences to burnish their bawdery; and you diuinite to couer your knauerye. But tell mee truth, Gosson, speakest thou as thou thinkest? what

coulers findest thou in a Poete not to be admitted? are
his speeches vnperfect? sauor they of inscience? I think,
if thou hast any shame, thou canst not but like and approue them: are their gods displesant vnto thee? doth
Saturne in his maiesty moue thee? doth Iuno with her
riches displease thee? doth Minerua with her weapon
discomfort thee? doth Apollo with his harping harme
thee?—thou mayst say nothing les then harme thee,
because they are not, and, I thinke so to, because thou
knowest them not. For wot thou that in the person of
Saturne our decaying yeares are signified; in the picture
of angry Iuno our affections are dissiphered; in the person of Minerua is our vnderstanding signified, both in
respect of warre as policie. When they faine that Pallas
was begotten of the braine of Iupiter, their meaning is
none other but that al wisedome (as the learned say) is
from aboue, and commeth from the father of Lights: in
the portrature of Apollo all knowledge is denotated. So
that, what so they wrot, it was to this purpose, in the way
of pleasure to draw men to wisedome: for, seing the world
in those daies was vnperfect, yt was necessary that they
like good Phisitions should so frame their potions that
they might be appliable to the quesie stomaks of their
werish patients. But our studientes by your meanes haue
made shipwrack of theyr labors; our schoolemaisters haue
so offended that by your iudgement they shall *subire
poenam capitis* for teaching poetry; the vniversitie is litle
beholding to you,—al their practices in teaching are friuolus.
Witt hath wrought that in you, that yeares and studie
neuer setled in the heads of our sagest doctors. No
meruel though you disprayse poetrye, when you know not
what it meanes.

Erasmus will make that the path waye to knowledge
which you disprayse; and no meane fathers vouchsafe in
their seriouse questiones of deuinitie to inserte poeticall

sensures. I think, if we shal wel ouerloke the philosophers, we shal find their iudgements not halfe perfect. Poetes, you saye, fayle in their fables, Philosophers in the verye secrets of Nature. Though Plato could wish the expulsion of Poetes from his well publiques, which he might doe with reason, yet the wisest had not all that same opinion: it had bene better for him to haue sercht more narowly what the soule was, for his definition was verye friuolus, when he would make it naught els but *Substantiam intellectu predictam.* If you say that Poetes did labour about nothing, tell me (I besech you) what wonders wroughte those your dunce Doctors in ther reasons *de ente, et non ente,* in theyr definition of no force, and les witt? how sweate they, power soules, in makinge more things then cold be? that I may vse your owne phrase, did not they spende one candle by seeking another? Democritus, Epicurus, with ther scholler Metrodorus, how labored they in finding out more worlds then one? Your Plato in midst of his presisnes wrought that absurdite that neuer may be redd in Poets, to make a yearthly creature to beare the person of the creator, and a corruptible substance an incomprehensible God! for, determining of the principall causes of all thinges, a made them naughte els but an Idea, which if it be conferred wyth the truth, his sentence will sauour of Inscience. But I speake for Poetes; I answeare your abuse; therefore I will disproue or disprayse naught, but wish you with the wise Plato to disprayse that thing you offend not in. Seneca sayth that the studdie of Poets is to make children ready to the vnderstanding of wisdom, and that our auncients did teache *artes Eleutherias, i. liberales,* because the instructed children by the instrument of knowledg in time became *homines liberi, i. Philosophye.* It may be that in reding of poetry it happened to you as it is with the Oyster, for she in her swimming receiueth no ayre, and

you in your reding lesse instruction. It is reported that
the shepe of Euboia want ther gale, and on the contrarye
side that the beastes of Naxus have *distentum fel.* Men
hope that scollers should have witt, brought vpp in the
Vniuersite; but your sweet selfe, with the cattell of
Euboia, since you left your College, have lost your learning. You disprayse Maximus Tirius pollicey, and that
thinge that he wrott to manifest learned Poets mening
you atribute to follye. O holy hedded man! why may
not Iuno resemble the ayre? why not Alexander valour?
why not Vlisses pollice? Will you have all for your
owne tothe? must men write that you maye know theyr
meaning? as though your wytt were to wrest all things?
Alas! simple Irus, begg at knowledge gate awhile; thou
haste not wonne the mastery of learning. Weane thy
selfe to wisdome, and vse thy tallant in zeale, not for
enuie; abuse not thy knowledge in dispraysing that which
is pereles. I shold blush from a Player to become an
enuiouse Preacher, if thou hadst zeale to preach; if for
Sions sake thou coldst not holde thy tongue, thy true
dealing were prayse worthy, thy reuolting woulde counsell me to reuerence thee. Pittie weare it that Poetrye
should be displaced; full little could we want Buchanan's
workes, and Boetius comfortes may not be banished.
What made Erasmus labor in Euripides tragedies? Did
he indeuour by painting them out of Greeke into Latine
to manifest sinne vnto vs? or to confirme vs in goodness?
Labor (I pray thee) in Pamphelets more prayse worthy:
thou haste not saued a Senator, therefore not worthye
a Lawrell wreth; thou hast not (in disprouing poetry) reproued an abuse, and therfore not worthy commendation.

Seneca sayth that *Magna vitae pars elabitur male agentibus, maxima nihil agentibus, tota aliud agentibus.* The
most of our life (sayd he) is spent ether in doing euill, or
nothing, or that wee should not; and I would wish you

weare exempted from this sensure. Geue eare but a little more what may be said for poetrie, for I must be briefe; you haue made so greate matter that I may not stay on one thing to long, lest I leaue another vntouched. And first, whereas you say that Tullie, in his yeres of more iudgement, despised Poetes, harke (I pray you) what he worketh for them in his Oration *pro Archia poeta*: but before you heare him, least you fayle in the incounter, I would wysh you to followe the aduise of the dasterdlye Ichneumon of Ægipt, who, when shee beholdeth the Aspis her enemye to drawe nighe, calleth her fellowes together, bismering herselfe with claye, agaynst the byting and stroke of the serpent: arme your selfe, call your witts together: want not your wepons, lest your imperfect iudgement be rewardede with Midas eares. You had neede play the night burd now, for you[r] day Owl hath misconned his parte, and for 'to who' now a dayes he cryes 'foole you': which hath brought such a sort of wondering birds about your eares, as I feare me will chatter you out of your Iuey bush. The worlde shames to see you, or els you are afrayde to shew your selfe. You thought poetrye should want a patron (I think) when you fyrste published this inuectiue, but yet you fynd al to many, euen *preter expectationem*; yea, though it can speake for its selfe, yet her patron Tullie now shall tell her tale. *Haec studia* (sayth he) *adolescentiam alunt, senectutem oblectant, secundas res ornant, aduersis perfugium ac solatium praebent, delectant domi, non impediunt foris, pernoctant nobiscum, peregrinantur, rusticantur.* Then will you disprayse that which all men commend? you looke only vpon the refuse of the abuse, nether respecting the importance of the matter nor the weigh[t]e of the wryter. Solon can fayne himselfe madde, to further the Athenians. Chaucer in pleasant vein can rebuke sin vncontrold; and, though he be lauish in the letter, his sence is serious. Who in

Rome lamented not Roscius death? and canst thou suck
no plesure out of thy M. Claudian's writings? Hark
what Cellarius a learned father attributeth to it; *Acuit
memoriam* (saith he), it profiteth the memory. Yea and
Tully atributeth it for prais to Archias that vpon any
theame he cold versify extempory. Who liketh not of the
promptnes of Ouid? who not vnworthely cold bost of
himself thus, *Quicquid conabar dicere versus erat.* Who
then doothe not wonder at poetry? who thinketh not that
it procedeth from aboue? what made the Chians and
Colophonians fal to such controuersy? Why seke the
Smirnians to recouer from the Salaminians the prais of
Homer? Al wold haue him to be of ther city: I hope
not for harme, but because of his knowledge. Themistocles
desireth to be acquainted with those who could
best discipher his praises. Euen Marius himselfe, tho
neuer so cruel, accompted of Plotinus poems. What
made Aphricanus esteme Ennius? Why did Alexander
giue prais to Achilles, but for the prayses which he found
written of him by Homer? Why estemed Pompie so
muche of Theophanes Mitiletus? or Brutus so greatlye
the wrytinges of Accius? Fuluius was so great a fauorer
of Poetry, that, after the Aetolian warres, he attributed to
the Muses those spoiles that belonged to Mars. In all
the Romaine conquest, hardest thou euer of a slayne
Poete? nay rather the Emperours honored them, beautified
them with benefites, and decked their sanctuaries
with sacrifice. Pindarus colledg is not fit for spoil of
Alexander ouercome; nether feareth poetry the persecutors
sword. What made Austin so much affectate that
heauenly fury? not folly, for, if I must needes speake,
illud non ausim affirmare, his zeale was in setting vp of
the house of God, not in affectate eloquence; he wrot not,
he accompted not, he honnored not so much that (famous
poetry) whyche we prayse, without cause, for, if it be true

that Horace reporteth in his booke *de Arte Poetica*, all the
answeares of the Oracles weare in verse. Among the precise Iewes you shall find Poetes; and for more maiestie
Sibilla will prophesie in verse. Beroaldus can witnes
with me that Dauid was a poet, and that his vayne was in
imitating (as S. Ierom witnesseth) Horace, Flaccus, and
Pindarus; somtimes his verse runneth in an Iambus foote,
anone he hath recourse to a Saphic vaine, and *aliquando
semipede ingreditur*. Ask Iosephus, and he wil tel you
that Esay, Iob, and Salomon voutsafed poetical practises,
for (if Origen and he fault not) theyre verse was Hexameter and pentameter. Enquire of Cassiodorus, he will
say that all the beginning of Poetrye proceeded from the
Scripture. Paulinus, tho the Byshop of Nolanum, yet
voutsafe[th] the name of a Poet; and Ambrose, tho he
be a patriarke in Mediolanum, loueth versifing. Beda
shameth not the science that shamelesse Gosson misliketh. Reade ouer Lactantius, his proofe is by poetry;
and Paul voutsafeth to ouerlooke Epimenides: let the
Apostle preach at Athens, he disdaineth not of Aratus
authorite. It is a pretye sentence, yet not so prety as
pithy, *Poeta nascitur, Orator fit*: as who should say,
Poetrye commeth from aboue, from a heauenly seate of
a glorious God, vnto an excellent creature man; an
Orator is but made by exercise. For, if we examine well
what befell Ennius amonge the Romans, and Hesiodus
among his contrimen the Grecians, howe they came by
theyr knowledge, whence they receued their heauenly
furye, the first will tell vs that, sleping on the Mount of
Parnassus, he dreamed that he received the soule of
Homer into him, after the which he became a Poete; the
next will assure you that it commeth not by labor,
nether that night watchings bringeth it, but that we must
haue it thence whence he fetched it, which was (he saith)
from a well of the Muses which Persius calleth Caballinus,

a draught whereof drewe him to his perfection; so of a
shephard he becam an eloquent Poet. Wel then you
see that it commeth not by exercise of play making, nether
insertion of gawds, but from nature, and from aboue: and
I hope that Aristotle hath sufficiently taught you that
Natura nihil fecit frustra. Persius was made a poete
Diuino furore percitus; and whereas the poets were sayde
to call for the Muses helpe, ther mening was no other, as
Iodocus Badius reporteth, but to call for heauenly inspiration from aboue to direct theyr endeuors. Nether were
it good for you to sette light by the name of a Poet, since
the offspring from whence he commeth is so heauenly.
Sibilla in her answers to Æneas against hir will, as the
poet telleth vs, was possessed with thys fury; ye[a], wey
consideratly but of the writing of poets, and you shal se
that when ther matter is most heauenly their stile is most
loftye, a strange token of the wonderfull efficacy of the
same. I would make a long discourse vnto you of Platoes
4 furies, but I leue them: it pitieth me to bring a rodd of
your owne making to beate you wythal.

But, mithinks, while you heare thys, I see you swallowe
down your owne spittle for reuenge, where (God wot) my
wryting sauoreth not of enuye. In this case I could wyshe
you fare farre otherwyse from your foe; yf you please,
I wyll become your frende, and see what a potion or re-
ceypt I can frame fytt for your diet. And herein I will
proue myselfe a practiser; before I purdge you, you shall
take a preparatiue to disburden your heuay hedde of those
grose follis you haue conceued: but the receipt is bitter,
therfore I would wysh you first to tasten your mouth with
the Sugar of perseuerance: for ther is a cold collop that
must downe your throate, yet such a one as shall chaunge
your complection quit. I wyll haue you therfore to tast
first of the cold riuer Phricus, in Thracia, which, as Aristotle reporteth, changeth blacke into white, or of Scaman-

dar, which maketh gray yalow, that is of an enuious man a wel minded person, reprehending of zeale that wherein he hath sinned by folly; and so being prepard, thy purgation wyll worke more easy, thy vnderstandinge wyll be more perfit, thou shalt blush at thy abuse, and reclaime thy selfe by force of argument; so wilt thou proue a clene recouered patient, and I a perfecte practiser in framing so good a potion. This broughte to passe, I with thee wil seeke out some abuse in poetry, which I wil seeke for to disproue by reason, first pronounced by no smal birde, euen Aristotle himselfe. *Poetae* (sayth he) *multa mentiuntur*; and to further his opinion seuer Cato putteth in his censure, *Admiranda canunt, sed non credenda, Poetae*. These were sore blemishes, if obiected rightly; and heare you may say the streme runnes a wronge; but, if it be so, by you[r] leue, I wyll bring him shortly in his right chanel. My answere shall not be my owne, but a learned father shall tell my tale; if you wil know his name, men call him Lactantius, who, in hys booke *de diuinis institutionibus*, reesoneth thus. I suppose (sayth he) Poets are full of credit, and yet it is requisite for those that wil vnderstand them to be admonished that among them not onely the name but the matter beareth a show of that it is not; for if, sayth he, we examine the Scriptures litterallye, nothing will seeme more falls, and, if we way Poetes wordes and not ther meaning, our learning in them wilbe very mene. You see nowe that your Catoes iudgement is of no force, and that all your obiections you make agaynst Poetrye be of no valor; yet, lest you should be altogether discoraged, I wyll helpe you forwarde a little more. It pities me to consider the weaknes of your cause; I wyll therfore make your strongest reason more strong, and, after I have builded it vp, destroy it agayn. Poets you confesse are eloquent, but you reproue them in their wantonnesse: they write of no wisedom; you may say their tales are friuolus, they prophane holy thinges, they seeke nothing to the perfection of our soules, theyr practise is in other things of lesse force. To this obiection I answer no otherwise then Horace doeth in his booke *de Arte Poetica*, where he wryteth thus.

> *Siluestres homines sacer interpresque deorum*
> *Caedibus et victu foedo deterruit Orpheus:*
> *Dictus ob hoc lenire tigres, rabidosque leones:*
> *Dictus et Amphion, Thebanae conditor vrbis,*
> *Saxa mouere sono testudinis, et prece blanda*
> *Ducere quo vellet: fuit haec sapientia quondam,*
> *Publica priuatis secernere, sacra profanis;*
> *Concubitu prohibere vago; dare iura maritis;*
> *Oppida moliri; leges incidere ligno.*

The holy spokesman of the Gods,
Wich heaue[n]ly Orpheus hight,
Did driue the sauage men from wods,
And made them liue aright;
And therefore is sayd the Tygers fierce
And Lyons full of myght
To ouercome: Amphion, he
Was sayd of Theabs the founder,
Who by his force of Lute did cause
The stones to part a sonder,
And by his speach them did derect,
Where he would haue them staye.
This wisedome this was it of olde
All strife for to allay;
To giue to euery man his owne;
To make the Gods be knowne;
To driue each lecher from the bed
That neuer was his owne;
To teach the law of mariage;
The way to build a towne;
For to engraue these lawes in woods—
This was these mens renowne.

I cannot leaue Tirtheus pollicy vntouched, who by force of his pen could incite men to the defence of theyr countrye. If you require of the Oracle of Apollo what successe you shal haue, *respondet bellicoso numine.*

Lo now you see your obiections [and] my answers; you behold or may perceiue manifestlye that Poetes were the first raysors of cities, prescribers of good lawes, mayntayners of religion, disturbors of the wicked, aduancers of the wel disposed, inuentors of laws, and lastly the very fot-paths to knowledge and vnderstanding; ye[a], if we shold beleue Hierome, he will make Plato's exiles honest men, and his pestiferous poets good preachers, for he accounteth Orpheus, Museus, and Linus Christians; therefore Virgil (in his 6 boke of Æneiados, wher he lernedly describeth the iourny of Æneas to Elis[i]um) asserteneth vs that, among them that were ther for the zeale they beare toward their country, ther wer found *Quique pii Vates, et Phoebo digna loqu*[*u*]*ti*: but I must answer al obiections, I must fil euery nooke. I must arme myself now, for here is the greatest bob I can gather out of your booke, forsoth Ouid's abuses, in descrybing whereof you labour very vehementlye, terming him letcher, and in his person dispraise all poems: but shall on[e] man's follye destroye a vniuersal commodity? what gift, what perfit knowledg hath ther bin emong the professors of which ther hath not bin a bad on[e]; the Angels haue sinned in heauen, Adam and Eue in earthly paradise, emong the holy Apostles vngratious Iudas. I reson not that al poets are holy, but I affirme that poetry is a heauenly gift, a perfit gift, then which I know not greater plesure. And surely, if I may speak my mind, I think we shal find but few Poets, if it were exactly wayd, what they oughte to be: your Muscouian straungers, your Scithian monsters wonderful, by one Eurus brought vpon one stage in ships made of Sheepe skins, wyll not proue you

a poet, nether your life alow you to bee of that learning.
If you had wisely wayed the abuse of poetry, if you had
reprehended the foolish fantasies of our Poets *nomine
non re* which they bring forth on stage, my self wold haue
liked of you and allowed your labor. But I perceiue nowe
that all red colloured stones are not Rubies, nether is
euery one Alexander that hath a scare in his cheke; al
lame men are not Vulcans, nor hooke nosed men Ciceroes,
nether each professor a poet. I abhore those poets that
sauor of ribaldry: I will with the zealous admit the ex-
pullcion of such enormities: poetry is dispraised not for
the folly that is in it, but for the abuse whiche manye ill
Wryters couller by it. Beleeue mee the magestrats may
take aduise (as I knowe wisely can) to roote out those
odde rymes which runnes in euery rascales mouth, sauoring of rybaldry. Those foolishe ballets that are admitted
make poets good and godly practises to be refused. I like
not of a wicked Nero that wyll expell Lucan, yet admit
I of a zealous gouernour that wil seke to take away the
abuse of poetry. I like not of an angrye Augustus which
wyll banishe Ouid for enuy. I loue a wise Senator, which
in wisedome wyll correct him, and with aduise burne his
follyes: vnhappy were we, yf like poore Scaurus we shoulde
find [a] Tiberius that wyll put vs to death for a tragedy
making; but most blessed were we, if we might find a
iudge that seuerely would amende the abuses of Tragedies.
But I leaue the reformation thereof to more wyser than
myselfe, and retourne to Gosson, whom I wyshe to be
fully perswaded in this cause; and therefore I will tell
hym a prety story, which Iustin wryteth in the prayse of
poetrye. The Lacedemonians, when they had loste many
men in diuers incountryes with theyr enemyes, soughte to
the Oracles of Apollo requiring how they myght recouer
theyr losses. It was answered, that they mighte ouercome
if so be that they could get an Athenian gouernor: Where-

upon they sent Orators vnto the Athenians, humbly requesting them that they woulde appoynt them out one of theyr best captaynes. The Athenians, owinge them old malice, sent them in steede of a *soldado vechio* a scholar of the Muses, in steede of a worthy warrior a poore poet, for a couragious Themistocles a silly Tirthetus, a man of great eloquence and singuler wytte, yet was he but a lame lymde captaine, more fit for the coche then the field. The Lacedemonians, trusting the Oracle, receued the champion, and, fearing the gouernment of a stranger, made him ther Citizen; which once don, and he obteining the Dukdome, he assended the theater, and ther very learnedly wyshing them to forget theyr folly and to thinke on victory, they, being acuate by his eloquence, waging battail, won the fielde.

Lo now you see that the framing of common welthes, and defence therof, proceedeth from poets, how dare you therfore open your mouth against them? how can you disprayse the preseruer of a countrye? You compare Homer to Methecus, cookes to Poetes, you shame your selfe in your vnreuerent similituds, you may see your follyes; *verbum sapienti sat.* Where as Homer was an ancient poet, you disalow him, and accompte of those of lesser iudgement. Strabo calleth poetry *primam sapientiam.* Cicero, in his firste of hys Tusculans, attributeth the inuencion of philosophy to poets. God keepe vs from a Plato that should expel such men: pittie were it that the memory of these valiant victours should be hidden, which haue dyed in the behalfe of ther countryes. Miserable were our state yf we wanted those worthy volumes of Poetry: could the learned beare the losse of Homer? or our younglings the wrytings of Mantuan? or you your volumes of Historyes? Belieue me, yf you had wanted your Mysteries of nature, and your stately storyes, your booke would haue scarce bene fedde wyth matter. If

therefore you will deale in things of wisdome, correct the
abuse, honor the science, renewe your schoole; crye out
ouer Hierusalem wyth the prophet the woe that he pronounced; wish the teacher to reforme hys lyfe, that his
weake scholler may proue the wyser; cry out against vn-
saciable desyre in rich men; tel the house of Iacob theyr
iniquities; lament with the Apostle the want of laborers in
the Lords vineyards; cry out on those dume doggs that
will not barke; wyll the mightye that they ouer mayster
not the poore; and put downe the beggars prowde heart
by thy perswasions. Thunder oute wyth the Prophete
Micha the mesage of the Lord, and wyth him desyre
the Iudges to heare thee, the Prynces of Iacob to hearken
to thee, and those of the house of Israell to vnderstande;
then tell them that they abhorre iudgement, and preuent
equitie, that they iudge for rewardes, and that theyr priests
teach for hyre, and the prophets thereof prophesie for
money, and yet that they saye the Lorde is wyth them,
and that no euil can befall them; breath out the sweete
promises to the good, the cursses to the badde, tell them
that a peace muste needes haue a warre, and that God
can rayse vp another Zenacharib; shew them that Sala-
mons kingdome was but for a season, and that aduersitie
cometh ere we espye it. These be the songes of Sion,
these be those rebukes which you oughte to add to abuses;
recouer the body, for it is sore; the appe[n]di:es thereof
will easely be reformed, if that we ar at a staye.

[*Lodge proceeds to discuss Gosson's Second Abuse—
Music*, 'which you vnaduisedly terme Pyping.' Homer
commended it. 'Looke vppon the harmonie of the
Heauens? hange they not by Musike?' Dauid sang
and praised the Lord with the harp: and the testimony
of the Greek philosophers is in fauour of its vse. 'But
as I like Musik, so admit I not of thos that depraue
the same: your Pipers are so odius to mee as yourselfe;

nether alowe I your harpinge merye beggars, although
I knewe you my self a professed play maker and a paltry
actor.']

Well, I leaue this poynt til I know further of your
mynde; mean while I must talke a little wyth you about
the thyrd abuse, for the cater cosens of Pypers, theyr
names (as you terme them), be Players, and I thinke as
you doe, for your experience is sufficient to enforme me;
but here I must loke about me, *quacunque te t[et]igeris vlcus
est*: here is a task that requireth a long treatis, and what
my opinion is of Players ye now shall plainly perceue.
I must now search my wits; I see this shall passe throughe
many seuere sensors handling; I must aduise me what
I write, and write that I would wysh. I way wel the
seriousnes of the cause, and regarde very much the
iudges of my endeuor, whom, if I could, I would perswade
that I woulde not nourish abuse, nether mayntaine that
which should be an vniversall discomoditye. I hope they
wil not iudge before they read, nether condemne without
occasion. The wisest wil alwais carry t[w]o eares, in that
they are to diserne two indifferent causes. I meane
not to hold you in suspenc[e] (seuere Iudges): if you
gredely expect my verdit, brefely this it is.

Demost[he]nes thoughte not that Phillip shoulde ouercome when he reproued hym, nether feared Cicero
Anthonies force when in the Senate hee rebuked hym.
To the ignorant ech thinge that is vnknowne semes vnprofitable, but a wise man can forsee and prayse by proofe.
Pythagoras could spy oute in women's eyes two kind of
teares, the one of grefe, the other of disceit; and those
of iudgement can from the same flower suck honey with
the bee, from whence the Spyder (I mean the ignorant)
take their poison. Men that haue knowledge what
comedies and tragedis be wil comend them, but it is
sufferable in the folish to reproue that they know not,

becaus ther mouthes will hardly be stopped. Firste therfore, if it be not tedious to GOSSON to harken to the lerned, the reder shal perceiue the antiquity of play-making, the inuentors of comedies, and therewithall the vse and comoditye of them. So that in the end I hope my labor shall be liked, and the learned wil soner conceue his folly. For tragedies and comedies, Donate the gramarian sayth, they wer inuented by lerned fathers of the old time to no other purpose but to yeelde prayse vnto God for a happy haruest or plentiful yeere. And that thys is trewe the name of Tragedye doth importe, for, if you consider whence it came, you shall perceiue (as Iodocus Badius reporteth) that it drewe his original of *Tragos, Hircus, et Ode, Cantus* (so called), for that the actors thereof had in rewarde for theyr labour a gotes skynne fylled wyth wyne. You see then that the fyrste matter of Tragedies was to giue thankes and prayses to God, and a gratefull prayer of the countrymen for a happye haruest, and this I hope was not discommendable. I knowe you will iudge i[t] farthest from abuse. But to wade farther, thys fourme of inuention being found out, as the dayes wherein it was vsed did decay, and the world grew to more perfection, so the witt of the younger sorte became more riper, for they leauing this fourme inuented an other, in the which they altered the nature but not the name; for, for sonnets in prayse of the gods, they did set forth the sower fortune of many exiles, the miserable fal of haples princes, the reuinous decay of many countryes; yet not content with this, they presented the liues of Satyers, so that they might wiselye, vnder the abuse of that name, discouer the follies of many theyr folish fellow citesens. And those monsters were then as our parasites are now adayes: suche as with pleasure reprehended abuse. As for Commedies, because they bear a more plesanter vain, I will leaue the other to speake of them. Tulley defines them thus: *Comedia* (saith he) is *imitatio vitae, speculum consuetudinis, et imago veritatis*; and it is sayde to be termed of *Comai* (emongste the Greekes), which signifieth *Pagos*, and *Ode, Cantus*; for that they were exercised in the fielde, they had they[r] beginning with tragedies, but their matter was more plessaunt, for they were suche as did réprehend, yet *quodam lepore*. These first very rudly were inuented by Susarion Bullus and Magnes, t[w]o aunciente poets, yet so that they were meruelous profitable to the reclamynge of abuse; whereupon Eupolis with Cratinus and Aristophanes began to write, and with ther eloquenter vaine and perfection of stil dyd more seuerely speak agaynst the abuses then they: which Horace himselfe witnesseth. For, sayth he, ther was no abuse but these men reprehended it; a thefe was loth to be seene [at] one [of] there spectacle[s], a coward was neuer present at theyr assemblies, a backbiter abhord that company; and I my selfe could not haue blamed you (Gosson) for exempting yourselfe from this theater; of troth I shoulde have lykt your pollicy. These therefore, these wer they that kept men in awe, these restrayned the vnbridled cominaltie; wherupon Horace wisely sayeth,

Oderunt peccare boni, virtutis amore:
Oderunt peccare mali, formidine poenae.

The good did hate al sinne for vertues loue:
The bad for feare of shame did sin remoue.

Yea, would God our realme could light vppon a Lucilius; then should the wicked bee poynted out from the good; a harlot woulde seeke no harbor at stage plais, lest she shold here her owne name growe in question, and the discourse of her honesty cause her to bee hated of the godly. As for you, I am sure of this one thing, he would paint you in your players ornaments, for they best becam you. But as these sharpe corrections were disanulde in Rome when they grewe to more licenciousnes, so I fear me if we shold practise it in our dayes the same intertainmente would followe. But in ill reformed Rome what comedies now? A poet's wit can correct, yet not offend. Philemon will mitigate the corrections of sinne by reprouing them couertly in shadowes. Menander dare not offend the Senate openly, yet wants he not a parasite to touch them priuely. Terence wyl not report the abuse of harlots vnder there proper stile, but he can finely girde them vnder the person of Thais. Hee dare not openly tell the Rich of theyr couetousnesse and seuerity towards their children, but he can controle them vnder the person of Durus Demeas. He must not shew the abuse of noble yong gentilmen vnder theyr owne title, but he wyll warne them in the person of Pamphilus. Wil you learne to knowe a parasite? Looke vpon his Dauus. Wyl you seke the abuse of courtly flatterers? Behold Gnato. And if we had some Satericall Poetes nowe a dayes to penn our commedies, that might be admitted of zeale to discypher the abuses of the worlde in the person of notorious offenders, I knowe we should wisely ryd our assemblyes of many of your brotherhod.

But, because you may haue a full scope to reprehende, I will ryp vp a rablement of play makers, whose wrightinges I would wishe you ouerlooke, and seeke out theyr abuses. Can you mislike of Cecilius? or dispise Plinius? or amend Neuius? or find fault with Licinius? Wherein offended Atilius? I am sure you can not but wonder at Terence? Wil it please you to like of Turpilius? or alow of Trabea? You muste needs make much of Ennius; for ouerloke al thes and you shal find ther volums ful of wit if you examin them; so that, if you had no other masters, you might deserue to be a doctor, wher now you are but a folishe scholemaister: but I wyll deale wyth

you very freendlye, I wil resolue eueri doubt that you
find; those instrumentes which you mislike in playes grow
of auncient custome, for, when Roscius was an Actor, be
sure that as with his tears he moued affections, so the
5 Musitian in the Theater before the entrance did morne-
fully record it in melody (as Seruius reporteth). The
actors in Rome had also gay clothing, and euery mans
aparel was apliable to his part and person. The old men
in white, the rich men in purple, the parasite disguisedly,
10 the yong men in gorgeous coulours, ther wanted no deuise
nor good iudgement of the comedy, where I suppose our
players both drew ther plaies and fourme of garments.
As for the appointed dayes wherin comedies wer showen,
I reede that the Romaynes appoynted them on the festiual
15 dayes; in such reputation were they had at that time.
Also Iodocus Badius will assertain you that the actors for
shewing pleasure receued some profite. But let me apply
those dayes to ours, their actors to our players, their
autors to ours. Surely we want not a Roscius, nether
20 ar ther great scarsity of Terence's profession, but yet our
men dare not nowe a dayes presume so much as the old
Poets might, and therfore they apply ther writing to the
peoples vain; wheras, if in the beginning they had ruled,
we should now adaies have found smal spectacles of folly.
25 But (of truth) I must confes with Aristotle that men are
greatly delighted with imitation, and that it were good to
bring those things on stage that were altogether tending
to vertue: all this I admit and hartely wysh, but you say
vnlesse the thinge be taken away the vice will continue.
30 Nay, I say if the style were changed the practise would
profit, and sure I thinke our theaters fit that Ennius,
seeing our wanton Glicerium, may rebuke her. If our
poetes will nowe become seuere, and for prophane things
write of vertue, you I hope shoulde see a reformed state
35 in those thinges; which I feare me yf they were not, the

idle hedded commones would worke more mischiefe. I wish
as zealously as the best that all abuse of playinge weare
abolished; but for the thing, the antiquitie causeth me to
allow it, so it be vsed as it should be. I cannot allow the
prophaning of the Sabaoth. I praise your reprehension
in that; you did well in discommending the abuse, and
surely I wysh that that folly wer disclaymed; it is not to
be admitted, it maks those sinne, whiche perhaps, if it
were not, would have binne present at a good sermon.
It is in the Magistrate to take away that order, and
appoynt it otherwyse. But sure it were pittie to abolish
that which hath so great vertue in it, because it is abused.
The Germanes, when the vse of preaching was forbidden
them, what helpe had they I pray you? Forsoth the
learned were fayne couertly in comedies to declare abuses,
and by playing to incite the people to vertues, when they
might heare no preaching. Those were lamentable dayes
you will say, and so thinke I; but was not this, I pray you,
a good help in reforming the decaying Gospel? You see
then how comedies (my seuere iudges) are requesit both
for ther antiquity and for ther commoditye, for the dignity
of the wrighters, and the pleasure of the hearers. But,
after your discrediting of playmaking, you salue vppon the
sore somewhat, and among many wise workes there be
some that fitte your vaine: the practice of parasites is one,
which I meruel it likes you so well, since it bites you so
sore. But sure in that I like your iudgement, and for the
rest to I approue your wit, but for the pigg of your owne
sow (as you terme it) assuredly I must discommend your
verdit. Tell me, GOSSON, was all your owne you wrote
there? did you borow nothing of your neyghbours? Out
of what booke patched you out Cicero's Oration? Whence
fet you Catilin's Inuectiue. Thys is one thing, *alienam olet
lucernam, non tuam*; so that your helper may wisely reply
vpon you with Virgil—

Hos ego versiculos feci: tulit alter honores.

I made these verses, other bear[s] the name.

Beleue me I should preferr Wilson's: Shorte and sweete, if I were iudge, a peece surely worthy prayse, the practice of a good scholler; would the wiser would ouerlooke that, they may perhaps cull some wisedome out of a player's toye. Well, as it is wisedome to commend where the cause requireth, so it is a poynt of folly to praise without deserte. You dislike players very much, theyr dealings be not for your commodity; whom if I myghte aduise, they should learne thys of Iuuenal.

Viuendum est recte, cum propter plurima, tum his
Praecipue causis, vt linguas mancipiorum
Contemnas. Nam lingua mali pars pessima serui.

> We ought to leade our liues aright,
> For many causes moue.
> Especially for this same cause,
> Wisedom doth vs behoue
> That we may set at nought those blames
> Which seruants to vs lay;
> For why, the tongue of euel slaue
> Is worst, as wisemen euer say.

Methinks I heare some of them verifiing these verses vpon you; if it be so that I hear them, I will concele it: as for the statute of apparell and the abuses therof, I see it manifestly broken, and, if I should seeke for example, you cannot but offend my eyes. For, if you examine the statuts exactly, a simple cote should be fitted to your backe, we shold bereue you of your brauerye, and examine your auncestry, and by profession, in respect of that statute, we should find you cater cosens with a, (but hush) you know my meaning: I must for pitie fauor your credit, in that you weare once a scholler.

[*Lodge then refers briefly to Gosson's attack on* 'Carders, Dicers, Fencers, Bowlers, Daunsers, and Tomblers,' *and closes his* Defence *with these words*—]

And because I think my selfe to haue sufficiently answered that I supposed, I conclude wyth this : God preserue our peaceable Princes, and confound her enemies : God enlarge her wisedom, that like Saba she may seeke after a Salomon : God confounde the imaginations of her enemies, and perfit his graces in her, that the daies of her rule may be continued in the bonds of peace, that the house of the chosen Isralites may be maynteyned in happinesse : lastly, I frendly bid GOSSON farwell, wyshinge him to temper his penn with more discretion.

EDMUND SPENSER

AND

GABRIEL HARVEY

(*LETTERS ON REFORMED VERSIFYING, &c.*)

1579-80

[Letters I and II, dated 5 [? 16] Oct. and 23 Oct. 1579 respectively, were printed at London in 1580 by H. Bynneman, 'dwelling in Thames streate, neere unto Baynardes Castell,' and entitled *Two other | very commendable Letters | of the same mens writing: | both touching the foresaid | Artificiall Versifying, and certain other Particulars || More lately deliuered vnto the | Printer*. The later letters, III and IV, dated April 1580, were printed earlier in the same year by the same printer, and, with a third (placed second in the book-order), constituted the *Three Proper | and wittie familiar Letters: | lately passed betweene two V-|niuersitie men: touching the Earth-|quake in Aprill last, and our | English refourmed Versifying. || With a Preface of a well willer to them both*. The second letter in the earlier publication, which is omitted here, contains Gabriel Harvey's reflections on the recent earthquake. The text has been copied from the rare volume in the British Museum, C 40. d. 16, pp. 51 and 61 (I and II), and pp. 1 and 31 (III and IV). The concluding extracts, which have a direct bearing on this correspondence, are from the Letter-Book of Gabriel Harvey (1573-1580) B. M. Sloane 93.]

[I]

TO THE WORSHIPFULL HIS VERY SINGULAR GOOD FRIEND, MAISTER G. H., FELLOW OF TRINITIE HALL IN CAMBRIDGE.

GOOD Master G., I perceiue by your most curteous
and frendly Letters your good will to be no lesse
in deed than I alwayes esteemed. In recompence wherof,

think, I beseech you, that I wil spare neither speech nor wryting, nor aught else, whensoeuer and wheresoeuer occasion shal be offred me: yea, I will not stay till it be offred, but will seeke it in al that possibly I may. And that you may perceiue how much your Counsel in al things preuaileth with me, and how altogither I am ruled and ouerruled thereby, I am nowe determined to alter mine owne former purpose, and to subscribe to your aduizement, being notwithstanding resolued stil to abide your farther resolution. My principal doubts are these. First, I was minded for a while to haue intermitted the vttering of my writings, leaste, by ouermuch cloying their noble eares, I should gather a contempt of my self, or else seeme rather for gaine and commoditie to doe it, for some sweetnesse that I haue already tasted. Then also me seemeth the work too base for his excellent Lordship, being made in Honour of a priuate Personage vnknowne, which of some ylwillers might be vpbraided not to be so worthie as you knowe she is: or the matter not so weightie that it should be offred to so weightie a Personage: or the like. The selfe former Title stil liketh me well ynough, and your fine Addition no lesse. If these and the like doubtes maye be of importaunce in your seeming to frustrate any parte of your aduice, I beeseeche you, without the leaste selfe loue of your own purpose, councell me for the beste: and the rather doe it faithfullye and carefully, for that in all things I attribute so muche to your iudgement, that I am euer more content to annihilate mine owne determinations in respecte thereof. And indeede for your selfe to, it fitteth with you now to call your wits and senses togither (which are alwaies at call), when occasion is so fairely offered of Estimation and Preferment. For, whiles the yron is hote, it is good striking; and minds of Nobles varie as their Estates. *Verum ne quid durius.*

Of Reformed Versifying, &c.

I pray you bethinke you well hereof, good Maister G., and forthwith write me those two or three special points and caueats for the nonce, *De quibus in superioribus illis mellitissimis longissimisque Litteris tuis.* Your desire to heare of my late beeing with hir Maiestie muste dye in it selfe. As for the twoo worthy Gentlemen, Master SIDNEY and Master DYER, they haue me, I thanke them, in some vse of familiarity: of whom, and to whome, what speache passeth for youre credite and estimation, I leaue your selfe to conceiue, hauing alwayes so well conceiued of my vnfained affection and zeale towardes you. And nowe they haue proclaimed in their ἀρείῳ πάγῳ a generall surceasing and silence of balde Rymers, and also of the verie beste to: in steade whereof, they haue, by autho[ri]tie of their whole Senate, prescribed certaine Lawes and rules of Quantities of English sillables for English Verse, hauing had thereof already greate practise, and drawen mee to their faction. Newe Bookes I heare of none, but only of one, that writing a certaine Booke, called THE SCHOOLE OF ABUSE, and dedicating it to Maister SIDNEY, was for hys labor scorned, if at leaste it be in the goodnesse of that nature to scorne. Suche follie is it not to regarde aforehande the inclination and qualitie of him to whome wee dedicate oure Bookes. Suche mighte I happily incurre, entituling my SLOMBER and the other Pamphlets vnto his honor. I meant them rather to MAISTER DYER. But I am, of late, more in loue wyth my Englishe Versifying than with Ryming; whyche I should haue done long since, if I would then haue followed your councell. *Sed te solum iam tum suspicabar cum Aschamo sapere: nunc Aulam video egregios alere Poëtas Anglicos.* Maister E. K. hartily desireth to be commended vnto your Worshippe: of whome what accompte he maketh youre selfe shall hereafter perceiue, by hys paynefull and dutifull Verses of your selfe.

Thus much was written at Westminster yesternight;
but comming this morning, beeyng the sixteenth of
October, to Mystresse *Kerkes*, to haue it deliuered to the
Carrier, I receyued youre letter, sente me the laste
weeke; whereby I perceiue you otherwhiles continue
your old exercise of Versifying in English: whych glorie
I had now thought shoulde haue bene onely ours heere
at London and the Court.

Truste me, your Verses I like passingly well, and enuye
your hidden paines in this kinde, or rather maligne and
grudge at your selfe that would not once imparte so
muche to me. But once or twice you make a breache
in Maister DRANTS Rules: *quod tamen condonabimus
tanto Poëtae tuaeque ipsius maximae in his rebus autoritati.*
You shall see when we meete in London (whiche, when it
shall be, certifye vs) howe fast I haue followed after you
in that Course: beware leaste in time I ouertake you.
*Veruntamen te solum sequar (vt saepenumero sum professus),
nunquam sane assequar dum viuam.* And nowe requite
I you with the like, not with the verye beste, but with
the verye shortest, namely with a fewe *Iambickes*: I dare
warrant they be precisely perfect for the feete (as you
can easily iudge) and varie not one inch from the Rule.
I will imparte yours to Maister SIDNEY and Maister
DYER at my nexte going to the Courte. I praye you
keepe mine close to your selfe, or your verie entire
friendes, Maister PRESTON, Maister STILL, and the reste.

Iambicum Trimetrum.

Vnhappie Verse, the witnesse of my vnhappie state,
   Make thy selfe fluttring wings of thy fast flying
   Thought, and fly forth vnto my Loue, whersoeuer
      she be:
Whether lying reastlesse in heauy bedde, or else
   Sitting so cheerelesse at the cheerfull boorde, or else

Playing alone carelesse on hir heauenlie Virginals.
If in Bed, tell hir that my eyes can take no reste;
  If at Boorde, tell hir that my mouth can eate no meate;
5 If at hir Virginals, tel hir I can heare no mirth.
Asked why? say, Waking Loue suffereth no sleepe;
  Say that raging Loue dothe appall the weake stomacke;
  Say that lamenting Loue marreth the Musicall.
10 Tell hir that hir pleasures were wonte to lull me asleepe;
  Tell hir that hir beautie was wonte to feede mine eyes;
  Tell hir that hir sweete Tongue was wonte to make
15 me mirth.
Nowe doe I nightly waste, wanting my kindely reste;
  Nowe do I dayly starue, wanting my liuely foode;
  Nowe do I alwayes dye, wanting thy timely mirth.
And if I waste, who will bewaile my heauy chaunce?
20 And if I starue, who will record my cursed end?
  And if I dye, who will saye, *this was Immerito*?

I thought once agayne here to haue made an ende, with a heartie *Vale* of the best fashion; but loe an ylfauoured myschaunce. My last farewell, whereof I made great
25 accompt, and muche maruelled you shoulde make no mention thereof, I am nowe tolde (in the Diuels name) was thorough one mans negligence quite forgotten, but shoulde nowe vndoubtedly haue beene sent, whether I hadde come or no. Seing it can now be no otherwise,
30 I pray you take all togither, wyth all their faultes: and nowe I hope you will vouchsafe mee an answeare of the largest size, or else I tell you true you shall bee verye deepe in my debte, notwythstandyng thys other sweete but shorte letter, and fine but fewe Verses. But I woulde

rather I might yet see youre owne good selfe, and receiue a Reciprocall farewell from your owne sweete mouth.

Ad Ornatissimum virum, multis iamdiu nominibus clarissimum, G. H. IMMERITO *sui mox in Gallias nauigaturi* εὐτυχεῖν.

[*Here follow* 114 *lines of Latin verse.*]

I was minded also to haue sent you some English verses, or Rymes, for a farewell; but, by my Troth, I haue no spare time in the world to thinke on such Toyes, that you knowe will demaund a freer head than mine is presently. I beseeche you by all your Curtesies and Graces let me be answered ere I goe: which will be, (I hope, I feare, I thinke) the next weeke, if I can be dispatched of my Lorde. I goe thither, as sent by him, and maintained most what of him: and there am to employ my time, my body, my minde, to his Honours seruice. Thus, with many superhartie Commendations and Recommendations to your selfe and all my friendes with you, I ende my last farewell, not thinking any more to write vnto you before I goe; and withall committing to your faithfull Credence the eternall Memorie of our euerlasting friendship, the inuiolable Memorie of our vnspotted friendshippe, the sacred Memorie of our vowed friendship, which I beseech you Continue with vsuall writings, as you may; and of all things let me heare some Newes from you, as gentle M. SIDNEY, I thanke his good Worship, hath required of me, and so promised to doe againe. *Qui monet, vt facias, quod iam facis*; you knowe the rest. You may alwayes send them most safely to me by MISTRESSE KERKE, and by none other. So once againe, and yet once more, farewell most hartily, mine owne good MASTER H. and loue me, as I loue you, and thinke vpon poore IMMERITO, as he thinketh vppon you.

Leycester House. This 5 [? 16] of *October* 1579.

Per mare, per terras, Viuus mortuusque, Tuus Immerito.

[II]

TO MY VERIE FRIENDE
M. IMMERITO.

Liberalissimo Signor Immerito, in good soothe my poore Storehouse will presently affourd me nothing, either to recompence or counteruaile your gentle Masterships long, large, lauish, Luxurious, Laxatiue Letters withall (now, a Gods name, when did I euer in my life hunt the Letter before? but, belike, theres no remedie; I must needes be euen with you once in my dayes), but only, forsoothe, a fewe Millions of Recommendations and a running Coppie of the Verses enclosed. Which Verses (*extra iocum*) are so well done in Latin by two Doctors, and so well Translated into English by one odde Gentleman, and generally so well allowed of all that chaunced to haue the perusing of them, that, trust mee, G. H. was at the first hardly intreated to shame himselfe, and, truely, now blusheth to see the first Letters of his name stande so neere their Names, as of necessitie they must. You know the *Greeke* prouerb, πορφύρα περὶ πορφύραν διακριτέα, and many colours (as in a manner euery thing else), that seuerally by themselues seeme reasonably good and freshe ynough, beyng compared and ouermatched wyth their betters are maruellously disgraced, and, as it were, dashed quite oute of Countenaunce. I am at this instant very busilye and hotly employed in certaine greate and serious affayres: whereof, notwithstanding (for all youre vowed and long experimented secrecie), you are not like to heare a worde more at the moste, till I my selfe see a World more at the leaste. And, therefore, for this once I beseech you (notwithstanding your greate expectation of I knowe not what Volumes for an aunsweare) content your good selfe with these Presentes (pardon me, I came lately

out of a Scriueners shop) and, in lieu of many gentle
Farewels and goodly Godbewyes at your departure,
gyue me once againe leaue to playe the Counsaylour
a while, if it be but to iustifie your liberall Mastershippes,
Nostri Cato maxime saecli: and I coniure you by the
Contents of the Verses and Rymes enclosed, and by al
the good and bad Spirites that attende vpon the Authors
themselues, immediatly vpon the contemplation thereof
to abandon all other fooleries, and honour Vertue, the
onely immortall and suruiuing Accident amongst so manye
mortall and euer-perishing Substaunces. As I strongly
presume, so good a Texte, so clearkly handeled by three
so famous Doctours, as olde MAISTER WYTHIPOLE and
the other two bee, may easily and will fully perswade you,
howsoeuer you tush at the fourths vnsutable Paraphrase.
But a worde or two to your large, lauishe, laxatiue
Letters, and then for thys time *Adieu*. Of my credite,
youre doubtes are not so redoubted as youre selfe ouer
suspiciously imagine; as I purpose shortely to aduize you
more at large. Your hotte yron is so hotte that it
striketh mee to the hearte; I dare not come neare to
strike it. The Tyde tarryeth no manne, but manye a good
manne is fayne to tarry the Tyde. And I knowe some,
whyche coulde be content to bee theyr own Caruers, that
are gladde to thanke other for theyr courtesie. But
Beggars, they saye, must be no choosers.

Your new-founded ἄρειον πάγον I honoure more than you
will or can suppose, and make greater accompte of the
twoo worthy Gentlemenne than of two hundreth *Dionisii
Areopagitae*, or the verye notablest Senatours that euer
Athens dydde affourde of that number.

Your Englishe *Trimetra* I like better than perhappes
you will easily beleeue, and am to requite them wyth
better, or worse, at more conuenient leysure. Marry, you
must pardon me, I finde not your warrant so sufficiently

good and substauntiall in Lawe that it can persuade me
they are all so precisely perfect for the feete, as your
selfe ouer-partially weene and ouer-confidently auouche:
especiallye the thirde, whyche hathe a foote more than
a Lowce (a wonderous deformitie in a righte and pure
SENARIE), and the sixte, whiche is also in the same
Predicament, vnlesse happly one of the feete be sawed
off wyth a payre of SYNCOPES: and then shoulde the
Orthographie haue testified so muche: and, in steade
of *Heauēnlĭ Virgĭnāls*, you should haue written *Heaūnlĭ
Virgnāls*, and *Virgnāls* againe in the ninth, and should
haue made a Curtoll of *Imměrĭtō* in the laste: being all
notwithstandyng vsuall, and tollerable ynoughe, in a mixte
and licentious IAMBICKE: and of two euilles better (no
doubte) the fyrste than the laste, a thyrde superfluous
sillable than a dull SPONDEE. Then me thinketh you
haue in my fancie somwhat too many SPONDEES beside:
and whereas TROCHEE sometyme presumeth in the firste
place, as namely in the second Verse, *Make thy*, whyche
thy by youre Maistershippes owne authoritie muste needes
be shorte, I shall be faine to supplye the office of the
Arte Memoratiue, and putte you in minde of a pretty
Fable in ABSTEMIO the Italian, implying thus much, or
rather thus little, in effect.

A certaine lame man, beyng inuited to a solempne
Nuptiall Feaste, made no more adoe, but sate me hym
roundlye downe foremoste at the hyghest ende of the Table.
The Master of the feast, suddainly spying his presumption,
and hansomely remoouing him from thence, placed me
this haulting Gentleman belowe at the nether end of the
bourd; alledging for his defence the common verse
Sedes nulla datur praeterquam sexta Trochaeo, and
pleasantly alluding to this foote, which, standing vppon
two syllables, the one long, the other short (much like,
of a like, his guestes feete), is alwayes thrust downe to the

last place in a true Hexameter, and quite thrust out of
doores in a pure and iust SENARIE. Nowe, Syr, what
thinke you I began to thinke with my selfe, when I began
to reade your warrant first, so boldly and venterously
set downe in so formall and autentique wordes as these,
PRECISELY PERFIT, AND NOT AN INCH FROM THE RULE?
Ah Syrrha, and Iesu Lord, thought I, haue we at the
last gotten one, of whom his olde friendes and Companions
may iustly glory *In eo solum peccat, quod nihil peccat*,
and that is yet more exacte and precise in his English
Comicall Iambickes than euer M. WATSON himselfe
was in his Latin Tragicall Iambickes, of whom M. *Ascham*
reporteth that he would neuer to this day suffer his famous
Absolon to come abrode, onely because *Anapaestus in locis
paribus* is twice or thrice vsed in steade of *Iambus*? A
small fault, ywisse, and such a one, in M. ASCHAMS owne
opinion, as perchaunce would neuer haue beene espyed,
no neither in *Italy* nor in *Fraunce*. But when I came to
the curious scanning and fingering of euery foote and
syllable: So here, quoth I, M. WATSONS *Anapaestus* for
all the worlde: A good horse, that trippeth not once in
a iourney: and M. IMMERITO doth but as M. WATSON,
and in a manner all other *Iambici* haue done before him:
marry, he might haue spared his preface, or, at the least,
that same restrictiue and streightlaced terme PRECISELY,
and all had been well enough: and I assure you, of my
selfe, I beleeue, no peece of a fault marked at all. But
this is the Effect of warrantes, and perhappes the Errour
may rather proceede of his Master M. DRANTES Rule
than of himselfe. Howsoeuer it is, the matter is not
great, and I alwayes was, and will euer continue, of this
Opinion, *Pauca multis condonanda vitia Virtutibus*,
especially these being no *Vitia* neither, in a common
and licencious IAMBICKE. *Verum ista obiter, non quidem
contradicendi animo aut etiam corrigendi mihi crede: sed*

Of Reformed Versifying, &c. 97

nostro illo Academico, pristinoque more ratiocinandi. And, to saye trueth, partely too to requite your gentle courtesie in beginning to me, and noting I knowe not what breache in your gorbellyed Maisters Rules: which Rules go for good, I perceiue, and keepe a Rule, where there be no better in presence. My selfe neither sawe them, nor heard of them before, and therefore will neither praise them, nor dispraise them nowe; but, vppon the suruiewe of them and farther conference (both which I desire), you shall soone heare one mans opinion too or fro. Your selfe remember I was wonte to haue some preiudice of the man; and I still remaine a fauourer of his deserued and iust commendation. Marry in these poyntes, you knowe, PARTIALITIE in no case may haue a foote: and you remember mine olde Stoicall exclamation, FIE ON CHILDISH AFFECTION, IN THE DIS-COURSING AND DECIDING OF SCHOOLE MATTERS. This I say, because you charge me with an vnknowne authoritie, which, for aught I know yet, may as wel be either vnsufficient or faultie as otherwise; and I dare more than halfe promise (I dare not saye warrant) you shall alwayes in these kinde of controuersies finde me nighe hande answerable in mine owne defence. *Reliqua omnia quae de hac supersunt Anglicorum versuum ratione in aliud tempus reseruabimus otiosum magis.* Youre Latine farewell is a goodly braue yonkerly peece of work, and, Goddilge yee, I am alwayes maruellously beholding vnto you for your bountifull Titles: I hope by that time I haue been resident a yeare or twoo in ITALY I shall be better qualifyed in this kind, and more able to requite your lauishe and magnificent liberalitie that way. . . . TRINITIE HALL, stil in my Gallerie, 23 Octob. 1579. In haste.

Yours, as you knowe,
G. H.

[III]

TO MY LONG APPROOUED AND SINGULAR GOOD FRENDE, MASTER G. H.

Good Master H. I doubt not but you haue some great important matter in hande, which al this while restraineth youre Penne and wonted readinesse in prouoking me vnto that wherein your selfe nowe faulte. If there bee any such thing in hatching, I pray you hartily lette vs knowe before al the worlde see it. But if happly you dwell altogither in Iustinians Courte, and giue your selfe to be deuoured of secreate Studies, as of all likelyhood you doe, yet at least imparte some your olde or newe, Latine or Englishe, Eloquent and Gallant Poesies to vs, from whose eyes, you saye, you keepe in a manner nothing hidden. Little newes is here stirred: but that olde greate matter still depending. His Honoure neuer better. I thinke the Earthquake was also there wyth you (which I would gladly learne) as it was here with vs, ouerthrowing diuers old buildings and peeces of Churches. Sure verye straunge to be hearde of in these Countries, and yet I heare some saye (I knowe not howe truely) that they haue knowne the like before in their dayes. *Sed quid vobis videtur magnis Philosophis?* I like your late English Hexameters so exceedingly well that I also enure my Penne sometime in that kind: whyche I fynd indeede, as I haue heard you often defende in worde, neither so harde, nor so harshe, that it will easily and fairely yeelde it selfe to oure Moother tongue. For the onely or chiefest hardnesse, whych seemeth, is in the Accente; whyche sometime gapeth, and, as it were, yawneth ilfauouredly, comming shorte of that it should, and sometime exceeding the measure of the Number, as in Carpenter the middle sillable, being vsed shorte in speache,

when it shall be read long in Verse, seemeth like a lame
Gosling that draweth one legge after hir: and Heauen,
beeing vsed shorte as one sillable, when it is in Verse
stretched out with a *Diastole*, is like a lame Dogge that
holdes vp one legge. But it is to be wonne with Custome,
and rough words must be subdued with Vse. For why,
a Gods name, may not we, as else the Greekes, haue the
kingdome of oure owne Language, and measure our Accentes by the sounde, reseruing the Quantitie to the
Verse? Loe, here I let you see my olde vse of toying
in Rymes turned into your artificial straightnesse of
Verse by this Tetrasticon. I beseech you tell me your
fancie without parcialitie.

    See yee the blindefoulded pretie God, that feathered
        Archer,
    Of Louers Miseries which maketh his bloodie Game?
    Wote ye why his Moother with a Veale hath cooured
        his Face?
    Trust me, least he my Looue happely chaunce to
        beholde.

Seeme they comparable to those two, which I translated
you *ex tempore* in bed, the last time we lay togither in
Westminster?

    That which I eate did I ioy, and that which I greedily
        gorged.
    As for those many goodly matters leaft I for others.

I would hartily wish you would either send me the Rules
and Precepts of Arte, which you obserue in Quantities,
or else followe mine, that M. Philip Sidney gaue me,
being the very same which M. Drant deuised, but enlarged
with M. Sidneys own iudgement, and augmented with my
Obseruations, that we might both accorde and agree in
one, leaste we ouerthrowe one an other and be ouerthrown

of the rest. Truste me, you will hardly beleeue what
greate good liking and estimation Maister Dyer had of
youre Satyricall Verses, and I, since the viewe thereof,
hauing before of my selfe had speciall liking of Englishe
Versifying, am euen nowe aboute to giue you some token,
and howe well therein I am able to doe: for, to tell you
trueth, I minde shortely at conuenient leysure to sette
forth a Booke in this kinde, whyche I entitle *Epithalamion
Thamesis*, whyche Booke I dare vndertake wil be very
profitable for the knowledge and rare for the Inuention
and manner of handling. For in setting forth the marriage
of the Thames I shewe his first beginning and offspring,
and all the Countrey that he passeth thorough, and also
describe all the Riuers throughout Englande whyche
came to this Wedding, and their righte names, and right
passage, &c. A worke, beleeue me, of much labour,
wherein notwithstanding Master *Holinshed* hath muche
furthered and aduantaged me, who therein hath bestowed
singular paines in searching oute their firste heades and
sources, and also in tracing and dogging oute all their
course til they fall into the Sea.

*O Tite, siquid ego,
Ecquid erit pretii?*

But of that more hereafter. Nowe, my *Dreames* and
Dying Pellicane being fully finished (as I partelye signified in my laste Letters) and presentlye to bee imprinted,
I wil in hande forthwith with my *Faery Queene*, whyche
I praye you hartily send me with al expedition; and your
frendly Letters and long expected Iudgement wythal,
whyche let not be shorte, but in all pointes suche as you
ordinarilye vse and I extraordinarily desire. *Multum vale.
Westminster, Quarto Nonas Aprilis* 1580. *Sed, amabo te,
meum Corculum tibi se ex animo commendat plurimum:
iam diu mirata, te nihil ad literas suas responsi dedisse.*

Vide quaeso, ne id tibi Capitale sit: Mihi certe quidem erit, neque tibi hercle impune, vt opinor, iterum vale, et quam voles saepe.

Yours alwayes to commaunde,

IMMERITO.

[IV]

A GALLANT FAMILIAR LETTER, CONTAINING AN ANSWERE TO THAT OF M. IMMERITO, WITH SUNDRY PROPER EXAMPLES AND SOME PRECEPTS OF OUR ENGLISH REFORMED VERSIFYING.

To my very friend M. *Immerito*.

Signor Immerito, to passe ouer youre needelesse complaint, wyth the residue of your preamble (for of your EARTHQUAKE I presuppose you haue ere this receyued my goodly discourse), and withall to let my late Englishe Hexametres goe as lightlye as they came, I cannot choose but thanke and honour the good Aungell (whether it were Gabriell or some other) that put so good a motion into the heads of those two excellent Gentlemen MR. SIDNEY and M. DYER, the two very Diamondes of hir Maiesties Courte for many speciall and rare qualities, as to helpe forwarde our new famous enterprise for the Exchanging of Barbarous and Balductum Rymes with Artificial Verses, the one being in manner of pure and fine Goulde, the other but counterfet and base ylfauoured Copper. I doubt not but their liuelie example and Practise wil preuaile a thousand times more in short space than the dead Aduertizement and persuasion of M. ASCHAM

to the same Effecte, whose SCHOLEMAISTER, notwithstanding, I reuerence in respect of so learned a Motiue.
I would gladly be acquainted with M. DRANTS Prosodye,
and I beseeche you commende me to good M. SIDNEYS
iudgement, and gentle M. IMMERITOS Obseruations. I
hope your nexte Letters, which I daily expect, wil bring
me in farther familiaritie and acquaintance with al three.
Mine owne Rules and Precepts of Arte I beleeue wil fal
out not greatly repugnant, though peraduenture somewhat
different: and yet I am not so resolute but I can be
content to reserue the Coppying out and publishing
thereof vntil I haue a little better consulted with my
pillowe, and taken some farther aduize of MADAME
SPERIENZA. In the meane, take this for a general
Caueat, and say I haue reuealed one great mysterie
vnto you: I am of Opinion there is no one more regular
and iustifiable direction, eyther for the assured and infallible Certaintie of our English Artificiall Prosodye
particularly, or generally to bring our Language into
Arte and to frame a Grammer or Rhetorike thereof,
than first of all vniuersally to agree vpon ONE AND THE
SAME ORTOGRAPHIE, in all pointes conformable and pro-
portionate to our COMMON NATURAL PROSODYE. Whether
SIR THOMAS SMITHES in that respect be the most perfit,
as surely it must needes be very good; or else some
other of profounder Learning and longer Experience
than SIR THOMAS was, shewing by necessarie demonstration wherin he is defectiue, wil vndertake shortely to
supplie his wantes and make him more absolute; my
selfe dare not hope to hoppe after him, til I see something
or other, too or fro, publickely and autentically established,
as it were by a generall Counsel or acte of Parliament:
and then peraduenture, standing vppon firmer grounde,
for Companie sake, I may aduenture to do as other do.
Interim, credit me, I dare geue no Preceptes, nor set

downe any CERTAINE GENERAL ARTE; and yet see my boldenesse. I am not greatly squaimishe of my PARTICULAR EXAMPLES, whereas he that can but reasonably skil of the one wil giue easily a shreude gesse at the other, considering that the one fetcheth his original and offspring from the other. In which respecte, to say troth, WE BEGINNERS haue the start and aduantage of our Followers, who are to frame and conforme both their Examples and Precepts according to that President which they haue of vs: as no doubt Homer or some other in *Greeke*, and ENNIUS or I know not who else in *Latine*, did preiudice and ouerrule those that followeth them, as well for the quantities of syllables as number of feete, and the like: their onely Examples going for current payment, and standing in steade of Lawes and Rules with the posteritie. In so much that it seemed a sufficient warrant (as still it doth in our Common Grammer Schooles) to make τι in τιμή and *v* in *Vnus* long, because the one hath τιμὴ δ' ἐκ διός ἐστί and the other *Vnus homo nobis*, and so consequently in the rest. But to let this by-disputation passe, which is already so throughly discoursed and canuassed of the best Philosophers, and namely ARISTOTLE, that poynt vs, as it were with the forefinger, to the very FOUNTAINES AND HEAD SPRINGES of Artes and Artificiall preceptes, in the ANALITIQUES and METAPHYSIKES: most excellently set downe in these FOURE GOLDEN TERMES, the famoussest Termes to speake of in all LOGIQUE and PHILOSOPHIE, ἐμπειρία, ἱστορία, αἴσθησις, ἐπαγωγή.

Shall I nowe by the way sende you a IANUARIE GIFT in APRILL, and, as it were, shewe you a CHRISTMAS GAMBOWLDE after EASTER? Were the manner so very fine, as the matter is very good, I durst presume of an other kinde of *Plaudite* and GRAMERCIE than now I will: but, being as it is, I beseeche you set parcialitie aside, and tell me your maisterships fancie.

A New yeeres Gift to my old friend Maister George Bilchaunger: in commendation of three most precious Accidentes, *Vertue*, *Fame*, and *Wealth*: and finally of the fourth, *a good Tongue*.

Vertue sendeth a man to *Renowne*; *Fame* lendeth *Aboundaunce*;
Fame with Aboundaunce maketh a man thrise blessed and happie;
So the Rewarde of Famous Vertue makes many wealthy,
And the Regard of Wealthie Vertue makes many blessed:
O blessed Vertue, blessed Fame, blessed Aboundaunce,
O that I had you three, with the losse of thirtie Comencementes.
Nowe farewell *Mistresse*, whom lately I loued aboue all.
These be my three bonny lasses, these be my three bonny Ladyes;
Not the like *Trinitie* againe, saue onely the Trinitie aboue all:
Worship and Honour first to the one and then to the other.
A thousand good leaues be for euer graunted *Agrippa*,
For squibbing and declayming against many fruitlesse
Artes and Craftes, deuisde by the *Diuls and Sprites* for a torment
And for a plague to the world: as both *Pandora*, *Prometheus*,
And that cursed *good bad Tree* can testifie at all times:
Meere Gewegawes and Bables, in comparison of these,
Toyes to mock Apes and Woodcockes, in comparison of these,
Iugling castes and knicknackes, in comparison of these.

Of Reformed Versifying, &c.

Yet behinde there is one thing, worth a prayer at all tymes,
A good Tongue in a mans Head, *A good Tongue* in a woomans.
And what so precious matter and foode for a good Tongue
As blessed Vertue, blessed Fame, blessed Aboundaunce.

L'Enuoy.

Maruell not that I meane to send these Verses at Euensong,
On *Neweyeeres* Euen, and Oldyeeres End, as a *Memento*:
Trust me, I know not a richer Iewell, newish or oldish,
Than blessed Vertue, blessed Fame, blessed Abundaunce.
O blessed Vertue, blessed Fame, blessed Aboundaunce,
O that you had these three, with the losse of *Fortie Valetes*.

> *He that wisheth you may liue to see a hundreth Good Newe yeares, euery one happier and merrier than other.*

Now to requite your BLINDFOLDED PRETIE GOD (wherin by the way I woulde gladly learne why *Thĕ* in the first, *Yĕ* in the first and thirde, *Hĕ* and *My* in the last, being shorte, Mē alone should be made longer in the very same). Imagin me to come into a goodly Kentishe *Garden* of your old Lords, or some other Noble man, and, spying a florishing Bay Tree there, to demaunde *ex tempore* as followeth. Thinke vppon Petrarches

> *Arbor vittoriosa, trionfale,*
> *Onor d'Imperadori e di Poeti,*

and perhappes it will aduance the wynges of your Imagination a degree higher: at the least if any thing can be added to the loftinesse of his conceite, who[m] gentle Mistresse *Rosalinde* once reported to haue all the Intelligences at commaundement, and an other time christened her *Segnior Pegaso*.

Encomium Lauri.

What might I call this Tree? *A Laurell*? O bonny Laurell:
Needes to thy bowes will I bow this knee, and vayle my bonetto.
Who, but thou, the renowne of Prince and Princely *Poeta*?
Th' one for Crowne, for Garland th' other thanketh *Apollo*.
Thrice happy *Daphne*, that turned was to the *Bay Tree*,
Whom such seruauntes serue, as challenge seruice of all men.
Who chiefe Lorde, and King of Kings, but th' *Emperour* only?
And *Poet* of right stampe ouerawith th' *Emperour* himselfe.
Who but knowes *Aretyne*, was he not halfe Prince to the Princes?
And many a one there liues, as nobly minded at all poyntes.
Now farewell *Bay Tree*, very Queene, and Goddesse of all trees,
Ritchest perle to the Crowne, and fayrest Floure to the Garland!
Faine wod I craue, might I so presume, some farther aquaintaunce;
O that I might? but I may not: woe to my destinie therefore.

Trust me, not one more loyall seruaunt longes to thy
    Personage.
But what says *Daphne*? *Non omni dormio*, worse
    lucke.
Yet Farewell, Farewell, the Reward of those that I
    honour:
Glory to *Garden*: Glory to *Muses*: Glory to *Vertue*.
   Partim Ioui et Palladi,
   Partim Apollini et Musis.

But seeing I must needes beuray my store, and set open
my shoppe wyndowes, nowe I pray thee, and coniure thee
by all thy amorous Regardes and Exorcismes of Loue,
call a Parliament of thy Sensible and Intelligible powers
together, and tell me, in Tom Trothes earnest, what *Il
fecondo & famoso Poeta* MESTER IMMERITO sayth to
this bolde Satyri[c]all Libell, lately deuised at the instaunce
of a certayne worshipfull Hartefordshyre Gentleman of
myne olde acquayntaunce *in Gratiam quorundam Illustrium* Anglofrancitalorum, *hic et ubique apud nos volitantium. Agedum vero, nosti homines, tanquam tuam ipsius
cutem.*

SPECULUM TUSCANISMI.

Since *Galateo* came in and *Tuscanisme* gan vsurpe,
Vanitie aboue all, Villanie next her, Statelynes Empresse;
No man but Minion, Stowte Lowte, Plaine swayne,
    quoth a Lording:
No wordes but valorous, no workes but woomanish onely.
For life Magnificoes, not a beck but glorious in shew,
In deede most friuolous, not a looke but Tuscanish
    alwayes:
His *cringing side necke, Eyes glauncing, Fisnamie
    smirking,*

With *forefinger kisse*, and braue *embrace to the foote-
warde*:
Largebelled Kodpeas'd Dublet, vnkodpeased halfe hose,
Straite to the dock, like a shirte, and close to the britch, like a diueling,
A little Apish Hatte, cowched fast to the pate, like an Oyster,
French Camarick Ruffes, deepe with a witnesse, starched to the purpose; 5
Euery one A per se A; his termes and braueries in Print,
Delicate in speach, queynte in araye, conceited in all poyntes:
In Courtly guyles a passing singular odde man;
For Gallantes a braue Myrrour, a Primerose of Honour;
A Diamond for nonce, a fellowe perelesse in England. 10
Not the like *Discourser* for Tongue and head to be found out,
Not the like *resolute Man* for great and serious affayres,
Not the like *Lynx* to spie out secretes and priuities of States,
Eyed like to *Argus*, *Earde* like to *Midas*, *Nosd* like to *Naso*,
Winged like to *Mercury*, fittst of a Thousand for to 15
be employde:
This, nay more than this, doth practise of *Italy* in one yeare.
None doe I name, but some doe I know, that a peece of a tweluemonth
Hath so perfited, outly and inly, both body, both soule,
That none for sense, and senses, halfe matchable with them.
A *Vulturs smelling*, *Apes tasting*, *sight* of an *Eagle*, 20

A *spiders touching, Hartes hearing, might* of a *Lyon*,
Compoundes of wisedome, witte, prowes, bountie, be-
hauiour,
All gallant Vertues, all qualities of body and soule:
O thrice tenne hundreth times blessed and happy,
Blessed and happy *Trauaile, Trauailer* most blessed
and happy.

Penatibus Hetruscis laribusque nostris
Inquilinis.

Tell me, in good sooth, doth it not too euidently appeare that this English Poet wanted but A GOOD PATTERNE before his eyes, as it might be some delicate and choyce elegant Poesie of good M. SIDNEY or M. DYERS (ouer very CASTOR and POLLUX for such and many greater matters) when this trimme geere was in hatching: Much like some GENTLE-WOOMEN I coulde name in England, who by all Phisick and Physiognomie too might as well haue brought forth all goodly faire children, as they haue now some ylfauored and deformed, had they, at the tyme of their CONCEPTION, had in sight the amiable and gallant beautifull Pictures of ADONIS, CUPIDO, GANYMEDES, or the like, which no doubt would haue wrought such deepe impression in their fantasies and imaginations, as their children, and per-happes their Childrens children too, myght haue thanked them for as long as they shall haue Tongues in their heades.

But myne owne leysure fayleth me, and, to say troth, I am lately become a maruellous great straunger at mayne olde MISTRESSE POETRIES, being newly entertayned and dayly employed in our Emperour IUSTINIANS SERUICE (sauing that I haue alreadie addressed a certaine pleasur-able, and Morall, Politique, Naturall, mixte deuise to his most Honourable Lordshippe in the same kynde, where-vnto my next Letter, if you please mee well, may perchaunce make you priuie): marrie nowe, if it lyke you in the meane while, for varietie sake, to see howe I taske a young Brother of myne (whom of playne IOHN our ITALIAN Maister hath Cristened his *Picciolo Giouannibattista*), Lo here (and God will) a peece of hollydayes exercise. In the morning I gaue him this THEAME out of OUID to translate, and varie after his best fashion.

> *Dum fueris felix, multos numerabis amicos;*
> *Tempora si fuerint nubila, solus eris.*
> *Aspicis, vt veniant ad candida tecta columbae?*
> *Accipiat nullas sordida turris aues.*

His translation, or rather Paraphrase, before dinner was first this:

1.

Whilst your Bearnes are fatte, whilst Cofers stuff'd with aboundaunce,
Freendes will abound: If bearne waxe bare, then adieu sir a Goddes name.
See ye the Dooues? they breede, and feede in gorgeous Houses:
Scarce one Dooue doth loue to remaine in ruinous Houses.

And then forsooth this, to make proofe of his facultie in Pentameters too, affecting a certain *Rithmus* withall:

2.

Whilst your Ritches abound, your friends will play the *Placeboes*;
If your wealth doe decay, friend, like a feend, will away.
Dooues light and delight in goodly fairetyled houses:
If your House be but olde, Dooue to remoue be ye bolde.

Of Reformed Versifying, &c.

And the last and largest of all, this:

3.

If so be goods encrease, then dayly encreaseth a goods friend.
If so be goods decrease, then straite decreaseth a goods friend.
Then G[o]od night goods friend, who seldome prooueth a good friend.
5 Giue me the goods, and giue me the good friend; take ye the goods friend.
Douehouse and Louehouse in writing differ a letter;
In deede scarcely so much, so resembleth an other an other.
Tyle me the Doouehouse trimly, and gallant: where the like storehouse?
Tyle me the Doouehouse; leaue it vnhansome: where the like poorehouse?
10 Looke to the Louehouse; where the resort is, there is a gaye showe:
Gynne port and mony fayle, straight sports and Companie faileth.

Beleeue me I am not to be charged with aboue one or two of the Verses, and a foure or fiue wordes in the rest. His afternoones THEAME was borrowed out of him, whom
15 one in your Coate, they say, is as much beholding vnto as any Planet or Starre in Heauen is vnto the Sunne, and is quoted, as your self best remember, in the Close of your October.

Giunto Alessandro a[l]la famosa tomba
20 *Del fero Achille, sospirando disse,*
O fortunato, che si chiara tromba
Trouasti.

Within an houre, or there aboutes, he brought me these

foure lustie Hexameters, altered since not past in a worde or two.

> Noble *Alexander*, when he came to the tombe of *Achilles*,
> Sighing spake with a bigge voyce: O thrice blessed *Achilles*,
> That such a Trump, so great, so loude, so glorious hast found,
> As the renowned and surprizing *Archpoet Homer*.

Vppon the viewe whereof: Ah my Syrrha, quoth I, here is a gallant exercise for you in deede: we haue had a little prettie triall of you[r] LATIN and ITALIAN Translation: Let me see now, I pray, what you can doo in your owne TONGUE. And with that, reaching a certaine famous Booke, called the newe SHEPHARDES CALENDER, I turned to WILLYES and THOMALINS EMBLEMES, in MARCHE, and bad him make them eyther better or worse in English verse. I gaue him an other howres respite; but, before I looked for him, he suddainely rushed vpon me, and gaue me his deuise, thus formally set downe in a faire peece of Paper.

1. Thomalins Embleme.

> Of Honny and of Gaule in Loue there is store:
> The Honny is much, but the Gaule is more.

2. Willyes Embleme.

> To be wize, and eke to Loue,
> Is graunted scarce to God aboue.

3. Both combined in one.

> Loue is a thing more fell, than full of Gaule, than of Honny.
> And to be wize, and Loue, is a worke for a God, or a Goddes peere.

Of Reformed Versifying, &c.

With a small voluntarie Supplement of his owne, on the other side, in commendation of hir most gratious and thrice excellent Maiestie:

> Not the like *Virgin* againe, in Asia, or Afric, or Europe,
> For Royall Vertues, for Maiestie, Bountie, Behauiour.
>   *Raptim, vti vides.*

In both not passing a worde or two corrected by mee. Something more I haue of his, partly that very day begun, and partly continued since: but yet not so perfitly finished that I dare committe the viewe and examination thereof to MESSER IMMERITOES Censure, whom after those same two incomparable and myraculous GEMINI, *omni exceptione maiores*, I recount and chaulk vppe in the Catalogue of our very principall Englishe ARISTARCHI. Howbeit, I am nigh halfe perswaded that in tyme (*siquidem vltima primis respondeant*) for length, bredth, and depth it will not come far behinde your *Epithalamion Thamesis*: the rather, hauing so fayre a president and patterne before his Eyes as I warrant him, and he presumeth, to haue of that: both MASTER COLLINSHEAD and M. HOLLI[N]SHEAD too being togither therein. But euer and euer, me thinkes, your great CATOES, *Ecquid erit pretii*, and our little CATOES, *Res age quae prosunt*, make suche a buzzing and ringing in my head, that I haue little ioy to animate and encourage either you or him to goe forward, vnlesse ye might make account of some certaine ordinarie wages, at the leastwise haue your meate and drinke for your dayes workes. As for my selfe, howsoeuer I haue toyed and trifled heretofore, I am nowe taught, and I trust I shall shortly learne (no remedie, I must of meere necessitie giue you ouer in the playne fielde) to employ my trauayle and tyme wholly, or chiefely, on those studies and practizes that carrie, as they saye, meate in their mouth, hauing euermore their eye vppon the Title *De pane lucrando*, and their hand vpon their halfpenny. For, I pray now, what saith M. Cuddie, *alias* you know who, in the tenth Æglogue of the foresaid famous new Calender:

> Piers, I haue piped erst so long with payne,
> That all myne oten reedes been rent and wore,
> And my poore Muse hath spent hir spared store,
> Yet little good hath got, and much lesse gayne.
> Such pleasaunce makes the Grashopper so poore,
> And ligge so layde, when winter doth her strayne.
> The Dapper Ditties, that I woont deuize
> To feede youthes fancie, and the flocking fry,
> Delighten much: what I the bett for-thy?
> They han the pleasure, I a sclender prize.
> I beate the bushe, the birdes to them doe flye.
> What good thereof to Cuddy can arise?

But Master Collin Cloute is not euery body, and albeit his olde Companions, Master Cuddy and Master Hobbinoll, be as little beholding to their Mistresse Poetrie as euer you wist; yet he, peraduenture, by the meanes of hir speciall fauour and some personall priuiledge, may happely liue by Dying Pellicanes, and purchase great landes and Lordshippes with the money which his Calendar and Dreames haue, and will, affourde him. *Extra iocum*, I like your Dreames passingly well: and the rather, bicause they sauour of that singular extraordinarie veine and inuention whiche I euer fancied moste, and in a manner admired onelye, in Lucian, Petrarche, Aretine, Pasquill, and all the most delicate and fine conceited Grecians and Italians (for the Romanes to speake of are but verye Ciphars in this kinde): whose chiefest endeuour and drifte was to haue nothing vulgare, but in some respecte or other, and especially in liuely Hyperbolicall Amplifications,

rare, queint, and odde in euery pointe, and, as a man
woulde saye, a degree or two at the leaste aboue the
reach and compasse of a common Schollers capacitie.
In which respecte notwithstanding, as well for the singularitie of the manner as the Diuinitie of the matter,
I hearde once a Diuine preferre SAINT JOHNS REUE-
LATION before al the veriest MÆTAPHYSICALL VISIONS
and iollyest conceited DREAMES or EXTASIES that euer
were deuised by one or other, howe admirable or superexcellent soeuer they seemed otherwise to the worlde.
And truely I am so confirmed in this opinion, that when
I bethinke me of the verie notablest and moste wonderful Propheticall or Poeticall Vision that euer I read or
hearde, me seemeth the proportion is so vnequall, that
there hardly appeareth anye semblaunce of Comparison:
no more in a manner (specially for Poets) than doth betweene the incomprehensible Wisedome of God and the
sensible Wit of Man. But what needeth this digression
betweene you and me: I dare saye you wyll holde your
selfe reasonably wel satisfied if youre DREAMES be but as
well esteemed of in Englande as PETRARCHES VISIONS be in
Italy: whiche I assure you is the very worst I wish you.
But see how I haue the Arte MEMORATIUE at commaundement. In good faith I had once again nigh forgotten
your FAERIE QUEENE: howbeit, by good chaunce, I haue
nowe sent hir home at the laste, neither in better nor
worse case than I founde hir. And must you of necessitie haue my Iudgement of hir in deede: To be plaine,
I am voyde of all iudgement, if your NINE COMŒDIES,
wherunto, in imitation of HERODOTUS, you giue the names
of the *Nine Muses* (and in one mans fansie not vn-
worthily), come not neerer ARIOSTOES COMŒDIES, eyther
for the finenesse of plausible Elocution or the rarenesse of
Poetical Inuention, than that the ELUISH QUEENE doth to
his ORLANDO FURIOSO, which, notwithstanding, you wil

needes seeme to emulate, and hope to ouergo, as you
flatly professed your self in one of your last Letters.
Besides, that you know it hath bene the vsual practise of
the most exquisite and odde wittes in all nations, and
specially in *Italie*, rather to shewe and aduaunce themselues that way than any other: as, namely, those three
notorious dyscoursing heads, BIBIENA, MACHIAUEL, and
ARETINE did (to let BEMBO and ARIOSTO passe) with the
great admiration and wonderment of the whole countrey:
being in deede reputed matchable in all points, both for
conceyt of Witte and eloquent decyphering of matters,
either with ARISTOPHANES and MENANDER in Greek or
with PLAUTUS and TERENCE in Latin, or with any other,
in any other tong. But I wil not stand greatly with you
in your owne matters. If so be the FAERYE QUEENE be
fairer in your eie than the NINE MUSES, and HOBGOBLIN
runne away with the Garland from APOLLO, Marke what
I saye, and yet I will not say that I thought; but there
an End for this once, and fare you well, till God or some
good Aungell putte you in a better minde.

And yet, bicause you charge me somewhat suspitiouslye
with an olde promise to deliuer you of that iealousie,
I am so farre from hyding mine owne matters from you,
that loe I muste needes be reuealing my friendes secreates,
now an honest Countrey Gentleman, sometimes a Scholler:
At whose request I bestowed this pawlting bungrely
Rime vpon him, to present his Maistresse withall. The
parties shall bee namelesse, sauing that the Gentle-
womans true, or counterfaite, Christen name must necessarily be bewrayed.

[*Here follow forty-two lines of burlesque verse*, 'To my
good Mistresse *Anne*, the very lyfe of my lyfe, and onely
beloued Mystresse.]

God helpe vs, you and I are wisely employed (are wee
not?) when our Pen and Inke, and Time and Wit, and all

runneth away in this goodly yonkerly veine: as if the world had nothing else for vs to do, or we were borne to be the only NONPROFICIENTS and NIHILAGENTS of the world. *Cuiusmodi tu nugis, atque nanis, nisi vna mecum (qui solemni quodam iureiurando atque voto obstringor, relicto isto amoris Poculo, iuris Poculum primo quoque tempore exhaurire) iam tandem aliquando valedicas, (quod tamen vnum tibi, credo,* τῶν ἀδυνάτων *videbitur*): *nihil dicam amplius: Valeas. E meo municipio. Nono Calendas Maias.*

But hoe I pray you, gentle sirra, a word with you more. In good sooth, and by the faith I beare to the Muses, you shal neuer haue my subscription or consent (though you should charge me wyth the authoritie of fiue hundreth Maister DRANTS) to make your *Carpēnter*, our *Carpĕnter*, an inche longer or bigger than God and his Englishe people haue made him. Is there no other Pollicie to pull downe Ryming and set vppe Versifying but you must needes correcte *Magnificat*: and againste all order of Lawe, and in despite of Custome, forcibly vsurpe and tyrannize vppon a quiet companye of wordes that so farre beyonde the memorie of man haue so peaceably enioyed their seuerall Priuiledges and Liberties, without any disturbance or the leaste controlement? What? Is HORACES *Ars Poetica* so quite out of our Englishe Poets head that he muste haue his Remembrancer to pull hym by the sleeue, and put him in mind of *Penes vsum*, and *ius*, and *norma loquendi*? Indeed I remember who was wont in a certaine brauerie to call our M. VALANGER Noble M. VALANGER. Else neuer heard I any that durst presume so much ouer the Englishe (excepting a fewe suche stammerers as haue not the masterie of their owne Tongues) as to alter the Quantitie of any one sillable, otherwise than oure common speache and generall receyued Custome woulde beare them oute. Woulde not I laughe, thinke you, to heare MESTER IMMERITO come in baldely with his *Maiĕstie, Royāltie, Honēstie, Sciēnces, Facŭlties, Excēllent, Tauērnour, Manfŭlly, Faithfŭlly*, and a thousande the like, in steade of *Maiĕstie, Royăltie, Honĕstie*, and so forth: And trowe you anye coulde forbeare the byting of his lippe or smyling in his Sleeue, if a iolly fellowe and greate Clarke (as it mighte be youre selfe) reading a fewe Verses vnto him, for his owne credit and commendation, should nowe and then tell him of *bargaīneth, follōwing, harrōwing, thoroŭghly*, or the like, in steade of *bargaĭneth, follŏwing, harrŏwing*, and the reste: Or will SEGNIOR IMMERITO, bycause, may happe, he hathe a fat-bellyed Archdeacon on his side, take vppon him to controll Maister Doctor WATSON for his *All Trauaïlers*, in a Verse so highly extolled of Master ASCHAM? or Maister ASCHAM himselfe, for abusing HOMER and corrupting our Tongue, in that he saith,

> *Quite throŭghe a Doore flĕwe a shafte with a brasse head?*

Nay, haue we not somtime, by your leaue, both the Position of the firste and Dipthong of the seconde concurring in one and the same sillable, which neuerthelesse is commonly and ought necessarily to be pronounced short? I haue nowe small time to bethink me of many examples. But what say you to the second in *Merchaŭndise*? to the third in *Couenaŭnteth*? and to the fourth in *Appurtenaŭnces*? Durst you aduenture to make any of them long, either in Prose or in Verse? I assure you I knowe who dareth not, and *suddaĭnly* feareth the displeasure of all true Englishemen if he should. Say you *suddaīnly*, if you like; by my *certaĭnly* and *certaĭnty* I wil not. You may perceiue by the *Premisses* (which very worde I woulde haue you note by the waye to) the Latine is no rule for vs: or imagine aforehande (bycause you are like to proue a great Purchaser, and leaue suche store of money and possessions behinde you) your *Execŭtors* wil deale *fraudulently* or *violently* with your *succēssour* (whiche in a maner is euery mans case), and it will fall oute a resolute pointe: the third in *Execūtores, fraudulenter, violenter*, and the seconde in *Succēssor*, being long in the one and shorte in the other, as in seauen hundreth more, suche as *discīple, recīted, excīted*: *tenĕment, orătour, laudĭble*, and a number of their fellowes are long in English, short in Latine, long in Latine, short in English. Howbeit, in my fancy such words as *violently, diligently, magnificently, indifferently* seeme in a manner reasonably indifferent, and tollerable either waye; neither woulde I greately stande with him that translated the Verse

Cur mittis violas? vt me violentius vras?

WHY SEND YOU VIOLETS? TO BURNE MY POORE HART VIOLĒNTLY.

Marry so, that being left common for verse, they are to be pronounced shorte in Prose, after the maner of the Latines, in suche wordes as these, *Cathedra, Volucres, mediocres, Celebres*.

And thus farre of your *Carpēnter* and his fellowes, wherin we are to be moderated and ouerruled by the vsuall and common receiued sounde, and not to deuise any counterfaite fantasticall Accent of oure owne, as manye, otherwise not vnlearned, haue corruptely and ridiculouslye done in the Greeke.

Nowe for your *Heauen, Seauen, Eleauen*, or the like, I am likewise of the same opinion, as generally in all words else: we are not to goe a little farther, either for the PROSODY or the ORTHOGRAPHY (and therefore your Imaginarie DIASTOLE nothing worthe) then we are licenced and authorized by the ordinarie vse, and custome, and proprietie, and Idiome, and, as it were, Maiestie of our speach: which I accounte the only infallible and soueraigne Rule of all Rules. And therefore, hauing respecte thereunto, and reputing it Petty Treason to reuolt therefro, dare hardly eyther in the Prosodie, or in the Orthography either, allowe them two sillables in steade of one, but woulde as well in Writing as in Speaking haue them vsed as *Monosyllaba*, thus: *heavn, seavn, a leavn*, as Maister Ascham in his Toxophilus doth Yrne, commonly written Yron:

Vp to the pap his string did he pull, his shafte to the harde yrne:

especially the difference so manifestly appearing by the Pronunciation betweene these two, *a leavn a clocke* and *a leaven of Dowe*, whyche *lea-ven* admitteth the Diastole you speake of. But see what absurdities thys yl fauoured Orthographye, or rather Pseudography, hathe ingendred, and howe one errour still breedeth and begetteth an other. Haue wee not *Mooneth* for *Moonthe, sithence* for *since, whilest* for *whilste, phantasie* for *phansie, euen* for *evn, Diuel* for *Divl, God hys wrath* for *Goddes wrath*, and a thousande of the same stampe, wherein the corrupte Orthography in the moste hathe beene the sole, or principall, cause of corrupte Prosodye in ouer many?

Marry, I confesse some wordes we haue indeede, as for example *fayer*, either for *beautifull* or for a *Marte, ayer*, bothe *pro aere* and *pro haerede*, for we say not *Heire* but plaine *Aire* for him to (or else Scoggins Aier were a poore iest), whiche are commonly and maye indifferently be vsed eyther wayes. For you shal as well and as ordinarily heare *fayer* as *faire*, and *Aier* as *Aire*, and bothe alike, not onely of diuers and sundrye persons but often of the very same, otherwhiles vsing the one, otherwhiles the other: and so *died* or *dyde, spied* or *spide, tryed* or *tride, fyer* or *fyre, myer* or *myre*, wyth an infinyte companye of the same sorte, sometime *Monosyllaba*, sometime *Polysyllaba*.

To conclude both pointes in one, I dare sweare priuately to your selfe, and will defende publiquely againste any, it is neither Heresie nor Paradox to sette downe and stande vppon this assertion (notwithstanding all the Preiudices and Presumptions to the contrarie, if they were tenne times as manye moe) that it is not either Position, or Dipthong, or Diastole, or anye like Grammer Schoole Deuice that doeth or can indeede either make long or short, or encrease, or diminish the number of Sillables, but onely the common allowed and receiued PROSODYE, taken vp by an vniuersall consent of all, and continued by a generall vse and Custome of all. Wherein neuerthelesse I grant, after long aduise and diligent obseruation of particulars, a certain Vniform Analogie and Concordance being in processe of time espyed out, sometime this, sometime that, hath been noted by good wits in their ANALYSES to fall out generally alyke, and, as a man woulde saye, regularly, in all or moste wordes: as Position, Dipthong, and the like: not as firste and essentiall causes of this or that effecte (here lyeth the point), but as Secundarie and Accidentall Signes of this or that Qualitie.

It is the vulgare and naturall Mother PROSODYE that alone worketh the feate, as the onely supreame Foundresse and Reformer of Position, Dipthong, Orthographie, or whatsoeuer else: whose Affirmatiues are nothing worth, if she once conclude the Negatiue: and whose *secundae intentiones* muste haue their whole allowance and warrante from hir *primae*. And therefore, in shorte, this is the verie shorte and the long: Position neither maketh shorte nor long in oure Tongue, but so farre as we can get hir good leaue. Peraduenture, vppon the diligent suruewe and examination of Particulars, some the like Analogie and Vniformity might be founde oute in some other respecte, that shoulde as vniuersally and Canonically holde amongst vs as Position doeth with the Latines and Greekes. I saye peraduenture, bycause, hauing not yet made anye speciall obseruation, I dare not precisely affirme any generall certaintie: albeit I presume, so good and sensible a Tongue as our is, beeyng wythall so like itselfe as it is, cannot but haue something equipollent and counteruaileable to the beste Tongues in some one such kinde of conformitie or other. And this forsooth is all the Artificial Rules and Precepts you are like to borrowe of one man at this time.

Sed amabo te, ad Corculi tui delicatissimas Literas, propediem, qua potero, accuratissime: tot interim illam exquisitissimis salutibus, atque salutationibus impertiens, quot habet in Capitulo, capillos semiaureos, semiargenteos, semigemmeos. Quid quaeris? Per tuam Venerem altera Rosalindula est: eamque non alter, sed idem ille, (tua, vt ante, bona cum gratia) copiose amat Hobbinolus. O mea Domina Immerito, mea bellissima Collina Clouta, multo plus plurimum salue, atque vale.

You knowe my ordinarie Postscripte: you may communicate as much or as little as you list of these Patcheries and fragments with the two Gentlemen: but there a straw, and you loue me: not with any else, friend or foe, or other: vnlesse haply you haue a special desire to imparte some parte hereof to my good friend *M. Daniel Rogers*, whose curtesies are also registred in my Marble booke. You know my meaning.

Nosti manum et stylum.

G.

FROM HARVEY'S 'LETTER-BOOK.'

What thoughe Italy, Spayne, and Fraunce, rauisshed with a certayne glorious and ambitious desier (your gallantshipp would peraduenture terme it zeale and deuotion) to sett oute and aduaunce ther owne languages aboue the very Greake and Lattin, if it were possible, and standinge altogither vppon termes of honour and exquisite formes of speaches, karriinge a certayne braue magnificent grace and maiestye with them, do so highly and honorablely esteeme of ther countrye poets, reposing on greate parte of their souraigne glory and reputation abroad in the worlde in the famous writings of their nobblist wittes? What though you and a thousand such nurrishe a stronge imagination amongst yourselues that Alexander, Scipio, Cæsar, and most of ower honorablist and worthyest captaynes had neuer bene that they were but for pore blinde Homer? What thoughe it hath vniversally bene the practisse of the floorishingist States and most politique commonwelthes, from whence we borrowe our substantiallist and most materiall præceptes and examples of wise and considerate gouernement, to make the very most of ther vulgare tunges, and togither with there seigniorye and dominions by all meanes possible to amplifye and enlarge them, deuisinge all ordinarye and extraordinarye helpes, both for the polisshinge and refininge of them at home, and alsoe for the spreddinge and dispersinge of them abroade? What though Il Magnifico Segnior Beniuolo hath notid this amongst his politique Discourses and matters of state and gouernemente, that the most couragious and valorous minds have euermore bene where was most furniture of eloquence, and greatist stoare of notable orators and famous Poets? What, a goddes name, passe we what was dun in ruinous

Athens or decayid Roome a thousand or twoe thousande yeares agoe? Doist thou not ouersensibely perceiue that the markett goith far otherwise in Inglande, wherein nothinge is reputid so contemptible, and so baselye and vilelye accountid of, as whatsoeuer is taken for Inglishe, whether it be handsum fasshions in apparrell, or seemely and honorable in behauiour, or choise wordes and phrases in speache, or anye notable thinge else in effecte that sauorith of our owne cuntrye and is not ether merely or mixtely outlandishe? Is it not cleerer then the sonne at noonedayes that oure most excellent Inglish treatises, were they neuer so eloquentlye contriued in prose, or curiously deuised in meeter, haue euer to this daye, and shall euer hereafter, be sibb to arithmetericians or Marchantes cownters, which nowe and then stande for hundreds and thowsands, by and bye for odd halfpens or farthinges, and otherwhiles for very nihils? Hath your monsieurshipp so soone forgottin our long Westminster conference the verie last Ester terme touchinge certayne odd peculiar qualities, appropriate in a manner to Inglishe heddes, and esspeciallye that same worthy and notorious βριταννικὴν ζηλοτυπίαν that Erasmus prettily playeth withall in a certayne gallant and braue politique epistle of his, written purposely to an Inglish gentleman, a courtier, to instructe him howe he mighte temporize and courte it best here in Inglande? Is not this the principall fundation and grande maxime of our cuntry Pollicy, not to be ouer hasty in occupying a mans talent, but to be very chary and circumspect in opening himselfe and reuealinge his giftes vnto others? Is it not on of the highest pointes of our Inglish experiencid wisdum, and, as a man would saye, the very profoundist mystery of our most deepe and stayd hedds, to haue euery on in continuall ielouzye lest he sitt ouer neere there schirtes or haue familiar insighte in ther commendable and discommendable qualityes?

Doth not silence couer and conceale many a want, and is it not both an easier and far surer way to maynetayne and nurrish the opinion of a mans excellency by noddinge and countenauncinge oute the matter ether with tunge or penne withoute thessame discoursing vagaries after a certayne solemne manner then by speakinge or writinge to purchisse creddit: Esspecially in Inglishe where Inglishe is contemnid, or in meeter where meeter goith a begginge? And canst thou tell me nowe, or doist thou at the last begin to imagin with thyselfe what a wonderfull and exceeding displeasure thou and thy Prynter have wroughte me, and howe peremptorily ye have preiudishd my good name for euer in thrustinge me thus on the stage to make tryall of my extemporall faculty, and to play Wylsons or Tarletons parte? I suppose thou wilt go nighe hande shortelye to sende my lorde Vawsis or my lord Ritches Players or sum other freshe starteupp comedanties vnto me for sum newe deuised interlude, or sum maltconceiuid comedye fitt for the Theater or sum other paintid stage, whereat thou and thy liuely copesmates in London maye lawghe ther mouthes and bellyes full for pence or twoepence apeece: by cause peraduenture thou imaginest Vnico Aretino and the pleasurable Cardinall Bibiena that way esspecially attraynid to be so singularly famous. And then perhappes not longe after vppon newe occasion (an God will) I must be M. Churchyards and M. Eldertons successours tooe, and finally cronycled for on of the most notorious ballat makers and Christmas carollers in the tyme of Her Maiestyes reigne. *Extra iocum,* In good troothe, and by the fayth of a most faythfull frende, I feare me exceedinglye thou haste alreddy hazardid that that will fall owte to your greatist . . .

In the nexte seate to thes hexameters, adonickes, and

iambicks I sett those that stand vppon the number, not in meter, sutch as my lorde of Surrey is sayde first to haue putt forthe in prynte, and my lorde Buckhurste and M. Norton in the Tragedye of Gorboduc, M. Gascoygnes Steele Glasse, an vncertayne autor in certayne cantions agaynst the wylde Irishe, and namelye Mack Morrice, an inuectiue agaynst Simmias Rhodius, a folishe idle phantasticall poett that first deuised this odd rimeinge with many other triflinge and childishe toyes to make verses, that shoulde in proportion represente the form and figure of an egg, an ape, a winge, and sutche ridiculous and madd gugawes and crockchettes, and of late foolishely reuiuid by sum, otherwise not vnlernid, as Pierius, Scaliger, Crispin, and the rest of that crue. Nothinge so absurde and fruteles but beinge once taken vpp shall haue sume imitatoures. The like veyne of those that hunte the letter; and I heard one Mr. Willes, a greate trauelour, very well lernid, and nowe of riper yeares and sownder iudgment, that hath vsid them himselfe, call them meere fooleryes, vices taken vpp for virtues, apish deuices, friuolous boyishe grammer schole trickes.

And heare will I take occasion to shewe you a peece of a letter that I lately receyuid from the Courte written by a frende of mine, that, since a certayn chaunce befallen vnto him, a secrett not to be reuealid, calleth himself Immerito.

'The twoe worthy gentlemen, Mr. Sidney and Mr. Dyer, haue me, I thanke them, in sum vse of familiaritye; of whome and to whome what speache passith for your creddite and estimation, I leaue yourselfe to conceyue, hauinge allwayes so well conceyuid of my vnfainid affection and good will towardes yow. And nowe they haue proclaymid in there ἀρείῳ πάγῳ.'

'E. K.'

(*The Epistle Dedicatory to the Shepheards Calender*)

1579

[This Epistle, addressed by 'E. K.' to Gabriel Harvey in commendation of Spenser's *Shepheards Calender*, is reprinted from the first edition of the *Calender*, issued by Hugh Singleton of Creed Lane near Ludgate, towards the close of 1579.]

TO THE MOST EXCELLENT AND LEARNED, BOTH ORATOR AND POETE, MAYSTER GABRIELL HARVEY, HIS VERIE SPECIAL AND SINGULAR GOOD FREND E. K. COMMENDETH THE GOOD
5 LYKING OF THIS HIS LABOUR, AND THE PATRONAGE OF THE NEW POETE.

UNCOVTHE, vnkiste, sayde the old famous Poete Chaucer: whom, for his excellencie and wonderfull skil in making, his scholler Lidgate, a worthy scholler
10 of so excellent a maister, calleth the Loadestarre of our Language, and whom our Colin Clout in his Æglogue calleth Tityrus the God of shepheards, comparing hym to the worthines of the Roman Tityrus, Virgile. Which prouerbe, myne owne good friend Ma. Haruey, as in that
15 good old Poete it serued well Pandares purpose for the bolstering of his baudy brocage, so very well taketh place in this our new Poete, who for that he is vncouthe (as said Chaucer) is vnkist, and vnknown to most men is regarded but of few. But I dout not, so soone as his name shall
20 come into the knowledg of men, and his worthines be sounded in the tromp of fame, but that he shall be not onely kiste, but also beloued of all, embraced of the most,

and wondred at of the best. No lesse, I thinke, deserueth
his wittinesse in deuising, his pithinesse in vttering, his
complaints of loue so louely, his discourses of pleasure so
pleasantly, his pastoral rudenesse, his morall wisenesse,
his dewe obseruing of Decorum euerye where, in personages, in seasons, in matter, in speach; and generally,
in al seemely simplycitie of handeling his matter and
framing his words: the which, of many thinges which in
him be straunge, I know will seeme the straungest, the
words them selues being so aunceint, the knitting of them
so short and intricate, and the whole Periode and compasse of speache so delightsome for the roundnesse, and
so graue for the straungenesse. And firste of the wordes
to speake, I graunt they be something hard, and of most
men vnused, yet both English, and also vsed of most
excellent Authors and most famous Poetes. In whom,
whenas this our Poet hath bene much traueiled and
throughly redd, how could it be (as that worthy Oratour
sayde) but that walking in the sonne, although for other
cause he walked, yet needes he mought be sunburnt; and,
hauing the sound of those aunceint Poetes still ringing in
his eares, he mought needes, in singing, hit out some of
theyr tunes. But whether he vseth them by such casualtye
and custome, or of set purpose and choyse, as thinking
them fittest for such rusticall rudenesse of shepheards,
eyther for that theyr rough sounde would make his rymes
more ragged and rustical, or els because such olde and obsolete wordes are most vsed of country folke, sure I think,
and think I think not amisse, that they bring great grace,
and, as one would say, auctoritie to the verse. For albe,
amongst many other faultes, it specially be obiected of
Valla against Liuie, and of other against Saluste, that with
ouer much studie they affect antiquitie, as coueting thereby
credence and honor of elder yeeres, yet I am of opinion,
and eke the best learned are of the lyke, that those aunceint

In praise of the New Poet

solemne wordes are a great ornament, both in the one and in the other; the one labouring to set forth in hys worke an eternall image of antiquitie, and the other carefully discoursing matters of grauitie and importaunce. For, if my memory faile not, Tullie, in that booke wherein he endeuoureth to set forth the paterne of a perfect Oratour, sayth that ofttimes an aunciest worde maketh the style seeme graue, and as it were reuerend, no otherwise then we honour and reuerence gray heares, for a certein religious regard which we haue of old age. Yet nether euery where must old words be stuffed in, nor the common Dialecte and maner of speaking so corrupted therby, that, as in old buildings, it seme disorderly and ruinous. But all as in most exquisite pictures they vse to blaze and portraict not onely the daintie lineaments of beautye, but also rounde about it to shadow the rude thickets and craggy clifts, that, by the basenesse of such parts, more excellency may accrew to the principall; for oftimes we fynde ourselues, I knowe not how, singularly delighted with the shewe of such naturall rudenesse, and take great pleasure in that disorderly order. Euen so doe those rough and harsh termes enlumine, and make more clearly to appeare, the brightnesse of braue and glorious words. So oftentimes a dischorde in Musick maketh a comely concordaunce: so great delight tooke the worthy Poete Alceus to behold a blemish in the ioynt of a wel shaped body. But if any will rashly blame such his purpose in choyse of old and vnwonted words, him may I more iustly blame and condemne, or of witlesse headinesse in iudging or of heedelesse hardinesse in condemning; for, not marking the compasse of hys bent, he wil iudge of the length of his cast: for in my opinion it is one special prayse of many whych are dew to this Poete, that he hath laboured to restore, as to theyr rightfull heritage, such good and naturall English words as haue ben long time out of vse and almost cleane disherited. Which is the onely cause that our Mother tonge, which truely of it self is both ful enough for prose and stately enough for verse, hath long time ben counted most bare and barrein of both. Which default when as some endeuoured to salue and recure, they patched up the holes with peces and rags of other languages, borrowing here of the French, there of the Italian, every where of the Latine; not weighing how il those tongues accorde with themselues, but much worse with ours: So now they haue made our English tongue a gallimaufray or hodgepodge of al other speches. Other some, no[t] so wel sene in the English tonge as perhaps in other languages, if they happen to here an olde word, albeit very naturall and significant, crye out streightway that we speak no English, but gibbrish, or rather such as in old time Euanders mother spake: whose first shame is, that they are not ashamed, in their own mother tonge, straungers to be counted and alienes. The second shame, no lesse then the first, that what so they vnderstand not they streight way deeme to be sencelesse and not at al to be vnderstode. Much like to the Mole in Æsopes fable, that, being blynd her selfe, would in no wise be perswaded that any beast could see. The last, more shameful then both, that of their owne country and natural speach, which together with their Nources milk they sucked, they haue so base regard and bastard iudgement, that they will not onely themselues not labor to garnish and beautifie it, but also repine that of other it shold be embellished. Like to the dogge in the maunger, that him selfe can eate no hay, and yet barketh at the hungry bullock that so faine would feede: whose currish kind, though it cannot be kept from barking, yet I conne them thanke that they refrain from byting.

Now, for the knitting of sentences, whych they call the ioynts and members therof, and for al the compasse of

In praise of the New Poet

the speach, it is round without roughnesse, and learned wythout hardnes, such indeede as may be perceiued of the leaste, vnderstoode of the moste, but iudged onely of the learned. For what in most English wryters vseth to be loose, and as it were vngyrt, in this Authour is well grounded, finely framed, and strongly trussed up together. In regard wherof, I scorne and spue out the rakehellye route of our ragged rymers (for so themselues vse to hunt the letter) which without learning boste, without iudgement iangle, without reason rage and fome, as if some instinct of Poeticall spirite had newly rauished them aboue the meanenesse of commen capacitie. And being in the middest of all theyr brauery, sodenly, eyther for want of matter or of ryme, or hauing forgotten theyr former conceipt, they seeme to be so pained and traueiled in theyr remembrance, as it were a woman in childebirth, or as that same Pythia when the traunce came vpon her: *Os rabidum fera corda domans*, &c.

Nethelesse, let them a Gods name feede on theyr owne folly, so they seeke not to darken the beames of others glory. As for Colin, vnder whose person the Authour selfe is shadowed, how furre he is from such vaunted titles and glorious showes, both him selfe sheweth, where he sayth,

   Of Muses, Hobbin[ol], I conne no skill,
and
   Enough is me to paint out my vnrest, &c:

And also appeareth by the basenesse of the name, wherein it semeth he chose rather to vnfold great matter of argument couertly then, professing it, not suffice thereto accordingly. Which moued him rather in Æglogues then other wise to write, doubting perhaps his habilitie, which he little needed, or mynding to furnish our tongue with this kinde wherein it faulteth; or following the example of the best and most auncient Poetes, which deuised this kind of wryting, being both so base for the matter and homely for the manner, at the first to trye theyr habilities, and, as young birdes that be newly crept out of the nest, by little first to proue theyr tender wyngs before they make a greater flyght. So flew Theocritus, as you may perceiue he was all ready full fledged. So flew Virgile, as not yet well feeling his winges. So flew Mantuane, as not being full somd. So Petrarque. So Boccace. So Marot, Sanazarus, and also diuers other excellent both Italian and French Poetes, whose foting this Author euery where followeth; yet so as few, but they be wel sented, can trace him out. So finally flyeth this our new Poete as a birde whose principals be scarce growen out, but yet as [one] that in time shall be hable to keepe wing with the best.

Now, as touching the generall dryft and purpose of his Æglogues, I mind not to say much, him selfe labouring to conceale it. Onely this appeareth, that his vnstayed yougth had long wandred in the common Labyrinth of Loue, in which time to mitigate and allay the heate of his passion, or els to warne (as he sayth) the young shepheards, .f. his equalls and companions, of his vnfortunate folly, he compiled these xij Æglogues, which, for that they be proportioned to the state of the xij monethes, he termeth the SHEPHEARDS CALENDAR, applying an olde name to a new worke. Hereunto haue I added a certain Glosse or scholion, for thexposition of old wordes and harder phrases; which maner of glosing and commenting, well I wote, wil seeme straunge and rare in our tongue: yet, for so much as I knew many excellent and proper deuises, both in wordes and matter, would passe in the speedy course of reading, either as vnknowen or as not marked, and that in this kind, as in other, we might be equal to the learned of other nations, I thought good to take the paines vpon me, the rather for that by meanes of some familiar acquaintaunce I was made priuie to his counsell and secret

meaning in them, as also in sundry other works of his, which albeit I know he nothing so much hateth as to promulgate, yet thus much haue I aduentured vpon his frendship, him selfe being for long time furre estraunged, hoping
5 that this will the rather occasion him to put forth diuers other excellent works of his which slepe in silence, as his *Dreames*, his *Legendes*, his *Court of Cupide*, and sondry others, whose commendations to set out were verye vaine, the thinges though worthy of many yet being knowen to
10 few. These my present paynes, if to any they be pleasurable or profitable, be you iudge, mine own good Maister Haruey, to whom I haue, both in respect of your worthinesse generally and otherwyse vpon some particular and special considerations, voued this my labour and the may-
15 denhead of this our commen frends Poetrie ; himselfe hauing already in the beginning dedicated it to the Noble and worthy Gentleman, the right worshipfull Ma. Phi. Sidney, a special fauourer and maintainer of all kind of learning. Whose cause, I pray you, Sir, yf Enuie shall stur vp
20 any wrongful accusasion, defend with your mighty Rhetorick and other your rare gifts of learning, as you can, and shield with your good wil, as you ought, against the malice and outrage of so many enemies, as I know wilbe set on fire with the sparks of his kindled glory. And thus recom-
25 mending the Author vnto you, as vnto his most special good frend, and my selfe vnto you both, as one making singuler account of two so very good and so choise frends, I bid you both most hartely farwel, and commit you and your most commendable studies to the tuicion of the greatest.

30   Your owne assuredly to be commaunded,

                                   E. K.

Post scr.

NOW I trust, M. Haruey, that vpon sight of your speciall frends and fellow Poets doings, or els for enuie of so many vnworthy Quidams which catch at the garlond which to you alone is dewe, you will be perswaded to pluck out of the hateful darknesse those so many excellent English poemes of yours which lye hid, and bring them forth to eternall light. Trust me, you doe both them great wrong, in depriuing them of the desired sonne, and also your selfe, in smoothering your deserued prayses, and all men generally, in withholding from them so diuine pleasures, which they might conceiue of your gallant English verses, as they haue already doen of your Latine Poemes, which, in my opinion, both for inuention and Elocution are very delicate and superexcellent. And thus againe I take my leaue of my good Mayster Haruey: from my lodging at London thys 10. of Aprill, 1579.

RICHARD STANYHURST

(*FROM THE TRANSLATION OF THE* AENEID)

1582

[The Dedication and the Preface ('Too thee Learned Reader') are prefixed to *Thee First Fov|re Bookes of Vir-|gil his Aeneis |transla|ted in too English Heroical Verse* ... || *Imprinted at Leiden in Holland by John Pates | Anno M.D.LXXXII.*

The following extracts are taken from the copy which was formerly in the Ashburnham Library, and is now in the British Museum. The only other known copy is preserved in the library at Britwell Court, Burnham, Bucks. The second (or 1583) edition, which is now hardly less rare, was a London reprint by Henry Bynneman, the printer of the Spenser and Harvey Letters (ante, p. 87). As the difference between these editions is entirely orthographical, it appeared, prima facie, to be desirable to take the London text, partly because it is more 'modern,' and partly because the earlier is accessible in Mr. Arber's excellent reprint (1880). Bynneman's text, on the other hand, was reprinted by James Maidment in 1836 in a private issue of fifty copies. But a collation of the British Museum text of 1582 with that of 1583, in the copy presented to the library of the University of Edinburgh in 1628 by the poet William Drummond, has made it clear that the former is the better. For though Pates speaks, in his Note 'To thee Cvrteovs Reader,' of 'thee nooueltye of imprinting English in theese partes, and thee absence of the author from perusing soom proofes,' his text is more consistent with Stanyhurst's rules, and seems, as far as the prefatory matter is concerned, to have been revised by the author. Bynneman, who is somewhat impatient of the 'newe Ortographie vsed in the booke (whether with the writers mind or the Printers fault, I know not)', sets himself to cut out most of the double 'e's and 'o's and other eccentricities of the text; but he retains Stanyhurst's account of these special forms. His rendering is therefore a botch, neither illustrating his author's theory nor conforming to contemporary English usage. Stanyhurst's orthography, like that of the *Ormulum*, must be considered as a necessary part of the writer's prosodic theory.

The Dedication is dated 'From Leiden in Holland, thee last of Iune 1582.']

TOO THEE RIGHT HONOVRABLE MY VERIE LOOVING BROOTHER THEE LORD BARON OF DVNSANYE.

WHAT deepe and rare poynctes of hydden secrets *Virgil* hath sealde vp in his twelue bookes of *Æneis* may easelye appeere too such reaching wyts as bend theyre endewours too thee vnfolding thereof, not onlye by gnibling vpon thee outward ryne of a supposed historie, but also by groaping thee pyth that is shrind vp wythin thee barck and bodye of so exquisit and singular a discourse. For where as thee chiefe prayse of a wryter consisteth in thee enterlacing of pleasure wyth profit, oure author hath so wiselye alayed thee one wyth thee oother as thee shallow reader may bee delighted wyth a smooth tale, and thee diuing searcher may bee aduantaged by sowning a pretiouse treatise. And certes this preheminencye of writing is chieflye (yf wee respect oure old latin Poëtes) too bee affurded too *Virgil* in this wurck, and too *Ouid* in his *Metamorphosis*. As for *Ennius*, *Horace*, *Iuuenal*, *Persius*, and thee rablement of such cheate Poëtes, theyre dooinges are, for fauoure of antiquitye, rather to be pacientlye allowed thean highlye regarded. Such leauinges as wee haue of *Ennius* his ragged verses are nothing current, but sauoure soomwhat nappy of thee spigget, as one that was neauer accustomed too strike vp thee drum, and too crye, in blazing martial exploytes, 'alarme,' but when hee were haulfe tipsye, as *Horace* recordeth. Thee oother three, ouer this that theyre Verses in camfering wise run harshe and rough, perfourme nothing in matter but biting quippes, taunting Darcklye certeyn men of state that liued in theyre age, beesprinckling theyre *inuectiues* with soom moral preceptes aunswerable too thee capacitye of eurie weake brayne. But oure *Virgil*, not content wyth such meigre stuffe, dooth laboure, in telling as yt were a *Cantorburye tale*, too ferret owt thee secretes of *Nature*, with woordes so fitlye coucht, wyth verses so smoothlye slyckte, with sentences so featlye orderd, with orations so neatlie burnisht, with similitudes so aptly applyed, with eeche *decorum* so duely obserued, as in truth hee hath in right purchased too hym self thee name of a surpassing poët, thee fame of an od oratoure, and thee admiration of a profound philosopher. Hauing therefore (mi good lord) taken vpon mee too execute soom part of mayster *Askam* his wyl, who, in his goulden pamphlet intituled *thee Schoolemayster*, dooth wish thee Vniuersitie students too applie theyre wittes in bewtifying oure English language with heroical verses, I heeld no *Latinist* so fit, too geeue thee onset on, as *Virgil*, who, for his peerelesse style and machlesse stuffe, dooth beare thee prick and price among al thee Roman Poëts. How beyt, I haue heere haulf a guesh that two sortes of carpers wyl seeme too spurne at this myne entreprise; thee one vtterlie ignorant, thee oother meanelye letterd. Thee ignorant wyl imagin that thee passage was nothing craggye, in as much as M. *Phaere* hath broken thee ice before mee: Thee meaner clarcks wyl suppose my trauail in theese heroical verses too carrye no great difficultie, in that yt lay in my choise too make what word I would short or long, hauing no English writer beefore mee in this kind of poëtrye with whose squire I should leauel my syllables. Too shape therefor an answer too thee first, I say they

are altogeather in a wrong box: considering that such
woordes as fit M. *Phaer* may bee very vnapt for mee,
which they would confesse, yf theyre skil were, so much
as spare, in theese verses. Further more, I stand so
nicelie on my pantofles that way, as yf I could, yeet I
would not renne on thee skore with M. *Phaer* or ennie
oother, by borrowing his termes in so copious and fluent
a language as oure English tongue is. And in good
sooth althogh thee gentleman hath translated *Virgil* in too
English rythme with such surpassing excellencie, as a verie
few (in my conceit) for pyckt and loftie wordes can burd
hym, none, I am wel assured, ouergoe hym: yeet hee hath
rather dubled then defalckt oght of my paines, by reason
that, in conferring his translation with myne, I was forced
too weede owt from my verses such choise woordes as
were forestald by him, vnlesse they were so feeling as
oothers could not countreuaile theyre signification: In
which case yt were no reason too sequester my pen from
theyre acquaintance, considering that, as M. *Phaer* was
not thee first founder, so hee may not bee accoumpted
thee only owner of such termes. Truely I am so far from
embeazling his trauailes, as that for thee honoure of thee
English I durst vndertake too renne ouer theese bookes
agayne, and too geeue theym a new liuerie in such different
wise, as they should not iet with M. *Phaer* his badges,
ne yeet bee clad with this apparaile, wherewith at this
present they coom furth atyred. Which I speake not of
vanitie, too enhaunce my coonning, but of meere veritie,
too aduaunce thee riches of oure speeche. More ouer
in soom poinctes of greatest price, where thee matter, as
yt were, doth bleede, I was mooued too shun M. *Phaer*
his enterpretation, and clinge more neere too thee meaning of myne authoure, in slising thee husk and cracking
thee shel, too bestow thee kernel vpon thee wyttye and
enquisitiue reader.

[*Stanyhurst then proceeds to discuss some points of difference between his version and Phaer's.*]

Now too coom too theym that guesh my trauaile too be easye by reason of thee libertye I had in English woordes (for as I can not deuine vpon such bookes that happlye rouke in studentes mewes, so I trust I offer no man iniurie yf I assume too my selfe thee maydenhed of al wurcks that hath beene beefore this tyme in print, too my knowlegde, diuulged in this kind of verse), I wil not greatly wrangle with theym therein: yeet this much they are too consider, that as thee first applying of a woord may ease mee in thee first place, so perhaps, when I am occasioned too vse thee selfe same woord els where, I may bee as much hyndered as at thee beginning I was furthred. For example: In thee first verse of *Virgil* I mak *season* long; in an oother place yt woul[d] steede mee percase more yf I made yt short, and yeet I am now tyed too vse yt as long. So that the aduantage that way is not verie great. But as for thee general facilitiee, this much I dare warrant yoong beginners, that when they shal haue soom firme footing in this kind of Poetrie, which by a litle payneful exercise may bee purchast, they shal find as easye a veyne in thee English as in thee Latin verses, yee, and much more easye than in the *English rythmes*. Touching myne owne trial, this much I wil discoouer. Thee three first bokes I translated by startes, as my leasure and pleasure would serue mee. In thee fourth booke I did task my self, and persued thee matter soomwhat hoatlie. M. *Phaer* tooke too thee making of that booke fifteene dayes. I hudled vp myne in ten. Wherein I coouet no prayse, but rather doe craue pardon. Fore lyke as forelittring biches whelp blynd puppies, so I may bee perhaps entwighted of more haste then good speede, as *Syr Thomas More* in lyke case gybeth at one that made vaunt of certeyn pild verses clowted vp *extrumpere*.

> *Hos quid te scripsisse mones ex tempore versus?*
> *Nam liber hoc loquitur, te reticente, tuus.*

But too leaue that too thee veredict of oothers (wherein
I craue thee good lyking of thee curteouse, and skorne
thee controlment of thee currish, as those that vsuallie
reprehend moste, and yeet can amend leaste), thee ods
beetweene *verses* and *rythme* is verye great. For, in thee
one, euerye *foote*, euerye *word*, euerye *syllable*, yea euerye
letter is too bee obserued: in thee oother, thee last *woord*
is onlye too bee heeded: As is very liuelye exprest by
thee *lawyer* in empaneling a iurye.

Johannes Doa:	*Iohannes Den:*	*Johannes Hye:*
Richardus Roa:	*Willielmus Fen:*	*Thomas Pye:*
Iohannes Myles:	*Willielmus Neile:*	*Richardus Leake:*
Thomas Giles:	*Iohannes Sneile:*	*Johannes Peake.*

Happlye such curious *makers* as youre lordship is wyl
accompt this but *rythme dogrel*; but wee may suite yt
wyth a more ciuil woord, by terming yt *rythme peale meale*—
yt rowles so roundlye in thee hyrer his eares. And are
there not diuerse skauingers of draftye poëtrye in this
oure age, that bast theyre papers wyth smearie larde
sauoring al too geather of thee frying pan? What *Tom
Towly* is so simple that wyl not attempt too bee a *rith-
moure?* Yf your Lordship stand in doubt thereof, what
thinck you of thee *thick skyn* that made this for a *fare wel*
for his *mystresse* vpon his departure from *Abingtowne?*

> *Abingtowne, Abingtowne, God bee wyth thee:*
> *For thou haste a steeple lyke a dagger sheathe.*

And an oother in thee prayse, not of a steeple, but of
a dagger.

> *When al is goane but thee black scabbard,*
> *Wel fare thee haft wyth thee duggeon dagger.*

Thee therd (for I wyl present your lordship with a leshe)
in thee commendacion of bacon.

Hee is not a king that weareth satten,
But hee is a king that eateth bacon.

Haue not theese men made a fayre speake? If they
had put in *Mightye Ioue*, and *Gods* in thee plural number,
and *Venus* wyth *Cupide thee blynd Boy*, al had beene in
thee nick, thee rythme had beene of a right stamp. For
a few such stiches boch vp oure newe fashion makers:
Prouyded not wythstanding alwayes that *Artaxerxes*, al
be yt hee bee spurgalde, beeing so much gallopt, bee
placed in thee dedicatorye epistle receauing a cuppe of
water of a swayne, or elles al is not wurth a beane. Good
God, what a frye of such *wooden rythmours* dooth swarme
in stacioners shops, who neauer enstructed in any grammar
schoole, not atayning too thee paringes of thee Latin or
Greeke tongue, yeet lyke blynd bayards rush on forward,
fostring theyre vayne conceites wyth such ouerweening
silly follyes, as they reck not too bee condemned of thee
learned for ignorant, so they bee commended of thee
ignorant for learned. Thee reddyest way therefore too
flap theese droanes from thee sweete senting hiues of
Poëtrye is for thee learned too applye theym selues wholye
(yf they be delighted wyth that veyne) too thee true making
of verses in such wise as thee *Greekes* and *Latins*, thee
fathers of knowledge, haue doone, and too leaue too theese
doltish coystrels theyre rude rythming and balducktoom
ballads. . . .

TOO THEE LEARNED READER.

IN thee obseruation of quantitees of syllables, soom
happlye wyl bee so stieflie tyed too thee ordinaunces of
thee Latins, as what shal seeme too swarue from theyre

maximes they wyl not stick too skore vp for errours. In
which resolution such curious *Priscianistes* dooe attribute
greater prerogatiue too thee Latin tongue than reason
wyl affurd, and lesse libertye too oure language than
nature may permit. For in as much as thee Latins haue
not beene authors of theese verses, but traced in thee
steps of thee Greekes, why should we with thee stringes
of thee Latin rules cramp oure tongue more than the
Latins doe fetter theyre speeche, as yt were wyth thee
chaynes of thee Greeke preceptes. Also that nature wyl
not permit vs too fashion oure wordes in al poinctes
correspondent too thee Latinistes, may easely appeere
in suche termes as we borrow of theym. For exemple:
The first of *Breuiter* is short, thee first of *briefly* wyth
vs must bee long. Lykewise, *sonans* is short, yeet
sowning in English must bee long, and much more yf
yt were *Sounding*, as thee ignorant generaly, but falslye,
dooe wryte; nay, that where at I woonder more, thee
learned trip theyre pennes at this stoane, in so much as
M. *Phaer* in thee verye first verse of Virgil mistaketh thee
woorde. Yeet *sound* and *sowne* differ as much in English
as *solidus* and *sonus* in Latin. Also in thee midest of
a woord wee differ soomtymes from the Romans. As in
Latin wee pronounce *Orātor, Audītor, Magīster* long: in
English, *Orătoure, Audĭtoure, Magĭstrat* short. Lykewise
wee pronounce *Præpăro, compăro* short in Latin, and
prepâred and *compâred* long in English. Agayne thee
infallibelist rule that thee Latins haue for thee quantitye
of middle syllables is this. *Penultima acuta producitur,
vt virtūtis; penultima grauata corripitur, vt sanguĭnis.*
Honoure in English is short, as wyth thee Latins; yeet
dishonour must bee long by thee formoure maxime: which
is contrary too an oother ground of thee Latins, whereby
they prescribe that thee *primatiue* and *deriuatiue*, thee
simple and *compound*, bee of one quantitye. But that rule

of al oothers must be abandoned from thee English, oother
wise al woordes in effcct should bee abridged. *Moother*
I make long; yeet *graundmother* must bee short. *Buckler*
is long; yeet *swashbuckler* is short. And albeyt that
woord bee long by *position*, yeet doubtlesse thee natural
dialect of English wyl not allow of that rule in middle
syllables, but yt must bee of force with vs excepted, where
thee natural pronuntiation wyl so haue yt. For ootherwise wee should bannish a number of good and necessarye
wordes from oure verses; as *M. Gabriel Haruye* (yf I
mystake not thee gentleman his name) hath verye wel
obserued in one of his familiar letters: where hee layeth
downe diuerse wordes straying from thee Latin preceptes,
as *Maiestye, Royaltye, Honestie, &c.* And soothly, too my
seeming, yf thee coniunction *And* were made common
in English, yt were not amisse, although yt bee long by
position: For thee Romans are greatly aduantaged by
theyre woordes *Et, Que, Quoque, Atque*: which were they
disioincted from thee Latin poëtrie, many good verses
would bee rauelde and dismembred that now cary a good
grace among theym, hauing theyre ioynctes knit with
theese copulatiue sinnewes. But too rip vp further thee
peculiar propretye of oure English, let vs listen too *Tullye*
his iudgement, wherein thogh hee seeme verie peremptorie,
yeet, with his fauoure, hee misheth thee cushen. Thus
in his booke intituled *Orator*, hee writeth, *Ipsa natura,
quasi modularetur hominum orationem, in omni verbo posuit
acutam vocem, nec vna plus, nec a postrema syllaba citra
tertiam.* In this saying Tullye obserueth three poinctes.
First, that by course of *Nature* euerye woord hath an
accent: next, one only: lastlye, that thee sayde *accent*
must be on thee last syllable, as *propè*, or on thee last
saluing one, as *Virtūtis*, or, at thee furthest, on thee therd
syllable, as *Omnîpotens*. Yeet this rule taketh no such
infallible effect with vs, althogh *Tully* maketh yt natural,

who by thee skyl of thee Greek and Latin dyd ayme at
oother languages too hym vnknowen, and therefor is too
bee borne wythal. As, *Peremtorie* is a woord of foure
syllables, and yeet thee *accent* is on thee first. So
Sêcundarie, órdinarie, Mâtrimonie, Pâtrimonie, Plânetarie,
imperatiue, Côsmographie, órtography, with many lyke.
For althogh thee ignorant pronounce *Impêratiue, Cosmô-*
graphie, Ortôgraphy, geeuing the *accent* too thee therd
syllable, yeet that is not thee true English pronuntiation.
Now put case thee cantel of thee Latin verse *Sapiens*
dominabitur astris were thus Englished, *Planetary woorck-*
inges thee wismans vertue represseth, albeyt thee middle
of *planeta* bee long with thee Romans, yeet I would not
make yt scrupulus too shorten yt in English, by reason
thee natural pronountiation would haue yt so. For thee
final eende of a verse is to please thee eare, which must
needes bee thee vmpyre of thee woord, and according too
that weight oure syllables must bee poysed. Wherefor
syth thee *poëtes* theymselues aduouch, *Tu nihil inuita facies*
dicesue Minerua, That nothing may bee doone or spoaken
agaynst nature, and that *Art* is also bound too shape yt
self by al imitation too *Nature,* wee must request theese
grammatical Precisians, that as euery countrye hath his
peculiar law, so they permit euerye language too vse
his particular loare. For my part I purpose not too beat
on euerye childish tittle that concerneth *Prosodia,* neither
dooe I vndertake too chalck owt any lines or rules too
oothers, but too lay downe too thee reader his view thee
course I tooke in this my trauaile. Such woordes as
proceede from thee Latin, and bee not altred by oure
English, in theym I obserue thee quantitie of thee Latin.
As *Honest, Honor*: a few I excepted, as thee first of
apeered, auenture, aproched I make short, althogh they
are long in Latin, as *Appareo, Aduenio, Appropinquo*:
for which, and percase a few such woordes, I must craue

pardon of thee curteous reader. For ootherwise yt were
lyke ynough that soom *grammatical pullet,* hacht in *Dispater*
his sachel, would stand clocking aganyst mee, as thogh
hee had found an horse nest, in laying that downe for
5 a falt that perhaps I dooe knowe better then hee. Yeet
in theese *diriuations* of termes I would not bee doomde
by euerye reaching herrault, that in roaming wise wyl
attempt too fetche thee petit degree of woordes, I know
not from what auncetoure. As I make thee first of *Riuer*
10 short, a Wrangler may imagin yt should bee long, by
reason of *Riuus,* of which yt seemeth too bee deriued.
And yeet forsooth *riuus* is but a *brooke,* and not a *riuer.*
Likewyse soom English woordes may bee read in soom
places long, in soom short, as *skyeward, seaward, searowme.*
15 Thee difference thereof groweth beecause they are but
compound woordes that may bee with good sense sunderd:
and thee last of *Sea* and *skye* beeing common breedeth
that diuersitie. Also thee self same woord may varye
beecause of thee signification. Thee first of *Felon* for
20 a *theefe* I make long, but when yt signifieth thee disease,
so named, I hold yt better too make yt short. Agayne
a woord that is short beeing deuided may bee long in
an oother place contracted. As thee first of. *Leaues,* yf
you deuide yt in two syllables, I make short; yf you
25 contract yt too one syllabe, I make yt long. So thee first
in *Crauing* is long, and thee therd person of thee verb,
too wyt, *Craues,* may seeme short, where the next woord
following beginneth with a vocal, yet yt is long by contraction: and so diuerse lyke woordes are too bee taken.
30 And truely such nice obseruations that *Grammarians* dooe
prescribe are not by thee choysest poëtes alwayes so preciselye put in execution: as in this oure authour I haue
by thee way marckt. In thee fore front of thee first
booke hee maketh thee first of *Lauin[i]um* long. In thee
35 same booke hee vseth yt for short. Likewise dooth he

varie thee first of *Sichæus*. So in thee therd booke thee midest of *Cyclopes* soomtyme is made long, soomtyme short. And in the same booke the coniunction *Que* is long, as

Liminaque laurusque Dei; totusque moueri:

And in thee fourth:

Cretesque Dryopesque fremunt, pictique Agathyrsi:

Also thee first of *Italia* is long: yeet in thee therd book *Italus* is short, as

Has autem terras, Italique hanc littoris oram.

Touching the *termination* of syllables, I made a *prosodia* too my selfe squaring soomwhat from thee Latin: in this wise.

A. *finita communia.* B. D. T. *breuia*: yeet theese woordes that eende lyke dipthonges are common: as *mouth, south, &c.* C. common. E. common: yf yt bee short, I wryte yt vsualy with a single E, as *the, me*; yf long with two, as *thee, mee*; althogh I would not wish thee quantitie of syllables too depend so much vpon thee gaze of thee eye as thee censure of thee eare. F. *breuia*. G. *breuia*: soomtyme long by *position* where D may bee enterserted, as *passage* is short, but yf you make yt long, *passadge* with D would bee written; albeyt, as I sayd right now, thee eare, not ortographie, must decyde thee quantitye as neere as is possible. I. common. K. common. L. *breuia, præter Hebræa, vt Michaël, Gabriel*. N. *Breuia*; yeet woordes eending in dipthongwise would bee common, as *playne, fayne, swayne*. O. common, *præter ô longum*. P. *Breuia*. R. *Breuia*, except woordes eending lyke dipthonges that may bee common, as *youre, oure, houre, soure, succour, &c*. As and Es common. Is *breuia*. Os common. Vs *breuia*. V. common. As for M. yt is either long by *position*, or els

clipt, yf thee next woord begyn with a vocal, as *fame*,
name: for albeyt E bee thee last letter, that must not
salue M from accurtation, beecause in thee eare M is
thee last letter, and E dooth noght els but leng[t]hen and
mollifye thee pronountiation.   As for I. Y. W., in as much
as they are moungrels, soomtyme consonantes, soomtyme
vocals, where they further I dooe not reiect theym,
where they hinder I doe not greatlye weigh theym: As
thee middle of *folowing* I make short, notwythstanding
thee W, and lykwise the first of *power*: But where
a consonant immediatly followeth the W, I make yt
alwayes long, as *fowling*.

This much I thoght good too acquaynt thee gentle
reader wythal, rather too discoouer wyth what priuat
preceptes I haue embayed my verses then too publish
a *directorye* too thee learned, who in theyre trauayls
may franckly vse theyre owne discretion wythowt my
direction.

SIR PHILIP SIDNEY

(*An Apologie for Poetrie*)

c. 1583 (printed 1595)

[Two editions of Sidney's famous essay (written c. 1583) appeared in 1595—(a) *The | Defence of | Poesie. | By Sir Phillip Sidney, | Knight || London. | Printed for William Ponsonby. |* 1595, and (b) *An | Apologie | for Poetrie. | Written by the right noble, vertu-|ous, and learned, Sir Phillip | Sidney, Knight. || Odi profanum vulgus, et arceo. || At London, | Printed for Henry Olney, and are to be sold at | his shop in Paules Church-yard, at the signe | of the George, neere to Cheap-gate. | Anno* 1595. Ponsonby's edition, which is extant in the unique copy in the collection of Mr. F. Locker, seems, from the evidence of the Stationers' Register[1], to have been the earlier of the two. It is the basis of the later texts from the folio of 1598, where the essay appears as an addition to the *Arcadia*. It has been reprinted by Dr. Ewald Flügel in his *Sir Philip Sidney's Astrophel and Stella und Defence of Poesie*, Halle 1889. Yet Olney's text is more carefully printed than Ponsonby's and his successors'. It was last reprinted by Mr. Arber in his *English Reprints* and by Mr. Shuckburgh in the *Pitt Press Series*. The present text has been taken from the copy of Olney's edition presented to the library of the University of Edinburgh by the poet William Drummond. The important differences between it and Mr. Locker's copy of Ponsonby's edition (ed. Flügel) are pointed out in the Notes.

It will be seen that there is bibliographical justification for either title—*Defence* or *Apologie*. The popularity of the later editions, founded on Ponsonby's, gave greater vogue to the former. Sidney himself speaks of his effort

[1] See Notes.

as a 'pittiful defence of poore Poetry': and the term was frequently employed by contemporary critics in their pamphlet feuds. But the title *Apologie*, of the 1595 edition, was perhaps not less common among Sidney's friends and successors, for we find Harington so styling the Essay in his *Briefe Apologie of Poetrie* (q. v.), which was printed four years before the first edition of Sidney's work. So also William Vaughan (q. v.).

The Essay is preceded in Olney's edition by four sonnets 'written by Henrie Constable to Sir Phillip Sidney's soule,' and by the following note 'To the Reader': —

'The stormie Winter (deere Chyldren of the Muses), which hath so long held backe the glorious Sunshine of diuine Poesie, is heere by the sacred pen-breathing words of diuine Sir *Phillip Sidney* not onely chased from our fame-inuiting Clyme, but vtterly for euer banisht eternitie: then graciously regreet the perpetuall spring of euer-growing inuention, and like kinde Babes, either enabled by wit or power, help to support me poore Midwife, whose daring aduenture hath deliuered from Obliuions wombe this euer-to-be-admired wits miracle. Those great ones who in themselues haue interr'd this blessed innocent wil with *Aesculapius* condemne me as a detractor from their Deities: those who Prophet-like haue but heard presage of his coming wil (if they wil doe wel) not onely defend but praise mee as the first publique bewrayer of Poesies *Messias*. Those who neither haue seene, thereby to interre, nor heard, by which they might be inflamed with desire to see, let them (of duty) plead to be my Champions, sith both theyr sight and hearing by mine incurring blame is reasoned. Excellent Poesie (so created by this Apologie), be thou my Defendresse; and if any wound mee, let thy beautie (my soules Adamant) recure mee; if anie commend mine endeuored hardiment, to them commend thy most diuinest fury as a winged incouragement; so shalt thou haue deuoted to thee, and to them obliged,

Henry Olney.]

AN APOLOGIE FOR POETRIE.

WHEN the right vertuous *Edward Wotton* and I were at the Emperors Court together, wee gaue our selues to learne horsemanship of *Iohn Pietro Pugliano*, one that with great commendation had the place of an Esquire in his stable. And hee, according to the fertilnes of the Italian wit, did not onely afoord vs the demonstration of his practise, but sought to enrich our mindes with the contemplations therein which hee thought most precious. But with none I remember mine eares were at any time more loden, then when (either angred with slowe paiment, or mooued with our learner-like admiration) he exercised his speech in the prayse of his facultie. Hee sayd, Souldiours were the noblest estate of mankinde, and horsemen the noblest of Souldiours. Hee sayde they were the Maisters of warre, and ornaments of peace; speedy goers, and strong abiders; triumphers both in Camps and Courts. Nay, to so vnbeleeued a poynt hee proceeded, as that no earthly thing bred such wonder to a Prince as to be a good horseman. Skill of gouernment was but a Pedanteria in comparison. Then would hee adde certaine prayses, by telling what a peerlesse beast a horse was; the onely seruiceable Courtier without flattery, the beast of most beutie, faithfulnes, courage, and such more, that if I had not beene a peece of a Logician before I came to him, I think he would haue perswaded mee to haue wished my selfe a horse. But thus much at least with his no fewe words hee draue into me, that selfe-loue is better then any guilding to make that seeme gorgious wherein our selues are parties. Wherein, if *Pugliano* his strong affection and weake arguments will not satisfie you, I wil giue you a neerer example of my selfe, who (I knowe not by what mischance) in these my not old yeres and idelest times, hauing slipt into the title of a Poet, am prouoked

to say somthing vnto you in the defence of that my vn-
elected vocation, which if I handle with more good will
then good reasons, beare with me, sith the scholler is to
be pardoned that foloweth the steppes of his Maister.
And yet I must say that as I haue iust cause to make
a pittiful defence of poore Poetry, which from almost the
highest estimation of learning is fallen to be the laughing-
stocke of children; so haue I need to bring some more
auaileable proofes: sith the former is by no man barred of
his deserued credite, the silly latter hath had euen the
names of Philosophers vsed to the defacing of it, with
great danger of ciuill war among the Muses. And first,
truly to all them that professing learning inueigh against
Poetry, may justly be objected, that they goe very neer to
vngratfulnes, to seek to deface that which, in the noblest
nations and languages that are knowne, hath been the first
light-giuer to ignorance, and first Nurse, whose milk by
little and little enabled them to feed afterwards of tougher
knowledges: and will they now play the Hedghog that,
being receiued into the den, draue out his host? or rather
the Vipers, that with theyr birth kill their Parents? Let
learned Greece in any of her manifold Sciences be able
to shew me one booke before *Musæus*, *Homer*, and
Hesiodus, all three nothing els but Poets. Nay, let any
historie be brought that can say any Writers were there
before them, if they were not men of the same skil, as
Orpheus, *Linus*, and some other are named: who, hauing
beene the first of that Country that made pens deliuerers
of their knowledge to their posterity, may iustly chalenge
to bee called their Fathers in learning: for not only in
time they had this priority (although in it self antiquity
be venerable) but went before them, as causes to drawe
with their charming sweetnes the wild vntamed wits to
an admiration of knowledge. So as *Amphion* was sayde
to moue stones with his Poetrie to build Thebes; and

Orpheus to be listened to by beastes, indeed stony and beastly people. So among the Romans were *Liuius, Andronicus,* and *Ennius.* So in the Italian language the first that made it aspire to be a Treasure-house of Science were the Poets *Dante, Boccace,* and *Petrarch.* So in our English were *Gower* and *Chawcer.*

After whom, encouraged and delighted with theyr excellent fore-going, others haue followed, to beautifie our mother tongue, as wel in the same kinde as in other Arts. This did so notably shewe it selfe, that the Phylosophers of Greece durst not a long time appeare to the worlde but vnder the masks of Poets. So *Thales, Empedocles,* and *Parmenides* sange their naturall Phylosophie in verses: so did *Pythagoras* and *Phocilides* their morral counsells: so did *Tirteus* in war matters, and *Solon* in matters of policie: or rather, they, beeing Poets, dyd exercise their delightful vaine in those points of highest knowledge, which before them lay hid to the world. For that wise *Solon* was directly a Poet it is manifest, hauing written in verse the notable fable of the Atlantick Iland, which was continued by *Plato.*

And truely, euen *Plato,* whosoeuer well considereth, shall find that in the body of his work, though the inside and strength were Philosophy, the skinne as it were and beautie depended most of Poetrie: for all standeth vpon Dialogues, wherein he faineth many honest Burgesses of Athens to speake of such matters, that, if they had been sette on the racke, they would neuer haue confessed them. Besides, his poetical describing the circumstances of their meetings, as the well ordering of a banquet, the delicacie of a walke, with enterlacing meere tales, as *Giges* Ring, and others, which who knoweth not to be flowers of Poetrie did neuer walke into *Apollos* Garden.

And euen Historiographers (although theyr lippes sounde of things doone, and veritie be written in theyr fore-heads) haue been glad to borrow both fashion and perchance weight of Poets. So *Herodotus* entituled his Historie by the name of the nine Muses: and both he and all the rest that followed him either stole or vsurped of Poetrie their passionate describing of passions, the many particularities of battailes, which no man could affirme, or, if that be denied me, long Orations put in the mouthes of great Kings and Captaines, which it is certaine they neuer pronounced. So that, truely, neyther Phylosopher nor Historiographer coulde at the first haue entred into the gates of populer iudgements, if they had not taken a great pasport of Poetry, which in all Nations at this day, wher learning florisheth not, is plaine to be seene: in all which they haue some feeling of Poetry. In Turky, besides their lawe-giuing Diuines, they haue no other Writers but Poets. In our neighbour Countrey Ireland, where truelie learning goeth very bare, yet are theyr Poets held in a deuoute reuerence. Euen among the most barbarous and simple Indians where no writing is, yet haue they their Poets, who make and sing songs, which they call *Areytos*, both of theyr Auncestors deedes and praises of theyr Gods: a sufficient probabilitie that if euer learning come among them, it must be by hauing theyr hard dull wits softned and sharpened with the sweete delights of Poetrie. For vntill they find a pleasure in the exercises of the minde, great promises of much knowledge will little perswade them that knowe not the fruites of knowledge. In Wales, the true remnant of the auncient Brittons, as there are good authorities to shewe the long time they had Poets, which they called *Bardes*, so thorough all the conquests of Romaines, Saxons, Danes, and Normans, some of whom did seeke to ruine all memory of learning from among them, yet doo their Poets, euen to this day, last; so as it is not more notable in soone beginning then in long continuing. But since the Authors of most of our Sciences were the Romans, and before them the Greekes, let vs a little stand vppon their authorities, but euen so farre as to see what names they haue giuen vnto this now scorned skill.

Among the Romans a Poet was called *Vates*, which is as much as a Diuiner, Fore-seer, or Prophet, as by his conioyned wordes *Vaticinium* and *Vaticinari* is manifest: so heauenly a title did that excellent people bestow vpon this hart-rauishing knowledge. And so farre were they carried into the admiration thereof, that they thought in the chaunceable hitting vppon any such verses great foretokens of their following fortunes were placed. Whereupon grew the worde of *Sortes Virgilianae*, when, by suddaine opening *Virgils* booke, they lighted vpon any verse of hys making: whereof the histories of the Emperors liues are full; as of *Albinus*, the Gouernour of our Iland, who in his childehoode mette with this verse,

Arma amens capio nec sat rationis in armis;

and in his age performed it: which although it were a very vaine and godles superstition, as also it was to think that spirits were commaunded by such verses—whereupon this word charmes, deriued of *Carmina*, commeth—so yet serueth it to shew the great reuerence those wits were helde in. And altogether not without ground, since both the Oracles of *Delphos* and *Sibillas* prophecies were wholy deliuered in verses. For that same exquisite obseruing of number and measure in words, and that high flying liberty of conceit proper to the Poet, did seeme to haue some dyuine force in it.

And may not I presume a little further, to shew the reasonablenes of this worde *Vates*? And say that the holy *Dauids* Psalmes are a diuine Poem? If I doo, I shall not do it without the testimonie of great learned men, both aunciently and moderne: but euen the name

Psalmes will speake for mee, which, being interpreted, is
nothing but songes. Then that it is fully written in meeter,
as all learned Hebricians agree, although the rules be not
yet fully found. Lastly and principally, his handeling his
prophecy, which is meerely poetical. For what els is the
awaking his musicall instruments; the often and free
changing of persons; his notable *Prosopopeias*, when he
maketh you, as it were, see God comming in his Maiestie;
his telling of the Beastes ioyfulnes, and hills leaping, but
a heauenlie poesie, wherein almost hee sheweth himselfe
a passionate louer of that vnspeakable and euerlasting
beautie to be seene by the eyes of the minde, onely
cleered by fayth? But truely nowe hauing named him,
I feare mee I seeme to prophane that holy name, applying
it to Poetrie, which is among vs throwne downe to so
ridiculous an estimation: but they that with quiet iudgements will looke a little deeper into it, shall finde the end
and working of it such, as beeing rightly applyed, deserueth
not to bee scourged out of the Church of God.

But now, let vs see how the Greekes named it, and
howe they deemed of it. The Greekes called him a Poet,
which name hath, as the most excellent, gone thorough
other Languages. It commeth of this word *Poiein*, which
is to make: wherein I know not, whether by lucke or
wisedome, wee Englishmen haue mette with the Greekes
in calling him a maker: which name, how high and
incomparable a title it is, I had rather were knowne by
marking the scope of other Sciences then by my partiall
allegation.

There is no Arte deliuered to mankinde that hath not
the workes of Nature for his principall obiect, without
which they could not consist, and on which they so
depend, as they become Actors and Players, as it were, of
what Nature will haue set foorth. So doth the Astronomer
looke vpon the starres, and, by that he seeth, setteth downe

what order Nature hath taken therein. So doe the
Geometrician and Arithmetician in their diuerse sorts of
quantities. So doth the Musitian in times tel you which
by nature agree, which not. The naturall Philosopher
thereon hath his name, and the Morrall Philosopher
standeth vpon the naturall vertues, vices, and passions of
man; and 'followe Nature' (saith hee) 'therein, and thou
shalt not erre.' The Lawyer sayth what men haue determined. The Historian what men haue done. The
Grammarian speaketh onely of the rules of speech; and
the Rethorician and Logitian, considering what in Nature
will soonest proue and perswade, thereon giue artificial
rules, which still are compassed within the circle of
a question, according to the proposed matter. The
Phisition waigheth the nature of a mans bodie, and the
nature of things helpful or hurtefull vnto it. And the
Metaphisick, though it be in the seconde and abstract
notions, and therefore be counted supernaturall, yet doth
hee indeede builde vpon the depth of Nature. Onely the
Poet, disdayning to be tied to any such subiection, lifted
vp with the vigor of his owne inuention, dooth growe in
effect another nature, in making things either better then
Nature bringeth forth, or, quite a newe, formes such as
neuer were in Nature, as the *Heroes, Demigods, Cyclops,
Chimeras, Furies,* and such like: so as hee goeth hand in
hand with Nature, not inclosed within the narrow warrant
of her guifts, but freely ranging onely within the Zodiack
of his owne wit.

Nature neuer set forth the earth in so rich tapistry
as diuers Poets haue done, neither with plesant riuers,
fruitful trees, sweet smelling flowers, nor whatsoeuer
els may make the too much loued earth more louely.
Her world is brasen, the Poets only deliuer a golden.
But let those things alone and goe to man, for whom
as the other things are, so it seemeth in him her vtter-

most cunning is imployed, and knowe whether shee haue
brought foorth so true a louer as *Theagines*, so constant
a friende as *Pilades*, so valiant a man as *Orlando*, so right
a Prince as *Xenophons Cyrus*, so excellent a man euery
way as *Virgils Aeneas*: neither let this be iestingly conceiued, because the works of the one be essentiall, the
other, in imitation or fiction; for any vnderstanding
knoweth the skil of the Artificer standeth in that *Idea*
or fore-conceite of the work, and not in the work it selfe.
And that the Poet hath that *Idea* is manifest, by deliuering
them forth in such excellencie as hee hath imagined them.
Which deliuering forth also is not wholie imaginatiue,
as we are wont to say by them that build Castles in the
ayre: but so farre substantially it worketh, not onely to
make a *Cyrus*, which had been but a particuler excellencie,
as Nature might haue done, but to bestow a *Cyrus* vpon
the worlde, to make many *Cyrus's*, if they wil learne aright
why and how that Maker made him.

Neyther let it be deemed too sawcie a comparison to
ballance the highest poynt of mans wit with the efficacie
of Nature: but rather giue right honor to the heauenly
Maker of that maker, who, hauing made man to his owne
likenes, set him beyond and ouer all the workes of that
second nature, which in nothing hee sheweth so much
as in Poetrie, when with the force of a diuine breath he
bringeth things forth far surpassing her dooings, with no
small argument to the incredulous of that first accursed
fall of *Adam*: sith our erected wit maketh vs know what
perfection is, and yet our infected will keepeth vs from
reaching vnto it. But these arguments wil by fewe be
vnderstood, and by fewer granted. Thus much (I hope)
will be giuen me, that the Greekes with some probabilitie
of reason gaue him the name aboue all names of learning.

Now let vs goe to a more ordinary opening of him, that
the trueth may be more palpable: and so I hope, though

we get not so vnmatched a praise as the Etimologie of his names wil grant, yet his very description, which no man will denie, shall not iustly be barred from a principall commendation.

(Poesie therefore is an arte of imitation,) for so *Aristotle* termeth it in his word *Mimesis*,)that is to say, a representing, counterfetting, or figuring foorth : to speake metaphorically, a speaking picture : with this end, to teach and delight. Of this haue beene three seuerall kindes.)

(The chiefe both in antiquitie and excellencie were they that did imitate the inconceiuable excellencies of GOD.) Such were *Dauid* in his Psalmes, *Salomon* in his song of Songs, in his Ecclesiastes, and Prouerbs, *Moses* and *Debora* in theyr Hymnes, and the writer of *Iob*; which, beside other, the learned *Emanuell Tremelius* and *Franciscus Iunius* doe entitle the poeticall part of the Scripture. Against these none will speake that hath the holie Ghost in due holy reuerence. In this kinde, though in a full wrong diuinitie, were *Orpheus*, *Amphion*, *Homer* in his hymnes, and many other, both Greekes and Romaines: and this Poesie must be vsed, by whosoeuer will follow S. *Iames* his counsell, in singing Psalmes when they are merry : and I knowe is vsed with the fruite of comfort by some, when, in sorrowfull pangs of their death-bringing sinnes, they find the consolation of the neuer-leauing goodnesse.

(The second kinde is of them that deale with matters Philosophicall ; eyther morrall, as *Tirteus*, *Phocilides*, and *Cato*; or naturall, as *Lucretius* and *Virgils Georgicks*; or Astronomicall, as *Manilius* and *Pontanus*; or historical, as *Lucan* : which who mislike, the faulte is in their iudgements quite out of taste, and not in the sweet foode of sweetly vttered knowledge.

But because thys second sorte is wrapped within the folde of the proposed subiect, and takes not the course of

his owne inuention, whether they properly be Poets or no
let Gramarians dispute: and goe to the thyrd, indeed right
Poets, of whom chiefly this question ariseth; betwixt whom
and these second is such a kinde of difference as betwixt
the meaner sort of Painters (who counterfet onely such
faces as are sette before them) and the more excellent, who,
hauing no law but wit, bestow that in cullours vpon you
which is fittest for the eye to see: as the constant though
lamenting looke of *Lucrecia*, when she punished in her selfe
an others fault; wherein he painteth not *Lucrecia* whom he
neuer sawe, but painteth the outwarde beauty of such a
vertue. For these third be they which most properly do
imitate to teach and delight, and to imitate borrow nothing
of what is, hath been, or shall be: but range, onely rayned
with learned discretion, into the diuine consideration of
what may be, and should be. These bee they that, as the
first and most noble sorte, may iustly bee termed *Vates*,
so these are waited on in the excellen[te]st languages and
best vnderstandings, with the fore described name of Poets:
for these indeede doo meerely make to imitate, and imitate
both to delight and teach, and delight to moue men to
take that goodnes in hande, which without delight they
would flye as from a stranger; and teach, to make them
know that goodnes whereunto they are mooued, which
being the noblest scope to which euer any learning was
directed, yet want there not idle tongues to barke at them.

These be subdiuided into sundry more speciall denomi-
nations. The most notable bee the *Heroick, Lirick, Tragick,
Comick, Satirick, Iambick, Elegiack, Pastorall*, and certaine
others, some of these being termed according to the
matter they deale with, some by the sorts of verses they
liked best to write in, for indeede the greatest part of
Poets have apparelled their poeticall inuentions in that
numbrous kinde of writing which is called verse: indeed
but apparelled, verse being but an ornament and no cause

to Poetry, sith there haue beene many most excellent
Poets that neuer versified, and now swarme many versifiers that neede neuer aunswere to the name of Poets.)
For *Xenophon*, who did imitate so excellently as to giue
vs *effigiem iusti imperii*, the portraiture of a iust Empire
vnder the name of *Cyrus* (as *Cicero* sayth of him), made
therein an absolute heroicall Poem; so did *Heliodorus*
in his sugred inuention of that picture of loue in *Theagines*
and *Cariclea*; and yet both these writ in Prose: which
I speak to shew that it is not riming and versing that
maketh a Poet, no more then a long gowne maketh an
Aduocate, who though he pleaded in armor should be
an Aduocate and no Souldier. But it is that fayning
notable images of vertues, vices, or what els, with that
delightfull teaching, which must be the right describing
note to know a Poet by:) although indeed the Senate of
Poets hath chosen verse as their fittest rayment, meaning, as in matter they passed all in all, so in maner
to goe beyond them: not speaking (table talke fashion
or like men in a dreame) words as they chanceably fall
from the mouth, but peyzing each sillable of each worde
by iust proportion according to the dignitie of the
subiect.

Nowe therefore it shall not bee amisse first to waigh
this latter sort of Poetrie by his works, and then by his
partes; and if in neyther of these Anatomies hee be
condemnable, I hope wee shall obtaine a more fauourable
sentence. This purifing of wit, this enritching of memory,
enabling of iudgment, and enlarging of conceyt, which
commonly we call learning, vnder what name soeuer it
com forth, or to what immediat end soeuer it be directed,
the final end is to lead and draw vs to as high a perfection
as our degenerate soules, made worse by theyr clayey
lodgings, can be capable of. This, according to the inclination of the man, bred many formed impressions. For some

that thought this felicity principally to be gotten by knowledge, and no knowledge to be so high and heauenly
as acquaintance with the starres, gaue themselues to
Astronomie; others, perswading themselues to be *Demi-*
gods if they knewe the causes of things, became naturall
and supernaturall Philosophers; some an admirable delight
drew to Musicke; and some the certainty of demonstration to the Mathematickes: But all, one and other,
hauing this scope—to knowe, and by knowledge to lift vp
the mind from the dungeon of the body to the enioying
his owne diuine essence. But when by the ballance of
experience it was found that the Astronomer looking
to the starres might fall into a ditch, that the enquiring
Philosopher might be blinde in himselfe, and the Mathematician might draw foorth a straight line with a crooked
hart; then loe, did proofe, the ouer ruler of opinions, make
manifest that all these are but seruing Sciences, which as
they haue each a priuate end in themselues, so yet are
they all directed to the highest end of the mistres Knowledge, by the Greekes called *Arkitecktonike*, which stands,
(as I thinke) in the knowledge of a mans selfe, in the
Ethicke and politick consideration, with the end of well
dooing and not of well knowing onely; euen as the
Sadlers next end is to make a good saddle, but his
farther end to serue a nobler facultie, which is horsemanship; so the horsemans to souldiery, and the Souldier not
onely to haue the skill, but to performe the practise of
a Souldier: so that, the ending end of all earthly learning
being vertuous action, those skilles that most serue to
bring forth that haue a most iust title to bee Princes ouer
all the rest. Wherein if wee can shewe the Poets noblenes,
by setting him before his other Competitors, among whom
as principall challengers step forth the morrall Philosophers, whom, me thinketh, I see comming towards mee
with a sullen grauity, as though they could not abide vice

by day light, rudely clothed for to witnes outwardly their
contempt of outward things, with bookes in their hands
agaynst glory, whereto they sette theyr names, sophisti-
cally speaking against subtility, and angry with any man
in whom they see the foule fault of anger: these men
casting larges as they goe of Definitions, Diuisions, and
Distinctions, with a scornefull interogatiue doe soberly
aske whether it bee possible to finde any path so ready
to leade a man to vertue as that which teacheth what
vertue is? and teacheth it not onely by deliuering forth
his very being, his causes, and effects; but also by making
known his enemie vice, which must be destroyed, and his
combersome seruant Passion, which must be maistered;
by shewing the generalities that contayneth it, and the
specialities that are deriued from it; lastly, by playne
setting downe, how it extendeth it selfe out of the limits
of a mans own little world to the gouernment of families,
and maintayning of publique societies.

The Historian scarcely giueth leysure to the Moralist
to say so much, but that he, loden with old Mouse-eaten
records, authorising himselfe (for the most part) vpon other
histories, whose greatest authorities are built vpon the
notable foundation of Heare-say, hauing much a-doe to
accord differing Writers and to pick trueth out of
partiality, better acquainted with a thousande yeeres
a goe then with the present age, and yet better knowing
how this world goeth then how his owne wit runneth,
curious for antiquities and inquisitiue of nouelties, a
wonder to young folkes and a tyrant in table talke,
denieth, in a great chafe, that any man for teaching of
vertue, and vertuous actions, is comparable to him. I am
*Lux vitae, Temporum magistra, Vita memoriae, Nuncia
vetustatis, &c.*

'The Phylosopher' (sayth hee) 'teacheth a disputatiue
vertue, but I doe an actiue: his vertue is excellent in

the dangerlesse Academie of *Plato*, but mine sheweth foorth her honorable face in the battailes of *Marathon*, *Pharsalia*, *Poitiers*, and *Agincourt*. Hee teacheth vertue by certaine abstract considerations, but I onely bid you follow the footing of them that haue gone before you. Olde-aged experience goeth beyond the fine-witted Phylosopher, but I giue the experience of many ages. Lastly, if he make the Song-booke, I put the learners hande to the Lute: and if hee be the guide, I am the light.'

Then woulde hee alledge you innumerable examples, conferring storie by storie, how much the wisest Senatours and Princes haue beene directed by the credite of history, as *Brutus*, *Alphonsus* of *Aragon*, and who not, if need bee? At length the long lyne of theyr disputation maketh a poynt in thys, that the one giueth the precept, and the other the example.

Nowe, whom shall wee finde (sith the question standeth for the highest forme in the Schoole of learning) to bee Moderator? Trulie, as mee seemeth, the Poet; and if not a Moderator, euen the man that ought to carrie the title from them both, and much more from all other seruing Sciences. Therefore compare we the Poet with the Historian, and with the Morrall Phylosopher, and, if hee goe beyond them both, no other humaine skill can match him. For as for the Diuine, with all reuerence it is euer to be excepted, not only for hauing his scope as far beyonde any of these as eternitie exceedeth a moment, but euen for passing each of these in themselues. And for the Lawyer, though *Ius* bee the Daughter of Iustice, and Iustice the chiefe of Vertues, yet because hee seeketh to make men good rather *Formidine poenae* then *Virtutis amore*, or, to say righter, dooth not indeuour to make men good, but that their euill hurt not others, hauing no care, so hee be a good Cittizen, how bad a man he be: Therefore, as our wickednesse maketh him necessarie, and necessitie maketh him honorable, so is hee not in the deepest trueth to stande in rancke with these who all indeuour to take naughtines away, and plant goodnesse euen in the secretest cabinet of our soules. And these foure are all that any way deale in that consideration of mens manners, which beeing the supreme knowledge, they that best breed it deserue the best commendation.

The Philosopher therfore and the Historian are they which would win the gole, the one by precept, the other by example. But both not hauing both, doe both halte. For the Philosopher, setting downe with thorny argument the bare rule, is so hard of vtterance, and so mistie to bee conceiued, that one that hath no other guide but him shall wade in him till hee be olde before he shall finde sufficient cause to bee honest: for his knowledge standeth so vpon the abstract and generall, that happie is that man who may vnderstande him, and more happie that can applye what hee dooth vnderstand. On the other side, the Historian, wanting the precept, is so tyed, not to what shoulde bee but to what is, to the particuler truth of things and not to the general reason of things, that hys example draweth no necessary consequence, and therefore a lesse fruitfull doctrine.

Nowe dooth the peerelesse Poet performe both: for whatsoeuer the Philosopher sayth shoulde be doone, hee giueth a perfect picture of it in some one, by whom hee presupposeth it was doone. So as hee coupleth the generall notion with the particuler example. A perfect picture I say, for hee yeeldeth to the powers of the minde an image of that whereof the Philosopher bestoweth but a woordish description: which dooth neyther strike, pierce, nor possesse the sight of the soule so much as that other dooth.

For as in outward things, to a man that had neuer

seene an Elephant or a Rinoceros, who should tell him
most exquisitely all theyr shapes, cullour, bignesse, and
perticular markes, or of a gorgeous Pallace the Architecture, with declaring the full beauties, might well make
5 the hearer able to repeate, as it were by rote, all hee had
heard, yet should neuer satisfie his inward conceits with
being witnes to it selfe of a true liuely knowledge: but the
same man, as soone as hee might see those beasts well
painted, or the house wel in moddel, should straightwaies
10 grow, without need of any description, to a iudicial comprehending of them: so no doubt the Philosopher with his
learned definition, bee it of vertue, vices, matters of
publick policie or priuat gouernment, replenisheth the
memory with many infallible grounds of wisdom, which,
15 notwithstanding, lye darke before the imaginatiue and
iudging powre, if they bee not illuminated or figured
foorth by the speaking picture of Poesie.

Tullie taketh much paynes, and many times not without
poeticall helpes, to make vs knowe the force loue of our
20 Countrey hath in vs. Let vs but heare old *Anchises*
speaking in the middest of Troyes flames, or see *Vlisses*
in the fulnes of all *Calipso's* delights bewayle his absence
from barraine and beggerly *Ithaca*. Anger, the *Stoicks*
say, was a short madnes: let but *Sophocles* bring you
25 *Aiax* on a stage, killing and whipping Sheepe and Oxen,
thinking them the Army of Greeks, with theyr Chiefe-
taines *Agamemnon* and *Menelaus*, and tell mee if you
haue not a more familiar insight into anger then finding
in the Schoolemen his *Genus* and difference. See whether
30 wisdome and temperance in *Vlisses* and *Diomedes*, valure
in *Achilles*, friendship in *Nisus* and *Eurialus*, euen to an
ignoraunt man carry not an apparent shyning: and, contrarily, the remorse of conscience in *Oedipus*, the soone
repenting pride of *Agamemnon*, the selfe-deuouring crueltie
35 in his Father *Atreus*, the violence of ambition in the two

Theban brothers, the sowre-sweetnes of reuenge in *Medœa*, and, to fall lower, the *Terentian Gnato* and our *Chaucers Pandar* so exprest that we nowe vse their names to signifie their trades: and finally, all vertues, vices, and passions so in their own naturall seates layd to the viewe, that wee seeme not to heare of them, but cleerely to see through them. But euen in the most excellent determination of goodnes, what Philosophers counsell can so redily direct a Prince, as the fayned *Cyrus* in *Xenophon*? or a vertuous man in all fortunes, as *Aeneas* in *Virgill*? or a whole Common-wealth, as the way of Sir *Thomas Moores Eutopia*? I say the way, because where Sir *Thomas Moore* erred, it was the fault of the man and not of the Poet, for that way of patterning a Common-wealth was most absolute, though hee perchaunce hath not so absolutely perfourmed it: for the question is, whether the fayned image of Poesie or the regular instruction of Philosophy hath the more force in teaching: wherein if the Philosophers haue more rightly shewed themselues Philosophers then the Poets haue obtained to the high top of their profession, as in truth,

Mediocribus esse poetis,
Non Di, non homines, non concessere Columnae,

it is, I say againe, not the fault of the Art, but that by fewe men that Arte can bee accomplished.) Certainly, euen our Sauiour Christ could as well haue giuen the morrall common places of vncharitablenes and humblenes as the diuine narration of *Diues* and *Lazarus*; or of disobedience and mercy, as that heauenly discourse of the lost Child and the gratious Father; but that hys through-searching wisdom knewe the estate of *Diues* burning in hell, and of *Lazarus* being in *Abrahams* bosome, would more constantly (as it were) inhabit both the memory and iudgment. Truly, for my selfe, mee

seemes I see before my eyes the lost Childes disdainefull
prodigality, turned to enuie a Swines dinner : which by
the learned Diuines are thought not historicall acts, but
instructing Parables. For conclusion, I say the Philosopher teacheth, but he teacheth obscurely, so as the
learned onely can vnderstande him, that is to say, he
teacheth them that are already taught; but the Poet is
the foode for the tenderest stomacks, the Poet is indeed
the right Popular Philosopher, whereof *Esops* tales giue
good proofe: whose pretty Allegories, stealing vnder the
formall tales of Beastes, make many, more beastly then
Beasts, begin to heare the sound of vertue from these
dumbe speakers.

But now may it be alledged that if this imagining of
matters be so fitte for the imagination, then must the
Historian needs surpasse, who bringeth you images of
true matters, such as indeede were doone, and not such
as fantastically or falsely may be suggested to haue been
doone. Truely, *Aristotle* himselfe, in his discourse of
Poesie, plainely determineth this question, saying that
Poetry is *Philosophoteron* and *Spoudaioteron*, that is to
say, it is more Philosophicall and more studiously
serious then history. His reason is, because Poesie
dealeth with *Katholou*, that is to say, with the vniuersall
consideration; and the history with *Kathekaston*, the perticuler: 'nowe,' sayth he, 'the vniuersall wayes what is fit
to bee sayd or done, eyther in likelihood or necessity,
(which the Poesie considereth in his imposed names), and
the perticuler onely marks whether *Alcibiades* did, or
suffered, this or that.' Thus farre *Aristotle*: which reason
of his (as all his) is most full of reason. For indeed, if
the question were whether it were better to haue a perticular acte truly or falsly set down, there is no doubt
which is to be chosen, no more then whether you had
rather haue *Vespasians* picture right as hee was, or at

the Painters pleasure nothing resembling. But if the
question be for your owne vse and learning, whether it
be better to haue it set downe as it should be, or as it
was, then certainely is more doctrinable the fained *Cirus*
in *Xenophon* then the true *Cyrus* in *Iustine*, and the
fayned *Aeneas* in *Virgil* then the right *Aeneas* in *Dares
Phrigius*. As to a Lady that desired to fashion her
countenance to the best grace, a Painter should more
benefite her to portraite a most sweet face, wryting
Canidia vpon it, then to paynt *Canidia* as she was, who,
Horace sweareth, was foule and ill fauoured.

If the Poet doe his part a-right, he will shew you in
Tantalus, *Atreus*, and such like, nothing that is not to
be shunned; in *Cyrus*, *Aeneas*, *Vlisses*, each thing to
be followed; where the Historian, bound to tell things
as things were, cannot be liberall (without hee will be
poeticall) of a perfect patterne, but, as in *Alexander* or
Scipio himselfe, shew dooings, some to be liked, some
to be misliked. And then how will you discerne what
to followe but by your owne discretion, which you had
without reading *Quintus Curtius*? And whereas a man
may say, though in vniuersall consideration of doctrine
the Poet preuaileth, yet that the historie, in his saying
such a thing was doone, doth warrant a man more in that
hee shall follow, the aunswere is manifest, that if hee
stande vpon that was—as if hee should argue, because it
rayned yesterday, therefore it shoulde rayne to day—then
indeede it hath some aduantage to a grose conceite; but
if he know an example onlie informes a coniectured likelihood, and so goe by reason, the Poet dooth so farre
exceede him, as hee is to frame his example to that which
is most reasonable, be it in warlike, politick, or priuate
matters, where the Historian in his bare *Was* hath
many times that which wee call fortune to ouer-rule
the best wisedome. Manie times he must tell euents

whereof he can yeelde no cause: or, if hee doe, it must
be poeticall.

For that a fayned example hath asmuch force to teach
as a true example (for as for to mooue, it is cleere, sith
the fayned may bee tuned to the highest key of passion),
let vs take one example wherein a Poet and a Historian
doe concur. *Herodotus* and *Iustine* do both testifie that
Zopirus, King *Darius* faithfull seruaunt, seeing his Maister
long resisted by the rebellious *Babilonians*, fayned himselfe in extreame disgrace of his King: for verifying of
which, he caused his own nose and eares to be cut off:
and so flying to the *Babylonians*, was receiued, and for
his knowne valour so far credited, that hee did finde
meanes to deliuer them ouer to *Darius*. Much like
matter doth *Liuie* record of *Tarquinius* and his sonne.
Xenophon excellently faineth such another stratageme,
performed by *Abradates* in *Cyrus* behalfe. Now would
I fayne know, if occasion bee presented vnto you to
serue your Prince by such an honest dissimulation, why
you doe not as well learne it of *Xenophons* fiction as
of the others verity: and truely so much the better, as
you shall saue your nose by the bargaine; for *Abradates*
did not counterfet so far. (So then the best of the Historian is subiect to the Poet; for whatsoeuer action, or
faction, whatsoeuer counsell, pollicy, or warre stratagem
the Historian is bound to recite, that may the Poet (if
he list) with his imitation make his own; beautifying it
both for further teaching, and more delighting, as it
pleaseth him ; hauing all, from *Dante* his heauen to hys
hell, vnder the authoritie of his penne.) Which if I be
asked what Poets haue done so, as I might well name
some, yet say I, and say againe, I speak of the Arte, and
not of the Artificer.

Nowe, to that which commonly is attributed to the prayse
of histories, in respect of the notable learning is gotten by

marking the successe, as though therein a man should see
vertue exalted and vice punished. Truely that commendation is peculiar to Poetrie, and farre of from History. For
indeede Poetrie euer setteth vertue so out in her best
cullours, making Fortune her wel-wayting hand-mayd, that
one must needs be enamored of her. Well may you see
Vlisses in a storme, and in other hard plights; but they
are but exercises of patience and magnanimitie, to make
them shine the more in the neere-following prosperitie.
And of the contrarie part, if euill men come to the stage,
they euer goe out (as the Tragedie Writer answered to
one that misliked the shew of such persons) so manacled
as they little animate folkes to followe them. But the
Historian, beeing captiued to the trueth of a foolish world,
is many times a terror from well dooing, and an incouragement to vnbrideled wickednes.

For see wee not valiant *Milciades* rot in his fetters?
The iust *Phocion* and the accomplished *Socrates* put to
death like Traytors? The cruell *Seuerus* liue prosperously?
The excellent *Seuerus* miserably murthered? *Sylla* and
Marius dying in theyr beddes? *Pompey* and *Cicero* slaine
then when they would haue thought exile a happinesse?
See wee not vertuous *Cato* driuen to kyll himselfe? and
rebell *Cæsar* so aduaunced that his name yet, after 1600
yeares, lasteth in the highest honor? And marke but euen
Cæsars own words of the fore-named *Sylla* (who in that
onely did honestly, to put downe his dishonest tyrannie),
Literas nesciuit, as if want of learning caused him to doe
well. Hee meant it not by Poetrie, which, not content
with earthly plagues, deuiseth new punishments in hel for
Tyrants: nor yet by Philosophie, which teacheth *Occi-
dendos esse*; but no doubt by skill in Historie, for that
indeede can affoord your *Cipselus*, *Periander*, *Phalaris*,
Dionisius, and I know not how many more of the same
kennell, that speede well enough in theyr abhominable

vniustice or vsurpation. I conclude, therefore, that hee excelleth Historie, not onely in furnishing the minde with knowledge, but in setting it forward to that which deserueth to be called and accounted good : which setting forward, and moouing to well dooing, indeed setteth the Lawrell crowne vpon the Poet as victorious, not onely of the Historian, but ouer the Phylosopher, howsoeuer in teaching it may bee questionable.

For suppose it be granted (that which I suppose with great reason may be denied) that the Philosopher, in respect of his methodical proceeding, doth teach more perfectly then the Poet, yet do I thinke that no man is so much *Philophilosophos* as to compare the Philosopher, in moouing, with the Poet.

And that moouing is of a higher degree then teaching, it may by this appeare, that it is wel nigh the cause and the effect of teaching. For who will be taught, if hee bee not mooued with desire to be taught? and what so much good doth that teaching bring forth (I speak still of morrall doctrine) as that it mooueth one to doe that which it dooth teach? for, as *Aristotle* sayth, it is not *Gnosis* but *Praxis* must be the fruit. And howe *Praxis* cannot be, without being mooued to practise, it is no hard matter to consider.

The Philosopher sheweth you the way, hee informeth you of the particularities, as well of the tediousnes of the way, as of the pleasant lodging you shall haue when your iourney is ended, as of the many by-turnings that may diuert you from your way. But this is to no man but to him that will read him, and read him with attentiue studious painfulnes. Which constant desire, whosoeuer hath in him, hath already past halfe the hardnes of the way, and therefore is beholding to the Philosopher but for the other halfe. Nay truely, learned men haue learnedly thought that, where once reason hath so much ouer-mastred passion

as that the minde hath a free desire to doe well, the inward
light each minde hath in it selfe is as good as a Philosophers booke; seeing in nature we know it is wel to doe
well, and what is well and what is euill, although not in
the words of Arte which Philosophers bestowe vpon vs.
For out of naturall conceit the Philosophers drew it; but
to be moued to doe that which we know, or to be mooued
with desire to knowe, *Hoc opus, hic labor est.*

Nowe therein of all Sciences (I speak still of humane,
and according to the humaine conceits) is our Poet the
Monarch. For he dooth not only show the way, but
giueth so sweete a prospect into the way, as will intice
any man to enter into it. Nay, he dooth, as if your
journey should lye through a fayre Vineyard, at the first
giue you a cluster of Grapes, that, full of that taste, you
may long to passe further. He beginneth not with obscure
definitions, which must blur the margent with interpretations, and load the memory with doubtfulnesse; but hee
commeth to you with words sent in delightfull proportion, either accompanied with, or prepared for, the well
inchaunting skill of Musicke; and with a tale forsooth he
commeth vnto you, with a tale which holdeth children
from play, and old men from the chimney corner. And,
pretending no more, doth intende the winning of the mind
from wickednesse to vertue: euen as the childe is often
brought to take most wholsom things by hiding them in
such other as haue a pleasant tast: which, if one should
beginne to tell them the nature of *Aloes* or *Rubarb* they
shoulde receiue, woulde sooner take their Phisicke at their
eares then at their mouth. So is it in men (most of which
are childish in the best things, till they bee cradled in their
graues): glad they will be to heare the tales of *Hercules*,
Achilles, *Cyrus*, and *Aeneas*; and, hearing them, must needs
heare the right description of wisdom, valure, and iustice;
which, if they had been barely, that is to say Philo-

sophically, set out, they would sweare they bee brought to schoole againe.

That imitation, wherof Poetry is, hath the most conueniency to Nature of all other, in somuch that, as *Aristotle* sayth, those things which in themselues are horrible, as cruell battailes, vnnaturall Monsters, are made in poeticall imitation delightfull. Truely, I haue knowen men, that euen with reading *Amadis de Gaule* (which God knoweth wanteth much of a perfect Poesie) haue found their harts mooued to the exercise of courtesie, liberalitie, and especially courage. Who readeth *Aeneas* carrying olde *Anchises* on his back, that wisheth not it were his fortune to perfourme so excellent an acte? Whom doe not the words of *Turnus* mooue? (the tale of *Turnus* hauing planted his image in the imagination)

> *Fugientem haec terra videbit?*
> *Vsque adeone mori miserum est?*

Where the Philosophers, as they scorne to delight, so must they bee content little to mooue, sauing wrangling whether Vertue bee the chiefe or the onely good, whether the contemplatiue or the actiue life doe excell: which *Plato* and *Boetius* well knew, and therefore made Mistres Philosophy very often borrow the masking rayment of Poesie. For euen those harde harted euill men who thinke vertue a schoole name, and knowe no other good but *indulgere genio*, and therefore despise the austere admonitions of the Philosopher, and feele not the inward reason they stand vpon, yet will be content to be delighted, which is al the good felow Poet seemeth to promise; and so steale to see the forme of goodnes (which seene they cannot but loue) ere themselues be aware, as if they tooke a medicine of Cherries. Infinite proofes of the strange effects of this poeticall inuention might be alledged; onely two shall serue, which are so often remembred, as I thinke all men knowe them.

The one of *Menenius Agrippa*, who, when the whole people of Rome had resolutely deuided themselues from the Senate, with apparant shew of vtter ruine, though hee were (for that time) an excellent Oratour, came not among them vpon trust of figuratiue speeches or cunning insinuations; and much lesse with farre fet *Maximes* of Phylosophie, which (especially if they were *Platonick*) they must haue learned Geometrie before they could well haue conceiued; but forsooth he behaues himselfe like a homely and familiar Poet. Hee telleth them a tale, that there was a time when all the parts of the body made a mutinous conspiracie against the belly, which they thought deuoured the fruits of each others labour: they concluded they would let so vnprofitable a spender starue. In the end, to be short, (for the tale is notorious, and as notorious that it was a tale) with punishing the belly they plagued themselues. This applied by him wrought such effect in the people, as I neuer read that euer words brought forth but then so suddaine and so good an alteration; for vpon reasonable conditions a perfect reconcilement ensued. The other is of *Nathan* the Prophet, who when the holie *Dauid* had so far forsaken God as to confirme adulterie with murther, when hee was to doe the tenderest office of a friende, in laying his owne shame before his eyes, sent by God to call againe so chosen a seruant, how doth he it but by telling of a man whose beloued Lambe was vngratefullie taken from his bosome? the applycation most diuinely true, but the discourse it selfe fayned; which made *Dauid* (I speake of the second and instrumentall cause) as in a glasse to see his own filthines, as that heauenly Psalme of mercie wel testifieth.

By these, therefore, examples and reasons, I think it may be manifest that the Poet, with that same hand of

An Apology for Poetry

delight, doth draw the mind more effectually then any other Arte dooth: and so a conclusion not vnfitlie ensueth, that as vertue is the most excellent resting place for all worldlie learning to make his end of, so Poetrie, beeing the most familiar to teach it, and most princelie to moue towards it, in the most excellent work is the most excellent workman. But I am content not onely to decipher him by his workes (although works in commendation or dispraise must euer holde an high authority), but more narrowly will examine his parts: so that (as in a man) though al together may carry a presence ful of maiestie and beautie, perchance in some one defectious peece we may find a blemish. Now in his parts, kindes, or *Species* (as you list to terme them), it is to be noted that some Poesies haue coupled together two or three kindes, as Tragicall and Comicall, wher-vpon is risen the Tragi-comicall. Some in the like manner haue mingled Prose and Verse, as *Sanazzar* and *Boetius*. Some haue mingled matters Heroicall and Pastorall. But that commeth all to one in this question, for, if seuered they be good, the coniunction cannot be hurtfull. Therefore perchaunce forgetting some, and leauing some as needlesse to be remembred, it shall not be amisse in a worde to cite the speciall kindes, to see what faults may be found in the right vse of them.

Is it then the Pastorall Poem which is misliked? (for perchance, where the hedge is lowest they will soonest leape ouer). Is the poore pype disdained, which sometime out of *Melibeus* mouth can shewe the miserie of people vnder hard Lords or rauening Souldiours? and again, by *Titirus*, what blessednes is deriued to them that lye lowest from the goodnesse of them that sit highest? sometimes, vnder the prettie tales of Wolues and Sheepe, can include the whole considerations of wrong dooing and patience; sometimes shew that contention for trifles can get but a trifling victorie. Where perchaunce a man may see that euen *Alexander* and *Darius*, when they straue who should be Cocke of thys worlds dunghill, the benefit they got was that the after-liuers may say,

> *Haec memini et victum frustra contendere Thirsin:*
> *Ex illo Coridon, Coridon est tempore nobis.*

Or is it the lamenting Elegiack, which in a kinde hart would mooue rather pitty then blame, who bewailes with the great Philosopher *Heraclitus* the weakenes of mankind and the wretchednes of the world: who surely is to be praysed, either for compassionate accompanying iust causes of lamentation, or for rightly paynting out how weake be the passions of wofulnesse? Is it the bitter but wholsome Iambick, which rubs the galled minde, in making shame the trumpet of villanie with bolde and open crying out against naughtines?. Or the Satirick, who

> *Omne vafer vitium ridenti tangit amico?*

who sportingly neuer leaueth vntil hee make a man laugh at folly, and, at length ashamed, to laugh at himselfe; which he cannot auoyd, without auoyding the follie; who, while

> *circum praecordia ludit,*

giueth vs to feele how many head-aches a passionate life bringeth vs to—how, when all is done,

> *Est Vlubris, animus si nos non deficit aequus?*

No, perchance it is the Comick, whom naughtie Playmakers and Stage-keepers haue iustly made odious. To the argument of abuse I will answer after. Onely thus much now is to be said, that the Comedy is an imitation of the common errors of our life, which he representeth in the most ridiculous and scornefull sort that may be;

so as it is impossible that any beholder can be content to be such a one.

Now, as in Geometry the oblique must bee knowne as wel as the right, and in Arithmetick the odde as well as the euen, so in the actions of our life who seeth not the filthines of euil wanteth a great foile to perceiue the beauty of vertue. This doth the Comedy handle so in our priuate and domestical matters, as with hearing it we get as it were an experience, what is to be looked for of a nigardly *Demea*, of a crafty *Dauus*, of a flattering *Gnato*, of a vaine glorious *Thraso*, and not onely to know what effects are to be expected, but to know who be such, by the signifying badge giuen them by the Comedian. And little reason hath any man to say that men learne euill by seeing it so set out: sith, as I sayd before, there is no man liuing but, by the force trueth hath in nature, no sooner seeth these men play their parts, but wisheth them in *Pistrinum*: although perchance the sack of his owne faults lye so behinde hys back that he seeth not himselfe daunce the same measure; whereto yet nothing can more open his eyes then to finde his own actions contemptibly set forth. So that the right vse of Comedy will (I thinke) by no body be blamed, and much lesse of the high and excellent Tragedy, that openeth the greatest wounds, and sheweth forth the Vlcers that are couered with Tissue; that maketh Kinges feare to be Tyrants, and Tyrants manifest their tirannicall humors; that, with sturring the affects of admiration and commiseration, teacheth the vncertainety of this world, and vpon how weake foundations guilden roofes are builded; that maketh vs knowe,

> *Qui sceptra saeuus duro imperio regit,*
> *Timet timentes, metus in auctorem redit.*

But how much it can mooue, *Plutarch* yeeldeth a notable

testimonie of the abhominable Tyrant *Alexander Pheraeus*; from whose eyes a Tragedy, wel made and represented, drewe aboundance of teares, who, without all pitty, had murthered infinite nombers, and some of his owne blood. So as he, that was not ashamed to make matters for Tragedies, yet coulde not resist the sweet violence of a Tragedie. And if it wrought no further good in him, it was that he, in despight of himselfe, withdrewe himselfe from harkening to that which might mollifie his hardened heart.

But it is not the Tragedy they doe mislike: For it were too absurd to cast out so excellent a representation of whatsoeuer is most worthy to be learned. Is it the Liricke that most displeaseth, who with his tuned Lyre, and wel accorded voyce, giueth praise, the reward of vertue, to vertuous acts? who giues morrall precepts, and naturall Problemes, who sometimes rayseth vp his voice to the height of the heauens, in singing the laudes of the immortall God. Certainly I must confesse my own barbarousnes: I neuer heard the olde song of *Percy* and *Duglas* that I found not my heart mooued more then with a Trumpet; and yet is it sung but by some blinde Crouder, with no rougher voyce then rude stile; which being so euill apparrelled in the dust and cobwebbes of that vnciuill age, what would it worke trymmed in the gorgeous eloquence of *Pindar*? In *Hungary* I haue seene it the manner at all Feasts, and other such meetings, to haue songes of their Auncestours valour; which that right Souldier-like Nation thinck the chiefest kindlers of braue courage. The incomparable *Lacedemonians* did not only carry that kinde of Musicke euer with them to the field, but euen at home, as such songs were made, so were they all content to bee the singers of them, when the lusty men were to tell what they dyd, the olde men what they had done, and the young men what they wold doe. And where a man may

say that *Pindar* many times prayseth highly victories of
small moment, matters rather of sport then vertue; as it
may be aunswered, it was the fault of the Poet, and not
of the Poetry; so indeede the chiefe fault was in the
tyme and custome of the Greekes, who set those toyes
at so high a price that *Phillip* of *Macedon* reckoned a
horse-race wonne at *Olimpus* among hys three fearefull
felicities. But as the vnimitable *Pindar* often did, so
is that kinde most capable and most fit to awake the
thoughts from the sleep of idlenes, to imbrace honorable
enterprises.

There rests the Heroicall, whose very name (I thinke)
should daunt all back-biters; for by what conceit can a
tongue be directed to speake euill of that which draweth
with it no lesse Champions then *Achilles, Cyrus, Aeneas,
Turnus, Tideus,* and *Rinaldo*? who doth not onely teach
and moue to a truth, but teacheth and mooueth to the
most high and excellent truth; who maketh magna-
nimity and iustice shine throughout all misty fearefulnes
and foggy desires; who, if the saying of *Plato* and
Tullie bee true, that who could see Vertue would be
wonderfully rauished with the loue of her beauty: this
man sets her out to make her more louely in her holyday
apparell, to the eye of any that will daine not to disdaine
vntill they vnderstand. But if any thing be already sayd
in the defence of sweete Poetry, all concurreth to the
maintaining (the Heroicall, which is not onely a kinde,
but the best and most accomplished kinde of Poetry.)
For as the image of each action styrreth and instructeth
the mind, so the loftie image of such Worthies most
inflameth the mind with desire to be worthy, and informes
with counsel how to be worthy. Only let *Aeneas* be
worne in the tablet of your memory; how he gouerneth
himselfe in the ruine of his Country; in the preseruing
his old Father, and carrying away his religious cere-

monies; in obeying the Gods commandement to leaue
Dido, though not onely all passionate kindenes, but euen
the humane consideration of vertuous gratefulnes, would
haue craued other of him; how in storms, howe in
sports, howe in warre, howe in peace, how a fugitiue,
how victorious, how besiedged, how besiedging, howe to
strangers, howe to allyes, how to enemies, howe to his
owne; lastly, how in his inward selfe, and how in his
outward gouernment; and I thinke, in a minde not
preiudiced with a preiudicating humor, hee will be found
in excellencie fruitefull, yea, euen as *Horace* sayth,

Melius Chrisippo et Crantore.

But truely I imagine it falleth out with these Poet-
whyppers, as with some good women, who often are sicke,
but in fayth they cannot tel where. So the name of
Poetrie is odious to them, but neither his cause nor
effects, neither the sum that contains him nor the particularities descending from him, giue any fast handle to their
carping disprayse.

Sith then Poetrie is of all humane learning the most
aunciant and of most fatherly antiquitie, as from whence
other learnings haue taken theyr beginnings; sith it is
so vniuersall that no learned Nation dooth despise it,
nor no barbarous Nation is without it; sith both Roman
and Greek gaue diuine names vnto it, the one of pro-
phecying, the other of making; and that indeede that
name of making is fit for him, considering that where
as other Arts retaine themselues within their subiect, and
receiue, as it were, their beeing from it, the Poet onely
bringeth his owne stuffe, and dooth not learne a conceite
out of a matter, but maketh matter for a conceite; Sith
neither his description nor his ende contayneth any euill,
the thing described cannot be euill; Sith his effects be so
good as to teach goodnes and to delight the learners;

An Apology for Poetry

Sith therein (namely in morrall doctrine, the chiefe of all knowledges) hee dooth not onely farre passe the Historian, but, for instructing, is well nigh comparable to the Philosopher, and, for mouing, leaues him behind him; Sith the holy scripture (wherein there is no vncleannes) hath whole parts in it poeticall, and that euen our Sauiour Christ vouchsafed to vse the flowers of it; Sith all his kindes are not onlie in their vnited formes but in their seuered dissections fully commendable: I think (and think I thinke rightly) the Lawrell crowne appointed for tryumphing Captaines doth worthilie (of al other learnings) honor the Poets tryumph. But because wee haue eares aswell as tongues, and that the lightest reasons that may be will seeme to weigh greatly, if nothing be put in the counter-ballance, let vs heare, and aswell as wee can ponder, what obiections may bee made against this Arte, which may be worthy eyther of yeelding or answering.

First, truely I note not onely in these *Mysomousoi*, Poet-haters, but in all that kinde of people who seek a prayse by dispraysing others, that they doe prodigally spend a great many wandering wordes in quips and scoffes, carping and taunting at each thing, which, by styrring the Spleene, may stay the braine from a through beholding the worthines of the subiect.

Those kinde of obiections, as they are full of very idle easines, sith there is nothing of so sacred a maiestie but that an itching tongue may rubbe it selfe vpon it, so deserue they no other answer, but, in steed of laughing at the iest, to laugh at the iester. Wee know a playing wit can prayse the discretion of an Asse, the comfortablenes of being in debt, and the iolly commoditie of beeing sick of the plague. So of the contrary side, if we will turne *Ouids* verse,

Vt lateat virtus proximitate mali,

that good lye hid in neerenesse of the euill, *Agrippa* will be as merry in shewing the vanitie of Science as *Erasmus* was in commending of follie. Neyther shall any man or matter escape some touch of these smyling raylers. But for *Erasmus* and *Agrippa*, they had another foundation then the superficiall part would promise. Mary, these other pleasant Fault-finders, who wil correct the Verbe before they vnderstande the Noune, and confute others knowledge before they confirme theyr owne, I would haue them onely remember that scoffing commeth not of wisedom. So as the best title in true English they gette with their merriments is to be called good fooles, for so haue our graue Fore-fathers euer termed that humorous kinde of iesters. But that which gyueth greatest scope to their scorning humors is ryming and versing. It is already sayde (and, as I think, trulie sayde) it is not ryming and versing that maketh Poesie. One may bee a Poet without versing, and a versifyer without Poetry. But yet presuppose it were inseparable (as indeede it seemeth *Scaliger* iudgeth) truelie it were an inseparable commendation. For if *Oratio* next to *Ratio*, Speech next to Reason, bee the greatest gyft bestowed vpon mortalitie, that can not be praiselesse which dooth most pollish that blessing of speech, which considers each word, not only (as a man may say) by his forcible qualitie but by his best measured quantitie, carrying euen in themselues a Harmonie (without, perchaunce, Number, Measure, Order, Proportion be in our time growne odious). But lay a side the iust prayse it hath, by beeing the onely fit speech for Musick (Musick I say, the most diuine striker of the sences), thus much is vndoubtedly true, that if reading bee foolish without remembring, memorie being the onely treasurer of knowled[g]e, those words which are fittest for memory are likewise most conuenient for knowledge.

Now, that Verse farre exceedeth Prose in the knitting

vp of the memory, the reason is manifest; the words (besides theyr delight, which hath a great affinitie to memory) beeing so set as one word cannot be lost but the whole worke failes: which accuseth it selfe, calleth the remembrance backe to it selfe, and so most strongly confirmeth it; besides, one word so, as it were, begetting another, as, be it in ryme or measured verse, by the former a man shall haue a neere gesse to the follower: lastly, euen they that haue taught the Art of memory haue shewed nothing so apt for it as a certaine roome deuided into many places well and throughly knowne. Now, that hath the verse in effect perfectly, euery word hauing his naturall seate, which seate must needes make the words remembred. But what needeth more in a thing so knowne to all men? who is it that euer was a scholler that doth not carry away some verses of *Virgill*, *Horace*, or *Cato*, which in his youth he learned, and euen to his old age serue him for howrely lessons? But the fitnes it hath for memory is notably proued by all deliuery of Arts: wherein for the most part, from Grammer to Logick, Mathematick, Phisick, and the rest, the rules chiefely necessary to bee borne away are compiled in verses. So that, verse being in it selfe sweete and orderly, and beeing best for memory, the onely handle of knowledge, it must be in iest that any man can speake against it.

Nowe then goe wee to the most important imputations laid to the poore Poets: for ought I can yet learne, they are these. First, that there beeing many other more fruitefull knowledges, a man might better spend his tyme in them then in this. Secondly, that it is the mother of lyes. Thirdly, that it is the Nurse of abuse, infecting vs with many pestilent desires; with a Syrens sweetnes, drawing the mind to the Serpents tayle of sinfull fancy. And heerein, especially, Comedies giue the largest field to erre, as *Chaucer* sayth: howe both in other Nations and in ours, before Poets did soften vs, we were full of courage, giuen to martiall exercises, the pillers of manlyke liberty, and not lulled a sleepe in shady idlenes with Poets pastimes. And lastly, and chiefely, they cry out with an open mouth, as if they out shot *Robin Hood*, that *Plato* banished them out of hys Common-wealth. Truely, this is much, if there be much truth in it. First to the first: that a man might better spend his tyme is a reason indeede: but it doth (as they say) but *Petere principium*: for if it be, as I affirme, that no learning is so good as that which teacheth and mooueth to vertue, and that none can both teach and moue thereto so much as Poetry, then is the conclusion manifest that Incke and Paper cannot be to a more profitable purpose employed. And certainly, though a man should graunt their first assumption, it should followe (me thinkes) very vnwillingly, that good is not good because better is better. But I still and vtterly denye that there is sprong out of earth a more fruitefull knowledge. To the second therefore, that they should be the principall lyars, I aunswere paradoxically, but, truely, I thinke truely, that of all Writers vnder the sunne the Poet is the least lier, and, though he would, as a Poet can scarcely be a lyer. The Astronomer, with his cosen the Geometrician, can hardly escape, when they take vpon them to measure the height of the starres. How often, thinke you, doe the Phisitians lye, when they auer things good for sicknesses, which afterwards send *Charon* a great number of soules drownd in a potion before they come to his Ferry? And no lesse of the rest, which take vpon them to affirme. Now, for the Poet, he nothing affirmes, and therefore neuer lyeth. For, as I take it, to lye is to affirme that to be true which is false. So as the other Artists, and especially the Historian, affirming many things, can, in the cloudy knowledge of mankinde, hardly escape from many lyes.

But the Poet (as I sayd before) neuer affirmeth. The
Poet neuer maketh any circles about your imagination,
to coniure you to beleeue for true what he writes. Hee
citeth not authorities of other Histories, but euen for hys
entry calleth the sweete Muses to inspire into him a good
inuention; in troth, not labouring to tell you what is, or is
not, but what should or should not be: and therefore,
though he recount things not true, yet because hee telleth
them not for true, he lyeth not, without we will say that
Nathan lyed in his speech, before alledged, to *Dauid*.
Which as a wicked man durst scarce say, so think I
none so simple would say that *Esope* lyed in the tales of
his beasts: for who thinks that *Esope* writ it for actually
true were well worthy to haue his name cronicled
among the beastes hee writeth of. What childe is there
that, comming to a Play, and seeing *Thebes* written in
great Letters vpon an olde doore, doth beleeue that it
is *Thebes*? If then a man can ariue, at that childs age,
to know that the Poets persons and dooings are but
pictures what should be, and not stories what haue
beene, they will neuer giue the lye to things not affirma-
tiuely but allegorically and figuratiuelie written. And
therefore, as in Historie, looking for trueth, they goe
away full fraught with falshood, so in Poesie, looking for
fiction, they shal vse the narration but as an imaginatiue
groundplot of a profitable inuention.

But heereto is replyed, that the Poets gyue names to
men they write of, which argueth a conceite of an actuall
truth, and so, not being true, prooues a falshood. And
doth the Lawyer lye then, when vnder the names of *Iohn
a stile* and *Iohn a noakes* hee puts his case? But that is
easily answered. Theyr naming of men is but to make
theyr picture the more liuely, and not to builde any
historie; paynting men, they cannot leaue men namelesse.
We see we cannot play at Chesse but that wee must giue

names to our Chesse-men; and yet, mee thinks, hee were a very partiall Champion of truth that would say we lyed for giuing a peece of wood the reuerend title of a Bishop. The Poet nameth *Cyrus* or *Aeneas* no other way then to shewe what men of theyr fames, fortunes, and estates should doe.

Their third is, how much it abuseth mens wit, trayning it to wanton sinfulnes and lustfull loue: for indeed that is the principall, if not the onely abuse I can heare alledged. They say the Comedies rather teach then reprehend amorous conceits. They say the Lirick is larded with passionate Sonnets: The Elegiack weepes the want of his mistresse: And that euen to the Heroical *Cupid* hath ambitiously climed. Alas, Loue, I would thou couldest, as well defende thy selfe as thou canst offende others. I would those, on whom thou doost attend, could eyther put thee away, or yeelde good reason why they keepe thee. But grant loue of beautie to be a beastlie fault (although it be very hard, sith onely man, and no beast, hath that gyft to discerne beauty). Grant that louely name of Loue to deserue all hatefull reproches (although euen some of my Maisters the Phylosophers spent a good deale of theyr Lamp-oyle in setting foorth the excellencie of it). Grant, I say, what soeuer they wil haue granted; that not onely loue, but lust, but vanitie, but (if they list) scurrilitie, possesseth many leaues of the Poets bookes: yet thinke I, when this is granted, they will finde theyr sentence may with good manners put the last words foremost, and not say that Poetrie abuseth mans wit, but that mans wit abuseth Poetrie.

For I will not denie but that mans wit may make Poesie (which should be *Eikastike*, which some learned haue defined, figuring foorth good things) to be *Phantastike*: which doth, contrariwise, infect the fancie with vnworthy obiects. As the Painter, that shoulde giue to the eye eyther some excellent perspectiue, or some fine picture, fit for building or fortification, or contayning in it some notable example, as *Abraham* sacrificing his Sonne *Isaack*, *Iudith* killing *Holofernes*, *Dauid* fighting with *Goliah*, may leaue those, and please an ill-pleased eye with wanton shewes of better hidden matters. But what, shall the abuse of a thing make the right vse odious? Nay truely, though I yeeld that Poesie may not onely be abused, but that beeing abused, by the reason of his sweete charming force, it can doe more hurt then any other Armie of words, yet shall it be so far from concluding that the abuse should giue reproch to the abused, that contrariwise it is a good reason, that whatsoeuer, being abused dooth most harme, beeing rightly vsed (and vpon the right vse each thing conceiueth his title), doth most good.

Doe wee not see the skill of Phisick (the best rampire to our often-assaulted bodies) beeing abused, teach poyson, the most violent destroyer? Dooth not knowledge of Law, whose end is to euen and right all things being abused, grow the crooked fosterer of horrible iniuries? Doth not (to goe to the highest) Gods word abused breed heresie? and his Name abused become blasphemie? Truely, a needle cannot doe much hurt, and as truely (with leaue of Ladies be it spoken) it cannot doe much good. With a sword thou maist kill thy Father, and with a sword thou maist defende thy Prince and Country. So that, as in their calling Poets the Fathers of lyes they say nothing, so in this theyr argument of abuse they prooue the commendation.

They alledge heere-with, that before Poets beganne to be in price our Nation hath set their harts delight vpon action, and not vpon imagination: rather doing things worthy to bee written, then writing things fitte to be done. What that before tyme was, I thinke scarcely *Sphinx* can tell: Sith no memory is so auncient that hath the precedence of Poetrie. And certaine it is that, in our plainest homelines, yet neuer was the *Albion* Nation without Poetrie. Mary, thys argument, though it bee leaueld against Poetrie, yet is it indeed a chaine-shot against all learning, or bookishnes, as they commonly tearme it. Of such minde were certaine *Gothes*, of whom it is written that, hauing in the spoile of a famous Citie taken a fayre librarie, one hangman (bee like fitte to execute the fruites of their wits), who had murthered a great number of bodies, would haue set fire on it: 'no,' sayde another very grauely, 'take heede what you doe, for whyle they are busie about these toyes, wee shall with more leysure conquer their Countries.'

This indeede is the ordinary doctrine of ignorance, and many wordes sometymes I haue heard spent in it: but because this reason is generally against all learning, aswell as Poetrie, or rather, all learning but Poetry; because it were too large a digression to handle, or at least to superfluous (sith it is manifest that all gouernment of action is to be gotten by knowledg, and knowledge best by gathering many knowledges, which is reading), I onely, with *Horace*, to him that is of that opinion,

Iubeo stultum esse libenter:

for as for Poetrie it selfe, it is the freest from thys obiection. For Poetrie is the companion of the Campes.

I dare vndertake, *Orlando Furioso*, or honest King *Arthur*, will neuer displease a Souldier: but the quiddity of *Ens* and *Prima materia* will hardely agree with a Corslet: and therefore, as I said in the beginning, euen Turks and Tartares are delighted with Poets. *Homer*, a Greek, florished before Greece florished. And if to a slight coniecture a coniecture may be opposed, truly it may seeme, that as by him their learned men tooke

An Apology for Poetry

almost their first light of knowledge, so their actiue men receiued their first motions of courage. Onlie *Alexanders* example may serue, who by *Plutarch* is accounted of such vertue, that Fortune was not his guide but his footestoole: whose acts speake for him, though *Plutarch* did not; indeede the Phœnix of warlike Princes. This *Alexander* left his Schoolemaister, liuing *Aristotle*, behinde him, but tooke deade *Homer* with him: he put the Philosopher *Calisthenes* to death for his seeming philosophicall, indeed mutinous, stubburnnes; but the chiefe thing he euer was heard to wish for was that *Homer* had been aliue. He well found he receiued more brauerie of minde bye the patterne of *Achilles* then by hearing the definition of Fortitude: and therefore, if *Cato* misliked *Fuluius* for carying *Ennius* with him to the fielde, it may be aunswered that, if *Cato* misliked it, the noble *Fuluius* liked it, or els he had not doone it: for it was not the excellent *Cato Vticensis* (whose authority I would much more haue reuerenced), but it was the former, in truth a bitter punisher of faults, but else a man that had neuer wel sacrificed to the Graces. Hee misliked and cryed out vpon all Greeke learning, and yet, being 80 yeeres olde, began to learne it; be-like fearing that *Pluto* vnderstood not Latine. Indeede, the Romaine lawes allowed no person to be carried to the warres but hee that was in the Souldiers role: and therefore, though *Cato* misliked his vnmustered person, hee misliked not his worke. And if hee had, *Scipio Nasica*, iudged by common consent the best Romaine, loued him. Both the other *Scipio* Brothers, who had by their vertues no lesse surnames then of *Asia* and *Affrick*, so loued him that they caused his body to be buried in their Sepulcher. So as *Cato* his authoritie being but against his person, and that aunswered with so farre greater then himselfe, is heerein of no validitie.

But now indeede my burthen is great; now *Plato* his name is layde vpon mee, whom, I must confesse, of all Philosophers I haue euer esteemed most worthy of reuerence, and with great reason, sith of all Philosophers he is the most poeticall. Yet if he will defile the Fountaine out of which his flowing streames haue proceeded, let vs boldly examine with what reasons hee did it. First truly, a man might maliciously obiect that *Plato*, being a Philosopher, was a naturall enemie of Poets: for indeede, after the Philosophers had picked out of the sweete misteries of Poetrie the right discerning true points of knowledge, they forthwith, putting it in method, and making a Schoole-arte of that which the Poets did onely teach by a diuine delightfulnes, beginning to spurne at their guides, like vngratefull Prentises, were not content to set vp shops for themselues, but sought by all meanes to discredit their Maisters. Which by the force of delight beeing barred them, the lesse they could ouerthrow them, the more they hated them. For indeede, they found for *Homer* seauen Cities stroue who should haue him for their Citizen; where many Cities banished Philosophers as not fitte members to liue among them. For onely repeating certaine of *Euripides* verses, many *Athenians* had their lyues saued of the *Siracusians*; when the *Athenians* themselues thought many Philosophers vnwoorthie to liue. Certaine Poets, as *Simonides* and *Pindarus*, had so preuailed with *Hiero* the first, that of a Tirant they made him a iust King, where *Plato* could do so little with *Dionisius*, that he himselfe of a Philosopher was made a slaue. But who should doe thus, I confesse, should requite the obiections made against Poets with like cauillation against Philosophers, as likewise one should doe that should bid one read *Phædrus* or *Symposium* in *Plato*, or the discourse of loue in *Plutarch*, and see whether any Poet doe authorize abhominable filthines, as they doe.

An Apology for Poetry 191

Againe, a man might aske out of what Common-wealth *Plato* did banish them? insooth, thence where he himselfe alloweth communitie of women. So as belike this banishment grewe not for effeminate wantonnes, sith little should poeticall Sonnets be hurtfull when a man might haue what woman he listed. But I honor philosophicall instructions, and blesse the wits which bred them: so as they be not abused, which is likewise stretched to Poetrie.

S. *Paule* himselfe, who (yet for the credite of Poets) alledgeth twise two Poets, and one of them by the name of a Prophet, setteth a watch-word vpon Philosophy, indeede vpon the abuse. So dooth *Plato* vpon the abuse, not vpon Poëtrie. *Plato* found fault that the Poets of his time filled the worlde with wrong opinions of the Gods, making light tales of that vnspotted essence; and, therefore, would not haue the youth depraued with such opinions. Heerin may much be said: let this suffice: the Poets did not induce such opinions, but dyd imitate those opinions already induced. For all the Greek stories can well testifie that the very religion of that time stoode vpon many, and many-fashioned, Gods, not taught so by the Poets, but followed according to their nature of imitation. Who list may reade in *Plutarch* the discourses of *Isis* and *Osiris*, of the cause why Oracles ceased, of the diuine prouidence, and see whether the Theologie of that nation stood not vpon such dreames which the Poets indeed supersticiously obserued, and truly (sith they had not the light of Christ) did much better in it then the Philosophers, who, shaking off superstition, brought in Atheisme. *Plato* therefore (whose authoritie I had much rather iustly conster then vniustly resist) meant not in general of Poets, in those words of which *Iulius Scaliger* saith, *Qua authoritate barbari quidam atque hispidi abuti velint ad Poetas e republica exigendos*; but only meant to driue out those wrong opinions of the Deitie (whereof now, without further law, Christianity hath taken away all the hurtful beliefe), perchance (as he thought) norished by the then esteemed Poets. And a man need goe no further then to *Plato* himselfe to know his meaning: who, in his Dialogue called *Ion*, giueth high and rightly diuine commendation to Poetrie. So as *Plato*, banishing the abuse, not the thing, not banishing it, but giuing due honor vnto it, shall be our Patron and not our aduersarie. For indeed I had much rather (sith truly I may doe it) shew theyr mistaking of *Plato* (vnder whose Lyons skin they would make an Asse-like braying against Poesie) then goe about to ouerthrow his authority, whom the wiser a man is the more iust cause he shall find to haue in admiration; especially sith he attributeth vnto Poesie more then my selfe doe, namely, to be a very inspiring of a diuine force, farre aboue mans wit, as in the afore-named Dialogue is apparant.

Of the other side, who wold shew the honors haue been by the best sort of iudgements granted them, a whole Sea of examples woulde present themselues: *Alexanders, Cæsars, Scipios*, al fauorers of Poets; *Lelius*, called the Romane *Socrates*, him selfe a Poet, so as part of *Heautontimorumenos* in *Terence* was supposed to be made by him. And euen the Greek *Socrates*, whom *Apollo* confirmed to be the onely wise man, is sayde to haue spent part of his old tyme in putting *Esops* fables into verses. And therefore, full euill should it become his scholler *Plato* to put such words in his Maisters mouth against Poets. But what need more? *Aristotle* writes the Arte of Poesie: and why, if it should not be written? *Plutarch* teacheth the vse to be gathered of them, and how, if they should not be read? And who reades *Plutarchs* eyther historie or philosophy shall finde hee trymmeth both theyr garments with gards of Poesie. But I list not to

An Apology for Poetry

defend Poesie with the helpe of her vnderling Historiography. Let it suffise that it is a fit soyle for prayse to dwell vpon; and what dispraise may set vpon it, is eyther easily ouer-come, or transformed into iust commendation. So that, sith the excellencies of it may be so easily and so iustly confirmed, and the low-creeping obiections so soone troden downe; it not being an Art of lyes, but of true doctrine; not of effeminatenes, but of notable stirring of courage; not of abusing mans witte, but of strengthning mans wit; not banished, but honored by *Plato*; let vs rather plant more Laurels for to engarland our Poets heads (which honor of beeing laureat, as besides them onely tryumphant Captaines weare, is a sufficient authority to shewe the price they ought to be had in) then suffer the ill-fauouring breath of such wrong-speakers once to blowe vpon the cleere springs of Poesie.

But sith I haue runne so long a careere in this matter, me thinks, before I giue my penne a fulle stop, it shalbe but a little more lost time to inquire why England (the Mother of excellent mindes) should bee growne so hard a step-mother to Poets, who certainly in wit ought to passe all other; sith all onely proceedeth from their wit, being indeede makers of themselues, not takers of others. How can I but exclaime,

Musa mihi causas memora, quo numine laeso.

Sweete Poesie, that hath aunciently had Kings, Emperors, Senators, great Captaines, such as, besides a thousand others, *Dauid, Adrian, Sophocles, Germanicus*, not onely to fauour Poets, but to be Poets. And of our neerer times can present for her Patrons a *Robert*, king of Sicil, the great king *Francis* of France, King *Iames* of Scotland. Such Cardinals as *Bembus* and *Bibiena*. Such famous Preachers and Teachers as *Beza* and *Melancthon*. So learned Philosophers as *Fracastorius* and *Scaliger*. So great Orators as *Pontanus* and *Muretus*. So piercing wits as *George Buchanan*. So graue Counsellors as, besides many, but before all, that *Hospitall* of Fraunce, then whom (I thinke) that Realme neuer brought forth a more accomplished iudgement, more firmly builded vpon vertue. I say these, with numbers of others, not onely to read others Poesies, but to Poetise for others reading. That Poesie, thus embraced in all other places, should onely finde in our time a hard welcome in England, I thinke the very earth lamenteth it, and therfore decketh our Soyle with fewer Laurels then it was accustomed. For heertofore Poets haue in England also florished; and, which is to be noted, euen in those times when the trumpet of *Mars* did sounde loudest. And now that an ouer-faint quietnes should seeme to strew the house for Poets, they are almost in as good reputation as the *Mountibancks* at *Venice*. Truly euen that, as of the one side it giueth great praise to Poesie, which like *Venus* (but to better purpose) hath rather be troubled in the net with *Mars* then enioy the homelie quiet of *Vulcan*; so serues it for a peece of a reason why they are lesse gratefull to idle England, which nowe can scarce endure the payne of a pen. Vpon this necessarily followeth, that base men with seruile wits vndertake it: who think it inough if they can be rewarded of the Printer. And so as *Epaminondas* is sayd, with the honor of his vertue, to haue made an office, by his exercising it, which before was contemptible, to become highly respected; so these, no more but setting their names to it, by their owne disgracefulnes disgrace the most gracefull Poesie. For now, as if all the Muses were gotte with childe, to bring foorth bastard Poets, without any commission they doe poste ouer the banckes of *Helicon*, tyll they make the readers more weary then Post-horses; while, in the mean tyme, they,

Queis meliore luto finxit praecordia Titan,

are better content to suppresse the out-flowing of their wit, then by publishing them to bee accounted Knights of the same order. But I that, before euer I durst aspire vnto the dignitie, am admitted into the company of the Paper-blurrers, doe finde the very true cause of our wanting estimation is want of desert; taking vpon vs to be Poets in despight of *Pallas*. Nowe, wherein we want desert were a thanke-worthy labour to expresse: but if I knew, I should haue mended my selfe. But I, as I neuer desired the title, so haue I neglected the meanes to come by it. Onely, ouer-mastred by some thoughts, I yeelded an inckie tribute vnto them. Mary, they that delight in Poesie it selfe should seeke to knowe what they doe, and how they doe; and, especially, looke themselues in an vnflattering Glasse of reason, if they bee inclinable vnto it. For Poesie must not be drawne by the eares; it must bee gently led, or rather it must lead. Which was partly the cause that made the auncient-learned affirme it was a diuine gift, and no humaine skill: sith all other knowledges lie ready for any that hath strength of witte: A Poet no industrie can make, if his owne *Genius* bee not carried vnto it: and therefore is it an old Prouerbe, *Orator fit, Poeta nascitur*. Yet confesse I alwayes that as the firtilest ground must bee manured, so must the highest flying wit haue a *Dedalus* to guide him. That *Dedalus*, they say, both in this and in other, hath three wings to beare it selfe vp into the ayre of due commendation: that is, Arte, Imitation, and Exercise. But these, neyther artificiall rules nor imitatiue patternes, we much cumber our selues withall. Exercise indeede wee doe, but that very fore-backwardly: for where we should exercise to know, wee exercise as hauing knowne: and so is oure braine deliuered of much matter which neuer was begotten by knowledge. For, there being two principal parts, matter to be expressed by wordes and words to expresse the matter, in neyther wee vse Arte or Imitation rightly. Our matter is *Quodlibet* indeed, though wrongly perfourming *Ouids* verse

Quicquid conabar dicere versus erat:

neuer marshalling it into an assured rancke, that almost the readers cannot tell where to finde themselues.

Chaucer, vndoubtedly, did excellently in hys *Troylus and Cresseid*; of whom, truly, I know not whether to meruaile more, either that he in that mistie time could see so clearely, or that wee in this cleare age walke so stumblingly after him. Yet had he great wants, fitte to be forgiuen in so reuerent antiquity. I account the *Mirrour of Magistrates* meetely furnished of beautiful parts; and in the Earle of Surries *Liricks* many things tasting of a noble birth, and worthy of a noble minde. The *Sheapheards Kalender* hath much Poetrie in his Eglogues: indeede worthy the reading, if I be not deceiued. That same framing of his stile to an old rustick language I dare not alowe, sith neyther *Theocritus* in Greeke, *Virgill* in Latine, nor *Sanazar* in Italian did affect it. Besides these, doe I not remember to haue seene but fewe (to speake boldely) printed, that haue poeticall sinnewes in them: for proofe whereof, let but most of the verses bee put in Prose, and then aske the meaning; and it will be found that one verse did but beget another, without ordering at the first what should be at the last; which becomes a confused masse of words, with a tingling sound of ryme, barely accompanied with reason.

Our Tragedies and Comedies (not without cause cried out against), obseruing rules neyther of honest ciuilitie nor of skilfull Poetrie, excepting *Gorboduck* (againe, I say, of those that I haue seene), which notwithstanding, as it is full of stately speeches and well sounding Phrases,

clyming to the height of *Seneca* his stile, and as full of
notable moralitie, which it doth most delightfully teach,
and so obtayne the very end of Poesie, yet in troth it
is very defectious in the circumstaunces, which greeueth
mee, because it might not remaine as an exact model of
all Tragedies. For it is faulty both in place and time,
the two necessary companions of all corporall actions.
For where the stage should alwaies represent but one
place, and the vttermost time presupposed in it should
be, both by *Aristotles* precept and common reason, but
one day, there is both many dayes, and many places,
inartificially imagined. But if it be so in *Gorboduck*, how
much more in al the rest? where you shal haue *Asia*
of the one side, and *Affrick* of the other, and so many
other vnder-kingdoms, that the Player, when he commeth
in, must euer begin with telling where he is, or els
the tale wil not be conceiued. Now ye shal haue three
Ladies walke to gather flowers, and then we must beleeue the stage to be a Garden. By and by, we heare
newes of shipwracke in the same place, and then wee
are to blame if we accept it not for a Rock. Vpon
the backe of that, comes out a hidious Monster, with
fire and smoke, and then the miserable beholders are
bounde to take it for a Caue. While in the meantime
two Armies flye in, represented with foure swords and
bucklers, and then what harde heart will not receiue it
for a pitched fielde? Now, of time they are much more
liberall, for ordinary it is that two young Princes fall in
loue. After many trauerces, she is got with childe,
deliuered of a faire boy; he is lost, groweth a man, falls
in loue, and is ready to get another child; and all this in
two hours space: which how absurd it is in sence euen
sence may imagine, and Arte hath taught, and all aunctient
examples iustified, and, at this day, the ordinary Players
in Italie wil not erre in. Yet wil some bring in an

example of *Eunuchus* in *Terence*, that containeth matter of two dayes, yet far short of twenty yeeres. True it is, and so was it to be playd in two daies, and so fitted to the time it set forth. And though *Plautus* hath in one place done amisse, let vs hit with him, and not misse with him. But they wil say, how then shal we set forth a story, which containeth both many places and many times? And doe they not knowe that a Tragedie is tied to the lawes of Poesie, and not of Historie? not bound to follow the storie, but, hauing liberty, either to faine a quite newe matter, or to frame the history to the most tragicall conueniencie. Againe, many things may be told which cannot be shewed, if they knowe the difference betwixt reporting and representing. As, for example, I may speake (though I am heere) of *Peru*, and in speech digresse from that to the description of *Calicut*; but in action I cannot represent it without *Pacolets* horse: and so was the manner the Auncients tooke, by some *Nuncius*, to recount thinges done in former time or other place. Lastly, if they wil represent an history, they must not (as *Horace* saith) beginne *Ab ouo*, but they must come to the principall poynt of that one action which they wil represent. By example this wil be best expressed. I haue a story of young *Polidorus*, deliuered for safeties sake, with great riches, by his Father *Priamus* to *Polimnestor*, king of *Thrace*, in the Troyan war time. Hee after some yeeres, hearing the ouer-throwe of *Priamus*, for to make the treasure his owne, murthereth the child; the body of the child is taken vp by *Hecuba*; shee the same day findeth a slight to bee reuenged most cruelly of the Tyrant: where nowe would one of our Tragedy writers begin, but with the deliuery of the childe? Then should he sayle ouer into *Thrace*, and so spend I know not how many yeeres, and trauaile numbers of places. But where dooth *Euripides*? Euen with the finding of the body, leauing the rest to be tolde by the spirit of *Polidorus*. This need no further to be inlarged; the dullest wit may conceiue it.

But besides these grosse absurdities, how all theyr Playes be neither right Tragedies, nor right Comedies; mingling Kings and Clownes, not because the matter so carrieth it, but thrust in Clownes by head and shoulders, to play a part in maiesticall matters, with neither decencie nor discretion: So as neither the admiration and commiseration, nor the right sportfulnes, is by their mungrell Tragycomedie obtained. I know *Apuleius* did some-what so, but that is a thing recounted with space of time, not represented in one moment: and I knowe the Auncients haue one or two examples of Tragy-comedies, as *Plautus* hath *Amphitrio*. But, if we marke them well, we shall find, that they neuer, or very daintily, match Horn-pypes and Funeralls. So falleth it out that, hauing indeed no right Comedy, in that comicall part of our Tragedy we haue nothing but scurrility, vnwoorthy of any chast eares, or some extreame shew of doltishnes, indeed fit to lift vp a loude laughter, and nothing els: where the whole tract of a Comedy shoulde be full of delight, as the Tragedy shoulde be still maintained in a well raised admiration. But our Comedians thinke there is no delight without laughter; which is very wrong, for though laughter may come with delight, yet commeth it not of delight, as though delight should be the cause of laughter; but well may one thing breed both together: nay, rather in themselues they haue, as it were, a kind of contrarietie: for delight we scarcely doe but in things that haue a conueniencie to our selues or to the generall nature: laughter almost euer commeth of things most disproportioned to our selues and nature. Delight hath a ioy in it, either permanent or present. Laughter hath onely a scornful tickling. For example, we are rauished with delight to see a faire woman, and yet are far from being moued to laughter.

We laugh at deformed creatures, wherein certainely we cannot delight. We delight in good chaunces, we laugh at mischaunces; we delight to heare the happines of our friends, or Country, at which he were worthy to be laughed at that would laugh; wee shall, contrarily, laugh sometimes to finde a matter quite mistaken and goe downe the hill agaynst the byas, in the mouth of some such men, as for the respect of them one shalbe hartely sorry, yet he cannot chuse but laugh; and so is rather pained then delighted with laughter. Yet deny I not but that they may goe well together; for as in *Alexanders* picture well set out wee delight without laughter, and in twenty mad Anticks we laugh without delight, so in *Hercules*, painted with his great beard and furious countenance, in womans attire, spinning at *Omphales* commaundement, it breedeth both delight and laughter. For the representing of so strange a power in loue procureth delight: and the scornefulnes of the action stirreth laughter. But I speake to this purpose, that all the end of the comicall part bee not vpon such scornefull matters as stirreth laughter onely, but, mixt with it, that delightful teaching which is the end of Poesie. And the great fault euen in that point of laughter, and forbidden plainely by *Aristotle*, is that they styrre laughter in sinfull things, which are rather execrable then ridiculous: or in miserable, which are rather to be pittied then scorned. For what is it to make folkes gape at a wretched Begger, or a beggerly Clowne? or, against lawe of hospitality, to iest at straungers, because they speake not English so well as wee doe? what do we learne? sith it is certaine

Nil habet infelix paupertas durius in se,
Quam quod ridiculos homines facit.

But rather a busy louing Courtier, a hartles threatening *Thraso*, a selfe-wise-seeming schoolemaster, a awry-trans-

formed Traueller : These if wee sawe walke in stage
names, which wee play naturally, therein were delightfull
laughter, and teaching delightfulnes : as in the other,
the Tragedies of *Buchanan* doe iustly bring forth a diuine
admiration. But I haue lauished out too many wordes
of this play matter. I doe it because as they are excel-
ling parts of Poesie, so is there none so much vsed in
England, and none can be more pittifully abused. Which
like an vnmannerly Daughter, shewing a bad education,
causeth her mother Poesies honesty to bee called in
question.

Other sorts of Poetry almost haue we none, but that
Lyricall kind of Songs and Sonnets : which, Lord, if he
gaue vs so good mindes, how well it might be imployed,
and with howe heauenly fruite, both priuate and publique,
in singing the prayses of the immortall beauty, the
immortall goodnes of that God who gyueth vs hands to
write and wits to conceiue ; of which we might well want
words, but neuer matter; of which we could turne our
eies to nothing, but we should euer haue new budding
occasions. But truely many of such writings as come
vnder the banner of vnresistable loue, if I were a Mistres,
would neuer perswade mee they were in loue ; so coldely
they apply fiery speeches, as men that had rather red
Louers writings, and so caught vp certaine swelling
phrases, which hang together like a man which once
tolde mee the winde was at North West, and by South,
because he would be sure to name windes enowe,—then
that in truth they feele those passions, which easily (as
I think) may be bewrayed by that same forciblenes, or
Energia (as the Greekes cal it), of the writer. But let
this bee a sufficient though short note, that wee misse the
right vse of the materiall point of Poesie.

Now, for the out-side of it, which is words, or (as
I may tearme it) *Diction*, it is euen well worse. So is

that honny-flowing Matron Eloquence apparelled, or
rather disguised, in a Curtizan-like painted affectation:
one time with so farre fette words, they may seeme Monsters, but must seeme straungers to any poore English
man; another tyme, with coursing of a Letter, as if
they were bound to followe the method of a Dictionary;
an other tyme, with figures and flowers, extreamelie
winter-starued. But I would this fault were only peculier
to Versifiers, and had not as large possession among
Prose-printers, and (which is to be meruailed) among
many Schollers, and (which is to be pittied) among
some Preachers. Truly I could wish, if at least I might
be so bold to wish in a thing beyond the reach of my
capacity, the diligent imitators of *Tullie* and *Demosthenes*
(most worthy to be imitated) did not so much keep
Nizolian Paper-bookes of their figures and phrases, as by
attentiue translation (as it were) deuoure them whole,
and make them wholly theirs. For nowe they cast Sugar
and Spice vpon euery dish that is serued to the table;
like those Indians, not content to weare eare-rings at
the fit and naturall place of the eares, but they will thrust
Iewels through their nose and lippes, because they will
be sure to be fine. *Tullie*, when he was to driue out
Catiline, as it were with a Thunder-bolt of eloquence,
often vsed that figure of repitition, *Viuit. viuit? imo in
Senatum venit &c.* Indeed, inflamed with a well-grounded
rage, hee would haue his words (as it were) double out
of his mouth; and so doe that artificially which we see
men doe in choller naturally. And wee, hauing noted
the grace of those words, hale them in sometime to a
familier Epistle, when it were too much choller to be
chollerick.

Now for similitudes, in certaine printed discourses, I
thinke all Herbarists, all stories of Beasts, Foules, and
Fishes are rifled vp, that they come in multitudes to waite

vpon any of our conceits; which certainly is as absurd a
surfet to the eares as is possible: for the force of a similitude not being to prooue anything to a contrary Disputer
but onely to explane to a willing hearer, when that is done,
the rest is a most tedious pratling, rather ouer-swaying
the memory from the purpose whereto they were applyed
then any whit informing the iudgement, already eyther
satisfied, or by similitudes not to be satisfied. For my
part, I doe not doubt, when *Antonius* and *Crassus*, the
great forefathers of *Cicero* in eloquence, the one (as *Cicero*
testifieth of them) pretended not to know Arte, the other
not to set by it, because with a playne sensiblenes they
might win credit of popular eares; which credit is the
neerest step to perswasion; which perswasion is the chiefe
marke of Oratory;—I doe not doubt (I say) but that they
vsed these tracks very sparingly, which who doth generally
vse any man may see doth daunce to his owne musick;
and so be noted by the audience more careful to speake
curiously then to speake truly.

Vndoubtedly (at least to my opinion vndoubtedly)
I haue found in diuers smally learned Courtiers a more
sounde stile then in some professors of learning: of which
I can gesse no other cause, but that the Courtier, following
that which by practise hee findeth fittest to nature, therein
(though he know it not) doth according to Art, though
not by Art: where the other, vsing Art to shew Art, and
not to hide Art (as in these cases he should doe), flyeth
from nature, and indeede abuseth Art.

But what? me thinkes I deserue to be pounded for
straying from Poetrie to Oratorie: but both haue such
an affinity in this wordish consideration, that I thinke
this digression will make my meaning receiue the fuller
vnderstanding: which is not to take vpon me to teach
Poets howe they should doe, but onely, finding my selfe
sick among the rest, to shewe some one or two spots of

the common infection growne among the most part of
Writers: that, acknowledging our selues somewhat awry,
we may bend to the right use both of matter and manner;
whereto our language gyueth vs great occasion, beeing
indeed capable of any excellent exercising of it. I know
some will say it is a mingled language. And why not
so much the better, taking the best of both the other?
Another will say it wanteth Grammer. Nay truly, it hath
that prayse, that it wanteth not Grammer: for Grammer
it might haue, but it needes it not; beeing so easie of it
selfe, and so voyd of those cumbersome differences of
Cases, Genders, Moodes, and Tenses, which I thinke
was a peece of the Tower of *Babilons* curse, that a man
should be put to schoole to learne his mother-tongue.
But for the vttering sweetly and properly the conceits
of the minde, which is the end of speech, that hath it
equally with any other tongue in the world: and is parti-
culerly happy in compositions of two or three words
together, neere the Greeke, far beyond the Latine: which
is one of the greatest beauties can be in a language.

(Now, of versifying there are two sorts, the one Aunceint,
the other Moderne :) the Auncient marked the quantitie
of each silable, and according to that framed his verse;
the Moderne obseruing onely number (with some regarde
of the accent), the chiefe life of it standeth in that lyke
sounding of the words, which wee call Ryme.) Whether
of these be the most excellent, would beare many speeches.
The Auncient (no doubt) more fit for Musick, both words
and tune obseruing quantity, and more fit liuely to expresse
diuers passions, by the low and lofty sounde of the well-
weyed silable. The latter likewise, with hys Ryme,
striketh a certaine musick to the eare: and, in fine, sith
it dooth delight, though by another way, it obtaines the
same purpose: there beeing in eyther sweetnes, and
wanting in neither maiestie. Truely the English, before

An Apology for Poetry

any other vulgar language I know, is fit for both sorts: for, for the Ancient, the Italian is so full of Vowels that it must euer be cumbred with *Elisions*; the Dutch so, of the other side, with Consonants, that they cannot yeeld the sweet slyding fit for a Verse; the French, in his whole language, hath not one word that hath his accent in the last silable, sauing two, called *Antepenullima*; and little more hath the Spanish: and, therefore, very gracelesly may they vse *Dactiles*. The English is subiect to none of these defects.

Nowe, for the ryme, though wee doe not obserue quantity, yet wee obserue the accent very precisely: which other languages eyther cannot doe or will not doe so absolutely. That *Cæsura*, or breathing place in the middest of the verse, neither Italian nor Spanish haue, the French, and we, neuer almost fayle of. Lastly, euen the very ryme it selfe the Italian cannot put in the last silable, by the French named the Masculine ryme, but still in the next to the last, which the French call the Female, or the next before that, which the Italians terme *Sdrucciola*. The example of the former is *Buono*, *Suono*, of the *Sdrucciola*, *Femina*, *Semina*. The French, of the other side, hath both the Male, as *Bon*, *Son*, and the Female, as *Plaise*, *Taise*. But the *Sdrucciola* hee hath not: where the English hath all three, as *Due*, *True*, *Father*, *Rather*, *Motion*, *Potion*; with much more which might be sayd, but that I finde already the triflingnes of this discourse is much too much enlarged.

So that sith the euer-praise-worthy Poesie is full of vertue-breeding delightfulnes, and voyde of no gyfte that ought to be in the noble name of learning: sith the blames laid against it are either false or feeble; sith the cause why it is not esteemed in Englande is the fault of Poet-apes, not Poets; sith, lastly, our tongue is most fit to honor Poesie, and to bee honored by Poesie; I coniure you all

that haue had the euill lucke to reade this incke-wasting
toy of mine, euen in the name of the nyne Muses, no
more to scorne the sacred misteries of Poesie, no more
to laugh at the name of Poets, as though they were next
inheritours to Fooles, no more to iest at the reuerent
title of a Rymer; but to beleeue, with *Aristotle*, that they
were the auncient Treasurers of the Græcians Diuinity.
To beleeue, with *Bembus*, that they were first bringers
in of all ciuilitie. To beleeue, with *Scaliger*, that no
Philosophers precepts can sooner make you an honest
man then the reading of *Virgill*. To beleeue, with *Clauserus*,
the Translator of *Cornutus*, that it pleased the
heauenly Deitié, by *Hesiod* and *Homer*, vnder the vayle
of fables, to giue vs all knowledge, Logick, Rethorick,
Philosophy, naturall and morall; and *Quid non*? To
beleeue, with me, that there are many misteries contained
in Poetrie, which of purpose were written darkely, least
by prophane wits it should bee abused. To beleeue, with
Landin, that they are so beloued of the Gods that whatsoeuer they write proceeds of a diuine fury. Lastly, to
beleeue themselues, when they tell you they will make
you immortall by their verses.

Thus doing, your name shal florish in the Printers
shoppes; thus doing, you shall bee of kinne to many
a poeticall Preface; thus doing, you shall be most fayre,
most ritch, most wise, most all; you shall dwell vpon
Superlatiues. Thus dooing, though you be *Libertino patre
natus*, you shall suddenly grow *Herculea proles*,

Si quid mea carmina possunt.

Thus doing, your soule shal be placed with *Dantes
Beatrix*, or *Virgils Anchises*. But if (fie of such a but)
you be borne so neere the dull making *Cataphract* of
Nilus that you cannot heare the Plannet-like Musick of
Poetrie, if you haue so earth-creeping a mind that it

cannot lift it selfe vp to looke to the sky of Poetry, or rather, by a certaine rusticall disdaine, will become such a Mome as to be a *Momus* of Poetry; then, though I will not wish vnto you the Asses eares of *Midas*, nor to bee driuen by a Poets verses (as *Bubonax* was) to hang himselfe, nor to be rimed to death, as is sayd to be doone in Ireland; yet thus much curse I must send you, in the behalfe of all Poets, that while you liue, you liue in loue, and neuer get fauour for lacking skill of a *Sonnet*; and when you die, your memory die from the earth for want of an *Epitaph*.

KING JAMES VI

(*ANE SCHORT TREATISE CONTEINING SOME REVLIS AND CAUTELIS
TO BE OBSERUIT AND ESCHEWIT IN SCOTTIS POESIE*)

1584

[*Ane schort | Treatise, | conteining some revlis | and cautelis to be obseruit and | eschewit in Scottis | Poesie*, was issued in the volume of *The Essayes of a Prentise, in the Divine Art of Poesie*, printed at Edinburgh by Thomas Vautroullier in 1584. The text is taken from the copy which was formerly in the possession of the poet William Drummond of Hawthornden, and was presented by him to the Library of the University of Edinburgh (De. 2. 57). The *Treatise* begins at sig. K. On the back of the special title-page is printed 'A Qvadrain of Alexandrin Verse, declaring to qvhome the Authour hes directit his labour.

> *To ignorants obdurde, quhair wilful errour lyis,*
> *Nor yit to curious folks, quhilks carping dois deiect thee,*
> *Nor yit to learned men, quha thinks thame onelie wyis,*
> *Bot to the docile bairns of knawledge I direct thee.'*

The incorporation in a book of *Elizabethan* texts of a tract on Scots verse, by a Scottish king, requires no apology, especially when its relation to earlier Southern work can be clearly shown (see *Introduction*).

THE PREFACE TO THE READER.

THE cause why (docile Reader) I haue not dedicat this short treatise to any particular personis (as commounly workis vsis to be) is, that I esteme all thais quha hes already some beginning of knawledge, with ane earnest 5

A short Treatise on Verse

desyre to atteyne to farther, alyke meit for the reading of this worke, or any vther, quhilk may help thame to the atteining to thair foirsaid desyre. Bot as to this work, quhilk is intitulit *The Reulis and cautelis to be obseruit and eschewit in Scottis Poesie*, ye may maruell parauenture quhairfore I sould haue writtin in that mater, sen sa mony learnit men, baith of auld and of late, hes already written thairof in dyuers and sindry languages: I answer that, nochtwithstanding, I haue lykewayis writtin of it, for twa caussis. The ane is: As for them that wrait of auld, lyke as the tyme is changeit sensyne, sa is the ordour of Poesie changeit. For then they obseruit not *Flowing*, nor eschewit not *Ryming in termes*, besydes sindrie vther thingis, quhilk now we obserue and eschew, and dois weil in sa doing: because that now, quhen the warld is waxit auld, we haue all their opinionis in writ, quhilk were learned before our tyme, besydes our awin ingynis, quhair as they then did it onelie be thair awin ingynis, but help of any vther. Thairfore, quhat I speik of Poesie now, I speik of it as being come to mannis age and perfectioun, quhair as then it was bot in the infancie and chyldheid. The vther cause is: That as for thame that hes written in it of late, there hes neuer ane of thame written in our language. For albeit sindrie hes written of it in English, quhilk is lykest to our language, yit we differ from thame in sindrie reulis of Poesie, as ye will find be experience. I haue lykewayis omittit dyuers figures, quhilkis are necessare to be vsit in verse, for twa causis. The ane is, because they are vsit in all languages, and thairfore are spokin of be *Du Bellay*, and sindrie vtheris, quha hes written in this airt. Quhairfore, gif I wrait of them also, it sould seme that I did bot repete that quhilk they haue written, and yit not sa weil as they haue done already. The vther cause is that they are figures of Rhetorique and Dialectique, quhilkis airtis I professe nocht, and thairfore will apply to my selfe the counsale quhilk *Apelles* gaue to the shoomaker, quhen he said to him, seing him find falt with the shankis of the Image of *Venus*, efter that he had found falt with the pantoun, *Ne sutor vltra crepidam*.

I will also wish yow (docile Reidar) that, or ye cummer yow with reiding thir reulis, ye may find in your self sic a beginning of Nature as ye may put in practise in your verse many of thir foirsaidis preceptis, or euer ye sie them as they are heir set doun. For gif Nature be nocht the cheif worker in this airt, Reulis wilbe bot a band to Nature, and will mak yow within short space weary of the haill airt: quhair as, gif Nature be cheif, and bent to it, reulis will be ane help and staff to Nature. I will end heir, lest my preface be langer nor my purpose and haill mater following: wishing yow, docile Reidar, als gude succes and great proffeit by reiding this short treatise as I tuke earnist and willing panis to blok it, as ye sie, for your cause. Fare weill.

I haue insert in the hinder end of this Treatise maist kyndis of versis quhilks are not cuttit or brokin, bot alyke many feit in euerie lyne of the verse, and how they are commounly namit, with my opinioun for quhat subiectis ilk kynde of thir verse is meitest to be vsit.

To knaw the quantitie of your lang or short fete in they lynes, quhilk I haue put in the reule quhilk teachis yow to knaw quhat is *Flowing*, I haue markit the lang fute with this mark —, and abone the heid of the shorte fute I haue put this mark ◡.

SONNET OF THE AVTHOVR

TO THE READER.

SEN for your saik I wryte vpon your airt,
Apollo, Pan, and ye O Musis nyne,
And thou, O Mercure, for to help thy pairt
I do implore, sen thou be thy ingyne,
Nixt efter Pan had found the quhissill, syne
Thou did perfyte that quhilk he bot espyit:
And efter that made Argus for to tyne
(Quha kepit Io) all his windois by it.
Concurre ye Gods, it can not be denyit,
Sen in your airt of Poësie I wryte.
Auld birds to learne by teiching it is tryit:
Sic docens discens, gif ye help to dyte.
   Then Reidar sie of nature thou haue pairt,
   Syne laikis thou nocht bot heir to reid the airt.

SONNET DECIFRING

THE PERFYTE POETE.

ANE rype ingyne, ane quick and walkned witt,
With sommair reasons, suddenlie applyit,
For euery purpose vsing reasons fitt,
With skilfulnes, where learning may be spyit,
With pithie wordis, for to expres yow by it
His full intention in his proper leid,
The puritie quhairof weill hes he tryit,
With memorie to keip quhat he dois reid,
With skilfulnes and figuris, quhilks proceid
From Rhetorique, with euerlasting fame,
With vthers woundring, preassing with all speid
For to atteine to merite sic a name:
All thir into the perfyte Poëte be.
Goddis, grant I may obteine the Laurell trie.

THE REVLIS AND CAVTELIS TO BE OBSERVIT AND ESCHEWIT IN SCOTTIS POESIE.

Chap. I.

First, ye sall keip iust cullouris, quhairof the cautelis are thir.

That ye ryme nocht twyse in ane syllabe. As for exemple, that ye make not *proue* and *reproue* ryme together, nor *houe*, for houeing on hors bak, and *behoue*.

That ye ryme ay to the hinmest lang syllabe (with accent) in the lyne, suppose it be not the hinmest syllabe in the lyne, as *bakbyte yow* and *out flyte yow*. It rymes in *byte* and *flyte*, because of the lenth of the syllabe, and accent being there, and not in *yow*, howbeit it be the hinmest syllabe of ather of the lynis. Or *question* and *digestion*: It rymes in *ques* and *ges*, albeit they be bot the antepenult syllabis, and vther twa behind ilkane of thame.

Ye aucht alwayis to note that, as in thir foirsaidis or the lyke wordis, it rymes in the hinmest lang syllabe in the lyne, althoucht there be vther short syllabis behind it, sa is the hinmest lang syllabe the hinmest fute, suppose there be vther short syllabis behind it, quhilkis are eatin vp in the pronounceing and na wayis comptit as fete.

Ye man be war likewayis (except necessitie compell yow) with *Ryming in Termis*, quhilk is to say, that your first or hinmest word in the lyne exceid not twa or thre syllabis at the maist, vsing thrie als seindill as ye can. The cause quhairfore ye sall not place a lang word first in the lyne is that all lang words hes ane syllabe in them sa verie lang, as the lenth thairof eatis vp in the pronouncing euin the vther syllabes quhilks ar placit lang in the same word, and thairfore spillis the flowing of that lyne. As for exemple in this word, *Arabia*, the second syllable (*ra*) is sa lang that it eatis vp in the prononcing (*a*), quhilk is the hinmest syllabe of the same word. Quhilk (*a*) althocht it be in a lang place, yit it kythis not sa, because of the great lenth of the preceding syllabe (*ra*). As to the cause quhy ye sall not put a lang word hinmest in the lyne, it is because that the lenth of the secound syllabe (*ra*), eating vp the lenth of the vther lang syllabe (*a*), makis it to serue bot as a tayle vnto it, together with the short syllabe preceding. And because this tayle nather seruis for cullour nor fute, as I spak before, it man be thairfore repetit in the nixt lyne ryming vnto it, as it is set doune in the first: quhilk makis that ye will scarcely get many wordis to ryme vnto it, yea nane at all will ye finde to ryme to sindrie vther langer wordis. Thairfore cheifly be warre of inserting sic lang wordis hinmest in the lyne, for the cause quhilk I last allegit. Besydis that, nather first nor last in the lyne, it keipis na *Flowing*. The reulis and cautelis quhairof are thir, as followis.

Chap. II.

First, ye man vnderstand that all syllabis are deuydit in thrie kindes: That is, some schort, some lang, and some indifferent. Be indifferent I meane they quhilk are ather lang or short, according as ye place thame.

The forme of placeing syllabes in verse is this. That your first syllabe in the lyne be short, the second lang, the thrid short, the fourt lang, the fyft short, the sixt lang, and sa furth to the end of the lyne. Alwayis tak heid that the nomber of your fete in euery lyne be euin, and nocht odde: as four, six, aucht, or ten, and not thrie, fyue, seuin, or nyne, except it be in broken verse, quhilkis are out of reul and daylie inuentit be dyuers Poetis. Bot gif ye wald ask me the reulis quhairby to knaw euerie ane of thir thre foirsaidis kyndis of syllabes, I answer your eare man be the onely iudge and discerner thairof. And to proue this, I remit to the iudgement of the same, quhilk of thir twa lynis following flowis best,

Into the Sea then Lucifer vpsprang,

In the Sea then Lucifer to vpsprang.

I doubt not bot your eare makkis you easilie to persaue that the first lyne flowis weil and the vther nathing at all. The reasoun is because the first lyne keips the reule abone written—to wit, the first fute short, the secound lang, and sa furth, as I shewe before—quhair as the vther is direct contrair to the same. Bot specially tak heid, quhen your lyne is of fourtene, that your *Sectioun* in aucht be a lang monosyllabe, or ellis the hinmest syllabe of a word alwais being lang, as I said before. The cause quhy it man be ane of thir twa is for the Musique, because that quhen your lyne is ather of xiiij or xij fete it wilbe drawin sa lang in the singing, as ye man rest in the middes of it, quhilk is the *Sectioun*: sa as, gif your *Sectioun* be nocht ather a monosyllabe, or ellis the hinmest syllabe of a word, as I said before, bot the first syllabe of a polysyllabe, the Musique sall make yow sa to rest in the middes of that word, as it sall cut the ane half of the word fra the vther, and sa sall mak it seme twa different wordis, that is bot ane. This aucht onely to be obseruit in thir foirsaid lang lynis: for the shortnes of all shorter lynis then thir before mentionat is the cause that the Musique makis na rest in the middes of thame, and thairfore thir obseruationis seruis nocht for thame. Onely tak heid that the *Sectioun* in thame kythe something langer nor any vther feit in that lyne, except the secound and the last, as I haue said before.

Ye man tak heid lykewayis that your langest lynis

A short Treatise on Verse

exceid nochte fourtene fete, and that your shortest be nocht within foure.

Remember also to mak a *Sectioun* in the middes of euery lyne, quhether the lyne be lang or short. Be *Sectioun* I mean, that gif your lyne be of fourtene fete, your aucht fute man not only be langer then the seuint, or vther short fete, but also langer nor any vther lang fete in the same lyne, except the secound and the hinmest. Or gif your lyne be of twelf fete, your *Sectioun* to be in the sext. Or gif of ten, your *Sectioun* to be in the sext also. The cause quhy it is not in fyue is because fyue is odde, and euerie odde fute is short. Or gif your lyne be of aucht fete, your *Sectioun* to be in the fourt. Gif of sex, in the fourt also. Gif of four, your *Sectioun* to be in twa.

Ye aucht likewise be war with oft composing your haill lynis of monosyllabis onely (albeit our language haue sa many as we can nocht weill eschewe it), because the maist pairt of thame are indifferent, and may be in short or lang place, as ye like. Some wordis of dyuers syllabis are likewayis indifferent, as

Thairfore, restore.

I thairfore, then.

In the first *thairfore*, (*thair*) is short and (*fore*) is lang; in the vther, (*thair*) is lang and (*fore*) is short; and yit baith flowis alike weill. Bot thir indifferent wordis, composit of dyuers syllabes, are rare, suppose in monosyllabes commoun. The cause then quhy ane haill lyne aucht nocht to be composit of monosyllabes only is that, they being for the maist pairt indifferent, nather the secound, hinmest, nor *Sectioun* will be langer nor the other lang fete in the same lyne. Thairfore ye man place a word composit of dyuers syllabes, and not indifferent, ather in the secound, hinmest, or *Sectioun*, or in all thrie.

Ye man also tak heid that quhen thare fallis any short

syllabis efter the last lang syllabe in the lyne, that ye
repeit thame in the lyne quhilk rymis to the vther, even as
ye set them downe in the first lyne: as for exempill, ye
man not say

> *Then feir nocht*
> *Nor heir ocht,*

Bot
> *Then feir nocht*
> *Nor heir nocht,*

repeting the same *nocht* in baith the lynis: because this
syllabe *nocht*, nather seruing for cullour nor fute, is bot
a tayle to the lang fute preceding, and thairfore is repetit
lykewayis in the nixt lyne quhilk rymes vnto it euin as
it [is] set doun in the first.

There is also a kynde of indifferent wordis asweill as of
syllabis, albeit few in nomber. The nature quhairof is
that gif ye place thame in the begynning of a lyne they
are shorter be a fute nor they are gif ye place thame
hinmest in the lyne, as

> *Sen patience I man haue perforce,*
> *I liue in hope with patience.*

Ye se there are bot aucht fete in ather of baith thir lynis
abone written. The cause quhairof is that *patience* in the
first lyne, in respect it is in the beginning thairof, is bot
of twa fete, and in the last lyne of thrie, in respect it is
the hinmest word of that lyne. To knaw and discerne
thir kynde of wordis from vtheris, your eare man be the
onely iudge, as of all the vther parts of *Flowing*, the verie
twichestane quhairof is Musique.

I haue teachit yow now shortly the reulis of *Ryming*,
Fete, and *Flowing*. There restis yet to teache yow the
wordis, sentences, and phrasis necessair for a Poete to
vse in his verse, quhilk I haue set doun in reulis, as efter
followis.

Chap. III.

First, that in quhatsumeuer ye put in verse, ye put in na wordis ather *metri causa* or yit for filling furth the nomber of the fete, bot that they be all sa necessare as ye sould be constrainit to vse thame in cace ye were speiking the same purpose in prose. And thairfore that your wordis appeare to haue cum out willingly, and by nature, and not to haue bene thrawin out constrainedly, be compulsioun.

That ye eschew to insert in your verse a lang rable of mennis names, or names of tounis, or sik vther names, because it is hard to mak many lang names all placit together to flow weill. Thairfore, quhen that fallis out in your purpose, ye sall ather put bot twa or thrie of thame in euerie lyne, mixing vther wordis amang thame, or ellis specifie bot twa or thre of them at all, saying (*With the laif of that race*), or (*With the rest in thay pairtis*), or sic vther lyke wordis: as for example,

> *Out through his cairt, quhair Eous was eik*
> *With other thre, quhilk Phaëton had drawin.*

Ye sie thair is bot ane name there specifeit, to serue for vther thrie of that sorte.

Ye man also take heid to frame your wordis and sentencis according to the mater: As in Flyting and Inuectiues your wordis to be cuttit short, and hurland ouer heuch. For thais quhilkis are cuttit short, I meane be sic wordis as thir,

> *Iis neir cair,*

for

> *I sall neuer cair,* gif your subiect

were of loue, or tragedies. Because in thame your words man be drawin lang, quhilkis in Flyting man be short.

Ye man lykewayis tak heid that ye waill your wordis

according to the purpose: as in ane heich and learnit purpose to vse heich, pithie, and learnit wordis.

Gif your purpose be of loue, to vse commoun language, with some passionate wordis.

Gif your purpose be of tragicall materis, to vse lamentable wordis, with some heich, as rauishit in admiratioun.

Gif your purpose be of landwart effairis, to vse corruptit and vplandis wordis.

And finally, quhatsumeuer be your subiect, to vse *vocabula artis*, quhairby ye may the mair viuelie represent that persoun quhais pairt ye paint out.

This is likewayis neidfull to be vsit in sentences, als weill as in wordis. As gif your subiect be heich and learnit, to vse learnit and infallible reasonis, prouin be necessities.

Gif your subiect be of loue, to vse wilfull reasonis, proceding rather from passioun nor reasoun.

Gif your subiect be of landwart effaris, to vse sklender reasonis, mixt with grosse ignorance, nather keiping forme nor ordour. And sa furth, euer framing your reasonis according to the qualitie of your subiect.

Let all your verse be *Literall*, sa far as may be, quhatsumeuer kynde they be of, bot speciallie *Tumbling* verse for flyting. Be *Literall* I meane that the maist pairt of your lyne sall rynne vpon a letter, as this tumbling lyne rynnis vpon F.

Fetching fude for to feid it fast furth of the Farie.

Ye man obserue that thir *Tumbling* verse flowis not on that fassoun as vtheris dois. For all vtheris keipis the reule quhilk I gaue before, to wit, the first fute short, the secound lang, and sa furth. Quhair as thir hes twa short and ane lang throuch all the lyne, quhen they keip ordour: albeit the maist pairt of thame be out of ordour, and keipis na kynde nor reule of *Flowing*, and for that cause are callit *Tumbling* verse: except the short lynis of aucht in the hinder end of the verse, the quhilk flowis as vther verses dois, as ye will find in the hinder end of this buke, quhair I giue exemple of sindrie kyndis of versis.

Chap. IIII.

MARK also thrie speciall ornamentis to verse, quhilkis are *Comparisons, Epithetis*, and *Prouerbis*.

As for *Comparisons*, take heid that they be sa proper for the subiect that nather they be ouer bas, gif your subiect be heich, for then sould your subiect disgrace your *Comparisoun*, nather your *Comparisoun* be heich quhen your subiect is basse, for then sall your *Comparisoun* disgrace your subiect. Bot let sic a mutuall correspondence and similitude be betwix them as it may appeare to be a meit *Comparisoun* for sic a subiect, and sa sall they ilkane decore vther.

As for *Epithetis*, it is to descryue brieflie, *en passant*, the naturall of euerie thing ye speik of, be adding the proper adiectiue vnto it, quhairof there are twa fassons. The ane is to descryue it be making a corruptit worde, composit of twa dyuers simple wordis, as

Apollo gyde-Sunne.

The vther fasson is be *Circumlocution*, as

Apollo, reular of the Sunne.

I esteme this last fassoun best, because it expressis the authoris meaning als weill as the vther, and yit makis na corruptit wordis, as the vther dois.

As for the *Prouerbis*, they man be proper for the subiect, to beautifie it, chosen in the same forme as the *Comparisoun*.

Chap. V.

It is also meit, for the better decoratioun of the verse, to vse sumtyme the figure of Repetitioun, as

>   *Quhylis ioy rang,*
>   *Quhylis noy rang. &c.*

Ye sie this word *quhylis* is repetit heir. This forme of repetitioun, sometyme vsit, decoris the verse very mekle. Yea, quhen it cummis to purpose, it will be cumly to repete sic a word aucht or nyne tymes in a verse.

Chap. VI.

Ye man also be warre with composing ony thing in the same maner as hes bene ower oft vsit of before. As in speciall, gif ye speik of loue, be warre ye descryue your *Loues* makdome, or her fairnes. And siclyke that ye descryue not the morning and rysing of the Sunne in the Preface of your verse; for thir thingis are sa oft and dyuerslie writtin vpon be Poëtis already, that gif ye do the lyke it will appeare ye bot imitate, and that it cummis not of your awin *Inuentioun*, quhilk is ane of the cheif properteis of ane Poete. Thairfore, gif your subiect be to prayse your *Loue*, ye sall rather prayse hir vther qualiteis, nor her fairnes or hir shaip; or ellis ye sall speik some lytill thing of it, and syne say that your wittis are sa smal, and your vtterance sa barren, that ye can not discryue any part of hir worthelie; remitting alwayis to the Reider to iudge of hir, in respect sho matches, or rather excellis, *Venus,* or any woman, quhome to it sall please yow to compaire her. Bot gif your subiect be sic as ye man speik some thing of the morning or Sunne rysing, tak heid that, quhat name ye giue to the Sunne, the Mone, or vther starris the ane tyme, gif ye happin to wryte thairof another tyme, to change thair names. As gif ye call the Sunne *Titan* at a tyme, to call him *Phœbus* or *Apollo* the vther tyme; and siclyke the Mone, and vther Planettis.

Chap. VII.

Bot sen *Inuention* is ane of the cheif vertewis in a Poete, it is best that ye inuent your awin subiect your self, and not to compose of sene subiectis. Especially translating any thing out of vther language, quhilk doing, ye not onely essay not your awin ingyne of *Inuentioun*, bot be the same meanes ye are bound, as to a staik, to follow that buikis phrasis quhilk ye translate.

Ye man also be war of wryting any thing of materis of commoun weill, or vther sic graue sene subiectis (except Metaphorically, of manifest treuth opinly knawin, yit nochtwithstanding vsing it very seindil), because nocht onely ye essay nocht your awin *Inuentioun*, as I spak before, bot lykewayis they are to graue materis for a Poet to mell in. Bot because ye can not haue the *Inuentioun*, except it come of Nature, I remit it thairvnto, as the cheif cause not onely of *Inuentioun* bot also of all the vther pairtis of Poesie. For airt is onely bot ane help and a remembraunce to Nature, as I shewe yow in the Preface.

Chap. VIII.

TUICHING THE KYNDIS OF VERSIS MENTIONAT IN THE PREFACE.

First, there is ryme quhilk seruis onely for lang historeis, and yit are nocht verse. As for exemple,

In Maii when that the blissefull Phœbus bricht,
The lamp of ioy, the heauens gemme of licht,
The goldin cairt, and the etheriall King,
With purpour face in Orient dois spring,

> *Maist angel-lyke ascending in his sphere,*
> *And birds with all thair heauenlie voces cleare*
> *Dois mak a sweit and heauinly harmony,*
> *And fragrant flours dois spring vp lustely:*
> *Into this season, sweitest of delyte,* 5
> *To walk I had a lusty appetyte.*

And sa furth.

¶ For the descriptioun of Heroique actis, Martiall and knichtly faittis of armes, vse this kynde of verse following, callit *Heroicall*, as 10

> *Meik mundane mirrour, myrrie and modest,*
> *Blyth, kynde, and courtes, comelie, clene, and chest,*
> *To all exemple for thy honestie,*
> *As richest rose, or rubie, by the rest,*
> *With gracis graue, and gesture maist digest,* 15
> *Ay to thy honnour alwayis hauing eye,*
> *Were fassons fliemde, they micht be found in the:*
> *Of blissings all, be blyth, thow hes the best;*
> *With euerie berne belouit for to be.*

¶ For any heich and graue subiectis, specially drawin out of learnit authouris, vse this kynde of verse following, callit *Ballat Royal*, as

> *That nicht he ceist, and went to bed, bot greind*
> *Yit fast for day, and thocht the nicht to lang.*
> *At last Diana doun her head recleind* 25
> *Into the sea. Then Lucifer vpsprang,*
> *Auroras post, whome sho did send amang*
> *The Ieittie cludds, for to foretell ane hour,*
> *Before sho stay her tears, quhilk Ouide sang*
> *Fell for her loue, quhilk turnit in a flour.* 30

¶ For tragicall materis, complaintis, or testamentis, vse this kynde of verse following, callit *Troilus* verse, as

A short Treatise on Verse

To thee, Echo, and thow to me agane,
In the desert, amangs the wods and wells,
Quhair destinie hes bound the to remane,
But company, within the firths and fells,
Let vs complein, with wofull youtts and yells,
A shaft, a shotter, that our harts hes slane:
To thee, Echo, and thow to me agane.

¶ For flyting, or Inuectiues, vse this kynde of verse following, callit *Rouncefallis* or *Tumbling* verse.

In the hinder end of haruest, vpon Alhallow ene,
Quhen our gude nichtbors rydis (nou gif I reid richt),
Some bucklit on a benwod, and some on a bene,
Ay trottand into troupes fra the twylicht:
Some sadland a sho ape, all grathed into grene:
Some hotcheand on a hemp stalk, hovand on a heicht:
The king of Fary with the Court of the Elf quene,
With many elrage Incubus, rydand that nicht:
   There ane elf on ane ape ane vnsell begat,
   Besyde a pot baith auld and worne:
   This bratshard in ane bus was borne:
   They fand a monster, on the morne,
     War facit nor a Cat.

¶ For compendious praysing of any bukes, or the authouris thairof, or ony argumentis of vther historeis, quhair sindrie sentences and change of purposis are requyrit, vse *Sonet* verse, of fourtene lynis, and ten fete in euery lyne. The exemple quhairof I neid nocht to shaw yow, in respect I haue set doun twa in the beginning of this treatise.

¶ In materis of loue, vse this kynde of verse, quhilk we call *Commoun* verse, as

Quhais answer made thame nocht sa glaid
That they sould thus the victors be,

As euen the answer quhilk I haid
Did greatly ioy and confort me:
Quhen lo, this spak Apollo myne,
All that thou seikis, it sall be thyne.

¶ Lyke verse of ten fete, as this foirsaid is of aucht, ye may vse lykewayis in loue materis: as also all kyndis of cuttit and brokin verse, quhairof new formes are daylie inuentit according to the Poëtes pleasour, as

Quha wald haue tyrde to heir that tone,
Quhilk birds corroborat ay abone
   Throuch schouting of the Larkis!
They sprang sa heich into the skyes,
Quhill Cupide walknis with the cryis
   Of Naturis chapell Clarkis.
Then, leauing all the Heauins aboue,
   He lichted on the eard.
Lo! how that lytill God of loue
   Before me then appeard,
So myld-lyke,
And chyld-lyke,   *With bow thre quarters skant*
So moylie
And coylie,   *He lukit lyke a Sant.*

And sa furth.

¶ This onely kynde of brokin verse abonewrittin man of necessitie, in thir last short fete, as *so moylie and coylie*, haue bot twa fete and a tayle to ilkane of thame, as ye sie, to gar the cullour and ryme be in the penult syllabe.

¶ And of thir foirsaidis kyndes of ballatis of haill verse, and not cuttit or brokin as this last is, gif ye lyke to put ane owerword till ony of thame, as making the last lyne of the first verse to be the last lyne of euerie vther verse in that ballat, [will] set weill for loue materis.

A short Treatise on Verse

Bot besydis thir kyndes of brokin or cuttit verse, quhilks ar inuentit daylie be Poetis, as I shewe before, there are sindrie kyndes of haill verse, with all thair lynis alyke lang, quhilk I haue heir omittit, and tane bot onelie thir few kyndes abone specifeit as the best, quhilk may be applyit to ony kynde of subiect, bot rather to thir quhairof I haue spokin before.

WILLIAM WEBBE

(*A Discourse of English Poetrie*)

1586

[*A Discourse of Eng|lish Poetrie. || Together with the Authors| iudgment, touching the re-|formation of our Eng-|lish Verse. || By William Webbe | Graduate* was printed at London in 1586 by John Charlewood for Robert Walley (1 vol. 4to). The text is taken from the rare copy in the Bodleian (Malone 708). Webbe dedicated this 'draught of English Poetry' to Edward Suliard, of Flemyngs, in the parish of Runwell, Essex, to whose sons Edward and Thomas he had been tutor. 'I sende it into your sight, not as anie wyttie peece of worke that may delight you, but being a sleight somewhat compyled for recreation in the intermyssions of my daylie businesse (euen thys Summer Eueninges), as a token of that earnest and vnquenchable desyre I haue to shewe my selfe duetifull and welwylling towardes you[1].']

A PREFACE TO THE NOBLE POETS OF ENGLANDE.

AMONG the innumerable sortes of Englyshe Bookes, and infinite fardles of printed pamphlets, wherewith thys Countrey is pestered, all shoppes stuffed, and euery study furnished, the greatest part I thinke, in any one kinde, are such as are either meere Poeticall, or which tende in some respecte (as either in matter or forme) to

---

[1] Warton informs us that Edward Hake wrote a tract entitled *The Touch-stone of Wittes* (12mo, black letter; London, Edmund Botifaunt, 1588), 'chiefly compiled with some slender additions from William Webbe's *Discourse of English Poetrie*' (*Hist.* iv. 97). He quotes one sentence from it: 'Then haue we the Mirrour of Magistrates lately augmented by my friend mayster Iohn Higgins, and penned by the choysest learned wittes, which, for the stately-proportioned uaine of

Of English Poetry

Poetry. Of such Bookes therfore, sith I haue beene one that haue had a desire to reade not the fewest, and because it is an argument which men of great learning haue no leysure to handle, or at least hauing to doo with more serious matters doo least regarde, if I write something concerning what I thinke of our English Poets, or aduenture to sette downe my simple iudgement of English Poetrie, I trust the learned Poets will giue me leaue, and vouchsafe my Booke passage, as beeing for the rudenesse thereof no preiudice to their noble studies, but euen (as my intent is) an *instar cotis* to stirre vppe some other of meete abilitie to bestowe trauell in this matter: whereby I thinke wee may not onelie get the meanes, which wee yet want, to discerne betweene good writers and badde, but perhappes also challenge from the rude multitude of rusticall Rymers, who will be called Poets, the right practise and orderly course of true Poetry.

It is to be wondred at of all, and is lamented of manie, that where as all kinde of good learning haue aspyred to royall dignitie and statelie grace in our English tongue, being not onelie founded, defended, maintained, and enlarged, but also purged from faultes, weeded of errours, and pollished from barbarousnes, by men of great authoritie and iudgement, onelie Poetrie hath founde fewest frends to amende it, those that can reseruing theyr skyll to themselues, those that cannot running headlong vppon it, thinking to garnish it with their deuises, but more corrupting it with fantasticall errours. What shoulde be the cause that our English speeche, in some of the wysest mens iudgements, hath neuer attained to anie sufficient ripenes, nay not ful auoided the reproch of

the heroick style and good meetly proportion of uerse, may challenge the best of Lydgate, and all our late rhymers.' This is all we know of Hake's volume. Warton does not tell us where he saw the text. No copy is known to be preserved.

barbarousnes in Poetry? The rudenes of the Countrey, or basenesse of wytts; or the course *Dialect* of the speeche? Experience vtterlie disproueth it to be anie of these. What then? Surelie the canckred enmitie of curious custome: which as it neuer was great freend to any good learning, so in this hath it grounded in the most such a negligent perswasion of an impossibilitie in matching the best, that the finest witts and most diuine heades haue contented themselues with a base kinde of fingering, rather debasing theyr faculties in setting forth theyr skyll in the coursest manner, then for breaking custome they would labour to adorne their Countrey and aduaunce their style with the highest and most learnedst toppe of true Poetry. The rudenes or vnaptnesse of our Countrey to be either none or no hinderaunce, if reformation were made accordinglie, the exquisite excellency in all kindes of good learning nowe flourishing among vs, inferiour to none other nation, may sufficiently declare.

That there be as sharpe and quicke wittes in England as euer were among the peerelesse Grecians or renowmed Romaines, it were a note of no witte at all in me to deny. And is our speeche so course, or our phrase so harshe, that Poetry cannot therein finde a vayne whereby it may appeare like it selfe? Why should we think so basely of this? rather then of her sister, I meane Rhetoricall *Eloquution*? which as they were by byrth Twyns, by kinde the same, by originall of one descent, so no doubt, as Eloquence hath founde such fauourers in the English tongue, as she frequenteth not any more gladly, so would Poetrye, if there were the like welcome and entertainment gyuen her by our English Poets, without question aspyre to wonderfull perfection, and appeare farre more gorgeous and delectable among vs. Thus much I am bolde to say in behalfe of Poetrie, not that I meane to call in question the reuerend and learned workes of Poetrie written in

Of English Poetry

our tongue by men of rare iudgement and most excellent Poets, but euen as it were by way of supplication to the famous and learned Lawreat Masters of Englande, that they would but consult one halfe howre with their heauenly Muse what credite they might winne to theyr natiue speeche, what enormities they might wipe out of English Poetry, what a fitte vaine they might frequent, wherein to shewe forth their worthie faculties if English Poetrie were truely reformed, and some perfect platforme or *Prosodia* of versifying were by them ratified and sette downe, eyther in immitation of Greekes and Latines, or, where it would skant abyde the touch of theyr Rules, the like obseruations selected and established by the naturall affectation of the speeche. Thus much I say, not to perswade you that are the fauourers of Englishe Poetry, but to mooue it to you: beeing not the firste that haue thought vpon this matter, but one that by consent of others haue taken vpon me to lay it once again in your wayes, if perhaps you may stumble vppon it, and chance to looke so lowe from your diuine cogitations, when your Muse mounteth to the starres and ransacketh the Spheres of heauen: whereby perhaps you may take compassion of noble Poetry, pittifullie mangled and defaced by rude smatterers and barbarous immitatours of your worthy studies. If the motion bee worthy your regard, it is enough to mooue it; if not, my wordes woulde simply preuaile in perswading you; and therefore I rest vppon thys onely request, that of your courtesies you wyll graunt passage, vnder your fauourable corrections, for this my simple censure of English Poetry, wherein, if you please to runne it ouer, you shall knowe breefely myne opinion of the most part of your accustomed Poets, and particularly, in his place, the lyttle somewhat which I haue sifted out of my weake brayne concerning thys reformed versifying.

W. W.

A DISCOURSE OF ENGLISHE POETRIE.

INTENDING to write some discourse of English Poetrie, I thinke it not amysse if I speake something generally of Poetrie, as, what it is, whence it had the beginning, and of what estimation it hath alwayes beene and ought to be among al sorts of people. Poetrie, called in Greeke ποετρια beeing deriued from the Verbe ποιέω, which signifieth in Latine *facere*, in English to make, may properly be defined the arte of making: which word, as it hath alwaies beene especially vsed of the best of our English Poets to expresse the very faculty of speaking or wryting Poetically, so doth it in deede containe most fitly the whole grace and property of the same, the more fullye and effectually then any other English Verbe. That Poetry is an Arte (or rather a more excellent thing then can be contayned wythin the compasse of Arte), though I neede not stande long to prooue, both the witnes of *Horace*, who wrote *de arte Poetica*, and of *Terence*, who calleth it *Artem Musicam*, and the very naturall property thereof may sufficiently declare. The beginning of it, as appeareth by *Plato*, was of a vertuous and most deuout purpose; who witnesseth that by occasion of meeting of a great company of young men, to solemnize the feasts which were called *Panegeryca*, and were wont to be celebrated euery fift yeere, there they that were most pregnant in wytt, and indued with great gyfts of wysedome and knowledge in Musicke aboue the rest, did vse commonly to make goodly verses, measured according to the sweetest notes of Musicke, containing the prayse of some noble vertue, or of immortalitie, or of some such thing of greatest estimation: which vnto them seemed so heauenly and ioyous a thing, that, thinking such men to be inspyrde with some diuine instinct from heauen, they called them *Vates*. So when other among them of the finest wits and aptest capacities beganne in imitation of these to frame ditties of lighter matters, and tuning them to the stroake of some of the pleasantest kind of Musicke, then began there to growe a distinction and great diuersity betweene makers and makers. Whereby (I take it) beganne thys difference: that they which handled in the audience of the people graue and necessary matters were called wise men or eloquent men, which they meant by *Vates*; and the rest which sange of loue matters, or other lighter deuises alluring vnto pleasure and delight, were called *Poetæ* or makers. Thus it appeareth both Eloquence and Poetrie to haue had their beginning and originall from these exercises, beeing framed in such sweete measure of sentences and pleasant harmonie called Ῥυθμός, which is an apt composition of wordes or clauses, drawing as it were by force the hearers eares euen whether soeuer it lysteth, that *Plato* affirmeth therein to be contained γοητεία an inchauntment, as it were to perswade them anie thing whether they would or no. And heerehence is sayde that men were first withdrawne from a wylde and sauadge kinde of life to ciuillity and gentlenes and the right knowledge of humanity by the force of this measurable or tunable speaking.

This opinion shall you finde confirmed throughout the whole workes of *Plato* and *Aristotle*: and that such was the estimation of this Poetry at those times, that they supposed all wisdome and knowledge to be included mystically in that diuine instinction wherewith they thought their *Vates* to bee inspyred. Wherevpon, throughout the noble workes of those most excellent Philosophers before named, are the authorities of Poets very often alledged. And *Cicero* in his *Tusculane* questions is of that minde, that a Poet cannot expresse verses aboundantly. sufficiently, and fully, neither his eloquence can flowe pleasauntly, or his wordes sounde well and plenteously, without celestiall instinction: which Poets themselues doo very often and gladlie witnes of themselues, as namely *Ouid* in 6. *Fasto*: *Est deus in nobis; agitante calescimus illo, etc.* Wherevnto I doubt not equally to adioyne the authoritye of our late famous English Poet who wrote the *Sheepheards Calender*, where, lamenting the decay of Poetry at these dayes, saith most sweetely to the same:

Then make thee winges of thine aspyring wytt,
And, whence thou camest, flye back to heauen apace, etc.

Whose fine poeticall witt and most exquisite learning, as he shewed aboundantly in that peece of worke, in my iudgment inferiour to the workes neither of *Theocritus* in Greeke nor *Virgill* in Latine, whom he narrowly immitateth: so I nothing doubt but if his other workes were common abroade, which are as I thinke in the close custodie of certaine his freends, we should haue of our owne Poets whom wee might matche in all respects with the best. And, among all other his workes whatsoeuer, I would wysh to haue the sight of hys *English Poet*, which his freend *E. K.* did once promise to publishe, which whether he performed or not, I knowe not: if he did, my happe hath not beene so good as yet to see it.

But to returne to the estimation of Poetry. Besides the great and profitable fruites contained in Poetry, for the instruction of manners and precepts of good life (for that was cheefly respected in the first age of Poetry), this is also added to the eternall commendations of that noble faculty: that Kinges and Princes, great and famous men, did euer encourage, mayntaine, and reward Poets in al ages, because they were thought onely to haue the whole power in their handes of making men either immortally famous for their valiaunt exploytes and vertuous exercises,

or perpetually infamous for their vicious liues. Where-
vppon it is said of *Achilles* that this onely vantage he
had of *Hector*, that it was his fortune to be extolled and
renowmed by the heauenly verse of *Homer*. And as *Tully*
recordeth to be written of *Alexander*, that with natural
teares he wept ouer *Achilles* Tombe, in ioy that he conceiued at the consideration howe it was his happe to be
honoured wyth so diuine a worke as *Homers* was. *Aristotle*, a most prudent and learned Philosopher, beeing
appointed Schoolemaster to the young Prince *Alexander*,
thought no worke so meete to be reade vnto a King as the
worke of *Homer* : wherein the young Prince, being by
him instructed throughly, found such wonderfull delight
in the same when hee came to maturity, that hee would
not onely haue it with him in all his iourneyes, but in his
bedde also vnder his pyllowe, to delight him and teache
him both nights and dayes. The same is reported of
noble *Scipio*, who, finding the two Bookes of *Homer* in the
spoyle of Kyng *Darius*, esteemed them as wonderfull
precious Iewelles, making one of them his companion for
the night, the other for the day. And not onely was he
thus affected to that one peece or parte of Poetry, but so
generally he loued the professors thereof, that in his most
serious affayres, and hottest warres against *Numantia* and
Carthage, he could no whitte be without that olde Poet
Ennius in his company. But to speake of all those noble
and wyse Princes, who bare speciall fauour and countenaunce to Poets, were tedious, and would require a
rehearsall of all such in whose time there grewe any to
credite and estimation in that faculty. Thus farre therefore may suffice for the estimation of Poets. Nowe
I thinke most meete to speake somewhat concerning
what hath been the vse of Poetry, and wherin it rightly
consisted, and whereof consequently it obteyned such
estimation.

To begin therefore with the first that was first worthelye memorable in the excellent gyft of Poetrye, the best wryters agree that it was *Orpheus*, who by the sweete gyft of his heauenly Poetry withdrew men from raungyng vncertainly and wandring brutishly about, and made them gather together and keepe company, make houses, and keep fellowshippe together, who therefore is reported (as *Horace* sayth) to asswage the fiercenesse of Tygers and mooue the harde Flynts. After him was *Amphion*, who was the first that caused Citties to bee builded, and men therein to liue decently and orderly according to lawe and right. Next was *Tyrtæus*, who began to practise warlike defences, to keepe back enemies and saue themselues from inuasion of foes. In thys place I thinke were most conuenient to rehearse that aunceient Poet *Pyndarus*; but of the certaine time wherein he flourished I am not very certaine; but of the place where he continued moste, it shoulde seeme to be the City of *Thebes*, by *Plinie*, who reporteth that *Alexander* in sacking the same Cittie woulde not suffer the house wherein he dwelt to be spoyled as all the rest were. After these was *Homer*, who as it were in one summe comprehended all knowledge, wisedome, learning, and pollicie that was incident to the capacity of man. And who so liste to take viewe of hys two Bookes, one of his *Iliades*, the other his *Odissea*, shall throughly perceiue what the right vse of Poetry is: which indeede is to mingle profite with pleasure, and so to delight the Reader with pleasantnes of hys Arte, as in the mean time his mind may be well instructed with knowledge and wisedome. For so did that worthy Poet frame those his two workes, that in reading the first, that is his *Iliads*, by declaring and setting forth so liuely the Grecians assembly against Troy, together with their prowesse and fortitude against their foes, a Prince shall learne not onely courage and valiantnesse, but discretion also and pollicie to encounter with his enemies, yea a perfect forme of wyse consultations with his Captaines and exhortations to the people, with other infinite commodities.

Agayne, in the other part, wherein are described the manifold and daungerous aduentures of *Vlisses*, may a man learne many noble vertues; and also learne to escape and auoyde the subtyll practises and perrilous entrappinges of naughty persons; and not onely this, but in what sort also he may deale to knowe and perceiue the affections of those which be neere vnto him, and most familiar with him, the better to put them in trust with his matters of waight and importaunce. Therefore I may boldly sette downe thys to be the truest, auncientest, and best kinde of Poetry, to direct ones endeuour alwayes to that marke, that with delight they may euermore adioyne commoditie to theyr Readers: which because I grounde vpon *Homer*, the Prince of all Poets, therefore haue I alledged the order of his worke, as an authority sufficiently proouing this assertion.

Nowe what other Poets which followed him, and beene of greatest fame, haue doone for the moste parte in their seuerall workes I wyll briefely, and as my slender ability wyll serue me, declare. But, by my leaue, I must content my selfe to speake not of all, but of such as my selfe haue seene and beene best acquainted withall, and those not all nor the moste part of the auncient Grecians, of whom I knowe not how many there were, but these of the Latinists, which are of greatest fame and most obuious among us.

Thus much I can say, that *Aristotle* reporteth none to haue greatly flourished in Greece, at least wyse not left behynd them any notable memoriall, before the time of *Homer*. And *Tully* sayth as much, that there were none wrytt woorth the reading twyce in the Romaine tongue, before the Poet *Ennius*. And surely as the very summe or cheefest essence of Poetry dyd alwayes for the most part consist in delighting the readers or hearers wyth pleasure, so, as the number of Poets increased, they styll inclyned thys way rather then the other, so that most of them had speciall regarde to the pleasantnesse of theyr fine conceytes, whereby they might drawe mens mindes into admiration of theyr inuentions, more then they had to the profitte or commoditye that the Readers shoulde reape by their works. And thus, as I suppose, came it to passe among them that, for the most part of them, they would not write one worke contayning some serious matter: but for the same they wold likewise powre foorth as much of some wanton or laciuious inuention. Yet some of the auncientest sort of Grecians, as it seemeth, were not so much disposed to vayne delectation: as *Aristotle* sayth of *Empedocles*, that in hys iudgment he was onley a naturall Philosopher, no Poet at all, nor that he was like vnto *Homer* in any thing but hys meeter or number of feete, that is, that hee wrote in verse. After the time of *Homer* there began the firste Comedy wryters, who compyled theyr workes in a better stile, which continued not long before it was expelled by penalty, for scoffing too broade at mens manners, and the priuie reuengements which the Poets vsed against their ill wyllers. Among these was *Eupolis*, *Cratinus*, and *Aristophanes*; but afterward the order of thys wryting Comedies was reformed and made more plausible: then wrytte *Plato* (*Comicus*), *Menander*, and I knowe not who more.

There be many most profitable workes, of like antiquity, or rather before them, of the Tragedy writers: as of *Euripides* and *Sophocles*; then was there *Phocilides* and *Theagines*, with many other: which Tragedies had their inuention by one *Thespis*, and were pollished and amended by *Æschilus*. The profitte or discommoditie which aryseth by the vse of these Comedies and Tragedies, which is most, hath beene long in controuersie, and is sore vrged among vs at these dayes: what I thinke of the same, perhaps I shall breefely declare anon.

Nowe concerning the Poets which wrote in homely manner, as they pretended, but indeede with great pythe and learned iudgment, such as were the wryters of Sheepeheards talke and of husbandly precepts, who were among the Grecians that excelled, besides *Theocritus* and *Hesiodus*, I know not; of whom the first, what profitable workes he left to posterity, besides hys *Idillia* or contentions of Goteheards, tending most to delight and pretty inuentions, I can not tell. The other, no doubt for his Argument he tooke in hande, dealt very learnedly and profitably, that is, in precepts of Husbandry, but yet so as he myxed much wanton stuffe among the rest.

The first wryters of Poetry among the Latines shoulde seeme to be those which excelled in the framing of Commedies, and that they continued a long time without any notable memory of other Poets. Among whom the cheefest that we may see or heare tell of were these: *Ennius, Caecilius, Naeuius, Licinius, Attilius, Turpilius, Trabea, Luscius, Plautus*, and *Terens*. Of whom these two last named haue beene euer since theyr time most famous, and to these dayes are esteemed as greate helpes and furtheraunces to the obtayning of good Letters. But heere cannot I stay to speake of the most famous, renowmed, and excellent that euer writte among the Latine Poets, *P. Virgill*, who performed the very same in that tongue which *Homer* had doone in Greeke, or rather better, if better might, as *Sex. Propert.* in his *Elegies* gallantly recordeth in his praise, *Nescio quid magis nascitur Iliade*. Vnder the person of *Æneas* he expresseth the valoure of a worthy Captaine and valiaunt Gouernour, together with the perrilous aduentures of warre, and polliticke deuises at all assayes. And as he immitateth *Homer* in that worke, so doth he likewyse followe the very steps of *Theocritus*, in his most pythy inuentions of his *Æglogues*: and likewyse *Hesiodus* in hys *Georgicks* or bookes of Husbandry, but yet more grauely, and in a more decent style. But, notwithstanding hys sage grauity and wonderfull wisedome, dyd he not altogether restrayne his vayne, but that he would haue a cast at some wanton and skant comely an Argument, if indeede such trifles as be fathered vppon him were his owne. There followed after him very many rare and excellent Poets, wherof the most part writt light matters, as *Epigrammes* and *Elegies*, with much pleasant dalliance, among whom may be accounted *Propertius*, *Tibullus*, *Catullus*, and diuers whom *Ouid* speaketh of in diuers places of his workes. Then are there two Hystoricall Poets, no lesse profitable then delightsome to bee read, *Silius* and *Lucanus*: the one declaring the valiant prowesse of two noble Captaines, one enemie to the other, that is, *Scipio* and *Haniball*; the other, likewise, the fortitude of two expert warriours (yet more lamentably then the other, because these warres were ciuill), *Pompey* and *Cæsar*. The next in tyme, but (as most men doo account, and so did he himselfe) the second in dignity, we wyll adioyne *Ouid*, a most learned and exquisite Poet. The worke of greatest profitte which he wrote was his Booke of *Metamorphosis*, which though it consisted of fayned Fables for the most part, and poeticall inuentions, yet beeing moralized according to his meaning, and the trueth of euery tale beeing discouered, it is a worke of exceeding wysedome and sounde iudgment. If one lyst in like manner to haue knowledge and perfect intelligence of those rytes and ceremonies which were obserued after the Religion of the Heathen, no more profitable worke for that purpose then his bookes *De fastis*. The rest of his dooinges, though they tende to the vayne delights of loue and dalliaunce (except his *Tristibus* wherein he bewayleth hys exile), yet surely are mixed with much good counsayle and profitable

Of English Poetry

lessons, if they be wisely and narrowly read. After his time I know no worke of any great fame till the time of *Horace*, a Poet not of the smoothest style, but in sharpnesse of wytt inferiour to none, and one to whom all the rest both before his time and since are very much beholding. About the same time *Iuuenall* and *Persius*, then *Martial*, *Seneca*, a most excellent wryter of Tragedies, *Boetius*, *Lucretius*, *Statius*, *Val: Flaccus*, *Manilius*, *Ausonius*, *Claudian*, and many other, whose iust times and seuerall workes to speake of in this place were neither much needefull, nor altogeather tollerable, because I purposed an other argument. Onely I will adde two of later times, yet not farre inferiour to the most of them aforesayde, *Pallengenius* and *Bap. Mantuanus*; and, for a singuler gyft in a sweete Heroicall verse, match with them *Chr. Oclan*, the Authour of our *Anglorum Prœlia*. But nowe, least I stray too farre from my purpose, I wyl come to our English Poets, to whom I would I were able to yeelde theyr deserued commendations: and affoorde them that censure which I know many woulde, which can better if they were nowe to write in my steede.

I know no memorable worke written by any Poet in our English speeche vntill twenty yeeres past: where, although Learning was not generally decayde at any time, especially since the Conquest of King *William* Duke of *Normandy*, as it may appeare by many famous works and learned bookes (though not of this kinde) wrytten by Byshoppes and others, yet surelye that Poetry was in small price among them, it is very manifest, and no great maruayle, for euen that light of Greeke and Latine Poets which they had they much contemned, as appeareth by theyr rude versifying, which of long time was vsed (a barbarous vse it was), wherin they conuerted the naturall property of the sweete Latine verse to be a balde kinde of ryming, thinking nothing to be learnedly written in verse which fell not out in ryme, that is, in wordes whereof the middle worde of eche verse should sound a like with the last, or of two verses the ende of both should fall in the like letters as thus:

O male viuentes, versus audite sequentes.

And thus likewyse:

Propter haec et alia dogmata doctorum
Reor esse melius et magis decorum:
Quisque suam habeat, et non proximorum.

This brutish Poetrie, though it had not the beginning in this Countrey, yet so hath it beene affected heere that the infection thereof would neuer (nor I thinke euer will) be rooted vppe againe: I meane this tynkerly verse which we call ryme. Master *Ascham* sayth that it first began to be followed and maintained among the *Hunnes* and *Gothians* and other barbarous Nations, who, with the decay of all good learning, brought it into *Italy*: from thence it came into *Fraunce*, and so to *Germany*; at last conueyed into *England*, by men indeede of great wisedome and learning, but not considerate nor circumspect in that behalfe. But of this I must intreate more heereafter.

Henry the first King of that name in England is wonderfully extolled, in all aunciendt Recordes of memory, for hys singuler good learning in all kinde of noble studies, in so much as he was named by his surname *Beaucleark*, as much to say as *Fayreclerke* (whereof perhappes came the name of *Fayreclowe*). What knowledge hee attained in the skyll of Poetry, I am not able to say. I report his name for proofe that learning in this Country was not little esteemed of at that rude time, and that like it is, among other studies, a King would not neglect the faculty of Poetry. The first of our English Poets that I haue

Of English Poetry

heard of was *Iohn Gower*, about the time of king *Rychard* the seconde, as it should seeme by certayne coniectures bothe a Knight and questionlesse a singuler well learned man: whose workes I could wysh they were all whole and perfect among vs, for no doubt they contained very much deepe knowledge and delight; which may be gathered by his freend *Chawcer*, who speaketh of him oftentimes in diuers places of hys workes. *Chawcer*, who for that excellent fame which hee obtayned in his Poetry was alwayes accounted the God of English Poets (such a tytle for honours sake hath beene giuen him), was next after if not equall in time to *Gower*, and hath left many workes, both for delight and profitable knowledge farre exceeding any other that as yet euer since hys time directed theyr studies that way. Though the manner of hys stile may seeme blunte and course to many fine English eares at these dayes, yet in trueth, if it be equally pondered, and with good iudgment aduised, and confirmed with the time wherein he wrote, a man shall perceiue thereby euen a true picture or perfect shape of a right Poet. He by his delightsome vayne so gulled the eares of men with his deuises, that, although corruption bare such sway in most matters that learning and truth might skant bee admitted to shewe it selfe, yet without controllment myght hee gyrde at the vices and abuses of all states, and gawle with very sharpe and eger inuentions, which he did so learnedly and pleasantly that none therefore would call him into question. For such was his bolde spyrit, that what enormities he saw in any he would not spare to pay them home, eyther in playne words, or els in some prety and pleasant couert, that the simplest might espy him.

Neere in time vnto him was *Lydgate*, a Poet surely for good proportion of his verse and meetely currant style, as the time affoorded, comparable with *Chawcer*, yet more occupyed in supersticious and odde matters then was requesite in so good a wytte: which, though he handled them commendably, yet, the matters themselues beeing not so commendable, hys estimation hath beene the lesse. The next of our auncient Poets that I can tell of I suppose to be *Pierce Ploughman*, who in hys dooinges is somewhat harshe and obscure, but indeede a very pithy wryter, and (to hys commendation I speake it) was the first that I haue seene that obserued the quantity of our verse without the curiosity of Ryme.

Since these I knowe none other tyll the time of *Skelton*, who writ in the time of Kyng *Henry* the eyght, who as indeede he obtayned the Lawrell Garland, so may I wyth good ryght yeelde him the title of a Poet: hee was doubtles a pleasant conceyted fellowe, and of a very sharpe wytte, exceeding bolde, and would nyppe to the very quicke where he once sette holde. Next hym I thynke I may place master *George Gaskoyne*, as painefull a Souldier in the affayres of hys Prince and Country as he was a wytty Poet in his wryting: whose commendations, because I found in one of better iudgment then my selfe, I wyl sette downe hys wordes, and suppresse myne owne: of hym thus wryteth *E. K.*, vppon the ninth *Æglogue* of the new Poet. 'Master *George Gaskoyne*, a wytty Gentleman and the very cheefe of our late rymers, who, and if some partes of learning wanted not (albe it is well knowne he altogether wanted not learning), no doubt would haue attayned to the excellencye of those famous Poets. For gyfts of wytt and naturall promptnes appeare in him aboundantly.'

I might next speake of the dyuers workes of the olde Earle of *Surrey*, of the L. *Vaus*, of *Norton* of *Bristow*, *Edwardes*, *Tusser*, *Churchyard*, *Wyl. Hunnis, Haiwood, Sand, Hyll, S. Y., M. D.*, and many others; but to speake of their seuerall gyfts and aboundant skyll shewed forth by them in many pretty and learned workes woulde make my discourse much more tedious.

I may not omitte the deserued commendations of many honourable and noble Lordes and Gentlemen in her Maiesties Courte, which in the rare deuises of Poetry haue beene and yet are most excellent skylfull, among whom the right honourable Earle of *Oxford* may challenge to him selfe the tytle of the most excellent among the rest. I can no longer forget those learned Gentlemen which tooke such profitable paynes in translating the Latine Poets into our English tongue, whose desertes in that behalfe are more then I can vtter. Among these I euer esteemed, and while I lyue in my conceyt I shall account, Master *D. Phaer* without doubt the best: who, as indeede hee had the best peece of Poetry whereon to sette a most gallant verse, so performed he it accordingly, and in such sort, as in my conscience I thinke would scarcely be doone againe, if it were to doo again. Notwithstanding, I speak it but as myne own fancy, not preiudiciall to those that list to thinke otherwyse. Hys worke, whereof I speake, is the englishing of *Æneidos* of *Virgill*, so farre foorth as it pleased God to spare him life, which was to the halfe parte of the tenth Booke, the rest beeing since wyth no lesse commendations finished by that worthy scholler and famous Phisition, Master *Thomas Twyne*.

Equally with him may I well adioyne Master *Arthur Golding*, for hys labour in englishing *Ouids Metamorphosis*, for which Gentleman surely our Country hath for many respects greatly to gyue God thankes: as for him which hath taken infinite paynes without ceasing, trauelleth as yet indefatigably, and is addicted without society by his continuall laboure to profit this nation and speeche in all kind of good learning. The next very well derueth Master *Barnabe Googe* to be placed, as a painefull furtherer of learning: hys helpe to Poetry, besides hys owne deuises, as the translating of *Pallengenius Zodiac.* *Abraham Flemming*, as in many prety Poesis of hys owne, so in translating hath doone to hys commendations. To whom I would heere adioyne one of hys name, whom I know to haue excelled as well in all kinde of learning as in Poetry most especially, and would appeare so if the dainty morselles and fine poeticall inuentions of hys were as common abroade as I knowe they be among some of hys freendes. I wyl craue leaue of the laudable Authors of *Seneca* in English, of the other partes of *Ouid*, of *Horace*, of *Mantuan*, and diuers other, because I would hasten to ende thys rehearsall, perhappes offensyue to some, whom eyther by forgetfulnes or want of knowledge I must needes ouer passe.

And once againe, I am humbly to desire pardon of the learned company of Gentlemen Schollers and students of the Vniuersities and Innes of Courte, yf I omitte theyr seuerall commendations in this place, which I knowe a great number of them haue worthely deserued, in many rare deuises and singuler inuentions of Poetrie: for neither hath it beene my good happe to haue seene all which I haue hearde of, neyther is my abyding in such place where I can with facility get knowledge of their workes.

One Gentleman notwithstanding among them may I not ouerslyppe, so farre reacheth his fame, and so worthy is he, if hee haue not already, to weare the Lawrell wreathe, Master *George Whetstone*, a man singularly well skyld in this faculty of Poetrie. To him I wyl ioyne *Anthony Munday*, an earnest traueller in this arte, and in whose name I haue seene very excellent workes, among which, surely, the most exquisite vaine of a witty poeticall heade is shewed in the sweete sobs of Sheepheardes and Nymphes; a worke well worthy to be viewed, and to bee

esteemed as very rare Poetrie. With these I may place
Iohn Graunge, Knyght, Wylmott, Darrell, F. C., F. K.,
G. B., and many other, whose names come not nowe to my
remembraunce.

This place haue I purposely reserued for one, who, if
not only, yet in my iudgement principally, deserueth the
tytle of the rightest English Poet that euer I read, that
is, the Author of the Sheepeheardes Kalender, intituled
to the woorthy Gentleman Master *Phillip Sydney*: whether
it was Master *Sp.* or what rare Scholler in Pembrooke
Hall soeuer, because himself and his freendes, for what
respect I knowe not, would not reueale it, I force not
greatly to sette downe: sorry I am that I can not find
none other with whom I might couple him in this *Catalogue* in his rare gyft of Poetry: although one there is,
though nowe long since seriously occupied in grauer
studies (Master *Gabriell Haruey*), yet as he was once his
most special freende and fellow Poet, so because he hath
taken such paynes, not onely in his Latin Poetry (for
which he enioyed great commendations of the best both
in iudgment and dignity in thys Realme), but also to
reforme our English verse and to beautify the same with
braue deuises, of which I thinke the cheefe lye hidde in
hatefull obscurity: therefore wyll I aduenture to sette
them together, as two of the rarest witts and learnedst
masters of Poetrie in England. Whose worthy and
notable styl in this faculty I would wysh, if their high
dignities and serious businesses would permit, they would
styll graunt to bee a furtheraunce to that reformed kinde
of Poetry, which Master *Haruey* did once beginne to
ratify: and surely in mine opinion, if hee had chosen
some grauer matter, and handled but with halfe that skyll
which I knowe he could haue doone, and not powred it
foorth at a venture, as a thinge betweene iest and earnest,
it had taken greater effect then it did.

As for the other Gentleman, if it would please him or hys freendes to let those excellent *Poemes*, whereof I know he hath plenty, come abroad, as his Dreames, his Legends, his Court of *Cupid*, his English Poet, with other, he shoulde not onely stay the rude pens of my selfe and others, but also satisfye the thirsty desires of many which desire nothing more then to see more of hys rare inuentions. If I ioyne to Master *Haruey* hys two Brethren, I am assured, though they be both busied with great and waighty callinges (the one a godly and learned Diuine, the other a famous and skylfull Phisition), yet if they lysted to sette to their helping handes to Poetry, they would as much beautify and adorne it as any others.

If I let passe the vncountable rabble of ryming Ballet makers and compylers of sencelesse sonets, who be most busy to stuffe euery stall full of grosse deuises and vnlearned Pamphlets, I trust I shall with the best sort be held excused. For though many such can frame an Alehouse song of fiue or sixe score verses, hobbling vppon some tune of a Northen Iygge, or Robyn hoode, or La lubber etc., and perhappes obserue iust number of sillables, eyght in one line, sixe in an other, and there withall an A to make a iercke in the ende: yet if these might be accounted Poets (as it is sayde some of them make meanes to be promoted to the Lawrell) surely we shall shortly haue whole swarmes of Poets: and euery one that can frame a Booke in Ryme, though for want of matter it be but in commendations of Copper noses or Bottle Ale, wyll catch at the Garlande due to Poets; whose potticall, poeticall (I should say), heades I would wyshe at their worshipfull comencements might in steede of Lawrell be gorgiously garnished with fayre greene Barley, in token of their good affection to our Englishe Malt. One speaketh thus homely of them, with whose words I wyll content my selfe for thys time, because

I woulde not bee too broade wyth them in myne owne speeche.

'In regarde' (he meaneth of the learned framing the newe Poets workes which writt the Sheepheardes Calender) 'I scorne and spue out the rakehelly rout of our ragged Rymers (for so themselues vse to hunt the Letter) which without learning boaste, without iudgment iangle, without reason rage and fume, as if some instinct of poeticall spyrite had newlie rauished them aboue the meanesse of common capacity. And beeing in the midst of all their brauery, suddainly, for want of matter or of Ryme, or hauing forgotten their former conceyt, they seeme to be so payned and trauelled in theyr remembraunce, as it were a woman in Chyldbyrth, or as that same *Pythia* when the traunce came vpon her: *Os rabidum fera corda domans etc.*'

Thus farre foorth haue I aduentured to sette downe parte of my simple iudgement concerning those Poets, with whom for the most part I haue beene acquainted through myne owne reading: which though it may seeme something impertinent to the tytle of my Booke, yet I trust the courteous Readers wyll pardon me, considering that poetry is not of that grounde and antiquity in our English tongue, but that speaking thereof only as it is English would seeme like vnto the drawing of ones pycture without a heade.

Nowe therefore, by your gentle patience, wyll I wyth like breuity make tryall what I can say concerning our Englishe Poetry, first in the matter thereof, then in the forme, that is, the manner of our verse; yet so as I must euermore haue recourse to those times and wryters, whereon the English poetry taketh as it were the discent and proprietye.

English Poetry therefore, beeing considered according

to common custome and aunctient vse, is where any
worke is learnedly compiled in measurable speeche, and
framed in wordes contayning number or proportion of
iust syllables, delighting the readers or hearers as well
by the apt and decent framing of wordes in equall resemblance of quantity, commonly called verse, as by the
skyllfull handling of the matter whereof it is intreated.
I spake somewhat of the beginning of thys measuring of
wordes in iust number, taken out of *Plato*: and indeede
the regarde of true quantity in Letters and syllables
seemeth not to haue been much vrged before the time of
Homer in Greece, as *Aristotle* witnesseth.

The matters whereof verses were first made were
eyther exhortations to vertue, dehortations from vices,
or the prayses of some laudable thing. From thence
they beganne to vse them in exercises of immitating
some vertuous and wise man at their feastes: where as
some one shoulde be appointed to represent an other
mans person of high estimation, and he sang fine ditties
and wittie sentences, tunably to their Musick notes. Of
thys sprang the first kinde of Comedyes, when they
beganne to bring into these exercises more persons then
one, whose speeches were deuised Dyalogue wise, in
aunswering one another. And of such like exercises, or,
as some wyll needes haue it, long before the other, began
the first Tragedies, and were so called of τράγος, because
the Actor, when he began to play his part, slewe and
offered a Goate to their Goddesse: but Commedies tooke
their name of κωμάζειν καὶ ᾄδειν, *comessatum ire*, to goe
a feasting, because they vsed to goe in procession with
their sport about the Citties and Villages, mingling much
pleasaunt myrth wyth theyr graue Religion, and feasting
cheerefully together wyth as great ioy as might be deuised.
But not long after (as one delight draweth another) they
began to inuent new persons and newe matters for their

Comedies, such as the deuisers thought meetest to please the peoples vaine: And from these they beganne to present in shapes of men the natures of vertues and vices, and affections and quallities incident to men, as Iustice, Temperance, Pouerty, Wrathe, Vengeaunce, Sloth, Valiantnes, and such like, as may appeare by the aunciente workes of *Aristophanes*. There grewe at last to be a greater diuersitye betweene Tragedy wryters and Comedy wryters, the one expressing onely sorrowfull and lamentable Hystories, bringing in the persons of Gods and Goddesses, Kynges and Queenes, and great states, whose partes were cheefely to expresse most miserable calamities and dreadfull chaunces, which increased worse and worse, tyll they came to the most wofull plight that might be deuised. The Comedies, on the other side, were directed to a contrary ende, which, beginning doubtfully, drewe to some trouble or turmoyle, and by some lucky chaunce alwayes ended to the ioy and appeasement of all parties. Thys distinction grewe, as some holde opinion, by immitation of the workes of *Homer*; for out of his *Iliads* the Tragedy wryters founde dreadfull euents, whereon to frame their matters, and the other out of hys *Odyssea* tooke arguments of delight, and pleasant ending after dangerous and troublesome doubtes.

So that, though there be many sortes of poeticall wrytings, and Poetry is not debarred from any matter which may be expressed by penne or speeche, yet for the better vnderstanding and breefer method of thys discourse, I may comprehende the same in three sortes, which are Comicall, Tragicall, Historiall. Vnder the first may be contained all such *Epigrammes*, *Elegies*, and delectable ditties, which Poets haue deuised respecting onely the delight thereof: in the seconde, all dolefull complaynts, lamentable chaunces, and what soeuer is poetically expressed in sorrow and heauines. In the third we may comprise the reste of all such matters which is indifferent betweene the other two, [which] doo commonly occupy the pennes of Poets: such are the poeticall compyling of Chronicles, the freendly greetings betweene freendes, and very many sortes besides, which for the better distinction may be referred to one of these three kindes of Poetry. But once againe, least my discourse runne too farre awry, wyll I buckle my selfe more neerer to English Poetry: the vse wherof, because it is nothing different from any other, I thinke best to confirme by the testimony of *Horace*, a man worthy to beare authority in this matter, whose very opinion is this, that the perfect perfection of poetrie is this, to mingle delight with profitt in such wyse that a Reader might by his reading be pertaker of bothe; which though I touched in the beginning, yet I thought good to alledge in this place, for more confirmation thereof, some of hys owne wordes. In his treatise *de arte Poetica*, thus hee sayth:

> *Aut prodesse volunt, aut delectare poetae,*
> *Aut simul et iucunda et idonea dicere vitae.*

As much to saie: All Poets desire either by their works to profitt or delight men, or els to ioyne both profitable and pleasant lessons together for the instruction of life.

And againe:

> *Omne tulit punctum qui miscuit vtile dulci,*
> *Lectorem delectando pariterque monendo.*

That is, He misseth nothing of his marke which ioyneth profitt with delight, as well delighting his Readers as profiting them with counsell. And that whole Epistle which hee wryt of his Arte of Poetrie, among all the parts thereof, runneth cheefelie vppon this, that whether the argument which the Poet handleth be of thinges doone or fained inuentions, yet that they should beare such an Image of trueth that as they delight they may likewise profitt. For these are his wordes: *Ficta voluptatis causa sint proxima veris.* Let things that are faigned for pleasures sake haue a neere resemblance of the truth. This precept may you perceiue to bee most duelie obserued of *Chawcer*: for who could with more delight prescribe such wholsome counsaile and sage aduise, where he seemeth onelie to respect the profitte of his lessons and instructions? or who coulde with greater wisedome, or more pithie skill, vnfold such pleasant and delightsome matters of mirth, as though they respected nothing but the telling of a merry tale? So that this is the very grounde of right poetrie, to giue profitable counsaile, yet so as it must be mingled with delight. For among all the aunciente workes of poetrie, though the most of them incline much to that part of delighting men with pleasant matters of small importaunce, yet euen in the vainest trifles among them there is not forgotten some profitable counsaile, which a man may learne, either by flatte precepts which therein are prescribed, or by loathing such vile vices, the enormities whereof they largelie discouer. For surelie I am of this opinion that the wantonest Poets of all, in their most laciuious workes wherein they busied themselues, sought rather by that meanes to withdraw mens mindes (especiallie the best natures) from such foule vices then to allure them to imbrace such beastly follies as they detected.

Horace, speaking of the generall dueties of Poets, sayth, *Os tenerum pueri balbumque poeta figurat*, and manie more wordes concerning the profitte to be hadde out of Poets: which because I haue some of them comprised into an English translation of that learned and famous knight, Sir *Thomas Elyot*, I wyll set downe his wordes.

> The Poet fashioneth by some pleasant meane
> The speeche of children stable and vnsure:
> Gulling their eares from wordes and thinges vncleane,
> Giuing to them precepts that are pure:
> Rebuking enuy and wrath if it dure:
> Thinges well donne he can by example commend:
> To needy and sicke he doth also his cure
> To recomfort, if ought he can amende.

And manie other like wordes are in that place of *Horace* to like effect. Therefore poetrie, as it is of it selfe, without abuse is not onely not vnprofitable to the liues and studies of menne, but wonderfull commendable and of great excellencie. For nothing can be more acceptable to men, or rather to be wished, then sweete allurements to vertues and commodious caueates from vices; of which Poetrie is exceeding plentifull, powring into gentle witts, not roughly and tirannicallie, but as it were with a louing authoritie. Nowe, if the ill and vndecent prouocations, whereof some vnbridled witts take occasion by the reading of laciuious Poemes, bee obiected—such as are *Ouids* loue Bookes and *Elegies*, *Tibullus*, *Catullus*, and *Martials* workes, with the Comedies for the most part of *Plautus* and *Terence*—I thinke it easily aunswered. For though it may not iustlie be denied that these workes are indeede very Poetrie, yet that Poetrie in them is not the essentiall or formall matter or cause of the hurt therein might be affirmed, and although that reason should come short, yet this might be sufficient, that the workes themselues doo not corrupt, but the abuse of the vsers, who, vndamaging their owne dispositions by reading the discoueries of vices, resemble foolish folke who, comming into a Garden without anie choise or circumspection, tread downe the fairest flowers and wilfullie thrust their fingers among the nettles.

And surelie to speake what I verelie thinke, this is

mine opinion: that one hauing sufficient skyll to reade and vnderstand those workes, and yet no staie of him selfe to auoyde inconueniences, which the remembraunce of vnlawfull things may stirre vppe in his minde, he, in
5 my iudgement, is wholy to bee reputed a laciuious disposed personne, whom the recitall of Sins whether it be in a good worke or a badde, or vppon what occasion soeuer, wyll not staie him but prouoke him further vnto them. Contrariwise, what good lessons the warie and
10 skylful Readers shall picke out of the very worst of them, if they list to take anie heede, and reade them not of an intent to bee made the worse by them, you may see by these fewe sentences, which the foresayd Sir *Thomas Elyott* gathered as he sayth at all aduentures, intreating
15 of the like argument. First, *Plautus* in commendations of vertue hath such like wordes:

Verely vertue doth all thinges excell,
For if liberty, health, liuing, or substaunce,
Our Country, our parents, and children doo well,
20 It hapneth by vertue; she doth all aduaunce;
Vertue hath all thinges vnder gouernaunce:
And in whom of vertue is founde great plenty
Any thing that is good may neuer be dainty.

Terence, in Eunucho, hath a profitable speeche, in blasing
25 foorth the fashions of harlots before the eyes of young men. Thus sayth *Parmeno*:

In thys thing I tryumphe in myne owne conceite,
That I haue found for all young men the way,
Howe they of Harlots shall know the deceite,
30 Their witts and manners, that thereby they may
Them perpetuallie hate; for so much as they
Out of their owne houses be fresh and delicate,
Feeding curiously, at home all day
Lyuing beggerlie in most wretched estate.

And many more wordes of the same matter, but which may be gathered by these fewe.

Ouid, in his most wanton Bookes of loue, and the remedies thereof, hath very many pithie and wise sentences, which a heedefull Reader may marke and chose out from the other stuffe. This is one.

> Tyme is a medicine if it shall profitt;
> Wine gyuen out of tyme may be annoyaunce.
> And man shall irritat vice, if he prohibitt
> When time is not meete vnto his vtteraunce.
> Therfore, if thou yet by counsayle art recuperable,
> Fly thou from idlenes and euer be stable.

Martiall, a most dissolute wryter among all other, yet not without many graue and prudent speeches as this, is one worthy to be marked of these fond youthes which intangle theyr wytts in raging loue, who, stepping once ouer shoes in theyr fancyes, neuer rest plunging till they be ouer head and eares in their follie.

> If thou wylt eschewe bitter aduenture,
> And auoyde the annoyance of a pensifull hart,
> Set in no one person all wholly thy pleasure;
> The lesse maist thou ioy, but the lesse shalt thou smart.

These are but fewe gathered out by happe, yet sufficient to shewe that the wise and circumspect Readers may finde very many profitable lessons dispersed in these workes, neither take any harme by reading such Poemes, but good, if they wil themselues. Neuertheles, I would not be thought to hold opinion that the reading of them is so tollerable, as that there neede no respect to be had in making choyse of readers or hearers: for if they be prohibited from the tender and vnconstant wits of children and young mindes, I thinke it not without great reason: neyther am I of that deuillish opinion, of which some

there are, and haue beene, in England, who, hauing charge of youth to instruct them in learning, haue especially made choyse of such vnchildish stuffe to reade vnto young Schollers, as it shoulde seeme of some filthy pur-
5 pose, wylfully to corrupt theyr tender mindes and prepare them the more ready for theyr loathsome dyetts.

For, as it is sayd of that impudent worke of *Luciane*, a man were better to reade none of it then all of it, so thinke I that these workes are rather to be kept alto-
10 gether from children then they should haue free liberty to reade them, before they be meete either of their owne discretion or by heedefull instruction to make choyse of the good from the badde. As for our Englishe Poetrie, I know no such perilous peeces (except a fewe balde
15 ditties made ouer the Beere potts, which are nothing lesse then Poetry) which anie man may vse and reade without damage or daunger: which indeede is lesse to be meruailed at among vs then among the olde Latines and Greekes, considering that Christianity may be a staie to
20 such illecibrous workes and inuentions as among them (for their Arte sake) myght obtaine passage.

Nowe will I speake somewhat of that princelie part of Poetrie, wherein are displaied the noble actes and valiant exploits of puissaunt Captaines, expert souldiers, wise
25 men, with the famous reportes of auncient times, such as are the Heroycall workes of *Homer* in Greeke and the heauenly verse of *Virgils Æneidos* in Latine: which workes, comprehending as it were the summe and grounde of all Poetrie, are verelie and incomparably the best of
30 all other. To these, though wee haue no English worke aunswerable in respect of the glorious ornaments of gallant handling, yet our auncient Chroniclers and reporters of our Countrey affayres come most neere them: and no doubt, if such regarde of our English speeche and
35 curious handling of our verse had beene long since thought

vppon, and from time to time been pollished and bettered by men of learning, iudgement, and authority, it would ere this haue matched them in all respects. A manifest example thereof may bee the great good grace and sweete vayne which Eloquence hath attained in our speeche, because it hath had the helpe of such rare and singuler wits, as from time to time myght still adde some amendment to the same. Among whom I thinke there is none that will gainsay but Master *Iohn Lilly* hath deserued moste high commendations, as he which hath stept one steppe further therein then any either before or since he first began the wyttie discourse of his *Euphues*. Whose workes, surely in respecte of his singuler eloquence and braue composition of apt words and sentences, let the learned examine and make tryall thereof thorough all the partes of Rethoricke, in fitte phrases, in pithy sentences, in gallant tropes, in flowing speeche, in plaine sence, and surely, in my iudgment, I thinke he wyll yeelde him that verdict which *Quintilian* giueth of bothe the best Orators *Demosthenes* and *Tully*, that from the one nothing may be taken away, to the other nothing may be added. But a more neerer example to prooue my former assertion true (I meane the meetnesse of our speeche to receiue the best forme of Poetry) may bee taken by conference of that famous translation of Master D. *Phaer* with the coppie it selfe, who soeuer please with courteous iudgement but a little to compare and marke them both together, and weigh with himselfe whether the English tongue might by little and little be brought to the verye maiesty of a ryght Heroicall verse. First you may marke how *Virgill* always fitteth his matter in hande with wordes agreeable vnto the same affection which he expresseth: as in hys Tragicall exclamations, what pathe[ti]call speeches he frameth? in his comfortable consolations, howe smoothely hys verse runnes? in his dreadfull battayles and dreery bycker-

Of English Poetry

ments of warres, howe bygge and boystrous his wordes
sound? and the like notes in all partes of his worke may
be obserued. Which excellent grace and comely kind of
choyse, if the translatour hath not hitte very neere in our
course English phrase, iudge vprightly: wee wyll conferre
some of the places, not picked out for the purpose, but
such as I tooke turning ouer the Booke at randon.
When the Troyans were so tost about in tempestious
wether, caused by *Æolus* at *Iunoes* request, and driuen
vpon the coaste of *Affrick* with a very neere scape of their
liues, *Æneas* after hee had gone a land and kylled plenty
of victuals for his company of Souldiours, hee deuided the
same among them, and thus louinglie and sweetely he
comforted them (*Æn. Lib. i*):

> *et dictis maerentia pectora mulcet:*
> *O socii (neque enim ignari sumus ante malorum),*
> *O passi grauiora: dabit deus his quoque finem.*
> *Vos et Scyllaeam rabiem penitusque sonantes*
> *Accestis scopulos: vos et Cyclopea saxa*
> *Experti. Reuocate animos, maestumque timorem*
> *Mittite. Forsan et haec olim meminisse iuuabit.*
> *Per varios casus, per tot discrimina rerum,*
> *Tendimus in Latium: sedes vbi fata quietas*
> *Ostendunt. Illic fas regna resurgere Troiae.*
> *Durate, et vosmet rebus seruate secundis.*
> *Talia voce refert: curisque ingentibus aeger*
> *Spem vultu simulat, premit altum corde dolorem.*

Translated thus:

> And then to cheere their heauy harts with these words he him bent,
> O Mates, (quoth he) that many a woe haue bidden and borne ere thys,
> Worse haue we seene, and this also shall end when Gods wyll is.

Through *Sylla* rage (ye wott) and through the roaring rocks we past;
Though *Cyclops* shore was full of feare, yet came we through at last.
Plucke vppe your harts, and driue from thence both feare and care away;
To thinke on this may pleasure be perhapps another day.
By paynes and many a daunger sore, by sundry chaunce we wend, 5
To come to *Italy*, where we trust to find our resting ende,
And where the destnyes haue decreed *Troyes* Kingdome eft to ryse.
Be bold and harden now your harts, take ease while ease applies.
Thus spake he tho, but in his hart huge cares had him opprest;
Dissembling hope with outward eyes, full heauy was his brest. 10

Againe, marke the wounding of *Dido* in loue with *Æneas*, with howe choyse wordes it is pithily described, both by the Poet and the translator, in the beginning of the fourth booke.

> *At regina graui iamdudum saucia cura* 15
> *Vulnus alit venis, et caeco carpitur igni, etc.*

By this time perced satte the Queene so sore with loues desire,
Her wound in euery vayne she feedes, she fryes in secrete fire.
The manhood of the man full oft, full oft his famous lyne
She doth reuolue, and from her thought his face cannot vntwyne. 20

His countnaunce deepe she drawes and fixed fast she
  beares in brest
His words also; nor to her carefull hart can come no
  rest.

And in many places of the fourth booke is the same
matter so gallantly prosecuted in sweete wordes, as in
5 mine opinion the coppy it selfe goeth no whit beyond it.

Compare them likewise in the woefull and lamentable
cryes of the Queene for the departure of *Æneas*, towards
the ende of that Booke.

> *Terque quaterque manu pectus percussa decorum*
> 10 *Flauentesque abscissa comas, proh Iupiter, ibit*
> *Hic ? ait, et nostris illuserit aduena regnis? etc.*

Three times her hands she bet, and three times strake
  her comely brest,
Her golden hayre she tare and frantiklike with moode
  opprest;
She cryde, O *Iupiter*, O God, quoth she, and shall
  a goe?
15 Indeede? and shall a flowte me thus within my kingdome so?
Shall not mine Armies out, and all my people them
  pursue?
Shall they not spoyle their shyps and burne them vp
  with vengance due?
Out people, out vppon them, follow fast with fires and
  flames,
Set sayles aloft, make out with oares, in ships, in
  boates, in frames.
20 What speake I? or where am I? what furies me doo
  thus inchaunt?
O *Dydo*, wofull wretch, now destnyes fell thy head
  dooth haunt.

And a little after preparing to kyll her owne selfe:

> But *Dydo* quaking fierce with frantike moode and griesly hewe,
> With trembling spotted cheekes, her huge attempting[s] to persue,
> Besides her selfe for rage, and towards death with visage wanne,
> Her eyes about she rolde; as redde as blood they looked than.

At last ready to fall vppon *Æneas* sworde:

> O happy (welaway) and ouer happy had I beene,
> If neuer Troian shyps (ahlas) my Country shore had seene.
> Thus sayd, she wryde her head. And vnreuenged must we die?
> And let vs boldly die (quoth shee); thus, thus to death I ply.

Nowe likewise for the braue warlike phrase and bygge sounding kynd of thundring speeche, in the hotte skyrmyshes of battels, you may confer them in any of the last fiue Bookes: for examples sake, thys is one about the ninth Booke.

> *It clamor totis per propugnacula muris:*
> *Intendunt acris arcus, amentaque torquent.*
> *Sternitur omne solum telis: tum scuta cauaeque*
> *Dant sonitum flictu galeae: pugna aspera surgit, etc.*

> A clamarous noyse vpmounts on fortresse tops and bulwarks towres;
> They strike, they bend their bowes, they whirle from strings sharp shoting showres.
> All streetes with tooles are strowed, than helmets, skulles, with battrings marrd;
> And shieldes dishyuering cracke, vpriseth roughnesse byckring hard.

> Looke how the tempest storme when wind out wrastling blowes at south,
> Raine ratling beates the grownde, or clowdes of haile from Winters mouth
> Downe dashyng headlong driues, when God from skyes with griesly steuen
> His watry showres outwrings, and whirlwind clowdes downe breakes from heauen.

And so foorth much more of the like effect.

Onely one comparison more will I desire you to marke at your leysures, which may serue for all the rest, that is, the description of Fame, as it is in the 4. booke, towardes the end, of which it followeth thus.

Monstrum horrendum ingens, cui quot sunt corpore plumae
Tot vigiles oculi, etc.

> Monster gastly great, for euery plume her carkasse beares
> Like number learing eyes she hath, like number harkning eares,
> Like number tongues and mouthes she wagges, a wondrous thing to speake;
> At midnight foorth shee flyes, and vnder shade her sound dooth squeake.
> All night she wakes, nor slumber sweete doth take nor neuer sleepes;
> By dayes on houses tops shee sits, or gates of Townes she keepes.
> On watching Towres she clymbes, and Citties great she makes agast:
> Both trueth and falshood forth she telles, and lyes abroade doth cast.

But what neede I to repeate any more places? There is not one Booke among the twelue which wyll not yeelde you most excellent pleasure in conferring the translation

with the Coppie, and marking the gallant grace which
our Englishe speeche affoordeth. And in trueth the like
comparisons may you choose out through the whole translations of the *Metamorphosis* by Master *Golding*, who (considering both their Coppyes) hath equally deserued
commendations for the beautifying of the English speeche.
It would be tedious to stay to rehearse any places out of
him nowe : let the other suffice to prooue that the English
tongue lacketh neyther variety nor currantnesse of phrase
for any matter.

I will nowe speake a little of an other kinde of
poetical writing, which might notwithstanding for the
variablenesse of the argument therein vsually handled
bee comprehended in those kindes before declared : that
is, the compyling *Eglogues*, as much to say as Goteheardes tales, because they bee commonly Dialogues or
speeches framed or supposed betweene Sheepeheardes,
Neteheardes, Goteheardes, or such like simple men; in
which kind of writing many haue obtained as immortall
prayse and commendation as in any other.

The cheefest of these is *Theocritus* in Greeke; next
him, and almost the very same, is *Virgill* in Latin. After
Virgyl in like sort writ *Titus Calphurnius* and *Baptista
Mantuan*, wyth many other both in Latine and other languages very learnedlye. Although the matter they take
in hand seemeth commonlie in appearaunce rude and
homely, as the vsuall talke of simple clownes, yet doo
they indeede vtter in the same much pleasaunt and profitable delight. For vnder these personnes, as it were in
a cloake of simplicitie, they would eyther sette foorth the
prayses of theyr freendes, without the note of flattery, or
enueigh grieuously against abuses, without any token of
bytternesse.

Somwhat like vnto these works are many peeces of

Chawcer, but yet not altogether so poeticall. But nowe yet at the last hath England hatched vppe one Poet of this sorte, in my conscience comparable with the best in any respect: euen Master *Sp:*, Author of the *Sheepeheardes Calender*, whose trauell in that peece of English Poetrie I thinke verely is so commendable, as none of equall iudgment can yeelde him lesse prayse for hys excellent skyll and skylfull excellency shewed foorth in the same then they would to eyther *Theocritus* or *Virgill*, whom in mine opinion, if the coursenes of our speeche (I meane the course of custome which he woulde not infringe) had beene no more let vnto him then theyr pure natiue tongues were vnto them, he would haue (if it might be) surpassed them. What one thing is there in them so worthy admiration whereunto we may not adioyne some thing of his of equall desert? Take *Virgil* and make some little comparison betweene them, and iudge as ye shall see cause.

Virgill hath a gallant report of *Augustus* couertly comprysed in the first *Æglogue*; the like is in him of her Maiestie, vnder the name of *Eliza*. *Virgill* maketh a braue coloured complaint of vnstedfast freendshyppe in the person of *Corydon*; the lyke is him in his 5 *Æglogue*. Agayne, behold the pretty Pastorall contentions of *Virgill* in the third *Æglogue*; of him in the eight *Eglogue*. Finally, either in comparison with them, or respect of hys owne great learning, he may well were the Garlande, and steppe before the best of all English Poets that I haue seene or hearde; for I thinke no lesse 'deserueth' (thus sayth *E. K.* in hys commendations) 'hys wittinesse in deuising, his pithinesse in vttering, his complaintes of loue so louely, his discourses of pleasure so pleasantly, his Pastrall rudenes, his Morrall wysenesse, his due obseruing of *decorum* euery where, in personages, in season[s], in matter, in speeche, and generally in all seemely simplicity of handling hys matter and framing hys wordes.'

The occasion of his worke is a warning to other young men, who, being intangled in loue and youthful vanities, may learne to looke to themselues in time, and to auoyde inconueniences which may breede if they be not in time preuented. Many good Morrall lessons are therein contained, as the reuerence which young men owe to the aged, in the second *Eglogue*: the caueate or warning to beware a subtill professor of freendshippe, in the fift *Eglogue*: the commendation of good Pastors, and shame and disprayse of idle and ambitious Goteheardes, in the seauenth: the loose and retchlesse lyuing of Popish Prelates, in the ninth: the learned and sweete complaynt of the contempt of learning vnder the name of Poetry, in the tenth. There is also much matter vttered somewhat couertly, especially the abuses of some whom he would not be too playne withall: in which, though it be not apparent to euery one what hys speciall meaning was, yet so skilfully is it handled, as any man may take much delight at hys learned conueyance, and picke out much good sence in the most obscurest of it. Hys notable prayse deserued in euery parcell of that worke, because I cannot expresse as I woulde and as it should, I wyll cease to speake any more of, the rather because I neuer hearde as yet any that hath reade it, which hath not with much admiration commended it. One only thing therein haue I hearde some curious heades call in question, *viz*: the motion of some vnsauery loue, such as in the sixt *Eglogue* he seemeth to deale withall, which (say they) is skant allowable to English eares, and might well haue beene left for the Italian defenders of loathsome beastlines, of whom perhappes he learned it: to thys obiection I haue often aunswered (and I thinke truely) that theyr nyce opinion ouer shooteth the Poets meaning, who though hee in that as in other thinges immitateth the auncient Poets, yet doth not meane, no more did they before hym, any disordered

loue, or the filthy lust of the deuillish *Pederastice* taken
in the worse sence, but rather to shewe howe the dissolute
life of young men, intangled in loue of women, doo neglect
the freendshyp and league with their olde freendes and
familiers. Why (say they) yet he shold gyue no occasion
of suspition, nor offer to the viewe of Christians any
token of such filthinesse, howe good soeuer hys meaning
were: wherevnto I oppose the simple conceyte they haue
of matters which concerne learning or wytt, wylling them
to gyue Poets leaue to vse theyr vayne as they see good:
it is their foolysh construction, not hys wryting that is
blameable. Wee must prescrybe to no wryters (much
lesse to Poets) in what sorte they should vtter theyr conceyts.
But thys wyll be better discussed by some I hope
of better abillity.

One other sorte of Poeticall wryters remayneth yet to
bee remembred, that is, The precepts of Husbandry,
learnedly compiled in Heroycall verse. Such were the
workes of *Hesiodus* in Greeke, and *Virgils Georgickes* in
Latine. What memorable worke hath beene handled in
immitation of these by any English Poet I know not (saue
onely one worke of M. *Tusser*, a peece surely of great wytt
and experience, and wythal very prettilye handled). And
I thinke the cause why our Poets haue not trauayled in that
behalfe is, especially, for that there haue beene alwayes
plenty of other wryters that haue handled the same argument
very largely. Among whom Master *Barnabe Googe*,
in translating and enlarging the most profitable worke of
Heresbachius, hath deserued much commendation, as well
for hys faythfull compyling and learned increasing the
noble worke as for hys wytty translation of a good part
of the *Georgickes* of *Virgill* into English verse.

Among all the translations which hath beene my fortune
to see, I could neuer yet finde that worke of the
Georgicks wholly performed. I remember once Abraham

Flemming in his conuersion of the *Eglogues* promised to translate and publishe it; whether he dyd or not I knowe not, but as yet I heard not of it. I my selfe wott well I bestowed some time in it two or three yeeres since, turning it to that same English verse which other such workes were in, though it were rudely: howe beit, I did it onely for mine owne vse, and vppon certayne respectes towardes a Gentleman mine especiall freende, to whom I was desirous to shewe some token of duetifull good wyll, and not minding it should goe farre abroade, considering howe slenderly I ranne it ouer: yet, since then, hath one gott it in keeping, who, as it is told me, eyther hath or wyll vnaduisedly publishe it: which iniury though he meanes to doo me in myrth, yet I hope he wyll make me some suffycient recompence, or els I shall goe neere to watch hym the like or a worse turne.

But concerning the matter of our Englysh wryters lett thys suffice: nowe shall ye heare my simple skyl in what I am able to say concerning the forme and manner of our Englyshe verse.

The most vsuall and frequented kind of our English Poetry hath alwayes runne vpon and to this day is obserued in such equall number of syllables and likenes of wordes that in all places one verse either immediatly, or by mutuall interposition, may be aunswerable to an other both in proportion of length and ending of lynes in the same Letters. Which rude kinde of verse, though (as I touched before) it rather discrediteth our speeche, as borrowed from the *Barbarians*, then furnisheth the same with any comely ornament, yet beeing so ingraffed by custome, and frequented by the most parte, I may not vtterly dissalowe it, least I should seeme to call in question the iudgement of all our famous wryters, which haue wonne eternall prayse by theyr memorable workes compyled in that verse.

For my part, therefore, I can be content to esteeme it as a thing the perfection whereof is very commendable, yet so as wyth others I could wysh it were by men of learning and ability bettered, and made more artificiall, according to the woorthines of our speeche.

The falling out of verses together in one like sounde is commonly called, in English, Ryme, taken from the Greeke worde ῥυθμός, which surely in my iudgment is verye abusiuelye applyed to such a sence: and by thys the vnworthinesse of the thing may well appeare, in that wanting a proper name wherby to be called, it borroweth a word farre exceeding the dignitye of it, and not appropriate to so rude or base a thing. For Ryme is properly the iust proportion of a clause or sentence, whether it be in prose or meeter, aptly comprised together: wherof there is both an naturall and an artificiall composition, in any manner or kynde of speeche, eyther French, Italian, Spanish, or English, and is propper not onely to Poets, but also to Readers, Oratours, Pleaders, or any which are to pronounce or speake any thing in publike audience.

The first begynning of Ryme (as we nowe terme it), though it be somewhat aunctient, yet nothing famous. In Greece (they say) one *Symias Rhodius*, because he would be singuler in somthing, wryt poetically of the Fable, contayning howe *Iupiter* beeing in shape of a Swanne begatte the Egge on Leda, wherof came Castor, Pollux, and Helena, whereof euery verse ended in thys Ryme, and was called therefore ᾠόν; but thys foolyshe attempt was so contemned and dispysed that the people would neither admitte the Author nor Booke any place in memory of learning. Since that it was not hearde of till the time the *Hunnes* and *Gothians* renued it agayne, and brought it into Italie. But howsoeuer or wheresoeuer it beganne, certayne it is that in our Englishe tongue it beareth as good grace, or rather better, then in any other; and is a faculty whereby many may and doo deserue great prayse and commendation, though our speeche be capable of a farre more learned manner of versifying, as I wyl partly declare heereafter.

There be three speciall notes necessary to be obserued in the framing of our accustomed English Ryme. The first is, that one meeter or verse be aunswerable to an other, in equall number of feete or syllables, or proportionable to the tune whereby it is to be reade or measured. The seconde, to place the words in such sorte as none of them be wrested contrary to the naturall inclination or affectation of the same, or more truely the true quantity thereof. The thyrd, to make them fall together mutually in Ryme, that is, in wordes of like sounde, but so as the wordes be not disordered for the Rymes sake, nor the sence hindered. These be the most pryncipall obseruations which I thinke requisite in an English verse: for as for the other ornaments which belong thereto, they be more properly belonging to the seuerall gyfts of skylfull Poets then common notes to be prescribed by me: but somewhat perhaps I shall haue occasion to speake heereafter.

Of the kyndes of English verses which differ in number of syllables there are almost infinite, which euery way alter according to hys fancy, or to the measure of that meeter wherein it pleaseth hym to frame hys ditty. Of the best and most frequented I wyll rehearse some. The longest verse in length which I haue seene vsed in English consisteth of sixteene syllables, eache two verses ryming together, thus,

> Wher vertue wants and vice abounds, there wealth is but a bayted hooke
> To make men swallow down their bane, before on danger deepe they looke.

Thys kynde is not very much vsed at length thus, but is commonly deuided, eche verse into two, whereof eche shal

containe eyght syllables, and ryme crosse wyse, the first
to the thyrd, and the second to the fourth, in this manner,

> Great wealth is but a bayted hooke,
> Where vertue wants, and vice aboundes:
> Which men deuoure before they looke,
> So them in daungers deepe it drownes.

An other kynd next in length to thys is where eche
verse hath fourteene syllables, which is the most accustomed of all other, and especially vsed of all the translatours of the Latine Poets, for the most part thus,

> My mind with furye fierce inflamde of late, I know not
> howe,
> Doth burne Parnassus hyll to see, adorned wyth, Lawrell
> bowe.

Which may likewyse, and so it often is deuyded, eche
verse into two, the first hauing eyght sillables, the second
sixe, wherof the two sixes shall alwayes ryme, and sometimes the eyghtes, sometimes not, according to the wyll of
the maker.

> My minde with furye fierce inflamde
> Of late, I knowe not howe,
> Doth burne *Pernassus* hyll to see,
> Adornd wyth Lawrell bowe.

There are nowe wythin this compasse as many sortes
of verses as may be deuised differences of numbers:
wherof some consist of equall proportions, some of long
and short together, some of many rymes in one staffe (as
they call it), some of crosse ryme, some of counter ryme,
some ryming wyth one worde farre distant from another,
some ryming euery thyrd or fourth word, and so likewyse
all manner of dytties applyable to euery tune that may be
sung or sayd, distinct from prose or continued speeche.
To auoyde therefore tediousnesse and confusion, I wyll

repeate onely the different sortes of verses out of the *Sheepeheardes Calender*, which may well serue to beare authoritie in thys matter.

There are in that worke twelue or thirteene sundry sorts of verses which differ eyther in length or ryme, of destinction of the staues; but of them which differ in length or number of sillables, not past sixe or seauen. The first of them is of tenne sillables, or rather fiue feete in one verse, thus,

> A Sheepheards boy (no better doo him call),
> When Winters wastfull spight was almost spent.

Thys verse he vseth commonly in hys sweete complayntes and mornefull ditties, as very agreeable to such affections.

The second sort hath naturally but nine syllables, and is a more rough or clownish manner of verse, vsed most commonly of him if you mark him in hys satyricall reprehensions and his Sheepeheardes homelyest talke, such as the second *Æglogue* is.

> Ah for pitty! wyll rancke Winters rage
> These bytter blasts neuer gynne to asswage?

The number of nine sillables in thys verse is very often altered, and so it may without any disgrace to the same, especially where the speeche should be most clownish and simple, which is much obserued of hym.

The third kynd is a pretty rounde verse, running currantly together, commonly seauen sillables or sometime eyght in one verse, as many in the next, both ryming together: euery two hauing one the like verse after them, but of rounder wordes, and two of them likewyse ryming mutually. That verse expresseth, notably, light and youthfull talke, such as is the thyrde *Æglogue* betweene two Sheepheardes boys concerning loue.

> *Thomalin*, why sitten we so,
> As weren ouerwent with woe
> Vpon so fayre a morrowe?
> The ioyous time now nigheth fast,
> That wyll allay this bitter blast
> And slake the Winter sorrow.

The fourth sort containeth in eche staffe manie vnequall verses, but most sweetelie falling together, which the Poet calleth the tune of the waters fall. Therein is his song in prayse of *Eliza*.

> Ye daintie Nymphes, which in this blessed brooke
>   doo bathe your brest,
> Forsake your watrie bowres, and hether looke,
>   at my request.
> And eke yee Virgins that on *Parnass* dwell,
> Whence floweth *Helicon*, the learned Well,
>   helpe me to blaze
>   her woorthy praise,
> That in her sex doth all excell. etc.

The fift is a deuided verse of twelue sillables into two verses, whereof I spake before, and seemeth most meete for the handling of a Morrall matter, such as is the praise of good Pastors, and the dispraise of ill, in the seauenth *Æglogue*.

The sixt kinde is called a round, beeing mutuallie sung betweene two: one singeth one verse, the other the next; eche rymeth with himselfe.

> Per. It fell vppon a holie eue,
> Wyl. Hey ho holliday!
> Per. When holie fathers wont to shrieue;
> Wyl. Thus ginneth our Rondelay. etc.

The seauenth sorte is a verie tragicall mournefull measure,

wherein he bewayleth the death of some freend vnder the person of *Dydo*.

> Vp then *Melpomene*! the mournfulst Muse of nyne,
> such cause of mourning neuer hadst afore:
> Vp griesly ghostes! and vp my mournfull ryme!
> matter of myrth now shalt thou haue no more.
> > *Dydo*, my deere, alas! is dead,
> > Dead, and lyeth wrapt in leade:
> > > O heauie hearse!
> Let streaming teares be powred out in store:
> > O carefull vearse!

These sortes of verses for breuities sake haue I chosen foorth of him, whereby I shall auoide the tedious rehearsall of all the kindes which are vsed: which I thinke would haue beene vnpossible, seeing they may be altered to as manie formes as the Poets please: neither is there anie tune or stroke which may be sung or plaide on instruments, which hath not some poetical ditties framed according to the numbers thereof, some to Rogero, some to Trenchmore, to downe right Squire, to Galliardes, to Pauines, to Iygges, to Brawles, to all manner of tunes which euerie Fidler knowes better then my selfe, and therefore I will let them passe.

Againe, the diuersities of the staues (which are the number of verses contained with the diuisions or partitions of a ditty) doo often times make great differences in these verses. As when one staffe containeth but two verses, or (if they bee deuided) foure; the first or the first couple hauing twelue sillables, the other fourteene, which versifyers call Powlters measure, because so they talle their wares by dozens. Also, when one staffe hath manie verses, whereof eche one rimeth to the next, or mutuallie crosse, or distant by three, or by foure, or ended contrarye to the beginning, and a hundred sortes, whereof to shewe seuerall examples would bee too troublesome. Nowe for the second point.

The naturall course of most English verses seemeth to run vppon the olde Iambicke stroake, and I may well thinke by all likelihoode it had the beginning thereof. For if you marke the right quantitie of our vsuall verses, ye shall perceiue them to containe in sound the very propertie of Iambick feete, as thus,

I that my slender oaten pipe in verse was wont to sounde.

For transpose anie of those feete in pronouncing, and make short either the two, foure, sixe, eight, tenne, twelue sillable, and it will (doo what you can) fall out very absurdly.

Againe, though our wordes can not well bee forced to abyde the touch of *Position* and other rules of *Prosodia*, yet is there such a naturall force or quantity in eche worde, that it will not abide anie place but one, without some foule disgrace: as for example try anie verse, as thys,

Of shapes transformde to bodies strange I purpose to intreate.

Make the first sillable long, or the third, or the fift, and so foorth, or, contrariwise, make the other sillables to admitte the shortnesse of one of them places, and see what a wonderfull defacing it wil be to the wordes, as thus,

Of strange bodies transformd to shapes purpose I to intreate.

So that this is one especiall thing to be taken heede of in making a good English verse, that by displacing no worde bee wrested against his naturall propriety, where-vnto you shal perceyue eche worde to be affected, and may easilie discerne it in wordes of two sillables or aboue, though some there be of indifferencie, that wyll stand in

any place. Againe, in chouching the whole sentence, the
like regarde is to be had that wee exceede not too boldly
in placing the verbe out of his order and too farre behinde
the nowne: which the necessitie of Ryme may oftentimes
vrge. For though it be tollerable in a verse to sette
wordes so extraordinarily as other speeche will not admitt,
yet heede is to be taken least by too much affecting that
manner we make both the verse vnpleasant and the sence
obscure. And sure it is a wonder to see the folly of
manie in this respect, that vse not onely too much of
thys ouerthwart placing, or rather displacing of wordes,
in theyr Poemes and verses, but also in theyr prose or
continued writings; where they thinke to rolle most
smoothlie and flow most eloquently, there by this means
come foorth theyr sentences dragging at one anothers tayle
as they were tyde together with poynts, where often you
shall tarrie (scratching your heade) a good space before
you shall heare hys principall verbe or speciall word,
leaste hys singing grace, which in his sentence is contained, shouid be lesse and his speeche seeme nothing
poeticall.

The thyrd obseruation is the Ryme or like ending of
verses, which, though it is of least importance, yet hath
won such credite among vs that of all other it is most
regarded of the greatest part of Readers. And surely, as
I am perswaded, the regarde of wryters to this hath beene
the greatest decay of that good order of versifying which
might ere this haue beene established in our speeche. In
my iudgment, if there be any ornament in the same, it is
rather to be attributed to the plentifull fulnesse of our
speeche, which can affoorde ryming words sufficient for
the handling of any matter, then to the thing it selfe for
any beautifying it bringeth to a worke, which might bee
adorned with farre more excellent collours then ryming is.
Notwithstanding I cannot but yeelde vnto it (as custome

Of English Poetry

requireth) the deserued prayses, especially where it is with good iudgement ordered. And I thinke them right worthy of admiration for their readines and plenty of wytt and capacity, who can with facility intreate at large and, as we call it, *extempore*, in good and sencible ryme, vppon some vnacquainted matter.

The ready skyll of framing anie thing in verse, besides the naturall promptnesse which many haue therevnto, is much helped by Arte, and exercise of the memory: for, as I remember, I reade once among *Gaskoynes* workes a little instruction to versifying, where is prescribed, as I thinke, thys course of learning to versifye in Ryme.

When ye haue one verse well setled and decently ordered, which you may dispose at your pleasure, to ende it with what word you wyll, then, what soeuer the word is, you may speedilie runne ouer the other wordes which are aunswerable therevnto (for more readines through all the letters Alphabetically), whereof you may choose that which wyll best fitte the sence of your matter in that place: as for example, if your last worde ende in Booke, you may straightwayes in your minde runne them ouer thus, Brooke, Cooke, crooke, hooke, looke, nooke, pooke, rooke, forsooke, tooke, awooke, etc. Nowe it is twenty to one but alwayes one of these shall iumpe with your former worde and matter in good sence. If not, then alter the first.

And indeede I thinke that, next to the Arte of memory, thys is the readyest way to attaine to the faculty of ryming well Extempore, especially if it be helped with thus much paynes. Gather together all manner of wordes, especially *Monasillables*, and place them Alphabetically in some note, and either haue them meetely perfectly by hart (which is no verye laboursome matter) or but looke them diligently ouer at some time, practising to ryme indifferent often, whereby I am perswaded it wil soone be learned, so as the party haue withall any reasonable gyft of knowledge and learning, whereby hee want not bothe matter and wordes altogether.

What the other circumstaunces of Ryming are, as what wordes may tollerably be placed in Ryme, and what not; what words doo best become a Ryme, and what not; how many sortes of Ryme there is; and such like; I wyll not stay nowe to intreate. There be many more obseruations and notes to be prescribed to the exacte knowledge of versifying, which I trust wilbe better and larger laide forth by others, to whom I deferre manie considerations in this treatise, hoping that some of greater skill will shortlie handle this matter in better sorte.

Nowe the sundry kindes of rare deuises and pretty inuentions which come from the fine poeticall vaine of manie in strange and vnacustomed manner, if I could report them, it were worthie my trauell: such are the turning of verses, the infolding of wordes, the fine repititions, the clarklie conueying of contraries, and manie such like. Whereof though I coulde sette downe manie, yet because I want bothe manie and the best kindes of them, I will ouerpasse, onelie pointing you to one or two which may suffice for example.

Looke vppon the rufull song of *Colin* sung by *Cuddie* in the *Sheepheardes Calender*, where you shall see a singuler rare deuise of a dittie framed vpon these six wordes *Woe, sounde, cryes, part, sleep, augment,* which are most prettilie turned and wounde vppe mutually together, expressing wonderfully the dolefulnesse of the song. A deuise not much vnlike vnto the same is vsed by some who, taking the last wordes of a certaine number of verses as it were by the rebound of an *Echo*, shall make them fall out in some prettie sence.

Of this sorte there are some deuised by *Iohn Graunge*, [of] which, because they be not long, I wyll rehearse one.

> If feare oppresse, howe then may hope me shielde?
> Denyall sayes, vayne hope hath pleased well;
> But as such hope thou wouldest not be thine,
> So would I not the like to rule my hart.
> 5 For, if thou louest, it bidds thee graunt forthwith;
> Which is the ioy whereof I liue in hope.

Here if you take the last worde of euerie verse, and place them orderlie together, you shall haue this sentence: *Shielde well thyne hart with hope.* But of these *Echoes* I knowe indeede verie daintie peeces of worke, among some of the finest Poets this day in London, who for the rarenesse of them keepe them priuelie to themselues and wil not let them come abroad.

A like inuention to the last rehearsed, or rather a better, haue I seene often practised in framing a whole dittie to the Letters of ones name, or to the wordes of some two or three verses, which is very witty: as for example, this is one of *W. Hunnis*, which for the shortnes I rather chusde then some that are better.

> 20   If thou desire to liue in quiet rest,
> Gyue eare and see, but say the best.

These two verses are nowe, as it were, resolued into dyuers other, euery two wordes or sillables being the beginning of an other like verse, in this sort.

25 *If thou*   ⎧ delight in quietnes of life,
Desire   ⎪ to shunne from brawles, debate, and strife,
To liue ⎬ in loue with GOD, with freend and foe,
In rest ⎩ shalt sleepe when other cannot so.

Gyue eare ⎧ to all, yet doo not all beleeue,
30 *And see* ⎪ the end and then thy sentence gyue:
But say ⎬ For trueth of happy liues assignde
The best ⎩ hath he that quiet is in minde.

Thus are there infinite sortes of fine conueiances (as they may be termed) to be vsed, and are much frequented by versifyers, as well in composition of their verse as the wittines of their matter: which all I will referre to the consideration of euerie pleasant headded Poet in their proper gifts; onelie I sett downe these fewe sortes of their formes of versifying, which may stand in steede to declare what manie others may be deuised in like sorte.

But nowe to proceede to the reformed kind of English verse, which manie haue before this attempted to put in practise and to establish for an accustomed right among English Poets, you shall heare in like manner my simple iudgment concerning the same.

I am fully and certainlie perswaded that if the true kind of versifying in immitation of Greekes and Latines had beene practised in the English tongue, and put in vre from time to tyme by our Poets, who might haue continually beene mending and pollyshing the same, euery one according to their seuerall giftes, it would long ere this haue aspyred to as full perfection as in anie other tongue whatsoeuer. For why may I not thinke so of our English, seeing that among the Romaines a long time, yea euen till the dayes of *Tully*, they esteemed not the Latine Poetrie almost worth any thing in respecte of the Greeke, as appeareth in the Oration *pro Archia Poeta*; yet afterwardes it increased in credite more and more, and that in short space, so that in *Virgilles* time wherein were they not comparable with the Greekes? So likewise now it seemeth not currant for an English verse to runne vpon true quantity and those feete which the Latines vse, because it is straunge, and the other barbarous custome, beeing within compasse of euery base witt, hath worne it out of credite or estimation. But if our wryters, beeing of learning and iudgment, would rather infringe thys curious custome then omitte the occasion of inlarging the credite

Of English Poetry

of their natiue speeche, and theyr owne prayses, by practising that commendable kind of wryting in true verse, then
no doubt, as in other partes of learning, so in Poetry
shoulde not stoupe to the best of them all in all maner
of ornament and comlinesse. But some obiect that our
wordes are nothing resemblaunt in nature to theirs, and
therefore not possible to bee framed with any good grace
after their vse: but cannot we then, as well as the Latines
did, alter the cannon of the rule according to the quality
of our worde, and where our wordes and theyrs wyll agree,
there to iumpe with them, where they will not agree, there
to establish a rule of our owne to be directed by? Likewise, for the tenor of the verse, might we not (as *Horace*
dyd in the Latine) alter their proportions to what sortes
we listed, and to what we sawe wold best become the
nature of the thing handled or the quallity of the words?
Surely it is to be thought that if any one, of sound iudgment and learning, shoulde putt foorth some famous worke,
contayning dyuers formes of true verses, fitting the
measures according to the matter, it would of it selfe
be a sufficient authority, without any prescription of rules,
to the most part of Poets for them to follow and by
custome to ratify. For sure it is that the rules and
principles of Poetry were not precisely followed and
obserued of the first beginners and wryters of Poetry,
but were selected and gathered seuerally out of theyr
workes for the direction and behoofe of their followers.
And indeede, he that shall with heedefull iudgment make
tryall of the English wordes shall not finde them so grosse
or vnapt but that they wyll become any one of the most
accustomed sortes of Latine or Greeke verses meetely, and
run thereon somewhat currantly.

I my selfe, with simple skyll, I confesse, and farre vnable
iudgment, haue ventured on a fewe, which notwithstanding
the rudenes of them may serue to shewe what better might

bee brought into our speeche, if those which are of meete
abilitye woulde bestowe some trauell and endeuour there-
uppon. But before I sette them downe, I wyll speake
somewhat of such obseruations as I could gather necessary
to the knowledge of these kinde of verses, least I should
seeme to runne vpon them rashly, without regarde either
of example or authority.

The speciall poyntes of a true verse are the due obseruations of the feete and place of the feete.

The foote of a verse is a measure of two sillables, or of
three, distinguished by time which is eyther long or short.
A foote of two sillables is eyther simple or mixt, that is,
of like time or of diuers. A simple foote of two sillables
is likewise twofolde, eyther of two long sillables, called
Spondæus, as − − *goodnesse*, or of two short, called
Pyrrichius, as ∪ ∪ *hyther*. A myxt foote of 2 sillables is
eyther of one short and one long, called *Iambus*, as
∪ − *dying*, or of one long and one short, called *Choreus*,
as − ∪ *gladly*. A foote of 3 sillables in like sorte is either
simple or myxt. The simple is eyther *Molossus*, that is
of three long, as − − − *forgiuenes*, or *Tribrachys*, that is of
3 short, as ∪ ∪ ∪ *merylie*. The mixt is of 6 diuers sortes,
1. *Dactylus*, of one long and two short, as − ∪ ∪ *happily*;
2. *Anapæstus*, of two shorte and one long, as ∪ ∪ −
t[r]*auelers*; 3. *Bacchius*, of one short and two long, as
∪ − − *remembrers*; 4. *Palimbachius*, of two long and one
short, as − − ∪ *accorded*; 5. *Creticus*, of a long, a short,
and a long, [as] − ∪ − *daungerous*; 6. *Amphibrachus*, of
a short, a long, and a short, as ∪ − ∪ *reioyced*.

Many more deuisions of feete are vsed by some, but
these doo more artificially comprehende all quantities
necessary to the skanning of any verse, according to
Tallæus in hys Rethorique. The place of the feete is
the disposing of them in theyr propper roomes, whereby
may be discerned the difference of eche verse which is

Of English Poetry

the right numbring of the same. Now as for the quantity of our wordes, therein lyeth great difficultye, and the cheefest matter in this faculty. For in truth there being such diuersity betwixt our words and the Latine, it cannot stande indeede with great reason that they shoulde frame, wee beeing onelie directed by such rules as serue for onely Latine words; yet notwithstanding one may well perceiue by these fewe that these kinde of verses would well become the speeche, if so bee there were such Rules prescribed as woulde admitt the placing of our aptest and fullest wordes together. For indeede, excepting a fewe of our *Monasyllables*, which naturally shoulde most of them be long, we haue almost none that wyll stande fitlie in a short foote: and therfore, if some exception were made against the precise obseruation of *Position* and certaine other of the rules, then might we haue as great plenty and choyse of good woordes to furnish and sette foorth a verse as in any other tongue.

Likewise, if there were some derection in such wordes as fall not within the compasse of Greeke or Latine rules, it were a great helpe, and therefore I had great misse in these few which I made. Such as is the last sillable in these wordes, *able*, *noble*, or *possible*, and such like: againe for the nature and force of our *W*, of our *th*, of our *oo*, and *ee*, of our wordes which admytte an *e* in the ende after one or two Consonantes, and many other. I for my part, though (I must needes confesse) many faultes escaped me in these fewe, yet tooke I as good heede as I coulde, and in trueth did rather alwaies omitt the best wordes and such as would naturally become the speech best then I wolde committe any thing which shoulde notoriously impugne the Latine rules, which herein I had onely for my direction. Indeede most of our *Monasyllables* I am forced to make short, to supply the want of many short wordes requisite in these verses. The Participle *A*, being but the English article adioyned to Nownes, I alwayes make short, both alone and in composition, and likewise the wordes of one sillable ending in *E*, as *the*, when it is an article, *he*, *she*, *ye*, etc. *We* I thinke should needes be alwayes long because we pronounce continually *VVe*. *I*, beeing alone standing for the Pronowne *Ego*, in my iudgment might well be vsed common; but because I neuer sawe it vsed but short I so obserued it. Words ending in *y* I make short without doubt, sauing that I haue marked in others one difference which they vse in the same, that is to make it short in the ende ⏑ of an Aduerb, as *gladly*, and long in the ende — of an Adiectiue, as *goodly*: but the reason is, as I take it, because the Adiectiue is or should be most commonly written thus, *goodlie*. *O*, beeing an Aduerbe, is naturally long: in the ende of wordes, both *Monasyllables* and other, I thinke it may be vsed common. The first of *Pollisyllables* I directed according to the nature of the worde, as I thought most aunswerable to Latine examples, sauing that somewhere I am constrayned to straine curtesy with the preposition of a worde compounded or such like, which breaketh no great square, as in *defence* or *depart*, etc. The myddle sillables, which are not very many, come for the most part vnder the precinct of *Position*, whereof some of them will not possibly abide the touch, and therfore must needes be a little wrested: such are commonly the Aduerbs of three sillables, as *mournfully*, *spyghtfully*, and such like words, deriued of this Adiectiue *full*: and therfore if there be great occasion to vse them, they must be reformed by detracting onely (*l*) and then they stand meetely currant, as *mournfuly*. The last sillables I wholly directed so neere as I could to the touch of common rules.

The most famous verse of all the rest is called *Hexametrum Epicum*, which consisteth of sixe feete, wherof the first foure are indifferently either *Spondæi* or *Dactyli*,

the fift is euermore a *dactyl*, and the sixt a *Spondæ*, as
thus,

Tyterus happily thou liest tumbling vnder a beetchtree.

Thys kinde of verse I haue onely seene to be practised
in our English speeche; and indeede wyll stand somewhat more orderlye therein then any of the other kindes,
vntill we haue some tolleration of wordes made by
speciall rule. The first that attempted to practise thys
verse in English should seeme to be the Earle of *Surry*,
who translated some part of *Virgill* into verse indeede, but
without regard of true quantity of sillables. There is one
famous *Distichon*, which is common in the mouthes of all
men, that was made by one Master *Watson*, fellowe of
S. *Iohns* Colledge in Cambrydge, about 40. yeeres past,
which for the sweetnes and gallantnes therof in all
respects doth mat[c]h and surpasse the Latine coppy of
Horace, which he made out of *Homers* wordes, *qui mores
hominum etc.*

All trauellers doo gladlie report great praise to Vlisses,

For that he knewe manie mens maners, and saw many citties.

Which two verses, if they be examined throughout, all
the rules and obseruations of the best versifying shall bee
founde to attaine the very perfection of them all. There
be two other not much inferiour to these, which I found in
the Glosse of *E. K.* vppon the fift *Æglogue* of the newe
Poet: which Tully translated out of Greeke into Latine,
Haec habui quae edi etc.

All that I eate did I ioy and all that I greedilie gorged.

As for those manie goodlie matters left I for others.

Which though they wyll not abide the touch of *Synalæpha*
in one or two places, yet perhappes some English rule,

which might wyth good reason be established, would make
them currant enough, and auoyde that inconuenience
which is very obuious in our wordes. The great company
of famous verses of thys sort which Master *Haruey* made
is not vnknowne to any, and are to be viewed at all times.
I for my part, so farre as those examples would leade me,
and mine owne small skyll affoorde me, haue blundered
vppon these fewe, whereinto I haue translated the two
first Æglogues of Virgil, because I thought no matter of
mine owne inuention nor any other of antiquitye more
fitte for tryal of thys thyng, before there were some more
speciall direction which might leade to a lesse troublesome
manner of wryting.

[*Then follow Webbe's versions of the first and second
Eclogues, of which the opening verses are*—

Melibaeus. Tityrus.

Tityrus, happilie thou lyste tumbling vnder a beech tree,
All in a fine oate pipe these sweete songs lustilie chaunting:
We, poore soules, goe to wracke, and from these coastes be remooued,
And fro our pastures sweete: thou Tityr, at ease in a shade plott,
Makst thicke groues to resound with songes of braue Amarillis.

Tityrus.

O Melibaeus, he was no man but a God who releeude me:
Euer he shalbe my God: from this same Sheepcot his alters
Neuer a tender Lambe shall want, with blood to bedew them.
This good gift did he giue, to my steeres thus freelie to wander,
And to my selfe (thou seest) on pipe to resound what I listed.]

I durst not enterpryse to goe any further with this rude
translation, beeing for the respects aforesayd a troublesome and vnpleasant peece of labour: And therefore these
shall suffice till further occasion shall serue to imploy some
profitable paynes in this behalfe.

Of English Poetry

The next verse in dignity to the *Hexameters* is the *Carmen Elegiacum*, which consisteth of foure feete and two od sillables, viz: the two first feete, eyther *Dactyli* or *Spondæi* indifferent, the one long sillable, next two *Dactyli* and an other long sillable − − − ⌣ ⌣ − − ⌣ ⌣ − ⌣ ⌣ − : some doo measure it in this sorte (and more truely yet not so readily to all) accounting first two indifferently either *Dactyli* or *Spondæi*, then one *Spondæ* and two *Anapæsti*. But it commeth all to one reckoning. Thys verse is alwayes vnseperably adioyned vnto the Hexameter, and serueth especially to the handling of loue and dalliances, whereof it taketh the name. It will not frame altogether so currantlye in our English as the other, because the shortnesse of the seconde *Penthimimer* will hardly be framed to fall together in good sence after the Latine rules. I haue not seene very many of them made by any, and therefore one or two for example sake shall be sufficient.

This *Distichon* out of *Ouid*,

> *Ingenium quondam fuerat pretiosius auro;*
> *At nunc barbaria grandis habere nihil.*

may thus be translated,
Learning once was thought to be better then any gold was;
Now he that hath not wealth is but a barbarian.

And thys,

> *Omnia sunt hominum tenui pendentia filo:*
> *Et subito casu quae valuere ruunt.*

Tis but a slender thread, which all mens states do depend on:
And most goodly thinges quickly doo fall to decay.

As for the verses *Phalaecium* and *Iambicum*, I haue not as yet made any tryall in them: but the *Sapphic* I assure you, in my iudgment, wyl doo very pretty, if the wants which I speake were once supplied. For tryall of which I haue turned the new Poets sweete song of *Eliza* into such homely *Sapphick* as I coulde.

Thys verse consisteth of these fiue feete, one *Chore*, one *spondæ*, one *dactyl*, and two *Choreis*, with this addition, that after euery third verse be sette one *Adonium* verse, which consisteth of a *dactyl* and a *spondæ*. It is more troublesome and tedious to frame in our speeche by reason they runne without difference, euery verse being a like in quantity throughout, yet in my iudgement standeth meetely well in the same. I pray looke the Coppy which I haue translated in the fourth *Æglogue* of the *Sheepheardes Calender*—the song of *Colins* making which *Hobbinoll* singeth in prayse of the Queenes maiesty vnder the name of *Eliza*.

> Ye dainty Nymphes, that in this blessed brooke
>   doo bathe your brest,
> Forsake your watry bowres, and hether looke,
>   at my request.
> And onely you Virgins that on *Parnass* dwell,
> Whence floweth *Helicon*, the learned well,
>   helpe me to blase
>   her worthy praise,
> That in her sex doth all excell.
>
> Of fayre *Eliza* be your siluer song,
>   that blessed wight:
> The flowre of Virgins, may she flourish long
>   in princely plight.
> For she is *Syrinx* daughter without spott,
> Which *Pan*, the Sheepheards God, on her begot:
>   so sprang her grace
>   of heauenly race,
> No mortall blemish may her blott.
>
> See where she sittes, etc.

The *Saphick* Verse.

```
— ᴗ — — — ᴗ ᴗ — ᴗ — —
— ᴗ — — — ᴗ ᴗ — ᴗ — —
— ᴗ — — — ᴗ ᴗ — ᴗ — —
              — ᴗ ᴗ — —
```

O ye Nymphes most fine, who resort to this brooke,
For to bathe there your pretty breasts at all times,
Leaue the watrish bowres, hyther and to me come
      at my request nowe.

And ye Virgins trymme, who resort to *Parnass*,
Whence the learned well *Helicon* beginneth,
Helpe to blase her worthy deserts, that all els
      mounteth aboue farre.

Nowe the siluer songes of *Eliza* sing yee,
Princely wight, whose peere not among the virgins
Can be found: that long she may remaine among vs,
      now let vs all pray.

For *Syrinx* daughter she is, of her begotten
Of the great God *Pan*; thus of heauen aryseth
All her exlent race; any mortall harde happe
      cannot aproche her.

See, she sittes most seemely in a grassy greene plott,
Clothed in weedes meete for a princely mayden,
Boste with Ermines white, in a goodly scarlett
      brauely beseeming.

Decked is that crowne that vpon her head standes
With the red Rose and many Daffadillies;
Bayes, the Primrose, and violetts be sette by: how
      ioyfull a sight ist.

Say, behold did ye euer her Angelike face,
Like to *Phœbe* fayre? or her heauenly hauour,
And the princelike grace that in her remaineth,
      haue yee the like seene?

Medled ist red rose with a white together,
Which in either cheeke do depeinct a trymme cheere;
Her maiestie and eye to behold so comely, her
      like who remembreth?

Phœbus once peept foorth with a goodly guilt hewe, 5
For to gaze; but when he sawe the bright beames
Spread abroade fro' her face with a glorious grace,
      it did amaze him.

When another sunne he behelde belowe heere,
Blusht he red for shame, nor againe he durst looke: 10
Would he durst bright beames of his owne with hers match,
      for to be vanquisht.

Shew thy selfe now, *Cynthia*, with thy cleere rayes,
And behold her: neuer abasht be thou so:
When she spreades those beames of her heauenly beauty, 15
 how
      thou art in a dump dasht?

But I will take heede that I match not her grace
With the *Laton* seede; *Niobe* that once did,
Nowe she doth therefore in a stone repent; to all
      other a warning. 20

Pan he may well boaste that he did begit her,
Such a noble wight; to *Syrinx* is it ioy
That she found such lott with a bellibone trym
      for to be loaden.

When my younglinges first to the dammes doo bleat out, 25
Shall a milke white Lambe to my Lady be offred:
For my Goddesse shee is, yea I my selfe her Heardgrome,
      though but a rude Clowne.

Vnto that place *Caliope* dooth high her,
Where my Goddesse shines: to the same the Muses 30
After her, with sweete Violines about them
      cheerefully tracing.

Is not it Bay braunche that aloft in handes they haue,
Eune to giue them sure to my Lady *Eliza*:
O so sweete they play—and to the same doo sing too:
                    heaunly to heare ist.

5 See, the Graces trym to the stroake doo foote it,
Deftly dauncing, and meriment doo make them,
Sing to the instruments to reioyce the more, but
                    wants not a fourth grace?

Then the daunce wyll be eune, to my Lady therefore
10 Shalbe geune that place, for a grace she shall be
For to fill that place, that among them in heaune she
                    may be receiued.

Thys beuy of bright Nymphes, whether ist goe they now,
Raunged all thus fine in a rowe together?
15 They be Ladies all i' the Lake behight soe;
                    they thether all goe.

One, that is there chiefe that among the rest goes,
Called is *Chloris*; of Olyues she bears a
Goodly Crownett, meete for a Prince that in peace
20   euer abideth.

All ye Sheepheardes maides that about the greene dwell,
Speede ye there to her grace; but among ye take heede
All be Virgins pure that aproche to deck her,
                    duetie requireth.

25 When ye shall present ye before her in place,
See ye not your selues doo demeane too rudely:
Bynd the fillets, and to be fine the waste gyrt
                    fast with a tawdryne.

Bring the Pinckes, therewith many Gelliflowers sweete,
30 And the Cullambynes: let vs haue the Wynesops,
With the Cornation that among the loue laddes
                    wontes to be worne much.

Daffadowndillies all a long the ground strowe,
And the Cowslyppe with a prety paunce let heere lye;
Kyngcuppe, and Lillies so beloude of all men,
                And the deluce flowre.

One verse there remaineth vntranslated as yet, with some other of this sorte, which I meant to haue finished, but by reason of some let which I had, I am constrained to defer to some other time, when I hope to gratify the Readers with more and better verses of this sort; for in trueth I am perswaded a little paine taking might furnish our speeche with as much pleasaunt delight in this kinde of verse as any other whatsoeuer.

Heere followe the Cannons or generall cautions of Poetry, prescribed by Horace, first gathered by *Georgius Fabricius Chemnicensis*: which I thought good to annex to thys Treatise, as very necessary obseruations to be marked of all Poets.

IN HIS EPISTLE *AD PISONES DE ARTE POETICA.*

First, let the inuention be meete for the matter, not differing, or straunge, or monstrous. For a womans head, a horse necke, the bodie of a dyuers coloured Byrd, and many members of sundry creatures compact together, whose legges ending like a Fyshes tayle, this in a picture is a wonderful deformitie; but if there be such diuersitye in the frame of a speeche, what can be more vncomely or ilfauoured?

2. The ornaments or colours must not bee too many, nor rashly aduentured on; neither must they be vsed euery where and thrust into euery place.

3. The proprietie of speeche must bee duely obserued

that wayghty and great matters be not spoken slenderly or matters of length too briefly: for it belongeth much both to the comlinesse and nature of a matter that in big matters there be lykewise vsed boysterous wordes.

4. In Poeticall descriptions the speeche must not exceede all credite, nor any thing fainedlie brought in against all course of nature.

5. The disposing of the worke must be such that there be no offence committed, as it were by too exquisite dilligence: for many thinges may be oft committed, and some thing by too curious handling be made offenciue. Neyther is it in one part to be well furnished, and in another to be neglected. Which is prooued by example of a Caruer, who expressed very artificially the heade and vpper part of a body, but the rest hee could not make an ende of. Againe, it is prooued thus, that a body should not be in other partes beautifull, and yet bee deformed in the crooked nose; for all the members in a well shapen bodie must be aunswerable, sound, and well proportioned.

6. He that taketh in hande to write any thing must first take heede that he be sufficient for the same: for often vnwary fooles through their rashnes are ouertooke with great want of ability.

7. The ornament of a worke consisteth in wordes, and in the manner of the wordes; [they] are either simple or mixt, newe or olde, propper or translated. In them all good iudgment must be vsed and ready wytt. The chiefest grace is in the most frequented wordes, for the same reason holdeth in wordes as doth in coynes, that the most vsed and tried are best esteemed.

8. The kinde of verse is to be considered and aptly applied to the argument, in what measure is most meete for euery sort. The most vsuall kindes are foure, the *Heroic*, *Elegiac*, *Iambick*, and *Lyric*.

9. One must vse one kynde of speeche alike in all

wrytings. Sometime the *Lyric* ryseth aloft, sometime the comicall. To the Tragicall wryters belong properly the bygge and boysterous wordes. Examples must be interplaced, according fitly to the time and place.

10. Regarde is to be had of affections: one thing becommeth pleasant persons, an other sadde, an other wrathfull, an other gentle, which must all be heedefully respected. Three thinges therefore are requisite in verses, beauty, sweetnes, and the affection. *Theophrastus* sayth that this beauty or delectablenesse is a deceyt, and Aristotle called it τυραννίδα ὀλιγοχρόνιον, a momentany tyrany. Sweetnesse retayneth a Reader; affection moueth him.

11. Euery person must be fitted accordingly, and the speeche well ordered: wherein are to be considered the dignity, age, sex, fortune, condition, place, Country, &c. of eche person.

12. The personnes are eyther to be fayned by the Poets them selues, or borrowed of others. If he borrow them, then must hee obserue τὸ ὅμοιον, that is, that he folow that Author exactly whom he purposeth to immitate and whereout he bringeth his examples. But if he fayne newe personnes, then must he keepe his τὸ ὁμαλόν, that is equallie: so bringing them in eche place, that it be alwayes agreeable, and the last like vnto the first, and not make one person nowe a bolde boaster, and the same straightwaies a wise warie man, for that is passing absurd. Againe, euery one must obserue τὸ ἁρμοστόν, which is interpreted *conuenientiam*, fitnesse: as it is meete and agreeable euery where a man to be stoute, a woman fearefull, a seruant crafty, a young man gentle.

13. Matters which are common may be handled by a Poet as they may be thought propper to himselfe alone. All matters of themselues are open to be intreated of by any man: but if a thing be handled of some one in such sort as he thereby obtaine great prayse, he maketh it his

owne or propper to himselfe; as many did write of the Troiane war, but yet *Homer* made matter which was common to all propper to himselfe.

14. Where many thinges are to be taken out of auncienter tongues, as the Latines tooke much out of the Greekes, the wordes are not so preciselie to be followed but that they bee altered according to the iudgment and will of the Immitator; which precept is borrowed of Tully, *Non verbum verbo necesse est reddere*.

15. The beginning must not be foolishly handled, that is, straungly or too long.

16. The proposition or narration let it not be far fetched or vnlikely, and in the same forget not the differences of ages and persons.

17. In a Comedie it is [not] needfull to exhibite all the actions openlie, as such as are cruell, vnhonest, or ougly; but such thinges may better bee declared by some meete and handsome wordes, after what sorte they are supposed to bee doone.

18. If a Commedye haue more Actes then fiue, it is tedious; if fewer, it is not sufficient.

It fytteth not to bring in the personnes of Gods but in verie great matters. *Ciccro* sayth, when the Tragedy wryters cannot bring theyr matters to good passe, they runne to God. Let not more personnes speake together then foure, for auoyding confusion.

The *Chori* must be well garnished and sette foorth: wherein eyther menne are admonished, or reprehended, or counsayled vnto vertue. Such matter must bee chosen for the *Chorus* as may bee meete and agreeable to that which is in hand. As for instruments and singing, they are Reliques of olde simplicitye. For the Musicke commonlye vsed at Theaters and the licenciousnesse of theyr songes, which together wyth theyr wealth increased among the Romaines, is hurtfull to discipline and good manners.

19. In a *Satyr* the clownish company and rurall Gods are brought in to temperate the Heauinesse of Tragedies wyth some myrth and pastyme. In iesting it must be obserued that it bee not lacyuious, or Rybaldlike, or slaunderous; which precept holdeth generallie in all sortes of wrytynges.

In a *Satyr* greate heede is to be taken of the place, of the day, and of the personnes: as of *Bacchus*, *Silenus*, or the *Satyres*. Againe of the vnmeetnesse or inconuenience of the matter, and of the wordes that they be fitted according to the persons: of *Decorum*, that he which represented some noble personage in the Tragedie bee not some busy foole in the *Satyr*: finallie of the hearers, least they bee offended by myxing filthy matters with iestes, wanton toyes wyth vnhonest, or noysome with merry thinges.

20. The feete are to be applied propper to euery kinde of verse, and therin a Poet must not vse too much licence or boldnes. The auncient writers in *Iambick* verses vsed at first pure *Iambicks*: Afterwards *Spondæus* was admitted into *Locos impares*, but at last such was the licentious custome, that they woulde both *Spondæus* where they listed, and other feete without regarde.

21. In compyling of verses great care and circumspection must be vsed.

Those verses which be made Extempore are of no great estimation: those which are vnartificiall are vtterly repelled as too foolish. Though many doo lightlie regard our verses, yet ought the Carelesnesse of the hearers to bee no cause in vs of errour and negligence. Who desireth to make any thing worthy to be heard of learned eares, let hym reade Greeke Authors heedefullie and continually.

22. Artes haue their increasinges euen as other things, beeing naturall: so haue Tragedies, which were first rudely

inuented by *Thespis*, at last were much adorned by *Æschylus*: at the first they were practised in Villages of the Countrey, afterwardes brought to stages in great Citties.

23. Some Artes doo increase; some doo decay by a certayne naturall course. The olde manner of Commedies decayde by reason of slaundering which therein they vsed against many, for which there was a penaltie appointed, least their bitternes should proceede to farre: In place of which, among the Latines, came the *Satyres*.

The auncient Authors of Comedies were *Eupolis, Cratinus*, and *Aristophanes*; of the middle sorte *Plato Comicus*; of the last kinde *Menander*, which continued and was accounted the most famous.

24. A Poet should not content himselfe onely with others inuentions, but himselfe also by the example of old wryters sholde bring something of his owne industry which may bee laudable. So did they which writte among the Latines the Comedies called *Togatae*, whose arguments were taken from the Greekes, and the other which wrytt the *Pretextatae*, whereof the arguments were Latine.

25. Heedefulnesse and good composition maketh a perfecte verse, and that which is not so may be reprehended. The faculty of a good witte exceedeth Arte.

26. A Poet, that he may be perfect, hath neede to haue knowledge of that part of Philosophy which informeth the life to good manners. The other which pertaineth to naturall thinges is lesse plausible, hath fewer ornaments, and is not so profitable.

27. A Poet to the knowledge of Philosophie shoulde also adde greater experience, that he may know the fashions of men and dispositions of people. Thys profit is gott by trauelling, that whatsoeuer he wryteth he may so expresse and order it that hys narration may be formable.

28. The ende of Poetry is to wryte pleasant thinges, and profitable. Pleasant it is which delighteth by beeing not

too long or vneasy to be kept in memory, and which is somewhat likelie and not altogether forged. Profitable it is which styrreth vppe the mindes to learning and wisedome.

29. Certaine escapes are to be pardoned in some Poets, specially in great workes. A faulte may bee committed either in respect of hys propper Arte or in some other Arte: that a Poet shoulde erre in precepts of hys owne arte is a shamefull thing; to committe a faulte in another Arte is to be born withal: as in *Virgil*, who fayneth that Æneas comming into *Affrica* slew with hys darte certaine Stagges, whereas indeede *Affrica* hath in it none of those beastes. Such errours doo happen eyther by vnheedefulnes, when one escapeth them by negligence; or by the common fragility of man, because none there is which can know all thinges. Therefore this last kinde of errour is not to be stucke vppon.

30. A good Poet should haue respect to thys, how to retaine hys Reader or hearer. In a picture some thing delighteth beeing sette farre of, something neerer, but a Poet should delight in all places as well in sunne as shaddowe.

31. In a Poet is no meane to be admitted, which, if hee bee not [t]he [best] of all, is the worst of all.

32. A Poeme if it runne not sweetely and smoothly is odious; which is proued by a *simile* of the two senses, hearing and tasting, as in sweete and pleasaunt meates. And the Poem must bee of that sorte, that for the sweetenesse of it may bee acceptable and continue like it selfe vnto the ende, least it wearye or driue away a Reader.

33. He that would wryte any thing worthy the posteritye, let him not enterprise any thing whereunto his nature is not agreeable. *Mercury* is not made of wood (as they say), neyther doth *Minerua* fauour all studies in euery one. In all Artes nature is the best helpe, and

learned men vse commonly to say that *A Poet is as well
borne as made a Poet.*

34. Let no man esteeme himselfe so learned but that
he may submytte hys wrytinges to the iudgments of
others, and correct and thoroughly amend the same
himselfe.

35. The profitte of Poetry sprang thus, for that the
auncient wyse men set downe the best things that per-
tained to mans life, manners, or felicity, and, examining
and proouing the same by long experience of time, when
they were aged they published them in wrytinges. The
vse of Poetry, what it was at the first, is manifest by the
examples of the moste learned men: as of *Orpheus*, who
first builded houses; of *Amphion*, who made Citties; of
Tyrtæus, who first made warre; of *Homer*, who wryt most
wysely.

36. In an artificiall Poet three thinges are requisite,
nature, Arte, and dilligence.

37. A wryter must learne of the learned, and he must
not sticke to confesse when he erreth; that the worse
he may learne to auoyde, and knowe howe to follow the
better.

The confession of an errour betoken[eth] a noble and a
gentle minde. *Celsus* and *Quintillian* doo report of *Hippocrates* that, least he should deceiue his posterity, he confessed certayne errours, as it well became an excellent
minded man and one of great credite. For (as sayth
Celsus) light witts, because they haue nothing, wyll haue
nothing taken from them.

38. In making choise of such freendes as should tell vs
the trueth and correct our wrytinges, heedefull iudgment
must bee vsed; least eyther we choose vnskylfull folke,
or flatterers, or dissemblers. The vnskilfull know not how
to iudge; flatterers feare to offende; dissemblers in not
praysing doo seeme to commende.

39. Let no man deceiue himselfe, or suffer himselfe to be deceiued, but take some graue learned man to be iudge of his dooing, and let him according to hys counsayle change and put out what hee thinketh good.

40. He which will not flatter and is of ability to iudge, let him endeuour to nothing so much as to the correction of that which is wrytten, and that let be doone with earnest and exquisite iudgment. He which dooth not thus, but offendeth wilfully in breaking his credite too rashly, may be counted for a madde, furious, and franticke foole.

41. The faultes commonly in verses are seauen, as either they be destitute of Arte, of facility, or ornament, or els they be superfluous, obscure, ambicious, or needelesse.

OUT OF THE EPISTLES *AD MAECENATEM, AUGUSTUM, ET FLORUM.*

42. An immitation should not be too seruile or superstitious, as though one durst not varry one iotte from the example: neyther should it be so sencelesse or vnskilfull as to immitate thinges which are absurde and not to be followed.

43. One should not altogether treade in the steppes of others, but sometime he may enter into such wayes as haue not beene haunted or vsed of others. *Horace* borrowed the *Iambick* verse of *Archilocus,* expressing fully his numbers and elegantly, but his vnseemely wordes and pratling tauntes hee moste wyselye shunned.

44. In our verses we should not gape after the phrases of the simpler sorte, but striue to haue our writings allowable in the iudgments of learned menne.

45. The common peoples iudgments of Poets is seldome true, and therefore not to be sought after. The vulgar sort in *Rome* iudged *Pacuuius* to be very learned; *Accius*

to bee a graue wryter; that *Affranius* followed *Menander*,
Plautus Epicharmus; that *Terence* excelled in Arte,
Caecilius in grauity: but the learned sorte were not of
this opinion. There is extant in *Macrobius* (I knowe not
whether *Angellius*) the like verdite concerning them which
wryt *Epigrammes*: That *Catullus* and *Caluus* wrytt fewe
thinges that were good, *Naeuius* obscure, *Hortensius* vncomely, *Cynna* vnpleasant, and *Mummius* rough.

46. The olde wryters are so farre to be commended
as nothing be taken from the newe: neyther may we
thinke but that the way lyeth open styll to others to attaine
to as great matters. Full well sayd *Sidonius* to *Eucherius*,
'I reuerence the olde wryters, yet not so as though
I lesse esteemed the vertues and desertes of the wryters
in this age.'

47. Newnes is gratefull if it be learned: for certaine
it is Artes are not bothe begunne and perfected at once,
but are increased by time and studie; which notwithstanding, when they are at the full perfection, doo debate and
decrease againe.

Cic. de orat. There is nothing in the world which
bursteth out all at once and commeth to light all wholly
together.

48. No man should dare to practise an Arte that is
daungerous, especially before he haue learned the same
perfectly; so doo guyders of Shyppes, so doo Phisitions,
but so did not manie Romaine Poets (yea so doo not too
many English wryters) who in a certaine corragious heate
gaped after glory by wryting verses, but fewe of them
obtayned it.

49. A Poet should be no lesse skylfull in dealing with
the affectes of the mynde then a tumbler or a Iuggler
shoulde bee ready in his Arte. And with such pyth
shoulde he sette foorth hys matters that a Reader
shoulde seeme not onely to heare the thing, but to see

and be present at the dooing thereof. Which faculty *Fabius* calleth ὑποτύπωσιν, and *Aristotle* πρὸ ὀμμάτων θέσιν ἢ ποίησιν.

50. Poets are either such as desire to be liked of on stages, as Commedie and Tragedie wryters, or such as woulde bee regestered in Libraries. Those on stages haue speciall respect to the motions of the minde, that they may stirre bothe the eyes and eares of their beholders. But the other, which seeke to please priuately with[in] the walles, take good aduisement in their workes, that they may satisfy the exact iudgments of learned men in their studies.

51. A Poet shoulde not bee too importunate, as to offende in vnseasonable speeches; or vngentle, as to contemne the admonitions of others; or ambicious, as to thinke too well of his owne dooinges; or too wayward, as to thinke reward enough cannot be gyuen him for his deserte; or, finally, too proude, as to desyre to be honoured aboue measure.

52. The emendations of Poemes be very necessary, that in the obscure poyntes many thinges may be enlightned, in the baser partes many thinges may be throughly garnished. Hee may take away and put out all vnpropper and vnseemely words; he may with discretion immitate the auncient wryters; he may abridge thinges that are too lofty, mittigate thynges that are too rough, and may vse all remedies of speeche throughout the whole worke. The thinges which are scarce seemely he may amende by Arte and methode.

53. Let a Poet first take vppon him as though he were to play but an Actors part, as he may bee esteemed like one which wryteth without regarde; neyther let him so pollish his works but that euery one for the basenesse thereof may think to make as good. Hee may likewyse exercise the part of gesturer, as though he seemed to

meddle in rude and common matters, and yet not so deale
in them, as it were for variety sake, nor as though he had
laboured them thoroughly, but tryfled with them, nor as
though he had sweat for them, but practised a little. For
so to hyde ones cunning, that nothing should seeme to bee
laborsome or exquisite, when, notwithstanding, euery part
is pollished with care and studie, is a speciall gyft which
Aristotle calleth κρύψιν.

54. It is [not] onely a poynt of wysedome to vse many
and choyse elegant wordes, but to vnderstand also and to
set foorth thinges which pertaine to the happy ende of
mans life. Whereuppon the Poet *Horace* calleth the Arte
poeticall, without the knowledge of learning and philosophy,
a *prating vanity*. Therfore a good and allowable Poet
must be adorned with wordes, plentious in sentences, and,
if not equall to an Orator, yet very neere him, and a special
louer of learned men.

EPILOGUS.

This small trauell (courteous Reader) I desire thee take
in good worth: which I haue compyled, not as an exquisite censure concerning this matter, but (as thou mayst
well perceiue, and in trueth to that onely ende) that it
might be an occasion to haue the same throughly and
with greater discretion taken in hande and laboured by
some other of greater abilitie: of whom I knowe there be
manie among the famous Poets in London, who, bothe for
learning and leysure, may handle this Argument far more
pythilie then my selfe. Which if any of them wyll vouchsafe to doo, I trust wee shall haue Englishe Poetry at
a higher price in short space: and the rabble of balde
Rymes shall be turned to famous workes, comparable
(I suppose) with the best workes of Poetry in other tongues.

In the meane time, if my poore skill can sette the same any thing forwarde, I wyll not cease to practise the same towardes the framing of some apt English *Prosodia*, styll hoping and hartelie wishing to enioy first the bene-fitte of some others iudgment, whose authority may beare greater credite, and whose learning can better performe it.

ABRAHAM FRAUNCE

(*THE ARCADIAN RHETORIKE*)

1588

[Abraham Fraunce issued, in 1588, from the press of Thomas Orwin, *The Arcadian Rhetorike:* | *Or* | *The Præcepts of Rhetorike made plaine* | *by examples, Greeke, Latin, English, Ita|lian, French, Spanish, out of* || *Homers Ilias, and Odissea,* | *Virgils Æglogs, Georgikes, and Æneis* | *Sir Philip Sydneis Arcadiæ, Songs, and Sonets,* | *Torquato Tassoes Gosfredo, Aminta, Torrismondo,* | *Salust his Judith, and both his Se-maines,* | *Boscan and Garcilassoes Sonets and Æglogs.* || Only one copy is preserved, that in the Bodleian (Malone 514). Sheet B 1–8 (eight leaves) is missing. A MS. note on the fly-leaf states that the tract was entered on the Stationers' Books by T. Gubbyn and J. Newman on June 11, 1588.

A summary and a few extracts are here given in place of the complete text, which consists almost entirely of quotations from the authors named above. The rhetorical plan of the book is less elaborate than that of the contemporary *Arte of Englishe Poesie* (q. v. vol. ii. p. 1). The volume is dedicated 'To the Right excellent and most honorable Ladie, the Ladie Marie, Countesse of Pembroke,' in words which are printed thus[1]:

'Voi, pia nympha, tuum quem tolse, la morte, Philippum.
AEdentem llenas cœlesti melle palabras.
Italicum lumen, flowre of Fraunce, splendor Iberus,
Italicus Tasso, French Salust, Boscan Iberus,

---

[1] The lines are reprinted here exactly as they are in the original.

Τῆς Ρομης Ρομη Virgil, τῆς Ελλαδος Ελλας,
Greekish Homer, tanto læti iunguntur ἑταιρῷ.

    Your Honors most affectionate
       ABRAHAM FRAUNCE.'

The first book contains thirty-six chapters, and extends to Sig. H 6. The second book begins on H 6 v°, and has but six chapters.

Bk. I. chap. 1 defines 'What Rhetorike is,' as two parts, 'Eloqution & Pronuntiation.' 'Eloqution is the first part of Rhetorike, concerning the ordering & trimming of speach. It hath also two parts, Congruitie and Brauerie.' Congruitie includes 'grammaticall rules'—which Fraunce omits. 'Brauerie of speech consisteth in tropes or turnings: and in figures or fashionings. A trope or turning is when a word is turned,' &c. .... 'So much of the general proprieties of tropes: now to the divers kindes thereof.'

Chap. 2 to chap. 5 treat of the Metonymia of the subject and adjunct, &c.; chap. 6 of Ironia. Then comes the break in the text, which resumes in the midst of chap. 14, on feet and poetical dimensions, and the different sorts of verse, with examples. Chap. 15 is on the dimension for Orators; chap. 16, of Epizeuxis; chap. 17, of Anadiplosis; chap. 18, of Climax; chap. 19, of Anaphora; chap. 20, of Epistrophe; chap. 21, of Symploce; chap. 22, of Epanalepsis; chap. 23, of Epanodos; chap. 24, of Paronomasia; chap. 25, of Polyptoton (a long chapter); chap. 26, of Figures of Sentences; chap. 27, of Exclamation (with many classified examples); chap. 28, of Epanorthosis; chap. 29, of Aposiopesis; chap. 30, of Apostrophe; chap. 31, of Prosopopoia; chap. 32, of Addubitation; chap. 33, of Communication; chap. 34, of Præoccupation; chap. 35, of Sufferance; chap. 36, of Graunting. The Second Book consists of these chapters :—chap. 1, 'of utterance or pronunciation'; chap. 2, 'of the application of the voyce to severall affections'; chap. 3, 'of action or gesture of the whole bodie'; chap. 4, 'of the gesture of the head, eyes, lipps, &c.'; chap. 5, 'of the gesture of the arme, hand, fingers, &c.; chap. 6, Of the gesture of other parts of the bodie.

Chap. 19, 'Of Anaphora,' may be quoted as an average example of Fraunce's method:—

'Chap. 19. *Of Anaphora.*

Thus much of the continued repetition of the same word in one or diuers sentences; now followeth the severed repetition of the same sound, and that either in the same place, or in divers. In the same place, either simple or conioined. Simple, *Anaphora* and *Epistrophe.* Anaphora, a bringing back of the same sound, is when the same sound is iterated in the beginning of the sentence.'

Then follow quotations from Homer (*Iliad* I), Virgil (*Georg.* IV, *Eclog.* I, *Aen.* III), Sir Philip Sidney, Tasso, Du Bartas (four passages from the *Semaines*), Boscan, and Garcilasso.

In the volume there are three quotations from Spenser's works: (*a*) fol. C 4, to illustrate mixed iambics and spondees, the lines beginning, 'Vnhappie verse, the witnes of my vnhappie state (see Spenser's letter to Harvey, *ante*, p. 90): (*b*) fol. D 7, v^{o}, where the author, after giving some illustrations of *Polyptoton*, says, 'Before I leaue of to talk of these figures of woords, I will here confusedlie insert a number of conceited verses, sith all their grace and delicacie proceedeth from the figures afore-named. Theocritus hath expressed the forme of an egge and an alter in verse; so hath Willy represented the figure of a swoard, and an old Abbot the image of the crosse, in verie laboured and intangled verses: but let them passe, and come we to such as are more plausible;' and, among several examples, he quotes, 'Ye wastfull woods, beare witnesse of my woe,' &c. (*Sheph. Cal., August*): and (*c*), fol. E 3, in further illustration of 'conceipted kindes of verses,' he quotes Spenser, 'in his Fairie Queene, 2 booke, cant. 4'—

'Wrath, iealousie, griefe, loue, doo thus expell,' &c.

to the end of the stanza. The last quotation has the special interest of having been made before the publication of the *Faerie Queene,* and of being probably the first lines of the poem to appear in print. The MS. was already in circulation among Spenser's intimate friends, and the poet made no secret of it even in more general society (see Ludovick Bryskett's introduction to his *Discourse of Civill Life,* 1606, but written before 1589).]

THOMAS NASH

(I. PREFACE TO GREENE'S *MENAPHON*;
II. FROM *THE ANATOMIE OF ABSURDITIE*)

1589

I.

[The Preface *To the Gentlemen Students of both Universities* is prefixed to Robert Greene's *Menaphon: Camillas alarum to slumbering Euphues in his melancholie Cell at Silexedra*, London, printed by T. O. for Sampson Clarke, 1589. The text is printed from the copy in the British Museum, which is deficient at the end, from the words 'ere long to their juggling (p. 319, l. 35).' The lost portion is supplied from the copy of the edition of 1610, also in the British Museum.]

TO THE GENTLEMEN STUDENTS OF BOTH VNIUERSITIES.

CVRTEOVS and wise, whose iudgements (not entangled with enuie) enlarge the deserts of the Learned by
5 your liberall censures, vouchsafe to welcome your schollerlike Shepheard with such Vniuersitie entertainement as either the nature of your bountie or the custome of your common ciuilitie may affoord. To you he appeales that knew him *ab extrema pueritia*, whose *placet* he accounts the
10 *plaudite* of his paines; thinking his daie labour was not altogether lauisht *sine linea*, if there be anie thing of all in it that doth *olere atticum* in your estimate. I am not ignorant how eloquent our gowned age is growen of late, so that euerie mœchanicall mate abhorres the english he

was borne too, and plucks with a solemne periphrasis his *vt vales* from the inkhorne: which I impute not so much to the perfection of arts as to the seruile imitation of vainglorious tragœdians, who contend not so seriouslie to excell in action as to embowell the clowdes in a speach of comparison; thinking themselues more than initiated in poets immortalitie if they but once get *Boreas* by the beard, and the heauenlie bull by the deaw-lap. But herein I cannot so fully bequeath them to follie, as their idiote art-masters, that intrude themselues to our eares as the alcumists of eloquence, who (mounted on the stage of arrogance) think to outbraue better pens with the swelling bumbast of a bragging blanke verse. Indeed, it may be the ingrafted ouerflow of some kilcow conceipt, that ouercloieth their imagination with a more than drunken resolution, beeing not extemporall in the inuention of anie other meanes to vent their manhood, commits the digestion of their cholerick incumbrances to the spacious volubilitie of a drumming decasillabon. Mongst this kinde of men that repose eternitie in the mouth of a player, I can but ingrosse some deepe read Grammarians, who, hauing no more learning in their scull than will serue to take vp a commoditie, nor Arte in their brain than was nourished in a seruing mans idlenesse, will take vpon them to be the ironicall censors of all, when God and Poetrie doth know they are the simplest of all.

To leaue these to the mercie of their mother tongue, that feed on nought but the crummes that fal from the translators trencher, I come (sweet friend) to thy *Arcadian Menaphon*, whose attire, though not so statelie, yet comelie, dooth entitle thee aboue all other to that *temperatum dicendi genus* which *Tullie* in his *Orator* tearmeth true eloquence. Let other men (as they please) praise the mountaine that in seauen yeares brings foorth a mouse, or the Italianate pen that of a packet of pilfries affoordeth

the presse a pamphlet or two in an age, and then in disguised arraie vaunts *Ouids* and *Plutarchs* plumes as their owne; but giue me the man whose extemporall vaine in anie humor will excell our greatest Art-masters deliberate
5 thoughts, whose inuention, quicker than his eye, will challenge the proudest Rethoritian to the contention of like perfection with like expedition. What is he amongst Students so simple that cannot bring forth (*tandem aliquando*) some or other thing singular, sleeping betwixt
10 euerie sentence? Was it not *Maros* xij. years toyle that so famed his xij. *Æneidos*? Or *Peter Ramus* xvj. yeares paines that so praised his pettie Logique? Howe is it, then, our drowping wits should so wonder at an exquisite line that was his masters day labour? Indeede, I must
15 needes say the descending yeares from the Philosophers *Athens* haue not been supplied with such present Orators as were able in anie English vaine to be eloquent of their owne, but either they must borrow inuention of *Ariosto* and his Countreymen, take vp choyce of words by ex-
20 change in *Tullies Tusculane* and the Latine Historiographers store-houses, similitudes, nay whole sheetes and tractats *verbatim*, from the plentie of *Plutarch* and *Plinie*, and, to conclude, their whole methode of writing from the libertie of Comical fictions that haue succeeded to our
25 Rethoritians by a second imitation: so that well may the Adage, *Nil dictum quod non dictum prius*, bee the most iudiciall estimate of our latter Writers.

But the hunger of our vnsatiate humorists, beeing such as it is, readie to swallowe all draffe without indifference,
30 that insinuates it selfe to their senses vnder the name of delight, imployes oft times manie thred bare witts to emptie their inuention of their Apish deuices, and talke most superficiallie of Pollicie, as those that neuer ware gowne in the Vniuersitie; wherein they reuiue the olde
35 saide Adage, *Sus Mineruam*, & cause the wiser to quippe

them with *Asinus ad Lyram.* Would Gentlemen & riper iudgements admit my motion of moderation in a matter of follie, I wold perswade them to phisicke their faculties of seeing & hearing, as the *Sabæans* doo their dulled senses with smelling; who (as *Strabo* reporteth), ouer-cloyed with such odoriferous sauours as the naturall encrease of their Countrey (Balsamum, Amomum, with Myrrhe and Frankencense) sends foorth, refresh their nosthrills with the vnsauorie sent of the pitchie slime that *Euphrates* casts vp, and the contagious fumes of Goates beardes burnt; so woulde I haue them, beeing surfetted vnawares with the sweete satietie of eloquence which the lauish of our copious Language maie procure, to vse the remedie of contraries, and recreate their rebated witts not, as they did, with the senting of slyme or Goates beardes burnt, but with the ouer-seeing of that *sublime dicendi genus*, which walkes abroad for wast paper in each seruing mans pocket, and the otherwhile perusing of our Gothamists barbarisme; so shoulde the opposite comparison of *Puritie* expell the infection of absurditie, and their ouer-rackte Rhethorique bee the Ironicall recreation of the Reader. But so farre discrepant is the idle vsage of our vnexperienst punies from this prescription, that a tale of Ihon a Brainfords will and the vnluckie furmentie wilbe as soon interteined into their libraries as the best poeme that euer *Tasso* eternisht: which, being the effect of an vndescerning iudgement, makes drosse as valuable as gold, and losse as welcome as gaine, the Glowworme mentioned in *Æsops* fables, namelie the apes follie, to be mistaken for fire, when, as God wot, poore soules, they haue nought but their toyle for their heate, their paines for their sweate, and (to bring it to our english prouerbe) their labour for their trauaile. Wherin I can but resemble them to the Panther, who is so greedie of mens excrements that, if they be hangd vp in a vessell higher than his reach, he sooner

killeth himselfe with the ouer-stretching of his windlesse
bodie than he wil cease from his intended enterprise. Oft
haue I obserued what I now set downe; a secular wit, that
hath liued all daies of his life by what doo you lacke, to
bee more iudiciall in matters of conceit than our quadrant
crepundios that spit *ergo* in the mouth of euerie one they
meete: yet those & these are so affectionate to dogged
detracting, as the most poysonous *Pasquil* anie durtie
mouthed *Martin* or *Momus* euer composed is gathered vp
with greedinesse before it fall to the ground, and bought
at the deerest, though they smell of the friplers lauander
halfe a yeere after: for I know not how the minde of the
meanest is fedde with this follie, that they impute singularitie to him that slanders priuelie, and count it a great
peece of arte in an inkhorne man, in anie tapsterlie tearmes
whatsoeuer, to oppose his superiours to enuie. I will not
denie but in scholler-like matters of controuersie a quicker
stile may passe as commendable, and that a quippe to an
asse is as good as a goad to an oxe; but when an irregular
idiot, that was vp to the eares in diuinitie before euer he
met with *probabile* in the Vniuersitie, shall leaue *pro &
contra* before he can scarcely pronounce it, and come to
correct Common weales, that neuer heard of the name of
Magistrate before he came to *Cambridge*, it is no meruaile
if euery alehouse vaunt the table of the world turned
vpside down; since the childe beats his father, & the asse
whippes his master. But least I might seeme with these
night crowes *Nimis curiosus in aliena republica*, I'le turne
backe to my first text, of studies of delight, and talke a
little in friendship with a few of our triuiall translators.

It is a common practise now a daies amongst a sort of
shifting companions, that runne through euery arte and
thriue by none, to leaue the trade of *Nouerint*, whereto they
were borne, and busie themselues with the indeuors of Art,
that could scarcelie latinize their necke-verse if they should

haue neede; yet English *Seneca* read by candle light yeeldes manie good sentences, as *Bloud is a begger*, and so foorth; and, if you intreate him faire in a frostie morning, he will affoord you whole *Hamlets*, I should say handfulls of tragical speaches. But O griefe! *tempus edax rerum*, what's that will last alwaies? The sea exhaled by droppes will in continuance be drie, and *Seneca* let bloud line by line and page by page at length must needes die to our stage: which makes his famisht followers to imitate the Kidde in *Æsop*, who, enamored with the Foxes newfangles, forsooke all hopes of life to leape into a new occupation, and these men, renowncing all possibilities of credit or estimation, to intermeddle with Italian translations: wherein how poorelie they haue plodded (as those that are neither prouenzall men nor are able to distinguish of Articles), let all indifferent Gentlemen that haue trauailed in that tongue discerne by their twopenie pamphlets: & no meruaile though their home-born mediocritie be such in this matter, for what can be hoped of those that thrust *Elisium* into hell, and haue not learned, so long as they haue liued in the spheares, the iust measure of the Horizon without an hexameter. Sufficeth them to bodge vp a blanke verse with ifs and ands, & other while for recreation after their candle stuffe, hauing starched their beardes most curiouslie, to make a peripateticall path into the inner parts of the Citie, & spend two or three howers in turning ouer French *Doudie*, where they attract more infection in one minute than they can do eloquence all dayes of their life by conuersing with anie Authors of like argument.

But least in this declamatorie vaine I should condemne all & commend none, I will propound to your learned imitation those men of import that haue laboured with credit in this laudable kinde of Translation. In the forefront of whom I cannot but place that aged Father *Erasmus*, that inuested most of our Greeke Writers in the roabes of the auncient

Romaines; in whose traces *Philip Melancthon*, *Sadolet*, *Plantine*, and manie other reuerent Germaines insisting haue reedified the ruines of our decayed Libraries, and merueilouslie inriched the Latine tongue with the expence of their toyle. Not long after, their emulation beeing transported into *England*, euerie priuate Scholler, *William Turner* and who not, beganne to vaunt their smattering of Latine in English Impressions. But amongst others in that Age, Sir *Thomas Eliots* elegance did seuer it selfe from all equalls, although Sir *Thomas Moore* with his Comicall wit at that instant was not altogether idle: yet was not Knowledge fullie confirmed in hir Monarchie amongst vs till that most famous and fortunate Nurse of all learning, Saint *Iohns* in *Cambridge*, that at that time was as an Vniuersitie within it selfe—shining so farre aboue all other Houses, Halls, and Hospitalls whatsoeuer, that no Colledge in the Towne was able to compare with the tythe of her Students; hauing (as I haue hearde graue men of credite report) more candles light in it euerie Winter Morning before fowre of the clocke than the fowre of clocke bell gaue stroakes—till Shee (I saie), as a pittying Mother, put too her helping hande, and sent from her fruitefull wombe sufficient Schollers, both to support her owne weale as also to supplie all other inferiour foundations defects, and namelie that royall erection of *Trinitie Colledge*, which the Vniuersitie Orator, in an Epistle to the Duke of *Somerset*, aptlie tearmed *Colona diducta* from the Suburbes of *Saint Iohns:* In which extraordinarie conception, *vno partu in rempublicam prodiere* the Exchequer of eloquence Sir *Iohn Cheeke*, a man of men, supernaturally traded in al tongues, Sir *John Mason*, Doctor *Watson*, *Redman*, *Aschame*, *Grindall*, *Leuer*, *Pilkington*, all which haue, either by their priuate readings or publique workes, repurged the errors of Arts expelde from their puritie, and set before our eyes a more perfect Methode of Studie.

But howe ill their preceptes haue prospered with our idle Age, that leaue the fountaines of sciences, to follow the riuers of Knowledge, their ouer-fraught Studies with trifling Compendiaries maie testifie: for I knowe not howe it comes to passe by the doating practise of our Diuinitie dunces, that striue to make their Pupills pulpet men before they are reconciled to *Priscian*, but those yeares which shoulde bee employed in *Aristotle* are expired in Epitomes; and well too they maye haue so much Catechisme vacation to rake vp a little refuse Philosophie. And heere could I enter into a large fielde of inuectiue against our abiect abbreuiations of Artes, were it not growen to a newe fashion amongst our Nation to vaunt the pride of contraction in euerie manuarie action: in so much, that the *Pater noster*, which was woont to fill a sheete of paper, is written in the compasse of a pennie; whereupon one merelie affirmed that prouerb to be deriued, *No pennie, no pater noster*; which their nice curtailing puts me in mind of the custome of the *Scythians*, who, if they be at any time distressed with famin, take in their girdles shorter & swaddle themselues streighter, to the intent, no *vacuum* beeing left in their intrayles, hunger should not so much tirannize ouer their stomacks; euen so these men, opprest with a greater penurie of Art, do pound their capacitie in barren Compendiums, and bound their base humors in the beggerly straites of a hungry Analysis, least, longing after that *infinitum* which the pouertie of their conceit cannot compasse, they sooner yeeld vp their youth to destinie than their heart to vnderstanding. How is it, then, such bungling practitioners in principles shuld euer profite the Common wealth by their negligent paines, who haue no more cunning in Logique or Dialogue Latine than appertains to the literall construction of either: neuerthelesse, it is daily apparant to our domesticall eyes that there is none so forward to publish their imperfections, either in

A General Censure 315

the trade of glose or translations, as those that are more
vnlearned than ignorance and lesse conceiuing than
infants. Yet dare I not impute absurditie to all of that
societie, though some of them haue set their names to
their simplicitie. Who euer my priuate opinion condemneth as faultie, Master *Gascoigne* is not to bee abridged
of his deserued esteeme, who first beate the path to that
perfection which our best Poets haue aspired too since his
departure; whereto he did ascend by comparing the Italian
with the English, as *Tullie* did *Græca cum Latinis*. Neither
was Master *Turberuile* the worst of his time, although in
translating he attributed too much to the necessitie of rime.
And, in this page of praise, I cannot omit aged *Arthur
Golding*, for his industrious toile in Englishing *Ouids
Metamorphosis*, besides manie other exquisite editions of
Diuinitie, turned by him out of the French tongue into
our own. Master *Phaer* likewise is not to be forgot in
regard of his famous *Virgil*, whose heauenly verse had it
not bin blemisht by his hautie thoghts, *England* might haue
long insulted in his wit, and *corrigat qui potest* haue been
subscribed to his workes. But fortune, the Mistres of
change, with a pitying compassion respecting Master
Stanihursts praise, would that *Phaer* shoulde fall that hee
might rise, whose heroicall Poetrie, infired, I should say
inspired, with an hexameter furie, recalled to life whateuer
hissed barbarisme hath bin buried this hundred yeare,
and reuiued by his ragged quill such carterlie varietie as
no hodge plowman in a countrie but would haue held as
the extremitie of clownerie; a patterne whereof I will
propounde to your iudgements, as neere as I can, being
parte of one of his descriptions of a tempest, which is thus:

*Then did he make heauens vault to rebounde, with rounce
   robble hobble*
Of ruffe raffe roaring, with thwick thwack thurlery bouncing.

Which strange language of the firmament, neuer subiect before to our common phrase, makes vs, that are not vsed to terminate heauens moueings in the accents of any voice, esteeme of their triobulare interpreter as of some Thrasonical huffe snuffe, for so terrible was his stile to all milde eares, as would haue affrighted our peaceable Poets from intermedling hereafter with that quarrelling kinde of verse, had not sweete Master *France*, by his excellent translation of Master *Thomas Watsons* sugred *Amintas*, animated their dulled spirits to such high witted endeuors. But I knowe not how their ouer timerous cowardise hath stoode in awe of enuie, that no man since him durst imitate any of the worste of those Romane wonders in english, which makes me thinke that either the louers of medocritie are verie many or that the number of good Poets are very small: and in trueth, Master *Watson* except (whom I mentioned before), I knowe not almost any of late dayes that hath shewed himselfe singular in any speciall Latin Poëm, whose *Amintas* and translated *Antigone* may march in equipage of honour with any of our ancient Poets. I will not say but wee had a *Haddon* whose pen would haue challenged the Lawrell from *Homer*, together with *Carre*, that came as nere him as *Virgil* to *Theocritus*. But *Tho. Newton* with his *Leyland*, and *Gabriell Haruey*, with two or three other, is almost all the store that is left vs at this hower. Epitaphers and position Poets haue wee more than a good many, that swarme like Crowes to a dead carcas, but flie, like Swallows in the Winter, from any continuate subiect of witte. The efficient whereof I imagine to issue from the vpstart discipline of our reformatorie Churchmen, who account wit vanitie, and poetrie impietie; whose error, although the necessitie of Philosophie might confute, which lies couched most closely vnder darke fables profounditie, yet I had rather referre it as a disputatiue plea to diuines than set it downe as a determinate position, in my vnexperienst opinion. But how euer their dissentious iudgements should decree in their afternoone sessions of *an sit*, the priuat trueth of my discouered Creede in this controuersie is this, that as that beast was thought scarce worthie to bee sacrifised to the Ægiptian *Epaphus*, who had not some or other blacke spotte on his skinne, so I deeme him farre vnworthie of the name of scholler, & so, consequentlie, to sacrifice his endeuors to art, that is not a Poet, either in whole or in a parte. And here, peraduenture, some desperate quipper will canuaze my proposed comparison *plus vltra*, reconciling the allusion of the blacke spot to the blacke pot; which makes our Poets vndermeale Muses so mutinous, as euerie stanzo they pen after dinner is full poynted with a stabbe. Which their dagger drunkennesse, although it might be excused with *Tam Marti quam Mercurio*, yet will I couer it as well as I may with that prouerbial *fœcundi calices*, that might wel haue been doore keeper to the kanne of *Silenus*, when, nodding on his Asse trapt with iuie, hee made his moist nosecloth the pausing intermedium twixt euerie nappe. Let frugale scholares and fine fingerd nouices take their drinke by the ownce and their wine by the halpe-worthes, but it is for a Poet to examine the pottle pottes and gage the bottome of whole gallons; *qui bene vult* ποιεῖν, *debet ante* πίνειν. A pot of blew burning ale, with a fierie flaming tost, is as good as *Pallas* with the nine Muses on *Parnassus* top: without the which, in vaine may they crie, 'O thou, my muse, inspire mee with some pen,' when they want certaine liquid sacrifice to rouze her foorth her denne. Pardon me, Gentlemen, though somewhat merely I glaunce at their imoderate follie, who affirme that no man can write with conceit, except he takes counsell of the cup: nor would I haue you thinke that *Theonino dente* I arme my stile against all, since I doo knowe the

moderation of many Gentlemen of that studie to be so
farre from infamie as their verse from equalitie: whose
sufficiencie, were it as well seene into, by those of higher
place, as it wanders abroade vnrewarded in the mouthes
of vngratefull monsters, no doubte but the remembrance
of *Mæcenas* liberalitie extended to *Maro*, and men of like
qualitie, would haue lefte no memorie to that prouerb of
pouertie, *Si nihil attuleris, ibis Homere foras*. 'Tut,' saies
our English Italians, 'the finest witts our Climate sends
foorth are but drie braind doltes, in comparison of other
countries': whome if you interrupt with *redde rationem*,
they will tell you of *Petrarche, Tasso, Celiano*, with an
infinite number of others; to whome if I should oppose
Chaucer, Lidgate, Gower, with such like, that liued vnder
the tirranie of ignorance, I do think their best louers
would bee much discontented with the collation of contraries, if I should write ouer al their heads, Haile fellow
well met. One thing I am sure of, that each of these
three haue vaunted their meeters with as much admiration
in English as euer the proudest *Ariosto* did his verse in
Italian. What should I come to our court, where the
otherwhile vacations of our grauer Nobilitie are prodigall
of more pompous wit and choyce of words than euer
tragick *Tasso* could attaine too? But, as for pastorall
Poëmes, I will not make the comparison, least our
countrimens credit should bee discountenanst by the
contention, who, although they cannot fare with such
inferior facilitie, yet I knowe would carrie the bucklers
full easilie from all forreine brauers, if their *subiectum
circa quod* should sauor of any thing haughtie: and, should
the challenge of deepe conceit be intruded by an forreiner
to bring our english wits to the tutchstone of Arte, I would
preferre diuine Master *Spencer*, the miracle of wit, to
bandie line for line for my life in the honor of *England*,
gainst *Spaine, France, Italie*, and all the worlde. Neither

is he the only swallow of our summer (although *Apollo*,
if his *Tripos* were vp again, would pronounce him his
Socrates), but, he being forborne, there are extant about
London many most able men to reuiue Poetrie, though
it were executed ten thousand times, as in *Platos*, so in
Puritanes common wealth; as for example *Mathew Roydon*, *Thomas Atchelow*, and *George Peele*, the first of whome,
as hee hath shewed himselfe singular in the immortall
Epitaph of his beloued *Astrophel*, besides many other
most absolute comicke inuentions (made more publique
by euerie mans praise than they can bee by my speache),
so the second hath more than once or twise manifested
his deepe witted schollership in places of credit, and for
the last, thogh not the least of them all, I dare commend
him to all that know him as the chiefe supporter of
pleasance nowe liuing, the *Atlas* of Poetrie and *primus
verborum Artifex*, whose first encrease, the Arraignement of *Paris*, might plead to your opinions his pregnant
dexteritie of wit and manifold varietie of inuention,
wherein (*me iudice*) hee goeth a step beyond all that
write. Sundrie other sweete Gentlemen I know, that
haue vaunted their pens in priuate deuices, and trickt
vp a companie of taffata fooles with their feathers, whose
beautie if our Poets had not peecte with the supply of
their periwigs, they might haue antickt it vntill this time
vp and downe the countrey with the King of *Fairies*, and
dined euerie daie at the pease porredge ordinarie with
Delphrigus. But *Tolossa* hath forgot that it was sometime
sackt, and beggers that euer they caried their fardles on
footback: and in truth no meruaile, when as the deserued
reputation of one *Roscius* is of force to inrich a rabble
of counterfets; yet let subiects for all their insolence
dedicate a *De profundis* euerie morning to the preseruation of their *Cæsar*, least their encreasing indignities
returne them ere long to their iuggling to mediocrity,

and they bewaile in weeping blankes the wane of their Monarchie.

As Poetrie hath beene honoured in those her forenamed professours, so it hath not beene any whit disparaged by *William Warners* absolute *Albions*. And heere Authoritie hath made a full point: in whose reuerence insisting I cease to expose to your sport the picture of those Pamphleters and Poets, that make a patrimonie of *In speech*, and more than a younger brothers inheritance of their *Abcie*. Reade fauourably, to incourage me in the firstlings of my folly, and perswade your selues I will persecute those idiots and their heires vnto the third generation, that haue made Art bankerout of her ornaments, and sent Poetry a begging vp and downe the Countrey. It may be my *Anatomie* of *Absurdities* may acquaint you ere long with my skill in surgery, wherein the diseases of Art more merrily discouered may make our maimed Poets put together their blankes vnto the building of an Hospitall.

If you chance to meete it in *Paules*, shaped in a new suite of similitudes, as if, like the eloquent apprentice of *Plutarch*, it were propped at seuen yeares end in double apparell, thinke his master hath fulfilled couenants, and onely cancelled the Indentures of dutie. If I please, I will thinke my ignorance indebted vnto you that applaud it: if not, what rests but that I be excluded from your curtesie, like *Apocrypha* from your Bibles?

How euer, yours euer,
Thomas Nash.

II.

[The following extracts are taken from *The Anatomie of Absurditie* ... Compiled by *T. Nashe* ... At London, Printed by *I. Charlewood* for Thomas Hacket ... Ann. Dom. 1589, which may have been written before the Preface to Greene's *Menaphon*. The text is taken from the copy in the Bodleian (Malone 566). The last printed page (from 'me of,' p. 336, l. 32) is missing. It is added in MS., in a careful hand.]

ZEUXES, beeing about to drawe the counterfet of *Iuno*, assembled all the *Agrigentine* Maydes, whom after he pausing had viewed, he chose out fiue of the fayrest, that in their beautie he might imitate what was most
5 excellent: euen so it fareth with mee, who, beeing about to anatomize Absurditie, am vrged to take a view of sundry mens vanitie, a suruey of their follie, a briefe of their barbarisme, to runne through Authors of the absurder sort assembled in the Stacioners shop, sucking
10 and selecting out of these vpstart antiquaries somewhat of their vnsauery duncerie, meaning to note it with a *Nigrum theta*, that each one at the first sight may eschew it as infectious, to shewe it to the world that all men may shunne it. And euen as *Macedon Phillip*, hauing finished
15 his warres, builded a Cittie for the worst sorte of men, which hee called πονηρόπολις, *malorum Ciuitas*, so I, hauing laide aside my grauer studies for a season, determined with my selfe, beeing idle in the Countrey, to beginne in this vacation the foundation of a trifling subiect, which

might shroude in his leaues the abusiue enormities of
these our times. It fareth nowe a daies with vnlearned
Idiots as it doth with she Asses, who bring foorth all
their life long: euen so these brainlesse Bussards are
euery quarter bigge wyth one Pamphlet or other. But
as an Egge that is full beeing put into water sinketh to
the bottome, whereas that which is emptie floateth aboue,
so those that are more exquisitly furnished with learning
shroude themselues in obscuritie, whereas they that [are]
voide of all knowledge endeuour continually to publish
theyr follie.

Such and the very same are they that obtrude themselues vnto vs as the Authors of eloquence and fountains
of our finer phrases, when as they sette before vs nought
but a confused masse of wordes without matter, a Chaos
of sentences without any profitable sence, resembling
drummes, which beeing emptie within sound big without.
Were it that any Morrall of greater moment might be
fished out of their fabulous follie, leauing theyr words
we would cleaue to their meaning, pretermitting their
painted shewe we woulde pry into their propounded
sence; but when as lust is the tractate of so many leaues,
and loue passions the lauish dispence of so much paper,
I must needes sende such idle wits to shrift to the vicar
of S. Fooles, who in steede of a worser may be such a
Gothamists ghostly Father. Might *Ouids* exile admonish
such Idlebies to betake them to a new trade, the Presse
should be farre better employed; Histories of antiquitie
not halfe so much belyed; Minerals, stones, and herbes
should not haue such cogged natures and names ascribed
to them without cause; Englishmen shoulde not be halfe
so much Italianated as they are; finallie, loue woulde
obtaine the name of lust, and vice no longer maske vnder
the visard of vertue.

Are they not ashamed in their prefixed posies to adorne

A General Censure

a pretence of profit mixt with pleasure, when as in their bookes there is scarce to be found one precept pertaining to vertue, but whole quires fraught with amorous discourses kindling *Venus* flame in *Vulcans* forge, carrying *Cupid* in tryumph, alluring euen vowed *Vestals* to treade awry, inchaunting chaste mindes and corrupting the continenst? Henceforth, let them alter their posies of profit with intermingled pleasure, inserting that of Ouid insteed,

> *Si quis in hoc artem populo non nouit amandi,*
> *Me legat, & lecto carmine doctus amet.*

So shall the discreet Reader vnderstand the contents by the title, and their purpose by their posie: what els I pray you doe these bable bookemungers endeuor but to repaire the ruinous wals of *Venus* Court, to restore to the worlde that forgotten Legendary licence of lying, to imitate a fresh the fantasticall dreames of those exiled Abbie-lubbers, from whose idle pens proceeded those worne out impressions of the feyned no where acts of Arthur of the rounde table, Arthur of litle Brittaine, Sir Tristram, Hewon of Burdeaux, the Squire of low degree, the foure sons of Amon, with infinite others. It is not of my yeeres nor studie to censure these mens foolerie more theologicallie, but to shew how they to no Commonwealth commoditie tosse ouer their troubled imaginations to haue the praise of the learning which they lack. Many of them to be more amiable with their friends of the Feminine sexe blot many sheetes of paper in the blazing of Womens slender praises, as though in that generation there raigned and alwaies remained such singuler simplicitie that all posterities should be enioyned by duetie to fill and furnish their Temples, nay Townes and streetes, with the shrines of the Saints: Neuer remembring that as there was a loyall *Lucretia*, so there was a light a loue *Lais*, that as there was a modest

Medullina, so there was a mischiuous *Medea*, that as there was a stedfast *Timoclea*, so there was a trayterous *Tarpeya*, that as there was a sober *Sulpitia*, so there was a deceitful *Scylla*, that as there was a chast *Claudia*, so there was a wanton *Clodia*.

[*Nash then proceeds to discuss, in no friendly way, the character of woman, and to offer* (*in the words of the subtitle of the pamphlet*) 'a breefe confutation of the slender imputed prayses to feminine perfection.' *He rates the* 'idle heads' *for their* 'prodigall commendation,' *and for not consulting their credit* 'in the composition of some other more profitable contrary subiect.']

I leaue these in their follie, and hasten to other mens furie, who make the Presse the dunghill, whether they carry all the muck of their mellancholicke imaginations, pretending, forsooth, to anatomize abuses, and stubbe vp sin by the rootes, when as there waste paper, beeing wel viewed, seemes fraught with naught els saue dogge daies effects; who, wresting places of Scripture against pride, whoredome, couetousnes, gluttonie, and drunkennesse, extend their inuectiues so farre against the abuse that almost the things remaines not whereof they admitte anie lawfull vse: Speaking of pride, as though they were afraid some body should cut too large peniworthes out of their cloth; of couetousnes, as though in them that Prouerbe had beene verified, *Nullus ad amissas ibit amicus opes*; of gluttonie, as though their liuing did lye vppon another mans trencher; of drunkennesse, as though they had beene brought vppe all the dayes of their life with bread and water: and finally, of whoredome, as though they had beene Eunuckes from theyr cradle, or blind from the howre of their conception. But as the Stage player is nere the happier because hee represents oft times the persons of mightie men, as of Kings & Emperours, so I account such men neuer the holier because they place praise in painting foorth other mens imperfections.

These men resemble Trees, which are wont eftsoones to die if they be fruitfull beyond their wont; euen so they do die in vertue, if they once ouershoote themselues too much wyth inueighing against vice; to be brainsicke in workes, if they be too fruitfull in words. And euen as the Vultures slay nothing themselues, but pray vpon that which of other is slayne, so these men inueigh against no new vice which heeretofore by the censures of the learned hath not beene sharply condemned, but teare that peecemeale wise which long since by ancient wryters was wounded to the death, so that out of their forepassed paines ariseth their Pamphlets, out of theyr volumes theyr inuectiues. Good God, that those that neuer tasted of any thing saue the excrements of Artes, whose threddebare knowledge, beeing bought at the second hand, is spotted, blemished, and defaced through translaters rigorous rude dealing, shoulde preferre their sluttered sutes before other mens glittering gorgious array, should offer them water out of a muddie pit, who haue continually recourse to the Fountaine, or dregs to drink, who haue wine to sell. *At scire tuum nihil est, nisi te scire hoc sciat alter.* Thy knowledge bootes thee not a button, except another knowes that thou hast this knowledge. *Anacharsis* was wont to say that the Athenians vsed money to no other ende but to tell it: euen so these men make no other vse of learning but to shewe it. But as the Panther smelleth sweetelie but onely to brute beastes, which shee draweth vnto her to theyr destruction, not to men in like maner, so these men seeme learned to none but Idiots, whom, with a coloured shew of zeale, they allure vnto them to their illusion, and not to the learned in like sort. I know not howe it delighteth them to put theyr Oare in another mans boate, and their foote in another mans boote, to incurre that prouerbiall checke, *Ne sutor vltra crepidam*, or that oratoricall taunt, *Quam quisque norit artem in ea se exerceat*; with the Elephant to wade and wallowe in the shallow water, when they woulde sooner sincke then swym in the deepe Riuer; to be conuersant in those Authors which they cannot vnderstande but by the translatour their interpreter; to vaunte reading, when the sum of their diuinitie consists in twopennie Catichismes: and yet their ignoraunt zeale wyll presumptuously presse into the Presse, enquiring most curiouslie into euery corner of the Common wealth, correcting that sinne in others wherwith they are corrupted themselues. To prescribe rules of life belongeth not to the ruder sorte; to condemne those callings which are approoued by publique authoritie argueth a proude contempt of the Magistrates superiority. *Protogenes* knew *Apelles* by one lyne, neuer otherwise seene; and you may knowe these mens spirit by theyr speeche, their minds by their medling, their folly by their phrase. View their workes, and know their vanitie; see the Bookes bearing their name, and smile in thy sleeue at their shame. A small ship in a shallow Riuer seemes a huge thing, but in the sea a very litle vessell; euen so each trifling Pamphlet to the simpler sorte a most substantiall subiect, whereof the wiser lightly account & the learned laughing contemne. Therefore more earnestly I agrauate their faulte, because their crime is crept into credit, & their dooinges deemed deuotion, when as purposelie to some mans despight they bring into act their cholericke motions.

[*Then, after denouncing hypocritical Malcontents and those who* 'search curiouslie into the secrets of nature' *and publish portents for the superstitious, the pamphlet proceeds—*]

Hence come our babling Ballets, and our new found Songs & Sonets, which euery rednose Fidler hath at his fingers end, and euery ignorant Ale Knight will breath foorth ouer the potte, as soone as his braine waxeth hote. Be it a truth which they would tune, they enterlace it with a lye or two to make meeter, not regarding veritie so they may make vppe the verse: not vnlike to Homer, who cared not what he fained so hee might make his Countrimen famous. But as the straightest things beeing put into water seeme crooked, so the crediblest trothes if once they come within compasse of these mens wits seeme tales. Were it that the infamie of their ignoraunce did redound onlie vppon themselues, I could be content to apply my speech otherwise then to their *Apuleyan* eares; but sith they obtaine the name of our English Poets, and thereby make men thinke more baselie of the wittes of our Countrey, I cannot but turne them out of their counterfet liuerie and brand them in the foreheade, that all men may know their falshood. Well may that saying of *Campanus* be applyed to our English Poets, which hee spake of them in his time: 'They make,' saith he, 'Poetry an occupation; lying is their lyuing, and fables are their mooueables: if thou takest away trifles, sillie soules, they will famish for hunger.' It were to be wished that the acts of the ventrous and the praise of the vertuous were by publique Edict prohibited: by such mens merry mouthes to be so odiouslie extolde as rather breedes detestation then admiration, lothing then lyking. What politique Counsailour or valiant Souldier will ioy or glorie of this, in that some stitcher, Weauer, spendthrift, or Fidler hath shuffled or slubberd vp a few ragged Rimes, in the memoriall of the ones prudence or the others prowesse? It makes the learned sort to be silent, when as they see vnlearned sots so insolent.

These Bussards thinke knowledge a burthen, tapping it before they haue half tunde it, venting it before they haue filled it; in whom that saying of the Orator is verified, *Ante ad dicendum quam ad cognoscendum veniunt.*

They come to speake before they come to know. They contemne Arts as vnprofitable, contenting themselues with a little Countrey Grammer knowledge, god wote, thanking God with that abscedarie Priest in Lincolneshire, that he neuer knewe what that Romish popish Latine meant. Verie requisite were it that such blockheads had some *Albadanensis Appollonius* to send them to some other mechanicall Arte, that they might not thus be the staine of Arte. Such kind of Poets were they that *Plato* excluded from his Common wealth and *Augustine* banished *ex ciuitate Dei*, which the Romans derided, and the *Lacedæmonians* scorned, who wold not suffer one of Archilocus bookes to remaine in their Countrey: and amisse it were not, if these which meddle with the Arte they knowe not were bequethed to Bridwell, there to learne a new occupation: for as the Basiliske with his hisse driueth all other Serpents from the place of his aboad, so these rude Rithmours with their iarring verse allienate all mens mindes from delighting in numbers excellence, which they haue so defaced that wee may well exclaime with the Poet *Quantum mutatus ab illo*.

But least I should be mistaken as an enemie to Poetrie, or at least not taken as a friend to that studie, I haue thought good to make them priuie to my mind, by expressing my meaning. I account of Poetrie as of a more hidden & diuine kinde of Philosophy, enwrapped in blinde Fables and darke stories, wherin the principles of more excellent Arts and morrall precepts of manners, illustrated with diuers examples of other Kingdomes and Countries, are contained: for amongst the *Grecians* there were Poets before there were any Philosophers, who embraced entirely the studie of wisedome, as *Cicero* testifieth in his *Tusculanes*: whereas he saith that, of all sorts of men, Poets are most ancient, who, to the intent they might allure men with a greater longing to learning, haue

followed two things, sweetnes of verse and variety of
inuention, knowing that delight doth prick men forward
to the attaining of knowledge, and that true things are
rather admirde if they be included in some wittie fiction,
like to Pearles that delight more if they be deeper sette in
golde. Wherfore seeing Poetry is the very same with
Philosophy, the fables of Poets must of necessitie be
fraught with wisdome & knowledge, as framed of those
men which haue spent all their time and studies in the
one and in the other. For euen as in Vines the Grapes
that are fayrest and sweetest are couched vnder the
branches that are broadest and biggest, euen so in Poems
the thinges that are most profitable are shrouded vnder
the Fables that are most obscure: neither is there almost
any poeticall fygment wherein there is not some thing
comprehended, taken out either of Histories, or out of
the Phisicks or Ethicks; wher vpon *Erasmus Roterdamus*
very wittilie termes Poetry a daintie dish seasoned with
delights of euery kind of discipline. Nowe, whether
ryming be Poetry, I referre to the iudgment of the learned;
yea, let the indifferent Reader diuine what deepe misterie
can be placed vnder plodding meeter. Who is it that,
reading Beuis of Hampton, can forbeare laughing if he
marke what scambling shyft he makes to ende his verses
a like. I will propound three or foure payre by the way
for the Readers recreation.

> The Porter said, by my snout,
> It was Sir Beuis that I let out;

or this,

> He smote his sonne on the breast,
> That he neuer after spoke with Clark nor Priest;

or this,

> This almes, by my crowne,
> Gives she for Beuis of South-hamptoune;

or this,

Some lost a nose, some a lip;
And the King of Scots hath a ship.

But I let these passe as worne out absurdities, meaning not at this instant to vrge (as I might) the like instance of Authors of our time, least, in laying foorth their nakednesse, I might seeme to haue discouered my mallice, imitating *Aiax*, who, obiecting more irefully vnto Vlysses flattery, detected himselfe of follie.

As these men offend in the impudent publishing of witles vanitie, so others ouershoote themselues as much another waie, in sencelesse stoicall austeritie, accounting Poetrie impietie and witte follie. It is an old Question, and it hath beene often propounded, whether it were better to haue moderate affections, or no affections? The *Stoicks* said none. The *Peripaticians* answered to haue temperate affections: and in this respect I am a professed *Peripatician*, mixing profit with pleasure, and precepts of doctrine with delightfull inuention. Yet these men condemne them of lasciuiousnes, vanitie, and curiositie, who vnder fayned Stories include many profitable morrall precepts, describing the outrage of vnbridled youth hauing the reine in their owne hands, the fruits of idlenes, the ofspring of lust, and how auaileable good educations are vnto vertue. In which their preciser censure they resemble them that cast away the nutte for mislike of the shell, & are like to those which loath the fruite for the leaues, accounting the one sower because the other is bitter. It may be some dreaming dunce, whose bald affected eloquence making his function odious, better beseeming a priuie then a pulpit, a misterming Clowne in a Comedy then a chosen man in the Ministerie, will cry out that it breedes a scabbe to the conscience to peruse such Pamphlets, beeing indeed the display of their dun-

cerie, and breeding a mislike of such tedious dolts
barbarisme by the view of their rethoricall inuention.
Such trifling studies, say they, infect the minde and
corrupt the manners, as though the minde were only
conuersant in such toies, or shold continuallie stay where
the thoughts by chaunce doo stray. The Sunne beames
touching the earth remaine still from whence they came;
so a wyse mans mind, although sometimes by chance it
wandereth here and there, yet it hath recourse in staied
yeeres to that it ought. But graunt the matter to be
fabulous, is it therfore friuolous? Is there not vnder
Fables, euen as vnder the shaddowe of greene and
florishing leaues, most pleasant fruite hidden in secrete,
and a further meaning closely comprised? Did not
Virgill vnder the couert of a Fable expresse that diuine
misterie which is the subiect of his sixt Eglogue.

Iam noua progenies caelo demittitur alto.

I could send you to *Ouid*, who expresseth the generall
Deluge, which was the olde worldes ouerthrowe, in the
Fable of *Deucalion* and *Pirrha*: vnder which vndoubtedly
it is manifest (although diuers Authors are of contrarie
opinion) he meaneth *Noes* floode, in so much as there is
a place in *Lucian* in his booke *De Siria Dea*, by the which
it appeareth that by *Deucalions* Deluge is vnderstoode,
not (as some will) that Enundation, whereby in times past
Greece and Italie was ouerflowne and the Ile *Atlanta*
destroied, but that vniuersall flood which was in the time
of *Noe*. For thus *Lucian* writeth in that place, that it was
receiued for a common opinion among the *Grecians* that
this generation of men that nowe is hath not been from
the beginning, but that it which first was wholy perrished,
and this second sort of men which now are be of a newe
creation, growing into such a multitude by *Deucalion* and
Pirrhas meanes. . . .

Hetherto *Lucian* an Heathen Poet. *Plutarch* also recordeth, in his Treatise *De industria animalium,* that a Doue, beeing sent out of *Deucalions* Arke, shewed the waters ceasing. By these proofes it is euident that by *Deucalions* Deluge is vnderstoode *Noes* flood, because the very like thinges are sette downe in *Genesis,* of brute Beastes receiued by Noe into the Arke, and the Doue sent forth by him also. I trust, these probabilities beeing duely pondered, there is no man so distrustful to doubt that deeper diuinitie is included in Poets inuentions, and therefore not to be reiected, as though they were voide of all learning and wisedome.

I woulde not haue any man imagine that in praysing of Poetry I endeuour to approoue *Virgils* vnchast *Priapus,* or *Ouids* obscenitie: I commende their witte, not their wantonnes, their learning, not their lust: yet euen as the Bee out of the bitterest flowers and sharpest thistles gathers honey, so out of the filthiest Fables may profitable knowledge be sucked and selected. Neuerthelesse, tender youth ought to bee restrained for a time from the reading of such ribauldrie, least, chewing ouer wantonlie the eares of this Summer Corne, they be choaked with the haune before they can come at the karnell. Hunters, being readie to goe to their Game, suffer not their dogges to taste or smell of anything by the way, no carrion especially, but reserue them wholy to their approching disport; euen so youth, beeing ready to vndertake more waightier studies, ought in no case be permitted to looke aside to lasciuious toyes, least the pleasure of the one should breed a loathing of the profit of the other. I would there were not any, as there be many, who in Poets and Historiographers reade no more then serueth to the feeding of their filthy lust, applying those things to the pampering of their priuate *Venus* which were purposely published to the suppressing of

A General Censure

that common wandering *Cupid*. These be the Spyders
which sucke poyson out of the hony combe and corruption out of the holiest thinges, herein resembling those
that are troubled with a Feuer, in whome diuers things
haue diuers effects, that is to say, of hote things they waxe
cold, of cold things hote; or of Tygers, which by the
sound of melodious Instruments are driuen into madnesse,
by which men are wont to expell melancholie. He that
wil seeke for a Pearle must first learne to know it when
he sees it, least he neglect it when hee findes it, or make
a nought worth peeble his Jewell: and they that couet
to picke more precious knowledge out of Poets amorous
Elegies must haue a discerning knowledge before they can
aspire to the perfection of their desired knowledge, least
the obtaining of trifles be the repentant end of their
trauell.

Who so snatcheth vp follies too greedilie, making an
occupation of recreation, and delight his day labour, may
happes proue a wittome whiles he fisheth for finer witte,
and a Foole while hee findes himselfe laughing pastime
at other mens follies; not vnlike to him who drinking
Wine immoderately, besides that hee many times swal-
lowes downe dregs, at length prooues starke drunke.

There is no extremitie, either in actiue or contemplatiue
life, more outragious then the excessiue studies of delight,
wherwith young Students are so besotted that they forsake
sounder Artes to followe smoother eloquence, not vnlike
to him that had rather haue a newe painted boxe, though
there be nothing but a halter in it, then an olde bard
hutch with treasure inualuable; or *Æsops* Cocke, which
parted with a Pearle for a Barlie kurnell. Euen as a man
is inclined, so his studies are bended; if to vaineglorie, to
eloquence; if to profounde knowledge, to *Aristotle*; if
lasciuious, good in some English deuise of verse; to conclude, a passing potman, a passing Poet.

[*Then follows an attack on the* 'abusiue enormities' *practised in the name of knowledge, and a plea for the* 'suppression of the rauenous rable' *who discredit learning.* 'There be three things which are wont to slack young Students endeuour: Negligence, want of Wisedome, & Fortune.' 'Nothing is so great an enemie to a sounde iudgment as the pride of a peeuish conceit, which causeth a man both in life and beliefe either to snatch vppe or hatch newfangles.']

There is no such discredit of Arte as an ignoraunt Artificer,—men of meaner iudgement measuring oft times the excellencie of the one by the ignoraunce of the other. But as hee that censureth the dignitie of Poetry by *Cherillus* paultry paines, the maiestie of Rethorick by the rudenesse of a stutting *Hortensius*, the subtiltie of Logique by the rayling of *Ramus*, might iudge the one a foole in writing he knewe not what, the other tipsie by his stammering, the thirde the sonne of Zantippe by his scolding: so he that estimats Artes by the insolence of Idiots, who professe that wherein they are Infants, may deeme the Vniuersitie nought but the nurse of follie, and the knowledge of Artes nought but the imitation of the Stage. This I speake to shew what an obloquie these impudent incipients in Arts are vnto Art.

Amongst all the ornaments of Artes, Rethorick is to be had in highest reputation, without the which all the rest are naked, and she onely garnished: yet some there be who woulde seperate Arts from Eloquence, whose [opinion we] oppugne, because it abhorres from common experience. Who doth not know that in all tongues taske eloquence is odious if it be affected, and that attention is altogether wanting where it is reiected? A man may baule till his voice be hoarse, exhort with teares till his tongue ake and his eyes be drie, repeate that hee woulde perswade til his stalenes dooth secretlie call for a Cloake bagge, and yet moue no more then if he had been all that while mute, if his speech be not seasoned with eloquence and adorned with elocutions assistance. Nothing is more odious to the Auditor then the artlesse tongue of a tedious dolt, which dulleth the delight of hearing, and slacketh the desire of remembring; and I know not how it comes to passe, but many are so delighted to heare themselues that they are a cumber to the eares of all other, pleasing their Auditors in nothing more then in the pause of a ful point, when as by their humming and hawking respit they haue leisure to gesture the mislike of his rudenes. To the eschewing therefore of the lothing hatred of them that heare them, I would wish them to learne to speake many things in few, neither to speake all things which to theyr purpose they may speake, least those things be lesse profitably spoken which they ought to speake; neither would I haue them ouershoote themselues with an imitation of breuitie, so that striuing to be very short they should prooue very long, namelie, when as they endeuor to speake many things breefelie. Perswade one point throughlie rather then teach many things scatteringly; that which we thinke let vs speake, and that which we speake let vs thinke; let our speeche accorde with our life. Endeuour to adde vnto Arte Experience: experience is more profitable voide of arte then arte which hath not experience. Of it selfe arte is vnprofitable without experience, and experience rashe without arte. In reading thou must with warie regard learne as wel to discerne thy losse as thy gaine, thy hurt as good, least, being wonne to haue a fauorable like of Poets wanton liues, thou be excited vnto the imitation of their lust. It is very vnseemely that nobler wits shoulde be discredited with baser studies, and those whom high and mightie callings doo expect shold be hindered by the inticements of pleasure and vanitie. Young men are not

so much delighted with solide substances as with painted
shadowes, following rather those thinges which are goodly
to the viewe then profitable to the vse; neither doo they
loue so much those things that are dooing as those things
that are sounding, reioycing more to be strowed with
flowers then nourished with frute. How many be there
that seeke truth, not in truth but in vanitie, and find that
they sought not according to trueth but according to
vanitie, and that, which is most miserable, in the words
of life they toile for the merchandise of death. Hence
commeth it to passe that many make toyes their onelie
studie; storing of trifles, when as they neglect most precious treasures: and, hauing left the Fountaines of truth,
they folow the Riuers of opinions. I can but pittie their
folly, who are so curious in fables and excruciate themselues about impertinent questions, as about *Homers*
Countrey, parentage, and sepulcher, whether *Homer* or
Hesiodus were older, whether *Achilles* or *Patroclus* more
ancient, in what apparrell *Anacharsis* the *Scithian* slept,
whether *Lucan* is to be reckoned amongst the Poets or
Historiographers, in what Moneth in the yere *Virgill*
died, with infinite other, as touching the Letters of the
Hiacinth, the Chestnut tree, the children of *Niobe*, the
trees where *Latona* brought foorth *Diana*, in all which
idle interrogatories they haue left vnto vs not thinges
found, but things to be sought, and peraduenture they
had founde necessary things if they had not sought superfluous thinges.

[*So too in Philosophy there are* 'innumerable such vnnecessary questions.']

I know the learned wil laugh me to scorne for setting
down such Rams horne rules of direction, and euen nowe
I begin to bethinke me of *Mulcasters Positions*, which
makes my penne heere pause as it were at a full point:
which pause hath changd my opinion, and makes me

rather refer you to Aschame, the antienter of the two: whose prayses seeing Maister Grant hath so gloriously garnished, I will referre you to his workes, and more especially to his Schoolemaster, where he hath most learnedly censured both our Latine and Greeke Authors. As for lighter studies, seeing they are but the exercise of youth to keepe them from idlenes, and the preparation of the minde to more weightie meditations, let vs take heede least, whiles we seeke to make them the furthering helps of our finall profession, they proue not the hindering harmes of our intended vocation, that we dwell not so long in Poetry that wee become Pagans, or that we make not such proceedinges in Aristotle that we prooue proficients in Atheisme. Let not learning, which ought to be the Leuell whereby such as liue ill ought to square theyr crooked waies, be the occasion vnto them of farther corruption who haue already sucked infection, least thair knowledge way them downe into hell, when as the ignorant goe the direct way to heauen.

And thus I ende my Anatomie, least I might seeme to haue beene too tedious to the Reader in enlarging a Theame of Absurditie, desiring of the learned pardon, and of Women patience, which may encourage me heereafter to endeuour in some other matter of more moment, as well to be answerable to the expectation of the one as to make amends to the other. In the meane time I bidde them both farewell.

APPENDIX

FROM E. HOBY'S TRANSLATION OF COIGNET'S *POLITIQUE DISCOURSES*
1586

[The following passage is the thirty-fifth chapter of *Politique Discourses on trueth and lying. An instruction to Princes to keepe their faith and promise.... Translated out of French ... by Sir E. Hoby. R. Newberrie. London* 1586. 4°. (B. M. 523. g. 13). The original, by Matthieu Coignet, appeared in Paris in 1584, with the title *Instruction aux Princes pour garder la Foy promise: contenant un sommaire de la philosophie Chrestienne et morale ... en plusieurs discours.*]

THAT LYING HATH MADE POETS AND PAINTERS TO BE BLAMED, AND OF THE GARNISHING OF HOUSES.

PLATO wrote that Poetrie consisted in the cunning inuention of fables, which are a false narration resembling a true, and that therein they did often manifest sundrie follies of the gods; for this cause he banished and excluded them out of his common wealth, as men that mingled poyson with honie. Besides thorough their lying and wanton discourses they corrupt the manners of youth, and diminish that reuerence which men ought to carrie towards their superiors and the lawes of God, whom they faine to be replenished with passions & vice. And the principall ornament of their verses are tales made at pleasure, & foolish & disorderly subiectes, cleane disguising the trueth & hystorie, to the end they might the more delight; and for this cause haue they bin thrust out of sundry cities. Among other, after that *Archilocus* came into *Sparta*, he was presently thrust out, as soon as they had vnderstood how he had written in his poemes, that it was better to lose a mans weopens than his life, & forbad euer after al such deceitful

poesies. Hence grew the common prouerb, that al Poets are
lyers. And it was written of *Socrates*, that hee was yl brought
vp to poesie because he loued the truth. And a man mought
say that this moued *Caligula* to condemne *Virgils* & *Homers*
books, because of their prophane fables, which S. *Paul* exhorted *Timothie* to cast away. *Plutarque* telleth of a Lacedemonian, who, when he was demanded what he thought of
the Poet *Tirteus*, answered that he was very good to infect yong
mens wits. And *Hieron* of *Siracusa* condemned *Epicarmus* the
Poet in a great fine, because in his wiues presence he had
repeated certaine lasciuious verses. And *Viues* writeth that
Ouid was most iustly sent into banishment, as an instrument
of wantonnesse. He which first inuented the *Iambique* versifying, to byte and quippe, was the first that felt the smart.
And *Archilocus* the Poet fell into confusion through his own
detractions, as *Horace* and sundry other haue written; and
Aulus Gellius reporteth that *Orpheus, Homer*, and *Hesiodus* gaue
names & honours to the gods. And *Pithagoras* saide that their
soules hong in hel vpon a tree, still pulled of euery side by
serpents, for their so damnable inuention. And *Domitian*
banished *Juvenal*: and Pope *Paull* 2 and *Adrian* 6 held them
as enimies to religion. *Eusebius* in his 8 booke & first Chapter
de Preparatione Euangelica setteth down an example of a Poet,
who, for hauing lewdly applyed a peece of Scripture to a fable,
suddenly lost his naturall sight; and, after that he had done
penance, it was restored to him againe. And as touching
Painters, they haue beene greatly misliked of, for representing such fictions & Poetical deceits. For as *Simonides* saide:
Painting is a dumme Poesie, and a Poesie is a speaking painting: & the actions which the Painters set out with visible
colours and figures the Poets recken with wordes, as though
they had in deede beene perfourmed. And the end of eche is
but to yeeld pleasure by lying, not esteeming the sequele and
custome, or impression, which hereby giue to the violating of
the lawes and corruption of good manners. For this cause the
Prophets called the statuas, images, and wanton pictures, the
teachers of vanitie, of lyes, deceite, & abhomination. And
Lactantius writeth, that a counterfait tooke the name of counterfaiting, and all deceit (as wee before declared) springeth from
falshood and lying. This was it which mooued S. *John*, in the
ende of his first Epistle, to warne men to *keepe themselues from*

images: for an image doeth at their fansie counterfait the bodie of a man dead, but is not able to yeelde the least gaspe of breath. And idolatrie is properly such seruice as is done vnto Idoles. Wee reade howe God especially forbad it in the first table, and how long the *Romanes* and *Persians* liued without any vse thereof: and howe the *Lacedemonians* coulde neuer abyde that an image should stand in their Senate. There hath beene in sundrye councels mention made thereof & S. *Athanasius* more at large discoursed thereof in a sermon he made against Idols: and S. Augustin in his booke *de fide & Simbolo*, and vppon 150 Psalm, & in his eighth book of the citie of God, & *Damascene* in his 4 book & 8 c. The occasion of so free passage giuen to Poets is, for that their fables flyde awaye easily, and cunningly turne them selues to tickel at pleasure, whereas the trueth plainly setteth downe the matter as it is indeede, albeit the euent thereof bee not verie pleasant. *Plato* in like sort compared the disputes in Poetrie to the banquets of the ignorant, who vse Musike in steede of good discourse, and, in his thirde booke of his commonwealth, he forbiddeth Poets or painters to set downe or represent any thinge dishonest or wanton, for feare of corrupting of good manners. And *Aristotle* in his Politiques, the thirde booke and 17 Chapter, would haue all vyle wordes to be banished. And Saint *Paul* to the *Ephesians*, that any vncleannesse, foolish iesting, or talking shoulde bee once named among them. And *Tertullian*, an auncient doctor of the Church, called Poets, and certaine Philosophers, the Patriarches of heretiques. This which I haue spoken of must not be vnderstood of Poesies wherein much trueth and instruction is contained, nor of pictures which represent the actes of holye and vertuous personnages, nor of fables taken out of hystories, whereof, there maye growe some edifying; but onely of that which is lasciuious, and grounded vpon naughtie argument, rendring youth effeminate, and men more giuen to wantonnesse, pleasures, passion, & vayne opinions, then to virtue, cleane turning away the honour that is due vnto God or to good edifying; for according vnto the commaundement of God, Cherubyns were made. The admonition which *Epictetus* gaue to such as were too curious in pictures ought by no meanes to be here forgotten : *Trim not thy house* (saith hee) *with tables and pictures, but paint it and guild it with Temperance: the one vainely feedeth the eyes, the other is an eternall ornament which cannot be defaced.* The same doeth *Plutarque* teache in the life of *Dion*, that more care is to bee taken for the hanging and adorning of the palace of the soule, then of the outwarde. And the same Philosopher did not muche out of the waye warne vs, that wee shoulde take heede that the skirt of our garments shoulde not carrie a stinche of life.

NOTES

NOTES

Ascham (pp. 1–45).

The story of the origin of the *Scholemaster* is told by Ascham in his *Preface to the Reader* (Mayor, pp. xiii–xxiii; Giles, iii. pp. 78–87). The purpose of the book is discussed at great length in a letter addressed by him to his friend Sturm in ? Dec. 1568 (Giles, ii. pp. 174–91). The latter document is chiefly concerned with 'Imitation,' which Ascham appears to have considered the main critical topic of his work. '*Scribis tu* de Imitatione, *et ego nonnihil cogito de eodem argumento: sed tu absolute, eruditis iam ac viris; ego inchoate, rudibus adhuc et pueris.*' After describing the plan of the book (see note, p. 358), and informing Sturm that he has written in English, he proceeds—

'*In loco de Imitatione longiusculus est* Praeceptor *meus. Fatetur se omnes fere et veteres et recentes, qui de Imitatione scripsere, cupide perlegisse: probare se multos, admirari vero neminem, praeter unum Sturmium. Aliqui certe recte, qui sint imitandi; sed quomodo instituenda sit ipsa imitandi ratio, solus docet Sturmius. Itaque, si cum illa perfectione praeceptorum, quae in* Literata *tua* Nobilitate *et* Amissa dicendi Ratione *plenissime tradita sunt, copiam etiam exemplorum coniunxisses; quid praeterea requirendum esset, non video. Namque, ut in vitae et morum sic in doctrinae et studiorum ratione omni, longe plus possunt exempla quam praecepta. In illarum vero rerum sive arte, sive facultate, quae sola imitatione perfici videntur, praecepta aut nullum aut perexiguum habent locum, quum exempla isthic vel solitaria plane regnant. Pictores, sculptores, scriptores hoc et prudenter intelligunt et perfecte praestant.*

'*Atque ut oratores etiam in horum numero collocem movet nonnulla ratio, iubet quae illa est* Quinctiliani *auctoritas: qui dicit, Ciceronem (nec Cicero de se hoc ipse tacet) iucunditatem Isocratis, copiam Platonis, vim Demosthenis effinxisse; et effingere, in imitatione necne propriam sedem habeat, omnes vident. Verum enimvero ostendere, et iudicare solum, ubi hoc facit Cicero, mediocris diligentiae, vulgaris et quotidiani est laboris. Hoc Perionius, Victorius, Stephanus, et alii in Cicerone: hoc Macrobius, Hessus, et nuper diligentissime omnium Fulvius Ursinus, in Virgilio: hoc accurate etiam Clemens Alexandrinus, quinto* στρωμάτων *in veteribus Graecis scriptoribus attentavit. Sed hi omnes perinde sunt, ut operarii et baiuli, qui, quum comportent materiam, deesse certe in opere faciundo non possunt, mercedem tamen ipsi perexiguam et laudem quidem non maximam promerentur.* (Cf. supra, p. 19.)

'*Atqui docere perspicue et perfecte, qua ratione Cicero vel Demosthenem vel Platonem imitatur; singularis, fateor, doctrinae, summi iudicii, et rarae laudis existit. Sed haec laus adhuc praeceptionis tota propria est. Aliud volo, plus requiro. Opifex nobis et architectus opus est, qui separata coniungere, rudia perpolire, et totum opus construere, artificiosa ratione noverit. Et illud, mea certe opinione, hoc modo. "Hinc Demosthenis locum, illinc Ciceronis produci cupio. Tum, digito artificis me primum duci volo ad ea, quae in utroque sunt aut eadem aut simillima. Deinde, quae sunt in hoc addita et quo consilio; tum, quae sunt ablata et quo iudicio. Postremo quae sunt commutata; et quo ac quam vario artificio; sive id in verborum delectu, sive in sententiarum forma, sive in membrorum circumductione, sive in argumentorum ratione consistat. Nec uno aut altero exemplo contentus ero. Numero multa, genera varia, ex Platone, ex Isocrate, ex Demosthene, et ex Aristotele in libris rhetoricis, exempla expeto.*" (Cf. supra, p. 9.)

'*Patior Praeceptorem parcum esse in praeceptorum traditione, modo liberalem se et largum in exemplorum non solum productione, quod laboris est et diligentiae, verum etiam tractatione, quod est doctrinae et iudicii, ostendat.* . . .

'*Equidem amplector unice Ciceronis imitationem: sed eam dico et primam ordine, et praecipuam dignitate, qua Cicero ipse Graecos; non qua Lactantius olim, Omphalius nuper, aut qua multo felicius quidam Itali, Galli, Lusitani, et Angli Ciceronem sunt secuti. . . . Non possum probare consilium Bartholomaei Riccii Ferrariensis, doctissimi licet viri; qui quum sic scripserit de recta imitandi ratione, ut quum a Sturmio discesseris, caeteris omnibus mea certe opinione anteponendus sit (praecepta enim eius omnia sunt Sturmiana, et ex tuis fontibus hausta atque derivata), exempla tamen maluit Longolii ex Cicerone, quam Ciceronis ex Platone sibi proponere; et Virgilii ex Catullo, quam Virgilii ex Homero producere . . .*

'*Si vero optarem ipse fieri alter Cicero (et optare quidem nefas non est), ut fierem, et qua ratione fierem, quem potius ad consilium mihi adhiberem, quam ipsum Ciceronem? . . . Ille enim sermo non in Italia natus est, sed e Graecorum disciplina in Italiam traductus. . . . Unde evenit, ut sola Ciceronis oratio inter reliquos omnes Romanos, qui illi aetate aut superiores, aut aequales, aut suppares fuere, non colore solum vernaculo pure tincta, sed raro et transmarino quodam plene imbuta, tam admirabiliter resplendesceret.*

'*Itaque, quum ipsa lingua Latina, felicissimo suo tempore, in ipsa Roma, in ipso Cicerone, ad summam perfectionem sine Graeca lingua non pervenit: cur quisquam in sola Latina quaerit, quod Cicero ipse absque Graeca non invenit? . . . Sed ait quis, "Recte quidem Cicero; nam ante eum, nemo fuit praeter Graecos, ad imitationem proponendus. Sed nunc habemus ipsum Ciceronem, eum quidem, cum universa Graecia, et cum singulo quoque Graecorum, in ea eloquentiae laude qua maxime quisque floruit, comparandum. Cur igitur non Ciceronem solum mihi, variis illis Graecis relictis, ad imitandum proponerem?" Aliquid est, quod dicis. Ipse enim Ciceronem praecipue imitandum volo; sed tuta via, sed recta ratione, suo ordine, suo loco. Et rationem meam, cur hoc volo, et quomodo hoc volo, aperte ostendam. Primum, si optarem ipse alter fieri Cicero (quod ante dixi), qua ratione potius fierem, quam ea ipsa, qua ipse Cicero factus est Cicero? Hanc viam certam, cognitam, et expeditam esse, optimus testis est ipse Cicero. . . .*

'*Et haec est illa via, mea certe opinione, qua ad Ciceronis imitationem recta pergendum est. Non, quomodo Riccius ostendit Longolium fecisse (hoc est ut ipse putat, excellenti ratione; ut ego existimo, valde laudabiliter; ut multi sentiunt, mediocriter et tolerabiliter; et Erasmus et Paulus Manutius iudicant, inepte, frigide, et pueriliter), sed qua ratione Sturmius Ciceronem imitandum esse, et praeceptis in* Literata Nobilitate *perfecte docet, et exemplis in* Quinctiana Explicatione *insigniter ostendit.* ...

'*Sed quorsum tantopere, mi Sturmi, laboramus de imitatione? quum non desunt, qui docti et prudentes videri volunt, qui imitationem vel nullam esse putant, vel nihili prorsus aestimant, vel omnem temere permiscent, vel eam totam, quaecunque sit, cuiuscunque sit, ut servilem et puerilem repudiant. Sed hi sunt et inertes et imperiti; laborem fugiunt, artem nesciunt.* ... *Artis enim et naturae dissidium faciunt, quicunque casu non delectu, fortuito non observatione, in literarum studiis versantur. Isti idem sentiunt de eleganti illa eloquentiae parte, quae in numerorum ratione collocata est; illam enim aut nullam esse volunt, aut inanem omnem iudicant. Et aurium sensum cum artificioso et intelligenti animi iudicio nihil commercii habere existimant.*'

He proceeds to lament the loss of the books of Dionysius of Halicarnassus, *De imitatione et oratoria et historica*, and to pass in review Christophorus Longolius, Budaeus, Erasmus, Paulus Manutius, Petrus Victorius, Jovita Rapicius, author of the *De Numero Oratorio*, Carolus Sigonius, Giambattista Pigna, and Angelio Pietro da Barga (Bargaeus). All, except Manutius, Pigna, and Bargaeus, appear in the English text (see notes); but of Manutius he says: *Gaudeo* Praeceptorem *meum loqui* Anglice: *ne, quum tam libere dissentit hac in re a Manutio, tantum hominem offenderet: tamen Manutium non nominat.* The references to Pigna are concerned only with his views on Horace's *Ars Poetica* (*aureolum Horatii librum*), Aristotle's *Rhetoric*, and *Quaestiones Sophocleae*. Ascham appears to be unaware of Pigna's more important apology for the methods of Ariosto in *I Romanzi* (1554), or is perhaps unwilling to dispute with him on these matters of 'bold bawdrye' (see p. 4). He names Bargaeus for his *doctissimos commentarios in eruditum illum Demetrii libellum de Elocutione*.

1. Εὐφυής. Lyly is indebted to this passage for his *Euphues*. Ascham's definition is built up from classical usage, e.g. Plato, Aristotle, and especially Plutarch (*Moralia*, ed. Xylander, p. 81 D), but in its completeness of application has some claim to originality. Cf. the companion definition in Estienne's *Thesaurus*, which appeared in 1572.

2. 20-9. Cf. *Toxophilus*, ed. Giles, ii. p. 150.

3. 36. 'In our forefathers tyme,' &c. Cf. the similar passage

in the Preface to *Toxophilus* ('To all Gentlemen and Yeomen of England'), ed. Giles, ii. pp. 7-8. See Nash, infra, p. 323; Gosson, *Playes Confuted*, Roxb. Libr. p. 172; Jonson, *New Inn*, i. 1. For the argument that Ascham in his attack on Italian books is thinking especially of Painter's *Palace of Pleasure*, see Mr. Jacobs's edition of Painter, i. xix, xxiv.

4. 3. *bold bawdrye*: apparently not Ascham's own phrase. Cf. Sir Thomas Elyot, speaking of those 'that suppose that in the warkes of poetes is contayned nothynge but baudry (suche is their foule worde of reproche) and unprofitable leasinges' (*The Gouernour*, ed. Croft, i. 123).

7. 30. *De Republica*, 393 D.

8. 27. See the *Epistolae*, No. 1708, and the Preface to his 'Demosthenes.'

30. See Macrobius, *Saturnalia*, Bk. V.

35. *Eobanus Hessus*. Helius Eobanus Hessus (1488-1540) here interests Ascham as the editor of Theocritus. Cf. infra, p. 18, l. 35, and p. 20, l. 15. His annotations on the *Bucolics* and *Georgics* were printed in 1529. He had considerable reputation as a poet. 'Potest et terra nostra Germania,' writes Lilius Gyraldus, 'gloriari Helio Eobano Hesso, poeta insigni, cuius complura passim leguntur poemata non in Germania modo, sed et in Italia et Gallia' (*De Poetis*, ed. Wotke, p. 69). His editions of the *Psalms* and his *Medicinae Laus* (*ex Erasmo*) were frequently reprinted. His Life is written by Camerarius.

9. 30. Kindly references to Sir John Cheke (1514-57) are very frequent in Ascham's writings. He had been Ascham's tutor (p. 39, l. 33). See pp. 21 (l. 31), 44 (l. 27 and note).

32. *Io. St.* Ioannes Sturmius. His *De Imitatione Oratoria Libri Tres* was printed at Strassburg in 1574. His *Poeticum primum* [*secundum* ... *sextum*] *volumen cum lemmatibus* (Strassburg, 1565) was very popular, and his nine-volume edition of Cicero (1557) and the earlier *In partitiones oratorias Ciceronis Dialogi duo* (Strassburg, 1539) gave him an authoritative standing in the Ciceronian controversy. See note to p. 13, l. 31.

10. 23. *piteling*. Cf. *pickling*, infra, p. 43, l. 25. The sense seems to be 'piddling' (cf. ii. p. 248, l. 31), but no other examples of these forms have been recorded.

35. *Ad Atticum*, iv. 13. 1.

11. 10. *Ep. ad P. L.* i. 9. 23 ; *Ep. ad Att.* iv. 16. 2 ; *De Orat.* i. 55, ii. 152, 153, 160.

25. *De Orat.* i. 7. 28.

32. *Epist.* iv. 16.

13. 2. *De Orat.* ii. 89, &c.

3. *Orat. ad Brutum*, 40, &c., 172, &c.

4. Cf. infra, p. 45, l. 14. See Cic. *Brut.* passim, also Quint. xii. 1.

10. Quint. x. 2.

16. Especially in his *Dialogus cui titulus Ciceronianus: sive de optimo genere dicendi.* See the Dedication.

17. *Longolius* (Christopher Longueil de Malines) wrote a Commentary on Cicero's *Rhetoric* (1541) and published an edition of the *Letters to Atticus* (1549), which with his own Letters gave him a high contemporary reputation as a Ciceronian. 'Audio Longolium iuvenem Macliniensem,' says Gyraldus, 'inter barbaros natum et altum ita bonas litteras amplecti, ut nisi adversa valetudo obstet, brevi sit Latinae linguae non parum adlaturus ornamenti' (ed. Wotke, p. 42). He edited Quintilian, and published in 1562 the *Libri Elegantiarum* of Lorenzo Valla. See the references in Ascham's letter to Sturm, supra, p. 348, and in Harvey, ii. p. 248, ll. 5, 7.

20. *Budæus* (Guillaume Budé, 1467–1540). Ascham refers to his *Commentarii linguae Graecae* (Paris, 1529) in the First Book (ed. Mayor, p. 6); here, and in his *Letters*, to the Commentaries on Cicero's Letters. His complete works, critical, philosophical (theological), and juridical, were collected by Coelius Secundus Curio (4 vols. fol. Basle, 1557).

24. *Philip Melancthon* (1497–1560) discusses Imitation in his *Elementorum Rhetorices Libri II* (Wittenberg, 1531).

25. *Camerarius* (Joachimus), 1500–74, published several editions of Greek and Latin classics, including Aesop, Cicero, Macrobius, Plautus, and Terence, and a volume *De Imitatione, Comment. in Tullii Tusculan.* His chief historical value lies in his Letters, his *Narratio de H. Eobano Hesso, comprehendens mentionem de compluribus illius aetatis doctis et eruditis viris* (Nuremb. 1553), and his *Life of Melancthon* (Leipzig, 1566).

27. *Io. Sambucus* (d. 1584). His book *De Imitatione Cicero-*

niana, Dialogi Tres (Paris, 1561) passed through many editions. An edition of Plautus appeared in 1566, and a commentary on Caesar in 1574. Earlier in the *Scholemaster* (ed. Mayor, p. 127) Ascham refers to his annotated paraphrase of the *Ars Poetica* (Antwerp, 1564). See also note to ii. p. 323, l. 4.

29. *Cortesius* (Paolo Cortese), 1465-1510, Bishop of Urbino, author of a commentary on Peter Lombard and a treatise on the Cardinalate. Cortesius's letter, which Ascham approves, is criticized at considerable length by Erasmus in his *Ciceronianus*. Gabriel Harvey in his *Ciceronianus* (24) takes the other side. The texts are printed in the editions of Politian's Letters. Paolo Cortese must not be confused with another Cortese (Gregorio, originally Giambattista), 1483-1548, also Bishop of Urbino, and of the same family, and author of a volume of Letters (Venice, 1573). Paolo had two brothers, Alessandro, a poet, and Lattanzio, who wrote a commentary on Caesar.

30. *Bembus ad Picum.* This letter on *Imitation* (*De imitatione sermonis*) and another by Pico are printed in the editions of the *Epistolae* of Bembo.

31. *Ioan. Sturmius*, &c. The *De amissa dicendi ratione et quomodo ea recuperanda sit*, his first original work, appeared in 1538. The *Nobilitas litterata* was printed at Strassburg in 1549, and was Englished by 'T. B.' in 1570. See also note to p. 9, l. 32.

14. 12. *Bartholomaeus Riccius Ferrariensis* (Bartolommeo Ricci of Lugo). His *De imitatione libri tres, ad Alfonsum Alestium principem*, &c. (i.e. his pupil, son of Duke Ercole II of Ferrara), was issued from the Aldine press at Venice in 1545. His Latin lexicon, *Apparatus Latinae Locutionis*, had appeared in 1533. He was a friend of Lilius Gyraldus, who refers to him at the beginning of his *De Poetis* (ed. Wotke, pp. 2-3). See the letter to Sturm, *supra*, p. 348.

21-2. Cf. p. 30, ll. 6-7. *good cheape*, cheaply. Fr. *à bon marché*. Cf. 1 Hen. IV, iii. 3. 51.

Cf. the *Scholemaster*, Bk. I, p. 59 (ed. Mayor), where, speaking of 'the pastimes that be fitte for Courtlie Jentlemen,' he adds, 'But of all kinde of pastimes fitte for a Jentleman, I will, God willing, in fitter place, more at large, declare fullie, in my booke of the Cockpitte.' Ascham's favourite amusement was well known to his literary contemporaries. Cf. Sir Thomas Smith to Haddon (Bordeaux, 6th April, 1565) '*Quid autem agit Aschamus tuus, item ac meus? . . . Credo vero gallos suos ita illum excantasse, ut amicorum suorum prorsum sit oblitus* (*Haddoni Epist.* 307). Fuller, in his *Worthies*, laments that 'in his old age he [Ascham] exchanged [Archery] for a worse pastime, neither so healthfull for his body, nor profitable for his purse, I mean Cock-fighting' (ed. 1662, p. 209).

16. 35. For the *loci* in the wrangle about the merits of Greek and Latin see the excellent note in Mr. Mayor's edition of the *Scholemaster* (1863), pp. 244-8.

17. 26, &c. Cf. *Nizolian Paper-bookes* in Sidney, infra, p. 202, l. 16 (note).

31. *one labour.* See Erasmus, *Adagia, s.* 'Herculei labores.'

32. *namelie*, i.e. 'especially.' Cf. p. 45, l. 9.

Chiliades, Apophthegmata, and *Similia,* i.e. *Adagiorum Chiliades tres* (1508); *Apophthegmatum Opus* (1531), printed, in English, by Grafton, in 1542; and *Parabolarum sive Similium liber* (?1520).

18. 7. *De Orat.* iii. 28.

29. *Perionius* (*Ioachimus*) is best known by his edition of Aristotle (1563) and his *Dialogi de linguae gallicae origine eiusque cum Graeca cognatione* (Paris, 1555). He printed selections from Plato and Livy. Ascham probably refers to his *De optimo genere interpretandi* (Paris, 1540). See Ascham's letter to Sturm, supra, p. 347; and Harvey, ii. p. 245, l. 9.

Henr. Stephanus in dictionario Ciceroniano, i.e. Henri Estienne (second of the name) in his *Ciceronianum Lexicon Graecolatinum*, 1557.

P. Victorius . . . de varia lectione. Pietro Vettori (the elder), 1499-1585, printed his *Variarum Lectionum libri XXV* at Florence in 1553. By 1582 it had been expanded to thirty-eight books. His work was mainly editorial (Aristotle, Cicero, Terence, Varro, Sallust, &c.).

35. *Macrobius, Hessus.* Cf. p. 8, ll. 30, 35.

19. 14. Cf. Ascham's letter to Sturm, ed. Giles, ii. p. 189.

20. 32. Mr. Mayor appears to be right in saying 'There is no statement of the kind in Diogenes' (*Scholemaster*, p. 249).

21. 18. *Tomitanus,* Bernardino Tomitano (1506-76), a physician and scholar of Padua, wrote *Introductiones ad Sophisticos Elenchos*

Aristotelis, but is best known by his vernacular works *Quattro libri della lingua Thoscana* (Venice, 1545), *Ragionamenti della lingua Toscana* (1545), and *Discorso intorno all' eloquenza* (1554).

31. *Redman*, Dr. John (1499–1551), of St. John's College, Cambridge, first Master of Trinity. See p. 313, l. 30.

Cheke. See note to p. 9, l. 30, and p. 44, l. 27.

Smith, Sir Thomas (1513–77), Regius Professor of Civil Law, who with Cheke shared the honour of upholding Classical scholarship at Cambridge: one of 'The two eyes of this University' (Harvey in his *Ciceronianus*, 43)—'duo propugnacula, duo ornamenta eruditionis, literarum, Academiae Angliae' (*Vita Aschami*, 30). See note to p. 102, l. 24.

Haddon, Walter (1516–72).

Watson, Thomas (1513–84), Master of St. John's, Bishop of Lincoln, author of *Absolon* (see p. 23, l. 31, note); not to be confounded with the author of the Ἑκατομπαθία, *or the Passionate Centurie of Love*. See note to p. 316, l. 8, and Index.

23. 3. Cf. ante, p. 21, l. 31, note. See also Ascham's Letters to Cheke, passim.

7. *these three.* Cf. Quintil. xii. 10 (§ 636). See also Scaliger, *Poetice*, iv. chaps. xvi–xxi.

31. *Watson . . . Tragedie of* Absalon, in Latin (ante, p. 21). See other references by Index. He also translated the first book of the *Odyssey* into English verse. See the *Scholemaster*, Bk. I (ed. Mayor, p. 71), where Ascham gives a specimen.

33. Is this the first known reference in English to Aristotle's *Poetics*?

24. 7. The *Iephthes* of George Buchanan (1506–81), written not later than 1554, was printed at the Plantin Press and by the Stephani in 1566, and often later. See Freebairn's edition of the Works, 1715. Cf. Sidney, infra, p. 201, l. 4.

24. 8, &c. Mr. E. K. Chambers thinks this may be John Christopherson, afterwards Bishop of Chichester (see *Mediaeval Stage*, ii. 195, note).

22. The MS. is said to have been at Penshurst in 1860 (see Halliwell, *Dict. of Old English Plays*, p. 2); but Mr. E. K. Chambers points out that it is not recorded in the Hist. MSS. Comm. Report (iii. App. 227), and that it is probably identical with the B.M. Stowe MS. 957 (*Mediaeval Stage*, u. s., ii. 458).

Notes

25. 13. *Carolus Sigonius hath written of late.* Carlo Sigonio, also known as (Bernardinus) Lauredanus, 1524-84, printed his *De Dialogo* at Venice in 1561. The *Orationes Septem C. Sigonii* appeared in the previous year (Aldus, Venice), and his *Disputationum patavinarum lib.* [*ii*] at Padua in 1562. He translated Aristotle's *Rhetoric* into Latin. His complete works were edited by Muratori (6 vols., Milan, 1732-7). See ii. p. 246, l. 24.

15. 'Notes of Sturm's lectures, which Ascham procured in London, A.D. 1547 (*Epist.* 14); they have not been printed' (Mayor, *Scholemaster*, p. 261).

25. Περὶ ἰδεῶν, i. 1. Sturm's very popular edition of Hermogenes, the rhetorician, was probably the quarry for most of the references to that writer.

26. 23, &c. '*At oratio ac vis forensis, perfectumque prosae eloquentiae decus, ut idem separetur Cato, ... ita universa sub principe operis sui erupit Tullio, ut delectari ante eum paucissimis, mirari vero neminem possis, nisi aut ab illo visum, aut qui illum viderit.*' Vell. Pat. *Hist. Rom.* i. 17.

27. 30. *Three thinges.* Cf. p. 35, ll. 18-19.

28. 20. Cf. *Epist. ad Att.* vii. 3. 10. Cf. also Quintil. x. 1 (*licet Terentii scripta ad Scipionem Africanum referantur*).

29. 14. Quintil. x. 1 (§ 513).

16. *Ars Poet.* 268-9.

30. *beggerly ryming,* &c. See also bk. i (ed. Arber, p. 73). Cf. the Spenser-Harvey Letters, Webbe, Campion, and Daniel, by Index. Blenerhasset in his *Induction* in the *Mirror for Magistrates* speaks of the 'Gotish kinde of ryming.'

31. Cf. p. 32, l. 21.

30. 6. Cf. ante, p. 14, ll. 21-2.

8. Ascham calls Chaucer 'our English Homer' in *Toxophilus* (Giles, ii. 42), and adds, 'I ever thought his sayings to have as much authority as either Sophocles or Euripides in Greek.'

8. *Thomas Norton of Bristow*; not to be confounded with Sackville's collaborator. Cf. Webbe (p. 242, l. 32). He wrote in 1477 a poem entitled *The Ordinal, or Manual of Chemical Art.* See the article in the *D. N. B.*: also Warton, ed. 1824, ii. 447.

9. *Thomas Phaer.* See note to p. 137, l. 29, and cf. Gascoigne, Webbe, and Puttenham, by Index.

10. *Palingenius (Marcellus)*, i.e. Pietro Angelo Manzolli. The *Zodiacus Vitae pulcherrimum opus M. Palingenii Stellati poetae* (? Venice, 1531), of which there are innumerable editions, was translated by B. Googe in 1560 (*First three books*), 1561 (*First six books*), and 1565 (*The Zodiacke of Life* . . .).

20. *wordes of one syllable.* See Index for references in these volumes to the monosyllabic character of English (s. v. Monosyllables). Cf. Dryden, *Discourse concerning Satire* (ed. Scott and Saintsbury, xiii. 121).

26. Quintil. ix. 3 (§ 478).

33. *Carmen Exametrum . . . in our English tong.* Yet Ascham in his *Toxophilus* gives a few examples from his own pen.

31. 5. Probably a reference to the passage in Cicero's *Brutus*, 51.

32. 11. *Simmias Rhodius . . . ᾠόν.* See Webbe and Puttenham, by Index. The title refers only to the *shape* of the verse, and not, as Ascham and his copiers have it, to the subject. Nor is the piece in rhyme.

21. *Hunnes and Gothians.* See p. 29, l. 31.

24. See note to p. 283, l. 9.

25. *Gonsaluo Periz . . . in translating the Vlisses of Homer.* Gonçalo Perez issued his translation in 1553 (*La Vlyxea de Homero . . . traduzida . . . en Romance Castellano*). It was several times reprinted in the sixteenth century. Meres borrows this passage (see vol. ii. p. 314, l. 33). See letter from Ascham to G. Periz, Feb. 20, 1565 (Giles, ii. 108).

33. 11. *Senese Felice Figliucci*, i.e. Felice Figliucci, Sanese (of Sienna), whose volume, *Della filosofia morale* a commentary in Italian on the *Ethics*, appeared at Rome in 1551. He also translated the *Philippics* of Demosthenes (Rome, 1551). See Tiraboschi, vii. 837, 2323. The plea for classical metres was fully advanced earlier by Claudio Tolomei in his *Versi e Regole della Nuova Poesia Toscana*, 1539, and by his friends of the *Accademia della Nuova Poesia*. Daniel notes this (see infra, ii. p. 368, l. 34).

26. And yet the Prologues of Ariosto's *Negromante* and *Cassaria* are in classical form. Earlier examples by Leonardo Dati and others are extant.

34. 20-1. Cic. *Epist. ad Att.* iv. 16 (towards end).

Notes

25. '*Sed nos veri iuris, germanaeque iustitiae solidam et expressam effigiem nullam tenemus: umbra et imaginibus utimur: eas ipsas utinam sequeremur! feruntur enim ex optimis naturae et veritatis exemplis.*' *De Officiis*, iii. 17 (§ 69).

36. 18. Cf. the similar metaphor in *Toxophilus* (Giles, ii. 147).

38. 32. *in these wordes*. *Acad. Quaest.* i. 3, § 9.

39. 3. 'Fabricius (*Bibl. Gr.* Harles, iv. 383, note d) has pointed out Ascham's error in confounding the historian with Varro's freedman of the same name (*Epist.* 9), an error common to him with Fras. Philelphus. Dionysius says himself (i. 7) that he came to Rome "in *Augustus* dayes"; but for Ascham's statement respecting Varro's library (here and *Epist.* 9) there seems to be no other ground than his occasional citations from Varro' (Mayor, p. 265).

20. *Civ. Dei*, vi. 2.

40. 6. See the section '*Qui primi legendi*' in Quintil. ii. 5 (86).

16. Quintil. x. 3 (525). Cf. Saintsbury, *Hist. of Crit.* ii. 151.

29, &c. 'He that will write well in any tongue must follow this counsel of Aristotle, to speak as the common people do, to think as wise men do.' *Toxophilus*, 'To all Gentlemen and Yeomen of England' (Giles, ii. 7).

41. 19, 26. See Quintil. viii. 3 (§§ 391, 393).

33. So Gellius, i. 15. 18 ('*novator verborum*'). Ascham appears to be borrowing from him here. Cf. *exacte* (l. 35), which is not Sallustian.

42. 21. Quintilian (from whom Ascham borrows) gives this example in the section '*Graecanicae figurae*' (ix. 3).

43. 25. *pickling*. See note to p. 10, l. 23.

44. 4 and 9. *Epist. ad Att.* vii. 3.

27. *those reules*. A supplement to these critical remarks is found in Cheke's letter to Thomas Hoby, July 16, 1557 (printed at the end of *The Courtier*, 1561):—'... I am of this opinion that our own tung shold be written cleane and pure, vnmixt and vnmangeled with borowing of other tunges, wherein if we take not heed bi tijm, euer borowing and neuer payeng, she shall be fain to keep her house as bankrupt. For then doth our tung naturallie and praisablie vtter her meaning, when she bouroweth no conterfeitness of other tunges to attire her self withall, but vseth plainlie her own with such shift, as nature

craft, experiens, and folowing of other excellent doth lead her vnto: and if she want at ani tijm (as being vnperfight she must), yet let her borow with suche bashfulnes, that it mai appeer that, if either the mould of our own tung could serue us to fascion a woord of our own, or if the old denisoned wordes could content and ease this neede, we wold not boldly venture of vnknowen wordes. This I say not for reproof of you, who haue scarslie and necessarily vsed whear occasion serueth a strange word so, as it seemeth to grow out of the matter and not to be sought for; but for mijn own defens, who might be counted ouerstraight a deemer of thinges, if I gaue not thys accompt to you, mi freend and wijs, of mi marring this your handiwork...'
This passage and the conversation reported by Ascham are the only critical deliverances by Cheke preserved in the vernacular.

45. 3. *mase and muse.* Cf. Heywood, *Epigrammes,* 'Brought to this tricker nother muse nor mase' (ed. Spens. Soc., p. 107).

26. *example to follow,* i.e. Cicero (ante, p. 25, l. 32).

The *Scholemaster,* as we have it, is incomplete, and was probably left unfinisharlie by Ascham, though he had promised to discuss 'particularlie of everie one' of the six sections named ante, p. 5. According to the plan which he communicated to Sturm about Dec. 1568, there were to be eight divisions. '*Gradus sunt hi; primus, linguarum versio .... Sequuntur reliqui Gradus, Paraphrasis, Metaphrasis, Epitome, Imitatio, Commentatio, Scriptio, et Declamatio*' (Giles, ii. 177).

WILLES (footnote, pp. 46–7).

47. Cf. Harvey, infra, i. p. 126; Fraunce, infra, i. p. 305; and Puttenham, infra, ii. p. 95 et seq.

GASCOIGNE (pp. 46–57)

[The notes in Gabriel Harvey's hand are here marked (H.): others, on the same copy, which appear to be in a hand rather older than Harvey's, are marked (N.). I am indebted to Miss Toulmin Smith for the collation of the text and for a copy of these manuscript jottings.]

Notes

46. 4. 'Aduertisements, worth the reading & examining' (H.).

47. 7. 'Pregnant & notable points' (H.).

Cf. Ronsard, *Abrégé de l'art poétique françois* (1565), 'Tu auras en premier lieu les conceptions hautes, grandes, belles, et non traînantes à terre. Car le principal poinct est l'invention, laquelle vient tant de la bonne nature, que par la leçon des bons et anciens autheurs,' &c. See the notes to James VI's *Reulis*, infra, p. 210, ll. 5–13, p. 221, ch. vii.

9. *Inuentio salsa. Aliquid lautum, rarum, et singulare* (N.).

11. Prologue to *Persones Tale* (Oxford Chaucer, IV. p. 568: and see note, vol. v. p. 446).

48. 5. *Inventio rara, non vulgaris* (N.). *Contemnenda Musa vulgaris: praesertim in tanta messe exquisitorum Ingeniorum* (H.).

a tale of a tubbe. For early examples of this phrase see Mr. Ward's *Eng. Dram. Lit.* ii. 379, note.

10–12. '*Nota*' (H.): in margin, '*In hoc genere Lucianus excellebat; et post eum plerique Itali: maxime Poetae* (N.)—apparently referring to the words *trita et obuia*.

17, &c. '*Aretinus voluit albis equis praecurrere, et esse Vnicus in suo quodam hyperbolico genere: Petrarcha, Ariostus, Tassus, plus habent et civilis ingenii et heroici animi. Nouissime etiam Sallustius Bartasius, in lingua Gallica, ipse est Homerus diuinus. Nihil unquam tale in Gallia*' (H.).

35. '*A non sequitur*' (H.). *Indecorum.* See note to p. 59, l. 33.

49. 3 (Top margin) 'The difference of the last verse from the rest in euerie stanza, a grace in the Faerie Queen' (H.).

(Side margin) 'The measure all one thoroughowte' (N.).

7. (Bottom margin) 'His aptest partition had bene into precepts of { Invention.
Elocution. And the seueral rules of both, to be sorted and marshialled in their proper places. He doth prettily well: but might easely haue don much better, both in the one, and in the other: especially by the direction of Horaces and Aristotles *Ars Poetica*' (H.).

13, 16. xij, xiiij, xiiij. (In margin) 'An errour (if an error) in sum few Eclogues of Sir Philip Sidney' (H.).

19. Over '*emphasis*' H. writes 'Prosodie.' (In the margin)

'The naturall and ordinary Emphasis of euery word, as uiolĕntly: not uiolēntly' (N.). Cp. note to p. 102, l. 23.

34. 'As I haue heard sum straungers, and namely Frenchmen, pronounce it Treasūre, *sed inepte*' (N.).

50. 4-5. Cf. l. 27, and see note to p. 267, ll. 6-15.

6. 'The onlie verse in esse' (H.).

9. 'The reason of menie a good uerse marred in Sir Philip Sidney, M. Spenser, M. Fraunce, and in a manner all owr excellentest poets: in such words as hēauĕn, ĕuĭl, dĭuĕl, and the like; made dyssyllables, contrarie to their natural pronunciation' (H.).

19. *to the eare.* 'So M. Spenser and Sir Philip, for the most part' (H.). 'Our poems only Rymes; & not verses, Aschami querela (N.): et mea post illum Reformatio; post me Sidneius, Spenserus, Francius' (H.).

51. 18, &c. '*Non placet*. A greater grace and Maiesty in longer wordes, so they be current Inglish. Monasyllables ar good to make vpp a hobling and hudling uerse' (N.).

22. Cf. Gascoigne's *Steel Glas* (ed. Arber, p. 77):—

'That *Grammer* grudge not at our english tong,
Bycause it stands by *Monosyllaba*.'

24. *Inkehorne.* The common Elizabethan phrase 'inkhorn termes' was perhaps established by Wilson in his *Arte of Rhetorique* (1553), though it occurs earlier (see *N. E. D.*). 'Inkhornism' is frequent in Nash and Harvey (cf. vol. ii. p. 431) and Hall. Florio uses 'inkpot tearmes' in his definition of 'pedantaggine.'

28. 'Sir Philip Sidney and M. Spenser, of mie opinion' (H.).

30-1. '*Idem ante in 2 Regula*' (N.).

52. 10. 'A pithie rule in Sir Philips Apologie for Poetrie. The Inuention must guide & rule the Elocution: *non contra*' (H.).

14, &c. Sidney is thinking of such methods in *Astrophel and Stella*, quoted infra, in note to p. 202, ll. 3-8.

22. (At end of § 7) '*Elocution*' (H.).

23. 'Tropes and figures lende an especiall grace to a uerse' (N.).

26. 'Gallant & fine' (H.).

'Persecuting of our figure too mutely: bald, and childish' (N.).

Ne quid nimis. See ii. p. 161, l. 15.

53. 3. (At end of § 9) 'Spenser hath reuiued *uncouth, whilom, of yore, forthy*' (H.).

4–9. (In margin of § 10) 'The stile sensible and significant; gallant & flowing' (H.).

10–32. (In margin of § 11) 'And yet we use to say, " He is of the *bludd royal*," and not " He is of the roiall bludd ": he is *heier apparant* to the Crowne, and not he is apparant heier to the Crowne: Rime *Roiall*, in regula 13 et 14 (N.), not royal ryme' (H.).

54. 1. *turkeneth*, altereth. Cf. Gascoigne: 'And for the rest you shall find it now in this second imprinting so turquened and turned, so clensed from all unclenly wordes...' (*Posies*, 'Epist. to Reuerend Diuines,' 1575). This rare word occurs at least twice in Golding's *De Mornay* (1587), pp. 353, 368 ('If they chaunce to stumble vpon some good saying for maners or for the life of man, they turkin it a thousand waies to make it seem good for thir purpose'), and once in Rogers's 39 *Articles* (1607), pref. p. 24. See Prof. Skeat's article in *Notes and Queries*, 6th Ser. v. 165 (4 Mar. 1882). The etymology is uncertain. Such a formation from Fr. *torquer*, L. *torqueo* would be unusual.

3. 'dissyllaba pro monosyllabis' (N.).

7. (End of § 12) 'All theise in Spenser and manie like: but with discretion: & tolerably, though sumtime not greatly commendably' (H.).

12. *Musicians.* Cf. Ronsard (apropos of masculine and feminine rhymes) in his *Abrégé*. With him *cesure* is practically elision ('une certaine cesure de la voyelle *e*').

21. (End of § 13) 'A special note in Sir Philips *Apologie for Poetrie*' (H.).

22. 'The Inglish Pentameter' (H.).

31. 'Ryme Royal still carrieth the credit for a gallant & stately verse' (H.).

55. 24. Gascoigne is of course out in his etymology. The older French form *vireli* was falsely associated with *virer* and *lai*.

30. 'Rather better than the royal' (H.).

34. *Gascoignes voyage into Holland* (1572).

35. 'Sir Philip vseth this kind often: as in Astrophil, Arcadia' (H.).

56. 6. N. writes opposite 'Poulters measure.'

11. (End of § 14) 'Mr. Phaers Virgil in a braue long verse, stately and flowing: the King of owr Inglish metricians' (H.). See note to p. 30, l. 9.

22. (Bottom) '*Gaudent breuitate moderni.* Spenser doth sumtime otherwise, and commendably, as the matter leadeth, the verse floweth, or other circumstance will beare it owt' (H.).

25. Gascoigne, it will be noted, does not give a formal definition of 'riding rime,' as he does in other cases.

33, &c. 'The difference of rymes, according to the difference of the matters subject' (H.).

57. 9. 'Or sum heroical discourse, or statelie argument' (H.).

12. *affying*, trusting, confiding.

WHETSTONE (pp. 58–60).

58. 8. Sir Humphrey Gilbert (? 1539–83) the navigator, stepbrother of Sir Walter Raleigh. Cf. Harvey, ii. 261, 28, &c.

Whetstone's friend Gascoigne had published, in 1576, *A Discourse of a new Passage to Cataia* [Cathay]: *Written by Sir Humfrey Gilbert, Knight.* Gascoigne informs us, in the Preface, that he had interested himself in the matter 'because I vnderstode that M. Fourboiser [i.e. Frobisher] (a kinsman of mine) did pretend to trauaile in the same *Discouerie*.'

15. *Promos and Cassandra* is based on the eighty-fifth novel of Giraldi Cintio's *Hecatommithi*, which Whetstone also translated in his *Heptameron of Ciuill Discourses* (1582). Shakespeare's *Measure for Measure* is founded on Whetstone's play.

59. 15. Cp. p. 79, l. 31; p. 332, l. 17, and ii. p. 309, l. 13.

21. *Germaine.* Cf. p. 84, l. 13. Mr. A. W. Ward (*Eng. Dram. Lit.* i. 216, &c.) points out that the objection to the *Germaine* is the same as that brought against English plays by Northbrooke in his *Treatise* (infra, p. 61).

27. Cf. p. 197, l. 29; ii. p. 389, l. 22. So Boileau in his *Art Poétique*, iii. 41, apropos of the Spanish drama; and D'Aubignac

in his *Pratique du Théâtre*, ii. 7, giving a sketch of a play in which the hero is born and 'gets children.'

33. Cf. Sidney, infra, 199. 5. Also Hall, *Satires*, i. 3; and *The Pilgrimage to Parnassus*, v (l. 671, &c.). Whetstone uses *Indecorum* (60. 1) in the specific sense intended by the generality of Renaissance critics. See *Decorum*, by Index.

[In 1584 Whetstone published his *Touchstone for the Time* (see p. 63), in which he allies himself with the anti-stage pamphleteers.]

THOMAS LODGE (pp. 61-86).

62. (Headnote) *Playes Confuted*. Gosson calls Lodge *William* on the title-page and in the text (p. 171).

63. (Headnote) The list may be supplemented by *The French Academie ... by Peter de la Primaudaye ... newly translated into English by T*[homas] *B*[owes], London, 1586. 'And I think it wil not be far from the matter, if we say that it is a shameful thing to suffer amongst us, or to loose time that ought to be so precious unto us, in beholding and in hearing plaiers, actors of Interludes and Comedies, who are as pernitious a plague in a common wealth as can be imagined. For nothing marreth more the behavior, simplicitie, and natural goodnes of any people than this, bicause they soone receiue into their soules a liuely impression of that dissolutenes and villanie which they see and heare, when it is ioyned with words, accents, gestures, motions, & actions, wherewith players and iuglers know how to inrich, by all kind of artificiall sleights, the filthiest and most dishonest matters, which commonly they make choice of. And to speek freely in few wordes, we may truely say, that the theatre of players is a school of all unchastnes, uncleannes, whoredom, craft, subtletie, and wickednes (p. 216).'

1. The allusion to Protogenes and Apelles is based upon the story in Pliny, xxxv. 10. See also Carlo Dati's *Vite de' Pittori Antichi*, Florence, 1730 ('Vita di Protogene'). Cf. Nash, infra, p. 326, l. 16.

63. 5. Cf. ii. p. 270, ll. 1-2.

64. 5. Gosson's *Schoole of Abuse* (see p. 61) was entered at

Stationers' Hall on July 22, 1579 (Arber). It was followed on Nov. 7 by his composite volume, *Ephemerides of Phialo* and *A Short Apologie* (see p. 62), in the first portion of which he attacks the *Straunge News out of Affrick* (ib.), and in the second defends the thesis of his *Schoole of Abuse*. Towards the close of the latter he refers to Lodge's counterblast (ib.), and concludes, 'but I stay my handes till I see his booke; when I haue perusd it I will tell you more.' He fulfils his promise in the *Playes Confuted* (ib.), dealing with Lodge's tract (which 'came not to my handes in one whole yeere after the priuy printing thereof' (p. 169)), and the defence entitled *The Play of Playes* (ib.). Lodge therefore had only the *Schoole of Abuse* before him when he wrote this *Defence*. He returned to the attack later (1584) in his Preface to *An Alarum against Vsurers*, in which he denounces the personalities of the *Playes Confuted*.

23-6. Cf. Sidney, infra, p. 189, ll. 7-8. The persistency of the allusion in Elizabethan literature is jocularly referred to in *The Returne from Parnassus*, Pt. i, Act iv, sc. 1 (1224).

33-4. '*Virgill* sweates in describyng his Gnat: *Ouid* bestirreth him to paint out his Flea: the one shewes his art in the lust of *Dido*, the other his cunning in the inceste of *Myrrha*, and that trumpet of Baudrie, the Craft of Loue' (*Schoole of Abuse*, ed. Arber, p. 19). The pseudo-Ovidian *De Pulice* is often referred to. Cf. Marlowe, *Dr. Faustus*, vi. l. 116.

65. 10. Cf. the *Schoole of Abuse*, passim. The reference is not verbal.

16. Cf. Nash, 331. 12.

21. *Campanus.* Giovannantonio Campano (c. 1429-1477), humanist and poet, pupil of Demetrius Chalcondylas, successively bishop of Crotona and of Teramo. (See Fabricius, *Bibl. med. et inf. Latin.* I. 326; Tiraboschi, VI. 1393, &c.; Gyraldus, *De Poetis*, u.s., p. 19; and G. Lesca, *Giovannantonio Campano*, Pontedera, 1892.) His books, other than his volumes of poems, are chiefly editorial. The reference here may be to a popular edition of Aesop in which he collaborated. His complete works appeared at Venice, n. d. (? 1495). See infra, p. 327, l. 17.

31. This common Latin proverb is a favourite with the Elizabethan pamphleteers. Cf. 'nodum in serpo querere' in the *Seruingman's Comfort*, 1598 (Roxb. Libr.).

Notes

32. *inco[n]u[en]iences*, improprieties, offences. See Webbe, infra, p. 253. 3 : and p. 294. 9 (with Latin on p. 418). Cf. Genevan Bible (1560) *Numbers, Argt.* 'That either they fall not to such inconueniences, or else return to him quickly by true repentance.' The Shakespeare Soc. edit. proposes 'incontinencies.'

66. 2. *inscience*. Cf. 67. 25. This word had just come into vogue. See *N. E. D.*

14. *as*: perhaps a misprint for 'and,' but not wrong.

18. Orig. ' denocated.'

23. *quesie*, unsettled (or easily unsettled), nauseated, squeamish; of common occurrence in Elizabethan books. Cf. Gosson, u. s., p. 31, and *Playes Confuted* (Roxb. Libr.), p. 168; Harvey, infra, ii. p. 231, l. 32; Chapman, infra, ii. p. 295, l. 14; *Euphues* (ed. Landmann, p. 20); Shakespeare, *M. Ado*, ii. 1. 399 ; Greene, *Friar Bacon*, x. 130.

24. *werish*, here = sick. It is generally applied to food: 'savourless,' *mal savouré* (Palsgrave). Cf. Sc. *wersh*.

67. 4. *Though Plato*, &c. Gosson applies this well-worn argument twice in his *Schoole* (ed. Arber, pp. 20, 21).

5. *well publiques*. Cf. Stanyhurst, 'with a iagged *hystorie* of a ragged Weale publicke' (Epistle in *Description of Ireland*, Arber's 'Stanyhurst,' p. 12).

68. 2. *gale*, gall.

7, &c. *Maximus* [orig. *Maximinus*] *Tirius*, &c. 'Maximus Tyrius taketh vppon him to defend the discipline of these Doctors vnder the name of *Homer*, wresting the rashnes of *Aiax* to valour, the cowardice of *Vlisses* to Policie, the dotage of *Nestor* to graue counsell, and the battaile of *Troy* too the woonderfull conflict of the foure elements; where *Iuno*, which is counted the ayre, settes in her foote to take vp the strife, and steps boldly betwixt them to part the fray. It is a Pageant woorth the sight, to beholde how he labors with Mountaines to bring foorth Mise.' Gosson, *Schoole of Abuse*, p. 21. Cf. also ib. pp. 29, 40.

14. *Irus*, the proverbial 'poor man,' after the beggar in the house of Ulysses. Cf. ii. p. 45, l. 21.

23. *Buchanan* (p. 24, l. 7, note). Gosson retorts in his *Playes Confuted* that the reference to 'Buchanans booke' is 'an old wormeaten obiection,' and that 'neither Players nor their friends

are able to proue' that it or the 'Playe of Christ' by Nazianzenus was performed on the stage. He argues that they were prepared 'dialoguewise, as Plato and Tullie did their Philosophye, to be reade, not to be played' (pp. 189–197).

24. *Boetius comfortes*, i.e. the *De Consolatione* of Boetius or Boethius (fl. 525).

25. *Erasmus* 'interpreted' or translated *Hecuba* and *Iphigenia*. Lodge's reference to these, to Buchanan, and to Donatus (p. 80) suggests the idea that he was familiar with a popular edition of *Tragœdiæ selectæ* issued by Henri Estienne, printer to Huldrich Fugger (1567, &c.), which contains the interpretations of *Hecuba* and *Iphigenia* by Erasmus (pp. 5–117), the tract by Donatus *De Tragœdia et Comœdia* (pp. 118–28), the interpretations of the *Medea* and *Alcestis* (pp. 129-213), and of the *Ajax*, *Antigone*, and *Electra* of Sophocles, by Georgius Rotallerus.

69. 5. 'Tullie accustomed to read them with great diligence in his youth, but when hee waxed grauer in studie, elder in yeares, riper in iudgement, hee accompted them the fathers of lyes, Pipes of vanitie, and Schooles of Abuse [*Tusc.* 1. 2],' Gosson, *Schoole of Abuse*, p. 21.

25. Cicero, *Pro Archia*, xxvi. 7.

70. 3. *Cellarius*. Probably (as suggested by the editor of the Shakes. Soc. reprint) a printer's error for Cassiodorus (cf. p. 71, l. 12): but I have failed to find the passage in the collected works (Geneva, 1609). He cannot be 'James Cellarius, editor of Cicero,' as stated in the Index of the Hunterian Club edition of Lodge's works, for *he*, Jacob Keller, Jesuit, *alias* 'Hercynianus (Fabius),' did not produce his edition of the *Thesaurus Ciceronianus* of Nizolius (see p. 202, l. 16, note) till 1613.

8. *Quicquid*, &c. A favourite line. Cf. ii. 323. 17.

16. Gosson had said that Marius 'doubted the abuses of those Schooles, where Poets were euer the head Maisters' (*Schoole of Abuse*, p. 23). Lodge's list of examples is in direct retort to Gosson's list of persons who held poets in no honour (ib.).

71. 1. Horace, *Ars Poetica*, 403.

4. *Orig.* 'Hiroaldus,' a misprint for Beroaldus, of which

name there were two poets (Filippo Beroaldo). The elder (1453–1505), humanist and commentator, is here referred to. See Gyraldus, *De Poetis*, u.s., p. 31.

12. *Cassiodorus* (Magnus Aurelius C., *b.* 468), author of *De Institutione Divinarum Scripturarum*. See note 70. 3.

14. *Paulinus ... Byshop of Nolanum.* Saint Paulinus (Meropius Pontius Anicius Paulinus), 353–431. His *Epistolae et Poema'a* was printed by Badius Ascensius in 1516.

15. *Ambrose ... in Mediolanum.* St. Ambrose (*b.* 340).

16. Probably a reference to the well-known chapter of Bæda's *Eccles. Hist.* (iv. 24), 'Quod in monasterio eius fuerit frater cui donum canendi sit diuinitus concessum'; perhaps also to Bæda's *Death-Song*.

18. See p. 73, l. 19. Gosson, in his *Apologie* (Arber, p. 70), quotes Lactantius as a condemner of plays 'without any manner of exception, thinking them, the better they are penned or cunninglier handled, the more to be fled.'

19-20. Epimenides of Crete, *Titus* i. 12, from the lost work '*On Oracles*': Aratus of Cilicia, *Acts* xvii. 28, from the *Phaenomena* (see Stobaeus, *Eclog*. i. 3. 3). Cf. Sidney, p. 191, l. 10, and note.

22. *Poeta nascitur*, &c. See note to p. 195, l. 23.

35. The original print reads 'well of the Muses which Cabelimus calleth Porum,' a strange but explicable travesty of Lodge's MS. See Persius, *Prol.* i.

72. 9. *Iodocus Badius* (1462–1535), the famous printer, also a satiric poet: generally known as Iod. Bad. Ascensius, from Aasche, near Brussels, where he was born.

73. 19. *Lactantius* (Firmianus), *d. c.* 325. See p. 342, and by Index.

74. 6. *Ars Poetica*, ll. 391–9.

75. 1. Tyrtæus. Ib., l. 402. Cf. infra, p. 77, l. 6, &c.

6. *that Poetes were*: the mediaeval conception of poetry, adopted by sixteenth-century criticism.

18. *Aen.* vi. 662.

22. See the quotation from Gosson, supra (note to 64. 33–4). Elsewhere Gosson speaks of Ovid as the 'high martial of Venus' and the 'amorous scholemaister' (*Schoole*, p. 29). Cf. also pp. 34–5 (ed. Arber).

33. Gosson is fond of making complimentary allusions to the Scythians throughout his *Schoole*. Cf. 'Poetrie in *Scythia* without vice, as the *Phœnix* in Arabia without a fellow' (side-note, p. 22). He praises the olden times in England, when there were 'men in valure not yeelding to *Scithia*' (p. 34). See other references by Index.

76. 7. *scare*. The clue to this allusion is to be found in the *Epistle Dedicatorie* to *Euphues*. 'Alexander hauing a Skar in his cheeke helde his finger vpon it that Appelles might not paint it. Appelles painted him with his finger cleauing to his face. "Why," quod Alexander, "I layde my finger on my Skarre, bicause I would not haue thee see it." "Yea," sayd Appelles, "and I drew it there, bicause none els should perceiue it; for if thy finger had bene away, either thy Skarre would haue been seene, or my arte mislyked."' Is this one of Lyly's inventions? There appears to be no record of the scar in the authorities cited by Overbeck in *Die antiken Schriftquellen*.

17–25. '*Tiberius* the Emperour sawe somewhat, when he iudged *Scaurus* to death for writing a Tragidie: *Augustus*, when hee banished *Ouid*: and *Nero* when he charged *Lucan* to put vp his pipes, to stay his penne and write no more' (Gosson, *Schoole*, p. 23).

30, &c. Justinus, *Hist.* iii. 5.

77. 19, &c. 'I may well liken *Homer* to *Mithecus*, and Poets to Cookes: the pleasures of the one winnes the body from labor, and conquereth the sense; the allurement of the other drawes the mind from vertue, and confoundeth wit' (Gosson, *Schoole*, p. 22).

35. Orig. 'ledde.'

78. 30. Gosson himself had said, 'Pythagoras bequeathes them a Clookebagge and condemns them for fooles, that iudge Musicke by sounde and eare. If you will bee good Scholars and profite well in the Arte of Musicke, shutte your Fidels in their cases, and looke vp to heauen: the order of the Spheres, the vnfallible motion of the Planets, the iuste course of the yeere, and varietie of seasons, the concorde of the Elementes and their qualyties, Fyre, Water, Ayre, Earth, Heate, Colde, Moysture, and Drought, concurring togeather

to the constitution of earthly bodies and sustenance of euery creature' (*Schoole*, p. 26). He returns to the subject in *Playes Confuted* (ed. Roxb. Libr., p. 168).

79. 2. *Gosson in the Schoole* refers to *Catilins Conspiracies*, which he dismisses as 'knowen too be a Pig of myne own Sowe' (p. 40), and elsewhere informs us that he had written *The Comedie of Captaine Mario*, and a 'moral,' *Praise at Parting*: but 'since the first printing of my Inuectiue, to this day, I neuer made Playe' (*Playes Confuted*, 'To the Universities, &c.'). He explains his changed attitude thus: 'Now if any man aske me why my selfe haue penned Comedyes in time paste, and inveigh so egerly against them here, let him knowe that *semel insaniuimus omnes*: I haue sinned, and am sorry for my fault: hee runnes farre that neuer turnes; better late than neuer' (*Schoole*, p. 41).

79. 31. Cf. p. 59, l. 15; p. 332. l. 17, and ii. p. 309, l. 13. This passage is in close parallel with Chettle's *Kind-Harts Dreame*, 64.

80. 7. In the opening words of his tract *De Tragœdia* &c. (see note to p. 68, l. 25): '*Initium Tragœdiæ & Comœdiæ a rebus diuinis est inchoatum: quibus pro fructibus vota soluentes operabantur antiqui.*'

13. *Iodocus Badius*. Supra, p. 72, l. 9, note.

81. 1. *Tulley defines*. Probably borrowed from Donatus (edit. u. s., p. 123), who is responsible for the ascription of the phrase to Cicero. It is very common, with, and without, reference to its origin; cf. *Every Man out of his Humour*, iii. 1, and *Hamlet*, iii. 2. 23. It is quoted by Minturno, *De Poeta*, p. 44, Jacques Grévin, *Brief Discours* (1562), and referred to by Cervantes, *Don Quix*. pt. I, ch. xlviii.

Of this passage Gosson says in his *Playes Confuted*: 'Yonge Master Lodge, thinking to iett vpon startoppes, and steale an ynche of his hight by the bare name of Cicero, allegeth from him, that a Play is the Schoolmistresse of life, the lookinge glasse of manners, and the image of trueth. But finding him selfe too weeke in the knees to stand it out, neither alleadging the place where Tullie saith it, nor bringing any reason of his owne to proue it, hee flittes from this to the Etymologie of Plaies, from thence to the inuentors, and so gallops his wisedome out of breath. It seemeth that Master Lodge saw this in Tullie with other folkes eyes, and not his owne. For to my remembrance I neuer read it in him, neither doe I thinke that Master Lodge can shewe it me. [*He then refers to passages in* Tusc. Orat. *where Cicero* 'misliketh playes' *and to others where* 'he is sharpe set against them'.] But because Master Lodge will needes father these wordes vpon Tullie that neuer spake them, I will first sette downe the matter, and the persons of both kindes of playes, then rippe vp every part of this definition, that you may see how this Gentleman, like the Foxe at the banquet of the Storke, lickes the outside of the glasse with an empty stomacke, when his heade will not suffer him to enter in.... Master Lodge, finding some peevish index or gatherer of Tullie to be a sleepe, is very wel contented to winke for company, and thinking his worde so currant to goe for payment, woulde gladly persuade vs vpon Tullies credite that a Play is the Schoolmistres of life. Wherein I perceive hee is no changeling, for hee disputeth as soundly, being from the vniversitie and out of exercise, as hee did when hee was there, and at his booke.' (Roxburghe Library, ed. Hazlitt, pp. 179-83.)

9. *Susarion Bullus and Magnes*, probably Lodge's printer's misreading of 'Susario, Myllus, and Magnes.' For an account of these three early writers of Comedy see Meineke, *Historia Critica Comicorum Graecorum*, i. pp. 18-35.

11. *Eupolis with Cratinus*. Cf. Webbe, infra, p. 236. See Meineke, u. s., pp. 104-46, 43-58.

24. Epist. I. xvi. 53, but altered.

82. 5. *Philemon* of Soli, a Greek comic poet, contemporary with Menander.

7. *Menander*, the Greek comic poet, the model of Terence (see *Andria*, Prol.).

11, &c. *Thais* in the *Eunuchus*; *Demeas* (Demea, Δημέας) in the *Adelphi*; *Pamphilus* in the *Andria* and *Hecyra*; *Dauus* 'the slave' in Terence and Plautus, e. g. in the *Andria* (cf. p. 65, l. 26) and *Phormio*; *Gnatho* in the *Eunuchus* (cf. p. 65, l. 28).

27, &c. *Cecilius*, Caecilius Statius, contemporary with Ennius; *Plinius*, for Livius Andronicus (?); *Neuius*, Cn. Naevius, epic and dramatic poet; *Licinius*, Licinius Imbrex; *Atilius* (in original text printed *Actilius*); *Turpilius*, Sextus Turpilius, the comic poet, and friend of Terence; *Trabea*, the Roman comic poet.

83. 6. *as Seruius reporteth.* Servius Honoratus Maurus, grammarian, best known by his commentary on Virgil.

16. *Iodocus Badius*, supra, p. 72, l. 9, note.

32. *Glicerium.* Glycerium (Γλυκέριον): *Andria*, i. 1. 108.

84. 13. *The Germanes*, supra, p. 59, l. 21, note.

28. 'The last [*Catilins Conspiracies*], because it is knowen too be a Pig of myne owne Sowe, I will speake the lesse of it' (*Schoole*, p. 40). Cf. Harvey's *Letter-Book* (ed. Scott, p. 59), 'And nowe in bestowing uppon myselfe a misshapin illfavorid freshe copy of my precious poems, as it were a pigg of myne owne sowe.' Gosson's unfortunate phrase was not readily forgotten.

85. 1. See the Life of Virgil by Tib. Claudius Donatus. Cf. Puttenham, infra, ii. p. 58.

3. *Wilson*, Robert, the elder (*d.* 1600), comedian and playwright; the fellow of Tarlton, and frequently named with him. See Harvey, infra, i. 125. 15, and Meres, infra, ii. 320. 16, 323. 24. His play of *Catiline* is not extant. It may have been the basis of a play with that title which Henslowe, in his *Diary* (p. 132), tells us was prepared by a Robert Wilson (probably R. W. junior) and Chettle. (See the article on Wilson by Mr. S. Lee in *D. N. B.*)

12. Juvenal, *Sat.* ix. 118.

25. *statute of apparrell.* Cf. *Schoole of Abuse* (p. 39) 'How often hath her Maiestie ... sette downe the limits of apparell to euery degree, and how soone againe hath the pride of our harts ouerflowen the chanel.'

30, &c. The flout is explained in one of the verses by Barnabe Rich, prefixed to Lodge's later *Alarum against Vsurers* (Shakespeare Society, 1853):—

'If thus it be, good Lodge, continue still;
Thou needst not feare Goose sonne, or Gander's hisse,
Whose rude reportes, part from a slaundrous quill,
  Will be determind but in reading this,
  Of whom the wiser sort will thinke amis
To slaunder him whose birth and life is such
As false report his fame can never tuch.'

See also *Tarlton's Jests*, ed. Halliwell, p. xxi.

Spenser and Harvey (pp. 87–126).

According to Nash, Harvey 'publiquely diuulged these letters,' and Spenser was 'no way priuie to the committing of them to print' (*Foure Letters Confuted* in Grosart's edition of Nash, ii. 231, 233). Cf. also his *Haue with you to Saffron-Walden* (ib. iii. 188).

88. 11, &c. Presumably referring to the *Shepheardes Calender*. Spenser, still hesitating to publish his poem, is doubtful of its welcome by Sidney and the common friends who were received at Penshurst and Leicester House. Cf. p. 112, l. 12 (note).

19. *she*. Cf. p. 106, l. 2.

89. 7. *Master Dyer*. Sir Edward Dyer (*d.* 1607), courtier and poet. See note to p. 94, l. 29. Sidney and Dyer are grouped together in the prefatory verses to Watson's Ἑκατομπαθία—

'Hic quoque seu subeas Sydnaei, siue Dyeri
Scrinia, qua Musis area bina patet.'

12. Orig. ἀρειωπαγῷ. Cf. p. 94, l. 27 (orig. ἀρειόνπαγον). Of this *Areopagus* we know little. It was probably an informal society, perhaps unknown by that name except to one or two of its members. 'Academies' were in the air; and it may be that the young writers had Baïf's recent project in mind. It has been suggested that the title was borrowed from 'the Florentine Academy in the time of Lorenzo, which bore the same name' (Einstein, *Ital. Renaissance in England* (1902), p. 357), but it is more probably a direct adaptation from classical history. 'Areopagites' frequently occurs in the ordinary sense.

20. *Schoole of Abuse*. See p. 61, and notes to Lodge's *Defence*, passim.

25. *Slomber* is not known. It may be *A senights slumber*, referred to in the printer's preface to the *Complaints* (1591). See also the *Dreames*, p. 100, l. 24.

32. *Maister E. K.* See p. 127, and note.

90. 3. *Mystresse Kerkes*. See the note on 'E. K.', p. 127.

13. *Maister Drants Rules*. These, if ever committed to writing, are not extant. The references throughout these letters (e.g. pp. 96, 97, 99, 102), and elsewhere, do not preclude the possibility that Drant had merely conveyed his

views to his friends in conversation, and had persuaded them to carry them out in their verse-making.

Thomas Drant (*d.* ? 1578), Archdeacon of Lewes, is known as the author of *A Medicinable Morall*, 1566, and of *Horace his arte of Poetrie, pistles & satyrs Englished*, 1567. In neither is there any critical material. His recognition in later literary history is undoubtedly due to the allusions in these letters (especially Spenser's), and is as undoubtedly in excess of his deserts, even as a contributor to the narrow controversy about the English hexameter.

27. *Maister Preston.* Thomas Preston (1537-98), Master of Trinity Hall, Cambridge, author of *Cambises* (1569).

Maister Still. John Still (? 1543-1608), Bishop of Bath and Wells, and the reputed author, on very doubtful evidence, of *Gammer Gurton's Needle* (1575). See note, ii. p. 443.

91. 21. *Immerito.* Cf. p. 92, l. 4, p. 93, l. 3, &c. Spenser so signs the prefatory verses to his *Shepheardes Calender.*

92. 29. *Mistresse Kerke.* See note to p. 127.

93. 11. *extra iocum*, a favourite phrase of Harvey's. Cf. p. 114.

94. 13. *Maister Wythipole.* Gascoigne entitled a set of verses *Councel giuen to Master Bartholomew Withipoll a little before his latter iourney to Geane, 1572* (*Works*, Roxb. Libr. i. 372). Harvey in his *Letter-Book* introduces these lines (Camden Soc. ed. p. 57)—

'But preythe see where Withipolls cum,
Daniel and Bath both at onse.'

See the verses in Haslewood, ii. 302-3, which associate Harvey with two Wythipolls, father and son.

29. *twoo worthy Gentlemenne.* See pp. 89. ll. 7, 101. 22, 109. 11, 113. 11.

95. 12. *Curtoll*, curtal; here a 'docked' or 'clipped' word.

23. *Abstemio.* Laurentius Abstemius (Lorenzo Abstémio). His *Fabulae nuper compositae* was printed at Venice in 1495, and was often reprinted.

96. 11. *Watson*, ante, p. 354.

29. *Drantes Rule*, supra, p. 90, l. 13, note.

97. 4. *gorbellyed*, corpulent. Here applied to Drant, as again by Harvey on p. 118, l. 11.

26. *Goddilge yee* (= God yield you!).

98. 7. *in Iustinians Courte.* The clue to this is found in a

letter in Harvey's *Letter-Book* addressed to Sir Thomas Smith. 'Your wurship mai marvel mutch that to haue absentid mi self thus long time from you, having so great and iust occasion to resort unto you, as I haue had. But suerly, sir, mi lets and hinderances eueri wai haue bene sutch, that I could not possibely do that I purposid fully, and wuld willingly haue dun for mi better proffiting in the ciuil lawe. It were too long a thing to declare them al severally and at larg; but truly, what for sicknes and priuate busines, I could scars reade ouer thre titles in Justinian before Lent, and euer sins the beginning of Lent, at the instant and importunate request of M. Church, mi verri frend, I haue red the rhetorick lecture in the schooles; so that the prouiding for mi lecture, togither with the reading to mi pupils, the doing of ordinari acts in the howse, and disputing in the schooles, haue made me so unprouidid for Justinian, that, to sai troth, I haue bene ashamid to cum unto you' (Camden Soc. edit. pp. 176–7).

14. *the Earthquake*, April 6, 1580. Thomas Twyne, the translator of the Aeneid, was also prompted to write *A shorte and pithie Discourse* concerning it and earthquakes generally; and Anthony Munday, too, wrote a *Short Discourse*.

27. Orig. '*pawneth*.'

99. 21–22. These lines, with minor differences, appear in 'E. K.'s gloss on 'May' in the *Shepheardes Calender*. Dr. O. Sommer finds proof in this that 'E. K.' was Spenser himself (*Sh. Cal.* p. 23). But see note on 'E. K.', p. 127. The lines are quoted by Webbe, infra, p. 283.

100. 8. *Epithalamion Thamesis* is unknown. Cf. p. 113, l. 16.

22. Cicero, *De Senect.* i. 1. Generally *praemii*.

24. *my Dreames and Dying Pellicane*. The former is referred to in a postscript to this letter (printed in the 'Globe' *Spenser*, p. 709), and in 'E. K.'s preface (see p. 133, l. 7); the latter in the printer's preface to the *Complaints* (1591). Both appear to have been ready for press: but no copies are known. Some have endeavoured to identify the *Dreames* with *Muiopotmos* and the *Visions of Bellay*.

101. 23. *Balductum*, trashy, a favourite word of Harvey's. Cf. Nash, ii. p. 242, l. 26, and Stanyhurst, p. 141, l. 27. Literally a posset or curd, L. Lat. *balducta*.

Notes

102. 3. *Drants Prosodye*, supra, p. 372.

13. 'Mistresse Experience.' Cf. Harvey's *Letter-Book*, p. 130, and infra, ii. p. 283, l. 33.

23. *Prosodye.* Harvey appears to use this word, throughout this letter, in the restricted and special sense of the *pronunciation* of a word or syllable (in verse). See note to p. 49, l. 19; and p. 121.

24. *Sir Thomas Smithes* (Orthography): a reference to his *De recta & emendata Linguae Anglicae Scriptione*, Paris, 1568. Harvey had recently written his elegy, *Smithus, vel Musarum lachrymae: pro obitu Thomae Smithi* (1578). See note to p. 21, l. 31.

103. 6-20. Cf. Puttenham, infra, ii. p. 122, l. 34, &c.: and Du Bellay, *Defense*, I. ix.

31. *Gambowlde*, toy, plaything.

104. 21. *Bables*, baubles. Cf. ii. 331. 12.

105. 15. See p. 99, l. 14.

23. Petrarch, Sonnet CCV (225). This is quoted in 'E. K.'s gloss. on 'April' in the *Shepheardes Calender*. Dr. Sommer cites this in support of the theory that 'E. K.' is Spenser. Here, however, it would be as fair to say that 'E. K.' is Gabriel Harvey; and more reasonable to believe that Kirke had heard the lines from Spenser. But see note to p. 127.

106. 2. *Rosalinde.* Cf. p. 88, l. 19, and, more fully, the *Shepheardes Calender*, passim. The name, as 'E. K.' tells us, is an anagram. For an account of editorial guesses on this subject see Mr. Herford's edition of the *Calender*, pp. xvi-xvii. All the solutions assume, quite unnecessarily, that 'Rose' is one of the words, and overlook the choice of such excellent Elizabethan names as Eliza, Delia, Alis. But the matter is of small concern.

107. 19, &c. Harvey's *Letter-Book* (f. 51 b) introduces 'A short poetic discourse to my gentle masters the readers, conteyning a garden communication or dialogue in Cambridge betwene Master G. H. and his cumpanye at a Midsumer Comencement, togither with certayne delicate sonnetts and epigraumes in Inglish verse of his makinge.' Of the last the verses here printed form a part. (See Camd. Soc. edit. p. 98.) With *Anglofrancitalorum* (l. 16), cf.

'O tymes, O manners, O French, O Italish Inglande'
(ib. p. 97).

Galateo. The *Galateo* (Venice 1558, Milan 1559, Florence 1560) of Giovanni della Casa (1503-56), archbishop of Benevento, shared popular favour with Castiglione's *Courtier*, Guazzo's *Conversations*, and other books of courtesy. It was Englished in 1576, but it was known in a French edition of 1562.

There is an interesting passage in Harvey's *Letter-Book* (pp. 78-9) which describes the reading of his day. 'They have gotten Philbertes Philosopher of the Courte [Englished by G. North, 1575], the Italian Archebysshoppies braue Galateo [u.s.], Castiglioes fine Cortegiano [Eng. by Hoby, 1561], Bengalassoes Ciuil Instructions to his Nephewe Seignor Princisca [? Francesca] Ganzar, Guatzoes new Discourses of curteous behauiour [Eng. by G. Pettie & B. Young, 1586], Jouios and Rassellis Emblemes in Italian, Paradines in Frenche, Plutarche in Frenche, Frontines Stratagemes [Eng. Morysine, 1539], Polyenes Stratagemes, Polonica, Apodemica, Guigiardine [Guicciardini's *Istoria*, Eng. by Fenton, 1579], Philipp de Comines [not Eng. till 1596, by Danett], and I know not how many owtlandishe braveryes besides of the same stampe.'

24. *Tuscanish* : 'Italish' (Letter-Book).

107-8. Harvey's description of the Italianate Englishmen is, according to Nash, directed against the Earl of Oxford, who had just come home from Italy. But see note to ii. 239. 10-12.

108. 5. *with a witnesse*, excessively.

17—109. 5. Not in the Letter-Book text.

109. 11. *ouer very Castor*, &c. See note to p. 94, l. 29.

28. See note, p. 98, l. 7.

110. 3. John Harvey (1564-92). See Index.

8. Ovid, *Tristia*, i. 8. 5.

111. 17. On fol. 43 of the original edition of the *Shepheardes Calender*, again referred to on p. 112, l. 12. The lines are from Petrarch, Sonnet CXXXV (154).

112. 12. Though this allusion to the *Shepheardes Calender* is more obvious than Spenser's own (p. 88), and though both were clear enough to the two friends, it must not be forgotten that the authorship remained a mystery to Spenser's admirers for several years to come. Cf. Webbe, p. 245, and Puttenham, vol. ii. p. 65.

113. 11. *two incomparable*, &c. See note to p. 94, l. 29.

16. *Epithalamion Thamesis*. See supra, p. 100, l. 8.

21. *Ecquid*, &c. See p. 100, l. 23.

114. 3. *alias you know who*. See the gloss to 'October' of the *Shepheardes Calender*. The lines are quoted by Harvey from fol. 40 b of the original edition.

22. *Dying Pellicanes*. See supra, p. 100, l. 24 (note).

25. *Extra iocum*. See p. 93, l. 11, and p. 125, l. 29.

116. 7. *Bibiena* (Bernardo), Cardinal (1470–1560).

8. *Bembo* (Piero), Cardinal (1470–1547). Harvey had been inspired by him in his early lectures at Cambridge (see the *Ciceronianus*).

26. *pawlting*, hesitating or lame: *bungreley*, slovenly (bungling).

117. 10, &c. Harvey's general argument, and his claim, among other things, for a true orthography, is supported by an interesting passage, addressed to the 'Reader' of *The First Booke of the Preservation of King Henry the VII*, written in so-called English hexameters (1599)—printed by Collier in his *Illust. of O. E. Lit.* (1866) II. No. 3, and by Mr. Arber, in his preface to Stanyhurst's *Aeneis*.

'Right honored, worshipfull, and gentell Reader, these Hexameters and Pentameters in Englishe are misliked of many, because they are not yet come to their full perfection, and specially of some that are accounted and knowne to be Doctors and singularly well learned and great Linguistes; but especially of the plaine Rythmer, that scarce knowes the footed quantitie or metricall scanning thereof, muche lesse to reade them with a grace according to the same. But for him, I say thus; *Scientia nullum habet inimicum praeter ignorantem.* Whose bookes are stuft with lines of prose, with a rythme in the end; which euery fidler or piper can make vpon a theame giuen. Neuerthelesse, I confesse and acknowledge that we haue many excellent and singular good Poets in this our age, as Maister *Spencer*, that was, Maister *Gowlding*, Doctor *Phayer*, Maister *Harrington, Daniell*, and diuers others, whom I reuerence in that kinde of prose-rythme; wherein *Spencer* (without offence spoken) hath surpassed them all. I would to God they had done so well in trew Hexameters; for they had then beautified our language. For the *Greekes* and *Latines* did in a manner abolish quite that kinde of rythme-prose: And why should not we doe the like in Englishe? ....

For, at the first, Maister *Askam* had much ado to make two or three verses in English: but now euery scholler can make some. What language so hard, harsh, or barbarous, that time and art will not amend? ....

This trew kinde of Hexametred and Pentametred verse will bring vnto vs foure commodities. First, it will enrich our speach with good and significant wordes: Secondly, it will bring a delight and pleasure to the skilfull Reader, when he seeth them formally compyled: And, thirdly, it will incourage and learne the good and godly Students that affect Poetry, and are naturally enclyned thereunto, to make the like: Fourthly, it will direct a trew Idioma, and will teach trew Orthography. For as gould surpasseth leade, so the Hexameters surpasse rythme prose.' Yet the author does not 'utterly discommend' this 'prose-rhythme.'

18. *correcte Magnificat*. Cf. Ronsard, *Préface de la Franciade*, 'J'atteste les Muses que je ne suis point ignorant, et ne crie point en langage vulgaire, comme ces nouveaux venus qui veulent corriger le *Magnificat* ....' Cf. also Harington, infra, ii. p. 219, and the Epistle to the *Cobler of Canterburie* (1608), in the Appendix to *Tarlton's Jests* (Shakespeare Soc. 1844, p. 107).

26. Horace, *Ars Poet.* 71, 72. Cf. p. 121, l. 10.

118. 11. *Fat-bellyed Archdeacon*. See note to p. 97, l. 4.

17. Ascham, *Toxophilus*, Bk. II (ed. Giles, *Works*, ii. 129). Cf. infra, p. 283. See *Toxophilus*, too, for line quoted on p. 120.

20 (121. 4, 22–33). Cf. Webbe, i. p. 281, l. 15, and note.

120. 24. *Scoggins Aier*. See *The Jests of Scoggin* in Hazlitt's *Old English Jest-Books* (ii. 93).

121. 4. *Position*. Cf. l. 27, p. 281. 15. See Quintil. i. 5, ix. 4.

20. *Prosodye*. See note to p. 102, l. 23.

122. 12. *Rosalindula*. Cf. supra, p. 106, l. 2.

22. *M. Daniel Rogers* (? 1538–91), courtier and diplomatist. He is frequently referred to in the correspondence of Sidney and Languet (ed. Pears, 1845). See also his correspondence with Buchanan (Edin., 1715, vol. ii).

124. 14. *arithmetericians*. Probably a slip for 'arithmet[r]icians.'

Notes

124. 22. Erasmus, *Epistolae*, cxlii.

34. *sitt ... schirtes.* Cf. note to ii. p. 186, l. 18.

125. 15. *Wylsons or Tarletons.* See supra, p. 85, l. 3, note. Harvey is probably referring to his share of the *Letters*, supra, p. 87, &c.

18. *comedanties* = 'comediantes,' comedians: probably a press error. Cf. Sidney's *Apology*, p. 199, l. 23, where we have 'comedients' in Ponsonby's text (see p. 148).

23. *Vnico Aretino.* This is Bernardo Accolti (*d.* 1534) famed as an *improvvisatore*. He is spoken of by Bembo, Harvey's favourite. See Tiraboschi, vi. pp. 1249-52.

26. *M. Churchyard.* Thomas Churchyard (? 1520-1604), a writer of broadsides. Cf. infra, p. 242, l. 33, note; ii. 280, l. 15.

27. *M. Elderton.* William Elderton (*d.* ? 1592), ballad writer. See Harvey, ii. 253, l. 5; 273, l. 16, &c.; and cf. 246, ll. 28-34. There are many references to his heavy drinking (e.g. his 'ale crammed nose,' Nash, *Apol. for Pierce Pennilesse*).

126. 2. *Surrey is sayde first,* i.e. in his *Certain Bokes* [II and IV] *of Virgiles Aenœis turned into English meter* (1557). In Day's reprint of the Fourth Book (n. d.) the title describes the translation as *drawn into a strange meter*.

3. *Buckhurste* [Thomas, Lord Buckhurst] *and M. Norton in ... Gorboduc* (acted 1561, printed 1565). See Shakespeare Soc. reprint, 1847.

4. *Gascoygnes Steele Glasse* (1576). See Mr. Arber's reprint.

5. *cantions,* songs. Cf. *Sheph. Cal.* 'October' (Gloss).

6. *namelye,* especially.

13. *Pierius.* Giampetro Valeriano (Pierius Valerianus), *b.* 1477. His *Poemata* appeared at Basle in 1538; his *Amorum lib. V et alia poemata* at Venice in 1549. He was attracted by the subject of symbols, and wrote *Hieroglyphica, siue de sacris Aegyptiorum aliarumque gentium litteris commentariorum lib. LVIII* (Basle, 1556).

17. *Mr. Willes.* See p. 47, note (col. 2). Harvey's description here is explained by the fact that Willes, after quitting New College, Oxford, travelled in France, Germany, and Italy, graduated at Mainz (1565) and was admitted a Jesuit, thereafter lectured at Perugia and at Trier, and on his return to England, where he abjured Catholicism, was incorporated at

Cambridge. He is probably the co-editor of a *History of Travel in the West and East Indies* (1577) and the author of three papers in Hakluyt's *Collections of Voyages*.

26-33. See p. 89, ll. 6-12.

'E. K.' (pp. 127-34).

The identification of 'E. K.', the author of this 'Epistle Dedicatory' and of the Glosses in the *Shepheardes Calender*, remains a vexed question; but the evidence, such as it is, is in favour of the traditional view that the writer was Edward Kirke or Kerke (1553-1613) of Pembroke Hall, Cambridge. The argument that 'E. K.' is Spenser in masquerade has been fully worked out by Uhlemann in *Jahresbericht No. xiii des K. Kaiser Wilhelms Gymnasium zu Hannover*, 1888, and by O. Sommer in his reprint of the *Shepheardes Calender*, 1890 (pp. 15-25). See Mr. Herford's exhaustive reply to the latter in his edition of the *Sh. Cal.* 1895 (pp. xxii-xxvi), and Mr. Sidney Lee's article in *D. N. B.* This is not the place for further discussion, but it is perhaps excusable to point out that the references to 'Mistresse Kerke' in Spenser's letter (ante, pp. 90, l. 3, and 92, l. 29) have a strong circumstantial value in the argument for a real 'E. K.' They at least show that some one of the name was actually known to Spenser and Harvey; and it may well be that she was the mother of their College contemporary, and had received them as her son's friends at her house in London[1].

127. 7. Chaucer, *Troilus and Criseyde*, i. 809—
  'Unknowe, unkist, and lost that is un-sought.'
See 'E. K.'s eulogy of Chaucer in his gloss to 'June' of the *Shepheardes Calender*. John Heywood (1562) has two epigrams 'Of kissing,' beginning 'Unknowen vnkist' (Spenser Soc. ed., p. 148).

9. Lydgate, passim: and all the 'Chaucerians,' English and Scottish.

11. *in his Æglogue*. See 'Februarie,' l. 92, and 'E. K.'s gloss.

16. *brocage*, procuracy (by a 'go-between' or 'broker').

---

[1] All were of Pembroke Hall. Spenser was admitted in 1569, and Kirke in 1571. Harvey was elected a Fellow in 1570. His seniority may partly explain his general attitude to Spenser.

128. 32. *Valla against Liuie.* See his *Emendationes in Livium de bello Punico*, in the Paris edition of Livy, 1573.

other against Saluste. Cf. *Ascham*, ante, p. 39, &c.

130. 12. *gallimaufray or hodgepodge.* Cf. ii. 253. 12, and note.

131. 7, &c. Quoted by Webbe, infra, p. 247.

132. 7. *full somd*, full fledged.

21. *ſ.* = *scilicet*.

133. 7. *His Dreames, his Legendes, his Court of Cupide.* For the *Dreames*, see note to p. 100, l. 24. The others are also unknown. It has been suggested that they were incorporated in the *Faerie Queene*.

Postscript. Cf. 'E. K.'s gloss to 'September' of *The Shepheardes Calendar*, where he speaks of Gabriel Harvey, 'of whose speciall commendation as well in Poetrye as Rhetorike and other choyce learning we haue lately had a sufficient tryall in diuerse his workes, but specially in his *Musarum Lachrymae* [1578: see note to p. 102, l. 24], and his late *Gratulation[es] Valdinens[es]* [1578] . . . . Beside other his sundrye most rare and very notable writings, partely vnder vnknown Tytles, and partly vnder counterfayt names, as hys *Tyrannomastix*, his *Ode Natalitia*, his *Rameidos*, and esspecially that parte of *Philomusus*, his diuine *Anticosmopolita*, and diuers other of lyke importance.' See also note to p. 284, l. 4 infra.

STANYHURST (pp. 135-47).

136. 20. *cheate Poëtes*, impostors of poets. 'Cheate' (sb.) is used attributively.

137. 3. *in camfering wise.* Unexplained in *N. E. D.*, which quotes Shropshire '*campering*' = mettlesome, high-spirited.

15. *od* = famous, distinguished, rare. Cf. Ascham, *Scholemaster*, ii (ed. Mayor, p. 113), 'For our tyme the odde man to performe all . . . is . . . *Joannes Sturmius*.' See *N. E. D.*, s. v. 'Odd,' ii. 6.

19. See p. 1.

29. *M. Phaere.* Thomas Phaer's translation, which Stanyhurst criticizes, appeared in 1558 (*The Seuen first Bookes of the Eneidos of Virgill*). Two books were added in 1562 (*The nyne fyrst Bookes . . . with so much of the tenth Booke as since his Death* [i.e.

in 1560] *could be found*). The translation of the twelve books was completed by Thomas Twyne in 1573, and republished ten years later with the addition of a version of the thirteenth book (by Maphaeus Vegius).

34. *squire* = square (carpenter's). See Palsgrave.

140. 1. *Mori Epigg.*, p. 261, ed. 1518.

12. *Johannes Doa*, &c. See note to p. 185, l. 30.

20. *draftye*, rubbishy, vile. Cf. vol. ii, pp. 399, l. 11, 400, l. 14, and Hall's *Satires*, v. 2 (ed. Singer, p. 134). *N.E.D.* (q. v.) explains 'draftye' as an early misreading of 'drasty', dreggy.

32. *duggeon dagger*, a dudgeon-hilted dagger. Dudgeon is a hard wood used for handles of knives, &c. Cf. ii. p. 394, l. 16.

141. 27. *balducktoom*. See supra, p. 101, l. 23, note.

142. 2. *Priscianistes*, grammarians (after Priscian).

143. 12. Ante, p. 118, l. 1.

25. *misheth thee cushen*, misseth the cushion, aim, or mark (*Euphues*, ed. Landmann, p. 68). Cf. 'beside the cushion,' 'to put beside the cushion' (to deprive one of place), also common Elizabethan usages. The phrase 'bore with a cushion' is not clear (see ii. p. 271, l. 21, infra).

26. Cicero, *Orator* xviii. 58.

144. 10. *Now put case*, now suppose.

19. Horace, *Ars Poet.* l. 385.

146. 5. *Aen.* iii. 91.

7. *Aen.* iv. 146.

10. *Aen.* iii. 396.

SIDNEY (pp. 148–207).

Headnote—Olney's text has been reprinted also by Mr. E. Rhys in the first volume of his *Literary Pamphlets* (London, 1897). Mr. Albert S. Cook's edition, *The Defense of Poesy, otherwise known as An Apology for Poetry* (Boston, U.S.A., 1890, 1898), contains a modernized text based on both the editions of 1595.

Rodenburg's *Eglentiers Poëtens Borst-weringh*, which appeared in 1619, is in part a paraphrase of the *Apologie* (see Jonckbloet, *Geschiedenis der Nederlandsche Letterkunde*, 1889, iii. p. 200, &c.). Charles Gildon in his *Complete Art of Poetry* (1718)

Notes

incorporates long passages without acknowledgment (see Dialogue I, pp. 48-74).

150. 1. *Edward Wotton* (1548-1626), afterwards first Baron Wotton. Sir Henry Wotton was his half-brother.

3. *Iohn Pietro Pugliano*, an Equerry of the Emperor Maximilian II, held in high repute as an exponent of knightly exercises on horseback. Sidney shows his enthusiasm for these fashionable accomplishments in an elaborate passage in the *Arcadia* (bk. ii), in *Astrophel and Stella*, Sonnets 41 and 49, and in a letter to his brother Robert, Oct. 18, 1580, in which he recommends the study of Grisone's work on horsemanship (*Correspondence*, ed. Pears, 1845, p. 202). Castiglione, Sidney's model of manners, said that all gentlemen should ride well. Cf. Harvey, ii. p. 263; and see Einstein's *Italian Renaissance in England* (1902), pp. 69-70.

14-18. *Souldiours . . . Camps and Courts.* See note to p. 188, l. 26.

21. *Pedanteria.* The Italian form is significant.

151. 13, &c. Cf. Daniello, *Della Poetica*, pp. 12 and 21.

17. *first Nurse*, &c. Cf. Minturno: 'Io ho sempre stimato ... la Poesia non pur esser di tutte le scienze reina, ma lor madre anchora; e le Muse non solamente di tutte l'arti eccellenti inuentrici, ma etiandio gouernatrici di tutte le cose.' (*L'Arte Poet.* Preface.) See Harington, infra, ii. p. 194, l. 10.

20. *or rather the Vipers.* Cf. ii. p. 373, l. 11. Perhaps a playful hit at Gosson's *Schoole of Abuse* (ed. Arber, p. 46); but the simile is common, especially in the Euphuistic writers (cf. *Euphues*, ed. Arber, p. 215). It was taken from Pliny (cf. Wilson, *Arte of Rhetorique*, ed. 1553, fol. 69), who may have borrowed it from Herodotus iii. 109.

22. Sidney's plea for the antiquity of poetry and the selection of the names which follow seem to be directly inspired by Minturno's passage, *Poeticae vetustas*, and his list of illustrations on pp. 9, 13, and 15 of the *De Poeta*.

152. 22-5. Cf. Daniello, u.s., p. 22. Cf. p. 190, l. 4.

30-1. Plato, *Symposium* (passim); *Phaedrus*, 230 B; *De Rep.* ii. 359, &c.

34, &c. Cf. Sidney's letter to his brother Robert (Oct. 18, 1580), in which, in speaking of the writing of history, he says:

'This I think in haste, a story is either to be considered as a story, or as a treatise, which, besides that, addeth many things for profit and ornament: as a story, he is nothing but a narration of things done, with the beginnings, causes, and appendances therof . . . and thus much as a very historiographer. Besides this, the historian makes himself a discourser for profit, and an orator, yea a poet, sometimes for ornament. An orator, in making excellent orations, " e re nata," which are to be marked, but marked with the note of rhetorical remembrances: a poet, in painting forth the effects, the motions, the whisperings of the people, which, though in disputation one might say were true, yet who will mark them well shall find them taste of a poetical vein, and in that kind are gallantly to be marked: for though perchance they were not so, yet it is enough they might be so. The last point which tends to teach profit is of a discourser, which name to give to whosoever speaks "non simpliciter de facto, sed de qualitatibus et circumstantiis facti . . ."' Sidney adds: 'This write I to you in great haste, of method without method, but with more leisure and study (if I do not find some book that satisfies), I will venture to write more largely of it unto you.' (*Correspondence*, ed. Pears, 1845, pp. 199-201.)

153. 12. *which in all Nations*, &c. Cf. Minturno: 'Quibus de causis cum ita prodesset, tamquam oblectaret Poësis, nulla unquam profecto natio, nullaque omnino gens fuit, quae non eam libentissime sinu complexuque suo receperit . . . Quod denique genus hominum est tam barbarum, tamque agreste, quod a Poësi fuerit alienum?' (*De Poeta*, Bk. I. p. 9). In the same passage he refers to the Welsh Bards (cf. ll. 28, 30).

21. *Areytos*. Sp. *aréito*, adopted from the West Indians, describing a mixed form of dancing and singing. Puttenham apparently borrows Sidney's reference, infra, ii. 10. 32. For an account of these song-dances see Oviedo, *Hist. Gen. de las Indias*, v. 1 (quoted by A. S. Cook), and Guniston's translation of Jos. de Acosta's *Hist. of the Indies*, ed. Markham, ii. 445 (quoted by Shuckburgh).

154. 5. *a Poet was called Vates*, i. e. in the very earliest and in the post-Virgilian periods. Sidney may be recalling Minturno (though he transposes the premisses) : 'Quapropter qui apud

priscos illos veteres essent interpretes Deorum & sacerdotes, qui sapientes, qui eloquentes haberentur, qui recte ac prudenter in publicis rebus versarentur, omnes Poetae dicebantur' (p. 15); but the similarity of phrase suggests that he had Sir Thomas Elyot's words before him: 'in poetes was supposed to be science misticall and inspired, and therefore in Latine they were called *Vates*, which worde signifyeth as moche as prophetes. And therefore Tulli in his Tusculane questyons supposeth that a poete can nat abundantly expresse verses sufficient and complete, or that his eloquence may flowe without labour, wordes wel souninge and plentuouse, without celestiall instruction' (*Gouernour*, ed. Croft, i. 122). With the last words cf. ll. 26-9. Cf. p. 159, l. 17. Webbe (infra, p. 231) distinguishes between *Vates* and *Poetae*.

16-18. *Albinus*, &c. This anecdote of Albinus is taken from the popular *Sex Scriptores Historiae Augustae* (referred to by Sidney as 'the histories of the Emperors liues'). See the account in Fabricius, *Bibl. Latina*, pp. 546-53. Several Paris editions appeared in Sidney's lifetime.

32, &c. *Dauids Psalmes.* Cf. Lodge, p. 71, l. 5; Puttenham, ii. p. 10, l. 3; Harington, ii. p. 207, l. 20.

155. 5. *meerely*, wholly.

26. *Maker*, as a technical term, synonymous with 'Poet,' was used more frequently in our northern literature, and especially by the Scottish Chaucerians. Cf. Scaliger's complaint of the lack of the vernacular term in Latin: 'Quod nomen Graeci sapientes vbi commodissime παρὰ τὸ ποιεῖν effinxissent: miror maiores nostros sibi tam iniquos fuisse: vt Factoris vocem, quae illam exprimeret, maluerint oleariorum cancellis circumscribere: eum enim solum qui oleum facit, quum pro consuetudine caste, tum pro significatione stulte appellare licet' (*Poetice*, I. i). Cf. also Uberto Folieta, *De Similitudine Normae Polybianae* (*Artis Penus Historicae*, 1579, ii. 450*).

Sidney's argument here, and on p. 156, appears to be based on this chapter in Scaliger, especially on the portion immediately preceding the above quotation.

34. *So doth the Astronomer*, &c. The illustrative details in this passage appear to be suggested by Minturno, *De Poeta*, pp. 87-100, where they occur in almost identical order.

157. 2. *Theagines*, in the romance by Heliodorus. See infra, p. 160, l. 10, and note.

3. *Orlando*, in Ariosto's *Orlando Furioso*. Harington's English version did not appear till 1591. See infra, ii. p. 194.

19 &c. Cf. Scaliger, *Poet.* i. 1 'At poeta & naturam alteram & fortunas plures etiam ac demum sese isthoc ipso perinde ac Deum alterum efficit. Nam quae omnium opifex condidit, eorum reliquae scientiae tanquam actores sunt. Poetica vero, quum & speciosius quae sunt, & quae non sunt, eorum speciem ponit: videtur sane res ipsas, non ut aliae, quasi histrio, narrare, sed velut alter deus condere: vnde cum eo commune nomen ipsi non a consensu hominum, sed a naturae prouidentia inditum videatur.' See also Minturno, *De Poeta*, pp. 87, &c.

158. 5-6. *Poesie . . . Mimesis*. Aristotle, *Poetics*, i. 2, &c. It is more probable that Sidney is drawing here, as he does frequently throughout the essay, from Scaliger's *Poetice*. The succeeding words, 'to teach and delight,' are reminiscent of Bk. I. c. i, where, speaking of *Poesis*, Scaliger says: 'Quamobrem tota in imitatione sita fuit. Hic enim finis est medius ad illum vltimum, qui est docendi cum delectatione.' Sidney, like his contemporaries, is Horatian rather than Aristotelian in his co-ordination of the *utile* with the *dulce*. See also note to p. 197, l. 3.

8. *a speaking picture* (cf. p. 165, l. 17), a commonplace of Elizabethan and Renaissance criticism (cf. the verses in Puttenham, iii. ed. Arber, p. 218; E. Hoby, infra, p. 342, l. 29; Daniel's *Musophilus*, 178; Jonson's *Discoveries*, ed. Cunningham, iii. 409), borrowed from Plutarch, *De Aud. Poetis*, 3, who refers to it as an established metaphor. Cf. Horace, *Ars Poet.* 361. Vives, in his account of Comedy, utilizes the figure thus: 'Venit in scenam poesis populo ad spectandum congregato, et ibi sicut pictor tabulam proponit multitudini spectandam, ita poeta imaginem quandam vitae, ut merito Plutarchus de his dixerit, poema esse picturam loquentem, et picturam poema tacens, ita magister est populi, et pictor, et poeta' (*De Causis Corrupt. Artium*, p. 367, ed. 1555). Mambrun in his *De Carmine Epico*, 1652 (pp. 155, 284), mentions it as 'illud Simonidis dictum, quod a Plutarcho lib. de aud. poet. accepimus, ζωγραφίαν, &c. Poesin pictura loquaci et picturam poesi tacita definiri.' (Cf. Jonson, u.s.) Mambrun also says: 'Poesis est vocalis pictura,

quae etiam comparatio Aristoteli familiaris fuit,' which, if not a random association, may perhaps be explained in the light of the passages referred to in Mr. Butcher's *Aristotle's Theory of Poetry*, 3rd ed., p. 187, note. Cf. Scaliger's reference to poetry, 'veluti aurium pictura quadam' (*P.* i. 1). See Mr. Courthope's *Life in Poetry*, &c., p. 172, for an interesting passage on the later influence of the saying of Simonides. The definition of Painting reappears in the ' muda poesia' of Camoens, *Lus.* vii. 76. Horace's phrase suggested the opening lines of Du Fresnoy's *De Arte Graphica* (1658), which are freely quoted in the eighteenth century. The metaphor is the basis of Lessing's *Laokoon* (see especially the *Preface*). His statement that the ancients were careful to inculcate that each art had its own objects and modes of imitation will not, however, describe the practice of Renaissance writers.

9. *three seuerall kinds*, &c. Sidney's division is as in Scaliger: 'Primum est Theologorum: cuiusmodi Orpheus & Amphion . . . Secundum genus Philosophorum: idque duplex Naturale, quale Empedocles, Nicander, Aratus, Lucretius: Morale secundum suas partes, vt Politicum ab Solone & Tyrtaeo; Oeconomicum ab Hesiodo; Commune a Phocilide, Theognide, Pythagora. Tertio loco ponentur ii, de quibus omnibus mox' (*Poetice*, i. 2). It may be compared also with Minturno's parallel division, *De Poeta*, Bk. I. pp. 53-4.

14. *Exodus* xv; *Deut.* xxxii; *Judges* v.

15-16. *Emanuell Tremelius* or *Tremellius* (text *Tremilius*) (1510-80), a Jew of Ferrara, converted to Catholic Christianity by Cardinal Pole and Marcantonio Flaminio, and later to Protestantism by Peter Martyr. He devoted himself to Oriental studies and produced a Latin Bible with the collaboration of Franciscus Iunius.

Franciscus Iunius (1545-1602), a French protestant who taught Theology at Neustadt, Heidelberg (where he assisted Tremelius with his translation), and Leyden. Sidney refers to the title-page of the 2nd vol. of their Bible, containing the five 'poetical books.'

23. Perhaps a reference to the translation of the Psalms begun by him, and completed by the Countess of Pembroke.

29. *Cato*. The *Disticha de moribus*, ascribed to a certain

Dionysius Cato. The book, which is referred to by John of Salisbury (*Policraticus*, vii), was frequently printed towards the close of the fifteenth century, and was edited by Erasmus and praised by Luther. See Fabricius, *Bibl. Latina*, pp. 682-5. It was used as a textbook in Elizabethan schools (cf. Drayton, *To Henry Reynolds*; Peele, *Edward I*, ed. Bullen, i. 169).

30. *Pontanus*, J. Jovianus, author of the *Urania* (see ii. p. 315, l. 9, note). Scaliger devotes a considerable portion of Chap. II (*Poetae recentiores*) in the 6th Book of his *Poetice* to a criticism of his work.

159. 5. Cf. Cicero, *Orator* ii. 3.

17. See p. 154, l. 4.

35. *verse being but an ornament*, &c. See p. 182, ll. 17-18 and note, and ll. 19-20, note. Cf. Castelvetro, *Poetica*, pp. 23, &c., 190. For a discussion of this question from the Aristotelian and Sidneian points of view see Mr. Courthope's *Life in Poetry*, pp. 68, &c., and Mr. Butcher's *Aristotle's Theory of Poetry* (3rd edit.), pp. 143, &c.

The contrast between poets and versifiers had been noted by Elyot in the *Gouernour* ('semblably they that make verses, expressynge therby none other lernynge but the craft of versifyeing, be nat of aunctient writers named poetes, but onely called versifyers,' ed. Croft, i. 120). Cf. Puttenham, infra, ii. 3. 16-17. The distinction is of course as old as Quintilian.

160. 8. *Theagines and Cariclea*. Supra, p. 157, l. 2. Probably borrowed from Scaliger, who also instances *Theagines and Cariclea* as an epic in prose. See *Poetice*, iii. 95.

13-16. This is in agreement with Minturno's general theory and may even be an echo of his phrases, e.g. 'aut vitia aut virtutes effingunt,' *De Poeta*, p. 27. Cf. also pp. 11 and 35. Mr. Spingarn points out, in support of this contention, that Sidney, like Minturno, makes poets feign images of *virtues and vices*, not merely *actions*, as Aristotle does.

161. 12. Plato, *Theaetetus*, 174. Sidney uses the metaphor again in the 19th Sonnet of *Astrophel and Stella*.

20. *Arkitecktonike* (ἀρχιτεκτονική). Arist. *Eth*. i. 1. 4; with which compare Sidney's ensuing words (ll. 23, &c.).

31. I follow the original text in not making a new paragraph here, though the Philosophers deserve one equally with the

Historians. The following anacoluthon suggests a run-on idea. Ponsonby's text reads: 'wherin if we can shew, the Poet is worthy to haue it before anyother competitors: among whom principall challengers . . .'

162. 2, &c. So Cicero, *Pro Arch.* 11; *Tusc.* i. 15.

32. From Cicero, *De Orat.* ii. 9. 36 'Historia vero testis temporum, lux veritatis, vita memoriae, magistra vitae, nuntia vetustatis . . .'

163. 13. *Alphonsus of Aragon.* Alphonso V of Aragon and I of Sicily (1416–58).

29, &c. For a parallel comparison of poetry with ethics and law in Varchi's *Lezioni* (Florence, 1590), see Spingarn's *Lit. Crit.* pp. 50–1.

31–2. Horace, *Epist.* i. 16. 52–3.

164. 12–13. Cf. Daniello, u.s., p. 19; also Minturno, *De Poeta* 39 ('quae severius asperiusque quam opus fit philosophi disputant').

24. Orig. 'fruitlesse.'

25, &c. Cf. the passage in Minturno, *De Poeta* (I. p. 38), concluding 'Sed tamen docendus erat populus, & ad virtutem informandus, non praeceptis philosophorum, sed exemplis, quae non historici, sed poetae protulissent.' Cf. also Varchi, as above. The continuation of Sidney's argument, on to p. 168, follows Minturno's defence, *De Poeta*, pp. 38–40, both in general drift and in the citation of certain examples. For proof of a direct point of contact, compare Sidney, p. 167, ll. 8–10, with 'Quod autem fabulas illi fingerent eas, quae populo placerent, exprimerentque; non alia, quam quae populo probarentur; num adeo philosophi hallucinati ab hominum consuetudine mentis aciem abducebant, vel, ut verius dicam, ita mente capti e statu suo dimouebantur, ut non viderent, nisi esset oratio ad eorum, qui audirent, opinionem accommodanda, nullum esse genus oratorum oportere' (p. 38). And again, 'At enim poeta non ita populo seruit, non ita se vulgo addictum putat, ut praeter id omne, quod probet multitudo, nihil aliud proferre possit' (p. 39). Minturno returns to this on p. 106. See Harington, infra, ii. p. 199, ll. 2–3.

165. 17. Cf. p. 158, l. 8.

24. Orig. 'maddesse.' Hor. *Epist.* i. 2. 62 'Ira furor brevis est.' Cf. Seneca, *De Ira*, i. 1.

25. Sidney refers to the dramatic situation generally, for the audience did not see the 'killing and whipping.'

166. 2. *Chaucers Pandar*, in *Troilus and Criseyde*.

12. *Eutopia*. Perhaps a misprint, though Mr. Shuckburgh points out that in the prefatory verses to the Latin editions of the *Utopia* there is a punning distinction made between 'Utopia' and 'Eutopia' (ed. *Apologie*, p. 96).

22-4. Horace, *Ars Poet.* ll. 372-3 ('Non homines, non di,' &c.).

26. Cf. Harington, infra, ii. p. 205, l. 35.

167. 9. *Popular*. So Plutarch. See note to p. 164, l. 25, &c.

19-30. See Aristotle's *Poetics*, 9.

31. *full of reason*. Cf. p. 168, l. 32, and p. 197, l. 10. See Mr. Spingarn's section on the growth of Rationalism in Renaissance criticism (*Lit. Crit.* pp. 150, &c., 246, &c.).

168. 11. Horace, *Sat.* i. 8; *Epod.* v.

170. 10-15. Cf. Giraldi Cintio, *Dei Romanzi* (ed. Daelli, i. p. 66).

11. See Plutarch, *De Aud. Poetis*, iv.

17. *Milciades* (Miltiades), the victor at Marathon.

18. See Plutarch's *Life of Phocion*.

19-20. Septimius Severus (193-211) and Alexander Severus (222-35).

28. Suetonius, *Julius Caesar*, 77.

33. *Cipselus, Periander*. Herodotus, v. 92.

Phalaris, tyrant of Agrigentum. Cf. Cicero, *De Off.* ii. 7.

26. See Harington, infra, ii. p. 210, l. 16.

Dionysius, tyrant of Syracuse. Cf. Cicero, *Tusc.* 5. 20.

171. 13. *Philophilosophos* (φιλοφιλόσοφος—Ponsonby's text): a Renaissance form, perhaps Sidney's own. Cf. *Mysomousoi*, p. 181, l. 19.

14, 15. *moouing*. Cf. Minturno, *De Poeta*, p. 106; Varchi, *Lezzioni*, 576.

21. *not Gnosis but Praxis*. Aristotle, *Ethics*, i.

172. 9, &c. Cf. Varchi, passim. (See note to p. 163, l. 29, &c.)

21-3. *with a tale*, &c. Borrowed by Harington, infra, ii. p. 208, ll. 6-8.

25-30. For this common Renaissance simile, see Minturno, *De P.* p. 49, and Daniello, *De P.* p. 19. See also Harington's reference to Plutarch and his quotation from Tasso, infra, ii. pp. 198-9, and p. 208, l. 1; Lyly's *Euphues* (Arber, p. 328); and Nash (ed. Grosart, ii. p. 90). It is not probable that Sidney is thinking (as Mr. A. S. Cook suggests) of a passage in the Preface to Part III of the edition of the Bible by Junius and Tremellius (to whom Sidney refers, supra, p. 158). There the figure is the smearing of the mouth of a vessel with honey, as it is in Lucretius, i. 936, &c.—a fact noted by Giulio Guastauino and Scipio Gentili in the 1590 Genoa edition of Tasso, where a parallel is given from Lactantius, *Institutiones*, v. If Sidney be directly indebted to any one, he may be recalling Gosson's *Schoole of Abuse* (ed. Arber, p. 20).

173. 5. *as Aristotle*. *Poetics*, 4.

17-18. *Aen.* xii. 645-6.

26. Persius, *Sat.* v. 151.

174. 3, &c. *Menenius Agrippa*. Livy, ii. 32. Cf. Shakespeare, *Coriolanus*, i. 1. 94.

8. *farre fet*. A favourite phrase with Sidney. Cf. p. 202, l. 3, and note; and Puttenham, infra, ii. 169, l. 7, &c.

23. *Nathan*. (2 *Sam.* xii.) Cf. p. 185, l. 10. This is borrowed by Harington, infra, ii. p. 205, l. 27.

175. 16, &c. *the Tragicomicall*. Cf. p. 199, ll. 9, 13.

18. In the *Arcadia* and in the *Consolatio*.

176. 5-6. Virgil, *Eclog.* vii. 69-70.

17 and 23. Persius, *Sat.* 1. 116-117:—

> 'Omne vafer vitium ridenti Flaccus amico
> Tangit et admissus circum praecordia ludit.'

26. Horace, *Epist.* i. 11. 30 'Est Ulubris, animus si te non deficit aequus.'

27. *No, perchance*. A direct reference to the particular attack of the *Schoole of Abuse* and like pamphlets (supra, p. 61 et seq.).

30. *Comedy is an imitation*, &c. Sidney's definition of the function of comedy is analogous to (if not derived from) Trissino's (*Opere*, ii. 127, &c.) and Cicero's (*De Orat.* ii. 58-9), and may be compared with Elyot's statement in the *Gouernour* (1531), ed. Croft, i. 124-5. See also notes to p. 81, l. 1, and ii. p. 389, ll. 35-6. Sidney distinguishes the 'common errors of

our life' and the 'domestical matters' as the special material for the laughter which is to beget 'admiratio' (see below) in the breasts of the spectators. The delightfulness of comedy cannot be found in the greater evils and sorrows which belong to tragedy: and laughter is an accident and nowise an essential condition of effective comedy. Cf. Jonson's *Discoveries*, apropos of Aristotle's views on laughter.

177. 10–11. *Demea*, &c. See supra, p. 370.

18. *Pistrinum*, the 'mill' for troublesome slaves.

24–5. See Introduction, p. lxxxvi.

28. *affects*, feelings. Cf. Sidney's *Arcadia*, p. 351 (ed. 1622).

'Admiration' is used in the technical sense first established by Minturno, who added it to the Horatian 'instruction' and 'delight' as the third function of Poetry. See *De Poeta*, p. 102: 'Verum, ut quae proposita sunt exponamus, erit Poetae sic dicere versibus, ut doceat, ut delectet, ut moueat. Qui non ita dicet, ut haec tria assequi debeat nunquam, mea quidem sententia, hoc nomine appellabitur'; p. 106, 'Illud autem ne te praetereat velim, sic poetis esse dicendum, ut siue doceant, siue oblectent, siue moueant, haec singula statim admiratio legentis, audientisue consequatur'; and p. 107 (with the marginalia). So too Scaliger, *Poetice*, III. xcvi ('sed & docendi & mouendi & delectandi'). See Mr. Spingarn's exposition of Minturno's doctrine (*Lit. Crit.* pp. 52–3). Though in some passages of Elizabethan criticism the term is, as here, conjoined with 'commiseration' as the equivalent of the Aristotelian 'pity' and 'fear' of tragedy, it defines, in part, the function of poetry *per se* and in all its kinds. Though 'Admiration' was ultimately raised to the level of Pity and Terror, its critical place is with 'instruction' and 'delight' in the general definition of the purpose of Poetry. The narrowing down comes later, in Corneille, Boileau, and Saint-Évremond, with whom 'Admiration is a tragic passion.' See the important letter from Boileau to Ch. Perrault (1700): 'Pouvez-vous nier que ce ne soit dans Tite-Live ... que M. de Corneille a pris ses plus beaux traits, a puisé ces grandes idées qui lui ont fait inventer un nouveau genre de tragédie inconnu à Aristote? Car c'est sur ce pied, à mon avis, qu'on doit regarder quantité de ses plus belles pièces de théâtre, où, se mettant au-dessus des règles de ce philosophe, il n'a point songé, comme les poètes de l'ancienne tragédie, à émouvoir la pitié et la terreur, mais à exciter dans l'âme des spectateurs, par la sublimité des pensées et par la beauté des sentiments, une certaine admiration, dont plusieurs personnes, et les jeunes gens surtout, s'accommodent souvent beaucoup mieux que des véritables passions tragiques.'

32–3. Seneca, *Œdipus*, 705. (Orig. '*authorem.*')

178. 1. Plutarch, *Life of Pelopidas*, 29.

16. *naturall Problemes*, i.e. 'problems' based on, or dealing with, natural history. 'Problem' here and elsewhere is equivalent to 'figure,' 'illustration.' Cf. *Astrophel and Stella*, iii. ll. 6, 10 (ed. Flügel, p. 2).

20. *Percy and Duglas*, a reference to the older version of *Chevy Chase*, or perhaps (as Mr. Child has suggested) to the *Battle of Otterbourne*.

30, &c. See Plutarch's *Lycurgus*, 21.

179. 7. *three fearefull felicities.* Plutarch's *Alexander*, 3.

21. *Plato and Tullie.* See *De Finibus*, ii. 16, and *De Officiis*, i. 5. Cicero refers to Plato in both passages.

28. Cf. Puttenham, infra, ii. p. 43, ll. 21–2, note.

180. 12. Horace, *Epist.* i. 2. 4.

181. 10, 11. See note to p. 188, l. 26.

19. *Mysomousoi*: μυσομουσοι (for μισομουσοι) in Ponsonby's text. Perhaps Sidney's own word. Cf. note to p. 171, l. 13.

35. Ovid, *Ars Amat.* ii. 662, altered of purpose by Sidney:

'Dic habilem, quaecumque brevis; quae turgida, plenam:
Et lateat vitium proximitate boni.'

182. 1. Henricus Cornelius Agrippa. See Harington, infra, ii. p. 199, l. 27, &c. Sidney here refers to Agrippa's *De vanitate et incertitudine scientiarum*. The objections against poetry stated on p. 183 are probably inspired by this work, which speaks of *architectrix mendaciorum et cultrix perversorum dogmatum*.

17–18. See p. 159, l. 35. Cf. Ronsard, 'Tous ceux qui escrivent en carmes, tant doctes puissent-ils estre, ne sont pas poëtes. Il y a autant de différence entre un poëte et un versificateur,' &c. (*Préface de la Franciade*).

19–20. Scaliger, *Poetice*, i. 2 'Poetae igitur nomen non a

fingendo, vt putarunt, quia fictis vteretur; sed initio a faciendo versu dictum est.'

21. *Oratio ... Ratio*: following Quintilian, ii. 16 (109). Cf. Cicero, *De Officiis*, i. 16. This is a common Renaissance theme. Cf. J. J. Pontanus, *De Sermone*, lib. i (*Opera*, Aldus, 1518, iii. 185 v°).

183. 18. '... hourely lessons; as *Percontatorem fugito, nam garrulus idem est, Dum tibi quisque placet credula turba sumus.* But the fitnes ...' (Ponsonby's text). Hor. *Epist.* i. 18, and Ovid, *Rem. Amoris*, 686.

26. Sidney now addresses himself directly to answer Gosson.

35. *erre* (Ponsonby, *eare*) = 'to plough.' Sidney's reference to Chaucer is merely verbal, not as an argument about Comedies. See the passage in *The Knightes Tale*, 28, 'I have, God woot, a large feeld to ere,' which is borrowed from the *Rom. de la Rose*, 21481.

in other Nations, &c. So Gosson's *Schoole of Abuse*, passim.

184. 5. *out shot Robin Hood*. See ii. p. 219, l. 21, note.

5–6. *Plato*. Cf. Gosson and Lodge, supra.

22. Cf. Harington, infra, ii. p. 201, l. 19.

185. 10. *Nathan*, supra, p. 174, l. 23.

30–1. *Iohn a stile and Iohn a noakes* (orig. 'John atte stile,' i.e. John who dwells at the stile, and 'John atten Oke,' i.e. John who dwells at the oak), fictitious names in a legal action. See infra, ii. p. 270, l. 14, and the passage in *The Returne from Parnassus*, pt. II. iv. i. 1537 et seq. Cf. 'John Doe' and 'John Roe' (supra, p. 140); now obsolete in English law, though still retained in American law.

186. 13. Cf. Harington, infra, ii. p. 209, l. 3.

30. ib. ll. 13–14.

32, 33. *Eikastike—Phantastike*. See Plato, *Sophist.* 235–6. Cf. *phantasticall* in Puttenham, infra, ii. p. 19, l. 11.

187. 17. *rampire*, 'rampart,' defence.

35. *before*, previous, earlier.

188. 24. Horace, *Sat.* i. 1. 63:

'Quid facias illi? iubeas miserum esse, libenter
Quatenus id facit.'

26. *companion of the Campes* (cf. pp. 150, ll. 14–18, 181, ll. 10–11). So Sidney throughout, both in his life and in his writings. Cf. the more academic Buchanan, esteemed by Sidney, who in the Preface to his *Jephthes*, dedicated to the Maréchal de Brissac, writes 'Absurdam fortasse rem facere quibusdam videbor, qui ad te, hominem ab ineunte aetate militaribus imbutum studiis, & inter arma tubasque semper versatum, munusculum hoc literarium mittam: sed ii fere hoc absurdum existimaturi sunt, qui aut harum rerum inter se consensionem non satis animadvertunt, aut tuum ingenium parum habent perspectum. Neque enim inter rei militaris & literarum studium ea est, quam plerique falso putant, discordia: sed summa potius concordia, et occulta quaedam naturae conspiratio.' This concord is a favourite Renaissance topic. Cf. the controversy between Muzio (*Il Gentiluomo*) and Mora (*Il Cavaliere*) as to whether letters or arms better befit a gentleman; the sixth dialogue (*Del Paragone dell' Arme & delle Lettere*) of Guazzo's *Dialoghi piaceuoli*; and N. Breton's *Discourse of a Scholler and a Souldier* (1599), which argues for and against the superiority of 'learning' over 'martiall discipline.' Nash laments, in the Epistle to his *Anatomie of Absurditie*, 'that England afforded many mediocrities, but neuer saw anything more singuler then worthy Sir *Philip Sidney*, of whom it might truely be saide *Arma virumque cano*.' Cf. also Daniel's *Funeral Poem on the Earl of Devonshire*, ll. 120–2 (Grosart, i. 176).

189. 3. Plutarch, *De seu Fortuna seu virtute Alexandri*.

7–8. See note to p. 64, ll. 23–6.

14–16. In answer to Gosson's *Schoole of Abuse*, p. 21.

190. 4. *sith*, &c. Cf. supra, p. 152, l. 22, and note.

9. *naturall enemie of Poets*. Cf. Minturno's passage on the dissension between poets and philosophers, 'Fui quondam inter poeticam et philosophiam non leuis dissensio,' &c. (*De P.* p. 36). See also Plato's *Republic*, x. 607.

33–5. Cf. Scaliger, *Poetice*, i. 2 'Respiciat ipse sese, quot ineptas quot spurcas fabellas inserat: quas Graecanicum scelus olentes sententias identidem inculcet. Certe Symposium & Phaedrum atque alia monstra operae pretium fuerit nunquam legisse.'

191. 10. Cf. supra, p. 71, ll. 19–20, and note. The other

'two' are said to be Cleanthes (*Hymn to Zeus*), also in the *Acts* xvii. 28, and Menander (*Thais*) in 1 Cor. xv. 33. (See Mr. Cook's note, ed. *Apologie*, p. 109.) Ponsonby's text omits the note—' S. Paule himselfe sets a watchword.'

Cf. Lodge, supra, p. 71, ll. 19-20.

31. *conster*, construe.

33. Scaliger, *Poetice*, i. 2. See note to p. 193, l. 34.

192. 5-6. Sidney borrows the reference from Scaliger, u. s.

15-18. Plato, *Ion*, 534; elaborated in Minturno, *De Poeta*, passim, especially pp. 67, 74-6. See also later in the *Apologie*, p. 195, ll. 19-20, and Harington's reference, infra, ii. p. 197, ll. 6-7. Cf. too the 'Argument' of 'October' in the *Shepheardes Calender* : ' No arte, but a diuine gift and heauenly instinct not to bee gotten by laboure and learning, but adorned with both ; and poured into the witte by a certaine ἐνθουσιασμός and celestiall inspiration.' Of this, the writer of the Argument continues, 'the author els where discourseth in his book called the English Poete, which booke being lately come to my hands, I mynde also by Gods grace vpon further aduisement to publish.' Spenser's treatise is not extant. (See note to p. 232, l. 21.)

22-4. Cf. Kyd's *Householder's Philosophie* (transl. from Tasso): ed. Boas, p. 267, ll. 37-9.

24. Orig. '*Heautontimorumenon*.'

27. Plato, *Phaedo*, 61.

193. 25. Virgil, *Aen.* i. 12.

28, &c. Hadrian, author of *Animula vagula, blandula*.

30-1. Robert II of Anjou (1309-43); Francis I (1515-47). *King Iames of Scotland* is generally identified with James I, King of Scots (1394-1437), author of the *Kingis Quair*; but Sidney is not likely to have known of James's reputation as a poet, except through Buchanan's *History* which had just been published (1582)[1]. [If this be so, we have a clue to the date of the *Apologie*.] Can he refer to James VI, whose *juvenilia* were collected in 1584 (infra, pp. 208, 404)?

32. *Bembus and Bibiena*, supra, p. 377.

34. *Fracastorius*, Hieronymus (1483-1533), author of the dialogue *Naugerius, siue de Poetica*, and of *Syphilis* and other works in Latin verse. See Scaliger, *Poetice*, vi. 4, u. s.

[1] It is less likely that he knew Major's *De Gestis Scotorum* (1521).

Scaliger, Julius Caesar (1484-1558), named above, p. 191, l. 33, &c. (See the Introduction p. lxxxiv, and Index.) 'Non solum soluta oratione, in qua nonnulla leguntur,' says Gyraldus, 'sed et versu quaedam cecinit, inter quae Elysius (poematis haec inscriptio est), in quo insulam Padi Belvedere Ferrariae ducis eleganti carmine descripsit et omnem fere Estensium genealogiam' (ed. Wotke, p. 84).

194. 1. *Pontanus.* See supra, p. 158, l. 30, note.

Muretus, M. Antonius (1526-85): the *Juvenilia* written at Rome, and the *Hymns* of his old age.

2. *Buchanan*, George. See supra, p. 24, ll. 5-7: infra, p. 201, l. 4.

3. *Hospitall of Fraunce*, Michel de l'Hôpital (1505-73), Chancellor of France.

15. Cf. *Arcadia*, i. (p. 38), where Sidney speaks of men 'disused with a long peace'—significant references by the poet-soldier to the political situation before the coming of the Armada.

17. *Mountibancks.* Cf. Sidney's letter to his brother Robert (*Correspondence*, ed. Pears, 1845, p. 196).

35. Juvenal, xiv.

195. 23. Cf. p. 71, l. 22. The proverb does not appear to be classical, in form at least, and has not as yet been traced further back than the *Lectiones Antiquae* of Coelius Rhodiginus (1450-1525). See Mr. Shuckburgh's note, ed. *Apologie*, p. 144. The genealogy of the more common form *Poeta nascitur, non fit*, is also doubtful, though it may have been suggested by the passage in Florus, *De Qualitate Vitae*, Fragm. viii (quoted by Ben Jonson in his *Discoveries*, ed. Cunningham, iii. p. 420). Cf. Webbe, infra, p. 297, ll. 1-2, and the original Latin of Fabricius in the notes (p. 420).

196. 4. Ovid, *Trist.* iv. 10. 26; printed in the original text, *Quicquid conabor discere versus erit*. A favourite quotation. Cf. Meres, infra, ii. p. 323, l. 17.

13. *Mirrour of [for] Magistrates.* The first edition, with nineteen 'legends' contributed by Baldwin, Ferrers, Phaer, Challoner, and others, appeared in 1559. For the later sixteenth-century issues, see Corser's *Collectanea*, viii. p. 418.

14. *the Earle of Surries Liricks* appeared first in *Tottel's Miscellany* (1557).

16. *The Sheapheards Kalender* was dedicated to Sidney (title-page, and 'To his Booke'). Sidney's criticism may be compared with 'E. K.'s defence, supra.

32. *Gorboduck* (*Tragedie of*), by Thomas Sackville (Lord Buckhurst) and Thomas Norton, 1565 (acted 1561), reprinted [? 1570] with the title, *The Tragidie of Ferrex and Porrex*.

197. 3. *The very end of Poesie*, cf. p. 200, l. 22. See Scaliger, *Poetice*, vii. 2 (p. 831) 'Quamobrem dicendum est Poetae finem esse docere cum delectatione ... Poetae finem esse docere cum iucunditate': and cf. Giraldi Cintio, u. s. (ed. Daelli), i. 61. See also note to p. 158, ll. 5–6.

6, &c. *in place and time*, &c. This is the earliest known reference in English to the doctrine of 'the Three Unities,' first formulated by Castelvetro in 1570. 'La mutatione tragica non può tirar con esso seco se non vna giornata & vn luogo' (*Poetica*, 1576, p. 534, ll. 20–1). See also ib. pp. 109, 168, &c., and cf. the reference in 1572 by Jean de la Taille in his *Art de la Tragédie*. Sidney drew direct from Castelvetro.

The canon of the Three Unities was a Renaissance development from the single Aristotelian Unity of Action, first by the adoption of the Unity of Time by the Italians Giraldi Cintio, Robortello, Segni, Maggi, Minturno, Scaliger, and Trissino, and later by the addition of the Unity of Place by Castelvetro in Italy, Jean de la Taille in France, and Sidney in England. In Maggi, Scaliger, and Minturno, there is, as Mr. Spingarn has pointed out, a forecast of the third unity which Castelvetro first made absolute. It should be borne in mind that the title 'the three unities' does not occur till well on in the seventeenth century. They had been treated individually, as shown above, and to some extent by Mairet in his Preface to *Silvanire*, ? 1625 (whose attitude is the same as Scaliger's, iv. 97, ed. 1617, p. 334), but it was left to Chapelain to bind them together in a code. Corneille knew nothing of this triple rule when he began to write, nor did Richelieu until he was told of it by Chapelain. It should be added that though Jean de la Taille supplies an interesting hint of the Unity of Place, he exerted no influence in France and was soon forgotten; and that the later establishment of the canon of the three Unities was directly due to the study of Castelvetro and the Italians. The frequent references to Castelvetro in Chapelain's correspondence would seem to narrow down the channel of influence to Chapelain himself, though he too naively says, in his *Démonstration de la Règle des vingt-quatre heures* (1630), that he has no defence to offer but 'la pratique des anciens, suiuie d'un consentement vniuersel par tous les Italiens,' and that he does not remember 'si Aristote l'a traitté, ou aucun de ses commentateurs.'

For the history of the growth of the theory see Breitinger's *Les unités d'Aristote avant le Cid de Corneille* (Geneva, 1879), and his important correction in the *Revue critique*, December 27, 1879 (pp. 478-80); Lintilhac's *De J.-C. Scaligeri Poetice*, Paris, 1887, and his articles in the *Nouvelle Revue*, May 15 and June 1, 1890 (lxiv. 541); Arnaud's *Études ... sur les Théories Dramatiques au XVIIe Siècle* (1887); Ebner's *Beitrag zu einer Geschichte der dramatischen Einheiten in Italien*, Erlangen, 1898; Spingarn's *Literary Criticism in the Renaissance*, pp. 73, 89-101, 206-10; Saintsbury's *History of Criticism*, ii. Bks. iv and v, passim; Butcher's *Aristotle's Theory of Poetry*, 3rd edit., ch. vii.

It is not pedantic to protest against the popular title, 'The Unities of Aristotle' (as in M. Breitinger's book, referred to above), though the 'Dramatic Unities' *were* evolved in the study of the *Poetics*; or hypercritical to disclaim M. Lintilhac's 'Unités scaligériennes,' now that Mr. Spingarn has stated Scaliger's position and established Castelvetro's claim.

10. See note to p. 167, l. 31.

17, &c. Cf. Whetstone, supra, p. 59, ll. 24, &c.; Ben Jonson, infra, ii. p. 389. Cf. also Shakespeare, Prologue to *Henry V*, and the passage (parallel even in details) in *Don Quixote*, Pt. i. ch. xlviii. I am reminded by Mr. Spingarn that Rodenburg (supra, p. 382) in paraphrasing this passage, in 1619, quotes Lope de Vega's similar theory (*Arte nuevo de hacer comedias*), and adds ''t z'eve ghebruyken oock alle de Poëten in Enghelandt' (cited by Jonckbloet, u. s., iii. 201, note). This idea he probably got from Sidney; but it is an interesting early foreign comment on the practice of the Elizabethan dramatists.

35. *some*, &c. Cf. Castelvetro, *Poetica*, p. 109, l. 30 'Per la qual cosa veggansi Plauto & Terentio, come si possono scusare di non hauere errato, che in alcune comedie loro hanno fatto rappresentare l' attione più lunga d' un giorno': and Scaliger,

Poetice, vi. 3. See also Dryden's reference to Scaliger on the *Heautontimorumenos* (*Essay of Dramatic Poesy, Works*, ed. Scott and Saintsbury, xv. p. 307). Sidney's mention of the *Eunuchus* is a slip. The 'time' of Terence's play was a fruitful topic of discussion by, among others, Muretus, Vossius, Mambrun, d'Aubignac, and Ménage. (See d'Aubignac's *Térence justifié* and *Pratique du Théâtre*.)

198. 17. *Pacolets horse*. See the Romance of *Valentine and Orson* for the story of the magic horse of the dwarf Pacolet. Cf. Rabelais, ii. 24.

21. Horace, *Ars Poet.* 147.

199. 5. *mingling Kings and Clownes*. See Whetstone, supra, p. 58, l. 19; p. 59, ll. 33-4; p. 60, l. 1, and notes; and 'E. K.', p. 128, l. 5. Cf. Scaliger, *Poetice*, I. xi (end).

9. *mungrell Tragy-comedie*. Cf. p. 175, l. 16. See the Prologue to *Amphitruo*, 59.

13-14. Cf. Scaliger, 'Festiue (vt solet) Plautus Amphitruonem suam Tragicomoediam appellauit : in qua personarum dignitas atque magnitudo Comoediae humilitati admistae essent' (*Poet*. i. 7, p. 31). See supra, p. 175, l. 16, &c.

200. 22. See note to p. 197, l. 3.

24. Aristotle, *Poetics*, v. 1. On Laughter, cf. Trissino, *Opere*, ii. 127 et seq.

31-2. Juvenal, *Sat.* iii. 152-3.

34. *Thraso*, in the *Eunuchus* of Terence.

awry-transformed Traueller. Cf. Ascham, *Scholemaster* (ed. Mayor, i. p. 74), 'returned out of *Italie* worse transformed.' The sentiment is, of course, an Elizabethan commonplace.

201. 4. *Buchanan*, supra, p. 194.

6-10. *this play matter*. Cf. p. 176, l. 27 (note).

24-25. Cf. Sidney's *Astrophel and Stella*, i. 7-8; lxxiv. 8.

31. *Energia* (ἐνέργεια, Arist. *Rhet*. iii. 11. 2, &c.; Quintil. 401). See note in *N.E.D.*, s. v. 'Energy.' Sidney may be recalling Scaliger's chapter on '*Efficacia*' (*Poetice*, iii. 26), which begins 'Efficaciam Graeci ἐνέργειαν vocant.'

202. 1-2. A retort to Gosson's 'chaste Matrons apparel on common Curtesans' (*Schoole of Abuse*, ed. Arber, p. 20).

3-8. Cf. the identity of phrase in Sidney's fifteenth Sonnet in *Astrophel and Stella* (ed. Flügel, 1899, p. 7):—

'You that doe search for euery purling spring,
Which from the rybs of old *Pernassus* flowes,
And euery flower (not sweete perhaps) which growes
Neere there about, into your Poems wring.
You that doe dictionary method bring
Into your rymes, running in ratling rowes,
You that old *Petrarchs* long deceased woes
With new borne sighes and wit disguised sing,
You take wrong wayes; those far-fet helps be such
As doe bewray a want of inward tutch;
And sure at length stolne goods doe come to light.
But if both for your loue & skill you[r] name
You seeke to nurse at fullest brest of Fame,
Stella behold, and then begin to write.'

Cf. also the third Sonnet (ib. p. 2).

8-12. Apparently a reference to Gosson, and probably, as Mr. A. S. Cook suggests, a direct parody of his style.

16. *Nizolian Paper-bookes*, i.e. on the model of the *Thesaurus Ciceronianus* of Marius Nizolius (1498-? 1576). The style of these collections of annotations is described by Ascham, supra, p. 17, ll. 26, &c.

16-18. Mr. A. S. Cook compares Du Bellay, *Defense* (1549), i. 7: '[Les Romains] imitant les meilleurs auteurs grecs, se transformant en eux, les devorant; et, après les avoir bien digerez, les convertissant en sang et nourriture.' The metaphor is, however, very common.

25. Cicero, *In Catil.* i. 2, slightly altered.

32. '. . . to be challericke. How well store of *Similiter Cadenses* doth sounde with the grauitie of the Pulpit, I woulde but inuoke Demosthenes soule to tell: who with a rare daintinesse vseth them. Truly they haue made mee thinke of the Sophister, that with too much subtilitie would proue two Egges three, and though he might be counted a Sophister, had none for his labour. So these men bringing in such a kinde of eloquence, well may they obtaine an opinion of a seeming finenesse, but perswade few, which should be the ende of their finenesse, Now for Similitudes . . .' (Ponsonby's text). See Flügel's edition, p. 107.

34, &c. *all Herbarists*, &c. A gibe at the excesses of Euphuism, and more directly at Gosson's style. Cf. Sidney's third Sonnet in *Astrophel and Stella* :—

> 'Or with straunge similes, inricht each line,
> Of hearbes or beastes, which *Inde* or *Affricke* hold.'

See i. p. 322, l. 28, note, and ii. p. 269.

203. 10. *as Cicero. De Oratore*, ii. 1. 4.

20-2. Ronsard, on the contrary, gives the advice not to affect the style of courts, as courtiers fight more, and better, than they write (ed. Blanchemain, vii. 322).

204. 18. Sidney is fond of this mannerism, especially in his *Arcadia*. Cf. Hall, *Satires*, Bk. vi. 255, &c. (ed. Grosart) :—

> 'He knows the grace of that new elegance
> Which sweet *Philisides* fetch't of late from *France*,
> That well beseem'd his high-stil'd *Arcady*,
> Tho others marre it with much liberty;
> In Epithets to ioyne two words in one,
> Forsooth, for Adiectiues cannot stand alone;
> As a great Poet could of *Bacchus* say,
> That he was *Semele-femori-gena*.'

21. Cf. the Spenser-Harvey Correspondence, passim.

205. 11. *ryme*; here = 'rhythm' (cf. Webbe, infra, p. 267, ll. 13, &c.). Contrast the meaning in ll. 17-18, and cf. Webbe, u.s., ll. 6-7. Cf. also Gascoigne, supra, p. 50, ll. 4-5, 27-8, and p. 52, l. 16. For a kindred Renaissance discussion of these themes cf. Du Bellay, *Defense*, ii. chs. 7 and 8.

For the form *rhythme*=rhyme, see the quotation from the *Preservation of King Henry the VII*, supra, p. 377.

11-12. Cf. Daniel, infra, ii. p. 360, ll. 24-5.

14. *Cæsura*, cf. Gascoigne, supra, p. 54, l. 9, &c.

206. 6. Not in Aristotle; but probably taken from Boccaccio, *De Geneal. Deorum*, XV. viii (edit. 1532, pp. 392-3), which refers to Aristotle's testimony.

8. *Bembus*, supra, p. 396.

9-11. Scaliger, *Poet*. iii. c. 19 'Nullis profecto Philosophorum praeceptis aut melior aut ciuilior euadere potes quam ex Virgiliana lectione.'

11-12. *Clauserus, the Translator of Cornutus*. Sidney refers to the Preface of the Latin translation, by Conrad Clauser, of the περὶ τῆς τοῦ θεοῦ φύσεως of Annaeus Cornutus.

16–18. Borrowed by Harington, infra, ii. p. 203, ll. 5–10.

19. *Landin* (Cristoforo Landino), 1424–? 1504. The fullest account will be found in the *Specimen Literaturae Florentinae saeculi xv*, by Ang. Bandinio, 2 vols. Florence, 1747. The list of his works is given in ii. p. 179, &c. Sidney probably refers to the *Disputationes Camaldulenses*.

For the doctrine of 'divine fury,' here associated with Landin, see supra, p. 192, ll. 15–18, note.

27. Cf. Horace, *Sat.* i. 6. 6.

29. Virgil, *Aen.* ix. 446.

32–3. This common figure will be found in Cicero's *Somnium Scipionis*, 5. Cf. Overbury, *Characters*, 'A Quacksalver' (ed. Rimbault, p. 141).

207. 3. Will become such a fool as to be a dull critic of poetry.

5. *Bubonax.* 'Sidney is referring to the tale of *Hipponax* (an Iambic poet of Ephesus about B.C. 500), of whom one story was that he satirized the statuary *Bupalus* so bitterly that he hanged himself. By some confusion ... he has combined the two names' (Shuckburgh, ed. *Apologie*, p. 176). Cf. Hor. *Epod.* vi. 14.

10–11. Cf. *The Pilgrimage to Parnassus*, Act. V (ll. 538–9).

KING JAMES VI (pp. 208–25).

209. 7, &c. James's references to his sources are put darkly. From the writers 'of auld,' whether classical or mediaeval, he could draw little help in his study of Scots prosody; and, as his statement that nothing had been written on the subject in Scots (l. 23) is still valid, the possible originals are narrowed down to English and French. It is difficult to interpret the phrase 'sindrie hes written of it in English' as we do not have, except in one case, any evidence, external or internal, how far the youthful author was then familiar with the criticism of Spenser and his friends and the other tracts printed in this volume, or whether he is referring in a general way to more technical rhetorical works such as Wilson's (cf. ll. 34, 35). The exception is Gascoigne's *Certayne Notes* (supra, pp. 46–57), though

James does not name it. The similar purpose of the two books and the parallelisms noted below seem to prove this, unless it be that in some places James, like Gascoigne (see note to p. 47, l. 7), has drawn direct from the French. He mentions Du Bellay (l. 30); and the 'sindrie others' may reasonably include Ronsard (see note to l. 30).

It has been surmised that the material of the volume of *Essayes of a Prentise in the Divine Art of Poesie*, in which this tract appears, was selected from the school-exercises which James had done when he was Buchanan's pupil at Stirling. It may be that his effort towards an *Ars Poetica* was directly inspired by his master's *De Prosodia* and his annotations on Vives (*Opera*, Edin. 1715, vol. ii).

12. *Flowing*, i.e. rhythm. Cf. p. 210, l. 26; p. 216, l. 28; p. 218, l. 34.

13. *Ryming in termes*: defined on p. 212, l. 25.

30. *Du Bellay*. See *La Defense et Illustration de la langue françoise* (1st edit. 1549), the *Epistre au Lecteur* prefixed to *L'Olive* (1st edit. 1549), the shorter poems *Discours au Roy sur la Poësie* and *Le Poëte courtisan* (added to *L'Olive*), and the *Epistre* to *Vers traduits* (1552).

See also Ronsard, *Préface de la Franciade* and *Abrégé de l'Art poétique françois* (1565).

210. 1-4. Cf. Thomas Randolphe's letter to Buchanan (Mar. 15, 1579): 'No lesse famous then *Apelles* Table was, & as voyde of Comptrollment as his Worke was, howe curiouse soeuer the Souter would seme to be' (Buchanan, *Opera*, 1715, ii; *Epist.* xxi). James's misquotation—and from his favourite Pliny (*N. H.* xxxv. (36) 10)—would show that the popular substitution of *ultra* for *supra* had been already accepted.

pantoun. Cf. Watson, 'Εκατομπαθία, 'To the Reader': '[say] to the second that though *Venus* be in my verse, yet her slipper is left out' (Spenser Soc. ed., p. 6).

5-13. Cf. Du Bellay, *Defense*, chap. xi; and Gascoigne, ante, p. 47 and note. See infra, p. 221, chap. vii. And cf. Wilson, *Arte of Rhetorique* [1553], fol. 3 v°: and Ben Jonson: 'But all this in vain, without a natural wit and a poetical nature in chief' (*Discoveries*, in *Works*, ed. Cunningham, iii. 421).

17. *blok*, plan, 'block out.' Cf. James's preface to the

Uranie, 'I haue put in the French on the one side of the leif, and my blocking on the other' (ed. Arber, p. 21).

24. *fete*; for *syllable,* though James uses the latter too (e. g. p. 212, l. 27; p. 213, l. 21).

211. 19-32. The characteristics of the poet here given are exclusively external and technical, as in Ronsard and Du Bellay. In some portions the resemblance may be due to direct suggestion (cf. Ronsard, *Préf. de la Franciade*; Du Bellay, *Le Poëte courtisan,* ll. 75-80, 113).

212. 5. *cullouris* (pl.), i.e. rhythm or metre—a Scots usage, to be distinguished from that other sense, 'figures,' 'ornaments,' 'rhetorical modes,' deduced from Cicero, Quintilian, and Horace, through Scaliger, *Poetice,* iii. 30. For the former sense cf., perhaps, Jonson, *Conversations,* XV; for the latter supra, p. 65, l. 32, Chaucer, *Squieres Tale,* ll. 30-1. Wilson, *Arte of Rhetorique* [1553], f. 94 v⁰. For the sing. form in the sense here, see p. 213, l. 11.

213. 21-4. Cf. Gascoigne, ante, p. 49, ll. 23-5.

26. This exclusive choice of the iamb may be, as has been suggested (Saintsbury, *Hist. Crit.* ii. 178), additional proof of French influence in this tract, but the limitation was already recognized. See Gascoigne, ante, p. 50, ll. 6-10, 23-7, the Spenser-Harvey correspondence, passim, and Webbe, p. 273, l. 4.

32. Cf. p. 224, l. 7.

214. 1-11. Obviously modelled on Gascoigne, ante, p. 50, l. 30-p. 51, l. 17. James's example is less happy.

12, &c. *Sectioun,* i.e. caesura.

215. 3-14. Contrast Gascoigne's placing of the caesura, ante, p. 54, § 13.

16. *monosyllabis.* Contrast Gascoigne, ante, p. 51, § 5.

26. *suppose,* though.

216. 29. Cf. Ronsard, *Abrégé de l'Art poétique,* u. s., p. 344.

217. 1-3. Cf. Gascoigne, ante, p. 48, ll. 31-3, and p. 51, § 6; Ronsard, u. s., p. 351.

10-11. James had many examples to choose from in mediaeval literature or in sixteenth-century Scots: and he may have been thinking of such passages as the opening lines of Du Bellay's *Exécration sur l'Angleterre.*

24. *Flyting*. This is a common sixteenth-century Scots form of poetic invective, allied to the older *tenson* and *estrif*, and analogous in excessive abuse to the Medicean *tenzone*.

25. *hurland ouer heuch*, i.e. dashing (driven violently) over craggy steeps.

33. *waill*, choose.

218. 1-10. *vocabula artis*. Cf. Gascoigne's 'apt vocables,' ante, p. 47, l. 12.

18-20. Cf. the Glosse on 'his name' in 'July' of the *Shepheardes Calender*. Contrast the 'indecorous' learning of the shepherds in the *Complaynt of Scotlande* (1549).

23, &c. *Tumbling verse*. See note to p. 223, l. 9.

219. 4. Orig. 'giue.'

9. *as for Comparisons*. Cf. Ronsard, *Préf. de la Franciade*, u.s., p. 188.

18. Ronsard speaks of epithets (*Abrégé*, u.s., p. 350), but against those which are unnecessary (e.g. *rivière courante*).

28. *corruptit wordis*. Cf. Sidney, supra, note to p. 204, l. 18.

220. 20-8. Cf. Gascoigne, ante, p. 48, ll. 9-23.

30-2. An anacoluthon: 'that ... *ye*' or '[that] ... to.'

221. 1. As James does in his *Phoenix*, e.g. p. 45 (ed. Arber).

5. *Inuention*. Cf. p. 210, ll. 5-13 (note).

10. Cf. Du Bellay, *Vers traduits* (*Epistre*), p. 4.

12, &c. Cf. ii. p. 33, ll. 18-19.

26. Cf. Gascoigne's 'ryding rime' and remarks thereon, ante, p. 56, § 16. Also Puttenham, Campion, and Daniel, by the Index.

222. 21. *learnit*. The example chosen will be found among James's poems in the *Lusus Regius* (ed. Rait, p. 17).

22. *Ballat Royal*, ballade royal, originally of seven lines of ten syllables, *a b a b b c c*, as in the *Kingis Quair* of James I, King of Scots; later, according to James VI, as here, with an additional line inserted between the sixth and seventh, *a b a b b c b c*. This is not the true *ottava rima*; nor is it the true *rhyme-royal*, though it frequently bears the name, and is historically related through it to the older French *chant-royal*. See next note.

32. *Troilus verse*, so-called from Chaucer's use of the seven-lined stanza in his *Troilus*, is the true *rhyme-royal*. This is Gascoigne's *rythme royall*, defined ante, p. 54, § 14. Chaucer,

it should be noted, uses *three* rhymes (*a b a b b c c*). James's example is from Alexander Montgomerie's *Echo* (S. T. S. edit. p. 138).

223. 9. *Rouncefallis or Tumbling verse.* The origin of the term *rouncefal*, which James VI here applies prosodically, is not clear. Stanyhurst uses it in the same sense, 'to tumble'—

'thee tree
At leingth with rounsefal, from stock vntruncked, yt harssheth'

(*Aen.*, ed. Arber, p. 63: see also p. 92). Dekker has 'Dost roare? th'ast a good rouncivall voice to cry Lanthorne and candle-light' (*Satiromastix*, 1602, p. 243). T. Heywood in the *Golden Age* (ii. 1) speaks of a 'bona roba, a rounceval, a virago, or a good manly lass'; and Gayton in 1654 (*Notes upon Don Quixote*, III. ii. 72) describes a certain woman as a 'more rare sight then we exhibit at Bartholomew Faire (take in to help it the reaking sweating Rouncifolds of Py-Corner too).' The underlying notion of a hoydenish, rough-and-tumble, 'falling-away' manner is well expressed in the line, and in the rush and bob of the stanza. I am indebted to Mr. W. A. Craigie for the above quotations from the collections for *N. E. D.*

The example is from Montgomerie's *Polwart and Montgomerie's Flyting* (S. T. S. edit. p. 69).

26-7. Cf. Gascoigne, ante, p. 55, l. 16.

31. *Commoun verse.* This stave is Gascoigne's *Ballade* (ante, p. 54, l. 35), which he also gives to 'matters of loue' (ib. p. 57, l. 1).

224. 3. *this*, thus (Middle Scots usage).

7. Cf. ante, p. 213, l. 32.

9. Montgomerie's *Cherrie and the Slae* (S. T. S. edit. p. 6).

WEBBE (pp. 226-302).

227. 27. *deuises.* Sir Egerton Brydges would find here an allusion to *The Paradyse of Daynty Deuices* (1578). See his edition, p. xxiv.

229. 16. *beeing not the firste.* Webbe refers (infra) to the critical opinions of, among others, Ascham, Gascoigne, Spenser, and Harvey; and has, indeed, small claim to originality in any portion of his Treatise.

30. *censure*, judgment, criticism (not necessarily adverse). Cf. p. 301, l. 21, note.

34. *thys reformed versifying.* See pp. 278 et seq.

230. 6. ποετρια. This impossible variant of ποίησις is the M. Lat. word *poetria* printed in Greek letters; the Greek word ποιήτρία means a poetess. *Poetria* was given currency by Geoffrey de Vinsauf's *Nova Poetria*, c. 1200. Webbe's scholarship throughout is not of the best, though he ventures on translation.

Cf. Sidney, ante, p. 155: and 'E. K.'s gloss to 'April' in the *Shepheardes Calender*.

18. *Phormio*, Prol. 18. Cf. also *Heaut.* Prol. 23. See infra, ii. p. 329, ll. 9-10, and ' E. K.'s gloss to 'December' of *The Shepheardes Calender*: 'Musick, that is Poetry, as Terence sayth . . ., speking of Poetes.'

24. *Panegeryca*, i.e. πανηγυρικά (συμπόσια, δεῖπνα). The whole passage (l. 20-p. 231, l. 5) is taken direct from 'E. K.'s gloss to 'October' of *The Shepheardes Calender*. Webbe omits 'E.K.'s clue to the passage in Plato (*Laws*, i).

231. 2. *Vates.* See ante, p. 154, l. 5, note. Webbe distinguishes between *Vates* and *Poeta*: just as Ronsard makes a further distinction between the original poets who conversed with oracles and prophets, and 'les seconds Poëtes' who were 'plus enflez d'artifice et labeur que de divinité' (*Abrégé*).

16. *Orig.* Ρ'ιθμος. Cf. p. 267, ll. 6-15.   20. *Orig.* λοητεία.

34. *Tusc.* i. 26 'sine caelesti aliquo mentis instinctu.' Cf. Webbe's words on the next page, ll. 2-3.

232. 5. *Fasti*, vi. 5. The emblem in 'October' of *The Shepheardes Calender*, from which Webbe quotes below.

7. *late*, recently.

10-11. *Shepheardes Calender*, ' October.'

21. *English Poet.* Cf. p. 246, l. 4, and note to p. 192, ll. 15-18. ' E. K.'s reference to this unknown work will be found in the argument to 'October' in *The Shepheardes Calender*. Grosart's '*soupçon* of suspicion' that it is 'incorporated or adapted' in Sidney's *Apologie* (ed. Spenser, i. pp. 99, 453) is probably of little value; and Collier's discovery of a reference to it in Nicholas Breton's 'Epitaph on Spenser' in his *Melancholike Humours* (ed. Spenser, i. cxlviii) is based on a misunderstanding of the

text. See Schelling's *Poetic and Verse Criticism of the Reign of Elizabeth*, Philadelphia, 1891, pp. 31-3.

234. 6, 7. *Orig.* 'made houses, and kept.'

235. 15. *delight . . . commoditie.* Cf. supra, p. 158, ll. 5-6, note, and p. 197, l. 3, note.

33. *none woorth the reading twyce* is said by Cicero of the plays of Livius Andronicus in particular ('Livianae fabulae vix satis dignae quae iterum legantur,' *Brutus*, 71): but his general drift in the passage is substantially what Webbe makes it.

236. 14. Aristotle, *Poetics*, i. 8. Webbe probably takes this at second-hand, as elsewhere in his references to the Aristotelian canon. He follows Horace not merely in the theory but in the historical illustrations, e.g. l. 24, where, with Lodge (supra, p. 81), he reproduces the order of *Sat.* i. 4 (though Cratinus is senior to the other two), and l. 26, where he recalls the association of Plato and Menander in *Sat.* ii. 3. In these examples he copies Fabricius Chemnicensis *verbatim*, whom he translates, infra, p. 295.

31. *Theagines.* Probably for the tragic poet Theognis (by confusion with the better known name of the hero in the *Aethiopica* of Heliodorus, supra, p. 388), of whose work but two words, φόρμιγξ ἄχορδος, survive. These are mentioned in Aristotle's *Rhetoric*, and in Demetrius, *De Elocutione*, 85. Aristophanes refers to him once or twice as a poet so dull and frigid (ψυχρός) that it snowed in Thrace when he brought out a play at Athens (Smith's *Class. Dict.*).

237. 20. Cf. Lodge, supra, p. 82.

30. Propertius ii. 32. 66. Quoted by Meres, infra, ii. p. 316, l. 3 (see note).

238. 15. C. Silius Italicus, author of the *Punica*.

239. 14. *Pallengenius.* See p. 30, l. 10, note.

Baptista Mantuanus. See p. 244, ll. 11-12, note.

15-16. Christopher Ocland, Master of Southwark and Cheltenham Schools, whose Latin poems appeared in 1582, in a volume entitled *Anglorum Praelia ab anno 1327 . . . vsque ad annum 1558. Item De Pacatissimo Angliae Statu imperante Elizabetha compendiosa Narratio.* The book was ordered by the Privy Council to be taught 'in all grammar and free schools within this realme.' Alexander Neville's *Kettus, sive de furoribus*

Norfolciensium Ketto Duce is included in the volume. Cf. Hall's *Satires* (ed. Grosart), iv. 3, ll. 16-17:—

> 'Or cyte olde *Oclands* verse, how they did weild
> The wars in *Turwin*, or in *Turney* field.'

240. 14. See supra, p. 29, ll. 31, &c.; p. 32, l. 21.

241. 4-5. Now in the edition by Mr. G. C. Macaulay, 4 vols., Oxford, 1899-1902.

10. *the God of English Poets*, &c. So Spenser, 'The God of Shepheards, *Tityrus*, is dead' (*Sh. Cal.*, 'June'); and 'E. K.' in his gloss '... by Tityrus is meant Chaucer, ... whom he calleth the God of Poetes for his excellencie.'

242. 9. *quantity*. Webbe's description of Langland's verse is not clear. If he be using 'quantity' as in p. 281, l. 1, his account is not less inadequate.

23. *ninth*; an error for the *eleventh* eclogue ('November') of the *Shepheardes Calender* (q. v.).

31. *the olde Earle of Surrey*. (See p. 126, l. 2, note.) The first collection of his poems appeared in *Tottel's Miscellany* (1557). See the editions by Nott (1815-16), Yeowell ('Aldine,' 1866), and Arber (1870, &c.).

32. L. Vaus, i.e. Thomas Vaux, second Baron Vaux of Harrowden (1510-56), whose poems appeared posthumously in *Tottel's Miscellany* (1557) and *The Paradyse of Daynty Deuises* (1576). See ii. p. 413.

Thomas Norton of Bristow. See supra, p. 30, l. 8, note.

33. Richard Edwardes (? 1523-66), Master of the Children of the Chapel Royal (1561), author of *Palamon and Arcite* (1566), and of the comedy *Damon and Pithias* (1571).

Thomas Tusser (? 1524-80), author of the popular *Hundreth Good Pointes of Husbandrie* (1st edit. 1557).

Thomas Churchyard (? 1520-1604), a contributor to *Tottel's Miscellany*, and chiefly known by his occasional booklets or broadsheets (*Churchyardes Chippes*, 1575, &c.).

William Hunnis (*d.* 1597), Master of the Children of the Chapel Royal (1566), author of *A Hyve full of Hunnye* (1578), and some metrical psalms. Webbe quotes from him on p. 277.

Haiwood. This may be either John Heywood the epigrammatist (see Index) or Jasper Heywood (1535-98), who contributed to the *Paradyse of Daynty Deuises*, and to the English *Seneca*. The context favours the latter ascription.

34. *Sand*. The 'D. S.' and 'D. Sand' of the *Paradyse of Daynty Deuises* have been identified, on slender evidence, with Dr. Edwin Sandys (?1516–88).

Hyll. Perhaps the 'R. Hill' (also printed 'Hall') of the *Paradyse of Daynty Deuises*.

S. Y. Is this the 'M. Yloop' (perhaps for Pooly), one of the contributors to the above (see title-page of edit. 1576)?

M. D. Is this 'Master Dyer' (see p. 89, l. 7, note)?

243. 7. *Earle of Oxford*, i.e. the seventeenth Earl (1550–1604). See notes to ii. p. 63, l. 32; p. 65, l. 26.

14. *D.* Phaer: an error for T[homas] Phaer, repeated on p. 256, l. 25. For Phaer and Twyne see note to p. 137, l. 29.

27. Arthur Golding's translation of the *Metamorphoses* appeared in 1565 (*The Fyrst Fower Bookes*) and in 1567 (*The XV Bookes*).

35. *Googe ... Pallengenius*. See supra, p. 30, l. 10, note.

244. 3. Abraham Fleming (?1552–1607). Cf. also p. 266, l. 1.

5. *one of hys name*. Is Webbe alluding to Samuel Fleming of King's College (see ii. p. 425)? Or, if he refers to the Christian name, can he be thinking of Abraham Fraunce?

11–12. *Seneca in English*. See note to p. 312, l. 1.

the other partes of Ouid, i.e. *The Heroycall Epistles*, by George Turberville, 1567 (see p. 315, l. 11, note), and the first three books of the *De Tristibus*, by Churchyard (1580).

Horace, by Drant (see note on p. 373).

Mantuan. *The Eglogs of the Poet B. Mantuan Carmelitan*, by George Turberville (1567). See p. 315, ll. 11–12, note.

29. *Whetstone*. See p. 58.

31. Anthony Munday (1553–1633). Cf. the allusion in ii. Appendix, p. 490, l. 13.

245. 2. Iohn Graunge (fl. 1577), author of *The Golden Aphroditis* (1577). Webbe quotes from him on p. 277.

Knyght. Mr. H. Morley suggests *Edward Knight*. 'Little is known of Edward Knight, whose initials "E. K., Gentleman," are before commendatory verses prefixed to Munday's *Mirror of Mutabilitie*, "Ed. Knight" being signed at the end. This must be Webbe's "Knyght" in the list of good poets—the only known person who might be the "E. K." of Spenser's *Shepheardes Calendar*, if he was not Edward Kirke' (*English Writers*, ix. 152).

Robert Wylmott (fl. 1568-1608), was to bring out, in 1591, a second edition of the Tragedy of *Tancred and Gismund* (written by 'The Gentlemen of the Inner Temple' and acted in 1568), in which the older decasyllabic rhymed quatrains are 'polished according to the decorum of these daies,' i.e. in blank verse. Webbe was interested in Wilmot's venture, and wrote an epistle for the revised version. There he speaks of the play as 'a work, either in stateliness of shew, depth of conceit, or true ornaments of poetical art, inferior to none of the best in that kind: no, were the Roman Seneca the censurer.' And again: 'Your commendable pains in disrobing him of his antique curiosity, and adorning him with the approved guise of our stateliest English terms (not diminishing, but more augmenting his artificial colours of absolute poesy, derived from his first parents) cannot but be grateful to most men's appetites, who upon our experience we know highly to esteem such lofty measures of sententiously confused tragedies.' (Dodsley, ed. 1825, ii. 160-4.)

Darrell? This can hardly be the antiquary William Darell (*d*. 1580). Googe's wife was a Darrell of Scotney, Kent.

F. C. Mr. H. Morley suggests that this is a misprint for *F. G.*, i.e. Fulke Greville.

F. K.? Francis Kinwelmersh (*d*. ?1580), who collaborated with Gascoigne and contributed to the *Paradyse of Daynty Deuises*.

G. B. Perhaps G. Bucke, who adds a Quatorzain in commendation of Thomas Watson in the Ἑκατομπαθία (Spens. Soc. edit. p. 11). A George Buc or Bucke (*d*. 1623), a minor poet, knighted in 1603, was Master of the Revels from 1608. Or is he the 'M. Bewe' who contributes to the *Paradyse of Daynty Deuices*, which Webbe has much in mind?

10. *Master Sp*. See note to p. 112, l. 12.

17. *Gabriell Haruey*. See note to p. 284, l. 4.

31-5. Cf. p. 284, ll. 3-5.

246. 3-4. *his Dreames, his Legends*, &c. See p. 100, l. 24 (note); p. 133, l. 7 (note); and p. 232, l. 21 (note).

8. *hys two brethren*: John Harvey (1564-92), and Richard Harvey (1560-1623).

Notes

246. 28-34. Probably a reference to Elderton. See ante, p. 125, l. 28 (note). With the pun in l. 30 cf. Nash, infra, p. 333, l. 35.

247. 3-16. Quoted from 'E. K.', ante, p. 131.

248. 26, &c. Webbe here repeats the mediaeval distinction between tragedy and comedy borrowed from Donatus and the neo-classical critics. Cf. Puttenham, infra, ii. p. 33 et seq. On the question of the influence of the *Iliad* and *Odyssey* in defining these kinds, see Scaliger, *Poetice*, i. 4.

250. 19-20. *Ars Poet.* ll. 333-4.

26-27. ib., ll. 343-4.

251. 4. ib., l. 338.

31. *Ep.* ii. 1. 126. [Orig. *fugitat.*]

35. Sir Thomas Elyot (1490 ?-1546).

252. 1-8. See Mr. Croft's edition of Elyot's *Gouernour*, i. 123. The third line reads 'Pullyng their eares from wordes unclene.'

17. Orig. 'but it is were.'

253. 3. *inconueniences.* Cf. p. 65, l. 32 (note).

255. 22, &c. Webbe's definition of the Epic may be compared with Puttenham's, infra.

256. 19. Quintil. x. 1 (514).

25. *D.* Phaer. See note to p. 243, l. 14.

257. 15, &c. *Aen.* i. 201-13. Webbe does not give the extracts from Phaer quite *verbatim*.

258. 15. *Aen.* iv. 1.

259. 9. Ib., l. 589.

260. 16. Ib., ix. 664.

261. 8-9. *towardes the end.* Not so; l. 181.

262. 4. *Golding.* See note to p. 243, l. 27.

15, &c. *Eglogues.* Cf. The General Argument of *The Shepheardes Calender*.

23. *Titus Calphurnius*, i.e. T. Julius Calpurnius, Sicilian, whose volume *Eclogae Septem* was printed first at Parma in 1478, and in many later editions with the Eclogues of Nemesianus. See Fabricius, *Bibl. Lat.* p. 554 et seq.

24. *Mantuan.* See p. 239, l. 14 (note), and p. 244, l. 12 (note).

263. 4. *Sp.* See p. 245, l. 10 (note).

29. See ante, p. 128, ll. 1-7.

264. 25-**265.** 5. Cf. 'E. K.' in Gloss to 'January' of *The Shepheardes Calender*.

265. 12-13. Cf. p. 279, l. 21. Webbe's wisdom is but Horace's, *Ars Poet.* 9 &c. and 465.

22. Tusser. Supra, p. 242, l. 33 (note).

27. Googe. Supra, p. 243, l. 35 (note).

29. Heresbachius, Conradus (1496-1576), author of *Rei Rusticae Libri Quatuor* (Cologne, 1570), Englished in 1577 by Googe in his *Foure Bookes of Husbandrie*.

266. 1. *Flemming.* Supra, p. 244, l. 3 (note).

4-16. There is no record of the separate publication of Webbe's pirated verses. He himself gives his version of the First and Second Eclogues, infra, p. 284.

27. Supra, p. 240.

267. 6-15. Cf. p. 231, l. 16. Cf. also Gascoigne, ante, p. 50, ll. 4-5, 27.

22, &c. Borrowed from Ascham, ante, p. 32. See also Willes, ante, p. 47 (footnote).

268. 5. The 'three speciall notes' are taken from Gascoigne. See ante, p. 49, §§ 3 and 4.

270. 9-10. 'January' eclogue.

271. 9. See the 'April' eclogue, before the 'Song.'

11-19. Repeated on p. 286.

28. 'August' eclogue.

272. 3-11 'November' eclogue.

19. *Rogero ... Trenchmore.* Cf. Gosson, *Schoole of Abuse*, 'neyther pyped *Rogero* nor *Turkelony*' (ed. Arber, p. 26).

30. *Powlters Measure*: borrowed from Gascoigne, ante, p. 56, l. 8.

273. 4. *the old Iambicke stroake.* See note to p. 213, l. 26.

10-13. Cf. Gascoigne, p. 51, and James VI, p. 214.

29. See ante, p. 268, l. 11 (and note).

274. 1. *chouching*, couching. See *N. E. D.*, s. v. *Couch* v.[1] § 15. It is difficult to account for this form.

15. *anothers* (orig. *Authors*).

275. 10, &c. A tardy acknowledgment to Gascoigne's *Certayne Notes*, printed supra, pp. 46-57. The passage here referred to will be found on p. 52.

276. 16-17. See Puttenham, infra, Book ii.

24. 'August' eclogue.

27. Orig. *pact*.

34. Iohn Graunge. See p. 245, l. 2.

277. 18. W. Hunnis. See p. 242, l. 33.

279. 21. *without any prescription of rules.* Cf. p. 265, ll. 12–15. Perhaps a sly reference to the much-talked-of 'Rules of Master Drant' (supra, p. 90, l. 13, note).

280. 18. *Choreus*: called later *Trochaeus*, which Webbe reserves for the tribrach. See next note.

21. *Tribrachys.* By a well-intentioned error of the press, this has been substituted for 'Trochaeus' in Webbe's text. The foot is a tribrach, but Webbe adopts the alternative usage allowed by Cicero (*Or.* 57. 193) and Quintilian (ix. 4. 82) by which *trochaeus* is a name of the tribrach. Puttenham and others follow the accepted rule.

25-6. For the reverse definition of *Bacchius* and *Palimbacchius* see Quintil. ix. 4 (484). See also Scaliger, *Poetice*, ii. 3, and Fabricius Chemnicensis, Bk. VI (p. 265 a).

33. *Tallæus.* Audomarus Tallaeus or Talaeus, editor of Cicero's *De Oratore* (1553), published his own *Rhetorica* at Paris in 1552. For other references see notes, infra, p. 309, l. 11; ii. p. 245, ll. 6 and 10.

281. 15. *Position.* Cf. Harvey (p. 118, l. 20; p. 121, l. 4, note, 22-33). For the place of 'Position' &c. in academic criticism, see Fabricius, *De Re Poetica*, i. 1, from which Webbe borrows the *Catholica*, infra, p. 290.

282. 7-8. From this it would appear that Webbe had not seen Stanyhurst's volume, where long 'I' is common. (See the article by Mr. R. B. McKerrow, in *The Modern Language Quarterly*, V. i. 7.)

283. 3. See the complete verse on p. 284.

9. This is a wrong-headed reference to Surrey's Virgil 'drawn into a strange meter' (ante, p. 32, l. 24).

12-20. Watson's lines were certainly 'in the mouthes of all men.' Cf. Ascham's *Scholemaster* (ed. Mayor, 71); Spenser and Harvey, supra, p. 118, l. 13; Kendall's *Flowers of Epigrammes* (1577). See Sidney's commentary on the Latin quotation in the letter to his brother Robert (*Correspondence*, ed. Pears, pp. 196–7).

28-9. See p. 99, ll. 21-2, and note.

284. 4. Cf. Webbe's passage on p. 245. See the specimens

in the Spenser-Harvey correspondence, ante, p. 87 et seq., and 'E. K.'s Postscript, ante, p. 134, and note.

284. 13. See note to p. 266, ll. 4-16.

285. 20-1. Ovid, *Amores*, iii. 8. 3-4.

26-7. Ovid, *Epist. ex Ponto*, iv. 3. 35-6.

30. Orig. *Phalocium*.

286. 2, &c. The verses are quoted by Webbe on p. 271.

289. 18. Orig. *Chores*: Webbe's (or his printer's) confusion with *Chore*, &c. on p. 286.

290. 13. *the Cannons . . . gathered by Georgius Fabricius Chemnicensis* (orig. *Cremnicensis*, in error). These are a translation of the concluding section of the 6th Book of the enlarged edition of Fabricius's *De Re Poetica Libri Septem* (printed in 1560). See pp. 300 a-305 b of the 1584 Paris edition, reprinted infra, as an Appendix to the Notes to Webbe (pp. 417-21). George Fabricius (1516-71) must not be confused with Jo. Albertus Fabricius who is referred to supra and infra. His Life (with a portrait) by Schreber appeared at Leipzig in 1717.

292. § 12. Cf. Arist. *Poetics*, xv.

293. 8-9. Cic. *De Opt. Gen. Orat.* 5 (14). Cf. Horace, *Ars Poet.* 133.

15. *In a Comedie*: 'In genere Dramatico' (G. Fabricius).

23-5. Cicero, *De Deorum Natura*, i. 20. 53.

294. 9. *inconuenience*. Cf. note to p. 253, l. 3.

295. 17-21. Cf. Scaliger, *Poetice*, i. 7.

297. 1. *A Poet is*, &c. Cf. Sidney, supra, p. 195, l. 23, and note.

299. 5. *Angellius*. Nic. Angellius edited Macrobius in 1515 (Basle). See J. A. Fabricius, *Bibl. Lat.* p. 622.

8. *Mummius*. Webbe follows the text of Fabricius in reading *Memmius*.

12. C. Sollius Apollinaris Sidonius (*d.* 482), Bishop of Auvergne (Clermont), whose *Carmina XXIV* and *Epistolarum libri IX* are extant (1st edit. Milan, 1498). See J. A. Fabricius, u.s., pp. 634-6.

21. *De Orat.* ii. 78.

300. 2. See Quintil. iv. 2. 191. Scaliger, *Poetice*, iii. 32.

301. 8. Webbe repeats the error in the text of Fabricius ($\kappa\rho\tilde{\eta}\psi\iota\nu$).

14. *Ars Poet.* l. 322.

21. *exquisite censure*, exact (careful) criticism.

Appendix to Notes on Webbe.

(See note to p. 290.)

Q. HORATII FLACCI DE *ARTE POETICA* CATHOLICA.

Ex Epistola ad Pisones.

I. *Inuentio sit ad materiam accommodata, non dissidens, non aliena, non monstrosa. Nam mulieris caput, ceruix equi, corpus auis varie coloratum, membra e variis animantibus collecta, pedes in caudam piscis exeuntes, in pictura monstrum deforme faciunt: quod si eadem sit in oratione diuersitas, quid potest dici mendosius?*

II. *Ornamenta nec nimia sint, nec temere quaesita, nec vbique adhibeantur aut ostententur.*

III. *Forma dicendi obseruanda, ne grauia tenuiter, prolixa breuiter dicantur, hoc ad decorum pertinet & ad materiam, vt cum rebus magis verba grandia consentiant.*

IV. *In descriptionibus poëticis, fidem ne excedat oratio, neve sit plane contra naturam inducta fictio.*

V. *Dispositio talis sit, ne peccetur exquisita sedulitate, aliqua omitti possunt, aliqua prolixitate nocent: nec est vna pars excolenda, & relinquenda altera. Id probat exemplo fabri, qui caput & superiorem corporis partem exprimebat artificiose, reliquum opus absoluere non poterat. Probat idem suo iudicio, quod nollet corporis parte reliqua esse pulcher, & naso esse adunco deformis. Omnia membra similia & composita sint oportet, in integro & bene formato corpore.*

VI. *Videndum est, num quis par esse possit ei materiae, quam tractandam suscipere cogitat. Ingenii enim vires saepe imprudentem vel incautum destituunt.*

VII. *Elocutio in verbis posita est, & in verborum formis. Verba sunt aut simplicia aut coniuncta, vetera aut noua, propria aut translata. In singulis vtendum iudicio & prudentia, & vsitatorum praecipuus honor est. Eadem enim ratio verborum, quae nummorum, vt vsitata & probata magis valeant.*

VIII. *Considerandum genus carminis, & accommodandum argumentis, & qui nuneri sint ad quoduis genus accommodati magis. Carminum genera vsitatissimorum quatuor, Heroicum, Elegiacum, Iambicum, Lyricum.*

IX. *Non vno orationis genere in omnibus scriptis est vtendum. Insurgunt interdum Lyrici, interdum Comici. Conueniunt autem grandia proprie tragicis, humilia comicis. Fit autem vt ideae misceantur, pro ratione temporis aut loci.*

X. *Affectuum habenda ratio est: aliud decet hilares, aliud tristes: aliud iracundos, aliud lenes, quare cum industria tractandi sunt. Requiruntur autem tria in carmine, pulchritudo, suauitas, animorum affectio. Theophrastus scripsit, pulchritudinem esse quandam deceptionem, & Aristoteles eam vocat τυραννίδα ὀλιγοχρόνιον. Suauitas retinet lectorem, affectus mouent.*

XI. *Personis danda sunt sua conuenientia, vt oratio sit bene morata.*

In hac parte consideranda dignitas, aetas, sexus, fortuna, conditio, prouincia, patria.

XII. *Personae sumuntur aut a poëtis aliis, aut finguntur a nobis. Si sumuntur ab aliis, obseruandum est* τὸ ὅμοιον, *hoc est, vt sequamur eum auctorem exacte, quem ad imitandum proposuimus, cuius rei ponuntur exempla. Sin finguntur nouae a nobis retinendum est* τὸ ὁμαλόν, *id est, aequale, vt ita personas introducamus, vt vbique sibi conueniant, & vt extrema primis respondeant, ne hominem modo audacem introducamus, modo prudentem, & cautum: id enim viciosum est. In vtroque seruandum* τὸ ἁρμόττον, *quod hoc loco vertit conuenientiam, vt conueniens est, virum esse fortem, mulierem timidam, seruum callidum, adolescentem ingenuum.*

XIII. *Quae communia sunt: ita tractentur, vt propria fiant. Materiae communes sunt, de quibus omnes possunt dicere, quas si ita quis tractet, vt praecipuam laudem consequatur, facit eas proprias & suas, vt multi scripserunt de bello Troiano, sed quod commune fuit, id sibi proprium fecit Homerus.*

XIV. *De Graecis quia sumenda multa, vt Latini omnes sumpserunt, non eadem verba vt interpreti sunt exprimenda, sed libertate quadam vtendum est, ingenii atque iudicii, qualis esse solet imitatoris.*

Hoc praeceptum de Cicerone transtulit, qui inquit, Non verbum verbo necesse est reddere.

XV. *Exordium ne sit ineptum, hoc est, alienum, aut tumidum.*

XVI. *Propositio vel narratio e propinquo petita & verisimilis sit. In narrando decorum aetatum ne negligatur.*

XVII. *In genere Dramatico, non necessarium est omnia facta palam exhibere, vt sunt crudelia, turpia, monstrosa: sed ea narrare ut gesta sunt, oratione commoda & pudica, multo rectius & speciosius est.*

XVIII. *In comoedia plures esse actus, quam quinque, molestum, pauciores illepidum.*

Deorum personas inducere non decet, nisi in rebus maximis. Cicero: 'Poëtae Tragici cum explicare argumenti exitum non possunt, ad Deum confugiunt.'

Plures personae quam quatuor ne loquantur propter confusionem.

Chori sint morati, in quibus aut admoneantur homines, aut reprehendantur, aut instituantur ad virtutem.

Chori materia eligatur eiusmodi, quae sit argumento praesenti apta atque congrua.

Instrumenta & cantus referantur ad simplicitatem vetustam.

Musica enim theatralis, & cantuum licentia, quae cum opibus Romanorum creuit, est perniciosa disciplinae & moribus.

XIX. *In Satyra grex rusticus, & dii agrestes producuntur ad temperandam ludo & iocis Tragoediae tristiciam. In iocis tenendum, ne sint lasciui, scurriles, maledici, quod praeceptum in genere ad alia scripta omnia pertinet.*

In satyra habenda ratio est loci, vt diei festi, personarum, vt Bacchi, Sileni, Satyrorum: argumenti ne misceantur inconuenientia: verborum, vt sint apta personis: decori, ne qui in Tragoedia fuit heros, in Satyra introducatur ardelio: auditorum denique, ne offendantur, si misceantur ridiculis foeda, turpibus lasciua, iocosis probrosa.

XX. *Eligendi pedes carminis vniuscuiusque proprii, in eoque nimia licentia non est vtendum.*

Veteres in Iambico vsi puris iambis, deinceps assumptus est spondeus in locis inaequalibus.

Secuta postea talis licentia est, vt & spondeo liberrime, & pedibus aliis peregrinis, nequaquam festiue vterentur.

XXI. *Adhibenda in carmine scribendo cura & attentio.*

Quae ex tempore fiunt carmina, tanquam operae leues habentur, quae sine arte fiunt, eiiciuntur vt ineptae. Hoc quamuis multi non curant, tamen incuria auditoris, esse non debet causa negligentiae & erroris.

Qui scribere digna eruditis auribus cupit, auctores Graecos studiose legat, nec vnquam deponat de manibus.

XXII. *Artes habent sua incrementa, vt caeterae in natura res. Ita Tragoedia, quae primum rudis fuit auctore Thespi, posteris temporibus ornamenta accepit ab Aeschylo, primum acta ruri in vicis, deinde in theatris vrbium magnarum.*

XXIII. *Artes quaedam oriuntur, quaedam intercidunt, naturali quadam vicissitudine. Intercidit Comoedia vetus, propter maledicentiam, qua aperte lacerabantur homines: ei petulantiae statuta poena est, ne nimium acerbitas progrederetur. In eius locum Satyra successit apud Latinos. Veteris Comoediae auctores fuerunt Eupolis, Cratinus, Aristophanes: mediae, Plato Comicus: recentioris, Menander, quae in vsu mansit, & celebris facta est.*

XXIV. *Non simus contenti aliorum inuentis, sed & ipsi exemplo veterum aliquid nostra industria proseramus, quod laude sit dignum. Hoc fecerunt, qui scripserunt apud Latinos Togatas, quae habebant argumenta Graeca: vel qui scripserunt Praetextatas, quae argumenta Latina.*

XXV. *Vt carmen sit perfectum, id efficit cura & compositio: ideo quod tale non est, merito reprehenditur. Ingenii facultas artem superat.*

XXVI. *Poëta vt perfectus fiat, eget cognitione eius philosophiae, quae mores efficit meliores. Quae ad naturam spectat, minus plausibilis est, & minus ornamentorum habet & minus est vtilis.*

XXVII. *Ad philosophiam maior addenda est poëtae scientia, vt nouerit mores hominum, & ingenia populorum: id fit peregrinando, vt quae scribenda sunt, ita exprimat, atque variet, vt fiant narrationes speciosae.*

XXVIII. *Finis poëticae est, vt scribantur iucunda & vtilia. Iucundum est, quod delectat, nempe quod non nimis prolixum, quodve memoria teneri potest, itaque quod verisimile, & non plane ficticium. Vtile est quod animos incitat doctrina & sapientia.*

XXIX. *Ignoscendum est delictis quibusdam, praesertim in magno opere. Errores committuntur aut in arte propria, aut in aliena. Errare poëtam in praeceptis, turpe est: in aliena arte errorem committere, magis ferendum, vt a Virgilio in aditu Africae fingitur Aeneas ceruos iaculatus, cum Africa ceruum non habeat. Errores iisdem contingunt, aut incuria, cum peccatur negligentia, aut communi hominum fragilitate, quia nemo inuentus, qui nouerit omnia. Itaque hi postremi errores etiam non sunt exagitandi.*

XXX. *Bonus poëta hoc agat, vt semper delectet, & auditorem lectoremve detineat. In pictura quaedam delectant longius posita, quaedam adhibita propius. Contra, poëta & in vmbra & in sole delectationem asserat.*

XXXI. *In poëta nihil admittitur mediocre, qui nisi excellentissimus sit, deterrimus est.*

XXXII. *Poema nisi sit dulce & aequale, ingratum est: id probatur sensibus duobus, vt auditu & gustatu in cibis iucundis. Ita igitur sit poema, vt suauitate sit gratum, & sui simile sit, vsque ad finem, ne quem a legendo moretur & absterreat.*

XXXIII. *Qui scripturus est aliquid posteritate dignum, ne id aggrediatur, natura non adiuuante.*

Non e ligno omni fit Mercurius, vt est in prouerbio, nec omnium studiis aut laboribus fauet Minerua. Praestantissima est in omni arte, natura, & poetam non tam fieri, quam nasci sermone eruditorum dicitur.

XXXIV. *Nemo tam doctum se existimet, quin aliorum iudiciis sua scripta subiiciat, & ea domi sapius retractet atque corrigat.*

XXXV. *Vtilitas poëticae inde propagata est, quia veteres scripserunt optima, ad hominum videlicet vitam, mores, & felicitatem pertinentia, suaque scripta longo tempore examinata, iam senes protulerunt.* Vsus poëticae quis olim fuerit, exemplis hominum doctissimorum constat. Orphei, qui primum villas condidit : Amphionis, qui vrbes: Tyrtaei, qui bella fortiter gessit: Homeri, qui scripsit sapienter.

XXXVI. *In poëta artifice tria requiruntur, natura, ars, & diligentia.*

XXXVII. *Discendum a peritis, & erroris confessio scribenti necessaria, vt quod malum est vitet, & meliora discat facere.*

Erroris confessio animi magni est & ingenui.

De Hippocrate medico scribunt Celsus & Quintilianus, quod errores quosdam, ne posteros deciperet, sit confessus, more scilicet magni viri, & fiduciam rerum magnarum habentis. Leuia enim ingenia, quia nihil habent, nihil sibi detrahunt, vt idem Celsus ait.

XXXVIII. *In eligendis amicis, qui verum nos doceant, & scripta emendent nostra, acri iudicio vtendum est: ne eligantur imperiti, adulatores fraudulenti, imperiti iudicare nesciunt, adulatores metuunt offendere, fraudulenti non laudanda solent commendare.*

XXXIX. *Nemo se ipse fallat, aut falli se ab aliis patiatur, sed ad emendationem scriptorum adhibeat grauem virum iudicem, eiusque consilio mutet ac deleat, quae corrigenda & expolienda videbuntur.*

XL. *Qui adulator non est, & post scriptionem iudicare nouit, rei nulli magis incumbat, quam emendationi, idque faciat graui studio & iudicio exquisito.* Id qui non facit, & hac in re qui peccat sponte, & famam temere prostituit : is pro insano & furioso & cer[r]ito habeatur.

XLI. *Vicia versuum sunt septem, vt eorum qui carent arte, facilitate, ornatu: item eorum, qui sunt superflui, obscuri, ambigui, otiosi.*

Ex Epistolis ad Maecenatem, Augustum, Florum.

XLII. *Imitatio non sit seruilis nec superstitiosa, quasi non audeas ab exemplo decedere, neque eadem sit fatua & imprudens, vt etiam imiteris non imitanda & viciosa.*

XLIII. *Alienis vestigiis non semper insistendum, viam enim interdum non tritam ab aliis & inusitatam, ingredi licet.*. Horatius carmen Iambicum mutuatus ab Archilocho est, eiusque numeros & elegantiam expressit: turpitudinem in verbis, & in conuiciis dicacitatem vitauit prudenter.

XLIV. *In carmine aura popularis non captanda, sed videndum, vt doctorum iudiciis probentur, ea quae scripta sunt.*

XLV. *Iudicium vulgi de poëtis raro verum, ideo non est sequendum.* Iudicauit autem vulgus Romae, quod Pacuuius esset doctus, Accius grandiloquus, quod Afranius imitator Menandri, Plautus Epicharmi, quod Terentius arte esset superior, Caecilius grauitate: sed non idem periti sentiebant. Extat apud Macrobium nescio an Angellium, de iis qui scripserunt epigrammata, simile iudicium, de Rhetoris Antonii Iuliani sententia, quod Catullus

& Caluus bona pauca, Neuius implicata, Hortentius inuenusta, Cinna illepida, Mummius dura scripserit.

XLVI. *Antiqui ita sunt laudandi ne nouis detrahatur, nec aliis putetur iter interclusum ad magna perueniendi. Scite Sidonius ad Eucherium, Veneror antiquos, non tamen ita, vt meorum aequaeuorum virtutes aut merita postponam.*

XLVII. *Nouitas grata est, si sit erudita: nam artes non simul inchoari & perfici certum est, sed tempore & studio excoluntur: quae tamen si ad summum peruenerint, rursus minuuntur & quasi decrescunt.*

Cic. de Orat. Nihil est in natura rerum omnium, quod se vniuersum profundat, & quod totum repente euolet.

XLVIII. *Artem nemo exercere audet in primis periculosam, qui eam non bene didicerit: id faciunt gubernatores, faciunt idem medici: sed hoc minime fecerunt poëtae quidam Romani, quos calor & impetus tantus tulit, vt scribendis carminibus fere omnes gloriam quaererent, pauci tamen assequerentur.*

XLIX. *Poëta affectuum tractandorum non sit minus peritus, quam funambulus aut magus artis suae esse solet: tum ea euidentia res describat, vt lector non audire, sed ipsis locis & negociis, vbi quid agitur, interesse videatur. Eam facultatem* ὑποτύπωσιν *Fabius,* πρὸ ὀμμάτων θέσιν ἢ ποίησιν *vocat Aristoteles.*

L. *Poëtae aut in theatris placere cupiunt, vt Comici & Tragici: aut in bibliothecis student reponi.*

Theatrales affectuum animi habeant rationem, vt permoueant spectatorum aures & oculos. Ii vero qui intra parietes placere expetunt, sumant ad scribendum otium, & ad expoliendum tempus, vt possint satisfacere politis virorum sapientissimorum iudiciis in vmbra.

LI. *Poëta non sit importunus, vt auditu intempestiuo offendat: non difficilis, vt aliorum admonitiones spernat, non ambitiosus, vt sua scripta nimis admiretur: non morosus vt satis praemiorum tribui sibi non posse existimet: non superbus denique, vt honorari vltra modum velit.*

LII. *Necessaria poëtae est emendatio, vt obscuris lucem, splendorem vulgatis addat. Omnia impropria, leuia, parum decora tollat atque deleat, antiquos, cum iudicio imitetur, nimis ambitiosa rescindat, aspera leuiget, sanitate sermonis in toto scripto vtatur, quae virtute carent, ea arte & ordine corrigat.*

LIII. *Suscipiat primum partes actoris poëta, vt sic habeatur, quasi non scribat attente, nec scripta sua expoliat, vt quiuis putet, se similia posse efficere, propter simplicitatem. Suscipiat praeterea partes histrionis, vt videatur vulgaria & vsitata agere: non tamen eadem agere propter varietatem: nec laborasse, sed lusisse, nec sudasse, sed exercuisse videatur. Nam artem sic celare, vt nihil appareat laboriosum aut exquisitum, cum tamen studio & cura expolita sint omnia, maxima virtus est, quam Aristoteles* κρύψιν *appellat.*

LIV. *Sapientia non ea sola est, vti verbis multis & elegantibus, sed ea etiam scire ac dicere, quae ad vitam bene beateque agendam pertinent, vnde artem poëticam sine cognitione & scientia philosophiae, nugas canoras supra nominauit. Itaque poëtam bonum & legitimum, oportet esse ornatum verbis, & sententiis sapientem, & oratori si non parem, certe maxime propinquum & philosopho amicissimum.*

Fraunce (pp. 303–6).

Fraunce's *Arcadian Rhetorike* and his earlier *Lawier's Logike* (1588), his other prose work in English, probably owe something, if only in inception, to Thomas Wilson's popular *Arte of Rhetorique* (1553) and his earlier *Rule of Reason, conteinyng the Arte of Logique* (1551). They belong to the same class, though, like Richard Sherry's *Treatise of Schemes and Tropes* (1550), or William Fulwood's *Enimie of Idlenesse* (1568), they are more exclusively devoted to the collection of illustrative passages from ancient and modern authors. *The Arcadian Rhetorike* shows an advance on these in respect of its wider range of comparison, and it is for this, and its incidental references to Spenser, rather than for any critical value, that it is remembered. The *Returne from Parnassus* (Pt. i, Act 4, Sc. 1) pokes fun at these books, perhaps at Fraunce's own title-page.

Fraunce's books of verse, *The Lamentations of Amintas*, a translation of Thomas Watson's *Amyntas* (1587), *The Countesse of Pembrokes Yvychurch* (Parts I and II, 1591; Part III, 1592), and *The Countess of Pembrokes Emanuell* (1591), are written in hexameters, but they do not contain any critical observations, even on their metrical form. In these, according to Ben Jonson (by Drummond's report), Fraunce 'was a foole,' but perhaps not a greater than many of his contemporaries who experimented in the 'English hexameter.'

303. ll. 20, &c. *Countesse of Pembroke*, &c. See the titles of the poems named above. Fraunce was Sidney's friend. In his *Lawier's Logike* he tells us that the book had grown out of an early discourse on logic in presence of Sir Philip Sidney. He gives passages from Sidney's *Arcadia* and *Sonnets* in the *Rhetorike*: and the title is probably a direct compliment to his hero.

305. 26. *forme of an egge*, &c. See ante, p. 32, l. 11, note; p. 47, note.

27. *Willy*. See p. 47, footnote, and p. 126, l. 17.

32. *Sheph. Cal.* In his *Lawier's Logike*, Fraunce says 'because many loue logike that neuer learne Lawe, I haue reteyned those ould examples of the new Shepheards Kalender which I first gathered.'

Nash (pp. 307-37).

I.

307. 11. *sine linea.* The proverbial *nulla dies sine linea*, explained in Pliny, xxxv. 10. 36, § 84.

308. 5-8. Nash's sarcasm generally contains covert attacks on individual authors and books (cf. p. 311, l. 31, &c.). Here, strangely enough, he appears to be referring to a passage in Greene's *Menaphon*: 'Wee had, answered *Doron*, an Eaw amongst our Rams, whose fleece was as white as the haires that grow on father *Boreas* chinne, or as the dangling deawlap of the siluer Bull, ... her face like *Mars* treading vpon the milke white cloudes.' Nash may be implying that 'better pens,' such as Greene's, are 'outbraued' by the 'bumbast' of the tragedians. Studioso in the *Parnassus* Plays delights to bring in Boreas.

13. *bumbast ... blanke verse.* Cf. the phrase in the famous Shakespearian passage in Greene's *Groatsworth of Wit* ('as well able to bumbast out a blanke verse as the best of you'), probably written in 1592.

14. *kilcow*, bragging, bullying. See *N. E. D.*

31. Cic. *Orat.* 28. Cf. *De Orat.* ii. 60.

309. 11. *Peter Ramus ... his pettie Logique.* The well-known logic of Pierre de La Ramée (*Dialecticae libri duo, A. Talaei praelectionibus illustrati.* Paris, 1560) was Englished in 1574 '*per M. R. Makylmenaeum Scotum.*' William Temple, afterwards Sir Philip Sidney's secretary, published an edition in 1584. See also ii. p. 245, l. 6, note; and *The Pilgrimage to Parnassus*, Acts 2 and 3.

35, &c. *Sus Mineruam.* This adage (a favourite with Cicero) is explained in Pompeius Festus (Müll., p. 310): 'Sus Mineruam in prouerbio est, ubi quis id docet alterum cuius ipse inscius est.' *Asinus ad Lyram*, spoken of a doltish or awkward person, is noted by Gellius, p. 3, l. 16. Nash is probably borrowing in both cases from school-day memories.

310. 7. *Amomum* (ἄμωμον), a fragrant herb, not carefully determined in older literary usage, though now restricted to the genus 'Zingiberaceae.' Turner, in his *Herbal* (1551), reports that it is sometimes identified with the Christmas Rose. Cf. *Euphues* (ed. Landmann, p. 85).

23-4. *Iyl of Braintford's Testament* was printed by Robert Copland, c. 1525.

furmentie, frumenty, a spiced dish of hulled wheat boiled in milk.

Brainford (Brentford), a holiday resort of the lower classes, frequently referred to in the Jest-Books and popular tracts. Cf. *The Jests of George Peele, with foure of his companions at Brainford* (*Shaks. Jest-Books*, ii), and Dekker, *Works*, ii. 322, iii. 130.

27-8. Note Nash's 'euphuistic' alliteration. See p. 322, ll. 28-34, note.

28-9. Cf. ii. p. 227, ll. 31-2.

33, &c. Cf. infra, p. 325, ll. 16, 28.

311. 8. *Pasquil.* See ii. p. 56, l. 29.

9. A reference to the Martinist controversy.

11. *friplers*, i.e. fripperer's, old-clothes man's.

15. *tapsterlie.* Cf. supra, p. 125, l. 28, note; p. 317, &c.

30, &c. Nash's reference to *triuiall translators*, and the allusions which he strews throughout the following sentences (down to l. 29 on p. 312), are now explained as an attack on Thomas Kyd. (See G. Sarrazin's *Thomas Kyd und sein Kreis* (1892), J. W. Cunliffe's *Influence of Seneca on Elizabethan Tragedy*, 1893, and the Introduction to F. S. Boas's edition of Kyd's *Works*, 1901.) Kyd had produced, in 1588, *The Householders Philosophie*, a translation of Tasso's *Padre di Famiglia* (printed by Boas, u. s., pp. 231-84). His *Cornelia* (Boas, u. s., pp. 101-60) was a translation, with modifications, of Garnier's *Cornélie*, as it appeared in the edition of 1585.

33. *Nouerint.* From the opening phrase of a scrivener's document: *Nouerint uniuersi per praesentes*, &c., as given infra ii. p. 238, l. 31, and in *The Returne from Parnassus*, Pt. ii. 4. 2, l. 1624. The usage is common. Cf. Greene's *Groatsworth of Wit*: 'for he had good experience in a *nouerint*' (l. 16).

35. This would appear to be a satirical exaggeration. (See Boas, u.s., p. lxv.)

312. 1. *English Seneca*, i.e. the translation of the *Tenne Tragedies*, which was issued by Thomas Newton in a collected edition in 1581, consisting of Jasper Heywood's version of the *Troas* (first printed 1559), the *Thyestes* (1560), the *Hercules Furens*

(1561), Alexander Nevyle's *Oedipus* (wr. 1560, pr. 1563), Thomas Nuce's *Octavia* (wr. 1562, pr. 1566), John Studley's *Medea and Agamemnon* (1566), Henry Denham's *Hippolytus* (lic. 1556), and Thomas Newton's *Thebais* (1581).

3-4. A reference to the earlier *Hamlet*, ascribed to Kyd, on which Shakespeare founded his play. (See Cunliffe, u.s., p. 5; Boas, u.s., pp. xlv-liv.)

10. Mr. Boas (u.s., p. xxiii) suggests that Nash borrowed the image not from Aesop but from the *Shepheardes Calender*. The likeness of Nash's phrase to Spenser's line, 'He was so enamored with the newell' (276), is striking.

13. *Italian.* See note to p. 311, l. 30.

18. Nash's charge of 'home-born mediocritie' is supported by Kyd's editor. (See Boas, u.s., xx.)

19-20.
                       'The middle path
  Which brought me to the faire Elizian greene . . .
  Here finding Pluto with his Proserpine
  I shewed my passport . . .'
                            The Spanish Tragedie, i. 1. 73-7.

Marlowe's line 'For he confounds hell in Elysium' (*Doctor Faustus*, iii. 60) had been connected by R. Simpson (*New Shaks. Soc. Trans.*, 1875-6, 168, note) with Nash's gibe: but the allusion to the foregoing passage is clear.

20-22. 'The sneer at those who "haue not learned the iust measure of the Horizon without (i.e. without the aid of) an hexameter" is directed (with a probable pun upon the various senses of "measure") at Kyd's borrowing the details of his picture of the lower world from the Sixth Book of the *Aeneid*.' (Boas, u.s., p. xxix.)

22-3.

'*Lorenzo.* Yet speake the truth, and I will guerdon thee,
    And shield thee from what euer can ensue,
    And will conceale what ere proceeds from thee;
    But if thou dally once againe, thou diest.
Pedringano. If Madame *Bel-Imperia* be in loue—
Lorenzo. What, Villaine, ifs and ands?'
                            The Spanish Tragedie, ii. 1. 72-7.

Nash's 'bodge up' is, of course, unjust.

26. *French Doudie.* See note to p. 311, l. 30. Mr. Boas suggests that there may be here a more special reference to Kyd's imitation in the Lord General's narrative (*Sp. Tr.* i. 2. 22 *et seq.*) of the Messenger's account in *Cornélie*, Act V, of the Battle of Thapsus (u.s., p. xxix).

313. 1. *Sadolet,* Cardinal Jacopo Sadoleto. See ii. p. 248, ll. 5-13, note.

2. *Plantine,* Christoffel Plantin, the famous printer.

6. *William Turner* (*d.* 1568), Dean of Wells, physician and writer on botanical subjects.

9. *Sir Thomas Eliot.* Ante, p. 413.

10-11. *with his Comicall wit,* in his *Utopia* ('Libellus vere aureus'), Louvain, 1516; afterwards translated, London, 1551 ('A frutefull and pleasaunt worke').

13. Cf. Ascham, supra, p. 21, and the passages printed in Mayor's edition, p. 162, &c. See also Ascham's letter to the Duke of Somerset, Nov. 21, 1547 (Giles, I. i. p. 138). Nash obviously knew his Ascham well; he refers to the *Scholemaster,* infra, pp. 336-7.

27. *Colona.* Read *Colonia,* as in Ascham (ed. Mayor, p. 162). 'Colony,' not 'Colonist,' is intended.

30. Sir John Cheke. Ante, i. p. 9, l. 30, &c.

31. Sir John Mason (1503-66), ambassador and statesman. Doctor Watson. See i. p. 21, l. 31, note.

32. Redman, John (1499-1551). See note to p. 21, l. 31.

Grindall. This is less likely to be the more notorious Edmund (? 1519-81), Archbishop of Canterbury, the 'Algrind' of the *Shepheardes Calender,* than William Grindal (*d.* 1548), Ascham's favourite pupil, who was a Fellow of St. John's, Cambridge, in 1543, and tutor to Queen Elizabeth. See Grant's *Vita Aschami* (Giles's *Ascham,* III).

Leuer, Thomas (1521-77), Fellow of St. John's, Cambridge, 1548.

Pilkington, James (? 1520-76), Master of St. John's, Cambridge, 1559, and first Protestant Bishop of Durham, 1561.

314. 14. *manuarie,* manual. Cf. *manuary craftes* (=handicrafts) in *Euphues* ('To the Gentlemen Schollers in Athens').

19. *Scythians.* Cf. note, supra, p. 75, l. 33.

Notes

315. 9. Gascoigne's *Supposes* (acted 1565) was an adaptation of Ariosto's *I Suppositi*.

10. *as Tullie.* See *Acad. Quaest.* i. 3. 10; *De Fin.* i. 3; *Tusc. Quaest.* i. 1, &c.

11-12. Turberuile (George), translator of Mantuan (1567), Ovid's Epistles (1567-8), Mancinus (1568), and the *Tragical Tales* from the Italian (1576). He tried blank verse in six of the Ovidian Epistles.

14. Golding. See p. 243, l. 27, note.

15. *editions of Diuinitie ... out of the French tongue.* He completed Sidney's translation of De Mornay (1589), and translated sermons and commentaries of Calvin, Beza, &c.

17. *Phaer,* supra, p. 137, l. 29, note.

23. *Stanihurst,* supra, p. 135.

30. *as neere as I can.* Nash takes great liberties with Stanyhurst's text. See the *Conceites,* pp. 137-8, in Arber's edition.

316. 4. *triobulare,* trifling, of small account (lit. 3 *oboli*, or a ½-drachm).

5. *huffe snuffe,* braggart. Nash is gibing at Stanyhurst in his own words—'Linckt was in wedlock a loftye Thrasonical huf snuffe' (ed. Arber, p. 143). See the parody in ii. p. 241, ll. 4-5. Cf. Hall's *Sat.* i. 3, 17: 'Graced with huf-cap termes and thundring threats', and Peele's *Old Wives Tale* (Bullen, i. p. 333).

8, &c. *France.* See Fraunce, supra, p. 303, note.

Thomas Watson (? 1557-92) is best known as the author of the Ἑκατομπαθία, *or a Passionate Centurie of Loue* (1582). His Latin translation of the *Antigone* appeared in 1581 (see ii. p. 322, l. 29, note); his Latin poem *Amyntas* in 1585. The last was 'paraphrastically translated' into English by Fraunce (see notes to i. p. 303, and ii. p. 321, ll. 7 and 11).

21. *Haddon, Walter.* See i. p. 21, l. 31. Cf. this list of names with Meres's, ii. p. 315, l. 14, &c.

23. *Carre, Nicholas* (1524-68), Regius Professor of Greek at Cambridge, 1547.

24. *Thomas Newton with his Leyland.* Thomas Newton (? 1542-1607) contributed in 1589 *Illustrium aliquot Anglorum Encomia* to Leland's *De Rebus Britannicis Collectanea*.

317. 13. *vndermeale,* afternoon.

16. *Tam Marti*, &c. A common motto: used by Gascoigne on his title-pages. See *The Returne from Parnassus*, Pt. i. 3. 1 (l. 951). Cf. the other form *Tam armis quam ingenio*, as in Kyd, *Sp. Trag.* ii. 1. 107.

18. Hor. *Epist.* i. 5. 19.

34-5. Hor. *Epist.* i. 18. 82.

318-19. Cf. Meres's lists, infra, ii. p. 319.

318. 12. Livio Celiano. (Cf. Meres, infra, ii. p. 319.) His *Rime* appeared in 1587. A paraphrase of one of his madrigals, as printed in John Wilbye's *Madrigals*, 1598, will be found in Mr. Bullen's *Lyrics from Elizabethan Song-books*, p. 64.

33. As yet Spenser had published only the *Epigrams* and *Sonnets* (the *Visions of Petrarch* and the *Visions of Bellay* of 1591), and the *Shepheardes Calender*.

319. 6, 9. *Mathew Roydon* (fl. 1580-1622). His *Elegie, or Friends passion for his Astrophill*, is printed in Spenser's *Colin Clout* (1595). See the 'Globe' *Spenser*, p. 568.

7. *Thomas Atchelow*, the 'ingenious Atchlow' of Dekker's *Knights Coniuring* (1607). Not in *D. N. B.*

George Peele's first work, the *Araygnement of Paris*, is dated 1584.

Roydon, Atchelow, and Peele are three of the five writers of commendatory verses in Watson's Ἑκατομπαθία (1582).

320. 1. *blankes*, i.e. blank verse. See note to l. 18.

5. William Warner (? 1558–1609). The first edition of his *Albions England* (Pt. I) is dated 1586; the second (Parts I and II), 1589.

10. *Abcie*, i.e. A B C. Cf. *Abscedarie*, infra, p. 328, l. 4, note.

18. *blankes*. Cf. l. 1. Is a pun intended here (*blank*, a small coin)?

II.

321. Grosart has endeavoured to explain the title of Nash's pamphlet as 'more likely fetched from Greene's *Anatomie of Flatterie* or from his *Arbasto, or Anatomie of Fortune* than from the *Anatomie of Abuses*,' because of 'his relations to and admiration of Robert Greene, and contrariwise his detestation of Stubbes as a grim Puritan.' The argument is, however, double-

edged: and we have sufficient evidence to prove that he has the Puritan in mind. See note to p. 324, l. 16.

1-5. This favourite story is given by Cicero, *De Invent.* ii. 1.

2. Cf. Ariosto, *O. F.* c. 11, st. 71; *The Complaynt of Scotlande*, ed. Murray, p. 11.

11. *duncerie*, a common word with Nash (cf. p. 331). See also *The Returne from Parnassus*, Pt. ii. 3. 1 (l. 1111). *N. E. D.* gives only later examples.

12. *Nigrum theta*, (Θ), a conventional critical mark indicating censure of a passage, derived from the Θ (the initial of θάνατος), placed on the Greek voting-tablets. See ii. p. 376, l. 4.

16. Orig. πουεσοπολις.

322. 27. *Idlebies*, idle fellows.

28-34. A direct hit at the Euphuistic vogue. Cf. Sidney, supra, p. 202, l. 33, note, and ii. p. 269. Note also *loue, lust ... vice, visard.* Cf. p. 310, ll. 27-8. See also the list of names on p. 323, l. 33, &c., and also p. 337, ll. 12-13.

323. 1. Sir Egerton Brydges sees here an allusion to the title-page of *The Paradyse of Daynty Deuices: Conteyning sundry pithy preceptes, learned Counsels, and excellent inuentions, right pleasant and profitable for all estates . . .* (1578).

9-10. Ovid, *Ars Amat.* i. 1.

15-21. Cf. Ascham, supra, pp. 3-4. See Nash, p. 329, *Abbie-lubber.* Cf. *Euphues* (ed. Landmann, p. 83).

33, &c. Cf. the parallel passage in *Euphues* ('To the graue Matrones and honest Maydens of Italy').

324. 16. An obvious allusion to Philip Stubbes's *Anatomie of Abuses* (1583). See note to p. 321.

26. *Nullus*, &c. Ovid, *Tristia*, i. 9. 6. Quoted by Greene in *Menaphon* (ed. Arber, p. 30), and as a motto in the *Paradyse of Daynty Devices* (ed. Brydges, p. 30*, No. 40).

325. 16 and 28. See note, supra, p. 310, l. 33, &c.

35. *boate, boote.* See note, p. 322, ll. 28-34.

*326. 1. *Ne sutor.* See note, supra, p. 210, ll. 1-4.

16-20. See Lodge, supra, p. 63, ll. 1-4.

21. *A small ship.* A common Elizabethan metaphor.

35. *rednose Fidler. . . . Ale Knight.* Cf. note to p. 125, l. 28.

327. 12. The *De Asino Aureo* of Apuleius supplies the figure.

17. *Campanus.* Cf. Lodge, p. 65, l. 21.

328. 4. *abscedarie*, illiterate (med. Lat. *abecedarium*, an alphabet or primer—'A B C D').

7. i. e. Alabandensis Apollonius. See Cic. *de Orat.* i. 28. 126.

21. *Aen.* ii. 274.

33. In the opening paragraphs of the *Tusculan Disputations*.

329. 18. *Poetry a daintie dish.* A common metaphor. See Introduction.

23. Cf. the list of Romances on p. 323.

331. 1. *duncerie.* See note, p. 321, l. 12.

12. Cf. Lodge, p. 65, l. 16.

16. *sixt.* It is in the *Fourth*, line 7.

332. 17. Cf. p. 59, l. 15; p. 79, l. 31, and ii. p. 309, l. 13.

19–23. Cf. Ascham, passim, and Webbe, pp. 254–5.

23. *haune*, awn.

333. 35. *potman . . . Poet.* Cf. Webbe, supra, p. 246, l. 30.

334. 9. Cf. p. 312, l. 10.

13. *Cherillus*, Choerilus, referred to by Horace, *Epist.* ii. 1. 233, and *Ars Poet.* 357. 'I rather take vpon me to write better then *Choerilus*, then once suppose to imitate Homer,' Thomas Watson Ἑκατομπαθία, 'To the Reader' (Spenser Soc. edit., p. 6). For other references, see Index.

16. *Ramus*, supra, p. 309, l. 11, note.

335. 12. *his.* Nash has confused his grammatical number.

336. 33. Mulcaster's *Positions wherein those primitiue circumstances be examined, which are necessarie for the training vp of Children, either for skill in their booke or health in their bodie* was printed in 1581. His *First Part of the Elementarie which entreateth chefelie of the writing of our English tung* followed in 1582.

The Bodleian text is missing after 'bethinke.' The concluding portion is added to the copy in a later hand.

35. See note to p. 313, l. 13.

337. 1. See *Eduardi Grant Oratio de Vita et Obitu R.A.* (printed by Giles, iii. pp. 294–355).

23. *of Women.* See supra, p. 324, ll. 6–9.

Appendix (pp. 341-4).

Sir Edward Hoby (1560-1617), son of Sir Thomas Hoby, the translator of Castiglione's *Cortegiano* ('The Courtyer').

342. 11. *Viues*, Ioannes Ludovicus (1492-1540), frequently referred to throughout these volumes (in text and notes). His English reputation was probably helped by the fact that he had been tutor to the Princess Mary, daughter of Henry VIII. He was a Fellow of Corpus Christi College, Oxford (see *D. N. B.*). Cf. ii. p. 245, l. 6, note.

28-9. See note to p. 158, l. 8.

38. See note to p. 71, l. 18.

END OF VOLUME I

ELIZABETHAN CRITICAL ESSAYS

EDITED WITH AN INTRODUCTION

BY

G. GREGORY SMITH

VOLUME II

OXFORD UNIVERSITY PRESS
LONDON : HUMPHREY MILFORD

First edition 1904
Reprinted photographically in Great Britain in 1937
by LOWE & BRYDONE, LONDON, from sheets of the
First edition

CONTENTS OF VOL. II

PUTTENHAM[1].   PAGE
   The Arte of English Poesie. 1589 1–193

SIR JOHN HARINGTON.
   A Preface, or rather a Briefe Apologie of Poetrie,
   prefixed to the translation of *Orlando Furioso.*
   1591 194–222

THOMAS NASH.
   Preface to Sidney's *Astrophel and Stella.* 1591 . 223–228

GABRIEL HARVEY.
   From *Foure Letters.* 1592 229–238

THOMAS NASH.
   From *Strange Newes,* or *Foure Letters Confuted.*
   1592 239–244

GABRIEL HARVEY.
   I. From *Pierce's Supererogation.* 1593. . . 245–282
   II. From *A New Letter of Notable Contents.* 1593 . 282–284

RICHARD CAREW.
   The Excellency of the English Tongue. ? 1595-6 . 285–294

GEORGE CHAPMAN.
   I. Preface to *Seaven Bookes of the Iliades of*
      Homere. 1598 295–297
   II. Dedication, &c. of *Achilles Shield.* 1598 . . 297–307

FRANCIS MERES.
   From *Palladis Tamia.* 1598 308–324

WILLIAM VAUGHAN.
   From *The Golden Grove.* 1600 325–326

[1] See note, p. 407.

Contents

	PAGE
THOMAS CAMPION.	
Observations in the Art of English Poesie. 1602	327–355
SAMUEL DANIEL.	
A Defence of Ryme. ? 1603	356–384
APPENDIX.	
I. BEN JONSON.	
i and ii. From *Every Man in his Humour*	387–390
iii. From *Every Man out of his Humour*	390–393
iv. From *The Poetaster*	393–397
II. *The Returne from Parnassus.* 1601. Part II, I. ii	398–403
NOTES TO TEXTS IN VOL. II	405–466
ADDITIONAL NOTES AND CORRECTIONS (VOLS. I AND II)	467
GENERAL INDEX TO VOLS. I AND II (TEXTS, INTRODUCTION, AND NOTES)	469–509

GEORGE PUTTENHAM

(*The Arte of English Poesie*)

1589

[*The Arte of English Poesie. Contriued into three Bookes: The first of Poets and Poesie, the second of Proportion, the third of Ornament* was published without the author's name, in 1589, by '*Richard Field, dwelling in the black-Friers, neere Ludgate.*' The text here printed follows Ben Jonson's copy, now in the British Museum. Many passages are underlined (especially in the opening chapters), and there are a few annotations; but it is extremely doubtful that any of these are by Ben Jonson. The copy also contains eight unnumbered pages on the 'Device' and 'Anagram' (see p. 105), which were withdrawn while the volume was passing through the press: and it has the substituted passage in Book III, chap. xix, in place of the criticism of the Flemings, which occurs in some copies of this edition (see Notes).

The *Arte of English Poesie* is anonymous, yet the evidence of Puttenham's authorship is, if not absolute, at least sufficiently strong to justify the ascription. It is dedicated (May 28, 1589) to Lord Treasurer Burghley by the printer Richard Field, who excuses his presumption and his author's 'slender subject' in these words:—'This Booke (right Honorable) comming to my handes, with his bare title without any Authours name or any other ordinarie addresse, I doubted how well it might become me to make you a present thereof, seeming, by many expresse passages in the same at large, that it was by the Authour intended to our Soueraigne Lady the Queene, and for her recreation and seruice chiefly deuised; in which case to make any other person her highnes partener in the honour of his guift it could not stand with my dutie, nor be without some preiudice to her Maiesties interest and his merrite. Perceyuing, besides, the title to purport so slender a subiect, as nothing almost could be more discrepant from the grauitie of your yeeres and Honorable function, whose contemplations are euery houre more seriously employed vpon the publicke administration and seruices, I thought it no condigne gratification nor scarce any good satisfaction for such a person as you. Yet when I considered, that bestowyng vpon your Lordship the first vewe of this mine impression (a feat of mine owne simple facultie) it could not scypher her Maiesties honour or prerogatiue in the guift, nor yet the Authour of his thanks, and seeing the thing it selfe to be a deuice of some noueltie (which commonly giueth euery good thing a speciall grace), and a noueltie so highly tending to the most worthy prayses of her Maiesties most excellent name (deerer to you I dare conceiue then any worldly thing besides), mee thought I could not deuise to haue presented your Lordship any gift more agreeable to your appetite, or fitter for my vocation and abilitie to bestow, your Lordship beyng learned and a louer of learning, my present a Booke, and my selfe a printer alwaies ready and desirous to be at your Honourable commaundement.']

THE FIRST BOOKE

OF POETS AND POESIE

CHAP. I.

WHAT A POET AND POESIE IS, AND WHO MAY BE WORTHILY
SAYD THE MOST EXCELLENT POET OF OUR TIME.

A POET is as much to say as a maker. And our English name well conformes with the Greeke word, for of ποιεῖν, to make, they call a maker *Poeta*. Such as (by way of resemblance and reuerently) we may say of God; who without any trauell to his diuine imagination made all the world of nought, nor also by any paterne or mould, as the Platonicks with their Idees do phantastically suppose. Euen so the very Poet makes and contriues out of his owne braine both the verse and matter of his poeme, and not by any foreine copie or example, as doth the translator, who therefore may well be sayd a versifier, but not a Poet. The premises considered, it giueth to the name and profession no smal dignitie and preheminence, aboue all other artificers, Scientificke or Mechanicall. And neuerthelesse, without any repugnancie at all, a Poet may in some sort be said a follower or imitator, because he can express the true and liuely of euery thing is set before him, and which he taketh in hand to describe: and so in that respect is both a maker and a counterfaitor: and Poesie an art not only of making, but also of imitation. And this science in his perfection can not grow but by some diuine instinct—the Platonicks call it *furor*; or by excellencie of nature and complexion; or by great subtiltie of the spirits & wit; or by much experience and obseruation

of the world, and course of kinde; or, peraduenture, by
all or most part of them. Otherwise, how was it possible
that *Homer*, being but a poore priuate man, and, as some
say, in his later age blind, should so exactly set foorth and
describe, as if he had bene a most excellent Captaine or
Generall, the order and array of battels, the conduct of
whole armies, the sieges and assaults of cities and townes?
or, as some great Princes maiordome and perfect Surueyour
in Court, the order, sumptuousnesse, and magnificence
of royal bankets, feasts, weddings, and enteruewes? or,
as a Polititian very prudent and much inured with the
priuat and publique affaires, so grauely examine the lawes
and ordinances Ciuill, or so profoundly discourse in matters
of estate and formes of all politique regiment? Finally,
how could he so naturally paint out the speeches, countenance, and maners of Princely persons and priuate, to wit,
the wrath of *Achilles*, the magnanimitie of *Agamemnon*,
the prudence of *Menelaus*, the prowesse of *Hector*, the
maiestie of king *Priamus*, the grauitie of *Nestor*, the pollicies
and eloquence of *Vlysses*, the calamities of the distressed
Queenes, and valiance of all the Captaines and aduenturous
knights in those lamentable warres of Troy? It is therefore of Poets thus to be conceiued, that if they be able to
deuise and make all these things of them selues, without
any subiect of veritie, that they be (by maner of speech)
as creating gods. If they do it by instinct diuine or
naturall, then surely much fauoured from aboue; if by
their experience, then no doubt very wise men; if by any
president or paterne layd before them, then truly the
most excellent imitators & counterfaitors of all others.
But you (Madame) my most Honored and Gracious, if
I should seeme to offer you this my deuise for a discipline
and not a delight, I might well be reputed of all others
the most arrogant and iniurious, your selfe being alreadie,
of any that I know in our time, the most excellent Poet;

forsooth by your Princely purse, fauours, and countenance, making in maner what ye list, the poore man rich, the lewd well learned, the coward couragious, and vile both noble and valiant: then for imitation no lesse, your person as a most cunning counterfaitor liuely representing *Venus* in countenance, in life *Diana*, *Pallas* for gouernement, and *Iuno* in all honour and regall magnificence.

CHAP. II.

THAT THERE MAY BE AN ART OF OUR ENGLISH POESIE, ASWELL AS THERE IS OF THE LATINE AND GREEKE.

Then as there was no art in the world till by experience found out, so if Poesie be now an Art, & of al antiquitie hath bene among the Greeks and Latines, & yet were none vntill by studious persons fashioned and reduced into a method of rules and precepts, then no doubt may there be the like with vs. And if th'art of Poesie be but a skill appertaining to vtterance, why may not the same be with vs aswel as with them, our language being no lesse copious, pithie, and significatiue then theirs, our conceipts the same, and our wits no lesse apt to deuise and imitate then theirs were? If againe Art be but a certaine order of rules prescribed by reason, and gathered by experience, why should not Poesie be a vulgar Art with vs aswell as with the Greeks and Latines, our language admitting no fewer rules and nice diuersities then theirs? but peraduenture moe by a peculiar, which our speech hath in many things differing from theirs; and yet, in the generall points of that Art, allowed to go in common with them: so as if one point perchance, which is their feete whereupon their measures stand, and in deede is all the beautie of their Poesie, and which feete we haue not, nor as yet neuer went about to frame (the nature of our language and wordes not permitting it), we haue in stead thereof twentie other curious points in that skill more then they euer had, by reason of our rime and tunable concords or simphonie, which they neuer obserued. Poesie therefore may be an Art in our vulgar, and that verie methodicall and commendable.

CHAP. III.

HOW POETS WERE THE FIRST PRIESTS, THE FIRST PROPHETS, THE FIRST LEGISLATORS AND POLITITIANS IN THE WORLD.

The profession and vse of Poesie is most ancient from the beginning, and not, as manie erroniously suppose, after, but before, any ciuil society was among men. For it is written that Poesie was th'originall cause and occasion of their first assemblies, when before the people remained in the woods and mountains, vagarant and dispersed like the wild beasts, lawlesse and naked, or verie ill clad, and of all good and necessarie prouision for harbour or sustenance vtterly vnfurnished, so as they litle diffred for their maner of life from the very brute beasts of the field. Whereupon it is fayned that *Amphion* and *Orpheus*, two Poets of the first ages, one of them, to wit *Amphion*, builded vp cities, and reared walles with the stones that came in heapes to the sound of his harpe, figuring thereby the mollifying of hard and stonie hearts by his sweete and eloquent perswasion. And *Orpheus* assembled the wilde beasts to come in heards to harken to his musicke, and by that meanes made them tame, implying thereby, how by his discreete and wholsome lesons vttered in harmonie and with melodious instruments he brought the rude and sauage people to a more ciuill and orderly life, nothing, as it seemeth, more preuailing or fit to redresse and edifie the cruell and sturdie courage of man then it. And as these two Poets, and *Linus* before them, and *Museus* also and *Hesiodus* in Greece and Archadia, so by all likelihood had mo Poets done in other places and in other ages before them, though there be no remembrance left of them, by reason of the Recordes by some accident of time perished and failing. Poets therfore are of great antiquitie. Then forasmuch as they were the first that entended to the obseruation of nature and her works, and specially of the Celestiall courses, by reason of the continuall motion of the heauens, searching after the first mouer, and from thence by degrees comming to know and consider of the substances separate & abstract, which we call the diuine intelligences or good Angels (*Demones*), they were the first that instituted sacrifices of placation, with inuocations and worship to them, as to Gods; and inuented and stablished all the rest of the obseruances and ceremonies of religion, and so were the first Priests and ministers of the holy misteries. And because for the better execution of that high charge and function it behoued them to liue chast, and in all holines of life, and in continuall studie and contemplation, they came by instinct diuine, and by deepe meditation, and much abstinence (the same assubtiling and refining their spirits) to be made apt to receaue visions, both waking and sleeping, which made them vtter prophesies and foretell things to come. So also were they the first Prophetes or seears, *Videntes*, for so the Scripture tearmeth them in Latine after the Hebrue word, and all the oracles and answers of the gods were giuen in meeter or verse, and published to the people by their direction. And for that they were aged and graue men, and of much wisedome and experience in th'affaires of the world, they were the first lawmakers to the people, and the first polititiens, deuising all expedient meanes for th'establishment of Common wealth, to hold and containe the people in order and duety by force and vertue of good and wholesome lawes, made for the preseruation of the publique peace and tranquillitie: the same peraduenture not purposely intended, but greatly furthered by the aw of their gods and such scruple of conscience as the terrors of their late inuented religion had led them into.

CHAP. IV.

HOW POETS WERE THE FIRST PHILOSOPHERS, THE FIRST ASTRONOMERS AND HISTORIOGRAPHERS AND ORATOURS AND MUSITIENS OF THE WORLD.

Vtterance also and language is giuen by nature to man for perswasion of others and aide of them selues, I meane the first abilite to speake. For speech it selfe is artificiall and made by man, and the more pleasing it is, the more it preuaileth to such purpose as it is intended for: but speech by meeter is a kind of vtterance more cleanly couched and more delicate to the eare then prose is, because it is more currant and slipper vpon the tongue, and withal tunable and melodious, as a kind of Musicke, and therfore may be tearmed a musicall speech or vtterance, which cannot but please the hearer very well. Another cause is, for that is briefer & more compendious, and easier to beare away and be retained in memorie, then that which is contained in multitude of words and full of tedious ambage and long periods. It is beside a maner of vtterance more eloquent and rethoricall then the ordinarie prose which we vse in our daily talke, because it is decked and set out with all maner of fresh colours and figures, which maketh that it sooner inuegleth the iudgement of man, and carieth his opinion this way and that, whither soeuer the heart by impression of the eare shalbe most affectionatly bent and directed. The vtterance in prose is not of so great efficacie, because not only it is dayly vsed, and by that occasion the eare is ouerglutted with it, but is also not so voluble and slipper vpon the tong, being wide and lose, and nothing numerous, nor contriued into measures and sounded with so gallant and harmonical accents, nor, in fine, alowed that figuratiue conueyance nor so great licence in choise of words and phrases as meeter is. So as the Poets were also from the beginning the best perswaders, and their eloquence the first Rethoricke of the world, euen so it became that the high mysteries of the gods should be reuealed & taught by a maner of vtterance and language of extraordinarie phrase, and briefe and compendious, and aboue al others sweet and ciuill as the Metricall is. The same also was meetest to register the liues and noble gests of Princes, and of the great Monarkes of the world, and all other the memorable accidents of time: so as the Poet was also the first historiographer. Then forasmuch as they were the first obseruers of all naturall causes & effects in the things generable and corruptible, and from thence mounted vp to search after the celestiall courses and influences, & yet penetrated further to know the diuine essences and substances separate, as is sayd before, they were the first Astronomers and Philosophists and Metaphisicks. Finally, because they did altogether endeuor them selues to reduce the life of man to a certaine method of good maners, and made the first differences betweene vertue and vice, and then tempered all these knowledges and skilles with the exercise of a delectable Musicke by melodious instruments, which withall serued them to delight their hearers, & to call the people together by admiration to a plausible and vertuous conuersation, therefore were they the first Philosophers Ethick, & the first artificial Musiciens of the world. Such was *Linus*,

Orpheus, Amphion, & *Museus,* the most ancient Poets and Philosophers of whom there is left any memorie by the prophane writers. King *Dauid* also & *Salomon* his sonne and many other of the holy Prophets wrate in meeters, and vsed to sing them to the harpe, although to many of vs, ignorant of the Hebrue language and phrase, and not obseruing it, the same seeme but a prose. It can not bee therefore that anie scorne or indignitie should iustly be offred to so noble, profitable, ancient, and diuine a science as Poesie is.

CHAP. V.

HOW THE WILDE AND SAUAGE PEOPLE VSED A NATURALL POESIE IN VERSICLE AND RIME AS OUR VULGAR IS.

And the Greeke and Latine Poesie was by verse numerous and metricall, running vpon pleasant feete, sometimes swift, sometime slow (their words very aptly seruing that purpose) but without any rime or tunable concord in th'end of their verses, as we and all other nations now vse. But the Hebrues & Chaldees, who were more ancient then the Greekes, did not only vse a metricall Poesie, but also with the same a maner of rime, as hath bene of late obserued by learned men. Wherby it appeareth that our vulgar running Poesie was common to all the nations of the world besides, whom the Latines and Greekes in speciall called barbarous. So as it was, notwithstanding, the first and most ancient Poesie, and the most vniuersall; which two points do otherwise giue to all humane inuentions and affaires no small credit. This is proued by certificate of marchants and trauellers, who by late nauigations haue surueyed the whole world, and discouered large countries and strange peoples wild and sauage, affirming that the American, the Perusine, and the very Canniball do sing and also say their highest and

holiest matters in certaine riming versicles, and not in
prose, which proues also that our maner of vulgar Poesie
is more ancient then the artificiall of the Greeks and
Latines, ours comming by instinct of nature, which was
before Art or obseruation, and vsed with the sauage and
vnciuill, who were before all science or ciuilitie, euen as
the naked by prioritie of time is before the clothed, and
the ignorant before the learned. The naturall Poesie
therefore, being aided and amended by Art, and not vtterly
altered or obscured, but some signe left of it (as the
Greekes and Latines haue left none), is no lesse to be
allowed and commended then theirs.

CHAP. VI.

HOW THE RIMING POESIE CAME FIRST TO THE GRECIANS
AND LATINES, AND HAD ALTERED AND ALMOST SPILT
THEIR MANER OF POESIE.

But it came to passe, when fortune fled farre from the
Greekes and Latines, & that their townes florished no
more in traficke, nor their Vniuersities in learning as
they had done continuing those Monarchies, the barbarous
conquerers inuading them with innumerable swarmes of
strange nations, the Poesie metricall of the Grecians and
Latines came to be much corrupted and altered, in so
much as there were times that the very Greekes and
Latines themselues tooke pleasure in Riming verses, and
vsed it as a rare and gallant thing. Yea, their Oratours
proses nor the Doctors Sermons were acceptable to
Princes nor yet to the common people, vnlesse it went
in manner of tunable rime or metricall sentences, as
appeares by many of the auncient writers about that
time and since. And the great Princes, and Popes, and
Sultans would one salute and greet an other sometime in

frendship and sport, sometime in earnest and enmitie, by ryming verses, & nothing seemed clerkly done, but must be done in ryme. Whereof we finde diuers examples from the time of th'Emperours Gracian & Valentinian downwardes: For then aboutes began the declination of the Romain Empire, by the notable inundations of the *Hunnes* and *Vandalles* in Europe, vnder the conduict of *Totila* & *Atila* and other their generalles. This brought the ryming Poesie in grace, and made it preuaile in Italie and Greece (their owne long time cast aside, and almost neglected), till after many yeares that the peace of Italie and of th'Empire Occidentall reuiued new clerkes, who, recouering and perusing the bookes and studies of the ciuiler ages, restored all maner of arts, and that of the Greeke and Latine Poesie withall, into their former puritie and netnes. Which neuerthelesse did not so preuaile but that the ryming Poesie of the Barbarians remained still in his reputation, that one in the schole, this other in Courts of Princes more ordinary and allowable.

CHAP. VII.

HOW IN THE TIME OF CHARLEMAINE AND MANY YEARES AFTER HIM THE LATINE POETES WROTE IN RYME.

And this appeareth euidently by the workes of many learned men who wrote about the time of *Charlemaines* raigne in the Empire *Occidentall,* where the Christian Religion became through the excessiue authoritie of Popes and deepe deuotion of Princes strongly fortified and established by erection of orders *Monastical,* in which many simple clerks for deuotion sake & sanctitie were receiued more then for any learning; by which occasion & the solitarinesse of their life waxing studious without discipline or instruction by any good methode, some of them grew to be historiographers, some Poets; and following either the barbarous rudenes of the time, or els their own idle inuentions, all that they wrote to the fauor or prayse of Princes they did it in such maner of minstrelsie, and thought themselues no small fooles when they could make their verses goe all in ryme, as did the schoole of *Salerne*, dedicating their booke of medicinall rules vnto our king of England, with this beginning.

> *Anglorum Regi scripsit schola tota Salerni*
> *Si vis incolumem, si vis te reddere sanum,*
> *Curas tolle graues, irasci crede prophanum,*
> *Nec retine ventrem nec stringas fortiter anum.*

And all the rest that follow throughout the whole booke more curiously then cleanely, neuerthelesse very well to the purpose of their arte. In the same time king *Edward* the iij., him selfe quartering the Armes of England and France, did discouer his pretence and clayme to the Crowne of Fraunce in these ryming verses.

> *Rex sum regnorum bina ratione duorum;*
> *Anglorum regno sum rex ego iure paterno;*
> *Matris iure quidem Francorum nuncupor idem:*
> *Hinc est armorum variatio facta meorum.*

Which verses *Phillip de Valois*, then possessing the Crowne as next heire male by pretexte of the law *Salique*, and holding out *Edward* the third, aunswered in these other of as good stuffe.

> *Praedo regnorum qui diceris esse duorum,*
> *Regno materno priuaberis atque paterno;*
> *Prolis ius nullum [est] vbi matris non fuit vllum:*
> *Hinc est armorum variatio stulta tuorum.*

It is found written of Pope *Lucius* for his great auarice and tyranny vsed ouer the Clergy thus in ryming verses.

> *Lucius est piscis, rex atque tyrannus aquarum,*
> *A quo discordat Lucius iste parum ;*
> *Deuorat hic homines, hic piscibus insidiatur,*
> *Esurit hic semper, hic aliquando satur.*
> *Amborum vitam si laus aequata notaret,*
> *Plus rationis habet qui ratione caret.*

And as this was vsed in the greatest and gayest matters of Princes and Popes by the idle inuention of Monasticall men then raigning al in their superlatiue, so did euery scholer and secular clerke or versifier, when he wrote any short poeme or matter of good lesson, put it in ryme ; whereby it came to passe that all your old Prouerbes and common sayinges, which they would haue plausible to the reader and easie to remember and beare away, were of that sorte as these.

> *In mundo mira faciunt duo nummus et ira;*
> *Mollificant dura, peruertunt omnia iura.*

And this verse in disprayse of the Courtiers life following the Court of Rome.

> *Vita palatina dura est animaeque ruina.*

And these written by a noble learned man.

> *Ire, redire, sequi regum sublimia castra*
> *Eximius status est, sed non sic itur ad astra.*

And this other which to the great iniurie of all women was written (no doubt by some forlorne louer, or els some old malicious Monke), for one womans sake blemishing the whole sexe.

> *Fallere, flere, nere, mentiri, nilque tacere,*
> *Haec quinque vere statuit Deus in muliere.*

If I might haue bene his Iudge, I would haue had him for his labour serued as *Orpheus* was by the women of Thrace : his eyes to be picket out with pinnes, for his so

deadly belying of them; or worse handled, if worse could be deuised. But will ye see how God raised a reuenger for the silly innocent women, for about the same ryming age came an honest ciuill Courtier somewhat bookish, and
5 wrate these verses against the whole rable of Monkes.

> *O Monachi, vestri stomachi sunt amphora Bacchi:*
> *Vos estis, Deus est testis, turpissima pestis.*

Anon after came your secular Priestes, as iolly rymers as the rest, who being sore agreeued with their Pope
10 *Calixtus*, for that he had enioyned them from their wiues, & railed as fast against him.

> *O bone Calixte, totus mundus perodit te;*
> *Quondam Presbiteri poterant vxoribus vti;*
> *Hoc destruxisti postquam tu Papa fuisti.*

15 Thus what in writing of rymes and registring of lyes was the Clergy of that fabulous age wholly occupied.

We finde some, but very few, of these ryming verses among the Latines of the ciuiller ages, and those rather hapning by chaunce then of any purpose in the writer, as
20 this *Distick* among the disportes of *Ouid*.

> *Quot coelum stellas tot habet tua Roma puellas;*
> *Pascua quotque haedos tot habet tua Roma Cinaedos.*

The posteritie taking pleasure in this manner of *Simphonie* had leasure as it seemes to deuise many other
25 knackes in their versifying that the aunciend and ciuill Poets had not vsed before, whereof one was to make euery word of a verse to begin with the same letter, as did *Hugobald* the Monke, who made a large poeme to the honour of *Carolus Caluus*, euery word beginning with *C*,
30 which was the first letter of the kings name, thus,

> *Carmina clarisonae Caluis cantate camenae.*

And this was thought no small peece of cunning, being

in deed a matter of some difficultie to finde out so many
wordes beginning with one letter as might make a iust
volume, though in truth it were but a phantasticall deuise,
and to no purpose at all more then to make them harmonicall to the rude eares of those barbarous ages.

Another of their pretie inuentions was to make a verse
of such wordes as by their nature and manner of construction and situation might be turned backward word by
word, and make another perfit verse, but of quite contrary
sence, as the gibing Monke that wrote of Pope *Alexander*
these two verses.

> *Laus tua non tua fraus, virtus non copia rerum,*
> *Scandere te faciunt hoc decus eximium.*

Which if ye will turne backwards, they make two other
good verses, but of a contrary sence, thus,

> *Eximium decus hoc faciunt te scandere, rerum*
> *Copia, non virtus, fraus tua non tua laus.*

And they called it *Verse Lyon*.

Thus you may see the humors and appetites of men
how diuers and chaungeable they be in liking new fashions,
though many tymes worse then the old, and not onely in
the manner of their life and vse of their garments, but
also in their learninges and arts, and specially of their
languages.

CHAP. VIII.

IN WHAT REPUTATION POESIE AND POETS WERE IN OLD
TIME WITH PRINCES AND OTHERWISE GENERALLY, AND
HOW THEY BE NOW BECOME CONTEMPTIBLE AND FOR
WHAT CAUSES.

For the respectes aforesayd in all former ages and in
the most ciuill countreys and commons wealthes, good
Poets and Poesie were highly esteemed and much fauoured

Of Poets and Poesy

of the greatest Princes. For proofe whereof we read how
much *Amyntas*, king of *Macedonia*, made of the Tragicall
Poet *Euripides*; and the *Athenians* of *Sophocles*; in
what price the noble poemes of *Homer* were holden with
Alexander the great, in so much as euery night they were
layd vnder his pillow, and by day were carried in the rich
iewell cofer of *Darius* lately before vanquished by him in
battaile. And not onely *Homer*, the father and Prince of
the Poets, was so honored by him, but for his sake all
other meaner Poets, in so much as *Cherillus*, one no very
great good Poet, had for euery verse well made a *Phillips*
noble of gold, amounting in value to an angell English,
and so for euery hundreth verses (which a cleanely pen
could speedely dispatch) he had a hundred angels. And
since *Alexander* the great, how *Theocritus* the Greeke poet
was fauored by *Tholomee*, king of Egipt, & Queene *Berenice*,
his wife; *Ennius* likewise by *Scipio*, Prince of the *Romaines*;
Virgill also by th'Emperour *Augustus*. And in later times,
how much were *Iehan de Mehune* & *Guillaume de Loris*
made of by the French kinges; and *Geffrey Chaucer*, father
of our English Poets, by *Richard* the second, who, as it
was supposed, gaue him the maner of new Holme in
Oxfordshire; and *Gower* [by] *Henry* the fourth; and
Harding [by] *Edward* the fourth. Also, how *Frauncis* the
Frenche king made *Sangelais*, *Salmonius Macrinus*, and
Clement Marot of his priuy Chamber for their excellent
skill in vulgare and Latine Poesie; and king *Henry*
the 8, her *Maiesties* father, for a few Psalmes of *Dauid*
turned into English meetre by Sternhold, made him
groome of his priuy chamber & gaue him many other
good gifts. And one *Gray*, what good estimation did he
grow vnto with the same king *Henry*, & afterward with the
Duke of Sommerset, Protectour, for making certaine merry
Ballades, whereof one chiefly was *The hunte is vp, the hunte
is vp*? And Queene *Mary*, his daughter, for one *Epithalamie*

or nuptiall song made by *Vargas*, a Spanish Poet, at her
mariage with king *Phillip* in Winchester, gaue him during
his life two hundred Crownes pension. Nor this reputation
was giuen them in aunceient times altogether in respect
that Poesie was a delicate arte, and the Poets them selues
cunning Princepleasers, but for that also they were thought
for their vniuersall knowledge to be very sufficient men
for the greatest charges in their common wealthes, were
it for counsell or for conduct; whereby no man neede to
doubt but that both skilles may very well concurre and be
most excellent in one person. For we finde that *Iulius
Caesar*, the first Emperour and a most noble Captaine,
was not onely the most eloquent Orator of his time, but
also a very good Poet, though none of his doings therein
be now extant. And *Quintus Catulus*, a good Poet, and
Cornelius Gallus, treasurer of Egipt; and *Horace*, the most
delicate of all the Romain *Lyrickes*, was thought meete
and by many letters of great instance prouoked to be
Secretarie of estate to *Augustus* th'Emperour, which
neuerthelesse he refused for his vnhealthfulnesse sake,
and, being a quiet mynded man and nothing ambitious
of glory, *non voluit accedere ad Rempublicam*, as it is
reported. And *Ennius* the Latine Poet was not, as some
perchaunce thinke, onely fauored by *Scipio* the *Africane*
for his good making of verses, but vsed as his familiar
and Counsellor in the warres for his great knowledge and
amiable conuersation. And long before that, *Antimenides*
and other Greeke Poets, as *Aristotle* reportes in his Politiques, had charge in the warres. And *Tyrtaeus* the Poet,
being also a lame man & halting vpon one legge, was
chosen by the Oracle of the gods from the *Athenians* to be
generall of the *Lacedemonians* armie, not for his Poetrie,
but for his wisedome and graue perswasions and subtile
Stratagemes, whereby he had the victory ouer his enemies.
So as the Poets seemed to haue skill not onely in the

subtilties of their arte but also to be meete for all maner of functions ciuill and martiall, euen as they found fauour of the times they liued in, insomuch as their credit and estimation generally was not small. But in these dayes, although some learned Princes may take delight in them, yet vniuersally it is not so. For as well Poets as Poesie are despised, & the name become of honorable infamous, subiect to scorne and derision, and rather a reproch than a prayse to any that vseth it: for commonly who so is studious in th'Arte or shewes him selfe excellent in it, they call him in disdayne a *phantasticall*; and a light headed or phantasticall man (by conuersion) they call a Poet. And this proceedes through the barbarous ignoraunce of the time, and pride of many Gentlemen and others, whose grosse heads not being brought vp or acquainted with any excellent Arte, nor able to contriue or in manner conceiue any matter of subtiltie in any businesse or science, they doe deride and scorne it in all others as superfluous knowledges and vayne sciences, and whatsoeuer deuise be of rare inuention they terme it *phantasticall*, construing it to the worst side: and among men such as be modest and graue, & of litle conuersation, nor delighted in the busie life and vayne ridiculous actions of the popular, they call him in scorne a *Philosopher* or *Poet*, as much to say as a phantasticall man, very iniuriously (God wot), and to the manifestation of their own ignoraunce, not making difference betwixt termes. For as the euill and vicious disposition of the braine hinders the sounde iudgement and discourse of man with busie & disordered phantasies, for which cause the Greekes call him φαντα- στικός, so is that part, being well affected, not onely nothing disorderly or confused with any monstruous imaginations or conceits, but very formall, and in his much multiformitie *vniforme*, that is well proportioned, and so passing cleare, that by it, as by a glasse or mirrour, are represented vnto the soule all maner of bewtifull visions, whereby the inuentiue parte of the mynde is so much holpen as without it no man could deuise any new or rare thing: and where it is not excellent in his kind, there could be no politique Captaine, nor any witty enginer or cunning artificer, nor yet any law maker or counsellor of deepe discourse, yea, the Prince of Philosophers stickes not to say *animam non intelligere absque phantasmate*; which text to another purpose *Alexander Aphrodis[i]ens[is]* well noteth, as learned men know. And this phantasie may be resembled to a glasse, as hath bene sayd, whereof there be many tempers and manner of makinges, as the *perspectiues* doe acknowledge, for some be false glasses and shew thinges otherwise than they be in deede, and others right as they be in deede, neither fairer nor fouler, nor greater nor smaller. There be againe of these glasses that shew thinges exceeding faire and comely; others that shew figures very monstruous & illfauored. Euen so is the phantasticall part of man (if it be not disordered) a representer of the best, most comely, and bewtifull images or apparances of thinges to the soule and according to their very truth. If otherwise, then doth it breede *Chimeres* & monsters in mans imaginations, & not onely in his imaginations, but also in all his ordinarie actions and life which ensues. Wherefore such persons as be illuminated with the brightest irradiations of knowledge and of the veritie and due proportion of things, they are called by the learned men not *phantastici* but *euphantasioti*, and of this sorte of phantasie are all good Poets, notable Captaines stratagematique, all cunning artificers and enginers, all Legislators, Polititiens, & Counsellours of estate, in whose exercises the inuentiue part is most employed, and is to the sound and true iudgement of man most needful. This diuersitie in the termes perchance euery man hath not noted, & thus much be said in defence of the Poets honour, to the end no noble and generous

minde be discomforted in the studie thereof, the rather
for that worthy & honorable memoriall of that noble
woman, twise French Queene, Lady *Anne* of Britaine,
wife first to king *Charles* the viij. and after to *Lewes* the
xij., who, passing one day from her lodging toward the
kinges side, saw in a gallerie *Maister Allaine Chartier*,
the kings Secretarie, an excellent maker or Poet, leaning
on a tables end a sleepe, & stooped downe to kisse him,
saying thus in all their hearings, 'we may not of Princely
courtesie passe by and not honor with our kisse the mouth
from whence so many sweete ditties & golden poems haue
issued.' But me thinks at these words I heare some
smilingly say, 'I would be loath to lacke liuing of my own
till the Prince gaue me a maner of new Elme for my
riming.' And another to say, 'I haue read that the Lady
Cynthia came once downe out of her skye to kisse the
faire yong lad *Endimion* as he lay a sleep: & many noble
Queenes that haue bestowed kisses vpon their Princes
paramours, but neuer vpon any Poets.' The third, me
thinks, shruggingly saith, 'I kept not to sit sleeping with
my Poesie till a Queene came and kissed me.' But what
of all this? Princes may giue a good Poet such conuenient
countenaunce and also benefite as are due to an excellent
artificer, though they neither kisse nor cokes them, and
the discret Poet lookes for no such extraordinarie fauours,
and aswell doth he honour by his pen the iust, liberall, or
magnanimous Prince as the valiaunt, amiable, or bewtifull,
though they be euery one of them the good giftes of God.
So it seemes not altogether the scorne and ordinarie disgrace offered vnto Poets [in] these dayes is cause why few
Gentlemen do delight in the Art, but for that liberalitie is
come to fayle in Princes, who for their largesse were wont
to be accompted th'onely patrons of learning and first
founders of all excellent artificers. Besides it is not perceiued that Princes them selues do take any pleasure in

this science, by whose example the subiect is commonly led, and allured to all delights and exercises, be they good or bad, according to the graue saying of the historian, *Rex multitudinem religione impleuit, quae semper regenti similis est.* And peraduenture in this iron and malitious age of ours Princes are lesse delighted in it, being ouer earnestly bent and affected to the affaires of Empire & ambition, whereby they are as it were inforced to indeuour them selues to armes and practises of hostilitie, or to entend to the right pollicing of their states, and haue not one houre to bestow vpon any other ciuill or delectable Art of naturall or morall doctrine, nor scarce any leisure to thincke one good thought in perfect and godly contemplation, whereby their troubled mindes might be moderated and brought to tranquillitie. So as it is hard to find in these dayes of noblemen or gentlemen any good *Mathematician*, or excellent *Musitian*, or notable *Philosopher*, or els a cunning Poet, because we find few great Princes much delighted in the same studies. Now also of such among the Nobilitie or gentrie as be very well seene in many laudable sciences, and especially in making or Poesie, it is so come to passe that they haue no courage to write, &, if they haue, yet are they loath to be a knowen of their skill. So as I know very many notable Gentlemen in the Court that haue written commendably, and suppressed it agayne, or els suffred it to be publisht without their owne names to it: as if it were a discredit for a Gentleman to seeme learned and to shew him selfe amorous of any good Art. In other ages it was not so, for we read that Kinges & Princes haue written great volumes and publisht them vnder their owne regall titles. As to begin with *Salomon*, the wisest of Kings, *Iulius Caesar*, the greatest of Emperours, *Hermes Trismegistus*, the holiest of Priestes and Prophetes. *Euax*, king of *Arabia*, wrote a booke of precious stones in verse, Prince *Auicenna*

Of Poets and Poesy

of Phisicke and Philosophie, *Alphonsus*, king of Spaine, his Astronomicall Tables, *Almansor*, a king of *Marrocco*, diuerse Philosophicall workes : and by their regall example our late soueraigne Lord, king *Henry* the eight, wrate a booke in defence of his faith, then perswaded that it was the true and Apostolicall doctrine; though it hath appeared otherwise since, yet his honour and learned zeale was nothing lesse to be allowed. Queenes also haue bene knowen studious, and to write large volumes, as Lady *Margaret* of Fraunce, Queene of *Nauarre*, in our time. But of all others the Emperour *Nero* was so well learned in Musique and Poesie, as, when he was taken by order of the Senate and appointed to dye, he offered violence to him selfe and sayd, *O quantus artifex pereo!* as much as to say, as how is it possible a man of such science and learning as my selfe should come to this shameful death? Th'emperour *Octauian*, being made executor to *Virgill*, who had left by his last will and testament that his bookes of the *Æneidos* should be committed to the fire as things not perfited by him, made his excuse for infringing the deads will by a nomber of verses most excellently written, whereof these are part,

> *Frangatur potius legum veneranda potestas,*
> *Quam tot congestos noctesque diesque labores*
> *Hauserit vna dies;*

and put his name to them. And before him his vncle & father adoptiue *Iulius Caesar* was not ashamed to publish vnder his owne name his Commentaries of the French and Britaine warres. Since therefore so many noble Emperours, Kings, and Princes haue bene studious of Poesie and other ciuill arts, and not ashamed to bewray their skils in the same, let none other meaner person despise learning, nor (whether it be in prose or in Poesie, if they them selues be able to write, or haue written any thing well or of rare inuention) be any whit

squeimish to let it be publisht vnder their names, for
reason serues it, and modestie doth not repugne.

CHAP. IX.

HOW POESIE SHOULD NOT BE IMPLOYED VPON VAYNE CONCEITS, OR VICIOUS, OR INFAMOUS.

Wherefore, the Nobilitie and dignitie of the Art considered aswell by vniuersalitie as antiquitie and the naturall excellence of it selfe, Poesie ought not to be abased and imployed vpon any vnworthy matter & subiect, nor vsed to vaine purposes; which neuerthelesse is dayly seene, and that is to vtter conceits infamous & vicious, or ridiculous and foolish, or of no good example & doctrine. Albeit in merry matters (not vnhonest) being vsed for mans solace and recreation it may be well allowed, for, as I said before, Poesie is a pleasant maner of vtteraunce, varying from the ordinarie of purpose to refresh the mynde by the eares delight. Poesie also is not onely laudable, because I said it was a metricall speach vsed by the first men, but because it is a metricall speach corrected and reformed by discreet iudgements, and with no lesse cunning and curiositie then the Greeke and Latine Poesie, and by Art bewtified & adorned & brought far from the primitiue rudenesse of the first inuentors: otherwise it may be sayd to me that *Adam* and *Eues* apernes were the gayest garmentes, because they were the first, and the shepheardes tente or pauillion the best housing, because it was the most auncient & most vniuersall; which I would not haue so taken, for it is not my meaning but that Art & cunning concurring with nature, antiquitie, & vniuersalitie, in things indifferent, and not euill, doe make them more laudable. And right so our vulgar riming Poesie, being by good wittes brought to that perfection, we see is worthily to be preferred before any other maner of vtterance in prose, for such vse and to such purpose as it is ordained, and shall hereafter be set downe more particularly.

CHAP. X.

THE SUBIECT OR MATTER OF POESIE.

Hauing sufficiently sayd of the dignitie of Poets and Poesie, now it is tyme to speake of the matter or subiect of Poesie, which to myne intent is what soeuer wittie and delicate conceit of man meet or worthy to be put in written verse, for any necessary vse of the present time, or good instruction of the posteritie. But the chief and principall is the laud, honour, & glory of the immortall gods (I speake now in phrase of the Gentiles): secondly, the worthy gests of noble Princes, the memoriall and registry of all great fortunes, the praise of vertue & reproofe of vice, the instruction of morall doctrines, the reuealing of sciences naturall & other profitable Arts, the redresse of boistrous & sturdie courages by perswasion, the consolation and repose of temperate myndes: finally, the common solace of mankind in all his trauails and cares of this transitorie life; and in this last sort, being vsed for recreation onely, may allowably beare matter not alwayes of the grauest or of any great commoditie or profit, but rather in some sort vaine, dissolute, or wanton, so it be not very scandalous & of euill example. But as our intent is to make this Art vulgar for all English mens vse, & therefore are of necessitie to set downe the principal rules therein to be obserued, so in mine opinion it is no lesse expedient to touch briefly all the chief points of this aunceint Poesie of the Greeks and Latines, so far forth as it conformeth with ours. So as it may be knowen what we

hold of them as borrowed, and what as of our owne
peculiar. Wherefore, now that we haue said what is the
matter of Poesie, we will declare the manner and formes
of poemes vsed by the auncients.

CHAP. XI.

OF POEMES AND THEIR SUNDRY FORMES, AND HOW THEREBY
THE AUNCIENT POETS RECEAUED SURNAMES.

As the matter of Poesie is diuers, so was the forme of
their poemes & maner of writing, for all of them wrote not
in one sort, euen as all of them wrote not vpon one matter.
Neither was euery Poet alike cunning in all, as in some
one kinde of Poesie, nor vttered with like felicitie. But
wherein any one most excelled, thereof he tooke a surname, as to be called a Poet *Heroick, Lyrick, Elegiack,
Epigrammatist*, or otherwise. Such therefore as gaue
themselues to write long histories of the noble gests of
kings & great Princes entermedling the dealings of the
gods, halfe gods, or *Heroes* of the gentiles, & the great &
waighty consequences of peace and warre, they called
Poets *Heroick*, whereof *Homer* was chief and most
auncient among the Greeks, *Virgill* among the Latines:
Others who more delighted to write songs or ballads of
pleasure, to be song with the voice, and to the harpe,
lute, or citheron, & such other musical instruments, they
were called melodious Poets (*melici*), or, by a more common
name, *Lirique* Poets: of which sort was *Pindarus, Anacreon*,
and *Callimachus*, with others among the Greeks, *Horace*
and *Catullus* among the Latines. There were an other
sort, who sought the fauor of faire Ladies, and coueted
to bemone their estates at large & the perplexities of loue
in a certain pitious verse called *Elegie*, and thence were
called *Elegiack*: such among the Latines were *Ouid*,

Tibullus, & *Propertius*. There were also Poets that wrote onely for the stage, I meane playes and interludes, to recreate the people with matters of disporte, and to that intent did set forth in shewes [&] pageants, accompanied with speach, the common behauiours and maner of life of priuate persons, and such as were the meaner sort of men, and they were called *Comicall* Poets: of whom among the Greekes *Menander* and *Aristophanes* were most excellent, with the Latines *Terence* and *Plautus*. Besides those Poets *Comick* there were other who serued also the stage, but medled not with so base matters, for they set forth the dolefull falles of infortunate & afflicted Princes, & were called Poets *Tragicall*: such were *Euripides* and *Sophocles* with the Greeks, *Seneca* among the Latines. There were yet others who mounted nothing so high as any of them both, but, in base and humble stile by maner of Dialogue, vttered the priuate and familiar talke of the meanest sort of men, as shepheards, heywards, and such like: such was among the Greekes *Theocritus*, and *Virgill* among the Latines; their poems were named *Eglogues* or shepheardly talke. There was yet another kind of Poet, who intended to taxe the common abuses and vice of the people in rough and bitter speaches, and their inuectiues were called *Satyres*, and them selues *Satyricques*: such were *Lucilius*, *Iuuenall*, and *Persius* among the Latines, & with vs he that wrote the booke called Piers plowman. Others of a more fine and pleasant head were giuen wholly to taunting and scoffing at vndecent things, and in short poemes vttered pretie merry conceits, and these men were called *Epigrammatistes*. There were others that for the peoples good instruction, and triall of their owne witts, vsed in places of great assembly to say by rote nombers of short and sententious meetres, very pithie and of good edification, and thereupon were called Poets *Mimistes*, as who would say, imitable and meet to be followed for

their wise and graue lessons. There was another kind
of poeme, inuented onely to make sport & to refresh
the company with a maner of buffonry or counterfaiting
of merry speaches, conuerting all that which they had
hard spoken before to a certaine derision by a quite
contrary sence, and this was done when *Comedies* or
Tragedies were a playing, & that betweene the actes when
the players went to make ready for another, there was
great silence, and the people waxt weary, then came in
these maner of conterfaite vices; they were called *Pantomimi*, and all that had before bene sayd, or great part of
it, they gaue a crosse construction to it very ridiculously.
Thus haue you how the names of the Poets were giuen
them by the formes of their poemes and maner of writing.

CHAP. XII.

IN WHAT FORME OF POESIE THE GODS OF THE GENTILES WERE PRAYSED AND HONORED.

The gods of the Gentiles were honoured by their
Poetes in hymnes, which is an extraordinarie and diuine
praise, extolling and magnifying them for their great
powers and excellencie of nature in the highest degree
of laude; and yet therein their Poets were after a sort
restrained, so as they could not with their credit vntruly
praise their owne gods, or vse in their lauds any maner
of grosse adulation or vnueritable report. For in any
writer vntruth and flatterie are counted most great
reproches. Wherfore to praise the gods of the Gentiles,
for that by authoritie of their owne fabulous records they
had fathers and mothers, and kinred and allies, and wiues
and concubines, the Poets first commended them by their
genealogies or pedegrees, their mariages and aliances,
their notable exploits in the world for the behoofe of

mankind, and yet, as I sayd before, none otherwise then
the truth of their owne memorials might beare, and in
such sort as it might be well auouched by their old
written reports, though in very deede they were not from
the beginning all historically true, and many of them verie
fictions, and such of them as were true were grounded
vpon some part of an historie or matter of veritie, the
rest altogether figuratiue & misticall, couertly applied to
some morall or natural sense, as *Cicero* setteth it foorth
in his bookes *de natura deorum*. For to say that *Iupiter*
was sonne to *Saturne*, and that he maried his owne sister
Iuno, might be true, for such was the guise of all great
Princes in the Orientall part of the world both at those
dayes and now is. Againe, that he loued *Danae, Europa,
Leda, Cal[l]isto*, & other faire Ladies, daughters to kings,
besides many meaner women, it is likely enough, because
he was reported to be a very incontinent person and
giuen ouer to his lustes, as are for the most part all the
greatest Princes; but that he should be the highest god
in heauen, or that he should thunder and lighten, and do
manie other things very vnnaturally and absurdly, also
that *Saturnus* should geld his father *Coelus*, to th'intent
to make him vnable to get any moe children, and other
such matters as are reported by them, it seemeth to be
some wittie deuise and fiction made for a purpose, or
a very no[ta]ble and impudent lye, which could not be
reasonably suspected by the Poets, who were otherwise
discreete and graue men, and teachers of wisedome to
others. Therefore either to transgresse the rules of their
primitiue records or to seeke to giue their gods honour
by belying them (otherwise then in that sence which
I haue alledged) had bene a signe not onely of an vnskilfull Poet but also of a very impudent and leude man.
For vntrue praise neuer giueth any true reputation. But
with vs Christians, who be better disciplined, and do

acknowledge but one God Almightie, euerlasting, and in
euery respect selfe suffizant, *autharcos*, reposed in all
perfect rest and soueraigne blisse, nor needing or exacting
any forreine helpe or good, to him we can not exhibit
ouermuch praise, nor belye him any wayes, vnlesse it be
in abasing his excellencie by scarsitie of praise, or by
misconceauing his diuine nature, weening to praise him
if we impute to him such vaine delights and peeuish
affections as commonly the frailest men are reproued
for: namely, to make him ambitious of honour, iealous
and difficult in his worships, terrible, angrie, vindicatiue,
a louer, a hater, a pitier, and indigent of mans worships,
finally, so passionate as in effect he shold be altogether
Anthropopathis. To the gods of the Gentiles they might
well attribute these infirmities, for they were but the
children of men, great Princes and famous in the world,
and not for any other respect diuine then by some resemblance of vertue they had to do good and to benefite
many. So as to the God of the Christians such diuine
praise might be verified; to th'other gods none, but
figuratiuely or in misticall sense, as hath bene said. In
which sort the ancient Poets did in deede giue them
great honors & praises, and made to them sacrifices,
and offred them oblations of sundry sortes, euen as the
people were taught and perswaded by such placations
and worships to receaue any helpe, comfort, or benefite to
them selues, their wiues, children, possessions, or goods.
For if that opinion were not, who would acknowledge any
God? the verie *Etimologie* of the name with vs of the
North partes of the world declaring plainely the nature
of the attribute, which is all one as if we sayd good, *bonus*,
or a giuer of good things. Therfore the Gentiles prayed
for peace to the goddesse *Pallas*; for warre (such as
thriued by it) to the god *Mars*; for honor and empire
to the god *Iupiter*; for riches & wealth to *Pluto*; for

eloquence and gayne to *Mercurie*; for safe nauigation to
Neptune; for faire weather and prosperous windes to
Eolus; for skill in musick and leechcraft to *Apollo*; for
free life & chastitie to *Diana*; for bewtie and good grace,
as also for issue & prosperitie in loue, to *Venus*; for
plenty of crop and corne to *Ceres*; for seasonable vintage
to *Bacchus*; and for other things to others. So many
things as they could imagine good and desirable, and to
so many gods as they supposed to be authors thereof, in
so much as *Fortune* was made a goddesse, & the feuer
quartaine had her aulters: such blindnes & ignorance
raigned in the harts of men at that time, and whereof
it first proceeded and grew, besides th'opinion hath bene
giuen, appeareth more at large in our bookes of *Ierotekni*,
the matter being of another consideration then to be
treated of in this worke. And these hymnes to the gods
was the first forme of Poesie and the highest & the
stateliest, & they were song by the Poets as priests, and
by the people or whole congregation, as we sing in our
Churches the Psalmes of *Dauid*, but they did it commonly
in some shadie groues of tall tymber trees: In which
places they reared aulters of green turfe, and bestrewed
them all ouer with flowers, and vpon them offred their
oblations and made their bloudy sacrifices (for no kinde
of gift can be dearer then life) of such quick cattaille, as
euery god was in their conceit most delighted in, or in
some other respect most fit for the misterie: temples or
churches or other chappels then these they had none at
those dayes.

CHAP. XIII.

IN WHAT FORME OF POESIE VICE AND THE COMMON ABUSES OF MANS LIFE WAS REPREHENDED.

Some perchance would thinke that next after the
praise and honoring of their gods should commence the

worshippings and praise of good men, and specially of
great Princes and gouernours of the earth in soueraignety
and function next vnto the gods. But it is not so, for
before that came to passe the Poets or holy Priests
chiefly studied the rebuke of vice, and to carpe at the
common abuses, such as were most offensiue to the
publique and priuate, for as yet for lacke of good ciuility
and wholesome doctrines there was greater store of lewde
lourdaines then of wise and learned Lords or of noble
and vertuous Princes and gouernours. So as next after
the honours exhibited to their gods, the Poets, finding in
man generally much to reproue & litle to praise, made
certaine poems in plaine meetres, more like to sermons or
preachings then otherwise, and when the people were
assembled togither in those hallowed places dedicate to
their gods, because they had yet no large halles or places
of conuenticle, nor had any other correction of their faults,
but such as rested onely in rebukes of wise and graue
men, such as at these dayes make the people ashamed
rather then afeard, the said aunceint Poets vsed for that
purpose three kinds of poems reprehensiue, to wit, the
Satyre, the *Comedie*, and the *Tragedie*. And the first and
most bitter inuectiue against vice and vicious men was the
Satyre: which, to th'intent their bitternesse should breede
none ill will, either to the Poets, or to the recitours (which
could not haue bene chosen if they had bene openly
knowen), and besides to make their admonitions and reproofs seeme grauer and of more efficacie, they made wise
as if the gods of the woods, whom they called *Satyres* or
Siluanes, should appeare and recite those verses of rebuke,
whereas in deede they were but disguised persons vnder
the shape of *Satyres*, as who would say, these terrene and
base gods, being conuersant with mans affaires, and spiers
out of all their secret faults, had some great care ouer
man, & desired by good admonitions to reforme the euill

of their life, and to bring the bad to amendment by those kinde of preachings; whereupon the Poets inuentours of the deuise were called *Satyristes*.

CHAP. XIV.

HOW VICE WAS AFTERWARD REPROUED BY TWO OTHER MANER OF POEMS, BETTER REFORMED THEN THE SATYRE, WHEREOF THE FIRST WAS COMEDY, THE SECOND TRAGEDIE.

But when these maner of solitary speaches and recitals of rebuke, vttered by the rurall gods out of bushes and briers, seemed not to the finer heads sufficiently perswasiue, nor so popular as if it were reduced into action of many persons, or by many voyces liuely represented to the eare and eye, so as a man might thinke it were euen now a doing, the Poets deuised to haue many parts played at once by two or three or foure persons, that debated the matters of the world, sometimes of their owne priuate affaires, sometimes of their neighbours, but neuer medling with any Princes matters nor such high personages, but commonly of marchants, souldiers, artificers, good honest housholders, and also of vnthrifty youthes, yong damsels, old nurses, bawds, brokers, ruffians, and parasites, with such like, in whose behauiors lyeth in effect the whole course and trade of mans life, and therefore tended altogither to the good amendment of man by discipline and example. It was also much for the solace & recreation of the common people by reason of the pageants and shewes. And this kind of poeme was called *Comedy*, and followed next after the *Satyre*, & by that occasion was somwhat sharpe and bitter after the nature of the *Satyre*, openly & by expresse names taxing men more maliciously and impudently then became, so as they were enforced for feare

of quarell & blame to disguise their players with strange
apparell, and by colouring their faces and carying hatts &
capps of diuerse fashions to make them selues lesse
knowen. But as time & experience do reforme euery
thing that is amisse, so, this bitter poeme called the old
Comedy being disused and taken away, the new *Comedy*
came in place, more ciuill and pleasant a great deale, and
not touching any man by name, but in a certaine generalitie
glancing at euery abuse, so as from thenceforth fearing
none illwill or enmitie at any bodies hands they left aside
their disguisings and played bare face, till one *Roscius
Gallus*, the most excellent player among the Romaines,
brought vp these vizards which we see at this day vsed,
partly to supply the want of players, when there were moe
parts than there were persons, or that it was not thought
meet to trouble & pester princes chambers with too many
folkes. Now by the chaunge of a vizard one man might
play the king and the carter, the old nurse & the yong
damsell, the marchant and the souldier, or any other part
he listed very conueniently. There be that say *Roscius*
did it for another purpose, for being him selfe the best
Histrien or buffon that was in his dayes to be found, insomuch as *Cicero* said *Roscius* contended with him by varietie
of liuely gestures to surmount the copy of his speach, yet
because he was squint eyed and had a very vnpleasant
countenance, and lookes which made him ridiculous or
rather odious to the presence, he deuised these vizards
to hide his owne ilfauored face. And thus much touching
the *Comedy*.

CHAP. XV.

IN WHAT FORME OF POESIE THE EUILL AND OUTRAGIOUS
BEHAUIOURS OF PRINCES WERE REPREHENDED.

But because in those dayes when the Poets first taxed
by *Satyre* and *Comedy* there was no great store of Kings

or Emperors or such high estats (al men being yet for the most part rude, & in a maner popularly egall), they could not say of them or of their behauiours any thing to the purpose, which cases of Princes are sithens taken for the highest and greatest matters of all. But after that some men among the moe became mighty and famous in the world, soueraignetie and dominion hauing learned them all maner of lusts and licentiousnes of life, by which occasions also their high estates and felicities fell many times into most lowe and lamentable fortunes: whereas before in their great prosperities they were both feared and reuerenced in the highest degree, after their deathes, when the posteritie stood no more in dread of them, their infamous life and tyrannies were layd open to all the world, their wickednes reproched, their follies and extreme insolencies derided, and their miserable ends painted out in playes and pageants, to shew the mutabilitie of fortune, and the iust punishment of God in reuenge of a vicious and euill life. These matters were also handled by the Poets, and represented by action as that of the *Comedies*: but because the matter was higher then that of the *Comedies*, the Poets stile was also higher and more loftie, the prouision greater, the place more magnificent; for which purpose also the players garments were made more rich & costly and solemne, and euery other thing apperteining, according to that rate: So as where the *Satyre* was pronounced by rusticall and naked *Syluanes* speaking out of a bush, & the common players of interludes called *Planipedes* played barefoote vpon the floore, the later *Comedies* vpon scaffolds, and by men well and cleanely hosed and shod. These matters of great Princes were played vpon lofty stages, & the actors thereof ware vpon their legges buskins of leather called *Cothurni*, and other solemne habits, & for a speciall preheminence did walke vpon those high corked shoes or pantofles, which now they call in

Spaine and Italy *Shoppini*. And because those buskins
and high shoes were commonly made of goats skinnes
very finely tanned, and dyed into colours, or for that, as
some say, the best players reward was a goate to be giuen
him, or for that, as other thinke, a goate was the peculiar
sacrifice of the god *Pan*, king of all the gods of the
woodes—forasmuch as a goate in Greeke is called *Tragos*,
therfore these stately playes were called *Tragedies*. And
thus haue ye foure sundry formes of Poesie *Drammatick*
reprehensiue, & put in execution by the feate and dexteritie
of mans body, to wit, the *Satyre*, old *Comedie*, new *Comedie*,
and *Tragedie*, whereas all other kinde of poems, except
Eglogue, whereof shalbe entreated hereafter, were onely
recited by mouth or song with the voyce to some melodious
instrument.

CHAP. XVI.

IN WHAT FORME OF POESIE THE GREAT PRINCES AND DOMINATORS OF THE WORLD WERE HONORED.

But as the bad and illawdable parts of all estates and
degrees were taxed by the Poets in one sort or an other,
and those of great Princes by Tragedie in especial, & not
till after their deaths, as hath bene before remembred, to
th'intent that such exemplifying (as it were) of their blames
and aduersities, being now dead, might worke for a secret
reprehension to others that were aliue, liuing in the same
or like abuses: so was it great reason that all good and
vertuous persons should for their well doings be rewarded
with commendation, and the great Princes aboue all others
with honors and praises, being for many respects of greater
moment to haue them good & vertuous then any inferior
sort of men. Wherfore the Poets, being in deede the
trumpetters of all praise and also of slaunder (not slaunder,
but well deserued reproch), were in conscience & credit

bound next after the diuine praises of the immortall gods
to yeeld a like ratable honour to all such amongst men as
most resembled the gods by excellencie of function, and
had a certaine affinitie with them, by more then humane
and ordinarie vertues shewed in their actions here vpon
earth. They were therfore praised by a second degree
of laude: shewing their high estates, their Princely genealogies and pedegrees, mariages, aliances, and such noble
exploites, as they had done in th'affaires of peace & of
warre to the benefit of their people and countries, by
inuention of any noble science or profitable Art, or by
making wholsome lawes or enlarging of their dominions
by honorable and iust conquests, and many other wayes.
Such personages among the Gentiles were *Bacchus, Ceres,
Perseus, Hercules, Theseus,* and many other, who thereby
came to be accompted gods and halfe gods or goddesses
(*Heroes*), & had their commendations giuen by Hymne
accordingly, or by such other poems as their memorie was
therby made famous to the posteritie for euer after, as shal
be more at large sayd in place conuenient. But first we
will speake somewhat of the playing places, and prouisions
which were made for their pageants & pomps representatiue
before remembred.

CHAP. XVII.

OF THE PLACES WHERE THEIR ENTERLUDES OR POEMES DRAMMATICKE WERE REPRESENTED TO THE PEOPLE.

As it hath bene declared, the *Satyres* were first vttered
in their hallowed places within the woods where they
honoured their gods vnder the open heauen, because they
had no other housing fit for great assemblies. The old
comedies were plaid in the broad streets vpon wagons or
carts vncouered, which carts were floored with bords &

made for remouable stages to passe from one streete of
their townes to another, where all the people might stand
at their ease to gaze vpon the sights. Their new comedies
or ciuill enterludes were played in open pauilions or tents
of linnen cloth or lether, halfe displayed that the people
might see. Afterward, when Tragidies came vp, they
deuised to present them upon scaffoldes or stages of
timber, shadowed with linen or lether as the other, and
these stages were made in the forme of a *Semicircle*, wherof
the bow serued for the beholders to sit in, and the string
or forepart was appointed for the floore or place where
the players vttered, & had in it sundrie little diuisions by
curteins as trauerses to serue for seueral roomes where
they might repaire vnto & change their garments and come
in againe, as their speaches & parts were to be renewed.
Also there was place appointed for musiciens to sing or to
play vpon their instrumentes at the end of euery scene, to
the intent the people might be refreshed and kept occupied.
This maner of stage in halfe circle the Greekes called
theatrum, as much to say as a beholding place, which was
also in such sort contriued by benches and greeces to
stand or sit vpon, as no man should empeach anothers
sight. But as ciuilitie and withall wealth encreased, so
did the minde of man growe dayly more haultie and superfluous in all his deuises, so as for their *theaters* in halfe
circle, they came to be by the great magnificence of the
Romain princes and people somptuously built with marble
& square stone in forme all round, & were called *Amphitheaters*, wherof as yet appears one among the ancient
ruines of Rome, built by *Pompeius Magnus*, for capasitie
able to receiue at ease fourscore thousand persons, as it is
left written, & so curiously contriued as euery man might
depart at his pleasure, without any annoyance to other.
It is also to be knowne that in those great *Amphitheaters*
were exhibited all maner of other shewes & disports for

the people, as their fence playes, or digladiations of naked men, their wrastlings, runnings, leapings, and other practises of actiuitie and strength, also their baitings of wild beasts, as Elephants, Rhinoceros, Tigers, Leopards, and others, which sights much delighted the common people, and therefore the places required to be large and of great content.

CHAP. XVIII.

OF THE SHEPHEARDS OR PASTORALL POESIE CALLED EGLOGUE, AND TO WHAT PURPOSE IT WAS FIRST INUENTED AND VSED.

Some be of opinion, and the chiefe of those who haue written in this Art among the Latines, that the pastorall Poesie which we commonly call by the name of *Eglogue* and *Bucolick*, a tearme brought in by the Sicilian Poets, should be the first of any other, and before the *Satyre*, *Comedie*, or *Tragedie*, because, say they, the shepheards and haywards assemblies & meetings when they kept their cattell and heards in the common fields and forests was the first familiar conuersation, and their babble and talk vnder bushes and shadie trees the first disputation and contentious reasoning, and their fleshly heates growing of ease the first idle wooings, and their songs made to their mates or paramours either vpon sorrow or iolity of courage the first amorous musicks; sometime also they sang and played on their pipes for wagers, striuing who should get the best game and be counted cunningest. All this I do agree vnto, for no doubt the shepheards life was the first example of honest felowship, their trade the first art of lawfull acquisition or purchase, for at those daies robbery was a manner of purchase. So saith *Aristotle* in his bookes of the Politiques; and that pasturage was before tillage, or fishing, or fowling, or any other predatory art or cheuisance.

And all this may be true, for before there was a shepheard keeper of his owne or of some other bodies flocke, there was none owner in the world, quick cattel being the first property of any forreine possession. I say forreine, because alway men claimed property in their apparell and armour, and other like things made by their owne trauel and industry, nor thereby was there yet any good towne, or city, or Kings palace, where pageants and pompes might be shewed by Comedies or Tragedies. But for all this, I do deny that the *Eglogue* should be the first and most auncient forme of artificiall Poesie, being perswaded that the Poet deuised the *Eglogue* long after the other *drammatick* poems, not of purpose to counterfait or represent the rusticall manner of loues and communication, but vnder the vaile of homely persons and in rude speeches to insinuate and glaunce at greater matters, and such as perchance had not bene safe to haue beene disclosed in any other sort, which may be perceiued by the Eglogues of *Virgill*, in which are treated by figure matters of greater importance then the loues of *Titirus* and *Corydon*. These Eglogues came after to containe and enforme morall discipline, for the amendment of mans behauiour, as be those of *Mantuan* and other moderne Poets.

CHAP. XIX.

OF HISTORICALL POESIE, BY WHICH THE FAMOUS ACTS OF PRINCES AND THE VERTUOUS AND WORTHY LIUES OF OUR FOREFATHERS WERE REPORTED.

There is nothing in man of all the potential parts of his mind (reason and will except) more noble or more necessary to the actiue life then memory; because it maketh most to a sound iudgement and perfect worldly wisedome, examining and comparing the times past with the present, and, by them both considering the time to come, concludeth with a stedfast resolution what is the best course to be taken in all his actions and aduices in this world. It came, vpon this reason, experience to be so highly commended in all consultations of importance, and preferred before any learning or science, and yet experience is no more than a masse of memories assembled, that is, such trials as man hath made in time before. Right so no kinde of argument in all the Oratorie craft doth better perswade and more vniuersally satisfie then example, which is but the representation of old memories, and like successes happened in times past. For these regards the Poesie historicall is of all other next the diuine most honorable and worthy, as well for the common benefit as for the speciall comfort euery man receiueth by it: no one thing in the world with more delectation reuiuing our spirits then to behold as it were in a glasse the liuely image of our deare forefathers, their noble and vertuous maner of life, with other things autentike, which because we are not able otherwise to attaine to the knowledge of by any of our sences, we apprehend them by memory, whereas the present time and things so swiftly passe away, as they giue vs no leasure almost to looke into them, and much lesse to know & consider of them throughly. The things future, being also euents very vncertaine, and such as can not possibly be knowne because they be not yet, can not be vsed for example nor for delight otherwise then by hope; though many promise the contrary, by vaine and deceitfull arts taking vpon them to reueale the truth of accidents to come, which, if it were so as they surmise, are yet but sciences meerely coniecturall, and not of any benefit to man or to the common wealth where they be vsed or professed. Therefore the good and exemplarie things and actions of the former ages were reserued only to the historicall reportes of wise and graue men: those of the

present time left to the fruition and iudgement of our
sences: the future, as hazards and incertaine euentes
vtterly neglected and layd aside for Magicians and
mockers to get their liuings by, such manner of men as by
negligence of Magistrates and remiss[n]es of lawes euery
countrie breedeth great store of. These historical men
neuerthelesse vsed not the matter so precisely to wish that
al they wrote should be accounted true, for that was not
needeful nor expedient to the purpose, namely to be vsed
either for example or for pleasure: considering that many
times it is seene a fained matter or altogether fabulous,
besides that it maketh more mirth than any other, works
no lesse good conclusions for example then the most true
and veritable, but often times more, because the Poet
hath the handling of them to fashion at his pleasure, but
not so of th' other, which must go according to their veritie,
and none otherwise, without the writers great blame.
Againe, as ye know, mo and more excellent examples may
be fained in one day by a good wit then many ages
through mans frailtie are able to put in vre; which made
the learned and wittie men of those times to deuise many
historicall matters of no veritie at all, but with purpose to
do good and no hurt, as vsing them for a maner of discipline and president of commendable life. Such was the
common wealth of *Plato*, and Sir *Thomas Moores Vtopia*,
resting all in deuise, but neuer put in execution, and
easier to be wished then to be performed. And you shall
perceiue that histories were of three sortes, wholly true,
and wholly false, and a third holding part of either, but for
honest recreation and good example they were all of
them. And this may be apparant to vs not onely by the
Poeticall histories but also by those that be written in
prose: for as *Homer* wrate a fabulous or mixt report of
the siege of Troy and another of *Ulisses* errors or
wandrings, so did *Museus* compile a true treatise of the

life & loues of *Leandér* and *Hero*, both of them *Heroick*,
and to none ill edification. Also, as *Theucidides* wrate
a worthy and veritable historie of the warres betwixt the
Athenians and the *Peloponeses*, so did *Zenophon*, a most
graue Philosopher and well trained courtier and counsellour, make another (but fained and vntrue) of the childhood
of *Cyrus*, king of *Persia*; neuertheless both to one effect,
that is for example and good information of the posteritie.
Now because the actions of meane & base personages tend
in very few cases to any great good example; for who
passeth to follow the steps and maner of life of a craftes
man, shepheard, or sailer, though he were his father or
dearest frend? yea how almost is it possible that such
maner of men should be of any vertue other then their
profession requireth? therefore was nothing committed to
historie but matters of great and excellent persons & things,
that the same by irritation of good courages (such as
emulation causeth) might worke more effectually, which
occasioned the story writer to chuse an higher stile fit for
his subiect, the Prosaicke in prose, the Poet in meetre,
and the Poets was by verse exameter for his grauitie and
statelinesse most allowable: neither would they intermingle him with any other shorter measure, vnlesse it
were in matters of such qualitie as became best to be song
with the voyce and to some musicall instrument, as were
with the Greeks all your Hymnes & *Encomia* of *Pindarus*
& *Callimachus*, not very histories, but a maner of historicall
reportes; in which cases they made those poemes in
variable measures, & coupled a short verse with a long to
serue that purpose the better. And we our selues who
compiled this treatise haue written for pleasure a litle
brief *Romance* or historicall ditty in the English tong, of
the Isle of great *Britaine*, in short and long meetres, and
by breaches or diuisions to be more commodiously song to
the harpe in places of assembly, where the company shalbe

desirous to heare of old aduentures & valiaunces of noble
knights in times past, as are those of king *Arthur* and his
knights of the round table, Sir *Beuys* of *Southampton, Guy*
of *Warwicke*, and others like. Such as haue not premonition hereof, and consideration of the causes alledged,
would peraduenture reproue and disgrace euery *Romance*
or short historicall ditty for that they be not written in
long meeters or verses *Alexandrins*, according to the
nature and stile of large histories; wherin they should do
wrong, for they be sundry formes of poems, and not
all one.

CHAP. XX.

IN WHAT FORME OF POESIE VERTUE IN THE INFERIOUR SORT WAS COMMENDED.

In euerie degree and sort of men vertue is commendable,
but not egally: not onely because mens estates are vnegall,
but for that also vertue it selfe is not in euery respect of
egall value and estimation. For continence in a king is
of greater merit then in a carter, th'one hauing all opportunities to allure him to lusts, and abilitie to serue his
appetites, th'other partly for the basenesse of his estate
wanting such meanes and occasions, partly by dread of
lawes more inhibited, and not so vehemently caried away
with vnbridled affections; and therfore deserue not in
th'one and th'other like praise nor equall reward, by the
very ordinarie course of distributiue iustice. Euen so
parsimonie and illiberalitie are greater vices in a Prince
then in a priuate person, and pusillanimitie and iniustice
likewise: for to th'one fortune hath supplied inough to
maintaine them in the contrarie vertues, I meane, fortitude,
iustice, liberalitie, and magnanimitie, the Prince hauing all
plentie to vse largesse by, and no want or neede to driue
him to do wrong; also all the aides that may be to lift vp
his courage and to make him stout and fearlesse: *augent*

animos fortunae, saith the *Mimist,* and very truly, for nothing pulleth downe a mans heart so much as aduersitie and lacke. Againe, in a meane man prodigalitie and pride are faultes more reprehensible then in Princes, whose high estates do require in their countenance, speech, & expence a certaine extraordinary, and their functions enforce them sometime to exceede the limites of mediocritie, not excusable in a priuat person, whose manner of life and calling hath no such exigence. Besides the good and bad of Princes is more exemplarie, and thereby of greater moment then the priuate persons. Therfore it is that the inferiour persons with their inferiour vertues haue a certaine inferiour praise to guerdon their good with, & to comfort them to continue a laudable course in the modest and honest life and behauiour. But this lyeth not in written laudes so much as ordinary reward and commendation to be giuen them by the mouth of the superiour magistrate. For histories were not intended to so generall and base a purpose, albeit many a meane souldier & other obscure persons were spoken of and made famous in stories, as we finde of *Irus* the begger, and *Thersites* the glorious noddie, whom *Homer* maketh mention of. But that happened (& so did many like memories of meane men) by reason of some greater personage or matter that it was long of, which therefore could not be an vniuersall case nor chaunce to euery other good and vertuous person of the meaner sort. Wherefore the Poet in praising the maner of life or death of anie meane person did it by some litle dittie, or Epigram, or Epitaph, in fewe verses & meane stile conformable to his subiect. So haue you how the immortall gods were praised by hymnes, the great Princes and heroicke personages by ballades of praise called *Encomia,* both of them by historicall reports of great grauitie and maiestie, the inferiour persons by other slight poemes.

CHAP. XXI.

THE FORME WHEREIN HONEST AND PROFITABLE ARTES AND SCIENCES WERE TREATED.

The profitable sciences were no lesse meete to be imported to the greater number of ciuill men for instruction of the people and increase of knowledge then to be reserued and kept for clerkes and great men onely. So as next vnto the things historicall such doctrines and arts as the common wealth fared the better by were esteemed and allowed. And the same were treated by Poets in verse *Exameter* sauouring the *Heroicall*, and for the grauitie and comelinesse of the meetre most vsed with the Greekes and Latines to sad purposes. Such were the Philosophicall works of *Lucretius Carus* among the Romaines, the Astronomicall of *Aratus* and *Manilius*, one Greeke, th'other Latine, the Medicinall of *Nicander*, and that of *Oppianus* of hunting and fishes, and many moe that were too long to recite in this place.

CHAP. XXII.

IN WHAT FORME OF POESIE THE AMOROUS AFFECTIONS AND ALLUREMENTS WERE VTTERED.

The first founder of all good affections is honest loue, as the mother of all the vicious is hatred. It was not therefore without reason that so commendable, yea honourable, a thing as loue well meant, were it in Princely estate or priuate, might in all ciuil common wealths be vttered in good forme and order as other laudable things are. And because loue is of all other humane affections the most puissant and passionate, and most generall to all sortes and ages of men and women, so as whether it be of the

yong or old, or wise or holy, or high estate or low, none
euer could truly bragge of any exemption in that case :
it requireth a forme of Poesie variable, inconstant, affected,
curious, and most witty of any others, whereof the ioyes
were to be vttered in one sorte, the sorrowes in an other,
and, by the many formes of Poesie, the many moodes and
pangs of louers throughly to be discouered; the poore
soules sometimes praying, beseeching, sometime honouring,
auancing, praising, an other while railing, reuiling, and
cursing, then sorrowing, weeping, lamenting, in the ende
laughing, reioysing, & solacing the beloued againe, with
a thousand delicate deuises, odes, songs, elegies, ballads,
sonets, and other ditties, moouing one way and another
to great compassion.

CHAP. XXIII.

THE FORME OF POETICALL REIOYSINGS.

Pleasure is the chiefe parte of mans felicity in this
world, and also (as our Theologians say) in the world to
come. Therefore, while we may (yea alwaies if it coulde
be), to reioyce and take our pleasures in vertuous and
honest sort, it is not only allowable but also necessary
and very naturall to man. And many be the ioyes and
consolations of the hart, but none greater than such as he
may vtter and discouer by some convenient meanes : euen
as to suppresse and hide a mans mirth, and not to haue
therein a partaker, or at least wise a witnes, is no little
griefe and infelicity. Therfore nature and ciuility haue
ordained (besides the priuate solaces) publike reioisings
for the comfort and recreation of many. And they be of
diuerse sorts and vpon diuerse occasions growne. One
& the chiefe was for the publike peace of a countrie, the
greatest of any other ciuill good; and wherein your

Maiestie (my most gracious Soueraigne) haue shewed your selfe to all the world, for this one and thirty yeares space of your glorious raigne, aboue all other Princes of Christendome, not onely fortunate, but also most sufficient, vertuous, and worthy of Empire. An other is for iust & honourable victory atchieued against the forraine enemy. A third at solemne feasts and pompes of coronations and enstallments of honourable orders. An other for iollity at weddings and marriages. An other at the births of Princes children. An other for priuate entertainments in Court, or other secret disports in chamber, and such solitary places. And as these reioysings tend to diuers effects, so do they also carry diuerse formes and nominations; for those of victorie and peace are called *Triumphall*, whereof we our selues haue heretofore giuen some example by our *Triumphals*, written in honour of her Maiesties long peace. And they were vsed by the auncients in like manner as we do our generall processions or Letanies, with bankets and bonefires and all manner of ioyes. Those that were to honour the persons of great Princes or to solemnise the pompes of any installment were called *Encomia*; we may call them carols of honour. Those to celebrate marriages were called songs nuptiall or *Epithalamies*, but in a certaine misticall sense, as shall be said hereafter. Others for magnificence at the natiuities of Princes children, or by custome vsed yearely vpon the same dayes, are called songs natall, or *Genethliaca*. Others for secret recreation and pastime in chambers with company or alone were the ordinary Musickes amorous, such as might be song with voice or to the Lute, Citheron, or Harpe, or daunced by measures, as the Italian Pauan and galliard are at these daies in Princes Courts and other places of honourable or ciuill assembly; and of all these we will speake in order and very briefly.

CHAP. XXIV.

THE FORME OF POETICALL LAMENTATIONS.

Lamenting is altogether contrary to reioising; euery man saith so, and yet is it a peece of ioy to be able to lament with ease, and freely to poure forth a mans inward sorrowes and the greefs wherewith his minde is surcharged. This was a very necessary deuise of the Poet and a fine, besides his poetrie to play also the Phisitian, and not onely by applying a medicine to the ordinary sicknes of mankind, but by making the very greef it selfe (in part) cure of the disease. Nowe are the causes of mans sorrowes many: the death of his parents, frends, allies, and children (though many of the barbarous nations do reioyce at their burials and sorrow at their birthes), the ouerthrowes and discomforts in battell, the subuersions of townes and cities, the desolations of countreis, the losse of goods and worldly promotions, honour and good renowne, finally, the trauails and torments of loue forlorne or ill bestowed, either by disgrace, deniall, delay, and twenty other wayes, that well experienced louers could recite. Such of these greefs as might be refrained or holpen by wisedome and the parties owne good endeuour, the Poet gaue none order to sorrow them. For first, as to the good renowne, it is lost for the more part by some default of the owner, and may be by his well doings recouered againe. And if it be vniustly taken away, as by vntrue and famous libels, the offenders recantation may suffise for his amends: so did the Poet *Stesichorus*, as it is written of him in his *Pallinodie* vpon the disprayse of *Helena*, and recouered his eye sight. Also, for worldly goods, they come and go, as things not long proprietary to any body, and are not yet subiect vnto fortunes dominion so but that we our selues are in great part accessarie to our own losses and hinder-

aunces by ouersight & misguiding of our selues and our
things; therefore, why should we bewaile our such voluntary
detriment? But death, the irrecouerable losse, death, the
dolefull departure of frendes, that can neuer be recontinued
by any other meeting or new acquaintance—besides our
vncertaintie and suspition of their estates and welfare in
the places of their new abode—seemeth to carry a reasonable pretext of iust sorrow. Likewise, the great ouerthrowes in battell and desolations of countreys by warres,
aswell for the losse of many liues and much libertie as for
that it toucheth the whole state, and euery priuate man
hath his portion in the damage. Finally, for loue, there is
no frailtie in flesh and bloud so excusable as it, no comfort
or discomfort greater then the good and bad successe
thereof, nothing more naturall to man, nothing of more
force to vanquish his will and to inuegle his iudgement.
Therefore of death and burials, of th'aduersities by warres,
and of true loue lost or ill bestowed are th'onely sorrowes
that the noble Poets sought by their arte to remoue or
appease, not with any medicament of a contrary temper,
as the *Galenistes* vse to cure *contraria contrariis*, but as the
Paracelsians, who cure *similia similibus*, making one dolour
to expell another, and, in this case, one short sorrowing
the remedie of a long and grieuous sorrow. And the
lamenting of deathes was chiefly at the very buriells of
the dead, also at monethes mindes and longer times, by
custome continued yearely, when as they vsed many offices
of seruice and loue towardes the dead, and thereupon are
called *Obsequies* in our vulgare; which was done not onely
by cladding the mourners their friendes and seruauntes in
blacke vestures, of shape dolefull and sad, but also by
wofull countenaunces and voyces, and besides by Poeticall
mournings in verse. Such funerall songs were called
Epicedia if they were song by many, and *Monodia* if they
were vttered by one alone, and this was vsed at the enter-

ment of Princes and others of great accompt, and it was
reckoned a great ciuilitie to vse such ceremonies, as at this
day is also in some countrey vsed. In Rome they accustomed to make orations funerall and commendatorie of the
dead parties in the publique place called *Pro rostris*: and
our *Theologians* in stead thereof vse to make sermons,
both teaching the people some good learning and also
saying well of the departed. Those songs of the dolorous
discomfits in battaile and other desolations in warre, or of
townes saccaged and subuerted, were song by the remnant
of the army ouerthrowen, with great skrikings and outcries,
holding the wrong end of their weapon vpwards in signe
of sorrow and dispaire. The cities also made generall
mournings & offred sacrifices with Poeticall songs to
appease the wrath of the martiall gods & goddesses. The
third sorrowing was of loues, by long lamentation in *Elegie*:
so was their song called, and it was in a pitious maner of
meetre, placing a limping *Pentameter* after a lusty *Exameter*,
which made it go dolourously, more then any other meeter.

CHAP. XXV.

OF THE SOLEMNE REIOYSINGS AT THE NATIUITIE OF PRINCES CHILDREN.

To returne from sorrow to reioysing, it is a very good
hap and no vnwise part for him that can do it; I say, therefore, that the comfort of issue and procreation of children
is so naturall and so great, not onely to all men but
specially to Princes, as duetie and ciuilitie haue made it
a common custome to reioyse at the birth of their noble
children, and to keepe those dayes hallowed and festiuall
for euer once in the yeare, during the parentes or childrens
liues; and that by publique order & consent. Of which
reioysings and mirthes the Poet ministred the first occasion

honorable, by presenting of ioyfull songs and ballades,
praysing the parentes by proofe, the child by hope, the
whole kinred by report, & the day it selfe with wishes of
all good successe, long life, health, & prosperitie for euer
to the new borne. These poemes were called in Greeke
Genet[h]liaca; with vs they may be called natall or birth
songs.

CHAP. XXVI.

THE MANER OF REIOYSINGS AT MARIAGES AND WEDDINGS.

As the consolation of children well begotten is great, no
lesse but rather greater ought to be that which is occasion
of children, that is honorable matrimonie, a loue by al
lawes allowed, not mutable nor encombred with such vaine
cares & passions, as that other loue, whereof there is no
assurance, but loose and fickle affection occasioned for the
most part by sodaine sights and acquaintance of no long
triall or experience, nor vpon any other good ground
wherein any suretie may be conceiued: wherefore the
Ciuill Poet could do no lesse in conscience and credit,
then as he had before done to the ballade of birth, now
with much better deuotion to celebrate by his poeme the
chearefull day of mariages aswell Princely as others, for
that hath alwayes bene accompted with euery countrey
and nation of neuer so barbarous people the highest &
holiest of any ceremonie apperteining to man; a match
forsooth made for euer and not for a day, a solace prouided
for youth, a comfort for age, a knot of alliance & amitie
indissoluble: great reioysing was therefore due to such
a matter and to so gladsome a time. This was done in
ballade wise, as the natall song, and was song very sweetely
by Musitians at the chamber dore of the Bridegroome and
Bride at such times as shalbe hereafter declared, and they
were called *Epithalamies*, as much to say as ballades at the

bedding of the bride : for such as were song at the borde at dinner or supper were other Musickes and not properly *Epithalamies*. Here, if I shall say that which apperteineth to th'arte, and disclose the misterie of the whole matter, I must and doe with all humble reuerence bespeake pardon of the chaste and honorable eares, least I should either offend them with licentious speach, or leaue them ignorant of the ancient guise in old times vsed at weddings, in my simple opinion nothing reproueable. This *Epithalamie* was deuided by breaches into three partes to serue for three seuerall fits or times to be song. The first breach was song at the first parte of the night, when the spouse and her husband were brought to their bed, & at the very chamber dore, where in a large vtter roome vsed to be (besides the musitiens) good store of ladies or gentle-women of their kinsefolkes, & others who came to honor the mariage ; & the tunes of the songs were very loude and shrill, to the intent there might no noise be hard out of the bed chamber by the skreeking and outcry of the young damosell feeling the first forces of her stiffe & rigorous young man, she being, as all virgins, tender & weake, and vnexpert in those maner of affaires. For which purpose also they vsed by old nurses (appointed to that seruice) to suppresse the noise by casting of pottes full of nuttes round about the chamber vpon the hard floore or pauement, for they vsed no mattes nor rushes as we doe now. So as the Ladies and gentlewomen should haue their eares so occupied what with Musicke, and what with their handes wantonly scambling and catching after the nuttes, that they could not intend to harken after any other thing. This was, as I said, to diminish the noise of the laughing lamenting spouse. The tenour of that part of the song was to congratulate the first acquaintance and meeting of the young couple, allowing of their parents good discretions in making the match, then afterward to sound cherfully to

the onset and first encounters of that amorous battaile, to
declare the comfort of children, & encrease of loue by that
meane cheifly caused: the bride shewing her self euery
waies well disposed, and still supplying occasions of new
lustes and loue to her husband by her obedience and
amorous embracings and all other allurementes. About
midnight or one of the clocke, the Musicians came again
to the chamber dore (all the Ladies and other women as
they were of degree hauing taken their leaue, and being
gone to their rest). This part of the ballade was to refresh
the faint and weried bodies and spirits, and to animate new
appetites with cherefull wordes, encoraging them to the
recontinuance of the same entertainments, praising and
commending (by supposall) the good conformities of them
both, & their desire one to vanquish the other by such
frendly conflictes; alledging that the first embracementes
neuer bred barnes, by reason of their ouermuch affection
and heate, but onely made passage for children and
enforced greater liking to the late made match; that the
second assaultes were lesse rigorous, but more vigorous
and apt to auance the purpose of procreation; that therefore they should persist in all good appetite with an
inuincible courage to the end. This was the second part
of the *Epithalamie*. In the morning when it was faire
broad day, & that by liklyhood all tournes were sufficiently
serued, the last actes of the enterlude being ended, & that
the bride must within few hours arise and apparell her
selfe, no more as a virgine but as a wife, and about dinner
time must by order come forth *Sicut sponsa de thalamo*
very demurely and stately to be sene and acknowledged
of her parents and kinsfolkes whether she were the same
woman or a changeling, or dead or aliue, or maimed by
any accident nocturnall, the same Musicians came againe
with this last part and greeted them both with a Psalme
of new applausions, for that they had either of them so

well behaued them selues that night, the husband to rob
his spouse of her maidenhead and saue her life, the bride
so lustely to satisfie her husbandes loue and scape with so
litle daunger of her person; for which good chaunce that
they should make a louely truce and abstinence of that
warre till next night, sealing the placard of that louely
league with twentie maner of sweet kisses; then by good
admonitions enformed them to the frugall & thriftie life
all the rest of their dayes, the good man getting and
bringing home, the wife sauing that which her husband
should get, therewith to be the better able to keepe good
hospitalitie, according to their estates, and to bring vp
their children (if God sent any) vertuously, and the better
by their owne good example; finally to perseuer all the
rest of their life in true and inuiolable wedlocke. This
ceremony was omitted when men maried widowes or such
as had tasted the frutes of loue before (we call them well
experienced young women), in whom there was no feare of
daunger to their persons, or of any outcry at all, at the
time of those terrible approches. Thus much touching
the vsage of *Epithalamie* or bedding ballad of the ancient
times, in which if there were any wanton or lasciuious
matter more then ordinarie, which they called *F[es]cenina
licentia*, it was borne withal for that time because of the
matter no lesse requiring. *Catullus* hath made of them
one or two very artificiall and ciuil; but none more
excellent then of late yeares a young noble man of
Germanie, as I take it, *Iohannes secundus*, who, in that
and in his poeme *De basiis*, passeth any of the auncient
or moderne Poetes in my iudgment.

CHAP. XXVII.

THE MANNER OF POESIE BY WHICH THEY VTTERED THEIR BITTER TAUNTS, AND PRIUY NIPS OR WITTY SCOFFES, AND OTHER MERRY CONCEITS.

But all the world could not keepe, nor any ciuill ordinance to the contrary so preuaile, but that men would and must needs vtter their splenes in all ordinarie matters also, or else it seemed their bowels would burst: therefore the poet deuised a prety fashioned poeme short and sweete (as we are wont to say) and called it *Epigramma*, in which euery mery conceited man might, without any long studie or tedious ambage, make his frend sport, and anger his foe, and giue a prettie nip, or shew a sharpe conceit in few verses: for this *Epigramme* is but an inscription or writting made as it were vpon a table, or in a windowe, or vpon the wall or mantell of a chimney in some place of common resort, where it was allowed euery man might come, or be sitting to chat and prate, as now in our tauernes and common tabling houses, where many merry heades meete, and scrible with ynke, with chalke, or with a cole, such matters as they would euery man should know & descant vpon. Afterward the same came to be put in paper and in bookes and vsed as ordinarie missiues, some of frendship, some of defiaunce, or as other messages of mirth. *Martiall* was the cheife of this skil among the Latines, & at these days the best Epigrammes we finde, & of the sharpest conceit, are those that haue bene gathered among the reliques of the two muet *Satyres* in Rome, *Pasquill* and *Marphorius*, which in time of *Sede vacante*, when merry conceited men listed to gibe & iest at the dead Pope or any of his Cardinales, they fastened them vpon those Images which now lie in the open streets, and were tollerated, but after that terme expired they were

Of Poets and Poesy 57

inhibited againe. These inscriptions or Epigrammes at their begining had no certaine author that would auouch them, some for feare of blame, if they were ouer saucy or sharpe, others for modestie of the writer, as was that *disticke* of *Virgil* which he set vpon the pallace gate of the emperour *Augustus*, which I will recite for the breifnes and quicknes of it, and also for another euente that fell out vpon the mater worthy to be remembred. These were the verses:

> *Nocte pluit tota, redeunt spectacula mane ;*
> *Diuisum imperium cum Ioue Caesar habet.*

Which I haue thus Englished:

> *It raines all night, early the shewes returne ;*
> *God and Caesar do raigne and rule by turne.*

As much to say, God sheweth his power by the night raines, Caesar his magnificence by the pompes of the day.

These two verses were very well liked, and brought to th'Emperours Maiestie, who tooke great pleasure in them, & willed the author should be knowen. A sausie courtier profered him selfe to be the man, and had a good reward giuen him, for the Emperour him self was not only learned, but of much munificence toward all learned men: whereupon *Virgill* seing him self by his ouermuch modestie defrauded of the reward, that an impudent had gotten by abuse of his merit, came the next night, and fastened vpon the same place this halfe metre, foure times iterated. Thus:

> *Sic vos non vobis*
> *Sic vos non vobis*
> *Sic vos non vobis*
> *Sic vos non vobis*

And there it remained a great while because no man

wist what it meant, till *Virgill* opened the whole fraude by this deuise. He wrote aboue the same halfe metres this whole verse *Exameter*:

Hos ego versiculos feci: tulit alter honores.

And then finished the foure half metres, thus:

Sic vos non vobis   nidificatis aues.
Sic vos non vobis   vellera fertis oues.
Sic vos non vobis   mellificatis apes.
Sic vos non vobis   fertis aratra boues.

And put to his name *Publius Virgilius Maro*. This matter came by and by to Th'emperours eare, who, taking great pleasure in the deuise, called for *Virgill*, and gaue him not onely a present reward, with a good allowance of dyet, a bouche in court as we vse to call it, but also held him for euer after, vpon larger triall he had made of his learning and vertue, in so great reputation as he vouchsafed to giue him the name of a frend (*amicus*), which among the Romanes was so great an honour and speciall fauour as all such persons were allowed to the Emperours table, or to the Senatours who had receiued them (as frendes), and they were the only men that came ordinarily to their boords, & solaced with them in their chambers and gardins when none other could be admitted.

CHAP. XXVIII.

OF THE POEME CALLED EPITAPH VSED FOR MEMORIALL OF THE DEAD.

An Epitaph is but a kind of Epigram only applied to the report of the dead persons estate and degree, or of his other good or bad partes, to his commendation or reproch, and is an inscription such as a man may commodiously write or engraue vpon a tombe in few verses, pithie, quicke, and sententious, for the passer-by to peruse and iudge vpon without any long tariaunce. So as if it exceede the measure of an Epigram, it is then (if the verse be correspondent) rather an Elegie then an Epitaph, which errour many of these bastard rimers commit, because they be not learned, nor (as we are wont to say) craftes masters, for they make long and tedious discourses and write them in large tables to be hanged vp in Churches and chauncells ouer the tombes of great men and others, which be so exceeding long as one must haue halfe a dayes leasure to reade one of them, & must be called away before he come halfe to the end, or else be locked into the Church by the Sexten, as I my selfe was once serued reading an Epitaph in a certain cathedrall Church of England. They be ignorant of poesie that call such long tales by the name of Epitaphes; they might better call them Elegies, as I said before, and then ought neither to be engrauen nor hanged vp in tables. I haue seene them neuertheles vpon many honorable tombes of these late times erected, which doe rather disgrace then honour either the matter or maker.

CHAP. XXIX.

A CERTAINE AUNCIENT FORME OF POESIE BY WHICH MEN DID VSE TO REPROCH THEIR ENEMIES.

As frendes be a rich and ioyfull possession, so be foes a continual torment and canker to the minde of man; and yet there is no possible meane to auoide this inconuenience, for the best of vs all, he that thinketh he liues most blamelesse, liues not without enemies, that enuy him for his good parts, or hate him for his euill. There be wise men, and of them the great learned man *Plutarch* tooke vpon them to perswade the benefite that men receiue by their enemies, which though it may be true in manner of *Paradoxe*, yet

I finde mans frailtie to be naturally such, and alwayes hath beene, that he cannot conceiue it in his owne case, nor shew that patience and moderation in such greifs, as becommeth the man perfite and accomplisht in all vertue: but either in deede or by word he will seeke reuenge against them that malice him, or practise his harmes, specially such foes as oppose themselues to a mans loues. This made the auncient Poetes to inuent a meane to rid the gall of all such Vindicatiue men : so as they might be awrecked of their wrong, & neuer bely their enemie with slaunderous vntruthes. And this was done by a maner of imprecation, or as we call it by cursing and banning of the parties, and wishing all euill to alight vpon them, and, though it neuer the sooner happened, yet was it great easment to the boiling stomacke. They were called *Dirae*, such as *Virgill* made aginst *Battarus*, and *Ouide* against *Ibis*: we Christians are forbidden to vse such vncharitable fashions, and willed to referre all our reuenges to God alone.

CHAP. XXX.

OF SHORT EPIGRAMES CALLED POSIES.

There be also other like Epigrammes that were sent vsually for new yeares giftes, or to be Printed or put vpon their banketting dishes of suger plate or of march paines, & such other dainty meates as by the curtesie & custome euery gest might carry from a common feast home with him to his owne house, & were made for the nonce. They were called *Nenia* or *apophoreta*, and neuer contained aboue one verse, or two at the most, but the shorter the better; we call them Posies, and do paint them now a dayes vpon the backe sides of our fruite trenchers of wood, or vse them as deuises in rings and armes and about such courtly purposes.

Of Poets and Poesy

So haue we remembred and set forth to your Maiestie very briefly all the commended fourmes of the auncient Poesie, which we in our vulgare makings do imitate and vse vnder these common names: enterlude, song, ballade, carroll, and ditty; borrowing them also from the French, al sauing this word 'song' which is our naturall Saxon English word: the rest, such as time and vsurpation by custome haue allowed vs out of the primitiue Greeke & Latine, as Comedie, Tragedie, Ode, Epitaphe, Elegie, Epigramme, and other moe. And we haue purposely omitted all nice or scholasticall curiosities not meete for your Maiesties contemplation in this our vulgare arte, and what we haue written of the auncient formes of Poemes we haue taken from the best clerks writing in the same arte. The part that next followeth, to wit of proportion, because the Greeks nor Latines neuer had it in vse nor made any obseruation, no more then we doe of their feete, we may truly affirme to haue bene the first deuisers thereof our selues, as $αὐτο\-δίδακτοι$, and not to haue borrowed it of any other by learning or imitation, and thereby trusting to be holden the more excusable if any thing in this our labours happen either to mislike or to come short of th'authors purpose, because commonly the first attempt in any arte or engine artificiall is amendable, & in time by often experiences reformed. And so no doubt may this deuise of ours be, by others that shall take the penne in hand after vs.

CHAP. XXXI.

WHO IN ANY AGE HAUE BENE THE MOST COMMENDED WRITERS IN OUR ENGLISH POESIE, AND THE AUTHORS CENSURE GIUEN VPON THEM.

It appeareth by sundry records of bookes both printed & written that many of our countreymen haue painfully trauelled in this part: of whose works some appeare to be but bare translations, other some matters of their owne inuention and very commendable, whereof some recitall shall be made in this place, to th'intent chiefly that their names should not be defrauded of such honour as seemeth due to them for hauing by their thankefull studies so much beautified our English tong as at this day it will be found our nation is in nothing inferiour to the French or Italian for copie of language, subtiltie of deuice, good method and proportion in any forme of poeme, but that they may compare with the most, and perchance passe a great many of them. And I will not reach aboue the time of king *Edward* the third and *Richard* the second for any that wrote in English meeter, because before their times, by reason of the late Normane conquest, which had brought into this Realme much alteration both of our langage and lawes, and there withall a certain martiall barbarousnes, whereby the study of all good learning was so much decayd as long time after no man or very few entended to write in any laudable science: so as beyond that time there is litle or nothing worth commendation to be founde written in this arte. And those of the first age were *Chaucer* and *Gower*, both of them, as I suppose, Knightes. After whom followed *Iohn Lydgate*, the monke of Bury, & that nameles, who wrote the *Satyre* called Piers Plowman; next him followed *Harding*, the Chronicler; then, in king *Henry* th'eights time, *Skelton*, (I wot not for what great worthines) surnamed the Poet *Laureat*. In the latter end of the same kings raigne sprong vp a new company of courtly makers, of whom Sir *Thomas Wyat* th'elder & *Henry* Earle of Surrey were the two chieftaines, who hauing trauailed into Italie, and there tasted the sweete and stately measures and stile of the Italian Poesie, as nouices newly crept out of the schooles of *Dante*, *Arioste*, and *Petrarch*, they greatly pollished our rude &

homely maner of vulgar Poesie from that it had bene
before, and for that cause may iustly be sayd the first
reformers of our English meetre and stile. In the same
time, or not long after, was the Lord *Nicholas Vaux*, a man
of much facilitie in vulgar makings. Afterward, in king
Edward the sixths time, came to be in reputation for the
same facultie *Thomas Sternehold*, who first translated into
English certaine Psalmes of Dauid, and *Iohn Heywood*,
the Epigrammatist, who for the myrth and quicknesse of
his conceits more then for any good learning was in him
came to be well benefited by the king. But the principall
man in this profession at the same time was Maister
Edward Ferrys, a man of no lesse mirth & felicitie that
way, but of much more skil & magnificence in his meeter,
and therefore wrate for the most part to the stage, in
Tragedie and sometimes in Comedie or Enterlude, wherein
he gaue the king so much good recreation as he had
thereby many good rewardes. In Queenes *Maries* time
florished aboue any other Doctour *Phaer*, one that was
well learned & excellently well translated into English
verse Heroicall certaine bookes of *Virgils Æneidos*. Since
him followed Maister *Arthure Golding*, who with no lesse
commendation turned into English meetre the Metamorphosis of *Ouide*, and that other Doctour, who made
the supplement to those bookes of *Virgils Æneidos* which
Maister *Phaer* left vndone. And in her Maiesties time
that now is are sprong vp an other crew of Courtly
makers, Noble men and Gentlemen of her Maiesties owne
seruauntes, who haue written excellently well, as it would
appeare if their doings could be found out and made
publicke with the rest; of which number is first that noble
Gentleman *Edward* Earle of Oxford, *Thomas* Lord of
Bukhurst, when he was young, *Henry* Lord Paget, Sir
Philip Sydney, Sir *Walter Rawleigh*, Master *Edward Dyar*,
Maister *Fulke Greuell, Gascon, Britton, Turberuille*, and

a great many other learned Gentlemen, whose names
I do not omit for enuie, but to auoyde tediousnesse, and
who haue deserued no little commendation. But of them
all particularly, this is myne opinion, that *Chaucer*, with
Gower, *Lidgat*, and *Harding*, for their antiquitie ought to
haue the first place, and *Chaucer*, as the most renowmed
of them all, for the much learning appeareth to be in him,
aboue any of the rest. And though many of his bookes
be but bare translations out of the Latin & French, yet
are they wel handled, as his bookes of *Troilus* and *Cresseid*,
and the Romant of the Rose, whereof he translated but
one halfe,—the deuice was *Iohn de Mehunes*, a French
Poet: the Canterbury tales were *Chaucers* owne inuention,
as I suppose, and where he sheweth more the naturall of
his pleasant wit then in any other of his workes; his
similitudes, comparisons, and all other descriptions are
such as can not be amended. His meetre Heroicall of
Troilus and *Cresseid* is very graue and stately, keeping
the staffe of seuen and the verse of ten; his other verses
of the Canterbury tales be but riding ryme, neuerthelesse
very well becomming the matter of that pleasaunt pilgrimage, in which euery mans part is playd with much decency.
Gower, sauing for his good and graue moralities, had
nothing in him highly to be commended, for his verse was
homely and without good measure, his wordes strained
much deale out of the French writers, his ryme wrested,
and in his inuentions small subtillitie: the applications of
his moralities are the best in him, and yet those many
times very grossely bestowed; neither doth the substance
of his workes sufficiently aunswere the subtilitie of his
titles. *Lydgat*, a translatour onely, and no deuiser of that
which he wrate, but one that wrate in good verse. *Harding*,
a Poet Epick or Historicall, handled himselfe well according to the time and maner of his subiect. He that wrote
the Satyr of Piers Ploughman seemed to haue bene a

malcontent of that time, and therefore bent himselfe wholy to taxe the disorders of that age, and specially the pride of the Romane Clergy, of whose fall he seemeth to be a very true Prophet; his verse is but loose meetre, and his termes hard and obscure, so as in them is litle pleasure to be taken. *Skelton*, a sharpe Satirist, but with more rayling and scoffery then became a Poet Lawreat: such among the Greekes were called *Pantomimi*, with vs Buffons, altogether applying their wits to Scurrillities & other ridiculous matters. *Henry* Earle of Surrey and Sir *Thomas Wyat*, betweene whom I finde very litle difference, I repute them (as before) for the two chief lanternes of light to all others that haue since employed their pennes vpon English Poesie: their conceits were loftie, their stiles stately, their conueyance cleanely, their termes proper, their meetre sweete and well proportioned, in all imitating very naturally and studiously their Maister *Francis Petrarcha*. The Lord *Vaux* his commendation lyeth chiefly in the facillitie of his meetre, and the aptnesse of his descriptions such as he taketh vpon him to make, namely in sundry of his Songs, wherein he sheweth the counterfait action very liuely & pleasantly. Of the later sort I thinke thus. That for Tragedie, the Lord of Buckhurst & Maister *Edward Ferrys*, for such doings as I haue sene of theirs, do deserue the hyest price: Th'Earle of Oxford and Maister *Edwardes* of her Maiesties Chappell for Comedy and Enterlude. For Eglogue and pastorall Poesie, Sir *Philip Sydney* and Maister *Challenner*, and that other Gentleman who wrate the late shepheardes Callender. For dittie and amourous *Ode* I finde Sir *Walter Rawleyghs* vayne most loftie, insolent, and passionate. Maister *Edward Dyar*, for Elegie most sweete, solempne, and of high conceit. *Gascon*, for a good meeter and for a plentifull vayne. *Phaer* and *Golding*, for a learned and well corrected verse, specially in translation

cleare and very faithfully answering their authours intent.
Others haue also written with much facillitie, but more
commendably perchance if they had not written so much
nor so popularly. But last in recitall and first in degree
is the Queene our soueraigne Lady, whose learned, delicate, 5
noble Muse easily surmounteth all the rest that haue
written before her time or since, for sence, sweetnesse,
and subtillitie, be it in Ode, Elegie, Epigram, or any
other kinde of poeme Heroick or Lyricke wherein it
shall please her Maiestie to employ her penne, euen by 10
as much oddes as her owne excellent estate and degree
exceedeth all the rest of her most humble vassalls.

THE SECOND BOOKE
OF PROPORTION POETICAL

CHAP. I.

OF PROPORTION POETICALL.

IT is said by such as professe the Mathematicall sciences, that all things stand by proportion, and that without it nothing could stand to be good or beautiful. The Doctors of our Theologie to the same effect, but in other termes, say that God made the world by number, measure, and weight; some for weight say tune, and peraduenture better. For weight is a kind of measure or of much conueniencie with it; and therefore in their descriptions be alwayes coupled together *statica et metrica*, weight and measures. Hereupon it seemeth the Philosopher gathers a triple proportion, to wit, the Arithmeticall, the Geometricall, and the Musicall. And by one of these three is euery other proportion guided of the things that haue conueniencie by relation, as the visible by light colour and shadow; the audible by stirres, times, and accents; the odorable by smelles of sundry temperaments; the tastible by sauours to the rate; the tangible by his obiectes in this or that regard. Of all which we leaue to speake, returning to our poeticall proportion, which holdeth of the Musical, because, as we sayd before, Poesie is a skill to speake & write harmonically: and verses or rime be a kind of Musicall vtterance, by reason of a certaine congruitie in sounds pleasing the eare, though not perchance so exquisitely as the harmonicall concents of the artificial Musicke, consisting in strained tunes, as is the vocall

Musike, or that of melodious instruments, as Lutes,
Harpes, Regals, Records, and such like. And this our
proportion Poeticall resteth in fiue points: Staffe, Measure,
Concord, Scituation, and Figure, all which shall be spoken
of in their places.

CHAP. II.

OF PROPORTION IN STAFFE.

Staffe in our vulgare Poesie I know not why it should
be so called, vnlesse it be for that we vnderstand it for
a bearer or supporter of a song or ballad, not vnlike
the old weake bodie that is stayed vp by his staffe,
and were not otherwise able to walke or to stand
vpright. The Italian called it *Stanza*, as if we should
say a resting place: and if we consider well the forme
of this Poeticall staffe, we shall finde it to be a certaine
number of verses allowed to go altogether and ioyne
without any intermission, and doe or should finish vp
all the sentences of the same with a full period, vnlesse
it be in som special cases, & there to stay till another
staffe follow of like sort: and the shortest staffe conteineth
not vnder foure verses, nor the longest aboue ten; if it
passe that number it is rather a whole ditty then properly
a staffe. Also for the more part the staues stand rather
vpon the euen number of verses then the odde, though
there be of both sorts. The first proportion then of a staffe
is by *quadrein* or foure verses. The second of fiue verses,
and is seldome vsed. The third by *sizeine* or sixe verses,
and is not only most vsual, but also very pleasant to
th'eare. The fourth is in seuen verses, & is the chiefe of
our ancient proportions vsed by any rimer writing any
thing of historical or graue poeme, as ye may see in
Chaucer and *Lidgate*, th'one writing the loues of *Troylus*
and *Cresseida*, th'other of the fall of Princes: both by

Of Proportion

them translated, not deuised. The fifth proportion is of eight verses very stately and *Heroicke*, and which I like better then that of seuen, because it receaueth better band. The sixt is of nine verses, rare but very graue. The seuenth proportion is of tenne verses, very stately, but in many mens opinion too long; neuerthelesse of very good grace & much grauitie. Of eleuen and twelue I find none ordinary staues vsed in any vulgar language, neither doth it serue well to continue any historicall report and ballade or other song, but is a dittie of it self, and no staffe; yet some moderne writers haue vsed it, but very seldome. Then last of all haue ye a proportion to be vsed in the number of your staues, as to a caroll and a ballade, to a song, & a round, or virelay. For to an historicall poeme no certain number is limited, but as the matter fals out: also a *distick* or couple of verses is not to be accompted a staffe, but serues for a continuance, as we see in Elegie, Epitaph, Epigramme, or such meetres, of plaine concord, not harmonically entertangled as some other songs of more delicate musick be.

A staffe of foure verses containeth in it selfe matter sufficient to make a full periode or complement of sence, though it doe not always so, and therefore may go by diuisions.

A staffe of fiue verses is not much vsed, because he that can not comprehend his periode in foure verses will rather driue it into six then leaue it in fiue, for that the euen number is more agreable to the eare then the odde is.

A staffe of sixe verses is very pleasant to the eare, and also serueth for a greater complement then the inferiour staues, which maketh him more commonly to be vsed.

A staffe of seuen verses, most vsuall with our auncient makers, also the staffe of eight, nine, and ten of larger complement then the rest, are onely vsed by the later

makers, &, vnlesse they go with very good bande, do not
so well as the inferiour staues. Therefore, if ye make your
staffe of eight by two fowers not entertangled, it is not
a huitaine or a staffe of eight, but two quadreins: so is it
in ten verses; not being entertangled, they be but two
staues of fiue.

CHAP. III.

OF PROPORTION IN MEASURE.

Meeter and measure is all one, for what the Greekes
called μέτρον, the Latines call *Mensura*, and is but the
quantitie of a verse, either long or short. This quantitie
with them consisteth in the number of their feete: & with
vs in the number of sillables, which are comprehended in
euery verse, not regarding his feete, otherwise then that
we allow, in scanning our verse, two sillables to make one
short portion (suppose it a foote) in euery verse. And
after that sort ye may say we haue feete in our vulgare
rymes, but that is improperly; for a foote by his sence
naturall is a member of office and function, and serueth to
three purposes, that is to say, to go, to runne, & to stand
still; so as he must be sometimes swift, sometimes slow,
sometime vnegally marching or peraduenture steddy.
And if our feete Poeticall want these qualities it can not
be sayd a foote in sence translatiue as here. And this
commeth to passe, by reason of the euident motion and
stirre which is perceiued in the sounding of our wordes
not alwayes egall, for some aske longer, some shorter
time to be vttered in, & so, by the Philosophers definition,
stirre is the true measure of time. The Greekes & Latines,
because their wordes hapned to be of many sillables, and
very few of one sillable, it fell out right with them to
conceiue and also to perceiue a notable diuersitie of
motion and times in the pronuntiation of their wordes,

Of Proportion

and therefore to euery *bissillable* they allowed two times, & to a *trissillable* three times, & to euery *polisillable* more, according to his quantitie, & their times were some long, some short, according as their motions were slow or swift. For the sound of some sillable stayd the eare a great while, and others slid away so quickly, as if they had not bene pronounced; then euery sillable being allowed one time, either short or long, it fell out that euery *tetrasillable* had foure times, euery *trissillable* three, and the *bissillable* two, by which obseruation euery word, not vnder that sise, as he ranne or stood in a verse, was called by them a foote of such and so many times, namely the *bissillable* was either of two long times, as the *spondeus*, or two short, as the *pir[ri]chius*, or of a long & a short as the *trocheus*, or of a short and a long as the *iambus*; the like rule did they set vpon the word *trissillable*, calling him a foote of three times, as the *dactilus* of a long and two short, the *molossus* of three long, the *tribracchus* of three short, the *amphibracchus* of two long and a short, the *amphimacer* of two short and a long. The word of foure sillables they called a foote of foure times, some or all of them, either long or short: and yet, not so content, they mounted higher, and, because their wordes serued well thereto, they made feete of sixe times; but this proceeded more of curiositie then otherwise, for whatsoeuer foote passe the *trissillable* is compounded of his inferiour, as euery number Arithmeticall aboue three is compounded of the inferiour number, as twise two make foure, but the three is made of one number, videl. of two and an vnitie. Now because our naturall & primitiue language of the *Saxon English* beares not any wordes (at least very few) of moe sillables then one (for whatsoeuer we see exceede commeth to vs by the alterations of our language growen vpon many conquestes and otherwise), there could be no such obseruation of times in the sound of our wordes, & for that

cause we could not haue the feete which the Greeks and
Latines haue in their meetres. But of this stirre & motion
of their deuised feete nothing can better shew the qualitie
then these runners at common games, who setting forth
from the first goale, one giueth the start speedely, & perhaps
before he come half way to th'other goale decayeth his
pace, as a man weary & fainting; another is slow at the
start, but by amending his pace keepes euen with his
fellow or perchance gets before him; another one while
gets ground, another while loseth it again, either in the
beginning or middle of his race, and so proceedes vnegally,
sometimes swift, somtimes slow, as his breath or forces
serue him; another sort there be that plod on & will neuer
change their pace, whether they win or lose the game: in
this maner doth the Greeke *dactilus* begin slowly and
keepe on swifter till th'end, for his race being deuided
into three parts, he spends one, & that is the first slowly,
the other twaine swiftly; the *anapestus* his two first parts
swiftly, his last slowly: the *Molossus* spends all three
parts of his race slowly and egally; *Bacchius* his first
part swiftly, & two last parts slowly; the *tribrachus* all
his three parts swiftly; the *antibacchius* his two first partes
slowly, his last & third swiftly; the *amphimacer* his first
& last part slowly & his middle part swiftly; the *amphibracus* his first and last parts swiftly, but his midle part
slowly; & so of others by like proportion. This was a pretie
phantasticall obseruation of them, and yet brought their
meetres to haue a maruelous good grace, which was in
Greeke called ῥυθμός; whence we haue deriued this word
ryme, but improperly & not wel, because we haue no such
feete or times or stirres in our meeters, by whose *simpathie*,
or pleasant conueniencie with th'eare, we could take any
delight: this *rithmus* of theirs is not therfore our rime,
but a certaine musicall numerositie in vtterance, and not
a bare number as that of the Arithmeticall computation is,

Of Proportion

which therfore is not called *rithmus* but *arithmus*. Take this away from them, I meane the running of their feete, there is nothing of curiositie among them more then with vs, nor yet so much.

CHAP. IV[1].

HOW MANY SORTS OF MEASURES WE VSE IN OUR VULGAR.

To returne from rime to our measure againe, it hath bene sayd that, according to the number of the sillables contained in euery verse, the same is sayd a long or short meeter, and his shortest proportion is of foure sillables, and his longest of twelue; they that vse it aboue passe the bounds of good proportion. And euery meeter may be aswel in the odde as in the euen sillable, but better in the euen, and one verse may begin in the euen, & another follow in the odde, and so keepe a commendable proportion. The verse that containeth but two silables, which may be in one word, is not vsuall: therefore many do deny him to be a verse, saying that it is but a foot, and that a meeter can haue no lesse then two feete at the least; but I find it otherwise, aswell among the best Italian Poets as also with our vulgar makers, and that two sillables serue wel for a short measure in the first place, and midle, and end of a staffe, and also in diuerse scituations and by sundry distances, and is very passionate and of good grace, as shalbe declared more at large in the Chapter of proportion by scituation.

The next measure is of two feete or of foure sillables, and then one word *tetrasillable* diuided in the middest makes vp the whole meeter, as thus, *Rēuē rēntlīe*; or a

[1] From this point onwards throughout the Second Book the Chapter numbers of the original are wrong. Here the number of the previous chapter ('III') is repeated.

trissillable and one monosillable, thus, *Soueraine God*; or
two bissillables, and that is plesant, thus, *Restore againe*;
or with foure monossillables, and that is best of all,
thus, *When I doe thinke*. I finde no fauour in a meetre
of three sillables, nor in effect in any odde; but they may
be vsed for varietie sake, and specially, being enterlaced
with others, the meetre of six sillables is very sweete and
delicate, as thus,

> O God, when I behold
> This bright heauen so hye,
> By thine owne hands of old
> Contriud so cunningly.

The meter of seuen sillables is not vsual, no more is
that of nine and eleuen; yet if they be well composed, that
is, their *Cesure* well appointed, and their last accent which
makes the concord, they are commendable inough, as in
this ditty, where one verse is of eight, an other is of seuen,
and in the one the accent vpon the last, in the other vpon
the last saue on.

> The smoakie sighes, the bitter teares,
> That I in vaine haue wasted,
> The broken sleepes, the woe and feares,
> That long in me haue lasted,
> Will be my death, all by thy guilt,
> And not by my deseruing,
> Since so inconstantly thou wilt
> Not loue, but still be sweruing.

And all the reason why these meeters in all sillable are
alowable is, for that the sharpe accent falles vpon the
penultima or last saue one sillable of the verse, which doth
so drowne the last, as he seemeth to passe away in maner
vnpronounced, & so make the verse seeme euen: but if
the accent fall vpon the last and leaue two flat to finish

Of Proportion

the verse, it will not seeme so; for the odnes will more
notoriously appeare, as for example in the last verse
before recited, *Not loue, but still be sweruing*, say thus,
Loue it is a maruelous thing. Both verses be of egall
quantitie, vidz. seauen sillables a peece, and yet the first
seemes shorter then the later, who shewes a more odnesse
then the former by reason of his sharpe accent which is
vpon the last sillable, and makes him more audible then if
he had slid away with a flat accent, as the word *swéruing*.

Your ordinarie rimers vse very much their measures
in the odde, as nine and eleuen, and the sharpe accent
vpon the last sillable, which therefore makes him go ill
fauouredly and like a minstrels musicke. Thus sayd one
in a meeter of eleuen very harshly in mine eare, whether
it be for lacke of good rime or of good reason, or of both,
I wot not.

Now sucke childe and sleepe childe, thy mothers owne ioy,
Her only sweete comfort, to drowne all annoy;
For beauty surpassing the azured skie,
I loue thee, my darling, as ball of mine eye.

This sort of composition in the odde I like not, vnlesse
it be holpen by the *Cesure* or by the accent, as I sayd
before.

The meeter of eight is no lesse pleasant then that of
sixe, and the *Cesure* fals iust in the middle, as this of the
Earle of Surreyes.

When raging loue, with extreme payne.

The meeter of ten sillables is very stately and Heroicall,
and must haue his *Cesure* fall vpon the fourth sillable, and
leaue sixe behinde him, thus,

I serue at ease, and gouerne all with woe.

This meeter of twelue sillables the French man calleth
a verse *Alexandrine*, and is with our moderne rimers most

vsuall; with the auncient makers it was not so. For
before Sir *Thomas Wiats* time they were not vsed in our
vulgar; they be for graue and stately matters fitter than
for any other ditty of pleasure. Some makers write in
verses of foureteene sillables, giuing the *Cesure* at the first
eight; which proportion is tedious, for the length of the
verse kepeth the eare too long from his delight, which
is to heare the cadence or the tuneable accent in the ende
of the verse. Neuerthelesse that of twelue, if his *Cesure*
be iust in the middle, and that ye suffer him to runne at
full length, and do not as the common rimers do, or their
Printer for sparing of paper, cut them of in the middest,
wherin they make in two verses but halfe rime, they
do very wel, as wrote the Earle of Surrey, translating the
booke of the preacher,

> Salomon Dauids sonne, king of Ierusalem.

This verse is very good *Alexandrine*, but perchaunce
woulde haue sounded more musically if the first word
had bene a dissillable or two monosillables, and not a
trissillable: hauing this sharpe accent vppon the *Antepenultima* as it hath, by which occasion it runnes like
a *Dactill*, and carries the two later sillables away so
speedily as it seemes but one foote in our vulgar measure,
and by that meanes makes the verse seeme but of eleuen
sillables, which odnesse is nothing pleasant to the eare.
Iudge some body whether it would haue done better if it
might haue bene sayd thus,

> Robóham Dauids sonne, king of Ierusalem,

letting the sharpe accent fall vpon *bo*; or thus,

> Restóre king Dáuids sónne vntó Ierúsalém.

For now the sharpe accent falles vpon *bo*, and so doth it
vpon the last in *restóre*, which was not in th'other verse.
But because we haue seemed to make mention of *Cesure*,

Of Proportion

and to appoint his place in euery measure, it shall not be
amisse to say somewhat more of it, & also of such pauses
as are vsed in vtterance, and what commoditie or delectation they bring either to the speakers or to the hearers.

CHAP. V.

OF CESURE.

There is no greater difference betwixt a ciuill and
brutish vtteraunce then cleare distinction of voices; and
the most laudable languages are alwaies most plaine
and distinct, and the barbarous most confuse and indis-
tinct: it is therefore requisit that leasure be taken in
pronuntiation, such as may make our wordes plaine &
most audible and agreable to the eare; also the breath
asketh to be now and then releeued with some pause or
stay more or lesse; besides that the very nature of speech
(because it goeth by clauses of seuerall construction &
sence) requireth some space betwixt them with intermission of sound, to th'end they may not huddle one
vpon another so rudly & so fast that th'eare may not
perceiue their difference. For these respectes the aunciant
reformers of language inuented three maner of pauses,
one of lesse leasure then another, and such seuerall
intermissions of sound to serue (besides easment to the
breath) for a treble distinction of sentences or parts of
speach, as they happened to be more or lesse perfect in
sence. The shortest pause or intermission they called
comma, as who would say a peece of a speach cut of.
The second they called *colon*, not a peece, but as it were
a member for his larger length, because it occupied twise
as much time as the *comma*. The third they called
periodus, for a complement or full pause, and as a resting
place and perfection of so much former speach as had

bene vttered, and from whence they needed not to passe
any further, vnles it were to renew more matter to enlarge
the tale. This cannot be better represented then by
example of these common trauailers by the hie ways,
where they seeme to allow themselues three maner of
staies or easements: one a horsebacke calling perchaunce
for a cup of beere or wine, and, hauing dronken it vp, rides
away and neuer lights; about noone he commeth to his
Inne, & there baites him selfe and his horse an houre or
more; at night, when he can conueniently trauaile no
further, he taketh vp his lodging, and rests him selfe till
the morrow; from whence he followeth the course of
a further voyage, if his businesse be such. Euen so our
Poet when he hath made one verse, hath as it were
finished one dayes iourney, & the while easeth him
selfe with one baite at the least, which is a *Comma* or
Cesure in the mid way, if the verse be euen and not odde,
otherwise in some other place, and not iust in the middle.
If there be no *Cesure* at all, and the verse long, the lesse
is the makers skill and hearers delight. Therefore in a
verse of twelue sillables the *Cesure* ought to fall right vpon
the sixt sillable; in a verse of eleuen vpon the sixt also,
leauing fiue to follow. In a verse of ten vpon the fourth,
leauing sixe to follow. In a verse of nine vpon the
fourth, leauing fiue to follow. In a verse of eight iust
in the middest, that is, vpon the fourth. In a verse of
seauen, either vpon the fourth or none at all, the meeter
very ill brooking any pause. In a verse of sixe sillables
and vnder is needefull no *Cesure* at all, because the breath
asketh no reliefe: yet if ye giue any *Comma*, it is to make
distinction of sense more then for any thing else; and
such *Cesure* must neuer be made in the middest of any
word, if it be well appointed. So may you see that the
vse of these pawses or distinctions is not generally with
the vulgar Poet as it is with the Prose writer, because the

Of Proportion

Poetes cheife Musicke lying in his rime or concorde to heare the Simphonie, he maketh all the hast he can to be at an end of his verse, and delights not in many stayes by the way, and therefore giueth but one *Cesure* to any
5 verse: and thus much for the sounding of a meetre. Neuerthelesse, he may vse in any verse both his *comma, colon,* and *interrogatiue* point, as well as in prose. But our auncient rymers, as *Chaucer, Lydgate,* & others, vsed these *Cesures* either very seldome, or not at all, or else
10 very licentiously, and many times made their meetres (they called them riding ryme) of such vnshapely wordes as would allow no conuenient *Cesure,* and therefore did let their rymes runne out at length, and neuer stayd till they came to the end: which maner though it were not
15 to be misliked in some sort of meetre, yet in euery long verse the *Cesure* ought to be kept precisely, if it were but to serue as a law to correct the licentiousnesse of rymers, besides that it pleaseth the eare better, & sheweth more cunning in the maker by following the rule of his restraint.
20 For a rymer that will be tyed to no rules at all, but range as he list, may easily vtter what he will: but such maner of Poesie is called, in our vulgar, ryme dogrell, with which rebuke we will in no case our maker should be touched. Therfore before all other things let his ryme and con-
25 cordes be true, cleare, and audible, with no lesse delight then almost the strayned note of a Musicians mouth, and not darke or wrenched by wrong writing, as many doe to patch vp their meetres, and so follow in their arte neither rule, reason, nor ryme. Much more might be sayd for the
30 vse of your three pauses, *comma, colon,* & *periode,* for perchance it be not all a matter to vse many *commas* and few, nor *colons* likewise, or long or short *periodes* for it is diuersly vsed by diuers good writers. But because it apperteineth more to the oratour or writer in prose then
35 in verse, I will say no more in it then thus, that they

be vsed for a commodious and sensible distinction of
clauses in prose, since euery verse is as it were a clause
of it selfe, and limited with a *Cesure* howsoeuer the sence
beare, perfect or imperfect, which difference is obseruable
betwixt the prose and the meeter.

CHAP. VI.

OF PROPORTION IN CONCORD, CALLED SYMPHONIE OR RIME.

Because we vse the word rime (though by maner of
abusion), yet to helpe that fault againe we apply it in our
vulgar Poesie another way very commendably & curiously.
For wanting the currantnesse of the Greeke and Latine
feete, in stead thereof we make in th' ends of our verses
a certaine tunable sound: which anon after with another
verse reasonably distant we accord together in the last fall
or cadence, the eare taking pleasure to heare the like tune
reported and to feel his returne. And for this purpose
serue the *monosillables* of our English Saxons excellently
well, because they do naturally and indifferently receiue
any accent, & in them, if they finish the verse, resteth the
shrill accent of necessitie, and so doth it not in the last of
euery *bissillable*, nor of euery *polisillable* word. But to the
purpose, *ryme* is a borrowed word from the Greeks by the
Latines and French, from them by vs Saxon angles, and
by abusion as hath bene sayd, and therefore it shall not
do amisse to tell what this *rithmos* was with the Greekes,
for what is it with vs hath bene already sayd. There is an
accomptable number which we call *arithmeticall* (*arithmos*)
as one, two, three. There is also a musicall or audible
number, fashioned by stirring of tunes & their sundry
times in the vtterance of our wordes, as when the voice
goeth high or low, or sharpe or flat, or swift or slow:

Of Proportion

& this is called *rithmos* or numerositie, that is to say, a certaine flowing vtteraunce by slipper words and sillables, such as the toung easily vtters, and the eare with pleasure receiuéth, and which flowing of words with much volubilitie smoothly proceeding from the mouth is in some sort *harmonicall* and breedeth to th'eare a great compassion. This point grew by the smooth and delicate running of their feete, which we haue not in our vulgare, though we vse as much as may be the most flowing words & slippery sillables that we can picke out: yet do not we call that by the name of ryme, as the Greekes did, but do giue the name of ryme onely to our concordes, or tunable consentes in the latter end of our verses, and which concordes the Greekes nor Latines neuer vsed in their Poesie till by the barbarous souldiers out of the campe it was brought into the Court and thence to the schoole, as hath bene before remembred; and yet the Greekes and Latines both vsed a maner of speach by clauses of like termination, which they called ὁμοιοτέλευτον, and was the nearest that they approched to our ryme, but is not our right concord; so as we in abusing this terme (*ryme*) be neuerthelesse excusable applying it to another point in Poesie no lesse curious then their *rithme* or numerositie, which in deede passed the whole verse throughout, whereas our concordes keepe but the latter end of euery verse, or perchaunce the middle and the end in meetres that be long.

CHAP. VII.

OF ACCENT, TIME, AND STIR PERCEIUED EUIDENTLY IN THE DISTINCTION OF MANS VOICE, AND WHICH MAKES THE FLOWING OF A MEETER.

Nowe because we haue spoken of accent, time, and stirre or motion in wordes, we will set you downe more at large what they be. The aunciente Greekes and Latines by reason their speech fell out originally to be fashioned with words of many sillables for the most part, it was of necessity that they could not vtter euery sillable with one like and egall sounde, nor in like space of time, nor with like motion or agility, but that one must be more suddenly and quickely forsaken, or longer pawsed vpon then another, or sounded with a higher note & clearer voyce then another; and of necessitie this diuersitie of sound must fall either vpon the last sillable, or vpon the last saue one, or vpon the third, and could not reach higher to make any notable difference. It caused them to giue vnto three different sounds three seuerall names: to that which was highest lift vp and most eleuate or shrillest in the eare they gaue the name of the sharpe accent; to the lowest and most base, because it seemed to fall downe rather then to rise vp, they gaue the name of the heauy accent; and that other which seemed in part to lift vp and in part to fall downe they called the circumflex, or compast accent, and, if new termes were not odious, we might very properly call him the windabout, for so is the Greek word. Then bycause euery thing that by nature fals down is said heauy, & whatsoeuer naturally mounts vpward is said light, it gaue occasion to say that there were diuersities in the motion of the voice, as swift & slow, which motion also presupposes time, bycause time is *mensura motus* by the Philosopher. So haue you the causes of their primitiue inuention and vse in our arte of Poesie. All this by good obseruation we may perceiue in our vulgar wordes if they be of mo sillables then one, but specially if they be *trissillables*; as, for example, in these wordes *altitude* and *heauinesse* the sharpe accent falles vpon *al* & *he* which be the *antepenultimaes*, the other two fall away speedily as if they were scarse sounded; in this *trissilable forsaken* the sharp accent fals vpon *sa*, which is the *penultima*, and in the other two is heauie and obscure. Againe, in these *bissillables*, *endure, vnsure, demure, aspire, desire, retire,* your sharpe accent falles vpon the last sillable; but in words *monosillable*, which be for the more part our naturall Saxon English, the accent is indifferent, and may be vsed for sharp or flat and heauy at our pleasure. I say Saxon English, for our Normane English alloweth vs very many *bissillables*, and also *trissillables*, as *reuerence, diligence, amorous, desirous,* and such like.

CHAP. VIII.

OF YOUR CADENCES BY WHICH YOUR MEETER IS MADE SYMPHONICALL, WHEN THEY BE SWEETEST AND MOST SOLEMNE IN A VERSE.

As the smoothnesse of your words and sillables running vpon feete of sundrie quantities make with the Greekes and Latines the body of their verses numerous or Rithmicall, so in our vulgar Poesie, and of all other nations at this day, your verses answering eche other by couples, or at larger distances in good *cadence,* is it that maketh your meeter symphonicall. This cadence is the fal of a verse in euery last word with a certaine tunable sound, which, being matched with another of like sound, do make a *concord.* And the whole cadence is contained sometime in one sillable, sometime in two, or in three at the most: for aboue the *antepenultima* there reacheth no accent (which is chiefe cause of the cadence), vnlesse it be by vsurpation in some English words, to which we giue a sharpe accent vpon the fourth, as *Hónorable, mátrimonie, pátrimonie, miserable,* and such other as would neither make a sweete cadence, nor easily find any word of like quantitie to match them. And the accented sillable with all the rest vnder him make the cadence, and no sillable aboue, as in these words, *Agíllitie, facíllitie, subiéction, diréction*, and these bissilables, *Ténder, slénder, trústie, lústie*; but alwayes the cadence which falleth vpon the last sillable of a verse is sweetest and most commendable; that vpon the *penultima* more light, and not so pleasant; but falling vpon the *antepenultima* is most vnpleasant of all, because they make your meeter too light and triuiall, and are fitter for the Epigrammatist or Comicall Poet then for the Lyrick and Elegiack, which are accompted the sweeter Musickes. But though we haue sayd that (to make good concord) your seuerall verses should haue their cadences like, yet must there be some difference in their orthographie, though not in their sound, as if one cadence be *constraine*, the next *restraine*, or one *aspire*, another *respire*, this maketh no good concord, because they are all one; but if ye will exchange both these consonants of the accented sillable, or voyde but one of them away, then will your cadences be good and your concord to, as to say, *restraine, refraine, remaine*; *aspire, desire, retire*; which rule neuerthelesse is not well obserued by many makers, for lacke of good iudgement and delicate eare. And this may suffise to shew the vse and nature of your cadences, which are in effect all the sweetnesse and cunning in our vulgar Poesie.

CHAP. IX.

HOW THE GOOD MAKER WILL NOT WRENCH HIS WORD TO HELPE HIS RIME, EITHER BY FALSIFYING HIS ACCENT, OR BY VNTRUE ORTHOGRAPHIE.

Now there can not be in a maker a fowler fault then to falsifie his accent to serue his cadence, or by vntrue orthographie to wrench his words to helpe his rime, for it is a signe that such a maker is not copious in his owne

Of Proportion

language, or (as they are wont to say) not halfe his crafts
maister: as for example, if one should rime to this word
Restore, he may not match him with *Doore* or *Poore*, for
neither of both are of like terminant, either by good
orthography or in naturall sound; therfore such rime
is strained; so is it to this word *Ram* to say *came*, or to
Beane, Den, for they sound not nor be written a like; &
many other like cadences which were superfluous to recite,
and are vsuall with rude rimers who obserue not precisely
the rules of *prosodie*; neuerthelesse in all such cases
(if necessitie constrained) it is somewhat more tollerable
to help the rime by false orthographie then to leaue an
vnplesant dissonance to the eare by keeping trewe orthographie and loosing the rime, as for example it is better to
rime *Dore* with *Restore* then in his truer orthographie,
which is *Doore*, and to this word *Desire* to say *Fier* then
fyre, though it be otherwise better written *fire*. For since
the cheife grace of our vulgar Poesie consisteth in the
Symphonie, as hath bene already sayd, our maker must
not be too licentious in his concords, but see that they go
euen, iust, and melodious in the eare, and right so in the
numerositie or currantnesse of the whole body of his verse,
and in euery other of his proportions. For a licentious
maker is in truth but a bungler and not a Poet. Such
men were in effect the most part of all your old rimers,
and specially *Gower*, who to make vp his rime would for
the most part write his terminant sillable with false orthographie, and many times not sticke to put in a plaine
French word for an English; & so, by your leaue, do many
of our common rimers at this day, as he that by all likelyhood hauing no word at hand to rime to this word *ioy*, he
made his other verse ende in *Roy*, saying very impudently
thus,

> *O mightie Lord of loue, dame Venus onely ioy,*
> *Who art the highest God of any heauenly Roy.*

Which word was neuer yet receiued in our language for an English word. Such extreme licentiousnesse is vtterly to be banished from our schoole, and better it might haue bene borne with in old riming writers, bycause they liued in a barbarous age, & were graue morall men but very homely Poets, such also as made most of their workes by translation out of the Latine and French toung, & few or none of their owne engine, as may easely be knowen to them that list to looke vpon the Poemes of both languages.

Finally, as ye may ryme with wordes of all sortes, be they of many sillables or few, so neuerthelesse is there a choise by which to make your cadence (before remembred) most commendable, for some wordes of exceeding great length, which haue bene fetched from the Latine inkhorne or borrowed of strangers, the vse of them in ryme is nothing pleasant, sauing perchaunce to the common people, who reioyse much to be at playes and enterludes, and, besides their naturall ignoraunce, haue at all such times their eares so attentiue to the matter, and their eyes vpon the shewes of the stage, that they take little heede to the cunning of the rime, and therefore be as well satisfied with that which is grosse, as with any other finer and more delicate.

CHAP. X.

OF CONCORDE IN LONG AND SHORT MEASURES, AND BY NEARE OR FARRE DISTAUNCES, AND WHICH OF THEM IS MOST COMMENDABLE.

But this ye must obserue withall, that, bycause your concordes containe the chief part of Musicke in your meetre, their distaunces may not be too wide or farre a sunder, lest th'eare should loose the tune and be defrauded of his delight; and whensoeuer ye see any

Of Proportion

maker vse large and extraordinary distaunces, ye must thinke he doth intende to shew himselfe more artificiall then popular, and yet therein is not to be discommended, for respects that shalbe remembred in some other place of this booke.

Note also that rime or concorde is not commendably vsed both in the end and middle of a verse, vnlesse it be in toyes and trifling Poesies, for it sheweth a certaine lightnesse either of the matter or of the makers head, albeit these common rimers vse it much, for, as I sayd before, like as the Symphonie in a verse of great length is, as it were, lost by looking after him, and yet may the meetre be very graue and stately, so on the other side doth the ouer busie and too speedy returne of one maner of tune too much annoy &, as it were, glut the eare, vnlesse it be in small & popular Musickes song by these *Cantabanqui* vpon benches and barrels heads, where they haue none other audience then boys or countrey fellowes that passe by them in the streete, or else by blind harpers or such like tauerne minstrels that giue a fit of mirth for a groat, & their matters being for the most part stories of old time, as the tale of Sir *Topas*, the reportes of *Beuis* of *Southampton*, *Guy* of *Warwicke*, *Adam Bell*, and *Clymme* of the *Clough*, & such other old Romances or historicall rimes, made purposely for recreation of the common people at Christmasse diners & brideales, and in tauernes & alehouses, and such other places of base resort; also they be vsed in Carols and rounds and such light or lasciuious Poemes, which are commonly more commodiously vttered by these buffons or vices in playes then by any other person. Such were the rimes of *Skelton*, vsurping the name of a Poet Laureat, being in deede but a rude rayling rimer & all his doings ridiculous: he vsed both short distaunces and short measures, pleasing onely the popular eare: in our courtly maker we banish

them vtterly. Now also haue ye in euery song or ditty
concorde by compasse & concorde entertangled and a
mixt of both: what that is and how they be vsed shalbe
declared in the chapter of proportion by *scituation*.

CHAP. XI.

OF PROPORTION BY SITUATION.

This proportion consisteth in placing of euery verse in
a staffe or ditty by such reasonable distaunces as may best
serue the eare for delight, and also to shew the Poets art
and variety of Musick. And the proportion is double:
one by marshalling the meetres, and limiting their distaunces, hauing regard to the rime or concorde how they
go and returne; another by placing euery verse, hauing
a regard to his measure and quantitie onely, and not to
his concorde, as to set one short meetre to three long, or
foure short and two long, or a short measure and a long,
or of diuers lengthes with relation one to another, which
maner of *Situation*, euen without respect of the rime, doth
alter the nature of the Poesie, and make it either lighter
or grauer, or more merry, or mournfull, and many wayes
passionate to the eare and hart of the hearer, seeming
for this point that our maker by his measures and concordes of sundry proportions doth counterfait the harmonicall tunes of the vocall and instrumentall Musickes.
As the *Dorien*, because his falls, sallyes, and compasse be
diuers from those of the *Phrigien*, the *Phrygien* likewise
from the *Lydien*, and all three from the *Eolien*, *Miolidien*, and
Ionien, mounting and falling from note to note such as be
to them peculiar, and with more or lesse leasure or preci-
p[it]ation; euen so by diuersitie of placing and scituation
of your measures and concords, a short with a long, and by

Of Proportion

narrow or wide distances, or thicker or thinner bestowing of them, your proportions differ, and breedeth a variable and strange harmonie not onely in the eare, but also in the conceit of them that heare it; whereof this may be an ocular example.

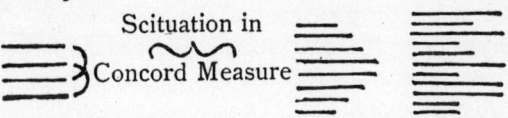

Where ye see the concord or rime in the third distance, and the measure in the fourth, sixth, or second distaunces, whereof ye may deuise as many other as ye list, so the staffe be able to beare it. And I set you downe an occular example, because ye may the better conceiue it. Likewise it so falleth out most times your occular proportion doeth declare the nature of the audible; for if it please the eare well, the same represented by delineation to the view pleaseth the eye well, and *e conuerso*; and this is by a naturall *simpathie* betweene the eare and the eye, and betweene tunes & colours, even as there is the like betweene the other sences and their obiects, of which it apperteineth not here to speake.

Now for the distances vsually obserued in our vulgar Poesie. They be in the first, second, third, and fourth verse, or, if the verse be very short, in the fift and sixt, and in some maner of Musickes farre aboue.

And the first distance for the most part goeth all by *distick* or couples of verses agreeing in one cadence, and do passe so speedily away and so often returne agayne, as their tunes are neuer lost nor out of the eare, one couple supplying another so nye and so suddenly: and this is the most vulgar proportion of distance or situation, such as vsed *Chaucer* in his Canterbury tales, and *Gower* in all his workes.

Second distance is when ye passe ouer one verse, and

ioyne the first and the third, and so continue
on till an other like distance fall in, and this is
also vsuall and common, as

Third distaunce is when your rime falleth vpon the first
and fourth verse, ouerleaping two: this maner is
not so common, but pleasant and allowable inough.
In which case the two verses ye leaue out are ready
to receiue their concordes by the same distaunce or any
other ye like better.

The fourth distaunce is by ouerskipping three verses
and lighting upon the fift: this maner is rare and
more artificiall then popular, vnlesse
it be in some speciall case, as when
the meetres be so little and short as
they make no shew of any great delay
before they returne. Ye shall haue example of both. And these ten litle meeters make but
one *Exameter* at length.

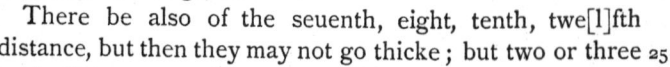

There be larger distances also, as when the
first concord falleth vpon the sixt verse, & is
very pleasant if they be ioyned with other distances not so large, as

There be also of the seuenth, eight, tenth, twe[l]fth
distance, but then they may not go thicke; but two or three
such distances serue to proportion
a whole song, and all betweene must
be of other lesse distances, and these
wide distaunces serue for coupling
of staues, or for to declare high and
passionate or graue matter, and
also for art: *Petrarch* hath giuen
vs examples hereof in his *Canzoni*,
and we by lines of sundry lengths
and distances, as followeth:

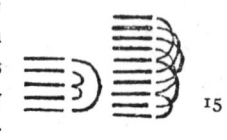
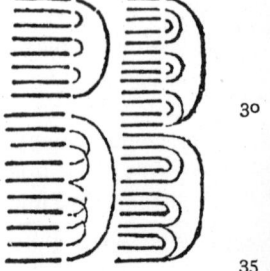

Of Proportion

And all that can be obiected against this wide distance is to say that the eare by loosing his concord is not satisfied. So is in deede the rude and popular eare, but not the learned; and therefore the Poet must know to whose eare he maketh his rime, and accommodate himselfe thereto, and not giue such musicke to the rude and barbarous, as he would to the learned and delicate eare.

There is another sort of proportion vsed by *Petrarche* called the *Seizino*, not riming as other songs do, but by chusing sixe wordes out of which all the whole dittie is made, euery of those sixe commencing and ending his verse by course, which restraint to make the dittie sensible will try the makers cunning, as thus:

Besides all this there is in *Situation* of the concords two other points, one that it go by plaine and cleere compasse not intangled, another by enterweauing one with another by knots, or, as it were, by band, which is more or lesse busie and curious, all as the maker will double or redouble his rime or concords, and set his distances farre or nigh, of all which I will giue you ocular examples, as thus:

Concord in

Plaine compasse  Entertangle.

And first in a *Quadreine* there are but two proportions, for foure verses in this last sort coupled are but two *Disticks*, and not a staffe *quadreine* or of foure.

The staffe of fiue hath seuen proportions, as

whereof some of them be harsher and vnpleasaunter to the eare then other some be.

The *Sixaine* or staffe of sixe hath ten proportions, wherof some be vsuall, some not vsuall, and not so sweet one as another.

The staffe of seuen verses hath seuen proportions, whereof one onely is the vsuall of our vulgar, and kept by our old Poets *Chaucer* and other in their historicall reports and other ditties: as in the last part of them that follow next.

The *huitain*, or staffe of eight verses, hath eight proportions such as the former staffe, and, because he is longer, he hath one more than the *settaine*.

The staffe of nine verses hath yet moe then the eight, and the staffe of ten more then the ninth, and the twelfth, if such were allowable in ditties, more then any of them all, by reason of his largenesse receiuing moe compasses and enterweauings, always considered that the very large distances be more artificiall then popularly pleasant, and yet do giue great grace and grauitie, and moue passion and affections more vehemently, as it is well to be obserued by *Petrarcha* his *Canzoni*.

Of Proportion

Now ye may perceiue by these proportions before described that there is a band to be giuen euery verse in a staffe, so as none fall out alone or vncoupled, and this band maketh that the staffe is sayd fast and not loose; euen as ye see in buildings of stone or bricke the mason giueth a band, that is a length to two breadths, & vpon necessitie diuers other sorts of bands to hold in the worke fast and maintaine the perpendicularitie of the wall: so, in any staffe of seuen or eight or more verses, the coupling of the moe meeters by rime or concord is the faster band, the fewer the looser band, and therfore in a *huiteine* he that putteth foure verses in one concord and foure in another concord, and in a *dizaine* fiue, sheweth him selfe more cunning, and also more copious in his owne language. For he that can find two words of concord can not find foure or fiue or sixe, vnlesse he haue his owne language at will. Sometime also ye are driuen of necessitie to close and make band more then ye would, lest otherwise the staffe should fall asunder and seeme two staues: and this is in a staffe of eight and ten verses: whereas without a band in the middle, it would seeme two *quadreins* or two *quintaines*, which is an error that many makers slide away with. Yet *Chaucer* and others in the staffe of seuen and sixe do almost as much a misse, for they shut vp the staffe with a *disticke*, concording with none other verse that went before, and maketh but a loose rime, and yet, bycause of the double cadence in the last two verses, serue the eare well inough. And as there is in euery staffe band giuen to the verses by concord more or lesse busie, so is there in some cases a band giuen to euery staffe, and that is by one whole verse running alone throughout the ditty or ballade, either in the middle or end of euery staffe. The Greekes called such vncoupled verse *Epimonie*, the Latines *Versus intercalaris*. Now touching the situation of measures, there are as

manie or more proportions of them which I referre to
the makers phantasie and choise, contented with two or
three ocular examples and no moe.

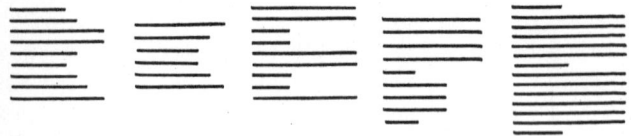

Which maner of proportion by situation of measures giueth
more efficacie to the matter oftentimes then the concords
them selues, and both proportions concurring together as
they needes must, it is of much more beautie and force
to the hearers mind.

To finish the learning of this diuision, I will set you
downe one example of a dittie written extempore with this
deuise, shewing not onely much promptnesse of wit in
the maker, but also great arte and a notable memorie.
Make me, saith this writer to one of the companie, so
many strokes or lines with your pen as ye would haue
your song containe verses; and let euery line beare his
seuerall length, euen as ye would haue your verse of
measure. Suppose of foure, fiue, sixe, or eight, or more
sillables, and set a figure of euerie number at th' end
of the line, whereby ye may knowe his measure. Then
where you will haue your rime or concord to fall, marke
it with a compast stroke or semicircle passing ouer those
lines, be they farre or neare in distance, as ye haue seene
before described. And bycause ye shall not thinke the
maker hath premeditated beforehand any such fashioned
ditty, do ye your selfe make one verse, whether it be of
perfect or imperfect sense, and giue it him for a theame
to make all the rest vpon. If ye shall perceiue the maker
do keepe the measures and rime as ye haue appointed
him, and besides do make his dittie sensible and ensuant

to the first verse in good reason, then may ye say he is
his crafts maister. For, if he were not of a plentiful
discourse, he could not vpon the sudden shape an entire
dittie vpon your imperfect theame or proposition in one
verse. And, if he were not copious in his language, he
could not haue such store of wordes at commaundement
as should supply your concords. And, if he were not
of a maruelous good memory, he could not obserue the
rime and measures after the distances of your limitation,
keeping with all grauitie and good sense in the whole
dittie.

CHAP. XII.

OF PROPORTION IN FIGURE.

Your last proportion is that of figure, so called for that
it yelds an ocular representation, your meeters being by
good symmetrie reduced into certaine Geometricall figures,
whereby the maker is restrained to keepe him within his
bounds, and sheweth not onely more art, but serueth also
much better for briefenesse and subtiltie of deuice; and
for the same respect are also fittest for the pretie amourets
in Court to entertaine their seruants and the time withall,
their delicate wits requiring some commendable exercise
to keepe them from idlenesse. I find not of this proportion vsed by any of the Greeke or Latine Poets, or in
any vulgar writer, sauing of that one forme which they
cal *Anacreons egge*. But being in Italie conuersant with
a certaine gentleman who had long trauailed the Orientall
parts of the world and seene the Courts of the great
Princes of China and Tartarie, I being very inquisitiue to
know of the subtillities of those countreyes, and especially
in matter of learning and of their vulgar Poesie, he told
me that they are in all their inuentions most wittie, and
haue the vse of Poesie or riming, but do not delight so

much as we do in long tedious descriptions, and therefore when they will vtter any pretie conceit, they reduce it into metricall feet, and put it in forme of a *Lozange* or square, or such other figure; and so engrauen in gold, siluer, or iuorie, and sometimes with letters of ametist, rubie, emeralde, or topas curiousely cemented and peeced together, they sende them in chaines, bracelets, collars, and girdles to their mistresses to weare for a remembrance. Some fewe measures composed in this sort this gentleman gaue me, which I translated word for word, and as neere as I could followed both the phrase and the figure, which is somewhat hard to performe, because of the restraint of the figure from which ye may not digresse. At the beginning they wil seeme nothing pleasant to an English eare, but time and vsage wil make them acceptable inough, as it doth in all other new guises, be it for wearing of apparell or otherwise. The formes of your Geometricall figures be hereunder represented.

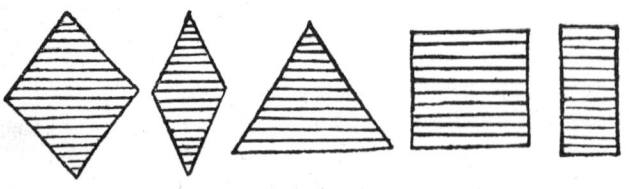

The Lozange, called Rombus.   The Fuzie or spindle, called Romboides.   The Triangle or Tricquet.   The Square or quadrangle.   The Pillaster or Cillinder.

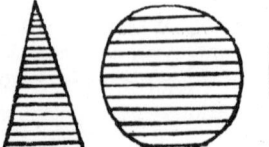
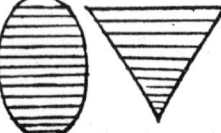
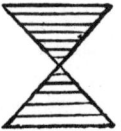

The Spire or taper, called piramis.   The Rondel or Sphere.   The egge or figure ouall.   The Tricquet reuerst.   The Tricquet displayed.

Of Proportion

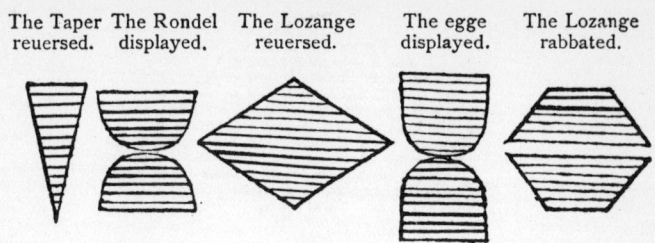

The Taper reuersed. The Rondel displayed. The Lozange reuersed. The egge displayed. The Lozange rabbated.

Of the Lozange.

The Lozange is a most beautifull figure, & fit for this purpose, being in his kind a quadrangle reuerst, with his point vpward like to a quarrell of glasse. The Greekes and Latines both call it *Rombus*, which may be the cause, as I suppose, why they also gaue that name to the fish commonly called the *Turbot*, who beareth iustly that figure. It ought not to containe aboue thirteene or fifteene or one & twentie meetres, & the longest furnisheth the middle angle, the rest passe vpward and downward, still abating their lengthes by one or two sillables till they come to the point. The Fuzie is of the same nature but that he is sharper and slenderer. I will giue you an example or two of those which my Italian friend bestowed vpon me, which as neare as I could I translated into the same figure, obseruing the phrase of the Orientall speach word for word.

A great Emperor in Tartary whom they cal *Can*, for his good fortune in the wars & many notable conquests he had made, was surnamed *Temir Cutzclewe*. This man loued the Lady *Kermesine*, who presented him returning from the conquest of *Corasoon* (a great kingdom adioyning) with this *Lozange* made in letters of rubies & diamants entermingled thus:

Sound,
O Harpe,
Shril lie out
Temir the stout
Rider who with sharpe
Trenching blade of bright steele
Hath made his fiercest foes to feele,
All such as wrought him shame or harme,
The strength of his braue right arme,
Cleauing hard downe vnto the eyes
The raw skulles of his enemies,
Much honor hath he wonne
By doughtie deedes done
In Cora soon
And all the
Worlde
Round.

To which *Can Temir* answered in *Fuzie*, with letters of Emeralds and Ametists artificially cut and entermingled, thus:

Fiue
Sore batailes
Manfully fought
In blouddy fielde
With bright blade in hand
Hath Temir won, & forst to yeld
Many a Captaine strong & stoute,
And many a king his Crowne to vayle,
Conquering large countreys and land,
Yet ne uer wanne I vi cto rie,
I speake it to my greate glo rie,
So deare and ioy full vn to me,
As when I did first con quere thee,
O Kerme sine, of all myne foes
The most cruell, of all myne woes
The smartest, the sweetest,
My proude Con quest,
My ri chest pray.
O once a daye
Lend me thy sight,
Whose only light
Keepes me
Aliue.

Of the Triangle or Triquet.

The Triangle is an halfe square, Lozange, or Fuzie parted vpon the crosse angles; and so, his base being brode and his top narrow, it receaueth meetres of many sizes, one shorter then another: and ye may vse this figure standing or reuersed, as thus.

A certaine great Sultan of Persia, called *Ribuska*, entertaynes in loue the Lady *Selamour*, sent her this triquet reue[r]st pitiously bemoning his estate, all set in merquetry,

Of Proportion

with letters of blew Saphire and Topas artificially cut
and entermingled.

>   *Selamour, dearer than his owne life,*
>   *To thy di stressed wretch, captiue*
>   *Ri buska, whome late ly erst*
>   *Most cru el ly thou perst*
>   *With thy dead ly dart,*
>   *That paire of starres*
>   *Shi ning a farre*
>   *Turne from me, to me*
>   *That I may & may not see*
>   *The smile, the loure,*
>   *That lead and driue*
>   *Me to die to liue,*
>   *Twise yea thrise*
>   *In one*
>   *houre.*

To which *Selamour*, to make the match egall, and the
figure entire, answered in a standing Triquet, richly engrauen
with letters of like stuffe.

>   *Power*
>   *Of death*
>   *Nor of life*
>   *Hath Selamour;*
>   *With Gods it is rife.*
>   *To geue and bereue breath.*
>   *I may for pitie perchaunce*
>   *Thy lost libertie re store,*
>   *Vpon thine othe with this penaunce,*
>   *That while thou liuest thou neuer loue no more.*

This condition seeming to Sultan *Ribuska* very hard
to performe, and cruell to be enioyned him, doeth by
another figure in Taper, signifying hope, answere the
Lady *Selamour*, which dittie for lack of time I translated not.

Of the Spire or Taper called Pyramis.

The Taper is the longest and sharpest triangle that
is, & while he mounts vpward he waxeth continually
more slender, taking both his figure and name of the
fire, whose flame, if ye marke it, is alwaies pointed, and
naturally by his forme couets to clymbe: the Greekes
call him *Pyramis*, of πῦρ. The Latines, in use of Architecture, called him *Obeliscus*. It holdeth the altitude of
six ordinary triangles, and in metrifying his base can

not well be larger then a meetre of six; therefore in his altitude he wil require diuers rabates to hold so many sizes of meetres as shall serue for his composition, for neare the toppe there wilbe roome litle inough for a meetre of two sillables, and sometimes of one to finish the point. 5 I haue set you downe one or two examples to try how ye can disgest the maner of the deuise.

Her Maiestie, for many parts in her most noble and vertuous nature to be found, resembled to the spire. Ye must begin beneath according to the nature of the deuice.

From God, the fountaine of all good, are deriued into the world all good things: and vpon her maiestie all the good fortunes any worldly creature can be furnished with. Reade downward according to the nature of the deuice.

Skie. 1

Azurd 2
in the
assurde,

And better, [3]
And richer,
Much greter,

Crown & empir
After an hier
For to aspire 4
Like flame of fire
In forme of spire
To mount on hie,

Con ti nu al ly
With trauel & teen
Most gratious queen,
Ye haue made a vow, 5
Shews vs plainly how
Not fained but true,
To euery mans vew,
Shining cleere in you
Of so bright an hewe,
Euen thus vertewe

Vanish out of our sight
Till his fine top be quite
To Taper in the ayre 6
Endeurs soft and faire
By his kindly nature
Of tall comely stature
Like as this faire figure

1 *God*
  On
  Hie
2 *From*
  Aboue
  Sends loue,
  Wisedome,
  Iu stice,
  Cou rage,
  Boun tie,
[3] *And doth geue*
  Al that liue
  Life & breath,
  Harts ese, helth,
  Children, welth,
  Beauty, strength,
  Restfull age,
  And at length
  A mild death,
4 *He doeth bestow*
  All mens fortunes
  Both high & low,
  And the best things
  That earth can haue
  Or mankind craue,
  Good queens & kings,
  Fi nally is the same
  Who gaue you (madam)
  Seyson of this Crowne
  With poure soueraigne,
5 *Impug nable right.*
  Redoubtable might,
  Most prosperous raigne,
  Eternall re nowme,
  And that your chiefest is
  Sure hope of heauens blis.

The Piller, Pillaster, or Cillinder.

The Piller is a figure among all the rest of the Geometricall most beawtifull, in respect that he is tall and 10 vpright and of one bignesse from the bottom to the toppe.

Of Proportion

In Architecture he is considered with two accessarie parts, a pedestall or base, and a chapter or head; the body is the shaft. By this figure is signified stay, support, rest, state, and magnificence. Your dittie then being reduced into the forme of the Piller, his base will require to beare the brea[d]th of a meetre of six or seuen or eight sillables; the shaft of foure; the chapter egall with the base. Of this proportion I will giue you one or two examples, which may suffise.

Her Maiestie resembled to the crowned pillar. Ye must read vpward.

 Is blisse with immortalitie.
  Her trymest top of all ye see
   Garnish the crowne,
   Her iust renowne
   Chapter and head,
   Part that maintain
   And   womanhead
   Her mayden raigne
   In te gri tie:
   In ho nour and
   With ve ri tie,
   Her roundnes stand
   Strengthen the state.
   By their increase
   With out de bate
   Concord and peace
   Of her sup port,
   They be the base
   With   stedfastnesse
   Vertue and grace
   Stay, and comfort;
   Of Albi ons rest,
   The sounde Pillar
  And seene a farre
  Is plainely exprest
 Tall stately and strayt
By this no ble pour trayt

Philo to the Lady Calia sendeth this Odelet of her prayse in forme of a Piller, which ye must read downeward.

Thy Princely port and Maiestie
Is my ter rene dei tie,
 Thy wit and sence
 The streame & source
 Of e lo quence
 And deepe discours,
 Thy faire eyes are
 My bright loadstarre,
 Thy speache a darte
 Percing my harte,
 Thy face, a las,
 My loo king glasse,
 Thy loue ly lookes
 My prayer bookes,
 Thy pleasant cheare
 My sunshine cleare,
 Thy ru full sight
 My darke midnight,
 Thy will the stent
 Of my con tent,
 Thy glo rye flour
 Of myne ho nour,
 Thy loue doth giue
 The lyfe I lyue,
 Thy lyfe it is
 Mine earthly blisse:
But grace & fauour in thine eies
My bodies soule & souls paradise.

The Roundell or Spheare.

The most excellent of all the figures Geometrical is the Round, for his many perfections. First, because he is euen & smooth, without any angle or interruption, most voluble and apt to turne, and to continue motion, which is the author of life: he conteyneth in him the commodious description of euery other figure, & for his

ample capacitie doth resemble the world or vniuers, & for
his indefinitenesse, hauing no speciall place of beginning
nor end, beareth a similitude with God and eternitie.
This figure hath three principall partes in his nature and
vse much considerable: the circle, the beame, and the
center. The circle is his largest compasse or circumference; the center is his middle and indiuisible point;
the beame is a line stretching directly from the circle to
the center, & contrariwise from the center to the circle.
By this description our maker may fashion his meetre
in Roundel, either with the circumference, and that is
circlewise, or from the circumference, that is like a beame,
or by the circumference, and that is ouerthwart and
dyametrally from one side of the circle to the other.

*A generall resemblance of the Roundell to God, the World,
and the Queene.*

> All and whole, and euer, and one,
> Single, simple, eche where, alone,
> These be counted, as Clerkes can tell,
> True properties of the Roundell.
> His still turning by consequence
> And change doe breede both life and sence.
> Time, measure of stirre and rest,
> Is also by his course exprest.
> How swift the circle stirre aboue,
> His center point doeth neuer moue:
> All things that euer were or be
> Are closde in his concauitie.
> And though he be still turnde and tost,
> No roome there wants, nor none is lost.
> The Roundell hath no bonch nor angle,
> Which may his course stay or entangle.
> The furthest part of all his spheare
> Is equally both farre and neare.
> So doth none other figure fare
> Where natures chattels closed are:

And beyond his wide compasse
There is no body nor no place,
Nor any wit that comprehends
Where it begins, or where it ends:
And therefore all men doe agree,
That it purports eternitie.
God aboue the heauens so hie
Is this Roundell; in world the skie;
Vpon earth she who beares the bell
Of maydes and Queenes is this Roundell:
All and whole, and euer alone,
Single, sans peere, simple, and one.

*A special and particular resemblance of her Maiestie
to the Roundell.*

First her authoritie regall
Is the circle compassing all,
The dominion great and large
Which God hath geuen to her charge:
Within which most spatious bound
She enuirons her people round,
Retaining them by oth and liegeance
Within the pale of true obeysance,
Holding imparked, as it were,
Her people like to heards of deere,
Sitting among them in the middes
Where she allowes and bannes and bids,
In what fashion she list and when,
The seruices of all her men.
Out of her breast as from an eye
Issue the rayes incessantly
Of her iustice, bountie, and might,
Spreading abroad their beames so bright,
And reflect not, till they attaine
The fardest part of her domaine.
And makes eche subiect clearely see
What he is bounden for to be
To God, his Prince, and common wealth,
His neighbour, kinred, and to himselfe.

> The same centre and middle pricke,
> Whereto our deedes are drest so thicke,
> From all the parts and outmost side
> Of her Monarchie large and wide,
> Also fro whence reflect these rayes 5
> Twentie hundred maner of wayes,
> Where her will is them to conuey
> Within the circle of her suruey.
> So is the Queene of Briton ground,
> Beame, circle, center of all my round. 10

Of the Square or Quadrangle equilater.

The Square is of all other accompted the figure of most solliditie and stedfastnesse, and for his owne stay and firmitie requireth none other base then himselfe, and therefore as the Roundell or Spheare is appropriat to the heauens, the Spire to the element of the fire, the Triangle to the ayre, and the Lozange to the water, so is the Square for his inconcussable steadinesse likened to the earth, which perchaunce might be the reason that the Prince of Philosophers, in his first booke of the *Ethicks*, termeth a constant minded man euen egal and direct on all sides, and not easily ouerthrowne by euery litle aduersitie, *hominem quadratum*, a square man. Into this figure may ye reduce your ditties by vsing no moe verses then your verse is of sillables, which will make him fall out square; if ye go aboue it wil grow into the figure *Trapezion*, which is some portion longer then square. I neede not giue you any example, bycause in good arte all your ditties, Odes, & Epigrammes should keepe & not exceede the nomber of twelue verses, and the longest verse to be of twelue sillables & not aboue, but vnder that number as much as ye will.

The figure Ouall.

This figure taketh his name of an egge, and also as it is thought his first origine, and is, as it were, a bastard or

imperfect rounde declining toward a longitude, and yet
keeping within one line for his periferie or compasse as
the rounde; and it seemeth that he receiueth this forme
not as an imperfection by any impediment vnnaturally
hindring his rotunditie, but by the wisedome and prouidence of nature for the commoditie of generation, in such
of her creatures as bring not forth a liuely body (as do
foure footed beasts), but in stead thereof a certaine quantitie
of shapelesse matter contained in a vessell, which, after it
is sequestred from the dames body, receiueth life and perfection, as in the egges of birdes, fishes, and serpents: for
the matter being of some quantitie, and to issue out at
a narrow place, for the easie passage thereof it must of
necessitie beare such shape as might not be sharpe and
greeuous to passe, as an angle, nor so large or obtuse as
might not essay some issue out with one part moe then
other, as the rounde; therefore it must be slenderer in
some part, & yet not without a rotunditie & smoothnesse
to giue the rest an easie deliuerie. Such is the figure
Ouall whom for his antiquitie, dignitie, and vse, I place
among the rest of the figures to embellish our proportions:
of this sort are diuers of *Anacreons* ditties, and those
other of the Grecian Liricks who wrate wanton amorous
deuises, to solace their witts with all; and many times
they would (to giue it right shape of an egge) deuide
a word in the midst, and peece out the next verse with the
other halfe, as ye may see by perusing their meetres[1].

*Of the Deuice or Embleme, and that other which the Greekes
call Anagramma, and we the Posie transposed.*

And besides all the remembred points of Metricall proportion, ye haue yet two other sorts of some affinitie with

[1] The two following paragraphs, 'Of the deuice or embleme' and 'Of the Anagrame,' are inserted in the British Museum copy. They occupy eight pages, but have no page-numbers.

them, which also first issued out of the Poets head, and whereof the Courtly maker was the principall artificer, hauing many high conceites and curious imaginations, with leasure inough to attend his idle inuentions: and these be the short, quicke, and sententious propositions, such as be at these dayes all your deuices of armes and other amorous inscriptions which courtiers vse to giue and also to weare in liuerie for the honour of their ladies, and commonly containe but two or three words of wittie sentence or secrete conceit till they [be] vnfolded or explaned by some interpretation. For which cause they be commonly accompanied with a figure or purtraict of ocular representation, the words so aptly corresponding to the subtilitie of the figure that aswel the eye is therwith recreated as the eare or the mind. The Greekes call it *Emblema*, the Italiens *Impresa*, and we, a Deuice, such as a man may put into letters of gold and sende to his mistresses for a token, or cause to be embrodered in scutchions of armes, or in any bordure of a rich garment to giue by his noueltie maruell to the beholder. Such were the figures and inscriptions the Romane Emperours gaue in their money and coignes of largesse, and in other great medailles of siluer and gold, as that of the Emperour *Augustus*, an arrow entangled by the fish *Remora*, with these words, *Festina lente*, signifying that celeritie is to be vsed with deliberation; all great enterprises being for the most part either ouerthrowen with hast or hindred by delay, in which case leasure in th'aduice and speed in th'execution make a very good match for a glorious successe.

Th'Emperour *Heliogabalus*, by his name alluding to the sunne, which in Greeke is *Helios*, gaue for his deuice the cœlestial sunne, with these words *Soli inuicto*: the subtilitie lyeth in the word *soli* which hath a double sense, viz. to the Sunne, and to him onely.

Of Proportion

We our selues attributing that most excellent figure, for his incomparable beauty and light, to the person of our Soueraigne lady, altring the mot, made it farre passe that of Th'Emperour *Heliogabalus* both for subtilitie and multiplicitie of sense, thus, *Soli nunquam deficienti*, To her onely that neuer failes, viz. in bountie and munificence toward all hers that deserue, or else thus, To her onely whose glorie and good fortune may neuer decay or wane. And so it inureth as a wish by way of resemblaunce in *Simile dissimile*, which is also a subtillitie, likening her Maiestie to the Sunne for his brightnesse, but not to him for his passion, which is ordinarily to go to glade, and sometime to suffer eclypse.

King *Edwarde* the thirde, her Maiesties most noble progenitour, first founder of the famous order of the Garter, gaue this posie with it, *Honi soit qui mal y pense*, commonly thus Englished, Ill be to him that thinketh ill, but in mine opinion better thus, Dishonored be he who meanes vnhonorably. There can not be a more excellent deuise, nor that could containe larger intendment, nor greater subtilitie, nor (as a man may say) more vertue or Princely generositie. For first he did by it mildly & grauely reproue the peruers construction of such noble men in his court as imputed the kings wearing about his neck the garter of the lady with whom he danced to some amorous alliance betwixt them, which was not true. He also iustly defended his owne integritie, saued the noble womans good renowme, which by licentious speeches might haue bene empaired, and liberally recompenced her iniurie with an honor, such as none could haue bin deuised greater nor more glorious or permanent vpon her and all the posteritie of her house. It inureth also as a worthy lesson and discipline for all Princely personages, whose actions, imaginations, countenances, and speeches should euermore correspond in all trueth and honorable simplicitie.

Charles the fift Emperour, euen in his yong yeares shewing his valour and honorable ambition, gaue for his new order the golden Fleece, vsurping it vpon Prince Iason and his Argonauts rich spoile brought from *Cholcos*. But for his deuice two pillers with this mot *Plus vltra*, as one not content to be restrained within the limits that *Hercules* had set for an vttermost bound to all his trauailes, viz. two pillers in the mouth of the straight *Gibraltare*, but would go furder: which came fortunately to passe, and whereof the good successe gaue great commendation to his deuice; for by the valiancy of his Captaines before he died he conquered great part of the west Indias, neuer knowen to *Hercules* or any of our world before.

In the same time (seeming that the heauens and starres had conspired to replenish the earth with Princes and gouernours of great courage and most famous conquerours) *Selim*, Emperour of Turkie, gaue for his deuice a croissant or new moone, promising to himself increase of glory and enlargement of empire til he had brought all Asia vnder his subiection, which he reasonably well accomplished. For in lesse then eight yeres which he raigned he conquered all Syria and Egypt, and layd it to his dominion. This deuice afterward was vsurped by *Henry* the second, French king, with this mot, *Donec totum compleat orbem*, till he be at his full; meaning it not so largely as did *Selim*, but onely that his friendes should knowe how vnable he was to do them good and to shew benificence vntil he attained the crowne of France, vnto which he aspired as next successour.

King *Lewis* the twelfth, a valiant and magnanimous prince, who because hee was on euery side enuironed with mightie neighbours, and most of them his enemies, to let them perceiue that they should not finde him vnable or vnfurnished (incase they should offer any vnlawfull hostillitie) of sufficient forces of his owne, aswell to offende as

to defend, and to reuenge an iniurie as to repulse it, he
gaue for his deuice the Porkespick with this posie, *pres &
loign*, both farre and neare. For the Purpentines nature
is, to such as stand aloofe, to dart her prickles from her,
and, if they come neare her, with the same as they sticke
fast to wound them that hurt her.

But of late yeares in the ransacke of the Cities of *Carta-
gena* and *S. Dominico* in the West Indias, manfully put in
execution by the prowesse of her Maiesties men, there was
found a deuice made peraduenture without King *Philips*
knowledge, wrought al in massiue copper, a king sitting
on horsebacke vpon a *monde* or world, the horse prauncing
forward with his forelegges as if he would leape of, with
this inscription, *Non sufficit orbis*, meaning, as it is to be
conceaued, that one whole world could not content him.
This immeasurable ambition of the Spaniards, if her
Maiestie by Gods prouidence had not with her forces
prouidently stayed and retranched, no man knoweth what
inconuenience might in time haue insued to all the Princes
and common wealthes in Christendome, who haue founde
them selues long annoyed with his excessiue greatnesse.

Atila, king of the Huns, inuading France with an army
of 300000 fighting men, as it is reported, thinking vtterly
to abbase the glory of the Romane Empire, gaue for his
deuice of armes a sword with a firie point and these words,
Ferro & flamma, with sword and fire. This very deuice,
being as ye see onely accommodate to a king or conquerour and not a coillen or any meane souldier, a certaine
base man of England, being knowen euen at that time
a bricklayer or mason by his science, gaue for his crest:
whom it had better become to beare a truell full of morter
then a sword and fire, which is onely the reuenge of
a Prince, and lieth not in any other mans abilitie to
performe, vnlesse ye will allow it to euery poore knaue
that is able to set fire on a thacht house. The heraldes

ought to vse great discretion in such matters: for neither
any rule of their arte doth warrant such absurdities, nor
though such a coat or crest were gained by a prisoner
taken in the field, or by a flag found in some ditch & neuer
fought for (as many times happens), yet is it no more
allowable then it were to beare the deuice of *Tamerlan*, an
Emperour in Tartary, who gaue the lightning of heauen,
with a posie in that language purporting these words, *Ira
Dei*, which also appeared well to answer his fortune. For
from a sturdie shepeheard he became a most mighty
Emperour, and with his innumerable great armies deso-
lated so many countreyes and people as he might iustly
be called *the wrath of God*. It appeared also by his strange
ende, for in the midst of his greatnesse and prosperitie
he died sodainly, & left no child or kinred for a successour
to so large an Empire, nor any memory after him more
then of his great puissance and crueltie.

But that of the king of China in the fardest part of the
Orient, though it be not so terrible, is no lesse admirable,
& of much sharpnesse and good implication, worthy for
the greatest king and conqueror: and it is, two strange
serpents entertangled in their amorous congresse, the
lesser creeping with his head into the greaters mouth,
with words purporting *ama & time*, loue & feare. Which
posie with maruellous much reason and subtillity implieth
the dutie of euery subiect to his Prince, and of euery
Prince to his subiect, and that without either of them both
no subiect could be sayd entirely to performe his liegeance,
nor the Prince his part of lawfull gouernement. For without feare and loue the soueraigne authority could not be
vpholden, nor without iustice and mercy the Prince be
renowmed and honored of his subiect. All which parts
are discouered in this figure: loue by the serpents amorous
entertangling; obedience and feare by putting the inferiours head into the others mouth hauing puissance to

Of Proportion

destroy. On th'other side, iustice in the greater to prepare and manace death and destruction to offenders; and if he spare it, then betokeneth it mercie, and a grateful recompence of the loue and obedience which the soueraigne receaueth.

It is also worth the telling how the king vseth the same in pollicie; he giueth it in his ordinarie liueries to be worne in euery vpper garment of all his noblest men and greatest Magistrats & the rest of his officers and seruants, which are either embrodered vpon the breast and the back with siluer or gold or pearle or stone more or lesse richly, according to euery mans dignitie and calling, and they may not presume to be seene in publick without them, nor also in any place where by the kings commission they vse to sit in iustice, or any other publike affaire; wherby the king is highly both honored and serued, the common people retained in dutie and admiration of his greatnesse, the noblemen, magistrats, and officers euery one in his degree so much esteemed & reuerenced, as in their good and loyall seruice they want vnto their persons litle lesse honour for the kings sake then can be almost due or exhibited to the king him selfe.

I could not forbeare to adde this forraine example to accomplish our discourse touching deuices. For the beauty and gallantnesse of it, besides the subtillitie of the conceit, and princely pollicy in the vse, more exact then can be remembred in any other of any *European* Prince; whose deuises I will not say but many of them be loftie and ingenious, many of them louely and beautifull, many other ambitious and arrogant, and the chiefest of them terrible and ful of horror to the nature of man, but that any of them be comparable with it, for wit, vertue, grauitie, and if ye list brauerie, honour, and magnificence, not vsurping vpon the peculiars of the gods—in my conceipt there is none to be found.

This may suffice for deuices, a terme which includes in his generality all those other, viz. liueries, cognizances, emblemes, enseigns, and impreses. For though the termes be diuers, the vse and intent is but one, whether they rest in colour or figure or both, or in word or in muet shew, and thit is to insinuat some secret, wittie, morall, and braue purpose presented to the beholder, either to recreate his eye, or please his phantasie, or examine his iudgement, or occupie his braine, or to manage his will either by hope or by dread, euery of which respectes be of no litle moment to the interest and ornament of the ciuill life, and therefore giue them no little commendation. Then hauing produced so many worthy and wise founders of these deuices, and so many puissant patrons and protectours of them, I feare no reproch in this discourse, which otherwise the venimous appetite of enuie by detraction or scorne would peraduenture not sticke to offer me.

Of the Anagrame, or Posie transposed.

One other pretie conceit we will impart vnto you and then trouble you with no more, and is also borrowed primitiuely of the Poet, or courtly maker we may terme him, the *posie transposed*, or in one word *a transpose*, a thing if it be done for pastime and exercise of the wit without superstition commendable inough and a meete study for Ladies, neither bringing them any great gayne nor any great losse, vnlesse it be of idle time. They that vse it for pleasure is to breed one word out of another, not altering any letter nor the number of them, but onely transposing of the same, wherupon many times is produced some gratefull newes or matter to them for whose pleasure and seruice it was intended: and bicause there is much difficultie in it, and altogether standeth vpon hap hazard, it is compted for a courtly conceit no lesse then the deuice

Of Proportion

before remembred. *Lycophron,* one of the seuen Greeke Lyrickes who when they met together (as many times they did) for their excellencie and louely concorde were called the seuen starres, *pleiades,* this man was very perfit & fortunat in these transposes, & for his delicate wit and other good parts was greatly fauoured by *Ptolome* king of Egypt and Queene *Arsinoe* his wife. He after such sort called the king ἀπομελίτος, which is letter for letter *Ptolomaeus,* and Queene *Arsinoe* he called ἴον ἤρας, which is *Arsinoe*: now the subtillitie lyeth not in the conuersion but in the sence, in this that *Apomelitos* signifieth in Greek *hony sweet,* so was *Ptolome* the sweetest natured man in the world both for countenance and conditions, and *Ioneras* signifieth the violet or flower of *Iuno,* a stile among the Greekes for a woman endued with all bewtie and magnificence; which construction, falling out grateful and so truly, exceedingly well pleased the King and the Queene, and got *Lycophron* no litle thanke and benefite at both their hands.

The French Gentlemen haue very sharpe witts and withall a delicate language, which may very easily be wrested to any alteration of words sententious, and they of late yeares haue taken this pastime vp among them, many times gratifying their Ladies, and often times the Princes of the Realme, with some such thankfull nouveltie. Whereof one made by *François de Vallois* thus, *De façon suis Roy,* who in deede was of fashion, countenance, and stature, besides his regall vertues, a very king, for in a world there could not be seene a goodlier man of person. Another found this by *Henry de Vallois, Roy de nulz hay,* a king hated of no man, and was apparant in his conditions and nature, for there was not a Prince of greater affabilitie and mansuetude than he.

I my selfe seeing this conceit so well allowed of in Fraunce and Italie, and being informed that her Maiestie

tooke pleasure sometimes in desciphring of names, and
hearing how diuers Gentlemen of her Court had essayed
but with no great felicitie to make some delectable transpose
of her Maiesties name, I would needs try my luck, for
cunning I [k]now not why I should call it, vnlesse it be
for the many and variable applications of sence, which
requireth peraduenture some wit & discretion more then
of euery vnlearned man; and for the purpose I tooke me
these three wordes (if any other in the world) containing
in my conceit greatest mysterie, and most importing good
to all them that now be aliue vnder her noble gouernement,

Elissabet Anglorum Regina.

Which orthographie (because ye shall not be abused) is
true & not mistaken, for the letter *zeta* of the Hebrewes &
Greeke and of all other toungs is in truth but a double *ss*,
hardly vttered, and *H* is but a note of aspiration onely
and no letter, which therefore is by the Greeks omitted.
Vpon the transposition I found this to redound:

Multa regnabis ense gloria.
By thy sword shalt thou raigne in great renowne.

Then transposing the word *ense* it came to be

Multa regnabis sene gloria.
Aged and in much glorie shall ye raigne.

Both which resultes falling out vpon the very first marshalling of the letters, without any darknesse or difficultie, and
so sensibly and well appropriat to her Maiesties person
and estate, and finally so effectually to mine own wish
(which is a matter of much moment in such cases), I took
them both for a good boding, and very fatallitie to her
Maiestie appointed by Gods prouidence for all our comfortes. Also I imputed it for no litle good luck and glorie
to my selfe to haue pronounced to her so good and pros-

Of Proportion

perous a fortune, and so thankefull newes to all England, which though it cannot be said by this euent any destinie or fatal necessitie, yet surely is it by all probabillitie of reason so likely to come to passe as any other worldly euent of things that be vncertaine, her Maiestie continuing the course of her most regal proceedings and vertuous life in all earnest zeale and godly contemplation of his word, & in the sincere administration of his terrene iustice, assigned ouer to her execution as his Lieutenant vpon earth within the compasse of her dominions.

This also is worth the noting, and I will assure you of it, that, after the first search whereupon this transpose was fashioned, the same letters being by me tossed & tranlaced fiue hundreth times, I could neuer make any other, at least of some sence & conformitie to her Maiesties estate and the case. If any other man by triall happen vpon a better omination, or what soeuer els ye will call it, I will reioyse to be ouermatched in my deuise, and renounce him all the thankes and profite of my trauaile[1].

When I wrate of these deuices, I smiled with my selfe, thinking that the readers would do so to, and many of them say, that such trifles as these might well haue bene spared, considering the world is full inough of them, and that it is pitie mens heades should be fedde with such vanities as are to none edification nor instruction, either of morall vertue or otherwise behooffull for the common wealth, to whose seruice (say they) we are all borne, and not to fill and replenish a whole world full of idle toyes. To which sort of reprehendours, being either all holy and mortified to the world, and therfore esteeming nothing that sauoureth not of Theologie, or altogether graue and worldly, and therefore caring for nothing but matters of pollicie & discourses of estate, or all giuen to thrift and passing for none art that is not gainefull and lucratiue, as the sciences

[1] The additional matter ends here. See p. 105, *note*.

of the Law, Phisicke, and marchaundise : to these I will giue none other answere then referre them to the many trifling poemes of *Homer, Ouid, Virgill, Catullus*, and other notable writers of former ages, which were not of any grauitie or seriousnesse, and many of them full of impudicitie and ribaudrie, as are not these of ours, nor for any good in the world should haue bene; and yet those trifles are come from many former siecles vnto our times, vncontrolled or condemned or supprest by any Pope or Patriarch or other seuere censor of the ciuill maners of men, but haue bene in all ages permitted as the conuenient solaces and recreations of mans wit. And as I can not denie but these conceits of mine be trifles, no lesse in very deede be all the most serious studies of man, if we shall measure grauitie and lightnesse by the wise mans ballance, who, after he had considered of all the profoundest artes and studies among men, in th'ende cryed out with this Epyphoneme, *Vanitas vanitatum & omnia vanitas*. Whose authoritie if it were not sufficient to make me beleeue so, I could be content with *Democritus* rather to condemne the vanities of our life by derision then as *Heraclitus* with teares, saying with that merrie Greeke thus,

> *Omnia sunt risus, sunt puluis, & omnia nil sunt.*
> *Res hominum cunctae, nam ratione carent.*

Thus Englished,

> All is but a iest, all dust, all not worth two peason :
> For why in mans matters is neither rime nor reason.

Now passing from these courtly trifles, let vs talke of our scholastical toyes, that is of the Grammaticall versifying of the Greeks and Latines, and see whether it might be reduced into our English arte or no.

CHAP. XIII.

HOW IF ALL MANER OF SODAINE INNOUATIONS WERE NOT VERY SCANDALOUS, SPECIALLY IN THE LAWES OF ANY LANGAGE OR ARTE, THE VSE OF THE GREEKE AND LATINE FEETE MIGHT BE BROUGHT INTO OUR VULGAR POESIE, AND WITH GOOD GRACE INOUGH.

Now neuerthelesse albeit we haue before alledged that our vulgar *Saxon English* standing most vpon wordes *monosillable*, and little vpon *polysillables*, doth hardly admit the vse of those fine inuented feete of the Greeks & Latines, and that for the most part wise and graue men doe naturally mislike with all sodaine innouations, specially of lawes (and this the law of our aunctient English Poesie), and therefore lately before we imputed it to a nice & scholasticall curiositie in such makers as haue sought to bring into our vulgar Poesie some of the aunctient feete, to wit the *Dactile* into verses *exameters*, as he that translated certaine bookes of *Virgils Eneydos* in such measures & not vncommendably—if I should now say otherwise, it would make me seeme contradictorie to my selfe: yet for the information of our yong makers, and pleasure of all others who be delighted in noueltie, and to th'intent we may not seeme by ignorance or ouersight to omit any point of subtillitie, materiall or necessarie to our vulgar arte, we will in this present chapter & by our own idle obseruations shew how one may easily and commodiously lead all those feete of the auncients into our vulgar langage; and if mens eares were not perchaunce to daintie, or their iudgementes ouer partiall, would peraduenture nothing at all misbecome our arte, but make in our meetres a more pleasant numerositie then now is. Thus farre therefore we will aduenture and not beyond, to th'intent to shew some singularitie in our arte that euery man hath not heretofore obserued, and (her maiesty good liking always had) whether we make the common readers to laugh or to lowre, all is a matter, since our intent is not so exactlie to prosecute the purpose, nor so earnestly, as to thinke it should by authority of our owne iudgement be generally applauded at to the discredit of our forefathers maner of vulgar Poesie, or to the alteration or peraduenture totall destruction of the same, which could not stand with any good discretion or curtesie in vs to attempt; but thus much I say, that by some leasurable trauell it were no hard matter to induce all their auncient feete into vse with vs, and that it should proue very agreable to the eare and well according with our ordinary times and pronunciation, which no man could then iustly mislike, and that is to allow euery word *polisillable* one long time of necessitie, which should be where his sharpe accent falls in our owne *ydiome* most aptly and naturally, wherein we would not follow the licence of the Greeks and Latines, who made not their sharpe accent any necessary prolongation of their times, but vsed such sillable sometimes long, sometimes short, at their pleasure; the other sillables of any word where the sharpe accent fell not to be accompted of such time and quantitie as his *ortographie* would best beare, hauing regard to himselfe or to his next neighbour word bounding him on either side, namely to the smoothnes & hardnesse of the sillable in his vtterance, which is occasioned altogether by his *ortographie* & scituation; as in this word *dáyly* the first sillable for his vsuall and sharpe accentes sake to be always long, the second for his flat accents sake to be always short, and the rather for his *ortographie*, bycause if he goe before another word commencing with a vowell not letting him to be eclipsed, his vtterance is easie & currant; in this trissillable *daūngĕrŏus* the first to be long, th'other two short for the same causes; in this word *dāngĕroŭsnēsse* the first & last to be both

Of Proportion

long, bycause they receiue both of them the sharpe accent, and the two middlemost to be short; in these words *remedie* & *remedilesse* the time to follow also the accent, so as if it please better to set the sharpe accent vpon *re* then vpon *dye* that sillable should be made long and *e conuerso*; but in this word *remedilesse*, bycause many like better to accent the sillable *me* then the sillable *les*, therfore I leaue him for a common sillable to be able to receiue both a long and a short time as occasion shall serue. The like law I set in these wordes *reuocable, recouerable, irreuocable, irrecouerable,* for sometime it sounds better to say *rĕuŏ cāblĕ* then *rĕ uōcăblĕ, rēcŏuĕr āblĕ* then *rĕcōuĕr ăblĕ*: for this one thing ye must alwayes marke that if your time fall either by reason of his sharpe accent or otherwise vpon the *penultima*, ye shal finde many other words to rime with him, bycause such terminations are not geazon, but if the long time fall vpon the *antepenultima* ye shall not finde many wordes to match him in his termination, which is the cause of his concord or rime, but if you would let your long time by his sharpe accent fall aboue the *antepenultima*, as to say *cōuĕrăblĕ*, ye shall seldome or perchance neuer find one to make vp rime with him, vnlesse it be badly and by abuse; and therefore in all such long *polisillables* ye doe commonly giue two sharpe accents, and thereby reduce him into two feete, as in this word *rēmŭ nĕrātĭŏn* which makes a couple of good *dactils*, and in this word *cōntrībūtĭŏn* which makes a good *spondeus* and a good *dactill*, and in this word *recāpĭtŭlātĭŏn* it makes two *dactills* and a sillable ouerplus to annexe to the word precedent to helpe peece vp another foote. But for wordes *monosillables* (as be most of ours), because in pronouncing them they do of necessitie retaine a sharpe accent, ye may iustly allow them to be all long if they will so best serue your turne, and, if they be tailed one to another, or th'one to a *dissillable* or *polyssillable*, ye ought to allow them that time that best serues your purpose and pleaseth your eare most, and truliest aunsweres the nature of the *ortographie*, in which I would as neare as I could obserue and keepe the lawes of the Greeke and Latine versifiers, that is to prolong the sillable which is written with double consonants or by dipthong or with single consonants that run hard and harshly vpon the toung, and to shorten all sillables that stand vpon vowels, if there were no cause of *elision*, and single consonants & such of them as are most flowing and slipper vpon the toung, as *n, r, t, d, l*; and for this purpose to take away all aspirations, and many times the last consonant of a word, as the Latine Poetes vsed to do, specially *Lucretius* and *Ennius*, as to say *finibu* for *finibus*; and so would not I stick to say thus *delite* for *delight*, *hye* for *high*, and such like, & doth nothing at all impugne the rule I gaue before against the wresting of wordes by false *ortographie* to make vp rime, which may not be falsified. But this omission of letters in the middest of a meetre to make him the more slipper helpes the numerositie and hinders not the rime. But generally the shortning or prolonging of the *monosillables* dependes much vpon the nature of their *ortographie*, which the Latin Grammariens call the rule of position; as for example, if I shall say thus,

> *Nōt mănĭe dayēs pāst.*   Twentie dayes after.

This makes a good *dactill* and a good *spondeus*, but if ye turne them backward it would not do so, as

> Many dayes, not past.

And the *distick* made all of *monosillables*:

> Būt nōne ōf ūs trūe mēn ānd frēe,
> Could finde so great good lucke as he.

Which words serue well to make the verse all *spondiacke* or *iambicke*, but not in *dactil*, as other words or the same

Of Proportion

otherwise placed would do, for it were an ill-fauored *dactil* to say,

Būt nŏne ŏf, ūs ăll trĕwe.

Therefore, whensoeuer your words will not make a smooth *dactil*, ye must alter them or their situations, or else turne them to other feete that may better beare their maner of sound and orthographie; or, if the word be *polysillable*, to deuide him, and to make him serue by peeces, that he could not do whole and entierly. And no doubt by like consideration did the Greeke & Latine versifiers fashion all their feete at the first to be of sundry times, and the selfe same sillable to be sometime long and sometime short, for the eares better satisfaction, as hath bene before remembred.

Now also wheras I said before that our old Saxon English for his many *monosillables* did not naturally admit the vse of the ancient feete in our vulgar measures so aptly as in those languages which stood most vpon *polisillables*, I sayd it in a sort truly, but now I must recant and confesse that our Normane English which hath growen since *William* the Conquerour doth admit any of the auncient feete, by reason of the many *polysillables*, euen to sixe and seauen in one word, which we at this day vse in our most ordinarie language; and which corruption hath bene occasioned chiefly by the peeuish affectation not of the Normans them selues, but of clerks and scholers or secretaries long since, who, not content with the vsual Normane or Saxon word, would conuert the very Latine and Greeke word into vulgar French, as to say innumerable for innombrable, reuocable, irreuocable, irradiation, depopulation, & such like, which are not naturall Normans nor yet French, but altered Latines, and without any imitation at all; which therefore were long time despised for inkehorne termes, and now be reputed the best & most delicat of any other. Of which & many other causes of corruption of our speach we haue in another place more amply discoursed; but by this meane we may at this day very well receiue the aunciect feete *metricall* of the Greeks and Latines, sauing those that be superflous, as be all the feete aboue the *trissillable*, which the old Grammarians idly inuented and distinguisht by speciall names, whereas in deede the same do stand compounded with the inferiour feete, and therefore some of them were called by the names of *didactilus, dispondeus,* and *disiambus*: all which feete, as I say, we may be allowed to vse with good discretion & precise choise of wordes and with the fauorable approbation of readers; and so shall our plat in this one point be larger and much surmount that which *Stanihurst* first tooke in hand by his *exameters dactilicke* and *spondaicke* in the translation of *Virgills Eneidos*, and such as for a great number of them my stomacke can hardly digest for the ill shapen sound of many of his wordes *polisillable*, and also his copulation of *monosillables* supplying the quantitie of a *trissillable* to his intent. And right so in promoting this deuise of ours, being (I feare me) much more nyce and affected, and therefore more misliked then his, we are to bespeake fauour, first of the delicate eares, then of the rigorous and seuere dispositions, lastly to craue pardon of the learned & auncient makers in our vulgar; for if we should seeke in euery point to egall our speach with the Greeke and Latin in their *metricall* obseruations it could not possible be by vs perfourmed, because their sillables came to be timed some of them long, some of them short, not by reason of any euident or apparant cause in writing or sounde remaining vpon one more then another, for many times they shortned the sillable of sharpe accent and made long that of the flat, & therefore we must needes say it was in many of their wordes done by preelection in the first Poetes, not hauing regard altogether to the *ortographie* and hardnesse or

Of Proportion

softnesse of a sillable, consonant, vowell, or dipthong, but at their pleasure, or as it fell out: so as he that first put in a verse this word *Penelope*, which might be *Homer* or some other of his antiquitie, where he made *pē* in both places long and *ně* and *lŏ* short, he might haue made them otherwise and with as good reason, nothing in the world appearing that might moue them to make such preelection more in th'one sillable then in the other, for *pe, ne,* and *lo* being sillables vocals be egally smoth and currant vpon the toung, and might beare aswel the long as the short time, but it pleased the Poet otherwise: so he that first shortned *ca* in this word *caňo*, and made long *tro* in *troia*, and *o* in *oris*, might haue aswell done the contrary, but because he that first put them into a verse found, as it is to be supposed, a more sweetnesse in his owne eare to haue them so tymed, therefore all other Poets who followed were fayne to doe the like, which made that *Virgill*, who came many yeares after the first reception of wordes in their seuerall times, was driuen of necessitie to accept them in such quantities as they were left him, and therefore said,

 ārmă ŭī rūmqŭe că nō trō iē quī prīmŭs ăb ōrĭs.

Neither truely doe I see any other reason in that lawe (though in other rules of shortning and prolonging a sillable there may be reason) but that it stands vpon bare tradition. Such as the *Cabalists* auouch in their mysticall constructions Theologicall and others, saying that they receaued the same from hand to hand from the first parent *Adam, Abraham,* and others; which I will giue them leaue alone both to say and beleeue for me, thinking rather that they haue bene the idle occupations or perchaunce the malitious and craftie constructions of the *Talmudists* and others of the Hebrue clerks, to bring the world into admiration of their lawes and Religion. Now peraduenture with vs Englishmen it be somewhat

too late to admit a new inuention of feete and times that
our forefathers neuer vsed nor neuer obserued till this
day, either in their measures or in their pronuntiation,
and perchaunce will seeme in vs a presumptuous part to
attempt, considering also it would be hard to find many
men to like of one mans choise in the limitation of times
and quantities of words, with which not one but euery
eare is to be pleased and made a particular iudge, being
most truly sayd that a multitude or comminaltie is hard
to please and easie to offend; and therefore I intend not
to proceed any further in this curiositie then to shew some
small subtillitie that any other hath not yet done, and not
by imitation but by obseruation, nor to th'intent to haue it
put in execution in our vulgar Poesie, but to be pleasantly
scanned vpon, as are all nouelties so friuolous and ridiculous
as it.

CHAP. XIV.

A MORE PARTICULAR DECLARATION OF THE METRICALL
FEETE OF THE ANCIENT POETS GREEKE AND LATINE, AND
CHIEFLY OF THE FEETE OF TWO TIMES.

Their Grammarians made a great multitude of feete,
I wot not to what huge number, and of so many sizes as
their wordes were of length, namely sixe sizes; whereas,
in deede, the metricall feete are but twelue in number,
wherof foure only be of two times, and eight of three
times, the rest compounds of the premised two sorts, euen
as the Arithmeticall numbers aboue three are made of two
and three. And if ye will know how many of these feete
will be commodiously receiued with vs, I say all the whole
twelue. For first for the foote *spondeus* of two long times,
ye haue these English wordes *mōrnīng, mīdnīght, mīs-
chāunce*, and a number moe whose ortographie may direct
your iudgement in this point: for your *trocheus* of a long

Of Proportion

and short, ye haue these wordes *mānĕr, brōkĕn, tākĕn, bōdiĕ, mēmbĕr*, and a great many moe, if their last sillables abut not vpon the consonant in the beginning of another word, and in these, whether they do abut or no, *wĭtlĭe,* *dĭtlĭe, sōrrŏw, mōrrŏw,* & such like, which end in a vowell. For your *iambus* of a short and a long, ye haue these wordes *rĕstōre, rĕmōrse, dĕsīre, ĕndūre*, and a thousand besides. For your foote *pirrichius* or of two short silables, ye haue these words *mănĭe, mŏnĕy, pĕnĭe, sĭlĭĕ*, and others of that constitution or the like. For your feete of three times, and first your *dactill*, ye haue these wordes & a number moe, *pātĭĕnce, tēmpĕrănce, wōmănheăd, iōlĭtĭe, dāungĕrŏus, dūetĭfŭll*, and others. For your *molossus* of all three long, ye haue a number of wordes also, and specially most of your participles actiue, as *pērsīstīng, dēspōilīng, ēndēntīng*, and such like in ortographie: for your *anapestus* of two short and a long, ye haue these words but not many moe, as *mănĭfōld, mŏnŭlēsse, rĕmănēnt, hŏlĭnēsse*. For your foote *tribracchus* of all three short, ye haue very few *trissillables*, because the sharpe accent will always make one of them long by pronunciation, which els would be by ortographie short, as *mĕrĭly, minion*, & such like. For your foote *bacchius* of a short & two long, ye haue these and the like words *trissillables, lămēntīng, rĕquēstīng, rĕnoūncīng, rĕpēntānce, ĕnūrīng*. For your foote *antibacchius* of two long and a short, ye haue these wordes, *fōrsākĕn, īmpūgnĕd*, and others many. For your *amphimacer*, that is a long, a short, and a long, ye haue these wordes and many moe, *éxcellént, īmĭnēnt*, and specially such as be proper names of persons or townes or other things, and namely Welsh wordes. For your foote *amphibracchus* of a short, a long, and a short, ye haue these wordes and many like to these, *rĕsīstĕd, dĕlīghtfŭll, rĕprīsăll, ĭnaūntĕr, ĕnămĭll*. So as for want of English wordes, if your eare be not to daintie and your rules to precise, ye neede not be without the *metricall* feete of the ancient Poets such as be most pertinent and not superfluous. This is (ye will perchaunce say) my singular opinion: then ye shall see how well I can maintaine it. First, the quantitie of a word comes either by preelection, without reason or force as hath bene alledged, and as the aunceint Greekes and Latines did in many wordes, but not in all; or by election, with reason as they did in some, and not a few. And a sound is drawen at length either by the infirmitie of the toung, because the word or sillable is of such letters as hangs long in the palate or lippes ere he will come forth, or because he is accented and tuned hier and sharper then another, whereby he somewhat obscureth the other sillables in the same word that be not accented so high— in both these cases we will establish our sillable long; contrariwise, the shortning of a sillable is when his sounde or accent happens to be heauy and flat, that is to fall away speedily and as it were inaudible, or when he is made of such letters as be by nature slipper & voluble and smoothly passe from the mouth. And the vowell is alwayes more easily deliuered then the consonant; and of consonants the liquide more then the mute, & a single consonant more then a double, and one more then twayne coupled together: all which points were obserued by the Greekes and Latines, and allowed for *maximes* in versifying. Now if ye will examine these foure *bissillables, rēmnānt, rĕmāine, rēndĕr, rĕnĕt*, for an example by which ye may make a generall rule, and ye shall finde that they aunswere our first resolution. First in *remnant, rem*, bearing the sharpe accent and hauing his consonant abbut vpon another, soundes long. The sillable *nant* being written with two consonants must needs be accompted the same, besides that *nant* by his Latin originall is long, viz. *remanēns*. Take this word *remaine*: because the last sillable beares the sharpe accent, he is long in the eare, and *re*, being the

Of Proportion

first sillable, passing obscurely away with a flat accent, is short, besides that *re* by his Latine originall and also by his ortographie is short. This word *render* bearing the sharpe accent vpon *ren* makes it long; the sillable *der*, falling away swiftly and being also written with a single consonant or liquide, is short, and makes the *trocheus*. This word *rĕnĕt* hauing both sillables sliding and slipper make[s] the foote *Pirrichius*, because, if he be truly vttered, he beares in maner no sharper accent vpon the one then the other sillable, but be in effect egall in time and tune, as is also the *Spondeus*. And because they be not written with any hard or harsh consonants, I do allow them both for short sillables, or to be vsed for common, according as their situation and place with other words shall be. And as I haue named to you but onely foure words for an example, so may ye find out by diligent obseruation foure hundred if ye will. But of all your words *bissillables* the most part naturally do make the foote *Iambus*, many the *Trocheus*, fewer the *Spondeus*, fewest of all the *Pirrichius*, because in him the sharpe accent (if ye follow the rules of your accent, as we haue presupposed) doth make a litle oddes: and ye shall find verses made all of *monosillables*, and do very well, but lightly they be *Iambickes*, bycause for the more part the accent falles sharpe vpon euery second word rather then contrariwise, as this of Sir *Thomas Wiats*,

I fīnde nŏ peāce ănd yēt mĭe wārre ĭs dōne,
I feare and hope, and burne and freese like ise.

And some verses where the sharpe accent falles vpon the first and third, and so make the verse wholly *Trochaicke*, as thus,

Worke not, no nor wish thy friend or foes harme;
Try, but trust not all that speake thee so faire.

And some verses made of *monosillables* and *bissillables* enterlaced, as this of th'Earles,

When raging loue with extreme paine.

And this,

A fairer beast of fresher hue beheld I neuer none.

And some verses made all of *bissillables*, and others all of *trissillables*, and others of *polisillables* egally increasing and of diuers quantities and sundry situations, as in this of our owne, made to daunt the insolence of a beautifull woman,

> Brittle beauty, blossome daily fading,
> Morne, noone, and eue, in age and eke in eld,
> Dangerous disdainefull, pleasantly perswading,
> Easie to gripe but combrous to weld,
> For slender bottome hard and heauy lading,
> Gay for a while, but little while durable,
> Suspicious, incertaine, irreuocable,
> O since thou art by triall not to trust,
> Wisedome it is, and it is also iust
> To sound the stemme before the tree be feld,
> That is, since death will driue vs all to dust,
> To leaue thy loue ere that we be compeld.

In which ye haue your first verse all of *bissillables* and of the foot *trocheus*; the second all of *monosillables*, and all of the foote *iambus*; the third all of *trissillables*, and all of the foote *dactilus*; your fourth of one *bissillable*, and two *monosillables* interlarded; the fift of one *monosillable* and two *bissillables* enterlaced; and the rest of other sortes and scituations, some by degrees encreasing, some diminishing: which example I haue set downe to let you perceiue what pleasant numerosity in the measure and disposition of your words in a meetre may be contriued by curious wits: & these with other like were the obseruations of the Greeke and Latine versifiers.

CHAP. XV.

OF YOUR FEET OF THREE TIMES, AND FIRST OF THE DACTIL.

Your feete of three times by prescription of the Latine Grammariens are of eight sundry proportions, for some notable difference appearing in euery sillable of three falling in a word of that size: but because aboue the *antepenultima* there was (among the Latines) none accent audible in any long word, therfore to deuise any foote of longer measure then of three times was to them but superfluous, because all aboue the number of three are but compounded of their inferiours. Omitting therefore to speake of these larger feete, we say that of all your feete of three times the *Dactill* is most vsuall and fit for our vulgar meeter, & most agreeable to the eare, specially if ye ouerlade not your verse with too many of them, but here and there enterlace a *Iambus* or some other foote of two times to giue him grauitie and stay, as in this *quadrein Trimeter* or of three measures.

    Rēndĕr ăgaīne mĭe lībĕrtĭe,
    ănd sēt yoŭr cāptĭue frēe.
    Glōrĭoŭs īs thĕ vīctŏrĭe
    Cōnquĕrŏurs ūse wĭth lēnĭtĭe.

Where ye see euery verse is all of a measure, and yet vnegall in number of sillables; for the second verse is but of sixe sillables, where the rest are of eight. But the reason is for that in three of the same verses are two *Dactils* a peece, which abridge two sillables in euery verse, and so maketh the longest euen with the shortest. Ye may note besides by the first verse, how much better some *bissillable* becommeth to peece out an other longer foote then another word doth; for in place of *render* if ye had sayd *restore*, it had marred the *Dactil* and of necessitie driuen him out at length to be a verse *Iambic* of foure feete, because *render* is naturally a *Trocheus* & makes the first two times of a *Dactil*. *Restore* is naturally a *Iambus*, & in this place could not possibly haue made a pleasant *Dactil*.

Now, againe, if ye will say to me that these two words *libertie* and *conquerours* be not precise *Dactils* by the Latine rule, so much will I confesse to, but since they go currant inough vpon the tongue, and be so vsually pronounced, they may passe wel inough for *Dactils* in our vulgar meeters; & that is inough for me, seeking but to fashion an art, & not to finish it: which time only & custom haue authoritie to do, specially in all cases of language, as the Poet hath wittily remembred in this verse,

si volet usus,
Quem penes arbitrium est & vis & norma loquendi.

The Earle of Surrey vpon the death of Sir *Thomas Wiat* made among other this verse *Pentameter* and of ten sillables,

What holy graue? alas, what sepulcher?

But if I had the making of him, he should haue bene of eleuen sillables and kept his measure of fiue still, and would so haue runne more pleasantly a great deale; for as he is now, though he be euen, he seemes odde and defectiue, for not well obseruing the natural accent of euery word; and this would haue bene soone holpen by inserting one *monosillable* in the middle of the verse, and drawing another sillable in the beginning into a *Dactil*, this word *holy* being a good *Pirrichius* and very well seruing the turne, thus,

Whāt hŏlĭe grāue? ă lās, whăt fīt sĕpūlchĕr?

Which verse if ye peruse throughout, ye shall finde him

Of Proportion

after the first *Dactil* all *Trochaick* & not *Iambic*, nor of any
other foot of two times. But perchance if ye would seeme
yet more curious, in place of these foure *Trocheus* ye might
induce other feete of three times, as to make the three
sillables next following the *Dactil* the foote *Amphimacer*, the
last word *sepulcher* the foote *Amphibracus*, leauing the other
midle word for a *Iambus* thus,

Whāt hŏlĭe grāue ? ă lās, whăt fĭt sĕpūlchĕr ?

If ye aske me further why I make *what* first long & after
short in one verse, to that I satisfied you before, that it is
by reason of his accent sharpe in one place and flat in
another, being a common *monosillable*, that is apt to receiue
either accent, & so in the first place receiuing aptly the
sharpe accent he is made long; afterward receiuing the
flat accent more aptly then the sharpe, because the sillable
precedent *las* vtterly distaines him, he is made short & not
long, & that with very good melodie; but to haue giuen
him the sharpe accent & plucked it from the sillable *las* it
had bene to any mans eare a great discord : for euermore
this word *alás* is accented vpon the last, & that lowdly &
notoriously as appeareth by all our exclamations vsed
vnder that terme. The same Earle of Surrey & Sir *Thomas
Wyat*, the first reformers & polishers of our vulgar Poesie,
much affecting the stile and measures of the Italian
Petrarcha, vsed the foote *dactil* very often but not many
in one verse, as in these,

Fūll mănĭe that in presence of thy līuelĭe hĕd.
Shed Cæsars teares vpon Pōmpĕiūs hĕd.
Th'ēnĕmĭe to life destroi er of all kinde.
If āmŏ rŏus faith in an hart vn fayned.
Myne old deēre ĕnĕ my my froward master.
Thē fŭrĭ ous gone in his most ra ging ire.

And many moe which if ye would not allow for *Dactils*
the verse would halt, vnlesse ye would seeme to helpe it

contracting a sillable by vertue of the figure *Syneresis*, which I thinke was neuer their meaning, nor in deede would haue bred any pleasure to the eare, but hindred the flowing of the verse. Howsoeuer ye take it, the *Dactil* is commendable inough in our vulgar meetres, but most plausible of all when he is sounded vpon the stage, as in these comicall verses shewing how well it becommeth all noble men and great personages to be temperat and modest, yea more then any meaner man, thus:

> Lēt nŏ nŏbīlĭtĭe, rĭchĕs, ŏr hērĭtăge,
> Hōnŏur, ŏr ēmpĭre, ŏr eārthlĭe dŏmīnĭŏn
> Brēed ĭn yŏur heād ănie pēeuish ŏpīnĭŏn
> That yĕ măy sāfĕr ăuōuch ănĭe ōutrāge.

And in this distique taxing the Prelate symoniake, standing all vpon perfect *Dactils*,

> Nōw mānīe bīe mōnēy pūruĕy prŏmōtĭŏn,
> For mony mooues any hart to deuotion.

But this aduertisement I will giue you withall, that if ye vse too many *Dactils* together ye make your musike too light and of no solemne grauitie such as the amorous *Elegies* in court naturally require, being alwaies either very dolefull or passionate as the affections of loue enforce, in which busines ye must make your choise of very few words *dactilique*, or them that ye can not refuse, to dissolue and breake them into other feete by such meanes as it shall be taught hereafter: but chiefly in your courtly ditties take heede ye vse not these maner of long *polisillables*, and specially that ye finish not your verse with them, as *retribution, restitution, remuneration, recapitulation*, and such like: for they smatch more the schoole of common players than of any delicate Poet, *Lyricke* or *Elegiacke*.

CHAP. XVI.

OF ALL YOUR OTHER FEETE OF THREE TIMES, AND HOW WELL THEY WOULD FASHION A MEETRE IN OUR VULGAR.

All your other feete of three times I find no vse of them in our vulgar meeters nor no sweetenes at all, and yet words inough to serue their proportions. So as though they haue not hitherto bene made artificiall, yet nowe by more curious obseruation they might be, since all artes grew first by obseruation of natures proceedings and custome. And first your *Molossus*, being of all three long, is euidently discouered by this word *pērmīttīng*; the *Anapestus*, of two short and a long, by this word *fŭrĭŏus*, if the next word beginne with a consonant; the foote *Bacchius*, of a short and two long, by this word *rĕsīstānce*; the foote *Antibac[c]hius*, of two long [and] a short, by this word *cōnquērĭng*; the foote *Amphimacer*, of a long a short & a long, by this word *cōnquĕrīng*; the foote *Amphibrachus*, of a short a long and a short, by this word *rĕmēmbĕr*, if a vowell follow. The foote *Tribrachus*, of three short times, is very hard to be made by any of our *trissillables*, vnles they be compounded of the smoothest sort of consonants or sillables vocals, or of three smooth *monosillables*, or of some peece of a long *polysillable*, & after that sort we may with wresting of words shape the foot *Tribrachus* rather by vsurpation then by rule, which neuertheles is allowed in euery primitiue arte & inuention : & so it was by the Greekes and Latines in their first versifying, as if a rule should be set downe that from henceforth these words should be counted al *Tribrachus*, *ĕnĕmĭe*, *rĕmĕdĭe*, *sĕlĭnĕs*, *mŏnĭlĕs*, *pĕnĭlĕs*, *crŭĕllĭe*, & such like, or a peece of this long word *rĕcōuĕrăblĕ*, *innŭmĕrăblĕ*, *rĕădĭlĭe*, and others. Of all which manner of apt wordes to make these stranger feet of three times which go not so currant with our eare

as the *Dactil*, the maker should haue a good iudgement to
know them by their manner of orthographie and by their
accent which serue most fitly for euery foote, or else he
shoulde haue alwaies a little calender of them apart to vse
readily when he shall neede them. But because in very
truth I thinke them but vaine & superstitious obseruations
nothing at all furthering the pleasant melody of our English
meeter, I leaue to speake any more of them, and rather
wish the continuance of our old maner of Poesie, scanning
our verse by sillables rather than by feete, and vsing most
commonly the word *Iambique* & sometime the *Trochaike*,
which ye shall discerne by their accents, and now and then
a *Dactill*, keeping precisely our symphony or rime without
any other mincing measures, which an idle inuentiue head
could easily deuise, as the former examples teach.

CHAP. XVII.

OF YOUR VERSES PERFECT AND DEFECTIUE, AND THAT WHICH THE GRAECIANS CALLED THE HALFE FOOTE.

The Greekes and Latines vsed verses in the odde
sillable of two sortes, which they called *Catalecticke* and
Acatalecticke, that is odde vnder and odde ouer the iust
measure of their verse, & we in our vulgar finde many of
the like, and specially in the rimes of Sir Thomas Wiat,
strained perchaunce out of their originall made first by
Francis Petrarcha: as these,

> Like vnto these immeasurable mountaines,
> So is my painefull life the burden of ire:
> For hie be they, and hie is my desire,
> And I of teares and they are full of fountaines.

Where in your first, second, and fourth verse ye may
find a sillable superfluous, and though in the first ye will

Of Proportion

seeme to helpe it by drawing these three sillables, *īm mĕ sŭ* into a *Dactil*, in the rest it can not be so excused; wherefore we must thinke he did it of purpose, by the odde sillable to giue greater grace to his meetre; and we finde in our old rimes this odde sillable, sometime placed in the beginning and sometimes in the middle of a verse, and is allowed to go alone & to hang to any other sillable. But this odde sillable in our meetres is not the halfe foote as the Greekes and Latines vsed him in their verses, and called such measure *pentimimeris* and *eptamimeris*, but rather is that which they called the *catalectik* or maymed verse. Their *hemimeris* or halfe foote serued not by licence Poeticall or necessitie of words but to bewtifie and exornate the verse by placing one such halfe foote in the middle *Cesure*, & one other in the end of the verse, as they vsed all their *pentameters elegiack*, and not by coupling them together, but by accompt to make their verse of a iust measure and not defectiue or superflous: our odde sillable is not altogether of that nature, but is in a maner drowned and supprest by the flat accent, and shrinks away as it were inaudible, and by that meane the odde verse comes almost to be an euen in euery mans hearing. The halfe foote of the auncients was reserued purposely to an vse, and therefore they gaue such odde sillable, wheresoeuer he fell, the sharper accent, and made by him a notorious pause as in this *pentameter*,

Nīl mĭ hī rēscrībàs āttămĕn īpsĕ vĕ nì.

Which in all make fiue whole feete, or the verse *Pentameter*. We in our vulgar haue not the vse of the like halfe foote.

CHAP. XVIII.

OF THE BREAKING YOUR BISSILLABLES AND POLYSILLABLES,
AND WHEN IT IS TO BE VSED.

But whether ye suffer your sillable to receiue his
quantitie by his accent, or by his ortography, or whether
ye keepe your *bissillable* whole, or whether ye breake him,
all is one to his quantitie, and his time will appeare the
selfe same still, and ought not to be altered by our makers,
vnlesse it be when such sillable is allowed to be common
and to receiue any of both times, as in the *dimeter*, made
of two sillables entier,

   ēxtrēame děsīre.

The first is a good *spondeus*, the second a good *iambus*;
and if the same wordes be broken thus it is not so
pleasant,
   ĭn ēx trēame dĕ sire.

And yet the first makes a *iambus*, and the second a *trocheus*,
ech sillable retayning still his former quantities.

And alwaies ye must haue regard to the sweetenes of
the meetre, so as if your word *polysillable* would not sound
pleasantly whole, ye should for the nonce breake him,
which ye may easily doo by inserting here and there one
monosillable among your *polysillables*, or by chaunging your
word into another place then where he soundes vn-
pleasantly, and, by breaking, turne a *trocheus* to a *iambus*,
or contrariwise, as thus,

  Hōllŏw vāllĕis ūndĕr hīĕst moūntaĭnes;
  Crāggĭe clīffes brĭng foōrth thĕ faīrĕst foūntaĭnes.

These verses be *trochaik*, and in mine eare not so sweete
and harmonicall as the *iambicque*, thus,

  Thĕ hōllŏwst vāls lĭe ūndĕr hīĕst moūntāines;
  Thĕ crāggĭst clīfs brĭng fōrth thĕ faīrĕst foūntāines.

Of Proportion

All which verses bee now become *iambicque* by breaking the first *bissillables*, and yet alters not their quantities though the feete be altered: and thus,

> Restlesse is the heart in his desires,
> Rauing after that reason doth denie.

Which being turned thus makes a new harmonie,

> The restlesse heart renues his old desires,
> Ay rauing after that reason doth it deny.

And following this obseruation, your meetres being builded with *polysillables* will fall diuersly out, that is some to be *spondaick*, some *iambick*, others *dactilick*, others *trochaick*, and of one mingled with another, as in this verse,

> Hēaui̯e īs thĕ būrdĕn of Prīncĕs īre.

The verse is *trochaick*, but being altered thus is *iambicque*,

> Fŭll hēaui̯e īs thĕ pāise ŏf Prīncĕs īre.

And as Sir *Thomas Wiat* song in a verse wholly *trochaick*, because the wordes do best shape to that foote by their naturall accent, thus,

> Fārewĕll lōue ănd āll thĭe lāwes fŏr ēuĕr.

And in this ditty of th'Erle of Surries, passing sweete and harmonicall, all be *Iambick*,

> When raging loue with extreme paine
> So cruelly doth straine my hart,
> And that the teares like fluds of raine
> Bear witnesse of my wofull smart.

Which beyng disposed otherwise or not broken would proue all *trochaick*, but nothing pleasant.

Now furthermore ye are to note that al your *monosyllables* may receiue the sharp accent, but not so aptly one as another, as in this verse where they serue well to make him *iambicque*, but not *trochaick*,

> Gŏd graūnt thĭs peāce măy lōng ĕndūre,

where the sharpe accent falles more tunably vpon *graunt, peace, long, dure,* then it would by conuersion, as to accent them thus,

> Gōd graŭnt—thīs peăce—māy lŏng—ēndūre,

And yet if ye will aske me the reason, I can not tell it, but that it shapes so to myne eare, and as I thinke to euery other mans. And in this meeter where ye haue whole words *bissillable* vnbroken, that maintaine (by reason of their accent) sundry feete, yet going one with another be very harmonicall.

Where ye see one to be a *Trocheus* another the *Iambus*, and so entermingled not by election but by constraint of their seuerall accents, which ought not to be altred, yet comes it to passe that many times ye must of necessitie alter the accent of a sillable, and put him from his naturall place, and then one sillable of a word *polysillable*, or one word *monosillable*, will abide to be made sometimes long, sometimes short; as in this *quadreyne* of ours playd in a mery moode,

> Gèue mé mìne ówne ànd whén I dó dèsíre,
> Geue others theirs, and nothing that is mine,
> Nòr gíue mè thát wherto all men aspire
> Then neither gold, nor faire women, nor wine.

Where in your first verse these two words, *giue* and *me*, are accented one high, th'other low; in the third verse the same words are accented contrary: and the reason of this exchange is manifest, because the maker playes with these two clauses of sundry relations, *giue me* and *giue others*, so as the *monosillable me*, being respectiue to the word *others*, and inferring a subtilitie or wittie implication, ought not to haue the same accent as when he hath no such respect; as in this *distik* of ours,

Of Proportion

Prōue mĕ (Madame) ere ye rēprŏue;
Meeke minds should ēcŭse not āccŭse.

In which verse ye see this word *reprooue*, the sillable *prooue* alters his sharpe accent into a flat, for naturally it is long in all his singles and compoundes *reproòue*, *approòue*, *disproòue*, & so is the sillable *cuse* in *excuse*, *accuse*, *recuse*, yet in these verses by reason one of them doth as it were nicke another, and haue a certaine extraordinary sence with all, it behoueth to remoue the sharpe accents from whence they are most naturall, to place them where the nicke may be more expresly discouered; and therefore in this verse where no such implication is, nor no relation, it is otherwise, as thus,

If ye rĕprōue my constancie,
I will excūse you curtesly.

For in this word *reproóue*, because there is no extraordinary sence to be inferred, he keepeth his sharpe accent vpon the sillable *proóue*, but in the former verses, because they seeme to encounter ech other, they do thereby merite an audible and pleasant alteration of their accents in those sillables that cause the subtiltie. Of these maner of nicetees ye shal finde in many places of our booke, but specially where we treate of ornament, vnto which we referre you, sauing that we thought good to set down one example more to solace your mindes with mirth after all these scholasticall preceptes, which can not but bring with them (specially to Courtiers) much tediousnesse, and so to end. In our Comedie intituled *Ginecocratia* the king was supposed to be a person very amorous and effeminate, and therefore most ruled his ordinary affaires by the aduise of women, either for the loue he bare to their persons or liking he had to their pleasant ready witts and vtterance. Comes me to the Court one *Polemon*, an honest plaine man of the country, but rich; and, hauing a suite to the

king, met by chaunce with one *Philino*, a louer of wine and
a merry companion in Court, and praied him in that he
was a stranger that he would vouchsafe to tell him which
way he were best to worke to get his suite, and who were
most in credit and fauour about the king, that he might
seeke to them to furder his attempt. *Philino*, perceyuing
the plainnesse of the man, and that there would be some
good done with him, told *Polemon* that if he would well
consider him for his labor he would bring him where he
should know the truth of all his demaundes by the sentence
of the Oracle. *Polemon* gaue him twentie crownes; *Philino*
brings him into a place where behind an arras cloth hee
himselfe spake in manner of an Oracle in these meeters,
for so did all the Sybils and sothsaiers in old times giue
their answers.

> Your best way to worke, and marke my words well,
> Not money; nor many;
> Nor any; but any;
> Not weemen; but weemen beare the bell.

Polemon wist not what to make of this doubtful speach, &,
not being lawfull to importune the oracle more then once
in one matter, conceyued in his head the pleasanter construction, and stacke to it: and hauing at home a fayre
young damsell of eighteene yeares old to his daughter,
that could very well behaue her selfe in countenance & also
in her language, apparelled her as gay as he could, and
brought her to the Court, where *Philino*, harkning daily
after the euent of this matter, met him, and recommended
his daughter to the Lords, who perceiuing her great beauty
and other good parts, brought her to the King, to whom
she exhibited her fathers supplication, and found so great
fauour in his eye, as without any long delay she obtained
her sute at his hands. *Polemon* by the diligent solliciting
of his daughter wanne his purpose: *Philino* gat a good

reward and vsed the matter so, as, howsoeuer the oracle had bene construed, he could not haue receiued blame nor discredit by the successe, for euery waies it would haue proued true, whether *Polemons* daughter had obtayned the
5 sute, or not obtained it. And the subtiltie lay in the accent and Ortographie of these two wordes *any* and *weemen*, for *any* being deuided sounds *a nie* or neere person to the king, and *weemen* being diuided soundes *wee men*, and not *weemen*, and so by this meane *Philino*
10 serued all turnes and shifted himselfe from blame; not vnlike the tale of the Rattlemouse who in the warres proclaimed betweene the foure footed beasts and the birdes, beyng sent for by the Lyon to be at his musters, excused himselfe for that he was a foule and flew with winges;
15 and beyng sent for by the Eagle to serue him, sayd that he was a foure footed beast; and by that craftie cauill escaped the danger of the warres, and shunned the seruice of both Princes, and euer since sate at home by the fires side, eating vp the poore husbandmans baken, halfe lost for
20 lacke of a good huswifes looking too.

THE THIRD BOOKE
OF ORNAMENT

CHAP. I.

OF ORNAMENT POETICALL.

AS no doubt the good proportion of any thing doth gretly adorne and commend it, and right so our late remembred proportions doe to our vulgar Poesie, so is there yet requisite to the perfection of this arte another maner of exornation, which resteth in the fashioning of our makers language and stile, to such purpose as it may delight and allure as well the mynde as the eare of the hearers with a certaine noueltie and strange maner of conueyance, disguising it no litle from the ordinary and accustomed; neuerthelesse making it nothing the more vnseemely or misbecomming, but rather decenter and more agreable to any ciuill eare and vnderstanding. And as we see in these great Madames of honour, be they for personage or otherwise neuer so comely and bewtifull, yet if they want their courtly habillements or at leastwise such other apparell as custome and ciuilitie haue ordained to couer their naked bodies, would be halfe ashamed or greatly out of countenaunce to be seen in that sort, and perchance do then thinke themselues more amiable in euery mans eye when they be in their richest attire, suppose of silkes or tyssewes & costly embroderies, then when they go in cloth or in any other plaine and simple apparell; euen so cannot our vulgar Poesie shew it selfe either gallant or gorgious, if any lymme be left naked and bare and not clad in his kindly clothes and coulours, such as may conuey them somwhat out of sight, that is from

the common course of ordinary speach and capacitie of
the vulgar iudgement, and yet being artificially handled
must needes yeld it much more bewtie and commendation. This ornament we speake of is giuen to it by figures
and figuratiue speaches, which be the flowers, as it were,
and coulours that a Poet setteth vpon his language of arte,
as the embroderer doth his stone and perle or passements
of gold vpon the stuffe of a Princely garment, or as
th'excellent painter bestoweth the rich Orient coulours
vpon his table of pourtraite: so neuerthelesse as if the
same coulours in our arte of Poesie (as well as in those
other mechanicall artes) be not well tempered, or not well
layd, or be vsed in excesse, or neuer so litle disordered or
misplaced, they not onely giue it no maner of grace at
all, but rather do disfigure the stuffe and spill the whole
workmanship, taking away all bewtie and good liking from
it, no lesse then if the crimson tainte, which should be laid
vpon a Ladies lips, or right in the center of her cheekes,
should by some ouersight or mishap be applied to her
forhead or chinne, it would make (ye would say) but
a very ridiculous bewtie; wherfore the chief prayse and
cunning of our Poet is in the discreet vsing of his figures,
as the skilfull painters is in the good conueyance of his
coulours and shadowing traits of his pensill, with a delectable varietie, by all measure and iust proportion, and in
places most aptly to be bestowed.

CHAP. II.

HOW OUR WRITING AND SPEACHES PUBLIKE OUGHT TO BE FIGURATIUE; AND, IF THEY BE NOT, DOE GREATLY DISGRACE THE CAUSE AND PURPOSE OF THE SPEAKER AND WRITER.

But as it hath bene alwayes reputed a great fault to
vse figuratiue speaches foolishly and indiscretly, so is it

esteemed no lesse an imperfection in mans vtterance to haue none vse of figure at all, specially in our writing and speaches publike, making them but as our ordinary talke, then which nothing can be more vnsauourie and farre from all ciuilitie. I remember in the first yeare of Queenes Maries raigne a Knight of Yorkshire was chosen speaker of the Parliament, a good gentleman and wise in the affaires of his shire and not vnlearned in the lawes of the Realme, but as well for some lack of his teeth as for want of language nothing well spoken, which at that time and businesse was most behooffull for him to haue bene; this man after he had made his Oration to the Queene, which ye know is of course to be done at the first assembly of both houses, a bencher of the Temple both well learned and very eloquent, returning from the Parliament house, asked another gentleman, his frend, how he liked M. Speakers Oration : 'mary,' quoth th'other, 'me thinks I heard not a better alehouse tale told this seuen yeares.' This happened because the good old Knight made no difference betweene an Oration or publike speach to be deliuered to th'eare of a Princes Maiestie and state of a Realme then he would haue done of an ordinary tale to be told at his table in the countrey, wherein all men know the oddes is very great. And though graue and wise counsellours in their consultations doe not vse much superfluous eloquence, and also in their iudiciall hearings do much mislike all scholasticall rhetoricks, yet in such a case as it may be (and as this Parliament was) if the Lord Chancelour of England or Archbishop of Canterbury himselfe were to speake, he ought to doe it cunningly and eloquently, which can not be without the vse of figures : and neuerthelesse none impeachment or blemish to the grauitie of their persons or of the cause : wherein I report me to them that knew Sir *Nicholas Bacon*, Lord keeper of the great Seale, or the now Lord Treasorer of England,

Of Ornament

and haue bene conuersant with their speaches made in
the Parliament house & Starrechamber. From whose
lippes I haue seene to proceede more graue and naturall
eloquence then from all the Oratours of Oxford or Cambridge; but all is as it is handled, and maketh no matter
whether the same eloquence be naturall to them or artificiall (though I thinke rather naturall), yet were they
knowen to be learned and not vnskilfull of th'arte when
they were yonger men. And as learning and arte teacheth
a schollar to speake, so doth it also teach a counsellour,
and aswell an old man as a yong, and a man in authoritie
aswell as a priuate person, and a pleader aswell as a
preacher, euery man after his sort and calling as best
becommeth: and that speach which becommeth one doth
not become another, for maners of speaches, some serue
to work in excesse, some in mediocritie, some to graue
purposes, some to light, some to be short and brief, some
to be long, some to stirre vp affections, some to pacifie
and appease them, and these common despisers of good
vtterance, which resteth altogether in figuratiue speaches,
being well vsed whether it come by nature or by arte or
by exercise, they be but certaine grosse ignorance, of
whom it is truly spoken *scientia non habet inimicum nisi
ignorantem*. I haue come to the Lord Keeper Sir *Nicholas
Bacon*, & found him sitting in his gallery alone with the
works of *Quintilian* before him; in deede he was a most
eloquent man, and of rare learning and wisedome, as euer
I knew England to breed, and one that ioyed as much
in learned men and men of good witts. A Knight of the
Queenes priuie chamber once intreated a noble woman
of the Court, being in great fauour about her Maiestie
(to th'intent to remoue her from a certaine displeasure,
which by sinister opinion she had conceiued against a
gentleman his friend), that it would please her to heare
him speake in his own cause, & not to condemne him

vpon his aduersaries report: 'God forbid,' said she, 'he is
to wise for me to talke with; let him goe and satisfie such
a man, naming him.' 'Why,' quoth the Knight againe, 'had
your Ladyship rather heare a man talke like a foole or
like a wise man?' This was because the Lady was a litle
peruerse, and not disposed to reforme her selfe by hearing
reason, which none other can so well beate into the
ignorant head as the well spoken and eloquent man.
And because I am so farre waded into this discourse of
eloquence and figuratiue speaches, I will tell you what
hapned on a time, my selfe being present, when certaine
Doctours of the ciuil law were heard in a litigious cause
betwixt a man and his wife, before a great Magistrat who
(as they can tell that knew him) was a man very well
learned and graue, but somewhat sowre, and of no
plausible vtterance. The gentlemans chaunce was to say:
'my Lord the simple woman is not so much to blame as
her lewde abbettours, who by violent perswasions haue
lead her into this wilfulnesse.' Quoth the iudge, 'what
neede such eloquent termes in this place.' The gentleman
replied, 'doth your Lordship mislike the terme *violent*, &
me thinkes I speake it to great purpose, for I am sure she
would neuer haue done it but by force of perswasion, &
if perswasions were not very violent, to the minde of man
it could not haue wrought so strange an effect as we read
that it did once in Ægypt,' & would haue told the whole
tale at large, if the Magistrate had not passed it ouer
very pleasantly. Now to tell you the whole matter as
the gentleman intended, thus it was. There came into
Ægypt a notable Oratour, whose name was *Hegesias*,
who inueyed so much against the incommodities of this
transitory life, & so highly commended death the dispatcher
of all euils, as a great number of his hearers destroyed
themselues, some with weapon, some with poyson, others
by drowning and hanging themselues, to be rid out of this

Of Ornament

vale of misery, in so much as it was feared least many moe of the people would haue miscaried by occasion of his perswasions, if king *Ptolome* had not made a publicke proclamation that the Oratour should auoyde the countrey and no more be allowed to speake in any matter. Whether now perswasions may not be said violent and forcible to simple myndes in speciall, I referre it to all mens iudgements that heare the story. At least waies, I finde this opinion confirmed by a pretie deuise or embleme that *Lucianus* alleageth he saw in the pourtrait of *Hercules* within the Citie of Marseills in Prouence, where they had figured a lustie old man with a long chayne tyed by one end at his tong, by the other end at the peoples eares, who stood a farre of and seemed to be drawen to him by the force of that chayne fastned to his tong, as who would say, by force of his perswasions. And to shew more plainly that eloquence is of great force and not (as many men thinke amisse) the propertie and gift of yong men onely, but rather of old men, and a thing which better becommeth hory haires then beardlesse boyes, they seeme to ground it vpon this reason: age (say they and most truly) brings experience, experience bringeth wisedome, long life yeldes long vse and much exercise of speach, exercise and custome with wisedome make an assured and volluble vtterance: so is it that old men more then any other sort speake most grauely, wisely, assuredly, and plausibly, which partes are all that can be required in perfite eloquence, and so in all deliberations of importance, where counsellours are allowed freely to opyne & shew their conceits, good perswasion is no lesse requisite then speach it selfe; for in great purposes to speake and not to be able or likely to perswade is a vayne thing. Now let vs returne backe to say more of this Poeticall ornament.

CHAP. III.

HOW ORNAMENT POETICALL IS OF TWO SORTES ACCORDING TO THE DOUBLE VERTUE AND EFFICACIE OF FIGURES.

This ornament then is of two sortes, one to satisfie & delight th'eare onely by a goodly outward shew set vpon the matter with wordes and speaches smothly and tunably running, another by certaine intendments or sence of such wordes & speaches inwardly working a stirre to the mynde. That first qualitie the Greeks called *Enargia*, of this word *argos*, because it geueth a glorious lustre and light. This latter they called *Energia*, of *ergon*, because it wrought with a strong and vertuous operation. And figure breedeth them both, some seruing to giue glosse onely to a language, some to geue it efficacie by sence; and so by that meanes some of them serue th'eare onely, some serue the conceit onely and not th'eare. There be of them also that serue both turnes as common seruitours appointed for th'one and th'other purpose, which shalbe hereafter spoken of in place; but because we haue alleaged before that ornament is but the good or rather bewtifull habite of language or stile, and figuratiue speaches the instrument wherewith we burnish our language, fashioning it to this or that measure and proportion, whence finally resulteth a long and continuall phrase or maner of writing or speach, which we call by the name of *stile*, we wil first speake of language, then of stile, lastly of figure, and declare their vertue and differences, and also their vse and best application, & what portion in exornation euery of them bringeth to the bewtifying of this Arte.

CHAP. IV.

OF LANGUAGE.

Speach is not naturall to man sauing for his onely habilitie to speake, and that he is by kinde apt to vtter all his conceits with sounds and voyces diuersified many maner of wayes, by meanes of the many & fit instruments he hath by nature to that purpose, as a broad and voluble tong, thinne and mouable lippes, teeth euen and not shagged, thick ranged, a round vaulted pallate, and a long throte, besides an excellent capacitie of wit that maketh him more disciplinable and imitatiue then any other creature: then as to the forme and action of his speach, it commeth to him by arte & teaching, and by vse or exercise. But after a speach is fully fashioned to the common vnderstanding, & accepted by consent of a whole countrey and nation, it is called a language, & receaueth none allowed alteration but by extraordinary occasions, by little & little, as it were insensibly, bringing in of many corruptions that creepe along with the time: of all which matters we haue more largely spoken in our bookes of the originals and pedigree of the English tong. Then when I say language, I meane the speach wherein the Poet or maker writeth, be it Greek or Latine, or as our case is the vulgar English, & when it is peculiar vnto a countrey it is called the mother speach of that people: the Greekes terme it *Idioma*: so is ours at this day the Norman English. Before the Conquest of the Normans it was the Anglesaxon, and before that the British, which, as some will, is at this day the Walsh, or as others affirme the Cornish: I for my part thinke neither of both, as they be now spoken and pronounced. This part in our maker or Poet must be heedyly looked vnto, that it be naturall, pure, and the most vsuall of all his countrey; and for the

same purpose rather that which is spoken in the kings
Court, or in the good townes and Cities within the land,
then in the marches and frontiers, or in port townes,
where straungers haunt for traffike sake, or yet in
Vniuersities where Schollers vse much peeuish affectation
of words out of the primatiue languages, or finally, in any
vplandish village or corner of a Realme, where is no
resort but of poore rusticall or vnciuill people: neither
shall he follow the speach of a craftes man or carter, or
other of the inferiour sort, though he be inhabitant or
bred in the best towne and Citie in this Realme, for such
persons doe abuse good speaches by strange accents or
ill shapen soundes and false ortographie. But he shall
follow generally the better brought vp sort, such as the
Greekes call *charientes*, men ciuill and graciously be-
hauoured and bred. Our maker therfore at these dayes
shall not follow *Piers plowman* nor *Gower* nor *Lydgate*
nor yet *Chaucer*, for their language is now out of vse with
vs; neither shall he take the termes of Northern-men,
such as they vse in dayly talke, whether they be noble
men or gentlemen or of their best clarkes, all is a matter;
nor in effect any speach vsed beyond the riuer of Trent,
though no man can deny but that theirs is the purer
English Saxon at this day, yet it is not so Courtly nor so
currant as our Southerne English is; no more is the far
Westerne mans speach. Ye shall therefore take the vsuall
speach of the Court, and that of London and the shires
lying about London within lx. myles, and not much aboue.
I say not this but that in euery shyre of England there
be gentlemen and others that speake, but specially write,
as good Southerne as we of Middlesex or Surrey do,
but not the common people of euery shire, to whom
the gentlemen, and also their learned clarkes, do for the
most part condescend; but herein we are already ruled
by th'English Dictionaries and other bookes written by

learned men, and therefore it needeth none other direction in that behalfe. Albeit peraduenture some small admonition be not impertinent, for we finde in our English writers many wordes and speaches amendable, & ye shall see in some many inkhorne termes so ill affected brought in by men of learning as preachers and schoolemasters, and many straunge termes of other languages by Secretaries and Marchaunts and trauailours, and many darke wordes and not vsuall nor well sounding, though they be dayly spoken in Court. Wherefore great heed must be taken by our maker in this point that his choise be good. And peraduenture the writer hereof be in that behalfe no lesse faultie then any other, vsing many straunge and vnaccustomed wordes and borrowed from other languages, and in that respect him selfe no meete Magistrate to reforme the same errours in any other person; but since he is not vnwilling to acknowledge his owne fault, and can the better tell how to amend it, he may seem a more excusable correctour of other mens: he intendeth therefore for an indifferent way and vniuersall benefite to taxe him selfe first and before any others.

These be words vsed by th'author in this present treatise: *scientificke*, but with some reason, for it answereth the word *mechanicall*, which no other word could haue done so properly, for when hee spake of all artificers which rest either in science or in handy craft, it followed necessarilie that *scientifique* should be coupled with *mechanicall*, or els neither of both to haue bene allowed but in their places—a man of science liberall and a handicrafts man, which had not bene so cleanly a speech as the other. *Maior-domo*, in truth this word is borrowed of the *Spaniard* and *Italian*, and therefore new and not vsuall but to them that are acquainted with the affaires of Court, and so for his iolly magnificence (as this case is) may be accepted among Courtiers, for whom this is specially written. A man might haue said in steade of *Maior-domo* the French word *maistre d'hostell*, but ilfauouredly, or the right English word *Lord Steward*. But me thinks for my owne opinion this word *Maior-domo*, though he be borrowed, is more acceptable than any of the rest; other men may iudge otherwise. *Politien*, this word also is receiued from the Frenchmen, but at this day vsuall in Court and with all good Secretaries; and cannot finde an English word to match him, for to haue said a man politique had not bene so wel, bicause in trueth that had bene no more than to haue said a ciuil person. *Politien* is rather a surueyour of ciuilitie than ciuil, & a publique minister or Counseller in the state. Ye haue also this worde *Conduict*, a French word, but well allowed of vs and long since vsuall; it soundes somewhat more than this word *leading*, for it is applied onely to the leading of a Captaine, and not as a little boy should leade a blinde man, therefore more proper to the case when he saide *conduict* of whole armies: ye finde also this word *Idiome*, taken from the Greekes, yet seruing aptly when a man wanteth to expresse so much vnles it be in two words, which surplussage to auoide we are allowed to draw in other words single, and asmuch significatiue. This word *significatiue* is borrowed of the Latine and French, but to vs brought in first by some Noblemans Secretarie, as I thinke, yet doth so well serue the turne, as it could not now be spared: and many more like vsurped Latine and French words, as, *Methode, methodicall, placation, function, assubtiling, refining, compendious, prolixe, figuratiue, inueigle*, a terme borrowed of our common Lawyers, *impression*, also a new terme, but well expressing the matter and more than our English word. These words, *Numerous, numerositee, metricall, harmonicall*, but they cannot be refused, specially in this place for description of the arte. Also ye finde these words, *Penetrate, pene-*

trable, indignitie, which I cannot see how we may spare them, whatsoeuer fault wee finde with Ink-horne termes, for our speach wanteth wordes to such sence so well to be vsed; yet in steade of *indignitie* yee haue vnworthinesse, and for *penetrate* we may say *peerce,* and that a French terme also, or *broche,* or enter into with violence, but not so well sounding as *penetrate.* Item, *sauage,* for wilde; *obscure,* for darke. Item, these words, *declination, delineation, dimention* are scholasticall termes in deede, and yet very proper. But peraduenture (& I could bring a reason for it) many other like words borrowed out of the Latin and French were not so well to be allowed by vs, as these words, *audacious,* for bold, *facunditie,* for eloquence, *egregious,* for great or notable, *implete,* for replenished, *attemptat,* for attempt, *compatible,* for agreeable in nature, and many more. But herein the noble Poet *Horace* hath said inough to satisfie vs all in these few verses.

*Multa renascentur quae iam cecidere cadentque
Quae nunc sunt in honore vocabula, si volet vsus,
Quem penes arbitrium est & vis & norma loquendi.*

Which I haue thus englished, but nothing with so good grace, nor so briefly as the Poet wrote.

Many a word yfalne shall eft arise,
And such as now bene held in hiest prise
Will fall as fast, when vse and custome will,
Onely vmpiers of speach, for force and skill.

CHAP. V.

OF STILE.

Stile is a constant & continual phrase or tenour of speaking and writing, extending to the whole tale or processe of the poeme or historie, and not properly to any peece or member of a tale, but is, of words, speeches, and sentences together, a certaine contriued forme and qualitie, many times naturall to the writer, many times his peculier by election and arte, and such as either he keepeth by skill, or holdeth on by ignorance, and will not or peraduenture cannot easily alter into any other. So we say that *Ciceroes* stile and *Salusts* were not one, nor *Cesars* and *Liuies*, nor *Homers* and *Hesiodus*, nor *Herodotus* and *Theucidides*, nor *Euripides* and *Aristophanes*, nor *Erasmus* and *Budeus* stiles. And because this continuall course and manner of writing or speech sheweth the matter and disposition of the writers minde more than one or few words or sentences can shew, therefore there be that haue called stile the image of man, *mentis character*; for man is but his minde, and as his minde is tempered and qualified, so are his speeches and language at large, and his inward conceits be the mettall of his minde, and his manner of vtterance the very warp & woofe of his conceits, more plaine, or busie and intricate, or otherwise affected after the rate. Most men say that not any one point in all *Phisiognomy* is so certaine as to iudge a mans manner by his eye; but more assuredly in mine opinion, by his dayly maner of speech and ordinary writing. For if the man be graue, his speech and stile is graue; if lightheaded, his stile and language also light; if the minde be haughtie and hoate, the speech and stile is also vehement and stirring; if it be colde and temperate, the stile is also very modest; if it be humble, or base and meeke, so is also the language and stile. And yet peraduenture not altogether so, but that euery mans stile is for the most part according to the matter and subiect of the writer, or so ought to be and conformable thereunto. Then againe may it be said as wel, that men doo chuse their subiects according to the mettal of their minds, & therfore a high minded man chuseth him high & lofty matter to write of;

Of Ornament

the base courage, matter base & lowe; the meane &
modest mind, meane & moderate matters after the rate.
Howsoeuer it be, we finde that vnder these three principall
complexions (if I may with leaue so terme them), high,
meane, and base stile, there be contained many other
humors or qualities of stile, as the plaine and obscure,
the rough and smoth, the facill and hard, the plentifull
and barraine, the rude and eloquent, the strong and
feeble, the vehement and cold stiles, all which in their
euill are to be reformed, and the good to be kept and
vsed. But generally, to haue the stile decent & comely
it behooueth the maker or Poet to follow the nature of
his subiect, that is if his matter be high and loftie that
the stile be so to, if meane, the stile also to be meane,
if base, the stile humble and base accordingly: and they
that do otherwise vse it, applying to meane matter hie
and loftie stile, and to hie matters stile eyther meane or
base, and to the base matters the meane or hie stile, do
vtterly disgrace their poesie and shew themselues nothing
skilfull in their arte, nor hauing regard to the decencie,
which is the chiefe praise of any writer. Therefore to
ridde all louers of learning from that errour, I will, as
neere as I can, set downe which matters be hie and
loftie, which be but meane, and which be low and base,
to the intent the stiles may be fashioned to the matters,
and keepe their *decorum* and good proportion in euery
respect. I am not ignorant that many good clerkes be
contrary to mine opinion, and say that the loftie style
may be decently vsed in a meane and base subiect &
contrariwise, which I do in parte acknowledge, but with
a reasonable qualification. For *Homer* hath so vsed it in
his trifling worke of *Batrachomyomachia*, that is in his
treatise of the warre betwixt the frogs and the mice:
Virgill also in his *bucolickes*, and in his *georgicks*, whereof
the one is counted meane, the other base, that is the

husbandmans discourses and the shepheards. But hereunto serueth a reason in my simple conceite: for first to that trifling poeme of *Homer*, though the frog and the mouse be but litle and ridiculous beasts, yet to treat of warre is an high subiect, and a thing in euery respect terrible and daungerous to them that it alights on; and therefore of learned dutie asketh martiall grandiloquence, if it be set foorth in his kind and nature of warre, euen betwixt the basest creatures that can be imagined: so also is the Ante or pismire, and they be but little creeping things, not perfect beasts, but *insect*, or wormes: yet in describing their nature & instinct, and their manner of life approching to the forme of a common-welth, and their properties not vnlike to the vertues of most excellent gouernors and captaines, it asketh a more maiestie of speach then would the description of an other beastes life or nature, and perchance of many matters perteyning vnto the baser sort of men, because it resembleth the historie of a ciuill regiment, and of them all the chiefe and most principall, which is *Monarchie*. So also in his *bucolicks*, which are but pastorall speaches and the basest of any other poeme in their owne proper nature, *Virgill* vsed a somewhat swelling stile when he came to insinuate the birth of *Marcellus*, heire apparant to the Emperour *Augustus* as child to his sister, aspiring by hope and greatnes of the house to the succession of the Empire, and establishment thereof in that familie; whereupon *Virgill* could no lesse then to vse such manner of stile, whatsoeuer condition the poeme were of, and this was decent, & no fault or blemish to confound the tennors of the stiles for that cause. But now when I remember me againe that this *Eglogue* (for I haue read it somewhere) was conceiued by *Octauian* th'Emperour to be written to the honour of *Pollio*, a citizen of Rome & of no great nobilitie, the same was misliked againe as an

Of Ornament 157

implicatiue, nothing decent nor proportionable to *Pollio* his fortunes and calling, in which respect I might say likewise the stile was not to be such as if it had bene for the Emperours owne honour and those of the bloud imperiall, then which subiect there could not be among the *Romane* writers an higher nor grauer to treat vpon. So can I not be remoued from mine opinion, but still me thinks that in all decencie the stile ought to conforme with the nature of the subiect, otherwise if a writer will seeme to obserue no *decorum* at all, nor passe how he fashion his tale to his matter, who doubteth but he may in the lightest cause speake like a Pope, & in the grauest matters prate like a parrat, & finde wordes & phrases ynough to serue both turnes, and neither of them commendably; for neither is all that may be written of Kings and Princes such as ought to keepe a high stile, nor all that may be written vpon a shepheard to keepe the low, but according to the matter reported, if that be of high or base nature; for euery pety pleasure and vayne delight of a king are not to [be] accompted high matter for the height of his estate, but meane and perchaunce very base and vile. Nor so a Poet or historiographer could decently with a high stile reporte the vanities of *Nero*, the ribaudries of *Caligula*, the idlenes of *Domitian*, and the riots of *Heliogabalus*; but well the magnanimitie and honorable ambition of *Caesar*, the prosperities of *Augustus*, the grauitie of *Tiberius*, the bountie of *Traiane*, the wisedome of *Aurelius*, and generally all that which concerned the highest honours of Emperours, their birth, alliaunces, gouernement, exploits in warre and peace, and other publike affaires; for they be matter stately and high, and require a stile to be lift vp and aduaunced by choyse of wordes, phrases, sentences, and figures, high, loftie, eloquent, & magnifik in proportion. So be the meane matters, to be caried with all wordes and speaches of smothnesse and pleasant moderation, & finally the base things to be holden within their teder, by a low, myld, and simple maner of vtterance, creeping rather than clyming, & marching rather then mounting vpwardes, with the wings of the stately subiects and stile.

CHAP. VI.

OF THE HIGH, LOW, AND MEANE SUBIECT.

The matters therefore that concerne the Gods and diuine things are highest of all other to be couched in writing; next to them the noble gests and great fortunes of Princes, and the notable accidents of time, as the greatest affaires of war & peace: these be all high subiectes, and therefore are deliuered ouer to the Poets *Hymnick* & historicall who be occupied either in diuine laudes or in *heroicall* reports. The meane matters be those that concerne meane men, their life and busines, as lawyers, gentlemen, and marchants, good housholders and honest Citizens, and which sound neither to matters of state nor of warre, nor leagues, nor great alliances, but smatch all the common conuersation, as of the ciuiller and better sort of men. The base and low matters be the doings of the common artificer, seruingman, yeoman, groome, husbandman, day-labourer, sailer, shepheard, swynard, and such like of homely calling, degree, and bringing vp. So that in euery of the sayd three degrees not the selfe same vertues be egally to be praysed nor the same vices egally to be dispraised, nor their loues, mariages, quarels, contracts, and other behauiours be like high nor do require to be set fourth with the like stile, but euery one in his degree and decencie, which made that all *hymnes* and histories and Tragedies were written in the high stile, all Comedies and Enterludes and other common Poesies of loues and such like in the meane stile, all *Eglogues* and pastorall poemes in the low and base stile; otherwise they had bene vtterly disproporcioned. Likewise for the same cause some phrases and figures be onely peculiar to the high stile, some to the base or meane, some common to all three, as shalbe declared more at large hereafter when we come to speake of figure and phrase: also some wordes and speaches and sentences doe become the high stile that do not become th'other two, and contrariwise, as shalbe said when we talke of words and sentences: finally, some kinde of measure and concord doe not beseeme the high stile, that well become the meane and low, as we haue said speaking of concord and measure. But generally the high stile is disgraced and made foolish and ridiculous by all wordes affected, counterfait, and puffed vp, as it were a windball carrying more countenance then matter, and can not be better resembled then to these midsommer pageants in London, where, to make the people wonder, are set forth great and vglie Gyants marching as if they were aliue, and armed at all points, but within they are stuffed full of browne paper and tow, which the shrewd boyes vnderpeering do guilefully discouer and turne to a great derision : also all darke and vnaccustomed wordes, or rusticall and homely, and sentences that hold too much of the mery & light, or infamous & vnshamefast, are to be accounted of the same sort, for such speaches become not Princes, nor great estates, nor them that write of their doings to vtter or report and intermingle with the graue and weightie matters.

CHAP. VII.

OF FIGURES AND FIGURATIUE SPEACHES.

As figures be the instruments of ornament in euery language, so be they also in a sorte abuses or rather trespasses in speach, because they passe the ordinary limits of common vtterance, and be occupied of purpose to deceiue the eare and also the minde, drawing it from plainnesse and simplicitie to a certaine doublenesse, whereby our talke is the more guilefull & abusing. For what els is your *Metaphor* but an inuersion of sence by transport; your *allegorie* by a duplicitie of meaning or dissimulation vnder couert and darke intendments; one while speaking obscurely and in riddle called *Ænigma*; another while by common prouerbe or Adage called *Paremia*; then by merry skoffe called *Ironia*; then by bitter tawnt called *Sarcasmus*; then by periphrase or circumlocution when all might be said in a word or two; then by incredible comparison giuing credit, as by your *Hyperbole*; and many other waies seeking to inueigle and appassionate the mind: which thing made the graue iudges *Areopagites* (as I find written) to forbid all manner of figuratiue speaches to be vsed before them in their consistorie of Iustice, as meere illusions to the minde, and wresters of vpright iudgement, saying that to allow such manner of forraine & coulored talke to make the iudges affectioned were all one as if the carpenter before he began to square his timber would make his squire crooked; in so much as the straite and vpright mind of a Iudge is the very rule of iustice till it be peruerted by affection. This no doubt is true and was by them grauely considered; but in this case, because our maker or Poet is appointed not for a iudge, but rather for a pleader, and that of pleasant & louely causes and nothing perillous, such as be those for the triall of life, limme, or liuelyhood, and before iudges neither sower nor seuere, but in the eare of princely dames, yong ladies, gentlewomen, and courtiers, beyng all for the most part either meeke of nature, or of pleasant humour, and that all his abuses tende but to dispose the hearers to mirth and sollace by pleasant conueyance and efficacy of speach, they are not in truth to be accompted vices but for vertues in the poetical science very commendable. On the other side, such trespasses in speach (whereof there be many) as geue dolour and disliking to the eare & minde by any foule indecencie or disproportion of sounde, situation, or sence, they be called and not without cause the vicious parts or rather heresies of language: wherefore the matter resteth much in the definition and acceptance of this word *decorum*, for whatsoeuer is so cannot iustly be misliked. In which respect it may come to passe that what the Grammarian setteth downe for a viciositee in speach may become a vertue and no vice; contrariwise his commended figure may fall into a reprochfull fault: the best and most assured remedy whereof is generally to follow the saying of *Bias*: *ne quid nimis*. So as in keeping measure, and not exceeding nor shewing any defect in the vse of his figures, he cannot lightly do amisse, if he haue besides (as that must needes be) a speciall regard to all circumstances of the person, place, time, cause, and purpose he hath in hand; which being well obserued, it easily auoideth all the recited inconueniences, and maketh now and then very vice goe for a formall vertue in the exercise of this Arte.

CHAP. VIII.

SIXE POINTS SET DOWNE BY OUR LEARNED FOREFATHERS FOR A GENERALL REGIMENT OF ALL GOOD VTTERANCE, BE IT BY MOUTH OR BY WRITING.

But before there had bene yet any precise obseruation made of figuratiue speeches, the first learned artificers of language considered that the bewtie and good grace of vtterance rested in [s]o many pointes; and whatsoeuer transgressed those lymits, they counted it for vitious; and thereupon did set downe a manner of regiment in all speech generally to be obserued, consisting in sixe pointes. First, they said that there ought to be kept a decent proportion in our writings and speach, which they termed *Analogia*. Secondly, that it ought to be voluble vpon the tongue, and tunable to the eare, which they called *Tasis*. Thirdly, that it were not tediously long, but briefe and compendious, as the matter might beare, which they called *Syntomia*. Fourthly, that it should cary an orderly and good construction, which they called *Synthesis*. Fiftly, that it should be a sound, proper, and naturall speach, which they called *Ciriologia*. Sixtly, that it should be liuely & stirring, which they called *Tropus*. So as it appeareth by this order of theirs that no vice could be committed in speech, keeping within the bounds of that restraint. But, sir, all this being by them very well conceiued, there remayned a greater difficultie to know what this proportion, volubilitie, good construction, & the rest were, otherwise we could not be euer the more relieued. It was therefore of necessitie that a more curious and particular description should bee made of euery manner of speech, either transgressing or agreeing with their said generall prescript. Whereupon it came to passe that all the commendable parts of speech were set foorth by the name of figures, and all the illaudable partes vnder the name of vices or viciosities, of both which it shall bee spoken in their places.

CHAP. IX.

HOW THE GREEKS FIRST, AND AFTERWARD THE LATINES, INUENTED NEW NAMES FOR EUERY FIGURE, WHICH THIS AUTHOR IS ALSO ENFORCED TO DOO IN HIS VULGAR.

The Greekes were a happy people for the freedome & liberty of their language, because it was allowed them

Of Ornament

to inuent any new name that they listed, and to peece many words together to make of them one entire, much more significatiue than the single word. So among other things did they to their figuratiue speeches deuise certaine names. The Latines came somewhat behind them in that point, and for want of conuenient single wordes to expresse that which the Greeks could do by cobling many words together, they were faine to vse the Greekes still, till after many yeares that the learned Oratours and good Grammarians among the Romaines, as *Cicero*, *Varro*, *Quintilian*, & others, strained themselues to giue the Greeke wordes Latin names, and yet nothing so apt and fitty. The same course are we driuen to follow in this description, since we are enforced to cull out for the vse of our Poet or maker all the most commendable figures. Now to make them knowen (as behoueth), either we must do it by th'original Greeke name or by the Latine, or by our owne. But when I consider to what sort of Readers I write, & how ill faring the Greeke terme would sound in the English eare, then also how short the Latines come to expresse manie of the Greeke originals, finally, how well our language serueth to supplie the full signification of them both, I haue thought it no lesse lawfull, yea peraduenture, vnder licence of the learned, more laudable, to vse our owne naturall, if they be well chosen and of proper signification, than to borrow theirs. So shall not our English Poets, though they be to seeke of the Greeke and Latin languages, lament for lack of knowledge sufficient to the purpose of this arte. And in case any of these new English names giuen by me to any figure shall happen to offend, I pray that the learned will beare with me and to thinke the straungenesse thereof proceedes but of noueltie and disaquaintance with our eares, which in processe of tyme and by custome will frame very well: and such others as are not learned in the primitive languages, if they happen to hit vpon any new name of myne (so ridiculous in their opinion) as may moue them to laughter, let such persons yet assure themselues that such names go as neare as may be to their originals, or els serue better to the purpose of the figure then the very originall, reseruing alwayes that such new name should not be vnpleasant in our vulgar nor harsh vpon the tong; and where it shall happen otherwise, that it may please the reader to thinke that hardly any other name in our English could be found to serue the turne better. Againe, if to auoid the hazard of this blame I should haue kept the Greek or Latin, still it would haue appeared a little too scholasticall for our makers, and a peece of worke more fit for clerkes then for Courtiers, for whose instruction this trauaile is taken; and if I should haue left out both the Greeke and Latine name, and put in none of our owne neither, well perchance might the rule of the figure haue bene set downe, but no conuenient name to hold him in memory. It was therfore expedient we deuised for euery figure of importance his vulgar name, and to ioyne the Greeke or Latine originall with them; after that sort much better satisfying aswel the vulgar as the learned learner, and also the authors owne purpose, which is to make of a rude rimer a learned and a Courtly Poet.

CHAP. X.

A DIUISION OF FIGURES, AND HOW THEY SERUE IN EXORNATION OF LANGUAGE.

And because our chiefe purpose herein is for the learning of Ladies and young Gentlewomen, or idle Courtiers, desirous to become skilful in their owne mother tongue, and for their priuate recreation to make now & then ditties of pleasure, thinking for our parte none other science so

Of Ornament

fit for them & the place as that which teacheth *beau semblant*, the chiefe profession aswell of Courting as of poesie, since to such manner of mindes nothing is more combersome then tedious doctrines and schollarly methodes of discipline, we haue in our owne conceit deuised a new and strange modell of this arte, fitter to please the Court then the schoole, and yet not vnnecessarie for all such as be willing themselues to become good makers in the vulgar, or to be able to iudge of other mens makings: wherefore, intending to follow the course which we haue begun, thus we say that, though the language of our Poet or maker be pure & clenly, &, not disgraced by such vicious parts as haue bene before remembred in the Chapter of language, be sufficiently pleasing and commendable for the ordinarie vse of speech, yet is not the same so well appointed for all purposes of the excellent Poet as when it is gallantly arrayed in all his colours which figure can set vpon it; therefore we are now further to determine of figures and figuratiue speeches. Figuratiue speech is a noueltie of language euidently (and yet not absurdly) estranged from the ordinarie habite and manner of our dayly talke and writing, and figure it selfe is a certaine liuely or good grace set vpon wordes, speaches, and sentences to some purpose and not in vaine, giuing them ornament or efficacie by many maner of alterations in shape, in sounde, and also in sence, sometime by way of surplusage, sometime by defect, sometime by disorder, or mutation, & also by putting into our speaches more pithe and substance, subtilitie, quicknesse, efficacie, or modera- tion, in this or that sort tuning and tempring them, by amplification, abridgement, opening, closing, enforcing, meekening, or otherwise disposing them to the best pur- pose: whereupon the learned clerks who haue written methodically of this Arte in the two master languages, Greeke and Latine, haue sorted all their figures into three rankes, and the first they bestowed vpon the Poet onely, the second vpon the Poet and Oratour indifferently, the third vpon the Oratour alone. And that first sort of figures doth serue th'eare onely and may be therefore called *auricular*: your second serues the conceit onely and not th'eare, and may be called *sensable*, not sensible nor yet sententious: your third sort serues as well th'eare as the conceit, and may be called *sententious figures*, because not only they properly apperteine to full sentences, for bewtifying them with a currant & pleasant numerositie, but also giuing them efficacie and enlarging the whole matter besides with copious amplifications. I doubt not but some busie carpers will scorne at my new deuised termes *auricular* and *sensable*, saying that I might with better warrant haue vsed in their steads these words *orthographicall* or *syntacticall*, which the learned Grammarians left ready made to our hands, and do importe as much as th'other that I haue brought. Which thing peraduenture I deny not in part, and neuerthelesse for some causes thought them not so necessarie: but with these maner of men I do willingly beare, in respect of their laudable endeuour to allow antiquitie and flie innouation. With like beneuolence I trust they will beare with me writing in the vulgar speach and seeking by my nouelties to satisfie not the schoole but the Court: whereas they know very well all old things soone waxe stale & lothsome, and the new deuises are euer dainty and delicate, the vulgar instruction requiring also vulgar and communicable termes, not clerkly or vncouthe, as are all these of the Greeke and Latine languages primitiuely receiued, vnlesse they be qualified or by much vse and custome allowed and our eares made acquainted with them. Thus then I say that *auricular* figures be those which worke alteration in th'eare by sound, accent, time, and slipper volubilitie in vtterance, such as for that respect was called by the

auncients numerositie of speach. And not onely the whole
body of a tale in a poeme or historie may be made in such
sort pleasant and agreable to the eare, but also euery
clause by it selfe, and euery single word carried in a clause
may haue their pleasant sweetenesse apart. And so long
as this qualitie extendeth but to the outward tuning of
the speach, reaching no higher then th'eare and forcing the
mynde little or nothing, it is that vertue which the Greeks
call *Enargia* and is the office of the *auricular* figures to
performe. Therefore, as the members of language at large
are whole sentences, and sentences are compact of clauses,
and clauses of words, and euery word of letters and
sillables, so is the alteration (be it but of a sillable or letter)
much materiall to the sound and sweetenesse of vtterance.
Wherefore beginning first at the smallest alterations which
rest in letters and sillables, the first sort of our figures
auricular we do appoint to single words as they lye in
language; the second to clauses of speach; the third to
perfit sentences and to the whole masse or body of the
tale, be it poeme or historie, written or reported.

[*Puttenham then proceeds to a detailed description of the
grammatical and rhetorical tropes and figures included in
his general scheme. In each case he gives a definition and
illustrates it by quotations or by anecdotes, but he seldom
adds any matter of purely critical value. The more interesting
points are indicated in the following summary of the chapters
and figures.*]

CHAP. XI. OF AURICULAR FIGURES APPERTEINING TO SINGLE
WORDES AND WORKING BY THEIR DIUERS SOUNDES AND AUDIBLE
TUNES, ALTERATION TO THE EARE ONELY AND NOT THE MYNDE.

CHAP. XII. OF AURICULAR FIGURES PERTAINING TO CLAUSES OF
SPEECH AND BY THEM WORKING NO LITTLE ALTERATION TO
THE EARE. *These include—Eclipsis*, or the Figure of Default; *Zeugma*, or the Single Supply; *Prozeugma*, or the
Ringleader; *Mezozeugma*, or the Middlemarcher; *Hypozeugma*, or the Rerewarder; *Sillepsis*, or the Double

Supply; *Hypozeuxis*, or the Substitute; *Aposiopesis*, or the Figure of Silence, otherwise called the Figure of Interruption; and *Prolepsis*, or the Propounder.

CHAP. XIII. OF YOUR FIGURES AURICULAR WORKING BY DISORDER. *These are*—*Hiperbaton*, or the Trespasser; *Parenthesis*, or the Insertour; and *Histeron proteron*, or the Preposterous.

CHAP. XIV. OF YOUR FIGURES AURICULAR THAT WORKE BY SURPLUSAGE.

CHAP. XV. OF AURICULAR FIGURES WORKING BY EXCHANGE, namely—*Enallage*, or the Figure of Exchange, and *Hipallage*, or the Changeling.

CHAP. XVI. OF SOME OTHER FIGURES WHICH, BECAUSE THEY SERUE CHIEFLY TO MAKE THE MEETERS TUNABLE AND MELODIOUS, AND AFFECT NOT THE MINDE BUT VERY LITTLE, BE PLACED AMONG THE AURICULAR. *These are*—*Omoiotele[u]ton*, or the Like Loose; *Parimion*, or the Figure of Like Letter; *Asyndeton*, or the Loose Language; *Polisindeton*, or the Coople Clause; *Irmus*, or the Long Loose; *Epitheton*, or the Qualifier; and *Endiadis*, or the Figure of Twinnes.

Under the first we read: 'For a rime of good simphonie should not conclude his concords with one & the same terminant sillable, as *less, less, less*, but with diuers and like terminants, as *les, pres, mes*, as was before declared in the chapter of your cadences, and your clauses in prose should neither finish with the same nor with the like terminants, but with the contrary, as hath bene shewed before in the booke of proportions; yet many vse it otherwise, neglecting the Poeticall harmonie and skill. And th'Earle of *Surrey* with Syr *Thomas Wyat*, the most excellent makers of their time, more peraduenture respecting the fitnesse and ponderositie of their wordes then the true cadence or simphonie, were very licencious in this point. We call this figure, following the originall, the *like loose*, alluding to th'Archers terme who is not said to finish the feate of his shot before he giue the loose and deliuer his arrow from his bow; in which respect we vse to say marke the loose of a thing for marke the end of it.'

CHAP. XVII. OF THE FIGURES WHICH WE CALL SENSABLE,

BECAUSE THEY ALTER AND AFFECT THE MINDE BY ALTERA-
TION OF SENSE; AND FIRST IN SINGLE WORDES. *These
include*—*Metaphora*, or the Figure of Transport; *Catachresis*, or the Figure of Abuse; *Metonymia*, or the Misnamer; *Antonomasia*, or the Surnamer; *Onomatopeia*,
or the Newnamer; *Epitheton*, or the Qualifier, otherwise
called the Figure of Attribution; *Metalepsis*, or the Far-fet;
Emphasis, or the Renforcer; *Liptote*, or the Moderatour;
Paradiastole, or the Curry fauell, otherwise called the
Soother; *Meiosis*, or the Disabler; *Tapinosis*, or the Abbaser; and *Synecdoche*, or the Figure of Quick Conceite.

In speaking of Epitheton, Puttenham says: 'Some of our
vulgar writers take great pleasure in giuing Epithets, and
do it almost to euery word which may receiue them, and
should not be so, yea though they were neuer so propre
and apt, for sometimes wordes suffered to go single do
giue greater sence and grace than words quallified by attri-
butions do.'

CHAP. XVIII. OF SENSABLE FIGURES ALTERING AND AFFECTING
THE MYNDE BY ALTERATION OF SENCE OR INTENDEMENTS IN
WHOLE CLAUSES OR SPEACHES. *These are*—*Allegoria*, or
Figure of False Semblant; *Enigma*, or the Riddle; *Pari-
mia*, or the Prouerb; *Ironia*, or the Drie Mock; *Sarcasmus*,
or the Bitter Taunt; *Asteismus*, or the Merry Scoffe, other-
wise the Ciuill Iest; *Micterismus*, or the Fleering Frumpe;
Antiphrasis, or the Broad Floute; *Charientismus*, or the
Priuie Nippe; *Hiperbole*, or the Ouerreacher, otherwise the
Loud Lyer; *Periphrasis*, or the Figure of Ambage; and
Synecdoche, or the Figure of Quick Conceit (see l. 11), *which*
'may be put vnder the speeches *allegoricall*, because of the
darkenes and duplicitie of his sence.'

CHAP. XIX. OF FIGURES SENTENTIOUS, OTHERWISE CALLED
RHETORICALL. *This long chapter deals with*—*Anaphora*,
or the Figure of Report; *Antistrophe*, or the Counterturne;
Symploche, or the Figure of Replie; *Anadiplosis*, or the
Redouble; *Epanalepsis*, or the Eccho Sound, otherwise the
Slow Returne; *Epizeuxis*, or the Vnderlay, or Cuckowspell;
Ploche, or the Doubler, otherwise called the Swift Repeate;
Prosonomasia, or the Nicknamer; *Traductio*, or the Tran-
lacer; *Antipophora*, or the Figure of Responce; *Syneciosis*,

or the Crosse-couple; *Antanaclasis*, or the Rebounde; *Clymax*, or the Marching Figure; *Antimetauole*, or the Counterchange; *Insultatio*, or the Disdainefull; *Antitheton*, or the Quarreller, otherwise called the Ouerthwart or Renconter; *Erotema*, or the Questioner; *Ecphonisis*, or the Outcrie; *Brachiologia*, or the Cutted Comma; *Parison*, or the Figure of Euen; *Sinonimia*, or the Figure of Store; *Metanoia*, or the Penitent; *Antenagoge*, or the Recompencer; *Epiphonema*, or the Surclose, or Consenting Close; *Auxesis*, or the Auancer; *Meiosis*, or the Disabler; *Epanodis*, or the Figure of Retire; *Dialisis*, or the Dismembrer; *Merismus*, or the Distributor; *Epimone*, or the Loueburden; *Paradoxon*, or the Wondrer; *Aporia*, or the Doubtfull; *Epitropis*, or the Figure of Reference; *Parisia*, or the Licentious; *Anachinosis*, or the Impartener; *Paramologia*, or the Figure of Admittance; *Etiologia*, or the Tell-cause, or the Reason Rend; *Dichologia*, or the Figure of Excuse; *Noema*, or the Figure of Close Conceit; *Orismus*, or the Definer by Difference; *Procatalepsis*, or the Presumptuous; *Paralepsis*, or the Passager; *Commoratio*, or the Figure of Abode; *Metastasis*, or the Flitting Figure, or the Remoue; *Parecnasis*, or the Stragler; *Expeditio*, or the Speedie Dispatcher; *Dialogismus*, or the Right Reasoner; *Gnome*, or the Director; *Sententia*, or the Sage Sayer; *Sinathrismus*, or the Heaping Figure; *Apostrophe*, or the Turne Tale; *Hypotiposis*, or the Counterfait Representation; *Prosopographia*, or Counterfait Countenance; *Prosopopeia*, or the Counterfait in Personation; *Cronographia*, or the Counterfait Time; *Topographia*, or the Counterfait Place; *Pragmatographia*, or the Counterfait Action; *Omoiosis*, or Resemblance; *Icon*, or Resemblance by Imagerie; *Parabola*, or Resemblance misticall; and *Paradigma*, or Resemblance by Example. (*For the cancelled passage on the Flemings, see Notes.*)

CHAP. XX. THE LAST AND PRINCIPALL FIGURE OF OUR POETICALL ORNAMENT, i.e. *Exargasia*, or The Gorgious. 'In a worke of ours, intituled *Philocalia*, we have strained to shew the vse and application of this figure and al others mentioned in this booke, to which we referre you. I find none example in English meetre so well maintayning this figure as that ditty of her Maiesties owne making passing sweete

Of Ornament 171

& harmonicall.' *Then follow the verses on the disloyalty of the supporters of the Scots Queen, beginning*
'The doubt of future foes exiles my present ioy.'

CHAP. XXI. OF THE VICES OR DEFORMITIES IN SPEACH AND WRITING PRINCIPALLY NOTED BY AUNCIENT POETS.

Puttenham promises to speak briefly of the 'viciosities' of language, 'leauing no little to the Grammarians for maintenaunce of the scholasticall warre and altercations.'

CHAP. XXII. SOME VICES IN SPEACHES AND WRITING ARE ALWAYES INTOLLERABLE, SOME OTHERS NOW AND THEN BORNE WITHALL BY LICENCE OF APPROUED AUTHORS AND CUSTOME.

The 'intollerable vices' are Barbarismus or Forrein Speech, *Solecismus* or Incongruitie, *Cacozelia* or Fonde Affectation, *Soraismus* or the Mingle Mangle, and *Cacosintheton* or the Misplacer. *Less serious 'vices' are Cacemphaton* or the Figure of Foule Speech, *Tautologia* or the Figure of Selfe Saying, *Histeron Proteron* or the Preposterous, *Acyron* or the Vncouthe. *Then there are the 'Vices of Surplusage,'* viz. *Pleonasmus* or Too full Speech, *Macrologia* or Long Language, *Periergia* or Ouer labour, or The Curious; *after these, Tapinosis* or The Abbaser, *Bomphiologia* or Pompous Speech, and *Amphibologia* or the Ambiguous.

When speaking of the affectation of foreign terms, Puttenham says: ' Another [writer] of reasonable good facilitie in translation finding certaine of the hymnes of *Pyndarus* and of *Anacreons* odes and other *Lirickes* among the Greekes very well translated by *Rounsard* the French Poet, and applied to the honour of a great Prince in France, comes our minion and translates the same out of French into English, & applieth them to the honour of a great noble man in England (wherein I commend his reuerent minde and duetie), but doth so impudently robbe the French Poet both of his prayse and also of his French termes, that I cannot so much pitie him as be angry with him for his iniurious dealing, our sayd maker not being ashamed to vse these French wordes *freddon, egar, superbous, filanding, celest, calabrois, thebanois,* and a number of others, for English wordes, which haue no maner of conformitie with our language either by custome or deriuation which may make them tollerable: and in the end (which is worst of all)

makes his vaunt that neuer English finger but his hath
toucht *Pindars* string, which was neuerthelesse word by
word as *Rounsard* had said before by like braggery. ...
This man deserues to be endited of pety *larceny* for pilfering
other mens deuises from them & conuerting them to his
owne vse, for in deede as I would wish euery inuentour,
which is the very Poet, to receaue the prayses of his
inuention, so would I not haue a translatour to be ashamed
to be acknowen of his translation.'

And speaking of Periergia, Puttenham alludes to
'one of our late makers, who in the most of his things
wrote very well, in this (to mine opinion) more curiously
than needed, the matter being ripely considered; yet is
his verse very good, and his meetre cleanly. His intent
was to declare how vpon the tenth day of March he crossed
the riuer of Thames, to walke in Saint *Georges* field; the
matter was not great, as ye may suppose.

> The tenth of March when Aries receiued
> Dan Phoebus raies into his horned head,
> And I my selfe by learned lore perceiued
> That Ver approcht and frosty winter fled,
> I crost the Thames to take the cheerefull aire
> In open fields—the weather was so faire.

First, the whole matter is not worth all this solemne
circumstance to describe the tenth day of March; but if
he had left at the two first verses, it had bene inough. But
when he comes with two other verses to enlarge his
description, it is not only more than needes, but also very
ridiculous, for he makes wise as if he had not bene a man
learned in some of the mathematickes (by learned lore)
that he could not haue told that the x of March had fallen
in the spring of the yeare; which euery carter and also
euery child knoweth without any learning. Then also,
when he saith *Ver approcht and frosty winter fled*, though
it were a surplusage (because one season must needes
geue place to the other), yet doeth it well inough passe
without blame in the maker. These and a hundred more
of such faultie and impertinent speeches may yee finde
amongst vs vulgar Poets, when we be carelesse of our
doings.'

CHAP. XXIII.

WHAT IT IS THAT GENERALLY MAKES OUR SPEACH WELL PLEASING & COMMENDABLE, AND OF THAT WHICH THE LATINES CALL DECORUM.

In all things to vse decencie, is it onely that giueth euery thing his good grace & without which nothing in mans speach could seeme good or gracious, in so much as many times it makes a bewtifull figure fall into a deformitie, and on th'other side a vicious speach seeme pleasaunt and bewtifull: this decencie is therfore the line & leuell for al good makers to do their busines by. But herein resteth the difficultie, to know what this good grace is, & wherein it consisteth, for peraduenture it be easier to conceaue then to expresse. We wil therfore examine it to the bottome, & say that euery thing which pleaseth the mind or sences, & the mind by the sences as by meảns instrumentall, doth it for some amiable point or qualitie that is in it, which draweth them to a good liking and contentment with their proper obiects. But that cannot be if they discouer any illfauorednesse or disproportion to the partes apprehensiue: as for example, when a sound is either too loude or too low or otherwise confuse, the eare is ill affected; so is th'eye if the coulour be sad or not luminous and recreatiue, or the shape of a membred body without his due measures and simmetry; and the like of euery other sence in his proper function. These excesses or defectes or confusions and disorders in the sensible obiectes are deformities and vnseemely to the sence. In like sort the mynde for the things that be his mentall obiectes hath his good graces and his bad, whereof th'one contents him wonderous well, th'other displeaseth him continually, no more nor no lesse then ye see the discordes of musicke do to a well tuned eare. The Greekes call this good grace of

euery thing in his kinde τὸ πρέπον, the Latines *decorum*;
we in our vulgar call it by a scholasticall terme *decencie*;
our owne Saxon English terme is *seemelynesse*, that is to
say, for his good shape and vtter appearance well pleasing
the eye; we call it also *comelynesse*, for the delight it
bringeth comming towardes vs, and to that purpose may
be called *pleasant approche*. So as euery way seeking to
expresse this πρέπον of the Greekes and *decorum* of the
Latines, we are faine in our vulgar toung to borrow
the terme which our eye onely for his noble prerogatiue
ouer all the rest of the sences doth vsurpe, and to apply
the same to all good, comely, pleasant, and honest things,
euen to the spirituall obiectes of the mynde, which stand
no lesse in the due proportion of reason and discourse
than any other materiall thing doth in his sensible bewtie,
proportion, and comelynesse.

Now because his comelynesse resteth in the good conformitie of many things and their sundry circumstances,
with respect one to another, so as there be found a iust
correspondencie betweene them by this or that relation,
the Greekes call it *Analogie* or a conuenient proportion.
This louely conformitie, or proportion, or conueniencie,
betweene the sence and the sensible hath nature her selfe
first most carefully obserued in all her owne workes, then
also by kinde graft it in the appetites of euery creature
working by intelligence to couet and desire, and in their
actions to imitate & performe; and of man chiefly before
any other creature aswell in his speaches as in euery other
part of his behauiour. And this in generalitie and by an
vsuall terme is that which the Latines call *decorum*. So
albeit we before alleaged that all our figures be but trans-
gressions of our dayly speech, yet if they fall out decently
to the good liking of the mynde or eare and to the bewtifying of the matter or language, all is well; if indecently,
and to the eares and myndes misliking (be the figure of it

selfe neuer so commendable), all is amisse: the election is
the writers, the iudgement is the worlds, as theirs to whom
the reading apperteineth. But since the actions of man
with their circumstances be infinite, and the world likewise
replenished with many iudgements, it may be a question
who shal haue the determination of such controuersie as
may arise whether this or that action or speach be decent
or indecent: and verely it seemes to go all by discretion,
not perchaunce of euery one, but by a learned and experienced discretion, for otherwise seemes the *decorum* to
a weake and ignorant iudgement then it doth to one of
better knowledge and experience; which sheweth that it
resteth in the discerning part of the minde; so as he who
can make the best and most differences of things by
reasonable and wittie distinction is to be the fittest iudge
or sentencer of *decencie*. Such generally is the discreetest
man, particularly in any art the most skilfull and discreetest, and in all other things for the more part those
that be of much obseruation and greatest experience. The
case then standing that discretion must chiefly guide all
those businesse, since there be sundry sortes of discretion
all vnlike, euen as there be men of action or art, I see no
way so fit to enable a man truly to estimate of *decencie* as
example, by whose veritie we may deeme the differences
of things and their proportions, and by particular discussions come at length to sentence of it generally, and
also in our behauiours the more easily to put it in
execution. But by reason of the sundry circumstances
that mans affaires are, as it were, wrapt in, this *decencie*
comes to be very much alterable and subiect to varietie,
in[so]much as our speach asketh one maner of *decencie* in
respect of the person who speakes, another of his to whom
it is spoken, another of whom we speake, another of what
we speake, and in what place and time and to what purpose.
And as it is of speach, so of al other our behauiours. We

wil therefore set you down some few examples of euery circumstance how it alters the decencie of speach or action. And by these few shal ye be able to gather a number more to confirme and establish your iudgement by a perfit discretion.

This decencie, so farfoorth as apperteineth to the consideration of our art, resteth in writing, speech, and behauiour. But because writing is no more then the image or character of speech, they shall goe together in these our obseruations. And first wee wil sort you out diuers points, in which the wise and learned men of times past haue noted much decency or vndecencie, euery man according to his discretion, as it hath bene said afore; but wherein for the most part all discreete men doe generally agree, and varie not in opinion, whereof the examples I will geue you be worthie of remembrance; & though they brought with them no doctrine or institution at all, yet for the solace they may geue the readers, after such a rable of scholastical precepts which be tedious, these reports being of the nature historicall, they are to be embraced; but olde memories are very profitable to the mind, and serue as a glasse to looke vpon and behold the euents of time, and more exactly to skan the trueth of euery case that shall happen in the affaires of man; and many there be that haply doe not obserue euery particularitie in matters of decencie or vndecencie, and yet when the case is tolde them by another man they commonly geue the same sentence vpon it. But yet whosoeuer obserueth much shalbe counted the wisest and discreetest man, and whosoeuer spends all his life in his owne vaine actions and conceits, and obserues no mans else, he shal in the end prooue but a simple man. In which respect it is alwaies said, one man of experience is wiser than tenne learned men, because of his long and studious obseruation and often triall.

Of Ornament

And your decencies are of sundrie sorts, according to the many circumstances accompanying our writing, speech, or behauiour, so as in the very sound or voice of him that speaketh there is a decencie that becommeth, and an vndecencie that misbecommeth vs; which th'Emperor *Anthonine* marked well in the Orator *Philiseus*, who spake before him with so small and shrill a voice as the Emperor was greatly annoyed therewith, and, to make him shorten his tale, said, 'by thy beard thou shouldst be a man, but by thy voice a woman.'

[*Here Puttenham inserts a number of merry tales illustrative of his 'sundrie sorts of undecencies,' concluding with a story of a Herald of Charles V.*]

A Herald at armes sent by *Charles* the fifth Emperor to *Fraunces* the first French king, bringing him a message of defiance, and thinking to qualifie the bitternesse of his message with words pompous and magnificent for the kings honor, vsed much this terme *sacred Maiestie*, which was not vsually geuen to the French king, but to say for the most part *Sire*. The French king neither liking of his errant, nor yet of his pompous speech, said somewhat sharply, 'I pray thee, good fellow, clawe me not where I itch not with thy sacred maiestie, but goe to thy businesse, and tell thine errand in such termes as are decent betwixt enemies, for thy master is not my frend'; and turned him to a Prince of the bloud, who stoode by, saying, 'me thinks this fellow speakes like Bishop *Nicholas*,' for on Saint *Nicholas* night commonly the Scholars of the Countrey make them a Bishop, who, like a foolish boy, goeth about blessing and preaching with so childish termes as maketh the people laugh at his foolish counterfaite speeches.

And yet in speaking or writing of a Princes affaires & fortunes there is a certaine *Decorum*, that we may not vse the same termes in their busines as we might very wel doe in a meaner persons, the case being all one, such

reuerence is due to their estates. As for example, if an
Historiographer shal write of an Emperor or King, how
such a day hee ioyned battel with his enemie, and being
ouer-laide ranne out of the fielde, and tooke his heeles,
or put spurre to his horse and fled as fast as hee could,
the termes be not decent; but of a meane souldier or
captaine it were not vndecently spoken. And as one
who translating certaine bookes of *Virgils Æneidos* into
English meetre said that *Æneas* was fayne to trudge out
of Troy; which terme became better to be spoken of
a beggar, or of a rogue, or a lackey, for so wee vse to
say to such maner of people 'be **trudg**ing hence.'

Another Englishing this word of *Virgill, fato profugus*,
called *Æneas by fate a fugitiue*, which was vndecently
spoken, and not to the Authours intent in the same word:
for whom he studied by all means to auaunce aboue all
other men of the world for vertue and magnanimitie, he
meant not to make him a fugitiue. But by occasion of his
great distresses, and of the hardnesse of his destinies, he
would haue it appeare that *Æneas* was enforced to flie
out of Troy, and for many yeeres to be a romer and
a wanderer about the world both by land and sea, *fato
profugus*, and neuer to find any resting place till he came
into *Italy*; so as ye may euidently perceiue in this terme
fugitiue a notable indignity offred to that princely person,
and by th'other word (a wanderer) none indignitie at all,
but rather a terme of much loue and commiseration. The
same translatour when he came to these words: *Insignem
pietate virum, tot voluere casus tot adire labores compulit*,
hee turned it thus, 'what moued *Iuno* to tugge so great
a captaine as *Æneas*,' which word 'tugge' spoken in this
case is so vndecent as none other coulde haue bene deuised, and tooke his first originall from the cart, because
it signifieth the pull or draught of the oxen or horses, and
therefore the leathers that beare the chiefe stresse of the

Of Ornament

draught the cartars call them tugges, and so wee vse to say that shrewd boyes tugge each other by the eares, for pull.

Another of our vulgar makers spake as illfaringly in this verse written to the dispraise of a rich man and couetous, 'Thou hast a misers minde, thou hast a princes pelfe'—a lewde terme to be spoken of a princes treasure, which in no respect nor for any cause is to be called pelfe, though it were neuer so meane; for pelfe is properly the scrappes or shreds of taylors and skinners, which are accompted of so vile price as they be commonly cast out of dores or otherwise bestowed vpon base purposes, and carrieth not the like reason or decencie as when we say in reproch of a niggard, or vserer, or worldly couetous man that he setteth more by a little pelfe of the world than by his credit, or health, or conscience. For in comparison of these treasours, all the gold or siluer in the world may by a skornefull terme be called pelfe, & so ye see that the reason of the decencie holdeth not alike in both cases. Now let vs passe from these examples to treate of those that concerne the comelinesse and decencie of mans behauiour.

And some speech may be whan it is spoken very vndecent, and yet the same hauing afterward somewhat added to it may become prety and decent, as was the stowte worde vsed by a captaine in Fraunce, who sitting at the lower end of the Duke of *Guyses* table among many, the day after there had bene a great battaile foughten, the Duke finding that this captaine was not seene that day to do any thing in the field, taxed him priuily thus in al the hearings. 'Where were you, Sir, the day of the battaile, for I saw ye not?' The captaine answered promptly, 'where ye durst not haue bene': and the Duke began to kindle with the worde, which the Gentleman perceiuing, said spedily: 'I was that day among the carriages, where

your excellencie would not for a thousand crownes haue
bene seene.' Thus from vndecent it came by a wittie
reformation to be made decent againe.

The like hapned on a time at the Duke of Northumber-
landes bourd, where merry *Iohn Heywood* was allowed to
sit at the tables end. The Duke had a very noble and
honorable mynde alwayes to pay his debts well, and when
he lacked money would not stick to sell the greatest part
of his plate : so had he done few dayes before. *Heywood*,
being loth to call for his drinke so oft as he was dry,
turned his eye toward the cupbord and sayd 'I finde great
misse of your graces standing cups': the Duke, thinking he
had spoken it of some knowledge that his plate was lately
sold, said somewhat sharpely, 'why, Sir, will not those
cuppes serue as good a man as your selfe.' *Heywood*
readily replied : 'Yes if it please your grace, but I would
haue one of them stand still at myne elbow full of drinke,
that I might not be driuen to trouble your men so often
to call for it.' This pleasant and speedy reuers of the
former wordes holpe all the matter againe, whereupon
the Duke became very pleasaunt and dranke a bolle of
wine to *Heywood*, and bid a cup should alwayes be standing by him.

It were to busie a peece of worke for me to tell you of
all the parts of decencie and indecency which haue bene
obserued in the speaches of man & in his writings, and
this that I tell you is rather to solace your eares with
pretie conceits after a sort of long scholasticall preceptes
which may happen haue doubled them, rather then for
any other purpose of institution or doctrine, which to any
Courtier of experience is not necessarie in this behalfe.
And as they appear by the former examples to rest in
our speach and writing, so do the same by like proportion
consist in the whole behauiour of man, and that which
he doth well and commendably is euer decent, and the

contrary vndecent, not in euery mans iudgement alwayes one, but after their seuerall discretion and by circumstance diuersly, as by the next Chapter shalbe shewed.

CHAP. XXIV.

OF DECENCIE IN BEHAUIOUR, WHICH ALSO BELONGS TO
THE CONSIDERATION OF THE POET OR MAKER.

And there is a decency to be obserued in euery mans action & behauiour aswell as in his speach & writing, which some peraduenture would thinke impertinent to be treated of in this booke, where we do but informe the commendable fashions of language and stile: but that is otherwise, for the good maker or poet, who is in decent speach & good termes to describe all things, and with prayse or dispraise to report euery mans behauiour, ought to know the comelinesse of an action aswell as of a word, & thereby to direct himselfe both in praise & perswasion or any other point that perteines to the Oratours arte. Wherefore some examples we will set downe of this maner of decency in behauiour, leauing you for the rest to our booke which we haue written *de Decoro*, where ye shall see both partes handled more exactly. And this decencie of mans behauiour aswell as of his speach must also be deemed by discretion, in which regard the thing that may well become one man to do may not become another, and that which is seemely to be done in this place is not so seemely in that, and at such a time decent, but at another time vndecent, and in such a case and for such a purpose, and to this and that end, and by this and that euent, perusing all the circumstances with like consideration.

[*This chapter is devoted to anecdotes illustrative of 'decencie' in giving and taking, in manner of life at different ages*

[and in different classes, in choice of occasion, in apparel and fashion, in expressions of friendship, in sorrow and laughter, and in the bearing of the Prince and his Courtiers. Puttenham tells the story of the architect Dinocrates and Alexander the Great to illustrate the exception, when 'singularities' may have 'good liking and good successe.' The chapter concludes as follows.]

And with these examples I thinke sufficient to leaue, geuing you information of this one point, that all your figures Poeticall or Rhethoricall are but obseruations of strange speeches, and such as without any arte at al we should vse, & commonly do, euen by very nature without discipline; but more or lesse aptly and decently, or scarcely, or aboundantly, or of this or that kind of figure, & one of vs more then another, according to the disposition of our nature, constitution of the heart, & facilitie of each mans vtterance: so as we may conclude that nature her selfe suggesteth the figure in this or that forme, but arte aydeth the iudgement of his vse and application; which geues me occasion, finally and for a full conclusion to this whole treatise, to enforme you in the next chapter how art should be vsed in all respects, and specially in this behalfe of language, and when the naturall is more commendable then the artificiall, and contrariwise.

CHAP. XXV.

THAT THE GOOD POET OR MAKER OUGHT TO DISSEMBLE HIS ARTE, AND IN WHAT CASES THE ARTIFICIALL IS MORE COMMENDED THEN THE NATURALL, AND CONTRARIWISE.

And now (most excellent Queene) hauing largely said of Poets & Poesie, and about what matters they be employed; then of all the commended fourmes of Poemes;

Of Ornament

thirdly of metricall proportions, such as do appertaine to
our vulgar arte; and last of all set forth the poeticall
ornament consisting chiefly in the beautie and gallantnesse
of his language and stile, and so haue apparelled him
to our seeming, in all his gorgious habilliments, and
pulling him first from the carte to the schoole, and from
thence to the Court, and preferred him to your Maiesties
seruice, in that place of great honour and magnificence
to geue enterteinment to Princes, Ladies of honour, Gentlewomen, and Gentlemen, and by his many moodes of skill
to serue the many humors of men thither haunting and
resorting, some by way of solace, some of serious aduise,
and in matters aswell profitable as pleasant and honest:
Wee haue in our humble conceit sufficiently perfourmed
our promise or rather dutie to your Maiestie in the description of this arte, so alwaies as we leaue him not vnfurnisht
of one peece that best beseemes that place of any other,
and may serue as a principall good lesson for al good
makers to beare continually in mind in the vsage of this
science; which is, that being now lately become a Courtier
he shew not himself a craftsman, & merit to be disgraded
& with scorne sent back againe to the shop or other
place of his first facultie and calling, but that so wisely
& discreetly he behaue himselfe as he may worthily retaine
the credit of his place and profession of a very Courtier,
which is, in plaine termes, cunningly to be able to dissemble. But (if it please your Maiestie) may it not seeme
inough for a Courtier to know how to weare a fether,
and set his cappe a slaunt, his chaine *en écharpe*, a straight
buskin *al inglese*, a loose *alo Turquesque*, the cape *alla
Spaniola*, the breech *à la Françoise*, and by twentie maner
of new fashioned garments to disguise his body, and his
face with as many countenances, whereof it seemes there
be many that make a very arte, and studie who can
shew himselfe most fine, I will not say most foolish and

ridiculous? or perhaps rather that he could dissemble his
conceits as well as his countenances, so as he neuer
speake as he thinkes, or thinke as he speaks, and that
in any matter of importance his words and his meaning
very seldome meete: for so as I remember it was con- 5
cluded by vs setting foorth the figure *Allegoria*, which
therefore not impertinently we call the Courtier or figure
of faire semblant? Or is it not perchance more requisite
our courtly Poet do dissemble not onely his countenances
& conceits, but also all his ordinary actions of behauiour, 10
or the most part of them, whereby the better to winne
his purposes & good aduantages, as now & then to haue
a iourney or sicknesse in his sleeue, thereby to shake of
other importunities of greater consequence, as they vse
their pilgrimages in Fraunce, the Diet in Spaine, the 15
baines in Italy? and when a man is whole to faine himselfe
sicke to shunne the businesse in Court, to entertaine time
and ease at home, to salue offences without discredite,
to win purposes by mediation in absence, which their
presence would eyther impeach or not greatly preferre, 20
to harken after the popular opinions and speech, to entend
to their more priuate solaces, to practize more deepely
both at leasure & libertie, &, when any publique affaire
or other attempt & counsaile of theirs hath not receaued
good successe, to auoid therby the Princes present reproofe, 25
to coole their chollers by absence, to winne remorse by
lamentable reports, and reconciliation by friends intreatie?
Finally, by sequestring themselues for a time fro the Court,
to be able the freelier & cleerer to discerne the factions
and state of the Court and of al the world besides, no 30
lesse then doth the looker on or beholder of a game
better see into all points of auauntage, then the player
himselfe? and in dissembling of diseases, which I pray
you? for I haue obserued it in the Court of Fraunce,
not a burning feuer or a plurisie or a palsie, or the 35

hydropick and swelling gowte, or any other like disease, for if they be such as may be either easily discerned or quickly cured, they be ill to dissemble and doo halfe handsomly serue the turne.

But it must be either a dry dropsie, or a megrim, or letarge, or a fistule *in ano*, or some such other secret disease, as the common conuersant can hardly discouer, and the Phisition either not speedily heale, or not honestly bewray; of which infirmities the scoffing *Pasquil* wrote, *Vlcus vesicae, renum dolor, in pene scirrus.* Or, as I haue seene in diuers places, where many make themselues hart whole, when in deede they are full sicke, bearing it stoutly out to the hazard of their health, rather then they would be suspected of any lothsome infirmity, which might inhibit them from the Princes presence or enterteinment of the ladies. Or, as some other do, to beare a port of state & plentie when they haue neither penny nor possession, that they may not seeme to droope, and be reiected as vnworthy or insufficient for the greater seruices, or to be pitied for their pouertie, which they hold for a marueilous disgrace, as did the pocre Squire of Castile, who had rather dine with a sheepes head at home & drinke a cruse of water to it then to haue a good dinner giuen him by his friend who was nothing ignorant of his pouertie. Or, as others do, to make wise they be poore when they be riche, to shunne thereby the publicke charges and vocations, for men are not now a dayes (specially in states of *Oligarchie* as the most in our age) called somuch for their wisedome as for their wealth; also to auoyde enuie of neighbours or bountie in conuersation, for whosoeuer is reputed rich cannot without reproch but be either a lender or a spender. Or, as others do, to seeme very busie when they haue nothing to doo, and yet will make themselues so occupied and ouerladen in the Princes affaires, as it is a great matter to haue a couple of wordes

with them, when notwithstanding they lye sleeping on
their beds all an after noone, or sit solemnly at cardes
in their chambers, or enterteyning of the Dames, or laughing and gibing with their familiars foure houres by the
clock, whiles the poore suter desirous of his dispatch is
aunswered by some Secretarie or page, '*Il fault attendre,
Monsieur* is dispatching the kings businesse into Langue-
dock, Prouence, Piemont,'—a common phrase with the
Secretaries of France. Or, as I haue obserued in many
of the Princes Courts of Italie, to seeme idle when they
be earnestly occupied & entend to nothing but mischieuous
practizes, and do busily negotiat by coulor of otiation.
Or, as others of them that go ordinarily to Church and
neuer pray to winne an opinion of holinesse, or pray
still apace but neuer do good deede, and geue a begger
a penny and spend a pound on a harlot, to speake faire
to a mans face and foule behinde his backe, to set him
at his trencher and yet sit on his skirts, for so we vse to
say by a fayned friend, then also to be rough and churlish
in speach and apparance but inwardly affectionate and
fauouring, as I haue sene of the greatest podestates
and grauest iudges and Presidentes of Parliament in
Fraunce.

These & many such like disguisings do we find in
mans behauiour, & specially in the Courtiers of forraine
Countreyes, where in my youth I was brought vp, and
very well obserued their maner of life and conuersation,
for of mine owne Countrey I haue not made so great
experience. Which parts, neuerthelesse, we allow not
now in our English maker, because we haue geuen him
the name of an honest man, and not of an hypocrite: and
therefore leauing these manner of dissimulations to all
base-minded men, & of vile nature or misterie, we doe
allow our Courtly Poet to be a dissembler only in the
subtilties of his arte, that is, when he is most artificiall,

Of Ornament

so to disguise and cloake it as it may not appeare, nor seeme to proceede from him by any studie or trade of rules, but to be his naturall; nor so euidently to be descried, as euery ladde that reades him shall say he is a good scholler, but will rather haue him to know his arte well, and little to vse it.

And yet peraduenture in all points it may not be so taken, but in such onely as may discouer his grossenes or his ignorance by some schollerly affectation; which thing is very irkesome to all men of good trayning, and specially to Courtiers. And yet for all that our maker may not be in all cases restrayned, but that he may both vse and also manifest his arte to his great praise, and need no more be ashamed thereof than a shomaker to haue made a cleanly shoe, or a Carpenter to haue buylt a faire house. Therefore to discusse and make this point somewhat cleerer, to weete, where arte ought to appeare and where not, and when the naturall is more commendable than the artificiall in any humane action or workmanship, we wil examine it further by this distinction.

In some cases we say arte is an ayde and coadiutor to nature, and a furtherer of her actions to good effect, or peraduenture a meane to supply her wants, by renforcing the causes wherein shee is impotent and defectiue, as doth the arte of phisicke, by helping the naturall concoction, retention, distribution, expulsion, and other vertues, in a weake and vnhealthie bodie; or, as the good gardiner seasons his soyle by sundrie sorts of compost, as mucke or marle, clay or sande, and many times by bloud, or lees of oyle or wine, or stale, or perchaunce with more costly drugs, and waters his plants, and weedes his herbes or floures, and prunes his branches, and unleaues his boughes to let in the sunne, and twentie other waies cherisheth them and cureth their infirmities, and so makes that neuer or very seldome any of them miscarry, but bring foorth their flours and fruites in season. And in both these cases it is no smal praise for the Phisition & Gardiner to be called good and cunning artificers.

In another respect arte is not only an aide and coadiutor to nature in all her actions but an alterer of them, and in some sort a surmounter of her skill, so as by meanes of it her owne effects shall appeare more beautifull or straunge and miraculous, as in both cases before remembred. The Phisition by the cordials hee will geue his patient shall be able not onely to restore the decayed spirites of man and render him health, but also to prolong the terme of his life many yeares ouer and aboue the stint of his first and naturall constitution. And the Gardiner by his arte will not onely make an herbe, or flowr, or fruite, come forth in his season without impediment, but also will embellish the same in vertue, shape, odour, and taste, that nature of her selfe woulde neuer haue done, as to make single gillifloure, or marigold, or daisie, double, and the white rose redde, yellow, or carnation, a bitter mellon sweete, a sweete apple soure, a plumme or cherrie without a stone, a peare without core or kernell, a goord or coucumber like to a horne or any other figure he will: any of which things nature could not doe without mans help and arte. These actions also are most singular when they be most artificiall.

In another respect we say arte is neither an aider nor a surmounter but onely a bare immitatour of natures works, following and counterfeyting her actions and effects, as the Marmesot doth many countenances and gestures of man; of which sorte are the artes of painting and keruing, whereof one represents the naturall by light colour and shadow in the superficiall or flat, the other in a body massife expressing the full and emptie, euen, extant, rabbated, hollow, or whatsoeuer other figure and passion

Of Ornament

of quantitie. So also the Alchimist counterfeits gold, siluer, and all other mettals; the Lapidarie pearles and pretious stones by glasse and other substances falsified and sophisticate by arte. These men also be praised for
5 their craft, and their credit is nothing empayred to say that their conclusions and effects are very artificiall.

Finally, in another respect arte is, as it were, an encountrer and contrary to nature, producing effects neither like to hers, nor by participation with her operations, nor
10 by imitation of her paternes, but makes things and produceth effects altogether strange and diuerse, of such forme & qualitie (nature alwaies supplying stuffe) as she neuer would nor could haue done of her selfe, as the carpenter that builds a house, the ioyner that makes a table or
15 a bedstead, the tailor a garment, the Smith a locke or a key, and a number of like, in which case the workman gaineth reputation by his arte, and praise when it is best expressed & most apparant, & most studiously. Man also in all his actions that be not altogether naturall,
20 but are gotten by study, discipline, or exercise, as to daunce by measures, to sing by note, to play on the lute, and such like, it is a praise to be said an artificiall dauncer, singer, & player on instruments, because they be not exactly knowne or done, but by rules & precepts or
25 teaching of schoolemasters. But in such actions as be so naturall & proper to man, as he may become excellent therein without any arte or imitation at all (custome and exercise excepted, which are requisite to euery action not numbred among the vitall or animal), and wherein nature
30 should seeme to do amisse and man suffer reproch, to be found destitute of them: in those to shew himselfe rather artificiall then naturall were no lesse to be laughed at then for one that can see well inough to vse a paire of spectacles, or not to heare but by a trunke put to his eare,
35 nor feele without a paire of ennealed glooues, which things

in deede helpe an infirme sence, but annoy the perfit, and
therefore, shewing a disabilitie naturall, mooue rather to
scorne then commendation, and to pitie sooner then to
prayse. But what else is language, and vtterance, and
discourse, & persuasion, and argument in man, then the
vertues of a well constitute body and minde, little lesse
naturall then his very sensuall actions, sauing that the
one is perfited by nature at once, the other not without
exercise & iteration? Peraduenture also it wilbe granted
that a man sees better and discernes more brimly his collours and heares and feeles more exactly by vse and often
hearing and feeling and seing, & though it be better to
see with spectacles then not to see at all, yet is their
praise not egall nor in any mans iudgement comparable:
no more is that which a Poet makes by arte and precepts rather then by naturall instinct, and that which
he doth by long meditation rather then by a suddaine
inspiration, or with great pleasure and facillitie then
hardly and (as they are woont to say) in spite of Nature
or Minerua, then which nothing can be more irksome
or ridiculous.

And yet I am not ignorant that there be artes and
methodes both to speake and to perswade and also to
dispute, and by which the naturall is in some sorte relieued,
as th'eye by his spectacle. I say relieued in his imperfection, but not made more perfit then the naturall, in
which respect I call those artes of *Grammer*, *Logicke*, and
Rhetorick, not bare imitations, as the painter or keruers
craft and worke in a forraine subiect, viz. a liuely purtraite
in his table of wood, but by long and studious obseruation
rather a repetition or reminiscens naturall, reduced into
perfection, and made prompt by vse and exercise. And
so whatsoeuer a man speakes or perswades he doth it
not by imitation artificially, but by obseruation naturally
(though one follow another), because it is both the same

Of Ornament

and the like that nature doth suggest: but if a popingay speake, she doth it by imitation of mans voyce artificially and not naturally, being the like but not the same that nature doth suggest to man. But now because our maker or Poet is to play many parts and not one alone, as first to deuise his plat or subiect, then to fashion his poeme, thirdly to vse his metricall proportions, and last of all to vtter with pleasure and delight, which restes in his maner of language and stile as hath bene said, whereof the many moodes and straunge phrases are called figures, it is not altogether with him as with the crafts man, nor altogether otherwise then with the crafts man; for in that he vseth his metricall proportions by appointed and harmonicall measures and distaunces he is like the Carpenter or Ioyner, for, borrowing their tymber and stuffe of nature, they appoint and order it by art otherwise then nature would doe, and worke effects in apparance contrary to hers. Also in that which the Poet speakes or reports of another mans tale or doings, as *Homer* of *Priamus* or *Vlisses*, he is as the painter or keruer that worke by imitation and representation in a forrein subiect; in that he speakes figuratiuely, or argues subtillie, or perswades copiously and vehemently: he doth as the cunning gardiner that, vsing nature as a coadiutor, furders her conclusions, & many times makes her effectes more absolute and straunge. But for that in our maker or Poet which restes onely in deuise and issues from an excellent sharpe and quick inuention, holpen by a cleare and bright phantasie and imagination, he is not as the painter to counterfaite the naturall by the like effects and not the same, nor as the gardiner aiding nature to worke both the same and the like, nor as the Carpenter to worke effectes vtterly vnlike, but even as nature her selfe working by her owne peculiar vertue and proper instinct and not by example or meditation or exercise as all other artificers

do, is then most admired when he is most naturall and
least artificiall: and in the feates of his language and
vtterance, because they hold aswell of nature to be suggested and vttered as by arte to be polished and reformed.
Therefore shall our Poet receaue prayse for both, but
more by knowing of his arte then by vnseasonable vsing
it, and be more commended for his naturall eloquence
then for his artificiall, and more for his artificiall well
disembled then for the same ouermuch affected and
grossely or vndiscretly bewrayed, as many makers and
Oratours do.

The Conclusion.

And with this (my most gratious soueraigne Lady)
I make an end, humbly beseeching your pardon in that
I haue presumed to hold your eares so long annoyed with
a tedious trifle, so as, vnlesse it proceede more of your
owne Princely and naturall mansuetude then of my merite,
I feare greatly least you may thinck of me as the
Philosopher Plato did of *Aniceris*, an inhabitant of the
Citie *Cirene*, who, being in troth a very actiue and artificiall man in driuing of a Princes Charriot or Coche (as
your Maiestie might be), and knowing it himselfe well
enough, comming one day into Platos schoole, and hauing
heard him largely dispute in matters Philosophicall, 'I pray
you' (quoth he) 'geue me leaue also to say somewhat of
myne arte,' and in deede shewed so many trickes of his
cunning, how to lanche forth, and stay, and chaunge pace,
and turne and winde his Coche, this way and that way,
vphill, downe hill, and also in euen or rough ground, that
he made the whole assemblie wonder at him. Quoth
Plato, being a graue personage, 'verely in myne opinion
this man should be vtterly vnfit for any seruice of greater
importance then to driue a Coche. It is a great pitie that
so prettie a fellow had not occupied his braynes in studies

Of Ornament

of more consequence.' Now I pray God it be not thought so of me in describing the toyes of this our vulgar art. But when I consider how euery thing hath his estimation by oportunitie, and that it was but the studie of my yonger yeares, in which vanitie raigned; also that I write to the pleasure of a Lady and a most gratious Queene, and neither to Priestes nor to Prophetes or Philosophers; besides finding by experience that many times idlenesse is lesse harmefull then vnprofitable occupation, dayly seeing how these great aspiring mynds and ambitious heads of the world seriously searching to deale in matters of state be often times so busie and earnest that they were better be vnoccupied, and peraduenture altogether idle; I presume so much vpon your Maiesties most milde and gracious iudgement, howsoeuer you conceiue of myne abilitie to any better or greater seruice, that yet in this attempt ye wil allow of my loyall and good intent, alwayes endeuouring to do your Maiestie the best and greatest of those seruices I can.

SIR JOHN HARINGTON

(Preface to the Translation of *Orlando Furioso*)

1591

[The following essay, entitled *A Preface, or rather a Briefe Apologie of Poetrie, and of the Author and Translator*, is prefixed to Harington's translation of *Orlando Furioso* 'in English Heroicall verse,' 1591. It is reprinted from the copy in the British Museum.]

THE learned *Plutarch* in his Laconicall Apothegmes tels of a Sophister that made a long and tedious Oration in praise of *Hercules*, and expecting at the end thereof for some great thanks and applause of the hearers, a certaine Lacedemonian demanded him who had dis- praised *Hercules*. Me thinkes the like may be now said to me, taking vpon me the defence of Poesie, for surely if learning in generall were of that account among vs, as it ought to be among all men, and is among wise men, then should this my Apologie of Poesie (the verie first nurse and ancient grandmother of all learning) be as vaine and superfluous as was that Sophisters, because it might then be aunswered, and truly answered, that no man disgraced it. But sith we liue in such a time, in which nothing can escape the enuious tooth and backbiting tongue of an impure mouth, and wherein euerie blind corner hath a squint eyed *Zoilus* that can looke a right vpon no mans doings, (yea sure there be some that will not sticke to call *Hercules* himselfe a dastard, because forsooth he fought with a club and not at the rapyer and dagger), therefore I thinke no man of iudgement will iudge this my labour

A Brief Apology for Poetry

needlesse, in seeking to remoue away those slaunders that either the malice of those that loue it not, or the folly of those that vnderstand it not, hath deuised against it; for indeed as the old saying is, *Scientia non habet inimicum praeter ignorantem,* Knowledge hath no foe but the ignorant. But now because I make account I haue to deale with three sundrie kindes of reproouers, one of those that condemne all Poetrie, which (how strong head soeuer they haue) I count but a verie weake faction; another of those that allow Poetrie, but not this particular Poem, of which kind sure there cannot be manie; a third of those that can beare with the art, & like of the worke, but will finde fault with my not well handling of it, which they may not onely probably, but I doubt too truely do, being a thing as commonly done as said, that where the hedge is lowest, there doth euery man go ouer: therfore against these three I must arme me with the best defensiue weapons I can, and if I happen to giue a blow now and then in mine owne defence, and as good fensers vse to ward & strike at once, I must craue pardon of course, seing our law allowes that is done *se defendendo* and the law of nature teacheth *vim vi repellere.*

First therfore of Poetrie it selfe, for those few that generally disallow it might be sufficient to alledge those many that generally approue it, of which I could bring in such an army, not of souldiers, but of famous kings & captaines, as not only the sight, but the verie sound of them were able to vanquish and dismay the final forces of our aduersaries. For who would once dare to oppose himselfe against so many *Alexanders, Cæsars, Scipios* (to omit infinite other princes, both of former and later ages, and of forraine and nearer countries), that with fauour, with studie, with practise, with example, with honor, with giftes, with preferments, with great and magnificent cost, haue encoraged and aduanced Poets and Poetry? as witnes the huge Theaters and Amphitheaters, monuments of stupendious charge, made onely for Tragedies and Comedies, the workes of Poets, to be represented on: but all these aids and defences I leaue as superfluous. My cause I count so good, and the euidence so open, that I neither neede to vse the countenance of any great state to boulster it, nor the cunning of anie little lawyer to enforce it: my meaning is plainly and *bona fide*, confessing all the abuses that can truely be objected against some kind of Poets, to shew you what good vse there is of Poetrie. Neither do I suppose it to be greatly behoofull for this purpose to trouble you with the curious definitions of a Poet and Poesie, & with the subtill distinctions of their sundrie kinds; nor to dispute how high and supernatural the name of a Maker is, so christned in English by that vnknowne God-father that this last yeare saue one, viz. 1589, set forth a booke called the Art of English Poetrie: and least of all do I purpose to bestow any long time to argue whether *Plato*, *Zenophon*, and *Erasmus* writing fictions and Dialogues in prose may iustly be called Poets, or whether *Lucan* writing a story in verse be an historiographer, or whether Master *Faire* translating *Virgil*, Master *Golding* translating *Ouids* Metamorphosis, and my selfe in this worke that you see, be any more then versifiers, as the same *Ignoto* termeth all translators: for as for all, or the most part of such questions, I will refer you to Sir *Philip Sidneys* Apologie, who doth handle them right learnedly, or to the forenamed treatise where they are discoursed more largely, and where, as it were, a whole receit of Poetrie is prescribed, with so manie new named figures as would put me in great hope in this age to come would breed manie excellent Poets—saue for one obseruation that I gather out of the verie same book. For though the poore gentleman laboreth greatly to proue, or rather to make Poetrie an art, and reciteth as you may see, in the plurall number, some pluralities of patterns and parcels of his owne Poetrie, with diuerse pieces of Partheniads and hymnes in praise of the most praisworthy, yet whatsoeuer he would proue by all these, sure in my poore opinion he doth proue nothing more plainly then that which M. *Sidney* and all the learneder sort that haue written of it do pronounce, namely that it is a gift and not an art. I say he proueth it, because making himselfe and manie others so cunning in the art, yet he sheweth himselfe so slender a gift in it, deseruing to be commended as *Martiall* praiseth one that he compares to *Tully*.

Carmina quod scribis musis & Apolline nullo
Laudari debes: hoc Ciceronis habes.

But to come to the purpose, and to speake after the phrase of the common sort that terme all that is written in verse Poetrie, and, rather in scorne then in praise, bestow the name of a Poet on euerie base rymer and balladmaker, this I say of it, and I thinke I say truly, that there are many good lessons to be learned out of it, many good examples to be found in it, many good vses to be had of it, and that therfore it is not nor ought not to be despised by the wiser sort, but so to be studied and imployed as was intended by the first writers and deuisers thereof, which is to soften and polish the hard and rough dispositions of men, and make them capable of vertue and good discipline.

I cannot denie but to vs that are Christians, in respect of the high end of all, which is the health of our soules, not only Poetrie but al other studies of Philosophy are in a manner vaine and superfluous, yea (as the wise man saith) whatsoeuer is under the sunne is vanitie of vanities, and nothing but vanitie. But sith we liue with men & not with saints, and because few men can embrace this strict and stoicall diuinitie, or rather, indeed, for that the

holy scriptures, in which those high mysteries of our
saluation are contained, are a deepe & profound studie
and not subiect to euerie weake capacitie, no nor to the
highest wits and iudgments, except they be first illu-
minat by Gods spirit or instructed by his teachers and
preachers: therefore we do first read some other authors,
making them as it were a looking glasse to the eyes of our
minde, and then after we haue gathered more strength,
we enter into profounder studies of higher mysteries,
hauing first as it were enabled our eyes by long beholding
the sunne in a bason of water at last to looke vpon the
sunne it selfe. So we read how that great *Moses*, whose
learning and sanctitie is so renowned ouer all nations, was
first instructed in the learning of the Egyptians before he
came to that high contemplation of God and familiaritie
(as I may so terme it) with God. So the notable Prophet
Daniel was brought vp in the learning of the Chaldeans,
& made that the first step of his higher vocation to be
a Prophet. If then we may by the example of two such
special seruants of God spend some of our young yeares
in studies of humanitie, what better and more meete
studie is there for a young man then Poetrie? specially
Heroicall Poesie, that with her sweet statelinesse doth
erect the mind & lift it vp to the consideration of the
highest matters, and allureth them that of themselues
would otherwise loth them to take and swallow & digest
the holsome precepts of Philosophie, and many times
even of the true diuinitie. Wherefore *Plutarch*, hauing
written a whole treatise of the praise of *Homers* workes,
and another of reading Poets, doth begin this latter with
this comparison, that as men that are sickly and haue
weake stomakes or daintie tastes do many times thinke
that flesh most delicate to eate that is not flesh, and those
fishes that be not fish, so young men (saith he) do like
best that Philosophy that is not Philosophie, or that is not

deliuered as Philosophie, and such are the pleasant writings of learned Poets, that are the popular Philosophers and the popular diuines. Likewise *Tasso* in his excellent worke of Jerusalem *Liberata* likeneth Poetrie to the Phisicke that men giue vnto little children when they are sick; his verse is this in Italian, speaking to God with a pretie Prosopopeia,

> *Sai, che là corre il mondo, oue più versi*
> *Di sue dolcezze il lusinghier Parnaso,*
> *E che 'l vero condito in molli versi*
> *I più schiui allettando hà persuaso.*
> *Così à l'egro fanciul porgiamo aspersi*
> *Di soaue licor gli orli del vaso:*
> *Succhi amari ingannato intanto ei beue,*
> *E da l'inganno suo vita riceue.*

Thou knowst, the wanton worldlings euer runne
To sweete *Parnassus* fruites, how otherwhile
The truth well saw'st with pleasant verse hath wonne
Most squeamish stomakes with the sugred stile:
So the sicke child that Pocions all doth shunne
With comfets and with sugar we begile,
And cause him take a holsome sowre receit:
He drinkes, and saues his life with such deceit.

This is then that honest fraud in which (as *Plutarch* saith) he that is deceiued is wiser than he that is not deceiued, & he that doth deceiue is honester than he that doth not deceiue.

But briefly to answere to the chiefe objections: *Cornelius Agrippa*, a man of learning & authoritie not to be despised, maketh a bitter inuectiue against Poets and Poesie, and the summe of his reproofe of it is this (which is al that can with any probability be said against it), that it is a nurse of lies, a pleaser of fooles, a breeder of dangerous errors, and an inticer to wantonnes. I might here warne those that wil vrge this mans authoritie to the disgrace of Poetrie, to take heed (of what calling so euer they be) least with the same weapon that they thinke to giue Poetrie a blow they giue themselues a maime. For *Agrippa* taketh his pleasure of greater matters then Poetrie; I maruel how he durst do it, saue that I see he hath done it; he hath spared neither myters nor scepters. The courts of Princes where vertue is rewarded, iustice maintained, oppressions relieued, he cals them a Colledge of Giants, of Tyrants, of oppressors, warriors: the most noble sort of noble men he termeth cursed, bloodie, wicked, and sacrilegious persons. Noble men (and vs poore Gentlemen) that thinke to borrow praise of our auncestors deserts and good fame, he affirmed to be a race of the sturdier sort of knaues and lycencious liuers. Treasurers & other great officers of the common welth, with graue counsellors whose wise heads are the pillers of the state, he affirmeth generally to be robbers and peelers of the realme, and priuie traitors that sell their princes fauours and rob weldeseruing seruitors of their reward. I omit, as his *peccadilia*, how he nicknameth priests, saying for the most part they are hypocrites, lawyers, saying they are all theeues, phisicians, saying they are manie of them murtherers: so as I thinke it were a good motion, and would easily passe by the consent of the three estates, that this mans authoritie should be vtterly adnihilated, that dealeth so hardly and vniustly with all sorts of professions. But for the reiecting of his writings, I refer it to others that haue powre to do it, and to condemne him for a generall libeller; but for that he writeth against Poetrie, I meane to speake a word or two in refuting thereof.

And first for lying, I might if I list excuse it by the rule of *Poetica licentia*, and claime a priuiledge giuen to Poet[s], whose art is but an imitation (as *Aristotle* calleth it), & therefore are allowed to faine what they list, according to that old verse,

> *Iuridicis, Erebo, fisco, fas viuere [r]apto;*
> *Militibus, medicis, tortori, occidere ludo est;*
> *Mentiri astronomis, pictoribus atque poetis,*

which, because I count it without reason, I will English without rime.

> Lawyers, Hell, and the Checquer are allowed to liue on spoile;
> Souldiers, Phisicians, and Hangmen make a sport of murther;
> Astronomers, Painters, and Poets may lye by authoritie.

Thus you see that Poets may lye if they list *Cum priuelegio*. But what if they lye least of all other men? what if they lye not at all? then I thinke that great slaunder is verie vniustly raised upon them. For in my opinion they are said properly to lye that affirme that to be true that is false: and how other arts can free themselues from this blame, let them look that professe them: but Poets neuer affirming any for true, but presenting them to vs as fables and imitations, cannot lye though they would: and because this obiection of lyes is the chief, and that vpon which the rest be grounded, I wil stand the longer vpon the clearing thereof.

The ancient Poets haue indeed wrapped as it were in their writings diuers and sundry meanings, which they call the senses or mysteries thereof. First of all for the litterall sence (as it were the vtmost barke or ryne) they set downe in manner of an historie the acts and notable exploits of some persons worthy memorie: then in the same fiction, as a second rine and somewhat more fine, as it were nearer to the pith and marrow, they place the Morall sence profitable for the actiue life of man, approuing vertuous actions and condemning the contrarie. Manie times also vnder the selfesame words they comprehend some true vnderstanding of naturall Philosophie, or somtimes of politike gouernement, and now and then of diuinitie : and these same sences that comprehend so excellent knowledge we call the Allegorie, which *Plutarch* defineth to be when one thing is told, and by that another is vnderstood. Now let any man iudge if it be a matter of meane art or wit to containe in one historicall narration, either true or fained, so many, so diuerse, and so deepe conceits : but for making the matter more plaine I will alledge an example thereof.

Perseus sonne of Iupiter is fained by the Poets to haue slaine *Gorgon*, and, after that conquest atchieued, to haue flown vp to heauen. The Historicall sence is this, *Perseus* the sonne of *Iupiter*, by the participation of *Iupiters* vertues which were in him, or rather comming of the stock of one of the kings of Creet, or Athens so called, slew *Gorgon*, a tyrant in that countrey (*Gorgon* in Greeke signifieth earth), and was for his vertuous parts exalted by men vp vnto heauen. Morally it signifieth this much : *Perseus* a wise man, sonne of Iupiter, endewed with vertue from aboue, slayeth sinne and vice, a thing base & earthly signified by Gorgon, and so mounteth vp to the skie of vertue. It signifies in one kind of Allegorie thus much : the mind of man being gotten by God, and so the childe of God killing and vanquishing the earthlinesse of this Gorgonicall nature, ascendeth vp to the vnderstanding of heauenly things, of high things, of eternal things, in which contemplacion consisteth the perfection of man : this is the natural allegory, because man [is] one of the chiefe works of nature. It hath also a more high and heauenly Allegorie, that the heauenly nature, daughter of *Iupiter*, procuring with her continuall motion corruption and mortality in the inferiour bodies, seuered it selfe at last from these earthly bodies, and flew vp on high, and there remaineth for euer. It hath also another Theological Allegorie : that the angelicall nature, daughter of the most high God the creator of all things, killing & ouercomming all bodily substance, signified by *Gorgon*, ascended into heauen. The like infinite Allegories I could pike out of other Poeticall fictions, saue that I would auoid tediousnes. It sufficeth me therefore to note this, that the men of greatest learning and highest wit in the auncient times did of purpose conceale these deepe mysteries of learning, and, as it were, couer them with the vaile of fables and verse for sundrie causes: one cause was that they might not be rashly abused by prophane wits, in whom science is corrupted, like good wine in a bad vessell; another cause why they wrote in verse was conseruation of the memorie of their precepts, as we see yet the generall rules almost of euerie art, not so much as husbandrie, but they are oftner recited and better remembred in verse then in prose; another, and a principall cause of all, is to be able with one kinde of meate and one dish (as I may so call it) to feed diuers tastes. For the weaker capacities will feede themselues with the pleasantnes of the historie and sweetnes of the verse, some that haue stronger stomackes will as it were take a further taste of the Morall sence, a third sort, more high conceited then they, will digest the Allegorie: so as indeed it hath bene thought by men of verie good iudgement, such manner of Poeticall writing was an excellent way to preserue all kinde of learning from that corruption which now it is come to since they left that mysticall writing of verse. Now though I know the example and authoritie of *Aristotle* and *Plato* be still vrged against this, who took to themselues another manner of writing, first I may say indeed that lawes were made for poore men and not for Princes, for these two great Princes of Philosophie brake that former allowed manner of writing, yet *Plato* still preserued the fable, but refuseth the verse. *Aristotle*, though reiecting both, yet retained still a kind of obscuritie, in so much he aunswered *Alexander*, who

reproued him in a sort for publishing the sacred secrets
of Philosophie, that he had set forth his bookes in a sort,
and yet not set them forth, meaning that they were so
obscure that they would be vnderstood of few, except they
came to him for instructions, or else without they were
of verie good capacitie and studious of Philosophie. But
(as I say) *Plato* howsoeuer men would make him an enimie
of Poetrie (because he found indeed iust fault with the
abuses of some comicall Poets of his time, or some that
sought to set vp new and strange religions), yet you see he
kept still that principall part of Poetrie, which is fiction
and imitation; and as for the other part of Poetrie which
is verse, though he vsed it not, yet his master *Socrates* euen
in his old age wrote certaine verses, as *Plutarke* testifieth.

But because I haue named the two parts of Poetrie,
namely inuention or fiction and verse, let vs see how
well we can authorise the vse of both these. First for
fiction, against which, as I told before, many inueigh,
calling it by the foul name of lying, though notwithstanding, as I then said, it is farthest from it. *Demosthenes*,
the famous and renowned Orator, when he would persuade
the Athenians to warre against *Philip*, told them a solemne
tale how the wolues on a time sent Ambassadors to the
sheepe, offering them peace if they would deliuer vp the
dogs that kept their folds, with al that long circumstance
(needlesse to be repeated), by which he perswaded them
far more strongly then if he should haue told them in
plain termes that *Philip* sought to bereaue them of their
chief bulwarks & defences, to haue the better abilitie to
ouerthrow them. But what need we fetch an authority so
far of from heathen authors, that haue many neerer hand
both in time & in place? Bishop *Fisher*, a stout Prelate
(though I do not praise his Religion), when he was assaied
by king *Henrie* the eight for his good will and assent for
the suppression of Abbeys, the king alledging that he would

but take away their superfluities and let the substance stand still, or at least see it be conuerted to better and more godly vses, the graue Bishop answered it in this kind of Poeticall parable. He said there was an axe that, wanting a helue, came to a thicke and huge ouergrowne wood, & besought some of the great okes in that wood to spare him so much timber as to make him a handle or helue, promising that if he might finde that fauour he would in recompence thereof haue great regard in preseruing that wood, in pruning the braunches, in cutting away the vnprofitable and superfluous boughes, in paring away the bryers and thornes that were combersome to the fayre trees, and make it in fine a groue of great delight and pleasure: but when this same axe had obtained his suit, he so laid about him, & so pared away both timber and top and lop, that in short space of a woodland he made it a champion, and made her liberalitie the instrument of her ouerthrow.

Now though this Bishop had no very good successe with his parable, yet it was so farre from being counted a lye, that it was plainly seen soone after that the same axe did both hew down those woods by the roots & pared off him by the head, and was a peece of Prophecie as well as a peece of Poetrie: and indeed Prophets and Poets haue been thought to haue a great affinitie, as the name *Vates* in Latin doth testifie. But to come again to this maner of fiction or parable, the Prophet *Nathan*, reprouing King *Dauid* for his great sinne of adulterie and murther, doth he not come to him with a pretie parable of a poore man and his lambe that lay in his bosome and eate of his bread, and the rich man, that had whole flocks of his own, would needs take it from him? in which, as it is euident, it was but a parable, so it were vnreuerent and almost blasphemous to say it was a lye. But to goe higher, did not our Sauiour himselfe speake in parables? as that diuine

parable of the sower, that comfortable parable of the
Prodigall sonne, that dreadfull parable of *Diues* and
Lazarus, though I know of this last many of the fathers
hold that it is a storie indeed and no parable. But in the
rest it is manifest that he was all holinesse, all wisedome,
all truth, vsed parables, and euen such as discreet Poets
vse, where a good and honest and wholesome Allegorie
is hidden in a pleasaunt and pretie fiction; and therefore
for that part of Poetry of Imitation, I thinke no body will
make any question but it is not onely allowable, but godly
and commendable, if the Poets ill handling of it doe not
marre and peruert the good vse of it.

The other part of Poetrie, which is Verse, as it were the
clothing or ornament of it, hath many good vses. Of the
helpe of memorie I spake somewhat before; for the words
being couched together in due order, measure, and number,
one doth as it were bring on another, as my selfe haue often
proued, & so I thinke do many beside (though for my own
part I can rather bost of the marring a good memorie then
of hauing one), yet I have euer found that Verse is easier to
learne and farre better to preserue in memorie then is
prose. An other speciall grace in Verse is the forcible
manner of phrase, in which, if it be well made, it farre
excelleth loose speech or prose. A third is the pleasure
and sweetnesse to the eare which makes the discourse
pleasaunt vnto vs often time when the matter it selfe is
harsh and vnacceptable: for myne owne part I was neuer
yet so good a husband to take any delight to heare one of
my ploughmen tell how an acre of wheat must be fallowd
and twyfallowed, and how cold land should be burned, and
how fruitfull land must be well harrowed; but when I heare
one read *Virgill*, where he saith,

> *Saepe etiam steriles incendere profuit agros,*
> *Atque leuem stipulam crepitantibus vrere flammis.*

> *Siue inde occultas vires & pabula terrae*
> *Pinguia concipiunt: siue illis omne per ignem*
> *Excoquitur vitium, atque exsudat inutilis humor*, &c.,

and after,

> *Multum adeo, rastris glebas qui frangit inertes,*
> *Vimineasque trahit crates iuuat arua ;*

with many other lessons of homly husbandrie, but deliuered in so good Verse that me thinkes all that while I could find in my hart to driue the plough. But now for the authoritie of Verse, if it be not sufficient to say for them that the greatest Philosophers and grauest Senatours that euer were haue vsed them both in their speeches and in their writings, that precepts of all Arts haue been deliuered in them, that verse is as auncient a writing as prose, and indeed more auncient in respect that the oldest workes extant be verse, as *Orpheus, Linus, Hesiodus,* & others beyond memory of man or mention almost of history; if none of these will serue for the credit of it, yet let this serue that some part of the Scripture was written in verse, as the Psalmes of *Dauid,* & certain other songs of *Deborah,* of *Salomon,* & others, which the learnedest diuines do affirme to be verse and find that they are in meeter, though the rule of the Hebrew verse they agree not on. Suffiseth it me only to proue that by the authoritie of sacred Scriptures both parts of Poesie, inuention or imitation and verse, are allowable, & consequently that great obiection of lying is quite taken away & refuted.

Now the second obiection is pleasing of fooles. I haue already showed how it displeaseth not wise men. Now if it haue this vertue to, to please the fooles and ignorant, I would thinke this an article of prayse not of rebuke: wherefore I confesse that it pleaseth fooles, and so pleaseth them that, if they marke it and obserue it well, it will in time make them wise, for in verse is both goodnesse and

sweetnesse, Rubarb and Sugercandie, the pleasaunt and
the profitable. Wherefore, as *Horace* sayth, *Omne tulit
punctum qui miscuit vtile dulci,* he that can mingle the
sweete and the wholesome, the pleasaunt & the profitable, he is indeed an absolute good writer: and such be
Poets, if any be such; they present vnto vs a pretie tale,
able to keepe a childe from play, and an old man from the
chimnie corner; Or, as the same *Horace* sayth to a
couetous man,

> *Tantalus a labris sitiens fugientia captat
> Flumina. Quid rides? mutato nomine de te
> Fabula narratur.*

One tels a couetous man a tale of *Tantalus* that sits vp to
the chinne in water, and yet is plagued with thirst. This
signifies the selfe same man to whom the tale is told, that
wallows in plentie, and yet his miserable minde barres
him the vse of it: As my selfe knew, and I am sure many
remember, Iustice *Randall* of London, a man passing impotent in body but much more in mind, that, leauing behind
him a thousand pounds of gold in a chest ful of old boots
& shoes, yet was so miserable that at my Lord Maiors
dinner they say he would put vp a widgen for his supper,
& many a good meale he did take of his franke neighbour
the widdow *Penne.* But to come to the matter, this same
great sinne that is layd to Poetrie of pleasing fooles is
sufficiently answered if it be worth the answering.

Now for the breeding of errours which is the third Obiection, I see not why it should breed any when none is bound
to beleeue that they write, nor they looke not to haue their
fictions belieued in the litterall sence; and therefore he
that well examines whence errours spring shall finde the
writers of prose & not of verse the authors and main-
tainers of them; and this point I count so manifest as it
needes no proofe.

The last reproofe is lightnes & wantonnes. This is indeed an Obiection of some importaunce, sith, as Sir *Philip Sidney* confesseth, *Cupido* is crept euen into the Heroicall Poemes, & consequently makes that also subiect to this reproofe. I promised in the beginning not partially to prayse Poesie, but plainly and honestly to confesse that that might truely be obiected against it, and, if any thing may be, sure it is this lasciuiousnesse : yet this I will say, that of all kinde of Poesie the Heroicall is least infected therewith. The other kindes I will rather excuse then defende, though of all the kindes of Poesie it may bee sayd where any scurrilitie and lewdnesse is founde, there Poetry doth not abuse vs, but writers haue abused Poetrie.

And brieflie to examine all the kindes. First, the Tragicall is meerly free from it, as representing onely the cruell & lawlesse proceedings of Princes, mouing nothing but pitie or detestation. The Comicall, whatsoeuer foolish playmakers make it offend in this kind, yet being rightly vsed, it represents them so as to make the vice scorned and not embraced. The Satyrike is meerly free from it, as being wholly occupied in mannerly & couertly reprouing of all vices. The Elegie is still mourning. As for the Pastorall with the Sonnet or Epigramme, though many times they sauour of wantonnes and loue and toying, and, now and then breaking the rules of Poetry, go into plaine scurrilitie, yet euen the worst of them may be not ill applied, and are, I must confesse, too delightfull, in so much as *Martiall* saith,

Laudant illa, sed ista legunt,

and in another place,

Erubuit posuitque meum Lucrecia librum,
Sed coram Bruto; Brute recede; leget.

Lucrecia (by which he signifies any chast matron) will blush and be ashamed to read a lasciuious booke. But how? not except *Brutus* be by, that is if any graue man should see her read it. But if *Brutus* turne his backe, she will go to it agayne and read it all.

But to end this part of my Apologie, as I count and conclude Heroicall Poesie allowable and to be read and studied without all exception, so I may as boldly say that Tragedies well handled be a most worthy kinde of Poesie, that Comedies may make men see and shame at their owne faults, that the rest may be so written and so read as much pleasure and some profite may be gathered out of them. And for myne owne part, as *Scaliger* writeth of *Virgill*, so I beleeue that the reading of a good Heroicall Poeme may make a man both wiser and honester. And for Tragedies, to omit other famous Tragedies, that that was played at S. *Iohns* in Cambridge, of *Richard the* 3, would moue (I thinke) *Phalaris* the tyraunt, and terrifie all tyrannous minded men from following their foolish ambitious humors, seeing how his ambition made him kill his brother, his nephews, his wife, beside infinit others, and, last of all, after a short and troublesome raigne, to end his miserable life, and to haue his body harried after his death. Then, for Comedies, how full of harmeles myrth is our Cambridge *Pedantius*? and the Oxford *Bellum Grammaticale*? or, to speake of a London Comedie, how much good matter, yea and matter of state, is there in that Comedie cald the play of the Cards, in which it is showed how foure Parasiticall knaues robbe the foure principall vocations of the Realme, *videl.* the vocation of Souldiers, Schollers, Marchants, and Husbandmen? Of which Comedie I cannot forget the saying of a notable wise counseller that is now dead, who when some (to sing *Placebo*) aduised that it should be forbidden, because it was somewhat too plaine, and indeed as the old saying is, *sooth boord is no boord*, yet he would haue it allowed, adding it was fit that *They which doe that they should not should heare that they would not.* Finally, if

In Praise of Ariosto

Comedies may be so made as the beholders may be bettered by them, without all doubt all other sortes of Poetrie may bring their profit as they do bring delight, and if all, then much more the chiefe of all, which by all mens consent is the Heroicall. And thus much be sayd for Poesie.

Now for this Poeme of *Orlando Furioso*, which, as I haue heard, hath been disliked by some (though by few of any wit or iudgement), it followes that I say somewhat in defence thereof, which I will do the more moderately and coldly; by how much the paynes I haue taken, it (rising as you may see to a good volume) may make me seeme a more partiall prayser. Wherefore I will make choise of some other Poeme that is allowed and approued by all men, and a litle compare them together. And what worke can serue this turne so fitly as *Virgils Æneados*, whom aboue all other it seemeth my authour doth follow, as appeares both by his beginning and ending? The tone begins,

> *Arma virumque cano.*

The tother,

> *Le donne, i cauallier, l'arme, gli amori,*
> *Le cortesie, l'audaci imprese io canto.*

Virgill endes with the death of *Turnus*,

> *Vitaque cum gemitu fugit indignata sub vmbras.*

Ariosto ends with the death of *Rodomont*,

> *Bestemmiando fuggi l'alma sdegnosa,*
> *Che fu sì altera al mondo, e sì orgogliosa.*

Virgill extolled *Æneas* to please *Augustus*, of whose race he was thought to come; *Ariosto* prayeth *Rogero* to the honour of the house of *Este*: *Æneas* hath his *Dido* that retaineth him; *Rogero* hath his Alcina: finally, least I should note euery part, there is nothing of any speciall obseruation in *Virgill* but my author hath with great felicitie imitated it, so as whosoeuer wil allow *Virgil* must *ipso facto* (as they say) admit *Ariosto*. Now of what account *Virgil* is reckned, & worthily reckned, for auncient times witnesseth *August*. C. verse of him:

> *Ergone supremis potuit vox improba verbis*
> *Tam dirum mandare nefas?* &c.,

concluding thus,

> *Laudetur, placeat, vigeat, relegatur, ametur.*

This is a great prayse comming from so great a Prince. For later times, to omit *Scaliger*, whom I recited before, that affirmeth the reading of *Virgill* may make a man honest and vertuous, that excellent Italian Poet *Dant* professeth plainly that when he wandred out of the right way, meaning thereby when he liued fondly and looslie, *Virgill* was the first that made him looke into himselfe and reclaime himselfe from that same daungerous and lewd course. But what need we further witnes, do we not make our children read it commonly before they can vnderstand it, as a testimonie that we do generally approue it? And yet we see old men study it, as a proofe that they do specially admire it: so as one writes very pretily, that children do wade in *Virgill*, and yet strong men do swim in it.

Now to apply this to the prayse of myne author, as I sayd before so I say still, whatsoeuer is prayseworthy in *Virgill* is plentifully to be found in *Ariosto*, and some things that *Virgill* could not haue, for the ignoraunce of the age he liued in, you finde in my author, sprinckled ouer all his worke, as I will very briefly note and referre you for the rest to the booke it selfe. The deuout and Christen demeanor of Charlemayne in the 14 booke, with his prayer,

> *Non uoglia tua bontà per mio fallire,*
> *Che 'l tuo popol fedele habbia à patire.* &c.

In Praise of Ariosto

And in the beginning of the xvii booke, that would beseeme any pulpit,

Il giusto Dio, quando i peccati nostri.

But, aboue all, that in the xli. booke of the conuersion of
Rogero to the Christen Religion, where the Hermit speaketh to him, contayning in effect a full instruction against presumption and dispaire, which I haue set downe thus in English,

> Now (as I sayd) this wise that Hermit spoke,
> And part doth comfort him, and part doth checke;
> He blameth him that in that pleasaunt yoke
> He had so long defer'd to put his necke,
> But did to wrath his maker still prouoke,
> And did not come at his first call and becke,
> But still did hide himselfe away from God
> Vntill he saw him comming with his rod;
> Then did he comfort him and make him know
> That grace is near denyde to such as aske,
> As do the workemen in the Gospell show
> Receauing pay alike for diuers taske.

And so after, concluding,

> How to Christ he must impute
> The pardon of his sinnes, yet near the later
> He told him he must be baptisde in water.

These and infinit places full of Christen exhortation, doctrine, & example I could quote out of the booke, saue that I hasten to an ende, and it would be needles to those that will not read them in the booke it selfe, and superfluous to those that will: but most manifest it is & not to be denyed, that in this point my author is to be preferred before all the auncient Poets, in which are mentioned so many false Gods, and of them so many fowle deeds, their contentions, their adulteries, their incest, as were both obscenous in recitall and hurtful in example: though indeed those whom they termed Gods were certaine great Princes that committed such enormous faults, as great Princes in late ages (that loue still to be cald Gods of the earth) do often commit. But now it may be & is by some obiected that although he write Christianly in some places, yet in other some he is too lasciuious, as in that of the baudy Frier, in *Alcina* and *Rogeros* copulation, in *Anselmus* his *Giptian*, in *Richardetto* his metamorphosis, in mine hosts tale of Astolfo, & some few places beside. Alas, if this be a fault, pardon him this one fault, though I doubt too many of you (gentle readers) wil be to exorable in this point: yea, me thinks, I see some of you searching already for these places of the booke, and you are halfe offended that I haue not made some directions that you might finde out and read them immediatly. But I beseech you stay a while, and as the Italian sayth *Pian piano*, fayre and softly, & take this caueat with you, to read them as my author ment them, to breed detestation and not delectation. Remember, when you read of the old lecherous Frier, that a fornicator is one of the things that God hateth; when you read of *Alcina*, thinke how *Joseph* fled from his intising mistres; when you light on *Anselmus* tale, learne to loth bestly couetousnes; when on *Richardetto*, know that sweet meate wil haue sowre sawce; when on mine hostes tale, (if you will follow my counsell) turne ouer the leafe and let it alone, although euen that lewd tale may bring some men profit, and I haue heard that it is already (and perhaps not vnfitly) termed the comfort of cuckolds. But as I say, if this be a fault, then *Virgill* committed the same fault in *Dido* and *Æneas* intertainement, and if some will say he tels that mannerly and couertly, how will they excuse that where *Vulcan* was intreated by *Venus* to make an armour for *Æneas*?

> *Dixerat, & niueis hinc atque hinc diua lacertis*
> *Cunctantem amplexu molli fouet: ille repente*

*Accepit solitam flammam, notusque per artus
Intrauit calor.*

And a little after:

*Ea verba locutus
Optatos dedit amplexus, placitumque petiuit
Coniugis infusus gremio per membra soporem.*

I hope they that vnderstand Latin will confesse this is plaine enough, & yet with modest words & no obscenous phrase: and so I dare take vpon me that in all *Ariosto* (and yet I thinke is as much as three *Æneades*,) there is not a word of ribaldry or obscenousness; farther there is so meet a decorum in the persons of those that speake lasciuiously, as any of iudgement must needs allow. And therfore, though I rather craue pardon then prayse for him in this point, yet me thinkes I can smile at the finesse of some that will condemne him, and yet not onely allow but admire our *Chawcer*, who both in words & sence incurreth far more the reprehension of flat scurrilitie, as I could recite many places, not onely in his millers tale, but in the good wife of Bathes tale, & many more, in which onely the decorum he keepes is that that excuseth it and maketh it more tolerable.

But now whereas some will say *Ariosto* wanteth art, reducing all heroicall Poems vnto the methode of *Homer* and certain precepts of *Aristotle*, for Homer I say that that which was commendable in him to write in that age, the times being changed, would be thought otherwise now, as we see both in phrase & in fashions the world growes more curious each day then other. *Ouid* gaue precepts of making loue, and one was that one should spill wine on the boord & write his mistresse name therewith. This was a quaynt cast in that age; but he that should make loue so now, his loue would mocke him for his labour, and count him but a slouenly sutor. And if it be thus chaunged since *Ouids* time, much more since *Homers* time. And yet for *Ariostos* tales that many thinke vnartificially brought in, *Homer* him selfe hath the like: as in the Iliads the conference of *Glaucus* with *Diomedes* vpon some acts of *Bellerophon*, & in his Odysse as the discourse of the hog with *Vlysses*.

Further, for the name of the booke, which some carpe at because he called it *Orlando Furioso* rather then *Rogero*, in that he may also be defended by example of *Homer*, who, professing to write of *Achilles*, calleth his book Iliade of Troy, and not *Achillide*.

As for Aristotles rules, I take it he hath followed them verie strictly.

Briefly, *Aristotle* and the best censurers of Poesie would haue the *Epopeia*, that is the heroicall Poem, should ground on some historie, and take some short time in the same to bewtifie with his Poetrie: so doth mine Author take the storie of k. *Charls* the great, and doth not exceed a yeare or therabout in his whole work. Secondly, they hold that nothing should be fayned vtterly incredible. And sure *Ariosto* neither in his inchantments exceedeth credit (for who knowes not how strong the illusions of the deuill are?) neither in the miracles that *Altolfo* by the power of S. Iohn is fayned to do, since the Church holdeth that Prophetes both aliue and dead haue done mightie great miracles. Thirdly, they would haue an heroicall Poem (aswell as a Tragedie) to be full of *Peripet[e]ia*, which I interpret an agnition of some vnlooked for fortune either good or bad, and a sudden change thereof: of this what store there be the reader shall quickly find. As for apt similitudes, for passions well expressed of loue, of pitie, of hate, of wrath, a blind man may see, if he can but heare, that this worke is full of them.

There follows only two reproofs, which I rather interpret two peculiar praises of this writer aboue all that wrate before him in this kind. One, that he breaks off narrations verie abruptly, so as indeed a loose vnattentiue reader will hardly carrie away any part of the storie: but this doubtlesse is a point of great art, to draw a man with a continuall thirst to reade out the whole worke, and toward the end of the booke to close vp the diuerse matters briefly and clenly. If S. *Philip Sidney* had counted this a fault, he would not haue done so himselfe in his Arcadia. Another fault is, that he speaketh so much in his own person by digression, which they say also is against the rules of Poetrie, because neither *Homer* nor *Virgill* did it. Me thinks it is a sufficient defence to say, *Ariosto* doth it. Sure I am it is both delightfull and verie profitable, and an excellent breathing place for the reader, and euen as if a man walked in a faire long alley, to haue a seat or resting place here and there is easie and commodious: but if at the same seat were planted some excellent tree, that not onely with the shade shoulde keepe vs from the heat, but with some pleasant and right wholsom fruite should allay our thirst and comfort our stomacke, we would thinke it for the time a litle paradice. So are *Ariostos* morals and pretie digressions sprinkled through his long worke to the no lesse pleasure then profit of the reader. And thus much be spoken for defence of mine Author, which was the second part of my Apologie.

Now remaines the third part of it, in which I promised to speake somwhat for my selfe, which part, though it haue most need of an Apologie both large & substantiall, yet I will runne it ouer both shortly & slightly, because indeed the nature of the thing it self is such that the more one doth say, the lesse he shall seeme to say; and men are willinger to praise that in another man which himselfe shall debase then that which he shall seeme to maintaine. Certainly if I shold confesse or rather professe that my verse is vnartificiall, the stile rude, the phrase barbarous, the meeter vnpleasant, many more would beleeue it to be so, then would imagine that I thought them so: for this same φιλαυτία or self pleasing is so common a thing, as the more a man protests himself to be free from it, the more we wil charge him with it. Wherfore let me take thus much vpon me that admit it haue many of the fore-named imperfections, & many not named, yet as writing goes now a dayes it may passe among the rest; and as I haue heard a friend of mine (one verie iudicious in the bewtie of a woman) say of a Ladie whom he meant to praise, that she had a low forhead, a great nose, a wide mouth, a long visage, and yet all these put together she seemed to him a verie well fauoured woman, so I hope and I find alreadie some of my partiall friends that what seuerall imperfections soeuer they find in this translation, yet taking all together they allow it, or at least wise they reade it, which is a great argument of their liking.

Sir Thomas Moore, a man of great wisdome & learning, but yet a litle enclined (as good wits are many times) to scoffing, when one had brought him a booke of some shallow discourse, and preassed him very hard to haue his opinion of it, aduised the partie to put it into verse. The plaine meaning man in the best maner he could did so, and a twelue-month after at the least came with it to *Sir Thomas*, who, slightly perusing it, gaue it this *encomium*, that now there was rime in it, but afore it had neither rime nor reason. If any man had ment to serue me so, yet I haue preuented him; for sure I am he shall find rime in mine, and, if he be not voyd of reason, he shall find reason to. Though for the matter I can challenge no praise, hauing but borowed it; & for the verse I do challenge none, being a thing that euery body that neuer scarce bayted their horse at the Vniuersitie take vpon them to make. It is possible that, if I would haue employed that time that I haue done vpon this vpon some inuention of mine owne, I could haue by this made it haue

risen to a iust volume, &, if I wold, haue done, as many
spare not to do, flowne very high with stolen fethers.
But I had rather men should see and know that I borrow
all then that I steale any: and I would wish to be called
rather one of the worst translators then one of the meaner
makers, specially sith the Earle of Surrey and *Sir
Thomas Wiat*, that are yet called the first refiners of the
English tong, were both translators out of Italian. Now
for those that count it such a contemptible and trifling
matter to translate, I wil but say to them as *M. Bartholomew Clarke*, an excellent learned man, and a right good
translator, saith in maner of a pretie challenge, in his
Preface (as I remember) vpon the Courtier, which booke
he translated out of Italian into Latin. 'You,' saith he,
'that thinke it such a toy, lay aside my booke, and take
my author in your hand, and trie a leafe or such a matter,
and compare it with mine.' If I should say so, there
would be inow that would quickly put me down perhaps:
but doubtlesse he might boldly say it, for I thinke none
could haue mended him. But as our English prouerb
saith, many talke of *Robin Hood* that neuer shot in his bow,
and some correct *Magnificat* that know not *quid significat*.

For my part I will thanke them that will mend any thing
that I haue done amisse, nor I haue no such great conceipt
of that I haue done but that I thinke much in it is to be
mended; & hauing dealt plainly with some of my plaine
dealing frends, to tell me frankly what they heard spoken
of it (for indeed I suffred some part of the printed copies
to go among my frends, & some more perhaps went
against my will), I was told these in effect were the faults
were found with it. Some graue men misliked that I should
spend so much good time on such a trifling worke as
they deemed a Poeme to be. Some more nicely found
fault with so many two sillabled and three sillabled
rimes. Some (not vndeseruedly) reproued the fantasti-

calnes of my notes, in which they say I haue strained my
selfe to make mention of some of my kindred and frends
that might very well be left out. And one fault more
there is which I will tell my selfe, though many would
neuer find it, and that is, I haue cut short some of his
Cantos, in leauing out many staues of them, and sometimes
put the matter of two or three staues into one. To these
reproofes I shall pray you gentle and noble Readers
with patience heare my defence, and then I will end.

For the first reproofe, either it is alreadie excused or
it will neuer be excused; for I haue I thinke sufficiently
proued both the art to be allowable and this worke to be
commendable. Yet I will tell you an accident that happened vnto my selfe. When I was entred a pretie way
into the translation, about the seuenth booke, comming to
write that where *Melissa*, in the person of *Rogeros* Tutor,
comes and reproues *Rogero* in the 4 staffe,

> Was it for this that I in youth thee fed
> With marrow? &c.,

and againe,

> Is this a meanes or readie way you trow,
> That other worthie men haue trod before,
> A *Cæsar* or a *Scipio* to grow? &c.,

straight I began to thinke that my Tutor, a graue and
learned man, and one of a verie austere life, might say
to me in like sort, 'was it for this that I read *Aristotle*
and *Plato* to you, and instructed you so carefully both in
Greek & Latin, to haue you now become a translator of
Italian toyes?' But while I thought thus, I was aware
that it was no toy that could put such an honest and
seriouse consideration into my mind.

Now for them that find fault with polysyllable meeter,
me thinke they are like those that blame men for putting

An Answer to Critics

suger in their wine, and chide to bad about it, and say they marre all, but yet end with Gods blessing on their hearts. For indeed if I had knowne their diets, I could haue saued some of my cost, at least some of my paine: for when a verse ended with *ciuillitie*, I could easier, after the auncient maner of rime, haue made *see*, or *flee*, or *decree* to aunswer it, leauing the accent vpon the last syllable, then hunt after three syllabled wordes to answere it with *facillitie, gentillitie, tranquillitie, hostillitie, scurillitie, debillitie, agillitie, fragillitie, nobillitie, mobillitie*, which who mislike may tast lamp oyle with their eares. And as for two syllabled meeters, they be so approued in other languages, that the French call them the feminine rime, as the sweeter, & the one syllable the masculin. But in a word to answer this, & to make them for euer hold their peaces of this point, Sir *Philip Sidney*, not only vseth them, but affecteth them—*signifie, dignifie, shamed is, named is, blamed is, hide away, bide away*. Thogh if my many blotted papers that I haue made in this kind might affoord me authoritie to giue a rule of it, I would say that to part them with a one syllable meeter between them wold giue it best grace. For as men vse to sow with the hand and not with the whole sacke, so I would haue the eare fed but not cloyed with these pleasing and sweet falling meeters.

For the third reproofe about the notes, sure they were a worke (as I may so call it) of supererogation, and I would wish sometimes they had bin left out, & the rather if I be in such faire possibilitie to be thought a foole or fantasticall for my labour. True it is I added some notes to the end of euery canto, euen as if some of my frends and my selfe reading it together (and so it fell out indeed many times) had after debated vpon them what had bene most worthie consideration in them, and so oftimes immediatly I set it downe. And wheras I make mention here & there of some of mine owne frends & kin, I did it the rather because *Plutarke* in one place speaking of *Homer*, partly lamenteth, and partly blameth him, that writing so much as he did, yet in none of his works there was any mention made, or so much as inkling to be gathered, of what stocke he was, of what kindred, of what towne, nor, saue for his language, of what countrey. Excuse me then if I in a worke that may perhaps last longer then a better thing, and being not ashamed of my kindred, name them here and there to no mans offence, though I meant not to make euery body so far of my counsell why I did it, till I was told that some person of some reckening noted me of a litle vanitie for it: and thus much for that point.

For my omitting and abreuiating some things, either in matters impertinent to vs, or in some to tediouse flatteries of persons that we neuer heard of, if I haue done ill I craue pardon: for sure I did it for the best. But if anie being studious of the Italian would for his vnderstanding compare them, the first sixe bookes, saue a litle of the third, will stand him in steed. But yet I would not haue any man except that I should obserue his phrase so strictly as an interpreter, nor the matter so carefully as if it had bene a storie, in which to varie were as great a sinne as it were simplicitie in this to go word for word.

But now to conclude, I shall pray you all that haue troubled yourselues to read this my triple apologie to accept my labors and to excuse my errors, if with no other thing, at least with the name of youth (which commonly hath need of excuses); and so presuming this pardon to be graunted, we shall part good frends. Only let me intreate you in reading the booke ensuing not to do me that iniurie that a Potter did to Ariosto.

THOMAS NASH

(The Preface to Sidney's *Astrophel and Stella*)

1591

[This Preface appears in the first quarto edition of Sir Philip
 Sidney's *Astrophel and Stella*, printed at London by Thomas
 Newman in 1591. The text is taken from the copy in the
 British Museum.]

TEMPUS adest plausus; aurea pompa venit: so endes
the Sceane of Idiots, and enter *Astrophel* in pompe.
Gentlemen, that haue seene a thousand lines of folly, drawn
forth *ex vno puncto impudentiae*, & two famous Mountains
5 to goe to the conception of one Mouse, that haue had your
eares defned with the eccho of Fames brasen towres when
only they haue been toucht with a leaden pen, that haue
seene *Pan* sitting in his bower of delights & a number
of *Midasses* to admire his miserable hornepipes, let not
10 your surfeted sight, new come from such puppet play,
think scorne to turn aside into this Theater of pleasure,
for here you shal find a paper stage streud with pearle, an
artificial heau'n to ouershadow the fair frame, & christal
wals to encounter your curious eyes, while the tragicom-
15 mody of loue is performed by starlight. The chiefe Actor
here is *Melpomene*, whose dusky robes, dipt in the ynke of
teares, as yet seeme to drop when I view them neere. The
argument cruell chastitie, the Prologue hope, the Epilogue
dispaire; *videte, quaeso, et linguis animisque fauete*. And

here, peraduenture, my witles youth may be taxt with
a margent note of presumption for offering to put vp any
motion of applause in the behalfe of so excellent a Poet
(the least sillable of whose name sounded in the eares of
iudgment is able to giue the meanest line he writes a dowry
of immortality); yet those that obserue how iewels oftentimes com to their hands that know not their value, &
that the cockcombes of our days, like *Esop's* Cock, had
rather haue a Barly kernell wrapt vp in a Ballet then they
wil dig for the welth of wit in any ground that they know
not, I hope wil also hold me excused though I open the gate
to his glory & inuite idle eares to the admiration of his
melancholy.

Quid petitur sacris nisi tantum fama poetis?

Which although it be oftentimes imprisoned in Ladyes
casks & the president bookes of such as cannot see
without another man's spectacles, yet at length it breakes
foorth in spight of his keepers, and vseth some priuate
penne (in steed of a picklock) to procure his violent
enlargement. The Sunne for a time may maske his
golden head in a cloud, yet in the end the thicke vaile
doth vanish, and his embellished blandishment appeares.
Long hath *Astrophel* (Englands Sunne) withheld the
beames of his spirite from the common view of our darke
sence, and night hath houered ouer the gardens of the
nine Sisters, while *Ignis fatuus* and grosse fatty flames
(such as commonly arise out of Dunghilles) haue tooke
occasion, in the middest eclipse of his shining perfections,
to wander a broade with a wispe of paper at their tailes
like Hobgoblins, and leade men vp and downe in a circle
of absurditie a whole weeke, and neuer know where they
are. But now that cloude of sorrow is dissolued which
fierie Loue exhaled from his dewie haire, and affection
hath vnburthened the labouring streames of her wombe in

the lowe cesterne of his Graue; the night hath resigned
her iettie throne vnto *Lucifer*, and cleere daylight possesseth the skie that was dimmed; wherfore breake off your
daunce, you Fayries and Elues, and from the fieldes with
5 the torne carcases of your Timbrils, for your kingdome
is expired. Put out your rush candles, you Poets and
Rimers, and bequeath your crazed quaterzayns to the
Chaundlers; for loe, here he cometh that hath broke
your legs. *Apollo* hath resigned his Iuory Harp vnto
10 *Astrophel*, & he, like *Mercury*, must lull you a sleep with
his musicke. Sleepe *Argus*, sleep Ignorance, sleep Impudence, for *Mercury* hath *Io*, & onely *Io Pæan* belongeth
to *Astrophel*. Deare *Astrophel*, that in the ashes of thy
Loue liuest againe like the *Phœnix*, O might thy bodie (as
15 thy name) liue againe likewise here amongst vs! but the
earth, the mother of mortalitie, hath snacht thee too soone
into her chilled colde armes, and will not let thee by any
meanes be drawne from her deadly imbrace; and thy
diuine Soule, carried on an Angel's wings to heauen, is
20 installed in *Hermes* place, sole *prolocutor* to the Gods.
Therefore mayest thou neuer returne from the Elisian
fieldes like *Orpheus*; therefore must we euer mourne for
our *Orpheus*.

Fayne would a seconde spring of passion heere spend it
25 selfe on his sweet remembrance; but Religion, that
rebuketh prophane lamentation, drinkes in the riuers of
those dispaireful teares which languorous ruth hath out-
welled, & bids me looke back to the house of honor,
where from one and the selfe same root of renowne I shal
30 find many goodly branches deriued, & such as, with the
spreading increase of their vertues, may somewhat ouershadow the Griefe of his los. Amongst the which, fayre
sister of *Phœbus*, and eloquent secretary to the Muses, most
rare Countesse of *Pembroke*, thou art not to be omitted,
35 whom Artes doe adore as a second *Minerua*, and our Poets

extoll as the Patronesse of their inuention; for in thee the *Lesbian Sappho* with her lirick Harpe is disgraced, and the Laurel Garlande which thy Brother so brauely aduaunst on his Launce is still kept greene in the Temple of *Pallas*. Thou only sacrificest thy soule to contemplation, thou only entertainest emptie handed *Homer*, & keepest the springs of *Castalia* from being dryed vp. Learning, wisedom, beautie, and all other ornaments of Nobilitie whatsoeuer seeke to approue themselues in thy sight and get a further seale of felicity from the smiles of thy fauour:

O Joue digna viro ni Joue nata fores.

I feare I shall be counted a mercenary flatterer for mixing my thoughts with such figuratiue admiration, but generall report that surpasseth my praise condemneth my rhetoricke of dulnesse for so colde a commendation. Indeede, to say the truth, my stile is somewhat heauie gated, and cannot daunce, trip, and goe so liuely, with 'oh! my loue, ah! my loue, all my loues gone,' as other Sheepheards that haue beene fooles in the Morris time out of minde; nor hath my prose any skill to imitate the Almond leape verse, or sit tabring fiue yeres together nothing but 'to bee, to hee,' on a paper drum. Onely I can keepe pace with Grauesend barge, and care not if I haue water enough to lande my ship of fooles with the Tearme (the tyde I shoulde say). Now euery man is not of that minde; for some, to goe the lighter away, will take in their fraught of spangled feathers, golden Peebles, Straw, Reedes, Bulrushes, or anything, and then they beare out their sayles as proudly as if they were balisted with Bulbiefe. Others are so hardly bested for loading that they are faine to retaile the cinders of *Troy*, and the shiuers of broken trunchions, to fill vp their boate that else should goe empty; and if they haue but a pound

weight of good Merchandise, it shall be placed at the
poope, or pluckt in a thousand peeces to credit their
carriage. For my part, euery man as he likes, *mens
cuiusque is est quisque*. 'Tis as good to goe in cut-fingerd
Pumps as corke shooes, if one were Cornish diamonds on
his toes. To explain it by a more familiar example, an
Asse is no great statesman in the beastes common-wealth,
though he weare his eares *vpseuant muffe*, after the
Muscouy fashion, & hange the lip like a Capcase halfe
open, or look as demurely as a sixpenny browne loafe, for
he hath some imperfections that do keepe him from the
common Councel; yet of many he is deemed a very
vertuous member, and one of the honestest sort of men
that are. So that our opinion (as *Sextus Empiricus* affirmeth) giues the name of good or ill to euery thing.
Out of whose works (latelie translated into English for
the benefit of vnlearned writers) a man might collect a
whole booke of this argument, which no doubt woulde
proue a worthy commonwealth matter, and far better
than wits waxe karnell: much good worship haue the
Author.

Such is this golden age wherein we liue, and so re-
plenisht with golden asses of all sortes, that, if learning
had lost it selfe in a groue of Genealogies, wee neede doe
no more but sette an olde goose ouer halfe a dozen pottle
pots (which are as it were the egges of inuention), and wee
shall haue such a breede of bookes within a little while
after, as will fill all the world with the wilde fowle of good
wits. I can tell you this is a harder thing then making
golde of quick siluer, and will trouble you more then the
Morrall of *Æsop's* Glow-worme hath troubled our English
Apes, who, striuing to warme themselues with the flame
of the Philosopher's stone, haue spent all their wealth in
buying bellowes to blowe this false fyre. Gentlemen,
I feare I haue too much presumed on your idle leysure,

and beene too bold to stand talking all this while in an other mans doore; but now I will leaue you to suruey the pleasures of *Paphos*, and offer your smiles on the Aulters of *Venus*.

Yours in all desire to please,

THO: NASHE.

GABRIEL HARVEY

(From *Foure Letters*)

1592

[The following extracts are taken from Gabriel Harvey's Third
and Fourth Letters in *Fovre Letters | and certaine Sonnets: |
Especially touching Robert Greene, and | other parties, by him
abused: || But incidently of diuers excellent persons, | and some
matters of note. || To all courteous mindes, that will voutch-
safe the reading. || London | Imprinted by Iohn Wolfe, | 1592.*
(British Museum, C. 40. d. 14.)

This long-drawn invective against Greene was caused
by a slighting reference to Harvey's father in *A Quip for
an Upstart Courtier: or A Quaint Dispute between Velvet-
Breeches and Cloth-breeches*. Harvey deals with this 'Monarch
of Crossbiters and very Emperor of Shifters' in the second,
third, and fourth letters, which are chiefly remarkable for
their virulent abuse. In the *Second Letter*, addressed to
Christopher Bird of Walden, in which, among other vindic-
tive statements, he mentions Greene's death-bed charge to
Doll, he enters a plea for moderation. 'Oratours have
challenged a speciall Liberty, and Poets claimed an absolute
Licence; but no Liberty without boundes, nor any Licence
without limitation. Inuectiues by fauour haue bene too
bolde, and Satyres by vsurpation too presumptuous: I
ouerpasse *Archilochus, Aristophanes, Lucian, Iulian, Aretine,*
and that whole venemous and viperous brood of old &
new Raylers; euen *Tully* and *Horace* otherwhiles ouer-
reched; and I must needes say Mother Hubbard in heat
of choller, forgetting the pure sanguine of her sweete Feary
Queene, wilfully ouer-shott her malcontented selfe, as elsewhere I haue specified at larg, with the good leaue of
vnspotted friendshipp. Examples in some ages doe exceeding much hurt. *Salust* and *Clodius* learned of *Tully*

to frame artificiall Declamations and patheticall Inuectiues
against *Tully* himselfe, and other worthy members of that
most florishing State: if mother Hubbard, in the vaine of
Chawcer, happen to tel one Canicular tale, father *Elderton*
and his sonne *Greene*, in the vaine of *Skelton*, or *Scoggin*,
will counterfeit an hundred dogged Fables, Libles, Calum-
nies, Slaunders, Lies for the whetstone, what not, & most
currishly snarle & bite where they should most kindly
fawne and licke. Euery priuate excesse is daungerous;
but such publike enormities incredibly pernitious and in-
suportable: and who can tell what huge outrages might
amount of such quarrellous and tumultuous causes?']

FROM *THE THIRD LETTER*.

IT were pittie but wonderous wits (giue enemies their due)
shoulde become more woonderous by comparison;
conference maketh excellent things appeare more admirable: & I am so far from being a Saturnist by nature,
or a Stoick by discipline, that I can easily frame a certaine
pleasurable delight vnto my selfe, by ministring some
matter vnto them that now are faine to make something
of nothing, and wittily to plaie with their own shadowes.
It goeth somewhat hard in my harsh Legend, when the
father of Musicke must be mocked—not Tubulcain, as he
mistearmeth him, but Tuball, whom Genesis voutsafeth
honourable mention—and the Hexameter verse flouted:
whereof neither Homer in Greeke, nor Virgill in Latine
(how valorous Autors!), nor Alexander in conquest,
nor Augustus in maiesty (how puissant Princes!) were
ashamed, but accompted it the onely gallant trompet of
braue and Heroicall Actes. And I wis the English is
nothing too good to imitat the Greeke, or Latine, or other
eloquent Languages that honour the Hexameter as the
soueraigne of verses and the high Controwler of Rimes. If
I neuer deserue anye better remembraunce, let mee rather
be epitaphed, The Inuentour of the English Hexameter—

whome learned M. Stanihurst imitated in his Virgill, and
excellent Sir Phillip Sidney disdained not to follow in his
Arcadia & elsewhere—then be chronicled, The greene
maister of the Blacke Arte, or the founder of vgly oathes,
or the father of misbegotten *Infortunatus*, or the Scriuener
of Crosbiters, or, as one of his owne sectaries termed
him, the Patriarch of shifters. Happy man I, if these two
be my hainousest crimes and deadliest sinnes: To bee
the Inuentour of the English Hexameter, and to bee
orderlie clapt in the Fleete for the foresaide Letters;
where he that sawe me sawe me at Constantinople. . . .

I will not condemne or censure his [Greene's] works,
which I neuer did so much as superficially ouer-runne,
but as some fewe of them occursiuly presented themselues
in Stationers shops and some other houses of my acquaintaunce. But I pray God they haue not done more
harme by corruption of manners then good by quickening
of witte: and I would some Buyers had either more
Reason to discerne, or lesse Appetite to desire such
Nouels. The world is full inough of fooleries, though the
humor be not feasted with such luxurious and riotous
Pamphlets. Howe vnlike *Tullies* sweete Offices; or *Isocrates* pithy instructions; or *Plutarches* holesome Morrals;
or the delicate Dialogues of *Xenophon* and *Plato*; or the
sage Tragedies of *Sophocles* and *Euripides*; or the fine
Comedies of the dainetiest Atticke wittes; or other excellent monumentes of antiquity, neuer sufficientlie perused!
Yet the one as stale as oldest fashions; and what more
freshly current for awhile then the other? Euen *Guicciardines* siluer Historie and *Ariostos* golden Cantoes grow
out of request, & the Countesse of Pembrookes Arcadia
is not greene inough for queasie stomackes; but they
must haue *Greenes* Arcadia, and, I beleeue, most eagerlie
longed for *Greenes* Faerie Queene. . . .

Great and small things may in some proportion be compared together: and beholde as miserable a spectacle in their kinde. Flourishing Mr. *Greene* is most wofully faded: and whilest I am bemoaning his ouer-pittious decay, & discoursing the vsuall successe of such ranke wittes, Loe, all on the suddaine, his sworne brother, M. *Pierce Pennie-lesse* (still more paltery; but what remedy? we are already ouer shoes and must now goe through), Loe his inwardest companion, that tasted of the fatall herringe, cruelly pinched with want, vexed with discredite, tormented with other mens felicitie, and ouerwhelmed with his owne misery, in a raving and franticke moode most desperately exhibiteth his supplication to the Diuell. A strange title, an od wit, and a mad hooreson I warrant him: doubtles it wil proue some dainty deuise, queintly contriued by way of humble Supplication To the high and mighty Prince of Darkenesse; not Dunsically botched-vp, but right-formally conueied, according to the stile and tenour of Tarletons president, his famous play of the seauen Deadly sinnes. Which most dea[d]ly, but most liuely, playe I might haue seene in London, and was verie gently inuited thereunto at Oxford by *Tarleton* himselfe. Of whome I merrily demaunding which of the seauen was his owne deadlie sinne, he bluntly aunswered after this manner, 'By God, the sinne of other Gentlemen, Lechery.' 'Oh but that, M. Tarleton, is not your part vpon the stage; you are too blame that dissemble with the world & haue one part for your frends pleasure, an other for your owne.' 'I am somewhat of Doctor Pernes religion,' quoth he; and abruptlie tooke his leaue. Surely it must needes bee current in matter, and autentical in forme, that had first such a learned president, and is now pleasantlie interlaced with diuers new-founde phrases of the Tauerne, and patheticallie intermixt with sundry dolefull pageants of his own ruinous & beggerlie experience. For the poore

Tennement of his Purse (quoth himselfe, grammercy, good
Tarleton) hath bene the Diuels Dauncing schoole, anie
time this halfe yeare; and I pray God (quoth another) the
poore Tennement of his Heart hath not also beene the
Diuels Fencing Schoole twise as long. Particulars and
Circumstances are tedious, especially in sorrowfull and
forlorne causes. The summe of summes is, he tost his
imagination a thousand waies, and, I beleeue, searched
euery corner of his Grammer-schoole witte (for his margine
is as deepelie learned as *Fauste precor gelida*) to see if he
coulde finde anie meanes to relieue his estate; but all his
thoughtes and marginal notes consorted to his conclusion
that the worlde was vncharitable, and he ordained to be
miserable. It were cruelty to ad affliction to affliction:
what flinty Heart would not sigh, or rather melt, to heare
the bewailefull moane of that sobbing and groning Muse,
the daughter of most pregnant, but most wretched, *Niobe*?

> Why ist damnation to despaire, and die,
> When Life is my true happines disease?

And a little after:

> Diuines and dying men may talke of Hell:
> But in my Heart her seueral tormentes dwell.

And so foorth, most hideouslie, for the Text is much more
dolefull then the Glosse. And who woulde not be moued
with more pittifull compunction to heare the lamentable
Farewell,

> England, adieu! the soile that brought me foorth:
> Adieu vnkinde! where Skill is nothing worth:

then to read that profound Quotation,

> *Hei mihi, quam paucos haec mea dicta mouent?*

Which was thought Patheticall out of crie.

> Forgiue him God, although he curse his Birth,
> Since Miserie hath dawnted all his Mirth.

... Good sweete Oratour, be a deuine Poet indeede; and vse heauenly Eloquence indeede; and employ thy golden talent with amounting vsance indeede; and with heroicall Cantoes honour right Vertue, & braue valour indeede; as noble Sir Philip Sidney and gentle Maister Spencer haue done, with immortall Fame; and I will bestow more complements of rare amplifications vpon thee then euer any bestowed vppon them, or this Tounge euer affoorded, or any Aretinish mountaine of huge exaggerations can bring foorth. Right artificiality (whereat I once aimed to the vttermost power of my slender capacity) is not mad-brained, or ridiculous, or absurd, or blasphemous, or monstrous, but deepe conceited, but pleasurable, but delicate, but exquisite, but gratious, but admirable; not according to the fantasticall mould of *Aretine* or *Rabelays*, but according to the fine modell of *Orpheus, Homer, Pindarus*, & the excellentest wittes of Greece, and of the Lande that floweth with milke and hony. For what Festiuall Hymnes so diuinely dainty as the sweete Psalmes of King Dauid, royally translated by *Buchanan*? or what sage Gnomes so profoundly pithy as the wise Prouerbes of King Salomon, notably also translated. But how few Buchanans? Such liuely springes of streaming Eloquence & such right-Olympicall hilles of amountinge witte I cordially recommend to the deere Louers of the Muses; and namely to the professed Sonnes of the same, *Edmond Spencer, Richard Stanihurst, Abraham France, Thomas Watson, Samuell Daniell, Thomas Nash*, and the rest; whome I affectionately thancke for their studious endeuours, commendably employed in enriching & polishing their natiue Tongue, neuer so furnished or embellished as of late. For I dare not name the Honorabler Sonnes & Nobler Daughters of the sweetest & diuinest Muses that euer sang in English or other language, for feare of suspition of that which I abhorre;

and their owne most delectable and delicious Exercises
(the fine handy worke of excellent Nature and excellenter
Arte combined) speake incomparably more then I am able
briefly to insinuate. Gentle mindes and flourishing wittes
were infinitely to blame, if they should not also for curious
imitation propose vnto themselues such faire Types of
refined and engraced Eloquence. The right Noouice of pregnante and aspiring conceit wil not ouerskippe any precious
gemme of Inuention or any beautifull floure of Elocution
that may richly adorne or gallantly bedecke the trimme
garland of his budding stile. I speake generally to euery
springing wit, but more specially to a few, and at this
instante singularly to one, whom I salute with a hundred
blessings, and entreate with as many prayers, to loue them
that loue all good wittes, and hate none but the Diuell, and
his incarnate Impes, notoriously professed. I protest it was
not thy person that I any way disliked, but thy rash and
desperate proceeding against thy well-willers; which in
some had bene vnsufferable; in an youth was more
excusable; in a reformed youth is pardonable, and rather
matter of concordance then of aggrieuance.

FROM *THE FOURTH LETTER*.

Pregnant Rules auail much, but visible Examples amount
incredibly: Experience, the onely life of perfection, &
onely perfection of life. Whatsoeuer occasion causeth me
to be mistaken, as ouer-much addicted to Theory, without
respect of action (for that is one of the especiallest points,
which I am importuned to resolue), I neuer made account
of any study, meditation, conference, or Exercise that
importeth not effectual vse, & that aymeth not altogether
at action, as the singuler marke, whereat euery Arte &
euery vertue is to leuell. I loue Method, but honour
Practise: must I shew the difference? Either Arte is

obscure, or the quickest capacity dull and needeth Methode, as it were the bright Moone, to illuminate the darkesome night: but Practise is the bright Sun that shineth in the day, & the soueraigne Planet that gouerneth the world: as elsewhere I haue copiously declared. To excell, ther is no way but one: to marry studious Arte to diligent Exercise: but where they must be vnmarried, or diuorced, geue me rather Exercise without Arte then Arte without Exercise. Perfect vse worketh masteries, and disgraceth vnexperienced Arte. Examples are infinite, and dayly display themselues. A world without a Sunne; a Boddy without a Soule; Nature without Arte; Arte without Exercise—sory creatures. Singular practise the only singuler and admirable woorkeman of the world.

Must I dispatch the rest that is exacted? It is no fit place; and the least little wil seme too much. As in other thinges, so in Artes; formality doth well, but materiality worketh the feat. Were Artists as skillfull as Artes are powerfull, wonders might be atchieued by Arte emprooued; but they that vnderstand little write much; and they that know much write little. The vayne Peacocke with his gay coullours, and the prattling Parrat with his ignorant discourses (I am not to offend any but the Peacocke and the Parrat) haue garishly disguised the worthiest Artes, and deepely discredited the profoundest Artistes, to the pitifull defacement of the one and the shamefull preiudice of the other. *Rodolph Agricola, Philip Melancthon, Ludouike Viues, Peter Ramus,* and diuers excellent schollers haue earnestly complaned of Artes corrupted, and notably reformed many absurdities: but still corruption ingendreth one vermine or other, and still that pretious Trainement is miserably abused which should be the fountaine of skill, the roote of vertue, the seminary of gouernment, the foundation of all priuate and publike good.

The Methodist & Discourser might be more materiall;

the Theorist and Practitioner more formall: all fower
more effectuall: or how cometh it to passe that much more
is professed but much lesse perfourmed then in former
ages? especially in the Mathematikes, and in naturall
Magic, which being cunningly and extensiuely imployed
(after the manner of *Archimedes, Archytas, Apollonius,
Regiomontanus, Bacon, Cardan*, and such like industrious
Philosophers, the Secretaries of Art and Nature) might
wonderfully bestead the Commonwealth with many puissant engins and other commodious devises for warre and
peace. In actuall Experimentes and Polymechany, nothing
too profound: a superficiall slightnesse may seeme fine for
sheetes, but proueth good for nothinge: as in other businesse, so in learninge, as good neuer a whit, according to
the Prouerbe, as neuer the better: one perfect Mechanician
worth ten vnperfect Philosophers: an ignorant man lesse
shameth himselfe, lesse beguileth his frend, lesse disableth
the Common-wealth, then a putatiue Artiste: a whole
naturall wit more seruiceable, and more sufficient, then
a Demi-scholler, who presuming on that which he hath not
abateth the force of that which he hath. He must not
dreame of perfection that emproueth not the perfectest
Art with most perfect industrie. A snatch and away, with
Neoptolemus and the common sort of studentes, may please
a little, but profiteth nothing. It is the Body, not the
shadow, that dispatcheth the businesse. The flower
delighteth to-day, and fadeth to-morrow: the fruite edifieth
and endureth: the visard, the painted sheath, and such
terrible braueries, can best report their owne entertainment:
the peacock and the parrat haue good leaue to prancke
vppe themselues, and leysure inough to reuiue and repolish
their expired workes. 'What can last allwayes?' quoth the
neat Tayler, when his fine seames began to cracke their
credite at the first drawing-on. I appeale to Poules Churchyard, whether lines be like vnto seames: and whether

the Deft writer be as sure a workman as the neat Tayler.
There may be a fault in the Reader, aswell as in the weauer:
but euery manne contente himselfe to beare the burthen
of his owne faultes; and, good sweete Autors, infourme your
selues before you vndertake to instruct other...

God helpe, when Ignorance and want of Experience,
vsurping the chayre of scrupulous and rigorous Iudgement, will in a fantasticall Imagination, or percase in
a melancholy moode, presume farther, by infinite degrees,
then the learnedest men in a ciuill Common-wealth, or the
sagest counsellours in a Princes Court. Our new-new
writers, the Loadstones of the Presse, are wonderfully
beholdinge to the Asse; in a manner the only Autor,
which they alledge. The world was euer full inough of
fools, but neuer so full of Asses in print; the very Elephant,
a great Asse; the Camell, a huge Asse; the Beare,
a monstrous Asse; the Horse, an absurd Asse; the Fox
himselfe, a little Asse, or, for variety, an Ape: who not an
Asse or an Ape in good plaine English, that chanceth to
come in the wise Asse-makers & mighty Ape-dubbers
way? They are fine men, & haue many sweete phrases:
it is my simplicity that I am so slenderly acquainted with
that dainty stile, the only new fashion of current Eloquence
in Esse, far surpassing the stale vein of *Demosthenes* or
Tully, Iewel or *Harding, Whitgift* or *Cartwright, Sidney* or
Spencer. But I could wish Ignorance would fauour it
selfe: & it were not amisse that want of Experience should
be content to be a little modest or somewhat quiet: & both
enforce les occasion to be termed, as they will needes
notoriously proclaime themselues, as it were, with a publike 'Oh-is,' or a generall *Nouerint vniuersi per praesentes*.
For if any thing indeede be a right Asse in print, it is the
one; and if any thing indeede be a right Calfe in print, it
is the other: Ignorance, the famousest Asse; and want of
Experience, the notablest Calfe in the world.

THOMAS NASH

(From *Strange Newes*, or *Foure Letters Confuted*)

1592

[These extracts are taken from *Strange Newes of the intercepting certaine Letters, and a Conuoy of Verses, as they were going Priuilie to victual the Low Countries*, London. ? 1592. The pamphlet is otherwise known, from the headline of each page, as *Foure Letters Confuted*. The text is that of the British Museum copy (96. b. 16).]

O HEATHENISTS and Pagan Hexamiters, come thy waies down from thy *Doctourship*, & learne thy Primer of Poetry ouer again; for certainly thy pen is in state of a Reprobate with all men of iudgement and reckoning. . . .

5 *The tickling and stirring inuectiue vaine, the puffing and swelling Satiricall spirit* came vpon him, as it came on *Coppinger* and *Arthington*, when they mounted into the pease-cart in Cheapeside and preacht. Needes hee must cast vp certayne crude humours of English Hexameter
10 Verses that lay vppon his stomacke; a Noble-man stoode in his way as he was vomiting, and from top to toe he all to berayd him with *Tuscanisme*. . . .

Tubalcan, alias Tuball, first founder of Farriers Hall, heere is a great complaint made, that *Vtriusque Academiae*
15 *Robertus Greene* hath mockt thee, because hee saide that as thou wert the first inuenter of Musicke, so *Gabriell Howliglasse* was the first inuenter of English Hexameter

verses. *Quid respondes?* canst thou brooke it; yea or
no? Is it any treason to thy well tuned hammers to say
they begat so renowmed a childe as Musicke? Neither
thy hammers nor thou I knowe, if they were put to their
booke oaths, will euer say it.

The Hexamiter verse I graunt to be a Gentleman of an
aunceint house (so is many an english begger); yet this
Clyme of ours hee cannot thriue in. Our speech is too
craggy for him to set his plough in; hee goes twitching
and hopping in our language like a man running vpon
quagmiers, vp the hill in one Syllable, and downe the dale
in another, retaining no part of that stately smooth gate
which he vaunts himselfe with amongst the Greeks and
Latins.

Homer and Virgil, two valorous Authors, yet were they
neuer knighted, they wrote in Hexameter Verses: *Ergo*,
Chaucer and *Spencer*, the *Homer* and *Virgil* of England,
were farre ouerseene that they wrote not all their Poems
in Hexamiter verses also. In many Countries veluet and
Satten is a commoner weare than cloth amongst vs: *Ergo*
wee must leaue wearing of cloth, and goe euerie one in
veluet and satten, because other Countries vse so.

The Text will not beare it, good *Gilgilis Hobberdehoy*.
Our english tongue is nothing too good, but too bad *to imitate
the Greeke and Latine*.

Master *Stannyhurst* (though otherwise learned) trod
a foule, lumbring, boystrous, wallowing, measure in his
translation of *Virgil*. He had neuer been praisd by
Gabriel for his labour, if therein hee had not bin so
famously absurd. . . .

Let Maister *Butler* of Cambridge his testimoniall end
this controuersie, who at that time that thy ioyes were in
the Fleeting, and thou crying for the Lords sake out at an
iron window, in a lane not farre from Ludgate hill, questiond some of his companions verie inquisitiuelie that were

newlie come from London, what nouelties they brought home with them. Amongst the rest he broke into this Hexamiter interrogatory very abruptlie.

But ah! what newes do you heare of that good Gabriel
huffe snuffe,
Knowne to the world for a foole, and clapt in the Fleete
for a Rimer?

... Thy Hexameter Verses, or thy hue and cry after *a person as cleare as Christall*, I do not so deeply commend, for al *Maister* Spencer *long* since imbrast it with an ouerlouing sonnet.

Why should friends dissemble one with another: they are very vgly and artlesse. You will neuer leaue your olde trickes of drawing M. *Spencer* into euerie pybald thing you do. If euer he praisd thee, it was because he had pickt a fine vaine foole out of thee, and he would keepe thee still by flattring thee, til such time as he had brought thee into that extreame loue with thy selfe, that thou shouldst run mad with the conceit, and so be scorned of all men. ...

As for *Flores Poetarum*, they are flowers that yet I neuer smelt too. Ile pawne my hand to a halfepenny, I haue readd more good Poets thorough than thou euer hardst off.

The floures of your *Foure Letters* it may be I haue ouerlookt more narrowlie, and done my best deuoire to assemble them together into patheticall posie, which I will here present to Maister Orator Edge for a Newyeares gift, leauing them to his *wordie* discretion to be censured whether they be currant in inkehornisme or no: *Conscious mind; canicular tales; egregious an argument*—when as egregious is neuer vsed in English but in the extreame ill part; *Ingenuitie; Iouiall mind; valorous Authors; inckehorne aduentures; inckehorne pads; putatiue opinions;*

putatiue artists; energeticall persuasions; Rascallitie; materi-
allitie; artificiallitie; Fantasticallitie; diuine Entelechy; loud
mentery; deceitfull perfidy; addicted to Theory; the worlds
great Incendiarie; sirenized furies; soueraigntie immense;
abundant Cauteles; cautelous and aduentrous; cordiall 5
liquor; Catilinaries and Phillipicks; perfunctorie discourses;
Dauids sweetnes olimpique; The Idee; high and deepe Abisse
of excellence; the only Vnicorne of the Muses; the Aretinish
mountaine of huge exaggerations; the gratious law of Amnesty;
amicable termes; amicable end; effectuate; addoulce his 10
melodie; Mag[ic] polimechany; extensiuely emploid; precious
Traynment; Nouellets; Notorietie; negotiation; mechanician.

Nor are these all, for euerie third line hath some of this
ouer-rackt absonisme. Nor do I altogether scum off all
these as the new ingendred fome of the English, but 15
allowe some of them for a neede to fill vp a verse; as
Traynment, and one or two wordes more, which the
libertie of prose might well haue spar'd. In a verse,
when a worde of three sillables cannot thrust in but
sidelings, to ioynt him euen, we are oftentimes faine to 20
borrowe some lesser quarry of elocution from the Latine,
alwaies retaining this for a principle, that a leake of indesinence, as a leake in a shippe, must needly bee stopt
with what matter soeuer.

Chaucers authoritie I am certaine shal be alleadgd for 25
a many of these balductums. Had *Chaucer* liu'd to this
age, I am verily perswaded hee would haue discarded the
tone halfe of the harsher sort of them.

They were the Oouse which ouerflowing barbarisme,
withdrawne to her Scottish Northren chanell, had left 30
behind her. Art, like yong grasse in the spring of *Chaucers*
florishing, was glad to peepe vp through any slime of
corruption, to be beholding to she car'd not whome for
apparaile, trauailing in those colde countries. There is
no reason that shee, a banisht Queene into this barraine 35

soile, hauing monarchizd it so long amongst the Greeks
and Romanes, should (although warres furie had humbled
her to some extremitie) still be constrained, when she had
recouerd her state, to weare the robes of aduersitie [&] iet
it in her old rags, when she is wedded to new prosperitie.
Vtere moribus praeteritis, saith *Caius Caesar* in *Aulus Gellius,
loquere verbis praesentibus.* . . .

Wherein I haue borrowed from *Greene* or *Tarlton,* that
I should thanke them for all I haue? Is my stile like
Greenes, or my ieasts like *Tarltons*? Do I talke of any
counterfeit birds, or hearbs, or stones, or rake vp any
new-found poetry from vnder the wals of *Troy*? If I do,
trip mee with it; but I doe not, therefore Ile be so saucy
as trip you with the grand lie. Ware stumbling of whet-
stones in the darke there, my maisters.

This I will proudly boast (yet am I nothing a kindred
to the three brothers) that the vaine which I haue (be it
a *median* vaine, or a madde vaine) is of my owne begetting,
and cals no man father in England but my selfe, neyther
Euphues, nor *Tarlton,* nor *Greene.* Not *Tarlton* nor *Greene*
but haue beene contented to let my simple iudgement
ouerrule them in some matters of wit. *Euphues* I readd
when I was a little ape in Cambridge, and then I thought
it was *Ipse ille*; it may be excellent good still for ought
I know, for I lookt not on it this ten yeare: but to imitate
it I abhorre, otherwise than it imitates *Plutarch, Ouid,* and
the choisest Latine Authors.

If you be auisde I tooke *shortest vowels and longest mutes*
in the beginning of my booke as suspitious of being accessarie to the making of a Sonnet wherto Maister *Christopher
Birds* name is set, there I saide that you mute forth many
such phrases in the course of your booke which I would
point at as I past by. Heere I am as good as my word,
for I note that thou, beeing afraide of beraying thy selfe
with writing, *wouldest faine bee a mute,* when it is too late

to repent. Againe, thou reuiest on vs, and saist *that mutes are coursed and vowels haunted.* Thou art no mute, yet shalt thou be haunted and coursed to the full. I will neuer leaue thee as long as I am able to lift a pen.

Whether I seeke to bee counted a terrible bulbegger or no, Ile baite thee worse than a bull, so that the[n] thou shalt desire some body on thy knees to helpe thee with letters of commendation to *Bull* the hangman, that he may dispatch thee out of the way before more affliction come vpon thee.

GABRIEL HARVEY

(From *Pierce's Supererogation* and *A New Letter of Notable Contents*)

1593

[The text of I, including the 'Aduertisement for Pap-hatchet,' is taken from *Pierce's Supererogation | or | A New Prayse of the | Old Asse. || A Preparatiue to certaine Discourses, intituled | Nashes S. Fame*, printed at London by John Wolfe in 1593 (British Museum C. 40. d. 9). Gabriel Harvey's preface to the book is dated July 16, 1593. The text of II will be found in Harvey's *New Letter of | notable contents | with a straunge Sonet, intituled | Gorgon, | Or the wonderfull years*, also printed by Wolfe in 1593. The passage is part of the Letter 'To my loving friend, John Wolfe, Printer to the Cittie' (British Museum C. 40. d. 10).]

I.

THERE was a time when I floted in a sea of encountring waues, and deuoured many famous confutations with an eager and insatiable appetite; especially Aristotle against Plato and the old Philosophers, diuers excellent Platonistes,
5 indued with rare & diuine wittes (of whome elsewhere at large); Iustinus Martyr, Philoponus, Valla, Viues, Ramus, against Aristotle; oh, but the great maister of the schooles and high Chauncellour of Vniuersities could not want pregnant defence, Perionius, Gallandius, Carpentarius,
10 Sceggius, Lieblerus, against Ramus; what? hath the royall Professour of Eloquence and Philosophy no fauourites? Talaeus, Ossatus, Freigius, Minos, Rodingus,

Scribonius, for Ramus against them; and so foorth, in
that hott contradictory course of Logique and Philosophy.
But alas, silly men, simple Aristotle, more simple Ramus,
most simple the rest, either ye neuer knew what a sharpe-
edged & cutting Confutation meant, or the date of your
stale oppositions is expired, and a new-found land of confuting commodities discouered by this braue Columbus
of tearmes and this onely marchant venturer of quarrels,
that detecteth new Indies of Inuention & hath the winds
of Æolus at commaundement. Happy you flourishinge
youthes that follow his incomparable learned steps, and
vnhappy we old Dunses that wanted such a worthy
President of all nimble and liuely dexterities! What
should I appeale infinite other to their perpetuall shame,
or summon such and such to their foule disgrace? Erasmus
in Latine and Sir Thomas More in English were supposed
fine and pleasant Confuters in their time, and were accordingly embraced of the forwardest and trimmest wittes;
but alacke how vnlike this dainty minion! Agrippa was
reputed a gyant in confutation, a demi-god in omni-
sufficiency of knowledge, a diuell in the practise of horrible
Artes: oh, but Agrippa was an vrcheon, Copernicus a
shrimpe, Cardan a puppy, Scaliger a baby, Paracelsus
a scab, Erastus a patch, Sigonius a toy, Cuiacius a bable
to this Termagant, that fighteth not with simple wordes,
but with dubble swordes; not with the trickling water of
Helicon, but with piercing Aqua fortis; not with the sorry
powder of Experience, but with terrible gunpowder; not
with the small shott of contention, but with the maine
ordinaunce of fury.

For breuity I ouerskip many notable men and valorous
Confuters in their seuerall vaines, had not affection otherwhiles swinged their reason, where reason should haue
swayed their affection. But Partiality was euer the busiest
Actour, and Passion the whottest Confuter, whatsoeuer

plausible cause otherwise pretended: and hee is rather to bee esteemed an Angell then a man, or a man of Heauen, not of Earth, that tendereth integrity in his hart, equity in his tongue, and reason in his penne. Flesh and bloud are fraile Creatures, and partiall discoursers; but he approacheth neerest vnto God, & yeeldeth sweetest fruite of a diuine disposition, that is not transported with wrath or any blinde passion, but guided with cleere and pure Reason, the soueraigne principle of sound proceeding. It is not the Affirmatiue or Negatiue of the writer, but the trueth of the matter written, that carryeth meat in the mouth and victory in the hande. There is nothing so exceeding foolish but hath beene defended by some wise man; nor any thinge so passing wise but hath bene confuted by some foole. Mans will no safe rule, as Aristotle sayth; good Homer sometime sleepeth; S. Augustine was not ashamed of his retractations; S. Barnard saw not all thinges; and the best chart may eftsoones ouerthrow. He that taketh a Confutation in hand must bringe the standard of Iudgement with him, & make Wisedome the moderatour of Wit.

But I might aswell haue ouerpassed the censure as the persons: & I haue to do with a party that valueth both alike, and can phansy no Autor but his owne phansy. It is neyther reason, nor rime, nor witt, nor arte, nor any imitation, that hee regardeth; hee hath builded towers of Supererrogation in his owne head; and they must stand, whosoeuer fall. Howbeit, I cannot ouerslipp some without manifest iniury, that deserue to haue their names enrolled in the first rancke of valiant Confuters; worthy men, but subiect to imperfections, to errour, to mutuall reproofe, some more, some lesse, as the manner is. Harding and Iewell were our Eschines and Demosthenes; and scarsely any language in the Christian world hath affoorded a payre of aduersaries equiualent to Harding and Iewell, two

thundring and lightning Oratours in diuinity; but now at
last infinitely ouermatched by this hideous thunderbolt in
humanity, that hath the onely right tearmes inuectiue, and
triumpheth ouer all the spirites of Contradiction. You
that haue read Luther against the Pope; Sadolet, Longolius, Omphalius, Osorius against Luther; Caluin against
Sadolet; Melanchthon against Longolius; Sturmius against
Omphalius; Haddon against Osorius; Baldwin againste
Caluin; Beza againste Baldwin; Erastus against Beza;
Trauers against Erastus; Sutcliff against Trauers; and
so foorth (for there is no ende of endlesse controuersies:
nor Bellarmine shall euer satisfye the Protestantes; nor
Whittaker contente the Papistes; nor Bancroft appease
the Precisians; nor any reason pacify affection; nor any
authority resolue obstinacy); you that haue most diligently
read these, and these, and sundry other reputed excellente
in their kindes, cast them all away, and read him alone
that can schoole them all in their tearmes inuectiue, and
teacheth a new-found Arte of confuting, his all-onely Arte.
Martin himselfe but a meacocke, and Papp-hatchet himselfe but a milkesop to him, that inditeth with a penne of
fury and the incke of vengeance, and hath cartloades of
papershot and chainshot at commaundement. Tush, no
man can blason his Armes but himselfe. Behold the
mighty Champion, the dubble swordbearer, the redowtable
fighter with both handes, that hath robbed William Conquerour of his surname, and in the very first page of his
Straunge Newes choppeth off the head of foure Letters at
a blow. Hee it is that hath it rightly in him indeede, and
can roundly doe the feate with a witnesse. Why, man,
he is worth a thousand of these pidlinge and driblinge
Confuters that sitt all day buzzing vpon a blunt point or
two, and with much adoe drisle out as many sentences in
a weeke as he will powre downe in an howre. It is not
long since the goodlyest graces of the most noble Common-

wealthes vpon Earth, Eloquence in speech and Ciuility in manners, arriued in these remote parts of the world: it was a happy resolution of the heauens, and worthy to be chronicled in an English Liuy, when Tiberis flowed into
5 the Thames, Athens remoued to London, pure Italy and fine Greece planted themselues in rich England, Apollo with his delicate troupe of Muses forsooke his old mountaines and riuers and frequented a new Parnassus and an other Helicon nothinge inferiour to the olde, when they
10 were most solemnely haunted of diuine wittes that taught Rhetorique to speake with applause, and Poetry to sing with admiration. But euen since that flourishing transplantation of the daintiest and sweetest lerning that humanitie euer tasted, Arte did but springe in such as
15 Sir Iohn Cheeke and M. Ascham, & witt budd in such as Sir Phillip Sidney & M. Spencer, which were but the violetes of March or the Primeroses of May, till the one began to sprowte in M. Robart Greene, as in a sweating Impe of the euer-greene Laurell, the other to blossome in
20 M. Pierce Pennilesse, as in the riche garden of pore Adonis, both to growe to perfection in M. Thomas Nashe, whose prime is a haruest, whose Arte a misterie, whose witt a miracle, whose stile the onely life of the presse and the very hart-blood of the Grape. There was a kind of
25 smooth, and clenly, and neate, and fine elegancy before (proper men, handsome giftes), but alacke nothing liuelie and mightie like the braue *vino de monte*, till his frisking penne began to playe the Sprite of the buttry, and to teache his mother tongue such lusty gambolds as may
30 make the gallantest French, Italian, or Spanish gagliards to blushe for extreame shame of their ideot simplicitie.

The difference of wittes is exceeding straung and almost incredible. Good lord, how may one man passe a thousand, and a thousande not compare with one? Arte may giue
35 out precepts and directoryes *in communi forma*; but it is

superexcellent witt that is the mother pearle of precious
Inuention, and the goulden mine of gorgeous Elocution.
Na, it is a certaine pregnant and liuely thing without
name, but a queint mistery of mounting conceit, as it were
a knacke of dexterity, or the nippitaty of the nappiest
grape, that infinitly surpasseth all the Inuention and
Elocution in the world, and will bunge Demosthenes
owne mouth with new-fangled figures of the right stampe,
maugre all the thundering and lightninge Periodes of his
eloquentest orations, forlorne creatures. I haue had some
prettie triall of the finest Tuscanisme in graine, and haue
curiously obserued the cunningest experiments and brauest
complements of aspiring emulation, but must geeue the
bell of singularity to the humorous witt, and the garland
of victory to the *dominiering Eloquence*. I come not yet
to the Praise of the olde Asse : it is young Apuleius that
feedeth vpon this glory : and hauing enclosed these rancke
commons to the proper vse of himselfe & the capricious
flocke, adopteth whom he listeth without exception; as
Alexander the great had a huge intention to haue all men
his subiectes, and all his subiectes called Alexanders. It
was strange newes for some to be so assefied; and a
worke of Supererogation for him so bountifully to vouchsafe his golden name the appropriate cognisance of his
noble stile. God-night, poore Rhetorique of sorry bookes!
adieu, good old Humanity! gentle Artes and Liberall
Sciences, content your selues! Farewell my deere moothers,
sometime floorishing Vniuersities ! Some that haue long
continued your sonnes in Nature, your apprentises in
Arte, your seruauntes in Exercise, your louers in affection, and your vassalles in duety, must either take their
leaues of their sweetest freendes, or become the slaues of
that dominiering eloquence that knoweth no Art but the
cutting Arte, nor acknowledgeth any schoole but the
Curtisan schoole. The rest is pure naturall, or wondrous

supernaturall. Would it were not an infectious bane or an incroching pocke! Let me not bee mistaken by sinister construction, that wreasteth and wrigleth euery sillable to the worst. I haue no reference to my selfe, but to my
5 superiours by incomparable degrees. To be a Ciceronian is a flowting stocke: poore Homer, a wofull wight, may put his finger in a hole, or in his blind eye: the excellentest histories and woorthiest Chronicles (inestimable monumentes of wisdome and valour) what but stale Antickes?
10 the flowers and fruites of delicate humanity, that were wont to be dainetily and tenderly conserued, now preserued with dust, as it were with sugar, and with hoare, as it were with hoony! That frisking wine, & that liuely knacke in the right capricious veine, the onely booke that
15 holdeth out with a countenance, and will be heard, when woorme-toungued Oratours, dust-footed Poets, and weatherwise historians shall not bee allowed a woord to cast at a dogg! There is a fatall Period of whatsoeuer wee terme flourishinge: the worlde runneth on wheeles, and there
20 must be a vent for all thinges. The Ciceronian may sleepe til the Scogginist hath plaid his part; one sure Conny-catcher woorth twenty Philosophers; a phantasticall rimester more vendible then the notablest Mathematician; no profession to the faculty of rayling; all harsh
25 or obscure that tickleth not idle phantasies with wanton dalliance or ruffianly iestes. Robin Good-fellow the meetest Autor for Robin Hoodes Library; the lesse of Cambridge or Oxforde the fitter to compile woorkes of Supererogation; and wee that were simply trayned after the Athenian and
30 Romane guise must bee contente to make roome for roisters that know their place and will take it. Titles and tearmes are but woordes of course; the right fellow that beareth a braine can knocke twenty titles on the head at a stroke, and with a iugling shift of that same inuincible
35 knacke defende himselfe manfully at the Paper-barre.

Though I be not greatly employed, yet my leisure will scarsely serue to moralize Fables of Beares, Apes, and Foxes (some men can giue a shrewd gesse at a courtly allegory), but where Lordes in expresse tearmes are magnifically contemned, Doctours in the same stile may be courageously confuted. Liberty of Tongue and Pen is no Bondman; nippitaty will not be tied to a post; there is a cap of maintenaunce called Impudency; and what say to him that in a superabundaunce of that same odd capricious humour findeth 'no such want in England as of an Aretine, that might stripp these golden Asses out of their gay trappinges, and, after he had ridden them to death with rayling, leaue them on the dunghill for carrion'? A frolicke mind and a braue spirit to be employed with his stripping instrument, in supply of that onely want of a diuine Aretine, the great rider of golden Asses! Were his penne as supererogatory a woorkeman as his harte, or his liues such transcendentes as his thoughtes, Lord, what an egregious Aretine should we shortly haue, how excessiuely exceeding Aretine himselfe, that bestowed the surmountingest amplifications at his pleasure, and was a meere Hyperbole incarnate! Time may worke an accomplishment of woonders, and his graund intentions seeme to prognosticate no lesse then the vttermost possibilities of capacity or fury extended. Would God, or could the Diuell, giue him that vnmeasurable allowance of witt and Arte that he extreamely affecteth, and infinitely wanteth, there were no encounter but of admiration and honour. . . .

But when againe I lift vp mine eyes, and behold the glorious picture of that most-threatning Slassher, is it possible so couragious a Confuter should bee less terrible then the Basiliske of Orus Apollo, that with his onely hissing killed the poore snakes, his neighbours? Can any

Letters liue, that hee will slay? Were not Patience, or
Submission, or any course better then farther discourse?
What fonder businesse then to troble the Printe with
Pamphlets, that cannot possibly liue whiles the Basiliske
hisseth death? Was I woont to iest at Eldertons bal-
latinge, Gascoignes sonnettinge, Greenes pamphletting,
Martins libelling, Holinsheads engrosing, some-bodies
abridging, and whatchicaltes translating, & shall I now
become a scribling Creature with fragmentes of shame,
that might long sethence haue beene a fresh writer with
discourses of applause? The very whole matter, what
but a thinge of nothinge? the Methode, what but a hotchpott for a gallymafry? by the one or other, what hope of
publike vse or priuate credite? Socrates minde could as
lightly digest poison as Mithridates boddy; and how
easely haue the greatest stomackes of all ages, or rather
the valiantest courages of the worlde, concocted the
harshest and rankest iniuries? Politique Philip, victorious
Alexander, inuincible Scipio, triumphant Cæsar, happy
Augustus, magnificent Titus, and the flower of the noblest
mindes that Immortality honoureth, with a sweete facility
gaue many bitter reprehensions the slip, and finely ridd
their handes of roughest obloquies. Philosophy professeth
more, and the Philosopher of Emperours, or rather the
Emperour of Philosophers, Marcus Antoninus, when he
deserued best could with felicity heare the woorst. . . .

But without more circumlocution, pryde hath a fall: and
as of a Catt, so of Pierce himselfe, howsoeuer inspired or
enraged, you can haue but his skinne, puffed vp with
winde and bumbasted with vanitye. Euen when he stryueth
for life to shewe himselfe brauest in the flaunt-aflaunt of
his courage, and when a man would verily beleeue he
should nowe behold the stately personage of heroicall
Eloquence face to face, or see such an vnseene Frame of

the miracles of Arte as might amaze the heauenly eye of
Astronomy: holla sir, the sweete Spheres are not too-
prodigall of their soueraine influences. Pardon mee,
S. Fame. What the first pang of his diuine Furie but
notable Vanitie? what the seconde fitte but woorthy
vanitye? what the thirde career but egregious vanity?
what the glory of his ruffian Rhetorique and curtisan
Philosophy but excellent villany? That, that is Pierces
Supererogation: and were Penniles a person of any
reckoning, as he is a man of notorious fame, that, that
perhaps, in regarde of the outragious singularity, might be
supposed a Tragicall or Heroicall villany, if euer any
villany were so intituled. The present consideration of
which singularity occasioneth me to bethinke me of One
that this other day very soberlie commended some extraordinary giftes in Nashe; and when he had grauelie
maintayned that in the resolution of his conscience he was
such a fellowe as some wayes had few fellowes, at last
concluded somewhat more roundly:

'Well, my maisters, you may talke your pleasures of
Tom Nash, who yet sleepeth secure, not without preiudice
to some that might be more ielous of their name; but
assure your selues if M. Penniles had not bene deepely
plunged in a profound extasie of knauery, M. Pierce had
neuer written that famous worke of Supererogation, that
now stayneth all the bookes in Paules churchyard and
setteth both the vniuersites to schoole. Till I see your
finest humanitie bestow such a liberall exhibition of
conceit and courage vpon your neatest wittes, pardon me
though I prefer one smart Pamflet of knauery before ten
blundring volumes of the nine Muses. Dreaming and
smoke amount alike: Life is a gaming, a iugling, a
scoulding, a lawing, a skirmishing, a warre, a Comedie,
a Tragedy; the sturring witt, a quintessence of quicksiluer; and there is noe deade fleshe in affection or

courage. You may discourse of Hermes ascending spirit,
of Orpheus enchanting harpe, of Homers diuine furie, of
Tyrtæus enraging trumpet, of Pericles bounsinge thunder-
claps, of Platos enthusiasticall rauishment, and I wott not
what maruelous egges in mooneshine, but a flye for all
your flying speculations when one good fellow with his
odd iestes, or one madd knaue with his awke hibbergibber, is able to putt downe twentye of your smuggest
artificiall men that simper it so nicely and coylie in their
curious pointes. Try, when you meane to be disgraced;
& neuer giue me credit if Sanguine witt putt not Melancholy Arte to bedd. I had almost said all the figures of
Rhetorique must abate me an ace of Pierces Supererogation; and Penniles hath a certayne nimble and climbinge
reach of Inuention, as good as a long pole and a hooke
that neuer fayleth at a pinch. It were vnnaturall, as the
sweete Emperour Marcus Antoninus said, that the fig-tree
should euer want iuice. You that purpose with great
summes of studdy & candles to purchase the worshipfull
names of Dunses & Dodipoles may closely sitt or sokingly
ly at your bookes; but you that intende to be fine com-
panionable gentlemen, smirking wittes, and whipsters in
the world, betake yee timely to the liuely practis of the
minion profession, and enure your Mercuriall fingers to
frame semblable workes of Supererogation. Certes, other
rules are fopperies; and they that will seeke out the
Archmistery of the busiest Modernistes shall find it
nether more nor lesse then a certayne pragmaticall secret,
called Villany, the verie science of sciences, and the
Familiar Spirit of Pierces Supererogation. Coosen not
yourselues with the gay nothings of children & schollers:
no priuitie of learning, or inspiration of witt, or reuelation
of misteryes, or Arte Notory, counteruayleable with
Pierces Supererogation; which, hauing none of them,
hath them all, and can make them all Asses at his

pleasure. The Book-worme was neuer but a pickgoose:
it is the Multiplying spirit, not of the Alchimist but of
the villanist, that knocketh the naile one the head, and
spurreth outt farther in a day then the quickest Artist in
a weeke. Whiles other are reading, wryting, conferring,
arguing, discoursing, experimenting, platforminge, musing,
buzzing, or I know not what, that is the spirrit that with
a woondrous dexterity shapeth exquisite workes, and
atchieueth puissant exploites of Supererogation. O my
good frends, as ye loue the sweete world, or tender your
deare selues, be not vnmindfull what is good for the
aduauncement of your commendable partes. All is nothing
without aduancement. Though my experience be a Cipher
in these causes, yet hauing studiously perused the newe
Arte-notory, that is, the foresaid Supererogation, and
hauing shaken so manie learned asses by the eares, as it
were by the hands, I could say no lesse, and might think
more.'

Something else was vttered the same time by the same
Gentleman, aswell concerning the present state of France,
which he termed the most vnchristian kingdome of the
most christian kinge, as touching certaine other newes
of I wott not what dependence; but my minde was running
on my halfpeny, and my head so full of the foresaid round
discourse, that my hand was neuer quyet vntill I had
altered the tytle of this Pamphlet, and newlie christened it
Pierces Supererogation: aswell in remembrance of the
saide discourse as in honour of the appropriate vertues of
Pierce himselfe; who aboue all the writers that euer
I knew shall go for my money where the currantest
forgery, impudency, arrogancy, phantasticalitie, vanity,
and great store of little discretion may go for payment, and
the filthiest corruption of abhominable villany passe vn-
launced. His other miraculous perfections are still in
abeyance; and his monstrous excellencyes in the predica-

ment of Chimera. The birde of Arabia is longe in
hatchinge ; and mightye workes of Supererogation are not
plotted & accomplished att once. It is pittie so hyperbolicall a conceite, ouerhawty for the surmounting rage of
Tasso in his furious agony, should be humbled with so
diminitiue a witt, base enough for Elderton and the riffe-
raffe of the scribling rascality. I haue heard of many
disparagementes in felowship, but neuer saw so great
Impudency married to so little witt, or so huge presumption
allyed to so petty performance. I must not paint, though
hee dawbe. Pontan, decipher thy vauntinge Alopantius
Ausimarchides a new; and Terence, display thy boastinge
Thraso a new; and Plautus, addresse thy vain-glorious
Pyrgopolinices anew: heere is a bratt of Arrogancy,
a gosling of the Printing-house that can teach your brag-
gardes to play their partes in the Printe of woonder, &
to exploit redowtable workes of Supererogation, such as
neuer were atchieued in Latin or Greeke. Which deserue
to bee looked for with such a longing expectation as the
Iewes looke for their kingly Messias, or as I looke for
Agrippas dreadfull Pyromachy; for Cardans multiplied
matter that shall delude the force of the Canon; for
Ancontius perfect Arte of fortifieng little townes against
the greatest Battery; for the Iliades of all Courtly Stratagems that Antony Riccobonus magnifically promiseth;
for his vniuersall Repertory of all Histories, contayning
the memorable actes of all ages, all places, and all persons;
for the new Calepine of all learned and vulgar languages,
written or spoken, whereof a loud rumour was lately
published at Basill; for a generall Pandectes of the Lawes
and statutes of all nations and commonwealthes in the
worlde, largely promised by Doctor Peter Gregorius, but
compendiously perfourmed in his *Syntagma Iuris vniuersi*; for sundry such famous volumes of hugy miracles
in the cloudes. Do not such Arch-woondermentes of

supernaturall furniture deserue arch-expectation? What
should the Sonnes of Arte dreame of the Philosophers
Stone, that, like Midas, turneth into golde whatsoeuer it
toucheth : or of the soueraine and diuine Quintessence,
that, like Esculapius, restoreth health to sicknesse; like
Medea, youth to Olde-age ; like Apollonius, life to Death?
No Philosophers Stone or soueraine Quintessence, howsoeuer preciously precious, equiualent to such diuine
woorkes of supererogation! O high-minded Pierce, hadd
the traine of your woordes and sentences bene aunswear-
able to the retinue of your bragges and threates, or the
robes of your apparaunce in person suteable to the
weedes of your ostentation in tearmes, I would surely haue
beene the first that should haue proclaimed you the most
singuler Secretary of this language, & the heauenliest
creature vnder the Spheres. Sweete M. Ascham, that was
a flowing spring of humanity, and worthy Sir Phillip
Sidney, that was a florishing spring of nobility, must haue
pardoned me : I would directly haue charged my conscience. But you must giue plaine men leaue to vtter
their opinion without courtinge : I honor high heads that
stand vpon low feet; & haue no great affection to the
gay fellows that build vp with their clambring hartes, and
pull downe with their vntoward hands. Giue me the man
that is meeke in spirit, lofty in zeale, simple in presumption, gallant in endeuor, poore in profession, riche in
performance. Some such I knowe; and all such I value
highly. They glory not of the golden stone, or the youthfull Quintessence : but Industrie is their goulden Stone ;
Action their youthfull Quintessence ; and Valour their
diuine worke of Supererogation. . . .

I will not heere decipher thy vnprinted packet of bawdye
and filthy Rymes in the nastiest kind : there is a fitter
place for that discouery of thy foulest shame, & the whole

ruffianisme of thy brothell Muse, if she still prostitute her
obscene ballatts, and will needes be a younge Curtisan of
ould knauery. Yet better a Confuter of Letters then a
confounder of manners; and better the dogges-meate of
Agrippa or Cattes-meate of Poggius then the swines-meate
of Martial or goates-meate of Arretine. Cannot an Italian
ribald vomit out the infectious poyson of the world but an
Inglishe horrel-lorrel must lick it vp for a restoratiue, and
attempt to putrify gentle mindes with the vilest impostumes
of lewde corruption? ...

Euen amorous Sonnets, in the gallantest and sweetest
ciuil veine, are but daintyes of a pleasurable witt, or iunkets
of a wanton liuer, or buddes of an idle head; whatsoeuer
sprowteth farther would be lopped. Petrarckes Inuention
is pure Loue it selfe, and Petrarckes Elocution pure
Bewty it selfe: his *Laura* was the Daphne of Apollo,
not the Thisbe of Pyramus; a delitious Sappho, not
a lasciuious Lais; a sauing Hester, not a destroying
Helena; a nimph of Diana, not a Curtisan of Venus.
Aretines muse was an egregious bawd, & a haggishe witch
of Thessalia; but Petrarcks verse, a fine loouer, that
learneth of Mercury to exercise his fayrest giftes in a faire
subiect, & teacheth Wit to be inamored vpon Beautye, as
Quicksiluer embraseth gold, or as vertue affecteth honour,
or as Astronomy gazeth vpon heauen, to make Arte more
excellent by contemplation of excellentest Nature. Petrarck
was a delicate man, and with an elegant iudgement gra-
tiously confined Loue within the limits of Honour, Witt
within the boundes of Discretion, Eloquence within the
termes of Ciuility; as not many yeares sithence an Inglishe
Petrarck did, a singular Gentleman, and a sweete Poet,
whose verse singeth as valour might speake, and whose
ditty is an Image of the Sun voutsafing to represent his
glorious face in a clowde. All posterity honour Petrarck,

that was the harmony of heauen, the lyfe of Poetry, the grace of Arte, a precious tablet of rare conceits, & a curious frame of exquisite workemanship; nothing but neate Witt, and refined Eloquence. Were the amorous muse of my enemy such a liuely Spring of sweetest flowres & such a liuing Haruest of ripest fruits, I would abandon other loues, to dote vpon that most louely muse, and would debase the Dyamant in comparison of that most Dyamant muse. But out vpon ranke & lothsome ribaldry that putrifieth where it should purify, and presumeth to deflowre the most florishinge wittes with whom it consorteth, eyther in familiarity or by fauour! One Ouid was too much for Roome, and one Greene too much for London, but one Nashe more intollerable then both, not bicause his witt is anye thinge comparable, but bicause his will is more outragious. Ferraria could scarcely brooke Manardus, a poysonous Phisitian; Mantua hardly beare Pomponatius, a poysonous Philosopher; Florence more hardly tollerate Macchiauel, a poysonous politician; Venice most hardly endure Arretine, a poysonous ribald: had they liued in absolute Monarchies, they would haue seemed vtterly insupportable. Germany, Denmarke, Sweden, Polony, Boemia, Hungary, Moscouy, are noe soiles of any such wittes; but neither Fraunce, nor Spaine, nor Turky, nor any puissant kingdom in one or other Monarchy of the old or new world could euer abide any such pernicious writers, deprauers of common discipline.

Ingland, since it was Ingland, neuer bred more honorable mindes, more aduenturous hartes, more valorous handes, or more excellent wittes then of late: it is enough for Filly-folly to intoxicate it selfe, though it be not suffered to defyle the lande, which the water enuironeth, the Earth enritcheth, the aier ensweeteneth, and the Heauen blesseth. The bounteous graces of God are sowen thicke, but come vp thin; corruption hath little need to be fostred; wanton-

nesse wilbe a nurse, a bawde, a Poet, a Legend to itselfe;
vertue hath much-a-doe to hold out inuiolably her purposed
course; Resolution is a forward fellow, and Valour a braue
man; but affections are infectious, and appetite must sometime haue his swinge. Were Appetite a loyall subiect to
Reason, and Will an affectionate seruant to Wisdom, as
Labour is a dutifull vassal to Commodity, and Trauail a
flying post to Honour, O heauens, what exploites of worth,
or rather what miracles of excellency might be atcheeued
in an age of Pollicy & a world of Industry! The date of
idle vanityes is expired: awaye with these scribling
paltryes. There is an other Sparta in hande that indeede
requireth Spartan Temperance, Spartan Frugality, Spartan
exercise, Spartan valiancye, Spartan perseuerance, Spartan
inuincibility, and hath no wanton leasure for the Comedyes
of Athens, nor anye bawdy howers for the songes of
Priapus or the rymes of Nashe. Had he begun to
Aretinize when Elderton began to ballat, Gascoine to
sonnet, Turberuile to madrigal, Drant to versify, or
Tarleton to extemporise, some parte of his phantasticall
bibble-bables and capricious panges might haue bene tollerated in a greene and wild youth; but the winde is
chaunged, & there is a busier pageant vpon the stage.
M. Aschams Toxophilus long sithence shot at a fairer
marke; and M. Gascoigne himselfe, after some riper experience, was glad to trye other conclusions in the Lowe
Countryes, and bestowed an honorable commendation
vpon Sir Humfrye Gilbertes gallant discourse of a discouery for a newe passage to the East Indyes. But read
the report of the worthy Westerne discoueries, by the
said Sir Humfry Gilbert; the report of the braue West-
Indian voyage by the conduction of Sir Frauncis Drake;
the report of the horrible Septentrionall discoueryes by
the trauail of Sir Martin Forbisher; the report of the
politique discouery of Virginia by the Colony of Sir Walter

Raleigh; the report of sundry other famous discoueryes &
aduentures, published by M. Rychard Hackluit in one
volume, a worke of importance; the report of the hoatt
wellcom of the terrible Spanishe Armada to the coast of
Inglande, that came in glory and went in dishonour; the
report of the redoubted voyage into Spaine and Portugall,
whence the braue Earle of Essex and the twoo valorous
Generals, Sir Iohn Norris and Sir Frauncis Drake, returned with honour; the report of the resolute encounter
about the Iles Azores, betwixt the Reuenge of Ingland
and an Armada of Spaine, in which encounter braue Sir
Richard Grinuile most vigorously & impetuously attempted
the extreamest possibilities of valour and fury. For breuity
I ouerskipp many excellent Traicts of the same or the like
nature: but reade these, and M. William Borrowghes
notable discourse of the variation of the compas or mag-
neticall needle, annexed to the new Attractiue of Robert
Norman, Hydrographer; vnto which two Ingland in some
respectes is as much beholding as Spayne vnto Martin
Cortes & Peter de Medina for the Arte of Nauigation:
and when you haue obserued the course of Industry,
examined the antecedents and consequents of Trauail,
compared Inglish and Spanish valour, measured the Forces
of both parties, weighed euery circumstance of Aduantage,
considered the Meanes of our assurance, and finally found
proffit to be our pleasure, prouision our security, labour
our honour, warfare our welfare—who of reckoning can
spare anye lewde or vaine tyme for corrupt pamphlets, or
who of iudgment will not cry away with these paultringe
fidle-faddles? . . .

Were some demaunded whether Greenes or Nashes
Pamflets were better penned, I beleeue they would
aunsweare: Sir Roger Williams Discourse of War for
Militare Doctrine in Esse, and M. Thomas Digges Stra-

tioticos for Militare Discipline in Esse. And whiles I
remember the Princely care of Gelo, a famous Tyrant of
Sicill (many tyrants of Sicill were very politique) that com-
maunded his great horse to be brought into the banquet-
ting house, where other Lordes called for the Harpe, other
Knightes for the Waites, I cannot forget the gallant dis-
course of Horsemanship penned by a rare gentleman,
M. Iohn Asteley of the Court, whome I dare intitle our
Inglish Xenophon, and maruell not that Pietro Bizzaro, a
learned Italian, proposeth him for a perfect Patterne of
Castilios Courtier. And, thinking vpon worthy M. Asteley,
I cannot ouerpasse the like labour of good M. Thomas
Blundeuil without due commendation, whose painefull
and skillfull bookes of Horsemanship deserue also to be
registred in the Catalogue of Xenophontian woorkes.
What should I speake of the two braue Knightes, Musidorus and Pyrocles, combined in one excellent knight,
Sir Philip Sidney, at the remembrance of whose woorthy
and sweete Vertues my hart melteth? Will you needes
haue a written Pallace of Pleasure, or rather a printed
Court of Honour? Read the Countesse of Pembrookes
Arcadia, a gallant Legendary, full of pleasurable accidents
and proffitable discourses; for three thinges especially
very notable—for amorous Courting (he was young in
yeeres), for sage counselling (he was ripe in iudgement),
and for valorous fighting (his soueraine profession was
Armes); and delightfull pastime by way of Pastorall exercises may passe for the fourth. He that will Looue, let
him learne to looue of him that will teach him to Liue,
& furnish him with many pithy and effectuall instructions,
delectably interlaced by way of proper descriptions of
excellent Personages and common narrations of other
notable occurrences, in the veine of Salust, Liuy, Cornelius
Tacitus, Iustine, Eutropius, Philip de Comines, Guicciardine, and the most sententious Historians that haue

powdred their stile with the salt of discretion, and seasoned
their iudgement with the leauen of experience. There
v. ant not some suttle Stratagems of importance, and some
politique Secretes of pruitie; and he that would skilfully
and brauely manage his weapon with a cunning Fury may
finde liuely Precepts in the gallant Examples of his
valiantest Duellists; especially of Palladius and Dai-
phantus, Zelmane and Amphialus, Phalantus and Amphialus, but chiefly of Argalus and Amphialus, Pyrocles
and Anaxius, Musidorus and Amphialus, whose lusty
combats may seeme Heroicall Monomachies. And that
the valor of such redoubted men may appeere the more
conspicuous and admirable by comparison and interview
of their contraries, smile at the ridiculous encounters of
Dametas & Dorus, of Dametas and Clinias; and euer
when you thinke vpon Dametas remember the Confuting
Champion, more surquidrous then Anaxius, and more
absurd then Dametas; and if I should alwayes hereafter
call him Dametas, I should fitt him with a name as naturally
proper vnto him as his owne. Gallant Gentlemen, you
that honor Vertue and would enkindle a noble courage in
your mindes to euery excellent purpose, if Homer be not
at hand (whome I haue often tearmed the Prince of Poets
and the Poet of Princes), you may read his furious Iliads
& cunning Odysses in the braue aduentures of Pyrocles
and Musidorus; where Pyrocles playeth the dowty fighter,
like Hector or Achilles, Musidorus the valiant Captaine,
like Pandarus or Diomedes, both the famous errant
Knightes, like Æneas or Vlysses. Lord, what would him
selfe haue prooued in fine, that was the gentleman of
Curtesy, the Esquier of Industry, and the Knight of Valour
at those yeeres? Liue euer sweete Booke, the siluer
Image of his gentle witt, and the golden Pillar of his noble
courage, and euer notify vnto the worlde, that thy Writer
was the Secretary of Eloquence, the breath of the Muses, the

hoony-bee of the dayntiest flowers of Witt and Arte, the
Pith of morall & intellectuall Vertues, the arme of Bellona
in the field, the toung of Suada in the chamber, the spirite of
Practise in esse, and the Paragon of Excellency in Print.
And now whiles I consider what a Trompet of Honour
Homer hath bene to sturre vp many woorthy Princes,
I cannot forget the woorthy Prince that is a Homer to
himselfe, a Golden spurre to Nobility, a Scepter to Vertue,
a Verdure to the Spring, a Sunne to the day, and hath
not onely translated the two diuine Poems of Salustius du
Bartas, his heauenly Vrany, and his hellish Furies, but
hath readd a most valorous Martial Lecture vnto himselfe
in his owne victorious Lepanto, a short, but heroicall,
worke, in meeter, but royal meeter, fitt for a Dauids harpe
—Lepanto, first the glory of Christendome against the
Turke, and now the garland of a soueraine crowne.
When young Kings haue such a care of their flourishing
Prime, and, like Cato, are ready to render an accompt of
their vacant howers, as if Aprill were their Iuly, and May
their August, how should gentlemen of yeeres employ the
golden talent of their Industry and trauaile? with what
feruency, with what vigour, with what zeale, with what
incessant and indefatigable endeuour? Phy vpon fooleries:
there be honourable woorkes to doe, and notable workes
to read. The afore-named Bartas (whome elsewhere I
haue stiled the Treasurer of Humanity and the Ieweller
of Diuinity), for the highnesse of his subiect and the maiesty
of his verse nothing inferiour vnto Dante (whome some
Italians preferre before Virgil or Homer), a right inspired
and enrauished Poet, full of chosen, graue, profound,
venerable, and stately matter, euen in the next Degree to
the sacred and reuerend stile of heauenly Diuinity it selfe;
in a manner the onely Poet whome Vrany hath voutsafed
to Laureate with her owne heauenly hand, and worthy to
bee alleadged of Diuines and Counsellours, as Homer is

quoted of Philosophers & Oratours. Many of his solemne verses are oracles; & one Bartas, that is, one French Salomon, more weighty in stern and mighty counsell then the Seauen Sages of Greece. Neuer more beauty in vulgar Languages; but his stile addeth fauour and grace to beauty, and in a goodly Boddy representeth a puissant Soule. How few verses carry such a personage of state? or how few argumentes such a spirite of maiesty? Or where is the diuine instincte that can sufficiently commend such a volume of celestiall inspiration? What a iudgement hath the noble youth, the haruest of the Spring, the sapp of Apollos tree, the diademe of the Muses, that leaueth the enticingest flowers of delite, to reape the fruites of wisdome? ...

He can raile (what mad Bedlam cannot rail?), but the sauour of his railing is grosely fell, and smelleth noysomly of the pumpe, or a nastier thing. His gayest floorishes are but Gascoignes weedes, or Tarletons trickes, or Greenes crankes, or Marlowes brauados; his iestes but the dregges of common scurrilitie, or the shreds of the theater, or the of-scouring of new Pamflets; his freshest nippitatie but the froth of stale inuentions, long since lothsome to quick tastes; his shrouing ware but lenten stuff, like the old pickle herring; his lustiest verdure but ranke ordure, not to be named in Ciuilitie or Rhetorique; his only Art, & the vengeable drift of his whole cunning, to mangle my sentences, hack my arguments, chopp and change my phrases, wrinch my wordes, and hale euery sillable most extremely, euen to the disioynting and maiming of my whole meaning. O times, O pastimes, O monstrous knauerie! The residue whatsoeuer hath nothing more in it then is vsuallie in euery ruffianly Copesmate that hath bene a Grammar schollar, readeth riotous bookes, hanteth roisterly companie, delighteth in rude scoffing,

& karrieth a desperate minde. Let him be thorowly perused by any indifferent reader whomsoeuer that can iudiciously discerne what is what, and will vprightly censure him according to his skill, without partialitie *pro* or *contra*, and I dare vndertake he will affirme no lesse, vpon the credit of his iudgement, but will definitiuely pronounce him the very Baggage of new writers. I could nominate the person that vnder his hand-writing hath stiled him the cockish challenger, the lewd scribler, the offal of corruptest mouthes, the draff of filthiest pennes, the bag-pudding of fooles, & the very pudding-pittes of the wise or honest. He might haue read of foure notable thinges which many a iollie man weeneth he hath at will, when he hath nothing lesse—much knowledge, sound wisedome, great power, & many frends. . . .

You haue heard some worthie Premisses: behold a braue conclusion.

'Awaite the world, the Tragedy of Wrath:
What next I paint shall tread no common Path':

with an other doubble *Aut*, for a gallant Embleme or a glorious Farewell, *Aut nunquam tentes aut perfice*: Subscribed with his owne hand, *Thomas Nash*. Not expect or attend, but *a wait*: not some few, or the Citty, or the Vniuersity, or this Land, or Europe, but *the World*: not a Comedy, or a Declamation, or an Inuectiue, or a Satire, or any like Elencticall discourse, but a *Tragedy*, and the very *Tragedy of Wrath*, that shall dash the direfullest Tragedies of Seneca, Euripides, or Sophocles out of Conceit. *The next peece*, not of his Rhetorique, or Poetry, but of his *Painture* shall *not treade* the way to Poules, or Westminster, or the Royall Exchange, but at least shall perfect the Venus face of Apelles, or sett the world an euerlasting Sample of inimitable artificiality. Other mens writing in prose or verse may plodd on as before, but *his Painting* will now *tread a rare Path*, and, by the way, bestow a new Lesson vppon Rhetorique, how to continue a metaphor or vphold an Allegory with aduauntage. *The treading of that rare Path* by that exquisite *Painting* (his woorkes are miracles, and his *Painting* can *treade*, like his dauncing, or frisking, *no common, but a proper Path*), who expecteth not with an attentiue, a seruiceable, a coouetous, a longing expectation? *Await world*, and Apelles tender thy most affectionate deuotion, to learne a wonderfull peece of curious workemanship, when it shall please his next *Painting to tread the path* of his most singular singularity.

AN ADUERTISEMENT FOR PAP-HATCHET, AND MARTIN MAR-PRELATE

Pap-hatchet (for the name of thy good nature is pittyfully growen out of request) thy olde acquaintance in the Sauoy, when young Euphues hatched the egges that his elder freendes laide (surely Euphues was someway a pretty fellow: would God, Lilly had alwaies bene Euphues, and neuer Pap-hatchet), that old acquaintance, now somewhat straungely saluted with a new remembrance, is neither lullabied with thy sweete Papp nor scarre-crowed with thy sower hatchet. And although in selfe-conceit thou knowest not thy selfe, yet in experience thou mightest haue knowen him that can vnbutton thy vanity and vnlase thy folly, but in pitty spareth thy childish simplicity, that in iudgement scorneth thy roisterly brauery, and neuer thought so basely of thee, as since thou began'st to dis-

guise thy witt and disgrace thy arte with ruffianly foolery.
He winneth not most abroad that weeneth most at home:
and, in my poore fancy, it were not greatly amisse euen
for the pertest and gayest companions (notwithstanding
whatsoeuer courtly holly-water, or plausible hopes of preferment) to deigne their olde familiars the continuance of
their former courtesies, without contempt of the barrainest
giftes or empeachment of the meanest persons. The
simplest man in a parish is a shrewd foole, and Humanity
an Image of Diuinity, that pulleth downe the hawty and
setteth vp the meeke. Euphues, it is good to bee merry:
and, Lilly, it is good to bee wise: and, Papp-hatchet, it
is better to loose a new iest then an olde frend that can
cramme the capon with his owne Papp, and hewe downe
the woodcocke with his owne hatchet. Bolde men and
marchant Venturers haue sometime good lucke; but happ-
hazard hath oftentimes good leaue to beshrow his owne
pate, and to imbarke the hardy foole in the famous Shipp
of wisemen. I cannot stand nosing of Candlesticks, or
euphuing of Similes, *alla Sauoica*: it might happly be done
with a trice; but euery man hath not the guift of *Albertus
Magnus*; rare birdes are dainty; and they are queint
creatures that are priuiledged to create new creatures.
When I haue a mint of precious stones, & straunge Foules,
beastes, and fishes of mine owne coyning (I could name
the party, that in comparison of his owne naturall Inuentions tearmd Pliny a barraine woombe), I may peraduenture blesse you with your owne crosses, & pay you
with the vsury of your owne coyne. In the meane while
beare with a plaine man, as plaine as olde Accursius, or
Barthol. de Saxoferrato, that wil make his Censure good
vpon the carrion of thy vnsauory and stincking Pamflett,
a fitt booke to be ioyned with Scoggins woorkes, or the
French Mirrour of Madnesse. The very Title discouereth
the wisedome of the young man; as an olde Fox not long

since bewrayed himselfe by a flap of his taile; and a Lion, they say, is soon descried by his pawe, a Cocke by his combe, a Goat by his bearde, an Asse by his eare, a wise-man by his tale, an artist by his tearmes.

Papp with an hatchet.
Alias,
A Figg for my God-sonne.
Or
Cracke me this nutt.
Or
A Country Cuffe, that is, a sound boxe of the
eare, & *cetera.*

VVritten by one that dares call a dog a dog.

Imprinted by *Iohn Anoke*, and *Iohn Astile*, for the Bayly of Withernam *Cum priuilegio perennita-tis*, and are to be sold at the signe of the Crabb-tree Cudgell in Thwack-coate Lane.

What deuise of Martin, or what inuention of any other, could haue sett a fairer Orientall Starre vpon the forhead of that foule libell? Now you see the brande and know the Blackamore by his face, turne ouer the leafe, and, by the wittinesse of his first sentence, aime at the rest. Milke is like milke, hoony is like hoony, Papp like Papp, and hee like himselfe; in the whole a notable ruffler, and in euery part a dowty braggard. 'Roome for a roister: so that's well said: itch a little further for a good fellow:

now haue at you all, my gaffers of the rayling religion :
tis I that must take you a pegg lower : Ile make such
a splinter runne into your wittes,'—and so foorth in the
same lusty tenour. A very artificiall beginning to mooue
attention or to procure good liking in the reader, vnlesse
he wrote onely to roister-doisters & hacksters, or at-
least to iesters and vices. Oh, but in his Preamble to the
indifferent reader he approueth himselfe a maruellous,
discreet, and modest man of the soberest sort, were he
not prouoked in conscience to aunsweare contrary to his
nature and manner. You may see how graue men may
be made light to defend the Church. I perceiue they
were wise that at riotous times, when youth was wanton-
nest and knauery lustiest, as in Christmas, at Shrofetide,
in May, at the ende of Haruest, and by such wilde fittes,
created a certaine extraordinary Officer, called a Lord of
Misrule, as a needefull gouernour or Dictatour, to set
thinges in order and to rule vnruly people; with whome
otherwise there were no 'Ho So,' when Reuell-rout
beginneth to be a current Autour or Hurly-burly a **busy**
Promotour. *Roome for a roister*, that will bore them
thorough the noses with a cushion, that will bung vp
their mouthes with a Collyrium of all the stale iestes in
a country, that will suffer none to play the Rex but himselfe ! For that is the very depth of his plot ; and who
euer began with more roisterly tearmes, or proceeded
with more ruffianly scoffes, or concluded with more haire-
brain'd trickes, or wearied his reader with more thread-
bare iestes, or tired himselfe with more weather-beaten
cranckes? What scholler or gentleman can reade such
alehouse and tinkerly stuffe without blushing? They
were much deceiued in him at Oxford, and in the Sauoy,
when Master Absolon liued, that tooke him onely for
a dapper & deft companion, or a pert conceited youth that
had gathered together a fewe prettie sentences and could

handsomly helpe young Euphues to an old *Simile*, & neuer
thought him any such mighty doer at the sharpe. ...

When I first tooke a glancing vewe of *Ile, Ile, Ile*, &
durst scarsely be so hardy to looke the hatchet in the
face, methought his Imagination was hedded like a Saracen,
his stomack bellyed like the great Globe of Orontius, & his
breath like the blast of Boreas in the great Mapp of Mer-
cator. But when we began to renue our old acquaintance,
and to shake the handes of discontinued familiaritie, alas,
good Gentleman, his mandillion was ouercropped, his witt
paunched like his wiues spindle, his art shanked like a lath,
his conceit as lank as a shotten herring, and that same
blustering eloquence as bleake and wan as the Picture of a
forlorne Loouer. Nothing but pure Mammaday and a fewe
morsels of fly-blowne Euphuisme, somewhat nicely minced
for puling stomackes! But there be Painters enough, though
I goe roundly to worke; and it is my onely purpose to
speake to the purpose. I long sithence founde by experience how Dranting of Verses, and Euphuing of sentences,
did edifie. But had I consulted with the Prognostication
of Iohn Securis, I might peraduenture haue saued some
loose endes for afterclapps. Now his nephew Hatchet
must be content to accept of such spare intertainment as
he findeth. ...

So he may soone make vp the autenticall Legendary
of his *Hundred merrie Tales*, as true, peraduenture, as
Lucians true narrations, or the heroicall historyes of
Rabelais, or the braue Legendes of Errant Knights, or
the egregious prankes of Howleglasse, Frier Rush, Frier
Tuck, and such like, or the renowned *Bugiale* of Poggius,
Racellus, Luscus, Cincius, and that whole Italian crew of
merry Secretaryes in the time of Pope Martin the fift, of
whom our worshipfull Clarkes of the whetstone, Doctour

Clare, Doctour Bourne, M. Scoggin, M. Skelton, M. Wakefield, diuers late Historiologers, and haply this new Talefounder himselfe, learned their most wonderfull facultie. *Committing of matrimonie, carousing the sapp of the Church,* *cutting at the bumme Carde of conscience, besmearing of conscience, spelling of Our Father in a horne booke, the railing Religion,* and a whole sinke of such arrant phrases, sauour whotly of the same Lucianicall breath, & discoouer the minion Secretarie aloofe. 'Faith,' quoth himselfe, 'thou wilt be caught by thy stile.' Indeede, what more easie then to finde the man by his humour, the Midas by his eares, the Calfe by his tongue, the goose by his quill, the Play-maker by his stile, the hatchet by the Pap? Albertus Secrets, Poggius Fables, Bebelius iestes, Scoggins tales, Wakefield's lyes, Parson Darcyes knaueries, Tarletons trickes, Eldertons Ballats, Greenes Pamflets, Euphues Similes, double V^s phrases, are too well knowen to go vnknowen. Where the veine of Braggadocio is famous, the arterie of Pappadocio cannot be obscure. Gentlemen, I haue giuen you a tast of his Sugerloafe, that weeneth Sidneyes daintyes, Aschams comfites, Cheekes succats, Smithes conserues, and Mores iunkets, nothing comparable to his pap. Some of you dreamed of Electuaryes of Gemmes, and other precious restoratiues, of the quintessence of Amber and Pearle dissolued, of I wott not what incredible delicacies, but his Gemmemint is not alwayes current, and, as busie men, so painted boxes and gallipots must haue a Vacation. . . .

Would fayre Names were spelles and charmes against fowle Affections! and in some respectes I could wish that Diuinitie would giue Humanitie leaue to conclude otherwise then I must. I could in curtesie be content, and in hope of Reconciliation desirous, to mitigate the harshest sentences and mollifie the hardest termes. But can Truth

lye, or Discretion approoue follie, or Iudgement allowe
Vanitie, or Modestie abide Impudencie, or good manners
sooth bad speeches? He that penned the abooue-men-
tioned *Cock-alilly* saw reason to display the Black Artist in
his collier coolours, and thought it most vnreasonable to
suffer such light and emptie vessels to make such a lowde
and prowde rumbling in the ayre. Other had rather heare
the learned Nightingale then the Vnlearned Parrat, or tast
the wing of a Larke then the legge of a Rauen. The
finest wittes preferre the loosest period in M. Ascham or
Sir Philip Sidney before the tricksiest page in Euphues or
Pap-hatchet. The Muses shame to remember some fresh
quaffers of Helicon: and which of the Graces or Vertues
blusheth not to name some lustie tospots of Rhetorique?
The stately Tragedie scorneth the trifling Comedie; and
the trifling Comedie flowteth the new Ruffianisme. Wantonnesse was neuer such a swill-bowle of ribaldry, nor
Idlenesse euer such a carowser of knauerie. What honest
mynde or Ciuill disposition is not accloied with these
noisome & nasty gargarismes? Where is the polished
& refined Eloquence that was wont to bedeck and embellish Humanity? Why should learning be a niggard of
his excellent gifts, when Impudencie is so prodigall of his
rascall trish-trash? What daintie or neat Iudgement
beginneth not to hate his old looue, and loath his auncient
delight, the Presse, the most honorable Presse, the most
villanous Presse? Who smileth not at those, and those
trim-trammes of gawdie wittes, how floorishing Wittes, how
fading witts? Who laugheth not at *Ile, Ile, Ile*, or gibeth
not at some hundred Pibalde fooleryes in that harebrained
Declamation? They whom it neerelyest pincheth cannot
silence their iust disdaine: and I am forcibly vrged to
intimate my whole Censure, though without hatred to the
person, or derogation from any his commendable gift, yet
not without speciall dislike of the bad matter, and generall

condemnation of the vile forme: the whole Worke, a bald Toy, full of stale and wooden Iestes, and one of the most paltry thinges that euer was published by graduate of either Vniuersitie; good for nothing but to stop mustard pottes, or rub gridirons, or feather rattes neastes, or such like homely vse. For Stationers are already too full of such Realmes and Commonwealthes of Wast-paper, and finde more gaine in the lillypot blanke then in the lillypot Euphued—a day or two fine for sheetes, and afterward good for grosers. . . .

He is of no reading in comparison, that doth not acknowledge euery terme in those Letters to be autenticall English, and allow a thousand other ordinary Pragmaticall termes, more straunge then the straungest in those Letters, yet current at occasion. The ignorant Idiot (for so I will prooue him in very truth) confuteth the artificiall wordes which he neuer read; but the vayne fellow (for so he prooueth himselfe in word and deede) in a phantasticall emulation presumeth to forge a mishapen rablement of absurde and ridiculous wordes, the proper bodges of his new fangled figure, called Foolerisme: such as *Inkhornisme, Absonisme, the most copious Carminist, thy Carminicall art, a Prouiditore of young Schollars, a Corrigidore of incongruitie, a quest of Caualieros, Inamoratos on their workes, a Theologicall Gimpanado, a Dromidote Ergonist, sacrilegiously contaminated, decrepite capacitie, fictionate person, humour vnconuersable, merriments vnexilable, the horrisonant pipe of inueterate antiquitie,* and a number of such Inkhornish phrases, as it were a pan of outlandish collops, the very bowels of his profoundest Schollerisme. For his Eloquence passeth my intelligence, that cleapeth himselfe a *Calimunco*, for pleading his Companions cause in his owne Apology, and me a Pistlepragmos, for defending my frendes in my Letters; and very artificially *interfuseth*

Finicallitie, sillogistrie, disputatiue right, hermaphrodite phrases, declamatorie stiles, censoriall moralizers, vnlineall vsurpers of iudgement, infamizers of vice, new infringement to destitute the inditement, deriding dunstically, banging abominationly, vnhandsoming of diuinityship, absurdifying of phrases, ratifying of truthable and eligible English, a calme dilatement of forward harmefulnesse and backward irefulnesse, and how many sundry dishes of such dainty fritters? rare iunkets and a delicate seruice for him that compiled the most delitious Commentaries *De optimitate triparum.* And what say you Boyes, the flatteringest hope of your moothers, to *a Porch of Panim Pilfryes, Pestred with Prayses.* Dare the pertest or deftest of you hunt the letter, or hauke a metaphor, with such a *Tite-tute-tate*? He weeneth himselfe a speciall penman, as he were the headman of the Pamfletting crew, next, and immediately after Greene: and although he be a harsh Oratour with his toungue (euen the filed Suada of Isocrates wanted the voyce of a Siren or the sound of an Eccho), yet would he seeme as fine a Secretary with his penne as euer was Bembus in Latin, or Macchiauell in Italian, or Gueuara in Spanish, or Amiot in French; and with a confidence preasseth into the rowte of that humorous ranke that affected the reputation of supreme Singularity. But he must craue a little more acquaintance at the hand of Arte, and serue an apprentishood of some nine or ten yeares in the shop of curious Imitation (for his wild Phantasie will not be allowed to maintaine comparison with curious Imitation) before he will be hable to performe the twentith or fortith part of that sufficiency, whereunto the cranknesse of his Imagination already aspireth, as more exquisite then the Atticisme of Isocrates, or more puissant then the fury of Tasso.

But how insolently soeuer grose Ignorance presumeth of itselfe (none so hawty as the basest Bussard), or how desperatly soeuer foole-hardy Ambition aduaunceth his

owne colours (none so foole-hardy as the blindest Hobb),
I haue seldome read a more garish and pibald stile in any
scribling Inkhornist, or tasted a more vnsauory slaumpaump of wordes and sentences in any sluttish Pamfletter
that denounceth not defiance against the rules of Oratory
and the directions of the English Secretary: which may
here and there stumble vpon some tolerable sentence,
neighbourly borrowed, or featly picked out of some fresh
Pamflet, but shall neuer finde three sentences togither
worth any allowance; and as for a fine or neat period, in
the dainty and pithy Veyne of Isocrates or Xenophon,
marry, that were a periwig of a Siren, or a wing of the
very bird of Arabia, an inestimable relique. Tush, a
point: neither curious Hermogenes, nor trim Isocrates,
nor stately Demosthenes, are for his tooth, nor painting
Tully, nor caruing Cæsar, nor purple-dying Liuy for his
humour. It is for Cheeke or Ascham to stand leuelling of
Colons, or squaring of Periods, by measure and number:
his penne is like a spigot, and the Wine presse a dullard
to his Ink-presse. There is a certaine liuely and frisking
thing of a queint and capricious nature, as peerlesse as
namelesse, and as admirable as singular, that scorneth
to be a booke-woorme, or to imitate the excellentest artificiality of the most renowned worke-masters that antiquity
affourdeth. The witt of this & that odd Modernist is their
owne; & no such minerall of richest Art as prægnant
Nature, the plentifullest woombe of rare Inuention, and
exquisite Elocution. Whuist Art! and Nature aduaunce
thy precious Selfe in thy most gorgeous and magnificent
robes! and if thy new descant be so many notes aboue
old Æla, Good-now be no niggard of thy sweet accents
& heauenly harmony, but teach the antike muses their
right Leripup! Desolate Eloquence and forlorne Poetry,
thy most humble Suppliants *in forma pauperum*, cladd in
mournefull and dreery weedes, as becommeth their lament-

able case, lye prostrate at thy dainty foote, and adore the
Idoll-excellency of thy monstrous Singularity! O stately
Homer, and lofty Pindarus, whose witt mounteth like
Pegasus, whose verse streameth like Nilus, whose Inuention flameth like Ætna, whose Elocution rageth like
Sirius, whose passion blustereth like Boreas, whose
reason breatheth like Zephirus, whose nature sauoureth like
Tempe, and whose Art perfumeth like Paradise: O the
mightiest Spirites of couragious Vigour, of whom the
delicate Grecian, worthy Roman, and gallant Vulgar
Muses learned their shrillest tunes and hyperbolicall
notes: O the fiercest Trompets of heroicall Valour, that
with the straunge Sympathy of your diuine Fury, and with
thossame piercing motions of heauenly inspiration were
woont to rauish the affections, and euen to mealt the bowels
of brauest mindes; see, see what a woondrous quaime!

But peace, milkemaide, you will still be shaming yourselfe
and your bringing-vpp! Hadst thou learned to discerne
the fairest face of Eloquence from the fowlest visage of
Barbarisme, or the goodlyest frame of Method from the
ill-fauoredest shape of Confusion, as thou canst descry the
finest flower from the coursest branne, or the sweetest
creame from the sowrest whey, peraduenture thou wouldest
dote vpon the bewtifull and dainty feature of that naturall
stile, that appropriate stile, vpon which himselfe is so
deepely inamored. I would it were out of peraduenture:
no man more greedy to behold that miraculous Art of
emprooued Nature. He may malapertly bragge in the
vaine ostentation of his owne naturall conceit, and, if it
please him, make a Golden Calfe of his woodden stuffe,
but shewe me any halfe page without piperly phrases and
tinkerly composition, and say I am the simplest Artist that
euer looked fayre Rhetorique or sweet Poetry in the face.
It is the destiny of our language to be pestred with a
rablement of botchers in Print; but what a shamefull

shame is it for him that maketh an Idoll of his owne
penne, and raiseth vpp an huge expectation of paper-
miracles (as if Hermes Trismegist were newly risen from
the dead, and personally mounted vpon Danters Presse),
to emprooue himselfe as ranke a bungler in his mightiest
worke of Supererogation as the starkest Patch-pannell of
them all, or the grosest hammer-drudge in a country. He
disdaineth Thomas Delone, Philip Stubs, Robert Armin,
and the common Pamfletters of London, euen the pain-
fullest Chroniclers tooe, bicause they stand in his way,
hinder his scribling traffique, obscure his resplendishing
Fame, or haue not Chronicled him in their Catalogues of
the renowned moderne Autors, as he meritoriously meriteth,
and may peraduenture be remembred hereafter. But may
not Thomas Delone, Philip Stubs, Robert Armin, and the
rest of those misused persons more disdainfully disdaine
him, bicause he is so much vayner, so little learneder, so
nothing eleganter then they; and they so much honester,
so little obscurer, so nothing contemptibler then he?
Surely, Thomas, it were pollicy to boast lesse with Thomas
Delone, or to atchieue more with Thomas More ...

He that remembreth Humfrey Cole, a Mathematicall
Mechanician, Matthew Baker, a ship wright, Iohn Shute,
an Architect, Robert Norman, a Nauigatour, William
Bourne, a Gunner, Iohn Hester, a Chimist, or any like
cunning and subtile Empirique (Cole, Baker, Shute,
Norman, Bourne, Hester will be remembred when greater
Clarkes shalbe forgotten) is a prowd man if he contemne
expert artisans or any sensible industrious Practitioner,
howsoeuer Vnlectured in Schooles or Vnlettered in bookes.
Euen the Lord Vulcan himselfe, the supposed God of the
forge and thunder-smith of the great king Iupiter, tooke
the repulse at the handes of the Lady Minerua, whom he
would in ardent looue haue taken to wife. Yet what witt

or Pollicy honoreth not Vulcan? and what profounde
Mathematician, like Digges, Hariot, or Dee, esteemeth not
the pregnant Mechanician? Let euery man in his degree
enioy his due; and let the braue enginer, fine Dædalist,
skilfull Neptunist, maruelous Vulcanist, and euery Mercuriall occupationer, that is, euery Master of his craft and
euery Doctour of his mystery, be respected according to
the vttermost extent of his publique seruice or priuate
industry. I cannot stand to specific particularities. Our
late writers are as they are; and albeit they will not suffer
me to ballance them with the honorable Autors of the
Romanes, Grecians, and Hebrues, yet I will craue no
pardon of the highest to do the simplest no wrong. In
Grafton, Holinshed, and Stowe; in Heywood, Tusser, and
Gowge; in Gascoigne, Churchyarde, and Floide; in Ritch,
Whetstone, and Munday; in Stanyhurst, Fraunce, and
Watson; in Kiffin, Warner, and Daniell; in an hundred
such vulgar writers many things are commendable, diuers
things notable, somethings excellent. Fraunce, Kiffin,
Warner, and Daniell, of whom I haue elsewhere more
especiall occasion to entreate, may haply finde a thankefull
remembraunce of their laudable trauailes. For a polished
and garnished stile, fewe go beyonde Cartwright, and the
chiefest of his Confuters, furnished writers: and how few
may wage comparison with Reinolds, Stubbes, Mulcaster,
Norton, Lambert, and the Lord Henry Howarde, whose
seuerall writings the siluer file of the workeman recom-
mendeth to the plausible interteinement of the daintiest
Censure? Who can deny but the Resolution and Mary
Magdalens funerall teares are penned elegantly and pathe-
tically? Scottes discouery of Witchcraft dismasketh
sundry egregious impostures, and in certaine principall
Chapters & speciall passages hitteth the nayle on the head
with a witnesse: howsoeuer I could haue wished he had
either dealt somewhat more curteously with Monsieur

Bodine, or confuted him somwhat more effectually. Let
me not forget the Apology of sundry proceedings by Iuris-
diction Ecclesiasticall, or the Aunswere to an Abstract of
certaine Actes of Parliament, Iniunctions, Canons, consti-
tutions, and Synodals Prouinciall: vnlesse I will skip two
of the most materiall and most formall Treatises that any
English Print hath lately yeelded. Might I respectiuely
presume to intimate my slender opinion without flattery
or other vndecency, methought euer Doctour Whitgift
(whom I name with honour) in his Sermons was pithy,
Doctour Hutton profound, Doctour Young piercing to the
quick, Doctour Chaderton copious, M. Curtes elegant,
M. Wickam sententious, M. Drant curious, M. Deering
sweet, Doctor Still sound, Doctor Vnderhill sharpe, Doctor
Matthew fine, M. Lawherne gallant, M. Dooue eloquent,
M. Andrewes learned, M. Chaderton methodicall, M. Smith
patheticall, sundry other in their proper veyne notable,
some exquisite, a few singular. Yet which of the best
hath all perfections (*nihil omni ex parte beatum*), or which
of the meanest hath not some excellency? I cannot read
ouer all: I haue seldome heard some (it was neuer my
happ to heare Doctour Cooper, Doctour Humfry, or
Doctor Fletcher, but in Latin): and I would be loth to
iniury or preiudice any that deserueth well, *viua voce*, or
by pen. I deeme him wise that maketh choice of the best,
auoideth the worst, reapeth fruite by both, despiseth
nothing that is not to be abhorred, accepteth of any thing
that may be tollerated, interteineth euery thing with commendation, fauour, contentment, or amendment. Lucians
asse, Apuleius asse, Agrippas asse, Macchiauels asse,
miself since I was dubbed an asse by the only Monarch of
asses, haue found sauory herbes amongst nettles, roses
amongst prickles, berryes amongst bushes, marrow amongst
bones, graine amongst stubble, a little corne amongst a
great deal of chaff. The *abiectest naturalls* haue their

specificall properties and some wondrous vertues; and
Philosophy will not flatter the *noblest or worthiest naturals*
in their venoms or impurities. True Alchimy can alledge
much for her Extractions and quintessences; & true
Phisique more for her corrections and purgations. In the
best I cannot commende the badd, and in the baddest I
reiect not the good, but precisely play the Alchimist in
seeking pure and sweet balmes in the rankest poisons.
A pithy or filed sentence is to be embraced, whosoeuer is
the Autor; and for the lest benefit receiued, a good
minde will render dutifull thankes, euen to his greatest
enemy. . . .

II.

Some I know in *Cambridge*, some in *Oxford*, some in
London, some *elsewhere*, died in the purest graine of *Art*
& *Exercise*; but a few in either, and not many in all, that
vndoubtedly can do excellently well, exceedingly well.
And were they thoroughly employed according to the possibility of their *Learning* & *Industry*, who can tell what
comparison this tongue might wage with the most-floorish-
ing Languages of Europe, or what an inestimable crop of
most noble and soueraine fruite the hand of *Art* and the
spirite of *Emulation* might reape in a rich and honorable
field? Is not the Prose of *Sir Philip Sidney* in his sweet
Arcadia the embrodery of finest *Art* and daintiest *Witt*?
Or is not the Verse of M. *Spencer* in his braue Faery
Queene the Virginall of the diuinest Muses and gentlest
Graces? Both delicate Writers, alwayes gallant, often
braue, continually delectable, sometimes admirable. What
sweeter tast of Suada then the Prose of the One; or what
pleasanter relish of the Muses then the Verse of the
Other? *Sir Iohn Cheekes* stile was the hony-bee of Plato,
and M. *Aschams* Period the Syren of Isocrates. His, and

his breath, the balme and spicknard of the delightfullest *Tempe*. You may gesse whose meter I would intitle the harpe of Orpheus, or the dulcimers of Sappho. And which of the Golden Riuers floweth more currently then the siluer streame of the *English Ariosto*? Oh that we had such an *English Tasso*: and oh that the worthy *du Bartas* were so endenisoned! The *sky-coloured Muse* best commendeth her owne heauenly harmony; and who hath sufficiently praysed the hyacinthine & *azure die* but itselfe? What colours of astonishing *Rhetorique* or rauishing *Poetry* more deeply engrained then some of his amazing deuises, the fine dittyes of another *Petrarch*, or the sweet charmes of pure enchantment? What *Dia-margariton* or *Dia-ambre* so comfortatiue or cordiall as *Her Electuary of Gemmes* (for though the furious Tragedy *Antonius* be a bloudy chaire of estate, yet the diuine *Discourse of life and Death* is a restoratiue Electuary of Gemmes), whom I do not expresly name, not because I do not honour *Her* with my hart, but because I would not dishonour *Her* with my pen, whom I admire and cannot blason enough. Some other *Paragons* of bewtifullest Eloquence, and Mirrours of brightest witt, not so much for breuities sake as for like Honours sake, I ouerskip: whose onely imperfection is that they are touched with no imperfection. Yet *Hope* is a *Transcendent* & will not easely be imprisoned or impounded in any Predicament of aunctient or moderne *Perfection*: which it may honour with due reuerence, but will not serue with base homage. *Excellency* hath in all ages affected singularity: & *Ambition* how impetuously buckled for the mastery! And albeit *witt* haue a quicke sent that wil not be coosened, and *Iudgement* a sharpe eye that cannot be bleared (the Morning Starre of *Discretion* and the Euening Starre of *Experience* haue a deepe insight in the merites of euery cause), yet still *Hope* hath reason to continue *Hope*, and is a white Angell sent from heauen, aswell to enkindle Vigorous Zeale as to awaken lasie *Slougth*. A wan or windy Hope is a notable breake-necke vnto itselfe; but the grounded and winged Hope, which I someway perceiue in a few other, no way conceiue in miselfe, is the ascending scale and *Milk-way* to heauenly excellency.

RICHARD CAREW

(*THE EXCELLENCY OF THE ENGLISH TONGUE*)

? 1595-6

[The following text is taken from the MS. of Carew's *Epistle on the Excellency of the English Tongue*, preserved in the British Museum (Cott. F. xi, f. 265). It was printed by Camden in the 1614 edition of his *Remains*, with the heading, 'The Excellencie of the English tongue, by R. C. of Anthony Esquire to W. C.']

THE EXCELLENCY OF THE ENGLISH TONGUE. BY R. C., ESQ.

IT were most fittinge (in respect of discretion) that men should first waye matters with Iudgement, and then
encline their affection where the greatest reason swayeth, but ordinarilye it falleth out to the conntrarie; for either by nature or by Custome wee first settle our affection, and then afterwards drawe in those arguments to approue it, which should haue foregone to perswade ourselfes. This
preposterous course, seing antiquitye from our Elders and vniuersalitye of our neighbours doe entitle with a right, I hould my selfe the more freely warranted *delirare*, not only *cum Vulgo* but also *cum Sapientibus*, in seekinge out with what Commendacions I may attire our English
Languadge, as *Stephanus* hath done for the French and diuers others for theirs.

Four pointes requisite in a Languadge.

Locutio is defined *Animi sensus per vocem expressio*. On which grounde I builde these Consequences, that the first and principall point sought in euery Languadge is that wee maye expresse the meaning of our mindes aptlye ech to other; next, that we may doe it readilye without great adoo; then fullye, so as others maye thoroughlie conceiue vs; and, last of all, handsomely, that those to whome we speake maye take pleasure in hearing vs: soe as what soeuer tongue will gaine the race of perfection must runn on those fower wheeles, *Significancye*, *Easynes*, *Copiousnes*, & *Sweetnes*, of which the two foremost importe a necessitye, the two latter a delight. Nowe if I can proue that our English Langwadge for all or the most is macheable, if not preferable, before any other in vogue at this daye, I hope the assent of any impartiall reeder will passe on my side. And howe I endeuoure to performe the same this short laboure shall manyfest.

Significancye.

To beginn then with the significancye, it consisteth in the lettres, wordes, and phrases; and because the Greeke and Latyne haue euer borne awaye the prerogatiue from all other tongues, they shall serue as touchstones to make our tryall by.

Letters.

For letters, wee haue Q. more then the Greekes; K. and Y. more then the Latynes; and W. more then them both, or the French and Italians; for those Commone to them and vs, wee haue the vse of the Greek B. in our V: of our B. they haue none; soe haue wee of their Δ. and Θ. in our Th. which in *That* and *Things* expresseth both, but of our D. they haue none. Likewise there Υ. wee turne to another vse in yeeld then they cann, and as for C. G. and I. neither Greekes nor Latynes cann make perfitt of them as we doe in these wordes *ech, edge, ioye*. Trew it is that wee in pronouncing the Latyne vse them alsoe after this manner; but the same in regard of the auncient and right Romayne deliuerye altogether abusiuely, as maye appeare by Scaliger, Sir Tho. Smith, Lipsius, and others.

Now for significancye of wordes, as euery *indiuiduum* is but one, soe in our natiue Saxon language wee finde many of them suitablye expressed by woordes of one syllable; those consisting of more are borrowed from other nations; the examples are infinite, and therefore I will omitt them, as sufficiently notorious. *Woords.*

Againe, for expressing our passions, our interiections are very apt and forcible: as findeinge ourselues somewhat agreeued, wee cry *Ah*; yf more deeply, *Oh*; when we pittie, *Alas*; when wee bemone, *Alacke*; neither of them soe effeminate as the Italyane *Deh* or the French *hélas*. In detestation wee saye *Phy*, as if there withall wee should spitt; in attention, *Haa*; i[n] calling, *whowp*; in hallowinge, *wahahowe*: all which (in my eare) seeme to be deriued from the very natures of those seuerall affections. *Interiections.*

Growe from hence to the Compositione of wordes, and therein our Languadge hath a peculier grace, a like significancy, and more shorte then the Greekes; for example in *Moldwarp* wee expresse the nature of that beast; in *handkercher* the thing and his vse; in *vpright*, that vertue by a *Metaphore*; in *Wisedome* and *Domsdaye*, soe many sentences as wordes; and soe of the rest, for I geeue only a tast that may direct others to a fuller obseruation of what my soddaine memorye cannott represent vnto mee. It may passe allsoe the musters of this significancy that in a manner all the proper names of our people doe importe somewhat which, from a peculier note at first of some one of the Progenitors, in proces of tyme inuested it selfe [in] a possession of the posteritye, euen as wee see the like often befall to those whose fathers bare some vncouth Christian names. Yeat for the most parte wee avoyed the blemishe geuen by the Romanes in like cases, who distinguished the persones by the imperfections *Compositione of Wordes.*

of their bodyes, from whence grew their *Nasones, Labeones,*
Frontones, Dentones, and such like, how euer *Macrobius*
Equiuoca. coloreth the same. Yea, soe significant are our wordes,
that amongst them sundry single ones serue to expresse
diuers thinges; as by *Bill* are ment a weapon, a scroll,
and a birdes beake; by *Graue,* sober, a tombe, and to
carue; and by *light, marcke, match, file, sore,* & *praye,* the
semblable.

Againe, some sentences in the same wordes carrye
a diuers sence, as *till, desert, grounde;* some signifie one
thing forward, and another backward, as *Feeler I was no*
fo: of on saw I releef. Some signifie one self thinge forward
and backward, as *Ded deemed, I ioi, reuiuer,* & this, *eye did*
Madam erre. Some carry a conntrarye sence backwarde
to that they did foreward, as *I did leuell ere veu ; veu ere*
leuell did I.

Some deliuer a conntrarye sence by the diuers pointing,
as the Epistle in Doctor Wilsons Rethorick, and many
such like, which a curious head, leasure, & tyme might
picke out.

Prouerbs. Neither maye I omitt the significancy of our prouerbes,
concise in wordes but plentifull in number, breiffly pointing
at many great matters, and vnder the circuite of a few
syllables prescribing soundry auayleable caueats.

Meta-
phors. Lastly our speech doth not consist only of wordes, but
in a sorte euen of deedes, as when wee expresse a matter
by Metaphors, wherin the English is very frutefull and
forcible.

Easynes
to be
learned. And soe much for the significancye of our Language
in meaning; nowe for his easynes in learning. The same
shooteth oute into towe braunches: the one of others
learning our languadge, the second of our learning that of
others. For the first the most parte of our wordes (as I haue
touched) are Monasillables, and soe the fewer in tale, and
the sooner reduced to memorye; neither are we loden

with those declensions, flexions, and variations, which are incydent to many other tongues, but a few articles gouerne all our verbes and Nownes, and so wee neede a very shorte grammar.

For easye learning of other Languages by ours, lett these serue as prooffes; there are many Italyan wordes which the Frenchmen cannot pronounce, as *accio*, for which hee sayes *ashio*; many of the French which the Italian cann hardly come awaye withall, as *bayller, chagrin, postillon*; many in ours which neither of them cann vtter, as *Hedge, Water*. Soe that a straunger though neuer soe long conuersant amongest vs carryeth euermore a watch woorde vppon his tongue to descrye him by, but turne ann Inglishmann at any time of his age into what countrey soeuer, alloweing him dew respite, and you shall see him perfitt soe well that the Imitation of his vtteraunce will in nothing differ from the patterne of that natiue Languadge: the wante of which towardnes cost the Ephramites their skynnes. Neither doth this crosse my former assertione of others easye learninge our Language, for I meane of the sence & wordes & not touching the pronounciation. <small>To learne others.</small>

But I must nowe enter into the lardge feild of our tongues copiousnes, and perhapps longe wander vp and downe without finding easye way off issew, and yeat leaue many partes thereof vnsuruayed. <small>Copiousnes.</small>

My first prooff of our plentye I borowe from the choice which is geuen vs by the vse of diuers languages. The grounde of our owne apperteyneth to the old Saxon, little differing from the present low Dutch, because they more then any of their neighbours haue hitherto preserued that speach from any greate forrayne mixture. Heer amongst, the Brittons haue left diuers of their wordes entersowed, as it weere therby making a continuall clayme to their Auncient possession. Wee maye also trace the footestepps of the Danish bytter (though not longe duringe) soueraignty <small>Borrowing of others.</small>

in these partes: and the Romaine also imparted vnto vs of
his Latyne riches with noe sparing hand. Our neighbours
the French haue been likewise. contented wee should take
vp by retayle aswell their tearmes and their fashions, or
rather wee retaine yeat but some remnant of that which
once heere bare all the swaye, and daylye renewe the
store. Soe haue our Italyan trauilers brought vs acquainted
with their sweet relished phrases which (soe their con-
dicions crept not in withall) weere the better tollerable.
Yea euen wee seeke to make our good of our late Spanish
enymye, and feare as little the hurt of his tongue as the
dinte of his sworde. Seeing then wee borowe (and that
not shamfully) from the Dutch, the Breton, the Romaine,
the Dane, the French, Italyan, & Spanyard, how cann our
stocke bee other then exceeding plentifull? It may be
obiected that such patching maketh Littletons hotchpot
of our tongue, and in effect bringes the same rather to
a Babellish confusione then any one entyre Language.

Answere. It may againe be aunswered that this thefte of woordes is
not lesse warranted by the priuilidge of a prescription,
auncient and Vniuersall, then was that of goodes amongst
the *Lacedemonians* by an enacted lawe, for soe the Greekes
robbed the Hebrues, the Latynes the Greekes (which
filching *Cicero* with a large discourse in his booke *de
Oratore* defendeth), and (in a manner) all other Christiane

Words one in diuers Languages. Nations the Latyne. For Euidence hereof, many sentences
may be produced consisting of wordes that in their
oryginall are Latyne, and yeat (saue some smale varyaunce
in their termynacions) fall out all one with the French,
Dutch, and English, as *Ley Ceremonious persons, offer
prelate preest, cleere Candels flame, in Temples Cloistre, in
Cholerick Temperature, clisters purgation is pestilent, pulers
preseruatiue, subtill factors, aduocates, Notaries, practize,
Papers, libells, Registers, Regents, Maiesty in pallace hath
triumphant Throne, Regiments, Scepter, Vassalls supplica-*

tion, and such like. Then euen as the Italyane Potentates of those dayes make noe difference in their pedigrees and successions betwne the bed lawfull or vnlawfull, where either an vtter wante or a better deserte doth force or entice them thervnto, so maye the consenting practise of these nations passe for a Iust Legitimation of those bastard wordes which either necessitye or conueniencye hath induced them to adopt.

For our owne partes, we imploye the borrowed ware soe far to our aduantag that we raise a profitt of new woordes from the same stock, which yeat in their owne countrey are not merchantable; for example, wee deduce diuers wordes from the Latine which in the Latyne self cannot be yealded, as the verbes To *Aire, beard, cross, flame*, and their deriuations *ayring, ayred, bearder, bearding, bearded*, &c., as alsoe *closer, closely, closnes, glosingely, hourely, maiesticall, maiestically*. In like sort wee graffe vppon Frentch wordes those buddes to which that soyle affordeth noe growth, as *cheiffly, faulty, slauish, precisenes*. Diuers wordes alsoe wee deriue out of the Latyne at second hand by the French and make good English, though both Latyne and French haue their handes closed in that behalfe, as verbes *Praye, Pointe, Paze, Prest, Rent*, &c., and alsoe in the aduerbs *carpingly, currantly, actiuely, colourably*, &c.

Encrease in borrowinge.

Of Latyne in the French.

Againe, in other languages there fall out defectes while they want meanes to deliuer that which another tongue expresseth, as (by *Ciceroes* obseruation) you cannot interpret *ineptus* (vnapt, vnfitt, vntoward) in Greek, neither *Porcus, Capo, Vervex*, a barrow hogg, a Capon, a wether, as Cuiacius noteth *ad Tit. de verb. signif.*; noe more cann you *to stand* in *French, to Tye* in *Cornish*, nor *Knaue* in *Latyne*, for *Nebulo* is a cloudye fellow, or in *Irishe*; whereas you see our abillitye extendeth hereunto. Moreouer, the Copiousnes of our Languadge appeareth in the diuersitye

Defects of other tongues.

of our dialectes, for wee haue court, and wee haue countrye
Englishe, wee haue Northern and Southerne, grosse and
ordinary, which differ ech from other, not only in the
terminacions, but alsoe in many wordes, termes, and
phrases, and expresse the same thinges in diuers sortes,
yeat all right Englishe alike; neither cann any tongue (as
I am perswaded) deliuer a matter with more varietye then
ours, both plainely and by prouerbes and Metaphors; for
example, when wee would be rid of one, wee vse to saye
Bee going, trudge, pack, be faring, hence, awaye, shifte, and,
by circumlocution, *rather your roome then your companye,
Letts see your backe, com againe when I bid you, when you
are called, sent for, intreated, willed, desiered, inuited, spare
vs your place, another in your steede, a shipp of salte for you,
saue your credite, you are next the doore, the doore is open
for you, theres noe bodye holdes you, no bodie teares your
sleeue*, &c. Likewise this worde *fortis* wee maye *synnonomize*
after all these fashions, stoute, hardye, valiaunt, doughtye,
Couragious, aduenturous, &c.

<small>All sortes of Verses.</small>
And in a worde, to close vp these prooffes of our
copiousnes, looke into our Imitacione of all sortes of
verses affoorded by any other Language, and you shall
finde that S^r. *Phillip Sidney*, M^r. *Stanihurst*, and diuers
moe, haue made vse how farre wee are within compasse
of a fore imagined impossibility in that behalff.

<small>Sweetnes.</small>
I com nowe to the last and sweetest point of the sweetnes
of our tongue, which shall appeare the more plainelye yf,
like towe Turkeyes, or the *London Drapers*, wee match it
with our neighboures. The Italyan is pleasante but with-
<small>Compared with others.</small>
out synewes, as to stillye fleeting water; the French
delicate but ouer nice, as a woman scarce daring to open
her lipps for feare of marring her countenaunce; the
Spanishe maiesticall, but fullsome, running to much on the
O, and terrible like the deuill in a playe; the Dutch
manlike, but withall very harshe, as one ready at euery

The Excellency of English

worde to picke a quarrell. Now wee in borrowing from
them geue the strength of Consonantes to the Italyan,
the full sounde of wordes to the French, the varietye of
termi[na]cions to the Spanish, and the mollifieinge of more
vowells to the Dutch; and soe (like bees) gather the
honye of their good properties and leaue the dreggs to
themselfes. And thus, when substantiallnes combyneth
with delightfullnes, fullnes with fynes, seemelynes with
portlynes, and courrantnes with staydnes, howe canne the
languadge which consisteth of all these sounde other then Mixture.
most full of sweetnes? Againe, the longe wordes that wee
borrowe, being intermingled with the shorte of our owne
store, make vp a perfitt harmonye, by culling from out
which mixture (with Iudgment) yow maye frame your
speech according to the matter you must worke on,
maiesticall, pleasaunte, delicate, or manly, more or lesse,
in what sorte you please. Adde hereunto, that what Verse and
soeuer grace any other Languadge carryeth, in Verse or Prose.
Prose, in Tropes or Metaphors, in Ecchoes or Agnomina-
tions, they maye all be liuely and exactly represented in
ours. Will you haue *Platos* vayne? reede Sir *Thomas
Smith*: *The Ionick*? Sir *Tho. Moor*: *Ciceros*? *Aschame*:
Varro? *Chaucer*: *Demosthenes*? Sir *Iohn Cheeke* (who
in his treatise to the Rebells hath comprised all the figures
of Rhetorick). Will yow reade Virgill? take the *Earll of
Surrey*: *Catullus*? *Shakespheare*, and *Marlowes* fragment:
Ouid? *Daniell*: *Lucane*? *Spencer*: *Martiall*? Sir *Iohn
Dauis* and others. Will yow haue all in all for prose and
verse? take the miracle of our age Sir *Philip Sydney*.

And thus, if myne owne Eyes be not blinded by affection,
I haue made yours to see that the most renowned of other
nations haue laied vp, as in Treasure, and entrusted the
Diuisos orbe Britannos with the rarest Iewelles of their
lipps perfections, whether yow respect the vnderstanding
for significancye, or the memorye for Easynes, or the

conceipt for plentifullnes, or the Eare for pleasauntnes: wherin if inough be diliuered, to add more then Inough weare superfluous; if to little, I leaue it to bee supplied by better stored capacityes; if ought amisse, I submitte the same to the disciplyne of euery able and Impartiall censurer.

GEORGE CHAPMAN

(I. Preface to *Seaven Bookes of the Iliades*:
II. Dedication, etc. of *Achilles Shield*)

1598

I.

[This Preface 'To the Reader' appeared in the first draft of Chapman's translation of Homer, entitled *Seauen Bookes of the Iliades of Homere* (i. e. Bks. i, ii, vii–xi), which was printed by John Windet in 1598. The text is that of the copy in the Bodleian Library (Mason, H. 70).]

TO THE READER

I SUPPOSE you to be no meare reader, since you intend to reade Homer; and therefore wish I may walke free from their common obiections that can onelie reade. When my disorder is seene, that fower bookes are skipped (as a man would say) and yet the Poem continued according to the Greeke alphabet, viz. that for *Gamma* which is *Eta*, and that for *Delta* which is *Theta*, &c., then comes my knowne condemnation more greeuously then charitie would wish; especially with those that, hauing no eyes to peruse and iudge of the translation and whatsoeuer the maine matter deserues, will be glad to shew they see something, in finding fault with that forme; and peraduenture finde their queasie stomackes turnde at whatsoeuer is merited in the much laborde worke.

But to him that is more then a reader I write; and so consequentlie to him that will disdaine those easie ob-

iections which euery speller may put together. The
worth of a skilfull and worthy translator is to obserue the
sentences, figures, and formes of speech proposed in his
author, his true sence and height, and to adorne them
with figures and formes of oration fitted to the originall in
the same tongue to which they are translated: and these
things I would gladlie haue made the questions of whatsoeuer my labors haue deserued; not slighted with the slight
disorder of some bookes, which if I can put in as fit place
hereafter without checke to your due vnderstanding and
course of the Poet, then is their easie obiection answerde,
that, I expect, wilbe drounde in the fome of their eager
and emptie spleanes. For likelyhood of which habilitie
I haue good authoritie that the bookes were not set together
by Homer himselfe: Licurgus first bringing them out
of Ionia in Greece as an entire Poeme, before whose time
his verses were sung disseuered into many workes, one
calde the battaile fought at the fleete, another Doloniades,
another Agamemnon's fortitude, another the Catalogue of
ships, another Patroclus death, another Hectors redemp-
tion, an other the funerall games, &c. All which are the
titles of seuerall Iliades: and, if those were ordred by
others, why may not I chalenge as much authority, reseruing the right of my president? But to omit what
I can say further for reason to my present alteration, in
the next edition, when they come out by the dosen, I will
reserue the ancient and common receiued forme: in the
meane time do me the encouragement to confer that which
I haue translated with the same in Homer, and, according
to the worth of that, let this first edition passe: so shall
you do me but lawfull fauor, and make me take paines to
giue you this Emperor of all wisedome (for so Plato will
allow him) in your owne language, which will more hônor
it (if my part bee worthily discharged) then anything else
can be translated. In the meane time peruse the pamphlet

of errors in the impression, and helpe to point the rest with your iudgement; wherein, and in purchase of the whole seauen, if you be quicke and acceptiue, you shall in the next edition haue the life of Homer, a table, a prettie comment, true printing, the due praise of your mother tongue aboue all others for Poesie: and such demonstratiue proofe of our english wits aboue beyond sea-muses (if we would vse them), that a proficient wit should be the better to heare it.

II.

[Later in 1598 Chapman published a further instalment of his translation of Homer, entitled *Achilles Shield, Translated as the other seuen Bookes of Homer out of his eighteenth booke of Iliades* (also printed by John Windet). The following passages constitute the prefatory matter, which, like the Note 'To the Reader' given above, were not reprinted in the later and more complete issues of 1609 and 1611. The text is that of the British Museum copy (C. 39, d. 54), which is bound up with a copy of the *Seaven Bookes* and was once in the possession of Ben Jonson.]

TO THE MOST HONORED EARLE, *EARLE MARSHALL*.

Spondanus, one of the most desertfull Commentars of Homer, cals all sorts of all men learned to be iudicial beholders of this more then Artificiall and no lesse then *Diuine Rapture*, then which nothing can be imagined more full of soule and humaine extraction: for what is here prefigurde by our miraculous Artist but the vniuersall world, which, being so spatious and almost vnmeasurable, one circlet of a Shield representes and imbraceth? In it heauen turnes, the starres shine, the earth is enflowered, the sea swelles and rageth, Citties are built, one in the happinesse and sweetnesse of peace, the other in open

warre & the terrors of ambush, &c.: and all these so
liuely proposde, as not without reason many in times past
haue belieued that all these thinges haue in them a kind of
voluntarie motion, euen as those Tripods of *Vulcan* and
that *Dedalian Venus* αὐτοκίνητος. Nor can I be resolu'd that
their opinions be sufficiently refuted by *Aristonicus*, for so
are all things here described by our diuinest Poet as if
they consisted not of hard and solid mettals, but of a truely
liuing and mouing soule. The ground of his inuention he
shews out of *Eustathius*, intending by the Orbiguitie of the
Shield the roundnesse of the world, by the foure mettalles
the foure elementes, viz. by gold fire, by brasse earth, for
the hardnes, by Tinne water, for the softnes and inclination to fluxure, by siluer Aire, for the grosnes & obscuritie
of the mettal before it be refind. That which he calls
ἄντυγα τρίπλακα μαρμαρέην he vnderstands the Zodiack, which
is said to be triple for the latitude it contains, & shining by
reason of the perpetual course of the Sun made in that
circle, by ἀργύρεον τελαμῶνα the Axletree, about which
heauen hath his motion, &c. Nor do I deny (saith
Spondanus) *Eneas* arms to be forged with an exceeding
height of wit by *Virgil*, but comparde with these of *Homer*
they are nothing. And this is it (most honorde) that
maketh me thus sodainely translate this Shield of
Achilles, for since my publication of the other seuen
bookes comparison hath beene made betweene *Virgill* and
Homer; who can be comparde in nothing with more
decysall & cutting of all argument then in these two
Shieldes. And whosoeuer shall reade *Homer* throughly
and worthily will know the question comes from a superficiall and too vnripe a reader; for *Homers* Poems were
writ from a free furie, an absolute & full soule, *Virgils* out
of a courtly, laborious, and altogether imitatorie spirit:
not a *Simile* hee hath but is *Homers*: not an inuention,
person, or disposition, but is wholly or originally built

vpon *Homericall* foundations, and in many places hath the
verie wordes *Homer* vseth: besides, where *Virgill* hath
had no more plentifull and liberall a wit then to frame
twelue imperfect bookes of the troubles and trauailes of
Æneas, *Homer* hath of as little subiect finisht eight & fortie
perfect. And that the triuiall obiection may be answerd,
that not the number of bookes but the nature and excellence
of the worke commends it—all *Homers* bookes are such
as haue beene presidents euer since of all sortes of Poems;
imitating none, nor euer worthily imitated of any. Yet
would I not be thought so ill created as to bee a malicious
detracter of so admired a Poet as *Virgill*, but a true
iustifier of *Homer*, who must not bee read for a few lynes
with leaues turned ouer *caprichiously* in dismembred
fractions, but throughout, the whole drift, weight, & height
of his workes set before the apprensiue eyes of his
iudge: the maiestie he enthrones and the spirit he in-
fuseth into the scope of his worke so farre outshining
Virgill, that his skirmishes are but meere scramblings
of boyes to *Homers*; the silken body of *Virgils* muse curiously drest in guilt and embrodered siluer, but *Homers* in
plaine massie and vnualued gold; not onely all learning,
gouernment, and wisedome being deduc't as from a bottom-
lesse fountaine from him, but all wit, elegancie, disposition,
and iudgement. Ὅμηρος πρῶτος διδάσκαλος καὶ ἡγεμών, &c.;
Homer (saith *Plato*) was the Prince and maister of all
prayses and vertues, the Emperour of wise men, an host
of men against any deprauer in any principle he held. All
the ancient and lately learned haue had him in equall
estimation. And for anie to be now contrarilie affected, it
must needes proceed from a meere wantonnesse of witte,
an Idle vnthriftie spirit, wilfull because they may choose
whether they will think otherwise or not, & haue power
and fortune enough to liue like true men without truth; or
els they must presume of puritanicall inspiration, to haue

that with delicacie & squemishnes, which others with as good means, ten times more time, and ten thousand times more labour could neuer conceiue. But some will conuey their imperfections vnder his Greeke Shield, and from thence bestowe bitter arrowes against the traduction, affirming their want of admiration grows from defect of our language, not able to expresse the coppie and elegancie of the originall. But this easie and traditionall pretext hides them not enough: for how full of height and round-nesse soeuer Greeke be aboue English, yet is there no depth of conceipt triumphing in it, but, as in a meere admirer it may bee imagined, so in a sufficient translator it may be exprest. And *Homer* that hath his chiefe holi-nesse of estimation for matter and instruction would scorne to haue his supreame worthinesse glosing in his court-shippe and priuiledge of tongue. And if Italian, French, & Spanish haue not made it daintie, nor thought it any presumption to turne him into their languages, but a fit and honorable labour and (in respect of their countries profit and their poesies credit) almost necessarie, what curious, proud, and poore shamefastnesse should let an English muse to traduce him, when the language she workes withall is more conformable, fluent, and expressiue; which I would your Lordship would commaunde mee to proue against all our whippers of their owne complement in their countries dialect.

O what peeuish ingratitude and most vnreasonable scorne of our selues we commit to bee so extrauagant and forreignely witted to honour and imitate that in a strange tongue which wee condemne and contemne in our natiue! For if the substance of the Poets will be exprest, and his sentence and sence rendred with truth and elocution, hee that takes iudiciall pleasure in him in Greeke cannot beare so rough a browe to him in English, to entombe his ac-ceptance in austeritie.

A defence of Homer

But thou soule-blind Scalliger, that neuer hadst anything but place, time, and termes to paint thy proficiencie in learning, nor euer writest any thing of thine owne impotent braine but thy onely impalsied diminuation of *Homer* (which I may sweare was the absolute inspiration of thine owne ridiculous Genius), neuer didst thou more palpably damn thy drossy spirit in al thy all-countries-exploded filcheries, which are so grossely illiterate that no man will vouchsafe their refutation, then in thy sencelesse reprehensions of *Homer*, whose spirit flew asmuch aboue thy groueling capacitie as heauen moues aboue *Barathrum*. But as none will vouchsafe repetition nor answere of thy other vnmanly fooleries, no more will I of these, my Epistle being too tedious to your Lo. besides, and no mans iudgement seruing better (if your high affaires could admit their deligent perusall) then your Lo. to refute and reiect him. But alas *Homer* is not now to bee lift vp by my weake arme, more then he is now deprest by more feeble oppositions. If any feele not their conceiptes so rauisht with the eminent beauties of his ascentiall muse, as the greatest men of all sorts and of all ages haue beene. Their most modest course is (vnlesse they will be powerfully insolent) to ascribe the defect to their apprehension, because they read him but sleightly, not in his surmised frugalitie of obiect, that really and most feastfully powres out himselfe in right diuine occasion. But the chiefe and vnanswerable meane to his generall and iust acceptance must be your Lo. high and of all men expected president, without which hee must, like a poore snayle, pull in his English hornes, that out of all other languages (in regard of the countries affection, and royaltie of his Patrones) hath appeared like an Angell from a clowde, or the world out of Chaos, when no language can make comparison of him with ours if he be worthily conuerted; wherein before he should haue beene borne so lame and defectiue, as the

French midwife hath brought him forth, he had neuer
made question how your Lo. would accept him: and yet
haue two of their Kings embraced him as a wealthy ornament to their studies, and the main battayle of their
armies.

If then your bountie would do me but the grace to conferre my vnhappie labours with theirs so successfull &
commended (your iudgement seruing you much better then
your leysure, & yet your leisure in thinges honourable
being to bee inforced by your iudgement), no malitious &
dishonorable whisperer that comes armed with an army of
authority and state against harmeles & armeles vertue
could wrest your wonted impression so much from it self
to reiect (with imitation of tiranous contempt) any affection
so zealous & able in this kind to honor your estate as
mine. Onely kings & princes haue been *Homers* Patrones,
amongst whom *Ptolomie* wold say, he that had sleight
handes to entertayne *Homer* had as sleight braines to rule
his common wealth. And an vsuall seueritie he vsed, but
a most rationall (how precise and ridiculous soeuer it may
seeme to men made of ridiculous matter), that, in reuerence
of the pietie and perfect humanitie he taught, whosoeuer
writ or committed any proud detraction against *Homer* (as
euen so much a man wanted not his malitious deprauers),
hee put him with torments to extreamest death. O high
and magically raysed prospect, from whence a true eye
may see meanes to the absolute redresse, or much to be
wished extenuation, of all the vnmanly degeneracies now
tyranysing amongst vs! For if that which teacheth happinesse and hath vnpainefull corosiues in it (being entertayned and obserued) to eate out the hart of that raging
vlcer, which like a *Lernean Fen* of corruption furnaceth
the vniuersall sighes and complaintes of this transposed
world, were seriously and as with armed garrisons defended and hartned, that which engenders & disperseth

A defence of Homer

that wilfull pestilence would bee purged and extirpate;
but that which teacheth being ouerturned, that which is
taught is consequently subiect to euersion; and if the
honour, happinesse, and preseruation of true humanitie
consist in obseruing the lawes fit for mans dignitie, and
that the elaborate prescription of those lawes must of
necessitie be authorised, fauoured, and defended before
any obseruations can succeed, is it vnreasonable to punish
the contempt of that mouing prescription with one mans
death, when at the heeles of it followes common neglect of
obseruation, and in the necke of it an vniuersall ruine?
This my Lord I enforce only to interrupt in others that
may reade this vnsauorie stuffe, the too open mouthed
damnation of royall & vertuous *Ptolomies* seueritie. For
to digest, transforme, and sweat a mans soule into rules
and attractions to societie, such as are fashioned and
tempered with her exact and long laborde contention of
studie, in which she tosseth with her impertiall discourse
before her all cause of fantasticall obiections and reproofes,
and without which she were as wise as the greatest number
of detractors that shall presume to censure her, and yet
by their flash and insolent castigations to bee sleighted
and turnde ouer their miserably vaine tongues in an
instant, is an iniurie worthy no lesse penaltie then
Ptolomie inflicted. To take away the heeles of which
running prophanation, I hope your Lo. honourable countenance will be as the Vnicorns horne, to leade the way
to English *Homers* yet poysoned fountaine: for till that
fauour be vouchsafed, the herde will neuer drinke, since
the venemous galles of their fellowes haue infected it,
whom alas I pittie. Thus confidently affirming your name
and dignities shall neuer bee more honored in a poore
booke then in English *Homer*, I cease to afflict your Lordshippe with my tedious dedicatories, and to still sacred
Homers spirit through a language so fitte and so fauourles;

humbly presenting your Achilleian vertues with *Achilles*
Shield; wishing as it is much more admirable and diuine,
so it were as many times more rich then the Shield the
Cardinall pawned at Anwerp.

By him that wisheth all the degrees of iudgement, and
honour, to attend your deserts to the highest.

                                GEORGE CHAPMAN.

TO THE VNDERSTANDER

You are not euery bodie; to you (as to one of my very
few friends) I may be bold to vtter my minde; nor is it
more empaire to an honest and absolute mans sufficiencie
to haue few friendes then to an Homericall Poeme to haue
few commenders, for neyther doe common dispositions
keepe fitte or plausible consort with iudiciall and simple
honestie, nor are idle capacities comprehensible of an
elaborate Poeme. My Epistle dedicatorie before my seuen
bookes is accounted darke and too much laboured: for the
darkenes there is nothing good or bad, hard or softe, darke
or perspicuous but in respect, & in respect of mens light,
sleight, or enuious perusalles (to whose loose capacities
any worke worthily composde is knit with a riddle); & that
the stile is materiall, flowing & not ranke, it may perhaps
seeme darke to ranke riders or readers that haue no more
soules then burbolts: but to your comprehension, & in it
selfe, I know it is not. For the affected labour bestowed
in it, I protest two morninges both ended it and the
Readers Epistle: but the truth is, my desire & strange
disposition in all thinges I write is to set downe vncommon
and most profitable coherents for the time, yet further
remoued from abhorde affectation then from the most
popular and cold disgestion. And I euer imagine that as

A defence of Homer

Italian & French Poems to our studious linguistes win much of their discountryed affection, as well because the vnderstanding of forreigne tongues is sweete to their apprehension as that the matter & inuention is pleasing, so my farre fetcht and, as it were, beyond sea manner of writing, if they would take as much paines for their poore countrimen as for a proud stranger when they once vnderstand it, should be much more gracious to their choice conceiptes then a discourse that fals naked before them, and hath nothing but what mixeth it selfe with ordinarie table talke. For my varietie of new wordes, I haue none Inckepot I am sure you know, but such as I giue pasport with such authoritie, so significant and not ill sounding, that if my countrey language were an usurer, or a man of this age speaking it, hee would thanke mee for enriching him. Why, alas, will my young mayster the reader affect nothing common, and yet like nothing extraordinarie? Swaggering is a new worde amongst them, and rounde headed custome giues it priuiledge with much imitation, being created as it were by a naturall *Prosopopeia* without etimologie or deriuation; and why may not an elegancie authentichly deriued, & as I may say of the vpper house, bee entertayned as well in their lower consultation with authoritie of Arte as their owne forgeries lickt up by nature? All tongues haue inricht themselues from their originall (onely the Hebrew & Greeke which are not spoken amongst vs) with good neighbourly borrowing, and as with infusion of fresh ayre and nourishment of newe blood in their still growing bodies, & why may not ours? *Chaucer* (by whom we will needes authorise our true english) had more newe wordes for his time then any man needes to deuise now. And therefore for currant wits to crie from standing braines, like a broode of Frogs from a ditch, to haue the ceaselesse flowing riuer of our tongue turnde into their Frogpoole, is a song farre from

their arrogation of sweetnes, & a sin wold soone bring the
plague of barbarisme amongst vs; which in faith needes
not bee hastned with defences of his ignorant furtherers,
since it comes with mealemouth'd toleration too sauagely
vpon vs. To be short, since I had the reward of my
labours in their consummation, and the chiefe pleasure of
them in mine owne profit, no young preiudicate or castigatorie braine hath reason to thinke I stande trembling vnder
the ayry stroke of his feuerie censure, or that I did euer
expect any flowing applause from his drie fingers; but the
satisfaction and delight that might probably redound to
euerie true louer of vertue I set in the seat of mine owne
profit and contentment; and if there be any one in whome
this successe is enflowred, a few sprigges of it shall bee
my garland. Since then this neuer equald Poet is to
bee vnderstood, and so full of gouernment and direction
to all estates, sterne anger and the affrights of warre
bearing the mayne face of his subiect, soldiers shall neuer
spende their idle howres more profitablie then with his
studious and industrious perusall; in whose honors his
deserts are infinite. Counsellors haue neuer better oracles
then his lines: fathers haue no morales so profitable for
their children as his counsailes; nor shal they euer giue
them more honord iniunctions then to learne *Homer* without book, that, being continually conuersant in him, his
height may descend to their capacities, and his substance
proue their worthiest riches. Husbands, wiues, louers,
friends, and allies hauing in him mirrors for all their
duties; all sortes of which concourse and societie in other
more happy ages haue in steed of sonnets & lasciuious
ballades sung his Iliades. Let the length of the verse
neuer discourage your endeuours; for talke our quidditicall
Italianistes of what proportion soeuer their strooting lips
affect, vnlesse it be in these coopplets into which I haue
hastely translated this Shield, they shall neuer doe *Homer*

A defence of Homer

so much right, in any octaues, canzons, canzonets, or with whatsoeuer fustian Epigraphes they shall entitle their measures. Onely the extreame false printing troubles my conscience, for feare of your deserued discouragement
5 in the empaire of our Poets sweetnes; whose generall diuinitie of spirit, clad in my willing labours (enuious of none nor detracting any), I commit to your good nature and solid capacitie.

FRANCIS MERES

(*PALLADIS TAMIA*)

1598

[Meres's *Palladis Tamia, Wits Treasury* was printed in 1598 as the second instalment of the series of literary commonplace-books beginning with Bodenham's *Politeuphuia, Wits Commonwealth* (See Notes).

The earlier sections of Meres's work are concerned with topics of religion, morality, conduct, and the like; and the later with music, painting, and other subjects. The sections immediately preceding the passages here printed deal with *Bookes* (ff. 265-6), *Reading of bookes* (ff. 266-7), *A choice is to be had in Reading of Bookes* (ff. 267-8), *The vse of reading many bookes* (f. 268), and *Philosophie and Philosophers* (ff. 268-75). Of Books he says, 'As cherries be fulsome when they bee through ripe, because they be plenty: so bookes be stale when they be printed, in that they be common.' In the chapter on the choice of Books he draws up a list of books 'to be censured of.' 'As the Lord de la Noue in the sixt Discourse of his *Politike and Military Discourses* censureth of the bookes of *Amadis de Gaul*, which, he saith, are no lesse hurtfull to youth than the workes of Machiavell to age: so these bookes are accordingly to be censured of whose names follow—*Beuis of Hampton, Guy of Warwicke, Arthur of the Round Table, Huon of Burdeaux, Oliver of the Castle, The Foure Sonnes of Aymon, Gargantua, Gireleon, The Honour of Chiualrie, Primaleon of Greece, Palermin de Oliua, The 7 Champions, The Myrror of Knighthood, Blancherdine, Meruin, Howleglasse*, The Stories of *Palladyne and Palmendos, The Blacke Knight, The Maiden Knight*, The History of

Cælestina, The Castle of Fame, Gallian of France, Ornatus and Artesia, &c.'

The text of the following pages is that of the copy in the Bodleian Library.]

POETRIE.

AS in a Vine clusters of grapes are often hidde vnder the broade and spacious leaues: so in deepe conceited and well couched poems, figures and fables, many things verie profitable to be knowne, do passe by a yong scholler. *Plut.*

As, according to Philoxenus, that flesh is most sweete which is no flesh, and those the delectablest fishes which are no fishes: so that Poetrie dooth most delight which is mixt with Philosophie, and that Philosophie which is mixt with Poetrie. *Plutarchus in Commentario, quomodo adolescens Poetas audire debet.*

As a Bee gathereth the sweetest and mildest honie from the bitterest flowers and sharpest thornes: so some profite may bee extracted out of obscene and wanton Poems and fables. *idem.*

Albeit many be drunke with wine, yet the Vines are not to bee cut downe, as *Lycurgus* did, but Welles and Fountaines are to be digged neare vnto them: so although many abuse poetrie, yet it is not to bee banished, but discretion is to be vsed, that it may bee made holesome. *idem.*

As Mandrake growing neare Vines doth make the wine more mild: so philosophie bordering vppon poetrie dooth make the knowledge of it more moderate. *idem.*

As poyson mixt with meate is verie deadlie: so lasciuiousnesse and petulancie in poetrie mixt with profitable and pleasing matters is very pestilent. *idem.*

As we are delighted in deformed creatures artificiallye painted: so in poetrie, which is a liuely adumbration of things, euil matters ingeniously contriued do delight.

As Phisitians vse for medicine the feete and wings of
the flies *Cantharides*, which flies are deadly poyson: so
we may gather out of the same poem that may quell the
hurtfull venome of it; for poets do alwaies mingle somewhat in their Poems, wherby they intimate that they condemne what they declare. *idem.*

As our breath doth make a shiller sound being sent
through the narrow channell of a Trumpet then if it be
diffused abroad into the open aire: so the well knitte and
succinct combination of a Poem dooth make our meaning
better knowen and discerned then if it were deliuered at
random in prose. *Seneca.*

As he that drinkes of the Well *Clitorius* doth abhorre
wine: so they that haue once tasted of poetry cannot away
with the study of philosophie. After the same maner holdes
the contrarie.

As the Anabaptists abhorre the liberall artes and humane
sciences: so puritanes and precisians detest poetrie and
poems.

As eloquence hath found many preachers & oratours
worthy fauourers of her in the English tongue: so her
sister poetry hath found the like welcome and entertainment giuen her by our English poets, which makes our
language so gorgeous & delectable among vs.

As Rubarbe and sugarcandie are pleasant & profitable:
so in poetry ther is sweetnes and goodness. *M. John
Haring.*, in his *Apologie for Poetry* before his translated
Ariosto.

Many cockney and wanton women ar often sicke, but in
faith they cannot tell where: so the name of poetrie is
odious to some, but neither his cause nor effects, neither
the summe that contains him nor the particularities descending from him, giue any fast handle to their carping dispraise. *Sir Philip Sidney*, in his *Apologie for Poetry*.

POETS.

As some do vse an Amethist in compotation agaynst drunkennes: so certain precepts are to be vsed in hearing and reading of poets, least they infect the mind. *Plut. & Plin.* lib. 37. cap. 9.

As in those places where many holsome hearbes doe growe there also growes many poysonfull weedes: so in Poets there are many excellent things and many pestilent matters. *Plut.*

As *Simonides* sayde that the *Thessalians* were more blockish then that they could be deceiued of him: so the riper and pregnanter the wit is the sooner it is corrupted of Poets. *idem.*

As *Cato* when he was a scholler woulde not beleeue his maister, except hee rendered a reason of what he taught him: so wee are not to beleeue Poets in all that they write or say, except they yeelde a reason. *idem.*

As in the same pasture the Bee seaseth on the flower, the Goate grazeth on the shrub, the swine on the root, & Oxen, Kine, & Horses on the grasse: so in Poets one seeketh for historie, an other for ornament of speech, another for proofe, & an other for precepts of good life. *idem.*

As they that come verie suddainlie out of a very darke place are greatly troubled, except by little & little they be accustomed to the light: so, in reading of Poets, the opinions of Phylosophers are to bee sowne in the mindes of young schollers, least many diuersities of doctrines doe afterwardes distract their mindes. *idem.*

As in the portraiture of murder or incest we praise the Art of him that drewe it, but we detest the thing it selfe: so in lasciuious Poets let vs imitate their elocution but execrate their wantonnes. *idem.*

Some thinges that are not excellent of themselues are

good for some, bicause they are meet for them: so some things are commended in Poets which are fit and correspondent for the persons they speak of, although in themselues they bee filthy and not to be spoken; As lame *Demonides* wished that the shoes that were stolne from him might fit his feet that had stoln them. *idem.*

As that ship is endaungered where all leane to one side, but is in safetie one leaning one way and another another way: so the dissensions of Poets among themselues doth make them that they lesse infect their readers. And for this purpose our Satyrists Hall, the Author of *Pigmalion's Image* and *Certaine Satyres,* Rankins, and such others are very profitable.

As a Bee doth gather the iuice of honie from flowres, whereas others are onely delighted with the colour and smel: so a Philosopher findeth that among Poets which is profitable for good life, when as others are tickled only with pleasure. *Plut.*

As wee are delighted in the picture of a viper or a spider artificially enclosed within a precious iewell: so Poets do delight vs in the learned & cunning depainting of vices.

As some are delighted in counterfet wines confected of fruites, not that they refresh the hart but that they make drunke; so some are delighted in Poets only for their obscenity, neuer respecting their eloquence, good grace, or learning.

As Emperors, Kings, & princes haue in their handes authority to dignifie or disgrace their nobles, attendants, subiects, & vassals: so Poets haue the whole power in their handes to make men either immortally famous for their valiant exploites and vertuous exercises, or perpetually infamous for their vicious liues.

As *God giueth* life vnto man: so a Poet giueth ornament vnto it.

As the Greeke and Latine Poets haue wonne immortall

credit to their natiue speech, beeing encouraged and graced
by liberall patrones and bountifull Benefactors: so our
famous and learned Lawreat masters of England would
entitle our English to far greater admired excellency if
either the Emperor Augustus, or Octauia his sister, or
noble Mecænas were aliue to rewarde and countenaunce
them; or if our witty Comedians and stately Tragedians
(the glorious and goodlie representers of all fine witte,
glorified phrase, and queint action) bee still supported and
vphelde, by which meanes for lacke of Patrones (O in-
gratefull and damned age) our Poets are soly or chiefly
maintained, countenaunced, and patronized.

In the infancy of Greece they that handled in the
audience of the people graue and necessary matters were
called wise men or eloquent men, which they ment by
Vates: so the rest, which sang of loue matters, or other
lighter deuises alluring vnto pleasure and delight, were
called Poets or makers.

As the holy Prophets and sanctified apostles could
neuer haue foretold nor spoken of such supernaturall
matters vnlesse they had bin inspired of God: so *Cicero*
in his Tusculane questions is of that minde, that a Poet
cannot expresse verses aboundantly, sufficiently, and fully,
neither his eloquence can flow pleasantly, or his wordes
sound well and plenteously, without celestiall instruction;
which Poets themselues do very often and gladly witnes of
themselues, as namely *Ouid in* 6 *Fast.*

Est Deus in nobis; agitante calescimus illo. &c.

And our famous English Poet Spenser, who in his
Sheepeheards Calender, lamenting the decay of Poetry at
these dayes, saith most sweetly to the same,

'Then make the wings of thine aspiring wit,
And whence thou camest fly backe to heauen apace.' &c.

As a long gowne maketh not an Aduocate, although a gowne be a fit ornament for him: so riming nor versing maketh a Poet, albeit the Senate of Poets hath chosen verse as their fittest rayment; but it is the faining notable images of vertues, vices, or what else, with that delightfull teaching, which must bee the right describing note to knowe a Poet by. *Sir Philip Sidney* in his *Apology for Poetry*.

A COMPARATIUE DISCOURSE OF OUR ENGLISH POETS WITH THE GREEKE, LATINE, AND ITALIAN POETS.

As Greece had three poets of great antiquity, Orpheus, Linus, and Musæus, and Italy other three aunceint poets, Liuius Andronicus, Ennius, and Plautus: so hath England three aunceint poets, Chaucer, Gower, and Lydgate.

As Homer is reputed the Prince of Greek poets, and Petrarch of Italian poets: so Chaucer is accounted the God of English poets.

As Homer was the first that adorned the Greek tongue with true quantity: so *Piers Plowman* was the first that obserued the true quantitie of our verse without the curiositie of rime.

Ouid writ a Chronicle from the beginning of the world to his own time, that is, to the raign of Augustus the Emperor: so hath Harding the Chronicler (after his maner of old harsh riming) from Adam to his time, that is, to the raigne of King Edward the fourth.

As Sotades Maronites, the Iambicke Poet, gaue himself wholy to write impure and lasciuious things: so Skelton (I know not for what great worthines surnamed the Poet Laureat) applied his wit to scurrilities and ridiculous matters; such among the Greeks were called *Pantomimi*, with vs, buffons.

As Consaluo Periz, that excellent learned man, and

A Comparison of English Poets

Secretary to King Philip of Spayne, in translating the
'Ulysses' of Homer out of Greeke into Spanish, hath
by good iudgement auoided the faulte of ryming, although
not fully hit perfect and true versifying: so hath Henrie
Howarde, that true and noble Earle of Surrey, in translating the fourth book of Virgil's *Æneas*; whom Michael
Drayton in his *England's heroÿcall Epistles* hath eternized
for an *Epistle to his fair Geraldine*.

As these Neoterickes, Iouianus Pontanus, Politianus,
Marullus Tarchaniota, the two Strozæ, the father and the
son, Palingenius, Mantuanus, Philelphus, Quintianus Stoa,
and Germanus Brixius have obtained renown and good
place among the ancient Latine poets: so also these
Englishmen, being Latine poets, Gualter Haddon, Nicholas
Car, Gabriel Haruey, Christopher Ocland, Thomas Newton with his *Leyland*, Thomas Watson, Thomas Campion,
Brunswerd, and Willey haue attained good report and
honourable aduancement in the Latin empyre.

As the Greeke tongue is made famous and eloquent by
Homer, Hesiod, Euripedes, Æschylus, Sophocles, Pindarus, Phocylides, and Aristophanes; and the Latine
tongue by Virgill, Ouid, Horace, Silius Italicus, Lucanus,
Lucretius, Ausonius, and Claudianus: so the English
tongue is mightily enriched and gorgeously inuested in
rare ornaments and resplendent abiliments by Sir Philip
Sydney, Spencer, Daniel, Drayton, Warner, Shakespeare,
Marlow, and Chapman.

As Xenophon, who did imitate so excellently as to giue
vs *effigiem iusti imperii*, 'the portraiture of a iust empyre,'
vnder the name of *Cyrus* (as Cicero saieth of him), made
therein an absolute heroicall poem; and as Heliodorus
writ in prose his sugred inuention of that picture of Loue
in *Theagines and Cariclea*; and yet both excellent admired
poets: so Sir Philip Sidney writ his immortal poem, *The*

Countess of Pembrooke's Arcadia in Prose; and yet our rarest Poet.

As Sextus Propertius said, *Nescio quid magis nascitur Iliade*: so I say of Spencer's *Fairy Queene*, I knowe not what more excellent or exquisite Poem may be written.

As Achilles had the aduantage of Hector, because it was his fortune to bee extolled and renowned by the heauenly verse of Homer: so Spenser's *Eliza, the Fairy Queen*, hath the aduantage of all the Queenes in the worlde, to be eternized by so diuine a Poet.

As Theocritus is famoused for his *Idyllia* in Greeke, and Virgill for his *Eclogs* in Latine: so Spencer their imitator in his *Shepheardes Calender* is renowned for the like argument, and honoured for fine Poeticall inuention and most exquisit wit.

As Parthenius Nicæus excellently sung the praises of his *Arete*: so Daniel hath diuinely sonetted the matchlesse beauty of his *Delia*.

As euery one mourneth when hee heareth of the lamentable plangors of Thracian Orpheus for his dearest *Euridice*: so euery one passionateth when he readeth the afflicted death of Daniel's distressed *Rosamond*.

As Lucan hath mournefully depainted the ciuil wars of Pompey and Cæsar: so hath Daniel the civill wars of Yorke and Lancaster, and Drayton the civill wars of Edward the second and the Barons.

As Virgil doth imitate Catullus in the like matter of *Ariadne* for his story of Queene *Dido*: so Michael Drayton doth imitate Ouid in his *England's Heroical Epistles*.

As Sophocles was called a Bee for the sweetnes of his tongue: so in Charles Fitz-Iefferies *Drake* Drayton is termed 'golden-mouth'd' for the purity and pretiousnesse of his stile and phrase.

As Accius, M. Atilius, and Milithus were called *Tragaediographi*, because they writ tragedies: so may wee truly

A Comparison of English Poets

terme Michael Drayton *Tragaediographus* for his passionate penning the downfals of valiant Robert of Normandy, chast Matilda, and great Gaueston.

As Joan. Honterus, in Latine verse, writ three bookes of Cosmography, with geographicall tables: so Michael Drayton is now in penning, in English verse, a Poem called *Poly-olbion*, Geographicall and Hydrographicall of all the forests, woods, mountaines, fountaines, riuers, lakes, flouds, bathes, and springs that be in England.

As Aulus Persius Flaccus is reported among al writers to be of an honest life and vpright conuersation: so Michael Drayton, *quem toties honoris et amoris causa nomino*, among schollers, souldiours, Poets, and all sorts of people is helde for a man of vertuous disposition, honest conuersation, and well gouerned cariage; which is almost miraculous among good wits in these declining and corrupt times, when there is nothing but rogery in villanous man, and when cheating and craftines is counted the cleanest wit, and soundest wisedome.

As Decius Ausonius Gallus, *in libris Fastorum*, penned the occurrences of the world from the first creation of it to his time, that is, to the raigne of the Emperor Gratian: so Warner, in his absolute *Albion's Englande*, hath most admirably penned the historie of his own country from Noah to his time, that is to the raigne of Queen Elizabeth. I haue heard him termd of the best wits of both our Vniuersities our English Homer.

As Euripedes is the most sententious among the Greek Poets: so is Warner among our English Poets.

· As the soule of Euphorbus was thought to liue in Pythagoras: so the sweete wittie soule of Ouid liues in mellifluous and hony-tongued Shakespeare, witnes his *Venus and Adonis*, his *Lucrece*, his sugred *Sonnets* among his priuate friends, &c.

As Plautus and Seneca are accounted the best for

Comedy and Tragedy among the Latines: so Shakespeare among the English is the most excellent in both kinds for the stage. For Comedy, witnes his *Gentlemen of Verona*, his *Errors*, his *Loue Labors Lost*, his *Loue Labours Wonne*, his *Midsummers Night Dreame*, and his *Merchant of Venice*; For Tragedy, his *Richard the* 2, *Richard the* 3, *Henry the* 4, *King Iohn, Titus Andronicus*, and his *Romeo and Iuliet*.

As Epius Stolo said that the Muses would speake with Plautus tongue if they would speak Latin: so I say that the Muses would speak with Shakespeares fine filed phrase if they would speak English.

As Musæus, who wrote the loue of Hero and Leander, had two excellent schollers, Thamaras and Hercules: so hath he in England two excellent poets, imitators of him in the same argument and subiect, Christopher Marlow and George Chapman.

As Ouid saith of his work,

> *Iamque opus exegi, quod nec Iouis ira, nec ignis,*
> *Nec poterit ferrum, nec edax abolere vetustas;*

and as Horace saith of his,

> *Exegi monumentum aere perennius*
> *Regalique situ pyramidum altius,*
> *Quod non imber edax, non Aquilo impotens*
> *Possit diruere, aut innumerabilis*
> *Annorum series, et fuga temporum:*

so I say seuerally of Sir Philip Sidney's, Spenser's, Daniel's, Drayton's, Shakespeare's, and Warner's workes,

> *Non Iovis ira, imbres, Mars, ferrum, flamma, senectus,*
> *Hoc opus vnda, lues, turbo, venena ruent.*
> *Et quanquam ad pulcherrimum hoc opus euertendum,*
> *tres illi Dii conspirabunt, Chronus, Vulcanus, et Pater ipse gentis.*

Non tamen annorum series, non flamma, nec ensis;
Aeternum potuit hoc abolere Decus.

As Italy had Dante, Boccace, Petrarch, Tasso, Celiano, and Ariosto: so England had Matthew Roydon, Thomas Atchelow, Thomas Watson, Thomas Kid, Robert Greene, and George Peele.

As there are eight famous and chiefe languages, Hebrew, Greek, Latine, Syriack, Arabicke, Italian, Spanish, and French: so there are eight notable seuerall kindes of Poets, Heroicke, Lyricke, Tragicke, Comicke, Satiricke, Iambicke, Elegiacke, and Pastoral.

As Homer and Virgil among the Greeks and Latines are the chiefe Heroick Poets: so Spencer and Warner be our chiefe heroicall Makers.

As Pindarus, Anacreon, and Callimachus among the Greekes, and Horace and Catullus among the Latines are the best Lyrick poets: so in this faculty the best among our poets are Spencer (who excelleth in all kinds), Daniel, Drayton, Shakespeare, Bretton.

As these Tragicke Poets flourished in Greece, Æschylus, Euripedes, Sophocles, Alexander Ætolus, Achæus Erithriœus, Astydamas Atheniensis, Apollodorus Tarsensis, Nicomachus Phrygius, Thespis Atticus, and Timon Apolloniates; and these among the Latines, Accius, M. Atilius, Pompon[i]us Secundus, and Seneca: so these are our best for Tragedie, The Lorde Buckhurst, Doctor Leg of Cambridge, Doctor Edes of Oxford, Master Edward Ferris, the author of the *Mirror for Magistrates*, Marlow, Peele, Watson, Kid, Shakespeare, Drayton, Chapman, Decker, and Beniamin Iohnson.

As M. Anneus Lucanus writ two excellent tragedies, one called *Medea*, the other *De incendio Troiae cum Priami calamitate*: so Doctor Leg hath penned two famous tragedies, the one of *Richard the* 3, the other of *The Destruction of Ierusalem.*

The best Poets for Comedy among the Greeks are these, Menander, Aristophanes, Eupolis Atheniensis, Alexis Terius, Nicostratus, Amipsias Atheniensis, Anaxandrides Rhodius, Aristonymus, Archippus Atheniensis, and Callias Atheniensis; and among the Latines, Plautus, Terence, Næuius, Sextus Turpilius, Licinius Imbrex, and Virgilius Romanus: so the best for Comedy amongst vs bee Edward, Earle of Oxforde, Doctor Gager of Oxforde, Master Rowley, once a rare scholler of learned Pembrooke Hall in Cambridge, Maister Edwardes, one of Her Maiesties Chappell, eloquent and wittie Iohn Lilly, Lodge, Gascoyne, Greene, Shakespeare, Thomas Nash, Thomas Heywood, Anthony Mundye, our best plotter, Chapman, Porter, Wilson, Hathway, and Henry Chettle.

As Horace, Lucilius, Iuuenall, Persius, and Lucullus are the best for Satyre among the Latines: so with vs, in the same faculty, these are chiefe, *Piers Plowman*, Lodge, Hall of Imanuel Colledge in Cambridge, the Author of *Pigmalion's Image* and *certain Satyrs*, the Author of *Skialetheia.*

Among the Greekes I will name but two for Iambicks, Archilochus Parius and Hipponax Ephesius: so amongst vs I name but two Iambical Poets, Gabriel Haruey and Richard Stanyhurst, bicause I haue seene no mo in this kind.

As these are famous among the Greeks for Elegie, Melanthus, Mymnerus Colophonius, Olympius Mysius, Parthenius Nicæus, Philetas Cous, Theogenes Megarensis, and Pigres Halicarnassæus; and these among the Latines, Mæcenas, Ouid, Tibullus, Propertius, C. Valgius, Cassius Seuerus, and Clodius Sabinus: so these are the most passionate among vs to bewaile and bemoane the perplexities of loue, Henrie Howard, Earle of Surrey, Sir

A Comparison of English Poets

Thomas Wyat the elder, Sir Francis Brian, Sir Philip Sidney, Sir Walter Rawley, Sir Edward Dyer, Spencer, Daniel, Drayton, Shakespeare, Whetstone, Gascoyne, Samuell Page, sometimes Fellowe of Corpus Christi Colledge in Oxford, Churchyard, Bretton.

As Theocritus in Greek, Virgil and Mantuan in Latine, Sanazar in Italian, and the Authour of *Amintæ Gaudia* and *Walsingham's Melibœus* are the best for Pastorall: so amongst vs the best in this kind are Sir Philip Sidney, Master Challener, Spencer, Stephen Gosson, Abraham Fraunce, and Barnefield.

These and many other Epigrammatists the Latin tongue hath, Q. Catulus, Porcius Licinius, Quintus Cornificius, Martial, Cnœus Getulicus, and wittie Sir Thomas Moore: so in English we have these, Heywood, Drante, Kendal, Bastard, Dauies.

As noble Mæcenas, that sprang from the Hetruscan Kinges, not onely graced Poets by his bounty but also by beeing a Poet himself; and as Iames the 6, nowe King of Scotland, is not only a fauorer of Poets but a Poet, as my friend Master Richard Barnefielde hath in this disticke passing well recorded,

> The King of Scots now liuing is a Poet,
> As his *Lepanto* and his *Furies* show it:

so Elizabeth, our dread Souereign and gracious Queene, is not only a liberal Patrone vnto Poets, but an excellent Poet herselfe, whose learned, delicate, and noble Muse surmounteth, be it in Ode, Elegy, Epigram, or in any other kind of poem, Heroicke or Lyricke.

Octauia, sister vnto Augustus the Emperour, was exceeding bountifull vnto Virgil, who gaue him for making 26 verses, 1,137 pounds, to wit, tenne *sestertiæ* for euerie verse (which amounted to aboue 43 pounds for euery verse): so learned Mary, the honourable Countesse of

Pembrook, the noble sister of immortall Sir Philip Sidney, is very liberall vnto Poets; besides, shee is a most delicate Poet, of whome I may say, as Antipater Sidonius writeth of Sappho,

> *Dulcia Mnemosyne demirans carmina Sapphus,*
> *Quaesiuit decima Pieris vnde foret.*

Among others, in times past, Poets had these fauourers, Augustus, Mæcenas, Sophocles, Germanicus, an Emperor, a Nobleman, a Senatour, and a Captaine: so of later times Poets haue these patrones, Robert, King of Sicil, the great King Francis of France, King Iames of Scotland, and Queene Elizabeth of England.

As in former times two great Cardinals, Bembus and [Bib]biena, did countenance Poets: so of late yeares two great preachers haue giuen them their right hands in fellowship, Beza and Melancthon.

As the learned philosophers Fracastorius and Scaliger haue highly prized them: so haue the eloquent Orators Pontanus and Muretus very gloriously estimated them.

As Georgius Buchananus' *Iepthæ* amongst all moderne Tragedies is able to abide the touch of Aristotle's precepts and Euripedes's examples: so is Bishop Watson's *Absalon*.

As Terence for his translations out of Apollodorus and Menander, and Aquilius for his translation out of Menander, and C. Germanicus Augustus for his out of Aratus, and Ausonius for his translated *Epigrams* out of Greeke, and Doctor Iohnson for his *Frogge-fight* out of Homer, and Watson for his *Antigone* out of Sophocles, have got good commendations: so these versifiers for their learned translations are of good note among vs, Phaer for Virgil's *Æneads*, Golding for Ouid's *Metamorphosis*, Harington for his *Orlando Furioso*, the Translators of Seneca's *Tragedies*, Barnabe Googe for Palingenius, Turberuile for Ouid's

Epistles and Mantuan, and Chapman for his inchoate Homer.

As the Latines haue these Emblematists, Andreas Alciatus, Reusnerus, and Sambucus: so we haue these, Geffrey Whitney, Andrew Willet, and Thomas Combe.

As Nonnus Panapolyta writ the *Gospell* of Saint Iohn in Greeke hexameters: so Iervis Markham hath written Salomon's *Canticles* in English verse.

As C. Plinius writ the life of Pompon[i]us Secundus: so young Charles Fitz-Ieffrey, that high touring Falcon, hath most gloriously penned *The honourable Life and Death of worthy Sir Francis Drake.*

As Hesiod writ learnedly of husbandry in Greeke: so hath Tusser very wittily and experimentally written of it in English.

As Antipater Sidonius was famous for extemporall verse in Greeke, and Ouid for his *Quicquid conabar dicere versus erat*: so was our Tarleton, of whome Doctor Case, that learned physitian, thus speaketh in the Seuenth Booke and seuenteenth chapter of his *Politikes: Aristoteles suum Theodoretum laudauit quendam peritum Tragaediarum actorem, Cicero suum Roscium: nos Angli Tarletonum, in cuius voce et vultu omnes iocosi affectus, in cuius cerebroso capite lepidae facetiae habitant.* And so is now our wittie Wilson, who for learning and extemporall witte in this facultie is without compare or compeere, as, to his great and eternall commendations, he manifested in his challenge at the *Swanne* on the Banke Side.

As Achilles tortured the deade bodie of Hector, and as Antonius and his wife Fuluia tormented the liuelesse corps of Cicero: so Gabriell Haruey hath shewed the same inhumanitie to Greene, that lies full low in his graue.

As Eupolis of Athens vsed great libertie in taxing the vices of men: so doth Thomas Nash, witnesse the broode of the Harueys!

As Actæon was wooried of his owne hounds: so is
Tom Nash of his *Isle of Dogs*. Dogges were the death
of Euripedes; but bee not disconsolate, gallant young
Iuuenall, Linus, the sonne of Apollo, died the same death.
Yet God forbid that so braue a witte should so basely
perish! Thine are but paper dogges, neither is thy banish-
ment like Ouid's, eternally to conuerse with the barbarous
Getæ. Therefore comfort thyselfe, sweete Tom, with
Cicero's glorious return to Rome, and with the counsel
Æneas giues to his seabeaten soldiors, *Lib.* 1, *Æneid*.

> Pluck vp thine heart, and driue from thence both
>   feare and care away!
> To thinke on this may pleasure be perhaps another
>   day.
> *Durate et temet rebus seruate secundis.*

As Anacreon died by the pot: so George Peele by the
pox.

As Archesilaus Prytanœus perished by wine at a drunken
feast, as Hermippus testifieth in *Diogenes*: so Robert
Greene died of a surfet taken at pickeld herrings and
Rhenish wine, as witnesseth Thomas Nash, who was at
the fatall banquet.

As Iodelle, a French tragical poet, beeing an epicure
and an atheist, made a pitifull end: so our tragicall poet
Marlow for his Epicurisme and Atheisme had a tragical
death. You may read of this Marlow more at large in the
Theatre of God's judgments, in the 25th chapter entreating
of *Epicures and Atheists*.

As the poet Lycophron was shot to death by a certain
riual of his: so Christopher Marlow was stabd to death by
a bawdy Servingman, a riual of his in his lewde loue.

WILLIAM VAUGHAN

(*THE GOLDEN GROVE*)

1600

[William Vaughan's book, entitled *The Golden-groue, moralized in three books: a work very necessary for all such as would know how to gouerne themselues, their houses, or their country*, appeared in 1600 (12mo, unpaged). The extracts have been taken from the copy preserved in the Bodleian Library (Wood, 743). In the note 'To the Reader,' Vaughan says:—'If any man delight to haue himselfe shine with a glorious shewe of virtue, I haue giuen him the toppes of moral behauior; if to haue his house and family wel beautified, I haue yeelded him diuers braunches for that purpose; if to haue his countrey flourish, I haue sent him the deep-grounded stemme of policy.' There are three books, containing respectively sixty-nine, thirty, and seventy chapters. The following notes include all the more important references to literary matters.

Book i, chap. 51, entitled 'Whether Stage Playes ought to be suffred in a Commonwealth?' is a diatribe against plays as mere folly and wickedness: the literary problem is not discussed.

In Bk. iii, chap. 39, ' Of Grammar,' chap. 40, ' Of Logick,' and chap. 41, ' Of Rhetoricke and the abuse thereof,' Vaughan follows the traditional line of description and commendation of these studies. Chap. 42 is headed 'Of Poetry, and of the excellency thereof.' This shows that Moses and Deborah were the most ancient poets, that poetry was the chief cause of the heathen's 'ciuility,' and that poets were the first to 'obserue the secrete operations of nature,' and to offer oblations, sacrifices, and prayers. Vaughan mentions the characteristics of poetry, opposes those who say that the Gentiles first

founded poetry, and that therefore it ought to be rejected,
and stands forth in its defence, drawing on classic names
and examples, and referring especially to Homer. 'Sundry
times haue I beene conuersant with such as blasphemed
Poetry, by calling it mincing and lying Poetry. But it is
no maruel that they thus deride Poetry, sith they sticke
not in this out-worne age to abuse the ministers of God by
terming them bookish fellowes and Puritanes, they themselues not knowing what they meane.' After the classics
he names modern poets. 'Ieffery Chaucer, the English
Poet, was in great account with King Richard the second,
who gaue him, in reward of his poems, the manour of
Newelme in Oxfordshire.' He refers to the story of Alain
Chartier's being kissed by the French Queen, and tells that
Francis I made 'those famous poets Dampetrus and Macrinus' of the Privy Council. 'King Henrie the eight, for a
few Psalmes of Dauid turned into English meeter by
Sternhold, made him Groome of his priuie chamber and
rewarded him with many great gifts besides. Moreouer,
hee made Sir Thomas Moore Lord Chauncelour of this
Realme, whose poeticall works are as yet in great regard.'
Queen Mary gave a pension to Vergoza the Spaniard for
a poem on her marriage with Philip, Queen Elizabeth
made Dr. Haddon Master of Requests. Princely poets
of former times were Julius Caesar, 'a very good poet,'
Augustus, Euax, King of Arabia, and Cornelius Gallus,
treasurer of Egypt. He then adds: 'Neither is our
owne age altogether to bee dispraysed. For the old
Earle of Surrey composed bookes in verse. Sir Philip
Sidney excelled all our English Poets in rarenesse of stile
and matter. King James the sixt of Scotland, that now
raigneth, is a notable Poet, and daily setteth out most
learned poems, to the admiration of all his subiects.'
Vaughan refers to Sidney's defence of Poetry in the
Apology, and sums up 'Take away the abuse, which is
meerely accidental, and let the substance of Poetrie stand
still. . . I conclude that many of our English rimers and
ballet-makers deserue for their baudy sonnets and amorous
allurements to bee banished, or seuerely punished: and
that Poetrie it selfe ought to bee honoured and made much
of, as a precious Iewell and a diuine gift.']

THOMAS CAMPION

(*OBSERVATIONS IN THE ART OF ENGLISH POESIE*)

1602

[Campion's tract, in 12mo, bears the title-page *Obseruations in the Art of English Poesie. By Thomas Campion. Wherein it is demonstratiuely prooued, and by example confirmed, that the English toong will receiue eight seuerall kinds of numbers, proper to it selfe, which are all in this booke set forth, and were neuer before this time by any man attempted. Printed at London by Richard Field for Andrew Wise. 1602.* It is dedicated by Campion to Lord Buckhurst, in these words:

'In two things (right honorable) it is generally agreed that man excels all other creatures, in reason and speech: and in them by how much one man surpasseth an other, by so much the neerer he aspires to a celestiall essence.

'Poesy in all kind of speaking is the chiefe beginner and maintayner of eloquence, not only helping the eare with the acquaintance of sweet numbers, but also raysing the mind to a more high and lofty conceite. For this end haue I studyed to induce a true forme of versefying into our language: for the vulgar and vnarteficiall custome of riming hath, I know, deter'd many excellent wits from the exercise of English poesy. The obseruations which I haue gathered for this purpose I humbly present to your Lordship, as to the noblest iudge of Poesy, and the most honorable protector of all industrious learning; which if your Honour shall vouchsafe to receiue, who both in your publick and priuate Poemes haue so deuinely crowned your fame, what man will dare to repine? or not striue to imitate them? Wherefore with all humility I subiect my selfe and them to your gratious fauour, beseeching you in the noblenes of your mind to take in worth so simple a present, which by some worke drawne from my more

serious studies I will hereafter endeuour to excuse.' Then
follow these lines, entitled 'The Writer to his Booke':

Whether thus hasts my little booke so fast?
To Paules Churchyard. What? in those cels to stand,
With one leafe like a rider's cloke put vp
To catch a termer? or lie mustie there
With rimes a terme set out, or two, before?
Some will redeeme me. Fewe. Yes, reade me too.
Fewer. Nay loue me. Now thou dot'st, I see.
Will not our English *Athens* arte defend?
Perhaps. Will lofty courtly wits not ayme
Still at perfection? If I graunt? I flye.
Whether? To Pawles. Alas, poore booke, I rue
Thy rash selfe-loue. Goe, spread thy pap'ry wings:
Thy lightnes cannot helpe or hurt my fame.

The text is that of the copy in the Bodleian Library
(Douce, C. 359). Two leaves which are missing (see footnotes, pp. 332, 341) are supplied from the quarto.]

OBSERVATIONS IN THE ART OF ENGLISH POESY.

THE FIRST CHAPTER, INTREATING OF NUMBERS IN GENERALL.

THERE is no writing too breefe that, without obscuritie, comprehends the intent of the writer. These my late obseruations in English Poesy I haue thus briefely gathered, that they might proue the lesse troublesome in perusing, and the more apt to be retayn'd in memorie. And I will first generally handle the nature of Numbers. Number is *discreta quantitas*: so that when we speake simply of number, we intend only the disseruer'd quantity; but when we speake of a Poeme written in number, we consider not only the distinct number of the sillables, but also their value, which is contained in the length or shortnes of their sound. As in Musick we do not say a straine of so many notes, but so many sem'briefes (though some-

times there are no more notes then sem'briefes), so in
a verse the numeration of the sillables is not so much to
be obserued as their waite and due proportion. In ioyning
of words to harmony there is nothing more offensiue to
the eare then to place a long sillable with a short note, or
a short sillable with a long note, though in the last the
vowell often beares it out. The world is made by Simmetry
and proportion, and is in that respect compared to Musick,
and Musick to Poetry: for *Terence* saith, speaking of Poets,
artem qui tractant musicam, confounding Musick and Poesy
together. What musick can there be where there is no
proportion obserued? Learning first flourished in *Greece*;
from thence it was deriued vnto the *Romaines*, both diligent
obseruers of the number and quantity of sillables, not
in their verses only but likewise in their prose. Learning, after the declining of the *Romaine* Empire and the
pollution of their language through the conquest of the
Barbarians, lay most pitifully deformed till the time of
Erasmus, Rewcline, Sir *Thomas More,* and other learned
men of that age, who brought the Latine toong again to
light, redeeming it with much labour out of the hands of
the illiterate Monks and Friers: as a scoffing booke,
entituled *Epistolae obscurorum virorum,* may sufficiently
testifie. In those lack-learning times, and in barbarized
Italy, began that vulgar and easie kind of Poesie which
is now in vse throughout most parts of Christendome,
which we abusively call Rime and Meeter, of *Rithmus* and
Metrum, of which I will now discourse.

THE SECOND CHAPTER, DECLARING THE VNAPTNESSE
OF RIME IN POESIE.

I am not ignorant that whosoeuer shall by way of reprehension examine the imperfections of Rime must encounter
with many glorious enemies, and those very expert and

ready at their weapon, that can if neede be extempore (as
they say) rime a man to death. Besides there is growne
a kind of prescription in the vse of Rime, to forestall the
right of true numbers, as also the consent of many nations,
against all which it may seeme a thing almost impossible
and vaine to contend. All this and more can not yet de-
terre me from a lawful defence of perfection, or make me
any whit the sooner adheare to that which is lame and
vnbeseeming. (For custome I alleage that ill vses are to
be abolisht, and that things naturally imperfect can not be
perfected by vse. (Old customes, if they be better, why
should they not be recald, as the yet florishing custome of
numerous poesy vsed among the *Romanes* and *Grecians*?
But the vnaptnes of our toongs and the difficultie of
imitation dishartens vs: againe, the facilitie and popularitie
of Rime creates as many Poets as a hot sommer flies.

But let me now examine the nature of that which we
call Rime. [By Rime is vnderstoode that which ends in
the like sound, so that verses in such maner composed
yeeld but a continual repetition of that Rhetoricall figure
which we tearme *similiter desinentia*, and that, being but
figura verbi, ought (as *Tully* and all other Rhetoritians
haue iudicially obseru'd) sparingly to be vs'd, least it
should offend the eare with tedious affectation) Such was
that absurd following of the letter amongst our English so
much of late affected, but now hist out of Paules Churchyard: which foolish figuratiue repetition crept also into
the Latine toong, as it is manifest in the booke of Ps called
praelia porcorum, and another pamphlet all of Fs which
I haue seene imprinted; but I will leaue these follies to
their owne ruine, and returne to the matter intended.
(The eare is a rationall sence and a chiefe iudge of proportion; but in our kind of riming what proportion is there
kept where there remaines such a confused inequalitie of
sillables? *Iambick* and *Trochaick* feete, which are opposed

On English Verse

by nature, are by all Rimers confounded·; nay, oftentimes they place instead of an *Iambick* the foot *Pyrrychius*, consisting of two short sillables, curtalling their verse, which they supply in reading with a ridiculous and vnapt drawing of their speech. As for example :

> Was it my desteny, or dismall chaunce?

In this verse the two last sillables of the word *Desteny*, being both short, and standing for a whole foote in the verse, cause the line to fall out shorter then it ought by nature. The like impure errors haue in time of rudenesse bene vsed in the Latine toong, as the *Carmina prouerbialia* can witnesse, and many other such reuerend bables. But the noble *Grecians* and *Romaines*, whose skilfull monuments outliue barbarisme, tyed themselues to the strict obseruation of poeticall numbers, so abandoning the childish titillation of riming that it was imputed a great error to *Ouid* for setting forth this one riming verse,

> *Quot caelum stellas tot habet tua Roma puellas.*

For the establishing of this argument, what better confirmation can be had then that of Sir *Thomas Moore* in his booke of Epigrams, where he makes two sundry Epitaphs vpon the death of a singing-man at *Westminster*, the one in learned numbers and dislik't, the other in rude rime and highly extold: so that he concludes, *tales lactucas talia labra petunt*, like lips like lettuce.

But there is yet another fault in Rime altogether intollerable, which is, that it inforceth a man oftentimes to abiure his matter and extend a short conceit beyond all bounds of arte; for in Quatorzens, methinks, the poet handles his subiect as tyrannically as *Procrustes* the thiefe his prisoners, whom, when he had taken, he vsed to cast vpon a bed, which if they were too short to fill, he would stretch them longer, if too long, he would cut them shorter. Bring before me now any the most self-lou'd Rimer, and

let me see if without blushing he be able to reade his lame
halting rimes. Is there not a curse of Nature laid vpon
such rude Poesie, when the Writer is himself asham'd of
it, and the hearers in contempt call it Riming and Ballat-
ing? What Deuine in his Sermon, or graue Counsellor
in his Oration, will alleage the testimonie of a rime? But
the deuinity[1] of the *Romaines* and *Gretians* was all written
in verse; and *Aristotle, Galene,* and the bookes of all the
excellent Philosophers are full of the testimonies of the
old Poets. By them was laid the foundation of all humane
wisdome, and from them the knowledge of all antiquitie
is deriued. I will propound but one question, and so
conclude this point. If the *Italians, Frenchmen,* and
Spanyards, that with commendation have written in Rime,
were demaunded whether they had rather the bookes they
haue publisht (if their toong would beare it) should remaine
as they are in Rime or be translated into the aunciet
numbers of the Greekes and Romaines, would they not
answere into numbers? What honour were it then for
our English language to be the first that after so many
yeares of barbarisme could second the perfection of the
industrious *Greekes* and *Romaines*? which how it may be
effected I will now proceede to demonstrate.

The third Chapter: of our English numbers in generall.

There are but three feete which generally distinguish
the Greeke and Latine verses, the *Dactil*, consisting of
one long sillable and two short, as $v\bar{\imath}u\breve{e}r\breve{e}$; the *Trochy*,
of one long and one short, as $v\bar{\imath}t\breve{a}$; and the *Iambick* of one
short and one long, as $\breve{a}m\bar{o}r$. The *Spondee* of two long,
the *Tribrach* of three short, the *Anapæstick* of two short
and a long, are but as seruants to the first. Diuers other

---

[1] From this point to l. 17 (to the word 'remayne') on p. 333 the text is supplied from a later edition (see head-note).

On English Verse

feete I know are by the Grammarians cited, but to little purpose. (The *Heroicall* verse that is distinguisht by the *Dactile* hath bene oftentimes attempted in our English toong, but with passing pitifull successe; and no wonder, seeing it is an attempt altogether against the nature of our language.) For both the concurse of our monasillables make our verses vnapt to slide, and also, if we examine our polysillables, we shall finde few of them, by reason of their heauinesse, willing to serue in place of a *Dactile*. Thence it is that the writers of English heroicks do so often repeate *Amyntas, Olympus, Auernus, Erinnis*, and suchlike borrowed words, to supply the defect of our hardly intreated *Dactile*. I could in this place set downe many ridiculous kinds of *Dactils* which they vse, but that it is not my purpose here to incite men to laughter. If we therefore reiect the *Dactil* as vnfit for our vse (which of necessity we are enforst to do), there remayne only the *Iambick* foote, of which the *Iambick* verse is fram'd, and the *Trochee*, from which the *Trochaick* numbers haue their originall. Let vs now then examine the property of these two feete, and try if they consent with the nature of our English sillables. And first for the *Iambicks*, they fall out so naturally in our toong, that, if we examine our owne writers, we shall find they vnawares hit oftentimes vpon the true *Iambick* numbers, but always ayme at them as far as their eare without the guidance of arte can attain vnto, as it shall hereafter more euidently appeare. The *Trochaick* foote, which is but an *Iambick* turn'd ouer and ouer, must of force in like manner accord in proportion with our Brittish sillables, and so produce an English *Trochaicall* verse. Then hauing these two principall kinds of verses, we may easily out of them deriue other formes, as the Latines and Greekes before vs haue done: whereof I will make plaine demonstration, beginning at the *Iambick* verse.

THE FOURTH CHAPTER: OF THE IAMBICK VERSE.

I haue obserued, and so may any one that is either practis'd in singing, or hath a naturall eare able to time a song, that the Latine verses of sixe feete, as the *Heroick* and *Iambick*, or of fiue feete, as the *Trochaick*, are in nature all of the same length of sound with our English verses of fiue feet; for either of them being tim'd with the hand, *quinque perficiunt tempora*, they fill vp the quantity (as it were) of fiue sem'briefs; as for example, if any man will proue to time these verses with his hand.

A pure *Iambick*.
Suis et ipsa Roma viribus ruit.

A licentiate *Iambick*.
Ducunt volentes fata, nolentes trahunt.

An *Heroick* verse.
Tityre, tu patulae recubans sub tegmine fagi.

A *Trochaick* verse.
Nox est perpetua vna dormienda.

English *Iambicks* pure.

The more secure, the more the stroke we feele
Of vnpreuented harms; so gloomy stormes
Appeare the sterner, if the day be cleere.

Th' English *Iambick* licentiate.

Harke how these winds do murmur at thy flight.

The English *Trochee*.

Still where Enuy leaues, remorse doth enter.

The cause why these verses differing in feete yeeld the same length of sound, is by reason of some rests which either the necessity of the numbers or the heauiness of the sillables do beget. For we find in musick that often-times the straines of a song cannot be reduct to true

number without some rests prefixt in the beginning and
middle, as also at the close if need requires. Besides,
our English monasillables enforce many breathings which
no doubt greatly lengthen a verse, (so that it is no wonder
if for these reasons our English verses of fiue feete hold
pace with the *Latines* of sixe.) The pure *Iambick* in
English needes small demonstration, because it consists
simply of *Iambick* feete; (but our *Iambick* licentiate offers
itselfe to a farther consideration, for in the third and fift
place we must of force hold the *Iambick* foote, in the first,
second, and fourth place we may vse a *Spondee* or *Iambick*
and sometime a *Tribrack* or *Dactile*, but rarely an *Anapestick* foote, and that in the second or fourth place.) But
why an *Iambick* in the third place? I answere, that the
forepart of the verse may the gentlier slide into his
Dimeter, as, for example sake, deuide this verse:

Harke how these winds do murmure at thy flight.

Harke how these winds, there the voice naturally affects
a rest; then *murmur at thy flight*, that is of itselfe a perfect
number, as I will declare in the next Chapter; and therefore the other odde sillable betweene them ought to be
short, least the verse should hang too much betweene the
naturall pause of the verse and the *Dimeter* following; the
which *Dimeter* though it be naturally *Trochaical*, yet it
seemes to haue his originall out of the *Iambick* verse.
But the better to confirme and expresse these rules, I will
set downe a short Poeme in *Licentiate Iambicks*, which
may giue more light to them that shall hereafter imitate
these numbers.

Goe, numbers, boldly passe, stay not for ayde
Of shifting rime, that easie flatterer,
Whose witchcraft can the ruder eares beguile.
Let your smooth feete, enur'd to purer arte,

> True measures tread. What if your pace be slow,
> And hops not like the Grecian elegies?
> It is yet gracefull, and well fits the state
> Of words ill-breathed and not shap't to runne.
> Goe then, but slowly, till your steps be firme;   5
> Tell them that pitty or peruersely skorne
> Poore English poesie as the slaue to rime,
> You are those loftie numbers that reuiue
> Triumphs of Princes and sterne tragedies:
> And learne henceforth t'attend those happy sprights   10
> Whose bounding fury height and waight affects.
> Assist their labour, and sit close to them,
> Neuer to part away till for desert
> Their browes with great *Apollos* bayes are hid.
> He first taught number and true harmonye;   15
> Nor is the lawrell his for rime bequeath'd.
> Call him with numerous accents paisd by arte,
> He'le turne his glory from the sunny clymes
> The North-bred wits alone to patronise.
> Let France their *Bartas*, Italy *Tasso* prayse;   20
> *Phœbus* shuns none but in their flight from him.

Though, as I said before, the naturall breathing-place of our English *Iambick* verse is in the last sillable of the second foote, as our *Trochy* after the manner of the Latine *Heroick* and *Iambick* rests naturally in the first of the third foote, yet no man is tyed altogether to obserue this rule, but he may alter it, after the iudgment of his eare, which Poets, Orators, and Musitions of all men ought to haue most excellent. Againe, though I said peremtorily before that the third and fift place of our licentiate *Iambick* must alwayes hold an *Iambick* foote, yet I will shew you example in both places where a *Tribrack* may be very formally taken, and first in the third place:

> Some trade in *Barbary*, some in *Turky* trade.

On English Verse

An other example:

> Men that do fall to misery, quickly fall.

If you doubt whether the first of *misery* be naturally short or no, you may iudge it by the easy sliding of these two verses following:

The first:

> Whome misery cannot alter, time deuours.

The second:

> What more vnhappy life, what misery more?

Example of the *Tribrack* in the fift place, as you may perceiue in the last foote of the fourth verse:

> Some from the starry throne his fame deriues,
> Some from the mynes beneath, from trees or herbs:
> Each hath his glory, each his sundry gift,
> Renown'd in eu'ry art there liues not any.

To proceede farther, I see no reason why the English *Iambick* in his first place may not as well borrow a foote of the *Trochy* as our *Trochy*, or the Latine *Hendicasillable*, may in the like case make bold with the *Iambick*: but it must be done euer with this caueat, which is, that a *Sponde*, *Dactile*, or *Tribrack* do supply the next place; for an *Iambick* beginning with a single short sillable, and the other ending before with the like, would too much drinke vp the verse if they came immediatly together.

The example of the *Sponde* after the *Trochy*:

> As the faire sonne the lightsome heau'n adorns.

The example of the *Dactil*:

> Noble, ingenious, and discreetly wise.

The example of the *Tribrack*:

> Beauty to ielousie brings ioy, sorrow, feare.

Though I haue set downe these second licenses as good and ayreable enough, yet for the most part my first rules are generall.

These are those numbers which Nature in our English destinates to the Tragick and Heroik Poeme: for the subiect of them both being all one, I see no impediment why one verse may not serue for them both, as it appeares more plainly in the old comparison of the two Greeke writers, when they say, *Homerus est Sophocles heroicus*, and againe *Sophocles est Homerus tragicus*, intimating that both Sophocles and Homer are the same in height and subiect, and differ onely in the kinde of their numbers.

The Iambick verse in like manner being yet made a little more licentiate, that it may thereby the neerer imitate our common talke, will excellently serue for Comedies; and then may we vse a *Sponde* in the fift place, and in the third place any foote except a *Trochy*, which neuer enters into our Iambick verse but in the first place, and then with his caueat of the other feete which must of necessitie follow.

THE FIFT CHAPTER: OF THE IAMBICK DIMETER, OR ENGLISH MARCH.

The *Dimeter* (so called in the former Chapter) I intend next of all to handle, because it seems to be a part of the *Iambick*, which is our most naturall and aunciente English verse. We may terme this our English march, because the verse answers our warlick forme of march in similitude of number. But call it what you please, for I will not wrangle about names, only intending to set down the nature of it and true structure. It consists of two feete and one odde sillable. The first foote may be made either a *Trochy*, or a *Spondee*, or an *Iambick*, at the pleasure of the composer, though most naturally that place affects a *Trochy* or *Spondee*; yet, by the example of *Catullus* in his *Hendicasillables*, I adde in the first place sometimes an *Iambick* foote. In the second place we must euer insert

a *Trochy* or *Tribrack*, and so leaue the last sillable (as in
the end of a verse it is alwaies held) common. Of this
kinde I will subscribe three examples, the first being a
peece of *Chorus* in a Tragedy.

        Rauing warre, begot
        In the thirstye sands
        Of the *Lybian* Iles,
        Wasts our emptye fields;
        What the greedye rage
        Of fell wintrye stormes
        Could not turne to spoile,
        Fierce *Bellona* now
        Hath laid desolate,
        Voyd of fruit, or hope.
        Th' eger thriftye hinde,
        Whose rude toyle reuiu'd
        Our skie-blasted earth,
        Himselfe is but earth,
        Left a skorne to fate
        Through seditious armes:
        And that soile, alive
        Which he duly nurst,
        Which him duly fed,
        Dead his body feeds:
        Yet not all the glebe
        His tuffe hands manur'd
        Now one turfe affords
        His poore funerall.
        Thus still needy liues,
        Thus still needy dyes
        Th' vnknowne multitude.

        An example *Lyrical*.

Greatest in thy wars,
Greater in thy peace,

Dread *Elizabeth*;
Our muse only Truth,
Figments cannot vse,
Thy ritch name to deck
That itselfe adorns:
But should now this age
Let all poesye fayne,
Fayning poesy could
Nothing faine at all
Worthy halfe thy fame.

An example *Epigrammaticall*.
Kind in euery kinde
This, deare Ned, resolue.
Neuer of thy prayse
Be too prodigall;
He that prayseth all
Can praise truly none.

THE SIXT CHAPTER: OF THE ENGLISH TROCHAICK VERSE.

Next in course to be intreated of is the English *Trochaick*, being a verse simple, and of itselfe depending. It consists, as the Latine *Trochaick*, of fiue feete, the first whereof may be a *Trochy*, a *Spondee*, or an *Iambick*, the other foure of necessity all *Trochyes*; still holding this rule authenticall, that the last sillable of a verse is always common. The spirit of this verse most of all delights in Epigrams, but it may be diuersely vsed, as shall hereafter be declared. I haue written diuers light Poems in this kinde, which for the better satisfaction of the reader I thought conuenient here in way of example to publish. In which though sometimes vnder a knowne name I haue shadowed a fain'd conceit, yet it is done without reference or offence to any person, and only to make the stile appeare the more English.

The first *Epigramme.*

Lockly spits apace, the rhewme he cals it,
But no drop (though often urgd) he straineth
From his thirstie iawes, yet all the morning
And all day he spits, in eu'ry corner;
At his meales he spits, at eu'ry meeting;
At the barre he spits before the Fathers;
In the Court he spits before the Graces;
In the Church he spits, thus all prophaning
With that rude disease, that empty spitting:
Yet no cost he spares, he sees the Doctors,
Keeps a strickt diet, precisely vseth
Drinks and bathes drying, yet all preuailes not.
'Tis not *China* (*Lockly*), *Salsa Guacum*,
Nor dry *Sassafras* can help, or ease thee;
'Tis no humor hurts, it is thy humor.

The second *Epigramme.*

Cease, fond wretch, to loue, so oft deluded,
[1] Still made ritch with hopes, still vnrelieued.
Now fly her delaies; she that debateth
Feeles not true desire; he that, deferred,
Others times attends, his owne betrayeth:
Learne t' affect thy selfe; thy cheekes deformed
With pale care reuiue by timely pleasure,
Or with skarlet heate them, or by paintings
Make thee louely; for such arte she vseth
Whome in vayne so long thy folly loued.

The third *Epigramme.*

Kate can fancy only berdles husbands,
Thats the cause she shakes off eu'ry suter,
Thats the cause she liues so stale a virgin,

---

[1] From this point to the end of l. 27 on p. 342 the text is supplied from a later edition, *u. s.*

For, before her heart can heate her answer,
Her smooth youths she finds all hugely berded.

The fourth *Epigramme*.

All in sattin Oteny will be suted,
Beaten sattin (as by chaunce he cals it);   5
Oteny sure will haue the bastinado.

The fift *Epigramme*.

Tosts as snakes or as the mortall *Henbane*
Hunks detests when huffcap ale he tipples,
Yet the bread he graunts the fumes abateth;   10
Therefore apt in ale, true, and he graunts it;
But it drinks vp ale, that *Hunks* detesteth.

The sixt *Epigramme*.

What though *Harry* braggs, let him be noble;
Noble *Harry* hath not half a noble.   15

The seauenth *Epigramme*.

Phœbe all the rights *Elisa* claymeth,
Mighty riuall, in this only diff'ring
That shees only true, thou only fayned.

The eight *Epigramme*.   20

Barnzy stiffly vows that hees no Cuckold,
Yet the vulgar eu'rywhere salutes him,
With strange signes of hornes, from eu'ry corner;
Wheresoere he commes, a sundry Cucco
Still frequents his eares; yet he's no Cuccold. 25
But this *Barnzy* knowes that his *Matilda*,
Skorning him, with *Haruy* playes the wanton.
Knowes it? nay desires it, and by prayers
Dayly begs of heau'n, that it for euer
May stand firme for him; yet hees no Cuccold. 30
And 'tis true, for *Haruy* keeps *Matilda*,

Fosters *Barnzy*, and relieues his houshold,
Buyes the Cradle, and begets the children,
Payes the Nurces, eu'ry charge defraying,
And thus truly playes *Matilda's* husband:
So that *Barnzy* now becomes a cypher,
And himselfe th' adultrer of *Matilda*.
Mock not him with hornes, the case is alterd;
Haruy beares the wrong, *he* proues the Cuccold.

The ninth *Epigramme*.

Buffe loues fat vians, fat ale, fat all things.
Keepes fat whores, fat offices, yet all men
Him fat only wish to feast the gallous.

The tenth *Epigramme*.

Smith, by sute diuorst, the knowne adultres
Freshly weds againe; what ayles the mad-cap
By this fury? euen so theeues by frailty
Of their hemp reseru'd, againe the dismal
Tree embrace, againe the fatall halter.

The eleuenth *Epigramme*.

His late losse the Wiueless *Higs* in order
Eu'rywhere bewailes to friends, to strangers;
Tels them how by night a yongster armed
Saught his Wife (as hand in hand he held her)
With drawne sword to force; she cryed; he mainely
Roring ran for ayde, but (ah) returning
Fled was with the prize the beawty-forcer,
Whome in vain he seeks, he threats, he followes.
Chang'd is *Hellen*, *Hellen* hugs the stranger,
Safe as *Paris* in the Greeke triumphing.
Therewith his reports to teares he turneth,
Peirst through with the louely Dames remembrance;
Straight he sighes, he raues, his haire he teareth,
Forcing pitty still by fresh lamenting.

Cease vnworthy, worthy of thy fortunes,
Thou that couldst so faire a prize deliuer,
For feare vnregarded, vndefended,
Hadst no heart I thinke, I know no liuer.

The twelfth *Epigramme*.

Why droopst thou, *Trefeild?* Will *Hurst* the Banker
Make dice of thy bones? By heau'n he cannot.
Cannot? What's the reason? Ile declare it:
Th'ar all growne so pockie and so rotten.

THE SEAUENTH CHAPTER: OF THE ENGLISH ELEGEICK VERSE.

The *Elegeick* verses challenge the next place, as being of all compound verses the simplest. They are deriu'd out of our own naturall numbers as neere the imitation of the *Greekes* and *Latines* as our heauy sillables will permit. The first verse is a meere licentiate *Iambick*; the second is fram'd of two vnited *Dimeters*. In the first *Dimeter* we are tyed to make the first foote either a *Trochy* or a *Spondee*, the second a *Trochy*, and the odde sillable of it alwaies long. The second *Dimeter* consists of two Trochyes (because it requires more swiftnes than the first) and an odde sillable, which, being last, is euer common. I will giue you example both of *Elegye* and *Epigramme*, in this kinde.

An *Elegy*.

Constant to none, but euer false to me,
   Traiter still to loue through thy faint desires,
Not hope of pittie now nor vaine redresse
   Turns my griefs to teares and renu'd laments.
Too well thy empty vowes and hollow thoughts
   Witnes both thy wrongs and remorseles hart.
Rue not my sorrow, but blush at my name;
   Let thy bloudy cheeks guilty thoughts betray.

On English Verse

My flames did truly burne, thine made a shew,
  As fires painted are which no heate retayne,
Or as the glossy *Pirop* faines to blaze,
  But toucht cold appeares, and an earthy stone.
5 True cullours deck thy cheeks, false foiles thy brest,
  Frailer then thy light beawty is thy minde.
None canst thou long refuse, nor long affect,
  But turn'st feare with hopes, sorrow with delight,
Delaying, and deluding eu'ry way
10   Those whose eyes are once with thy beawty chain'd.
Thrice happy man that entring first thy loue
  Can so guide the straight raynes of his desires,
That both he can regard thee and refraine:
  If grac't, firme he stands, if not, easely falls.

15 Example of *Epigrams*, in Elegeick verse.

The first *Epigramme*.

Arthure brooks only those that brooke not him,
  Those he most regards, and deuoutly serues:
But them that grace him his great brau'ry skornes,
20 Counting kindnesse all duty, not desert:
Arthure wants forty pounds, tyres eu'ry friend,
  But finds none that holds twenty due for him.

The second *Epigramme*.

If fancy can not erre which vertue guides,
25 In thee, *Laura*, then fancy can not erre.

The third *Epigramme*.

Drue feasts no Puritans; the churles, he saith,
  Thanke no men, but eate, praise God, and depart.

The fourth *Epigramme*.

30 A wiseman wary liues, yet most secure,
  Sorrowes moue not him greatly, nor delights:

Fortune and death he skorning, only makes
  Th' earth his sober Inne, but still heau'n his home.

The fifth *Epigramme*.

Thou tel'st me, *Barnzy*, *Dawson* hath a wife:
  Thine he hath, I graunt; *Dawson* hath a wife.

The sixt *Epigramme*.

Drue giues thee money, yet thou thank'st not him,
  But thankst God for him, like a godly man.
Suppose, rude Puritan, thou begst of him,
  And he saith God help, who's the godly man?

The seauenth *Epigramme*.

All wonders *Barnzy* speakes, all grosely faind:
  Speake some wonder once, *Barnzy*, speake the truth.

The eight *Epigramme*.

None then should through thy beawty, *Lawra*, pine,
  Might sweet words alone ease a loue-sick heart:
But your sweet words alone, that quit so well
  Hope of friendly deeds, kill the loue-sick heart.

The ninth *Epigramme*.

At all thou frankly throwst, while, *Frank*, thy wife,
  Bars not *Luke* the mayn; *Oteny* barre the bye.

THE EIGHT CHAPTER: OF DITTIES AND ODES.

To descend orderly from the more simple numbers to them that are more compounded, it is now time to handle such verses as are fit for *Ditties* or *Odes*; which we may call *Lyricall*, because they are apt to be soong to an instrument, if they were adorn'd with conuenient notes. Of that kind I will demonstrate three in this Chapter, and in the first we will proceede after the manner of the

Saphick, which is a *Trochaicall* verse as well as the *Hendicasillable* in Latine. The first three verses therefore in our English *Saphick* are meerely those *Trochaicks* which I handled in the sixt Chapter, excepting only that the first foote of either of them must euer of necessity be a *Spondee*, to make the number more graue. The fourth and last closing verse is compounded of three *Trochyes* together, to giue a more smooth farewell, as you may easily obserue in this Poeme made vpon a Triumph at Whitehall, whose glory was dasht with an vnwelcome showre, hindring the people from the desired sight of her Majestie.

The English *Sapphick*.

Faiths pure shield, the Christian *Diana*,
Englands glory crownd with all deuinenesse,
Liue long with triumphs to blesse thy people
    At thy sight triumphing.

Loe, they sound; the Knights in order armed
Entring threat the list, adrest to combat
For their courtly loues; he, hees the wonder
    Whome *Eliza* graceth.

Their plum'd pomp the vulgar heaps detaineth,
And rough steeds; let vs the still deuices
Close obserue, the speeches and the musicks
    Peacefull arms adorning.

But whence showres so fast this angry tempest,
Clowding dimme the place? Behold, *Eliza*
This day shines not here; this heard, the launces
    And thick heads do vanish.

The second kinde consists of *Dimeter*, whose first foote may either be a *Sponde* or a *Trochy*. The two verses following are both of them *Trochaical*, and consist of foure feete, the first of either of them being a *Spondee* or *Trochy*,

the other three only Trochyes. The fourth and last
verse is made of two *Trochyes*. The number is voluble,
and fit to expresse any amorous conceit.

The Example.

   Rose-cheekt *Lawra*, come
Sing thou smoothly with thy beawtie's
Silent musick, either other
     Sweetely gracing.

   Louely formes do flowe
From concent deuinely framed;
Heau'n is musick, and thy beawtie's
     Birth is heauenly.

   These dull notes we sing
Discords neede for helps to grace them;
Only beawty purely louing
     Knowes no discord,

   But still moues delight,
Like cleare springs renu'd by flowing,
Euer perfet, euer in them-
     selues eternall.

The third kind begins as the second kind ended, with
a verse consisting of two *Trochy* feete, and then as the
second kind had in the middle two *Trochaick* verses of
foure feete, so this hath three of the same nature, and ends
in a *Dimeter* as the second began. The *Dimeter* may
allow in the first place a *Trochy* or a *Spondee*, but no
Iambick.

The Example.

   Iust beguiler,
Kindest loue, yet only chastest,
Royall in thy smooth denyals,
Frowning or demurely smiling,
     Still my pure delight.

> Let me view thee
> With thoughts and with eyes affected,
> And if then the flames do murmur,
> Quench them with thy vertue, charme them
>   With thy stormy browes.
>
> Heau'n so cheerefull
> Laughs not euer, hory winter
> Knowes his season, euen the freshest
> Sommer mornes from angry thunder
>   Iet not still secure.

The ninth Chapter: of the *Anacreontick* Verse.

If any shall demaund the reason why this number, being in itselfe simple, is plac't after so many compounded numbers, I answere, because I hold it a number to licentiate for a higher place, and in respect of the rest imperfect; yet is it passing gracefull in our English toong, and will excellently fit the subiect of a *Madrigall*, or any other lofty or tragicall matter. It consists of two feete: the first may be either a *Sponde* or *Trochy*, the other must euer represent the nature of a *Trochy*, as for example:

> Follow, followe,
> Though with mischiefe
> Arm'd, like whirlewind
> Now she flyes thee;
> Time can conquer
> Loues vnkindnes;
> Loue can alter
> Times disgraces;
> Till death faint not
> Then but followe.
> Could I catch that
> Nimble trayter,

    Skornefull *Lawra*,
    Swift foote *Lawra*,
    Soone then would I
    Seeke auengement.
    Whats th' auengement?
    Euen submissely
    Prostrate then to
    Beg for mercye.

Thus haue I briefely described eight seueral kinds of English numbers simple or compound. The first was our *Iambick* pure and licentiate. The second, that which I call our *Dimeter*, being deriued either from the end of our *Iambick* or from the beginning of our *Trochaick*. The third which I deliuered was our English *Trochaick* verse. The fourth our English *Elegeick*. The fift, sixt, and seauenth were our English *Sapphick*, and two other *Lyricall* numbers, the one beginning with that verse which I call our *Dimeter*, the other ending with the same. The eight and last was a kind of *Anacreontick* verse, handled in this Chapter. These numbers which by my long obseruation I have found agreeable with the nature of our sillables, I haue set forth for the benefit of our language, which I presume the learned will not only imitate but also polish and amplifie with their owne inuentions. Some eares accustomed altogether to the fatnes of rime may perhaps except against the cadences of these numbers; but let any man iudicially examine them, and he shall finde they close of themselues so perfectly that the help of rime were not only in them superfluous but also absurd. Moreouer, that they agree with the nature of our English it is manifest, because they entertaine so willingly our owne British names, which the writers in English Heroicks could neuer aspire vnto, and euen our Rimers themselues haue rather delighted in

borrowed names than in their owne, though much more
apt and necessary. But it is now time that I proceede to
the censure of our sillables, and that I set such lawes
vpon them as by imitation, reason, or experience I can
confirme. ⸢Yet before I enter into that discourse, I will
briefely recite and dispose in order all such feete as are
necessary for composition of the verses before described.⸥
They are sixe in number, three whereof consist of two
sillables, and as many of three.

      Feete of two sillables.

  Iambick: ⎫   ⎧ rĕuēnge
  Trochaick: ⎬ as ⎨ bēawtie
  Sponde: ⎭   ⎩ cōnstānt

      Feete of three sillables.

  Tribrack: ⎫   ⎧ mĭsĕrie
  Anapestick: ⎬ as ⎨ mĭsĕrīes
  Dactile: ⎭   ⎩ dēstenie

THE TENTH CHAPTER: OF THE QUANTITY OF ENGLISH SILLABLES.

The *Greekes* in the quantity of their sillables were farre
more licentious than the *Latines*, as *Martiall* in his Epigramme of *Earinon* witnesseth, saying, *qui Musas colimus
seueriores*. But the English may very well challenge
much more licence than either of them, by reason it
stands chiefly vpon monasillables, which, in expressing
with the voyce, are of a heauy cariage, and for that cause
the *Dactil*, *Trybrack*, and *Anapestick* are not greatly mist
in our verses. But aboue all the accent of our words is
diligently to be obseru'd, for chiefly by the accent in any
language the true value of the sillables is to be measured.
Neither can I remember any impediment except position
that can alter the accent of any sillable in our English
verse. For though we accent the second of *Trumpington*

short, yet is it naturally long, and so of necessity must be held of euery composer. Wherefore the first rule that is to be obserued is the nature of the accent, which we must euer follow.

The next rule is position, which makes euery sillable long, whether the position happens in one or in two words, according to the manner of the *Latines*, wherein is to be noted that *h* is no letter.

Position is when a vowell comes before two consonants, either in one or two words. In one, as in *best*, *e* before *st* makes the word *best* long by position. In two words, as in *setled loue*, *e* before *d* in the last sillable of the first word and *l* in the beginning of the second makes *led* in *setled* long by position.

A vowell before a vowell is alwaies short, as *flīing, dīing, gŏing*, vnlesse the accent alter it, in *dĕnūing*.

The diphthong in the midst of a word is alwaies long, as *plaīing, deceīving*.

The *Synalœphas* or *Elisions* in our toong are either necessary to auoid the hollowness and gaping in our verse, as *to* and *the*, *t'inchaunt, th' inchaunter*, or may be vsd at pleasure, as for *let vs* to say *let's*; for *we will, wee'l*; for *euery, eu'ry*; for *they are, th'ar*; for *he is, hee's*; for *admired, admir'd*; and such like.

Also, because our English Orthography (as the French) differs from our common pronunciation, we must esteeme our sillables as we speake, not as we write; for the sound of them in a verse is to be valued, and not their letters, as for *follow* we pronounce *follo*; for *perfect, perfet*; for *little, littel*; for *loue-sick, loue-sik*; for *honour, honor*; for *money, mony*; for *dangerous, dangerus*; for *raunsome, raunsum*; for *though, tho*; and their like.

Deriuatiues hold the quantities of their primitiues, as *dĕvōut, dĕvōutelie*; *prŏphāne, prŏphānelie*; and so do the compositiues, as *dĕsēru'd, ūndĕsēru'd.*

In words of two sillables, if the last haue a full and
rising accent that sticks long vpon the voyce, the first
sillable is alwayes short, vnlesse position, or the diphthong,
doth make it long, as děsīre, prěsērue, děfīne, prŏphāne,
5 rěgārd, mănūre, and such like.

If the like dissillables at the beginning haue double consonants of the same kind, we may vse the first sillable as
common, but more naturally short, because in their pronunciation we touch but one of those double letters, as
10 ătēnd, ăpēare, ŏpōse. The like we may say when silent and
melting consonants meete together, as ădrēst, rědrēst, ŏprēst,
rěprēst, rětrīu'd, and such like.

Words of two sillables that in their last sillable mayntayne
a flat or falling accent, ought to hold their first sillable
15 long, as rīgŏr, glōrie, spīrĭt, fūrie, lābŏur, and the like: ăny,
măny, prěty, hŏly, and their like are excepted.

One obseruation which leades me to iudge of the difference
of these dissillables whereof I last spake, I take from the
originall monasillable; which if it be graue, as shāde, I hold
20 that the first of shādie must be long; so trūe, trūlie; hāue,
hāuĭng; tīre, tīrĭng.

Words of three sillables for the most part are deriued
from words of two sillables, and from them take the
quantity of their first sillable, as flōrĭsh, flōrĭshĭng long;
25 hŏlie, hŏlĭnes short; but mi in mīser being long hinders not
the first of mĭsery to be short, because the sound of the i is
a little altred.

De, di, and pro in trisillables (the second being short) are
long, as dēsŏlāte, dīlĭgēnt, prōdĭgāll.

30 Re is euer short, as rěmědie, rěfěrēnce, rědŏlēnt, rěuěrēnd.

Likewise the first of these trisillables is short, as the
first of běněfit, gěněrall, hĭděous, měmŏrie, nŭměrous, pěnětrāte,
sěpărat, tĭměrous, vărĭant, vărĭous; and so may we esteeme
of all that yeeld the like quicknes of sound.

35 In words of three sillables the quantity of the middle

sillable is lightly taken from the last sillable of the originall dissillable, as the last of *děuīne*, ending in a graue or long accent, makes the second of *děuīnīng* also long, and so *ēspīe, ēspīīng, děnīe, děnīīng*: contrarywise it falles out if the last of the dissillable beares a flat or falling accent, as *glōrĭe, glōrĭīng, ēnvĭīng*, and so forth.

Words of more sillables are eyther borrowed and hold their owne nature, or are likewise deriu'd and so follow the quantity of their primatiues, or are knowne by their proper accents, or may be easily censured by a iudiciall eare.

All words of two or more sillables ending with a falling accent in *y* or *ye*, as *faīrelĭe, děmurelĭe, beawŭe, pītĭe*, or in *ue*, as *vertŭe, rēscŭe*, or in *ow*, as *fōllŏw, hōllŏw*, or in *e*, as *parlĕ, Daphnĕ*, or in *a*, as *Mannă*, are naturally short in their last sillables: neither let any man cauill at this licentiate abbreuiating of sillables, contrary to the custome of the Latines, which made all their last sillables that ended in *u* long, but let him consider that our verse of fiue feete, and for the most part but of ten sillables, must equall theirs of sixe feete and of many sillables, and therefore may with sufficient reason aduenture vpon this allowance. Besides, euery man may obserue what an infinite number of sillables both among the *Greekes* and *Romaines* are held as common. But words of two sillables ending with a rising accent in *y* or *ye*, as *denye, descrye*, or in *ue*, as *ensue*, or in *ee*, as *foresee*, or in *oe*, as *forgoe*, are long in their last sillables, vnlesse a vowell begins the next word.

All monasillables that end in a graue accent are euer long, as *wrāth, hāth, thēse, thōse, tōoth, sōoth, thrōugh, dāy, plāy, feāte, speēde, strīfe, flōw, grōw, shēw*.

The like rule is to be obserued in the last of dissillables bearing a graue rising sound, as *deuine, delaie, retire, refuse, manure*, or a graue falling sound, as *fortune, pleasure, vampire*.

On English Verse

All such as haue a double consonant lengthning them, as *wărre, bărre, stărre, fŭrre, mŭrre,* appear to me rather long then any way short.

There are of these kinds other, but of a lighter sound, that, if the word following do begin with a vowell, are short, as *doth, though, thou, now, they, too, flye, dye, true, due, see, are, far, you, thee,* and the like.

These monasillables are alwayes short, as *ă, thĕ, thĭ, shĕ, wĕ, bĕ, hĕ, nŏ, tŏ, gŏ, sŏ, dŏ,* and the like.

But if *i* or *y* are ioyn'd at the beginning of a word with any vowell, it is not then held as a vowell, but as a consonant, as *ielosy, iewce, iade, ioy, Iudas, ye, yet, yel, youth, yoke.* The like is to be obseru'd in *w,* as *winde, wide, wood*: and in all words that begin with *va, ve, vi, vo,* or *vu,* as *vacant, vew, vine, voide,* and *vulture.*

All Monasillables or Polysillables that end in single consonants, either written or sounded with single consonants, hauing a sharp liuely accent and standing without position of the word following, are short in their last sillable, as *scăb, flĕd, pārtĕd, Gŏd, ŏf, ĭf, bāndŏg, ānguĭsh, sĭck, quĭck, rīuăl, wĭll, pēoplĕ, sīmplĕ, comĕ, somĕ, hĭm, thĕm, frŏm, sŭmmŏn, thĕn, prŏp, prōspĕr, hōnoŭr, lābouŕ, thĭs, hĭs, spēchĕs, gōddĕsse, pērfĕct, bŭt, whăt, thăt,* and their like.

The last sillable of all words in the plurall number that haue two or more vowels before *s* are long, as *vertūes, dutīes, miserīes, fellowēs.*

These rules concerning the quantity of our English sillables I haue disposed as they came next into my memory; others more methodicall, time and practise may produce. In the meane season, as the Grammarians leaue many sillables to the authority of the Poets, so do I likewise leaue many to their iudgments; and withall thus conclude, that there is no Art begun and perfected at one enterprise.

SAMUEL DANIEL

(*A Defence of Ryme*)

? 1603

[Daniel's reply to Campion is entitled *A Defence of Ryme, Against a Pamphlet entituled: 'Obseruations in the Art of English Poesie.' Wherein is demonstratiuely proued, that Ryme is the fittest harmonie of words that comportes with our Language. By Sa. D. At London: Printed by V. S. for Edward Blount.*

The text is printed from the copy (undated) in the Bodleian Library (CC. 23 art.) which is bound in at the end of *The Works of Samuel Daniel*, fol. 1601. The running head-line throughout is 'An apologie for Ryme' (*cf.* note, vol. i, pp. 148–9).]

To all the worthie Louers and learned Professors of Ryme within His Maiesties Dominions.

S. D.

WORTHIE Gentlemen, about a yeare since, vpon the great reproach giuen to the Professors of Rime and the vse thereof, I wrote a priuate letter, as a defence of mine owne vndertakings in that kinde, to a learned Gentleman, a great friend of mine, then in Court. Which I did rather to confirm my selfe in mine owne courses, and to hold him from being wonne from vs, then with any desire to publish the same to the world.

But now, seeing the times to promise a more regarde to the present condition of our writings, in respect of our Soueraignes happy inclination this way, whereby wee are rather to expect an incoragement to go on with what we do then that any innouation should checke vs with a shew of what it would do in an other kinde, and yet doe nothing but depraue, I haue now giuen a greater body to the same Argument, and here present it to your view, vnder the patronage of a noble Earle, who in bloud and nature is interessed to take our parte in this cause with others, who cannot, I know, but holde deare the monuments that haue beene left vnto the world in this manner of composition, and who I trust will take in good parte this my Defence, if not as it is my particular, yet in respect of the cause I vndertake, which I heere inuoke you all to protect.

SA. D.

To William Herbert, Erle of Pembrooke.

THE Generall Custome and vse of Ryme in this kingdome, Noble Lord, hauing beene so long (as if from a Graunt of Nature) held vnquestionable, made me to imagine that it lay altogither out of the way of contradiction, and was become so natural, as we should neuer haue had a thought to cast it off into reproch, or be made to thinke that it ill-became our language. But now I see, when there is opposition made to all things in the world by wordes, wee must nowe at length likewise fall to contend for words themselues, and make a question whether they be right or not. For we are tolde how that our measures goe wrong, all Ryming is grosse, vulgare, barbarous; which if it be so, we haue lost much labour to no purpose; and, for mine owne particular, I cannot but blame the fortune of the times and mine owne Genius, that cast me vppon so wrong a course, drawne with the current of custome and an vnexamined example. Hauing beene first incourag'd or fram'd thereunto by your most Worthy and Honorable Mother, and receiuing the first notion for the formall ordering of those compositions at *Wilton*, which I must euer acknowledge to haue beene my best Schoole, and thereof alwayes am to hold a feeling and gratefull Memory; afterward drawne farther on by the well liking and approbation of my worthy Lord, the fosterer of mee and my *Muse*; I aduentured to bestow all my whole powers therein, perceiuing it agreed so well, both with the complexion of the times and mine owne constitution, as I found not wherein I might better imploy me. But yet now, vpon the great discouery of these new measures, threatning to ouerthrow the whole state of Ryme in this kingdom, I must either stand out to defend, or els be forced to forsake my selfe and giue ouer all. And though irresolution and a selfe distrust be the most apparent faults of my nature, and that the least checke of reprehension, if it sauour of reason, will as easily shake my resolution as any man's liuing, yet in this case I know not how I am growne more resolued, and, before I sinke, willing to examine what those powers of iudgement are that must beare me downe and beat me off from the station of my profession, which by the law of Nature I am set to defend: and the rather for that this detractor (whose commendable Rymes, albeit now himselfe an enemy to ryme, haue giuen heretofore to the world the best notice of his worth) is a man of faire parts and good reputation; and therefore the reproach forcibly cast from such a hand may throw downe more at once then the labors of many shall in long time build vp againe, specially vpon the slippery foundation of opinion, and the world's inconstancy, which knowes not well what it would haue, and

A Defence of Rhyme

Discit enim citius meminitque libentius illud
Quod quis deridet, quam quod probat et veneratur.

And he who is thus become our vnkinde aduersarie must pardon vs if we be as iealous of our fame and reputation as hee is desirous of credite by his new-old arte, and must consider that we cannot, in a thing that concernes vs so neere, but haue a feeling of the wrong done, wherein euery Rymer in this vniuersall Iland, as well as myselfe, stands interressed. So that if his charitie had equally drawne with his learning, hee would haue forborne to procure the enuie of so powerfull a number vpon him, from whom he can not but expect the returne of a like measure of blame, and onely haue made way to his owne grace by the proofe of his abilitie, without the disparaging of vs, who would haue bin glad to haue stood quietly by him, and perhaps commended his aduenture, seeing that euermore of one science an other may be borne, and that these Salies made out of the quarter of our set knowledges are the gallant proffers onely of attemptiue spirits, and commendable, though they worke no other effect than make a Brauado : and I know it were *Indecens et morosum nimis alienae industriae modum ponere.*

We could well haue allowed of his numbers, had he not disgraced our Ryme, which both Custome and Nature doth most powerfully defend : Custome that is before all Law, Nature that is aboue all Arte. Euery language hath her proper number or measure fitted to vse and delight, which Custome, intertaininge by the allowance of the Eare, doth indenize and make naturall. All verse is but a frame of wordes confined within certaine measure, differing from the ordinarie speach, and introduced, the better to expresse mens conceipts, both for delight and memorie. Which frame of words consisting of *Rithmus* or *Metrum*, Number or measure, are disposed into diuers fashions, according to the humour of the Composer and the set of the time.

And these *Rhythmi*, as *Aristotle* saith, are familiar amongst
all Nations, and *e naturali et sponte fusa compositione*: and
they fall as naturally already in our language as euer Art
can make them, being such as the Eare of it selfe doth
marshall in their proper roomes; and they of themselues
will not willingly be put out of their ranke, and that in
such a verse as best comports with the nature of our
language. And for our Ryme (which is an excellencie
added to this worke of measure, and a Harmonie farre
happier than any proportion Antiquitie could euer shew vs)
dooth adde more grace, and hath more of delight then euer
bare numbers, howsoeuer they can be forced to runne in
our slow language, can possibly yeeld. Which, whether
it be deriu'd of *Rhythmus* or of *Romance*, which were
songs the *Bards* and *Druydes* about Rymes vsed, and
therof were called *Remensi*, as some Italians holde, or
howsoeuer, it is likewise number and harmonie of words,
consisting of an agreeing sound in the last sillables of
seuerall verses, giuing both to the Eare an Echo of a
delightful report, and to the Memorie a deeper impression
of what is deliuered therein. For as Greeke and Latine
verse consists of the number and quantitie of sillables,
so doth the English verse of measure and accent. And
though it doth not strictly obserue long and short sillables,
yet it most religiously respects the accent; and as the
short and the long make number, so the acute and graue
accent yeelde harmonie. And harmonie is likewise number;
so that the English verse then hath number, measure, and
harmonie in the best proportion of Musicke. Which,
being more certain and more resounding, works that effect
of motion with as happy successe as either the Greek or
Latin. And so naturall a melody is it, and so vniuersall,
as it seems to be generally borne with al the Nations of
the world as an hereditary eloquence proper to all mankind. The vniuersalitie argues the generall power of it:

for if the Barbarian vse it, then it shewes that it swais th'
affection of the Barbarian: if ciuil nations practise it, it
proues that it works vpon the harts of ciuil nations: if all,
then that it hath a power in nature on all. *Georgieuez de*
Turcarum moribus hath an example of the Turkish Rymes
iust of the measure of our verse of eleuen sillables, in
feminine Ryme; neuer begotten I am perswaded by any
example in *Europe*, but borne no doubt in *Scythia*, and
brought over *Caucasus* and *Mount Taurus*. The Scla-
uonian and Arabian tongs acquaint a great part of *Asia*
and *Affrique* with it; the Moscouite, Polacke, Hungarian,
German, Italian, French, and Spaniard vse no other
harmonie of words. The Irish, Briton, Scot, Dane, Saxon,
English, and all the Inhabiters of this Iland either haue
hither brought or here found the same in vse. And such
a force hath it in nature, or so made by nature, as the
Latine numbers, notwithstanding their excellencie, seemed
not sufficient to satisfie the eare of the world thereunto
accustomed, without this Harmonicall cadence: which
made the most learned of all nations labour with exceeding
trauaile to bring those numbers likewise vnto it: which
many did with that happinesse as neither their puritie
of tongue nor their materiall contemplations are thereby
any way disgraced, but rather deserue to be reuerenced
of all grateful posteritie, with the due regard of their
worth. And for *Schola Salerna*, and those *Carmina Pro-*
uerbialia, who finds not therein more precepts for vse,
concerning diet, health, and conuersation, then *Cato*,
Theognis, or all the Greekes and Latines can shew vs in
that kinde of teaching? and that in so few words, both
for delight to the eare and the hold of memorie, as they
are to be imbraced of all modest readers that studie to
know and not to depraue.

Me thinkes it is a strange imperfection that men should
thus ouer-runne the estimation of good things with so

violent a censure, as though it must please none else
because it likes not them : whereas *Oportet arbitratores
esse non contradictores eos qui verum indicaturi sunt,* saith
Arist., though he could not obserue it himselfe. And
milde charitie tells vs:

    ——— *Non ego paucis*
Offendar maculis quas aut incuria fudit
Aut humana parum cauit natura.

For all men haue their errours, and we must take the best
of their powers, and leaue the rest as not apperteining
vnto vs.

'Ill customes are to be left.' I graunt it; but I see not
howe that can be taken for an ill custome which nature
hath thus ratified, all nations receiued, time so long
confirmed, the effects such as it performes those office
of motion for which it is imployed; delighting the eare,
stirring the heart, and satisfying the iudgement in such
sort as I doubt whether euer single numbers will doe
in our Climate, if they shew no more worke of wonder
than yet we see. And if euer they prooue to become
anything, it must be by the approbation of many ages
that must giue them their strength for any operation,
as before the world will feele where the pulse, life, and
enargie lies; which now we are sure where to haue in our
Rymes, whose knowne frame hath those due staies for the
minde, those incounters of touch, as makes the motion
certaine, though the varietie be infinite.

Nor will the Generall sorte for whom we write (the wise
being aboue books) taste these laboured measures but as
an orderly prose when wee haue all done. For this kinde
acquaintance and continuall familiaritie euer had betwixt
our eare and this cadence is growne to so intimate a friendship, as it will nowe hardly euer be brought to misse it.
For be the verse neuer so good, neuer so full, it seemes
not to satisfie nor breede that delight, as when it is met

A Defence of Rhyme

and combined with a like sounding accent: which seemes
as the iointure without which it hangs loose, and cannot
subsist, but runnes wildely on, like a tedious fancie without
a close. Suffer then the world to inioy that which it
knowes, and what it likes: Seeing that whatsoeuer force
of words doth mooue, delight, and sway the affections
of men, in what Scythian sorte soeuer it be disposed or
vttered, that is true number, measure, eloquence, and the
perfection of speach: which I said hath as many shapes as
there be tongues or nations in the world, nor can with all
the tyrannicall Rules of idle Rhetorique be gouerned
otherwise then custome and present obseruation will
allow. And being now the trym and fashion of the
times, to sute a man otherwise cannot but giue a touch
of singularity; for when hee hath all done, hee hath but
found other clothes to the same body, and peraduenture
not so fitting as the former. But could our Aduersary
hereby set vp the musicke of our times to a higher note
of iudgement and discretion, or could these new lawes
of words better our imperfections, it were a happy attempt;
but when hereby we shall but as it were change prison,
and put off these fetters to receiue others, what haue we
gained? As good still to vse ryme and a little reason as
neither ryme nor reason, for no doubt, as idle wits will
write in that kinde, as do now in this, imitation wil after,
though it breake her necke. *Scribimus indocti doctique
poemata passim.* And this multitude of idle Writers can
be no disgrace to the good; for the same fortune in one
proportion or other is proper in a like season to all States
in their turne; and the same vnmeasurable confluence
of Scriblers hapned when measures were most in vse
among the Romanes, as we finde by this reprehension,

Mutauit mentem populus leuis, et calet vno
Scribendi studio; pueri[que] patresque seueri
Fronde comas vincti cenant et carmina dictant.

So that their plentie seemes to haue bred the same waste
and contempt as ours doth now, though it had not power
to disualew what was worthy of posteritie, nor keep backe
the reputation of excellencies destined to continue for
many ages. For seeing it is matter that satisfies the
iudiciall, appeare it in what habite it will, all these pretended
proportions of words, howsoeuer placed, can be but words,
and peraduenture serue but to embroyle our vnderstanding;
whilst seeking to please our eare, we enthrall our iudgement; to delight an exterior sense, wee smoothe vp a weake
confused sense, affecting sound to be vnsound, and all to
seeme *Servum pecus*, onely to imitate Greekes and Latines,
whose felicitie in this kinde might be something to themselues, to whome their owne *idioma* was naturall; but to vs
it can yeeld no other commoditie then a sound. We admire
them not for their smooth-gliding words, nor their measures,
but for their inuentions; which treasure if it were to be
found in Welch and Irish, we should hold those languages
in the same estimation; and they may thanke their sword
that made their tongues so famous and vniuersall as they
are. For to say truth, their Verse is many times but
a confused deliuerer of their excellent conceits, whose
scattered limbs we are faine to looke out and ioyne together,
to discerne the image of what they represent vnto vs. And
euen the Latines, who professe not to be so licentious as
the Greekes, shew vs many times examples, but of strange
crueltie in torturing and dismembering of words in the
middest, or disioyning such as naturally should be married
and march together, by setting them as farre asunder as
they can possibly stand: that sometimes, vnlesse the kind
reader out of his owne good nature wil stay them vp by
their measure, they will fall downe into flatte prose, and
sometimes are no other indeede in their naturall sound:
and then againe, when you finde them disobedient to their
owne Lawes, you must hold it to be *licentia poetica*, and

so dispensable. The striuing to shew their changable measures in the varietie of their Odes haue been verie painefull no doubt vnto them, and forced them thus to disturbe the quiet streame of their words, which by a naturall succession otherwise desire to follow in their due course.

But such affliction doth laboursome curiositie still lay vpon our best delights (which euer must be made strange and variable), as if Art were ordained to afflict Nature, and that we could not goe but in fetters. Euery science, euery profession, must be so wrapt vp in vnnecessary intrications, as if it were not to fashion but to confound the vnderstanding: which makes me much to distrust man, and feare that our presumption goes beyond our abilitie, and our Curiositie is more then our Iudgement; laboring euer to seeme to be more then we are, or laying greater burthens vpon our mindes then they are well able to beare, because we would not appeare like other men.

And indeed I haue wished that there were not that multiplicitie of Rymes as is vsed by many in Sonets, which yet we see in some so happily to succeed, and hath beene so farre from hindering their inuentions, as it hath begot conceit beyond expectation, and comparable to the best inuentions of the world: for sure in an eminent spirit, whome Nature hath fitted for that mysterie, Ryme is no impediment to his conceit, but rather giues him wings to mount, and carries him, not out of his course, but as it were beyond his power to a farre happier flight. Al excellencies being sold vs at the hard price of labour, it followes, where we bestow most thereof we buy the best successe: and Ryme, being farre more laborious than loose measures (whatsoeuer is obiected), must needs, meeting with wit and industry, breed greater and worthier effects in our language. So that if our labours haue wrought out a manumission from bondage, and that wee goe at libertie, notwithstanding these ties, wee are no longer the slaues of

Ryme, but we make it a most excellent instrument to serue vs. Nor is this certaine limit obserued in Sonnets, any tyrannicall bounding of the conceit, but rather reducing it in *girum* and a iust forme, neither too long for the shortest proiect, nor too short for the longest, being but onely imployed for a present passion. For the body of our imagination being as an vnformed *Chaos* without fashion, without day, if by the diuine power of the spirit it be wrought into an Orbe of order and forme, is it not more pleasing to Nature, that desires a certaintie and comports not with that which is infinite, to haue these clozes, rather than not to know where to end, or how farre to goe, especially seeing our passions are often without measure? and wee finde the best of the Latines many times either not concluding or els otherwise in the end then they began. Besides, is it not most delightfull to see much excellentlie ordred in a small roome, or little gallantly disposed and made to fill vp a space of like capacitie, in such sort that the one would not appeare so beautifull in a larger circuite, nor the other do well in a lesse? which often we find to be so, according to the powers of nature in the workman. And these limited proportions and rests of stanzes, consisting of six, seuen, or eight lines, are of that happines both for the disposition of the matter, the apt planting the sentence where it may best stand to hit, the certaine close of delight with the full bodie of a iust period well carried, is such as neither the Greekes or Latines euer attained vnto. For their boundlesse running on often so confounds the Reader, that, hauing once lost himselfe, must either giue off vnsatisfied, or vncertainely cast backe to retriue the escaped sence, and to find way againe into this matter.

Me thinkes we should not so soone yeeld our consents captiue to the authoritie of Antiquitie, vnlesse we saw more reason; all our vnderstandings are not to be built by the square of *Greece* and *Italie*. We are the children of nature

as well as they; we are not so placed out of the way of
iudgement but that the same Sunne of Discretion shineth
vppon vs; we haue our portion of the same virtues as well
as of the same vices: *Et Catilinam quocunque in populo*
videas, quocunque sub axe. Time and the turne of things
bring about these faculties according to the present estimation: and *Res temporibus non tempora rebus seruire oportet.*
So that we must neuer rebell against vse: *Quem penes*
arbitrium est et vis et norma loquendi. It is not the obseruing
of *Trochaicques* nor their *Iambicques* that wil make our
writings ought the wiser. All their Poesie, all their Philosophie is nothing, vnlesse we bring the discerning light of
conceipt with vs to apply it to vse. It is not bookes, but
onely that great booke of the world and the all-ouerspread-
ing grace of heauen that makes men truly iudiciall. Nor
can it be but a touch of arrogant ignorance to hold this or
that nation Barbarous, these or those times grosse, considering how this manifold creature man, wheresoeuer hee
stand in the world, hath alwayes some disposition of worth,
intertaines the order of societie, affects that which is most
in vse, and is eminent in some one thing or other that fits
his humour and the times. The Grecians held all other
nations barbarous but themselues; yet *Pirrhus* when he
saw the well ordered marching of the Romanes, which
made them see their presumptuous errour, could say it
was no barbarous manner of proceeding. The *Gothes,*
Vandales, and *Longobards,* whose comming downe like an
inundation ouerwhelmed, as they say, al the glory of
learning in *Europe,* haue yet left vs stil their lawes and
customes as the originalls of most of the prouinciall con-
stitutions of Christendome, which well considered with
their other courses of gouernement may serue to cleare
them from this imputation of ignorance. And though the
vanquished neuer yet spake well of the Conquerour, yet
even thorow the vnsound couerings of malidiction appeare

those monuments of trueth as argue wel their worth and
proues them not without iudgement, though without Greeke
and Latine.

Will not experience confute vs, if wee shoulde say the
state of *China*, which neuer heard of Anapestiques, Trochies,
and Tribracques, were grosse, barbarous, and vnciuille?
And is it not a most apparant ignorance, both of the
succession of learning in *Europe* and the generall course
of things, to say 'that all lay pittifully deformed in those
lacke-learning times from the declining of the Romane
Empire till the light of the Latine tongue was reuiued by
Rewcline, Erasmus, and Moore'? when for three hundred
yeeres before them, about the comming downe of *Tamburlaine* into *Europe*, *Franciscus Petrarcha* (who then no doubt
likewise found whom to imitate) shewed all the best notions
of learning, in that degree of excellencie both in Latine,
Prose and Verse, and in the vulgare Italian, as all the
wittes of posteritie haue not yet much ouer-matched him
in all kindes to this day: his great Volumes in Moral
Philosophie shew his infinite reading and most happy
power of disposition: his twelue Æglogues, his *Affrica*,
containing nine Bookes of the last Punicke warre, with
his three bookes of Epistles in Latine verse shew all
the transformations of wit and inuention that a Spirite
naturally borne to the inheritance of Poetrie and iudiciall
knowledge could expresse: all which notwithstanding
wrought him not that glory and fame with his owne Nation
as did his Poems in Italian, which they esteemè aboue al
whatsoeuer wit could haue inuented in any other forme
then wherein it is: which questionles they wil not change
with the best measures Greeks or Latins can shew them,
howsoeuer our Aduersary imagines. Nor could this very
same innouation in Verse, begun amongst them by
C. Tolomœi, but die in the attempt, and was buried as
soone as it came borne, neglected as a prodigious and

vnnaturall issue amongst them: nor could it neuer induce
Tasso, the wonder of Italy, to write that admirable Poem
of *Ierusalem*, comparable to the best of the ancients, in any
other forme than the accustomed verse. And with *Petrarch*
liued his scholar *Boccacius*, and neere about the same time
Iohannis Rauenensis, and from these, *tanquam ex equo
Troiano*, seemes to haue issued all those famous Italian
Writers, *Leonardus Aretinus, Laurentius Valla, Poggius,
Biondus*, and many others. Then *Emanuel Chrysolaras*,
a Constantinopolitan gentleman, renowmed for his learning
and vertue, being imployed by *Iohn Paleologus*, Emperour
of the East, to implore the ayde of Christian Princes for
the succouring of perishing *Greece*, and vnderstanding in
the meane time how *Baiazeth* was taken prisoner by
Tamburlan, and his country freed from danger, stayed still
at *Venice*, and there taught the Greeke tongue, discontinued
before in these parts the space of seauen hundred yeeres.
Him followed *Bessarion, George Trapezuntius, Theodorus
Gaza*, and others, transporting Philosophie, beaten by the
Turke out of *Greece*, into christendome. Hereupon came
that mightie confluence of Learning in these parts, which,
returning as it were *per postliminium*, and heere meeting
then with the new inuented stampe of Printing, spread it
selfe indeed in a more vniuersall sorte then the world euer
heeretofore had it; when *Pomponius Laetus, Aeneas Syluius,
Angelus Politianus, Hermolaus Barbarus, Iohannes Picus
de Mirandula*, the miracle and Phœnix of the world, adorned
Italie, and wakened other Nations likewise with this desire
of glory, long before it brought foorth *Rewclen, Erasmus*,
and *Moore*, worthy men, I confesse, and the last a great
ornament to this land, and a Rymer.

And yet long before all these, and likewise with these,
was not our Nation behinde in her portion of spirite and
worthinesse, but concurrent with the best of all this
lettered world; witnesse venerable *Bede*, that flourished

aboue a thousand yeeres since; *Aldelmus Durotelmus*, that liued in the yeere 739, of whom we finde this commendation registred: *Omnium Poetarum sui temporis facile primus, tantae eloquentiae, maiestatis, et eruditionis homo fuit, vt nunquam satis admirari possim vnde illi in tam barbara ac rudi aetate facundia accreuerit, vsque adeo omnibus numeris tersa, elegans, et rotunda, versus edidit cum antiquitate de palma contendentes.* Witnesse *Iosephus Deuonius*, who wrote *de bello Troiano* in so excellent a manner, and so neere resembling Antiquitie, as Printing his Worke beyond the seas they haue ascribed it to *Cornelius Nepos*, one of the Ancients. What should I name *Walterus Mape, Gulielmus Nigellus, Geruasius Tilburiensis, Bracton, Bacon, Ockam*, and an infinite Catalogue of excellent men, most of them liuing about foure hundred yeeres since, and haue left behinde them monuments of most profound iudgement and learning in all sciences! So that it is but the clowds gathered about our owne iudgement that makes vs thinke all other ages wrapt vp in mists, and the great distance betwixt vs that causes vs to imagine men so farre off to be so little in respect of our selues.

We must not looke vpon the immense course of times past as men ouer-looke spacious and wide countries from off high Mountaines, and are neuer the neere to iudge of the true Nature of the soyle or the particular syte and face of those territories they see. Nor must we thinke, viewing the superficiall figure of a region in a Mappe, that wee know strait the fashion and place as it is. Or reading an Historie (which is but a Mappe of Men, and dooth no otherwise acquaint vs with the true Substance of Circumstances then a superficiall Card dooth the Seaman with a Coast neuer seene, which alwayes prooues other to the eye than the imagination forecast it), that presently wee know all the world, and can distinctly iudge of times, men, and maners, iust as they were: When the

A Defence of Rhyme

best measure of man is to be taken by his owne foote
bearing euer the neerest proportion to himselfe, and is
neuer so farre different and vnequall in his powers, that
he hath all in perfection at one time, and nothing at
another. The distribution of giftes are vniuersall, and all
seasons haue them in some sort. We must not thinke
but that there were *Scipioes, Cæsars, Catoes,* and *Pompeies*
borne elsewhere then at *Rome*; the rest of the world hath
euer had them in the same degree of nature, though not of
state. And it is our weaknesse that makes vs mistake or
misconcieue in these deliniations of men the true figure
of their worth. And our passion and beliefe is so apt to
leade vs beyond truth, that vnlesse we try them by the
iust compasse of humanitie, and as they were men, we
shall cast their figures in the ayre, when we should make
their models vpon Earth. It is not the contexture of
words, but the effects of Action, that giues glory to the
times: we find they had *mercurium in pectore*, though not
in *lingua*; and in all ages, though they were not Ciceronians, they knew the Art of men, which onely is *Ars
Artium*, the great gift of heauen, and the chiefe grace and
glory on earth; they had the learning of Gouernement,
and ordring their State; Eloquence inough to shew their
iudgements. And it seemes the best times followed *Lycurgus* councell; *Literas ad vsum saltem discebant, reliqua
omnis disciplina erat vt pulchre pararent vt labores preferrent,
&c.* Had not vnlearned *Rome* laide the better foundation,
and built the stronger frame of an admirable state, eloquent *Rome* had confounded it vtterly, which we saw
ranne the way of all confusion, the plaine course of dissolution, in her greatest skill: and though she had not
power to vndoe herselfe, yet wrought she so that she
cast herselfe quite away from the glory of a common-
wealth, and fell vpon the forme of state she euer most
feared and abhorred of all other: and then scarse was

there seene any shadowe of pollicie vnder her first Emperours, but the most horrible and grosse confusion that could be conceued; notwithstanding it still indured, preseruing not onely a Monarchie, locked vp in her own limits, but therewithall held vnder her obedience so many Nations so farre distant, so ill affected, so disorderly commanded and vniustly conquered, as it is not to be attributed to any other fate but to the first frame of that commonwealth; which was so strongly ioynted, and with such infinite combinations interlinckt as one naile or other euer held vp the Maiestie thereof. There is but one learning, which *omnes gentes habent scriptum in cordibus suis*, one and the selfe-same spirit that worketh in all. We haue but one bodie of Iustice, one bodie of Wisdome thorowout the whole world; which is but apparelled according to the fashion of euery nation.

Eloquence and gay wordes are not of the substance of wit; it is but the garnish of a nice time, the Ornaments that doe but decke the house of a State, and *imitatur publicos mores*: Hunger is as well satisfied with meat serued in pewter as siluer. Discretion is the best measure, the rightest foote in what habit soeuer it runne. *Erasmus*, *Rewcline*, and *More* brought no more wisdome into the world with all their new reuiued wordes then we finde was before; it bred not a profounder Diuine then *S. Thomas*, a greater Lawyer then *Bartolus*, a more acute Logician then *Scotus*; nor are the effects of all this great amasse of eloquence so admirable or of that consequence, but that *impexa illa antiquitas* can yet compare with them.

Let vs go no further but looke vpon the wonderfull Architecture of this state of *England*, and see whether they were deformed times that could giue it such a forme: Where there is no one the least piller of Maiestie but was set with most profound iudgement, and borne vp with the iust conueniencie of Prince and people: no Court of

iustice but laide by the Rule and Square of Nature, and
the best of the best commonwealths that euer were in
the world: so strong and substantial as it hath stood
against al the storms of factions, both of beliefe and
ambition, which so powerfully beat vpon it, and all the
tempestuous alterations of humorous times whatsoeuer:
being continually in all ages furnisht with spirites fitte to
maintaine the maiestie of her owne greatnes, and to match
in an equall concurrencie all other kingdomes round
about her with whome it had to incounter.

But this innouation, like a Viper, must euer make way
into the world's opinion, thorow the bowelles of her owne
breeding, and is always borne with reproch in her
mouth; the disgracing others is the best grace it can put
on, to winne reputation of wit; and yet it is neuer so
wise as it would seeme, nor doth the world euer get so
much by it as it imagineth; which being so often deceiued,
and seeing it neuer performes so much as it promises,
me thinkes men should neuer giue more credite vnto it.
For, let vs change neuer so often, wee can not change
man; our imperfections must still runne on with vs. And
therefore the wiser Nations haue taught menne alwayes to
vse, *Moribus legibusque praesentibus etiamsi deteriores sint.*
The Lacedæmonians, when a Musitian, thincking to winne
himselfe credite by his new inuention and be before his
fellowes, had added one string more to his Crowde, brake
his fiddle and banished him the Citie, holding the Innouator,
though in the least things, dangerous to a publike societie.
It is but a fantastike giddinesse to forsake the way of
other men, especially where it lies tolerable: *Vbi nunc
est respublica, ibi simus potius quam dum illam veterem
sequimur simus in nulla.*

But shal we not tend to perfection? Yes: and that
euer best by going on in the course we are in, where we
haue aduantage, being so farre onward, of him that is but

now setting forth. For we shall neuer proceede, if wee be euer beginning, nor arriue at any certayne Porte, sayling with all windes that blowe—*non conualescit planta quae saepius transfertur*—and therefore let vs hold on in the course wee haue vndertaken, and not still be wandring. Perfection is not the portion of man ; and if it were, why may wee not as well get to it this way as another, and suspect those great vndertakers, lest they have conspired with enuy to betray our proceedings, and put vs by the honour of our attempts, with casting vs backe vpon another course, of purpose to ouerthrow the whole action of glory when we lay the fairest for it, and were so neere our hopes? I thanke God that I am none of these great Schollers, if thus their hie knowledges doe but giue them more eyes to looke out into vncertaintie and confusion, accounting my selfe rather beholding to my ignorance that hath set me in so lowe an vnder-roome of conceipt with other men, and hath giuen me as much distrust, as it hath done hope, daring not aduenture to goe alone, but plodding on the plaine tract I finde beaten by Custome and the Time, contenting me with what I see in vse.

And surely mee thinkes these great wittes should rather seeke to adorne than to disgrace the present ; bring something to it, without taking from it what it hath. But it is euer the misfortune of Learning to be wounded by her owne hand. *Stimulos dat emula virtus*, and where there is not abilitie to match what is, malice will finde out ingines, either to disgrace or ruine it, with a peruerse incounter of some new impression ; and, which is the greatest misery, it must euer proceed from the powers of the best reputation, as if the greatest spirites were ordained to indanger the worlde, as the grosse are to dishonour it, and that we were to expect *ab optimis periculum, a pessimis dedecus publicum*. Emulation, the strongest pulse that beats in high mindes, is oftentimes a winde, but of the worst effect ;

for whilst the soule comes disappoynted of the obiect it
wrought on, it presently forges another, and euen cozins
it selfe, and crosses all the world, rather than it will stay
to be vnder her desires, falling out with all it hath, to
flatter and make faire that which it would haue.

So that it is the ill successe of our longings that with
Xerxes makes vs to whippe the sea, and send a cartel
of defiance to Mount *Athos*: and the fault laide vpon
others weakenesse is but a presumptuous opinion of our
owne strength, who must not seeme to be maistered. But
had our Aduersary taught vs by his owne proceedings
this way of perfection, and therein fram'd vs a Poeme
of that excellencie as should haue put downe all, and
beene the maisterpeece of these times, we should all
haue admired him. But to depraue the present forme of
writing, and to bring vs nothing but a few loose and
vncharitable Epigrammes, and yet would make vs belieue
those numbers were come to raise the glory of our language,
giueth vs cause to suspect the performance, and to
examine whether this new Arte *constat sibi*, or *aliquid sit
dictum quod non sit dictum prius.*

First, we must heere imitate the Greekes and Latines,
and yet we are heere shewed to disobey them, euen in
theire owne numbers and quantities; taught to produce
what they make short, and make short what they produce;
made beleeue to be shewd measures in that forme we
haue not seene, and no such matter; tolde that heere is
the perfect Art of versifying, which in conclusion is yet
confessed to be vnperfect, as if our Aduersary, to be
opposite to vs, were become vnfaithfull to himselfe, and,
seeking to leade vs out of the way of reputation, hath
aduentured to intricate and confound him in his owne
courses, running vpon most vneuen groundes, with imperfect
rules, weake proofs, and vnlawful lawes. Whereunto
the world, I am perswaded, is not so vnreasonable as to

subscribe, considering the vniust authoritie of the Law-
giuer: for who hath constituted him to be the *Radaman-
thus*, thus to torture sillables and adiudge them their
perpetuall doome, setting his *Theta* or marke of condemnation vppon them, to indure the appoynted sentence of
his crueltie, as hee shall dispose? As though there were
that disobedience in our wordes, as they would not be
ruled or stand in order without so many intricate Lawes;
which would argue a great peruersenesse amongst them,
according to that *in pessima republica plurimae leges*, or
that they were so farre gone from the quiet freedome of
nature that they must thus be brought backe againe by
force. And now in what case were this poore state of
words, if in like sorte another tyrant the next yeere should
arise and abrogate these lawes and ordaine others cleane
contrary according to his humor, and say that they were
onely right, the others vniust? what disturbance were
there here, to whome should we obey? Were it not farre
better to holde vs fast to our olde custome than to stand
thus distracted with vncertaine Lawes, wherein Right
shall haue as many faces as it pleases Passion to make it,
that wheresoeuer mens affections stand, it shall still looke
that way? What trifles doth our vnconstant curiositie cal
vp to contend for? what colours are there laid vpon
indifferent things to make them seeme other then they áre,
as if it were but only to intertaine contestation amongst
men, who, standing according to the prospectiue of their
owne humour, seeme to see the selfe same things to
appeare otherwise to them than either they doe to other,
or are indeede in them selues, being but all one in nature?
For what adoe haue we heere? what strange precepts of
Arte about the framing of an Iambique verse in our language? which, when all is done, reaches not by a foote,
but falleth out to be the plaine ancient verse, consisting of
ten sillables or fiue feete, which hath euer beene vsed

A Defence of Rhyme

amongest vs time out of minde, and, for all this cunning and counterfeit name, can or will [not] be any other in nature then it hath beene euer heretofore: and this new *Dimeter* is but the halfe of this verse diuided in two, and no other then the *Caesura* or breathing place in the middest thereof, and therefore it had bene as good to haue put two lines in one, but only to make them seeme diuerse. Nay, it had beene much better for the true English reading and pronouncing thereof, without violating the accent, which now our Aduersarie hath heerein most vnkindely doone: for, being as wee are to sound it, according to our English March, we must make a rest, and raise the last sillable, which falles out very vnnaturall in *Desolate, Funerall, Elizabeth, Prodigall*, and in all the rest, sauing the Monosillables. Then followes the English *Trochaicke*, which is saide to bee a simple verse, and so indeede it is, being without Ryme: hauing here no other grace then that in sound it runnes like the knowne measure of our former ancient Verse, ending (as we terme it according to the French) in a feminine foote, sauing that it is shorter by one sillable at the beginning, which is not much missed, by reason it falles full at the last. Next comes the *Elegiacke*, being the fourth kinde, and that likewise is no other then our old accustomed measure of fiue feet: if there be any difference, it must be made in the reading, and therein wee must stand bound to stay where often we would not, and sometimes either breake the accent or the due course of the word. And now for the other foure kinds of numbers, which are to be employed for *Odes*, they are either of the same measure, or such as haue euer beene familiarly vsed amongst vs.

So that of all these eight seuerall kindes of new promised numbers, you see what we haue: Onely what was our owne before, and the same but apparelled in forraine Titles; which had they come in their kinde and naturall

attire of Ryme, wee should neuer haue suspected that
they had affected to be other, or sought to degenerate into
strange manners, which now we see was the cause why
they were turnd out of their proper habite, and brought in
as Aliens, onely to induce men to admire them as farre-
commers. But see the power of Nature; it is not all the
artificiall couerings of wit that can hide their natiue and
originall condition, which breakes out thorow the strongest
bandes of affectation, and will be it selfe, doe Singularitie
what it can. And as for those imagined quantities of
sillables, which haue bin euer held free and indifferent
in our language, who can inforce vs to take knowledge
of them, being *in nullius verba iurati*, and owing fealty to
no forraine inuention? especially in such a case where
there is no necessitie in Nature, or that it imports either
the matter or forme, whether it be so or otherwise. But
euery Versifier that wel obserues his worke findes in our
language, without all these vnnecessary precepts, what
numbers best fitte the Nature of her Idiome, and the
proper places destined to such accents as she will not
let in to any other roomes then in those for which they
were borne. As for example, you cannot make this fall
into the right sound of a verse—

None thinkes reward rendred worthy his worth,

vnlesse you thus misplace the accent vpon *Rendrèd* and
Worthìe, contrary to the nature of these wordes: which
sheweth that two feminine numbers (or Trochies, if so
you wil call them) will not succeede in the third and fourth
place of the Verse. And so likewise in this case,

Though Death doth consume, yet Vertue preserues,

it wil not be a Verse, though it hath the iust sillables,
without the same number in the second, and the altering
of the fourth place in this sorte,

Though Death doth ruine, Virtue yet preserues.

A Defence of Rhyme 379

Againe, who knowes not that we can not kindely answere a feminine number with a masculine Ryme, or (if you will so terme it) a *Trochei* with a *Sponde*, as *Weaknes* with *Confesse*, *Nature* and *Indure*, onely for that thereby wee shall wrong the accent, the chiefe Lord and graue Gouernour of Numbers? Also you cannot in a verse of foure feet place a *Trochei* in the first, without the like offence, as, *Yearely out of his watry Cell*; for so you shall sound it Yeareliè, which is vnnaturall. And other such like obseruations vsually occurre, which Nature and a iudiciall eare of themselues teach vs readily to auoyde.

But now for whom hath our Aduersary taken all this paines? For the Learned, or for the Ignorant, or for himselfe, to shew his owne skill? If for the Learned, it was to no purpose, for euerie Grammarian in this land hath learned his *Prosodia*, and alreadie knowes all this Arte of numbers: if for the Ignorant, it was vaine, for if they become Versifiers, wee are like to haue leane Numbers instead of fat Ryme; and if Tully would haue his Orator skilld in all the knowledges appertaining to God and man, what should they haue who would be a degree aboue Orators? Why then it was to shew his owne skill, and what himselfe had obserued; so he might well haue done without doing wrong to the fame of the liuing, and wrong to *England*, in seeking to lay reproach vpon her natiue ornaments, and to turne the faire streame and full course of her accents into the shallow current of a lesse vncertaintie, cleane out of the way of her knowne delight. And I had thought it could neuer haue proceeded from the pen of a Scholler (who sees no profession free from the impure mouth of the scorner) to say the reproach of others idle tongues is the curse of Nature vpon vs, when it is rather her curse vpon him, that knowes not how to vse his tongue. What, doth he think himselfe is now gotten so farre out of the way of contempt, that his numbers are gone beyond the reach of obloquie, and that, how friuolous or idle soeuer they shall runne, they shall be protected from disgrace? as though that light rymes and light numbers did not weigh all alike in the graue opinion of the wise. And that is not Ryme but our ydle Arguments that hath brought downe to so base a reckning the price and estimation of writing in this kinde; when the few good things of this age, by comming together in one throng and presse with the many bad, are not discerned from them, but ouerlooked with them, and all taken to be alike. But when after-times shall make a quest of inquirie; to examine the best of this Age, peraduenture there will be found in the now contemned recordes of Ryme matter not vnfitting the grauest Diuine and seuerest Lawyer in this kingdome. But these things must haue the date of Antiquitie to make them reuerend and authentical. For euer in the collation of Writers men rather weigh their age then their merite, and *legunt priscos cum reuerentia, quando coaetaneos non possunt sine inuidia*[1]. And let no writer in Ryme be any way discouraged in his endeuour by this braue allarum, but rather animated to bring vp all the best of their powers, and charge with all the strength of nature and industrie vpon contempt, that the shew of their reall forces may turne backe insolencie into her owne holde. For be sure that innouation neuer works any ouerthrow, but vpon the aduantage of a care-lesse idlenesse. And let this make vs looke the better to our feete, the better to our matter, better to our maners. Let the Aduersary that thought to hurt vs bring more profit and honor by being against vs then if he had stoode still on our side. For that (next to the awe of heauen) the best reine, the strongest hand to make men keepe their way, is that which their enemy beares vpon them: and let this be the benefite wee make by being oppugned, and the

[1] In the margin: *Simplicius longe posita miramur.*

meanes to redeeme backe the good opinion vanitie and idlenesse haue suffered to be wonne from vs; which nothing but substance and matter can effect. For *Scribendi recte sapere est et principium et fons.*

When we heare Musicke, we must be in our eare in the vtter-roome of sense, but when we intertaine iudgement, we retire into the cabinet and innermost withdrawing chamber of the soule: And it is but as Musicke for the eare *Verba sequi fidibus modulanda Latinis*; but it is a worke of power for the soule *Numerosque modosque ediscere vitae.* The most iudiciall and worthy spirites of this Land are not so delicate, or will owe so much to their eare, as to rest vppon the outside of wordes, and be intertained with sound; seeing that both Number, Measure, and Ryme is but as the ground or seate, whereupon is raised the work that commends it, and which may be easilie at the first found out by any shallow conceipt: as wee see some fantasticke to beginne a fashion, which afterward grauity itselfe is faine to put on, because it will not be out of the weare of other men, and *Recti apud nos locum tenet error vbi publicus factus est.* And power and strength that can plant it selfe any where hauing built within this compasse, and reard it of so high a respect, wee now imbrace it as the fittest dwelling for our inuention, and haue thereon bestowed all the substance of our vnderstanding to furnish it as it is. And therefore heere I stand foorth, onelie to make good the place we haue thus taken vp, and to defend the sacred monuments erected therein, which containe the honour of the dead, the fame of the liuing, the glory of peace, and the best power of our speach, and wherin so many honourable spirits haue sacrificed to Memorie their dearest passions, shewing by what diuine influence they haue beene moued, and vnder what starres they liued.

But yet notwithstanding all this which I haue heare

deliuered in the defence of Ryme, I am not so farre in
loue with mine owne mysterie, or will seeme so froward,
as to bee against the reformation and the better setling
these measures of ours. Wherein there be many things
I could wish were more certaine and better ordered, though
my selfe dare not take vpon me to be a teacher therein,
hauing so much neede to learne of others. And I must
confesse that to mine owne eare those continuall cadences
of couplets vsed in long and continued Poemes are verie
tyresome and vnpleasing, by reason that still, me thinks,
they run on with a sound of one nature, and a kinde of
certaintie which stuffs the delight rather then intertaines it.
But yet, notwithstanding, I must not out of mine owne
daintinesse condemne this kinde of writing, which peraduenture to another may seeme most delightfull; and
many worthy compositions we see to haue passed with
commendation in that kinde. Besides, me thinkes, sometimes to beguile the eare with a running out, and passing
ouer the Ryme, as no bound to stay vs in the line where
the violence of the matter will breake thorow, is rather
gracefull then otherwise. Wherein I finde my Homer-
Lucan, as if he gloried to seeme to haue no bounds, albeit
hee were confined within his measures, to be in my conceipt
most happy. For so thereby they who care not for Verse
or Ryme may passe it ouer with taking notice thereof, and
please themselues with a well measured Prose. And
I must confesse my Aduersary hath wrought this much
vpon me, that I thinke a Tragedie would indeede best
comporte with a blank Verse and dispence with Ryme,
sauing in the *Chorus*, or where a sentence shall require
a couplet. And to auoyde this ouer-glutting the eare with
that always certaine and full incounter of Ryme, I haue
assaid in some of my Epistles to alter the vsuall place of
meeting, and to sette it further off by one Verse, to
trie how I could disuse mine owne eare and to ease it of

this continuall burthen which indeede seemes to surcharge it a little too much: but as yet I cannot come to please my selfe therein, this alternate or crosse Ryme holding still the best place in my affection.

Besides, to me this change of number in a Poem of one nature fits not so wel as to mixe vncertainly feminine Rymes with masculine, which euer since I was warned of that deformitie by my kinde friend and countri-man Maister Hugh Samford, I haue alwayes so auoyded it, as there are not aboue two couplettes in that kinde in all my Poem of the Ciuill warres: and I would willingly if I coulde haue altered it in all the rest, holding feminine Rymes to be fittest for Ditties, and either to be set for certaine, or els by themselues. But in these things, I say, I dare not take vpon mee to teach that they ought to be so, in respect my selfe holds them to be so, or that I thinke it right: for indeed there is no right in these things that are continually in a wandring motion, carried with the violence of vncertaine likings, being but onely the time that giues them their power. For if this right or truth should be no other thing then that wee make it, we shall shape it into a thousand figures, seeing this excellent painter, Man, can so well lay the colours which himselfe grindes in his owne affections, as that hee will make them serue for any shadow and any counterfeit. But the greatest hinderer to our proceedings and the reformation of our errours is this Selfeloue, whereunto we Versifiers are euer noted to bee specially subiect; a disease of all other the most dangerous and incurable, being once seated in the spirits, for which there is no cure but onely by a spirituall remedie. *Multos puto ad sapientiam potuisse peruenire, nisi putassent se peruenisse*: and this opinion of our sufficiencie makes so great a cracke in our iudgement, as it wil hardly euer holde any thing of worth. *Caecus amor sui*; and though it would seeme to see all without it, yet certainely it discernes but little within. For there is not the simplest writer that will euer tell himselfe he doth ill, but, as if he were the parasite onely to sooth his owne doings, perswades him that his lines can not but please others which so much delight himselfe: *Suffenus est quisque sibi*

> *—neque idem vnquam*
> *Aeque est beatus, ac poema cum scribit.*
> *Tam gaudet in se tamque se ipse miratur.*

And the more to shew that he is so, we shall see him euermore in all places, and to all persons repeating his owne compositions; and

> *Quem vero arripuit, tenet, occiditque legendo.*

Next to this deformitie stands our affectation, wherein we alwayes bewray our selues to be both vnkinde and vnnaturall to our owne natiue language, in disguising or forging strange or vnusuall wordes, as if it were to make our verse seeme another kind of speach out of the course of our vsuall practise, displacing our wordes, or inuenting new, onely vpon a singularitie, when our owne accustomed phrase, set in the due place, would expresse vs more familiarly and to better delight than all this idle affectation of antiquitie or noueltie can euer doe. And I cannot but wonder at the strange presumption of some men, that dare so audaciously aduenture to introduce any whatsoeuer forraine wordes, be they neuer so strange, and of themselues, as it were, without a Parliament, without any consent or allowance, establish them as Free-denizens in our language. But this is but a Character of that perpetuall reuolution which wee see to be in all things that neuer remaine the same: and we must heerein be content to submit our selues to the law of time, which in few yeeres wil make al that for which we now contend *Nothing*.

APPENDIX

I

BEN JONSON

1598-1601

[The following passages from Ben Jonson's *Every Man in his Humour*, *Every Man out of his Humour*, and the *Poetaster* contain his earlier critical dicta and more important references to contemporary literature.]

I.

From *Every Man in his Humor*, Quarto 1601, Act v, Scene 1. (Bodleian Library. Malone, 229.) Omitted from the Folio 1616. The play was first acted in 1598 (or 1597).

Mat[heo]. Sir, heres the beginning of a sonnet I made to my mistresse.

Cle[ment]. That, that: who? To *Maddona Hesperida?* Is she your mistresse?

Pros[pero]. It pleaseth him to call her so, sir.

Clem. 'In Sommer time when Phœbus golden rayes.' You translated this too, did you not?

Pros. No, this is inuention; he found it in a ballad.

Mat. Fayth, sir, I had most of the conceite of it out of a ballad indeede.

Clem. Conceite: fetch me a couple of torches, sirha. I may see the conceite: quickly! its very darke!

Gui[lliano]. Call you this poetry?

Lo[renzo] iu[nior]. Poetry? nay, then call blasphemie religion; Call Diuels Angels; and Sinne pietie:
Let all things be preposterously transchangd.

Lo[renzo] se[nior]. Why, how now, sonne? what! are you
   startled now?
  Hath the brize prickt you, ha? go to; you see
  How abiectly your Poetry is ranckt,
  In generall opinion. 5
Lo. iu. Opinion! O God, let grosse opinion
  Sinck & be damnd as deepe as *Barathrum*.
  If it may stand with your most wisht content,
  I can refell opinion and approue
  The state of poesie, such as it is, 10
  Blessed, æternall, and most true deuine:
  Indeede, if you will looke on Poesie,
  As she appeares in many, poore and lame,
  Patcht vp in remnants and old worne ragges,
  Halfe starud for want of her peculiar foode, 15
  Sacred inuention, then I must conferme
  Both your conceite and censure of her merrite;
  But view her in her glorious ornaments,
  Attired in the maiestie of arte,
  Set high in spirite with the precious taste 20
  Of sweete philosophie, and, which is most,
  Crownd with the rich traditions of a soule
  That hates to haue her dignitie prophand
  With any relish of an earthly thought—
  Oh then how proud a presence doth she beare! 25
  Then is she like her selfe, fit to be seene
  Of none but graue and consecrated eyes.
  Nor is it any blemish to her fame
  That such leane, ignorant, and blasted wits,
  Such brainlesse guls, should vtter their stolne wares 30
  With such aplauses in our vulgar eares;
  Or that their slubberd lines haue currant passe,
  From the fat iudgements of the multitude;
  But that this barren and infected age
  Should set no difference twixt these empty spirits 35
  And a true Poet; then which reuerend name
  None can more adorne humanitie.   *Enter with torches.*
Clem. I, Lorenzo, but election is now gouernd altogether by the
   influence of humor, which, instead of those holy flames that
   should direct and light the soule to eternitie, hurles foorth 40
   nothing but smooke and congested vapours, that stifle her
   vp, and bereaue her of al sight & motion. But she must

haue store of *Ellebore* giuen her to purge these grosse
obstructions. Oh, thats well sayd. Giue me thy torch;
come lay this stuffe together. So, giue fire! there, see,
see, how our Poets glory shines brighter, and brighter!
still, still it increaseth! Oh, now its at the highest! and
now it declines as fast! You may see, gallants, *Sic transit
gloria mundi* . . .

II.

From *The Workes of Beniamin Ionson.*
Folio 1616. (Bodleian Library. Douce,
I. 302.)
This Prologue appears first in the
Folio, but may be dated 1598. Gifford's
evidence for 1596 is inconclusive.

PROLOGVE.

Though neede make many *Poets*, and some such
As art and nature haue not betterd much,
Yet ours, for want, hath not so lou'd the stage,
As he dare serue th' ill customes of the age,
Or purchase your delight at such a rate,
As, for it, he himselfe must iustly hate:
To make a child, now swadled, to proceede
Man, and then shoote vp, in one beard and weede,
Past threescore yeeres; or, with three rustie swords,
And helpe of some few foot-and-halfe-foote words,
Fight ouer *Yorke* and *Lancasters* long iarres,
And in the tyring-house bring wounds to scarres.
He rather prayes you will be pleas'd to see
One such to day, as other playes should be;
Where neither *Chorus* wafts you ore the seas;
Nor creaking throne comes downe, the boyes to please;
Nor nimble squibbe is seene, to make afear'd
The gentlewomen; nor roul'd bullet heard,
To say it thunders; nor tempestuous drumme
Rumbles, to tell you when the storme doth come;
But deedes, and language, such as men doe vse,
And persons, such as *Comœdie* would chuse,
When she would shew an Image of the times,
And sport with humane follies, not with crimes,
Except we make 'hem such, by louing still
Our popular errors, when we know th' are ill.

I meane such errors as you'll all confesse,
By laughing at them, they deserue no lesse:
Which when you heartily doe, there's hope left then,
You, that haue so grac'd monsters, may like men.

III.

From *Every Man out of his Humor*.
Quarto, 1600. (Bodleian Library. Malone,
229.) The play was produced in 1599.

INDVCTIO, SONO SECVNDO.
GREX.
ASPER, CORDATVS, MITIS.

. . . .

Mit[is]. In faith this Humor will come ill to some.
  You will be thought to be too peremptorie.
Asp[er]. This Humor? good; and why this Humor, *Mitis*?
  Nay, doe not turne, but answere.
Mit. Answere? what?
Asp. I will not stirre your patience: pardon me,
  I vrg'd it for some reasons, and the rather
  To giue these ignorant wel-spoken daies
  Some tast of their abuse of this word *Humor*.
Cor[datus]. O, doe not let your purpose fall, good *Asper*;
  It cannot but arriue most acceptable,
  Chiefely to such as haue the happinesse
  Daily to see how the poore innocent word
  Is rackt and tortur'd.
Mit. I; I pray you proceed.
Asp. Ha, what? what is't?
Cord. For the abuse of *Humor*.
Asp. O, I craue pardon, I had lost my thoughts.
  Why *Humor*, as 'tis *ens*, we thus define it
  To be a quality of aire or water,
  And in it selfe holds these two properties,
  Moisture and Fluxure: As, for demonstration,
  Poure water on this floore, 'twill wet and runne;
  Likewise the aire, forc't through a horne or trumpet,
  Flowes instantly away, and leaues behind
  A kinde of due; and hence we doe conclude,
  That what soe're hath fluxure and humiditie,

As wanting power to containe it selfe,
Is *Humor*: so in euery humane bodie
The choller, melancholy, flegme, and bloud,
By reason that they flow continually
5 In some one part, and are not continent,
Receiue the name of Humors. Now thus farre
It may, by Metaphore, apply it selfe
Vnto the generall disposition,
As when some one peculiar quality
10 Doth so possesse a man, that it doth draw
All his affects, his spirits, and his powers,
In their confluctions all to runne one way,
This may be truly said to be a Humor.
But that a Rooke in wearing a pide feather,
15 The cable hatband, or the three-pild ruffe,
A yard of shoe-tie, or the Switzers knot
On his French garters, should affect a Humor,
O, tis more than most ridiculous.
Cord. He speakes pure truth : Now if an Ideot
20 Haue but an Apish or Phantasticke straine,
It is his Humor.
Asp. Well, I will scourge those apes,
And to these courteous eies oppose a mirror,
As large as is the Stage whereon we act,
25 Where they shall see the times deformity
Anatomiz'd in euery Nerue and sinew,
With constant courage and contempt of feare.
Mit. Asp. (I vrge it as your friend) take heed ;
The daies are dangerous, full of exception,
30 And men are growne impatient of reproofe.
Asp. Ha, ha !
You might as well haue told me, yond' is heauen,
This earth, these men, and all had mou'd alike.
Doe not I know the times condition?
35 Yes, *Mitis*; and their soules, and who they be
That either will or can except against me :
None but a sort of fooles, so sicke in tast,
That they contemne all Physicke of the mind,
And, like gald Camels, kicke at euery touch.
40 Good men, and vertuous spirits, that loath their vices,
Will cherish my free labours, loue my lines,
And with the feruor of their shining grace

Make my braine fruitfull to bring forth more obiects
Worthy their serious and intentiue eies.
But why enforce I this? as fainting? no.
If any here chance to behold himselfe,
Let him not dare to challenge me of wrong;   5
For, if he shame to haue his follies knowne,
First he should shame to act 'hem: my strict hand
Was made to ceaze on vice, and with a gripe
Crush out the Humor of such spongie soules,
As licke vp euery idle vanity.   10

Cord. Why, this is right *Furor Poeticus.*
Kind gentlemen, we hope your patience
Will yet conceiue the best, or entertaine
This supposition, That a madman speakes.

. . . .   15

Mit. You haue seene his play, *Cordatus*? pray you, how is 't?
Cord. Faith sir, I must refraine to iudge, onely this I can say of
   it, 'tis strange, and of a perticular kind by it selfe, somewhat like *Vetus Comœdia*: a worke that hath bounteously
   pleased me: how it will answere the generall expectation,   20
   I know not.
Mit. Does he obserue all the lawes of Comedie in it?
Cord. What lawes meane you?
Mit. Why, the equall diuision of it into Acts and Scenes, accord-
   ing to the Terentian manner; his true number of Actors;   25
   the furnishing of the Scene with *Grex* or *Chorus*; and that
   the whole Argument fall within compasse of a daies
   efficiencie.
Cord. O no, these are too nice obseruations.
Mit. They are such as must be receiued by your fauour, or it   30
   cannot be Authentique.
Cord. Troth, I can discerne no such necessitie.
Mit. No?
Cord. No, I assure you, signior: if those lawes you speake of
   had beene deliuered vs *ab Initio*, and in their present vertue   35
   and perfection, there had beene some reason of obeying
   their powers; but 'tis extant that that which we call
   Comœdia was at first nothing but a simple and continued
   Satyre, sung by one only person, till *Susario* inuented
   a second; after him, *Epicharmus* a third; *Phormus* and   40
   Chionides deuised to haue foure Actors, with a *Prologue*
   and *Chorus*; to which *Cratinus* (long after) added fift and

sixt; *Eupolis* more; *Aristophanes* more than they: euery
man in the dignity of his spirit and iudgement supplied
something: and, though that in him this kind of Poeme
appeared absolute, and fully perfected, yet how is the face
of it chang'd since, in *Menander, Philemon, Cecilius, Plautus*,
and the rest; who haue vtterly excluded the *Chorus*,
altered the property of the persons, their names, and
natures, and augmented it with all libertie, according to
the elegancie and disposition of those times wherein they
wrote. I see not then but wee should enioy the same
Licentia or free power to illustrate and heighten our inuention
as they did; and not bee tied to those strict and
regular formes which the nicenesse of a fewe (who are
nothing but Forme) would thrust vpon vs.

Mit. Well, we will not dispute of this nowe: but what's his
Scene?

Cor. Mary, *Insula fortunata*, Sir.

Mit. O, the fortunate Iland? masse, he [h]as bound himselfe to
a strict law there.

Cor. Why so?

Mit. Hee cannot lightly a[l]ter the Scene, without crossing the
seas.

Cor. He needes not, hauing a whole Ilande to runne through,
I thinke.

Mit. No! howe comes it then, that in some one play wee see
so manye Seas, Countries, and Kingdomes past ouer with
such admirable dexteritie?

Cor. O, that but shewes how wel the Authors can trauaile in
their vocation, and out-run the apprehension of their
Auditory. But leauing this, I would they would begin
once: this protraction is able to sower the best-settled
patience in the Theatre.

IV.

From the *Poetaster or The Arraignment*,
Quarto 1620. (Bodleian Library. Malone,
213.) The play was produced in 1601.

ACTVS PRIMVS. SCENA SECVNDA.

. . . . .

Ouid. O sacred Poësy, thou spirit of *Arts*,
The soule of *Science*, and the Queene of Soules,

What prophane violence, almost sacriledge,
Hath here beene offered thy Diuinities!
Hmh! that thine owne guiltlesse Pouerty should arme
Prodigious Ignorance to wound thee thus!
For thence is all their force of Argument   5
Drawne foorth against thee; or from the abuse
Of thy great powers in Adultrate braines;
When, would men learne but to distinguish spirits,
And set true difference twixt those iaded wits
That runne a broken pase for common hire,   10
And the high Raptures of a happy soule,
Borne on the winges of her immortall thought,
That kickes at earth with a disdainefull heele,
And beates at Heauen gates with her bright hooues;
They would not then with such distorted faces,   15
And dudgeon Censures, stab at *Poesy*:
They would admire bright knowledge, and their minds
Should nere descend on so vnworthy obiects
As Gould or Titles; they would dread farre more
To be thought ignorant then be knowne poore.   20
The time was once, when wit drownd wealth: but now,
Your onely Barbarism 's to haue wit, and want.
No matter now in vertue who excells,
He that hath coyne hath all perfection else . . .

ACTVS QVINTVS.   SCENA PRIMA.   25

. . . . . .

[*Caesar.*] Say then, lou'd *Horace*, thy true thought of *Virgill*.
Hor[ace]. I iudge him of a rectified spirit,
  By many reuolutions of discourse
  (In his bright reasons influence) refin'd   30
  From all the tartarous Moodes of common Men;
  Bearing the Nature and similitude
  Of a right heauenly Bodie; most seuere
  In fashion and collection of himselfe;
  And, then, as cleare and confident as *Ioue*.   35
Gal[lus]. And yet so chast and tender is his Eare
  In suffering in any Syllable to passe,
  That he thinkes may become the honour'd name
  Of Issue to his so examin'd selfe,
  That all the lasting fruites of his full merit   40

In his owne *Poemes* he doth still distaste;
As if his mindes Peece, which he stroue to paint,
Could not with fleshly Pensils haue her right.
Tibul[*lus*]. But, to approue his workes of Soueraigne worth,
5 This Obseruation (me thinkes) more then serues,
And is not vulgar. That which he hath writ
Is with such iudgement labour'd, and distill'd
Through all the needefull vses of our liues,
That could a man remember but his Lines,
10 He should not touch at any serious point,
But he might breath his spirit out of him.
Cæsar. You meane, he might repeat part of his workes,
As fit for any conference he can vse?
Tib. Trew, Royall *Cæsar*.
15 *Cæsar*. 'Tis worthily obseru'd:
And a most worthie vertue in his workes.
What thinks Materiall *Horace* of his learning?
Hor. His Learning labours not the Schoole-like *Glosse*,
That most consists in *Ecchoing* Wordes and *Termes*,
20 And soonest wins a man an Empty name;
Nor any long or far-fetcht Circumstance,
Wrapt in the curious General'ties of *Artes*;
But a direct and *Analyticke* Summe
Of all the worth and first effectes of *Artes*.
25 And for his *Poësie*, 'tis so ramm'd with Life,
That it shall gather strength of Life with being,
And liue hereafter, more admir'd then now.
Cæsar. This one consent in all your doomes of him,
And mutuall Loues of all your seuerall merits,
30 Argues a truth of merit in you all. . . .

ACTVS QVINTVS. SCENA TERTIA.

Virgill. Before you goe together, worthy *Romanes*,
We are to tender our Opinion,
35 And giue you those Instructions that may adde
Vnto your euen Iudgement in the Cause;
Which thus we doe Commence. First, you must know
That where there is a true and perfect Merit,
There can be no Deiection; and the Scorne
40 Of humble Basenesse oftentimes so workes

In a high Soule vpon the grosser Spirit,
That to his bleared and offended Sense
There seemes a hideous Fault blaz'd in the Obiect,
When only the Disease is in his Eyes.
Here-hence it comes our *Horace* now stands taxt   5
Of *Impudence, Selfe-loue,* and *Arrogance*,
By these who share no merit in themselues,
And therefore thinke his Portion is as small.
For they, from their owne guilt, assure their Soules,
If they should confidently praise their workes,   10
In them it would appeare *Inflation*;
Which, in a full and well-digested man,
Cannot receiue that foule abusiue name,
But the faire Title of *Erection*.
And, for his trewe vse of *translating* Men,   15
It still hath beene a worke of as much Palme
In clearest Iudgements as t'*inuent* or *make*.
His *sharpnesse*—that is most excusable;
As being forc't out of a suffering Vertue,
Oppressed with the Licence of the Time;   20
And howsoeuer Fooles, or Ierking *Pedants*,
Players, or such like *Buffonary* wits,
May with their beggerly and barren trash
Tickle base vulgar eares, in their despight.
This, like *Ioues* Thunder, shall their pride controule. 25
'*The honest* Satyre *hath the happiest Soule.*'
Now, *Romanes*, you haue heard our thoughts. Withdrawe,
    when you please.

> [*Demetrius and Crispinus having been placed on trial, the
>   former confesses that mere envy had been his motive,*   30
>   *and is forgiven by Horace. To the latter Horace's pills*
>   '*mixt with the whitest kind of hellebore*' *are given to*
>   'purge
>   His braine and stomach of those tumorous heats.'
>   *The victim, like Lucian's Lexiphanes, rids himself pain-* 35
>   *fully of his rhetorical jargon* ('*terrible windy words*'),
>   *and the scene proceeds*—]

Virgill. These Pilles can but restore him for a Time;
Not cure him quite of such a Malady,
Caught by so many surfets, which haue fild   40
His Blood and Braine thus full of *Crudities*:

'Tis necessary, therefore, he obserue
A strict and holsome Diet. Looke you take
Each morning of old *Catoes* Principles
A good draught next your heart; that walke vpon,
5   Till it be well digested: Then come home
And taste a piece of *Terence*; sucke his *Phrase*
In steede of Licorice; and, at any hand,
Shun *Plautus* and old *Ennius*; they are meates
Too harsh for a weake Stomacke. Vse to read
10 (But not without a *Tutor*) the best *Greekes*,
As *Orpheus, Musœus, Pindarus,*
Hesiod, Callimachus, and *Theocrite,*
High *Homer*; but beware of *Lycophron*;
He is too darke and dangerous a Dish.
15 You must not hunt for wild out-landish Termes,
To stuffe out a peculiar *Dialect*;
But let your *Matter* runne before your *Words.*
And if, at any time, you chaunce to meete
Some *Gallo-Belgick* Phrase, you shall not straight
20 Racke your poor Verse to giue it entertainement,
But let it passe: and doe not thinke your selfe
Much damnified, if you doe leaue it out,
When nor your *Vnderstanding* nor the *Sense*
Could well receiue it. This faire Abstinence,
25 In time, will render you more sound and Cleare.
And thus haue I prescrib'd to you, in place
Of a strict Sentence: which till he performe,
Attire him in that Robe. And hence-forth learne
To beare your selfe more humbly; not to swell,
30 Or breath your insolent and idle Spight
On him whose Laughter can your worst affright.

II

THE RETURNE FROM PARNASSUS

1601

[The following extract is taken from the Second Part of the
   Returne from Parnassus, performed in St. John's College,
   Cambridge, in 1601. Two editions appeared in 1606
   (London: G. Eld for John Wright). Copies of these are
   preserved in the Malone Collection in the Bodleian Library.
   The three 'Parnassus' comedies have been edited by the
   Rev. W. D. Macray (*The Pilgrimage to Parnassus with
   the Two Parts of the Return from Parnassus*. Oxford. At
   the Clarendon Press. 1886). The passage is the second
   scene of the first Act.]

Enter INGENIOSO, IUDICIO.

Iud[*icio*]. What, *Ingenioso*, carrying a Vinegar bottle about thee,
   like a great schole-boy giuing the world a bloudy nose?
Ing[*enioso*]. Faith, *Iudicio*, if I carry the vineger bottle, it's great
   reason I should confer it vpon the bald pated world: and
   againe, if my kitchen want the vtensilies of viands, it's
   great reason other men should haue the sauce of vineger;
   and for the bloudy nose, *Iudicio*, I may chance indeed giue
   the world a bloudy nose, but it shall hardly giue me a
   crakt crowne, though it giues other Poets French crownes.
Iud. I would wish thee, *Ingenioso*, to sheath thy pen, for thou
   canst not be successefull in the fray, considering thy
   enemies haue the aduantage of the ground.
Ing. Or rather, *Iudicio*, they haue the grounds with aduantage,
   and the French crownes with a pox; and I would they had
   them with a plague too: but hang them, swadds, the basest
   corner in my thoughts is too gallant a roome to lodge

Appendix

them in. But say, *Iudicio*, what newes in your presse? did
you keepe any late corrections vpon any tardy pamphlets?

Iud. Veterem iubes renouare dolorem. Ingenioso, what ere befalls
thee, keepe thee from the trade of the corrector of the
presse.

Ing. Mary, so I will, I warrant thee; if pouerty presse not too
much, Ile correct no presse but the presse of the people.

Iud. Would it not grieue any good spirits to sit a whole
moneth nitting out a lousie beggarly Pamphlet, and like
a needy Phisitian to stand whole yeares, tossing and
tumbling the filth that falleth from so many draughty
inuentions as daily swarme in our printing house?

Ing. Come, I thinke, we shall haue you put finger in the eye,
and cry, *O friends, no friends*. Say man, what new paper
hobby horses, what rattle bables are come out in your late
May morrice daunce?

Iud. Slymy rimes as thick as flies in the sunne: I thinke there
be neuer an ale-house in England, not any so base a
maypole on a country greene, but sets forth some poets
petternels or demilances to the paper warres in Paules
Church-yard.

Ing. And well too may the issue of a strong hop learne to
hop all ouer England, when as better wittes sit like lame
coblers in their studies. Such barmy heads wil alwaies
be working, when as sad vineger wittes sit souring at the
bottome of a barrell: plaine Meteors, bred of the exhalation of Tobacco and the vapors of a moyst pot, that
soure vp into the open ayre, when as sounder wit keepes
belowe.

Iud. Considering the furies of the times, I could better endure
to see those young Can quaffing hucksters shoot of their
pellets so they would keepe them from these English
flores-poetarum; but now the world is come to that passe,
that there starts vp euery day an old goose that sits hatching vp those eggs which haue ben filcht from the nest[s]
of Crowes and Kestrells. Here is a booke, *Ing*: why, to
condemne it to cl[o]a[ca], the vsuall Tiburne of all misliuing
papers, were too faire a death for so foule an offender.

Ing. What's the name of it, I pray thee, *Iud.*?

Iud. Looke, its here—*Beluedere*.

Ing. What! a bel-wether in Paules Church-yeard, so cald
because it keeps a bleating, or because it hath the tinckling

bel of so many Poets about the neck of it? What is the rest
of the title?
Iud. *The garden of the Muses.*
Ing. 'What have we here? The Poett garish
    Gayly bedeckt like forehorse of the Parish.' 5
What followes?
Iud. *Quem referent musae, viuet dum robora tellus,*
    Dum caelum stellas, dum vehit amnis aquas.
[*Ing.*] Who blurres fayer paper with foule bastard rimes
    Shall liue full many an age in latter times; 10
Who makes a ballet for an ale-house doore
Shall liue in future times for euer more.
Then Antony, thy muse shall live so long
As drafty ballats to [the paile] are song.
But what's his deuise? Parnassus with the sunne and the 15
lawrel. I wonder this owle dares looke on the sunne, and
I maruaile this gose flies not: the laurell? his deuise
might haue bene better a foole going into the market place
to be seene, with this motto, *scribimus indocti*, or a poore
beggar gleaning of eares in the end of haruest, with this 20
word, *sua cuique gloria*.
Iud. Turne ouer the leafe, *Ing:*, and thou shalt see the paynes
of this worthy gentleman: Sentences gathered out of all
kind of Poetts, referred to certaine methodicall heads,
profitable for the vse of these times, to rime vpon any 25
occasion at a little warning. Read the names.
Ing. So I will, if thou wilt helpe me to censure them.

| *Edmund Spencer.* | *Michaell Drayton.* |
| *Henry Constable.* | *Iohn Dauis.* |
| *Thomas Lodge.* | *Iohn Marston.* | 30
| *Samuel Daniell.* | *Kit: Marlowe.* |
| *Thomas Watson.* | |

Good men and true, stand togither: heare your censure.
What's thy iudgement of *Spencer*?
Iud. A sweeter Swan then euer song in Poe, 35
A shriller Nightingale then euer blest
The prouder groues of selfe admiring Rome!
Blith was each vally, and each sheapeard proud,
While he did chaunt his rurall minstralsie;
Attentiue was full many a dainty eare; 40
Nay, hearers hong vpon his melting tong,
While sweetly of his Faiery Queene he song,

Appendix

    While to the waters fall he tun'd [he]r fame,
    And in each barke engrau'd Elizaes name.
    And yet, for all this, vnregarding soile
    Vnlac't the line of his desired life,
5 Denying mayntenance for his deare releife;
    Carelesse [e]re to preuent his exequy,
    Scarce deigning to shut vp his dying eye.
  Ing. Pity it is that gentler witts should breed,
    Where thick skin chuffes laugh at a schollers need.
10 But softly may our honours ashes rest,
    That lie by mery *Chaucers* noble chest.
    But I pray thee proceed breefly in thy censure, that I may be proud of my selfe; as in the first, so in the last, my censure may iumpe with thine. *Henry Constable, Samuel*
15 *Daniell, Thomas Lodg, Thomas Watson.*
  Iud. Sweete *Constable* doth take the wondring eare,
    And layes it vp in willing prisonment:
    Sweete hony dropping *Daniell* doth wage
    Warre with the proudest big Italian,
20 That melts his heart in sugred sonneting;
    Onely let him more sparingly make vse
    Of others wit, and vse his owne the more,
    That well may scorne base imitation.
    For *Lodge* and *Watson*, men of some desert,
25 Yet subiect to a Critticks marginall;
    Lodge for his oare in euery paper boate,
    He that turnes ouer *Galen* euery day,
    To sit and simper *Euphues* legacy.
  Ing. Michael Drayton.
30 [*Iud.*] *Draytons* sweete muse is like a sanguine dy,
    Able to rauish the rash gazers eye.
    How euer, he wants one true note of a Poet of our times, and that is this, hee cannot swagger it well in a Tauerne nor dominere in a hot house.
35 [*Ing.*] *Iohn Dauis.*
  [*Iud.*] Acute *Iohn Dauis*, I affect thy rymes,
    That ierck in hidden charmes these looser times;
    Thy plainer verse, thy vnaffected vaine,
    Is grac't with a faire and sooping trayne.
40 *Ing. Locke* and *Hudson.*
  Iud. Locke and *Hudson*, sleepe, you quiet shauers, among the shauings of the presse, and let your bookes lye in some

old nookes amongst old bootes and shooes, so you may auoide my censure.

Ing. Why then clap a lock on their feete, and turne them to commons.

  Iohn Marston.

Iud. What, *Monsier Kynsader*, lifting vp your legge and pissing against the world! put vp man, put vp for shame!

Me thinks he is a Ruffian in his stile,
Withouten bands or garters ornament;
He quaffes a cup of Frenchmans Helicon,
Then royster doyster in his oylie tearmes,
Cutts, thrusts, and foines at whomesoeuer he meets,
And strewes about Ram-ally meditations.
Tut, what cares he for modest close coucht termes,
Cleanly to gird our looser libertines.
Giue him plaine naked words stript from their shirts,
That might beseeme plaine dealing *Aretine*.
I, there is one that backes a paper steed
And manageth a pen-knife gallantly,
Strikes his poinado at a buttons breadth,
Brings the great battering ram of tearmes to towns,
And, at first volly of his Cannon shot,
Batters the walles of the old fustie world.

Ing. *Christopher Marlowe.*

Iud. *Marlowe* was happy in his buskind muse,
Alas! vnhappy in his life and end.
Pitty it is that wit so ill should dwell,
Wit lent from heauen, but vices sent from hell,

Ing. Our *Theater* hath lost, *Pluto* hath got,
A Tragick penman for a driery plot.

  Beniamin Iohnson.

Iud. The wittiest fellow of a Bricklayer in England.

Ing. A meere Empyrick, one that getts what he hath by obseruation, and makes onely nature priuy to what he indites; so slow an Inuentor that he were better betake himselfe to his old trade of Bricklaying; a bould whorson, as confident now in making a booke as he was in times past in laying of a brick.

  William Shakespeare.

Iud. Who loues [not] *Adons* loue or *Lucre*[*ce*] rape?
His sweeter verse contaynes hart [th]robbing li[n]e,

Could but a grauer subiect him content,
Without loues foolish lazy languishment.
Ing. Churchyard.
Hath not *Shor's* wife, although a light skirts she,
Giuen him a chast long lasting memory?
Iud. No, all light pamphlets once, I, finden shall
A Churchyard and a graue to bury all.
Inge. Thomas Nash.
I, heare is a fellow, *Iudicio*, that carryed the deadly stock-
ado in his pen, whose muse was armed with a gagtooth
and his pen possest with *Hercules* furies.
Iud. Let all his faultes sleepe with his mournfull chest,
And then for euer with his ashes rest!
His style was wittie, though he had some gal;
Something he might haue mended, so may all.
Yet this I say, that for a mother witt,
Few men haue euer seene the like of it.
Ing. Reades the rest.
Iud. As for these, they haue some of them beene the old
hedgstakes of the presse, and some of them are at this
instant the botts and glanders of the printing house.
Fellowes that stande only vpon tearmes to serue the
tearme with their blotted papers, write as men go to
stoole, for needes; and, when they write, they write as a
b[o]are pisses—now and then drop a pamphlet.
Ing. Durum telum necessitas. Good fayth they do as I do—
exchange words for mony. I haue some traffique this day
with *Danter*, about a little booke which I haue made; the
name of it is a Catalogue of *Cambrige* Cuckolds: but this
Beluedere, this methodicall asse, hath made me almost
forget my time. Ile now to Paules Churchyard; meete
me an houre hence, at the signe of the Pegasus in Cheapside, and Ile moyst thy temples with a cuppe of Claret,
as hard as the world goes.   *Ex.* IUDICIO.

NOTES

NOTES

PUTTENHAM (pp. 1-193).

1. The heading '*George* Puttenham' may reasonably be objected to, in the light of the evidence which Mr. Henry Crofts has brought forward in favour of an elder brother *Richard* (? 1520-? 1601), though that evidence is not conclusive. See *The Governour*, by Sir Thomas Elyot, ed. 1880, i. 182-9; Mr. Lee's article in *D. N. B.* (based on the preceding); and the Introduction to Mr. Arber's edition. The sheets were printed off before I had convinced myself that the traditional ascription to 'George' must be abandoned, and that a better heading would have been 'Richard Puttenham,' or simply 'Puttenham.' Mr. Croft would explain the anonymity by the fact that Richard Puttenham was a prisoner in very distressed circumstances, and 'had parted with the MS. of his work' in such a way that the printer did not know his name. The *Stationers' Registers* show that the book had already been licensed to Thomas Orwin on November 9, 1588.

There are several contemporary references to the book, e.g. by Harington, supra, p. 196, and by Meres, supra, pp. 314, 321; but the ascription to *a* Puttenham is not known to have been made before 1614, when Camden inserted the name in the text of Carew (see note to p. 292, l. 23). Edmund Bolton in his *Hypercritica* (first published by Dr. Anthony Hall in 1722) speaks of the 'witty and artificial book of the Art of English Poetry (the Work as the Fame is) of one of her Gentlemen Pensioners, Puttenham (p. 236).' Bolton's MS. may have been written in 1618. Harington refers to the author as 'that unknowne Godfather' and as 'Ignoto' (supra, p. 196). The absence of literary clue is the more remarkable, as the author has himself supplied, by references throughout his book, a goodly list of his other writings, including *The Eclogue of Elpine* (see Arber, p. 180), *Partheniades, Ierotekni* (supra, p. 31), *a ditty of Great*

Britaine (supra, p. 43), a comedy *Ginecocratia* (supra, p. 139), *Of the originals and pedigree of the English tong* (supra, p. 149), an interlude *Lustie London* (Arber, pp. 183, 208), another, *The Woer* (Arber, pp. 212, 233), a Hymn to the Queen, entitled *Minerua* (Arber, p. 244), *Triumphals* (Arber, p. 245), *Philocalia* (supra, p. 170, see note), *De Decoro* (supra, p. 181), &c. Only one of these has been preserved, *The Partheniades* (Cotton MSS. Vesp. E. viii). It is printed by Haslewood and (partly) by Nichols in his *Progresses of Queen Elizabeth*, and is edited by Dr. Furnivall in *Ballads from MSS.*, ii. 72 et seq. (Ballad Society Publ.).

l. 25. *expresse passages* : e.g. p. 182, l. 30. But cf. 'sir,' p. 162, l. 16.

3. 6, &c. *A poet ... a maker.* Cf. Sidney, i. p. 155, l. 26, note.

16. *a versifier.* See note to Sidney, supra, i. p. 159, l. 35.

4. 31. *Madame.* See note to p. 1, l. 25.

7. 8. Cf. Sidney, supra, i. 151.

28. Cf. Sidney, i. 154.

9. 10-25. Cf. Sidney, supra, i. passim.

34. *first Philosophers.* Cf. Sidney, i. pp. 151-2.

10. 1-8. Cf. Sidney, supra, i. p. 158.

32. *Perusine*, Peruvian.

12. 5-19. Cf. Ascham, supra, i. p. 29, l. 30.

13. 7, &c. A reference to the popular *Conseruandae bonae valetudinis praecepta*, written in 1100 for Robert, Duke of Normandy, son of William the Conqueror. Cf. ii. p. 361, l. 26, and Hall's *Satires*, iv. 4, 22-3 (ed. Grosart) :—

> 'Tho neuer haue I *Salerne* rimes profest
>   To be some Ladies trencher-criticke guest.'

Puttenham reads *Rege* and *tota schola* (an inversion of quantities), omits a fourth and fifth line, and alters the last line. (Cf. the Francfurt edition, 1573, f. 1.)

14. 1. Puttenham makes a false quantity of '&' by printing 'et' for 'atque.' He is not responsible for the other errors in quantity (e.g. sempēr, 4; nĕrē, 28; quinquē, 29, &c.).

15. 20-2. *the disportes of Ouid.* Cf. the quotation on p. 331, supra. The reference is probably to the Pseudo-Ovidius, not to P. Ovidius Naso, although the first line is found in some editions of the *Ars Amatoria*, i. 59.

Notes

27-30. Puttenham repeats this reference in Book III (see Arber, p. 261). Hucbald, monk of S. Amand, towards the close of the ninth century, wrote a poem in praise of bald heads, printed at Basle in 1516 and 1546. See the text in *Amphitheatrum Sapientiae Socraticae*, Hanau, 1619, and the account in *Histoire Lit. de la France*, vi. 215, and Ebert, iii. 167. See also Migne's *Patrologia*, cxxxii. 826.

16. 12-18. *Verse Lyon* cannot well be anything other than 'Leonine Verse' ('*versus Leonini*,' '*leonini rhythmi*,' '*rimes léonines*,' '*rimes doublettes*'), yet Puttenham's example does not illustrate the mediaeval form, viz. hexameters or alternate hexameters and pentameters in which the last word rhymes with the word immediately before the caesura. (See Scaliger, *Poetice*, ii. 29; Claude Fauchet, *Recueil* (1581), edit. 1610, pp. 552^r-3^r; Estienne Pasquier, *Les Recherches*, Bk. vii (edit. 1643); Buchler's recension of the *Instit. Poet.* of Jac. Pontanus, 69; Du Cange, s.v. '*Leonini versus*'; Langlois, *De Artibus Rhetoricae Rhythmicae*, 1890, p. 69, and *N.E.D.* s.v. 'Leonine.') Puttenham's quotation is an example of *versus reciproci* or *retrogradi*, verses which preserve the metre when the order of the words is reversed. See Scaliger, *Poetice*, ii. 30, and Buchler, u.s., who quotes the lines given by Puttenham.

17. 10. *Cherillus.* Cf. i. p. 334, l. 13.

19. Jean de Meun and Guillaume de Lorris; authors of the *Roman de la Rose*, of which the first part was written by the latter between 1225 and 1230 and the second by Jean de Meun over forty years later.

25. Sangelais, i.e. Melin de Saint-Gelais (1491-1559), son, or nephew, of the poet Octavien de Saint-Gelais who died in 1502.

Salmonius Macrinus, i.e. Jean Salmon, called 'Maigret' or 'Macrinus' (1490-1557), Latin poet, known to his contemporaries as the French Horace. See Gyraldus (ed. Wotke, u. s., p. 66).

26. Clement Marot (1495 or 1496-1544).

31. *one Gray*: probably William Gray (*d.* 1551), whose birthday verses to Somerset are printed by Dr. Furnivall in *Ballads from MSS.* (Ballad Soc. Public.), vol. i. pp. 310, 414 et seq.

18. 1. *Vargas.* See p. 326, l. 22, note. Is this the Balthasar de Vargas who wrote a verse account of the Duke of Alva's expedition to Flanders (1568)?

15. *Quintus Catulus*, i.e. C. Valerius Catullus.

27. *Antimenides*, brother of Alcaeus. See Aristotle, *Pol.* iii. 14. § 9.

19. 6, &c. Cf. Sidney, i. p. 151, l. 6, &c., and note.

1 & 30. Cf. Sidney, supra, i. p. 186, l. 33.

20. 27-8. See Quintil. vi. 2 (303). The text reads Euphantasio*te*, where *e* may stand for *œ*, a transliteration of Greek οι.

21. 3-12. This evergreen story of the Queen and Alain Chartier is not historical.

14. Cf. p. 17, l. 22.

22. 33. *Hermes Trismegistus*, Ἑρμῆς Τρισμέγιστος, second cent. A. D.

34. *Euax*, king of Arabia, is mentioned in a 'doubtful' passage in Pliny as the author of *De Simplicium Effectibus*. He is credited with the authorship of *De Nominibus et virtutibus Lapidum qui in Artem medicinae recipiuntur*, and is referred to by Marbodus in his *lapidarium* (*De Gemmis*).

35. *Auicenna*, i.e. Husain ibn 'Abd Allah, called Ibn Síná (or Avicenna), the commentator of Aristotle. See Buhle, i. 325.

23. 1. *Alphonsus*. See supra, i. p. 163, l. 13.

4. The reference is to Henry VIII's *Assertio Septem Sacramentorum* (1521), against Luther.

9. *Margaret . . of Nauarre* (1492-1549). Puttenham is probably thinking of her *Heptaméron* (2nd edit. 1559), rather than her verse (*Les Marguerites de la Marguerite des princesses, &c.*).

22-4. See the complete text in the *Scholastica in Virgilium* in Masvicius's Virgil, i.

27. 18. *heywards*, in sense of 'herdsmen.' Cf. p. 39, l. 18.

29. 22. Text, *Celius*.

30. 2. *autharcos*, αὐταρχος.

14. *Anthropopathis*, ἀνθρωποπαθής.

31. 14. *our bookes of Ierotekni*. These are not extant.

33. 18-19. Cf. Jas. VI, supra, i. p. 221.

22. *brokers*. See note on *brocage*, supra, i. p. 127, l. 16.

34. 5, &c. Cf. Scaliger, *Poetice*, i. 7.

22. *Histrien*, an erroneous form of 'histrion.' See *N. E. D.*

35. 28. *Planipedes* (text Plampedes). Cf. Scaliger, *Poetice*, i. 10, with this chapter.

36. 1. *Shoppini*, chopines (see art. in *N.E.D.*). Their use in England appears to have been confined to the stage.

Chap. xvi. Cf. Sidney, supra, i. p. 178, l. 15.

39. 33. *cheuisance*, device, expedient, resource, shift.

40. 10. *I do deny*.... Contrast Scaliger, *Poetice*, i. 4 and 5.

43. 4. *Zenophon*, a common Renaissance form. Cf. p. 196, l. 19.

21–2. *Poets=Poets stile*. For the sense of the passage cf. τὸ γὰρ ἡρωικὸν στασιμώτατον καὶ ὀγκωδέστατον τῶν μέτρων ἐστίν, Aristotle, *Poetics*, xxiv. 5. Cf. i. p. 179, l. 28; ii. p. 338, l. 2.

26–7. The references to Pindar and Callimachus are vague. Pindar wrote hymns, but none are extant. The Odes of Victory may be 'Encomia.' Callimachus's hymns (all but one, the *L. Palladis*) are in hexameters. Some of his complimentary epigrams might be called 'Encomia.'

32–3. *Romance . . . of the Isle of Great Britaine*. This is not extant.

44. 2–4. Cf. Ascham, i. p. 4, and Nash, i. 323.

45. 6. *extraordinary* (subs.): 'a certaine extraordinary'=something extraordinary, an extraordinary bearing.

21. *Irus*, supra, i. p. 68, l. 14.

22. *noddie*, fool.

25. *long of*, on account of, owing to. This O.E. and M.E. usage is found at least six times in Shakespeare. It still lingers in dialect.

46. 15. *the Astronomicall of Aratus and Manilius*. The Φαινόμενα of the former (cf. supra, p. 71, ll. 19-20, note) was translated into Latin by Cicero and by Caesar Germanicus, and was known to the Humanists in the *Metaphrasis Arati* of Avienus, which was first printed at Venice in 1488. The *Astronomica* of Manilius was frequently printed with it.

16. *the Medicinall of Nicander*. Nicander, physician and poet of Colophon, quoted by Macrobius, *Saturn*. v. 21, was the author of the Θηριακά and the 'Αλεξιφάρμακα. These were printed together by Estienne (the Second) in 1566.

17. *Oppianus* (text *Oprianus*). See Scaliger, *Poetice*, v. 9, which is probably the source of the many panegyrics of his piscatory and hunting poems, even as late as Thomas Browne and Pope Blount.

50. 21-2. *Galenistes* and *Paracelsians*. The distinction here implied appears to be much the same as between the later 'Allopaths' and Homœopaths; but the contrast in literary usage (when 'Galenist' was not a mere synonym of 'physician') was between those who held by vegetable cures and those who held by chemical cures. Cf. Nash 'This needie Gallaunt ... rayleth on our Galenists and calls them dull gardners and haymakers in a mans belly' (Grosart, iii. 249): and Dekker has 'What Galenist or Paracelsian in the world, by all his watercasting and minerall extractions . . .' (*Seven D. Sinnes*, ed. Arber, 46).

26. *monethes mindes*, remembrances of the dead a month after death. See quotation in Halliwell's *Dictionary*, 560.

51. 5. Text, *Procostris*.

52. 6. *Genetliaca* (γενεθλιακά). See Scaliger, *Poetice*, iii. 101.

33. *Epithalamies*. Puttenham here also borrows from Scaliger. See *Poetice*, iii. 100.

55. 23. Orig. *Ficenina*.

28-9. *Iohannes [Nicolaus] secundus*. His *Basia* was often reprinted. See the edition by Georg Ellinger, No. 14 of *Lateinische Litteraturdenkmäler* (Berlin, 1899).

56. 29. *Pasquill and Marphorius*. The *Dialogus Marphorii et Pasquilli* (Rome, c. 1552) had many imitations. Puttenham's uncle Sir Thomas Elyot, author of the *Governour*, had written in 1533 a dialogue entitled *Pasquil the Playne* (see Croft's Elyot, i. 98). Opposite the statue of Pasquin in the Piazzo di Pasquino in Rome (so named from its having been found below the booth of the cobbler or tailor Pasquino, who had a satirical vein) stood the statue of Marforio, which, in popular belief, conversed with its neighbour. Lampoons ('pasquinades,' 'pasquills') or papers of questions affixed to the pedestal of the former were answered on sheets placed on the base of the latter.

57. 5, &c. The story of the distich will be found in the Life of Virgil by Donatus.

58. 14. *bouche in court* (text *bonche*). *Bouch* is the allowance of victual &c. given by a king to members of his household or retinue. It is confined to the phrase 'to have bouch (lit. mouth) in court,' or 'bouch of court' ('*avoir bouche à*, or *en, cour*').

60. 11-19. See Scaliger, *Poetice*, i. 53.

Notes

28. *Nenia (Naenia)* or *apophoreta* (τὰ ἀποφόρητα).
See Scaliger, *Poetice*, i. 50 (and Quintilian, viii. 2 (383)).

61. 6. *Saxon English*. Cf. p. 80 and notes.

62. 3. Cf. Sidney's list and his statement, supra, i. p. 196, l. 21.

25. *that nameles* . Puttenham's accuracy in not taking Piers as the author is noteworthy, especially as the error is common with his contemporaries. Cf. Spenser, 'Epilogue' to *Shep. Cal.*; Webbe, supra, i. p. 242; Meres, infra, p. 314; &c.

63. 2. *the first reformers*. Cf. infra, p. 131, l. 23; also p. 219, l. 7.

4. *Lord .. Vaux*. Puttenham refers to his *'facilitie'* on p. 65, l. 19, and again on p. 247 of Mr. Arber's complete text of Bk. III ('a man otherwise of no great learning, but hauing herein a maruelous facillitie'). 'Nicholas' is a slip for 'Thomas.' See Index.

8. Text *Hoywood*. John Heywood (? 1497—? 1580). His *Proverbs* and *Epigrams* are printed by the Spenser Society (1867).

13. *Edward Ferrys* (or Ferrers). This appears to be an error (repeated by Meres and Anthony Wood) for George Ferrers, the dramatist. The description suits the latter. The form occurs again, p. 65, l. 24, and in association with Lord Buckhurst. See also Meres, infra, p. 319, l. 27. For notes on the only known 'Edwards,' see *D.N.B.* Evidence of a literary Edward Ferrers or Ferrys is entirely lacking.

18. *In Queenes Maries time*. Cf. infra, p. 144, l. 5. The form (if not a printer's error) is curious.

19. *Phaer*. Supra, i. p. 137, l. 29, note.

22. *Golding*. Supra, i. p. 243, l. 27, note.

24. *that other Doctour*, i. e. Thomas Twyne. See supra, i. p. 137, l. 29, note.

32. *Edward, Earle of Oxford* (cf. p. 65, l. 26). Puttenham quotes from him in Bk. III (Arber, p. 215). See i. p. 243, l. 7.

33. *Bukhurst*. Supra, i. p. 196, l. 32, &c.

Henry, Lord Paget. Have his 'doings' been 'found out'? I have failed to discover a clue to his literary work.

34. *Edward Dyar*. Supra, i. p. 89, l. 7, note.

35. *Fulke Greuell* (1554-1628).

Gascon, i. e. Gascoigne.

Britton, i.e. Nicholas Breton (? 1545—? 1626).

Turberuille. Supra, i. p. 315, ll. 11–12, note.

64. 6. Puttenham elsewhere (Arber, p. 246) shows an intimate acquaintance with Chaucer's works.

12. *Iohn de Mehunes.* Supra, ii. p. 17, l. 19, note.

20. *riding ryme.* Supra, i. p. 56, l. 25, note.

26. *much deale*=much. See *N. E. D.* (s. v. 'deal') and Stratmann (s. v. 'dael').

65. 8. *Pantomimi.* Cf. Scaliger, *Poetice*, i. 10.

12. *as before.* Supra, p. 63, l. 2.

18. *Vaux.* Supra, p. 63, l. 4. See note, p. 413.

24. *Ferrys.* See note to p. 63, l. 13.

26. Meres (p. 320, l. 10) repeats this statement that Edward, seventeenth Earl of Oxford (1550–1604) was known as a writer of comedy. No plays are extant.

Edwardes. Supra, i. p. 242, l. 33, note.

28. *Challener*, i.e. Sir Thomas Chaloner the elder (1521–65), referred to by Meres (infra, p. 321, l. 10). Most of his work is in Latin. His *De Repub. Anglorum instauranda* and other pieces appeared in one vol. in 1579.

29. *that other Gentleman*, Spenser. See note to i. p. 112, l. 12.

31. *insolent*: to be taken in a good sense, 'swelling.'

67. 21. *rate*, proportion, standard. Cf. *Faerie Queene*, IV. viii. 19, 5.

28. *concents*, i.e. 'musical' concords (Ital. and Span. *concento*).

68. 2. *Regals.* The 'regal' or 'regall' (It. *regale* or *ninfale*, Fr. *régale*) was a small organ or reed-piped musical instrument. See Grove's *Dict. of Music*, iii. p. 93. The *Record* or *Recorder* is a variety of flute, now obsolete. See ib. iii. p. 88.

26. Text, *quadrien*.

28. Cf. Gascoigne, supra, i. p. 55, l. 20; p. 57, l. 4.

31. ib. p. 54, l. 32.

70. Chap. iii. Cf. Scaliger, *Poetice*, ii. 2.

71. 30. *Saxon English.* Cf. p. 61, l. 6.

73. 18. Cf. James VI, supra, i. p. 215, l. 2.

74. 13–15. Gascoigne (i. p. 54), when discussing caesura, does not think of an odd number of syllables. On this topic see Van Dam and Stoffel's section on the 'Dogma of extra syllables' in

Chapters on English Printing, Prosody, and Pronunciation (1550–1700), Heidelberg, 1902.

75. 25. Cf. i. p. 54, l. 14.

29-30. Cf. i. p. 54, l. 15.

33. *Alexandrine.* See the chapter in Ronsard's *Abrégé.*

76. 4-6. Cf. i. p. 54, l. 19.

77. Chap. v. Cf. Gascoigne, i. p. 54, James VI, i. pp. 214-15, and notes.

10. *confuse*=confused. Cf. p. 173, l. 22.

78. 9. Cf. the metaphor in Campion, infra, p. 346, l. 2, and note.

79. 11. *riding ryme.* Cf. p. 64, l. 20, note.

80. 18. *monosillables.* Supra, i. pp. 51, 215, &c.

English Saxons. Cf. p. 61, l. 6; p. 71, l. 30.

19. Cf. i. p. 51, ll. 26-7.

24. *Saxon angles.* Cf. p. 61, l. 6; p. 71, l. 30; p. 80, l. 18.

27-32, 81-1, &c. Cf. Scaliger, *Poetice,* ii. 2.

81. 1 and 23. *rithmos* or *numerositie.* See Scaliger, *Poetice,* v. 1; and cf. Sidney's 'numbrous kinde of writing,' supra, i. p. 159, l. 34, and Puttenham again, p. 83, l. 16, and p. 152, l. 33.

19. ὁμοιοτέλευτον. Aristotle, *Rhet.* III. ix. 9. Cf. Scaliger, *Poetice,* iv. 41; Du Bellay, *Defense,* Chap. viii.

82. 13-19. Cf. Gascoigne, supra, i. 49, § 4.

20. Puttenham shows his fondness for 'new termes' in the ingenious catalogue of figures in his third book. See the summary on pp. 167-72.

83. 4, 7. *Saxon English, Normane English.* See p. 80, l. 24, note.

20. *cadence,* as defined here and by Bullokar (1616), 'the falling of the voice,' though Puttenham practically identifies it with rhyme. Elsewhere it frequently means rhythm. With Puttenham's account, cf. Morley's contemporary definition (1597) of the musical cadence (not *cadenza*): 'A cadence wee call that, when, coming to a close, two notes are bound together, and the following note descendeth' (*Introd. Mus.* 73; quoted in *N. E. D.*).

84. 10-20. Cf. James VI, supra, i. p. 216.

1-3. Cf. Gascoigne, i. p. 49, l. 19; Harvey, i. p. 120, l. 12 et seq., James VI.

86. 1-2. 'Roy' is found in Northern writings, and is, of course, a common word in Middle Scots.

87. 16. *Cantabanqui*, It. *cantambanchi*.

19. Cf. Sidney's 'blind crowder' (i. p. 178).

22-4. See supra, p. 44, ll. 2-4, note.

91. 10. *Seizino*. Cf. Gascoigne, supra, i. p. 55, l. 19, p. 57, l. 4.

93. 34. ἐπιμονή. See Scaliger, *Poetice*, ii. 32. The term is defined in the *Rhetoric* of Alexander (Spengel, *Rhet. Gr.* iii. 17). See also Longinus, xii. For *versus intercalares* see Scaliger, *Poetice*, ii. 30.

95. Chap. xii. Puttenham is in error in limiting the classical examples to the Figure of the Egg (l. 25: cf. i. p. 305, note). Scaliger (ii. 25) mentions the Axe of Simmias Rhodius, and the Wings; and adds 'Ouum quoque eiusdem memorant poema. Quod quia non extabat, nos duo dedimus animi gratia: alterum minusculum quasi Philomelae, alterum grandius, vt sit Cycni.' Puttenham, if he followed Scaliger, as is probable, had fixed his attention on the figured examples. An account of these figures will be found in the old Cambridge edition of the *Poetae Minores Graeci* by Winterton (ed. 1684, pp. 314-29), but more fully in Haeberlin's *Carmina Figurata Graeca* (Hanover, 1887).

For contemporary references and examples, cf. the 'Pasquine Piller,' entitled *My Love is Past*, in Watson's Ἑκατομπαθία (Spenser Soc. edit., pp. 94-5); Willes, supra, i. 47, note; Harvey's *Letter-Book*, supra, i. 126; James VI's Preface to *Phoenix* (ed. Arber, *Counterblaste*, pp. 40-1); Nash's *Haue with you to Saffron-Walden* (ed. Grosart, iii. 98).

96. 10. *translated*: presumably from the Italian (see p. 95, l. 26), though Puttenham, on p. 97, l. 16, professes to be careful of 'Oriental' idiom.

19. (p. 97, l. 12, &c.), *Fuzie*. Fr. *fuseau*, heraldic Fr. *fusée* (med. L. *fusus*, a spindle). *N. E. D.* does not give this form (see under *Fusil*).

99. 17. For an account of this etymology, see Liddell and Scott, s. v. πυραμίς.

100. 9-11. Yet the name is not always used in this sense. Cf. Watson, supra, note to Chap. xii (p. 95).

102. 31. *bonch*, bunch, protuberance. Not to be confounded with *bouche* (printed *bonche* in text, supra, p. 58, l. 14).

105. 23. *Liricks*, Lyrists, u. s.

106. 16. The Italian *Impresa* was either the emblem or device which was accompanied by a motto, or (later) the motto or saw itself. (See, for example, the fifth dialogue, *Delle Imprese*, of Guazzo's *Dialoghi piaceuoli*.) The fashion had already begun in English literature, but it was during the next century that it reached its height. See Daniel's *Worthy Tract of Paulus Ionius, contayning a Discourse of rare inuentions, both Militarie and Amorous, called Imprese* (1585), and especially the *Preface and Epistles* (reprinted by Grosart, *Daniel*, IV). There Daniel discusses 'the difference of *Emblemes* and *Impreses*,' and defines thus, '*Symbolum est genus, Emblema species*.' See also the *Discourse on Impresas* (and correspondence) in the 1711 edition of the Works of Drummond of Hawthornden, where, at p. 228, we have this distinction made : 'Though *Emblems* and *Impresa's* sometimes seem like other, ... the words of the *Emblem* are only placed to declare the figures of the *Emblem*; whereas, in an *Impresa*, the figures express and illustrate the one part of the author's intention, the word the other.'

109. 2. *Porkespick*, porcupine.

3. *Purpentines*, porcupines.

28. *coillen*, cullion, base fellow, rascal.

113. 6, &c. Puttenham borrows the stories of the anagrams of Ptolemy, Arsinoe, François de Valois, and Henri de Valois, direct from Du Bellay's *Defense*, Chap. viii.

114. 1. Cf. the anagram Rosalind, referred to by 'E. K.', supra, i. p. 375.

13, &c. Sir John Davies has twenty-six acrostics on *Elizabetha Regina*.

116. 27. *peason*, peas (M.E. plur. *pesen*).

117. 8. *our vulgar Saxon English*. Supra, p. 87, l. 5, note.

9. *monosillable*, &c. Supra, p. 80, l. 18, note.

17-19. Stanyhurst. Cf. p. 178, ll. 28-31, note.

119. 16. *geazon*, 'rare,' 'scarce,' a common Elizabethan word. Cf. Puttenham, 'The good is geazon, and short is his abode' (ed. Arber, p. 222); Lyly, *Euphues*, p. 21 (ed. Landmann); Spenser, *F. Q.* vi. p. 4, l. 37; and Greene's *Philomela's Second Ode*, ed. Dyce, ii. p. 302. Cotgrave gives it as a translation of Fr. *rare*.

120. 23. *the rule of position.* Cf. Webbe, supra, i. p. 273, l. 15, and note to i. p. 121, l. 4.

121. 15. *our old Saxon English*: 20. *our Normane English.* See p. 117, l. 8, note.

122. 12. *plat*, plan, outline, scheme. Cf. p. 191, l. 6. See 'The Platt' of Tarlton's *Seven Deadly Sins*, transcribed in Halliwell's Introduction to *Tarlton's Jests*, p. xxxv. Cf. *plot*, and *platform* as in 1 Henry VI, ii. 1. 77.

13-15. Cf. p. 117, ll. 17-19.

34, &c. *By preelection in the first Poetes.* Cf. i. p. 103, ll. 6-20, note.

127. 26-7. See Nott's edition of Wyatt and Surrey, ii. p. 9.

128. 1. Ibid. i. p. 5.

3. Ibid. i. p. 26.

130. 16-17. Horace, *Ars Poet.* 71-2. Puttenham repeats his reading of *vis* for *ius* in his quotation and translation on p. 153. Cf. p. 367, l. 8.

21. Nott, u. s., i. p. 45.

131. 23. *the first reformers.* See p. 63, l. 2.

132. 30. *smatch.* Cf. p. 158, l. 20.

134-5. Chap. xvii. This chapter is discussed in Van Dam and Stoffel's section on 'The Dogma of the extra Syllables' in *Chapters on English Printing, Prosody, and Pronunciation* (1550-1700), Heidelberg, 1902.

134. 26-9. Nott, u. s., ii. p. 13.

137. 21. Ib. ii. 17.

139. 23. See p. 142 et seq.

28. *Ginecocratia.* This 'Comedie,' of which Puttenham gives an account (pp. 139-41), is not extant.

140-1. For the common pun on *Weemen*, cf. Gascoigne, *Steele Glas* (Arber, p. 83); Breton, *Praise of Vertuous Ladies and Gentlemen* (1599); Barnfield, *The Combat betweene Conscience and Covetousnesse* (Grosart, p. 183); the verses from Robert Jones's *First Book of Songs and Airs*, 1601 (Bullen, *Lyrics*, p. 136); and Peele's *Edward I* (Bullen, i. p. 167).

143. 10. 'of' may be a misprint for 'or.'

10-26. 'Decorum.' See Introduction, p. xli, and Index.

144. 5. *Queenes.* See supra, p. 63, l. 18, note.

6. *Knight of Yorkshire*, &c. This appears to be an error

Notes

for the first Speaker of Queen *Elizabeth's* reign, Sir Thomas Gargrave, who represented the county of York in 1558. The first Speaker of Queen Mary's reign was Sir Charles Heigham, of Suffolk (see Manners's *Lives of the Speakers*).

34. Sir Nicholas Bacon (1509–79) Lord Keeper.

35. *Lord Treasorer.* See i. p. 1.

145. 23. Quoted in the passage printed on i. p. 377.

148. 9–12. *Enargia* (ἐνάργεια, a vivid description; Dion. Halic., *De Lysia*, vii); *Energia* (ἐνέργεια, efficiency, energy: Arist. *Rhet.* iii. 11. 2 et seq.). See Quintil. viii. 3 (396) and (401), and Scaliger, *Poetice*, iii. 26 ('*Efficacia*').

149. 20–1. See note to p. 1.

26. *Idioma.* Cf. Gascoigne, i. 53, § 11; and see p. 152, l. 19, infra.

28. *the Anglesaxon.* Cf. note to p. 87, l. 5.

29. *Walsh*, an error for 'Welsh.'

150. 15. *charientes* (οἱ χαρίεντες), contrasted with οἱ πολλοί: see Arist. *Pol.* ii. 7. 10. Cf. also Plato, *Rep.* 452 B, &c.

16–26. Another contribution to the problem of 'fitting vocabulary,' discussed by Gascoigne, James VI, Webbe, and others. The reference is more pointed,—perhaps to the *Shepheards Calender*.

152. 19. *Idiome.* See supra, p. 149, l. 26.

33. *Numerous, numerositee.* See supra, p. 81, l. 23, note.

153. 19–21. See p. 130, ll. 16–17, note.

154. 6, &c. Cf. Scaliger, *Poetice*, iv. 1 ('*Character*') 29–32: also Horace, *Ars Poetica*.

155. 26. *decorum.* Cf. p. 143, ll. 10–26 (and note), and p. 161, ll. 8–9.

157. 1. *implicatiue*, a statement implying more than is expressed.

158. 2. *teder*, tether.

20. *smatch.* Cf. p. 132, l. 30.

159. 23–9. Cf. Whetstone, i. p. 59, l. 33 et seq., and other passages for a like expression of the doctrine of 'decorum' in the drama. See Index.

160. 6–14. See the complete list on pp. 167–72.

161. 15. *ne quid nimis.* Cf. i. p. 52, l. 26.

162. 4, &c. ἀναλογία: Arist. *Rhet.* iii. 2 and 10, Dionys. Hal.

Ad Amm. viii. τάσις: Dionys. Hal. *De Compos. Verb.*, ed. Reiske, p. 133. συντομία: Arist. *Rhet.* iii. 6, Demetrius, *De Elocut.*, passim, Dionys. Hal., *Ad Pomp.* iii. σύνθεσις: Demetrius, *De Elocut.*, passim. κυριολογία: Longinus, xxviii. 1; cf. Arist. *Poet.* xxii. 8, *Rhet.* iii. 2; Dionys. Hal. *De Lysia*, iii, and Melanchthon *Rhet.* (1582) p. 387. τρόπος: Longinus, xii. 1, &c.

163. 13. *fitty*, fitting, suitable.

165. 1. *beau semblant.* Cf. *False Semblant*, p. 169, l. 22.

167. 1. *numerositie.* Infra, p. 180, l. 33, note.

    9. *Enargia.* Supra, p. 148, ll. 9-12, note.

    28. The complete text of Chapters xi-xxii, here given in epitome, will be found in Haslewood's edition, pp. 134-218, and Arber's, pp. 173, &c.

168. 25. Supra, p. 84.

    34. *th' Archers terme.* See Ascham's *Toxophilus*, ii (ed. Giles, ii. 145).

169. 12-18. Cf. James VI, supra, i. p. 219; Du Bellay, *Defense*, ii. 9.

    25. *Frumpe*, taunt, flout. It is thus described by Puttenham: 'as he that said to one whose wordes he beleeued not, "no doubt, Sir, of that." This fleering frumpe is one of the Courtly graces of *Hicke the scorner*' (Arber, p. 201). It is not uncommon in contemporary writings. Cp. *Euphues* (ed. Landmann), pp. 68, 86; Greene, *James IV*, ii, 'a frown, a scoff, a frump.'

    33. *Anaphora.* Cf. A. Fraunce, i. p. 305.

    35. *Anadiplosis.* Watson in his Ἑκατομπαθία (Spenser Soc., p. 55) gives a metrical example 'framed vpon a somewhat tedious or too much affected continuation of that figure in Rhetorique, whiche of the Greekes is called παλιλογία or ἀναδίπλωσις, of the Latines, *Reduplicatio*.'

170. 33. In the first copies, at the close of the section 'Of Paradigma,' Puttenham speaks disrespectfully of the Flemings ('a people very vnthankfull and mutable'), but in other copies a passage is substituted on the propriety of the English Queen's helping the Low Countries and rescuing them ftrom the Spanish seruitude.' See Mr. Arber's edition, pp. 252-3.

    36. '*Exargasia* or the Gorgious,' in the text of Chap. xx.

    37. *Philocalia.* This unknown work is again referred to by Puttenham in Book III: 'a worke of ours entituled *Philo*

Notes

Calia, where we entreat of the loues betwene prince *Philo* and Lady *Calia*, in their mutual letters, messages, and speeches' (see Arber, p. 256).

171. 24, &c. The writer referred to is John Southern, who published (before Constable) a volume of sonnets to his mistress Diana (*The Musyque of the Beautie of his Mistresse Diana*, 1584). See the account of this rare volume in *D. N. B.* In *N. E. D.* 'Egar' is quoted from Southern's *Pandora*. The quotations containing the words disliked by Puttenham will be found in Haslewood, p. 211, and Arber, p. 260.

172. 10-40. Cf. James VI, supra; Du Bellay, *Defense*, ii. 9.

173. Chap. xxiii. 'Of Decorum.' See infra, p. 181, l. 20.

22. *confuse.* Cf. p. 77, l. 10.

23. Text, *liminous*.

174. 3. *Saxon English.* Supra, p. 87, l. 5, &c.

5-6. *comelynesse ... comming.* See *N. E. D.* (s.v. 'comely'), to which this passage should be added.

21. *Analogie.* See p. 162, l. 4.

177. 5, 6. *th' Emperor Anthonine ... Orator Philiseus.* The original reads *Philiscus*. The story is found in Philostratus, *Vitae Sophistarum*, ii. 30. 'Anthonine' is the Emperor Caracalla.

32-5. Cf. supra, p. 157, l. 1 et seq.

178. 9. A reference to Stanyhurst's line (*Aen.* i. 7)—

'Lyke wandring pilgrim too famosed Italie trudging.'

Cf. line 26.

28-31.   'tot volvere casus
    Insignem pietate virum, tot adire labores
    Impulerit.'   (*Aen.* i. 13-15.)

The translation would appear to be a recollection of Stanyhurst's (l. 16)—

'Wyth sharp sundrye perils too tugge so famus a captayne,'

though the words 'the same translator' (l. 28) refer naturally to 'another' (l. 13).

179. 6. This may be Heywood's: but I have failed to find it.

181. Chap. xxiv. Cf. Ascham, supra, i. pp. 1-2, &c.; Lyly's *Euphues*, passim; Spenser, *Faerie Queene* ('Letter'), &c.

20. *our booke de Decoro.* This is not extant.

183. 30. *alo Turquesque.* Cf. Spenser, *M. Hubb. Tale,* l. 677. Cf. the whole description with that in Spenser, ibid. ll. 208 et seq.

184. 16. *baines,* baths.

185. 9. *Pasquil wrote.* See supra, ii. p. 56, l. 29, note.

186. 18. *sit on his skirts.* Cf.—

'Crosse me not Liza, neither be so perte,
For if thou dost, I'll sit upon thy skerte.
Tarlton cutt off all his skirts, because none should sit upon them.'

(Quoted in Halliwell's *Tarlton's Jests,* xxxii, from *The Abortiue of an Idle Howre,* 1620.) Cf. the phrase in i. p. 124, l. 34.

21. *podestates* (Ital. *podestà*).

187. 21 et seq. *arte* and *nature.* Cf. James VI, supra, i. p. 210, l. 221.

30. *stale,* urine.

190. 10. *brimly,* clearly, distinctly.

191. 6. *plat or subiect.* See p. 122, l. 12, note.

192. 19. *Plato . . . Aniceris.* The story comes from Aelian, *Varia Historia,* ii. 27.

HARINGTON (pp. 194–222).

194. 1–6. Σοφιστοῦ δὲ μέλλοντος ἀναγινώσκειν ἐγκώμιον Ἡρακλέους, ἔφη Τίς γὰρ αὐτὸν ψέγει;—Plut. *Apophthegmata,* 192 C.

10. *Apologie.* See head-note, i. 149. Harington borrows much from Sidney, and directly refers to his *Apologie* (p. 196, l. 27).

the verie nurse. See Sidney, i. p. 151, l. 17, note.

195. 30. *Alexanders, Cæsars, Scipios.* So Sidney, i. p. 192, l. 21.

196. 15, &c. A reference to Puttenham's *Arte of English Poetrie,* supra. See note to ii. p. 1.

the name of a Maker: a reference to Puttenham's opening words, ii. p. 3. But see Sidney, i. p. 155, l. 26, note, &c.

19. *Zenophon.* Cf. note to p. 43, l. 4, supra.

27. *Sidneys Apologie.* See i. 148 et seq. It must be remembered that Sidney's Essay was as yet unprinted.

197. 1–2. See the note to ii. p. 1.

Notes

6-7. See Sidney, i. p. 192, ll. 15-18, and note; and p. 195, ll. 19-20.

12-13. Martial, ii. 89. 3-4.

198. 23. *sweet statelinesse.* Cf. Puttenham, ii. p. 43, ll. 21-2, note.

30. *of reading Poets,* i. e. the *De Audiendis Poetis.*

199. 2-3. Cf. Sidney, i. p. 164, l. 25, note.

4-22. Cf. Sidney, i. p. 172, ll. 25-30, note. The passage here quoted is from *Gerusalemme Liberata,* c. i. st. 3.

199. 27. *De vanitate et incertitudine scientiarum,* cap. iv ('Of Poetrie,' in J. Sanford's translation, 1569 and 1575). See Sidney, i. p. 182.

32-3. Cf. Sidney, i. p. 183, l. 26 et seq., and notes.

201. 19. See Sidney, i. p. 184, l. 22.

202. 4. Plutarch, ii. 19 E.

10-12. Ovid, *Met.* iv. With Harington's argument cf. Lodge, i. p. 65, and Sidney, *passim.*

203. 5-10. A direct echo of Sidney, i. p. 206, ll. 16-18.

204. 6-14. Cf. Sidney, i. p. 173, l. 22, and especially ibid. p. 192, l. 7 et seq.

205. 25. *Vates.* Cf. Sidney, i. p. 154, l. 5, and note.

27. See Sidney, i. p. 174, l. 23.

35 et seq. Cf. Sidney, i. p. 166, l. 26 et seq.

206. 17. Cf. Sidney's phrase, i. p. 196, l. 25 (though the application is different).

33. Virgil, *Georg.* i. 84.

207. 5. Ibid. p. 94.

16. *Orpheus,* &c. The Horatian list, as in Lodge, Sidney, Webbe, Puttenham.

208. 1. *Rubarb.* Cf. Sidney's *Astrophel and Stella,* xiv. 5.

2. Horace, *Ars Poetica,* 343. This is Greene's favourite motto, on the title-pages of his prose works and as a colophon (e. g. in *Friar Bacon*). See note in Grosart's 'Greene,' i. 88; and cf. *The Returne from Parnassus* (1) I. i. 214.

6-8. From Sidney, i. p. 172, ll. 21-3.

10. Horace, *Sat.* i. 1. 68.

209. 3. See Sidney, i. p. 186, l. 13.

13-14. Ibid. p. 186, ll. 29-30.

16, 21. *nteerly,* wholly.

29. Martial, iv. 49. 10.

31. Martial, xi. 16.

210. 11. *Scaliger writeth of Virgill*: in the *Poetice*, passim.

15. This tragedy of Richard III is not the pre-Shakespearian *True Tragedie of Richard the Third* (which Mr. Fleay dates as early as 1587), but Thomas Legge's Latin tragedy, played at St. John's College, Cambridge, in 1579, and imitated by Henry Lacey in his Trinity College play (1586). The text is printed by the Shakespeare Society (1844). See Meres, infra, p. 319, l. 33, note.

16. *Phalaris*. See i. p. 170, l. 33.

23. *Pedantius*, a Latin comedy, acted in Trinity College, Cambridge, is ascribed by Nash, in *Strange Newes*, to 'M. Wingfield.' It was printed in 1631 (Halliwell). *Bellum Grammaticale, sive Nominum Verborumque Discordia Civilis*, by Spense, was played before Elizabeth in Christ Church, Oxford, on September 24, 1592. See the descriptive note in Mr. Ward's *Hist. of Dram. Lit.* iii. 187. It was printed in 1635.

25. *the play of the Cards*. This play does not appear to have been identified.

30. *In the margin* 'Sir Francis Walsingham.' He died in 1590.

211. 22-4. This is mentioned in Ruscelli's Commentary (edition of 1568).

25-6. C. xlvi, st. 140.

28. *prayeth*: a misprint for *prayseth*.

212. 5-6, 8. See the verses of Augustus Caesar in the *Scholastica in Virgilium*, referred to supra (ii. p. 23, l. 23, note).

10. See p. 210, l. 11.

12-16. *Inferno*, I.

32-3. C. xiv, st. 69.

213. 3. C. xvii, st. 1.

214. 34. *Aen.* viii. 387.

215. 4. *Aen.* viii. 404.

216. 17-18. Cf. Minturno, when speaking of the 'period' of *Scenica Poesia*: 'E chi ben mirerà nell' opere de' più pregiati authori antichi trouerà che la materia delle cose addutte in scena in un dì si termina, ò non trapassa lo spatio di duo giorni. *Si come dell' Epica più grande, e più lunga s' è detto, che non sia più d'uno anno*' (*L'Arte Poet.* p. 71).

18 et seq. Harington here appears to be acquainted with Minturno, *De Poeta*, p. 125 et seq. His definition of *Peripeteia* (περιπέτεια: Aristotle, *Poet.* xi. 1; *Rhet.* i. 11. 24) is based directly on the paragraphs there dealing with 'euentus inopinatus,' and 'Agnitio' (pp. 126-7), a reference which supplements Mr. Butcher's note on περιπέτεια in *Aristotle's Theory of Poetry and Fine Art*, third edition, pp. 323-4. See also Bucer, *Scripta Anglicana*, 1577 (c. liv, ' De honestis ludis'), and Heinsius, *De Tragœdiœ Constitutione*, chaps. vi and vii.

218. 2. Plut. ii. 40 F, &c.

18-19. Cf. Nash's epithet 'comique,' i. p. 313, l. 11.

219. 7. *the first refiners.* Cf. ii. p. 63, l. 2, note.

10. *Bartholomew Clarke* (? 1537-90). See *D. N. B.* (Clerke, B.). His Latin translation of the *Courtier* appeared in 1571.

219. 21. Cf. Heywood, *Proverbes* (Spenser Soc., p. 61):—

'But many a man speaketh of Robyn hood
That neuer shot in his bowe.'

See Sidney, supra, i. p. 184, l. 5.

22. *correct Magnificat.* See note to i. p. 117, l. 18.

220. 24. 'Samuel Flemming of kings colledge in Cambridge' (*Marginal note*). Cf. note to i. p. 244, l. 5.

221. 27. *supererogation*, a word much in vogue at this time. Cf. Harvey's book (1593), infra, p. 245 and note.

222. 26. *triple*, i.e. I. (An apology for Poetry), to p. 211, l. 5; II. (In praise of Ariosto), p. 211, l. 6 to p. 217, l. 23; III. (An answer to Critics), p. 217, l. 24 to end.

32. *that a Potter did to Ariosto.* Marginal note, 'In the life of Ariosto.' I cannot trace this story.

NASH (pp. 223-8).

For an account of the different issues of *Astrophel and Stella* in 1591, see Flügel's edition of *Sir Philip Sidney's Astrophel and Stella* (Halle, 1889), pp. lxxiv-lxxv. See also Grosart's reprint of *Nashe's Works*, i. pp. xxxix-xlv.

223. 1-10. Probably a reference by Nash *more suo* to some recent play: but the identification is not easy. Can it be to Lyly's *Mydas* (printed in 1592)? See note to p. 226, ll. 28-9.

224. 16. *casks*, caskets. Cf. Shakes., 2 Hen. VI, iii. 2. 409.

23. Sidney died in 1586.

31. *absurditie*, a favourite word with Nash. Cf. his *Anatomie of Absurditie*, ante, i. p. 321.

225. 33. Mary Sidney, Countess of Pembroke (? 1555–1621).

eloquent secretary to the Muses. Cf. p. 264, l. 35. The phrase is common. Cf. Daniel (ed. Grosart, iv. 7), who speaks of Pliny and others as the 'Secretaries of nature.'

226. 22. *Almond leape verse*. (Almond=Almain, i.e. German.) See Cotgrave, s.v. *Saut*, 'Trois pas & un saut, The Almonde Leape.' Cf. Jonson, *The Devil is an Ass*, i. 1. 104.

28–9. Is this a double reference to (*a*) the Euphuistic vocabulary generally (see supra, i. p. 202, l. 34, note), and (*b*) to Lyly's *Mydas* (especially Act i. Sc. 1)? With this and the passage referred to in the next note compare Nash's lines on p. 243, ll. 10–12.

31, &c. Is this a covert allusion to the Reformed versifying or so-called classical Prosody? See previous note.

227. 5. *Cornish diamonds*: crystals found in Cornish quartz; stones of inferior quality. Cf. Fuller's *Worthies*, 1662, p. 126.

8–9. *vpseuant muffe, after the Muscouy fashion*. This is a puzzling phrase; but the sense is helped by reference to the copy of the print of Sigismund I of Poland in Mr. Morfill's *Poland* ('Stories of the Nations'), where Sigismund is wearing a fur cap with turned-up points, which looks just like a muff. This was the Russian and Polish cap, called 'Yermolka.' (I am indebted to Mr. Morfill, through Mr. Doble, for this reference.) *Upseuant* is not clear, though it recalls Jonson's *vpsee*. Can it be a misprint for 'upslaunt'? (cf. p. 183, l. 29) or 'up-flaunt' (cf. p. 253, l. 31, note, and *N. E. D.* s.v. 'Flaunt')? Breton refers to the 'muff' in his *Pasquills Fooles-cap* (Grosart, i. 'f.', p. 24).

'Hee that puts fifteene elles into a Puffe,
    And seauenteene yards into a swagg'ring slappe [? flappe]:
And twentie thousand Crownes into a Muffe,
    And halfe his land into a hunting Cappe.'

9. *Capcase*, portmanteau, or, generally, any box or receptacle. Harvey in *Pierces Supererogation* (ed. Brydges, p. 149) speaks of the 'Capcase of *Strange News*' in association with 'an old urinal case.'

Notes

14. *Orig.* 'Sextus Empedocus.'

22-6. Is this a further reference to *Mydas* (see note to p. 223, ll. 1-10), perhaps a hit at Licio's speech, 'Ah, my girle, is not this a golden world?' Nine lines on, Licio says, 'Why, thou foole, what hen should lay that egge?' and Pipenetta replies, 'I warrant a goose.'

31-2. Cf. Nash, supra, i. 310, ll. 28-9.

HARVEY (pp. 229-38).

229. Three editions of *A Quippe for an Upstart Courtier* appeared in 1592, but that which contained the attack on the Harveys as sons of a ropemaker of Saffron Walden is not extant. There are one or two references to a 'Ropemaker' in the known text, but they are of small account. Nash, in his *Strange News*, maintains that the offending passage ran to only 'seven or eight lines.' See the reprint in Collier's Yellow Series, Hindley's reprint in 1871 (Reeves & Turner), and Grosart's in his edition of Greene. A handy bibliographical list of Greene's, Harvey's, and Nash's works will be found in Arber's edition of Greene's *Menaphon*, pp. vi-x.

Mother Hubbard's Tale. See p. 183, l. 30, note, and cf. Harvey's remarks on the *Faerie Queene* in his letter to Spenser, i. p. 115, l. 25.

230. *Elderton.* See i. p. 125, l. 28, note. *Scoggin.* See i. p. 120, l. 24, note.

5. *Saturnist.* Cf. Greene's *Menaphon*: 'The Feasts which the melancholy *Saturnists* founded in *Danuby* were neuer so quatted with silence but on their festiual daies they did frolicke amongst themselues with manie plesaunt parlies' (ed. Arber, p. 46).

21. et seq. Cf. the Spenser-Harvey correspondence in vol. i (pp. 87-122). It is fair to say, as Mr. Schelling has pointed out, that this passage, which has been so often quoted to Harvey's discredit as proof that he was the vainest of pedants, is, in its proper context, an apology, rather than ' a foolish boast.' (See *Poetic and Verse Criticism of the Reign of Elizabeth.* Publications of the University of Pennsylvania, 1891, pp. 25-6.)

231. 3. *greene*, a punning allusion to Robert Greene.

5. *father of misbegotten Infortunatus.* Is this a reference to : (1) Greene's own penitential writings, in which, as Harvey repeatedly reminds his opponent in the *Third Letter,* he laments his ill-fortune ('Remember thine owne Marginal Embleme, *Fortuna favet fatuis,*' and again, 'Yet who euer hearde me complaine of ill-luck, or once say *Fortune my Foe*'); or (2) Harvey's adversary Nash, whose first literary effort, the Preface to Greene's *Menaphon* (supra, i. 307), was written by Greene's request? Though Harvey, further over, speaks of Nash as Greene's 'sworne brother,' yet Nash's retort (p. 243, l. 19) to another gibe (see note to p. 241, l. 21) lends some support to the latter interpretation.

29. *Guicciardines siluer Historie.* Cf. note to i. p. 107.

Ariosto. See Harington, ii. p. 194 et seq.

32. *queasie.* See i. p. 66, l. 24, note.

232. 6. *Pierce Pennie-lesse,* i.e. Nash, author of *Pierce Pennilesse his Supplication to the Diuell* (1592). See l. 13.

9. i.e. *Greene.* See Meres, infra, p. 324, ll. 19-22.

19. *Tarleton.* See ii. p. 122, l. 12, note. His play of the *Seven Deadly Sins* is described by Collier from the original 'plat' in the library of Dulwich College (*History of the Stage*, iii. 394; reprinted in Halliwell's *Tarlton's Jests*, pp. xxxv-xxxviii).

29. *Doctor Pernes religion.* Andrew Perne (? 1519–89), dean of Ely and vice-chancellor of Cambridge, whose time-serving brought him the nicknames of 'old Andrew Turncoat,' 'Father Palinode,' and 'Andro Ambo,' and supplied his contemporaries with the verb 'perne,' i.e. 'to turn coat.' Harvey in this letter complains of him as a man who 'flattered' and 'overthuarted' him and 'alwaies plaied fast and loose'; and he speaks of 'a naturall Perne artificially emproued.' Perne is praised by Bishop Kennet. (See the extracts in Brydges's *Archaica*, II, 'Advertisement.')

233. 9-10. Mantuan, *Eclogae,* i. 1—

'Fauste, precor, gelida quando pecus omne sub umbra
Ruminat, antiquos paulum recitemus amores.'

See *Love's Labour's Lost,* iv. 2. 89, where Holofernes quotes the line. The early editions of Mantuan are 'deepelie learned' in notes: e.g., in the 1546 edition, the 'annotatiunculae' on this phrase run to three quarters of a page.

234. 9. *Aretinish*, a favourite gibe with Harvey.

21. *Gnomes*, γνῶμαι, maxims, sayings: not '*Tomes*,' as Ingleby suggests (*Shakspere Allusion-Books*, i. 36). Cf. p. 170, l. 23.

28. Watson died before the year (1592) was out.

Is the entry of Nash's name here a slip on the part of Harvey, or (more likely) a would-be compliment to add point to the retort? See also p. 249, ll. 20-1 (note).

235. 24, &c. *Experience*. Cf. supra, i. p. 102, l. 13, ii. p. 283, l. 33, and passim in Harvey.

236. 27. *Rodolph Agricola* (1443-85). See the letter quoted in Hallam's *Literary History*, i. 210.

28. *Ludouike Viues*. Supra, i. App. p. 342, l. 11, note, &c.

Peter Ramus. See i. p. 309, l. 11, note, and ii. p. 245, l. 6, note.

237. 7. On Regiomontanus (or Müller) and Jerome Cardan, see Hallam's *Literary History*, i. 190, 458-9.

Bacon, Roger (? 1214-94).

24. After the Alexandrian critic Neoptolemus of Parium.

238. 25. Jewel, John (1522-71), Bishop of Salisbury. See p. 247, l. 32, and p. 281, l. 22, note.

Thomas Harding (1516-72), theologian, in controversy with Jewel. He is not to be confused with the chronicler, p. 62, l. 26, p. 314, l. 24.

John Whitgift (? 1530-1604), Archbishop of Canterbury.

Thomas Cartwright (1535-1603), Puritan controversialist.

31. *Oh-is* 'oyez.'

Nouerint, &c. See i. p. 311, l. 33, note.

NASH (pp. 239-44).

239. 7. *Coppinger and Arthington* were fellow fanatics with William Hacket (*d.* 1591). Their mission of preparation for the Messiah developed into a plot to dethrone Elizabeth and to abolish episcopacy. They were tried after a riot in Cheapside, to which Nash here refers. Edmund Coppinger died in prison in 1592. Bishop Cosin or Cosins (see p. 281, l. 2) wrote *The Conspiracy for Pretended Reformation, viz. Presbyterial Discipline*

by *Hacket, Coppinger, and Arthington: with ... the life ... the arraignment and execution of Hacket* (1592).

10–12. This is explained by a passage in the previous letter (not printed in this volume): 'And that was all the Fleeting (see p. 231, l. 10) that euer I felt: sauing that an other company of speciall good fellowes ... would needs forsooth verye courtly perswade the Earl of Oxforde that some thing in those Letters, and namely the Mirrour of Tuscanismo, was palpably intended against him: whose noble Lordeship I protest I neuer meante to dishonour with the least preiudiciall word of my Tongue or pen, &c.' See supra, i. pp. 107–8, and note.

13. See p. 230, l. 10 et seq.

17. *Howliglasse* (Owl-glass): an uncomplimentary association with 'Tyl Eulenspiegel,' whose adventures had been printed in English, by W. Copland, in ? 1528 and ? 1530. Cf. p. 272, l. 29.

240. 19–20. The literary figure of 'velvet' and 'cloth' was used *ad nauseam* by the Martinists and their contemporaries. Cf. the sub-title of Greene's *Quip for an Upstart Courtier*—'*a Quaint Dispute between Veluet breeches and cloth-breeches.*'

23. *Gilgilis Hobberdehoy*, i. e. Gabriel Harvey, for whom Nash has many names. Cf. *Gabriel Hangtelow, Gregory Habberdine*, &c.

28. *praisd by Gabriel.* See p. 234, l. 27, and Harvey's letters in vol. i.

31. *Maister Butler.* Is this the eccentric physician, William Butler (1535–1618)? See *D. N. B.*

33. *Fleeting.* See p. 231, l. 10.

241. 4–7. A parody on Stanyhurst. See p. i. 316, l. 5, note. The sting is in the tail, for Harvey's attitude to rhyme was a commonplace.

9, &c. The verses, twelve in number, will be found in Harvey's *Third Letter.* The first is—

'Where shud I find, that I seeke, A person cleere as a Christal?'

To these Harvey adds, 'And so foorth: for the verse is not vnknowen: and runneth in one of those vnsatyricall Satyres, which Mr. *Spencer* long since embraced with an overloouing Sonnet: A token of his Affection, not a Testimony of hys Iudgement.' Nash seldom fails to attack Harvey's claim to

Spenser's regard. Spenser's Sonnet is printed in the 'Globe' edition, p. 607, and in Brydges's *Archaica*, ii. 69.

17. Read 'still a foole by flattring.'

21. 'What hee is improued since, excepting his good olde *Flores Poetarum* and Tarletons surmounting Rhetorique, with a little Euphuisme, and Greenesse inough, which were all prettily stale before he put hand to penne.' (Harvey's *Third Letter*.) See infra, p. 399, l. 33.

29. *inkehornisme*. Supra, i. p. 51, l. 24, note. Nash quotes from Harvey's vocabulary.

242. 14. *absonisme*, solecism. Harvey refers to this word on p. 275, l. 22.

17. *Traynment*. See p. 236, l. 32.

22. *indesinence*, want of fitting ending, of proper bounds. Cf. infra, p. 330, l. 21.

26. *balductums*. See i. p. 101, l. 23, note.

243. 8-27. See quotation in note to p. 241, l. 21, and see note to p. 231, ll. 5, 10-12. Cf. p. 226, l. 28—p. 227, l. 3, and notes.

18. Orig. 'madde man.'

30. *Christopher Bird* of Walden. The letter referred to, with the postscript containing the 'Sonnet,' is printed in Brydges's *Archaica*, ii. 1-2.

244. 1. *reuiest*, reviest, retortest. 'Revie,' a gaming word, means to respond to a challenge, ' return.'

5. *bulbegger*, bugbear, bogy. Nash refers to Harvey's taunt in the *Four Letters*—' Her redoutable bull-begging Knight.'

HARVEY (pp. 244-84).

245. *Pierce's Supererogation*. See p. 247, l. 27; p. 251, l. 28; p. 256, l. 15; also p. 221, l. 27, note.

6. Iustinus Martyr. His *Eversio falsorum Aristotelis dogmatum*, edited by G. Postellus, appeared at Paris in 1552.

Philoponus, Ioannes, i.e. John of Alexandria, the Grammarian (7th cent.), author of a life of Aristotle and editor of several Aristotelian books. See the list in Buhle's *Aristotle*, i. pp. 303-5.

Valla, i.e. Georgius (not Laurentius), editor and commentator of Aristotle, who interpreted the *Poetics* in 1515.

Ioannes Ludovicus Viues. Supra, ii. p. 236, l. 28, note. He published a summary of the *Nicomachean Ethics* in 1540.

Ramus (La Ramée). Supra, p. 236, l. 28, note. His *Animadversiones Aristotelicae* appeared in 1548, but Harvey is probably referring to his famous Logic (see i. p. 423), in which he is at variance with the Aristotelian view in the *Organon*. Harvey was an enthusiastic admirer of Ramus: see his *Rhetor* (1577), Sigs. E, E_2, H_3, &c., and his *Ciceronianus* (1577), 29, &c. He was probably influenced by the Ramist enthusiasm of William Temple. (See note to i. p. 309, l. 11.)

9. Perionius, Joachimus. See supra, i. p. 18, l. 29, note.

Gallandius, Petrus, author of *Contra novam Academiam P. Rami Oratio* (Paris, 1551).

Carpentarius, Jacobus (Claromontanus Bellovacus). His *Descriptio universae artis differendi ex Aristotelis logico organo collecta & in libros tres distincta* appeared at Paris in 1562, 1564. See note on Ossatus, infra.

10. *Sceggius*, i.e. Jacobus Schegkius (Deginus) the elder (1511–87), Aristotelian commentator.

Lieblerus, Georgius, author of an *Epitome philosophiae naturalis ex Aristotelis libris excerpta* (1561, &c.).

12. Talaeus, Audomarus, commentator. He associated himself with Ramus in several works, e.g. in the latter's *Dialecticae libri duo* (supra, i. p. 280, l. 33, note). Ascham mentions them together (*Scholemaster* ed. Mayor, pp. 101, 102).

Ossatus, i.e. Cardinal Arnaud d'Ossat. Harvey refers to his *Expositio in Disputationem Iacobi Carpentarii de Methodo*, Francfurt, 1583.

Freigius, Ioannes Thomas, author of *Rami praelectiones in Ciceronis orationes*, 1575. He edited Ramus's *Ciceronianus* in 1577.

Minos, i.e. Claude Mignault, editor of Cicero.

Rodingus, apparently an error for Rhodiginus (Lodovico Celio Rodigino, otherwise Ludovicus Coelius Richerius), commentator on Cicero. A certain Gulielmus Rodingus published two orations at Heidelberg in 1576, 1577; but it is unlikely that he is intended.

246. 1. Scribonius, Gulielmus Adolphus, author of the *Triumphus Logicae Rameae*, 2nd edit., Lond. 1583.

Notes

19. Agrippa. Supra, p. 199, l. 27, note.

22. Copernicus, Nicolas (1473–1543), astronomer.

23. Cardan. Supra, p. 429. See p. 435.

Paracelsus. See note, supra, i. p. 50, l. 21.

24. Erastus. See p. 248, ll. 9, 10, note.

Sigonius (Carlo Sigonio). See i. p. 25, l. 13, note.

Cuiacius, Jacobus, jurist. See p. 291, l. 31.

a bable. Cf. note, supra, i. p. 375.

247. 32. *Harding and Iewell*, u. s., p. 238, l. 25.

248. 5-13. Cardinal Jacopo Sadoleto (1477–1547). See Ascham's judgment on Sadolet, Omphalius, and Osorius in the *Scholemaster*, ed. Mayor, p. 110.

Longolius (cf. i. p. 13, l. 17, note). He is the author of an *Oratio ... ad Luterianos iam damnatos* (1524, 1529).

Omphalius, Jacobus (*d.* 1570). He was a Professor at Cologne, and was best known by his commentaries on *Cicero*.

Osorius, i. e. Jeronimo Osorio da Fonseca, Bishop of Silves. See note on Haddon, infra. He is frequently referred to by Harvey in his *Ciceronianus* and *Rhetor*. See Ascham's *Scholemaster* (ed. Mayor, pp. 129, 238-9, 271).

Sturmius. Cf. i. p. 9, l. 32, note.

Haddon (cf. i. p. 21, l. 31). Harvey refers to the book *Gualteri Haddoni pro Reformatione Anglicana epistola apologetica ad Hier. Osorium* (1562), a reply to Osorius's Latin book which was Englished by R. Shacklock in 1565. See note on Osorius, supra.

Balduin, François, who wrote more than one *Responsio* to Calvin and a *Responsio ad Calvinum et Bezam*, Cologne, 1564.

Erastus (see p. 246, l. 19, note), i. e. Thomas Lieber (1523–83), a physician of Heidelberg, who adopted the name *Erastus* at Basle in 1540. He was opposed to the study of astrology and to the doctrines of the Paracelsians (supra, p. 50, l. 21), and denied the penal right of the Church. Hence the term 'Erastian.'

Trauers, Walter (? 1548–1635), puritan divine, and friend of Beza.

Sutcliff, Matthew (?1550–1629), dean of Exeter and anti-Catholic controversialist.

Bellarmine, the famous Jesuit controversialist.

Whittaker, William (1548–95), Master of St. John's College, Cambridge, and Regius Professor of Divinity.

Bancroft, Richard (1544–1610), Archbishop of Canterbury.

14. *the Precisians*, the Puritans. The term was much in vogue. Cf. Marlowe, *Dr. Faustus*, sc. ii. 26, and the passage in the *Jew of Malta*, i. 2. See also Sir Thomas Overbury's 'character' *A Precisian*.

20. *meacocke*, an effeminate: a favourite term at this time, synonymous with 'milksop,' and often associated with it. Cf. *Euphues* (ed. Landmann, 81), 'I shall be accompted a Mecocke, a Milkesoppe': and Lodge's *Alarum* (Shakes. Soc. 51), 'The wisest by lewde love are made foolish, the mightiest by lust are become effeminate, the stoutest monarchs to miserable mecockes.'

Papp-hatchet, John Lyly, to whom the anonymous *Pappe with an hatchet* (1589), is generally given. See infra, p. 268, and the travestied title-page, p. 270.

28-9. See headnote, supra, p. 238, and p. 229.

249. 15. *Sir Iohn Cheeke.* See i. p. 9, l. 30 note, &c.

20-1. Did Harvey not know the identity of Pierce and Nash, or did he affect ignorance? See a like case, supra, p. 234, l. 28, note.

250. 5. *nippitaty* (cf. p. 252, l. 7), strong liquor. Halliwell gives the form *nippitato*, 'a cant term,' 'chiefly applied to ale.'

11. *Tuscanisme.* See supra, i. p. 107, l. 19, and note. *In grain*, thorough, downright, ineradicable.

22-3. See headnotes, pp. 239, 245.

251. 20. *Ciceronian*, not necessarily in the stricter sense derived from the Ciceronian controversy of the sixteenth century, but in the general sense of 'scholarly person' as opposed to a writer or reader of the intellectual level of Scogan, the court fool.

22. *Conny-catcher*, cheat, swindler (lit. one who catches conies, dupes); a side thrust at Greene's pamphlets on *Conny-catching* (three parts, 1591, 1591, 1592), and the *Disputation betweene a Hee Conny Catcher and Shee Conny catcher* (1592), which popularized the term.

22-3. In Gabriel's 'Philosophers' and 'Mathematician' there is perhaps a fraternal reference to the astrologers, John

Notes

Harvey (? 1563–92), and Richard Harvey (*d.* ? 1623), who had been dragged into the quarrel (see p. 229), and had suffered—the latter especially—at the hands of Nash. See Index.

252. 1–5. Is Harvey alluding—in his 'Apes and Foxes'—to Spenser's *Mother Hubberds Tale*, included in the volume of *Complaints* (1591)?

7. See p. 250, l. 5.

253. 5, &c. Cf. p. 261, l. 18 et seq.

7. *Martins libelling*, i.e. the lampooning of the *Martin Marprelate* controversy.

Holinsheads engrosing. Raphael Holinshead (*d.* ? 1580), author of the *Chronicles* of England, &c.

12. *a hotchpott for a gallymafry*. Cf. i. p. 130, l. 12; also *Mingle-mangle* in Puttenham, supra, ii. p. 171, l. 14. All were much in vogue. Cf. Lyly's *Mydas* (Prologue), 'what heretofore hath beene serued in seuerall dishes for a feast, is now minced in a charger for a gallimaufrey. If we present a mingle-mangle, our fault is to be excused, because the whole world is become an hodge-podge.' See also *The Returne from Parnassus*, pt. II. iv. ii. l. 1586 et seq.

31. *flaunt-aflaunt*, swagger. So Gascoigne, *Steele Glas*, Epilogue, l. 33 (Arber, p. 83), and Breton, *Flovrish upon Fancie*, 18 (ed. Grosart).

255. 5. *egges in mooneshine*. Cf. Shakespeare, *King Lear*, ii. 2. 32. For particulars of this once popular dish, see the quotation from May's *Accomplished Cook*, in Nares's *Glossary*, and *Notes and Queries*, 4th Ser., xii, July 19, 1873.

7. *awke*, untoward, clumsy: *hibbergibber*, gibberish.

256. 23. *was running on my halfpeny*, a common Elizabethan phrase. See *N. E. D.*, s.v. 'Halfpenny.'

257. 6. *Elderton*, supra, i. p. 125, l. 28, note.

21. *Agrippa*. Supra, p. 433.

Cardan. Probably Girolamo Cardano (1501–76), supra, p. 433; but to which work does Harvey refer?

23. *Ancontius*, an error for Acontius (Jacopo Aconzio)? 1500–? 66, whose *Ars Muniendorum Oppidorum* (in Lat. and Ital.) is said to have appeared at Geneva in 1585 (see Mazzuchelli and Watt).

25. *Antony Riccobonus*, i. e. Antonio Riccoboni, author of

De Historia Commentarius, Venice, 1568, and of a *Poëtica*, explaining Aristotle's Poetics (Vienna, 1585, Padua, 1591).

28. *Calepine*, dictionary, so called from Friar Ambrosio Calepino (of Calepio), 1435–1511, whose Latin Dictionary, which first appeared in 1502, was of great account during the sixteenth century, and was the basis of the not less famous Lexicon of Forcellini. Calepino's plan to give the meaning of the Latin words in more than one European tongue was rapidly developed in succeeding editions, till in the Basle edition of 1581 (to which Harvey probably refers) the dictionary had become a polyglot of no less than eleven languages. See Hallam, *Lit. Hist.* i. 258.

32–3. The full title of *Petrus Gregorius*'s work is *Syntagma Iuris universi atque Legum pene omnium gentium et rerum publicarum praecipuarum in tres partes digestum*.

258. 33. *filthy Rymes*. Cf. p. 261, ll. 16–17.

259. 8. *horrel-lorrel*, a reduplication of *lorrel*, a worthless fellow.

14, &c. Cf. Harvey, supra, i. p. 106.

30. *an Inglishe Petrarck*, i.e. Spenser. Cf. Clerke, in his *Polimanteia* (1595), 'Let other countries, sweet Cambridge, envy, yet admire ... thy Petrarch, sweet Spenser.'

260. 16. Manardus, Joannes (1462–1536), author of several medical works.

17. Pomponatius (Pietro Pomponazzi, nicknamed Peretto), 1462–? 1526, who stirred up controversy by his *De Immortalitate Animae*.

261. 18, &c. Cf. p. 253, l. 5, et seq. For Elderton, see i. p. 125, l. 28, note; Turberuile, i. p. 244, ll. 11–12, note; Drant, i. p. 90, l. 13, note; Tarlton, ii. p. 232, l. 19, note. Tarlton was notorious for his extempore rhyming as well as his jigs. Harvey elsewhere speaks of Greene's 'piperly extemporizing and Tarletonizing.'

22–3. A happy sentiment, but fuller in meaning to us than it can have been to Harvey and his contemporaries.

25–31. See note to i. p. 58, l. 5.

262. 2. *in one volume*, i.e. the first edition of 1589.

15. William Borough (1536–99). See *D. N. B.*

17. Robert Norman, mathematical instrument maker. See *D. N. B.*

Notes

33. Sir Roger Williams (? 1540–95). His *Brief Discourse of War* appeared in 1590.

34. Thomas Digges (*d.* 1595), mathematician, muster-master-general of the English troops in the Netherlands in 1586.

263. 8. Iohn Asteley (*d.* 1595), master of the Queen's jewel-house, published his *Art of Riding* in 1584. He is one of the dinner-party described in the Preface to Ascham's *Scholemaster*.

9. Pietro Bizzaro. See Tiraboschi, vii. 1468.

12. Thomas Blundevil, author of *The fower chiefyst offices belonging to Horsemanshippe* (1565-6) and other works.

16. *Musidorus and Pyrocles*, in Sidney's *Arcadia*. See p. 264.

20–1. Probably a reference to Painter's popular *Palace of Pleasure* (1st vol. 1566), and to the translation of *The Courtier* by Hoby (1561).

22. The *Arcadia* was first published in 1590.

34. Philip de Comines was not yet translated by Danett (1596). *Guicciardine*. See note, supra, i. p. 107, note.

264. 4. Read 'priuitie.'

35. *Secretary of Eloquence.* Cf. p. 225, l. 33.

265. 3. *Suada* (Πειθώ), the goddess of Persuasion.

7. James VI and I. Cf. i. p. 208 et seq. The *Uranie*, with Du Bartas's text, was printed in the *Essayes of a Prentise* (1584). James's volume of *Poeticall Exercises at vacant houres* (1591) contained a translation of the *Furies* of Du Bartas, 'his owne' *Lepanto*, and Du Bartas's version of the latter, *La Lepanthe*.

266. 18. *weedes.* Gascoigne's *Posies* consists of four parts, *Flowers, Herbs, Weeds,* and the *Notes of Instruction* (i. p. 46).

21. *nippitatie.* Supra, p. 250, l. 5, note.

23. *the old pickle herring.* Supra, p. 232, l. 9, note.

30. A Euphuistic punning translation of *O tempora O mores*.

32. *Copesmate,* fellow (in the contemptuous sense).

267. 18–19. Can it be that *The Pilgrimage to Parnassus* makes fun of these lines in its fourth act (l. 405)?

268. 16, &c. *Pap-hatchet.* Supra, p. 248, l. 20.

269. 5. *courtly holly-water.* Cf. *King Lear*, iii. 2. 10.

20. *alla Sauoica.* See p. 268, l. 18 ; p. 271, l. 32.

21. *Albertus Magnus.* Cf. p. 273, l. 14.

24, &c. *stones . . . Foules . . . beastes and fishes.* See note to i. p. 202, l. 33; and to p. 322, l. 28.

30. *olde Accursius*; probably the Glossator of Justinian, rather than M. Ang. Accorso (Accursius), born ? 1490, philologer and editor of *Cassiodorus*. The former wrote in a rough style and had small reputation for knowledge of classical literature. He is credited with the saying: *Graecum est; non legitur.*

31. *Bartholus de Saxoferrato* (1313–56), jurist, whose quaint plainspoken style may have attracted Harvey in his legal studies. One of his works is entitled *Processus Satanae contra Virginem coram iudice Iesu.* See infra, p. 460.

270. 1–2. Cf. Gosson and Lodge (i. p. 63, l. 5).

11. *Country Cuffe*, countercuff.

14. *Iohn Anoke*, &c. See note, supra, i. p. 185, ll. 30–1.

271. 21. *bore . . . cushion.* See note to i. p. 140, l. 25.

272. 4. *hatchet.* See p. 268, l. 16 et seq.

6. Orontius Finaeus (Oronce Finée), French mathematician, author of *Quadrans astrolabicus* (revised, 1534) and other works.

10. *mandillion*, a jacket or jerkin. 'The mandilion or mandevile was a kind of loose garment without sleeves, or, if with sleeves, having them hanging at the back' (Halliwell).

14. *Mammaday.* Cf. *The Courtier and the Countryman*, 1618 (Roxb. Libr.): 'Thy meat tasts all of mammaday pudding, which breaking at both ends, the stuffing runnes about the Pot.'

19. *Dranting.* See supra, i. p. 90, l. 13, note.

21. *Iohn Securis*, i.e. John Lyly ('Pap-hatchet').

26. *Hundred merrie Tales.* See *A C. Mery Talys* in Hazlitt's *Shakespeare Jest-Books*.

29. *Howleglasse.* See supra, ii. p. 239, l. 17, note.

30–2. Harvey is indebted to the concluding paragraphs of Poggio's *Facetiae*, where the latter speaks of his story-telling friends 'in secretiori aula Martini papae.' He says, 'Visum est mihi eum quoque nostris confabulationibus locum adiicere, in quo plures earum, tanquam in scaena, recitatae sunt. Is est Bugiale nostrum, hoc est mendaciorum veluti officina quaedam, olim a secretariis institutum, iocandi gratia. . . . Erat in eo princeps fabulator Raçellus Bononiensis, cuius nonnulla in confabulationes coniecimus. Antonius item Luscus, qui saepius inseritur, vir admodum facetus. Cinciusque Romanus & ipse iocis deditus. Nos quoque plura e nostris addidimus non insulsa. Hodie, cum illi diem suum obierint, desiit Bugiale, tum temporum tum hominum culpa, omnisque iocandi confabulandique consuetudo sublata' (edit. 1513).

273. 1. *Doctour Clare.*?

Doctour Bourne. Perhaps William Bourne, the almanac-maker, who died in 1583. See infra, p. 279, l. 25, and *D.N.B.*

M. Wakefield? Referred to again in l. 15.

4-7. A retort to Nash's list, supra, pp. 241-2.

5. *bumme Carde*, lit. a marked card for cheating at play. The reference is to *Pappe with a Hatchet*, Cij.: 'Hee'le cog the die of deceipt, & cutte at the bumme-carde of his conscience.'

14. Albertus, supra, p. 269, l. 21.

Poggius, supra, p. 272, ll. 30-2, note.

Bebelius (text ' Bebelices '). A reference to the *Facetiarum Libri Tres* of Heinrich Bebel, a popular contribution to Poggian literature, often reprinted with the *Facetiae* of Nic. Frischlin.

15. *Wakefield's.* See l. 1.

Parson Darcye, i.e. Brian Darcy, referred to in *Scot's Discouerie of Witchcraft*, 1584 (rep. p. 455).

17. *double V's*, i.e. 'W's': but whose initial is this?

22. *Cheeke, Smith.* See Ascham, supra, i. p. 9, l. 30, &c.

24-7. Cf. p. 283, l. 13 et seq. Probably a reference to such passages as supra, ii. p. 223, l. 12 et seq.

274. 20. *gargarisme*, lit. gargle.

29. Cf. p. 272, l. 3.

275. 2. *Toy*, frequently used in the special sense of a jest or anecdote, or bit of doggerel. Cf. *Tarltons Toyes*, 'a new booke in English verse,' licensed 10 Dec. 1576.

8. *lillypot*, in this pun, is an old size of paper with the 'lily-pot' as a watermark.

21 et seq. See note to p. 273, ll. 4-7.

22. *Absonisme.* See p. 242, l. 14.

32. *a Calimunco*, lit. a kind of fine stuff. See 'Calamanco,' *N.E.D.*, and Lyly's *Mydas*, passim.

276. 14. *Tite-tute-tate.* From the line of Ennius (*Annales*,

p. 113, Vahl.), 'O Tite, tute, Tati, tibi tanta, tyranne, tulisti,' given by Priscian, and copied and recopied in Renaissance Arts of Poetry. For example, it occurs twice in Buchler's recension of the *Institutio Poetica* of Jac. Pontanus, where it is described as something to be avoided ('cacophonus,' 'ridiculus,' 'insuavis,' &c.).

10. See the list of books in Rabelais, II. vii.

18. *filed Suada*, supra, p. 265, l. 3, note.

21. *Gueuara*, Antonio de (*d.* 1545), author of the *Marco Aurelio* (1st ed. 1529), which was translated by Lord Berners in his *Golden Booke of Marcus Aurelius* (1532), and, in its revised form (*Libro del Emperador Marco Aurelio con el Relox de Principes*), by Sir Thomas North in his *Diall of Princes* (1557). His *Epistolas Familiares* was rendered in the *Familiar Epistles* of Edward Hellowes in 1574, and was supplemented in 1575 by Geoffrey Fenton's version of the *Golden Epistles*. Sir Francis Bryan gave the *Libro llamado Menosprecio del Corte* in his *Dispraise of the Life of a Courtier* (1548), reprinted as *A Looking Glasse for the Courte* (1575).

22. *Amiot*, Jacques Amyot (1513–93), translated the *Theagenes and Chariclea* of Heliodorus (1547, revised 1559), seven books of Diodorus Siculus (1554), Longus (1559), and Plutarch's *Lives* (1559) and *Morals* (1572). His translation of Plutarch's *Lives* was Englished by Sir Thomas North in 1579.

277. 3. *slaumpaump*. Cf. Stanyhurst's *Aeneid* (ed. Arber, p. 116):—

'Quod she, "shal hee scape thus? shal a stranger geue me the slampam?
With such departure my regal segnorye frumping?"'

33. *Leripup*, lit. the tail of an academic hood = 'rôle,' 'lesson.' See *N. E. D.*, s. v. *Liripipe*.

278. 16. *quaime*, qualm.

279. 3. *Hermes Trismegist*, supra, p. 22, l. 33.

4. *Danters Presse*. See p. 403, l. 28. John Danter printed in London between 1591 and 1597, and his widow in 1599 and 1600. He is introduced in the second part of the *Returne from Parnassus* (Act I. Sc. iii). Cf. infra, p. 466.

8. Thomas Delone or Deloney (? 1543–? 1607), silkweaver,

a notorious ballad-maker and pamphleteer. Nash calls him 'the balleting silk-weaver.'

Philip Stubs or Stubbes, author of the *Anatomie of Abuses*. See supra, i. p. 63, and note to i. p. 321.

Robert Armin, actor and dramatist. (See *D.N.B.*) He had the honour of being known as the literary son and successor to Scogan.

22. Humfrey Cole (fl. 1575). See *D.N.B.*

23. Iohn Shute (fl. 1560), author of *The First and Chief Groundes of Architecture* (1563). See *D.N.B.*

24. Robert Norman. Supra, p. 262, l. 17, note.

William Bourne. See note to p. 273, l. 1.

25. Iohn Hester (*d.* 1593), distiller. See *D.N.B.*

280. 2. Digges. Supra, p. 262, l. 34, note.

Hariot, Thomas (1560-1621). See *D.N.B.*

Dee; the famous John Dee (1527-1608), astrologer.

9-12. Cf. Meres's scheme of comparison, infra, p. 314 et seq.

15. *Floide*, i.e. Ludovic or Lewis Lloyd, author of *The Pilgrimage of Princes*, 1573, &c. (See *Brit. Mus. Catalogue.*) The forms 'Lloyd' and 'Floyd' are interchangeable. Cf. Iohn F. or L., composer (*d.* 1523), and Sir Charles F. or L., royalist (*d.* 1661).

Ritch, i.e. Barnabe Rich (? 1540-? 1620), miscellaneous writer.

17. Kiffin, Maurice (*d.* 1599), author of *The Blessednes of Brytaine, or a Celebration of the Queenes Holyday*, 1587. He translated the *Andria* in 1588.

23. Cartwright, supra, p. 238, l. 25.

25. *Reinolds*. I have failed to identify him. The reference would appear to be too early for Henry Reynolds the translator of Tasso's *Aminta* and author of an essay on Poetry (1632), or for John Reynolds who published his *Epigrammata* in 1611. Can he be Iohn Rainolds (1549-1607) who was in high repute for his Oxford lectures on Aristotle, and translated the Prophets for the 'Authorized Version'?

Stubbes, supra, p. 279, l. 8, note.

Mulcaster, Richard (? 1530-1611), supra, i. p. 336, l. 32, note.

26. Norton, Thomas (1532-84), supra, i. p. 398. Besides

collaborating in *Gorboduc*, he wrote a number of prose works, including a translation of Calvin's *Institutes*.

Lambert. Is this the antiquary William Lambarde (1531–1601), the historian of Kent?

Lord Henry Howarde (1540–1614), first Earl of Northampton, second son of Henry Howard, Earl of Surrey.

29-30. *the Resolution*. Is this the poem of which the first part, entitled *The Mirrour of Mans Miserie*, was printed by Edward Allde in 1584?

Mary Magdalens funerall teares, by Robert Southwell ('S. W.'). The first known edition is dated 1594.

31. *Scottes discouery of Witchcraft* (1584). See Reginald or Reynold Scott (?1538–99), *D. N. B.*

Jean Bodine (b. 1530) wrote *De la Démonomanie des Sorciers* (Paris, 1580), which passed into many editions, and was translated into Latin (by Lotarius Philoponus, Basle, 1581), German, and Italian. Sidney deals with him not too kindly: 'You may read him and gather out of many words some matter' (*Correspondence*, ed. Pears, p. 199).

281. 2. This *Apology*, written by Richard Cosin, or Cosins, Bishop of Durham, was printed in 1591. See note to ii. p. 239, l. 7.

11. *Doctour Hutton*. Brydges, in *Archaica*, ii. 233, identifies him with Leonard Hutton the antiquary (see *D. N. B.*), but the reference is rather to Matthew Hutton (1529-1606), a Cambridge man, Master of Pembroke Hall, raised to the Archbishopric of York in 1596.

Doctour Young, i.e. John Young (?1534–1605), also Master of Pembroke Hall, Cambridge, and afterwards Bishop of Rochester. He is the 'Roffy' of Spenser's *Shepheardes Calender*.

12. *Doctour Chaderton*, i.e. William Chaderton (?1540–1608) of Pembroke College, Cambridge, Bishop of Chester, 1579-95, and afterwards of Lincoln.

M. Curtes, i.e. Richard Curteys (?1532–82) of St. John's College, Cambridge, and Bishop of Chichester (1570).

13. *M. Wickam*, i.e. William Wickham (1539–95), Bishop of Lincoln, and afterwards (1595) Bishop of Winchester.

M. Drant. Supra, i. p. 90, l. 13, note.

Notes 443

M. Deering, i.e. Edward Dering (? 1540-76) of Christ's College, Cambridge, a puritan divine who was appointed Prebendary of Salisbury, 1571.

14. *Doctor Still*, i.e. John Still (? 1543-1608) of Christ's College, Cambridge, appointed Bishop of Bath and Wells in 1593. *Gammer Gurton's Needle* has been attributed to him; but the claim of William Stevenson, also of Christ's, is better (see H. Bradley, in *Repres. Eng. Comedies*, 1903, i. 199, and Chambers, *Med. Stage*, ii. 457).

Doctor Vnderhill, i.e. John Underhill (? 1545-92), Bishop of Oxford, 1589-92.

15. *Doctor Matthew*, i.e. Tobie Matthew (1546-1628), Bishop of Durham in 1595, and Archbishop of York in 1606.

M. Lawherne (unidentified).

M. Dooue, i.e. John Dove (1561-1618), Rector of St. Mary Aldermary, London, author of *A Confutation of Atheism* (1605).

16. *M. Andrewes*, i.e. Lancelot Andrewes (1555-1626), Rector of St. Giles, Cripplegate, afterwards Bishop of Winchester, author of several learned works on patristic theology, and one of the makers of the 'Authorized Version.'

M. Chaderton, i.e. Laurence Chaderton (? 1536-1640), Master of Emmanuel College, Cambridge (1584), and a well-known preacher at Cambridge, of Protestant views. He did not obtain his doctorate till 1613. Cf. note on Dr. Chaderton (l. 12).

M. Smith: probably Henry Smith, 'silver-tongued Smith' (? 1550-91), the Puritan divine, who had great reputation as a preacher at St. Clement Danes, London.

22. *Doctour Cooper*, i.e. Thomas Cooper (? 1517-94), Bishop of Lincoln (1570), and Bishop of Winchester (1584). He compiled the books popularly known as Cooper's *Chronicle* and Cooper's *Latin Dictionary*. He was the object of the Martinist tract *Ha' ye any work for a Cooper?*, which he had provoked by an attack on 'Martin Marprelate.'

Doctour Humfry, i.e. Laurence Humphrey (? 1527-90), President of Magdalen College, Oxford, and Dean of Winchester (1580-90). He wrote a Latin life of Jewel (1573), and translated Origen and other Fathers of the Church.

23. *Doctor Fletcher*, i.e. Richard Fletcher (*d.* 1596), Bishop of Bristol (1589), of Worcester (1593), and of London (1594).

He was the father of John Fletcher, the dramatist, brother of Giles Fletcher, the elder, and uncle of Phineas Fletcher and Giles Fletcher, the younger.

282. 29. *Suada*, supra, p. 276, l. 18, note.

283. 7. *Endenisoned*. Cf. infra, p. 359, l. 29, note.

13. *Dia-margariton or Dia-ambre*, &c., cf. p. 273, l. 24 et seq. For the medical prefix *Dia-*, see *N. E. D.*

15. *Antonius*: so entitled in the edition of 1592, but generally the *Tragedie of Antonie*: by Mary, Countess of Pembroke (1590). See the reference to the play in Daniel's dedication to *Cleopatra*. The *Discourse of Life and Death* was translated by her from *Plessis de Mornay* (1593).

33. *Experience*, u.s., i. p. 102, l. 13, note, ii. p. 235, l. 24, note.

CAREW (pp. 285–94).

285. 15. *as Stephanus*. Henri Estienne (1528–98) had printed his *Projet du livre intitulé: de la Précellence du langage françois* in 1579 (Paris). This volume had been preceded in ? 1565 (Geneva) by the *Traité de la conformité du langage françois avec le grec*, in 1566 by the famous *Apologie pour Hérodote*, and in 1578 (Geneva) by *Deux Dialogues du langage françois italianisé*. The *Précellence* has been edited by Feugère, 1850, 1853, and by Huguet, 1896.

286. 14. *vogue*: 'use' (Camden's print).

287. 4. 'English-Saxon,' in Camden, as in Puttenham, supra, p. 61, l. 6, &c. See note to p. 292, l. 23.

27. 'masters' (Camden).

288. 18. This is Ralph's love-letter to Dame Christian Custance, misread by Matthew Merrygreek, in Nicholas Udall's *Roister Doister*. Thomas Wilson quotes it in his *Rule of Reason* (1551, p. 67), not in his *Arte of Rhetorique*, as 'an example of doubtfull writyng, whiche, by reason of poinctyng, maie haue double sense and contrary meanyng.'

290. 16. *Littletons hotchpot of our tongue*: a reference to Sir Thomas Littleton's (1402–81) famous treatise on *Tenures*, written in 'law-French.'

291. 31. Cuiacius *ad Tit. de verb. signif.* See p. 246, l. 24.

292. 23. Camden inserts 'Maister Puttenham' between 'Sidney'

Notes 445

and 'Stanihurst' in Carew's text, a fact which does not appear to have been noted in the discussions on Puttenham's authorship. See note to p. 1.

293. 19. *Agnomination*, generally, in rhetoric, a paronomasia or word-play, but here probably 'alliteration.' Camden (who prints Carew's tract) uses it in this sense in his *Remaines*, p. 27. See Hermogenes, *De Invent.* iv; Melanchthon, *Rhet.* ii; and Scaliger, *Poetice*, iii. 55.

J. J. Pontanus was perhaps the first to establish the word *alliteratio* for the older forms *agnominatio* or *adnominatio*. See Andreas Schottus: 'Budaeo adnominationem nobis resultationem nominare Latine liceat, ut in poetis antiquis, praesertim Marone, Iovianus Pontanus alliterationem solitus est appellare' (*Cicero a Calumniis vindicatus*, cap. x).

21. Sir Thomas Smith (cf. p. 287, l. 1). See Index.

26. 'Shakespheare': so, too, in Camden.

MS. and Camden read 'Barlowes.' The reference must be to Marlowe's fragment of *Hero and Leander*. See the bibliographical note in Mr. Bullen's edition, iii. 2.

CHAPMAN (pp. 295-307).

295. 14. *queasie stomackes*. Supra, i. p. 66, l. 24, note, &c.

297. 4, &c. See headnote to 'II' on the same page; also p. 300. The 1611-12 complete edition (*The Iliades of Homer, Prince of Poets*) contained the important verse preface 'To the Reader,' the essay 'Of Homer,' and the commentaries on the books.

12. *Spondanus*. Jean de Sponde (1557-95). Chapman refers to *Homeri quae extant opera ... cum Latina versione ... Perpetuis ... in Iliade simul et Odysseam, J. Spondani ... commentariis*, 1583.

298. 6. Aristonicus, in the περὶ σημείων Ἰλιάδος.

10. *out of Eustathius*, in the παρεκβολαὶ εἰς τὴν Ὁμήρου Ἰλιάδα, of which there were many sixteenth-century editions.

16, 19. Chapman's text, 'μαρμαρεω.' See *Iliad*, 18. 480.

21. Spondanus. See p. 297, l. 12, note.

299. 14. *caprichiously*. See *N.E.D.*, s.v. 'Caprice.'

301. 1, &c. Chapman's onslaught is directed chiefly against the long third chapter of the fifth book of Scaliger's *Poetice*,

which is devoted to a comparison of Virgil with Homer, to the disadvantage of the latter. There is some justice in Chapman's gibe that it is the only original part of the treatise, for, though neo-classic criticism had already exalted Virgil, the elaborateness of the comparison and its 'impalsied diminuation' give it a place apart from the more academic matters of 'place, time, and termes.' On Scaliger's attitude generally, see Hallam, ii. 300 et seq., and Saintsbury, *Hist. of Crit.* ii. 73 et seq.

11. *Barathrum.* See p. 388, l. 7, note.

302. 1. A reference to Arthur Hall's *Ten Books of Homers Iliades* (1581), the first Englishing of Homer. Hall used Hugues Salel's version of the ten books (Paris, 1545); his copy (1555), with his autograph dated 1556, is in the British Museum.

303. 35. *fauourles* (not a misprint for *sauourles*), 'out of favour.'

304. 24. *burbolts*, 'bird-bolts.'

306. 9. *feuerie*, feverish.

31. *The length of the verse*, i.e. in fourteen syllables in rhyming couplets.

32. *quidditicall*, quibbling, captious, subtle.

MERES (pp. 308-24).

[The text has been printed by Ingleby, *Shakspere Allusion-Books*, i. 152-65. The reprint by Arber (*English Garner*, ii) is a selection, with the paragraphs rearranged and the vocabulary modernized.]

308. 17. The *Discours politiques et militaires du Seigneur de la Noue: nouvellement recueillis & mis en lumière* was printed at Basle in 1587. An English version (*Politike and Militarie Discourses*) by 'E. A.' appeared in the same year.

Beuis of Hampton, &c. Cf. Ascham, i. 4; Nash, i. 323; Puttenham, ii. 44. The *Famous Historie of the Seauen Champions of Christendom* by Richard Johnson, the romance writer, had just appeared (entered 1596).

309. 13. Cf. i. p. 59, l. 15, p. 79, l. 31, p. 332, l. 17.

310. 25-8. *Rubarbe and sugarcandie*, &c. Supra, p. 208, l. 1.

29-34. See Sidney, i. p. 180, l. 13 et seq. Note that Meres changes 'some good' into 'many cockney and wanton.' *Cockney* (as applied to women), pampered, cockered, spoilt.

Cotgrave, defining Fr. *coquine*, gives 'cokney, simperdecockit, nice thing.'

312. 11. Joseph Hall (1574-1656), ed. Singer, 1824, Grosart, 1879.

John Marston's (? 1575-1634), *Metamorphosis of Pigmalions Image* appeared in 1598 and *The Scourge of Villanie* in 1598 and 1599. See infra, p. 465.

12. William Rankins had published his anti-stage attack, *A Mirrour of Monsters*, in 1587 (see i. p. 63). His *Seaven Satyres* appeared in 1598. *The English Ape* (1588) has been ascribed to him.

313. 13-33. Copied (for the most part *literatim*) from Webbe. See i. pp. 231-2.

314. 1-7. See Sidney, i. p. 160, ll. 10-16.

19-21. Copied from Webbe. See i. p. 242, ll. 8-10, note.

24. Harding. Supra, p. 62, l. 26. Cf. note to p. 238, l. 25.

27. Sotades of Maroneia (Σωτάδης Μαρωνείτης), B.C. 280.

29. *I know not*, &c. Taken from Puttenham. See ii. p. 62, l. 27.

31-2. Ib. p. 65, ll. 8-10.

33, &c. *Consaluo Periz*, &c. Copied from Ascham. See i. p. 32, l. 25 et seq.

315. 5. Surrey. Supra, i. p. 283, l. 9, note; and by Index.

9. *Iouianus Pontanus*, Giovanni Gioviano Pontano (1426-1503), Latin writer and poet, head of the Neapolitan Academy founded by Antonio Panormita, afterwards called the *Academia Pontani*. His best known poem was the *Urania*, which at once established itself as a model to the Renaissance poets (cf. Sannazzaro's *Poemata Selecta*, pp. 1-4, and Fracastoro's *Syphilis*, passim). See note to i. p. 158, l. 30. He is the 'Pontan' or 'Pontane' of English writers of the sixteenth and seventeenth centuries, and must not be confused with the Jesuit philologer Jacobus Pontanus (1542-1626), also referred to in these notes.

Politianus, i. e. Angelo Poliziano (1454-94), author of the vernacular *Stanze* and *Orfeo*. His chief Latin poem is the *Sylvae*, in four parts, *Nutricia, Rusticus, Manto, Ambra*.

10. *Marullus Tarchaniota*, Michael Tarchaniota Marullus, Latin poet, author of *Hymni & Epigrammata*, often reprinted, and edited, with the works of Angerianus and Secundus,

by Martellus (Paris, 1582), and by B. Albinus (Speier, 1595). The earliest edition in the British Museum is dated 1497. Scaliger gives a long account in his *Poetice*, vi. ch. iv. See *Correspondence of Sir Philip Sidney*, ed. Pears, p. 199.

the two Strozæ, i.e. Tito Vespasiano Strozzi (*d.* 1508) and his son Ercole Strozzi. See Lilius Gyraldus (ed. Wotke, p. 26) and Tiraboschi, vi. 1353-61. Their poems were often printed together in the sixteenth century.

11. *Palingenius.* Supra, i. p. 30, l. 10, note.

Mantuanus. Supra, i. p. 411, note, and by Index.

Philelphus, Francesco Filelfo (1426-81). See L. Gyraldus (u.s.), p. 23, Tiraboschi, vi. 1523; and Symonds, ii. 202, for an account of his *Satires* and *Odes*.

Quintianus Stoa. Gianfrancesco Quinziano Stoa (1484-1557. See L. Gyraldus, u.s., p. 74, Scaliger, *Poetice*, vi. 4. The best account is in Tiraboschi, vii. 2252-61.

12. Germanus Brixius. See L. Gyraldus, u.s., 65.

13. Meres's Latin poets are hardly 'ancient'; all, with the exception of the last, appear in Scaliger's chapter on 'Poetae Recentiores' in the sixth book of his *Poetice*.

14, &c. Meres's list may be compared with Nash's in i. p. 316. See notes.

15. Christopher Ocland. See i. p. 239, l. 15, note.

16. Thomas Campion (*d.* 1619). See infra, p. 327.

17. *Brunswerd*, i.e. John Brownswerd (?1540-89), master of Macclesfield Grammar School, author of Latin verses.

Willey, i.e. Richard Willes or Willey. See vol. i. pp. 46, 47, and 305.

28-34. Copied from Sidney. See i. p. 160, ll. 4-9. Meres turns Sidney's argument for prose-poetry (i. pp. 159-60) in favour of Sidney himself.

316. 3. Meres probably takes the quotation direct from Webbe, i. p. 237, l. 30 (see note).

16. Παρθένιος of Nicaea (reign of Augustus).

18-24. Samuel Daniel's *Delia, contayning certayne Sonnets* (1592). His *Complaint of Rosamund* was added to the second edition (also 1592). *The First Fowre Bookes of the Civile Wars* appeared in 1595: the extended poem, in eight books, in 1609.

25-9. Drayton's *Mortimeriados* (?1596) appeared in altered

Notes

form in 1603 as *The Barrons Wars*. *Englands Heroicall Epistles* (first edit., 1597) was conjoined with the *Barrons Wars* in the 1603 edition. See also note p. 317, ll. 2-3.

31. Charles Fitzgeffrey (? 1575-1638) published his poem on Drake in 1596. See p. 323, ll. 10-12, infra.

34. *Accius . . . Milithus* [Mitiletus]. Cf. Lodge, i. p. 70.

317. 2-3. *The Tragicall Legend of Robert, Duke of Normandie*, was issued in 1596 with revised editions of *Matilda, the faire & chaste daughter of Lord Rob. Fitzwater* (1594), and *The Legend of Peirs Gaueston* (? 1593).

4. *Joannes Honterus . . . Cosmography*, i. e. *Rudimentorum Cosmographicorum . . . Libri iii. cum tabellis geographicis.* Zurich, 1548.

6. *is now in penning.* The first edition of the first part appeared in ? 1612 : the second part in 1622.

23. William Warner's *Albion's Englande* appeared (first part) in 1586 and (first and second) in 1589; and in a third edition 'corrected,' 1592. Other editions followed. A complete edition appeared in 1612.

30-4. 'Mellifluous and hony-tongued' appears to have been a favourite epithet in contemporary references to the poet. Cf. Weever's 'Epigram to Shakespeare' and *Poems in Diuers humors,* 1598 (? by Rich. Barnfield), both printed in Ingleby's *Shakspere Allusion-Books,* i. pp. 182, 186; also T. Heywood's *Hierarchie of the Blessed Angels* (1635). It is, however, of common application in Elizabethan literature (cf. Sidney, supra, i. p. 202, l. 1, *Arcadia,* i. 3, &c.). Shakespeare has 'honey-tongued' in *L.L.L.* v. 2. 334, and kindred phrases elsewhere ; though he uses 'honey-mouthed' in *W. T.* ii. 2. 33 in the less common sarcastic sense—'If I proue hony-mouth'd, let my tongue blister.' See Ingleby's notes on the interpretation of the name *Melicertus* in Elizabethan literature (u. s., pp. xiii et seq.). The usage was probably fixed by the popularity of Boëthius, *De Consol.* (see v. 2. 2), rather than by direct knowledge of the classical $\mu\epsilon\lambda\iota\gamma\lambda\omega\sigma\sigma\sigma$ or $\mu\epsilon\lambda\iota\phi\omega\nu\sigma$ (see ii. p. 322, ll. 3-6, note).

318. 4. *Loue Labours Wonne.* This has been identified, by critics who hold that the play is not lost, with *L.L.L.,* with *M.N.D.,* with *The Tempest,* with *All's Well,* with *M. Ado,* and with the *Taming of the Shrew.* The latest contribution to the subject is A. H. Tolman's *What has Become of Shakespeare's Play 'Love's Labour's Won'*?, University of Chicago Press, 1903.

9. '*Epius Stolo*,' i.e. Aelius Stilo (Lucius Aelius Praeconius Stilo), who made the remark and was followed by Varro. 'Varro dicat *Musas*, Aelii Stilonis sententia, *Plautino sermone locuturas fuisse, si Latine loqui vellent*' (Quintil. x. 1 (513)). The passage is quoted by Ben Jonson in his *Discoveries* (*Works*, ed. Cunningham, iii. 421). [Some texts of Quintil. read *Stolonis*, which may partly excuse Meres's error.]

11. *fine filed phrase*, 'polished,' 'fine,' a common sixteenth-century usage. Jonson speaks of Shakespeare's 'well torned and true filed lines' (*To the Memory of my beloved Master William Shakespeare*, l. 68).

15. *imitators*, fellows; not to be taken in the chronological sense. Cf. p. 315, l. 26, where Meres places Shakespeare, Marlowe, and Chapman in the same order.

19-26. Ovid, *Met.* xv. 871-2; Horace, *Odes*, iii. 30. 1-5.

29-32. The lines are printed as in the original. Ingleby, u. s., p. 160, begins the fourth line with *conspirabunt*.

319. 3-6. Cf. the lists in Nash's Preface to *Menaphon*. Supra, i. pp. 318-19.

5. Thomas Kyd's association with these poets (and in parallel with Tasso) may be explained by the fact that, besides writing some non-dramatic verse in English and Latin, he had translated Tasso's prose *Padre di Famiglia* (*The Householders Philosophie*, 1588), and may have translated some of his verse. See Mr. Boas's *Kyd*, xxv, lxii, lxxviii.

26. *Doctor Leg of Cambridge*. See l. 33, infra.

27. *Doctor Edes of Oxford*, i. e. Richard Edes (1555-1604), Dean of Worcester, friend of Tobie Mathew (see ii. p. 281, l. 15). He is credited with a tragedy of *Julius Caesar*, acted at Christ Church in 1582.

Edward Ferris. Supra, ii. p. 63, l. 13, note.

33. Thomas Legge (1535-1607), Master of Caius College, Cambridge. His Latin tragedy of 'Richard III' was acted in 1579. See Harington, supra, p. 210, l. 15, note. The manuscript of his *Destruction of Jerusalem* was 'filched' by a 'Plageary'; but Fleay says it was acted at Coventry in 1577.

320. 10. *Edward, Earle of Oxforde*. See ii. p. 95, l. 26, note.

Notes

Doctor Gager of Oxforde, i.e. William Gager (fl. 1580–1619), who wrote five Latin plays which were acted at Oxford. He engaged in controversy with John Rainolds (see note, p. 441), who had denounced the acting of plays at Oxford.

11. *Master Rowley*. Is this Samuel Rowley, the dramatist (died ? 1633), though the reference to Pembroke Hall is a difficulty? *D. N. B.* suggests Ralph Rowley (died ? 1604), afterwards Rector of Chelmsford, 'who was the only student of Pembroke Hall of the name of Rowley during the second half of the sixteenth century.'

12. *Maister Edwardes*. See Webbe, i. p. 242, l. 33, note, and Puttenham, ii. p. 65, l. 26.

15. *our best plotter*. In Jonson's *Case is Altered* (I. i) Onion refers to this very passage when he says to Antonio Balladino (i.e. Anthony Munday), 'You are in print already for the best plotter.'

16. Porter, Henry (fl. 1596-9), author of *The Pleasant Historie of the two Angrië Women of Abington*. Four other plays are mentioned in Henslowe, but they are not extant.

Wilson. See note to i. p. 85, l. 3.

Hathway, Richard, one of the authors of *The First Part of the True and Honorable Historie of the Life of Sir John Oldcastle* (1599).

20-1. Cf. p. 312, ll. 11-12 (note).

21. *The Author of Skialetheia*, i.e. Edward Guilpin. *Skialetheia, or a Shadowe of Truth in certaine Epigrams and Satyres* appeared in 1598. It has been reprinted by Utterson (1843), Collier (1870), and Grosart (1878).

32. *C. Valgius* for *T.* Valgius Rufus, the poet. C. Valgius was a rhetorician.

321. 1. *Sir Francis Brian* (d. 1550) contributed anonymously to *Tottel's Miscellany* (1557). See note to ii. p. 275, l. 21.

2. *Sir Edward Dyer*. Puttenham speaks of him 'for elegie.' See i. p. 65, l. 32.

4. Samuel Page (1574-1630). His poem, *The Love of Amos and Laura*, was printed in *Alcilia* (1613).

7. *the Authour*, &c. Thomas Watson (? 1557-92), author of the Ἑκατομπαθία (see i. p. 316, l. 8, note). His *Amyntae Gaudia*, a Latin pastoral in hexameters, was printed posthumously (1592).

Walsingham's Meliboeus was written in honour of his patron Sir Francis Walsingham (1590). It was Englished by the author in the same year (*An Eclogue upon the death of ... Sir Fr. Walsingham*).

10. *Challener.* See p. 65, l. 28, note.

Gosson's claim as a pastoralist must be supported by material which is at present unknown.

11. Fraunce (supra, i. p. 303) appears here as the translator (1587) of Watson's Latin *Amyntas* (1585), which must not be confused with the *Amyntae Gaudia*, supra, l. 7. The *Amyntas* is a version of Tasso's *Aminta*. See *Anglia*, xi. 1-38.

Richard Barnfield's *Affectionate Shepheard* appeared in 1594.

15. *Drante.* Supra, i. p. 90, l. 13, note.

Timothy Kendal (fl. 1577), compiler of *Flowers of Epigrammes*.

16. Thomas Bastard (1566-1618), author of *Chrestoleros: Seuen Bookes of Epigrames* (1598).

Dauies, i.e. Sir John Davies (1569-1626), author of the *Nosce Teipsum*, who published a volume of *Epigrammes*, undated. It is reprinted in the Isham Tracts (ed. C. Edmonds, 1870).

21-4. See p. 265, l. 7, note.

26-9. Meres is in sorry plight when he has to borrow his praises of Eliza. See Puttenham, supra, p. 66.

322. 2. Cf. p. 225, l. 33; p. 264, l. 35.

3-6. Μναμοσύναν ἕλε θάμβος, ὅτ' ἔκλυε τᾶς μελιφώνου
Σαπφοῦς, μὴ δεκάταν Μοῦσαν ἔχουσι βροτοί.
Anth. Palat. ix. 66.

7-19. Borrowed from Sidney. See i. p. 193, l. 26—p. 194, l. 1. See note on 'King James,' i. p. 396.

20-3. Taken from Ascham. See i. p. 24, ll. 4-7.

28. *Christopher Iohnson* (? 1536-97), physician, and Latin poet of some repute, author of *Ranarum et murium pugna, Latina versione donata, ex Homero*, Lond. 1580.

29. *Watson for his Antigone*, i.e. Thomas Watson, author of the Ἑκατομπαθία (supra, i. p. 316, l. 8, note), whose Latin translation of the *Antigone* of Sophocles appeared in 1581. The

Notes

volume contains some allegorical pieces in Latin and some experiments in Latin metres. See also notes, ii. pp. 451, 452.

31, &c. See Webbe, i. p. 243, l. 9—p. 244, l. 15.

323. 1. *inchoate.* See ii. p. 295, note.

3. Andrea Alciati (1492-1550). See Tiraboschi, vi, pp. 1060-9). There were many editions of the *Emblematum Liber* (1531) during the sixteenth century.

4. *Reusnerus,* i.e. Nicolaus Reusner, author of a volume of *Emblemata* (1581).

Sambucus, Ioannes (cf. i. p. 13, l. 27, note). His volume of *Emblemata* was printed at the Plantin Press at Antwerp in 1564 (2nd edit. 1566, 3rd 1569, 4th 1584).

5. Geoffrey Whitney (? 1548-? 1601). His *Choice of Emblemes* was printed at Leyden in 1586. There is a facsimile reprint by H. Green (1866).

Andrew Willet (1562-1621), theologian and controversialist, author of *Sacrorum emblematum centuria,* Cambridge [1596?].

Thomas Combe.?

6. *Nonnus Panapolyta,* Νόννος of Panopolis (Egypt). The first printed edition of this work was issued by Aldus Manutius (Venice, 1501). There were many sixteenth-century editions.

7. Gervase Markham's version of the *Canticles* (*The Poem of Poems, or Sion's Muse*) appeared in 1596. He is known by his works on horsemanship and country life, and by his *Tragedie of Sir Richard Grinville* (1595). See *D.N.B.*: also note on Googe and Heresbachius, supra, i. p. 265, l. 22.

10-2. Charles Fitzgeffrey. See p. 316, l. 31, note.

16. Sidonius. Cf. p. 322, l. 3.

17. *Quicquid,* &c. See i. p. 196, l. 14, note.

18. *Doctor Case,* i.e. John Case (*d.* 1600), the commentator of Aristotle. He practised medicine at Oxford.

24. *our wittie Wilson.* See note to p. 320, l. 16.

31-2. See ii. p. 229, &c.

35. *the Harueys.* See note to p. 251, ll. 22-3.

324. 1-10. For particulars of Nash's troubles arising from his writing of the comedy *The Isle of Dogs* (1597), now lost, see Henslowe's *Diary* and the article in *D.N.B. Banishment* (l. 6) refers to Nash's retreat to Great Yarmouth (see *Nashes Lenten Stuffe*).

3. *young Iuuenall*, a common nickname of Nash, as in *Greene's Groatsworth of Wit*, Chettle's *Kind-Harts Dreame*, &c.

15. *Aen.* i. 211, *vosmet*.

20. See ii. p. 232, l. 9.

23. Iodelle, Étienne (1532-73), author of *Cléopâtre captive* (1552).

27. *the Theatre of Gods Iudgements* (1597), by Thomas Beard (*d*. 1632).

VAUGHAN (pp. 325-6).

325. 9-10. Cf. i. Appendix, p. 341.

326. 10-13. From Puttenham, ii. p. 17.

13-14. ibid. ii. p. 21.

15-16. ibid. ii. 17. Poems by Joannes Dampetrus are included in the *Delitiae C. poetarum Gallorum* ([Francfurt] 1609), edited by Ranutius Gherus (i.e. Janus Gruterus). Scaliger discusses his work in his *Poetice*, vi. 4.

16-19. ibid. ii. p. 17.

22. ibid. ii. p. 18. Puttenham reads 'Vargas.' See note.

24. ibid. ii. pp. 18, 22.

CAMPION (pp. 327-55).

327. There is perhaps some significance in the dedication to Thomas Sackville, now Lord Buckhurst, who had collaborated in the blank verse *Gorboduc*.

Campion's attack on Rhyme, which surprised Daniel (infra, p. 358, l. 27), is difficult to explain in the light of his own formal excellence and musical experience. His first song-book, *A Booke of Ayres*, had been printed in the preceding year.

328. [2 et seq.] These lines echo the opening lines of the first Satire of Persius.

[6.] *a termer*, one who goes to London for the season ('term-time').

11. *discreta quantitas*. See Scaliger, *Poetice*, iv. 1 and 45.

12. Read *disseuer'd*.

15. Campion's musical allusions are frequent. Cf. the quotations in the notes to p. 338, l. 2, and p. 340, l. 26.

329. 9-10. Cf. i. p. 230, l. 18, note.

16-28. Cf. Ascham, i, passim ; Webbe, i. p. 240.

John Reuchlin (1455-1522), German humanist.

23. *Epistolae obscurorum virorum* (1515). See Böcking's *Ulrich von Hutten* (7 vols., Leipzig, 1859-70), passim.

27-8. *Rithmus and Metrum.* Cf. ii. pp. 70-3.

330. 21. *similiter desinentia.* See Cic. *De Orat.* iii. 54 ; Quintil. ix. 3 (478). Cf. supra, ii. p. 242, note.

28-9. A reference to the popular *Pugna Porcorum per P. Porcium Poëtam*, which appeared in 1530 at ? Cologne or ? Antwerp. The writer was Joannes Leo Placentius. The book is a verse burlesque, in which every word begins with 'P.' Cf. Hucbald's verses beginning with 'C,' twice referred to by Puttenham, supra, p. 15, l. 29, and note.

331. 11. *Carmina prouerbialia* (cf. p. 361, l. 26), a quotation-book often reprinted in the sixteenth century. The title of the 1588 edition, London, 16mo, describes the collection thus : *Carmina prouerbialia totius humanae vitae statum breuiter deliniantia necnon vtilem de moribus doctrinam iucunde proponentia. Loci communes in gratiam inuentutis selecti.*

12. *bables*, baubles. Cf. i. p 104, l. 21.

17-18. See ii. p. 15, ll. 20-2.

20-5. More's *Epigrammata* (Basle, 1520). These verses on Henry Abyngdon were often quoted. They will be found in the collection of *Epitaphes* at the end of Stanyhurst's *Aeneis* (ed. Arber, pp. 155-6). Abyngdon was appointed Master of the Children of the Royal Chapel at Westminster in 1465.

29, &c. Mr. Bullen refers to the passage in Drummond's *Conversations*: 'He [Jonson] cursed Petrarch for redacting verses to Sonnets, which he said were like that Tirrant's bed, wher some who were too short were racked, others too long cut short.'

332. 8. Campion had more than a physician's interest in Galen. Cf. the Epistle to his *New way of making Four parts in Counter-point* (? 1617) : 'Galen either first, or next the first of physicians, became so expert a musician that he could not contain himself, but needs he must apply all the proportions of music to the uncertain motions of the pulse' (*Works*, ed. Bullen, xxiv).

334. 13. *licentiate Iambick.* See p. 335, l. 8 et seq.; and i. p. 95, l. 14.

336. 17. *paisd,* weighed.

337. 11. Orig. 'fift,' an error for 'fourth.'

32. *ayreable,* i.e. airable, capable of being set to music.

338. 2. *Heroik Poeme.* Campion, like his predecessors, gives the first place to it. Cf. the 'Preface to the Reader' in his first *Booke of Ayres* (1601). 'Nevertheless, as in poesy, we give the preeminence to the Heroical Poem; so in music, we yield the chief place to the grave and well invented Motet' (ed. Bullen, p. 5). See note to Puttenham, ii. p. 43, ll. 21-2. Cf. also Ronsard, *Abrégé*; Rapin, *Comparaison d'Homère et de Virgile* and *Réflexions sur la Poëtique d'Aristote*; and Dryden, *Apology for Heroic Poetry, A Discourse concerning Satire,* and *Dedication of the Æneis* (first sentence).

340. 26. Campion has left two books of Latin Epigrams (*Works,* ed. Bullen, pp. 263-366). In the Preface 'To the Reader' in his first *Booke of Ayres* (1601), he points to the analogy between epigrams and airs: 'What epigrams are in poetry, the same are airs in music: then in their chief perfection when they are short and well seasoned' (ed. Bullen, u.s., p. 4).

342. 5. *Beaten,* ?'figured,' embroidered, brocaded. Cf. Marlowe, 'No sirrah; in beaten silk and staves-acre' (*Dr. Faustus,* iv. p. 17); and see the quotation from *Ram Alley* in *N. E. D.,* s.v. 'Beaten, ppl. 5 c,' and Mr. Bullen's note (u. s., p. 247), where he quotes from Guilpin's *Skialetheia,* Epig. 53, 'He wears a jerkin cudgelled with gold lace' (which *N. E. D.* defines in the humorous sense of 'trimming laid on heavily').

21, &c. The references are perhaps, as Mr. Bullen suggests, to Barnabe Barnes (cf. also p. 346) and Gabriel Harvey, though the latter was generally called 'Gabriel' by friends and opponents. Campion satirizes the former in *Epigrammata,* ii. p. 80.

345. 3. *Pirop* (pyropus, πυρωπός), red or gold bronze. Cf. Ovid, *Met.* ii. 2.

21. *tyres.* Mr. Bullen proposes 'tries'; but the text may stand.

346. 2. *his Inne.* A favourite Elizabethan metaphor. Cf. ii. p. 78, l. 9, supra. Campion has the same phrase in 'The man of life upright' in the first *Booke of Ayres* (Bullen, pp. 21, 48).

349. 10. *Iet*, 'jet,' u. s., 'move proudly,' vaunt, 'trip it.'
   14. *to*, too.
351. 19. Martial, ix. xi. 17.
352. 5. *position.* Cf. i. p. 121, l. 4, note; ii. p. 120, l. 23.

DANIEL (pp. 356–84).

This essay may have appeared towards the close of 1602, the year in which Campion's attack on Rhyme was printed. Grosart (*Daniel*, vol. iv. pp. 33 et seq.) and Rhys (*Literary Pamphlets*, i. 190 et seq.) appear to have reprinted the text of the 1607 edition, which is in some respects inferior. The former, in his title and bibliographical note, i. pp. 221-2, confuses the *Defence* with the poem *Musophilus, containing a generall Defence of all Learning*, printed in 1599. The references to *Musophilus* in these notes are to Grosart's text (*Daniel*, i. pp. 225-56).

Ben Jonson was dissatisfied with the results of the controversy. In the Drummond *Conversations* we are told that he had written an epic: 'It is all in couplets, for he detesteth all other rimes.' 'Said he had written a Discourse of Poesie, both against Campion and Daniel, especially the last, wher he proues couplets to be the brauest sort of verses, especially when they are broken, like Hexameters; and that crosse rimes and stanzaes (becaus the purpose would lead him beyond 8 lines to conclude) were all forced.'

356. 8. This has been assumed to be Fulke Greville. But see Mr. Morris Croll's essay on the *Works of Fulke Greville*, Philadelphia, 1903, pp. 5-6.

357. 18. William Herbert, third Earl of Pembroke of the second creation (1580–1630), had succeeded in 1601. Daniel had been his tutor (cf. p. 358, ll. 6–7). His mother (p. 358, l. 4) was Mary, sister of Sir Philip Sidney.

359. 1–2. Horace, *Epist.* ii. 1. 262-3.

29. *indenize.* Grosart and Rhys read 'modernize.' Cf. Daniel, i. p. 277 (ed. Grosart):

'Here dost thou bring (my friend) a stranger borne
   To be indenized with us, and made our owne,'

and the word *Free-denizen*, infra, p. 384, l. 27. Florio (1598) defines *Patriare*, ' to endenize, or enfranchise into a countrie.' Cf. *endenisoned*, supra, p. 283, l. 7; and *denisoned*, in quotation in note to i. p. 44, l. 27.

360. 1. *as Aristotle saith.* Cf. *Poet*. iv. 6.

16. *Remensi*: wrongly assumed by Chalmers and Rhys to be an error of Daniel's. See Giraldi Cintio's *Discorso dei Romanzi*: '. . . quantunque vi sia alcuno che voglia che questa voce sia venuta da' Remensi, alcuni da Turpino il quale vogliono che più di ognuno abbia data materia a simili poesie colle sue scritture: perocchè essendo egli arcivescovo Remense, vogliono che state siano queste composizion' dette romanzi' (ed. Daelli, 1864, i. p. 7).

24-5. Cf. Sidney, supra, i. p. 205, ll. 11-12.

361. 4. *De Turcarum Moribus Epitome*, by Bartolomaeus Georgevicz (Rome, 1552), which was translated by Goughe in 1570. Dryden also explicitly refers (in the second edition of the *Essay of Dramatic Poesy*) to Daniel's tract when, speaking of the 'new way of poesy,' he says that 'we are able to prove that the Eastern people have used it from all antiquity.'

26. *Schola Salerna*. See ii. p. 13, l. 6, note.

Carmina Prouerbialia. Cf. ii. p. 331, l. 11, note.

362. 3. *saith Aristotle*. *Met*. x. 1.

6-8. Horace, *Ars Poet*. 351-3.

12. *Ill customes*, &c. Cf. Campion, supra, p. 330, ll. 9-10.

363. 7. *in what Scythian sorte*. Cf. note to i. p. 75, l. 33.

26. *Scribimus*, &c. Horace, *Epist*. ii. 1. 117.

33-5. Horace, ibid. 108-10.

364. 12. Horace, *Epist*. i. 19. 19.

365. 25. Cf. *Shepheards Calender*, 'October,' st. 14, which is frequently quoted, supra.

367. 8. Horace, *Ars Poet*. 72. For reading *vis* cf. p. 130, ll. 16-17, note, supra.

11-13. Cf. Gascoigne and James VI, supra, i. pp. 47, 210.

13, &c. Dryden expresses the same sentiment in his praise of Shakespeare in the *Essay of Dramatic Poesy*: 'He needed not the spectacles of books to read nature; he looked inwards, and found her there.'

368. 9-12. See Campion, supra, p. 329.

Notes 459

34. *C. Tolomœi.* Claudio Tolomei printed his *Versi e Regole della Nuova Poesia Toscana* in 1539.

369. 6. *Iohannis Rauenensis*, i.e. either Giovanni de' Malpaghini (da Ravenna), *d.* circa 1420, humanist, pupil and friend of Petrarch; or Giovanni da Ravenna, fl. 1399, author of an *Apologia*, an *Historia Elisiae*, and other works. See the elaborate discussion of the problem of identification in Tiraboschi, v. 946-58.

8. *Leonardus Aretinus*, i.e. Leonardo Bruni Aretino (1369-1444), author of a history of Florence and lives of Dante and Petrarch. He is not to be confused with Pietro Aretino, who is frequently referred to in these volumes (e.g. p. 402, l. 18); or with Unico Aretino (see i. p. 379).

Laurentius Valla (Lorenzo Valla, 1406-57), u.s.

Poggius (Poggio Bracciolini, 'fiorentino,' 1380-1459), u.s.

9. *Biondus* (generally Blondus, *Latine*), i.e. Flavio Biondo (1388-1463), antiquarian writer and historian.

Emanuel Chrysolaras (1355-1415), a Byzantine humanist in Italy.

18. *Bessarion*, Cardinal, patriarch of Constantinople (1389-1472), Italian humanist.

George Trapezuntius, i.e. of Trebizond (Τραπεζούντιος), 1396-1485, philologer and translator. See Fabricius, *Bibl. Graec.*

Theodorus Gaza (? 1400-78), another Byzantine philologer in Italy. See ibid.

25. *Pomponius Laetus* (? 1425-97), Italian humanist. His *Opera varia* appeared in one volume at Mainz in 1521.

Aeneas Syluius Piccolomini (1405-64), afterwards Pius II.

26. *Angelus Politianus* (1454-94), u.s.

Hermolaus Barbarus (Ermolao Barbaro), 1454-95, humanist and diplomatist.

Iohannes Picus de Mirandula (Giovanni Pico della Mirandola), 1463-94, Italian philosopher and theologian.

29. *Rewclen*, &c. See note, p. 368, l. 9.

370. 1. *Aldelmus Durotelmus*, i.e. Ealdhelm of Sherborne, who died in 709. In Bale's *Catalogus* he is described as *Durotellus seu Bladunius*, but this is not taken from Leland's *De Scriptoribus*, where no surname is given. Tanner says that Dempster gives *Durobellus*. Mr. R. L. Poole suggests that

Durotellus or Durobellus must be a pseudo-classical invention of the sixteenth century, and that the passage given in the text may have been got from Bostius, whom Bale quotes.

8-12. *Iosephus Deuonius*, i.e. Joseph of Exeter (Josephus Iscanus), fl. 1190. His *De Bello Troiano* had been held to be the work of Cornelius Nepos or of Dares Phrygius. See Fabricius, *Bibl. Latina*, 73, and Jusserand, *De Iosepho Exoniensi*, Paris, 1877). It does not appear to have been noted that Daniel anticipates Camden (*Remaines*) and Dresemius (edit. 1620) in ascribing the poem to Joseph of Exeter.

12. *Walterus Mape* (fl. 1200), author of the *De Nugis Curialium*.

13. *Gulielmus Nigellus*, i.e. Nigel, called 'Wireker' (fl. 1190), author of the *Speculum Stultorum*.

Geruasius Tilburiensis (fl. 1210), author of the *Otia Imperialia*.

Bracton, i.e. Henry de Bracton (*d.* 1268), author of *De Legibus et Consuetudinibus Angliae*.

14. Roger Bacon (? 1214-94), author of the *Opus Maius*.

Ockam, William (*d.* ? 1349), '*Doctor invincibilis*,' the second founder of Nominalism.

371. 19. *Ciceronians*. Cf. note to ii. p. 251, l. 20.

20-1. Cf. *Musophilus*, ll. 487-9.

372. 22. *Erasmus*, &c. Cf. p. 369, l. 29, note.

25. *S. Thomas*, i.e. Thomas Aquinas (1225-74), '*Doctor Angelicus*.'

26. *Bartolus* (1313-56), Italian jurist. See p. 438. He is often cited in association with Cuiacius (supra, p. 246, l. 24, &c.).

27. *Scotus*, i.e. Duns Scotus (1274-1308), '*Doctor Subtilis*.'

29. Tacitus, *Dialogus de Oratoribus*, 20.

373. 11. *like a Viper*. Cf. supra, i. p. 151, l. 21.

33, &c. Cf. *Musophilus*, ll. 259-62.

375. 15, &c. A reference to Campion, p. 340 et seq.

376. 4. *his Theta*. See i. p. 321, l. 13, note.

31. *For what adoe*. See Campion, supra, p. 334 et seq.

35. *which hath euer beene vsed*. Cf. supra, i. p. 405.

380. 12. *a quest of inquirie*. Cf. Florio, 'I in this search or quest of inquirie haue spent most of my studies' ('Epist. Ded.' to the *Dictionary*).

381. 3. *Scribendi recte*, &c. Horace, *Ars Poet.* 309.

9-10. *Verba sequi*, &c. Horace, *Epist.* ii. 2. 142-3.

382. 2. *mine owne mysterie*, apparently here = art, business. Cf. p. 365, l. 24, where a choice of meaning is possible. Cf. *Musophilus*, 64.

33. *in some of my Epistles*, as in *To The Lord Henrie Howard* in *Certaine Epistles* (Grosart, i. p. 199 et seq.).

383. 34. Horace, *Odes*, i. 18. 14.

384. 5, &c. Catullus, xxii.

12. Horace, *Ars Poet.* 474.

13-19. *affectation . . . singularitie.* Cf. p. 378, l. 9, and *Musophilus*, 82-5.

27. *Free-denizens.* Cf. note to p. 359, l. 29; and Peele's account of Harington in *Ad Maecenatem Prologus* (1593).

Appendix (pp. 387-403).

388. 2. *Hath the brize prickt you*? Cf. *Poetaster*, iii. 1. Brize, breeze (O. E. *briosa*), gad-fly. See *N.E.D.*, s.v. 'Breeze.'

5. *In generall opinion* is run on to line 3 in orig.

It is not known why Jonson omitted this passage on Poetry from the Folio. Mr. A. W. Ward has suggested that it may have been 'a mere stage-cut.' In its place in the Folio, Edward Knowell says, 'Sir, you have saved me the labour of a defence.'

7. *Barathrum* (βάραθρον), in the secondary sense of 'The Abyss,' Hell. Cf. p. 301, l. 11.

38. *I*, aye. Cf. p. 390, l. 27.

39. *humor.* See p. 462.

389. 22. *To make a child, now swadled, to proceede*, &c. Cf. i. p. 59, l. 27.

25. *foot-and-halfe-foote.* So the text, in the secondary sense of *Lat. sesquipedalis*, 'of excessive length.' Cf. Horace, *Ars Poet.* 97. Gifford and Cunningham read '*foot and half-foot.*'

26. *Fight ouer*, &c. Critical tradition has found a Shakespearian reference in this line, and an allusion to Marlowe's *Dr. Faustus* in the 'nimble squibbe.' The latter is doubtful, for the 'squib' often assisted in the stage cannonade of an historical play. Cf. also *Returne from Parnassus* (II), iii. 4

(l. 1361). The reference to the 'creaking throne' (μηχανή, *machina*) of the early stage is probably general.

37–8. *Comœdie... an Image of the times.* See Lodge, supra, i. p. 81, l. 1, note, and Sidney, i. p. 176, l. 30, note.

390. 10. *Grex*, Chorus. See p. 392, l. 26.

13. The *loci* in the history of the term 'Humour' in its dramatic association are these:—

(*a*) *Jonsonian.* (1) *Every Man in his Humour* (passim and espec. iii. 2). (2) *Every Man out of his Humour* (ante, and passim). (3) *Cynthia's Revels*, iv. i. (4) *The Poetaster*, iii. 1; iv. 4; v. 1. (5) *The Alchemist*, Prologue. (6) *The Magnetic Lady*, or *Humours reconciled* (Induction). (7) *The Case is Altered*, I. i. (8) Mayne's verses in *Jonsonius Virbius*. Cf. also the passage 'De Poetica' in *Discoveries*.

(*b*) *Contemporary allusions* (*in titles and by reference*). (1) Chapman's *Humorous Day's Mirth*, identified by Fleay (*Eng. Drama*, i. 55) with the *Comedy of Vmers* mentioned in Henslowe's Diary, May 11, 1597; printed 1599. (2) Dekker's *Satiromastix, or the Untrussing of the Humorous Poet* (1602). (3) John Day's *Humour out of Breath*, pr. 1608. Cf. also Fletcher's *Humorous Lieutenant* (acted 1619, pr. 1647) and Shirley's *Humorous Courtier* (pr. 1640). For the popular use, against which Jonson protests, cf. especially Shakespeare's *M.W.W.* i. Sc. 1 and 3.

(*c*) (1) Dryden's *Essay of Dramatic Poesy*, passim, especially the 'Examen of the *Silent Women*.' (2) William Cavendish's (Duke of Newcastle's) *The Humorous Lovers*, and *The Triumphant Widow, or the Medley of Humours*, both printed in 1677, but acted earlier. (3) Shadwell's *Sullen Lovers, or The Impertinents* (Preface), *The Humourists* (Preface and Epilogue), *The Virtuoso* (Epistle Dedicatory and Prologue)—all in vol. i of the 1720 edition. See also the 'Epilogue, spoken by one in deep mourning,' at the end of vol. iv of that edition. (4) Congreve's Letter to Dennis, 'Concerning Humour in Comedy,' July 10, 1695 (*Letters upon Several Occasions*, 1696, pp. 80–96; Dennis's *Select Works*, 1721, ii. pp. 514–25).

27. *I*, aye. Cf. p. 388, l. 38.

391. 11. *affects*, feelings, desires (cf. i. p. 392). Gifford reads *effects*.

12. *confluctions.* Text, *constructions.*

15. *cable hatband,* cord worn round the hat.

23-4. *mirror ... Stage.* Cf. p. 389, ll. 35-6, note.

392. 2. *intentiue,* intently directed, attentive.

11. *Furor Poeticus.* Cf. i. p. 72, l. 7; ii. p. 3, l. 27. Here, of course, the sense is somewhat quizzical. *Furor Poeticus* is introduced as a character in the second part of the *Returne from Parnassus,* Act i. Sc. vi.

19. *Vetus Comœdia.* Cf. ii. p. 34, l. 5.

24. *equall diuision ... into Acts ... Terentian manner,* &c. See Donatus, *De Tragoedia et Comoedia,* u.s.

27. *compasse of a daies efficiencie.* See note, i. p. 398.

39. *Susario,* &c. Cf. i. p. 81, l. 9 et seq. Gifford selects Athenaeus and Suidas, especially the former, as Jonson's quarries.

393. 25. *howe comes it then?* Gifford justly scoffs at Theobald's thinking this to be 'a flurt on Shakespeare.'

394. 11. *soule.* Gifford reads *muse.*

16. *dudgeon.* (Cf. note to i. p. 140, l. 32.) Gifford reads *desperate.*

21, 22. After Ovid, *Amor.* iii. 8. 3-4:—

'Ingenium quondam fuerat pretiosius auro:
   At nunc barbaries grandis, habere nihil.'

25. Caesar, earlier in the scene, speaks of Poetry—

'Of all the faculties on earth
The most abstract and perfect; if shee bee
True borne, and nurst with all the sciences.
Shee can so mould *Rome* and her monuments
Within the liquid marble of her lines,
That they shall stand fresh and miraculous,
Euen when they mixe with innouating dust;
In her sweet streames shall our braue *Roman* spirits
Chace, and swim after death, with their choise deeds
Shining on their white shoulders.'

395. 1. *distaste,* dislike.

2. *Peece,* piece.

4, &c. Gifford argues, very plausibly, that the 'Virgil' of the earlier paragraphs is here Shakespeare. Symonds takes the same view. 'I am persuaded,' Gifford adds, 'nothing but the ignorance of his numerous editors of the existence of such a passage has prevented its being taken for the motto to his works.' [*Like It*, iii. 3. 28.

17. *Materiall*, full of matter, full of good sense. Cf. *As You*

396. 6. *Impudence*, 15. *translating*, &c., quoted from Marston, whom Jonson had ridiculed. See note to p. 402, l. 34.

Demetrius is Dekker; Crispinus, Marston. Dekker replied in *Satiromastix* (1602). See Jonson's 'Dialogue' and 'To the Reader,' appended to the *Poetaster* (Ed. Gifford and Cunningham, i. pp. 262–70).

397. 3. *old Cato*, i.e. the author of the *Disticha* (see note to i. p. 158, l. 29).

8. *Shun Plautus*. Cf. i. p. 27.

15. *out-landish Termes*, &c. Cf. i, passim. See Introduction.

19. *Some Gallo-Belgick Phrase*. The *Mercurius Gallobelgicus* was an annual publication, in small octavo, giving accounts in Latin of recent affairs in Europe (Cologne 1588–1603, and thereafter Frankfurt). Cf. Jonson, *Epigrams*, xcii—

'They carry in their pockets Tacitus,
And the Gazetti, or Gallo-Belgicus.'

398. 29. *swadds*. Swad (lit. a peascod), a country lout or bumpkin. Cf. Greene: 'Let countrey swaines and silly swads be still' (*Perimedes*, quoted by Halliwell).

399. 3. *Veterem iubes*, &c. *Aen*. ii. 3.

11. *draughty*. See p. 400, l. 14, and note to i. p. 140, l. 20.

14. *O friends, no friends*: 'A parody on "O eyes, no eyes," *Span. Trag.*'—Malone's marginal note, quoted by Mr. Macray. See Kyd's *Spanish Tragedie*, iii. 2 (opening lines); also Tomkis's parody in *Albumazar* (1614), quoted in Mr. Boas's introduction to his edition of Kyd, pp. xcv–xcvi.

15. *bables*, baubles (see note to p. 331, l. 12). Mr. Macray follows the early prints, which read *babies*.

17. *Slymy rimes*. One of the early prints reads 'Flye my rimes.'

20. *petternels*, petronels, horse-pistols: in transferred sense, a braggart, as in the name 'Sir Petronel Flash.' See Halliwell.

demilances, short-shafted lances, or the horsemen carrying these: in transferred sense, a 'light horseman' or 'cavalier.'

Notes

28. *soure*, i.e. soar: not as in l. 25.

33. *flores-poetarum.* See supra, ii. p. 241, l. 21, note.

40. *Beluedere, or the Garden of the Muses*, of which John Bodenham has been credited with the editorship, appeared in 1600. It has been reprinted by the Spenser Society, 1875.

400. 4–5. The arrangement of these lines is from the Halliwell-Phillipps MS., as adopted by Mr. Macray.

7–8. Tibullus, i. 4. pp. 59–60. The motto on the title-page of *Belvedere* (u. s.).

13. *Antony*, presumably Anthony Munday, who may be the 'A. M.' of the prefatory sonnet to *Belvedere*. Mr. Macray proposes '[Bodenham],' but the reference to ballad-writing and the name 'Antony' point rather to Munday, the 'Antonio Balladino' of Jonson's *Case is Altered*.

14. *drafty.* See note to p. 399, l. 11.

The early prints read 'to thy praise are song'; but the line as given here, and first adopted by Mr. Macray, is supported by the line in the First Part of the *Returne* (v. 2 (l. 1534)), 'They maidens shall want sonnets at there pales,' and by that in Hall's *Satires* (iv. 6. 54), apropos of Elderton's drunken muse, 'Sung to the wheele and sung unto the payle.'

15. The sun and laurel constitute the device on the title-page of *Belvedere*.

401. 6. Mr. Macray reads *ere* for *care*, in the early prints.

10. *honours.* Mr. Macray reads *Homer's*, but the application of this epithet to Spenser is unusual. Ascham (see i. p. 30, l. 8, note) calls Chaucer (who is named in the next line) the 'English Homer.' Cf. Nash, supra, p. 240, l. 17.

18. *hony dropping.* Cf. note to p. 317, ll. 30-4.

34. *hot house*, brothel.

39. 'and a sooping,' in the early prints.

40. Henry Locke (?1553–?1608). See Grosart's *Miscellanies of the Fuller Worthies' Library*, vol. ii (1871), and *D.N.B.*

Robert Hudson. See *D.N.B.* and Montgomerie's *Poems*, ed. Cranstoun (S. T. S.), p. 337.

402. 6. *Monsier Kynsader.* Marston in his earliest work, *The Metamorphosis of Pigmalion's Image* (1598), gives the initials 'W. K.': in his second volume, *The Scourge of Villanie* (1598–

99), he adopts the full form 'William Kinsayder.' See *The Pilgrimage to Parnassus*, ii. 212. See supra, pp. 312, 320.

9, &c. I follow Mr. Macray's allocation of the speeches.

14. *Ram-ally*. A street of some disrepute, running from Fleet Street to the Temple. It gives the title to a comedy by Lodowick Barry (1611).

19. *I*, aye. See supra, p. 388, l. 38, note.

26, &c. Cf. ii. p. 324, l. 25, and note.

31. *driery*, dreary.

34. *by obseruation*, an echo of Jonson's dispute with Marston and Dekker. He had been characterized as 'a mere sponge, nothing but humours and observation.' See also note to ii. p. 396, l. 6.

41-2. The emendation of these lines is Mr. Macray's, from the evidence of the Halliwell-Phillipps MS. The early prints read 'who loves Adonis love or Lucre's rape.' Line 42 reads 'hart robbing life.'

403. 4. Thomas Churchyard's *Shore's Wife* appeared in 1563.

6. Mr. Macray (perhaps following the Halliwell-Phillipps MS.) reads '[one day]'. The text of the early prints is however quite clear. *Once*='one day' (see *N.E.D.* 'Once' 5); *I*=aye (see supra, p. 388, l. 38, note, and infra, l. 9).

8. The form 'Nashdo' in the early prints, which Mr. Macray notes and corrects to 'Nash,' is to be explained as the transfer of a syllable from 'stockado' in the next line, which is correspondingly imperfect.

9. *I*, aye. See note to p. 388, l. 38.

22-3. *tearmes to serue the tearme*. See note to ii. p. 328, ll. 6-7. One of the early prints reads *serue the turne*.

25. *beare*, in the early prints.

26. Cf. Livy, iv. 28.

28. *Danter*. See supra, ii. p. 279, l. 4, note.

34. *hard*, harsh, acid.

ADDITIONAL NOTES AND CORRECTIONS

Vol. I.

P. 106, ll. 6–7. These lines are parodied by Nash in *Strange Newes* (1592), D 3 (ed. McKerrow, i. p. 277).

Vol. II.

P. 233, l. 18 et seq. The verses from which these extracts are taken will be found at the beginning of Nash's *Pierce Penilesse his Supplication to the Diuell* (1592). Lines 32–33 are an adaptation by Harvey.

P. 239, l. 1. Read 'Heathenish.'

Nash's *Pierce Penilesse his Supplication to the Diuell*, also printed in 1592, contains a characteristic 'inuectiue against enemies of Poetrie.' See Mr. McKerrow's edition of the *Works*, i. pp. 192-5.

P. 241, l. 8 et seq. This paragraph follows the next ('As for *Flores Poetarum*') in the original.

P. 243, l. 3. For 'had' read 'hath.'
l. 8. Read 'haue I.'

P. 267, ll. 18–19 (and note, p. 437). These lines are the 'braue conclusion' to the 'Sonnetto' at the end of *Strange Newes* (ed. u. s., i. p. 334).

P. 272, l. 3. 'Ile' occurs frequently in the above 'Sonnetto,' and elsewhere in Nash.

P. 275, l. 33. *Pistlepragmos*. The reference is to *Strange Newes*, F 4^v (ed. u. s., i. p. 294).

P. 306, l. 7. 'preiudicate or castigatorie': apparently a favourite expression with Chapman. Cf. his Preface to *Andromeda Liberata*, 'To the preiudicate and peremptorie reader.'

P. 424 (note to 210. 23). Wingfield *or* Winkfield.

P. 426 (note to 227. 8). Cf., also from Nash—(*a*) 'his Cappe furd with cats skins, after the Muscouie fashion' (*Pierce Penilesse his Supplication to the Diuell*, B 1, ed. u. s., i. p. 166); (*b*) 'at no hand can I endure to haue my cheeks muffled vp in furre like a Muscouian' (*Strange Newes*: F 3, ib. p. 292).

P. 430 (note to 241. 9, &c.). A supplementary passage will be found on E 1, E 1^v (ed. u. s., i. pp. 281-2).

P. 436 (note to 260. 17). Perhaps referring also to Pomponazzi's *De Naturalium effectuum causis, sive de Incantationibus*, which appears to have been well known in England at this time.

INDEX

INDEX

'Abaser,' Figure of the, ii. 169, 171.
'Abode,' Figure of, ii. 170.
Absalon, i. 23, 24, 96, 354; ii. 271, 322. *See* Watson, Thomas.
Abstemio, Lorenzo, i. 95, 373.
'Abuse,' Figure of, ii. 169.
Abyndon, Henry, ii. 455.
Academy of Florence, i. 372.
Accent, Gascoigne on, i. 49; Stanyhurst on, i. 142 et seq.; Sidney on, i. 204 et seq.; Puttenham on, ii. 117 et seq. *See* Quantity, Verse.
Accius, i. 70, 298; ii. 316, 319.
Accolti Bernardo; *see* Aretino, Unico.
Accursius, ii. 269, 438.
Achaeus Erithrioeus, ii. 319.
Achilles Shield, Chapman's Dedication, &c. to, ii. 297-307.
Aconzio, Jacopo, ii. 257, 435.
Action, Unity of; *see* Unities.
Acutius, i. 82, 370.
'Acyron,' Figure of, ii. 171.
'Addubitation,' Figure of, ii. 304.
Adelphi, The, i. 28.
'Admiration,' p. lxxxiv; i. 392-3.
'Admittance,' Figure of, ii. 170.
Adrian; *see* Hadrian.
Advertisement for Pap-Hatchet and Martin Mar-Prelate, An, ii. 268 et seq.
Aelian, ii. 422.
Aeneas Sylvius Piccolomini, ii. 369, 459.
Aeneid, Stanyhurst's translation of, i. 135 et seq.; Surrey's, ii. 315. *See* Virgil.

Aeschines, ii. 247.
Aeschylus, i. 236, 295; ii. 315, 319.
Aesop, i. 63, 130, 167, 185, 192, 310, 312, 333, 425; ii. 224, 227.
Affranius, i. 299.
'Agnition,' p. lxxxiv; ii. 425.
'Agnomination,' ii. 445.
Agricola, Rodolph, ii. 236, 429.
Agrippa, H. Cornelius, pp. xxvii, lxxix; i. 182, 393; ii. 199, 200, 246, 257, 259, 281, 423, 433, 435.
Alamanni, Luigi, p. lxxxi.
Alarum against Usurers, An, i. 364, 371.
Albertus Magnus, ii. 269, 273, 438, 439.
Albinus, i. 154, 385.
Albions England, i. 320, 428; ii. 317, 449. *See* Warner, W.
Alcaeus, i. 129.
Alciati, Andrea, ii. 323, 453.
Alcilia, ii. 451.
Aldhelmus Durotelmus; *see* Ealdhelm.
Alexander, i. 64; ii. 17, 182, 203, 230, 253, &c.; his 'scar,' i. 76, 368.
Alexander Aetolus, ii. 319.
Alexander Aphrodisiensis, ii. 20.
Alexander (Pope), ii. 16.
Alexandrine Verse, p. lxxxix; i. 208; ii. 44, 75, 415.
Alexis Terius, ii. 320.
Allde, Edward, ii. 442.
Allegoria, ii. 160, 169, 184, 202, &c.
Allegory, Doctrine of, p. xxiv.
'Alliteration,' ii. 445.

Almanzor, ii. 23.
'Almond leape' verse, ii. 226, 426.
'Alopantius Ausimarchides,' ii. 257.
Alphonso V of Aragon, i. 163, 389; ii. 23, 410.
Amadis, i. 173; ii. 308.
'Ambage,' Figure of, ii. 169.
'Ambiguous,' Figure of the, ii. 171.
Ambrose, S., i. 71, 367.
American, the, ii. 10.
Aminta, Tasso's, ii. 441.
Amipsias Atheniensis, ii. 320.
'Amphibologia,' ii. 171.
Amphion, i. 151, 158, 234, 297; ii. 6, 10.
Amyntae Gaudia, ii. 321, 451, 452. See Watson, Thomas.
Amyntas, i. 316, 427; ii. 452. See Watson, Thomas.
Amyntas, King of Macedonia, ii. 17.
Amyot, Jacques, ii. 276, 440.
'Anachinosis,' ii. 170.
Anacreon, ii. 26, 105, 171, 319, 324.
Anacreon's Egg; *see* Figured Verses.
Anacreontic Verse, ii. 349 et seq.
Anacrisis, by Earl of Stirling, p. vi.
'Anadiplosis,' ii. 169, 304, 420.
Anagram, p. xxx; i. 375; ii. 1, 105 et seq., 112 et seq., 417.
Analogia, ii. 162, 174, 419.
Anapaest, i. 24, 96, &c.
'Anaphora,' ii. 169, 304, 305, 420.
Anatomie of Absurditie, Nash's, i. 321–37, 428–30; ii. 426.
Anatomie of Abuses, i. 63, 428, 429; ii. 441.
Anaxandrides Rhodius, ii. 320.
Ancontius (ii. 257) = Acontius. See Aconzio.
Andrewes, Lancelot, ii. 281, 443.
Andronicus, i. 152.
Angelio Pietro da Barga (Bargaeus), i. 349.

Angellius, Nic., i. 299, 416.
Anglo-Saxon Language, ii. 149, 419. See 'Saxon English.'
Anglofrancitali, i. 107.
Anglorum Proelia, i. 239; and note.
Aniceris, story of, ii. 192, 422.
Anne of Brittany, ii. 21.
'Antanaclasis,' ii. 170.
'Antenagoge,' ii. 170.
'Anthropopathis,' ii. 410.
Antigone, i. 427; ii. 322, 452. See Watson, Thomas.
Antimenides, ii. 18, 409.
'Antimetavole,' ii. 170.
Antipater Sidonius, ii. 322, 323.
'Antiphrasis,' ii. 169.
'Antipophora,' ii. 169.
Anti-Stage Pamphlets, i. 61 et seq.
'Antistrophe,' ii. 169.
'Antitheton,' ii. 170.
Antoninus, Marcus, i. 35; ii. 253, 255.
Antonius, tragedy of, ii. 283, 444.
'Antonomasia,' ii. 169.
Antony, i. 8–11, 39.
Apelles, i. 45, 63, 210, 326, 363, 368, 404; ii. 267, 268.
Apollodorus Tarsensis, ii. 319, 322.
Apollonius, ii. 237.
Apollonius, Alabandensis, i. 328, 430.
Apologie of Poetrie, A Briefe, by Harington, ii. 194–222, 310, 422–5. See Harington.
Apologie for Poetrie, An [*The Defence of Poesie*], pp. xi, xxi, lii, lxxiii, xci; i. 62, 63, 148–207, 360, 361, 382–403; ii. 196, 310, 314, 326. See Sidney.
Apology of Sundry proceedings . . . , ii. 281.
'Apology' and 'Defence,' On titles, p. xiv; 148–9.
Apophoreta, ii. 60.

Apophthegmata, Erasmus's, i. 17.
'Aporia,' ii. 170.
'Aposiopesis,' ii. 168, 304.
'Apostrophe,' ii. 170, 304.
Apuleius, i. 199, 429; ii. 281.
'young,' ii. 250.
Aquilius, ii. 322.
Aquinas. *See* Thomas quinas.
Aratus, i. 71, 367; ii. 46, 322, 411.
Araygnement of Paris, Peele's, i. 319, 428.
Arcadia, Sannazzaro's, i. 391.
    Sidney's, i. 148, 303, 362, 383, 392, 397, 402, 422; ii. 231, 263, 264, 282, 316, 437, 449.
Arcadian Rhetorike, The, i. 303-6, 422. *See* Fraunce.
Archaism, p. lv et seq.; i. 41, 52-3, 128 et seq., 196, &c.; ii. 86, 151, 397.
Archesilaus Prytanœus, ii. 324.
Archilocus, i. 298, 341, 342; ii. 229, 320.
Archimedes, ii. 237.
Archippus Atheniensis, ii. 320.
Archytas, ii. 237.
'Areopagus,' The, p. xlvi; i. 89, 94, 126, 372.
Areopagites (*general term*), ii. 160.
Arete, ii. 316.
'Aretine,' English, p. lxxxi (note).
'Aretinise,' ii. 261.
'Aretinish,' ii. 234, 429.
Aretino, Leonardo (Leonardo Bruni, aretino), ii. 369, 459.
    Pietro, i. 106, 114, 116; ii. 229, 234, 252, 259, 260, 402, 459.
    Unico (Accolti, Bernardo), i. 125, 379; ii. 459.
'Areytos,' i. 153, 384.
Ariosto, pp. xviii, xxix, xlv, lxi, lxvii, lxxvii, lxxxi; i. 33, 115, 116, 309, 318, 349, 356, 359, 386, 427, 429; ii. 62, 194-222 (passim), 231, 283, 310, 319, 322, 422-5, 428.

Aristonicus, ii. 298, 445.
Aristonymus, ii. 320.
Aristophanes, i. 23, 29, 81, 116, 236, 295; ii. 27, 154, 229, 315, 320, 393.
Aristotle, pp. xvi, xxiii, xxviii, xliii, xlv, lxxi, lxxiii, lxxiv, lxxv, lxxxiv; i. 7, 11, 13, 18, 19, 20, 21, 23, 24, 25, 33, 40, 72, 73, 83, 103, 158, 167, 171, 173, 189, 192, 197, 200, 206, 231, 233, 235, 236, 248, 292, 300, 301, 314, 333, 337, 343, 348, 349, 353, 354, 355, 357, 359, 386, 387, 388, 390, 392, 398, 399, 400, 402, 409; ii. 18, 39, 200, 203, 215, 216, 220, 245, 246, 247, 322, 323, 332, 360, 362, 411, 415, 419, 420, 431-2, 458. *See Poetics.*
arkitecktonike (ἀρχιτεκτονική), i. 161, 388.
Armin, Robert, ii. 279, 441.
ἁρμοστόν, τό, i. 292.
Arms and learning, p. lxxxvi; i. 395.
Ars Musica [= Poetry], i. 230; ii. 329.
Ars Poetica, Horace's, pp. lxxv, lxxxi, quoted passim: text of Fabricius's *Catholica*, i. 417-21. *See* Horace.
Arte of English Poesie, Puttenham's, ii. 1-193, 407-22; referred to by Harington, ii. 196. *See* Puttenham.
Arte of Logique (*Rule of Reason*), Wilson's, i. 422.
Arte of Rhetorique, Wilson's, p. xci; i. 383; ii. 288, 444.
Arte Poetica, Minturno's, p. lxxxiii et seq.
Arthington, ii. 239, 429.
Arthur, King, i. 4, 188, 323; ii. 44, 308.
Arthur of Little Britain, i. 323.
Artis Penus Historicae (1579), p. xxviii.

Index

Ascham (Askam), Roger, pp. vi, xiii, xviii, xix, xxi, xxxi, xxxii, xxxv, xxxviii, xli, xlii, xliii, l, lvii, lxiii, lxix, lxxiii, lxxiv, lxxvi, lxxx, lxxxi, lxxxvii, lxxxix, xci; 'Of Imitation,' i. 1–45; on rhyme, i. 29 et seq.; i. 89, 96, 101, 118, 120, 137, 240, 313, 337, 347–58, 360, 378, 381, 400, 407, 414, 415, 426, 429, 430; ii. 249, 258, 261, 273, 274, 277, 282, 293, 408, 420, 421, 432, 433, 437, 439, 446, 452, 455. *See Scholemaster, Toxophilus.*

'Asteismus,' ii. 169.

Asteley, John, ii. 263, 437.

Astrophel, Roydon's, i. 319.

Astrophel and Stella, Sidney's, p. xci; i. 148, 360, 362, 383, 393, 400, 402, 423; Nash's *Preface* to, ii. 223–8, 425–7.

Astydamas Atheniensis, ii. 319.

'Asyndeton,' ii. 168.

Atchelow, Thomas, i. 319, 428; ii. 319.

Athanasius, S., i. 343.

Athenaeus, ii. 463.

Atilius, i. 237; ii. 316, 319.

Atlantic Island, i. 152, 331.

Atticism, ii. 276.

Atticus, i. 44; *Epist. ad Att.*, i. 11.

'Attribution,' Figure of, ii. 169.

Augustine, S., p. xv; i. 39, 70, 328, 343; ii. 247.

Augustus, i. 8, 26, 76, 263; ii. 17, 18, 57, 211, 230, 253, 322, 326, 424.

Auricular Figures, ii. 166 et seq.

Ausonius, i. 239; ii. 315, 317, 322.

autharcos, ii. 30, 410.

'Auxesis,' ii. 170.

'Avancer,' Figure of the, ii. 170.

Avicenna, ii. 22, 410.

Avienus, ii. 411.

Bacon, Francis, pp. vi, liv.
  Sir Nicolas, ii. 144, 145, 419.
  Roger, ii. 237, 370, 429, 460.

Baeda (Bede), i. 367; ii. 369–70.

Baïf, Jean Antoine de, i. 372.

Bajazeth, ii. 369.

Baker, Matthew, ii. 279.

'balductum'; *see* i. 374, and ii. 431.

Balduin, François, ii. 24, 433.

Baldwin, William, i. 397.

Bale's *Catalogue*, ii. 459.

Ballade defined, i. 54–5.

Ballade-royal, i. 406; ballat royal, i. 222.

Bancroft, Richard, ii. 248, 434.

Bankside, The, ii. 323.

Barbarism, p. xxxiii; ii. 278, 394, 463, &c.

'Barbarismus,' Figure of, ii. 171.

Barbaro, Ermolao, ii. 369, 459.

Bards, The, i. 153; ii. 360.

Bargaeus; *see* Angelio Pietro da Barga.

Barnes, Barnabe, ii. 457.

Barnfield, Richard, ii. 321, 418, 449, 452.

Barrons Wars, Drayton's, ii. 316, 449.

Barry, Lodowick, ii. 466.

Bartholus de Saxoferrato, ii. 269, 372, 438.

Basia. See Joannes Secundus.

Bastard, Thomas, ii. 321, 452.

Batrachomyomachia, ii. 155.

Battle of Otterbourne, i. 393.

Beard, Thomas, ii. 454.

Beatrice, Dante's, i. 206. *See* Dante.

beau semblant, ii. 165, 420.

Bebel, Heinrich (Bebelius), ii. 273, 439.

Bede; *see* Baeda.

Bell, Adam, ii. 87.

Bellarmine, ii. 248, 433.

Bellum Grammaticale, ii. 210, 424.

Belvedere, or the Garden of the Muses, ii. 399–400, 403, 465.
Bembo, Pietro, p. lvi; i. 13, 116, 193, 206, 352, 377, 379, 396, 402; ii. 276, 322.
Bengalasso [? Galazzo], i. 376.
'Benivolo,' Signor, i. 123.
Bernard, S., ii. 247.
Berners, Lord, ii. 440.
Beroaldo, Filippo, i. 71, 366–7.
Bessarion (Cardinal), ii. 369, 459.
Bevis of Hampton, i. 329; ii. 44, 87, 308, 446.
Beza, i. 193, 427; ii. 248, 322.
Bibiena (Cardinal), i. 116, 125, 193, 377, 396; ii. 322.
Bible, The, i. 18, 158. See *Psalms, Song of Solomon*, &c.
Bilchaunger, George, i. 104.
Biondo, Flavio (Blondus), ii. 369, 459.
Bird, Christopher, ii. 229, 243, 431.
'Bitter Taunt,' Figure of the, ii. 169.
Bizarro, Pietro, ii. 263, 437.
Black Knight, The, ii. 308.
Blancherdine, ii. 308.
Blank Verse, p. xlix; ii. 454.
Blenerhasset, Thomas, pp. l, lxiii; i. 355.
Blondus; see Biondo.
Blount, Edward, bookseller, ii. 356.
Thomas Pope, ii. 411.
Blundevil, Thomas, ii. 263, 437.
Boccaccio, pp. xxii, xxvii, lxxviii–lxxix; i. 132, 152, 402; ii. 319, 369.
Bodenham, John, ii. 308, 465.
Bodine, Jean, ii. 281, 442.
Boethius (*De Consolatione*), i. 68, 173, 175, 239, 366, 391; ii. 449.
Boileau, i. 362, 392.
Bolton, Edmund, p. vi; ii. 402.
'Bomphiologia,' ii. 171.

Booke of Ayres, A, ii. 454.
Borough, William, ii. 262, 436.
Boscan, i. 303, 305.
Bossu, Le, p. xlvi.
Bostius, ii. 460.
Botifaunt, Edmund, printer, i. 226.
Bourne, William, ii. 273, 279, 439, 441.
'Brachiologia,' ii. 170.
Bracton, Henry de, ii. 370, 460.
'Brauerie' in Elocution, ii. 304.
Breton (Britton), Nicholas, i. 395, 408; ii. 63, 319, 321, 414, 418, 435.
Bridewell, i. 28, 328.
βριταννικὴν ζηλοτυπίαν, i. 124.
Britton; see Breton.
Brixius, Germanus, ii. 315, 448.
'Broad Floute,' Figure of the, ii. 169.
'brokin or cuttit verse,' i. 225.
Browne, Sir Thomas, ii. 411.
Brownswerd (Brunswerd), John, ii. 315, 448.
Bruni, Leonardo; see Aretino, Leonardo.
Brutus, i. 13, 45, 163.
Brutus, Cicero's, i. 28, 35.
Bryan (Brian), Sir Francis, ii. 321, 440, 451.
Bryskett, Ludovick, i. 306.
'Bubonax,' i. 207, 403.
Bucer, *De honestis ludis*, ii. 425.
Buchanan, George, pp. xi, xxx; i. 24, 194, 354, 365, 366, 378, 395, 397, 400, 404; ii. 234, 322.
Buchler, Johan, ii. 409.
? Bucke, G., i. 412.
Buckhurst, Lord; see Sackville, Thomas.
Bucolica, Virgil's, i. 9; ii. 155, 156.
Budé, Guillaume (Budaeus), i. 13, 349, 351; ii. 154.
Bugiale, ii. 272, 438–9.

Bull, the hangman, ii. 244.
'bumme carde,' ii. 439.
Burghley, Lord Treasurer, ii. 1, 144.
Butler, William, ii. 240, 430.
Bynneman, H., printer, i. 87, 135.

'Cabalists,' the, ii. 123.
'Cacemphaton,' ii. 171.
'Cacosintheton,' ii. 171.
'Cacozelia,' ii. 171.
Cadence, i. 401; ii. 83 et seq., 415.
Caecilius Statius, i. 29, 82, 237, 299, 370; ii. 393.
Caesar, Julius, i. 8; *Commentaries*, 25, 36, 38, 40, 41; Ascham's criticism of, 44–45, 170; ii. 18, 22, 23, 154, 277.
Caesura, p. lxxxix; i. 54, 205, 361, 402; ii. 74, 75, 76, 77 et seq., 414.
'Calamunco,' ii. 439.
'Calepine,' ii. 257, 436.
Calidius, i. 13.
Calixtus (Pope), ii. 15.
Callias Atheniensis, ii. 320.
Callimachus, ii. 26, 43, 319, 397, 411.
Callisthenes, i. 189.
Calphurnius, Titus Julius, i. 262, 413.
Calvin, i. 427; ii. 248, 433, 442.
Calvus, i. 13, 299.
Cambridge, Ascham on, i. 21, 311. *See* John's, St., Pembroke Hall, Trinity.
Camden, William, ii. 285, 402, 444–5, 460.
Camerarius, Joachimus, i. 13, 350, 351.
Camoens, i. 387.
Campano, Giovannantonio (Campanus), p. xxiv; i. 65, 327, 364, 429.
Campion, Thomas, pp. xi, xxxix, xlv, xlvii, xlviii, xlix, liii, lxiv; ii. 315, 415, 448, 457, 458, 460; *Observations in the Art of English Poesie*, 327–55, 454–7; answered by Daniel, 356–84.
'Cantabanqui,' ii. 416.
Canterbury Tales, The, i. 56; ii. 64, 89. 'A Cantorburye tale,' i. 137. *See* Chaucer.
Canticles. *See* Song of Solomon; Markham, Gervase.
Canzoni, Petrarch's, ii. 90, 92.
Caracalla (Emperor), ii. 421.
Cardan, Jerome, ii. 237, 246, 257, 429, 433.
Cards, The Play of the, ii. 424.
Carew, Richard, *The Excellency of the English Tongue*, pp. lvi, lxxxviii; ii. 285–94, 407, 444–5.
Carmina prouerbialia, ii. 331, 361, 455, 458.
Carpentarius, Jacobus, ii. 245, 432.
Carre, Nicholas, i. 316, 427; ii. 315.
Cartwright, Thomas, ii. 238, 280, 429, 441.
Case, John, ii. 323, 453.
Cassiodorus, i. 71, 366, 367.
Castelvetro, Lodovico, pp. lxxviii, lxxix, lxxxii; i. 388, 398, 399.
Castiglione, Baldassare, p. lxxxi; i. 376, 383, 431; ii. 263.
Castle of Fame, The, ii. 309.
'Catachresis,' ii. 169.
Catalectic verse, ii. 134 et seq.
Catilins Conspiracies, Gosson's, i. 369.
Cato, the Elder, i. 27, 38, 41, 73; ii. 311, 397.
— the Younger (Uticensis), i. 170, 189.
— Dionysius (author of the *Disticha*), i. 65, 158, 183, 387; ii. 361, 464.
'Cato,' a, i. 113.

Catullus, Q. Valerius, i. 14, 36, 238, 252, 299, 348; ii. 18, 26, 55, 116, 293, 316, 319, 321, 338, 410, 461.
Catulus, i. 11.
Cavendish, William (D. of Newcastle), ii. 462.
Celestina, ii. 309.
Celiano, Livio, p. lxxxii; i. 318, 428; ii. 319.
? Cellarius, i. 70, 366.
Celsus, i. 297.
Certaine Satyrs, ii. 312, 320.
Certayne Notes of Instruction, Gascoigne's, i. 46-57, 358-62, 403, 404, 405, 406, 407, 414. *See* Gascoigne.
Cervantes, i. 369, 399.
Chaderton, Laurence, ii. 281, 443.
William, ii. 281, 442.
Chaloner, Sir Thomas, the Elder, i. 397; ii. 65, 321, 414, 452.
'Changeling,' Figure of the, ii. 168.
'Chant-royal,' i. 406.
Chapelain, Jean, i. 398, 399.
Chapman, George, pp. xxii, xxiv, xxx (note), xxxix, liv, lix, lxv, lxvi, lxxi, lxxvii, lxxxv; Preface to *Seaven Bookes of the Iliades*, ii. 295-7; Dedication of *Achilles Shield*, &c., ii. 297-307, 315, 318, 319, 320, 323, 445-6, 450, 462.
charientes, ii. 150, 419.
'Charientismus,' ii. 169.
Charles the Bald, ii. 15.
Charlewood, John, printer, i. 226, 321.
Chartier, Alain, ii. 21, 326, 410.
Chaucer, pp. xvi, xviii, xlvii, lviii; i. 30, 31, 33, 47, 50, 56, 69, 127, 152, 166, 183, 196, 241, 263, 318, 355, 359, 380, 390, 394, 405, 406, 410; ii. 17, 62, 64, 68, 79, 89, 92, 93, 150, 215, 230, 240, 242, 293, 305, 314, 326, 401, 414, 465.

Cheke, Sir John, pp. xxxv, xxxviii, xlviii, lvii, lxvi, lxxiii, lxxvi; i. 9, 18, 21, 23, 26, 29, 40-4, 313, 350, 354, 357, 358, 426; ii. 249, 273, 277, 282, 293, 434, 439.
Chettle, Henry, i. 371; ii. 320, 454.
Chevy Chase, i. 393.
Chiliades, Erasmus's, i. 17, 353.
China, ii. 368.
Chionides, ii. 392.
Choerillus, i. 334, 430; ii. 17, 409.
'Chore,' i. 286.
Choreus *or* Trochaeus, i. 415.
Chorus, on the, ii. 392, 393, 462.
Christopherson, John, i. 354.
Christus, The, p. xxx; i. 366.
Chrysolaras, Emanuel, ii. 369, 459.
Chrysostom, p. xv.
Church, Master, i. 374.
Churchyard, Thomas, i. 125, 242, 379, 410, 411; ii. 280, 321, 403, 466.
Cicero, pp. xxi, lxxv, lxxvi; i. 7-45 passim, 69, 70, 75, 77, 79, 84, 129, 143, 160, 165, 170, 179, 202, 231, 233, 235, 256, 278, 283, 293, 299, 308, 309, 315, 328, 347-51 passim, 355-8 passim, 366, 369, 370, 374, 382, 388, 389, 390, 391, 393, 394, 398, 401, 402, 403, 405, 408, 409, 415, 416, 427, 429; ii. 29, 34, 154, 163, 197, 229, 231, 238, 277, 290, 291, 293, 313, 315, 323, 324, 330, 411, 432, 433, 455; wrongly referred to by Lodge, i. 81.
Ciceronians, the, i. 36; ii. 251, 371, 434.
Ciceronianus, Harvey's, i. 377; ii. 433, &c.
Cinna, C. Helvius, i. 299.
Cintio, Giraldi, pp. lxxviii, lxxix, lxxxii; i. 362, 390, 398; ii. 458.
Cinzio, ii. 272, 439.

Cipselus, i. 170.
Ciriologia, ii. 162, 420.
Civile Wars, Daniel's, ii. 316, 448.
'Civil Jest,' Figure of the, ii. 169.
Clare, Dr., ii. 273, 439.
Clarke, Bartholomew, ii. 219, 425.
    Sampson, bookseller, i. 307.
    See also Clerke.
Classical measures, Webbe on, i. 280; Puttenham on, ii. 124 et seq. *See* Hexameter, Quantity, Verse.
'Classical' purpose of Elizabethan criticism, p. xxxi et seq.
Classical tradition in Elizabethan criticism, p. lxxi et seq.
Claudian, i. 70, 239; ii. 315.
Clauser, Conrad, i. 206, 402–3.
Cleanthes, i. 396.
Clemens Alexandrinus, i. 347.
Clerke, William (*Polimanteia*), ii. 436.
'Climax,' Figure of, ii. 170.
Clodius Sabinus, ii. 229, 320.
'Close Conceit,' Figure of, ii. 170.
'Clown,' *Indecorum* of the, i. 59, 400.
Clymme of the Clough, ii. 87.
Cnoeus Getulicus, ii. 321.
Cobler of Canterburie, The, i. 378.
'Cockpit of learning,' i. 16, 352–3.
Coignet, Matthieu, *Instruction aux Princes*, translated by E. Hoby, i. 341–4.
Cole, Humphrey, ii. 279, 441.
Colin Clout, Spenser's, i. 428.
'colours,' i. 212, 213, 224, 405.
Columbus, ii. 246.
Combe, Thomas, ii. 323, 453.
Comedie of Captain Mario, Gosson's, i. 369.
Comedy, pp. xxx, xli; Whetstone on, i. 59; Lodge on, i. 80–1; Sidney on, i. 176 et seq., 391–2; Webbe on, i. 248 et seq.; Puttenham on, ii. 27, 33 et seq.; Harington on, ii. 209; Jonson on, ii. 392; Horace on, i. 293.
    The Laws of, ii, 392–3; Persons of, ii. 389; Iambic verse for, ii. 338; Shakespeare's the most excellent in English, ii. 318; Meres's list of writers of, ii. 320.
    The 'Old,' ii. 34, 392, 463; Greek, i. 236 et seq. *Also see* i. 23; ii. 210, 462.
Comedy of Errors, Shakespeare's, ii. 318.
comelynesse, ii. 174. *See* Decorum.
Commines, Philippe de, i. 376; ii. 263.
'Common' verse, i. 223, 407.
'Commoratio,' Figure of, ii. 170.
'Communication,' Figure of, ii. 304.
Comparative Discourse on our English Poets, A, ii. 314–24. *See* Meres.
Comparative Method, The, p. lxviii.
'Comparisons,' i. 219.
Complaint of Rosamund, Daniel's, ii. 316, 448.
Complaints, Spenser's, i. 372, 374; ii. 435.
Complaynt of Scotlande, i. 406, 429.
Compound words, i. 402.
Congreve, ii. 462.
'Congruity' in Elocution, i. 304.
'Conny-catcher,' ii. 434.
'Consenting Close,' Figure of the, ii. 170.
Constable, Henry, i. 149; ii. 400, 401.
convenientia, i. 292.
Cooper, Thomas, ii. 281, 443.
'Coople Clause,' Figure of the, ii. 168.
Copernicus, Nicolas, ii. 246, 433.
Coppinger, Edmund, ii. 239, 429.
Corneille, i. 398, 392.
Cornelius Gallus, ii. 326.

Cornificius, Quintus, ii. 321.
Cornish language, ii. 149.
Cornutus, Annaeus, i. 206, 403.
Cortese, Paolo (Cortesius), i. 13, 352.
Cortez, Martin, ii. 262.
Cosin *or* Cosins, Richard, ii. 429, 442.
'Counterfait Action,' Figure of, ii. 170.
'Counterfait Countenance,' Figure of, ii. 170.
'Counterfait in Personation,' Figure of, ii. 170.
'Counterfait Place,' Figure of, ii. 170.
'Counterfait Representation,' Figure of, ii. 170.
'Counterfait Time,' Figure of, ii. 170.
'Counter-change,' Figure of, ii. 170.
'Counter turne,' Figure of the, ii. 169.
Courtesy, Books of, p. lxxxi; i. 376.
Courtier, The (transl. by Clarke), ii. 219, 425.
    (transl. by Hoby), i. 357, 376, 431; ii. 263, 437.
Court of Cupide, Spenser's, i. 133, 246, 381.
Coxe, Leonard, pp. vi, xci (note).
Crassus, L., i. 11, 35.
Cratinus, i. 81, 236, 295, 370, 409; ii. 392.
Crispin, i. 126.
'Critical Temper' of the Elizabethan age, p. lxvi et seq.
Criticism, as a separate literary 'kind,' pp. xii, lxvi. *See* Classical, Elizabethan, Sources, &c.
'Cronographia,' ii. 170.
'Cross-couple,' Figure of the, ii. 170.
'Cuckowspell,' Figure of, ii. 169.

Cuiacius, Jacobus, ii. 246, 433, 444.
'Curiosity,' Daniel on, ii. 365.
'Curious,' Figure of the, ii. 171.
'Curry fauell,' Figure of the, ii. 169.
Curteys, Richard, ii. 281, 442.
'Custom,' On, i. 53, 99, 117; Daniel on, ii. 359.
'Cutted Comma,' Figure of the, ii. 170.
'Cylinder,' The, ii. 96, 100–1.
Cyprian, p. xv.
Cyrus, i. 157.

Dactyl, i. 30, 305; ii. 129 et seq., 131, 333.
Damascene, i. 343.
Dampetrus, Joannes, ii. 326, 454.
Danes, the, i. 153; ii. 361.
Danett, Thomas, i. 376; ii. 437.
Daniel, Samuel, pp. vi, vii, xiii, xxxiii, xl, xlvii, xlviii, xlix, liv, lvii, lix, lxi, lxii, lxiii, lxiv, lxv, lxviii, lxix, lxx, lxxiv, lxxx, lxxxii; *A Defence of Ryme*, ii. 356–84, 457–61; i. 356, 377, 386, 395, 402; ii. 234, 280, 293, 315, 316, 318, 319, 321, 400, 401, 417, 426, 444, 448. *See Delia, Complaint of Rosamond, Civile Wars, Musophilus, Defence of Ryme.*
Daniel (prophet), ii. 198.
Daniello, Bern., pp. lxxxi, lxxxiv; i. 383, 389, 390.
Dante, p. lxxxvii (note); i. 152, 169, 206; ii. 62, 212, 265, 319, 424.
Danter, John, ii. 403, 440, 466.
Darcy, Brian, ii. 273, 439.
Dares Phrygius, ii. 168; ii. 460.
Darrell, i. 245. *See* note i. 412.
Dati, Carlo, i. 363.
    Leonardo, i. 356.
D'Aubignac, l'Abbé, *Pratique du Théâtre*, i. 362, 400.

Davies, Sir John, ii. 293, 321, 400, 401, 452.
Day, John, playwright, ii. 462.
Daye, John, printer, i. 1.
De Antiquitatibus Romanorum, i. 39.
De Apparatu Linguae Lat., by B. Riccius Ferrariensis, i. 14.
De Bello Troiano, Joseph of Exeter's, ii. 370.
Deborah, Songs of, ii. 207.
'Decencie,' ii. 174, 175. *See Decorum.*
De Ciuitate Dei, St. Augustine's, i. 39, 328.
Declamatio, i. 5.
Decorum, pp. xli et seq., xlvii, lxxix; i. 19, 23, 48, 58, 59, 60, 128, 137, 197-9, 263, 294, 363; ii. 155, 157, 161, 173 et seq., 177, 419, 421.
De Decoro, by Puttenham, ii. 181.
Dee, John, ii. 280, 441.
'Default,' Figure of, ii. 167.
'Defence' and 'Apology' in titles, i. 148-9.
Defence of Poesie, The, by Sidney. See *Apologie for Poetrie, An.*
Defence of Poetry, A, by Lodge, i. 61-86, 363-71.
Defence of Ryme, A, by Daniel, ii. 356-84, 457-61.
'Definer by Difference,' Figure of the, ii. 170.
De Incendio Troiae, Lucan's, ii. 319.
Dekker, Thomas, i. 407, 424, 428; ii. 319, 412, 462, 464, 466.
de la Noue, 'Lord,' ii. 308, 446.
de la Primaudaye, Pierre, i. 363.
de la Ramée, Pierre (Petrus Ramus), i. 309, 334, 423; ii. 236, 245, 246, 429, 432.
de la Taille, Jean, p. lxxxviii; i. 398.
de l'Hôpital, Michel, i. 194, 397.

Delia, Daniel's, ii. 316, 448.
De Lingua Latina et Analogia, Varro's, i. 37.
della Casa, Giovanni, p. lxxxi; i. 376.
della Mirandola, G. Pico, i. 13, 352; ii. 369, 459.
Delone *or* Deloney, Thomas, ii. 279, 440.
Delphrigus, i. 319.
Demetrius Phalareus, *De Elocutione*, p. lxxiv; i. 349, 409; ii. 420.
Democritus, i. 67.
Demonides, ii. 312.
Démonomanie des Sorciers, De la, ii. 442. *See* Bodine.
Demosthenes, i. 8, 9, 15, 16, 18, 19, 20, 25, 45, 79, 202, 256, 347, 348; ii. 204, 238, 247, 250, 277, 293.
Denham, Henry, *A Second and Third Blast*, i. 62, 425.
Dennis, John, ii. 462.
De Nobilitate Literata, by Sturm, i. 13.
De Oratore, Cicero's, i. 11, 13, 299.
De Poeta, Minturno's, p. lxxxiii et seq.
De Ratione studii, Varro's, i. 38.
Dering, Edward, ii. 281, 443.
Deschamps, Eustache, p. lxxxvii.
Destruction of Jerusalem, Legge's, ii. 320, 450.
De Tragoedia &c., by Donatus (q.v.), i. 366, 369.
De vanitate et incertitudine scientiarum, i. 393. *See* Agrippa.
'Device,' Puttenham on, ii. 1, 105 et seq.
Dialect, Carew on, ii. 292; Jonson on, ii. 397. *See* Archaism, Vocabulary.
'Dialisis,' ii. 170.
Diall of Princes, ii. 440.
Dialoghi piacevoli, Guazzo's, i. 376, 395.

Index

'Dialogismus,' Figure of, ii. 170.
'Dichologia,' ii. 170.
'Diction,' p. lv et seq.; Sidney on, i. 201. *See* Vocabulary, Archaism, &c.
Dictionaries, English, ii. 151.
'Dictionary method,' i. 401.
Digges, Thomas, ii. 262, 280, 437, 441.
Dimeter verse, ii. 338 et seq., 377.
Dinocrates, ii. 182.
Diogenes Laertius, i. 20 (but *see* i. 353); ii. 324.
Dionysius of Halicarnassus, p. lxxiv; i. 13, 19, 20, 39, 349; ii. 419, 420.
Dionysius, the tyrant, i. 170.
'Director,' Figure of the, ii. 170.
'Disabler,' Figure of the, ii. 169, 170.
Discourse of Civill Life, Bryskett's, i. 306.
Discourse of English Poetrie, by W. Webbe, i. 226-302, 407-16.
Discourse of Life and Death, ii. 283, 444.
'Disdainefull,' Figure of the, ii. 170.
'Dismembrer,' Figure of the, ii. 170.
Disticha de moribus, i. 387. *See* Cato.
'Distributor,' Figure of the, ii. 170.
Ditties, Campion on, ii. 346 et seq.; Daniel on rhyme for, ii. 383.
'Dizain,' the, i. 55, 57.
'Doa, Ioannes,' i. 382, 394.
Donati, Edouardo, i. 46.
Donatus, Aelius, pp. lxxvi, lxxxv; i. 80, 366, 369, 371, 413; ii. 412, 463.
D'Ossat, Cardinal Arnaud (Ossatus), ii. 245, 432.
'Doubler,' Figure of the, ii. 169.
'Double Supply,' Figure of, ii. 167.
'Doubtfull,' Figure of the, ii. 170.
Dove, John, ii. 281, 443.
Drake, Sir Francis, ii. 261, 262;
Fitzgeffrey's poem on, ii. 316, 323, 449, 453.
Drama, p. xxx. *See* Comedy, Tragedy, Tragi-comedy, Unities.
Drant, Thomas, pp. l, lii, lv;
'Rules' of, i. 90, 96, 97, 99, 102, 117, 372-3, 375, 378, 411, 415; ii. 261, 281, 321, 436, 442, 452;
'Dranting of verses,' ii. 272.
Drayton, Michael, pp. vi, lviii, lix; i. 388; ii. 315, 316, 317, 318, 319, 321, 400, 401, 448, 449. See *Polyolbion, Barrons Wars, Englands Heroicall Epistles.*
Dreames, Spenser's, i. 100, 114, 115, 133, 246, 374, 381, 412.
Dresemius, ii. 460.
Druids, the, ii. 360.
Drummond, William, i. 135, 148, 208, 422; ii. 417, 455, 457.
Dryden, pp. vi, xii, xl, xli (note), xlvi, lxv; i. 356, 400; ii. 456, 458, 462.
'Dry Mock,' Figure of the, ii. 169.
Du Bartas (Saluste), i. 303, 305, 359; ii. 265, 266, 283, 336, 437.
Du Bellay, pp. lxxix, lxxxvii, lxxxviii, lxxxix; i. 209, 375, 401, 402, 404, 405, 406; ii. 415, 417, 420, 421.
Du Fresnoy, *De Arte Graphica*, i. 387.
Dunsanye, the Lord Baron of, i. 136.
Duns Scotus, ii. 460.
Dyer, Edward, i. 89, 90, 100, 101, 109, 114, 126, 372, 377, 411 (?); ii. 63, 65, 321, 451.

Ealdhelm of Sherborne, ii. 370, 459-60.
Earthquake of 1580, i. 87, 98, 101, 374.
Ecclesiastes, i. 158.
'Echo Sound,' Figure of the, ii. 169.
'Eclipsis,' ii. 167.

Eclogue, the, i. 131, 262; ii. 27, 40, 159; Virgil's, ii. 316.

'Ecphonisis,' ii. 170.

Edes, Richard, ii. 319, 450.

Edge, Master Orator, ii. 241.

Edwardes, Richard, i. 242, 410; ii. 65, 320, 451.

'Egg,' Figure of the, i. 305, 422; ii. 96, 416. *See* Figured Verses, ᾠόν.

'*Eikastike*,' i. 186, 394.

'E. K.', pp. xxxii, xxxiii, xxxiv, xlii, lxxxvii, lxxxviii, xc; identification of, i. 380; *Epistle Dedicatory to the Shepheards Calender*, i. 127–34, 380–2; ii. 232, 242, 263, 283, 372, 374, 375, 398, 400, 408, 413, 416.

Ἑκατομπαθία, *or a Passionate Centurie of Love*, p. lxxxvii (note); i. 427, 428, 430; ii. 416, 420, 452. *See* Watson, Thomas.

Eld, G., printer, ii. 398.

Elderton, William, p. xx; i. 125, 379, 413; ii. 230, 253, 257, 261, 273, 427, 435, 436, 465.

Elegiac Verse, pp. xxx, xlvi; i. 176, 249, 285; ii. 26, 209, 320-1, 344 et seq., 377.

Elizabeth, Queen, i. 263, 271; ii. 1–2, 4, 66, 114, 170, 182–3, 192, 193, 317, 321, 322, 347, 401, 417, 424, 429, 452.

Elizabethan Criticism; *see* Introduction (Table of Headings, p. ix); debt of seventeenth century to, pp. vi, xl.

Elyot, Sir Thomas, pp. xci; i. 251, 253, 313, 350, 388, 391, 413, 426; ii. 402, 412.

Emblematists, Meres's list of, ii. 323.

Emblems, i. 376; ii. 105 et seq., 417, 453.

Empedocles, i. 152, 236.

'Emphasis,' i. 49; ii. 169.

'Enallage,' ii. 168.

'*Enargia*,' p. lxxxv; i. 400; ii. 148, 167, 419, 420.

Encomia, ii. 43, 45, 411.

'*Energia*,' p. lxxxv; i. 201, 400; ii. 148, 419.

Englands Heroical Epistles, ii. 315, 316, 449.

'English Aretine,' p. lxxxi (note).

English Drama, Whetstone on, i. 59; Sidney on, i. 196 et seq. *See* Tragedy, Comedy, &c.

'English Hexameter,' Inventor of, ii. 230, 231, 239. *See* Hexameter.

'English Homer,' ii. 240, 465.

English Language, 'E. K.' on the, i. 130; Sidney on, i. 204; Carew on, ii. 285–94, 444–5. *See* Vocabulary.

'English March,' The [or Iambic Dimeter], ii. 338 et seq.

'English Petrarch,' ii. 436.

English Poet, The, by Spenser, i. 232, 246, 396, 408.

English Saxon, ii. 150, 415, 444, &c. *See* Anglo-Saxon.

English scholarship, Ascham on, i. 34.

English style, Harvey on, i. 123 et seq.

English wits, Harvey on, ii. 260 et seq.

English writers, influence of earlier, pp. lxxi, xc–xcii.

'*Enigma*,' ii. 160, 169.

Ennius, i. 29, 34, 71, 82, 83, 103, 136, 152, 189, 233, 235, 237; ii. 17, 18, 120, 314, 397, 439.

ἐνθουσιασμός, i. 396.

Eobanus Hessus; *see* Hessus.

Epaminondas, i. 194.

'Epanalepsis,' ii. 169, 304.

'Epanodis,' ii. 170.

'Epanorthosis,' ii. 304.

Ephemerides of Phialo, Gosson's, i. 62, 364.
Epic, p. xlvi; i. 23, 413. *See* Poetry, Heroic Verse.
Epicedia, ii. 50.
Epicharmus, i. 299, 342; ii. 392.
Epictetus, i. 343.
Epicurus, i. 67.
Epigram, the, pp. xxx, xlvi; i. 249; ii. 209; Puttenham on, ii. 56 et seq.; on Epigrammatists, ii. 27; Meres's list, ii. 321.
Epigrams, Campion's, ii. 341 et seq., 345 et seq., 375, 456. Spenser's, i. 428.
Epimenides, i. 71, 367.
ἐπιμονή, ii. 170, 416.
'Epimonie,' ii. 93.
'Epiphonema,' ii. 170.
Epist. ad Attic., Cicero's, i. 34.
Epist. Fam., Cicero's, i. 36.
Epistle to Henry Reynolds, pp. vi, lviii, lix.
'*Epistle to his fair Geraldine*,' Drayton's, ii. 315.
Epistolae virorum obscurorum, ii. 329.
'Epistrophe,' ii. 304, 305.
'Epitaph,' Puttenham on the, ii. 58 et seq.
Epithalamies, ii. 48, 52 et seq., 412.
Epithalamion Thamesis, Spenser's, i. 100, 113, 374, 377.
'Epitheton,' ii. 168, 169.
'Epithets,' i. 219, 406; ii. 169.
Epitome, i. 5.
'Epitropis,' ii. 170.
'Epizeuxis,' ii. 169, 304.
Epopeia, ii. 216. *See* Heroic Verse.
Erasmus, i. 8, 13, 17, 66, 68, 124, 182, 312, 329, 349, 352, 353, 366, 379, 388; ii. 154, 196, 246, 329, 368, 369, 372, 460.
Erastus; *see* Lieber, Thomas.

'Erotema,' Figure of, ii. 170.
Essayes of a Prentise, i. 208.
Estienne, Henri (II) (Stephanus), pp. lvi, lxxxviii; i. 18, 20, 347, 349, 353, 366; ii. 285, 411, 444.
'Etiologia,' ii. 170.
Eucherius, i. 299.
Eulenspiegel, Tyl; see *Howliglasse*.
Euphantasioti, ii. 20.
Εὐφυής, p. xxxv; i. 1-2, 349; ii. 19.
Euphues, i. 256, 349, 365, 368, 383, 423, 429; ii. 243, 268, 269, 272, 273, 274, 401, 420, 421, 434.
'Euphuing,' ii. 269, 272; 'euphued,' ii. 275.
Euphuism, pp. lix, lxviii; Sidney on, i. 202 et seq.; i. 402, 429; ii. 226 (?), 272, 426, 431, 437.
Eupolis, i. 81, 236, 295, 370; ii. 320, 323, 393.
Euripides, pp. xliii, lxxiii; i. 19, 20, 23, 24, 29, 33, 34, 68, 190, 198, 236, 355; ii. 17, 27, 154, 231, 267, 315, 317, 319, 322, 324.
Eusebius, i. 342.
Eustathius, ii. 298.
Eutropius, ii. 263.
Evax, king of Arabia, ii. 22, 326, 410.
'Even,' the Figure of, ii. 170.
Every Man in his Humour, ii. 387-90, 461-2.
Every Man out of his Humour, ii. 390-3, 462-3.
'Exargasia,' Figure of, ii. 170, 420.
Excellency of the English Tongue, Carew's, ii. 285-94.
'Exchange,' Figure of, ii. 168.
'Exclamation,' Fraunce on, ii. 304.
'Excuse,' Figure of, ii. 170.
'Exercise,' Harvey on, 235 et seq.
Expeditio, Figure of, ii. 170.

Fabius quoted, i. 300.

Fabricius Chemnicensis, Georgius, his *Catholica* translated by Webbe, pp. xlii, lxxv; i. 290-302, Latin text, 417-21; i. 397, 409, 415, 416.

Fabricius, Ioannes Albertus, i. 357, 385, 388, 413, 416; ii. 460.

Faerie Queene, Spenser's, pp. xv, xxxv; i. 100, 115, 116, 305-6, 359, 381; ii. 229, 231, 282, 316, 400, 414, 421, 427.

Falls of Princes, Lydgate's, ii. 68.

'False Semblant,' Figure of, ii. 169, 420.

Familiar Letters, Harvey's, i. 143.

'Far-fet,' Figure of the, ii. 169.

Fauchet, Claude, p. lxxxvii; ii. 409.

'F. C.', i. 245, 412.

Feet (metrical); *see* Gascoigne, James VI, Webbe, Puttenham, Campion, Daniel; 'foot' = syllable, i. 405.

Fenton, Geoffrey, ii. 440.

Ferrers, George, i. 397. *See* ii. 413.

'Ferrys,' Edward, ii. 63, 65, 319, 413, 414, 450. *See* previous entry.

Fescennina licentia, ii. 55.

Field, Richard, printer, ii. 1, 327.

Figliucci, Felice (of Sienna), i. 33, 356.

Figured Verses (*carmina figurata*), i. 32, 47, 267, 305; ii. 95 et seq., 416.

Figures, Rhetorical; *see* detailed list in Fraunce's text, i. 304-5, and in Puttenham's, ii. 164 &c., 167-72.

'filed,' ii. 318, 450.

Filelfo, Francesco, ii. 315, 448.

Finée, Oronce (Orontius Finaeus), ii. 272, 438.

First Book of the Preservation, &c.; *see* Preservation, &c.

First Foure Bookes of Virgil his Aeneis, Stanyhurst's, i. 135 et seq.

Fisher, Bishop, ii. 204.

Fitzgeffrey, Charles, author of *Sir Francis Drake, his honorable lifes commendation, and his tragicall Deathes lamentations*, ii. 316, 323, 449, 453.

'F. K.', i. 245.

Flaccus, Val., i. 71, 239.

'Fleering Frumpe,' Figure of the, ii. 169.

Fleetwoode, William, i. 58.

Flemings, Puttenham on the, ii. 1, 170, 420.

Flemming, Abraham, i. 244, 266, 411, 414.

— Samuel, i. 244 (?) (*see* note, p. 411); ii. 425.

Fletcher, Giles, the elder, p. lix; ii. 444.

— Giles, the younger, ii. 444.

— John, dramatist, ii. 443, 462.

— Phineas, ii. 444.

— Richard, Bishop of Bristol, ii. 281, 443.

'Flitting' Figure, the, ii. 170.

Floide; *see* Lloyd.

Flores Poetarum, ii. 241, 399, 431, 464.

Florio, i. 360.

Florus, i. 397.

'Flowing' verse, i. 209, 210, 213, 216, 218, 404. *See also* ii. 81.

'Flytings,' i. 217, 405-6.

Folieta, Uberto, i. 385.

'Fonde Affectation' (*Cacozelia*), ii. 171.

Foreign languages compared, ii. 292 et seq.

Foreign terms, ii. 151, 171, 289 et seq.; 304 et seq., 397. *See* Inkhorn, Italian, French, &c.

'Foule Speech,' Figure of, ii. 171.

Foure Letters, Harvey's, ii. 229-38, 241, 427-9.

Four Letters Confuted, i. 372; ii. 239-44.

Four Sons of Aymon, i. 323; ii. 308.

Fracastoro, Jeronimo, i. 193, 396; ii. 322, 447.

France (and French influence), pp. lxxi, lxxvii et seq.; i. 24, 29, 96, 123, 132, 403-4; ii. 64, 85, 402, 444. Whetstone on French Comedy, i. 59. The value of French analogies, p. lxxxviii.

Franciade; see Ronsard.

Francis I of France, i. 193, 396; ii. 322.

Fraunce, Abraham, p. liii; *The Arcadian Rhetorike*, i. 303-6, 422; i. 316, 360, 411 (?), 422, 427; ii. 234, 280, 321, 452.

Freigius, Ioannes, ii. 245, 432.

French Academie, The, i. 363.

Friar Rush, ii. 272.

Friar Tuck, ii. 272.

Frischlin, Nic., ii. 439.

Frobisher, Sir Martin, i. 362; ii. 261.

Frontine, i. 376.

'Frumpe,' ii. 420. *See also* 'Fleering Frumpe.'

Fulvius, i. 70.

Fulwood, William, *Enimie of Idlenesse*, vi. 422.

Furies, Du Bartas's, ii. 265, 321, 437.

'*Furor Poeticus*,' ii. 3, 297, 392, 463.

'Fuzie,' The, ii. 96 et seq., 416.

Gager, William, ii. 320, 451.

Galateo, i. 107, 376.

Galen, ii. 332, 401, 455.

Galenists, ii. 50, 412.

Gallandius, Petrus, ii. 245, 432.

Gallian of France, ii. 309.

'gallimaufry,' i. 130; ii. 253, 435.

Gallo-Belgicus, ii. 397, 464.

Gallus, Cornelius, ii. 18.

Gammer Gurton's Needle, i. 373; ii. 443.

Ganzar, Princisca [? Francesca], i. 376.

Garcilasso, i. 303, 305.

Gargantua, ii. 308. *See* Rabelais.

Gargrave, Sir Thomas, ii. 419.

Garnier's *Cornélie*, i. 424.

Gascoigne, George, pp. xiii, xlii, xliii, xlix, lix, lxxxix, xcii; *Certayne Notes of Instruction*, i. 46-57, 358-62; i. 55, 126, 242, 275, 315, 362, 379, 403, 404, 405, 406, 407, 412, 414, 427, 428; ii. 63, 65, 253, 261, 266, 280, 320, 321, 413, 414, 418, 435, 437, 458.

Gaza, Theodorus, ii. 369, 459.

'G. B.', i. 245 (*see* note).

Gellius, Aulus, i. 342, 357, 423; ii. 243.

γελοῖον, τὸ, p. lxxiv.

Genethliaca, ii. 48, 52, 412.

George of Trebizond (Trapezuntius), ii. 369, 459.

Georgevicz, Bartolomaeus, ii. 361, 458.

Georgics, Virgil's, i. 158, 265; ii. 155.

Germanicus, i. 193; ii. 322.

Germans and Germany, i. 24, 29, 59, 84, 313, 362.

Gerusalemme liberata by Tasso, ii. 199, 369.

Gervase of Tilbury, ii. 370, 460.

Giampetro Valeriano (Pierius), i. 126, 379.

Gilbert, Sir Humphrey, i. 58, 362; ii. 261.

Gildon, Charles, i. 382-3.

'Gilgilis Hobberdehoy,' ii. 430.

Ginecocratia, by Puttenham, ii. 139-41.

Giovanni de' Malpaghini, (?) ii. 459.
— da Ravenna, (?) ii. 459.

Giovio's *Emblems*, i. 376.
Giraldus; *see* Gyraldus.
Gireleon, ii. 308.
'Glorious,' Figure of the, ii. 170.
Glossing, 'E. K.' on, i. 132; 'trade of glose,' p. lxxxvii.
'Gnome,' Figure of, ii. 170.
'Gnomes,' ii. 429.
'Gnosis,' i. 171.
γοητεία, i. 231.
Golden Booke of Marcus Aurelius, ii. 440.
Golden Grove, Vaughan's, ii. 325–6, 454.
'Golden-mouth'd,' ii. 316.
Golding, Arthur, i. 243, 262, 315, 361, 377, 411, 413, 427; ii. 63, 65, 196, 322.
Googe, Barnabe, i. 243, 265, 356, 411, 414; ii. 280, 322.
Gorboduc, p. lv; i. 126, 196, 197, 398.
Gosson, Stephen, pp. xiv, xvii, xxix, xxx, lxviii; i. 62; i. 1, 63, 65, 76, 78, 80, 81, 84, 86, 89, 350, 363–71, 372, 383, 391, 394, 395, 400, 401; ii. 321, 438, 452; *Schoole of Abuse*, i. 61; *A Short Apologie of the Schoole of Abuse*, i. 62; *Playes confuted in five Actions*, i. 62.
Goths, Huns, and Vandals, 'influence' of, i. 29, 30, 32, 188, 240, 267; ii. 12, 367.
Gouernour, Elyot's, i. 350, 385, 391, 413.
Gower, i. 152, 241, 318, 410; ii. 17, 62, 64, 85, 89, 150, 314.
Grafton, Richard, ii. 280.
Grant, Edward, i. 337, 430.
'Granting,' Figure of, ii. 304.
Graunge, John, i. 245, 276, 411, 415.
Gray, William, ii. 17, 409.
Greek criticism, influence of, p. lxxii et seq.

Greek Poetry, Webbe on, i. 234 et seq.; Meres's comparisons with, ii. 314 et seq.; Greek proverb, i. 93. *See* under each author.
Greene, Robert, p. xci; i. 307, 365, 423–8, 429; ii. 229, 230, 231, 232, 239, 243, 249, 253, 260, 262, 266, 273, 276, 319, 320, 323, 324, 417, 420, 423, 427, 428, 434, 436, 454.
'Greenesse,' ii. 431.
Gregorius, Petrus, ii. 257, 436.
Grenville, Sir Richard, ii. 262.
Greville, Fulke, i. 412 (?); ii. 63, 457.
Grévin, Jacques, i. 369.
Grey de Wilton, Lord, i. 55.
Grindal, Edmund, (?) i. 313, 426.
    William, (?) i. 313, 426.
Grisone, F., i. 383.
Groatsworth of Wit, i. 423, 424. *See* Greene, Robert.
Guarini, Battista, p. lxxxi.
Guazzo, Stefano, p. lxxxi; i. 376, 395; ii. 417.
Gubbyn, T., bookseller, i. 303.
Guevara, Antonio de, p. xc; ii. 276, 440.
Guicciardini, Francesco, i. 376; ii. 231, 263, 437.
Guilpin, Edward, ii. 320, 451, 456.
Guy of Warwick, ii. 44, 87, 309.
Gyraldus, Lilius, pp. lxvii, lxxxvii; i. 350, 351, 352, 364, 367, 397; ii. 409, 448.

Hacket, Thomas, bookseller, i. 321.
    William, ii. 429.
Haddon, Walter, i. 21, 316, 353, 354, 427; ii. 248, 315, 326, 433.
Hadrian, i. 193, 396.
Hake, Edward (*The Touchstone of Wittes*), i. 226, 227.
Hakluyt, Richard, i. 380; ii. 262.
Half-feet, ii. 134–5.

Index

Hall, Arthur, ii. 446.

   Joseph, pp. vii, liv; i. 363, 402, 410, 427; ii. 312, 320, 408, 447, 465.

Hamlet, ascribed to Kyd, i. 312, 425.

Harding, Thomas, ii. 238, 247, 429, 433.

Hardyng, John, ii. 17, 62, 64, 314, 429, 447.

Harington, Sir John, pp. viii, xix, xx, xxii, xxiii, xxiv, xxviii, xxix, xxxi, xlv, lviii, lx, lxi, lxx, lxxiv, lxxvii, lxxxiv, lxxxv, xci, xcii; i. 149, 377, 378, 383, 386, 389; Preface to the translation of *Orlando Furioso*, ii. 194-222, 422-5, ii. 310, 322, 402, 450, 461.

Hariot, Thomas, ii. 280, 441.

Harvey, Gabriel, pp. v, xiii, xxxiii, xxxvii, xxxix, xlviii, xlix, l et seq., lvi, lxi, lxvii, lxviii, lxix, lxxi, lxxvii, lxxxi (note), xc, xcii; i. 87, 92, 93-7, 98, 101-22, 123-6, 127, 133, 134, 143, 245, 246, 284, 305, 316, 352, 354, 358-62, 371, 372-80, 380-1, 383, 402, 405, 407, 412, 415, 416; ii. 229-38, 239, 240, 241, 244-82, 282-4, 315, 320, 323, 342, 416, 425, 426, 427-9, 431-44, 456. His relations with Spenser, i. 380; ii. 430.

   John, i. 246, 376, 412; ii. 323, 427, 435, 453.

   Richard, i. 246, 412; ii. 323, 427, 435, 453.

Haslewood's *Ancient Critical Essays*, referred to, pp. v, xiii; i. 373; ii. 420, 421.

Hathway, Richard, ii. 320, 451.

Haue with you to Saffron-Walden, i. 372.

'Heaping Figure,' The, ii. 170.

Heautontimorumenos, i. 28, 192, 396, 400.

Hebrew Verse, ii. 207.

Hegesias, ii. 146.

Heinsius, Dan., ii. 425.

Heliodorus, i. 160, 386, 409; ii. 315, 440. See *Theagines and Cariclea*.

Hellowes, Edward, ii. 440.

'Hendiadys,' ii. 168.

Henry IV, Shakespeare's, ii. 318.

Henry VIII, ii. 17, 23, 204-5, 410.

Henslowe, i. 371; ii. 451, 453.

Heraclitus, i. 176; ii. 116.

Herbert, William, 3rd Earl of Pembroke, ii. 457.

Hercules: portrait of, ii. 147; Sophister on, ii. 194; story of, ii. 422.

Heresbachius, Conradus, i. 265, 414.

Hermes Trismegistus, ii. 22, 279, 418, 440.

Hermippus, ii. 324.

Hermogenes, i. 25, 355; ii. 277, 445.

Herodotus, i. 115, 153, 169, 390; ii. 154.

Heroic Verse, pp. xxx, xlv, xlvi; i. 30, 179 et seq., 222; ii. 26, 194, 198, 210 et seq., 319, 333, 456.

Hesiod, i. 71, 151, 206, 237, 238, 265, 336, 342; ii. 7, 154, 207, 315, 323, 397.

Hessus, Eobanus, i. 8, 18, 20, 347, 350.

Hester, John, ii. 279, 441.

Hexameter, pp. xli, xlvi et seq.; i. 30, 98, 125, 282 et seq., 356, 372-80; ii. 46, 51, 90, 230, 239, 240, 241, 427, 457. 'The inventor of the English Hexameter,' ii. 230, 239 (and note).

Heywood, Jasper, i. ?242, 424, ?410.

   John, i. ?242, 358, ?410; ii. 63, 180, 280, 321, 413, 421, 425.

   Thomas, i. 407; ii. 320, 449.

Hicke the Scorner, ii. 420.
Hiero of Syracuse, i. 8.
Higgins, John, i. 226.
Hill, R., i. ? 242, 411.
Hippocrates, i. 297.
Hipponax Ephesus, ii. 320.
'*Histeron Proteron*,' ii. 168, 171.
History: Poetry and, p. xxviii; Ascham's classification of, i. 24; Sidney on, i. 162 et seq., 184; Puttenham on historical poesy, ii. 40 et seq. The historical argument for poetry, p. xxi et seq.; the 'Historical Idea' in Criticism, p. lxii.
Hoby, Sir Edward, i. 341-4, 386, 431.
   Sir Thomas, pp. lvii, lviii; i. 357, 376, 431; ii. 437.
Holinshead, Raphael, i. 100, 113; ii. 253, 280, 435.
Homer, pp. xxiii, xxxix, lxxi, lxxvii, lxxxv; i. 8, 9, 14, 15, 20, 23, 29, 32, 33, 34, 64, 70, 71, 77, 78, 103, 118, 123, 151, 158, 188, 189, 190, 206, 233, 234, 235, 236, 237, 248, 249, 255, 283, 297, 316, 318, 336, 342, 348, 354, 356, 359; ii. 4, 17, 42, 45, 116, 123, 154, 155, 156, 191, 198, 215, 216, 217, 222, 226, 230, 234, 240, 247, 255, 264, 265, 278, 295-307, 314, 315, 316, 319, 322, 323, 326, 338, 397, 445-6, 452, 465.
   'English' (Chaucer); see 'English 'Homer.'
'Homer-Lucan,' ii. 382.
Honest Excuses, i. 62.
Honour of Chivalrie, The, ii. 308.
Honterus, Joannes, ii. 317, 449.
Horace, pp. xxiii, xxv, xlii, xliii, lxvii, lxxi, lxxiii, lxxiv et seq., lxxix; i. 8, 19, 20, 23, 29, 33, 35, 36, 71, 74, 81, 117, 136, 137, 168, 180, 183, 188, 198, 230, 234, 239, 244, 250, 251, 252, 279, 283, 290-302, 342, 349, 359, 378, 382, 386, 387, 389, 390, 391, 392, 393, 394, 400, 403, 405, 411, 413, 414, 416, 417-21, 428; ii. 18, 26, 208, 229, 315, 318, 319, 320, 418, 419, 423, 450, 457, 458, 460, 461. *See* Fabricius, G.; Webbe, William.
'Horace' (in *The Poetaster*), ii. 394 et seq.
Hortensius, i. 299, 334.
Howard, Lord Henry, ii. 280, 442. *See* Surrey, Earl of.
Howleglasse, ii. 272, 308, 430, 438.
Hudson, Robert, ii. 401, 465.
Hugobald (Hucbald), ii. 15, 409, 455.
huitain, ii. 92.
Humanistic influences in Elizabethan criticism, p. lxviii.
'Humours,' pp. xlii, xliv, xlv; Jonson on, ii. 390 et seq., 466; *loci* on, ii. 462.
Humphrey, Laurence, ii. 281, 443.
Hundred merrie Tales, ii. 272, 438.
Hungary, popular poetry in, i. 178.
Hunnis, William, i. 242, 277, 410, 415.
Huns. *See under* Goths.
Huon of Bordeaux, i. 323; ii. 308.
Hutton, Leonard; *see* note, ii. 442.
Hutton, Matthew, ii. 281, 442.
Hyll; *see* Hill.
'Hymnic' poets, ii. 158.
Hymns, metre for, i. 57.
'Hypallage,' ii. 168.
'Hyperbaton,' ii. 168.
'Hyperbole,' ii. 160, 169.
Hypercritica, Bolton's, p. vi; ii. 402.
'Hypotiposis,' ii. 170.
'Hypozeugma,' ii. 167.
'Hypozeuxis,' ii. 168.

Iambic verse, Iambus, i. 24, 30, 90, 176, 294, 342, 405; ii. 127, 129 et seq., 320, 330, 333, 334 et seq.; 'licentious iambic,' i. 95, 96; ii. 456; 'the old iambic stroke,' i. 273, 414.

'Icon,' Figure of, ii. 170.

Idioma, i. 53; ii. 149, 419.

Idyllia, Theocritus's, ii. 316.

Ierotekni, Puttenham's, ii. 31, 410.

Iliad, Chapman on the, ii. 295-307. *See* Homer.

Imitation, p. lv et seq.; Ascham on, i. 5-47; i. 158, 347-58; ii. 276 et passim.

'Immerito' (Spenser), i. 92, 93 &c., 96, 101, 107, 113, 117, 373.

'Impartener,' Figure of the, ii. 170.

Impresa, ii. 106, 417. *See* Emblem.

'Incongruity,' Vice of, ii. 171.

Indecorum; *see* Decorum.

Indians, i. 153, 202.

Inkhorn terms, Inkhornism, Inkhornist, p. lv et seq.; i. 51, 360; ii. 81, 241-2, 275-6, 277, 431.

'Insertor,' Figure of the, ii. 168.

Instruction aux Princes, by Coignet, i. 341.

'Insultatio,' Figure of, ii. 170.

'Interruption,' Figure of, ii. 168.

Invention, p. lxxxix; Gascoigne on, i. 47 et seq., 359; James VI on, i. 220, 221, 406.

'Ionic vein,' the, ii. 293.

Ireland, Irish, i. 126, 153; ii. 361, 364.

'Irmus,' Figure of, ii. 168.

'Irony,' ii. 160, 169.

Irus, i. 365.

Isle of Dogs, Nash's, ii. 324, 453.

Isocrates, i. 13, 18, 19, 20, 25, 43, 347, 348; ii. 231, 276, 277, 282.

Italy, Italian influences, &c., pp. xvii et seq., xxxvi, lix, lxx, lxxi, lxxii, lxxiv, lxxv, lxxviii et seq., lxxxix; i. 1, 2, 3-4, 24, 29, 33, 97, 116, 123, 308, 318, 375, 376, 400; ii. 62, 220, 259, 366 et seq.; Italian poets, i. 14, 132; Italian Comedy, i. 59; Rhyme in Italy, i. 29, 33; Scholarship in Italy, i. 34, 96. *See* under each author.

Jaggard, William, printer, p. vii.

James I, King of Scots, i. ?193, 406; ii. ?322. *See* note, ii. 396.

James VI, King of Scots (James I of England), pp. xiii, xxii, xxiii, xl, xlii, lxxxix, xcii; *Ane Schort Treatise*, &c., i. ?193, 208-25, 403-7; ii. 265, 321, ?322, 326, 410, 416, 437, 458. *See* note, ii. 396.

James, S., i. 158.

Jephthes, Buchanan's, i. 24, 354, 395; ii. 322.

Jerome, S., i. 71, 75.

Jewel, John, ii. 238, 247, 429, 433, 443.

Joannes Palaeologus, ii. 369.

Joannes Rauenensis, ii. 369, 459.

Joannes Secundus, ii. 55, 412, 447.

Job, Book of, i. 158.

Jodelle, Étienne, ii. 324, 454.

Jodocus Badius, i. 72, 80, 83, 367, 369, 371.

John, S., i. 342; *Revelation of*, i. 115.

'John a stile,' &c., i. 394.

Johnson, Christopher, ii. 322, 452.
    Richard, ii. 446.
    Dr. Samuel, pp. xl, lxv.

John's, St., Cambridge, i. 313; ii. 210, 398.

Jones, Robert, ii. 418.

Jonson, Ben, pp. vi, vii, xii, xix, xxxiii, xli, xliii, xlv, lvii, lxvi, lxvii, lxxi, lxxvi; i. 350, 386, 392, 397, 399, 404, 422; ii. 1, 297, 319, 387-

Jonson, Ben (*continued*)—
97, 402, 426, 450, 451, 461-4, 465, 466. See *Every Man in his Humour*; *Every Man out of his Humour*; Humours.

Joseph of Exeter (Josephus Devonius), ii. 370, 460.

Josephus, i. 71.

Judith, Du Bartas's, i. 303.

Julian, ii. 229.

Junius, Franciscus, i. 158, 387, 391. See also Philoponus, Lotarius.

Justinian, i. 98, 109, 373-4.

Justinus, i. 168, 169, 368; ii. 263.

Justinus Martyr, ii. 245, 431.

Juvenal, i. 85, 136, 239, 342, 371, 400; ii. 27, 320, 324. 'Young Juvenal' (i.e. Nash), ii. 324, 454.

Jyl of Brentford's Testament, i. 424.

κάθαρσις, p. lxxxvi.

Kendal, Timothy, i. 415; ii. 321, 452.

Kerke; see Kirk.

Kiffin, Maurice, ii. 280, 441.

King John, Shakespeare's, ii. 3, 18.

Kinwelmersh, Francis, i. ? 412.

Kirk, Edward; see 'E. K.' Also i. 412.

—— (Kerke), Mistress, i. 90, 92, 372, 373.

Knight, ? Edward, i. 245, 411.

κρύψις, i. 301.

Kyd, Thomas, p. lxviii; i. 312, 396, 424, 425, 426; ii. 319, 450, 464.

'Kynsader,' Monsieur, ii. 402, 465. See Marston, John.

Lacey, Henry, ii. 424.

Lactantius, pp. xv, xxviii; i. 71, 73, 342, 348, 367, 391.

Laelius, i. 26, 28.

'*La Lubber*' (tune), i. 246.

Lambarde, William, ? ii. 280, 442.

Lambert; see Lambarde.

Lamerock, Sir, i. 4.

Lancelot, Sir, p xviii; i. 4.

Landino, Cristoforo, p. lxxxi; i. 206, 403.

Langland, i. 242; ii. 62, 64, 150, 314, 320, 413. See *Piers the Plowman*.

Language, Puttenham on, ii. 149 et seq.; Carew on, ii. 444-5; Estienne on, ii. 444. See Archaism, Diction, Vocabulary.

Languet, H., i. 378.

Latin criticism, influence of, p. lxxii et seq.

Laudun, Pierre de, p. lxxxvii.

Lawherne, Mr., ii. 281, 443.

Lawier's Logike, Fraunce's, i. 422.

Legend of Peirs Gaueston, Drayton's, ii. 449.

Legendes, Spenser's, i. 133, 246, 381, 412.

Legge, Thomas, ii. 319, 424, 450.

Leland, *De Reb. Brit. Collect.*, i. 316, 427; ii. 315, 459.

Lentulum, Epist. ad P., i. 11.

Leonine Verse, ii. 409.

Leo Placentius, Joannes, ii. 455.

Lepanthe, La, ii. 437.

Lepanto, ii. 265, 321, 437.

Lessing's *Laokoon* cited, i. 387.

Letters on Reformed Versifying, i. 87-122.

Lever, Thomas, i. 313, 426.

Leyland; see Leland.

'Licentious,' The Figure of the, ii. 170.

Licinius Crassus, Lucius, i. 82, ? 237, 370.

Licinius Imbrex, ii. 320. See also Porcius Licinius.

Lieber, Thomas (Erastus), ii. 246, 248, 433.

Lieblerus, Georgius, ii. 245, 432.

'Like Letter,' Figure of the, ii. 168.
'Like Loose,' Figure of the, ii. 168.
'lilypot,' ii. 439.
Linus, i. 75, 151; ii. 7, 207, 314, 324.
'Liptotes,' ii. 169.
'Literal' Verse, i. 218.
Literata Nobilitas, &c.; *see Nobilitas*, &c.
Littleton, Thomas, ii. 444.
Livius Andronicus, i. 152, 409; ii. 314.
Livy, i. 19, 20, 25, 128, 169, 381, 391; ii. 154, 263, 277, 466.
Lloyd (Floide), Ludovic or Lewis, ii. 280, 441.
Locke, Henry, ii. 401, 465.
Lodge, Thomas, pp. vii, xiv, xxi, xxii, xxiv, xxviii, xxix, lxviii, lxxvi; *Defence of Poetry*, i. 61–86, 363–71, 372, 394, 409; ii. 320, 400, 401, 423, 434, 438.
Longinus, ii. 416, 420.
'Long Language,' Figure of, ii. 171.
'Long Loose, Figure of, ii. 168.
Longolius (Christopher Longueil de Malines), i. 13, 15, 348, 349, 351; ii. 248, 433.
'Loose Language,' Figure of, ii. 168.
Lope de Vega, ii. 399.
Lopez, Alonzo, p. xc.
'Lord of Misrule,' ii. 271.
Lorris, Guillaume de, ii. 17, 409.
Lot, King, i. 4.
'Loud Lyer,' Figure of the, ii. 169.
'Loveburden,' Figure of the, ii. 170.
Love's Labour's Lost, Shakespeare's, ii. 318.
Love's Labour's Won, Shakespeare's, ii. 318, 449–50.
'Lozange,' The, ii. 96 et seq.

Lucan, i. 76, 158, 238, 336; ii. 196, 293, 315, 316, 319.
Lucian, i. 114, 255, 331, 332; ii. 147, 229, 272, 281, 396.
Lucilius, i. 81; ii. 27, 320.
Lucius, Pope, ii. 13.
Lucrece, Shakespeare's, ii. 317, 402.
Lucretius, i. 36, 158, 239, 391; ii. 46, 120, 315.
Lucullus, ii. 320.
Luscius, i. 237.
Lusco, Antonio, ii. 272, 439.
Lusus Regius, i. 406.
Luther, i. 388; ii. 248.
Lycophron, ii. 113, 324, 397.
Lycurgus, ii. 296, 309, 371.
Lydgate, i. 127, 227, 241, 318, 380; ii. 62, 64, 68, 79, 150, 314.
Lyly, John, pp. xlvi, xci; i. 256, 349, 368; ii. 268, 269, 320, 425, 426, 434. See *Euphues, Mydas*, &c.
Lyric Poetry, i. 23; ii. 319; Puttenham on, ii. 26; Campion on, ii. 346 et seq.
Lysias, i. 25, 43.

Machiavelli, i. 116; ii. 260, 276, 281, 308.
'Mack Morrice,' i. 126.
Macrinus; *see* Salmon, Jean.
Macrobius, p. lxxvii; i. 8, 18, 20, 299, 347, 350; ii. 288, 411.
'Macrologia,' ii. 171.
'Madrigal,' the, ii. 349.
Maecenas, ii. 320, 321, 322.
Maggi, V, i. 398.
Magnes, i. 81, 370.
Maiden Knight, The, ii. 308.
Mairet, Jean, i. 398.
'Maker,' p. lxxxv; i. 385, &c.
Mambrun, *De Carmine Epico*, i. 386, 400.
Manardus, Joannes, ii. 260, 436.
Mancinus, i. 427.

Manilius, i. 158, 239; ii. 46, 411.

Mantuanus, Baptista, i. 77, 132, 239, 244, 262, 409, 411, 413, 427; ii. 40, 315, 321, 323, 428, 448.

Manutius, Paulus (Paolo Manuzio), i. 349.

Manzolli, Pietro Angelo (Palingenius), i. 30, 239, 244, 356, 409, 411; ii. 315, 322, 448.

Mape, Walter, ii. 370, 460.

Marbodus, ii. 410.

'Marching Figure,' The, ii. 170.

Marforio (Marphorius), ii. 56, 412.

Margaret of Navarre, ii. 23, 410.

Marius, i. 170.

Mark, King, i. 4.

Markham, Gervase, ii. 323, 453.

Marlowe, Christopher, i. 364, 425; ii. 266, 293, 315, 318, 319, 324, 400, 402, 445, 450, 456, 461.

Marot, Clément, i. 132; ii. 17, 409.

Marshal, The Earl, ii. 297.

Marston, John, ii. 400, 402, 447, 464, 465, 466.

Martial, i. 239, 252, 254; ii. 56, 197, 209, 259, 293, 321, 351, 423, 424.

'Martin,' 'Martinist,' &c., i. 311, 424; ii. 248, 253, 268, 270, 430, 435, 443.

Martin V, ii. 272.

Marullus, Michael Tarchianota, ii. 315, 447.

Mary Magdalens funerall teares, ii. 280, 442.

Mary, Princess, i. 431.

Mason, Sir John, i. 313, 426.

Matilda, Drayto's, ii. 449.

Matthew, Tobie, ii. 281, 443.

Maximus Tyrius, i. 68, 365.

'M.D.,' i. 242 (*see* note).

'meacocke,' ii. 434.

Medea, Lucan's, ii. 319.

Medina, Pedro de, ii. 262.

'Meiosis,' ii. 169, 170.

Melanchthon, Philip, p. lxxvi; i. 13, 193, 313, 351; ii. 236, 248, 322, 420, 445.

Melanthus, ii. 320.

'Melicertus,' ii. 449.

Melici, ii. 26 (cf. Ascham, i. 23). See Lyric.

'mellifluous,' ii. 317, 449.

Ménage, i. 400.

Menander, i. 8, 59, 82, 116, 236, 295, 299, 370, 396, 409; ii. 27, 320, 322, 393.

Menaphon, i. 307, 308, 321, 423-8, 429.

Menenius Agrippa, i. 174.

Merchant of Venice, Shakespeare's, ii. 318.

Meres, Francis, pp. vii, xiii, xxi, xxii, xxxi, lxviii, lxxxvii, xci; *Palladis Tamia*, ii. 308-24, 402, 441, 446-54.

'Merismus,' ii. 170.

Merlin (Meruin), ii. 308.

'Merry Scoff,' Figure of the, ii. 169.

'Metalepsis,' ii. 169.

'Metanoia,' ii. 170.

'Metaphor,' ii. 160, 169, 288. See Similes.

Metaphors and Similes, common Renaissance; see Similes.

Metaphrasis, i. 5.

'Metastasis,' ii. 170.

Methecus, i. 77, 368.

'Metonymia,' ii. 169, 304.

Metre; *see* Verse.

Metrodorus, i. 67.

Meun, Jean de, ii. 17, 64, 409, 414.

'Mezozeugma,' ii. 167.

'Micterismus,' ii. 169.

Middle Ages, the: Ascham on, i. 3; Nash on, i. 323; Puttenham on the literature of, ii. 12 et seq.; Daniel on, p. lxiv, ii. 380.

'Middlemarcher,' Figure of the, ii. 167.
Midsummer's Night's Dream, Shakespeare's, ii. 318.
Mignault, Claude (Minos), ii. 245, 432.
Milithus, ii. 316.
Miltiades, i. 170.
Milton, p. lxxxvi.
μίμησις, pp. xxiii, lxxiv; i. 158, 386. *See* Imitation.
Mimnerus Colophonius, ii. 320.
'Mingle Mangle,' the, ii. 171, 435.
Minos; *see* Mignault.
Minturno, Antonio, pp. lxxx, lxxxii et seq.; i. 369, 383, 384, 385, 386, 387, 388, 389, 390, 392, 395, 396, 398; ii. 424, 425.
Mirour for Magestrates of Cyties, A, i. 63.
Mirror for Magistrates, pp. l, lxiii; i. 196, 226, 397; ii. 319.
Mirror of Knighthood, The, ii. 308.
Mirror of Madness, 'the French,' ii. 269.
Mirrour of Monsters, A, by Rankins, i. 63; ii. 447.
'Misnamer,' Figure of the, ii. 169.
'Misplacer,' the, ii. 171.
'Moderator,' Figure of the, ii. 169.
'Modernists,' ii. 255, 277.
Momus, i. 207, 311.
Monodia, ii. 50.
Monosyllables, i. 30, 51, 275, 281, 356, 360, 405; ii. 80, 119, 120, 121, 288, 417.
Montgomerie, Alex., i. 407; ii. 465.
'Mora' (*Il Cavaliere*), i. 395.
Morality of Poetry, arguments against, p. xvi et seq.
More, Sir Thomas, i. 31, 139, 166, 313, 426; ii. 42, 218, 246, 273, 279, 293, 321, 326, 329, 331, 368, 369, 372, 455. *See* Utopia.

Mornay, Plessis de, i. 427; ii. 444.
Morte Arthur, i. 4, &c. *See* Arthur.
Mortimeriados, Drayton's, ii. 448.
Morysine, i. 376.
Mother Hubberds Tale, Spenser's, ii. 229, 230, 422, 427, 435.
'mountebanks,' i. 397.
Muiopotmos, Spenser's, i. 374.
Mulcaster, Richard, p. lvii; i. 336, 430; ii. 280, 441.
Mummius, i. 299, 416.
Munday, Anthony, i. 244, 374, 411; ii. 280, 320, ? 400, 451, 465.
Muretus, i. 194, 397, 400; ii. 322.
Musaeus, i. 75, 151; ii. 7, 10, 42, 314, 318, 397.
Muscovy, Muscovian, i. 75; ii. 227, 467.
Music (bearing of, and analogy from), p. xxvi; i. 54; Gosson's attack on, i. 78; i. 129, 172, 182, 206, 214, 230, 368; ii. 8, 9, 48, 52 et seq., 67, 79, 86, 230, 239-40, 328, 329, 373, 381, 454, 455, 456.
Musophilus, ii. 457-61.
'Muzio,' i. 395.
Mydas, Lyly's, ii. ? 222, 425, 426, 427.
'Mysomousoi,' i. 181, 393.

Naevius, Cn., i. 82, 237, 299, 370; ii. 320.
Nash or Nashe, Thomas, pp. v, xiii, xxi, xxvii, xxviii, xxix, xxxii, xxxiv, li, lvii, lxviii, lxix, lxxxi (note), xcii; Preface to Greene's *Menaphon*, i. 307-20, 423-8; *The Anatomie of Absurditie*, i. 321-37, 428-30; Preface to Sidney's *Astrophel and Stella*, ii. 223-8, 425-7; *Strange Newes*, or *Foure Letters Confuted*, ii. 239-44, 429-31; i. 350, 363, 372, 379, 391, 395; ii. 234, 249, 254, 261, 262, 267, 320, 323, 324,

Nash, Thomas (*continued*)—
403, 412, 416, 424, 427, 428, 429, 434, 435, 439, 441, 446, 448, 450, 453, 454, 465, 466, 467; Harvey's retort to Nash, ii. 282 et seq.
Nathan, i. 174, 185, 391, 394; ii. 205.
Nazianzen, p. xxx, i. 366.
'*Nenia*,' ii. 60.
Neoptolemus, ii. 237, 429.
Nepos, Cornelius, ii. 370, 460.
Nero, ii. 23.
Neville, Alexander, i. 409, 425.
Newberrie, R., printer, i. 341.
New Letter of Notable Contents, ii. 282-4, 444.
Newman, J., bookseller, i. 303.
Thomas, printer, ii. 223.
'Newnamer,' Figure of the, ii. 169.
Newton, Thos., i. 316, 424, 425, 427; ii. 315.
Nicander, ii. 46, 411.
Nicholas, S., ii. 177.
'Nicknamer,' Figure of the, ii. 169.
Nicomachus Phrygius, ii. 319.
Nicostratus, ii. 320.
Nigellus, Gulielmus ('Wireker'), ii. 370, 460.
Nigrum Theta; *see* Theta.
Nile, Cataract of, i. 206.
Nine Comœdies, Spenser's, i. 115.
Nine Muses, Spenser's, i. 115, 116.
'nippitaty,' ii. 434, 437.
Nizolius, i. 366, 401.
Nobilitas literata, &c., i. 347, 349, 352.
'Noema,' ii. 17.
Nonnus of Panopolis, ii. 323, 453.
Norman, Robert, ii. 262, 279, 437, 441.
Normans and 'Norman English,' i. 153; ii. 121, 149, 415, 418.
Norris, Sir John, ii. 262.
North, George, i. 376.

North, Sir Thomas, ii. 440.
Northbrooke, John, *Treatise*, i. 61.
Norton, Thomas (collaborator in *Gorboduc*), i. 126, 355, 379, 398; ii. 280, 441.
Norton of Bristow, Thomas, i. 30, 242, 355, 410.
Notes, Harington on editorial, ii. 221 et seq.
Nuce, Thomas, i. 425.
Number; *see* Verse.
'numerositie,' ii. 81, 415, 419, 420.

Obscenity, Harington on, ii. 213-5.
Observations in the Art of English Poesie, by Campion, ii. 327-55, 454-7.
Occam, William, ii. 370, 460.
Ocland, Christopher, i. 239, 409-10; ii. 315, 448.
Octavian, Emperor, ii. 23.
Odes, Campion on, ii. 346 et seq.
Odyssey; *see* Homer.
Oedipus, i. 165.
Officia, Cicero's, i. 25.
Οἰκονομία *et Decorum*, i. 19.
Oliver of the Castle, ii. 308.
Olney, Henry, bookseller, i. 148, 149.
Olympius Mysius, ii. 320.
ὁμαλόν, τὸ, i. 292.
ὅμοιον, τὸ, i. 292.
'Omoiosis,' Figure of, ii. 170.
'Omoioteleuton,' ii. 168.
Omphalius, Jacobus, i. 348; ii. 248, 433.
'Onomatopoeia,' ii. 169.
ᾠόν, i. 32, 267; ii. 416; *see* Figured Verses.
Oppianus, ii. 46, 411.
Orator, Cicero's, i. 143, 308.
Oratorical writings, Ascham's classification of, i. 25.
Oriental Figured Verses, ii. 96 et seq.

Origen, i. 71.
'Orismus,' ii. 170.
Orlando Furioso, i. 115, 157, 188, 386; Harington's Preface to translation of, 194, 211 et seq., 422–5; 322.
Ornament, Puttenham on Poetical, ii. 142–93.
Ornatus and Artesia, ii. 309.
Orontius; *see* Finée.
Orpheus, i. 75, 151, 152, 158, 234, 297, 342; ii. 6, 10, 14, 207, 225, 234, 255, 283, 314, 316, 397, 423.
'orthographical,' ii. 166.
Orthography, Harvey on, i. 95, 102, &c.; 119, 120; Puttenham on, ii. 84 et seq., 118, 122, 150; Campion on, ii. 352.
Orwin, Thomas, printer, i. 303, 306, 307.
Osorio da Fonseca, Jeronimo (Osorius), ii. 248, 433.
Ossatus; *see* D'Ossat.
'Outcrie,' Figure of the, ii. 170.
'Outlandish'; *see* Vocabulary.
'Oval,' The, ii. 96, 104–5; see Egg, ᾠόν.
Overbury's *Characters*, i. 403.
'Over Labour,' Figure of, ii. 171.
'Overreacher,' Figure of the, ii. 169.
'Oversea' Language, pp. lv et seq. *See* Vocabulary.
'Overthwart,' Figure of, ii. 170.
Ovid, i. 30, 64, 65, 70, 75, 76, 110, 136, 181, 232, 238, 243, 244, 252, 254, 285, 307, 315, 322, 323, 331, 332, 342, 367, 393, 394, 397, 411, 416, 427, 429; ii. 26, 60, 63, 116, 196, 215, 243, 260, 293, 313–8 passim, 320, 322, 323, 324, 423, 450, 463.
    Pseudo-, ii. 15, 331, 408.
Oxford, Edward, seventeenth Earl of, i. 243, 376, 411; ii. 63, 65, 320, 413, 414, 430, 450.

'Pacolet's Horse,' i. 198, 400.
Pacuvius, i. 298.
Page, Samuel, ii. 321, 451.
Paget, Henry Lord, ii. 63, 413.
Palace of Pleasure, William Painter's, i. 350; ii. 263, 437.
Paladin and Palmendos, ii. 308.
Palaeologus, Joannes; *see* Joannes.
Palingenius; *see* Manzoli, Pietro Angelo.
Palladis Tamia, ii. 308–24, 446–54. *See* Meres.
Palmerin, ii. 308.
Pandora, Southern's, ii. 421.
'panegeryca' (πανηγυρικά), i. 230, 408.
'Paphatchet,' ii. 248, 268, 269, 270, 272, 273, 274, 434.
'Parabola,' Figure of, ii. 170.
Paracelsians, ii. 50, 412, 433.
Paracelsus, ii. 246, 433.
'Paradiastole,' ii. 169.
'Paradigma,' Figure of, ii. 170, 420.
Paradine's *Emblems*, i. 376.
'Paradoxon,' ii. 170.
Paradyse of Daynty Devices, i. 407, 410, 411, 412, 429.
'Paralepsis,' ii. 170.
'Paramologia,' ii. 170.
Paraphrasis, i. 5.
'Parecnasis,' ii. 170.
Paremia, ii. 160.
'Parenthesis,' ii. 168.
'Parimia,' ii. 169.
'Parimion,' ii. 168.
'Parisia,' ii. 170.
'Parison,' ii. 170.
Parmenides, i. 152.
Parnassus Plays (*Pilgrimage to P. and Returne from P.*), pp. vii, xvii, lxxxviii; i. 363, 364, 403, 422, 423,

Parnassus Plays (*continued*)—
424, 429; ii. 398-403, 423, 435, 437, 440, 461, 463, 464-6.
'Paronomasia,' ii. 304.
Partheniades, Puttenham's, ii. 197, 403.
Parthenius of Nicaea, ii. 316, 320, 448.
Pasquier, Estienne, ii. 409.
Pasquil, i. 114, 311, 424; ii. 56, 185, 412, 422.
Pasquil the Playne, ii. 412.
'Passager,' Figure of the, ii. 170.
Pastoral Poetry, pp. xxx, xlvi; i. 175, 237, 262 et seq.; ii. 27, 39 et seq., 209, 321.
Pates, John, printer, i. 135.
Paul, S., i. 3, 71, 191, 342, 343, 396.
Paulinus, S., Bp. of Nolanum, i. 71, 367.
Pedantius, Comedy of, ii. 210, 424.
Peele, George, pp. vii, lx; i. 319, 388, 424, 428; ii. 319, 324, 418, 461.
Pelletier, Jacques, p. lxxxvii.
Pembroke Hall, Cambridge, i. 245, 380; ii. 320, 451.
Pembroke, Mary, Countess of, i. 303, 387, 422; ii. 225-6, 263, 283, 321, 358, 426, 444, 457.
—— William Herbert, Earl of, 357. *See also* Herbert.
'Penitent,' Figure of the, ii. 170.
Penne, the widow, ii. 208.
Percy and Douglas, 'Song' of, i. 178, 393.
Perez Gonçalo, p. lxxxix; i. 32, 356; ii. 314, 447.
Periander, i. 170.
Pericles, ii. 255.
'Periergia,' ii. 171, 172.
Peripeteia, p. lxxxiv; ii. 216, 425.
Perionius, Joachimus, i. 18, 20, 347, 353; ii. 245, 432.
'Periphrasis,' ii. 169.

Perne, Andrew, ii. 232, 428.
Perrault, Charles, i. 392-3.
Persius, i. 71, 72, 136, 239, 367, 391; ii. 27, 317, 320, 454.
Peruvian, the, ii. 10, 408.
Petrarch, pp. xviii, lxvii; i. 31, 33, 105, 111, 114, 115, 132, 152, 318, 359, 375, 376; ii. 62, 65, 90, 91, 92, 131, 134, 259-60, 283, 314, 319; Daniel on, 368, 369. 'English Petrarch,' p. lxxxi (note).
'Petrarchize,' p. lxxxi (note).
Pettie, G., i. 376.
Phaer, Thomas, p. lxviii; i. 30, 137-9, 142, 243, 256, 315, 355, 362, 377, 381, 397, 411, 413; ii. 63, 65, 196, 322.
Phalaris, the tyrant, i. 170; ii. 210.
'phantasticall,' ii. 19; 'phantastici,' ii. 20; 'phantastike,' i. 186, 394; φανταστικός, ii. 19.
Philemon of Soli, i. 82, 370; ii. 393.
Philetas Cous, ii. 320.
Philiseus, the Orator, ii. 177, 421.
Philocalia, Puttenham's, ii. 170, 420-1.
'Philophilosophos,' i. 390.
Philoponus, Joannes (of Alexandria), ii. 245, 431.
—— Lotarius (pseud. of Fr. Junius), ii. 442.
Philosophical writings, Ascham's classification of, i. 25.
Philosophy, Poetry and, p. xxviii; i. 162 et seq.
Philoxenus, ii. 309.
Phocilides, i. 152, 158, 236; ii. 315.
Phocion, i. 170.
Phoenix, James VI's, i. 406.
Phormus, ii. 392.
Pico; *see* della Mirandola.
Pierce Penielesse, Nash's, ii. 232, 248, 467.

Pierce's Supererogation, Harvey's, ii. 244-82, 254, 255, 256.

Pierius; *see* Giampetro Valeriano.

Piers the Plowman, i. 242; ii. 62, 64, 150, 314, 320, 413. *See* Langland.

Pigna, Giambattista, p. lxxxi; i. 349.

Pigres Halicarnassæus, ii. 320.

Pilgrimage to Parnassus; *see* Parnassus Plays.

Pilkington, i. 313, 426.

'Pilaster,' The, ii. 96, 100-1.

Pindar, i. 8, 19, 20, 23, 71, 178, 179, 190, 234; ii. 26, 43, 171, 172, 234, 278, 315, 319, 397, 411.

'Piramis,' The, ii. 96.

Piso, i. 41.

Place, 'Unity' of; *see* Unities.

Placentius; *see* Leo.

Plantin, Christoffel, i. 313, 426.

Plato, pp. xvi, xxiii, lxxi, lxxii, lxxvi (note), lxxix; i. 1, 7, 10, 11, 13, 15, 16, 17, 18, 19, 20, 21, 25, 34, 43, 45, 59, 67, 72, 75, 77, 152, 163, 173, 174, 179, 184; answered by Sidney, 190 et seq.; 230, 231, 248, 319, 328, 341, 343, 347, 348, 349, 350, 365, 366, 383, 388, 393, 394, 395, 396, 408, 409; ii. 42, 192, 196, 203, 204, 220, 231, 245, 255, 282, 293, 296, 299, 422.

(Comicus), i. 236, 295.

'Platonicks,' Platonists, ii. 3, 245.

Plautus, pp. xliii, lxxvi; i. 27, 28, 29, 34, 35, 59, 65, 116, 177, 198, 199, 237, 252, 253, 299, 399; ii. 27, 314, 317, 318, 320, 393, 397, 450.

Playes confuted in Five Actions, Gosson's, i. 62, 364, 365, 367.

Play of Playes, The, i. 62, 364.

Play of the Cards, The, ii. 210.

'*Pleasant approche*,' ii. 174. *See* Decorum.

Pléiade, The, p. lxxxviii.

'Pleonasmus,' ii. 171.

Pliny ('Senior' and 'Junior'), i. 82, 234, 309, 363, 370, 383, 404, 423; ii. 269, 311, 323, 410, 426.

'Ploche,' ii. 169.

Plotinus, i. 70.

Plutarch, pp. lxxii, lxxvi; i. 177, 189, 190, 191, 309, 320, 332, 342, 344, 349, 376, 386, 390, 391, 393, 395; ii. 59, 194, 198, 199, 202, 204, 222, 231, 243, 309, 311, 312, 422, 423, 440.

Poeta nascitur, &c., i. 397.

Poetaster, Jonson's, ii. 393-7, 463-4.

Poetical licence, i. 53; ii. 200.

Poetice, Scaliger's, pp. lxxxiii, lxxxiv et seq. *See* Scaliger.

Poetics, Aristotle's, p. lxxiii, and note; i. 23, 24, 192, 354, 359, 386, 390, 391, 400, 416; ii. 215, 216, 322, 411, 431, 436. *See* Aristotle.

Poetria; *see* note, i. 408.

Poetry, apologies for, p. xiv; Elizabethan defence of, p. xxi et seq.; criticism of contemporary, p. xxxii et seq.; defined by Puttenham, ii. 1 et seq.; the 'subject' or 'matter' of, ii. 25 et seq.; classification of kinds of, i. 23, 159 et seq., 201, 249; ii. 209 et seq., 319; antiquity of, i. 151-2; ii. 8 et seq., &c.; universality of, p. xxii; i. 153 et seq.; ii. 10 et seq., &c.; etymology of, i. 155, 230; Sidney on Poetry and Nature, i. 156 et seq.; Poetry and Verse, i. 160; Poet the 'monarch of all sciences,' i. 172 et seq.; imputations against, i. 183 et seq.; the honourers of, p. xxii et seq.; i. 193 et seq., 232 et seq.; ii. 16 et seq.; Webbe on, i. 407-16; Harington on, ii. 194-222; Meres on, ii. 309-14, 314-24; Vaughan on, ii.

Poetry (*continued*)—
325-6; Campion on, ii. 327-55 passim; Jonson on, ii. 387 et seq., 461, 463; Webbe on Latin, i. 237 et seq.; Poetry and History, &c., p. lxxiv (*see* History, Philosophy); Boccaccio on Poetry, p. lxxix; 'natural,' i. 158; 'philosophical,' ib.; 'sacred,' ib. *See* under each kind (e. g. Pastoral, Heroic, &c.).

Poggio Bracciolini, ii. 259, 272, 273, 369, 438, 459.

ποίησις, p. xxiii. *See* note, i. 408.

Polack, ii. 361.

Polimanteia, ii. 436.

Politeuphuia, ii. 308.

Politian; *see* Poliziano.

Politics, Aristotle's; *see* Aristotle; Case's translation, ii. 323.

Politike and Military Discourses, De la Nove's, ii. 308.

Politique Discourses, E. Hoby's, i. 341-4.

Poliziano, Angelo, i. 13, 352; ii. 315, 369, 447, 459.

Polybius, i. 19, 20.

Polyolbion, Drayton's, ii. 317.

'Polyptoton,' ii. 304, 305.

Polysyllabic metre, Harington on, ii. 220-1. *See* Monosyllables.

'Polysyndeton,' ii. 168.

Pomponazzi, Pietro (Pomponatius), ii. 260, 436, 467.

Pomponius Laetus, ii. 369, 459.

Pomponius Secundus, ii. 319.

'Pompous Speech,' Figure of the, ii. 171.

Ponsonby, William, bookseller, i. 148.

Pontano, Giovanni Gioviano (J. Jovianus Pontanus: 'Pontan'), i. 158, 194, 388, 394, 397; ii. 257, 315, 322, 445, 447.

Pontanus, Jacobus, ii. 409, 440, 447.

Pooly, ? i. 411.

Pope, Alexander, p. lxv.

Porcius Licinius, ii. 321.

Porter, Henry, ii. 320, 451.

Posies, Puttenham on, ii. 60 et seq.

'Posie transposed,' the, ii. 105 et seq., 112 et seq.

'Position,' p. li et seq.; i. 118, 121, 143, 273, 281, 282, 378, 415; ii. 418, 457.

'Poulters' measure,' i. 56, 272, 362, 414.

'Practise,' Harvey on, ii. 235 et seq.

'Praeoccupation,' Figure of, ii. 304.

Praetextatae, i. 295.

'Pragmatographia,' ii. 170.

Praise at Parting, i. 369.

'Praxis,' i. 171.

'Precisians,' The, ii. 434.

Preface or rather a Briefe Apologie of Poetrie . . . by Harington, ii. 194-222. *See* Harington.

πρέπον, τὸ, ii. 174.

'Preposterous,' Figure of the, ii. 168, 171.

Preservation of King Henry the VII, The First Booke of the, p. xlvii; i. 377-8, 402; ii. 419.

Preston, Thomas, i. 90, 373.

'Presumptuous,' Figure of the, ii. 170.

Primaleon of Greece, ii. 308.

Priscian, i. 314; ii. 440.

'Privie Nippe,' Figure of the, ii. 169.

'Procatalepsis,' ii. 170.

Procrustes, ii. 331 (*see* note).

'Prolepsis,' ii. 168.

Promos and Cassandra, Dedication, i. 58-60, 362.

Pronunciation, Carew on, ii. 289. *See* Prosody.

Propertius, i. 237, 228, 409; ii. 27, 316, 320.

Proportion, Puttenham on Poetical, ii. 67-141.

'Propounder,' Figure of the, ii. 168.

'Prose-rhythm,' i. 378.
Prosodia, Prosody, pp. xlvi et seq. *See* Verse; Italian Prosody, p. lxxx.
Prosody = Pronunciation, i. 375; 'Mother Prosodye,' i. 121.
'Prosonomasia,' ii. 169.
'Prosopographia,' ii. 170.
'Prosopopeia' ('Prosopopoia'), Figure of, ii. 170, 304.
Protogenes, i. 63, 326, 363.
'Proverb,' Figure of the, ii. 169.
Proverbs, Book of, i. 158; ii. 234.
'Prozeugma,' ii. 167.
Psalms, The, i. 154, 158, 385; ii. 31, 207, 234; Sidney's translation of, i. 387: metre for psalms, i. 57.
Ptolemy, ii. 17, 113, 147, 302, 303.
Pugliano, G. Pietro, i. 150, 383.
Pugna Porcorum, ii. 330, 455.
Punctuation, Puttenham on, ii. 77 et seq.
'Puritan Attack,' The, p. xiv et seq.
'Puritans,' i. 319; ii. 326, 345.
Puttenham (? Richard: *see* note, ii. 402), pp. xiii, xvi, xx, xxi, xxii, xxiii, xxv, xxvi, xxviii, xxix, xxxi, xxxiv, xxxv, xxxvii, xlii, xliv, xlv, xlvi, xlviii, liii, lv, lxii, lxiii, lxiv, lxv, lxvii, lxx, lxxii, lxxiv, lxxx (note), lxxxv, lxxxviii, lxxxix, xc, xcii; *Arte of English Poesie*, ii. 1–193 [*of Poets and Poesie*, 3–66; *of Proportion Poetical*, 67–141; *of Ornament*, 142–93]; ii. 196; list of works, ii. 402–3; 407–22, 423, 444, 445, 446, 452, 454, 455, 456.
Pygmalion's Image, ii. 312, 320, 465.
Pythagoras, i. 152, 342, 368; ii. 317.

Quadrain, ii. 68 et seq., 91, 93, 138.
'Qualifier,' Figure of the, ii. 168, 169.
Quantity, i. 89, &c., 99, 141 et seq., 204 et seq., 273 et seq., 410; ii. 117 et seq., 351 et seq., 454–7. *See* Accent, Hexameter, Verse.
'Quarreller,' Figure of the, ii. 170.
quatorzain, ii. 331.
'Questioner,' Figure of the, ii. 170.
'Quick Conceit,' Figure of the, ii. 169.
quintain, ii. 93.
Quintilian, pp. lxxv, lxxvi; i. 13, 29, 30, 41, 256, 297, 347, 355, 356, 357, 388, 394, 405, 415, 416; ii. 163, 410, 419, 450, 455.
Quintus Curtius, i. 168.
Quip for an Upstart Courtier, &c., A, ii. 229, 427.

Rabelais, ii. 234, 272, 430, 440. *See* Gargantua.
Raçellus, ii. 272, 438.
Raleigh, Sir Walter, i. 362; ii. 63, 65, 262, 321.
Ram Alley, ii. 466.
Ramus; *see* De la Ramée.
Randall, Justice, ii. 208.
Randolphe, Thomas, i. 404.
Rankins, William, i. 63; ii. 312, 447.
Rapicio, Giovita (Jovita Rapicius), i. 349.
Rapin, René, p. xlvi; ii. 456.
Rasselli; *see* Ruscelli, Geronimo.
'Reason'; *see* note, i. 390.
'Reason-Rend,' Figure of, ii. 170.
'Rebound,' Figure of the, ii. 170.
'Recompenser,' Figure of the, ii. 170.
Redman, John, i. 21, 313, 354, 426.
'Redouble,' Figure of the, ii. 169.
'Reduplicatio,' ii. 420.
'Reference,' Figure of, ii. 170.
Reformed Versifying, p. xlvi et seq.; i. 87–122, 278 et seq., 372–80 passim; ii. 426. *See* Accent, Hexameter, Quantity, Verse.

Regiomontanus, ii. 237, 429.
'Remensi,' p. lxxxii; ii. 360, 458.
'Remove,' Figure of the, ii. 170.
'Renconter,' Figure of, ii. 170.
'Renforcer,' Figure of the, ii. 169.
Rengifo, Diego Garcia, p. xc.
'Repetition,' Figure of, i. 220.
'Reply,' Figure of, ii. 169.
'Report,' Figure of, ii. 169.
'Rerewarder,' Figure of the, ii. 167.
'Resemblance,' Figure of, ii. 170.
'Resemblance by Example,' Figure of, ii. 170.
'Resemblance by Imagerie,' Figure of, ii. 170.
'Resemblance Misticall,' Figure of, ii. 170.
Resolution, The, ii. 280, 442.
'Response,' Figure of, ii. 169.
'Retire,' Figure of, ii. 170.
Returne from Parnassus; see *Parnassus* Plays.
Reuchlin, John, ii. 329, 368, 369, 372, 455, 459.
Reulis and Cautelis, James VI's, p. lxxxix; i. 403-7. See James VI.
Reusner, Nicolaus (Reusnerus), ii. 323, 453.
Reynolds, Henry, ii. 441.
   John, author of *Epigrammata*, ii. 441, 451.
   John (1549-1607), ii. 280(?), 441, 451.
Rhetor, Harvey's, ii. 433. See Harvey, Gabriel.
Rhetorical Figures, described by Fraunce, i. 304 et seq.; by Puttenham, ii. 167 et seq.
'Rhétoriqueurs,' The, p. lvi.
Rhodiginus; see Rodigino.
'Rhombus,' The, ii. 96 et seq. Cf. Romboides.
Rhyme, pp. xlvi et seq., lxxxviii; Ascham on, i. 29; Gascoigne on, i. 46 et seq.; Spenser and Harvey on, i. 87 et seq.; James VI on, i. 212 et seq.; Webbe on, i. 239 et seq., 266 et seq.; Puttenham on, ii. 11 et seq.; Campion on, ii. 327-55, 454-7; Daniel on, ii. 356-84, 457-61; *see also* i. 355, ii. 230, 315. Masculine and feminine, Webbe passim, ii. 221, 383.
   ='rhythm,' i. 205, 402.
   royal ('rhythm royal'), i. 54, 56, 361, 406.
   doggerel ('rhythme dogrel'), i. 140.
'rhyming in terms,' i. 209, 212, 404.
Rhythm, 'rithmes,' i. 50, 139; defined, i. 231. 'rhythme-prose,' i. 378; *Rithmus*, Campion on, ii. 329; Daniel on, ii. 359; Puttenham on rhythm, 'rime,' or 'numerositie,' ii. 80 et seq., 455. *See also* ii. 415.
Riccius (Bartholomaeus Riccius Ferrariensis), i. 14, 15, 348, 349, 352.
Riccoboni, Antonio, ii. 257, 435-6.
Rich, Barnabe, i. 371; ii. 280, 441.
Rich, Lord, i. 125.
Richard II, Shakespeare's, ii. 318.
Richard III (*Ricardus Tertius* by Legge), ii. 210, 320, 424, 450.
   by Henry Lacey, ii. 424.
   Shakespeare's, ii. 318.
Richelieu, i. 398.
'Riddle,' Figure of the, ii. 169.
'Riding rhyme,' i. 56, 362, 406; ii. 64, 414.
'Right Reasoner,' Figure of the, ii. 170.
'Ringleader,' Figure of the, ii. 167.
Robert of Sicily, p. lxxix (note); i. 193, 396; ii. 322.
'Robin Hood,' i. 184, 394; 219, 251; air of, i. 246.
Robortello, Francesco, i. 398.

Rodenburg, *Eglentiers Poëtens Borst-weringh*, i. 382, 399.
Rodigino, Lodovico Celio (Coelius Rhodiginus), i. 397; ii. 432.
Rodingus, ii. 245. *See* ii. 432.
'Rogero,' i. 272, 414.
Rogers, Daniel, i. 122, 378.
Roister Doister, ii. 288, 444.
Romance of the Isle of Great Britain, by Puttenham, 43.
Romance, attitude to Mediaeval, pp. xxix, xxxvi, lxiii; i. 323; ii. 43, 44, 87, 360.
Roman de la Rose, ii. 409; Chaucer's *Romaunt of the Rose*, ii. 64.
Romantic Qualities in Elizabethan Criticism, p. lx et seq.
Romanzi, I, by Pigna, i. 349.
'Romboides,' ii. 96. *See* Rhombus.
Romeo and Juliet, Shakespeare's, ii. 318.
rondelet, i. 55, 57.
'Rondell,' the, i. 96 et seq. *See* Roundel.
Ronsard, pp. lix, lxxxvii, lxxxviii, lxxxix; i. 359, 361, 378, 393, 402, 404, 405, 406, 408; ii. 75 (?), 171, 172, 415, 456.
'Rosalind,' Spenser's, i. 106, 122, 375, 378.
Roscius, i. 70, 83, 319; ii. 34, 323.
'Rouncefallis,' i. 223, 407. *See* Tumbling Verse.
'Roundel,' The, ii. 101-4. *See* Rondell.
Rowley, Ralph, ? ii. 320, 451.
Samuel, ? ii. 320, 451.
Roydon, Matthew, i. 319, 428; ii. 319.
Rule of Reason, ii. 444. *See* Wilson, Thomas.
Ruscelli, (?) Geronimo, i. 376.
Girolamo, ii. 424.
'Rym, Ram, Ruff,' i. 47.

S— V—, printer, ii. 356.
Sackville, Thomas, Lord Buckhurst, i. 126, 379, 398; ii. 63, 65, 319, 327, 413, 454.
Sadoleto, Jacopo, i. 313, 426; ii. 248, 433.
'Sage-Sayer,' Figure of the, ii. 170.
Saint-Évremond, i. 392.
Saint-Gelais (Sangelais), Melin de, ii. 17, 409.
Salel, Hugues, ii. 446.
Salerno, School of (*Schola Salerna*), ii. 13, 361, 408, 458.
Salisbury, John of, i. 388.
Sallust, p. lxvi; i. 8, 36; Ascham's (Cheke's) criticism of, i. 39-44, 128, 381; ii. 154, 229, 263.
Salmon, Jean ('Maigret'), Salmonius Macrinus, ii. 17, 326, 409.
Salust; *see* Du Bartas.
Sambucus, Joannes, i. 13, 351; ii. 323, 453.
Samford, Hugh, ii. 383.
Sand, ?, i. 242, 411.
Sandys, Edwin, i. 411 (?).
Sanford, J., ii. 423.
Sangelais; *see* Saint-Gelais, Melin de.
Sannazzaro, Jacopo, i. 132, 175, 196, 391; ii. 321, 447.
Sapphics, English, i. 285 et seq.; ii. 347.
Sappho, ii. 226, 259, 283, 322.
Sarcasm, 'Sarcasmus,' ii. 160, 169.
Satire, Satirical Poetry, pp. xxx, xlvi; i. 176, 294; ii. 27, 32 et seq., 209, 229, 320.
'Saturnist,' ii. 427.
Savoy, the, ii. 268, 269, 271, 438.
Saxon Angles, ii. 415.
English, ii. 121, 413, 414, 415, 417, 418, 421. *See* English Saxon.
'Saxon Language,' ii. 287.
Saxons, the, i. 153; ii. 361.

Scaevola, i. 11.

Scaliger, J. C., pp. xxiii, lxvi, lxvii, lxxiv (note), lxxvi (note), lxxvii, lxxx and note, lxxxii et seq., lxxxix; i. 126, 182, 191, 193, 206, 354, 385-8 passim, 392, 393, 395-400 passim, 402, 405, 413, 415, 416; ii. 210, 212, 246, 301, 322, 409-16 passim, 419, 424, 445-6, 448, 454.

Scaurus, i. 76.

Sceggius; *see* Schegkius.

Schegkius, Jacobus, ii. 432.

Scholarship, Ascham on English and Italian, i. 34.

Scholemaster, The, i. 1-45, 102, 137, 337, 347, 348; ii. 433, 437. *See* Ascham.

Schoole of Abuse, Gosson's, i. 61, 64, 89, 363 et seq.

Schottus, Andreas, ii. 445.

Scipio Africanus, i. 26, 28, 233; ii. 17, 18.

— Nasica, i. 189.

Scogan (Scoggin), John, ii. 230, 269, 273, 427, 441.

'Scogginist,' ii. 251.

'Scoggins air,' i. 120, 378.

Scot, Scotland, ii. 242, 361.

Scots Poetry; *see* James VI.

— Prosody, i. 403-7.

Scott, Reginald, ii. 280, 442.

Scotus, Duns, ii. 372.

Scribonius, Gulielmus, ii. 246, 432.

Scythia, i. 75, 314, 368, 426; ii. 361, 363, 458.

Seaven Bookes of the Iliades, Chapman's Preface to, ii. 295-7.

Seaven Champions of Christendom, ii. 308, 446.

Second and Third Blast of Retreat from Plays and Theatres, A, i. 62.

'Sectioun,' i. 214, 215, 405.

Secundus, J.; *see* Joannes Secundus.

Segni, Bernardo, i. 398.

'Self-Saying,' Figure of, ii. 171.

Semaines, Du Bartas's, i. 303. *See* Du Bartas.

'Senarie,' i. 95, 96.

Seneca, pp. xliii, lxxiii, lxxvi; i. 8, 19, 20, 23, 24, 30, 64, 67, 68, 197, 239, 244, 312, 389, 393; ii. 27, 267, 310, 317, 319, 322.

— 'English,' i. 312, 411, 424-5; ii. 322.

'Sensable' figures, ii. 166, 168 et seq.

'Sententia,' The Figure of, ii. 170.

'Sententious' Figures defined, ii. 166.

Servius, Honoratus Maurus, i. 83, 371.

'settaine,' ii. 92.

Seven Deadly Sins, Tarlton's, ii. 232, 418, 428. *See* Tarlton.

Seven; see also *Seaven*.

Severus, the 'cruel' and the 'excellent,' i. 170.

— Cassius, ii. 320.

Sextus Empiricus, ii. 227, 427.

Shacklock, R., ii. 433.

Shadwell, Thomas, ii. 462.

Shaftesbury's *Advice to an Author*, p. xli (note).

Shakespeare, i. 362, 365, 369, 391, 399, 425; ii. 293, 315; Meres's list of poems and plays, ii. 317-18; 319, 320, 321, 402-3, 424, 425, 428, 435, 437, 445, 449-50; 458, 461, 462, 463, 464; poems mentioned in the *Returne from Parnassus*, 466. *See under each play and poem.*

Shepheards Calender, pp. xxxv, xlii; i. 112, 114, 127-34, 196, 232, 245, 247, 263-5, 270 et seq., 276, 286 et seq., 305, 372, 374, 375, 376, 377, 379, 380-1, 396, 398, 406, 408, 410, 412, 413, 414, 422, 425, 428; ii. 65, 313, 316, 401, 419, 458. *See* Spenser.

Sherry, Richard, *Treatise of Schemes and Tropes*, p. vi; i. 422.
Shirley, James, ii. 462.
'Shoppini,' ii. 36, 411.
Shore's Wife, ii. 403, 466.
Short Apologie of the Schoole of Abuse, Gosson's, i. 62, 364.
Shute, John, ii. 279, 441.
Sibilet, Thomas, p. lxxxvii.
Sibilla, i. 71, 72.
Sidney, Sir Philip, pp. xi, xiii, xiv, xix, xx, xxi, xxii, xxiv, xxvi, xxvii, xxviii, xxix, xxx, xxxi, xxxii, xli, xliv, xlv, xlvi, lii, lvi, lix, lxi, lxiii, lxvii, lxix, lxx, lxxii, lxxiii, lxxiv, lxxix, lxxxi, lxxxiii, lxxxiv, lxxxv, lxxxvi, lxxxvii, lxxxviii, lxxxix, xci, xcii; i. 61, 62, 89, 90, 92, 99, 101, 102, 109, 126, 133; *Apologie for Poetrie*, 148–207; 245, 303, 305, 359, 360, 362, 363, 364, 367, 372, 378, 379, 382–403, 408, 415, 416, 422, 427; ii. 63, 65, 196, 197, 209, 217, 221; *Astrophel and Stella*, 223 et seq.; 231, 234, 238, 249, 258, 263, 273, 282, 292, 293, 310, 314, 315, 318, 321, 322, 326, 408, 410, 413, 416, 422–5, 425–7, 437, 444, 446, 447, 448, 449, 452, 457, 458. See *Apologie for Poetrie*, *Arcadia*, *Astrophel and Stella*.

Robert, i. 383–4, 397, 415.
Sidonius, C. S. Apollinaris, i. 299, 416; ii. 453.
Sigonio, Carlo (Sigonius), i. 25, 349, 355; ii. 246, 433.
'Silence,' the Figure of, ii. 168.
Silius Italicus, C., i. 238, 409; ii. 315.
'Sillepsis,' ii. 167.
Similes and Metaphors, common Renaissance, pp. xxiv, lxxxvi (*the list is not exhaustive*); Bee, i. 59, 79; ii. 309; Diet, 'Dish,' i. 72, 329, 430; Honey, i. 59, 79, 333, 390–1; ii. 309; Poison, i. 79; Potions, Medicine, i. 66, 72, 172, 390–1; ii. 199; Rhubarb, Aloes, &c., i. 172, 390–1; ii. 199, 208, 310, 423, 446; Spider, i. 79, 333; Sugar, Sugarcandy, i. 72, 172, 390–1; ii. 199, 208, 310, 446; Weeds, i. 59.
Similia, Erasmus's, i. 17.
Simmias Rhodius, i. 32, 126, 267, 356; ii. 416.
Simonides, pp. lxxvii, lxxxvi; i. 190, 342, 386–7; ii. 311.
'Sinathrismus,' ii. 170.
'Single Supply,' Figure of, ii. 167.
Singleton, Hugh, printer, i. 127.
'Situation,' Puttenham on, ii. 88 et seq.
'Six Points of Good Utterance,' Puttenham's, ii. 161–2.
sixain (syxaine, sizeine, seizino), i. 55, 57; ii. 68 et seq., 91, 92, 416.
Skelton, John, i. 242; ii. 62, 65, 87, 230, 273, 314.
Skialetheia, Guilpin's, ii. 320, 451, 456.
'slaumpaump,' ii. 440.
Slomber, Spenser's, i. 89, 372.
'Slow Returne,' Figure of, ii. 169.
Smith, Henry, ii. 281, 443.

Sir Thomas, i. 21, 102, 353, 354, 374, 375; ii. 273, 293, 439, 445.
Socrates, p. xxviii; i. 170, 192, 319, 342; ii. 204, 253.
Soldiers and Scholars, p. lxxxvi; i. 395.
'Solecismus,' ii. 171.
Solomon, ii. 10, 22. See *Song of Solomon*.
Solon, i. 69, 152.
Somerset, Protector, ii. 17.
Song of Solomon, i. 158; ii. 207; Markham's version, ii. 323.

Sonnet, the, i. 55, 57, 223; ii. 209.
Sonnets, James VI's, i. 211; Spenser's, i. 428; Shakespeare's, ii. 317.
'Soother,' Figure of the, ii. 169.
Sophocles, pp. xliii, lxxiii; i. 19, 20, 23, 24, 165, 193, 236, 349, 355; ii. 17, 27, 231, 267, 315, 316, 319, 322, 338.
'Soraismus,' ii. 171.
Sotades of Maroneia, ii. 314, 447.
Sources of Elizabethan critical ideas, pp. lxxi et seq.
Southern, John, ii. 171, 421.
Southwell, Robert, ii. 442.
Spain, i. 123; Whetstone on Spanish Comedy, i. 59; Homer in Spanish, i. 32. Estimate of Spanish influence on Elizabethan criticism, pp. lxxxix-xc.
Spanish Tragedie, The, i. 425. *See* Kyd.
'Speaking picture,' pp. lxxvii, lxxxvi; i. 158, 342, 386-7.
'Speedie Dispatcher,' Figure of the, ii. 170.
Spense, author of *Bellum Grammaticale*, ii. 424.
Spenser, Edmund, pp. xi, xxxiv, xxxvii, xlix, l, lix, lxviii, lxxxi, xc; correspondence with Gabriel Harvey on Reformed Versifying, i. 87-92, 98-101; 127-34, 196, 232, 245, 263-5, 305, 306, 318, 359, 360, 361, 362, 372-80, 380-1, 396, 402, 403, 405, 407, 410, 412, 413, 415, 416, 422, 425, 428; ii. 65, 234, 238, 240, 241, 249, 282, 293, 313, 315, 316, 318, 319, 321, 400, 413, 414, 421, 422, 427, 430, 431, 435, 436, 458, 465. *See* separate works.
Sponde, Jean de (Spondanus), p. xxiv; ii. 297, 298, 445.
Spondee, i. 95, 294; ii. 127.
Squire of low degree, The, i. 323.

Stage. *See* Anti-Stage Pamphlets.
Stanyhurst, Richard, pp. xxiv, xxxii, xl, xlii, lii, lxviii, xcii; prefatory matter to *Translation of the Aeneid*, i. 135-47; his rules, 135-6; 315, 365, 377, 381-2, 407, 415, 427; ii. 122, 231, 234, 240, 280, 292, 320, 417, 421, 430, 444, 455.
Stanza, Puttenham on the, ii. 68 et seq.
Statius, i. 239.
Staves, Puttenham on, ii. 68 et seq.
Steele Glas, i. 126, 360, 379.
Stephanus; *see* Estienne, H.
Sternhold, Thomas, ii. 17, 63.
Stesichorus, ii. 49.
Stevenson, William, ii. 443.
Still, John, i. 90, 373; ii. 281, 443.
Stilo, Lucius Aelius Praeconius (called 'Epius Stolo' by Meres), ii. 318, 450.
Stoa, Gianfrancesco Quinziano, ii. 315, 448.
Stolo, Epius; *see* Stilo.
'Store,' The Figure of, ii. 170.
Stow, John, ii. 280.
Strabo, i. 77, 310.
'Straggler,' Figure of the, ii. 170.
Strange Newes, Nash's, ii. 239-44, 248, 424, 429-31.
Strange News out of Affrick, i. 62, 364.
Strozzi, Ercole, ii. 315, 448.
Tito Vespaniano, ii. 315, 448.
Stub *or* Stubbes, Philip, i. 63, 428, 429; ii. 279, 280, 441.
Studley, John, i. 425.
Sturm, John, p. lxxvi; i. 9, 13, 14, 20, 21, 25, 347, 348, 349, 350-3 passim, 355, 358, 381; ii. 248, 433.
Style and Matter, i. 6; Harvey on English Style, i. 123 et seq.; Puttenham's definition of Style, ii. 153-4.

'Substitute,' Figure of the, ii. 168.
Suetonius, i. 390.
'Sufferance,' Figure of, ii. 304.
Suidas, ii. 463.
Suliard, Edward, i. 226.
Sulla, i. 170.
'Surclose,' Figure of the, ii. 170.
'Surnamer,' Figure of the, ii. 169.
Surrey, Henry Howard, Earl of, pp. xlix, l, lii, lxxxi; i. 30, 32, 126, 196, 242, 283, 379, 397, 410, 415; ii. 62, 65, 75, 76, 127, 128, 130, 131, 137, 168, 219, 293, 315, 320, 326, 447.
Susarion Bullus, i. 81, 370; ii. 392, 463.
Sutcliff, Matthew, ii. 248, 433.
'Swan,' The, ii. 323.
'Swift Repeat,' Figure of the, ii. 169.
'S. Y.', i. 242.
Sylvius, Aeneas, ii. 369.
'Symploce,' ii. 304.
Symposium, Plato's, i. 190.
'Synalæpha,' i. 283.
'Synecdoche,' ii. 169.
'Syneciosis,' ii. 169.
'Syneresis,' ii. 132.
'Synonymia,' ii. 170.
'syntactical,' ii. 166.
'Synthesis,' ii. 162, 419.
'Syntomia,' ii. 162, 419.

Tacitus, ii. 263, 460.
Talaeus, *or* Tallaeus, Audomarus, i. 280, 415, 423; ii. 245, 432.
Talmudists, the, ii. 123.
Tamburlaine, ii. 368, 369.
Tancred and Gismund, i. 412. *See* Wilmot.
'Taper,' The, ii. 96 et seq.
'Tapinosis,' ii. 169, 171.
Tarchaniota; *see* Marullus.
'Tarletonising,' ii. 436.
Tarlton (and *Tarlton's Jests*), pp. xx, xxci; i. 125, 371; ii. 232, 233, 243, 261, 266, 273, 323, 418, 422, 428, 431, 436. See *Seven Deadly Sins*.
Tasis, ii. 162, 419.
Tasso, Torquato, p. lxxxi; i. 303, 305, 310, 318, 359, 391, 424; ii. 199, 257, 276, 283, 319, 336, 369, 423, 441, 450.
'Tautologia,' ii. 171.
'Tell-cause,' Figure of the, ii. 170.
Temple, William, Sidney's Secretary, i. 423; ii. 432.
Tenne Tragedies (Seneca), i. 424-5.
Terence, pp. xliii, lxxvi; i. 8, 23, 27, 28, 29, 35, 59, 65, 82, 83, 116, 166, 177, 192, 198, 230, 237, 252, 253, 299, 371, 399, 400, 408; ii. 27, 257, 320, 322, 329, 397, 463.
Tertullian, p. xv; i. 343.
Thales, i. 152.
Thamaras, ii. 318.
Theagines (? Theognis, q.v.), i. 236, 409.
Theagines and Cariclea, i. 157, 160, 386, 388; ii. 315, 440. *See* Helidorus.
Theatre, pp. xvii, xxx. *See* Anti-Stage, Gosson, Lodge, Vaughan.
Theatre of God's Iudgements, ii. 324, 454.
The hunte is up, ii. 17.
Themistocles, i. 70.
Theocritus, i. 9, 132, 196, 232, 237, 262, 263, 316, 350; ii. 17, 27, 316, 321, 397.
Theodorus Gaza, ii. 369.
Theogenes Megarensis, ii. 320.
Theognis, i. 409; ii. 361. *See* Theagines (?).
Theophanes Mitiletus, i. 70.
Theophrastus, i. 292.
Thespis, i. 236; ii. 319.
Theta (*nigrum theta*), i. 321, 429; ii. 376, 460.

Thomas, S., ii. 372.
Thomas Aquinas, ii. 460.
Three Proper and wittie familiar letters, i. 87 et seq.
Thucydides, i. 19, 20, 40, 41, 42, 43; ii. 43, 154.
Tibullus, i. 238, 252; ii. 27, 320, 465.
Time, 'Unity' of; *see* Unities.
Timon Apolloniates, ii. 319.
Tirtaeus, Tirtheus; *see* Tyrtaeus.
'Tirthetus'; *see* Tyrtaeus.
'*Tite-tute-tate*,' ii. 439–40.
Titus Andronicus, Shakespeare's, ii. 318.
Tolomei, Claudio, p. lxxx; i. 356; ii. 368, 458.
Tomitano, Bernardino (Tomitanus), p. lxxx; i. 21, 353–4.
Tomkis, Thomas, ii. 464.
Topas, Sir, ii. 87.
'Topographia,' Figure of, ii. 176.
Tottel, Richard, bookseller, &c., i. 46.
Tottel's Miscellany, i. 397, 410; ii. 451.
Touchstone for the Time, A, by Whetstone, i. 63.
Touchstone of Wittes, The, i. 226.
Towly, Tom, i. 140.
Toxophilus, pp. l, lvi; i. 120, 349, 350, 355, 356, 357, 378; ii. 261, 420.
Trabea, i. 82, 237, 371.
'*Traductio*,' Figure of, ii. 169.
'Tragaediographus,' ii. 316, 317.
Tragedy, pp. xxx, xlii; Ascham on, i. 19, 23, 24; Lodge on, i. 80; Sidney on, i. 178 et seq.; Webbe on, i. 236 et seq., 413; Puttenham on, ii. 27, 36 et seq.; Harington on, ii. 209, 210; Meres's examples of, ii. 319; verse of, ii. 382; Shakespeare the most excellent in English, ii. 318.

Tragi-comedy, p. xliv; i. 175, 391, 400.
Translation, pp. xxx, lxxxi; i. 1, 3, 4, 5; ii. 217 et seq., 295–307 passim; Meres's list of translators, ii. 322–3.
'Transport,' Figure of, ii. 169.
Trapezuntius; *see* George of Trebizond.
Travers, Walter, ii. 248, 433.
Treatise of Daunses, &c., i. 62.
Treatise to the Rebels, Cheke's, ii. 293.
Treatise wherein Dicing Dauncing vaine Playes or Enterluds . . . are reproved, John Northbrooke's, i. 61.
Tremelius, *or* Tremellius, Emanuel, i. 158, 387, 391.
'Trenchmore,' i. 272.
'Trespasser,' Figure of the, ii. 168.
'Tribrachys'; *see* note i. p. 415.
'Tricquet,' the, ii. 96.
Trimetra, English, i. 94.
Trinity College, Cambridge, i. 313.
Trissino, Giangiorgio, p. lxxxii; i. 391, 398, 400.
Tristram, Sir, p. xviii; i. 4, 323.
Triumphals, by Puttenham, ii. 48.
Trochee, Trochaic Verse, i. 24, 95; ii. 340 et seq., 377. *Trochaeus* or *Tribrachys*, i. 415.
'Troilus verse,' i. 222, 406.
Tropes; *see* Sherry, Richard.
Tropus, ii. 162, 420.
Troylus and Cresseid, Chaucer's, i. 196; ii. 64, 68.
'Tumbling' verse, i. 218, 219, 407. *See* Rouncefallis.
Turbervile, George, i. 315, 411, 427; ii. 63, 261, 322, 436.
'Turbot,' The, ii. 97.
Turkey, Turks, i. 153; ii. 361, 458.
'Turn-Tale,' Figure of the, ii. 170.

Turner, William, i. 313, 423, 426.
Turpilius, Sextus, i. 82, 237, 371; ii. 320.
'Tuscanish,' i. 376.
Tuscanism, *Tuscanismo*, i. 107; ii. 239, 250, 430, 434.
Tusser, Thomas, i. 242, 265, 410, 414; ii. 280, 323.
'Twins,' The Figure of, ii. 168.
Two Gentlemen of Verona, Shakespeare's, ii. 318.
Two other very commendable Letters, &c., i. 87 et seq.
Twyne, Thomas, i. 243, 374, 382, 411; ii. 63, 413.
Tyrtaeus, i. 75, 77 ('Tirthetus'), 152, 158, 234, 297, 342; ii. 18, 255.

Udall, Nicholas, ii. 444.
Ulysses, i. 8, 14.
'Uncouth,' Figure of the, 171.
'Undecencie,' ii. 176, 177. See 'Decencie' and *Decorum*.
Underhill, John, ii. 281, 443.
'Underlay,' Figure of the, ii. 169.
Unities, Dramatic, pp. xli, xliv, xlv, lxxiv, lxxxiii, lxxxviii; Gascoigne on English disregard of time, i. 59; Sidney on, 197; i. 398-9, 400; ii. 301; Jonson on, ii. 389, 393; ii. 424, 461. See also *Decorum*.
ὑποτύπωσις, i. 300.
'upseuant muffe,' ii. 426. See ii. 467.
Urania, by Pontanus, ii. 447.
Uranie, Du Bartas's, i. 405; ii. 265, 437.
Ursinus, Fulvius, i. 347.
Utopia, More's, i. 166, 390, 426; ii. 42.

Valanger, Mr., i. 117.
Valentine and Orson, ii. 400.

Valgius, T., ii. 320, 451.
Valla, Giorgio, ii. 431.
— Lorenzo, i. 128, 381; ii. 245, 369, 459.
Varchi's *Lezzioni*, p. lxxxii; i. 389, 390.
Vargas, p. lxxxix; ii. 18, 410, 454. See Vergoza.
Varro, i. 36, 37-9, 357; ii. 163, 293, 450.
'Vates,' p. lxxv; i. 154, 159, 231, 284-5, 408; ii. 6 et seq., 205, 313, 423.
Vaughan, William, p. xix; i. 149; *The Golden Grove*, ii. 325-6, 454.
Vauquelin de la Fresnaye, Jean, p. lxxx.
Vautrollier, Thomas, printer, i. 280.
Vaux, Sir Nicholas, first Lord Vaux (*d.* 1523), ii. 63 (a slip by Puttenham for Thomas, q.v.), 413.
— Thomas, second Lord Vaux 1510-56), i. 242, 410; ii. 65 (cf. ii. 63 and note), 413.
— William, third Lord Vaux (? 1542-95), ? i. 125.
Velleius Paterculus, i. 26, 355.
'Velvet Breeches and Cloth Breeches,' ii. 430.
Venus and Adonis, Shakespeare's, ii. 317, 402.
Vergoza, ii. 326. See Vargas.
Verse, p. xlvi et seq.; Spenser and Harvey on Reformed Versifying (q.v.), i. 87-122; Verse and Poetry, i. 160, ii. 408; Stanyhurst on Latin and English, i. 141-7; Sidney on Verse and Prose, i. 182 et seq., 204; James VI on, i. 212 et seq.; Webbe on 'Reformation of English Verse,' i. 226, on English verse, 247 et seq., 266 et seq., 278 et seq.; Puttenham on Metre, ii. 70 et seq., on Classical Mea-

Verse (*continued*)—
sures, ii. 117 et seq.; Harington on, ii. 206; Carew on, ii. 292; Campion on, ii. 327-55; Daniel on, ii. 359 et seq.; Verse of Tragedy, i. 24. *See* under each kind (e. g. Heroical, Pastoral, &c.).

'figured,' ii. 416. (*See* Figured Verse); *versus intercalaris*, ii. 93; 'verse lyon,' ii. 16, 409; *versus reciproci* or *retrogradi*, ii. 409.

Vettori, Pietro (Petrus Victorius), i. 18, 20, 347, 349, 353.

'Vices in language, intolerable,' ii. 171.

'Vices of Surplusage,' the, ii. 171.

Victorius; *see* Vettori.

Vida, p. lxxix and note, p. lxxx and note.

'*Videntes*,' ii. 7.

Virelay, i. 55, 57.

Virgil, pp. xlv, lxvii, lxxvii, lxxx (note), lxxxv; i. 8, 9, 14, 15, 19, 20, 23, 29, 32, 33, 35, 36, 64, 65, 75, 84, 127, 132, 136, 137, 138, 139, 142, 154, 157, 158, 166, 168, 173, 183, 196, 206, 232, 237, 243, 255, 256, 257 et seq., 262, 263, 265, 284, 296, 305, 309, 316, 318, 331, 332, 336, 342, 347, 348, 371, 381, 382, 391, 396, 403, 413, 430; ii. 17, 23, 27, 40, 57, 58, 60, 63, 116, 117, 122, 123, 155, 156, 178, 196, 206, 210, 211, 212, 214, 217, 230, 231, 240, 265, 293, 298, 299, 315, 316, 319, 321, 322, 423, 424, 445, 454. *See* Surrey.

'English' [Spenser], ii. 240.

'Virgil' in the *Poetaster*, ii. 394 et seq.

Virgilius Romanus (*Comicus*), ii. 320.

Visions of Bellay, Spenser's, i. 374, 428.

Visions of Petrarch, Spenser's, i. 428.

Vives, Ioannes Ludovicus, i. 342, 404, 431; ii. 236, 245, 429, 432.

vocabula artis, i. 218; ii. 419.

Vocabulary, p. lv et seq.; compound words, i. 402; Jonson on the Poets', 397. *See* Archaism, Diction, Dictionary Method, Inkhorn, Oversea, Italian, French.

Vossius, i. 490.

Wakefield, Mr., ii. 273, 439.

Wales, i. 153. Welsh language, ii. 125, 149, 364. Welsh Bards, i. 384.

Walley, Robert, bookseller, i. 226.

Walsingham, Sir Francis, i. 62, 424, 452.

Walsingham's Meliboeus, ii. 321, 452.

Warner, William, i. 320, 428; ii. 280, 315, 317, 318, 319, 449. See *Albions England*.

Warton Thomas (*Hist. of Eng. Poetry*), i. 226 (note), 355.

Watson, Thomas (1513-18), author of *Absalon* (q.v.), pp. xi, l, lxxiii; i. 21, 23, 24, 29, 96, 118, 283, 313, 354, 373, 415, 426; ii. ? 319, 322.

(? 1557-92), author of 'Ἑκατομπαθία (q.v.), *Amyntas* (q.v.), *Walsingham's Meliboeus* (q.v.), *Amyntae Gaudia* (q.v.), transl. of *Antigone* (q.v.), p. lxxxvii (note); i. 316, 354, 372, 404, 422, 427, 428, 430; ii. 234, 280, 315, 319(2), 321, 322, 400, 401, 416, 420, 429, 451, 452.

Webbe, William, pp. vii, xxii, xxv, xxvi, xxx, xxxi, xxxii, xxxiii, xlii, xliv, xlv, xlvi, xlviii, xlix, lii, lxvii, lxxii, lxxiv, lxxv, xcii; *A Dis-*

course of English Poetrie, i. 226-302, 385, 407-16; ii. 447, 448, 453; on Wilmot, i. 412; his translation of Virgil's Eclogues, i. 284.

Weever, John, ii. 449.

Whetstone, George, *Dedication to Promos and Cassandra*, i. 58-60, 362-3; i. 244, 399, 400, 411; ii. 280, 321, 419; *A Touchstone for the Time*, i. 63.

Whitgift, John, ii. 238, 281, 429.

Whitney, Geoffrey, ii. 323, 453.

Whittaker, William, ii. 248, 434.

Wickham, William, ii. 281, 442.

Wilbye, John, i. 428.

Willes, *or* Willey, Richard, i. 46, 126, 358, 379, 414; ii. 315, 416, 448.

Willet, Andrew, ii. 323, 453.

Willey; *see* Willes.

Williams, Sir Roger, ii. 262, 437.

Wilmot, Robert, p. xliii; i. 245, 412.

Wilson, Robert, the elder (*d.* 1600), i. 85, 125, 371, 379; ii. 320, 323, 451, 453.

―― Thomas (? 1525-81), author of the *Arte of Rhetorique*, pp. vi, xxiv, lvii, xci; i. 383, 403, 405, 422; ii. 288, 444. *Rule of Reason, conteinyng the Arte of Logique*, i. 422.

Wilton, ii. 358.

Windet, John, printer, ii. 295, 297.

Wingfield, or Winkfield, Mr., ii. 424.

Wise, Andrew, bookseller, ii. 327.

Wolfe, John, printer, ii. 229, 245.

'Women,' Puns on word, ii. 418.

'Wondrer,' Figure of the, ii. 170.

Wotton, Edward, i. 150, 383.

―― Sir Henry, i. 383.

Wright, John, bookseller, ii. 398.

Wyatt, Sir Thomas, lxxxi; i. 30; ii. 62, 65, 76, 127, 130, 131, 134, 137, 168, 219, 321.

Wykeham, William of, i. 46.

Wylmott; *see* Wilmot.

Wythipole, Master, i. 94, 373.

Xenophon (Zenophon), i. 17, 18, 19, 20, 25, 40, 43, 157, 160, 166, 168, 169; ii. 43, 196, 231, 263, 277, 315, 411.

Yarmouth, i. 37; Great Yarmouth, ii. 453.

Yloop, S., ? 411.

Young, B., i. 376.

Young, John, ii. 281, 442.

'Zeugma,' ii. 167.

Zeuxis, i. 321.

Zodiac of Palingenius, i. 244, 356.

Zoilus, ii. 194.

END OF VOLUME II